Merriam-Webster's

Chinese-English Dictionary

Merriam-Webster's

Chinese-English Dictionary

Merriam-Webster, Incorporated
Springfield, Massachusetts

Merriam-Webster ISBN: 978-0-87779-259-8

Collins ISBN: 978-0-00-870303-5

Typeset by Davidson Publishing Solutions, Glasgow, Scotland

Printed in Canada

1st Printing: Marquis, Toronto, ON 07/2024

Contents

Preface

MERRIAM-WEBSTER'S CHINESE–ENGLISH DICTIONARY is a new dictionary designed to meet the needs of English and Chinese speakers in a time of ever-expanding communication among the countries of the world. It is intended for language learners, teachers, office workers, tourists, and business travelers – anyone who needs to communicate effectively in the Chinese and English languages as they are spoken and written today.

This dictionary provides accurate and up-to-date coverage of current vocabulary in both languages, as well as abundant examples of words used in context to illustrate usage. The dictionary includes Chinese words and phrases as they are spoken in China. The English vocabulary and spellings included here reflect American English usage. Entered words that we have reason to believe are trademarks have been designated as such with the symbol ®. However, neither the presence nor absence of such designation should be regarded as affecting the legal status of any trademark.

The front matter of this dictionary begins with an Introduction that includes notes about the structure and pronunciation of Chinese. It then has a section on how to use this dictionary followed by a list of abbreviations used in the dictionary. The list includes both Chinese and English abbreviations in a single list that gives both the Chinese and the English meanings of all of the abbreviations. This is followed by a listing of English irregular verbs and a table showing the symbols from the International Phonetic Alphabet (IPA) that are used in the dictionary for English. Finally, there is a Radical Index which helps you find the Chinese character you are looking for if you don't know how it is pronounced.

This dictionary is the result of a unique collaboration between Collins and Merriam-Webster. It is based on one of the most popular of the Collins Chinese–English databases and reflects the bilingual lexicographical expertise of Collins editors and contributors. In addition, it has been thoroughly reviewed by editors at Merriam-Webster to ensure its accurate treatment of American English spelling, vocabulary, and idioms. The editors of Collins and Merriam-Webster offer this new dictionary in the belief that it will serve well those who want a concise and handy guide to the Chinese and English languages of today.

Introduction

Learning Chinese is definitely a challenge. However, in some ways Chinese is not particularly complicated. Words do not change with gender, number or even tense, and there are not many complicated grammatical traps for the unwary. However, other things about it make it hard for native English speakers to learn.

Chinese pronunciation

The four tones

Chinese is a tonal language – the pitch of any syllable affects its meaning.

There are four tones: first tone (high, even pitch); second (rising pitch); third tone (falling and then rising) and fourth tone (falling pitch). There is also a fifth (or neutral) tone, which is pronounced so quietly and quickly that there is no discernible tone at all.

Tones are a very important part of the pronunciation – and wrong tones can cause real confusion.

Examples of differences in tones:

First tone	Second tone	Third tone	Fourth tone	Neutral tone
mā	má	mǎ	mà	ma
妈	麻	马	骂	吗
mother	hemp	horse	curse; swear	[question particle]

It may seem unnatural to native speakers of English to have pitch so rigidly attached to words, but the tone is as fundamental a part of any syllable as are its vowels and consonants.

Pinyin

Pinyin, the Chinese phonetic alphabet, was first introduced to help children learn to write characters, and foreigners and speakers of non-Mandarin dialects to pronounce Standard Chinese correctly. It is also very useful for dictionaries, as it provides an alphabetical order by which characters can be sorted. However, *pinyin* is not used much in China. Although signs in China are sometimes written in *pinyin*, do not expect people to understand *pinyin* as they would characters – in short, it should not be regarded as a substitute for learning Chinese characters. It is, however, a good, accurate guide to pronunciation.

Chinese characters

The Chinese script has a history that goes back at least three thousand years.

Although there are tens of thousands of known characters, a lot of these are archaic (some so old that even their meanings are unknown). An educated Chinese person will know roughly 4–6000 characters, and 2–3000 is considered sufficient for basic literacy (newspapers and the like).

Each character has to be learned individually – with the shape of the character, the sound of it and the meaning learned together as a unit.

There is no way of predicting the sound and meaning of an unknown Chinese character with any degree of accuracy. This does not mean, however, that there is no system behind the characters at all. All characters contain at least one of the component parts known as "radicals," and almost all radicals have an element of meaning; if you are familiar with these, not only will using a dictionary be much easier, it will also help you identify more of the building blocks of the characters you are trying to learn.

Simplified and complex characters

In the 1950s and 60s the government of the People's Republic of China simplified the Chinese script, in an effort to improve the literacy rate by making characters easier to write. It is these simplified characters which are used in this dictionary.

Chinese grammar

Compared to many languages, Chinese grammar is not particularly complicated. Words do not change according to gender, number or case the way they do in many European languages. Sentence structure is generally straightforward, and there are not many exceptions to the grammatical rules (unlike English).

Talking about time

It is sometimes said that Chinese has no tenses. This is not quite true, but speakers of Chinese talk about time in a way that is quite different from ours.

The English tense system is based on the idea of before and after the point of view of the narrator. Things that happened before the time in which we are talking take the past tense, those that are in the process of going on, the present, and things that have yet to take place, the future. This is shown by a change in the verbs. Chinese verbs, on the other hand, do not change with tense, but an aspect marker is placed before or after the verb. Some of the most common are 了 le (for completed actions – usually *but not always* in the past), 过 guò (for events that have already taken place), 要 yào (for things that are going to happen) and 在 zài (for things that are in the process of happening). These are no more than generalizations, however, and it is important not to use them indiscriminately as substitutes for English tenses, as that is not what they are for.

Adverbs of time are often used to show what time relation events have to each other, such as 已经 yǐjīng (already), 曾经 céngjīng (once), or specific times or dates.

明年我去中国。 Míngnián wǒ qù Zhōngguó. (literally: Next year I go China). I'm going to China next year.

Measure words

These are not unique to Chinese – you occasionally see something similar in English.

a *gaggle* of geese
a *piece* of fruit
six *pints* of milk etc.

They do not occur very often in English. In Chinese, however, measure words are mandatory when giving a number of nouns. It is important to remember to put them in – and also to get them right – as there are a lot of measure words in Chinese.

一只青蛙	yī zhī qīngwā	one frog
三部电影	sān bù diànyǐng	three films
五封信	wǔ fēng xìn	five letters

Different measure words are used for different types of objects. 张 zhāng is used for flat things, such as tickets, sheets and tables. 条 tiáo is used to talk about long, thin things such as ribbons, or fish. The most common measure word is 个 gè, and it is a useful "default setting" for when you cannot remember the exact term you need.

Word order

Because of the less specific nature of the Chinese view of time, the tendency to avoid redundancy and the lack of cases to show a word's function in the sentence, word order is important in Chinese. It generally follows a subject-verb-object pattern, although there are certain particles or rhetorical constructions that change the order slightly. If the word order is wrong, it can be very hard to unscramble the sense of a phrase or sentence.

All this may seem a little intimidating to a beginner. However, the challenge of learning Chinese is in direct proportion to the pleasure of being able to use it. Not only is it an absorbing and intriguing language, which can express both brutal frankness and extreme delicacy, it also brings with it great opportunities to learn about a new and very different country and culture. And there could be no better time to begin that exploration than now, when China is taking a greater role in the world.

Esther Tyldesley, University of Edinburgh

Explanatory Notes

On the following pages you will find an outline of how information is presented in this dictionary. We hope that this will help you to get the most out of your dictionary, not simply from its comprehensive wordlist, but also from the information provided in each entry.

Chinese–English side

Head entries

On the Chinese side, head entries are ordered traditionally, that is by single-character entries with multiple-character entries beginning with the same character nested below them.

标 biāo
标本 biāoběn
标点 biāodiǎn
标记 biāojì
标题 biāotí
标志 biāozhì
标准 biāozhǔn

表 biǎo
表达 biǎodá

Single character entries are ordered by pinyin, that is alphabetically and then by tone. In Chinese, there are four tones, each represented by a different mark above the relevant vowel:

¯	first tone	(flat tone)	mā
´	second tone	(rising tone)	má
ˇ	third tone	(falling rising tone)	mǎ
`	fourth tone	(falling tone)	mà
	light or no tone		ma

Where characters have the same pinyin and tone, they are ordered by the number of strokes in the character, with the smallest number of strokes first.

八　　bā
巴　　bā
芭　　bā
疤　　bā

Where characters have the same pinyin, tone, and number of strokes, they are ordered by the first stroke in the character, as follows:

一丨丿丶乛

The multiple-character entries nested below single-character entries are similarly ordered by the pinyin (including tone), and then by the number of strokes.

蒸　　zhēng
蒸气　zhēngqì
蒸汽　zhēngqì

Polyphones, that is characters with more than one pronunciation, are crossed-referenced to the alternative pinyin.

斗 [dǒu] N **1** (指容器) cup **2** (斗状物) ▶ 烟斗 [yāndǒu] pipe ▶ 漏斗 [lòudǒu] funnel

→ *see also*/另见 dòu

斗 [dòu] VB **1** (打斗) fight ▶ 斗鸡 [dòujī] cock fighting **2** (战胜) beat

→ *see also*/另见 dǒu

Radical and character index

If you do not know the pronunciation for the Chinese character that you are looking for, you can use the radical index before the start of the Chinese–English side. For further information on how to use this index, see the introduction to that section.

The structure of entries

On the Chinese side there are two levels of entry (single-character entries and multiple-character entries), both of which have essentially the same entry structure. Pinyin romanization is given for both types of entry.

Parts of speech are given in brackets after the pinyin. Where a word has more than one part of speech, Roman numerals are used. For a full list of all parts of speech used, see page 19a.

Where an entry has more than one meaning, it is divided into categories, which are shown by an Arabic numeral.

When expressing yourself in another language, it is important to be aware of when you can use certain words and expressions and with whom – you would communicate very differently with a business colleague than with a friend. To help you, we have labeled words and expressions appropriately throughout the dictionary.

A full list of field and register labels used in the dictionary is shown on page 19a–21a.

Examples

Word examples are preceded by a shaded arrow ▶. Fuller examples are preceded by an empty arrow ▷.

Translations

Translations are shown in normal roman type after the part of speech or indicator. In general, we have only given one translation per meaning, since we believe this is the most accurate and helpful approach.

In a few cases, there is no equivalent at all, and an explanation rather than a translation has to be given. In such cases it is shown in italics:

压岁钱 [yāsuìqián] N *traditional gifts of money given to children during the Spring Festival*

English–Chinese side

Headwords

The words you look up in the dictionary – 'headwords' – are listed alphabetically. Homographs (words which are written in the same way but have different pronunciations) are shown as separate headwords and differentiated by the use of superscript numbers. For example:

bow[1] [bəʊ] N [C] **1** (*knot*) 蝴蝶结 húdiéjié [个 gè] **2** (*weapon*) 弓 gōng [把 bǎ]
bow[2] [baʊ] **I** VI (*with head, body*) 鞠躬 jūgōng **II** VT (+ *head*) 低头 dītóu

Irregular past tenses and plural forms are also shown as headwords in their alphabetical position and cross-referenced to the base form. For example:

children [tʃɪldrən] N PL *of* **child**

went [wɛnt] PT *of* **go**

The structure of entries

Parts of speech are given in upper case after the phonetic spelling of the headword. We have used the notations C, U and S and PL in brackets after each noun to show whether nouns are countable, uncountable, singular or plural. C means that the noun is countable, and has a plural form (e.g. *I'm reading a book; she's bought several books*). U means that the noun is is not normally counted, and is not used in the plural (e.g. *Lesley refused to give me more information*). S (*for singular noun*) means the noun is always singular, and is usually preceded by *a*, *an* or *the* (e.g. *We need to persuade people to repect the environment).* PL means the noun is always plural, and is used with plural verbs or pronouns (e.g. *These clothes are ready to wear*). For a full list of all parts of speech used, see page 19a.

hairdryer [hɛ̲ərdraɪər] N [C] 吹风机 chuīfēngjī [个 gè]
hair gel N [U] 发胶 fàjiāo
kickoff [kɪ̲kɔf] N [S] 开场时间 kāichǎng shíjiān

Where an entry has more than one meaning, it is divided into categories, which are shown by an Arabic numeral. You will often find information in brackets and *italics* after the meaning category number. This information functions as a "signpost" to help the user select the right translation when there is more than one to choose from. This "signpost" or indicator may give a synonym of the headword, typical contexts in which the word might appear or a label indicating the subject field in which the word is used.

A full list of field and register labels used in the dictionary is shown on pages 19a–21a.

link [lɪ̲ŋk] **I** N [C] **1** (*between people, organizations*) 联系 liánxì [种 zhǒng] **2** (*Comput*) (*also*: **hyperlink**) 超链接 chāoliànjiē [个 gè] **II** VT **1** (+ *places, objects*) 连接 liánjiē **2** (+ *people, situations*) 联系 liánxì

Phrases

All phrases are given in bold and preceded by a shaded arrow ▶. For example:

half time (*Sport*) N [U] 半场 bànchǎng
▶ **at half-time** 半场时 bànchǎng shí

Translations

Translations are shown in normal roman type after the part of speech or indicator. In general, we have only given one translation per meaning, since we believe this is the most accurate and helpful approach. In a few cases, there is no equivalent at all, and an explanation rather than a translation has to be given.

au pair [oʊ pɛər] N [C] 为学习语言而住在当地人家里并提供家政服务的外国年轻人

Pinyin

Pinyin romanization is given for all translations, except where, as above, there is no real equivalent in Chinese and an explanation rather than a translation has been given.

Measure words

Measure words are given after translations of nouns which are countable and take a measure word. They are given in square brackets, with their pinyin. For more information on measure words, see the introduction on page 10a.

banknote [bæŋknoʊt] N [C] 纸币 zhǐbì [张 zhāng]

Keywords

Certain commonly used words, such as *have* and *do*, have been treated in special depth because they constitute basic elements of English and have very many uses and meaning. We have given them a special design to make it easier to find the meaning of construction you are looking for.

KEYWORD

have [həv, STRONG hæv] (*pt, pp* **had**) **I** VT **1** 有 yǒu ▸ **he has** *or* **he has got blue eyes/dark hair** 他长着蓝眼睛/黑头发 tā zhángzhe lán yǎnjīng/hēi tóufa ▸ **do you have** *or* **have you got a car/phone?** 你有车/电话吗? nǐ yǒu chē/diànhuà ma? ▸ **to have sth to do** 有必须得做的事 yǒu bìxū děi zuò de shì ▸ **she had her eyes closed** 她闭上了眼睛 tā bìshàng le yǎnjīng

Language notes

Language notes have been given at certain entries on the Chinese side, for example, 盏 zhǎn and 捌 bā. These are intended to give learners more information about certain important aspects of the Chinese language.

Cultural notes

A number of entries include cultural notes, giving an insight into Chinese life and culture. These notes cover many subject areas including political institutions and systems, national festivals and Chinese traditions and customs.

略语表
Abbreviations in This Work

Parts of speech — 词性

abbreviation	*ABBR*	简
adjective	*ADJ*	形
adverb	*ADV*	副
auxiliary verb	*AUX VB*	助动
conjunction	*CONJ*	连
compound	*CPD*	复合词
definite article	*DEF ART*	定冠词
indefinite article	*INDEF ART*	不定冠词
interjection	*INT*	叹
noun	*N*	名
noun abbreviation	*N ABBR*	名词缩写
singular noun	*N SING*	单数名词
noun (plural)	*N(PL)*	名（复数）
noun plural	*NPL*	复数名词
numeral	*NUM*	数
plural	*PL*	复数
plural adjective	*PL ADJ*	复数形容词
plural pronoun	*PL PRON*	复数代词
past participle	*PP*	过去分词
prefix	*PREFIX*	前缀
preposition	*PREP*	介
pres part	*PRES PART*	现在分词
pronoun	*PRON*	代
past tense	*PT*	过去时
suffix	*SUFFIX*	后缀
verb	*VB*	动
intransitive verb	*VI*	不及物动词
transitive verb	*VT*	及物动词
indicates that particle cannot be separated from the main verb	*VT FUS*	及物动词

Subject field labels — 专业学科领域

Administration	*Admin*	行政
Agriculture	*Agr*	农
Anatomy	*Anat*	解剖
Architecture	*Archit*	建筑
Art		艺术
Astrology	*Astrol*	占星术
Astronomy	*Astron*	天文
Automobiles	*Aut*	汽车

Subject field labels　专业学科领域

Aviation	*Aviat*	航空
Badminton		羽毛球
Baseball		棒球
Biology	*Bio*	生物
Bookkeeping		簿记
Botany	*Bot*	植物
Bowls		滚木球
Boxing		拳击
Cards		纸牌
Chemistry	*Chem*	化
Chess		国际象棋
Cinema	*Cine*	电影
Climbing		登山
Clothing		服饰
Commerce	*Comm*	商
Computing	*Comput*	计算机
Cricket		板球
Cooking	*Culin*	烹饪
Drawing		绘画
Drugs		药品
Economics	*Econ*	经济
Electricity	*Elec*	电子
Fencing		击剑
Finance	*Fin*	金融
Fishing		钓鱼
Football		足球
Geography	*Geo*	地理
Geology	*Geol*	地质
Geometry	*Geom*	几何
Golf		高尔夫
Grammar	*Gram*	语法
History	*Hist*	历史
Industry	*Ind*	工业
Insurance		保险
Law		法
Linguistics	*Ling*	语言
Literature	*Liter*	文学
Mathematics	*Math*	数
Medicine	*Med*	医
Meteorology	*Met*	气象
Military	*Mil*	军
Mining	*Min*	矿
Music	*Mus*	音
Mythology	*Myth*	神
Nautical	*Naut*	航海
Parliament	*Parl*	议会
Philosophy	*Phil*	哲

Subject field labels 专业学科领域

Photography	*Phot*	摄影
Physics	*Phys*	物
Physiology	*Physiol*	生理
Politics	*Pol*	政治
Police		警察
Post office	*Post*	邮政
Psychology	*Psych*	心理
Publishing		出版
Radio	*Rad*	广播
Railways	*Rail*	铁路
Religion	*Rel*	宗
Rugby		橄榄球
Science	*Sci*	科学
School	*Scol*	教育
	Sewing	缝纫
Sociology	*Sociol*	社会
Space		宇航
Sport		体育
Technical usage	*Tech*	术语
Telecommunications	*Tel*	电信
Tennis		网球
Texting		手机短信
Theater	*Theat*	戏剧
Television	*TV*	电视
University	*Univ*	大学
Zoology	*Zool*	动

Register labels 修辞色彩缩略语

dialect		方
euphemism		婉
formal	*frm*	正式
formerly		旧
humorous		诙谐
informal	*inf*	非正式
literary	*liter*	文
offensive		侮辱
old-fashioned	*o.f.*	过时
offensive	*inf!*	疑讳/讳
pejorative	*pej*	贬
humble		谦
respectful		敬
slang		俚
spoken language		口
written		书
polite		客套
literal	*lit*	字
figurative	*fig*	喻

不规则动词
English Irregular Verbs

present	pt	pp	present	pt	pp
arise	arose	arisen	**eat**	ate	eaten
awake	awoke	awoken	**fall**	fell	fallen
be (am, is,	was, were	been	**feed**	fed	fed
are; being)			**feel**	felt	felt
bear	bore	born(e)	**fight**	fought	fought
beat	beat	beaten	**find**	found	found
begin	began	begun	**fling**	flung	flung
bend	bent	bent	**fly**	flew	flown
bet	bet,	bet,	**forbid**	forbad(e)	forbidden
	betted	betted	**forecast**	forecast	forecast
bid *(at*	bid	bid	**forget**	forgot	forgotten
auction)			**forgive**	forgave	forgiven
bind	bound	bound	**freeze**	froze	frozen
bite	bit	bitten	**get**	got	got,
bleed	bled	bled			(US)
blow	blew	blown			gotten
break	broke	broken	**give**	gave	given
breed	bred	bred	**go** (goes)	went	gone
bring	brought	brought	**grind**	ground	ground
build	built	built	**grow**	grew	grown
burn	burned	burned	**hang**	hung	hung
	(*o* burnt)	(*o* burnt)	**hang**	hanged	hanged
burst	burst	burst	(execute)		
buy	bought	bought	**have**	had	had
can	could	(been	**hear**	heard	heard
		able)	**hide**	hid	hidden
cast	cast	cast	**hit**	hit	hit
catch	caught	caught	**hold**	held	held
choose	chose	chosen	**hurt**	hurt	hurt
cling	clung	clung	**keep**	kept	kept
come	came	come	**kneel**	knelt,	knelt,
cost	cost	cost		kneeled	kneeled
creep	crept	crept	**know**	knew	known
cut	cut	cut	**lay**	laid	laid
deal	dealt	dealt	**lead**	led	led
dig	dug	dug	**lean**	leaned	leaned
do (does)	did	done		(*o* leant)	(*o* leant)
draw	drew	drawn	**leap**	leaped	leaped
dream	dreamed,	dreamed,		(*o* leapt)	(*o* leapt)
	dreamt	dreamt	**learn**	learned	learned
drink	drank	drunk		(*o* learnt)	(*o* learnt)
drive	drove	driven	**leave**	left	left

present	**pt**	**pp**	**present**	**pt**	**pp**
lend	lent	lent	**smell**	smelled	smelled
let	let	let		(*o* smelt)	(*o* smelt)
lie (lying)	lay	lain	**sow**	sowed	sown,
light	lit,	lit,			sowed
	lighted	lighted	**speak**	spoke	spoken
lose	lost	lost	**speed**	sped,	sped,
make	made	made		speeded	speeded
may	might	–	**spell**	spelled	spelled
mean	meant	meant		(*o* spelt)	(*o* spelt)
meet	met	met	**spend**	spent	spent
mistake	mistook	mistaken	**spill**	spilt,	spilt,
mow	mowed	mown,		spilled	spilled
		mowed	**spin**	spun	spun
must	(had to)	(had to)	**spit**	spat	spat
pay	paid	paid	**spoil**	spoiled	spoiled
put	put	put		(*o* spoilt)	(*o* spoilt)
quit	quit,	quit,	**spread**	spread	spread
	quitted	quitted	**spring**	sprang	sprung
read	read	read	**stand**	stood	stood
rid	rid	rid	**steal**	stole	stolen
ride	rode	ridden	**stick**	stuck	stuck
ring	rang	rung	**sting**	stung	stung
rise	rose	risen	**stink**	stank	stunk
run	ran	run	**stride**	strode	stridden
saw	sawed	sawed,	**strike**	struck	struck
		sawn	**swear**	swore	sworn
say	said	said	**sweep**	swept	swept
see	saw	seen	**swell**	swelled	swollen,
sell	sold	sold			swelled
send	sent	sent	**swim**	swam	swum
set	set	set	**swing**	swung	swung
sew	sewed	sewn	**take**	took	taken
shake	shook	shaken	**teach**	taught	taught
shear	sheared	shorn,	**tear**	tore	torn
		sheared	**tell**	told	told
shed	shed	shed	**think**	thought	thought
shine	shone	shone	**throw**	threw	thrown
shoot	shot	shot	**thrust**	thrust	thrust
show	showed	shown	**tread**	trod	trodden
shrink	shrank	shrunk	**wake**	woke,	woken,
shut	shut	shut		waked	waked
sing	sang	sung	**wear**	wore	worn
sink	sank	sunk	**weave**	wove	woven
sit	sat	sat	**weep**	wept	wept
sleep	slept	slept	**win**	won	won
slide	slid	slid	**wind**	wound	wound
sling	slung	slung	**wring**	wrung	wrung
slit	slit	slit	**write**	wrote	written

英语发音指导
Guide to English Phonetics

Consonants / 辅音

[b] baby
[t] tent
[d] daddy
[k] cork kiss chord
[g] gag guess
[s] so rice kiss
[z] cousin buzz
[ʃ] sheep sugar
[ʒ] pleasure beige
[tʃ] church
[dʒ] judge general
[f] farm raffle
[v] very rev
[θ] thin math
[ð] that other
[l] little ball
[r] rat rare
[m] mommy comb
[n] no ran
[ŋ] singing bank
[p] puppy
[h] hat reheat
[x] loch

Semivowels / 半元音

[y]	yet
[w]	wet

Vowels / 元音

[i]	heel
[ɪ]	hit pity
[ɛ]	set tent
[æ]	bat apple
[ɑ]	car calm
[ʌ]	fun cousin
[ə]	over above
[ɜ]	urn fern work
[ɔ]	wash pot
[ʊ]	full soot
[u]	pool lewd

Diphthongs / 双元音

[ɪə]	beer tier
[ɛə]	tear fair there
[eɪ]	date plaice day
[aɪ]	life buy cry
[aʊ]	owl foul now
[ou]	low no
[ɔɪ]	boil boy oily
[ʊə]	poor tour

Radical Index

There is no way of predicting the sound and meaning of an unknown Chinese character with any degree of accuracy. This does not mean, however, that there is no system behind the characters at all. All characters contain at least one of the component parts known as radicals or head components, and almost all radicals will have an element of meaning; if you are familiar with these, not only will using a dictionary be much easier, it will also help you identify more of the building blocks you are trying to learn.

If you come across a character that you aren't familiar with, and so don't know the pronunciation of, you can look it up in the radical index, as follows:

1. Use the Radical Index on pages 26a–27a to identify the radical according to the number of strokes. Note the number preceding it.
2. In the Character Index on pages 28a–52a, use this number to find all the characters appearing in this dictionary which contain that radical. Characters are ordered according to the number of strokes (not including the radical). The pinyin given will lead you to the correct entry on the Chinese-English side of the dictionary.

1 stroke

1 一
2 丨
3 丿
4 丶
5 乙（乚乛）

2 strokes

6 二
7 匕
8 丷
9 十
10 厂
11 匚
12 刂
13 卜
14 冂
15 亻
16 八
17 人（入）
18 勹
19 几
20 儿
21 亠
22 冫
23 冖
24 讠
25 卩 *(on the left)*
26 阝 *(on the right)*
27 阝
28 凵
29 刀
30 力
31 厶
32 又
33 廴

3 strokes

34 巛
35 巳
36 工
37 土
38 士
39 扌
40 艹
41 寸 *(underneath)*
42 廾
43 大
44 尢
45 小
46 口
47 囗
48 巾
49 山
50 彳
51 彡
52 犭
53 夕
54 夂
55 饣
56 丬
57 广

58 忄
59 门
60 氵
61 宀
62 辶
63 彐（彑）
64 尸
65 弓
66 子
67 女
68 纟
69 马
70 幺

4 strokes

71 毋
72 王
73 韦
74 木
75 犬
76 歹
77 车
78 比
79 瓦
80 止
81 支
82 日
83 曰
84 水
85 贝
86 见
87 牛
88 手
89 毛
90 气
91 攵
92 片
93 斤
94 爪(爫)
95 父
96 月
97 欠
98 风
99 文
100 方
101 火
102 斗
103 灬
104 户
105 礻
106 心
107 肀(聿)
108 戈
109 毋

5 strokes

110 示
111 甘
112 石
113 龙
114 目
115 田
116 罒
117 皿
118 钅
119 矢
120 禾
121 白
122 瓜
123 鸟
124 疒
125 立
126 穴
127 衤
128 疋
129 皮
130 矛

6 strokes

131 耒
132 自
133 老（耂）
134 耳
135 西（覀）
136 页
137 虍
138 虫
139 缶
140 舌
141 竹（）
142 臼
143 血
144 舟
145 衣
146 羊
147 米
148 艮
149 羽
150 糸

7 strokes

151 赤
152 走
153 豆
154 酉
155 里
156 足（⻊）
157 身
158 采
159 豸
160 角
161 言（訁 see 讠）
162 辛

8 strokes

163 齿
164 谷
165 金
166 青
167 雨
168 隹
169 鱼

9 strokes

170 革
171 韭
172 骨
173 鬼
174 食

10 strokes

175 髟

11 strokes

176 麻

12 strokes

177 黑
178 黍

13 strokes

179 鼠

14 strokes

180 鼻

Character Index

13 strokes
舞 wǔ
疑 yí

14 strokes
靠 kào

4 丶

2 strokes
之 zhī

3 strokes
为 wéi

4 strokes
半 bàn
主 zhǔ
头 tóu

5 strokes
兴 xīng
农 nóng

6 strokes
良 liáng

7 strokes
学 xué

8 strokes
举 jǔ

5 乙（乚⺄）

2 strokes
乞 qǐ
也 yě
飞 fēi
习 xí
乡 xiāng

3 strokes
巴 bā
孔 kǒng
书 shū

5 strokes
买 mǎi

6 strokes
乱 luàn

7 strokes
乳 rǔ

6 二

二 èr

2 strokes
元 yuán
云 yún

6 strokes
些 xiē

7 匕

9 strokes
匙 chí

8 丷

3 strokes
兰 lán

5 strokes
兑 duì

8 strokes
兼 jiān

9 strokes
兽 shòu

9 十

十 shí

2 strokes
支 zhī

3 strokes
古 gǔ

4 strokes
考 kǎo
协 xié
毕 bì
华 huá

5 strokes
克 kè

6 strokes
卓 zhuō
卑 bēi
卖 mài

7 strokes
南 nán

8 strokes
真 zhēn

10 strokes
博 bó

10 厂

厂 chǎng

2 strokes
厄 è
历 lì
厅 tīng

4 strokes
压 yā
厌 yàn

6 strokes
厕 cè

7 strokes
厚 hòu

8 strokes
原 yuán
厘 lí

9 strokes
厩 jiù
厢 xiāng

10 strokes
厨 chú
夏 xià

11 匚

2 strokes
区 qū ōu

5 strokes
医 yī

8 strokes
匪 fěi
匿 nì

12 刂

3 strokes
刊 kān

4 strokes
创 chuāng chuàng
划 huá
刑 xíng
列 liè
刚 gāng

5 strokes
刨 bào
别 bié

利 lì
判 pàn
删 shān

6 strokes
刺 cì
到 dào
剂 jì
制 zhì
刮 guā
刻 kè
刹 shā
刷 shuā

7 strokes
剑 jiàn
前 qián
剃 tì
削 xuē

8 strokes
剥 bāo
剥 bō
剧 jù

9 strokes
副 fù

10 strokes
割 gē
剩 shèng

13 卜

3 strokes
卢 lú
占 zhān zhàn
外 wài

6 strokes
卧 wò

8 strokes
桌 zhuō

14 冂

2 strokes
冈 gāng
内 nèi

4 strokes
同 tóng
网 wǎng

15 亻

2 strokes
化 huà
仆 pú
什 shén shí
仍 réng
仁 rén
仅 jǐn

3 strokes
代 dài
付 fù
仪 yí
他 tā
仙 xiān

4 strokes
伊 yī
传 chuán zhuàn
份 fèn
伏 fú
仰 yǎng
伙 huǒ
价 jià
休 xiū
优 yōu
件 jiàn
伦 lún
任 rèn
伤 shāng
似 sì
伪 wěi
仲 zhòng

5 strokes
估 gū
何 hé
体 tǐ
但 dàn
伸 shēn
作 zuò
伯 bó
低 dī
你 nǐ
住 zhù
位 wèi
伴 bàn
佛 fó

6 strokes
供 gōng
拱 gǒng
使 shǐ
例 lì
侨 qiáo
侄 zhí
侧 cè
依 yī
侦 zhēn

7 strokes
俘 fú
侯 hóu hòu
俊 jùn
侵 qīn
修 xiū
保 bǎo
便 biàn pián
促 cù
俄 é
侮 wǔ
信 xìn

8 strokes
倘 tǎng
俯 fǔ
借 jiè
倦 juàn
倔 jué
值 zhí
倾 qīng
倒 dǎo
倍 bèi
健 jiàn
俱 jù

9 strokes
偿 cháng
假 jià
做 zuò
偶 ǒu
偏 piān
偷 tōu
停 tíng
假 jià

10 strokes
傲 ào
傧 bīn
储 chǔ

11 strokes
催 cuī
傻 shǎ

像 xiàng

13 strokes

僵 jiāng

14 strokes

16 八

0 strokes

八 bā

2 strokes

分 fēn

公 gōng

3 strokes

4 strokes

共 gòng

关 guān

5 strokes

兵 bīng

6 strokes

其 qí

具 jù

典 diǎn

卷 juǎn

单 chán dān

7 strokes

养 yǎng

首 shǒu

8 strokes

益 yì

9 strokes

黄 huáng

10 strokes

普 pǔ

曾 céng

17 人 (入)

人 rén

入 rù

1 stroke

个 gè

2 strokes

仓 cāng

介 jiè

从 cōng cóng

今 jīn

以 yǐ

3 strokes

令 lìng

4 strokes

全 quán

会 huì kuài

合 hé

企 qǐ

伞 sǎn

众 zhòng

5 strokes

余 yú

含 hán

6 strokes

舍 shě

8 strokes

拿 ná

9 strokes

盒 hé

10 strokes

舒 shū

18 勹

1 stroke

勺 sháo

2 strokes

勾 gōu

3 strokes

句 jù

匆 cōng

包 bāo

4 strokes

匈 xiōng

9 strokes

够 gòu

19 几

几 jī jǐ

2 strokes

凤 fèng

6 strokes

凭 píng

12 strokes

凳 dèng

20 儿

儿 ér

2 strokes

允 yǔn

3 strokes

兄 xiōng

4 strokes

光 guāng

先 xiān

9 strokes

兜 dōu

21 亠

2 strokes

六 liù

3 strokes

市 shì

4 strokes

交 jiāo

产 chǎn

充 chōng

亦 yì

6 strokes

京 jīng

享 xiǎng

夜 yè

7 strokes

亮 liàng

亭 tíng

8 strokes

高 gāo

旁 páng

9 strokes

商 shāng

10 strokes

就 jiù

12 strokes

豪 háo

15 strokes

赢 yíng

22 冫

4 strokes

次 cì

冲 chōng
决 jué
冰 bīng

5 strokes
冻 dòng
冷 lěng

8 strokes
准 zhǔn
凉 liáng

9 strokes
减 jiǎn

10 strokes
寒 hán

14 strokes
凝 níng

23 冖

2 strokes
冗 rǒng

3 strokes
写 xiě

4 strokes
军 jūn

7 strokes
冠 guàn

24 讠

2 strokes
讣 fù
讥 jī
计 jì
订 dìng
认 rèn

3 strokes
讨 tǎo
让 ràng
训 xùn
议 yì
记 jì
讯 xùn

4 strokes
讽 fěng
讲 jiǎng
诀 jué
许 xǔ
论 lúnlùn
设 shè
访 fǎng

5 strokes
词 cí
证 zhèng
评 píng
译 yì
词 cí
识 shí
诉 sù
诈 zhà
诊 zhěn
诅 zǔ

6 strokes
试 shì
诗 shī
诚 chéng
诡 guǐ
诙 huī
话 huà
询 xún
该 gāi
详 xiáng

7 strokes
诵 sòng
语 yǔ
误 wù
诱 yòu
说 shuō shuì

8 strokes
诺 nuò
谁 shéi
请 qǐng
课 kè
调 diào tiáo
谈 tán
谊 yì

9 strokes
谎 huǎng
谚 yàn
谜 mí

10 strokes
谢 xiè
谣 yáo
谦 qiān

11 strokes
谨 jǐn

25 卩

1 stroke
卫 wèi

3 strokes
印 yìn

4 strokes
危 wēi

5 strokes
卵 luǎn
却 què
即 jí

7 strokes
卸 xiè

26 阝

2 strokes
队 duì

4 strokes
邦 bāng
阳 yáng
阶 jiē
阴 yīn
防 fáng

5 strokes
陈 chén
陆 lù
阿 ā
阻 zǔ
附 fù

6 strokes
郁 yù
郎 láng
陋 lòu
陌 mò
降 jiàng
限 xiàn

7 strokes
陨 yǔn
除 chú
陡 dǒu
险 xiǎn
院 yuàn

8 strokes
陪 péi
陶 táo
陷 xiàn

9 strokes
随 suí
隐 yǐn

10 strokes
鄙 bǐ
障 zhàng

12 strokes
隧 suì

27 阝

4 strokes
邪 xié
那 nà

5 strokes
邻 lín
邮 yóu

6 strokes
耶 yē
郊 jiāo

8 strokes
部 bù

28 凵

2 strokes
凶 xiōng

3 strokes
凹 āo
击 jī

6 strokes
画 huà

7 strokes
幽 yōu

10 strokes
凿 záo

29 刀

刀 dāo

2 strokes
切 qiē

4 strokes
负 fù
色 sè

5 strokes
初 chū

6 strokes
兔 tù

9 strokes
剪 jiǎn
象 xiàng

30 力

力 lì

2 strokes
办 bàn

3 strokes
加 jiā

4 strokes
动 dòng
劣 liè

5 strokes
劳 láo
男 nán
努 nǔ
助 zhù

6 strokes
势 shì

7 strokes
勇 yǒng

9 strokes
勘 kān
勒 lè

31 厶

3 strokes
去 qù
台 tái

6 strokes
参 cān

8 strokes
能 néng

32 又

1 stroke
叉 chā

2 strokes
友 yǒu
劝 quàn
双 shuāng

3 strokes
发 fā
圣 shèng
对 duì

4 strokes
戏 xì
观 guān
欢 huān

5 strokes
鸡 jī

6 strokes
变 biàn
取 qǔ
叔 shū
受 shòu

7 strokes
叙 xù

8 strokes
难 nán
桑 sāng

33 廴

4 strokes
延 yán

6 strokes
建 jiàn

34 巛

8 strokes
巢 cháo

35 巳

6 strokes
巷 xiàng

36 工

工 gōng

1 stroke
巨 jù

2 strokes
左 zuǒ
巧 qiǎo

3 strokes
式 shì

4 strokes
攻 gōng
巫 wū

6 strokes
项 xiàng

---

37 土

土 tǔ

3 strokes
埃 āi
场 cháng
圭 guī
寺 sì
地 de dì
在 zài
至 zhì

4 strokes
坠 zhuì
址 zhǐ
坏 huài
均 jūn
坑 kēng
坟 fén
块 kuài
坚 jiān
坐 zuò
社 shè

5 strokes
垂 chuí
垃 lā
垄 lǒng
坡 pō
坦 tǎn
幸 xìng

6 strokes
型 xíng
城 chéng
垫 diàn

7 strokes
埋 mái

8 strokes
域 yù
堵 dǔ
堆 duī
堕 duò
培 péi
基 jī
堂 táng

9 strokes
堡 bǎo
堤 dī
塑 sù
塔 tǎ

10 strokes
塞 sài
墓 mù
填 tián

11 strokes
境 jìng
墙 qiáng
墅 shù

12 strokes
增 zēng
墨 mò

13 strokes
壁 bì

---

38 士

士 shì

3 strokes
壮 zhuàng

4 strokes
壳 ké
声 shēng

7 strokes
壶 hú

9 strokes
喜 xǐ

10 strokes
鼓 gǔ

---

39 扌

才 cái

1 stroke
扎 zhā

2 strokes
打 dá dǎ
扒 pá
扑 pū
扔 rēng

3 strokes
扣 kòu
执 zhí
扬 yáng
扩 kuò
扫 sǎo sào
托 tuō

4 strokes
把 bà
扳 bān
版 bǎn
扮 bàn
报 bào
抄 chāo
扯 chě
扼 è
扶 fú
抚 fǔ
护 hù
技 jì
拒 jù
抗 kàng
扭 niǔ
抛 pāo
找 zhǎo
批 pī
扰 rǎo
抢 qiǎng
折 shé zhé
抑 yì
抓 zhuā
投 tóu

5 strokes
抹 mò
拘 jū
招 zhāo
拔 bá
抱 bào
拨 bō
拆 chāi
抽 chōu

押 yā
拥 yōng
担 dān
抵 dǐ
拐 guǎi
拉 lā
拎 līn
抹 mā
拍 pāi
披 pī
拖 tuō

6 strokes

指 zhí
挣 zhēng
拱 gǒng
拮 jié
挪 nuó
按 àn
持 chí
挡 dǎng
挂 guà
挥 huī
挤 jǐ
括 kuò
拼 pīn
拾 shí
挑 tiāo tiǎo
指 zhǐ
挖 wā

7 strokes

捕 bǔ
换 huàn
捐 juān
捉 zhuō
挫 cuò
损 sǔn

8 strokes

掷 zhì
掉 diào
搅 jiǎo
接 jiē
捷 jié
控 kòng
排 pái
掐 qiā
授 shòu
探 tàn
推 tuī
掩 yǎn

9 strokes

揣 chuǎi
援 yuán
搓 cuō
提 dī tí
搭 dā
插 chā

10 strokes

摆 bǎi
搬 bān
摇 yáo
搞 gǎo
摄 shè
摊 tān

11 strokes

摧 cuī
撇 piě
摔 shuāi

12 strokes

播 bō
撞 zhuàng
撑 chēng
撬 qiào
撕 sī

13 strokes

操 cāo
擀 gǎn

14 strokes

擦 cā

20 strokes

攫 jué

---

40 艹

---

1 stroke

艺 yì

2 strokes

艾 ài
节 jié

3 strokes

芒 máng

4 strokes

芭 bā
苍 cāng
芳 fāng
芬 fēn
花 huā
芥 jiè
芦 lú
芹 qín
芜 wú
苏 sū
芯 xìn
芫 yuán

5 strokes

茅 máo
苛 kē
苦 kǔ
若 ruò
苹 píng
英 yīng
茄

6 strokes

茶 chá
茴 huí
茄 qié
荨 qián
草 cǎo
荒 huāng
荣 róng
药 yào
荫 yìn
荧 yíng

7 strokes

荷 hé
获 huò
莫 mò

8 strokes

菲 fēi
萎 wěi
菊 jú
萨 sà
著 zhù
萝 luó
菜 cài
菠 bō
营 yíng

9 strokes

葬 zàng
葱 cōng
董 dǒng
葡 pú
落 luò

10 strokes
蓟 jì
蓝 lán
蒲 pú
蒜 suàn
蒙 mēng
蒸 zhēng

12 strokes
蕃 fán
蕉 jiāo
蕨 jué
蔬 shū

13 strokes
薄 bò bù
薯 shǔ
薪 xīn

14 strokes
藏 cáng zàng

15 strokes
藤 téng

16 strokes
藻 zǎo

19 strokes
蘸 zhàn

41 寸

3 strokes
寻 xún
导 dǎo

6 strokes
封 fēng
耐 nài

7 strokes
射 shè

9 strokes
尊 zūn

42 廾

3 strokes
异 yì

4 strokes
弄 nòng lòng
弃 qì

43 大

大 dà

1 stroke
太 tài

3 strokes
夸 kuā
夹 jiā
尖 jiān

5 strokes
奔 bēn bèn
奉 fèng
奇 jī qí
态 tài

6 strokes
美 měi
奖 jiǎng

7 strokes
套 tào

8 strokes
奢 shē

9 strokes
奥 ào

44 尢

1 stroke
尤 yóu

2 strokes
龙 lóng

10 strokes
尴 gān

45 小

小 xiǎo

1 stroke
少 shǎo

3 strokes
当 dāng

6 strokes
省 shěng
尝 cháng

9 strokes
掌 zhǎng

46 口

口 kǒu

2 strokes
叨 dāo
号 hào
叫 jiào
另 lìng
司 sī
右 yòu
叹 tàn

3 strokes
吊 diào
吉 jí
吗 mǎ
吐 tù
吓 xià
吃 chī
吸 xī
各 gè

4 strokes
员 yuán
吧 bā
吵 chǎo
呃 è
君 jūn
吹 chuī
吨 dūn
否 fǒu
告 gào
吝 lìn
呕 ǒu
启 qǐ
吮 shǔn
听 tīng
吞 tūn
吟 yín

5 strokes
咕 gū
咔 kā
味 wèi
呼 hū
咖 gā kā
和 hé
咆 páo

6 strokes
哈 hā
咳 hāi ké
哪 nǎ

品 pǐn
虽 suī
咸 xián
哑 yǎ
响 xiǎng
咬 yǎo

7 strokes
哺 bǔ
唇 chún
哽 gěng
唤 huàn
哭 kū
唠 láo
哮 xiào
哲 zhé

8 strokes
唱 chàng
啤 pí
售 shòu
唯 wéi
唾 tuò
唷 yō

9 strokes
喊 hǎn
喀 kā
喧 xuān
喝 hē
喉 hóu
喷 pēn
善 shàn
喂 wèi

10 strokes
嗅 xiù

12 strokes
潮 cháo

13 strokes
嘴 zuǐ
器 qì
噪 zào

17 strokes
嚼 jiáo

19 strokes
囊 náng

47 口

2 strokes
囚 qiú
四 sì

3 strokes
因 yīn
回 huí
团 tuán

4 strokes
囤 tún
园 yuán
围 wéi
困 kùn

5 strokes
固 gù
国 guó
图 tú

7 strokes
圆 yuán

8 strokes
圈 juān quàn

48 巾

巾 jīn

2 strokes
布 bù

3 strokes
帆 fān

4 strokes
帐 zhàng
希 xī

5 strokes
帕 pà
贴 tiē tiě
帘 lián

6 strokes
帮 bāng
带 dài
帝 dì

8 strokes
常 cháng

9 strokes
帽 mào

10 strokes
幕 mù

49 山

山 shān

3 strokes
岁 suì
岛 dǎo

4 strokes
岔 chà

5 strokes
岸 àn
岳 yuè
岩 yán

7 strokes
峰 fēng

8 strokes
崩 bēng
崇 chóng
崭 zhǎn

9 strokes
崽 zǎi

50 彳

3 strokes
行 háng xíng

4 strokes
彻 chè

5 strokes
征 zhēng
往 wǎng

6 strokes
待 dāi
律 lù
很 hěn

7 strokes
徒 tú

8 strokes
徜 cháng
得 dé děi
徘 pái
徙 xǐ

9 strokes
循 xún
街 jiē

10 strokes
微 wēi

12 strokes
德 dé

14 strokes
徽 huī

51 彡

4 strokes
形 xíng

6 strokes
须 xū

8 strokes
彩 cǎi

12 strokes
影 yǐng

52 犭

2 strokes
犯 fàn
狂 kuáng

4 strokes
犹 yóu

5 strokes
狐 hú
狗 gǒu

6 strokes
狩 shòu
狮 shī
狡 jiǎo
狭 xiá
独 dú
狱 yù

7 strokes
狼 láng

8 strokes
猪 zhū
猎 liè
猫 māo
猛 měng

9 strokes
猩 xīng
猴 hóu

17 strokes
獾 huān

53 夕

3 strokes
多 duō

8 strokes
梦 mèng

54 夂

2 strokes
处 chǔ chù
冬 dōng

4 strokes
麦 mài
条 tiáo

5 strokes
备 bèi

7 strokes
夏 xià

8 strokes
敷 fū

55 饣

2 strokes
饥 jī

4 strokes
饮 yǐn
饭 fàn

5 strokes
饱 bǎo
饰 shì

6 strokes
饺 jiǎo
饼 bǐng

7 strokes
饿 è
馅 xiàn

8 strokes
馆 guǎn

9 strokes
搜 sōu

56 丬

4 strokes
状 zhuàng

57 广

广 guǎng

3 strokes
庄 zhuāng
庆 qìng

4 strokes
庇 bì
床 chuáng
库 kù
序 xù
应 yīng

5 strokes
店 diàn
底 dǐ
废 fèi
庞 páng

6 strokes
度 dù
庭 tíng

7 strokes
唐 táng
席 xí
座 zuò

8 strokes
康 kāng
廊 láng
鹿 lù

15 strokes
鹰 yīng

58 忄

3 strokes
忏 chàn
忙 máng

4 strokes
怀 huái
快 kuài

5 strokes
怜 lián
性 xìng
怕 pà
怪 guài

6 strokes
恢 huī
恰 qià
恨 hèn

恤 xù

7 strokes
离 lí
悚 sǒng

8 strokes
惯 guàn
悸 jì
惊 jīng
情 qíng

9 strokes
愠 yùn
愤 fèn
禽 qín
愉 yú

10 strokes
慎 shèn

11 strokes
慷 kāng
慢 màn

12 strokes
懂 dǒng
懊 ào
憎 zēng

13 strokes
憾 hàn
懒 lǎn

---

59 门

门 mén

2 strokes
闪 shǎn

3 strokes
闭 bì
闯 chuǎng
问 wèn

4 strokes
间 jiàn
闲 xián
闷 mēn

5 strokes
闹 nào
闸 zhá

6 strokes
阁 gé
闻 wén

7 strokes
阄 jiū
阅 yuè

8 strokes
阐 chǎn

9 strokes
阑 lán

---

60 氵

---

2 strokes
汉 hàn
汇 huì
汁 zhī

3 strokes
池 chí
汗 hàn
污 wū
汤 tāng

4 strokes
泛 fàn
沟 gōu
沐 mù
沙 shā
汽 qì
没 méi
沉 chén

5 strokes
沼 zhǎo
沾 zhān
泽 zé
波 bō
沸 fèi
沮 jǔ
浅 jiān qiǎn
法 fǎ
河 hé
油 yóu
泡 pāo pào
泣 qì
注 zhù
泳 yǒng
泥 ní
沿 yán
治 zhì

6 strokes
测 cè
洞 dòng
洪 hóng
活 huó
浇 jiāo
洁 jié
津 jīn
浏 liú
派 pài
洋 yáng
浓 nóng
洒 sǎ
洗 xǐ
洲 zhōu

7 strokes
涤 dí
浮 fú
海 hǎi
浣 huàn
浪 làng
浸 jìn
浴 yù
流 liú
酒 jiǔ
涉 shè
涂 tú
消 xiāo
涌 yǒng
涨 zhǎng

8 strokes
渍 zì
淡 dàn
淀 diàn
混 hùn
淋 lín
淹 yān
清 qīng
渔 yú
液 yè
深 shēn
添 tiān
淫 yín

9 strokes
猶 yóu
游 yóu
渡 dù
港 gǎng
滑 huá
溅 jiàn
渴 kě
溃 kuì

湖 hú
湿 shī
温 wēn
滋 zī

10 strokes
溢 yì
滤 lù
满 mǎn
溺 nì
溜 liū
滚 gǔn
溶 róng

11 strokes
滴 dī
漫 màn
演 yǎn
漏 lòu
漂 piāo piǎo piào
漆 qī
漱 shù

12 strokes
澳 ào
澄 chéng
潘 pān
潜 qián

13 strokes
激 jī

15 strokes
瀑 pù

17 strokes
灌 guàn

61 宀

2 strokes
宁 nìng
它 tā

3 strokes
安 ān
守 shǒu

4 strokes
宏 hóng
完 wán

5 strokes
宝 bǎo
定 dìng
宠 chǒng
官 guān
审 shěn
实 shí

6 strokes
宫 gōng
室 shì
宪 xiàn
客 kè

7 strokes
害 hài
宽 kuān
家 jiā
宾 bīn
宵 xiāo

8 strokes
寂 jì
寄 jì
宿 sù

9 strokes
富 fù
率 shuài

10 strokes
塞 sāi

11 strokes
寡 guǎ
赛 sài

62 辶

2 strokes
边 biān

3 strokes
过 guò
迂 yū

4 strokes
进 jìn
还 huán
连 lián
近 jìn
返 fǎn
迟 chí
违 wéi

5 strokes
迪 dí
迫 pò

6 strokes
逆 nì
迹 jī
送 sòng
适 shì
逃 táo
迷 mí
退 tuì

7 strokes
递 dì
逗 dòu
逛 guàng
速 sù
通 tōng
透 tòu
逍 xiāo

8 strokes
逮 dài

9strokes
遇 yù
逾 yú
道 dào

11 strokes
遮 zhē

13 strokes
避 bì

63 彐 (彑)

2 strokes
归 guī

4 strokes
灵 líng

5 strokes
录 lù

8 strokes
彗 huì

64 尸

尸 shī

1 stroke
尺 chǐ

2 strokes
尼 ní

3 strokes
尽 jǐn jìn

4 strokes
层 céng
尿 niào suī
屁 pì
尾 wěi
局 jú

5 strokes
居 jū

6 strokes
屏 píng
屋 wū

7 strokes
屑 xiè

8 strokes
屠 tú

9 strokes
属 shǔ

65 弓

弓 gōng

5 strokes
弥 mí

6 strokes
弯 wān

7 strokes
弱 ruò

8 strokes
弹 dàn tán

9 strokes
强 qiáng

66 子

3 strokes
存 cún
孙 sūn

5 strokes
孤 gū
孟 mèng

6 strokes
孩 hái
孪 luán

67 女

2 strokes
奴 nú

3 strokes
妆 zhuāng
妇 fù
如 rú
她 tā
好 hǎo
好 hào
妈 mā

4 strokes
姊 zǐ
妒 dù
妨 fáng
妓 jì
妥 tuǒ

5 strokes
姆 mǔ
妻 qī
姑 gū
姐 jiě
始 shǐ
委 wěi
姓 xìng

6 strokes
姜 jiāng
耍 shuǎ
威 wēi
姻 yīn

7 strokes
娘 niáng
娴 xián

8 strokes
婚 hūn
婆 pó

9 strokes
媒 méi

10 strokes
嫉 jí
嫁 jià

11 strokes
嫩 nèn

12 strokes
嬉 xī

68 纟

2 strokes
纠 jiū

3 strokes
红 hóng
纤 xiān
级 jí
纪 jì

4 strokes
纵 zòng
纯 chún
纺 fǎng
纲 gāng
纹 wén
纬 wěi

5 strokes
练 liàn
绅 shēn
细 xì
线 xiàn
终 zhōng
绊 bàn
经 jīng

6 strokes
绑 bǎng
绘 huì
结 jiē jié
给 gěi
绝 jué
绕 rào
绒 róng
统 tǒng

7 strokes
继 jì
绢 juàn

8 strokes
绷 bēng
绰 chuò
绵 mián
绳 shéng
维 wéi
绿 lù
续 xù

9 strokes
编 biān
缓 huǎn
缆 lǎn

10 strokes
缝 féng
缚 fù

11 strokes
缩 suō

69 马

马 mǎ

3 strokes
驰 chí
驯 xùn

4 strokes
驳 bó
驱 qū

5 strokes
驾 jià
驹 jū

6 strokes
骇 hài
骂 mà
骄 jiāo
骆 luò

8 strokes
骑 qí

9 strokes
骗 piàn
骚 sāo

11 strokes
骡 luó

70 幺

1 stroke
幻 huàn

5 strokes
段 duàn

9 strokes
毂 gū
毁 huǐ

11 strokes
毅 yì

71 毋

毋 wú

72 王

王 wáng

4 strokes
玩 wán
环 huán
现 xiàn
玫 méi

5 strokes
玻 bō
珐 fà
皇 huáng
珊 shān

6 strokes
班 bān
珠 zhū

7 strokes
琐 suǒ
球 qiú
理 lǐ
望 wàng

8 strokes
琥 hǔ

9 strokes
瑜 yú
瑞 ruì

10 strokes
璃 lí

73 韦

8 strokes
韩 hán

74 木

1 stroke
本 běn
术 shù

2 strokes
机 jī
权 quán
杀 shā

3 strokes
杓 sháo
杜 dù
极 jí
李 lǐ
杆 gān
杠 gāng
材 cái
村 cūn

4 strokes
杳 yǎo
杯 bēi
枫 fēng
杰 jié
林 lín
柜 guì
板 bǎn
松 sōng
枪 qiāng
果 guǒ
采 cǎi

5 strokes
柱 zhù
栅 zhà
柚 yòu
标 biāo
查 chá
柑 gān
柬 jiǎn
枯 kū
相 xiāng
柳 liǔ
栏 lán
染 rǎn
树 shù
亲 qīn
架 jià
柔 róu

6 strokes
桩 zhuāng
案 àn
柴 chái
档 dàng
桦 huà
桂 guì
格 gé
根 gēn
核 hé
框 kuàng
栗 lì
桥 qiáo
桃 táo
校 jiǎo xiào
栽 zāi

桅 wéi

7 strokes
梵 fàn
检 jiǎn
梁 liáng
梳 shū
梯 tī
桶 tǒng
梨 lí
械 xiè

8 strokes
棕 zōng
棒 bàng
椎 chuí
棺 guān
集 jí
棘 jí
棉 mián
棚 péng
棋 qí
森 sēn
椭 tuǒ
椰 yē

9 strokes
榆 yú
概 gài
楼 lóu

10 strokes
榨 zhà
榛 zhēn

11 strokes
槽 cáo
橄 gǎn
横 héng
槲 hú
橡 xiàng

12 strokes
橙 chéng
橱 chú
橘 jú
橇 qiāo

75 犬

犬 quǎn

6 strokes
臭 chòu

76 歹

2 strokes
死 sǐ

5 strokes
残 cán

10 strokes
殡 bìn

77 车

车 chē

2 strokes
轨 guǐ

4 strokes
轰 hōng
轮 lún
软 ruǎn

5 strokes
轻 qīng

6 strokes
轿 jiào
较 jiào
载 zǎi zài

7 strokes
辅 fǔ
辆 liàng

8 strokes
辉 huī

9 strokes
辐 fú
输 shū

78 比

比 bǐ

79 瓦

6 strokes
瓷 cí
瓶 píng

80 止

2 strokes
此 cǐ

3 strokes
步 bù

4 strokes
歧 qí
武 wǔ
肯 kěn

81 支

10 strokes
敲 qiāo

82 日

日 rì

3 strokes
旱 hàn
旷 kuàng
时 shí

4 strokes
昂 áng
昏 hūn
昆 kūn
旺 wàng
昔 xī

5 strokes
春 chūn
是 shì
显 xiǎn
星 xīng
香 xiāng
映 yìng

6 strokes
晒 shài

7 strokes
晨 chén
晚 wǎn

8 strokes
量 liáng
晾 liàng
晶 jīng
景 jǐng
晴 qíng
替 tì

9 strokes
暗 àn

10 strokes
暖 ài

11 strokes
暴 bào

83 曰

2 strokes
曲 qū

5 strokes
冒 mào

84 水

水 shuǐ

5 strokes
泵 bèng

6 strokes
泰 tài
浆 jiāng

85 贝

贝 bèi

3 strokes
财 cái
贡 gòng

4 strokes
败 bài
贬 biǎn
贩 fàn
购 gòu
贯 guàn
货 huò
贫 pín
贪 tān
质 zhì
贮 zhù

5 strokes
贷 dài
费 fèi
贵 guì
贺 hè
贸 mào
贻 yí

6 strokes
贿 huì

8 strokes
赌 dǔ
赔 péi
赏 shǎng

86 见

见 jiàn

4 strokes
规 guī

5 strokes
觉 jué
览 lǎn

87 牛

3 strokes
牢 láo

4 strokes
物 wù

6 strokes
特 tè
牺 xī

7 strokes
犁 lí

88 手

手 shǒu

4 strokes
承 chéng

6 strokes
拳 quán

15 strokes
攀 pān

89 毛

毛 máo

5 strokes
毡 zhān

7 strokes
毫 háo

8 strokes
毯 tǎn

90 气

气 qì

5 strokes
氢 qīng

6 strokes
氧 yǎng

8 strokes
氮 dàn
氯 lù

91 攵

2 strokes
收 shōu

3 strokes
攸 yōu
改 gǎi

5 strokes
故 gù

6 strokes
敌 dí
效 xiào

7 strokes
敢 gǎn
教 jiāo jiào
救 jiù

8 strokes
敞 chǎng
散 sǎn
敬 jìng

9 strokes
数 shù

92 片

片 piān

4 strokes
版 bǎn

8 strokes
牌 pái

93 斤

4 strokes
斧 fǔ
欣 xīn

7 strokes
断 duàn

8 strokes
斯 sī

9 strokes
新 xīn

94 爪(爫)

爪 zhuǎ

4 strokes
爬 pá

6 strokes
爱 ài

13 strokes
爵 jué

95 父

父 fù

2 strokes
爷 yé

4 strokes
爸 bà

96 月

2 strokes
肌 jī
肋 lèi

3 strokes
肠 cháng
肝 gān
肚 dǔ dù
肖 xiào
肘 zhǒu

4 strokes
肮 āng
肥 féi
肺 fèi
服 fú
膏 gāo
股 gǔ
肩 jiān
朋 péng
肾 shèn
胁 xié
肿 zhǒng

5 strokes
胞 bāo
背 bēi bèi
胆 dǎn
胛 jiǎ
胫 jìng
胡 hú
脉 mài
胜 shèng
胎 tāi
胃 wèi

6 strokes
脂 zhī
胺 àn
脆 cuì
胳 gē gé
脊 jǐ
胶 jiāo
朗 lǎng
脓 nóng
胰 yí

7 strokes
豚 tún
脚 jiǎo
脖 bó
脸 liǎn
脱 tuō

8 strokes
朝 cháo
腱 jiàn
脾 pí
期 qī
腌 yān
腋 yè

9 strokes
腾 téng
腹 fù
腼 miǎn
腮 sāi
腺 xiàn
腿 tuǐ

10 strokes
膀 bǎng páng

11 strokes
膝 xī

12 strokes
膨 péng
膳 shàn

13 strokes
臂 bì
臀 tún

97 欠

欠 qiàn

4 strokes
欧 ōu

8 strokes
款 kuǎn
欺 qī

10 strokes
歌 gē

98 风

风 fēng

11 strokes
飘 piāo

99 文

文 wén

2 strokes
齐 qí

6 strokes
斋 zhāi

8 strokes
斑 bān
斐 fěi

100 方

方 fāng

4 strokes
放 fàng
房 fáng

5 strokes
施 shī

6 strokes
旅 lǚ

7 strokes
族 zú

10 strokes
旗 qí

101 火

火 huǒ

2 strokes
灰 huī
灯 dēng

3 strokes
灶 zào

4 strokes
炒 chǎo
炊 chuī
炖 dùn
炉 lú

5 strokes
烂 làn
炼 liàn
炫 xuàn

6 strokes
烘 hōng
烤 kǎo
烦 fán
烧 shāo
烫 tàng
烛 zhú

9 strokes
煤 méi
煨 wēi

10 strokes
熔 róng
熄 xī

12 strokes
燃 rán

15 strokes
爆 bào

102 斗

6 strokes
料 liào

7 strokes
斜 xié

103 灬

5 strokes
点 diǎn

6 strokes
烈 liè
热 rè

7 strokes
烹 pēng

8 strokes
焦 jiāo
然 rán

9 strokes
煎 jiān

10 strokes
熬 áo

11 strokes
熟 shú

104 户 hù

4 strokes
所 suǒ

5 strokes
扁 biǎn

6 strokes
扇 shān

105 礻

1 stroke
礼 lǐ

4 strokes
祈 qí
视 shì

5 strokes
神 shén

9 strokes
福 fú

106 心

心 xīn

1 stroke
必 bì

3 strokes
忘 wàng
忍 rěn
志 zhì

4 strokes
忽 hū
忠 zhōng

5 strokes
急 jí
思 sī
怨 yuàn

6 strokes
恳 kěn
恐 kǒng
恶 ě è
恋 liàn
息 xī

7 strokes
患 huàn

8 strokes
悲 bēi

惩 chéng

9 strokes
愈 yù
慈 cí
想 xiǎng
感 gǎn

107 肀(聿)

108 戈

2 strokes
成 chéng

3 strokes
戒 jiè

4 strokes
或 huò

14 strokes
戳 chuō

109 毋

5 strokes
毒 dú

110 示

示 shì

6 strokes
祭 jì
票 piào

8 strokes
禁 jìn

111 甘

甘 gān

112 石

石 shídàn

3 strokes
矿 kuàng
码 mǎ

4 strokes
砍 kǎn
砂 shā

5 strokes
破 pò

6 strokes
硅 guī

7 strokes
确 què

8 strokes
碑 bēi
碰 pèng
碎 suì
碗 wǎn

9 strokes
碧 bì
磁 cí
碟 dié
碳 tàn

10 strokes
磅 páng

11 strokes
磨 mò

113 龙

6 strokes
袭 xí

114 目

2 strokes
盯 dīng

3 strokes
盲 máng
直 zhí

4 strokes
眨 zhǎ
盾 dùn
看 kān kàn
眉 méi

5 strokes
眩 xuàn

6 strokes
着 zhāo zháo zhuō

8 strokes
睫 jié
睡 shuì

9 strokes
睾 gāo

10 strokes
瞌 kē

11 strokes
瞠 chēng
瞥 piē

12 strokes
瞳 tóng
瞬 shùn

115 田

甲 jiǎ
田 tián

3 strokes
畅 chàng

4 strokes
界 jiè

5 strokes
畚 běn
留 liú

6 strokes
累 lèi
略 lüè

7 strokes
番 fān

116 罒

3 strokes
罗 luó

4 strokes
罚 fá

5 strokes
罢 bà

8 strokes
置 zhì
罩 zhào

117 皿

4 strokes
盆 pén

5 strokes
盎 àng
监 jiān

6 strokes
盗 dào
盔 kuī
盘 pán
盖 gài

11 strokes
盥 guàn

118 钅

2 strokes
钉 dìng

3 strokes
钓 diào

4 strokes
钝 dùn
钙 gài
钞 chāo
钢 gāng
钩 gōu

5 strokes
铀 yóu
钹 bó
钱 qián
钳 qián
铁 tiě
铃 líng
铅 qiān

6 strokes
铲 chǎn
铬 gè
铐 kào
铝 lǚ
铜 tóng

7 strokes
铸 zhù
锉 cuò
链 liàn
铺 pū pù
销 xiāo
锁 suǒ
锅 guō
锋 fēng
锌 xīn

8 strokes
锥 zhuī
锤 chuí
错 cuò
键 jiàn
锦 jǐn

锯 jū jù
锚 máo
锡 xī

9 strokes
镀 dù
锹 qiāo

10 strokes
镊 niè

11 strokes
镜 jìng

17 strokes
镶 xiāng

119 矢

3 strokes
知 zhī

4 strokes
矩 jǔ

6 strokes
矫 jiǎo

7 strokes
短 duǎn

8 strokes
矮 ǎi

120 禾

2 strokes
私 sī
秃 tū

3 strokes
季 jì

4 strokes
秋 qiū
科 kē

5 strokes
秘 bì
称 chēng
积 jī
称 chēng
秘 mì

7 strokes
程 chéng
税 shuì
稀 xī

8 strokes
稠 chóu

9 strokes
稳 wěn

10 strokes
稽 jī

12 strokes
黏 nián

121 白

白 bái

2 strokes
皂 zào

3 strokes
的 de dí

122 瓜

瓜 guā

11 strokes
瓢 piáo

123 鸟

3 strokes
鸣 míng

5 strokes
鸵 tuó

6 strokes
鸽 gē

7 strokes
鹅 é
鹈 tí

8 strokes
鹌 ān

10 strokes
鹤 hè

11 strokes
鹦 yīng

12 strokes
鹪 jiāo

13 strokes
鹭 lù

124 疒

2 strokes
疗 liáo

3 strokes
疟 nüè
疝 shàn

4 strokes
疣 yóu
疤 bā
疯 fēng
疫 yì

5 strokes
病 bìng
疾 jí
痉 jìng
疲 pí
疼 téng
疹 zhěn
症 zhēng zhèng

6 strokes
痕 hén
痔 zhì

7 strokes
痣 zhì
痛 tòng

8 strokes
痴 chī

9 strokes
瘦 shòu

10 strokes
瘫 tān

12 strokes
癌 ái

13 strokes
癞 lài

21 strokes
癫 diān

125 立

立 lì

4 strokes
竖 shù

5 strokes
竞 jìng

7 strokes
童 tóng

9 strokes
端 duān

126 穴

3 strokes
空 kōng

4 strokes
突 tū
穿 chuān
窃 qiè

5 strokes
容 róng

6 strokes
窒 zhì

7 strokes
窗 chuāng
窘 jiǒng
窝 wō

8 strokes
窦 dòu
窟 kū
窥 kuī

127 衤

2 strokes
补 bǔ

3 strokes
衬 chèn
衫 shān

5 strokes
被 bèi
袜 wà

7 strokes
裤 kù
裙 qún

8 strokes
裸 luǒ

9 strokes
褐 hè

128 疋

6 strokes
蛋 dàn

7 strokes
疏 shū

129 皮

皮 pí

5 strokes
皱 zhòu

130 矛

矛 máo

131 耒

4 strokes
耕 gēng
耙 pá

132 自

自 zì

133 老 (耂)

老 lǎo

134 耳

耳 ěr

4 strokes
耽 dān
耸 sǒng

5 strokes
聊 liáo

6 strokes
联 lián

8 strokes
聚 jù

9 strokes
聪 cōng

135 西 (覀)

西 xī

12 strokes
覆 fù

136 页 yè

2 strokes
顶 dǐng

3 strokes
顺 shùn

4 strokes
颁 bān
顾 gù
颂 sòng
顽 wán

5 strokes
领 lǐng
颊 jiá

7 strokes
频 pín

9 strokes
颚 è
题 tí
额 é

10 strokes
颠 diān

13 strokes
颤 chàn

137 虍

3 strokes
虐 nüè

138 虫

虫 chóng

2 stroke
虱 shī

3 strokes
虹 hóng
虾 xiā
蚂 mǎ

4 strokes
蚕 cán
蚝 háo
蚊 wén

5 strokes
蛆 qū
蛇 shé
蚱 zhà

6 strokes
蛮 mán
蛙 wā

7 strokes
蜂 fēng
蜗 wō

8 strokes
蜡 là
蜻 qīng
蜥 xī

9 strokes
蝙 biān
蝴 hú
蝌 kē
蝾 róng
蝎 xiē
蟑 zhāng

10 strokes
螃 páng
融 róng

11 strokes
螺 luó
蟋 xī

14 strokes
蠕 rú

139 缶

3 strokes
缸 gāng

4 strokes
缺 quē

8 strokes
罂 yīng

17 strokes
罐 guàn

140 舌

舌 shé

5 strokes
甜 tián

8 strokes
舔 tiǎn

141 竹 ( )

3 strokes
笃 dǔ

4 strokes
笔 bǐ
笑 xiào

5 strokes
笨 bèn
笛 dí
笼 lóng
符 fú
第 dì

6 strokes
策 cè
等 děng
答 dá
筏 fá
筋 jīn
筛 shāi
筒 tǒng

7 strokes
签 qiān
筷 kuài
简 jiǎn

8 strokes
箔 bó
箍 gū
算 suàn
管 guǎn

9 strokes
箭 jiàn
篓 lǒu
箱 xiāng

10 strokes
篝 gōu
篮 lán
篱 lí

142 臼

7 strokes
舅 jiù

143 血

血 xiě

144 舟

4 strokes
舱 cāng
航 háng
舰 jiàn

5 strokes
船 chuán
舵 duò

6 strokes
艇 tǐng

145 衣

4 strokes
衰 shuāi

5 strokes
袋 dài

6 strokes
裁 cái
裂 liè

146 羊

5 strokes
羚 líng

6 strokes
羡 xiàn

7 strokes
群 qún

13 strokes
羹 gēng

147 米

米 mǐ

3 strokes
类 lèi

4 strokes
粉 fěn

5 strokes
粗 cū
粘 nián

6 strokes
粥 zhōu

8 strokes
精 jīng

9 strokes
糊 hū hú

10 strokes
糙 cāo
糖 táng
糕 gāo

11 strokes
糠 kāng

148 艮

3 strokes
既 jì

149 羽

4 strokes
翅 chì

8 strokes
翠 cuì

12 strokes
翻 fān
耀 yào

150 糸

4 strokes
紧 jǐn
素 sù
索 suǒ

11 strokes
繁 fán

151 赤

赤 chì

152 走

3 strokes
赶 gǎn
起 qǐ

5 strokes
趋 qū
超 chāo

8 strokes
趟 tàng

153 豆

豆 dòu

5 strokes
登 dēng

154 酉

3 strokes
配 pèi

6 strokes
酱 jiàng

7 strokes
酵 jiào
酿 niàng
酸 suān

8 strokes
醋 cù

155 里

里 lǐ

156 足（⻊）

4 strokes
距 jù

5 strokes
跋 bá
跛 bǒ
跌 diē
跨 kuà
跚 shān
跑 pǎo

6 strokes
跷 qiāo
跳 tiào
跪 guì
路 lù
跟 gēn

8 strokes
踩 cǎi
踝 huái
踏 tà
踢 tī

9 strokes
蹄 tí

10 strokes
蹒 pán

11 strokes
蹦 bèng

12 strokes
蹲 dūn

157 身

身 shēn

6 strokes
躲 duǒ

8 strokes
躺 tǎng

158 采

5 strokes
释 shì

159 豸

5 strokes
貂 diāo

7 strokes
豹 bào

160 角

角 jiǎo jué

6 strokes
触 chù
解 jiě

161 言（⾔ see 讠）

7 strokes
誓 shì

8 strokes
读 dú

12 strokes
警 jǐng
谱 pǔ

13 strokes
譬 pì
谴 qiǎn

162 辛

辛 xīn

5 strokes
辜 gū

6 strokes
辞 cí

7 strokes
辣 là

9 strokes
辩 biàn
辨 biàn

10 strokes
辫 biàn

163 齿

齿 chǐ

5 strokes
龄 líng

164 谷

谷 gǔ

165 金

金 jīn

166 青

青 qīng

5 strokes
鉴 jiàn

6 strokes
静 jìng

167 雨

5 strokes
雷 léi
零 líng
雾 wù

7 strokes
霉 méi
震 zhèn

9 strokes
霜 shuāng

13 strokes
露 lù

168 隹

4 strokes
雇 gù

5 strokes
雏 chú

8 strokes
雕 diāo
难 nàn

169 鱼

6 strokes
鲜 xiān

7 strokes
鲨 shā

8 strokes
鲱 fēi
鲸 jīng
鲭 qīng

9 strokes
鳄 è

10 strokes
鳏 guān
鳍 qí

11 strokes
鳗 mán
鳕 xuě

12 strokes
鳟 zūn

170 革

革 gé

6 strokes
鞋 xié
鞍 ān

8 strokes
鞠 jū

9 strokes
鞭 biān

171 韭

韭 jiǔ

172 骨

骨 gǔ

4 strokes
骰 tóu

5 strokes
骷 kū

10 strokes
髋 kuān

173 鬼

鬼 guǐ

5 strokes
魅 mèi

174 食

食 shí

7 strokes
餐 cān

175 髟

176 麻

麻 má

177 黑

黑 hēi

4 strokes
默 mò

9 strokes
黯 àn

178 黍

3 strokes
黎 lí

179 鼠

鼠 shǔ

10 strokes
鼹 yǎn

180 鼻

鼻 bí

Chinese–English Dictionary

A

阿 [ā] PREFIX (方) ▶ 阿爸 [ābà] dad
阿拉伯 [Ālābó] N Arabia
阿拉伯数字 [Ālābó shùzì] N Arabic numerals (PL)
阿姨 [āyí] N (指年长妇女) auntie

啊 [ā] INT oh ▷ 啊！着火了！ [Ā! Zháohuǒ le!] Oh! It's caught fire!

哎 [āi] INT 1 (表示惊讶或不满) oh ▷ 哎！这么贵！ [Āi! Zhème guì!] Oh! It's so expensive! 2 (表示提醒) hey ▷ 哎！别踩了那朵花。 [Āi! Bié cǎi le nà duǒ huā.] Hey! Careful not to step on that flower.
哎呀 [āiyā] INT oh ▷ 哎呀，这条路真难走！ [Āiyā, zhè tiáo lù zhēn nán zǒu!] Oh, this road is hard going!

哀 [āi] ADJ (悲痛) sad
哀悼 [āidào] VB mourn

挨 [āi] VB 1 (靠近) be next to ▷ 两个孩子挨着门坐。 [Liǎng gè háizi āi zhe mén zuò.] The two children sat by the door. 2 (逐个) ▶ 挨个儿 [āigèr] one by one
→ *see also*/另见 ái

挨 [ái] VB 1 (遭受) suffer ▶ 挨饿 [ái'è] suffer from hunger ▶ 挨骂 [áimà] get told off 2 (艰难度过) endure
挨打 [áidǎ] VB be beaten up

癌 [ái] N cancer ▶ 癌症 [áizhèng] cancer

矮 [ǎi] ADJ 1 (指人) short 2 (指物) low

艾 [ài] N (植) mugwort
艾滋病 [àizībìng] N AIDS

爱 [ài] VB 1 (恋) love ▶ 爱人 [àiren] husband or wife, partner ▷ 我爱你。 [Wǒ ài nǐ.] I love you. 2 (喜欢) enjoy ▷ 爱上网 [ài shàngwǎng] enjoy surfing the net 3 (容易) ▷ 她爱晕车。 [Tā ài yùnchē.] She tends to get car sick.
爱好 [àihào] VB be keen on ▶ 她有广泛的爱好。 [Tā yǒu guǎngfàn de àihào.] She has many hobbies.
爱护 [àihù] VB take care of
爱情 [àiqíng] N love

安 [ān] I ADJ 1 (安定) quiet ▶ 不安 [bù'ān] anxious 2 (平安) safe ▶ 治安 [zhì'ān] public order II VB 1 (使安静) calm ▶ 安心 [ānxīn] calm the nerves 2 (安装) fit ▷ 门上安把锁 [mén shàng ān bǎ suǒ] fit a lock on the door
安定 [āndìng] I ADJ stable II VB stabilize ▷ 安定局面 [āndìng júmiàn] stabilize the situation
安家 [ānjiā] VB 1 (*also*: 安置家庭) settle 2 (结婚) get married
安检 [ānjiǎn] N security check
安静 [ānjìng] ADJ 1 (无声) quiet 2 (平静) peaceful
安乐死 [ānlèsǐ] N euthanasia
安排 [ānpái] VB arrange
安全 [ānquán] ADJ safe ▶ 注意安全。 [Zhùyì ānquán.] Be sure to take care. ▶ 人身安全 [rénshēn ānquán] personal safety
安全套 [ānquántào] N condom
安慰 [ānwèi] I VB comfort II ADJ reassured
安心 [ānxīn] VB (形容心情) stop worrying
安装 [ānzhuāng] VB install

鹌 [ān] *see below*/见下文
鹌鹑 [ānchún] N quail

鞍 [ān] N saddle ▶ 马鞍 [mǎ'ān] saddle

岸 [àn] N edge ▶ 河岸 [hé'àn] river bank ▶ 海岸 [hǎi'àn] seashore

按 [àn] I VB 1 (用手压) press ▷ 按电钮 [àn diànniǔ] press a button ▷ 按门铃 [àn ménlíng] push a doorbell 2 (人) push ... down 3 (抑制) restrain

▷ 按不住心头怒火 [àn bùzhù xīntóu nùhuǒ] be unable to restrain one's fury **II** PREP (依照) according to ▷ 按制度办事 [àn zhìdù bànshì] do things by the book

按揭 [ànjiē] N mortgage

按摩 [ànmó] VB massage

按照 [ànzhào] PREP according to ▷ 按照课本 [ànzhào kèběn] according to the textbook

---

案 [àn] N (案件) case ▶ 案子 [ànzi] case

案件 [ànjiàn] N case

暗 [àn] **I** ADJ (昏暗) dim ▷ 今晚月光很暗。 [Jīnwǎn yuèguāng hěn àn.] Tonight the moon is dim. **II** ADV secretly

暗号 [ànhào] N secret signal

暗杀 [ànshā] VB assassinate

暗示 [ànshì] VB hint

暗自 [ànzì] ADV secretly

肮 [āng] *see below*/见下文

肮脏 [āngzāng] ADJ **1** (不干净) filthy **2** (喻) (不道德) vile

盎 [àng] ADJ (书) abundant

盎司 [àngsī] MEAS ounce

熬 [áo] VB **1** (煮) stew ▶ 熬粥 [áozhōu] make oatmeal **2** (忍受) endure

熬夜 [áoyè] VB stay up late

袄 [ǎo] N coat ▶ 棉袄 [mián'ǎo] padded jacket

傲 [ào] ADJ proud

傲慢 [àomàn] ADJ arrogant

傲气 [àoqì] N arrogance

奥 [ào] ADJ profound

奥林匹克运动会 [Àolínpǐkè Yùndònghuì] N Olympic Games (PL)

澳 [ào] N bay

澳大利亚 [Àodàlìyà] N Australia

懊 [ào] ADJ **1** (后悔) regretful **2** (恼怒) annoyed

懊悔 [àohuǐ] VB regret

B

八 [bā] NUM eight ▶ 八月 [bāyuè] August

巴 [bā] N ▶ 下巴 [xiàbā] chin ▶ 尾巴 [wěibā] tail ▶ 嘴巴 [zuǐbā] mouth

巴士 [bāshì] N bus

巴掌 [bāzhang] N (手掌) palm

芭 [bā] N banana

芭蕾舞 [bāléiwǔ] N ballet

疤 [bā] N scar

捌 [bā] NUM eight

This is the complex character for eight, which is mainly used in banks, on receipts, etc.

拔 [bá] VB **1** (抽出) pull … up ▶ 拔草 [bá…cǎo] weed **2** (取下) pull … out ▷ 拔牙 [báyá] pull out a tooth **3** (挑选) choose ▷ 选拔人才 [xuǎnbá réncái] select talented people **4** (超出) exceed ▶ 海拔 [hǎibá] height above sea level

把 [bǎ] **I** VB **1** (握住) hold **2** (看守) guard **II** N (把手) handle **III** MEAS **1** ▷ 一把刀 [yī bǎ dāo] a knife ▷ 一把剪子 [yī bǎ jiǎnzi] a pair of scissors

measure word, used for objects with a handle

2 handful ▷ 一把米 [yī bǎ mǐ] a handful of rice

measure word, used for the quantity of something that can be held in a hand

3 ▷ 两把花 [liǎng bǎ huā] two bunches of flowers

measure word, used for something that can be bundled together

IV PREP ▷ 把门关好 [bǎ mén guān hǎo] shut the door ▷ 把作业做完 [bǎ zuòyè zuò wán] finish doing one's homework ▷ 她把书放在桌子上了。 [Tā bǎ shū fàngzài zhuōzi shàng le.] She put the book on the table.

把 bǎ is used to alter the word order of a sentence, especially when the verb is a complex one. The normal word order of Subject + Verb + Object, becomes Subject + 把 + Object + Verb. It is very commonly used when the verb implies a change of place, or when the verb is followed by certain complements. For instance, a word-for-word translation of the sentence, 我把书放在那儿。 Wǒ bǎ shū fàng zài nàr. (I put the book there) is 'I 把 book put there'.

把手 [bǎshou] N handle

把握 [bǎwò] **I** VB grasp ▷ 把握时机 [bǎwò shíjī] seize the opportunity **II** N certainty ▷ 没把握 [méi bǎwò] there is no certainty

爸 [bà] N father

爸爸 [bàba] N dad

吧 [ba] AUX WORD **1** (在句尾表示建议) ▷ 我们回家吧。 [Wǒmen huíjiā ba.] Let's go home. ▷ 吃吧！ [Chī ba!] Eat! ▷ 再想想吧。 [Zài xiǎngxiǎng ba.] Think about it again. **2** (在句尾表示对推测的肯定) ▷ 你听说了吧？ [Nǐ tīngshuō le ba?] You may have heard about this. ▷ 他明天走吧？ [Tā míngtiān zuǒ ba?] Is he leaving tomorrow?

Adding 吧 ba at the end of a sentence forms a suggestion, e.g. 我们走吧。 Wǒmen zǒu ba. (Let's go). But adding 吗 ma at the end of a sentence forms a question, e.g. 我们走吗？ Wǒmen zǒu ma? (Shall we go?)

白 [bái] **I** ADJ **1** (白色) white ▶ 白糖 [báitáng] white sugar ▶ 白领

[báilǐng] white-collar **2** (明亮) bright ▶ 白天 [báitiān] daytime **3** (平淡) plain ▶ 白开水 [bái kāishuǐ] boiled water ▶ 白米饭 [bái mǐfàn] boiled rice **II** ADV (无结果) in vain ▶ 白费 [báifèi] waste ▶ 白等 [báiděng] wait in vain

白菜 [báicài] N Chinese cabbage

白酒 [báijiǔ] N clear spirit

白人 [báirén] N White person

百 [bǎi] NUM hundred

百分之百 [bǎi fēn zhī bǎi] absolutely

百万 [bǎiwàn] NUM million

佰 [bǎi] N hundred

This is the character for hundred which is used in banks, on receipts, checks etc.

摆 [bǎi] VB **1** (放置) arrange ▶ 摆放 [bǎifàng] place **2** (摇动) wave ▶ 摆动 [bǎidòng] sway ▷ 她向我摆手。[Tā xiàng wǒ bǎi shǒu.] She waved her hand at me.

摆设 [bǎishè] VB furnish and decorate

败 [bài] VB (打败) defeat

败坏 [bàihuài] **I** VB corrupt **II** ADJ corrupt

败仗 [bàizhàng] N defeat

拜 [bài] VB (会见) pay a visit ▶ 拜访 [bàifǎng] visit

拜年 [bàinián] VB pay a New Year call

拜托 [bàituō] VB ▷ 拜托您给看会儿我女儿。[Bàituō nín gěi kān huìr wǒ nǚr.] Would you be kind enough to look after my daughter for a while?

班 [bān] **I** N **1** (班级) class ▶ 班长 [bānzhǎng] class monitor **2** (交通) scheduled trip ▶ 班机 [bānjī] scheduled flight ▶ 末班车 [mò bānchē] the last bus **3** (轮班) shift ▶ 上班 [shàngbān] go to work ▶ 下班 [xiàbān] finish work ▶ 晚班 [wǎnbān] night shift **4** (军) squad **II** MEAS ▷ 下一班船 [xià yī bān chuán] the next boat ▷ 错过一班飞机 [cuòguò yī bān fēijī] miss a flight

measure word, used for scheduled transportations

班级 [bānjí] N classes (PL)

搬 [bān] VB **1** (移动) take ... away ▷ 把这些东西搬走。[Bǎ zhèxiē dōngxi bān zuǒ.] Take these things away. **2** (迁移) move ▶ 搬家 [bānjiā] move house

板 [bǎn] **I** N (片状硬物) board **II** VB put on a stern expression

办 [bàn] VB **1** (处理) handle ▶ 办事 [bànshì] handle affairs ▷ 我们该怎么办？[Wǒmen gāi zěnme bàn?] What should we do? **2** (创设) set ... up ▷ 办工厂 [bàn gōngchǎng] set up a factory **3** (经营) run ▶ 办学 [bànxué] run a school **4** (展览) stage ▷ 办画展 [bàn huàzhǎn] stage an art exhibition

办法 [bànfǎ] N way ▷ 想办法 [xiǎng bànfǎ] find a way ▷ 联系办法 [liánxì bànfǎ] means of contact

办公 [bàngōng] VB work

办理 [bànlǐ] VB handle

半 [bàn] **I** NUM (二分之一) half ▷ 半价 [bàn jià] half price ▷ 半年 [bàn nián] half a year **II** N (在中间) middle ▶ 半夜 [bànyè] midnight **III** ADV partially ▷ 半新 [bàn xīn] almost new

半导体 [bàndǎotǐ] N **1** (指物质) semiconductor **2** (收音机) transistor radio

半岛 [bàndǎo] N peninsula

半径 [bànjìng] N radius

半球 [bànqiú] N hemisphere

半天 [bàntiān] N for quite a while ▷ 他等了半天。[Tā děng le bàntiān.] He waited for quite a while.

伴 [bàn] N company ▶ 做伴 [zuòbàn] keep company

拌 [bàn] VB (搅和) mix

绊 [bàn] VB (使跌倒) trip

瓣 [bàn] **I** N (指花儿) petal **II** MEAS ▷ 几瓣蒜 [jǐ bàn suàn] a few cloves of garlic ▷ 一瓣橘子 [yī bàn júzi] a segment of orange

measure word, used to describe flower petals and segments of fruits

帮 [bāng] VB (帮助) help ▷ 我帮他买票。 [Wǒ bāng tā mǎi piào.] I helped him get the tickets.

帮忙 [bāngmáng] VB help ▷ 请您帮我个忙。 [Qǐng nín bāng wǒ ge máng.] Please can you help me out?

帮助 [bāngzhù] VB help ▶ 谢谢您的帮助。 [Xièxie nín de bāngzhù.] Thank you for your help.

绑 [bǎng] VB tie up

榜 [bǎng] N list of names

榜样 [bǎngyàng] N model

棒 [bàng] **I** N (棍子) cudgel ▶ 棒子 [bàngzi] club **II** ADJ (口) great ▷ 他英语说得很棒。 [Tā Yīngyǔ shuō de hěn bàng.] He speaks great English.

傍 [bàng] VB be close to

傍晚 [bàngwǎn] N dusk

磅 [bàng] MEAS pound

镑 [bàng] N pound

包 [bāo] **I** VB **1** (包裹) wrap **2** (包含) include **3** (担保) guarantee **4** (约定专用) rent ▷ 包车 [bāo chē] rent a car ▷ 包飞机 [bāo fēijī] charter a plane **II** N **1** (包裹) parcel **2** (口袋) bag ▶ 背包 [bēibāo] backpack ▶ 钱包 [qiánbāo] billfold **3** (疙瘩) lump **III** MEAS pack, bag ▷ 一包烟 [yī bāo yān] a pack of cigarettes ▷ 一包衣服 [yī bāo yīfu] a bag of clothes

measure word, used to describe things that are wrapped up

包含 [bāohán] VB contain

包括 [bāokuò] VB include

包子 [bāozi] N *steamed stuffed bun*

包子 [bāozi]

包子 bāozi are bigger than 饺子 jiǎozi. Shaped like buns, they are usually stuffed with meat or vegetable fillings, and are steamed rather than boiled.

剥 [bāo] VB peel

雹 [báo] N hail ▶ 雹子 [báozi] hailstone

薄 [báo] ADJ **1** (不厚) thin **2** (冷淡) cold ▶ 我对她不薄。 [Wǒ duì tā bù báo.] I treat her very well.

宝 [bǎo] **I** N treasure **II** ADJ precious

宝贵 [bǎoguì] ADJ valuable

饱 [bǎo] ADJ full ▷ 我吃饱了。 [Wǒ chī bǎo le.] I am full.

保 [bǎo] VB **1** (保护) protect **2** (保持) keep ▶ 保密 [bǎomì] keep ... secret ▶ 保鲜膜 [bǎoxiān mó] Saran wrap® **3** (保证) ensure

保安 [bǎo'ān] N security guard

保持 [bǎochí] VB maintain ▷ 保持警惕 [bǎochí jǐngtì] stay vigilant

保存 [bǎocún] VB preserve

保护 [bǎohù] VB protect ▷ 保护环境 [bǎohù huánjìng] protect the environment

保龄球 [bǎolíngqiú] N (体育运动) bowling

保留 [bǎoliú] VB **1** (保存不变) preserve **2** (意见) hold back ▷ 你可以保留自己的意见。 [Nǐ kěyǐ bǎoliú zìjǐ de yìjiàn.] You can keep your opinions to yourself.

保姆 [bǎomǔ] N **1** (做家务的女工) domestic help **2** (保育员) nanny

保守 [bǎoshǒu] ADJ conservative

保卫 [bǎowèi] VB defend

保险 [bǎoxiǎn] **I** N insurance **II** ADJ safe

保证 [bǎozhèng] VB guarantee

保重 [bǎozhòng] VB take care of oneself

报 [bào] **I** VB (告诉) report **II** N **1** (报纸) newspaper ▶ 日报 [rìbào] daily ▶ 报社 [bàoshè] newspaper office **2** (刊物) periodical ▶ 画报 [huābào] glossy magazine

报仇 [bàochóu] VB take revenge

报酬 [bàochou] N pay

报到 [bàodào] VB register

报道 [bàodào] **I** VB report ▷ 电视台报道了这条新闻。 [Diànshì tái bàodào le zhè tiáo xīnwén.] The television station reported this item of news. **II** N report ▷ 一篇关于克隆人的报道 [yī piān guānyú kèlóng rén de bàodào] a report about human cloning

报复 [bàofù] VB retaliate

报告 [bàogào] **I** VB report ▷ 向主管部门报告 [xiàng zhǔguǎn bùmén bàogào] report to the department in charge **II** N report ▷ 在大会上作报告 [zài dàhuì shàng zuò bàogào] give a talk at the conference

报关 [bàoguān] VB declare

报刊 [bàokān] N newspapers and periodicals (PL)

报名 [bàomíng] VB sign up

报失 [bàoshī] VB report a loss

报销 [bàoxiāo] VB (费用) claim for

报纸 [bàozhǐ] N newspaper

抱 [bào] VB **1** (手臂围住) carry in one's arms **2** adopt **3** (心里存有) cherish ▷ 对某事抱幻想 [duì mǒushì bào huànxiǎng] have illusions about sth

抱歉 [bàoqiàn] **I** ADJ sorry **II** VB apologize

抱怨 [bàoyuàn] VB complain

豹 [bào] N leopard

暴 [bào] ADJ (猛烈) violent ▶ 暴雨 [bàoyǔ] rainstorm

爆 [bào] VB **1** (猛然破裂) explode ▶ 爆炸 [bàozhà] explode **2** (突然发生) break out ▶ 爆发 [bàofā] break out

杯 [bēi] **I** N **1** (杯子) cup ▶ 玻璃杯 [bōli bēi] glass ▶ 酒杯 [jiǔbēi] wineglass ▶ 杯子 [bēizi] cup **2** (奖杯) cup ▶ 世界杯 [Shìjièbēi] World Cup **II** MEAS cup, glass ▷ 一杯咖啡 [yī bēi kāfēi] a cup of coffee ▷ 两杯水 [liǎng bēi shuǐ] two glasses of water

背 [bēi] VB **1** (驮) carry ... on one's back **2** (担负) take ... on ▷ 背起重任 [bēi qǐ zhòngrèn] take on great responsibility
→ *see also*/另见 bèi

悲 [bēi] ADJ (悲伤) sad

悲惨 [bēicǎn] ADJ miserable

悲观 [bēiguān] ADJ pessimistic

悲伤 [bēishāng] ADJ sad

碑 [bēi] N tablet ▶ 纪念碑 [jìniànbēi] monument

北 [běi] N north ▶ 北方 [běifāng] the North ▶ 北京 [Běijīng] Beijing ▶ 北部 [běibù] the north

北极 [běijí] N the North Pole

备 [bèi] VB **1** (具备) have **2** (准备) prepare

备份 [bèifèn] VB (计算机) keep a backup copy

备用 [bèiyòng] VB backup ▷ 备用光盘 [bèiyòng guāngpán] backup CD

备注 [bèizhù] N (注解说明) notes (PL)

背 [bèi] **I** N **1** (指身体) back ▶ 背疼 [bèiténg] backache **2** (指反面) back ▶ 背面 [bèimiàn] reverse side **3** (指后面) behind ▶ 背后 [bèihòu] behind **II** VB (背诵) recite
→ *see also*/另见 bēi

背景 [bèijǐng] N (指景物, 情况) background

背诵 [bèisòng] VB recite

被 [bèi] I N comforter ▶ 被子 [bèizi] comforter II PREP ▷ 他被哥哥打了一顿。 [Tā bèi gēge dǎ le yī dùn.] He was beaten up by his elder brother. III AUX WORD ▷ 他被跟踪了。 [Tā bèi gēnzōng le.] He was followed.

倍 [bèi] N times (PL) ▷ 这本书比那本书厚三倍。 [Zhè běn shū bǐ nà běn shū hòu sānbèi.] This book is three times thicker than that one. ▷ 物价涨了两倍。 [Wùjià zhǎng le liǎngbèi.] Prices have doubled.

本 [běn] I N 1 (本子) book ▶ 笔记本 [bǐjìběn] notebook 2 (版本) edition ▶ 手抄本 [shǒuchāo běn] handwritten copy II ADJ 1 (自己的) one's own ▶ 本人 [běnrén] oneself 2 (现今) this ▶ 本月 [běnyuè] this month III ADV originally ▷ 我本想亲自去一趟。 [Wǒ běn xiǎng qīnzì qù yītàng.] I originally wanted to go myself. IV MEAS ▷ 几本书 [jǐ běn shū] a few books

measure word, used for counting books, magazines, dictionaries, etc.

本地 [běndì] N locality ▷ 她是本地人。 [Tā shì běndì rén.] She is a native of this place.

本科 [běnkē] N undergraduate course ▷ 本科生 [běnkē shēng] undergraduate

本来 [běnlái] I ADJ original ▷ 本来的打算 [běnlái de dǎsuàn] the original plan II ADV (原先) at first ▷ 我本来以为你已经走了。 [Wǒ běnlái yǐwéi nǐ yǐjīng zǒu le.] At first, I thought you had left.

本领 [běnlǐng] N skill

本身 [běnshēn] N itself

本事 [běnshi] N ability

本质 [běnzhì] N essence

笨 [bèn] ADJ 1 (不聪明) stupid 2 (不灵巧) clumsy ▷ 他嘴很笨。 [Tā zuǐ hěn bèn.] He's quite inarticulate.

蹦 [bèng] VB leap

逼 [bī] VB 1 (强迫) force 2 (强取) press for ▶ 逼债 [bīzhài] press for repayment of a debt 3 (逼近) close in on

逼近 [bījìn] VB close in on

逼迫 [bīpò] VB force

鼻 [bí] N (鼻子) nose

鼻涕 [bítì] N mucus

鼻子 [bízi] N nose

比 [bǐ] I VB 1 (比较) compare ▷ 比比过去, 现在的生活好多了。 [Bǐbǐ guòqù, xiànzài de shēnghuó hǎo duō le.] Life now is much better compared to the past. 2 (较量) compete ▷ 他们要比比谁游得快。 [Tāmen yào bǐbǐ shuí yóu de kuài.] They are competing to see who swims the fastest. II PREP 1 (指得分) ▷ 零比零 [líng bǐ líng] no score 2 (相对) ▷ 今年冬天比去年冷。 [Jīnnián dōngtiān bǐ qùnián lěng.] It is colder this winter than last winter.

比 bǐ is used to express comparisons: to say that X is taller than Y, simply say X 比 Y 高。 e.g. 上海比南京大。 Shànghǎi bǐ Nánjīng dà. (Shanghai is bigger than Nanjing.)

比方 [bǐfang] N analogy ▶ 比方说 [bǐfang shuō] for example

比分 [bǐfēn] N score

比基尼 [bǐjīní] N bikini

比较 [bǐjiào] I VB compare II ADV relatively ▷ 这里的水果比较新鲜。 [Zhèlǐ de shuǐguǒ bǐjiào xīnxiān.] The fruit here is relatively fresh.

比例 [bǐlì] N proportion

比率 [bǐlǜ] N ratio

比如 [bǐrú] CONJ for instance

比赛 [bǐsài] N match

彼 [bǐ] PRON **1** (那个) that **2** (对方) the other side

彼此 [bǐcǐ] PRON (双方) both sides

笔 [bǐ] **I** N **1** (工具) pen ▶ 圆珠笔 [yuánzhūbǐ] ball-point pen **2** (笔画) brush stroke **II** MEAS (款项) ▷ 一笔钱 [yī bǐ qián] a sum of money

measure word, used for money

笔记 [bǐjì] N (记录) note ▷ 记笔记 [jì bǐjì] take notes

笔记本电脑 [bǐjìběn diànnǎo] N laptop

币 [bì] N coin ▶ 货币 [huòbì] currency ▶ 外币 [wàibì] foreign currency

必 [bì] ADV **1** (必然) certainly **2** (必须) ▶ 必修课 [bìxiūkè] compulsory course

必然 [bìrán] **I** ADJ inevitable **II** N necessity

必须 [bìxū] ADV ▷ 你们必须准时来上班。 [Nǐmen bìxū zhǔnshí lái shàngbān.] You must start work on time.

必要 [bìyào] ADJ essential

毕 [bì] VB finish

毕业 [bìyè] VB graduate

避 [bì] VB **1** (躲开) avoid ▶ 避风 [bìfēng] shelter from the wind **2** (防止) prevent

避免 [bìmiǎn] VB avoid

避难 [bìnàn] VB take refuge

避孕 [bìyùn] VB use contraceptives ▷ 避孕药 [bìyùn yào] the pill

边 [biān] N **1** (边线) side ▷ 街两边 [jiē liǎngbiān] both sides of the street **2** (边缘) edge ▷ 路边 [lù biān] roadside **3** (边界) border **4** (旁边) side ▷ 在床边 [zài chuáng biān] by the bed

边…边… [biān…biān…] ▷ 边吃边谈 [biān chī biān tán] talk while eating

边疆 [biānjiāng] N border area

边界 [biānjiè] N border

边境 [biānjìng] N border

边缘 [biānyuán] N edge

编 [biān] VB **1** (编辑) edit ▶ 编程 [biānchéng] program **2** (创作) write ▷ 编歌词 [biān gēcí] write lyrics **3** (捏造) fabricate ▷ 编谎话 [biān huǎnghuà] fabricate a lie

编辑 [biānjí] **I** VB edit **II** N editor

蝙 [biān] *see below*/见下文

蝙蝠 [biānfú] N bat

鞭 [biān] N **1** (鞭子) whip **2** (爆竹) firecracker

鞭炮 [biānpào] N firecracker

鞭炮 [biānpào]

Firecrackers are believed by the Chinese to scare off evil spirits and attract the god of good fortune to people's doorsteps, especially in the celebration of the Spring Festival and at weddings.

贬 [biǎn] VB (降低) reduce ▶ 贬值 [biǎnzhí] depreciate

贬义词 [biǎnyì cí] N derogatory expression

扁 [biǎn] ADJ flat ▷ 自行车胎扁了。 [Zìxíngchē tāi biǎn le.] The bicycle tyre is flat.

变 [biàn] VB **1** (改变) change ▷ 小城的面貌变了。 [Xiǎochéng de miànmào biàn le.] The appearance of the town has changed. **2** (变成) become ▷ 他变成熟了。 [Tā biàn chéngshú le.] He's become quite grown up.

变化 [biànhuà] **I** VB change **II** N change

便 [biàn] **I** ADJ **1** (方便) convenient ▶ 轻便 [qīngbiàn] portable **2** (简单) simple ▶ 便饭 [biànfàn] simple meal **II** VB excrete ▶ 小便 [xiǎobiàn] urinate ▶ 大便 [dàbiàn] defecate **III** ADV ▷ 稍等片刻演出便开始。 [Shāoděng piànkè yǎnchū biàn kāishǐ.] The performance is about

to start in a moment.
→ *see also*/另见 pián

便利 [biànlì] **I** ADJ convenient **II** VB facilitate

便士 [biànshì] MEAS pence

便条 [biàntiáo] N note

便携式 [biànxiéshì] ADJ portable

便于 [biànyú] VB be easy to ▷ 便于联系 [biànyú liánxì] be easy to contact

---

遍 [biàn] **I** ADV all over ▷ 找了个遍 [zhǎo le ge biàn] searched high and low **II** MEAS ▷ 我说了两遍。 [Wǒ shuō le liǎng biàn.] I said it twice.

measure word, used for the number of times the same action takes place

---

辨 [biàn] VB distinguish ▶ 辨别 [biànbié] distinguish

辨认 [biànrèn] VB identify

辩 [biàn] VB debate ▶ 辩论 [biànlùn] argue

标 [biāo] **I** N **1** (记号) mark **2** (标准) standard **II** VB mark

标本 [biāoběn] N (样品) specimen

标点 [biāodiǎn] N punctuation

标记 [biāojì] N mark

标题 [biāotí] N **1** (指文章, 书) title **2** (指新闻) headline

标志 [biāozhì] N sign

标准 [biāozhǔn] N **I** standard ▷ 道德标准 [dàodé biāozhǔn] moral standard **II** ADJ standard ▷ 标准时间 [biāozhǔn shíjiān] standard time

---

表 [biǎo] N **1** (计时器) watch ▶ 手表 [shǒubiǎo] wristwatch **2** (计量器) meter ▶ 电表 [diànbiǎo] electricity meter **3** (表格) form ▷ 火车时间表 [huǒchē shíjiān biǎo] train timetable ▷ 填申请表 [tián shēnqǐng biǎo] fill in the application form **4** (指亲戚) cousin ▶ 表哥 [biǎogē] cousin

表达 [biǎodá] VB express

表格 [biǎogé] N form

表面 [biǎomiàn] N surface

表明 [biǎomíng] VB show

表示 [biǎoshì] **I** VB (表达) express **II** N **1** (言行或表情) gesture **2** (意见) attitude

表现 [biǎoxiàn] **I** VB (显出) show **II** N (指行为, 作风) performance

表演 [biǎoyǎn] **I** VB (演出) perform **II** N performance

表扬 [biǎoyáng] VB praise

别 [bié] **I** ADJ (其他) other **II** ADV (不要) ▷ 别忘了关灯。 [Bié wàng le guāndēng.] Don't forget to turn off the light.

别人 [biérén] N other people

别墅 [biéshù] N villa

别针 [biézhēn] N safety pin

宾 [bīn] N guest

宾馆 [bīnguǎn] N hotel

冰 [bīng] **I** N ice **II** VB **1** (使感觉寒冷) be freezing ▷ 这水冰手。 [Zhè shuǐ bīng shǒu.] This water is freezing. **2** (冰镇) cool ▶ 冰镇 [bīngzhèn] iced

冰淇淋 [bīngqílín] N ice cream

冰箱 [bīngxiāng] N fridge

兵 [bīng] N **1** (军队) the army ▷ 当兵 [dāng bīng] join the army **2** (士兵) soldier

---

饼 [bǐng] N (指面食) cake ▶ 月饼 [yuèbǐng] moon cake

饼干 [bǐnggān] N cookie

并 [bìng] **I** VB **1** (合并) merge **2** (并拢) bring ... together ▷ 把脚并起来 [bǎ jiǎo bìng qǐlái] bring your feet together **II** ADV (表示强调) really ▷ 他今晚并不想出去。 [Tā jīnwǎn bìng bù xiǎng chūqù.] He really doesn't want to go out this evening. **III** CONJ and ▷ 他会说法语, 并在学习西班牙语。 [Tā huì shuō Fǎ yǔ, bìng zài xuéxí Xībānyá yǔ] He can speak French, and he is studying Spanish at the moment.

并且 [bìngqiě] CONJ **1** (和) and ▷ 她聪明并且用功。 [Tā cōngmíng bìngqiě yònggōng.] She is clever and diligent. **2** (此外) also

病 [bìng] **I** N (疾病) disease ▶ 心脏病 [xīnzàng bìng] heart disease ▶ 生病 [shēngbìng] become ill ▷ 他去看病了。 [Tā qù kànbìng le.] He went to see a doctor. **II** VB be ill ▷ 他病得不轻。 [Tā bìng de bùqīng.] He was seriously ill.

病毒 [bìngdú] N virus

病房 [bìngfáng] N ward

病菌 [bìngjūn] N bacteria

病人 [bìngrén] N **1** (指医院里) patient **2** (指家里) invalid

波 [bō] N (指水, 声音, 电) wave

拨 [bō] VB **1** (号码) dial ▷ 拨电话号 [bō diànhuà hào] dial the phone number **2** (频道) change over to

玻 [bō] *see below*/见下文

玻璃 [bōlí] N glass

菠 [bō] *see below*/见下文

菠菜 [bōcài] N spinach

菠萝 [bōluó] N pineapple

播 [bō] VB (电视, 收音机) broadcast ▶ 播放 [bōfàng] broadcast

伯 [bó] N (伯父) uncle

伯伯 [bóbo] N **1** (伯父) uncle **2** (用于称呼) uncle

脖 [bó] N neck ▶ 脖子 [bózi] neck

博 [bó] ADJ abundant

博物馆 [bówùguǎn] N museum

补 [bǔ] VB **1** (衣服, 鞋, 车胎, 袜子) mend **2** (牙) fill **3** (增加) add

补充 [bǔchōng] **I** VB add **II** ADJ supplementary ▷ 补充说明 [bǔchōng shuōmíng] additional explanation

补考 [bǔkǎo] VB resit

补习 [bǔxí] VB take extra lessons

补助 [bǔzhù] N subsidy

捕 [bǔ] VB catch

捕捉 [bǔzhuō] VB **1** (抓住) seize **2** (捉拿) hunt down

不 [bù] ADV **1** (用于否定句) not ▷ 不诚实 [bù chéngshí] dishonest ▷ 他不抽烟。 [Tā bù chōuyān.] He doesn't smoke. **2** (用于否定回答) no ▷ "你累了吧?" — "不, 不累。" ["Nǐ lèi le ba?"—"Bù, bùlèi."] "Are you tired?" — "No, I'm not." **3** (客套) (不用) ▷ 不客气。 [Bù kèqi.] Please don't mention it. ▷ 不谢。 [Bù xiè.] You're welcome.

> Negating sentences in Chinese is very straightforward: just use 不 bù before the verb. E.g. 我不喝酒。 Wǒ bù hējiǔ (I don't drink alcohol). The only exception is the verb 有 yǒu, to have, for which you must use 没 méi. E.g. 我没有钱。 Wǒ méiyǒu qián. (I don't have any money). 不 bù is fourth tone unless it is followed by another fourth tone syllable, in which case it is usually pronounced as a second tone, eg. 不要 búyào. For more information on tones, please see the introduction.

不必 [bùbì] ADV ▷ 明天你们不必来了。 [Míngtiān nǐmen bùbì lái le.] You don't have to come tomorrow.

不但 [bùdàn] CONJ not only ▷ 这辆车的设计不但美观, 而且实用。 [Zhè liàng chē de shèjì bùdàn měiguān, érqiě shíyòng.] The design of this car is not only beautiful, it's also practical.

不得了 [bùdéliǎo] ADJ (表示程度) extreme ▷ 这孩子淘气得不得了。 [Zhè háizi táoqì de bùdéliǎo.] This child is terribly naughty.

不断 [bùduàn] ADV continually ▷ 沙漠不断扩大。 [Shāmò bùduàn kuòdà.] The desert is expanding all the time.

不敢 [bùgǎn] VB not dare

不管 [bùguǎn] CONJ ▷ 不管出什么事，我们都要保持镇定。[Bùguǎn chū shénme shì, wǒmen dōuyào bǎochí zhèndìng.] Whatever happens, we must remain calm.

不过 [bùguò] **I** ADV **1** (仅仅) only ▷ 不过是点小伤。[Bùguò shì diǎn xiǎoshāng.] It's only a slight injury. **2** (非常) can't be better ▷ 这是最简单不过的方法。[Zhè shì zuì jiǎndān bùguò de fāngfǎ.] This is by far the easiest method. **II** CONJ but ▷ 他很喜欢新学校，不过离家太远了。[Tā hěn xǐhuān xīn xuéxiào, bùguò lí jiā tài yuǎn le.] He really likes his new school, but it's a very long way from home.

不仅 [bùjǐn] ADV **1** (不止) not just ▷ 这不仅是学校的问题。[Zhè bùjǐn shì xuéxiào de wèntí.] This is not just the school's problem. **2** (不但) not only ▷ 这地毯不仅质量好，而且价格便宜。[Zhè dìtǎn bùjǐn zhìliàng hǎo, érqiě jiàgé piányi.] Not only is the carpet good quality, it's also cheap.

不久 [bùjiǔ] N ▶ 他们不久就要结婚了。[Tāmen bùjiǔ jiùyào jiéhūn le.] They are getting married soon.

不论 [bùlùn] CONJ no matter ▷ 不论是谁，都必须遵守法规。[Bùlùn shì shuí, dōu bìxū zūnshǒu fǎguī.] No matter who you are, you have to abide by the regulations.

不满 [bùmǎn] ADJ dissatisfied

不免 [bùmiǎn] ADV inevitably

不然 [bùrán] CONJ otherwise ▷ 多谢你提醒我，不然我就忘了。[Duōxiè nǐ tíxǐng wǒ, bùrán wǒ jiù wàng le.] Thanks very much for reminding me, or I would have forgotten about it.

不如 [bùrú] VB not be as good as ▷ 城里太吵，不如住在郊区。[Chénglǐ tài chǎo, bùrú zhùzài jiāoqū.] The city is too noisy, it's better living in the suburbs.

不少 [bùshǎo] ADJ a lot of ▷ 她有不少好朋友。[Tā yǒu bùshǎo hǎo péngyou.] She has a lot of good friends.

不同 [bùtóng] ADJ different

不幸 [bùxìng] **I** ADJ **1** (不幸运) unhappy **2** (出人意料) unfortunate **II** N disaster

不要紧 [bùyàojǐn] ADJ **1** (不严重) not serious ▷ 他的病不要紧。[Tā de bìng bùyàojǐn.] His illness is not serious. **2** (没关系) it doesn't matter

不一定 [bùyīdìng] ADV may not ▷ 她未必会回电话。[Tā wèibì huì huí diànhuà.] She may not return your call.

不止 [bùzhǐ] ADV **1** (不停地) incessantly ▷ 大笑不止 [dàxiào bùzhǐ] laugh incessantly **2** (多于) more than ▷ 不止一次 [bùzhǐ yīcì] on more than one occasion

---

布 [bù] N cloth

布置 [bùzhì] VB **1** (房间等) decorate **2** (任务，作业) assign

步 [bù] N **1** (脚步) step ▶ 步伐 [bùfá] pace **2** (阶段) stage ▶ 步骤 [bùzhòu] step **3** (地步) situation

步行 [bùxíng] VB go on foot

部 [bù] **I** N **1** (部分) part ▷ 东部 [dōng bù] the eastern part **2** (部门) department ▶ 总部 [zǒngbù] headquarters (PL) ▶ 部长 [bùzhǎng] department head ▷ 教育部 [jiàoyù bù] education department **II** MEAS ▷ 一部电话 [yī bù diànhuà] a telephone ▷ 三部电影 [sān bù diànyǐng] three films

measure word, used for films, phones, etc.

部队 [bùduì] N armed forces (PL)

部分 [bùfen] N part

部门 [bùmén] N department

部位 [bùwèi] N place

C

擦 [cā] VB **1** (抹) wipe ... clean **2** (指用水) wash **3** (皮鞋) polish **4** (摩擦) rub **5** (涂) apply **6** (火柴) strike **7** (破) scrape ▶ 擦伤 [cāshāng] scrape **8** (挨着) brush **9** (瓜果) shred

猜 [cāi] VB **1** (猜测) guess **2** (猜疑) suspect

猜测 [cāicè] **I** VB speculate **II** N speculation

猜想 [cāixiǎng] VB suppose

猜疑 [cāiyí] VB have unfounded suspicions about

才 [cái] **I** N **1** (才能) ability ▶ 多才多艺 [duōcái duōyì] multi-talented **2** (人才) talent ▶ 奇才 [qícái] extraordinary talent **II** ADV **1** (刚) just ▷ 我才到家，电话就响了。[Wǒ cái dào jiā, diànhuà jiù xiǎng le.] Just as I arrived home, the phone rang. **2** (表示晚) not ... until ▷ 我10点才到单位。[Wǒ shídiǎn cái dào dānwèi.] I didn't arrive at work until ten o'clock. **3** (表示条件) only ... if ▷ 学生只有用功，才能取得好成绩。[Xuéshēng zhǐyǒu yònggōng, cái néng qǔdé hǎo chéngjì.] Students will only be able to do well if they study hard. **4** (表示情况改变) only after ▷ 他解释后，我才明白了他为什么那么难过。[Tā jiěshì hòu, wǒ cái míngbai tā wèishénme nàme nánguò.] It was only after he explained that I understood why he was so sad. **5** (程度低) only ▷ 他才学会上网。[Tā cái xuéhuì shàngwǎng.] He has only just learned how to use the internet.

才华 [cáihuá] N talent

才能 [cáinéng] N ability

才子 [cáizǐ] N talented man

材 [cái] N (指物) material ▶ 教材 [jiàocái] teaching material

材料 [cáiliào] N **1** (原料) material **2** (资料) material **3** (人才) talent

财 [cái] N wealth

财富 [cáifù] N wealth

财政 [cáizhèng] N finance

裁 [cái] VB **1** (衣服，纸) cut **2** (减) cut ▶ 裁员 [cáiyuán] cut staff **3** (判断) decide

裁缝 [cáifeng] N **1** (指男装) tailor **2** (指女装) dressmaker

裁判 [cáipàn] **I** N judgment **II** VB make a decision

采 [cǎi] VB **1** (摘) pick **2** (选) choose **3** (开采) extract **4** (采集) gather

采访 [cǎifǎng] VB interview

采购 [cǎigòu] **I** VB purchase **II** N buyer

采取 [cǎiqǔ] VB adopt

采用 [cǎiyòng] VB adopt

彩 [cǎi] N (颜色) color

彩电 [cǎidiàn] N color TV

彩卷 [cǎijuǎn] N color film

彩排 [cǎipái] VB rehearse

彩票 [cǎipiào] N lottery ticket

彩色 [cǎisè] N color

踩 [cǎi] VB (脚) step on

菜 [cài] N **1** (植物) vegetable **2** (饭食) dish

菜单 [càidān] N menu

菜谱 [càipǔ] N **1** (菜单) menu **2** (指书) cookbook

参 [cān] VB (加入) join ▶ 参军 [cānjūn] enlist
→ *see also*/另见 shēn

参观 [cānguān] VB tour

参加 [cānjiā] VB take part in ▷ 参加新年晚会 [cānjiā xīnnián wǎnhuì] attend a New Year's party ▷ 参加了民主党 [cānjiā Mínzhǔ Dǎng] join the Democratic Party

参考 [cānkǎo] **I** VB consult **II** N reference ▷ 参考书 [cānkǎo shū] reference book

参谋 [cānmóu] I N 1 (顾问) advisor 2 (指军职) staff officer II VB give advice

参与 [cānyù] VB participate in

餐 [cān] I N meal II MEAS meal

餐车 [cānchē] N 1 (指推车) food trolley 2 (指车厢) dining car

餐巾 [cānjīn] N napkin

餐具 [cānjù] N eating utensils (PL)

餐厅 [cāntīng] N canteen

残 [cán] ADJ 1 (指器物) defective 2 (指人或动物) disabled 3 (剩余) remaining

残废 [cánfèi] VB be disabled

残疾 [cánjí] N disability ▷ 残疾人 [cánjí rén] people with disabilities

残酷 [cánkù] ADJ brutal

残忍 [cánrěn] ADJ cruel

蚕 [cán] N silkworm

惭 [cán] *see below*/见下文

惭愧 [cánkuì] ADJ ashamed

惨 [cǎn] ADJ (悲惨) tragic

灿 [càn] *see below*/见下文

灿烂 [cànlàn] ADJ glorious

仓 [cāng] N store

仓库 [cāngkù] N storehouse

苍 [cāng] ADJ (指鬓发) gray

苍白 [cāngbái] ADJ 1 (脸色) pale 2 (文章, 表演等) bland

苍蝇 [cāngying] N fly

舱 [cāng] N 1 (用于载人) cabin ▶ 头等舱 [tóuděngcāng] first-class cabin 2 (用于装物) hold ▶ 货舱 [huòcāng] cargo hold

藏 [cáng] VB 1 (隐藏) hide 2 (储存) store 3 (收集) collect ▶ 藏书 [cángshū] collect books → *see also*/另见 zàng

操 [cāo] N (体育活动) exercise

操场 [cāochǎng] N sports ground

操心 [cāoxīn] VB concern

操作 [cāozuò] VB operate

糙 [cāo] ADJ poor

草 [cǎo] N 1 (植物) grass ▶ 草地 [cǎodì] lawn, meadow 2 (用作材料) straw

草稿 [cǎogǎo] N rough draft

草帽 [cǎomào] N straw hat

草莓 [cǎoméi] N strawberry

草率 [cǎoshuài] ADJ rash

草原 [cǎoyuán] N grasslands (PL)

册 [cè] I N book ▶ 手册 [shǒucè] handbook ▶ 相册 [xiàngcè] photo album II MEAS 1 (指同一本书) copy 2 (指不同本书) volume

厕 [cè] N toilet ▶ 公厕 [gōngcè] public toilet

厕所 [cèsuǒ] N toilet

侧 [cè] I N side ▶ 两侧 [liǎngcè] both sides II VB turn ... away ▷ 我侧过脸去。 [Wǒ cè guò liǎn qù.] I turned my face away.

侧面 [cèmiàn] I ADJ 1 (非官方) unofficial 2 (指方位) side II N side

测 [cè] VB 1 (测量) measure 2 (推测) predict

测量 [cèliáng] I VB measure II N survey

测试 [cèshì] I VB test II N test

测验 [cèyàn] I VB test II N test

策 [cè] N suggestion

策划 [cèhuà] I VB design II N planning

策略 [cèlüè] I N strategy II ADJ strategic

层 [céng] I MEAS 1 (指建筑物) floor (指覆盖物) layer 3 (步) step 4 (指含义) layer II N (指物, 状态) layer

曾 [céng] ADV once

曾经 [céngjīng] ADV once

蹭 [cèng] VB 1 (摩擦) rub 2 (沾上) smear 3 (指速度) creep along

叉 [chā] N 1 (器具) fork 2 (餐具) fork 3 (符号) cross
叉子 [chāzi] N 1 (符号) cross 2 (餐具) fork

差 [chā] N difference
→ *see also*/另见 chà, chāi
差别 [chābié] N difference
差错 [chācuò] N 1 (错误) mistake 2 (意外) accident
差距 [chājù] N difference
差异 [chāyì] N difference

插 [chā] VB insert ▷ 我能不能插一句? [Wǒ néng bùnéng chā yījù?] Can I interrupt just a second?
插曲 [chāqǔ] N 1 (音乐) incidental music 2 (事件) interlude
插入 [chārù] VB insert
插图 [chātú] N illustration
插销 [chāxiāo] N 1 (闩) bolt 2 (插头) electrical plug
插嘴 [chāzuǐ] VB interrupt
插座 [chāzuò] N outlet

茶 [chá] N tea ▶ 红茶 [hóngchá] black tea ▶ 茶杯 [chábēi] teacup ▶ 茶壶 [cháhú] teapot ▶ 茶馆 [cháguǎn] teahouse ▷ 泡茶 [pào chá] make tea
茶具 [chájù] N tea set
茶叶 [cháyè] N tea leaves (PL)

查 [chá] VB 1 (检查) inspect 2 (调查) investigate 3 (字典, 词典) look ... up
查号台 [cháhàotái] N directory assistance
查阅 [cháyuè] VB look ... up
查找 [cházhǎo] VB look for

察 [chá] VB check ▶ 观察 [guānchá] observe
察觉 [chájué] VB detect

杈 [chà] N branch

差 [chà] I VB 1 (不相同) be different from ▷ 你比他差得远了。 [Nǐ bǐ tā chà de yuǎn le.] You are not nearly as good as him. 2 (缺欠) be short of ▷ 差3个人 [chà sān gè rén] be three people short II ADJ 1 (错误) mistaken 2 (不好) poor ▷ 质量差 [zhìliàng chà] poor quality
→ *see also*/另见 chā, chāi
差不多 [chà bu duō] I ADJ very similar II ADV almost

拆 [chāi] VB 1 (打开) tear ... open 2 (拆毁) dismantle

差 [chāi] VB send ▶ 出差 [chūchāi] go on a business trip
→ *see also*/另见 chā, chà
差事 [chāishi] N 1 (任务) assignment 2 (差使) position

柴 [chái] N firewood
柴油 [cháiyóu] N diesel

豺 [chái] N jackal

掺 [chān] VB mix

搀 [chān] VB 1 (搀扶) support ... by the arm 2 (混合) mix

馋 [chán] ADJ greedy

缠 [chán] VB 1 (缠绕) twine 2 (纠缠) pester

蝉 [chán] N cicada

产 [chǎn] VB 1 (生育) give birth to 2 (出产) produce
产量 [chǎnliàng] N yield
产品 [chǎnpǐn] N product
产权 [chǎnquán] N property rights (PL) ▷ 知识产权 [zhīshi chǎnquán] intellectual property
产生 [chǎnshēng] VB produce
产业 [chǎnyè] N 1 (财产) property 2 (工业生产) industry

铲 [chǎn] I N shovel II VB shovel

颤 [chàn] VB tremble
颤抖 [chàndǒu] VB shiver

长 [cháng] I ADJ long II N (长度) length
→ *see also*/另见 zhǎng
长城 [Chángchéng] N the Great Wall

长城 [Chángchéng]

As one of the longest man-made structures in the world, the Great Wall of China is nearly 4,000 miles in length, reaching from the border of Xinjiang province in the west to the eastern coast just north of Beijing. It is probably the most famous of China's landmarks, and was made a UNESCO World Heritage site in 1987. There are records of fortifications being built along the route which date from the 3rd century BC, although most of what remains today was built during the Ming dynasty (1368-1644). Built as a defence mechanism, its primary function was to withstand invasions by the northern tribes.

长处 [chángchu] N strong point

长度 [chángdù] N length

长江 [Cháng Jiāng] N the Yangtze

长久 [chángjiǔ] ADJ long-term

长跑 [chángpǎo] VB go long-distance running

长寿 [chángshòu] ADJ long-lived ▷ 祝您长寿！ [Zhù nín chángshòu!] Here's to a long life!

长寿面 [chángshòumiàn] N long-life noodles (PL)

长寿面 [chángshòumiàn]

In the Chinese tradition, long-life noodles are eaten on one's birthday. They are very long, thin noodles symbolizing longevity.

长途 [chángtú] ADJ long-distance ▷ 长途电话 [chángtú diànhuà] long-distance phone call ▷ 长途旅行 [chángtú lǚxíng] long journey

肠 [cháng] N intestines (PL)

肠子 [chángzi] N intestines (PL)

尝 [cháng] VB taste ▶ 品尝 [pǐncháng] taste

尝试 [chángshì] VB try

常 [cháng] I ADJ 1 (平常) common 2 (经常) frequent ▶ 常客 [chángkè] regular guest II ADV often

常常 [chángcháng] ADV often

常识 [chángshí] N 1 (非专业知识) general knowledge 2 (生活经验) common sense

偿 [cháng] VB 1 (归还) repay 2 (满足) fulfill ▶ 如愿以偿 [rúyuànyǐcháng] fulfill one's dreams

偿还 [chánghuán] VB repay

厂 [chǎng] N (工厂) factory

场 [chǎng] I N 1 (地方) ground ▶ 排球场 [páiqiúchǎng] volleyball court ▶ 市场 [shìchǎng] market 2 (舞台) stage ▶ 上场 [shàngchǎng] go on stage 3 (戏剧片段) scene 4 (物) field II MEAS 1 (比赛, 演出) ▷ 一场足球赛 [yī chǎng zúqiú sài] a soccer match ▷ 两场音乐会 [liǎng chǎng yīnyuèhuì] two concerts

measure word, used for games and shows

2 (病) ▷ 一场重病 [yī chǎng zhòngbìng] a serious illness

measure word, used for illnesses

3 (灾害, 战争, 事故) ▷ 一场火灾 [yī chǎng huǒzāi] a fire ▷ 一场战争 [yī chǎng zhànzhēng] a war ▷ 几场事故 [jǐ chǎng shìgù] several accidents

measure word, used for afflictions, wars, accidents, etc.

场地 [chǎngdì] N space ▷ 运动场地 [yùndòng chǎngdì] sports area

场合 [chǎnghé] N occasion

场所 [chǎngsuǒ] N place ▷ 公共场所 [gōnggòng chǎngsuǒ] public place

敞 [chǎng] I ADJ spacious ▶ 宽敞 [kuānchǎng] spacious II VB be open ▷ 大门敞着。 [Dàmén chǎng zhe.] The main door is open.

畅 [chàng] I ADJ 1 (无阻碍) smooth ▶ 畅通 [chàngtōng] unimpeded 2 (舒适) untroubled ▷ 他心情不畅。[Tā xīnqíng bùchàng.] He's troubled by something. II ADV uninhibitedly ▶ 畅饮 [chàngyǐn] drink one's fill

畅快 [chàngkuài] ADJ carefree

畅所欲言 [chàng suǒ yù yán] speak freely

畅通 [chàngtōng] VB be open

畅销 [chàngxiāo] VB have a ready market

倡 [chàng] VB initiate

倡议 [chàngyì] VB propose

唱 [chàng] VB (发出乐音) sing ▶ 独唱 [dúchàng] solo ▶ 合唱 [héchàng] chorus

唱歌 [chànggē] VB sing

唱戏 [chàngxì] VB perform opera

抄 [chāo] VB 1 (誊写) copy 2 (抄袭) plagiarize

抄袭 [chāoxí] VB (剽窃) plagiarize

钞 [chāo] N banknote

钞票 [chāopiào] N banknote

超 [chāo] I VB 1 (超过) exceed 2 (不受限制) transcend ▶ 超现实 [chāoxiànshí] surreal II ADJ super ▷ 超低温 [chāo dīwēn] ultra-low temperature

超级 [chāojí] ADJ super ▷ 超级大国 [chāojí dàguó] superpower ▷ 超级市场 [chāojí shìchǎng] supermarket

超人 [chāorén] N superman

超市 [chāoshì] N supermarket

超重 [chāozhòng] VB 1 (超过载重量) overload 2 (超过标准量) be overweight

巢 [cháo] N nest

朝 [cháo] I N (朝代) dynasty II VB face III PREP towards ▷ 他朝着我走过来。[Tā cháo zhe wǒ zǒu guòlai.] He was walking towards me.

朝鲜 [Cháoxiǎn] N North Korea

嘲 [cháo] VB ridicule

嘲笑 [cháoxiào] VB laugh at

潮 [cháo] I N 1 (潮汐) tide 2 (社会运动) movement ▶ 工潮 [gōngcháo] labor movement ▶ 思潮 [sīcháo] Zeitgeist II ADJ damp

潮流 [cháoliú] N 1 (水流) tide 2 (发展趋势) trend

潮湿 [cháoshī] ADJ damp

潮水 [cháoshuǐ] N tidal waters (PL)

吵 [chǎo] I VB 1 (发出噪音) make a racket 2 (争吵) squabble II ADJ noisy

吵架 [chǎojià] VB quarrel

吵闹 [chǎonào] VB 1 (争吵) bicker 2 (打扰) disturb

吵嘴 [chǎozuǐ] VB bicker

炒 [chǎo] VB 1 (烹调) stir-fry 2 (地皮，外汇等) speculate ▶ 炒股 [chǎogǔ] speculate in stocks and bonds 3 (方) (解雇) sack ▶ 炒鱿鱼 [chǎo yóuyú] be fired

车 [chē] N 1 (运输工具) vehicle ▶ 小汽车 [xiǎoqìchē] car ▶ 公共汽车 [gōnggòngqìchē] bus 2 (带轮的装置) wheel ▶ 风车 [fēngchē] windmill

车费 [chēfèi] N fare

车祸 [chēhuò] N traffic accident

车间 [chējiān] N workshop

车库 [chēkù] N garage

车辆 [chēliàng] N vehicle

车轮 [chēlún] N wheel

车胎 [chētāi] N tire

车厢 [chēxiāng] N coach

车站 [chēzhàn] N 1 (火车的) railroad station 2 (汽车的) bus stop

扯 [chě] VB (拉) pull

彻 [chè] VB penetrate ▶ 彻夜 [chèyè] all night

彻底 [chèdǐ] ADJ thorough

撤 [chè] VB 1 (除去) take ... away ▶ 撤职 [chèzhí] dismiss from one's job 2 (退) move away

撤退 [chètuì] VB withdraw
撤销 [chèxiāo] VB 1 (职务) dismiss 2 (计划) cancel 3 (法令) rescind

尘 [chén] N 1 (尘土) dirt ▶ 灰尘 [huīchén] dust 2 (尘世) the material world ▶ 尘世 [chénshì] worldly affairs (PL)
尘土 [chéntǔ] N dust

沉 [chén] I VB 1 (向下落) sink 2 (指情绪) become grave II ADJ 1 (指程度深) deep ▶ 昨晚我睡得很沉。[Zuówǎn wǒ shuì de hěn chén.] Last night I slept very deeply. 2 (重) heavy 3 (不舒服) heavy ▷ 我两条腿发沉。[Wǒ liǎng tiáo tuǐ fāchén.] My legs feel heavy.
沉静 [chénjìng] ADJ 1 (肃静) quiet 2 (指性格) placid
沉闷 [chénmèn] ADJ 1 (天气, 气氛) depressing 2 (心情) depressed 3 (指性格) introverted
沉没 [chénmò] VB sink
沉默 [chénmò] I ADJ taciturn II VB be silent
沉痛 [chéntòng] ADJ 1 (心情) grieving 2 (教训) bitter
沉稳 [chénwěn] ADJ 1 (稳重) steady 2 (安稳) peaceful
沉重 [chénzhòng] ADJ heavy
沉着 [chénzhuó] ADJ calm

陈 [chén] VB 1 (陈列) set ... out 2 (陈述) state
陈旧 [chénjiù] ADJ out-of-date
陈列 [chénliè] VB display
陈述 [chénshù] VB state

晨 [chén] N morning ▶ 早晨 [zǎochén] early morning

衬 [chèn] N lining ▶ 衬衫 [chènshān] shirt
衬托 [chèntuō] VB set ... off

称 [chèn] VB match ▶ 相称 [xiāngchèn] match ▶ 对称 [duìchèn] be symmetrical
→ *see also*/另见 chēng

称心 [chènxīn] VB be satisfactory

趁 [chèn] PREP ▷ 趁这个机会我讲几句话。[Chèn zhè ge jīhuì wǒ jiǎng jǐ jù huà.] I would like to take this opportunity to say a few words.

称 [chēng] I VB 1 (叫) call 2 (说) say 3 (测量) weigh II N name ▶ 简称 [jiǎnchēng] short form
→ *see also*/另见 chèn
称呼 [chēnghu] I VB call II N form of address
称赞 [chēngzàn] VB praise

撑 [chēng] VB 1 (抵住) prop ... up 2 (船) punt 3 (坚持住) keep ... up 4 (张开) open 5 (容不下) fill to bursting ▷ 少吃点吧, 别撑着! [Shǎo chī diǎn ba, bié chēng zhe!] Don't eat so much, you'll burst!

成 [chéng] I VB 1 (成功) accomplish ▷ 那件事成了。[Nà jiàn shì chéng le.] The job is done. 2 (成为) become II ADJ (可以) OK ▷ 成! 就这么定了。[Chéng! Jiù zhème dìng le.] OK, that's agreed.
成本 [chéngběn] N cost
成分 [chéngfèn] N 1 (组成部分) composition 2 (社会阶层) status
成功 [chénggōng] VB succeed
成果 [chéngguǒ] N achievement
成绩 [chéngjì] N success
成就 [chéngjiù] I N achievement II VB achieve
成立 [chénglì] VB 1 (建立) found 2 (有根据) be tenable
成年 [chéngnián] VB 1 (指动植物) mature 2 (指人) grow up
成人 [chéngrén] I N adult II VB grow up
成熟 [chéngshú] ADJ 1 (指果实) ripe 2 (指思想) mature 3 (指机会等) ripe
成为 [chéngwéi] VB become
成问题 [chéng wèntí] VB be a problem
成语 [chéngyǔ] N idiom

成员 [chéngyuán] N member

成长 [chéngzhǎng] VB grow up

诚 [chéng] ADJ honest ▶ 忠诚 [zhōngchéng] loyal ▶ 诚心 [chéngxīn] sincere

诚恳 [chéngkěn] ADJ sincere

诚实 [chéngshí] ADJ honest

承 [chéng] VB 1 (承受) bear 2 (承担) undertake

承担 [chéngdān] VB 1 (责任) bear 2 (工作) undertake 3 (费用) bear

承诺 [chéngnuò] I VB undertake II N commitment

承认 [chéngrèn] VB 1 (认可) acknowledge 2 (政权) recognize

承受 [chéngshòu] VB 1 (禁受) bear 2 (经受) experience

城 [chéng] N 1 (城墙) city wall ▶ 城外 [chéngwài] outside the city 2 (城市) city ▶ 进城 [jìnchéng] go to town 3 (城镇) town

城堡 [chéngbǎo] N castle

城市 [chéngshì] N city

乘 [chéng] VB 1 (搭坐) travel by ▷ 乘火车 [chéng huǒchē] travel by train 2 (利用) take advantage of 3 (几倍于) multiply ▷ 8乘5等于40。 [Bā chéng wǔ děngyú sìshí.] Eight times five is forty.

乘法 [chéngfǎ] N multiplication

乘方 [chéngfāng] N (数) power

乘客 [chéngkè] N passenger

乘务员 [chéngwùyuán] N conductor

盛 [chéng] VB 1 (装) ladle ... out 2 (容纳) contain
→ *see also*/另见 shèng

程 [chéng] N 1 (规矩) rule ▶ 章程 [zhāngchéng] constitution 2 (程序) procedure ▶ 议程 [yìchéng] agenda ▶ 课程 [kèchéng] curriculum 3 (距离) distance ▶ 路程 [lùchéng] journey 4 (道路) journey

程度 [chéngdù] N 1 (水平) level 2 (限度) extent

程式 [chéngshì] N form

程序 [chéngxù] N 1 (次序) procedure 2 (计算机) program

惩 [chéng] VB punish

惩罚 [chéngfá] VB punish

橙 [chéng] *see below*/见下文

橙子 [chéngzi] N orange

逞 [chěng] VB (夸耀) flaunt

逞能 [chěngnéng] VB show off

秤 [chèng] N scales

吃 [chī] VB 1 (咀嚼吞咽) eat ▶ 吃药 [chīyào] take medicine 2 (就餐) eat in 3 (依靠) live off ▷ 吃劳保 [chī láobǎo] live off welfare 4 (消灭) wipe ... out 5 (耗费) withstand ▶ 吃力 [chīlì] strenuous 6 (吸收) absorb

吃醋 [chīcù] VB be jealous

吃惊 [chījīng] VB surprise

吃苦 [chīkǔ] VB put up with hardship

吃亏 [chīkuī] VB 1 (受损失) lose out 2 (条件不利) be at a disadvantage

吃香 [chīxiāng] ADJ (口) popular

痴 [chī] I ADJ idiotic II N obsession

痴呆 [chīdāi] ADJ idiotic

痴迷 [chīmí] ADJ infatuated

池 [chí] N (池塘) pond ▶ 泳池 [yǒngchí] swimming pool

池塘 [chítáng] N pond

迟 [chí] ADJ 1 (慢) slow 2 (晚) late

迟到 [chídào] VB be late

迟钝 [chídùn] ADJ (贬) slow

迟早 [chízǎo] ADV sooner or later

持 [chí] VB 1 (拿着) hold 2 (支持) support ▶ 坚持 [jiānchí] maintain

持久 [chíjiǔ] ADJ protracted

持续 [chíxù] VB go on

匙 [chí] N spoon

尺 [chǐ] I MEAS *unit of length, equal to a third of a meter* II N ruler ▶ 尺子 [chǐzi] ruler

尺寸 [chǐcun] N **1** (长度) size **2** (口) (分寸) sense of propriety
尺码 [chǐmǎ] N (尺寸) size

齿 [chǐ] N (器官) tooth ▶ 牙齿 [yáchǐ] tooth

耻 [chǐ] N **1** (羞愧) shame **2** (耻辱) disgrace
耻辱 [chǐrǔ] N disgrace

赤 [chì] ADJ (红色) red
赤道 [chìdào] N the equator
赤裸裸 [chìluǒluǒ] ADJ **1** (光身子) stark naked **2** (喻) (毫无掩饰) undisguised

翅 [chì] N **1** (翅膀) wing **2** (鳍) fin
翅膀 [chìbǎng] N wing

冲 [chōng] VB **1** (向前闯) rush forward **2** (猛撞) clash ▶ 冲撞 [chōngzhuàng] collide **3** (浇) pour boiling water on **4** (冲洗) rinse **5** (指胶片) develop
→ *see also*/另见 chòng
冲刺 [chōngcì] VB (字) sprint
冲动 [chōngdòng] VB be impulsive
冲浪 [chōnglàng] N surf
冲突 [chōngtū] **I** VB **1** (激烈争斗) conflict **2** (相抵触) clash **II** N (矛盾) conflict
冲洗 [chōngxǐ] VB **1** (洗涤) wash **2** (指胶片) develop

充 [chōng] VB **1** (满) fill ▶ 充电 [chōngdiàn] charge a battery **2** (担任) act as **3** (假装) pass ... off as
充当 [chōngdāng] VB act as
充分 [chōngfèn] **I** ADJ ample **II** ADV fully
充满 [chōngmǎn] VB **1** (填满) fill **2** (有) brim with
充其量 [chōngqíliàng] ADV at best
充实 [chōngshí] **I** ADJ rich **II** VB enrich
充足 [chōngzú] ADJ sufficient

虫 [chóng] N insect ▶ 虫子 [chóngzi] insect

重 [chóng] **I** VB **1** (重复) repeat **2** (重叠) overlap **II** ADV again
→ *see also*/另见 zhòng
重叠 [chóngdié] ADJ overlapping
重逢 [chóngféng] VB reunite
重复 [chóngfù] VB repeat
重新 [chóngxīn] ADV again

崇 [chóng] ADJ high
崇拜 [chóngbài] VB worship
崇高 [chónggāo] ADJ lofty

宠 [chǒng] VB spoil
宠爱 [chǒng'ài] VB dote on
宠物 [chǒngwù] N pet

冲 [chòng] **I** ADJ **1** (指气味刺鼻) pungent **2** (劲儿足) vigorous **II** PREP **1** (对着) at **2** (凭) because of **III** VB (口) (正对) face
→ *see also*/另见 chōng

抽 [chōu] VB **1** (取出) take ... out **2** (取出部分) take ▷ 抽时间 [chōu shíjiān] find time **3** (吸) inhale ▶ 抽烟 [chōuyān] smoke ▶ 抽血 [chōuxiě] take blood **4** (抽缩) shrink **5** (打) whip
抽搐 [chōuchù] VB twitch
抽风 [chōufēng] VB **1** (指疾病) have convulsions **2** (喻) (不合常理) lose the plot
抽奖 [chōujiǎng] VB draw prizes
抽筋 [chōujīn] VB (口) (肌肉痉挛) have cramp
抽空 [chōukòng] VB find the time
抽签 [chōuqiān] VB draw lots
抽水 [chōushuǐ] VB **1** (吸水) pump water **2** (缩水) shrink
抽屉 [chōuti] N drawer
抽象 [chōuxiàng] ADJ abstract

仇 [chóu] N **1** (仇敌) enemy **2** (仇恨) hatred ▶ 报仇 [bàochóu] avenge
仇恨 [chóuhèn] VB hate

绸 [chóu] N silk ▶ 丝绸 [sīchóu] silk

酬 [chóu] VB (报答) reward
酬金 [chóujīn] N remuneration

酬劳 [chóuláo] **I** VB repay **II** N repayment
酬谢 [chóuxiè] VB repay

稠 [chóu] ADJ **1** (浓度大) thick **2** (稠密) dense
稠密 [chóumì] ADJ dense

愁 [chóu] VB be anxious ▶ 忧愁 [yōuchóu] be worried

丑 [chǒu] ADJ **1** (丑陋) ugly **2** (令人厌恶) disgraceful
丑陋 [chǒulòu] ADJ ugly
丑闻 [chǒuwén] N scandal

瞅 [chǒu] VB (方) look at

臭 [chòu] ADJ **1** (指气味) smelly **2** (惹人厌恶) disgusting **3** (拙劣) lousy

出 [chū] VB **1** (与入相对) go out ▶ 出国 [chūguó] go abroad ▶ 出游 [chūyóu] go sightseeing **2** (来到) appear ▶ 出庭 [chūtíng] appear in court **3** (超出) exceed ▶ 出轨 [chūguǐ] derail **4** (给) give out **5** (产生) produce **6** (发生) occur ▶ 出事 [chūshì] have an accident **7** (发出) come out ▶ 出血 [chūxiě] bleed ▶ 出汗 [chūhàn] sweat **8** (显露) appear ▶ 出名 [chūmíng] become famous
出版 [chūbǎn] VB publish
出差 [chūchāi] VB go away on business
出发 [chūfā] VB **1** (离开) set out **2** (表示着眼点) take ... as a starting point
出口 [chūkǒu] **I** VB (指贸易) export **II** N exit
出路 [chūlù] N **1** (指道路) way out **2** (前途) prospects (PL) **3** (销路) market
出名 [chūmíng] VB become famous
出勤 [chūqín] VB (按时到) show up on time ▶ 出勤率 [chūqínlǜ] ratio of attendance
出色 [chūsè] ADJ outstanding
出身 [chūshēn] **I** VB come from **II** N background
出生 [chūshēng] VB be born
出售 [chūshòu] VB sell
出席 [chūxí] VB attend
出现 [chūxiàn] VB appear
出院 [chūyuàn] VB leave hospital
出租 [chūzū] VB let ▷ 有房出租 [yǒu fáng chūzū] room to let
出租汽车 [chūzū qìchē] N taxi

初 [chū] **I** N original **II** ADJ **1** (第一) first ▶ 初恋 [chūliàn] first love **2** (最低) primary ▶ 初级 [chūjí] primary **3** (开始) early ▶ 初冬 [chūdōng] early winter
初步 [chūbù] ADJ fundamental
初期 [chūqī] N initial stage

除 [chú] **I** VB **1** (去掉) get rid of ▶ 开除 [kāichú] dismiss ▶ 去除 [qùchú] remove **2** (指算术) divide ▶ 除法 [chúfǎ] division ▷ 16除8等于2。 [Shíliù chú bā děngyú èr.] Sixteen divided by eight is two. **II** PREP **1** (表示绝对排除关系) except ▷ 除彼得外大家都来了。 [Chú Bǐdé wài dàjiā dōu lái le.] Everyone came except Peter. **2** (表示并非惟一) apart from
除非 [chúfēi] **I** CONJ unless ▷ 除非他要我去, 否则我不去。 [Chúfēi tā yào wǒ qù, fǒuzé wǒ bù qù.] I won't go unless he wants me to. **II** PREP other than
除了 [chúle] PREP **1** (表示不包括) except ▷ 除了你其他人都参加了会议。 [Chúle nǐ qítā rén dōu cānjiā le huìyì.] Everyone else attended the meeting except you. **2** (除此以外) apart from ▷ 他除了学习英语, 还学习日语。 [Tā chúle xuéxí Yīngyǔ, hái xuéxí Rìyǔ.] Apart from studying English, he also studies Japanese. **3** (表示非此即彼) apart from ... the only ... ▷ 他除了工作就是睡觉。 [Tā chúle gōngzuò jiùshì shuìjiào.] The only thing he does apart from work is sleep.
除夕 [chúxī] N New Year's Eve

厨 [chú] N **1** (厨房) kitchen ▶ 厨房 [chúfáng] kitchen **2** (厨师) cook

厨师 [chúshī] N cook

橱 [chú] N cabinet

橱窗 [chúchuāng] N **1** (指商店的展示窗) store window **2** (用于展览图片等) display case

处 [chǔ] VB **1** (在) be in **2** (办理) deal with **3** (处罚) penalize
→ *see also*/另见 chù

处罚 [chǔfá] VB punish

处方 [chǔfāng] N prescription

处分 [chǔfèn] **I** VB punish **II** N punishment

处境 [chǔjìng] N situation

处理 [chǔlǐ] VB **1** (解决) deal with **2** (减价) sell ... at a reduced price ▷ 处理品 [chǔlǐ pǐn] goods sold at a discount **3** (加工) treat

处于 [chǔyú] VB be in a position ▷ 处于困境 [chǔyú kùnjìng] be in a difficult position

储 [chǔ] VB store

储备 [chǔbèi] **I** VB store ... up **II** N reserve

储藏 [chǔcáng] VB **1** (保藏) store **2** (蕴藏) contain

储存 [chǔcún] VB stockpile

储蓄 [chǔxù] **I** VB save **II** N savings (PL)

处 [chù] N **1** (地方) place ▶ 益处 [yìchù] profit **2** (部门) department ▷ 人事处 [rénshì chù] human resources department
→ *see also*/另见 chǔ

畜 [chù] N livestock
→ *see also*/另见 xù

畜生 [chùsheng] N beast

触 [chù] VB **1** (接触) touch **2** (触动) move

触犯 [chùfàn] VB violate

触及 [chùjí] VB touch

触摸 [chùmō] VB touch

踹 [chuài] VB (踢) kick

川 [chuān] N (河流) river

穿 [chuān] VB **1** (破) (纸) pierce **2** (谎言, 事实) expose **3** (通过) pass through ▷ 穿过人群 [chuān guò rénqún] pass through the crowd ▷ 穿针 [chuān zhēn] thread a needle **4** (串) piece ... together ▷ 穿珍珠 [chuān zhēnzhū] string pearls together **5** (衣服, 鞋帽, 首饰等) wear **6** (表示透彻) penetrate

穿着 [chuānzhuó] N outfit

传 [chuán] VB **1** (交给) hand ... down **2** (传授) pass ... on **3** (传播) spread **4** (传导) conduct **5** (表达) express ▶ 传情 [chuánqíng] express one's feelings **6** (命令) summon **7** (传染) infect
→ *see also*/另见 zhuàn

传播 [chuánbō] VB disseminate

传达 [chuándá] **I** VB pass ... on **II** N receptionist ▷ 传达室 [chuándá shì] reception room

传单 [chuándān] N leaflet

传媒 [chuánméi] N (传播媒介) media (PL)

传票 [chuánpiào] N (传唤凭证) summons (SG)

传奇 [chuánqí] ADJ legendary

传染 [chuánrǎn] VB infect

传说 [chuánshuō] N legend

传统 [chuántǒng] **I** N tradition **II** ADJ **1** (世代相传) traditional **2** (保守) conservative

传真 [chuánzhēn] VB (指通讯方式) fax ▷ 给我发个传真吧。 [Gěi wǒ fā ge chuánzhēn ba.] Please send me a fax.

船 [chuán] N boat, ship

串 [chuàn] **I** VB **1** (连贯) string ... together **2** (勾结) conspire **3** (指信号) get mixed up **4** (走动) drop by **II** MEAS bunch ▷ 两串钥匙 [liǎng chuàn yàoshi] two bunches of keys ▷ 一串珍珠 [yī chuàng zhēnzhū] a string of pearls

创 [chuāng] N wound ▶ 创可贴 [chuāngkětiē] Band-Aid®
→ *see also*/另见 chuàng

创伤 [chuāngshāng] N 1 (指肉体) wound 2 (指精神) trauma

疮 [chuāng] N (指疾病) ulcer ▶ 口疮 [kǒuchuāng] mouth ulcer ▶ 冻疮 [dòngchuāng] chilblain

窗 [chuāng] N window ▶ 窗子 [chuāngzi] window

窗户 [chuānghu] N window

窗口 [chuāngkǒu] N 1 (字) window 2 (喻) (渠道) vehicle 3 (喻) (反映处) window

床 [chuáng] N bed ▶ 单人床 [dānrénchuáng] single bed ▶ 床单 [chuángdān] bed sheet ▶ 上床 [shàngchuáng] go to bed

闯 [chuǎng] VB 1 (冲) rush 2 (磨炼) steel oneself 3 (惹) stir ... up ▶ 闯祸 [chuǎnghuò] cause trouble

创 [chuàng] VB create ▶ 独创 [dúchuàng] make an original creation
→ *see also*/另见 chuāng

创建 [chuàngjiàn] VB establish

创立 [chuànglì] VB establish

创业 [chuàngyè] VB carve out a career

创意 [chuàngyì] N creativity

创造 [chuàngzào] VB create

创作 [chuàngzuò] I VB create II N work

吹 [chuī] VB 1 (出气) blow ▷ 吹蜡烛 [chuī làzhú] blow out a candle 2 (演奏) play ▷ 吹口琴 [chuī kǒuqín] play the harmonica 3 (夸口) boast 4 (口) (破裂) fall through ▷ 我和女友吹了。 [Wǒ hé nǚyǒu chuī le.] I've broken up with my girlfriend.

吹风 [chuīfēng] VB (吹干) blow-dry

吹牛 [chuīniú] VB brag

吹捧 [chuīpěng] VB flatter

吹嘘 [chuīxū] VB boast

炊 [chuī] VB cook ▶ 炊具 [chuījù] cooking utensil

垂 [chuí] VB (一头向下) hang down

垂直 [chuízhí] ADJ vertical

捶 [chuí] VB pound

锤 [chuí] I N hammer II VB hammer

春 [chūn] N (春季) spring

春节 [Chūn Jié] N Chinese New Year

春节 [Chūn Jié]

Chinese New Year, or Spring Festival, is the most important festival of the year and falls on the first day of the lunar calendar. Traditionally families gather together, children receive money in red envelopes, and in some parts of China everyone helps make and eat a festival feast. On greeting people over this festival it is traditional to wish them wealth and happiness, by saying 恭喜发财 gōngxǐ fācái.

春卷 [chūnjuǎn] N spring roll

春天 [chūntiān] N spring

纯 [chún] ADJ 1 (纯净) pure 2 (纯熟) skillful

纯粹 [chúncuì] I ADJ pure II ADV purely

纯洁 [chúnjié] I ADJ pure II VB purify

纯净 [chúnjìng] ADJ pure

唇 [chún] N lip

蠢 [chǔn] ADJ 1 (愚蠢) stupid 2 (笨拙) clumsy

戳 [chuō] I VB (穿过) poke II N seal

戳子 [chuōzi] N seal

辍 [chuò] VB stop

辍学 [chuòxué] VB give up one's studies

词 [cí] N 1 (语句) words (PL) ▶ 台词 [táicí] lines ▶ 闭幕词 [bìmùcí] closing speech 2 (指语言单位) word

词典 [cídiǎn] N dictionary
词汇 [cíhuì] N vocabulary
词语 [cíyǔ] N word
词组 [cízǔ] N phrase

瓷 [cí] N porcelain

辞 [cí] VB 1 (辞职) resign 2 (辞退) dismiss
辞职 [cízhí] VB resign

慈 [cí] ADJ kind
慈爱 [cí'ài] ADJ affectionate
慈善 [císhàn] ADJ charitable
慈祥 [cíxiáng] ADJ kind

磁 [cí] N (物) magnetism
磁场 [cíchǎng] N magnetic field
磁盘 [cípán] N disk

雌 [cí] ADJ female ▶ 雌性 [cíxìng] female

此 [cǐ] PRON (这) this ▶ 此时此刻 [cǐshí cǐkè] right now
此外 [cǐwài] CONJ apart from this

次 [cì] **I** N ranking ▶ 档次 [dàngcì] grade ▶ 名次 [míngcì] position **II** ADJ **1** (第二) second ▶ 次日 [cìrì] next day **2** (差) inferior ▶ 次品 [cìpǐn] inferior product **III** MEAS time ▶ 初次 [chūcì] first time ▶ 屡次 [lǚcì] repeatedly
次序 [cìxù] N order
次要 [cìyào] ADJ secondary

刺 [cì] N sting
刺耳 [cì'ěr] ADJ **1** (指声音) ear-piercing **2** (喻) (指言语) jarring
刺激 [cìjī] VB **1** (指生物现象) stimulate **2** (推动) stimulate **3** (打击) provoke
刺猬 [cìwei] N hedgehog

匆 [cōng] ADV hastily
匆忙 [cōngmáng] ADJ hurried

葱 [cōng] N green onion

聪 [cōng] **I** N hearing **II** ADJ **1** (指听力) acute **2** (聪明) clever
聪明 [cōngmíng] ADJ clever

从 [cóng] **I** VB **1** (跟随) follow **2** (顺从) comply with ▶ 服从 [fúcóng] obey **3** (从事) participate in **II** N follower **III** ADJ (从属) subordinate ▶ 从犯 [cóngfàn] accessory **IV** PREP **1** (起于) from ▷ 从明天起 [cóng míngtiān qǐ] from tomorrow onwards **2** (经过) ▷ 飞机从我们头顶飞过。 [Fēijī cóng wǒmen tóudǐng fēiguò.] The plane passed over our heads.
从此 [cóngcǐ] ADV after that
从而 [cóng'ér] CONJ thus
从来 [cónglái] ADV ▷ 她从来未说过。 [Tā cónglái wèi shuōguò.] She never said it.
从前 [cóngqián] N **1** (过去) past ▷ 希望你比从前快乐。 [Xīwàng nǐ bǐ cóngqián kuàilè.] I hope you are happier than you were before. **2** (很久以前) once upon a time
从事 [cóngshì] VB **1** (投身) undertake **2** (处理) deal with

凑 [còu] VB **1** (聚集) gather ... together **2** (碰) encounter **3** (接近) approach
凑合 [còuhe] VB **1** (聚集) gather ... together **2** (拼凑) improvise **3** (将就) get by
凑巧 [còuqiǎo] ADJ lucky

粗 [cū] ADJ **1** (横剖面大) thick **2** (颗粒大) coarse **3** (指声音) gruff **4** (糙) crude
粗暴 [cūbào] ADJ rough
粗糙 [cūcāo] ADJ **1** (不光滑) rough **2** (不细致) crude
粗话 [cūhuà] N obscene language
粗鲁 [cūlǔ] ADJ crude
粗心 [cūxīn] ADJ careless
粗野 [cūyě] ADJ rough

促 [cù] **I** ADJ urgent **II** VB **1** (催) press **2** (靠近) be near
促进 [cùjìn] VB promote
促使 [cùshǐ] VB press for

醋 [cù] N (指调味品) vinegar

催 [cuī] VB **1** (敦促) hurry ▶ 催促 [cuīcù] hurry **2** (加快) speed … up ▶ 催眠 [cuīmián] hypnotize

脆 [cuì] ADJ **1** (易碎) brittle **2** (指食物) crispy

脆弱 [cuìruò] ADJ fragile

村 [cūn] N village ▶ 村子 [cūnzi] village

存 [cún] VB **1** (存在) exist **2** (储存) store **3** (储蓄) save ▶ 存款 [cúnkuǎn] savings (PL) **4** (寄存) check … in ▷ 存行李 [cún xíngli] check in one's bags **5** (保留) retain **6** (心里怀着) harbor

存档 [cúndàng] VB file

存放 [cúnfàng] VB deposit

存心 [cúnxīn] ADV deliberately

存在 [cúnzài] VB exist

存折 [cúnzhé] N passbook

寸 [cùn] MEAS *unit of length, approximately 3 cm*

搓 [cuō] VB rub

撮 [cuō] VB (聚集) scoop … up

痤 [cuó] *see below*/见下文

痤疮 [cuóchuāng] N acne

挫 [cuò] VB (挫折) defeat ▶ 挫折 [cuòzhé] setback

措 [cuò] VB **1** (安排) handle **2** (筹划) make plans

措施 [cuòshī] N measure

错 [cuò] **I** ADJ (不正确) incorrect **II** VB (避开) miss **III** N fault ▷ 这是我的错。 [Zhè shì wǒ de cuò.] This is my fault.

错过 [cuòguò] VB miss ▷ 错过机会 [cuòguò jīhuì] miss an opportunity

错误 [cuòwù] **I** ADJ wrong **II** N mistake

D

搭 [dā] VB **1** (建造) put ... up ▷ 搭帐篷 [dā zhàngpeng] put up a tent **2** (挂) hang ▷ 我把大衣搭在胳膊上。 [Wǒ bǎ dàyī dā zài gēbo shàng.] I hung my overcoat over my arm. **3** (坐) take ▷ 他每个月搭飞机去上海。 [Tā méi ge yuè dā fēijī qù Shànghǎi.] He takes the plane to Shanghai every month. ▷ 搭便车 [dā biànchē] get a ride **4** (连接) join ▶ 搭伙 [dāhuǒ] join forces ▷ 两家公司终于搭上了关系。 [Liǎng jiā gōngsī zhōngyú dā shàng le guānxi.] The two companies finally joined forces. **5** (抬) carry

搭档 [dādàng] **I** N partner **II** VB team up

搭配 [dāpèi] VB **1** (安排) combine **2** (配合) pair up **3** (指语言) collocate

答 [dā] VB answer

→ *see also*/另见 dá

答理 [dāli] VB **1** (理睬) bother **2** (打招呼) acknowledge

答应 [dāying] VB **1** (回答) answer **2** (同意) agree **3** (承诺) promise

打 [dá] MEAS dozen

→ *see also*/另见 dǎ

达 [dá] VB **1** (数量, 目标) reach **2** (指时间) last **3** (通) ▶ 直达 [zhídá] non-stop journey **4** (表示) express ▶ 转达 [chuándá] convey

达到 [dádào] VB **1** (要求, 水平, 目的) achieve ▷ 达到目的 [dádào mùdì] achieve an aim ▷ 达到要求 [dádào yāoqiú] satisfy requirements **2** (指过程) reach

答 [dá] VB **1** (回答) answer **2** (还报) repay ▶ 报答 [bàodá] repay

→ *see also*/另见 dā

答案 [dá'àn] N answer

答复 [dáfù] VB respond

答卷 [dájuàn] **I** N answer sheet **II** VB answer exam questions

打 [dǎ] **I** VB **1** (指暴力) hit ▶ 殴打 [ōudǎ] beat up ▶ 打人 [dǎrén] beat sb up **2** (敲) beat ▷ 打鼓 [dǎ gǔ] beat a drum **3** (破) break ▷ 我把暖瓶给打了。 [Wǒ bǎ nuǎnpíng gěi dǎ le.] I broke the thermos. **4** (发出) send ▷ 打电话 [dǎ diànhuà] make a phone call ▷ 打手电 [dǎ shǒudiàn] shine a torch **5** (做游戏) play ▷ 打篮球 [dǎ lánqiú] play basketball **6** (表示动作) ▶ 打喷嚏 [dǎpēnti] sneeze ▶ 打滚 [dǎgǔn] roll about ▶ 打针 [dǎzhēn] have an injection **7** (建造) build ▷ 打基础 [dǎ jīchǔ] build the foundation **8** (涂抹) polish ▶ 打蜡 [dǎlà] wax **9** (交涉) deal with ▷ 打交道 [dǎ jiāodao] socialize ▷ 打官司 [dǎ guānsi] file a lawsuit **10** (制造) make ▷ 打家具 [dǎ jiājù] make furniture **11** (搅拌) beat ▷ 打两个鸡蛋 [dǎ liǎng ge jīdàn] beat two eggs **12** (编织) knit ▷ 打毛衣 [dǎ máoyī] knit a sweater **13** (捕捉) catch ▶ 打猎 [dǎliè] go hunting **14** (画) draw ▷ 打草稿 [dǎ cǎogǎo] draw up a draft **15** (举) hold ▶ 打伞 [dǎsǎn] hold an umbrella **16** (揭) open ▶ 打开 [dǎkāi] open **17** (穿凿) dig ▷ 打耳洞 [dǎ ěrdòng] pierce one's ears **18** (收割) gather ▶ 打柴 [dǎchái] gather firewood **19** (从事) do ▶ 打杂儿 [dǎzár] do odd jobs **20** (用) make ▷ 打比喻 [dǎ bǐyù] make a comparison **21** (捆) pack ▷ 打行李 [dǎ xíngli] pack one's bags **22** (拨动) flick ▶ 打字 [dǎzì] type ▶ 打字机 [dǎzìjī] typewriter **II** PREP from ▷ 打今儿起 [dǎ jīnr qǐ] from today

→ *see also*/另见 dá

打败 [dǎbài] VB defeat

打扮 [dǎban] VB make oneself up

打倒 [dǎdǎo] VB **1** (击倒在地) knock down **2** (指口号) down with **3** (推翻) overthrow

打的 [dǎ dī] VB take a taxi

打动 [dǎdòng] VB move

打赌 [dǎdǔ] VB bet

打发 [dǎfa] VB **1** (时间) while away **2** (哄走) get rid of **3** (派) send

打工 [dǎgōng] VB temp

打火机 [dǎhuǒjī] N lighter

打击 [dǎjī] **I** VB crack down on **II** N (指精神上) blow

打架 [dǎjià] VB have a fight

打开 [dǎkāi] VB **1** (开启) open **2** (扩展) expand **3** (开) turn ... on

打气 [dǎqì] VB (球, 轮胎) inflate

打扫 [dǎsǎo] VB clean

打算 [dǎsuan] **I** VB plan **II** N plan

打听 [dǎting] VB ask about

打印机 [dǎyìnjī] N printer

打仗 [dǎzhàng] VB fight a war

打招呼 [dǎ zhāohu] VB (问好) greet

打折 [dǎzhé] VB discount

大 [dà] ADJ **1** (数量, 体积, 面积) big ▸ 大街 [dàjiē] street ▸ 一大批 [yīdàpī] a large amount of **2** (指力气) great ▹ 他劲儿真大! [Tā jìnr zhēn dà!] He's so strong! **3** (重要) important **4** (强) strong ▹ 大风 [dà fēng] strong wind **5** (指声音) loud ▸ 大声 [dàshēng] loudly **6** (雨, 雪) heavy **7** (指年龄) old ▹ 你多大了? [Nǐ duōdà le?] How old are you? ▹ 他比我大。 [Tā bǐ wǒ dà.] He's older than me. **8** (指程度) ▸ 大笑 [dàxiào] roar with laughter **9** (老大) eldest ▹ 大姐 [dà jiě] eldest sister

→ *see also*/另见 dài

大胆 [dàdǎn] ADJ bold

大地 [dàdì] N the land

大方 [dàfang] ADJ **1** (慷慨) generous **2** (不拘束) natural **3** (不俗气) tasteful

大概 [dàgài] **I** N general idea **II** ADJ approximate **III** ADV probably

大伙儿 [dàhuǒr] PRON everybody

大家 [dàjiā] PRON everybody

大款 [dàkuǎn] N (贬) moneybags (SG)

大量 [dàliàng] ADJ (数量多) large amount of ▹ 大量资金 [dàliàng zījīn] a large investment ▹ 大量裁员 [dàliàng cáiyuán] lay off a large number of people

大陆 [dàlù] N **1** (指各大洲) continent **2** (指中国) the mainland ▹ 中国大陆 [Zhōngguó dàlù] mainland China

大米 [dàmǐ] N rice

大人 [dàren] N adult

大使 [dàshǐ] N ambassador

大使馆 [dàshǐguǎn] N embassy

大事 [dàshì] N important event

大提琴 [dàtíqín] N cello

大小 [dàxiǎo] N (尺寸) size

大写 [dàxiě] N (指字母) capital letter

大型 [dàxíng] ADJ large-scale

大选 [dàxuǎn] N general election

大学 [dàxué] N college

大学生 [dàxuéshēng] N college student

大雪 [dàxuě] N heavy snow

大衣 [dàyī] N overcoat

大雨 [dàyǔ] N downpour

大约 [dàyuē] ADV **1** (指数量) approximately **2** (可能) probably

大众 [dàzhòng] N the people (PL)

大自然 [dàzìrán] N nature

呆 [dāi] **I** ADJ **1** (傻) slow-witted **2** (发愣) blank ▸ 发呆 [fādāi] stare blankly **II** VB stay ▹ 我在北京呆了一个星期。 [Wǒ zài Běijīng dāi le yī ge xīngqī.] I stayed in Beijing for a week.

待 [dāi] VB stay ▹ 你再多待一会儿。 [Nǐ zài duō dāi yīhuìr.] Do stay a little longer.

→ *see also*/另见 dài

逮 [dǎi] VB catch

→ *see also*/另见 dài

大 [dài] *see below*/见下文

大夫 [dàifu] N doctor
→ *see also*/另见 dà

代 [dài] I VB 1 (替) do ... on behalf of 2 (指问候) send regards to ▷ 你见到他时, 代我问好。 [Nǐ jiàndào tā shí, dài wǒ wènhǎo.] When you see him, say hello from me. 3 (代理) act as ▷ 代校长 [dài xiàozhǎng] acting headmaster II N 1 (时代) times (PL) ▶ 古代 [gǔdài] ancient times 2 (辈分) generation 3 (朝代) dynasty ▷ 清代 [Qīng dài] Qing Dynasty

代表 [dàibiǎo] I N representative II VB 1 (代替) stand in for 2 (委托) represent 3 (指意义, 概念) be representative of III ADJ archetypal

代价 [dàijià] N cost

代理 [dàilǐ] VB 1 (暂时替代) act on behalf of 2 (委托) represent

代理人 [dàilǐrén] N agent

代码 [dàimǎ] N code

代数 [dàishù] N algebra

代替 [dàitì] VB substitute for

带 [dài] I N 1 (长条物) strap ▶ 皮带 [pídài] leather belt ▶ 磁带 [cídài] cassette ▶ 录像带 [lùxiàngdài] videotape 2 (轮胎) tire ▶ 车带 [chēdài] tire 3 (区域) zone ▶ 热带 [rèdài] the tropics II VB 1 (携带) take ▷ 别忘了带钱包! [Bié wàng le dài qiánbāo!] Don't forget to take your wallet! 2 (捎带) ▷ 你出去时带点牛奶回来, 好吗? [Nǐ chūqù shí dài diǎn niúnǎi huílai, hǎo ma?] Can you buy some milk when you're out? 3 (呈现) wear ▷ 面带笑容 [miàn dài xiàoróng] wear a smile on one's face 4 (含有) have 5 (连带) come with 6 (指导) direct 7 (领) lead 8 (养) bring ... up

带动 [dàidòng] VB (指进步) drive

带领 [dàilǐng] VB 1 (领着) guide 2 (指挥) lead

带头 [dàitóu] VB take the initiative

待 [dài] VB 1 (对待) treat 2 (招待) entertain 3 (等待) wait for
→ *see also*/另见 dāi

待业 [dàiyè] VB be unemployed

待遇 [dàiyù] N pay

贷 [dài] I VB 1 (指银行) lend 2 (指借钱方) take out a loan II N loan

贷款 [dàikuǎn] I VB lend II N loan

袋 [dài] I N bag II MEAS bag

袋鼠 [dàishǔ] N kangaroo

逮 [dài] VB capture
→ *see also*/另见 dǎi

逮捕 [dàibǔ] VB arrest

戴 [dài] VB (眼镜, 帽子, 小装饰品等) wear

单 [dān] I ADJ 1 (一个) single ▶ 单身 [dānshēn] single 2 (奇数) odd 3 (单独) solitary 4 (不复杂) simple 5 (薄弱) weak 6 (衣, 裤) thin II ADV only ▷ 成功不能单凭运气。 [Chénggōng bùnéng dān píng yùnqi.] To be successful you can't rely only on luck. III N 1 (单子) sheet ▶ 床单 [chuángdān] bed sheet 2 (列表) list ▶ 菜单 [càidān] menu

单程 [dānchéng] N single trip

单纯 [dānchún] I ADJ simple II ADV merely

单词 [dāncí] N word

单单 [dāndān] ADV only

单调 [dāndiào] ADJ monotonous

单独 [dāndú] ADJ 1 (独自) alone 2 (独立) unaided

单位 [dānwèi] N 1 (指标准量) unit 2 (机构) unit

单元 [dānyuán] N unit ▷ 单元房 [dānyuán fáng] self-contained apartment

单子 [dānzi] N 1 (指床上用品) sheet 2 (列表) list

担 [dān] VB 1 (挑) carry ... on one's shoulder 2 (负) take ... on
→ *see also*/另见 dàn

担保 [dānbǎo] VB guarantee

担当 [dāndāng] VB take ... on

担架 [dānjià] N stretcher
担任 [dānrèn] VB hold the post of
担心 [dānxīn] VB worry

耽 [dān] *see below*/见下文
耽误 [dānwu] VB delay

胆 [dǎn] N (胆量) courage
胆固醇 [dǎngùchún] N cholesterol
胆量 [dǎnliàng] N guts (PL)
胆子 [dǎnzi] N guts (PL)

掸 [dǎn] VB brush
掸子 [dǎnzi] N duster

但 [dàn] **I** CONJ but **II** ADV only ▶ 但愿 [dànyuàn] wish
但是 [dànshì] CONJ but ▷ 虽然下雨，但是不冷。 [Suīrán xiàyǔ, dànshì bù lěng.] Even though it's raining, it's not cold.

担 [dàn] N load
→ *see also*/另见 dān
担子 [dànzi] N (责任) responsibility

诞 [dàn] VB be born
诞生 [dànshēng] VB be born

淡 [dàn] ADJ **1** (指味道浓淡) weak **2** (指咸淡) bland **3** (颜色浅) light **4** (稀薄) light **5** (不热情) indifferent **6** (不红火) slack
淡季 [dànjì] N low season

蛋 [dàn] N (卵) egg ▶ 鸡蛋 [jīdàn] egg
蛋白质 [dànbáizhì] N protein
蛋糕 [dàngāo] N cake

弹 [dàn] N (子弹) bullet ▶ 子弹 [zǐdàn] bullet ▶ 原子弹 [yuánzǐdàn] atomic bomb
→ *see also*/另见 tán

当 [dāng] **I** PREP **1** (向) in front of ▶ 当众 [dāngzhòng] in public ▷ 当着全班 [dāng zhe quánbān] in front of the whole class **2** (正在) ▷ 当我们到时，电影已开始了。 [Dāng wǒmen dào shí, diànyǐng yǐ kāishǐ le.] When we arrived the film had already started. ▷ 当他在美国时，他爷爷去世了。 [Dāng tā zài Měiguó shí, tā yéye qùshì le.] His grandfather passed away while he was in America. **II** VB **1** (担任) act as ▷ 当经理 [dāng jīnglǐ] act as manager **2** (掌管) be in charge ▶ 当家 [dāngjiā] rule the roost
→ *see also*/另见 dàng
当场 [dāngchǎng] ADV there and then
当初 [dāngchū] N those days
当代 [dāngdài] N the present ▶ 当代文学 [dāngdài wénxué] contemporary literature
当地 [dāngdì] N locality ▷ 当地风俗 [dāngdì fēngsú] local customs
当今 [dāngjīn] N the present
当面 [dāngmiàn] VB do … face to face
当年 [dāngnián] N those days
当前 [dāngqián] **I** VB be faced with **II** N present ▷ 当前的目标 [dāngqián de mùbiāo] the present aim
当然 [dāngrán] **I** ADV of course **II** ADJ natural
当时 [dāngshí] N ▷ 我当时高兴极了。 [Wǒ dāngshí gāoxìng jí le.] I was ecstatic at the time.
当心 [dāngxīn] VB be careful

挡 [dǎng] VB (拦) keep off ▷ 别挡路！ [Bié dǎnglù!] Keep off the road!

党 [dǎng] N (政党) party ▶ 党员 [dǎngyuán] party member

当 [dàng] **I** ADJ appropriate ▶ 不当 [bùdàng] inappropriate **II** VB **1** (作为) treat … as **2** (认为) assume ▷ 我当你明白了。 [Wǒ dàng nǐ míngbai le.] I assumed you'd understood. **3** (抵押) pawn **4** (指时间和地点) ▶ 当天 [dàngtiān] that day ▶ 当场 [dàngchǎng] on the spot
→ *see also*/另见 dāng
当年 [dàngnián] N that same year
当铺 [dàngpù] N pawnshop

当作 [dàngzuò] VB regard … as

档 [dàng] N 1 (档案) file 2 (等级) grade
档案 [dàng'àn] N files (PL)
档次 [dàngcì] N grade

刀 [dāo] N (指工具) knife ▶ 刀子 [dāozi] knife

叨 [dāo] *see below*/见下文
叨唠 [dāolao] VB prattle on

导 [dǎo] VB 1 (引导) guide 2 (传导) conduct 3 (开导) give guidance 4 (导演) direct
导弹 [dǎodàn] N missile
导火线 [dǎohuǒxiàn] N 1 (字) fuze 2 (喻) trigger
导师 [dǎoshī] N 1 (字) tutor 2 (喻) mentor
导演 [dǎoyǎn] I VB direct II N director
导游 [dǎoyóu] I VB guide II N tour guide
导致 [dǎozhì] VB lead to ▷ 粗心导致她没考好。 [Cūxīn dǎozhì tā méi kǎo hǎo.] Because of her carelessness she failed the exam.

岛 [dǎo] N island ▶ 岛国 [dǎoguó] island nation ▶ 半岛 [bàndǎo] peninsula

倒 [dǎo] VB 1 (横躺) fall ▶ 摔倒 [shuāidǎo] fall down ▶ 卧倒 [wòdǎo] lie down 2 (失败) fail ▶ 倒闭 [dǎobì] go bankrupt 3 (食欲) spoil ▷ 倒胃口 [dǎo wèikǒu] lose one's appetite 4 (换) change ▶ 倒班 [dǎobān] change shifts
→ *see also*/另见 dào
倒霉 [dǎoméi] ADJ unlucky
倒塌 [dǎotā] VB collapse

捣 [dǎo] VB 1 (捶打) crush 2 (搅乱) make trouble
捣乱 [dǎoluàn] VB 1 (扰乱) disturb 2 (制造麻烦) make trouble

到 [dào] VB 1 (达到) arrive ▷ 火车到了。 [Huǒchē dào le.] The train has arrived. ▷ 到点了! [Dào diǎn le!] Time is up! 2 (去) go ▷ 我到厦门旅游。 [Wǒ dào Xiàmén lǚyóu.] I'm going to Xiamen on a tour. 3 (用作动词的补语) ▷ 听到这个消息我很吃惊。 [Tīngdào zhè ge xiāoxi wǒ hěn chījīng.] When I heard the news I was very surprised. ▷ 你的要求我办不到。 [Nǐ de yāoqiú wǒ bàn bù dào.] I can't handle your demands.
到处 [dàochù] N all places (PL)
到达 [dàodá] VB arrive
到底 [dàodǐ] I VB ▷ 坚持到底 [jiānchí dàodǐ] keep going until the end II ADV 1 (究竟) ▷ 你到底在干什么? [Nǐ dàodǐ zài gàn shénme?] What on earth are you up to? 2 (毕竟) after all 3 (终于) at last

倒 [dào] I VB 1 (颠倒) ▶ 他把地图挂倒了。 [Tā bǎ dìtú guà dào le.] He hung the map up upside down. ▶ 姓和名写倒了。 [Xìng hé míng xiě dào le.] The first name and surname were written the wrong way round. 2 (后退) reverse ▶ 倒车 [dàochē] reverse a car 3 (倾倒) empty out ▷ 倒垃圾 [dào lājī] empty out the trash ▷ 倒杯茶 [dào bēi chá] pour a cup of tea II ADV 1 (表示意料之外) unexpectedly 2 (反而) instead 3 (表示让步) ▷ 这房子地段倒好，就是太小。 [Zhè fángzi dìduàn dào hǎo, jiùshì tài xiǎo.] Although the location of the house is good, it's still too small. 4 (表示转折) but 5 (表示不耐烦) ▷ 你倒是说呀! [Nǐ dào shì shuō ya!] Can you get on with it please! 6 (表示责怪) ▷ 他说得倒漂亮。 [Tā shuō de dào piàoliang.] He's all talk.
→ *see also*/另见 dǎo
倒立 [dàolì] VB 1 (物) be upside down 2 (人) do a handstand
倒计时 [dàojìshí] VB count down
倒退 [dàotuì] VB go back
倒影 [dàoyǐng] N reflection

悼 [dào] VB mourn
悼念 [dàoniàn] VB mourn

盗 [dào] I VB rob ▶ 盗窃 [dàoqiè] steal II N robber ▶ 海盗 [hǎidào] pirate
盗版 [dàobǎn] I VB pirate ▶ 盗版软件 [dàobǎn ruǎnjiàn] pirated software II N pirate copy
盗贼 [dàozéi] N thieves (PL)

道 [dào] I N 1 (路) road ▶ 近道 [jìndào] shortcut 2 (方法) way ▶ 生财之道 [shēngcái zhī dào] the road to riches 3 (技艺) art ▶ 茶道 [chádào] tea ceremony 4 (道教) the Tao 5 (线) line ▶ 横道儿 [héngdàor] horizontal line 6 (水流途径) channel ▶ 下水道 [xiàshuǐdào] sewer II MEAS 1 ▷ 一道阳光 [yī dào yángguāng] a beam of sunlight ▷ 两道泪痕 [liǎng dào lèihén] two tear streaks

measure word, used for things in the shape of a long strip

2 ▷ 第二道门 [dì'èr dào mén] the second door ▷ 一道墙 [yī dào qiáng] a wall

measure word, used for doors, walls, etc.

3 ▷ 三道题 [sān dào tí] three questions ▷ 两道命令 [liáng dào mìnglìng] two orders

measure word, used for orders, questions, procedures, etc.

4 (次) ▷ 我还要办一道手续。 [Wǒ háiyào bàn yī dào shǒuxù] I still need to complete one formality. ▷ 刷了两道漆 [shuā le liǎng dào qī] paint two coats 5 ▷ 五道菜 [wǔ dào cài] five dishes

measure word, used for dishes or courses of a meal

道德 [dàodé] N morals (PL)
道教 [Dàojiào] N Taoism
道理 [dàoli] N 1 (规律) principle 2 (情理) sense
道路 [dàolù] N path
道歉 [dàoqiàn] VB apologize

得 [dé] I VB 1 (得到) get ▶ 得奖 [déjiǎng] win a prize 2 (病) catch ▷ 他得了流感。 [Tā dé le liúgǎn.] He caught flu. 3 (计算) equal ▷ 四减二得二。 [Sì jiǎn èr dé èr.] Four minus two equals two. 4 (完成) be ready ▷ 晚饭得了。 [Wǎnfàn dé le.] Dinner is ready. 5 (适合) be suitable ▶ 得体 [détǐ] appropriate II INT 1 (表示同意, 禁止) OK ▷ 得, 就这么决定了。 [Dé, jiù zhème juédìng le.] OK, that's settled then. 2 (表示无可奈何) Oh no! ▷ 得, 我又没考及格! [Dé, wǒ yòu méi kǎo jígé!] Oh no, I failed again! III AUX VB ▷ 版权所有, 不得转载。 [Bǎnquán suǒyǒu, bù dé zhuǎnzǎi.] All rights reserved, copying not allowed.
→ *see also*/另见 de, děi
得到 [dédào] VB get ▷ 得到帮助 [dédào bāngzhù] get help
得意 [déyì] ADJ pleased with oneself
得罪 [dézuì] VB offend

德 [dé] N 1 (品行) morality ▶ 品德 [pǐndé] moral character 2 (恩惠) kindness ▶ 恩德 [ēndé] kindness 3 (德国) Germany ▶ 德国 [Déguó] Germany ▶ 德语 [Déyǔ] German

地 [de] AUX WORD ▷ 刻苦地学习 [kèkǔ de xuéxí] study hard ▷ 努力地工作 [nǔlì de gōngzuò] work hard
→ *see also*/另见 dì

Use 地 de after adjectives to form adverbs.

的 [de] AUX WORD 1 (用于定语后) ▷ 昂贵的价格 [ánggui de jiàgé] high price ▷ 他的哥哥 [tā de gēge] his elder brother ▷ 经理的秘书 [jīnglǐ de mìshū] the manager's secretary 2 (名词化) ▷ 画画的 [huàhuà de] painter 3 (用于是…的强调结构) ▷ 我的嗓子是喊哑的。 [Wǒ de sǎngzi shì hǎnyǎ de.] My voice became

hoarse from shouting.
→ *see also*/另见 dí, dì

Use 的 de to link descriptive words, phrases and clauses to the noun they describe, e.g. 她是一个很漂亮的女人。 Tā shì yīgè hěn piàoliàng de nǚrén. (She is a very beautiful woman.); 这是他昨天给我的书。 Zhè shì tā zuótiān gěi wǒ de shū. (This is the book which he gave me yesterday.)

的话 [dehuà] AUX WORD ▷ 见到她的话, 替我问好。 [Jiàndào tā de huà, tì wǒ wènhǎo.] Please give her my regards if you see her.

得 [de] AUX WORD **1** (用于动词后面) ▷ 这种野菜吃得。 [Zhè zhǒng yěcài chī de.] This wild herb is edible. **2** (动词或补语中间) ▷ 她抬得动。 [Tā tái de dòng.] She can carry it. ▷ 我写得完。 [Wǒ xiě de wán.] I am able to finish writing it. **3** (动词和形容词后面) ▷ 他英语学得很快。 [Tā Yīngyǔ xué de hěn kuài.] He's learning English very quickly. ▷ 风大得很。 [Fēng dà de hěn.] The wind's very strong.
→ *see also*/另见 dé, děi

Most adverbial phrases follow the verb and are joined to it by 得 de. Such statements are often evaluations or judgments, and contain the idea of *to the extent of* or *to the degree that*, e.g. 她说得很流利。 Tā shuō de hěn liúlì. (She speaks very fluently.)

得 [děi] **I** VB (口) (需要) need ▷ 买房得多少钱? [Mǎifáng děi duōshao qián?] How much money do you need to buy a house? **II** AUX VB (口) **1** (必要) must ▷ 我们得6点出发。 [Wǒmen děi liùdiǎn chūfā.] We have to leave at six. **2** (表示推测) will ▷ 快走, 电影得开始了。 [Kuài zǒu, diànyǐng děi kāishǐ le.] Get a move on, the film's just about to start.
→ *see also*/另见 dé, de

灯 [dēng] N light ▶ 台灯 [táidēng] desk lamp ▶ 红绿灯 [hónglǜdēng] traffic lights (PL)

灯塔 [dēngtǎ] N lighthouse

登 [dēng] VB **1** (由低到高) go up **2** (刊登) publish **3** (踩踏板) pedal **4** (踩) get up onto

登记 [dēngjì] VB register

登录 [dēnglù] VB log in ▷ 登录网站 [dēnglù wǎngzhàn] log in to a website

蹬 [dēng] VB pedal

等 [děng] **I** N **1** (等级) grade ▶ 中等 [zhōngděng] medium ▷ 二等奖 [èr děng jiǎng] second prize **2** (类) kind **II** VB **1** (相同) equal ▶ 等于 [děngyú] be equal to **2** (等待) wait ▶ 等车 [děngchē] wait for a bus **III** CONJ (等到) when ▷ 等他来了, 我们再讨论。 [Děng tā lái le, wǒmen zài tǎolùn.] We'll talk about it when he comes. **IV** AUX WORD **1** (列举未尽的) etc. **2** (煞尾的) namely

等待 [děngdài] VB wait

等到 [děngdào] CONJ when

等等 [děngděng] AUX WORD and so on

等号 [děnghào] N (数) equals sign

等候 [děnghòu] VB expect

等级 [děngjí] N grade

等于 [děngyú] VB **1** (相等于) equal **2** (等同) be equivalent to

凳 [dèng] N stool ▶ 板凳 [bǎndèng] wooden stool ▶ 凳子 [dèngzi] stool

瞪 [dèng] VB **1** (表示生气) glare at **2** (睁大) open one's eyes wide

低 [dī] **I** ADJ **1** (指高度, 程度) low ▷ 他喜欢低声说话。 [Tā xǐhuan dī shēng shuōhuà.] He likes to speak quietly. **2** (指等级) junior ▶ 我比她低两届。 [Wǒ bǐ tā dī liǎngjiè.] I am two years below her. **II** VB (头) bend

低潮 [dīcháo] N low ebb
低调 [dīdiào] ADJ low-key
低级 [dījí] ADJ **1** (不高级) inferior **2** (庸俗) vulgar

堤 [dī] N dyke

提 [dī] VB carry
→ *see also*/另见 tí
提防 [dīfáng] VB guard against

滴 [dī] **I** VB drip **II** N drop ▸ 水滴 [shuǐdī] drop of water **III** MEAS drop ▹ 几滴墨水 [jǐ dī mòshuǐ] a few drops of ink

的 [dí] *see below*/见下文
→ *see also*/另见 de, dì
的确 [díquè] ADV really

迪 [dí] VB (书) enlighten
迪斯科 [dísikē] N disco

敌 [dí] **I** N enemy **II** VB oppose **III** ADJ equal
敌人 [dírén] N enemy

笛 [dí] N **1** (音) flute **2** (警笛) siren
笛子 [dízi] N bamboo flute

底 [dǐ] N **1** (最下部分) bottom ▸ 鞋底 [xiédǐ] sole ▸ 底下 [dǐxia] under **2** (末尾) end ▸ 年底 [niándǐ] the end of the year
底层 [dǐcéng] N **1** (指建筑) first floor **2** (最下部) bottom

抵 [dǐ] VB **1** (支撑) support **2** (抵抗) resist **3** (补偿) compensate for **4** (抵押) mortgage **5** (抵消) offset **6** (代替) be equal to
抵达 [dǐdá] VB reach
抵抗 [dǐkàng] VB resist
抵押 [dǐyā] VB mortgage

地 [dì] N **1** (地球) the Earth ▸ 地球 [dìqiú] the Earth **2** (陆地) land **3** (土地) fields (PL) **4** (地点) location ▸ 目的地 [mùdìdì] destination
→ *see also*/另见 de
地步 [dìbù] N **1** (处境) state, situation **2** (程度) extent
地带 [dìdài] N zone
地道 [dìdào] N tunnel
地道 [dìdao] ADJ **1** (真正) genuine **2** (纯正) pure **3** (指质量) well done
地点 [dìdiǎn] N location
地方 [dìfāng] N locality ▹ 地方政府 [dìfāng zhèngfǔ] local government
地方 [dìfang] N **1** (区域) place ▹ 你是哪个地方的人? [Nǐ shì nǎ ge dìfang de rén?] Where do you come from? **2** (空间) room **3** (身体部位) ▹ 我这个地方痛。 [Wǒ zhè ge dìfang tòng.] I ache here. **4** (部分) part ▹ 有不明白的地方吗? [Yǒu bù míngbai de dìfang ma?] Are there any parts that are not clear?
地理 [dìlǐ] N geography
地面 [dìmiàn] N **1** (地表) the Earth's surface **2** (指房屋) floor
地球仪 [dìqiúyí] N globe
地区 [dìqū] N area
地摊 [dìtān] N stall
地毯 [dìtǎn] N carpet
地铁 [dìtiě] N **1** (*also*: 地下铁道) subway **2** (列车) subway train ▹ 坐地铁 [zuò dìtiě] take the subway
地图 [dìtú] N map
地位 [dìwèi] N position ▹ 平等的地位 [píngděng de dìwèi] equal status ▹ 历史地位 [lìshǐ dìwèi] place in history
地下 [dìxià] N underground
地下室 [dìxiàshì] N basement
地震 [dìzhèn] N earthquake
地址 [dìzhǐ] N address ▹ 通信地址 [tōngxìn dìzhǐ] postal address
地址簿 [dìzhǐbù] N address book
地主 [dìzhǔ] N landlord

弟 [dì] N younger brother ▸ 表弟 [biǎodì] cousin ▸ 弟弟 [dìdi] younger brother
弟兄 [dìxiong] N brothers (PL)
弟子 [dìzǐ] N disciple

的 [dì] N target ▶ 目的 [mùdì] goal → *see also*/另见 de, dí

帝 [dì] N (君主) emperor
帝国 [dìguó] N empire

递 [dì] VB (传送) pass

第 [dì] N ▶ 第三产业 [dìsān chǎnyè] tertiary industry ▶ 第三世界 [dì sān shìjiè] the Third World ▶ 第一次世界大战 [dì yī cì shìjiè dàzhàn] the First World War
第六感觉 [dìliù gǎnjué] N sixth sense
第一手 [dìyīshǒu] ADJ first-hand

掂 [diān] VB weigh in one's hand

颠 [diān] VB **1** (颠簸) jolt **2** (跌落) fall
颠倒 [diāndǎo] VB ▷ 这张照片上下颠倒了。 [Zhè zhāng zhàopiàn shàngxià diāndǎo le.] The photo is upside down.

典 [diǎn] N **1** (标准) standard **2** (书籍) standard work ▶ 词典 [cídiǎn] dictionary **3** (典故) allusion **4** (典礼) ceremony
典礼 [diǎnlǐ] N ceremony ▷ 毕业典礼 [bìyè diǎnlǐ] graduation ceremony
典型 [diǎnxíng] ADJ (代表性) representative

点 [diǎn] **I** N **1** (时间单位) o'clock ▷ 早上8点 [zǎoshang bā diǎn] eight o'clock in the morning **2** (钟点) ▷ 到点了。 [Dào diǎn le.] It's time. **3** (小滴液体) drop ▶ 雨点 [yǔdiǎn] raindrops (PL) **4** (痕迹) stain **5** (指字, 画) dot **6** (指几何) point **7** (小数点) decimal point ▷ 五点六 [wǔ diǎn liù] five point six **8** (标志) point ▶ 终点 [zhōngdiǎn] end point **9** (方面) point ▶ 优点 [yōudiǎn] strong point ▶ 重点 [zhòngdiǎn] focal point **II** VB **1** (画点) make a dot **2** (头) nod ▶ 点头 [diǎntóu] nod one's head **3** (药水等) apply ▷ 点眼药 [diǎn yǎnyào] apply eye drops **4** (查对) check ▶ 点名 [diǎnmíng] call the register **5** (指定) select ▶ 点菜 [diǎncài] order food **6** (灯, 火, 烟等) light ▷ 点烟 [diǎn yān] light a cigarette **7** (点缀) decorate **III** MEAS **1** (少量) a little ▷ 有一点问题。 [Yǒu yī diǎn wèntí.] There is a bit of a problem. ▷ 她会说一点日语。 [Tā huì shuō yī diǎn Rìyǔ.] She can speak a little Japanese. **2** (事项) item ▷ 议事日程上有6点。 [Yìshì rìchéng shàng yǒu liù diǎn.] There are six items on the agenda. ▷ 我们有4点建议。 [Wǒmen yǒu sì diǎn jiànyì.] We have four recommendations.
点击 [diǎnjī] VB click
点头 [diǎntóu] VB nod
点心 [diǎnxin] N snack
点子 [diǎnzi] N **1** (关键部分) key point **2** (主意) idea

电 [diàn] **I** N **1** (能源) electricity ▶ 电能 [diànnéng] electric power ▶ 发电站 [fādiànzhàn] electric power station ▷ 停电了。 [Tíng diàn le.] There's been a power cut. **2** (电报) telegram **II** VB **1** (触电) get an electric shock **2** (发电报) send a telegram ▶ 电贺 [diànhè] congratulate by telegram
电报 [diànbào] N telegram
电池 [diànchí] N battery
电动 [diàndòng] ADJ electric
电话 [diànhuà] N **1** (电话机) telephone ▷ 办公室的电话占线。 [Bàngōngshì de diànhuà zhànxiàn.] The office phone is busy. ▷ 别挂电话！ [Bié guà diànhuà!] Don't hang up! **2** (打, 接, 回) call ▷ 接电话 [jiē diànhuà] answer the phone
电话号码 [diànhuà hàomǎ] N phone number
电脑 [diànnǎo] N computer ▷ 手提电脑 [shǒutí diànnǎo] laptop ▷ 平板电脑 [píngbǎn diànnǎo] tablet
电器 [diànqì] N electrical appliance
电视 [diànshì] N television, TV ▷ 彩色电视 [cǎisè diànshì] color television ▷ 看电视 [kàn diànshì]

watch television
电台 [diàntái] N station
电影 [diànyǐng] N movie
电影院 [diànyǐngyuàn] N movie theater
电子 [diànzǐ] N electron ▶ 电子表 [diànzǐ biǎo] digital watch ▶ 电子游戏 [diànzǐ yóuxì] electronic game ▶ 电子商务 [diànzǐ shāngwù] e-commerce ▶ 电子图书 [diànzǐ túshū] e-book ▶ 电子邮件 [diànzǐ yóujiàn] email

---

店 [diàn] N **1** (商店) store **2** (旅店) hotel

垫 [diàn] **I** N cushion ▶ 鞋垫 [xiédiàn] insole **II** VB **1** (铺) insert **2** (付钱) pay

---

惦 [diàn] *see below*/见下文
惦记 [diànjì] VB think about

殿 [diàn] N palace ▶ 宫殿 [gōngdiàn] palace

叼 [diāo] VB have ... in one's mouth

凋 [diāo] VB wither
凋谢 [diāoxiè] VB wither

雕 [diāo] **I** VB carve **II** N **1** (指艺术) sculpture ▶ 石雕 [shídiāo] stone sculpture **2** (鸟) vulture
雕刻 [diāokè] **I** VB carve **II** N carving
雕塑 [diāosù] N sculpture

吊 [diào] VB (悬挂) hang

钓 [diào] VB fish ▶ 钓鱼 [diàoyú] go fishing

调 [diào] **I** VB transfer **II** N **1** (口音) accent **2** (曲调) melody ▶ 走调 [zǒudiào] be out of tune **3** (音) key → *see also*/另见 tiáo
调查 [diàochá] VB investigate

掉 [diào] VB **1** (落下) fall **2** (落后) fall behind **3** (遗失) lose **4** (减少) reduce **5** (转回) turn ... round ▷ 把车头掉过来 [bǎ chētóu diào guòlai] turn the car round **6** (互换) swap ▶ 掉换 [diàohuàn] swap

---

跌 [diē] VB fall down

叠 [dié] VB **1** (一层加一层) pile ... up **2** (信, 纸, 衣, 被) fold

碟 [dié] *see below*/见下文
碟子 [diézi] N saucer

蝶 [dié] N butterfly ▶ 蝴蝶 [húdié] butterfly

叮 [dīng] VB (蚊虫) bite
叮嘱 [dīngzhǔ] VB warn

盯 [dīng] VB stare at

钉 [dīng] N nail

顶 [dǐng] **I** N top ▶ 头顶 [tóudǐng] top of one's head ▶ 山顶 [shāndǐng] mountain top **II** VB **1** (指用头) carry ... on one's head **2** (拱起) lift ... up **3** (支撑) prop ... up **4** (撞) butt **5** (迎着) face **6** (顶撞) be rude to **7** (承担) undertake **8** (相当) ▷ 他干活一个人能顶两个。 [Tā gànhuó yī ge rén néng dǐng liǎng ge.] He can do as much work as two people. **9** (顶替) take the place of **III** MEAS ▷ 一顶帽子 [yī dǐng màozi] a hat ▷ 一顶蚊帐 [yī dǐng wénzhàng] a mosquito net

measure word, used for things with a pointy tip, such as caps and hats

IV ADV extremely ▷ 顶棒 [dǐng bàng] extremely good
顶点 [dǐngdiǎn] N (最高点) top
顶峰 [dǐngfēng] N summit
顶替 [dǐngtì] VB **1** (替代) take the place of **2** (冒名) pose as
顶嘴 [dǐngzuǐ] VB answer back

订 [dìng] VB **1** (确立) draw ... up **2** (预订) order ▶ 订报 [dìngbào] subscribe to a newspaper **3** (校正) revise **4** (装订) fasten ... together
订单 [dìngdān] N order form
订购 [dìnggòu] VB order
订婚 [dìnghūn] VB get engaged
订货 [dìnghuò] VB order goods
订金 [dìngjīn] N deposit

定 [dìng] **I** ADJ **1** (平静) calm **2** (不变的) settled ▶ 定论 [dìnglùn] final conclusion **3** (规定的) fixed ▶ 定义 [dìngyì] definition **II** VB **1** (决定) decide ▷ 定计划 [dìng jìhuà] decide on a plan **2** (固定) settle **3** (预定) order **III** ADV definitely

定居 [dìngjū] VB settle

定期 [dìngqī] **I** VB set a date **II** ADJ fixed **III** ADV regularly

丢 [diū] VB **1** (遗失) lose **2** (扔掉) throw away **3** (投) toss

丢脸 [diūliǎn] VB lose face

丢人 [diūrén] VB lose face

东 [dōng] N **1** (方向) east ▶ 东南亚 [Dōngnányà] Southeast Asia **2** (主人) owner ▶ 股东 [gǔdōng] shareholder **3** (东道主) host

东道国 [dōngdàoguó] N host nation

东西 [dōngxi] N (物品) thing ▷ 今天他买了不少东西。 [Jīntiān tā mǎi le bùshǎo dōngxi.] He did quite a bit of shopping today.

冬 [dōng] N winter

冬眠 [dōngmián] VB hibernate

冬天 [dōngtiān] N winter

董 [dǒng] N director

董事 [dǒngshì] N director

董事会 [dǒngshìhuì] N (指企业) board of directors

懂 [dǒng] VB understand ▶ 懂得 [dǒngdé] understand

懂行 [dǒngháng] VB (方) know the ropes

动 [dòng] VB **1** (指改变位置) move ▷ 不许动! [Bùxǔ dòng!] Freeze! **2** (行动) act **3** (用作动补) ▷ 她太累了, 走不动。 [Tā tài lèi le, zǒu bù dòng.] She's too tired – she can't go on. **4** (使用) use ▷ 我们得动脑筋。 [Wǒmen děi dòng nǎojīn.] We must use our brains. **5** (触动) affect **6** (感动) move ▶ 动人 [dòngrén] moving

动机 [dòngjī] N motive

动静 [dòngjìng] N **1** (声音) sound **2** (情况) movement

动力 [dònglì] N **1** (指机械) power **2** (力量) strength

动脉 [dòngmài] N artery

动身 [dòngshēn] VB begin

动手 [dòngshǒu] VB **1** (开始做) get to work **2** (用手摸) touch ▷ 只许看, 不许动手。 [Zhǐxǔ kàn, bùxǔ dòngshǒu.] You can look, but don't touch. **3** (打人) strike a blow

动物 [dòngwù] N animal

动物园 [dòngwùyuán] N zoo

动员 [dòngyuán] VB mobilize

动作 [dòngzuò] **I** N movement **II** VB make a move

冻 [dòng] VB freeze ▶ 冻死 [dòngsǐ] freeze to death

洞 [dòng] N **1** (孔) hole **2** (穴) cave

洞穴 [dòngxué] N cave

都 [dōu] ADV **1** (全部) all ▷ 全体成员 [quántǐ chéngyuán] all the members **2** (表示理由) all ▷ 都是他才酿成了车祸。 [Dōu shì tā de cuò.] It's all his fault. **3** (甚至) even ▷ 老师待他比亲生父母都好。 [Lǎoshī dài tā bǐ qīnshēng fùmǔ dōu hǎo.] The teacher treated him even better than his parents. **4** (已经) already ▷ 都到冬天了! [Dōu dào dōngtiān le!] It's winter already!
→ *see also*/另见 dū

兜 [dōu] N **1** (衣袋) pocket ▶ 裤兜 [kùdōu] trouser pocket **2** (拎兜) bag ▶ 网兜 [wǎngdōu] string bag

兜风 [dōufēng] VB (游逛) go for a spin

兜圈子 [dōuquānzi] VB (喻) (拐弯抹角) beat about the bush

斗 [dǒu] N **1** (指容器) cup **2** (斗状物) ▶ 烟斗 [yāndǒu] pipe ▶ 漏斗 [lòudǒu] funnel
→ *see also*/另见 dòu

抖 [dǒu] VB **1** (颤抖) shiver **2** (甩动) shake

陡 [dǒu] ADJ steep

斗 [dòu] VB 1 (打斗) fight ▸ 斗鸡 [dòujī] cock fighting 2 (战胜) beat → *see also*/另见 dǒu

斗争 [dòuzhēng] VB 1 (努力战胜) struggle 2 (打击) combat 3 (奋斗) fight for

豆 [dòu] N bean

豆子 [dòuzi] N (豆类作物) bean

逗 [dòu] VB (引逗) tease

逗号 [dòuhào] N comma

逗留 [dòuliú] VB stay

都 [dū] N (首都) capital → *see also*/另见 dōu

都市 [dūshì] N metropolis

毒 [dú] I N poison II ADJ (有毒) poisonous

毒品 [dúpǐn] N drug

独 [dú] I ADJ only ▸ 独生子 [dúshēngzǐ] only son ▸ 独生女 [dúshēngnǚ] only daughter II ADV 1 (独自) alone 2 (惟独) only

独裁 [dúcái] VB dictate

独立 [dúlì] VB 1 (指国家) declare independence ▸ 独立宣言 [dúlì xuānyán] declaration of independence 2 (指个人) be independent

独身 [dúshēn] VB be single

独特 [dútè] ADJ distinctive

独自 [dúzì] ADV alone

读 [dú] VB 1 (朗读) read aloud 2 (阅读) read 3 (上学) go to school

读书 [dúshū] VB 1 (阅读) read 2 (学习) study 3 (上学) go to school

读者 [dúzhě] N reader

堵 [dǔ] I VB 1 (堵塞) block ▸ 堵车 [dǔchē] traffic jam 2 (发闷) suffocate II MEAS ▷ 一堵墙 [yī dǔ qiáng] a wall

measure word, used for walls

堵塞 [dǔsè] VB block up

赌 [dǔ] VB 1 (赌博) gamble 2 (打赌) bet

赌博 [dǔbó] VB gamble

赌注 [dǔzhù] N bet

肚 [dù] N belly

肚子 [dùzi] N (腹部) stomach

度 [dù] I N 1 (限度) limit 2 (气量) tolerance ▸ 大度 [dàdù] magnanimous 3 (考虑) consideration 4 (程度) degree ▸ 厚度 [hòudù] thickness II MEAS 1 (指经度或纬度) degree ▷ 北纬42度 [běiwěi sìshí'èr dù] latitude 42 degrees north 2 (指电量) kilowatt-hour 3 (指温度) degree ▷ 零下十度 [língxià shí dù] minus ten degrees 4 (指弧度或角度) degree 5 (次) time III VB spend

渡 [dù] VB 1 (越过) cross 2 (指用船只) ferry 3 (喻) (通过) survive ▷ 渡难关 [dù nánguān] go through a difficult time

端 [duān] I N 1 (头) end 2 (开头) beginning ▸ 开端 [kāiduān] beginning II VB carry

端午节 [Duānwǔjié] N Dragon Boat Festival

端午节 [Duānwǔjié]

Dragon Boat Festival is celebrated on the fifth day of the fifth month of the Chinese lunar calendar. The two main activities which take place at this time are dragon boat racing and eating 粽子 zòngzi.

端正 [duānzhèng] ADJ 1 (不歪斜) upright 2 (正派) proper

短 [duǎn] I ADJ short ▸ 短期 [duǎnqī] short-term II VB owe III N weakness

短处 [duǎnchu] N weakness

短裤 [duǎnkù] N 1 (指女式内裤) panties (PL) 2 (指男式内裤) briefs (PL) 3 (指夏装) shorts (PL)

短缺 [duǎnquē] VB lack

短信 [duǎnxìn] N text message

短暂 [duǎnzàn] ADJ brief

段 [duàn] MEAS 1 (用于长条物) ▷ 一段铁轨 [yī duàn tiěguǐ] a section of railroad ▷ 一段木头 [yī duàn mùtou] a chunk of wood

measure word, used for a part of something that is thin and long

2 (指时间) period ▷ 一段时间 [yī duàn shíjiān] a period of time 3 (指路程) stretch 4 (部分) piece

断 [duàn] VB 1 (分成段) break 2 (断绝) break ... off 3 (判断) decide

断定 [duàndìng] VB determine

断言 [duànyán] VB assert

缎 [duàn] N satin

锻 [duàn] VB forge

锻炼 [duànliàn] VB 1 (指身体) work out 2 (磨炼) toughen

堆 [duī] I VB pile ▷ 别把垃圾堆在这里。 [Bié bǎ lājī duī zài zhèli.] Don't pile the trash up here. II N pile III MEAS pile ▷ 一堆石头 [yī duī shítou] a pile of stones

队 [duì] N 1 (行列) line 2 (指集体) team ▶ 队长 [duìzhǎng] team leader ▶ 队员 [duìyuán] team member

队伍 [duìwu] N 1 (军队) troops (PL) 2 (指集体) contingent

对 [duì] I VB 1 (回答) answer 2 (对待) treat 3 (朝着) face 4 (接触) come into contact with 5 (投合) suit ▷ 对脾气 [duì píqi] suit one's temperament ▷ 今天的菜很对他的胃口。 [Jīntiān de cài hěn duì tā de wèikǒu.] Today's meal was definitely to his liking. 6 (调整) adjust 7 (核对) check ▷ 对表 [duì biǎo] set one's watch 8 (加进) add II ADJ 1 (对面) opposite 2 (正确) correct III PREP 1 (朝) at 2 (对于) ▷ 吸烟对健康有害。 [Xīyān duì jiànkāng yǒuhài.] Smoking is harmful to your health. IV MEAS pair ▷ 一对夫妻 [yī duì fūqī] a married couple

对比 [duìbǐ] VB contrast ▶ 鲜明的对比 [xiānmíng de duìbǐ] marked contrast

对不起 [duìbuqǐ] VB (愧疚) be sorry ▷ 对不起, 借过。 [Duìbuqǐ, jièguò.] Excuse me, may I just get through?

对称 [duìchèn] ADJ symmetrical

对待 [duìdài] VB treat

对方 [duìfāng] N other side

对付 [duìfu] VB 1 (应对) deal with 2 (将就) make do

对话 [duìhuà] I N dialogue II VB hold talks

对立 [duìlì] VB counter

对面 [duìmiàn] N 1 (对过) the opposite 2 (正前方) the front

对手 [duìshǒu] N 1 (指比赛) opponent 2 (指能力) match

对象 [duìxiàng] N 1 (目标) object 2 (指男女朋友) partner

对应 [duìyìng] VB correspond

对于 [duìyú] PREP ▷ 对于这篇文章, 大家理解不一。 [Duìyú zhè piān wénzhāng, dàjiā lǐjiě bù yī.] Not everyone understands this article in the same way.

兑 [duì] VB 1 (互换) exchange 2 (汇兑) cash

兑换 [duìhuàn] VB convert

吨 [dūn] MEAS ton

蹲 [dūn] VB (弯腿) squat

炖 [dùn] VB stew

钝 [dùn] ADJ 1 (不锋利) blunt 2 (不灵活) dim

顿 [dùn] I VB (停顿) pause II MEAS ▷ 一顿饭 [yī dùn fàn] a meal ▷ 挨了一顿打 [āi le yī dùn dǎ] take a beating

measure word, used for meals

顿时 [dùnshí] ADV immediately

多 [duō] I ADJ 1 (数量大) a lot of ▷ 很多书 [hěn duō shū] a lot of books

2 (相差大) more ▷ 我比你大多了。[Wǒ bǐ nǐ dà duō le.] I'm much older than you are. 3 (超出) too many ▷ 她喝多了。[Tā hē duō le.] She drank too much. 4 (过分) excessive ▶ 多疑 [duōyí] over-suspicious II NUM ▷ 2年多前 [liǎngnián duō qián] over two years ago III VB be more than ▷ 多个人就多份力量。[Duō ge rén jiù duō fèn lìliàng.] The more people we have, the stronger we will be. IV ADV 1 (用在疑问句中) how ▷ 从北京到上海有多远? [Cóng Běijīng dào Shànghǎi yǒu duō yuǎn?] How far is it from Beijing to Shanghai? ▷ 你儿子多大了? [Nǐ érzi duō dà le?] How old is your son? 2 (表示感叹) how ▷ 多美的城市! [Duō měi de chéngshì!] How beautiful this town is! 3 (表示任何一种程度) however ▷ 给我一把尺，多长都行。[Gěi wǒ yī bǎ chǐ, duō cháng dōu xíng.] Give me a ruler – any length will do.

多媒体 [duōméitǐ] N multimedia

多么 [duōme] ADV 1 (用于询问程度) how ▷ 他到底有多么聪明? [Tā dàodǐ yǒu duōme cōngming?] How clever is he really? 2 (用在感叹句) ▷ 多么蓝的天啊! [Duōme lán de tiān ya!] What a clear day! 3 (表示程度深) no matter how

多少 [duōshǎo] ADV 1 (或多或少) somewhat ▷ 这笔买卖多少能赚点钱。[Zhè bǐ mǎimai duōshaǒ néng zhuàn diǎn qián.] We're bound to earn some money from this deal. 2 (稍微) slightly

多少 [duōshao] I PRON (用于询问数量) ▷ 这台电视机多少钱? [Zhè tái diànshìjī duōshao qián?] How much is this television? ▷ 今天有多少人到会? [Jīntiān yǒu duōshao rén dàohuì?] How many people attended the meeting today? II NUM ▷ 你们有多少我们要多少。[Nǐmen yǒu duōshao wǒmen yào duōshao.] We want everything you've got.

多数 [duōshù] N the majority

多余 [duōyú] ADJ 1 (超出需要量的) surplus 2 (不必要的) redundant

哆 [duō] *see below*/见下文

哆嗦 [duōsuo] VB tremble

夺 [duó] VB 1 (抢) seize 2 (争取) compete for 3 (剥夺) deprive 4 (决定) resolve

夺取 [duóqǔ] VB 1 (武力强取) capture 2 (努力争取) strive for

朵 [duǒ] MEAS ▷ 朵朵白云 [duǒ duǒ báiyún] white clouds ▷ 几朵玫瑰 [jǐ duǒ méigui] some roses

measure word, used for clouds and flowers

躲 [duǒ] VB 1 (隐藏) hide 2 (避让) avoid

躲避 [duǒbì] VB 1 (回避) run away from 2 (躲藏) hide

躲藏 [duǒcáng] VB hide

剁 [duò] VB chop

堕 [duò] VB fall

堕落 [duòluò] VB go to the bad

堕胎 [duòtāi] VB have an abortion

跺 [duò] VB stamp

E

俄 [é] N (*also*: 俄罗斯) **Russia** ▶ 俄国 [Éguó] **Russia**

俄语 [Éyǔ] N **Russian language**

鹅 [é] N **goose**

蛾 [é] N **moth** ▶ 蛾子 [ézi] **moth**

额 [é] N **forehead** ▶ 额头 [étóu] **forehead**

恶 [ě] *see below*/见下文
→ *see also*/另见 è, wù

恶心 [ěxin] **I** VB **feel nauseous** **II** ADJ **nauseating**

恶 [è] **I** N **evil** **II** ADJ **1** (凶恶) **ferocious** **2** (恶劣) **evil**
→ *see also*/另见 ě, wù

恶劣 [èliè] ADJ **bad**

恶梦 [èmèng] N **nightmare**

饿 [è] **I** ADJ **hungry** ▷ 我很饿。 [Wǒ hěn è.] **I'm very hungry.** **II** VB **starve**

鳄 [è] N **crocodile, alligator** ▶ 鳄鱼 [èyú] **crocodile, alligator**

儿 [ér] N **1** (小孩子) **child** **2** (儿子) **son** ▶ 儿子 [érzi] **son**

儿女 [érnǚ] N **children** (PL)

儿童 [értóng] N **child**

而 [ér] CONJ **1** (并且) **and** ▷ 美丽而聪明 [měilì ér cōngming] **beautiful and clever** **2** (但是) **but** ▷ 浓而不烈 [nóng ér bù liè] **strong but not overpowering** ▷ 她不是学生，而是老师。 [Tā bù shì xuéshēng, ér shì lǎoshī.] **She isn't a student, but a teacher.**

而且 [érqiě] CONJ **and what's more** ▷ 他会讲英语, 而且讲得好。 [Tā huì jiǎng Yīngyǔ, érqiě jiǎng de hǎo.] **He can speak English, and what's more he speaks it very well.**

耳 [ěr] N (耳朵) **ear** ▶ 耳朵 [ěrduo] **ear**

二 [èr] NUM **two** ▶ 二月 [èryuè] **February** ▷ 第二次 [dì èr cì] **the second time**

二十 [èrshí] NUM **twenty**

贰 [èr] NUM **two**

This is the complex character for two, which is mainly used in banks, on receipts, etc.

F

发 [fā] VB **1** (送出) send ▷ 发工资 [fā gōngzī] pay wages **2** (发射) emit ▶ 发光 [fāguāng] shine **3** (产生) produce ▶ 发电 [fādiàn] generate electricity ▶ 发芽 [fāyá] sprout **4** (表达) express ▶ 发言 [fāyán] speak **5** (扩大) develop ▶ 发扬 [fāyáng] carry on **6** (兴旺) prosper ▶ 发家 [fājiā] make a family fortune **7** (使膨胀) ▶ 发面 [fāmiàn] leaven dough **8** (散开) spread ▶ 发散 [fāsàn] diverge **9** (揭开) uncover ▶ 发掘 [fājué] unearth ▶ 揭发 [jiēfā] expose **10** (变得) become ▶ 发霉 [fāméi] go moldy **11** (流露) ▶ 发愁 [fāchóu] worry ▷ 发脾气 [fā píqi] lose one's temper **12** (感到) feel **13** (起程) leave ▶ 出发 [chūfā] set out
→ *see also*/另见 fà

发表 [fābiǎo] VB **1** (宣布) announce **2** (刊登) publish

发财 [fācái] VB make a fortune

发出 [fāchū] VB **1** (发送) send out **2** (散发) give out

发达 [fādá] **I** ADJ developed **II** VB promote

发动 [fādòng] VB **1** (启动) start **2** (发起) launch **3** (鼓动) mobilize

发动机 [fādòngjī] N engine

发抖 [fādǒu] VB **1** (因恐惧等) tremble **2** (因寒冷等) shiver

发挥 [fāhuī] VB **1** (充分利用) bring ... into play **2** (详尽论述) elaborate

发火 [fāhuǒ] VB **1** (着火) catch fire **2** (爆炸) detonate **3** (发脾气) lose one's temper

发霉 [fāméi] VB go moldy

发明 [fāmíng] VB invent

发票 [fāpiào] N **1** (收据) receipt **2** (发货清单) invoice

发烧 [fāshāo] VB have a temperature

发生 [fāshēng] VB happen

发现 [fāxiàn] VB discover

发言 [fāyán] VB make a speech

发扬 [fāyáng] VB carry on

发音 [fāyīn] VB pronounce

发展 [fāzhǎn] VB **1** (变化) develop **2** (扩大) expand

罚 [fá] VB punish ▶ 罚款 [fákuǎn] fine

罚款 [fákuǎn] **I** VB fine **II** N fine

法 [fǎ] N **1** (法律) law **2** (方法) method ▶ 用法 [yòngfǎ] use **3** (标准) model **4** (佛理) Buddhism **5** (法术) magic ▶ 戏法 [xìfǎ] conjuring tricks

法国 [Fǎguó] N France

法律 [fǎlǜ] N law

法庭 [fǎtíng] N court

法语 [Fǎyǔ] N French

法院 [fǎyuàn] N court

发 [fà] N hair
→ *see also*/另见 fā

番 [fān] MEAS ▶ 三番五次 [sānfān-wǔcì] time and time again ▷ 经过几番挫折他明白了许多道理。 [Jīngguò jǐfān cuòzé tā míngbai le xǔduō dàoli.] After a few false starts he picked up quite a lot.

measure word, used for actions

番茄 [fānqié] N tomato

翻 [fān] VB **1** (换位置) turn over **2** (寻找) rummage **3** (推翻) reverse **4** (越过) get across **5** (增加) multiply **6** (翻译) translate **7** (翻脸) fall out

翻译 [fānyì] **I** VB translate **II** N translator

凡 [fán] **I** N **1** (人世间) mortal world **2** (大概) approximation **II** ADJ ordinary **III** ADV (总共) in all

---

烦 [fán] **I** N trouble **II** VB (谦) trouble **III** ADJ (厌烦) fed up

烦恼 [fánnǎo] ADJ worried

繁 [fán] **I** ADJ numerous **II** VB propagate

繁华 [fánhuá] ADJ bustling
繁忙 [fánmáng] ADJ busy
繁荣 [fánróng] ADJ flourishing
繁体字 [fántǐzì] N complex characters (PL)

繁体字 [fántǐzì]

Complex characters, also known as traditional Chinese characters, had been used as the Chinese script for centuries in all parts of China until 1956 when the government of the People's Republic of China carried out a program of simplifying these characters in an effort to improve the literacy rate by making characters easier to write. Since then, 简体字 jiǎntǐzì, "simplified characters," have become the dominant form of the Chinese script. However, for various cultural and political reasons, many Chinese-speaking regions and communities did not accept these changes, and continue to use the old system. Hong Kong and Taiwan are among these regions.

繁殖 [fánzhí] VB breed

反 [fǎn] I N 1 (相反) opposite 2 (造反) rebellion II VB 1 (转换) turn 2 (回) return 3 (反对) oppose 4 (背叛) rebel III ADJ opposite IV ADV 1 (相反地) on the contrary 2 (从反面) again ▶ 反思 [fǎnsī] review
反动 [fǎndòng] I ADJ reactionary II N reaction
反对 [fǎnduì] VB oppose
反复 [fǎnfù] ADV 1 (重复) repeatedly 2 (多变) capriciously
反抗 [fǎnkàng] VB resist
反面 [fǎnmiàn] I N other side II ADJ negative
反应 [fǎnyìng] N 1 (反响) response 2 (指机体) reaction 3 (指物理, 化学) reaction
反映 [fǎnyìng] VB 1 (反照) reflect 2 (汇报) report
反正 [fǎnzhèng] ADV anyway

返 [fǎn] VB return
返回 [fǎnhuí] VB come back

犯 [fàn] I VB 1 (违犯) violate 2 (侵犯) attack 3 (错误, 罪行等) commit II N criminal
犯法 [fànfǎ] VB break the law
犯规 [fànguī] VB break the rules
犯人 [fànrén] N prisoner
犯罪 [fànzuì] VB commit a crime

饭 [fàn] N 1 (餐) meal ▶ 晚饭 [wǎnfàn] supper 2 (米饭) rice
饭店 [fàndiàn] N 1 (住宿) hotel 2 (吃饭) restaurant
饭馆 [fànguǎn] N restaurant
饭厅 [fàntīng] N dining room

范 [fàn] N 1 (模范) model ▶ 典范 [diǎnfàn] model 2 (范围) limit ▶ 规范 [guīfàn] standard 3 (模子) pattern
范围 [fànwéi] N limit

方 [fāng] I N 1 (方向) direction ▶ 南方 [nánfāng] the South 2 (方形) square ▶ 长方形 [chángfāngxíng] rectangle 3 (方面) side 4 (方法) method 5 (地方) place 6 (方子) prescription 7 (数) (乘方) power II ADJ 1 (方形) square 2 (正直) honest
方案 [fāng'àn] N plan
方便 [fāngbiàn] ADJ 1 (便利) convenient 2 (适宜) appropriate
方法 [fāngfǎ] N method
方面 [fāngmiàn] N 1 (指人) side 2 (指物) aspect
方式 [fāngshì] N way
方向 [fāngxiàng] N direction
方言 [fāngyán] N dialect
方针 [fāngzhēn] N policy

防 [fáng] I VB 1 (防备) prevent 2 (防守) defend II N dyke
防止 [fángzhǐ] VB prevent

妨 [fáng] VB obstruct

妨碍 [fáng'ài] VB obstruct

房 [fáng] N **1** (房子) house **2** (房间) room ▶ 书房 [shūfáng] study **3** (家族) ▷ 远房亲戚 [yuǎnfáng qīnqi] a distant relative

房东 [fángdōng] N landlord

房屋 [fángwū] N building

仿 [fǎng] VB **1** (仿效) copy **2** (类似) be like

仿佛 [fǎngfú] **I** CONJ as if **II** ADJ similar

访 [fǎng] VB **1** (访问) call on ▶ 访谈 [fǎngtán] call in for a chat **2** (调查) investigate

访问 [fǎngwèn] VB visit

纺 [fǎng] **I** VB spin **II** N silk

纺织 [fǎngzhī] VB ▶ 纺织品 [fǎngzhīpǐn] textiles (PL)

放 [fàng] VB **1** (使自由) release ▶ 解放 [jiěfàng] free **2** (暂时停止) ▷ 放学了。 [fàngxué le.] School is now over. **3** (放纵) let oneself go **4** (赶牲畜吃草) graze **5** (驱逐) expel ▶ 流放 [liúfàng] banish **6** (发出) send out ▶ 放炮 [fàngpào] fire a gun **7** (点燃) set ... off **8** (借出收息) lend **9** (扩展) ▷ 把照片放大 [bǎ zhàopiàn fàngdà] enlarge a photo **10** (花开) bloom **11** (搁置) put ... to one side **12** (弄倒) cut down **13** (使处于) put **14** (加进) add **15** (控制自己) ▷ 放严肃点 [fàng yánsù diǎn] become more serious **16** (放映) project **17** (保存) leave

放大 [fàngdà] VB enlarge

放假 [fàngjià] VB go on vacation

放弃 [fàngqì] VB give ... up

放松 [fàngsōng] VB relax

放心 [fàngxīn] VB set one's mind at rest

放学 [fàngxué] VB finish school

飞 [fēi] **I** VB **1** (鸟, 虫, 飞机) fly **2** (空中游动) flutter **3** (挥发) evaporate **II** ADV swiftly

飞机 [fēijī] N airplane

飞行 [fēixíng] VB fly

非 [fēi] **I** N **1** (错误) wrong ▶ 是非 [shìfēi] right and wrong **2** (*also*: 非洲) Africa **II** VB **1** (非议) blame **2** (违反) run counter to ▶ 非法 [fēifǎ] illegal **3** (不是) not be **4** (强硬) insist on **III** ADV (必须) ▷ 我不让他去, 他非去不可。 [wǒ bù ràng tā qù, tā fēi qù bù kě.] I've tried to stop him, but he simply has to go.

非常 [fēicháng] **I** ADJ exceptional **II** ADV very

非典 [fēidiǎn] N (非典型性肺炎) SARS

非法 [fēifǎ] ADJ illegal

非洲 [Fēizhōu] N Africa

肥 [féi] **I** N fertilizer **II** VB **1** (使肥沃) fertilize **2** (暴富) get rich **III** ADJ **1** (脂肪多) fat **2** (肥沃) fertile **3** (肥大) loose

肥胖 [féipàng] ADJ fat

肥皂 [féizào] N soap

肺 [fèi] N lung

废 [fèi] **I** VB abandon **II** ADJ **1** (不用的) waste **2** (没用的) useless **3** (残废的) disabled

费 [fèi] **I** N fee ▷ 车费 [chēfèi] bus fare **II** ADJ expensive **III** VB spend

费用 [fèiyong] N expense

分 [fēn] **I** VB **1** (分开) divide ▶ 分离 [fēnlí] separate ▶ 分裂 [fēnliè] split **2** (分配) assign **3** (辨别) distinguish **II** N **1** (分支) branch **2** (分数) fraction ▶ 分母 [fēnmǔ] denominator **III** MEAS **1** (分数) fraction ▷ 四分之三 [sì fēn zhī sān] three quarters **2** (十分之一) one tenth **3** (指货币) *unit of Chinese currency, equal to a hundredth of a yuan* **4** (指时间) minute ▷ 5点过5分 [wǔ diǎn guò wǔ fēn] 5 minutes past 5 **5** (指弧度或角度) minute ▷ 36度20分角 [sānshíliù dù èrshí fēn jiǎo]

36 degrees 20 minutes 6 (百分之一) percent ▷ 月利1分 [yuèlì yī fēn] monthly interest of 1 percent
→ *see also*/另见 fèn

分别 [fēnbié] **I** VB **1** (离别) split up **2** (辨别) distinguish **II** N difference

分开 [fēnkāi] VB separate

分配 [fēnpèi] VB assign

分手 [fēnshǒu] VB **1** (告别) say goodbye **2** (指男女关系) break up

分数 [fēnshù] N mark

分析 [fēnxī] VB analyze

吩 [fēn] *see below*/见下文

吩咐 [fēnfù] VB instruct

纷 [fēn] ADJ **1** (多) numerous ▶ 纷繁 [fēnfán] numerous **2** (乱) confused ▶ 纷扰 [fēnrǎo] confusion

纷纷 [fēnfēn] **I** ADJ diverse **II** ADV one after another

坟 [fén] N grave

坟墓 [fénmù] N grave

粉 [fěn] **I** N **1** (粉末) powder **2** (粉丝) vermicelli **II** VB **1** (成碎末) crumble ▶ 粉碎 [fěnsuì] crush **2** (变成粉状) pulverize **III** ADJ **1** (白色) white **2** (粉红色) pink

粉笔 [fěnbǐ] N chalk

粉红 [fěnhóng] ADJ pink

粉末 [fěnmò] N powder

分 [fèn] N **1** (成分) component **2** (限度) limit ▶ 过分 [guòfèn] excessive **3** (情分) feelings (PL)
→ *see also*/另见 fēn

分量 [fènliàng] N weight

份 [fèn] **I** N **1** (一部分) part ▶ 股份 [gǔfèn] share **2** (指划分单位) ▶ 年份 [niánfèn] year **II** MEAS **1** (指食物) portion **2** (指报刊) copy

---

奋 [fèn] VB **1** (振作) exert oneself ▶ 勤奋 [qínfèn] diligent **2** (举起) raise

奋斗 [fèndòu] VB fight

愤 [fèn] ADJ indignant ▶ 气愤 [qìfèn] indignant

愤怒 [fènnù] ADJ angry

丰 [fēng] ADJ **1** (丰富) abundant **2** (大) great

丰富 [fēngfù] **I** ADJ abundant **II** VB enrich

丰收 [fēngshōu] VB have a good harvest

风 [fēng] **I** N **1** (指空气流动) wind **2** (风气) trend **3** (景象) scene ▶ 风光 [fēngguāng] scenery **4** (态度) manner ▶ 风度 [fēngdù] bearing **5** (消息) information **II** ADJ rumored **III** VB air ▶ 风干 [fēnggān] air-dry

风格 [fēnggé] N **1** (气度) manner **2** (特点) style

风景 [fēngjǐng] N scenery

风水 [fēngshuǐ] N feng shui

风俗 [fēngsú] N custom

风险 [fēngxiǎn] N risk

封 [fēng] **I** VB (封闭) seal **II** N envelope **III** MEAS ▷ 一封信 [yī fēng xìn] a letter

封建 [fēngjiàn] **I** N feudalism **II** ADJ feudal

疯 [fēng] **I** ADJ mad **II** ADV madly

疯子 [fēngzi] N lunatic

锋 [fēng] N **1** (尖端) point **2** (带头的) vanguard **3** (锋面) front

锋利 [fēnglì] ADJ **1** (工具) sharp **2** (言论) cutting

蜂 [fēng] **I** N **1** (黄蜂) wasp **2** (蜜蜂) bee **II** ADV in swarms

蜂蜜 [fēngmì] N honey

逢 [féng] VB come across

缝 [féng] VB sew
→ *see also*/另见 fèng

讽 [fěng] VB mock ▶ 讥讽 [jīfěng] satirize

讽刺 [fěngcì] VB ridicule

奉 [fèng] VB **1** (献给) present **2** (接受) receive **3** (尊重) respect **4** (信仰) believe in **5** (伺候) attend to

奉献 [fèngxiàn] VB dedicate

缝 [fèng] N 1 (接合处) seam 2 (缝隙) crack
→ *see also*/另见 féng

缝隙 [fèngxì] N crack

佛 [fó] N 1 (佛教) Buddhism 2 (佛像) Buddha

佛教 [fójiào] N Buddhism

否 [fǒu] I VB deny II ADV 1 (书) (不) no 2 (是, 能, 可) or not ▷ 他明天是否来参加聚会? [tā míngtiān shìfǒu lái cānjiā jùhuì?] Is he coming to the party tomorrow or not?

否定 [fǒudìng] I VB negate II ADJ negative

否认 [fǒurèn] VB deny

否则 [fǒuzé] CONJ otherwise

夫 [fū] N 1 (丈夫) husband 2 (男子) man 3 (劳动者) manual worker

夫妇 [fūfù] N husband and wife

夫妻 [fūqī] N husband and wife

夫人 [fūren] N Mrs.

扶 [fú] VB 1 (稳住) steady 2 (搀起) help up 3 (扶助) help

服 [fú] I N clothes (PL) II VB 1 (吃) take ▶ 服药 [fúyào] take medicine 2 (担任) serve ▶ 服役 [fúyì] serve in the army 3 (服从) comply with 4 (使信服) convince 5 (适应) adapt
→ *see also*/另见 fù

服从 [fúcóng] VB obey

服务 [fúwù] VB serve

服务员 [fúwùyuán] N 1 (指商店里) attendant 2 (指饭馆里) waiter, waitress 3 (指宾馆里) room attendant

服装 [fúzhuāng] N clothing

浮 [fú] I VB float II ADJ 1 (表面上) superficial 2 (可移动) movable 3 (暂时) temporary 4 (轻浮) slapdash 5 (空虚) empty ▶ 浮夸 [fúkuā] exaggerated 6 (多余) surplus

浮肿 [fúzhǒng] VB puff up

符 [fú] I N 1 (标记) mark 2 (图形) Daoist motif II VB be in keeping with

符号 [fúhào] N mark

符合 [fúhé] VB match

幅 [fú] I N 1 (指布) width 2 (泛指大小) size ▶ 幅度 [fúdù] range II MEAS ▷ 一幅画 [yī fú huà] a painting ▷ 三幅书法 [sān fú shūfǎ] three calligraphies

measure word, used for paintings, portraits and Chinese calligraphies

福 [fú] N good fortune

辅 [fǔ] VB complement

辅导 [fǔdǎo] VB coach

腐 [fǔ] I ADJ rotten II N bean curd

腐败 [fǔbài] I VB rot II ADJ corrupt

父 [fù] N 1 (父亲) father 2 (指男性长辈) *senior male relative* ▶ 祖父 [zǔfù] grandfather

父母 [fùmǔ] N parents

父亲 [fùqin] N father

付 [fù] VB 1 (事物) hand over ▶ 托付 [tuōfù] entrust 2 (钱) pay ▶ 偿付 [chángfù] pay back

付账 [fùzhàng] VB pay the bill

负 [fù] I VB 1 (书) (背) carry on one's back ▶ 负重 [fùzhòng] carry a heavy load 2 (担负) bear 3 (遭受) suffer 4 (享有) enjoy 5 (拖欠) be in arrears 6 (背弃) turn one's back on 7 (失败) lose II ADJ negative ▶ 负数 [fùshù] negative number

负担 [fùdān] I VB bear II N burden

负责 [fùzé] I VB be responsible II ADJ conscientious

妇 [fù] N 1 (妇女) woman ▶ 妇科 [fùkē] gynecology 2 (已婚妇女) married woman 3 (妻) wife

妇女 [fùnǚ] N woman

附 [fù] VB 1 (附带) attach 2 (靠近) get close to 3 (依从) depend on

附近 [fùjìn] I ADJ nearby II N

vicinity

服 [fù] MEAS dose
→ *see also*/另见 fú

复 [fù] **I** ADJ **1** (重复) duplicated ▶ 复制 [fùzhì] reproduce **2** (繁复) complex **II** VB **1** (转) turn **2** (回答) reply **3** (恢复) recover **4** (报复) take revenge **III** ADV again ▶ 复查 [fùchá] re-examine

复活节 [Fùhuó Jié] N (宗) Easter

复习 [fùxí] VB revise

复印 [fùyìn] VB photocopy

复杂 [fùzá] ADJ complex

副 [fù] **I** ADJ **1** (辅助) deputy **2** (附带) subsidiary ▶ 副业 [fùyè] subsidiary business **II** N assistant ▶ 大副 [dàfù] first mate **III** VB correspond to **IV** MEAS (套) pair ▷ 一副手套 [yī fù shǒutào] a pair of gloves ▷ 一副冷面孔 [yī fù lěng miànkǒng] a cold expression ▷ 一副笑脸 [yī fù xiàoliǎn] a smiling face

measure word, used for expressions

副作用 [fùzuòyòng] N side effect

富 [fù] **I** ADJ **1** (有钱) rich **2** (丰富) abundant **II** N wealth **III** VB enrich

富有 [fùyǒu] **I** ADJ wealthy **II** VB be full of

G

咖 [gā] *see below*/见下文
→ *see also*/另见 kā

咖喱 [gālí] N curry

该 [gāi] **I** VB **1** (应当) ought to **2** (轮到) be the turn of **3** (活该) serve … right ▶ 活该 [huógāi] serve … right **II** AUX VB **1** (应该) should ▷ 工作明天该完成了。 [Gōngzuò míngtiān gāi wánchéng le.] The work should be finished by tomorrow. **2** (表示推测) ▷ 再不吃的话，菜都该凉了。 [Zài bù chī dehuà, cài dōu gāi liáng le.] If we keep waiting the food is only going to get colder. **3** (用于加强语气) ▷ 要是他能在这儿该多好啊！ [Yàoshì tā néng zài zhèr gāi duō hǎo a!] It would be great if he could be here.

改 [gǎi] VB **1** (改变) change **2** (修改) alter **3** (改正) correct

改变 [gǎibiàn] VB change ▷ 我改变了主意。 [Wǒ gǎibiàn le zhǔyi.] I changed my mind.

改革 [gǎigé] VB reform ▷ 改革开放 [gǎigé kāifàng] reform and opening up

改善 [gǎishàn] VB improve

改正 [gǎizhèng] VB correct ▷ 改正缺点 [gǎizhèng quēdiǎn] mend one's ways

钙 [gài] N (化) calcium

盖 [gài] **I** N (指器皿) cover ▶ 盖子 [gàizi] lid **II** VB **1** (蒙上) cover **2** (遮掩) cover … up **3** (打上) stamp **4** (压过) block … out **5** (建造) build

概 [gài] N (大略) outline

概括 [gàikuò] **I** VB summarize **II** ADJ brief

概念 [gàiniàn] N concept

干 [gān] **I** VB have to do with ▷ 这不干我事。 [Zhè bù gān wǒ shì.] This has nothing to do with me. **II** ADJ **1** (无水) dry **2** (不用水) dry ▶ 干洗 [gānxǐ] dry-clean **3** (干涸) dried-up **III** N ▶ 豆腐干 [dòufugān] dried tofu ▶ 葡萄干 [pútaogān] raisin **IV** ADV (白白) in vain
→ *see also*/另见 gàn

干杯 [gānbēi] VB drink a toast ▷ "干杯！" ["Gānbēi!"] "Cheers!"

干脆 [gāncuì] ADJ direct

干旱 [gānhàn] ADJ arid

干净 [gānjìng] ADJ **1** (无尘) clean **2** (一点不剩) complete ▷ 请把汤喝干净。 [Qǐng bǎ tāng hē gānjìng.] Please finish your soup.

干扰 [gānrǎo] VB disturb

干预 [gānyù] VB interfere

干燥 [gānzào] ADJ dry

杆 [gān] N post

肝 [gān] N liver

竿 [gān] N pole ▶ 竿子 [gānzi] pole

赶 [gǎn] VB **1** (追) catch ▷ 赶公共汽车 [gǎn gōnggòng qìchē] catch a bus **2** (加快) rush ▷ 赶着回家 [gǎn zhe huíjiā] rush home **3** (驱赶) drive **4** (驱逐) drive … out

赶紧 [gǎnjǐn] ADV quickly

赶快 [gǎnkuài] ADV at once ▷ 我们得赶快走了！ [Wǒmen děi gǎnkuài zǒu le!] We must go at once!

赶上 [gǎnshàng] VB catch up with

赶忙 [gǎnmáng] ADV hurriedly

敢 [gǎn] VB **1** (有胆量) dare ▶ 敢于 [gǎnyú] dare to **2** (有把握) be sure

感 [gǎn] **I** VB **1** (觉得) feel **2** (感动) move ▶ 感人 [gǎnrén] moving **II** N sense ▷ 成就感 [chéngjiùgǎn] a sense of achievement ▷ 方向感 [fāngxiànggǎn] a sense of direction

感到 [gǎndào] VB feel ▷ 我感到幸运。 [Wǒ gǎndào xìngyùn.] I feel lucky.

感动 [gǎndòng] VB move ▷ 他容易被感动。 [Tā róngyì bèi gǎndòng.] He's very easily moved.

感恩节 [Gǎn'ēn Jié] N Thanksgiving

感激 [gǎnjī] VB appreciate

感觉 [gǎnjué] **I** N feeling **II** VB **1** (感到) feel **2** (认为) sense

感冒 [gǎnmào] VB catch a cold

感情 [gǎnqíng] N **1** (心理反应) emotion **2** (喜爱) feelings (PL)

感染 [gǎnrǎn] VB (传染) infect

感想 [gǎnxiǎng] N thoughts (PL)

感谢 [gǎnxiè] VB thank ▷ 感谢您的指导。 [Gǎnxiè nín de zhǐdǎo.] Thank you for your guidance.

感兴趣 [gǎn xìngqù] VB be interested in ▷ 他对绘画感兴趣。 [Tā duì huìhuà gǎn xìngqù.] He's interested in painting.

干 [gàn] VB **1** (做) do ▶ 干活 [gànhuó] work **2** (担任) act as ▷ 他干过队长。 [Tā gànguò duìzhǎng.] He acted as team leader.

→ *see also*/另见 gān

干部 [gànbù] N cadre

刚 [gāng] **I** ADJ strong **II** ADV **1** (恰好) just ▷ 水温刚好。 [Shuǐwēn gāng hǎo.] The temperature of the water was just right. **2** (仅仅) just ▷ 这儿刚够放一把椅子。 [Zhèr gāng gòu fàng yī bǎ yǐzi.] There is just enough room for a chair. **3** (不久以前) only just ▷ 小宝宝刚会走路。 [Xiǎo bǎobao gāng huì zǒulù.] The baby has only just started walking.

刚才 [gāngcái] N just now

刚刚 [gānggāng] ADV just

刚好 [gānghǎo] **I** ADJ just right **II** ADV luckily

钢 [gāng] N steel ▶ 钢铁 [gāngtiě] steel

钢笔 [gāngbǐ] N fountain pen

钢琴 [gāngqín] N piano

缸 [gāng] N (器物) vat ▶ 鱼缸 [yúgāng] fish bowl

港 [gǎng] N **1** (港湾) harbor **2** (香港) Hong Kong ▶ 香港 [Xiānggǎng] Hong Kong ▶ 港币 [gǎngbì] Hong Kong dollar

港口 [gǎngkǒu] N port

高 [gāo] ADJ **1** (指高度) tall ▶ 高楼 [gāolóu] tall building **2** (指标准或程度) high ▶ 高标准 [gāo biāozhǔn] high standard **3** (指等级) senior ▶ 高中 [gāozhōng] senior high school **4** (指声音) high-pitched **5** (指年龄) old **6** (指价格) high

高大 [gāodà] ADJ (字) huge

高档 [gāodàng] ADJ top quality

高等 [gāoděng] ADJ higher ▷ 高等教育 [gāoděng jiàoyù] higher education

高级 [gāojí] ADJ **1** (指级别) senior ▷ 高级法院 [gāojí fǎyuàn] high court **2** (超过一般) high-quality ▷ 高级英语 [gāojí Yīngyǔ] advanced English ▷ 高级宾馆 [gāojí bīnguǎn] luxury hotel

高考 [gāokǎo] N college entrance examination

高科技 [gāokējì] ADJ hi-tech

高速 [gāosù] ADJ rapid

高速公路 [gāosù gōnglù] N freeway

高兴 [gāoxìng] **I** ADJ happy **II** VB enjoy

高原 [gāoyuán] N plateau

高中 [gāozhōng] N (*also*: 高级中学) high school

糕 [gāo] N cake ▶ 蛋糕 [dàngao] cake

搞 [gǎo] VB **1** (干) do **2** (弄) get

告 [gào] VB **1** (陈述) tell **2** (控诉) sue

告别 [gàobié] VB say goodbye

告诉 [gàosu] VB tell

告状 [gàozhuàng] VB (抱怨) complain

哥 [gē] N **1** (哥哥) elder brother **2** (亲热称呼) brother

哥哥 [gēge] N elder brother
哥儿们 [gērmen] N (朋友) buddy

胳 [gē] *see below*/见下文
胳膊 [gēbo] N arm

鸽 [gē] N dove ▶ 鸽子 [gēzi] pigeon

搁 [gē] VB 1 (放) put 2 (搁置) put aside

割 [gē] VB cut

歌 [gē] I N song II VB sing
歌剧 [gējù] N opera
歌曲 [gēqǔ] N song
歌手 [gēshǒu] N singer

革 [gé] I N leather II VB (改变) change
革命 [gémìng] VB revolutionize ▷ 工业革命 [gōngyè gémìng] industrial revolution

格 [gé] N (格子) check
格式 [géshi] N format
格外 [géwài] ADV 1 (特别) especially 2 (额外) additionally

隔 [gé] VB 1 (阻隔) separate 2 (间隔) be apart
隔壁 [gébì] N next door ▷ 隔壁邻居 [gébì línjū] next-door neighbor

嗝 [gé] N 1 (饱嗝) burp ▶ 打饱嗝 [dǎ bǎogé] burp 2 (冷嗝) hiccup ▶ 打冷嗝 [dǎ lěnggé] have a hiccup

个 [gè] I N (指身材或大小) size ▶ 个头儿 [gètóur] build II MEAS (表示个数) ▷ 6个桃子 [liù gè táozi] six peaches ▷ 两个月 [liǎng gè yuè] two months

This is the most useful and common measure word, and can be used as the default measure word when you are unsure. It can be used for people, objects, fruits, countries, cities, companies, dates, weeks, months, ideas etc. (表示动量) ▷ 开个会 [kāi gè huì] have a meeting ▷ 冲个澡 [chōng gè zǎo] have a shower

the most useful measure word, used for actions

个别 [gèbié] ADJ 1 (单个) individual 2 (少数) a couple

个人 [gèrén] I N individual II PRON oneself ▷ 就他个人而言 [jiù tā gèrén éryán] as far as he's concerned ▷ 在我个人看来, 这是个好主意。 [Zài wǒ gèrén kànlái, zhè shì gè hǎo zhǔyi.] As far as I'm concerned this is a good idea.

个体 [gètǐ] N 1 (指生物) individual 2 (指经济形态) ▷ 个体经营 [gètǐ jīngyíng] private enterprise

个性 [gèxìng] N personality ▷ 他个性很强。 [Tā gèxìng hěn qiáng.] He has a very strong personality.

个子 [gèzi] N stature ▷ 高个子女人 [gāo gèzi nǚrén] a tall woman

各 [gè] I PRON each II ADV individually
各个 [gègè] I PRON each II ADV one by one
各种 [gèzhǒng] PRON all kinds
各自 [gèzì] PRON each

给 [gěi] I VB 1 (给予) give 2 (让) let II PREP 1 (为) for ▷ 我给妻子做早餐。 [Wǒ gěi qīzǐ zuò zǎocān.] I made breakfast for my wife. 2 (向) to ▷ 留给他 [liú gěi tā] leave it to him ▷ 递给我 [dì gěi wǒ] pass it to me

根 [gēn] I N (指植物) root ▶ 祸根 [huògēn] the root of the problem II MEAS ▷ 一根绳子 [yī gēn shéngzi] a rope ▷ 一根头发 [yī gēn tóufa] a hair

measure word, used for long thin objects, body parts and plants

根本 [gēnběn] I N root II ADJ fundamental III ADV 1 (完全) at all 2 (彻底) thoroughly ▷ 根本转变态度 [gēnběn zhuǎnbiàn tàidù] completely change one's attitude

根据 [gēnjù] I PREP according to II N basis

根源 [gēnyuán] N cause

跟 [gēn] **I** N heel **II** VB **1** (跟随) follow **2** (嫁) marry **III** PREP **1** (同) with ▷ 我跟朋友去公园了。 [Wǒ gēn péngyou qù gōngyuán le.] I went to the park with friends. **2** (向) ▷ 跟我说说这件事。 [Gēn wǒ shuōshuo zhè jiàn shì.] Tell me what happened. **3** (表示比较) as ▷ 他的教育背景跟我相似。 [Tā de jiàoyù bèijǐng gēn wǒ xiāngsì.] His educational background is similar to mine. **IV** CONJ and

跟随 [gēnsuí] VB follow

跟头 [gēntou] N fall ▷ 翻跟头 [fān gēntou] do a somersault

跟踪 [gēnzōng] VB tail

更 [gēng] VB (改变) change ▶ 更正 [gēngzhèng] correct
→ *see also*/另见 gèng

更改 [gēnggǎi] VB alter

更换 [gēnghuàn] VB change

更替 [gēngtì] VB replace

更新 [gēngxīn] VB **1** (事物) replace ▷ 更新网站内容 [gēngxīn wǎngzhàn nèiróng] update web content **2** (森林) renew

更衣室 [gēngyīshì] N fitting room

耕 [gēng] VB plow

耕地 [gēngdì] **I** VB plow **II** N cultivated land

更 [gèng] ADJ (更加) even more ▷ 天更黑了。 [Tiān gèng hēi le.] It's getting even darker.
→ *see also*/另见 gēng

更加 [gèngjiā] ADV even more

工 [gōng] N **1** (指人) worker ▶ 童工 [tónggōng] child labor **2** (指阶级) the working class **3** (工作或劳动) work **4** (工程) project **5** (工业) industry

工厂 [gōngchǎng] N factory

工程 [gōngchéng] N engineering project

工程师 [gōngchéngshī] N engineer

工夫 [gōngfu] N **1** (时间) time **2** (空闲) spare time

工具 [gōngjù] N **1** (器具) tool **2** (喻) instrument

工人 [gōngrén] N worker

工业 [gōngyè] N industry

工艺品 [gōngyìpǐn] N handicraft item

工资 [gōngzī] N pay

工作 [gōngzuò] N **1** (劳动) work **2** (职业) job **3** (业务) work

公 [gōng] **I** ADJ **1** (非私有) public ▶ 公共 [gōnggòng] public **2** (共识) general **3** (公正) fair **4** (雄性) male **II** N **1** (公务) official business **2** (敬) (老先生) ▷ 王公 [Wáng gōng] Mr. Wang **3** (丈夫的父亲) father-in-law ▶ 公公 [gōnggong] father-in-law

公安 [gōng'ān] N public security

公布 [gōngbù] VB announce

公厕 [gōngcè] N public toilet

公尺 [gōngchǐ] N meter

公费 [gōngfèi] N public expense

公分 [gōngfēn] N centimeter

公共 [gōnggòng] ADJ public

公共汽车 [gōnggòng qìchē] N bus

公共汽车站 [gōnggòng qìchēzhàn] N **1** (指总站) bus station **2** (指路边站) bus stop

公斤 [gōngjīn] N kilogram

公开 [gōngkāi] **I** ADJ public **II** VB make public

公里 [gōnglǐ] N kilometer

公路 [gōnglù] N freeway

公民 [gōngmín] N citizen

公平 [gōngpíng] ADJ fair

公社 [gōngshè] N commune

公司 [gōngsī] N company

公用 [gōngyòng] ADJ public

公寓 [gōngyù] N **1** (旅馆) boarding house **2** (楼房) apartment

公元 [gōngyuán] N A.D.

公园 [gōngyuán] N park

公正 [gōngzhèng] ADJ impartial

公众 [gōngzhòng] N public
公主 [gōngzhǔ] N princess

功 [gōng] N 1 (功劳) contribution 2 (成效) achievement
功夫 [gōngfu] N martial arts
功课 [gōngkè] N homework
功劳 [gōngláo] N contribution
功能 [gōngnéng] N function ▷ 多功能电话 [duōgōngnéng diànhuà] multi-functional telephone

攻 [gōng] VB (攻打) attack
攻击 [gōngjī] VB (进攻) attack

供 [gōng] VB 1 (供应) supply 2 (提供) provide
供给 [gōngjǐ] VB supply
供求 [gōngqiú] N supply and demand
供应 [gōngyìng] VB supply

宫 [gōng] N (皇宫) palace ▶ 宫殿 [gōngdiàn] palace

恭 [gōng] ADJ respectful
恭维 [gōngwei] VB flatter
恭喜 [gōngxǐ] VB congratulate

巩 [gǒng] *see below*/见下文
巩固 [gǒnggù] I ADJ solid II VB strengthen

共 [gòng] I ADJ common II VB share III ADV 1 (一齐) together 2 (总共) altogether IV N (*also*: 共产党) the communist party
共产党 [gòngchǎndǎng] N the communist party
共产主义 [gòngchǎnzhǔyì] N communism
共和国 [gònghéguó] N republic
共同 [gòngtóng] I ADJ common II ADV together

贡 [gòng] N tribute
贡献 [gòngxiàn] I VB devote II N contribution

沟 [gōu] N ditch
沟通 [gōutōng] VB communicate

钩 [gōu] I N 1 (钩子) hook 2 (符号) tick II VB 1 (用钩子挂) hook 2 (编织, 缝) crochet

狗 [gǒu] N dog

构 [gòu] I VB 1 (组成) compose 2 (结成) form 3 (建造) construct II N (结构) structure
构成 [gòuchéng] VB 1 (造成) constitute 2 (组成) compose
构造 [gòuzào] N structure

购 [gòu] VB buy
购买 [gòumǎi] VB buy
购物 [gòuwù] VB go shopping ▷ 她爱购物。 [Tā ài gòuwù.] She likes shopping.

够 [gòu] I ADJ enough ▷ 5个就够了。 [Wǔ gè jiù gòu le.] Five is enough. II VB reach

估 [gū] VB guess
估计 [gūjì] VB reckon

姑 [gū] N 1 (姑母) aunt 2 (丈夫的姐妹) sister-in-law
姑娘 [gūniang] N girl
姑姑 [gūgu] N aunt

孤 [gū] ADJ (孤单) alone
孤单 [gūdān] ADJ (寂寞) lonely
孤独 [gūdú] ADJ solitary
孤儿 [gū'ér] N orphan

古 [gǔ] I N ancient times (PL) II ADJ ancient
古代 [gǔdài] N antiquity
古典 [gǔdiǎn] I N classics (PL) II ADJ classical
古董 [gǔdǒng] N (古代器物) antique
古迹 [gǔjì] N historic site
古老 [gǔlǎo] ADJ ancient

股 [gǔ] I N 1 (指绳或线) strand 2 (股份) share II MEAS (气体) (气味) whiff
股票 [gǔpiào] N share
股市 [gǔshì] N stock market

骨 [gǔ] N bone

骨头 [gǔtou] N (字) bone

鼓 [gǔ] **I** N drum **II** VB **1** ▶ 鼓掌 [gǔzhǎng] applaud **2** (凸起, 胀大) bulge ▷ 他鼓着嘴。 [Tā gǔ zhe zuǐ.] He puffed his cheeks out. **III** ADJ bulging ▷ 她的书包鼓鼓的。 [Tā de shūbāo gǔgǔ de.] Her schoolbag was full to bursting.

鼓励 [gǔlì] VB encourage

鼓舞 [gǔwǔ] **I** VB inspire **II** ADJ inspiring

固 [gù] **I** ADJ strong ▶ 坚固 [jiāngù] solid ▶ 牢固 [láogù] firm **II** ADV (坚定) firmly

固定 [gùdìng] **I** ADJ fixed **II** VB fix

固体 [gùtǐ] N solid

固执 [gùzhí] ADJ stubborn

故 [gù] N **1** (变故) incident **2** (原因) reason

故宫 [gùgōng] N the Forbidden City

故宫 [gùgōng]

As the largest collection of ancient wooden structures in the world, 故宫 gùgōng formed the imperial palaces of the Ming (1368-1644) and Qing (1644-1911) dynasties. It is located at what was once the exact center of the old city of Beijing, just to the north of Tiananmen Square. It is now a major tourist attraction, both for the architecture of its 800-plus wooden buildings, and for the many artistic and cultural treasures which are housed within them. In 1987 it was declared a World Heritage Site by UNESCO.

故事 [gùshi] N story

故乡 [gùxiāng] N birthplace

故意 [gùyì] ADV deliberately

故障 [gùzhàng] N fault ▷ 这台机器出了故障。 [Zhè tái jīqì chū le gùzhàng.] This machine is faulty.

顾 [gù] VB **1** (看) look ▶ 回顾 [huígù] look back ▶ 环顾 [huángù] look around **2** (注意, 照管) attend to ▶ 照顾 [zhàogù] attend to

顾客 [gùkè] N customer

顾问 [gùwèn] N consultant

雇 [gù] VB **1** (雇佣) employ **2** (租赁) hire

雇员 [gùyuán] N employee

雇主 [gùzhǔ] N employer

瓜 [guā] N (植) melon

刮 [guā] VB **1** (指用刀) shave **2** (涂抹) smear **3** (风) blow

挂 [guà] VB **1** (悬) (吊) hang **2** (中断电话) hang up

挂号 [guàhào] **I** VB register **II** ADJ registered ▷ 挂号信 [guàhàoxìn] registered mail

挂历 [guàlì] N calendar

褂 [guà] N gown ▶ 褂子 [guàzi] gown

乖 [guāi] ADJ (听话) well-behaved

拐 [guǎi] **I** N **1** (拐杖) walking stick **2** (拐角处) turning **II** VB **1** (转变方向) turn ▷ 向左/右拐 [xiàng zuǒ/yòu guǎi] turn left **2** (拐骗) swindle

拐卖 [guǎimài] VB abduct and sell

怪 [guài] **I** ADJ strange **II** VB **1** (觉得奇怪) be surprised **2** (责怪) blame **III** ADV (口) really **IV** N monster

怪不得 [guàibude] CONJ no wonder

关 [guān] **I** VB **1** (合拢) close **2** (圈起来) imprison **3** (停业) close down **4** (中断) (终止) turn ... off ▷ 关灯 [guān dēng] turn off the light **5** (牵连) concern ▷ 这不关他的事。 [Zhè bù guān tā de shì.] This matter does not concern him. **II** N **1** (守卫处所) pass **2** (出入境收税处) customs (PL) ▶ 海关 [hǎiguān] customs (PL) **3** (转折点) critical point **4** (关联部分) ▶ 关节 [guānjié] joint ▶ 关键 [guānjiàn] key

关闭 [guānbì] VB **1** (合拢) close **2** (歇

业或停办) close down
关怀 [guānhuái] VB be concerned about
关税 [guānshuì] N customs duty
关系 [guānxì] I N (联系) relation II VB impact on
关心 [guānxīn] VB be concerned about
关于 [guānyú] PREP on
关照 [guānzhào] VB (关心照顾) look after
关注 [guānzhù] VB pay close attention to

观 [guān] I VB look ▸ 围观 [wéiguān] gather round to watch ▸ 旁观 [pángguān] look on II N view
观察 [guānchá] VB observe
观点 [guāndiǎn] N point of view
观看 [guānkàn] VB watch
观念 [guānniàn] N concept
观众 [guānzhòng] N spectator

官 [guān] N 1 (公职人员) official 2 (器官) organ
官司 [guānsi] N lawsuit
官员 [guānyuán] N official

管 [guǎn] I N 1 (管子) pipe ▸ 水管 [shuǐguǎn] water pipe ▸ 管子 [guǎnzi] tube 2 (乐器) wind instrument ▸ 双簧管 [shuānghuángguǎn] oboe 3 (管状物) tube II VB 1 (负责) be in charge of 2 (管辖) have jurisdiction over 3 (管教) discipline 4 (过问) interfere ▹ 这事不用你管。 [Zhè shì bù yòng nǐ guǎn.] It's no use you interfering in this. 5 (保证) guarantee ▸ 管保 [guǎnbǎo] guarantee 6 (提供) provide
管道 [guǎndào] N pipeline
管理 [guǎnlǐ] VB 1 (负责) be in charge 2 (保管) take care of 3 (看管) keep guard over ▸ 企业管理 [qǐyè guǎnlǐ] business management
管用 [guǎnyòng] ADJ effective

贯 [guàn] I VB 1 (贯穿) pass through 2 (连贯) keep following II N ancestral home ▸ 籍贯 [jíguàn] place of origin
贯彻 [guànchè] VB implement
贯穿 [guànchuān] VB run through

冠 [guàn] I VB crown II N crown
冠军 [guànjūn] N champion

惯 [guàn] VB 1 (习惯) be used to ▹ 我吃西餐已经惯了。 [Wǒ chī xīcān yǐjing guàn le.] I'm already used to Western food. 2 (纵容) spoil ▹ 惯孩子 [guàn háizi] spoil the children

灌 [guàn] VB 1 (灌溉) irrigate 2 (注入) pour … into

罐 [guàn] I N 1 (盛茶叶, 糖等) jar 2 (易拉罐) can 3 (煤气) cylinder ▸ 煤气罐 [méiqìguàn] gas cylinder II MEAS can ▹ 两罐啤酒 [liǎng guàn píjiǔ] two cans of beer ▹ 五罐苏打水 [wǔ guàn sūdǎshuǐ] five cans of soda water
罐头 [guàntou] N can ▹ 金枪鱼罐头 [jīnqiāngyú guàntou] canned tuna fish

光 [guāng] I N 1 (指物质) light ▸ 月光 [yuèguāng] moonlight ▸ 阳光 [yángguāng] sunlight 2 (景物) scenery ▸ 风光 [fēngguāng] scenery 3 (荣誉) glory ▸ 增光 [zēngguāng] bring glory II VB 1 (光大) glorify 2 (露出) bare III ADJ 1 (光滑) smooth ▸ 光滑 [guānghuá] smooth 2 (露着) bare ▸ 光脚 [guāngjiǎo] barefooted 3 (穷尽) used up ▹ 钱都用光了。 [Qián dōu yòng guāng le.] All the money's used up. IV ADV just ▹ 他光说不做。 [Tā guāng shuō bù zuò.] He's all talk.
光临 [guānglín] VB be present
光明 [guāngmíng] I N light II ADJ bright
光盘 [guāngpán] N CD
光荣 [guāngróng] ADJ glorious
光线 [guāngxiàn] N light

广 [guǎng] ADJ 1 (宽阔) broad 2 (多)

numerous

广播 [guǎngbō] VB broadcast

广场 [guǎngchǎng] N square

广大 [guǎngdà] ADJ 1 (宽广) vast 2 (众多) numerous

广泛 [guǎngfàn] ADJ wide-ranging ▶ 广泛开展活动 [guǎngfàn kāizhǎn huódòng] initiate a wide range of activities

广告 [guǎnggào] N advertisement

广阔 [guǎngkuò] ADJ broad

逛 [guàng] VB stroll

归 [guī] VB 1 (返回, 还给) return 2 (合并) group ... together ▶ 归类 [guīlèi] categorise 3 (属于) be under the charge of ▷ 这本书归他所有。 [Zhè běn shū guī tā suǒyǒu.] This book belongs to him.

归功于 [guīgōngyú] VB give credit to

归还 [guīhuán] VB return

龟 [guī] N tortoise ▶ 乌龟 [wūguī] tortoise

规 [guī] N 1 (工具) compasses (PL) 2 (规则) rule

规定 [guīdìng] I VB stipulate II N regulation

规范 [guīfàn] N standard ▶ 一定要规范市场秩序。 [yīdìng yaò guīfàn shìchǎng zhìxù] We must standardize the market economy.

规矩 [guīju] I N norm II ADJ well-behaved ▷ 他办事总是规矩。 [Tā bànshì zǒngshì guīju.] He always plays by the rules.

规律 [guīlǜ] N law

规模 [guīmó] N scale

规则 [guīzé] I N regulation II ADJ orderly

规章 [guīzhāng] N regulations (PL)

轨 [guǐ] N (轨道) rail ▶ 轨道 [guǐdào] track

鬼 [guǐ] N 1 (灵魂) ghost 2 (勾当) dirty trick 3 (不良行为者) ▶ 酒鬼 [jiǔguǐ] drunkard

鬼混 [guǐhùn] VB hang around

鬼脸 [guǐliǎn] N grimace ▷ 做鬼脸 [zuò guǐliǎn] make a funny face

柜 [guì] N (柜子) cupboard ▶ 衣柜 [yīguì] wardrobe ▶ 保险柜 [bǎoxiǎnguì] safe

柜台 [guìtái] N counter

贵 [guì] ADJ 1 (指价格) expensive 2 (值得珍视) valuable ▶ 贵宾 [guìbīn] VIP

贵重 [guìzhòng] ADJ valuable

贵族 [guìzú] N aristocrat

跪 [guì] VB kneel ▶ 跪下 [guìxià] kneel down

滚 [gǔn] I VB 1 (滚动) roll ▶ 滚动 [gǔndòng] roll 2 (走开) get lost ▶ 滚烫 [gǔntàng] boiling hot II ADJ 1 (滚动的) rolling 2 (沸腾的) boiling

棍 [gùn] N (棍子) stick ▶ 棍子 [gùnzi] stick

锅 [guō] N (指炊具) pot ▶ 炒菜锅 [chǎocàiguō] wok ▶ 火锅 [huǒguō] hotpot

国 [guó] I N country II ADJ (国家) national ▶ 国徽 [guóhuī] national emblem ▶ 国歌 [guógē] national anthem ▶ 国旗 [guóqí] national flag

国产 [guóchǎn] ADJ domestic

国画 [guóhuà] N traditional Chinese painting

国会 [guóhuì] N parliament

国籍 [guójí] N nationality

国际 [guójì] ADJ international

国家 [guójiā] N state

国力 [guólì] N national strength

国民 [guómín] N citizen

国内 [guónèi] ADJ domestic

国庆节 [guóqìngjié] N National Day

国庆节 [guóqìngjié]

国庆节 guóqìngjié (National Day) falls on October 1, and

commemorates the anniversary of the founding of the People's Republic of China in 1949. The PRC was declared by Chairman Mao Zedong, in Tiananmen Square in Beijing.

国王 [guówáng] N king

国务院 [guówùyuàn] N the State Council

国务院 [guówùyuàn]

国务院 guówùyuàn, the State Council, is the highest executive and administrative organ of the PRC government, headed by the Premier, and overseeing all the various ministries.

国营 [guóyíng] ADJ state-run

果 [guǒ] N **1** (果子) fruit ▶ 果子 [guǒzi] fruit **2** (结局) outcome ▶ 效果 [xiàoguǒ] result ▶ 成果 [chéngguǒ] achievement

果断 [guǒduàn] ADJ resolute

果然 [guǒrán] ADV really

果实 [guǒshí] N **1** (果子) fruit **2** (成果) fruits (PL)

果真 [guǒzhēn] ADV really

裹 [guǒ] VB (缠绕) wrap

过 [guò] **I** VB **1** (经过) pass through **2** (度过) spend ▷ 你假期怎么过的? [Nǐ jiàqī zěnme guò de?] How did you spend your vacation? **3** (过去) pass **4** (超过) be more than ▷ 年过半百 [nián guò bàn bǎi] over fifty years old **5** (生活) live ▷ 我们过得很好。 [Wǒmen guò de hěn hǎo.] We live well. **6** (庆祝) celebrate ▷ 过生日 [guò shēngrì] celebrate a birthday **II** N fault **III** PREP past ▷ 现在是9点过8分。 [Xiànzài shì jiǔ diǎn guò bā fēn.] It is now eight minutes past nine.

When 过 guò is used as a verb suffix to indicate a past action, it often corresponds to the present perfect tense (e.g. 'I have done') in English, stressing that the subject has experienced something, e.g. 我去过中国三次 Wǒ qùguo Zhōngguó sān cì (I have been to China three times).

过程 [guòchéng] N process

过道 [guòdào] N corridor

过分 [guòfèn] ADJ excessive

过后 [guòhòu] ADV later

过奖 [guòjiǎng] VB flatter ▷ 您过奖了。 [Nín guòjiǎng le.] I'm flattered.

过来 [guòlái] VB come over

过滤 [guòlǜ] VB filter

过敏 [guòmǐn] N (医) allergy

过期 [guòqī] VB expire

过年 [guònián] VB celebrate the new year

过去 [guòqù] N the past

过去 [guòqu] VB pass by

过日子 [guò rìzi] VB live

过时 [guòshí] ADJ outdated

过世 [guòshì] VB pass away

过头 [guòtóu] ADJ excessive

过瘾 [guòyǐn] VB do to one's heart's content

过于 [guòyú] ADV too

H

哈 [hā] **I** INT aha **II** ONO ha ha ▷ 哈哈大笑 [hā hā dàxiào] roar with laughter

还 [hái] ADV **1** (仍旧) still, yet ▷ 那家老饭店还很兴旺。 [Nà jiā lǎo fàndiàn hái hěn xīngwàng.] The old restaurant is still thriving. ▷ 她还没回来。 [Tā hái méi huílai.] She hasn't come back yet. **2** (更加) even more
→ *see also*/另见 huán

还是 [háishì] **I** ADV **1** (仍然) still **2** (最好) had better ▷ 你还是先完成作业吧。 [Nǐ háishì xiān wánchéng zuòyè ba.] You'd better finish your homework first. **II** CONJ or ▷ 你是去巴黎还是去伦敦? [Nǐ shì qù Bālí háishì qù Lúndūn?] Are you going to Paris or London?

孩 [hái] N child
孩子 [háizi] N child

海 [hǎi] N (海洋) ocean ▶ 地中海 [Dìzhōnghǎi] the Mediterranean Sea
海边 [hǎibiān] N coast
海拔 [hǎibá] N elevation
海报 [hǎibào] N poster
海滨 [hǎibīn] N seaside
海关 [hǎiguān] N customs (PL)
海军 [hǎijūn] N the navy
海绵 [hǎimián] N sponge
海滩 [hǎitān] N beach
海峡 [hǎixiá] N strait
海鲜 [hǎixiān] N seafood
海洋 [hǎiyáng] N ocean

害 [hài] **I** VB **1** (损害) harm **2** (杀害) kill **II** N harm ▶ 害处 [hàichu] harm ▶ 灾害 [zāihài] disaster **III** ADJ harmful ▶ 害虫 [hàichóng] pest
害怕 [hàipà] VB be afraid
害羞 [hàixiū] VB be shy

含 [hán] VB **1** (用嘴) keep ... in the mouth **2** (包含) contain
含量 [hánliàng] N content
含义 [hányì] N meaning

寒 [hán] ADJ (冷) cold ▶ 寒风 [hánfēng] chilly wind
寒假 [hánjià] N winter vacation
寒冷 [hánlěng] ADJ cold

韩 [hán] N *see below*/见下文
韩国 [Hánguó] N South Korea

喊 [hǎn] VB **1** (大声叫) shout ▶ 喊叫 [hǎnjiào] cry out **2** (叫) call

汉 [hàn] N (汉族) the Han (PL) ▶ 汉人 [Hànrén] the Han people (PL)
汉语 [Hànyǔ] N Chinese
汉字 [Hànzì] N Chinese characters (PL)
汉族 [Hànzú] N the Han (PL)

汗 [hàn] N sweat ▶ 汗水 [hànshuǐ] sweat

旱 [hàn] ADJ dry ▶ 旱灾 [hànzāi] drought

行 [háng] **I** N **1** (行列) row ▷ 第一行 [dìyī háng] first row **2** (行业) profession ▶ 同行 [tóngháng] people in the same profession **II** MEAS line ▷ 一行字 [yī háng zì] a line of words
→ *see also*/另见 xíng
行业 [hángyè] N industry

航 [háng] VB **1** (指船) sail **2** (指飞机) fly
航班 [hángbān] N (指客机) scheduled flight
航空 [hángkōng] VB fly ▷ 航空信 [hángkōngxìn] airmail ▷ 航空公司 [hángkōng gōngsī] airline

毫 [háo] N (千分之一) ▶ 毫米 [háomǐ] millimeter ▶ 毫升 [háoshēng] milliliter
毫不 [háobù] ADV not at all

毫无 [háowú] ADV without the slightest

豪 [háo] ADJ grand ▶ 豪华 [háohuá] luxurious

好 [hǎo] **I** ADJ **1** (令人满意) good ▷ 他脾气好。 [Tā píqì hǎo.] He's good-natured. **2** (容易) easy ▷ 这事不好办。 [Zhè shì bù hǎo bàn.] This won't be easy to manage. **3** (健康) well ▷ 你身体好吗？ [Nǐ shēntǐ hǎo ma?] Are you keeping well? **4** (亲密) good ▷ 我们是好朋友。 [Wǒmen shì hǎo péngyou.] We're good friends. **5** (表示问候) ▷ 你好！ [Nǐ hǎo!] Hello! ▷ 大家好。 [Dàjiā hǎo.] Hello everyone. **6** (表示完成) ▷ 工作找好了。 [Gōngzuò zhǎo hǎo le.] I've found work. ▷ 衣服洗好了。 [Yīfu xǐ hǎo le.] The clothes have been washed. **7** (表示答应, 结束等) ▷ 好，我们现在就去！ [Hǎo, wǒmen xiànzài jiù qù!] OK, let's go then! **II** ADV **1** (强调多或久) very ▷ 我等了好久她才来。 [Wǒ děng le hǎo jiǔ tā cái lái.] I'd waited for a long time before she arrived. **2** (表示程度深) ▷ 他话说得好快。 [Tā huà shuō de hǎo kuài.] He speaks so quickly. **III** N (问候) regards (PL) ▷ 请代我向你太太问好。 [Qǐng dài wǒ xiàng nǐ tàitai wènhǎo.] Please send my regards to your wife.
→ *see also*/另见 hào

好吃 [hǎochī] ADJ delicious

好处 [hǎochu] N **1** (益处) benefit **2** (利益) profit

好久 [hǎojiǔ] ADV for a long time

好看 [hǎokàn] ADJ **1** (漂亮) nice-looking **2** (精彩) good ▷ 这本书很好看。 [Zhè běn shū hěn hǎokàn.] This book is very good.

好受 [hǎoshòu] ADJ comfortable

好容易 [hǎoróngyì] ADV with great effort

好听 [hǎotīng] ADJ **1** (指声音, 音乐) lovely **2** (指言语) nice

好玩儿 [hǎowánr] ADJ fun

好像 [hǎoxiàng] ADV apparently

好笑 [hǎoxiào] ADJ funny

好些 [hǎoxiē] ADJ quite a great deal of

号 [hào] **I** N **1** (名称) name ▶ 外号 [wàihào] nickname **2** (商店) firm ▶ 商号 [shānghào] firm **3** (标记) sign ▶ 逗号 [dòuhào] comma **4** (次序) number **5** (日期) date ▷ 6月1号 [liùyuè yī hào] June first **6** (大小) size ▶ 大号 [dàhào] large-size **7** (乐器) brass instrument ▶ 小号 [xiǎohào] trumpet **II** VB (脉) take ▶ 号脉 [hàomài] take a pulse

号码 [hàomǎ] N number

号召 [hàozhào] VB appeal

好 [hào] VB **1** (喜爱) like **2** (容易) be easy
→ *see also*/另见 hǎo

好奇 [hàoqí] ADJ curious

喝 [hē] VB drink

合 [hé] VB **1** (闭) close **2** (合在一起) join ▶ 合资 [hézī] joint venture **3** (折合) be equal to **4** (符合) tally with

合并 [hébìng] VB merge

合唱 [héchàng] N chorus

合法 [héfǎ] ADJ legal

合格 [hégé] ADJ qualified

合理 [hélǐ] ADJ rational

合身 [héshēn] ADJ fitted

合适 [héshì] ADJ appropriate

合算 [hésuàn] VB be worthwhile

合同 [hétong] N contract

合作 [hézuò] VB cooperate

何 [hé] PRON (什么) ▶ 何时 [héshí] when ▶ 何人 [hérén] who ▶ 何地 [hédì] where

和 [hé] **I** CONJ and **II** PREP with ▷ 这事和你没关系。 [Zhè shì hé nǐ méi guānxi.] This has nothing to do with you. **III** N (总数) total **IV** VB draw ▷ 这场比赛和了。 [Zhè chǎng bǐsài hé le.] The match was a draw.

和蔼 [hé'ǎi] ADJ affable

和好 [héhǎo] VB reconcile

和睦 [hémù] ADJ harmonious

和平 [hépíng] N (指战争) peace

和气 [héqi] I ADJ polite II N peace

和数 [héshù] N sum

河 [hé] N (河) river

核 [hé] N (指水果) stone

盒 [hé] N box

盒子 [hézi] N box

贺 [hè] VB congratulate

贺卡 [hèkǎ] N greetings card

黑 [hēi] ADJ 1 (指颜色) black ▶ 黑板 [hēibǎn] blackboard 2 (暗) dark 3 (秘密) secret ▶ 黑市 [hēishì] black market 4 (反动) ▶ 黑社会 [hēishèhuì] gangland ▶ 黑手党 [hēishǒudǎng] the Mafia

黑暗 [hēi'àn] ADJ 1 (指光线) dark 2 (腐败) corrupt

黑人 [hēirén] N Black person

很 [hěn] ADV very

恨 [hèn] VB 1 (憎恶) hate 2 (后悔) regret

哼 [hēng] VB (唱) hum

横 [héng] I N horizontal II ADJ 1 (梁, 线, 行) horizontal 2 (左右向) sideways ▷ 横躺 [héngtǎng] lie sideways 3 (指横截) across ▶ 人行横道 [rénxíng héngdào] crosswalk III VB turn ... lengthways

红 [hóng] I ADJ 1 (指颜色) red ▶ 红旗 [hóngqí] red flag ▶ 红十字会 [Hóngshízìhuì] the Red Cross 2 (形容受欢迎) popular ▶ 走红 [zǒuhóng] be popular ▶ 红人 [hóngrén] rising star 3 (形容成功) successful ▶ 红运 [hóngyùn] lucky II N (红利) bonus ▶ 分红 [fēnhóng] get a bonus

红茶 [hóngchá] N black tea

红绿灯 [hónglǜdēng] N traffic lights (PL)

红色 [hóngsè] ADJ red

洪 [hóng] N (指洪水) flood ▶ 洪水 [hóngshuǐ] flood

喉 [hóu] N throat

喉咙 [hóulong] N throat

猴 [hóu] N monkey

猴子 [hóuzi] N monkey

后 [hòu] N 1 (背面) the back ▷ 房后有个车库。 [Fánghòu yǒu gè chēkù.] At the back of the house is a garage. 2 (指时间) ▶ 后天 [hòutiān] the day after tomorrow 3 (指次序) the last ▶ 后排 [hòupái] the last row

后边 [hòubian] N back

后代 [hòudài] N 1 (指时代) later generations (PL) 2 (子孙) offspring

后果 [hòuguǒ] N consequence

后悔 [hòuhuǐ] VB regret

后来 [hòulái] ADV afterwards ▷ 我后来再也没有见过他。 [Wǒ hòulái zài yě méi jiànguo tā.] I didn't see him again after that.

后门 [hòumén] N back door

后面 [hòumian] I N back II ADV later

后年 [hòunián] N the year after next

后退 [hòutuì] VB retreat

厚 [hòu] ADJ 1 (书, 衣服, 脸皮) thick 2 (雪, 土) deep 3 (指感情) profound

厚道 [hòudao] ADJ kind

呼 [hū] VB 1 (排气) exhale 2 (喊) shout ▶ 呼喊 [hūhǎn] shout 3 (叫) call ▶ 呼叫 [hūjiào] call ▶ 呼救 [hūjiù] call for help

呼机 [hūjī] N pager

呼噜 [hūlu] N (口) snore

呼吸 [hūxī] VB breathe

忽 [hū] ADV suddenly

忽然 [hūrán] ADV suddenly

忽视 [hūshì] VB ignore

狐 [hú] *see below*/见下文
狐狸 [húli] N fox

胡 [hú] **I** N **1** (髭) mustache **2** (长在下颚, 两腮) beard **II** ADV recklessly
胡乱 [húluàn] ADV **1** (随便) casually **2** (任意) wilfully
胡闹 [húnào] VB play around
胡说 [húshuō] VB talk nonsense
胡同 [hútòng] N lane
胡子 [húzi] N **1** (髭) mustache **2** (指长在下颚, 两腮) beard

壶 [hú] N pot

湖 [hú] N lake

蝴 [hú] *see below*/见下文
蝴蝶 [húdié] N butterfly

糊 [hú] VB paste
糊里糊涂 [húlihútu] confused
糊涂 [hútu] ADJ **1** (不明白) confused **2** (混乱) chaotic

虎 [hǔ] N tiger

互 [hù] ADV mutually
互联网 [hùliánwǎng] N the internet
互相 [hùxiāng] ADV mutually

户 [hù] N **1** (门) door **2** (住户) family **3** (户头) bank account ▶ 账户 [zhànghù] account
户口 [hùkǒu] N (户籍) registered permanent residence

护 [hù] VB (保护) protect
护理 [hùlǐ] VB nurse
护士 [hùshi] N nurse
护照 [hùzhào] N passport

花 [huā] **I** N **1** (指植物) flower **2** (烟火) fireworks (PL) **II** ADJ **1** (多彩) multi-colored **2** (有花的) floral ▶ 花篮 [huālán] flower basket **3** (模糊) blurred ▶ 头昏眼花 [tóuyūn yǎnhuā] muddle-headed and bleary-eyed **4** (虚假) superficial ▶ 花招 [huāzhāo] trick **III** VB spend ▷ 花钱 [huā qián] spend money ▷ 花工夫 [huā gōngfu] put in effort
花费 [huāfèi] VB spend ▶ 留学的花费很大。 [liúxué de huāfèi hěn dà.] It's very expensive to study abroad.
花生 [huāshēng] N peanut
花纹 [huāwén] N decorative design
花园 [huāyuán] N garden
花招 [huāzhāo] N trick

划 [huá] VB **1** (拨水) row **2** (合算) be worthwhile ▷ 划不来 [huábulái] not worth it **3** (擦) scratch
→ *see also*/另见 huà

华 [huá] N (中国) China ▶ 华人 [huárén] Chinese person
华丽 [huálì] ADJ resplendent
华侨 [huáqiáo] N overseas Chinese
华人 [huárén] N Chinese

滑 [huá] **I** ADJ **1** (光滑) slippery **2** (油滑) crafty **II** VB slip
滑冰 [huábīng] VB ice skate
滑动 [huádòng] VB slide
滑稽 [huájī] ADJ comical
滑坡 [huápō] VB **1** (字) slide **2** (喻) drop
滑雪 [huáxuě] VB ski

化 [huà] **I** N chemistry ▶ 化肥 [huàféi] chemical fertilizer **II** VB **1** (变化) change ▶ 化装 [huàzhuāng] disguise oneself **2** (消化) digest
化工 [huàgōng] N chemical industry
化石 [huàshí] N fossil
化学 [huàxué] N chemistry
化验 [huàyàn] VB test
化妆 [huàzhuāng] VB make oneself up

划 [huà] VB **1** (划分) demarcate ▶ 划分 [huàfēn] divide **2** (划拨) transfer **3** (计划) plan
→ *see also*/另见 huá

画 [huà] **I** VB **1** (用铅笔) draw **2** (用刷状) (笔画) paint **II** N **1** (用铅笔) drawing **2** (用刷状) (笔画) painting ▶ 油画 [yóuhuà] oil painting **3** (笔

画) stroke **III** ADJ painted
画报 [huàbào] N pictorial
画家 [huàjiā] N painter
画像 [huàxiàng] N portrait
画展 [huàzhǎn] N art exhibition

话 [huà] **I** N words (PL) ▶ 说话 [shuōhuà] talk ▶ 对话 [duìhuà] conversation ▶ 谎话 [huǎnghuà] lie **II** VB talk about ▶ 话旧 [huàjiù] reminisce
话剧 [huàjù] N stage play
话题 [huàtí] N subject

怀 [huái] **I** N **1** (胸前) bosom **2** (胸怀) mind **II** VB **1** (思念) think of **2** (存有) keep ... in mind **3** (有孕) become pregnant
怀念 [huáiniàn] VB yearn for
怀疑 [huáiyí] VB **1** (认为是真) suspect **2** (认为不可能) doubt
怀孕 [huáiyùn] VB be pregnant

坏 [huài] **I** ADJ **1** (不好) bad **2** (程度深) extreme **II** VB go off ▷ 空调坏了。[Kōngtiáo huài le.] The air-conditioning has broken down. **III** N dirty trick
坏处 [huàichu] N harm
坏蛋 [huàidàn] N (讳) bastard
坏话 [huàihuà] N (不利的话) bad words (PL)

欢 [huān] ADJ **1** (快乐) happy **2** (活跃) vigorous
欢呼 [huānhū] VB cheer
欢快 [huānkuài] ADJ cheerful
欢乐 [huānlè] ADJ joyful
欢心 [huānxīn] N favor
欢迎 [huānyíng] VB welcome ▷ 欢迎来中国。[Huānyín lái Zhōngguó.] Welcome to China.

还 [huán] VB **1** (回) return **2** (归还) return ▶ 还债 [huánzhài] repay a debt **3** (回报) repay ▶ 还价 [huánjià] haggle ▶ 还击 [huánjī] fight back
→ *see also*/另见 hái

环 [huán] **I** N **1** (圆圈) ring ▶ 耳环 [ěrhuán] earring **2** (环节) element ▶ 环节 [huánjié] element **II** VB surround
环保 [huánbǎo] N (*also*: 环境保护) environmental protection
环境 [huánjìng] N environment ▷ 生活环境 [shēnghuó huánjìng] living conditions (PL)
环绕 [huánrào] VB surround

缓 [huǎn] **I** ADJ **1** (慢) slow **2** (缓和) relaxed **II** VB **1** (推迟) delay **2** (恢复) revive
缓慢 [huǎnmàn] ADJ slow

幻 [huàn] ADJ unreal
幻想 [huànxiǎng] **I** VB dream **II** N fantasy

换 [huàn] VB **1** (交换) exchange **2** (更换) replace

唤 [huàn] N summon
唤醒 [huànxǐng] VB (叫醒) wake up

患 [huàn] **I** VB **1** (害) suffer from ▶ 患者 [huànzhě] sufferer **2** (忧虑) worry **II** N trouble

荒 [huāng] ADJ **1** (荒芜) waste **2** (荒凉) desolate **3** (短缺) short **4** (荒歉) famine

慌 [huāng] ADJ nervous
慌忙 [huāngmáng] ADJ hurried
慌张 [huāngzhāng] ADJ nervous

皇 [huáng] N emperor ▶ 皇帝 [huángdì] emperor ▶ 皇后 [huánghòu] empress
皇宫 [huánggōng] N palace

黄 [huáng] **I** ADJ **1** (指颜色) yellow **2** (色情) pornographic **II** N **1** (蛋黄) yolk **2** (黄金) gold
黄瓜 [huángguā] N cucumber
黄河 [Huánghé] N Yellow River
黄昏 [huánghūn] N dusk
黄金 [huángjīn] N gold
黄色 [huángsè] N **1** (指颜色) yellow **2** (色情) pornographic

黄油 [huángyóu] N butter

谎 [huǎng] N lie

谎言 [huǎngyán] N lie

晃 [huàng] VB shake

晃动 [huàngdòng] VB rock

灰 [huī] I N 1 (灰烬) ash 2 (尘土) dust 3 (石灰) lime II VB (消沉) be disheartened ▶ 灰暗 [huī'àn] gloomy

灰尘 [huīchén] N dust

灰色 [huīsè] N (指颜色) gray

灰心 [huīxīn] VB lose heart

恢 [huī] ADJ vast

恢复 [huīfù] VB recover

挥 [huī] VB 1 (挥舞) wave 2 (抹掉) wipe ... away 3 (指挥) command 4 (散出) scatter ▶ 挥发 [huīfā] evaporate

回 [huí] I VB 1 (旋转) circle 2 (还) return 3 (掉转) turn around ▶ 回头 [huítóu] turn one's head 4 (答复) reply ▶ 回信 [huíxìn] reply to a letter II MEAS 1 (次数) time ▷ 我去过两回。 [Wǒ qùguo liǎng huí.] I have been there twice. 2 (章) chapter

回报 [huíbào] VB (报答) repay

回避 [huíbì] VB avoid

回答 [huídá] VB answer

回复 [huífù] VB (答复) reply

回顾 [huígù] VB look back

回合 [huíhé] N round

回话 [huíhuà] VB reply

回扣 [huíkòu] N commission

回教 [Huíjiào] N Islam

回来 [huílai] VB come back

回去 [huíqu] VB go back

回声 [huíshēng] N echo

回收 [huíshōu] VB 1 (再利用) recycle 2 (收回) retrieve

回信 [huíxìn] VB write in reply

回忆 [huíyì] VB recall

毁 [huǐ] VB 1 (破坏) destroy 2 (诽谤) defame

毁坏 [huǐhuài] VB destroy

汇 [huì] I VB 1 (汇合) converge 2 (聚集) gather 3 (划拨) transfer II N 1 (外汇) foreign exchange 2 (聚集物) collection ▶ 词汇 [cíhuì] vocabulary

汇报 [huìbào] VB report

汇集 [huìjí] VB collect

汇率 [huìlǜ] N exchange rate

会 [huì] I VB 1 (聚合) assemble 2 (见面) meet ▶ 会客 [huìkè] receive a guest 3 (理解) understand ▶ 领会 [lǐnghuì] understand 4 (通晓) be able to ▷ 会武术 [huì wǔshù] be able to do martial arts II AUX VB 1 (能做) can ▷ 我不会下象棋。 [Wǒ bùhuì xià xiàngqí.] I can't play chess. 2 (擅长) ▷ 会过日子 [huì guò rìzi] know how to economize 3 (可能) might ▷ 明天会更热。 [Míngtiān huì gèng rè.] Tomorrow might be hotter. III N 1 (集会) gathering 2 (团体) association ▶ 学生会 [xuéshēnghuì] student union 3 (城市) city ▶ 大都会 [dàdūhuì] metropolis 4 (时机) opportunity ▶ 机会 [jīhuì] opportunity

→ *see also*/另见 kuài

Both 会 huì and 要 yào can be used to express the future tense. 会 huì is usually used to express a possible or probable outcome, e.g. 明天会下雨 míngtiān huì xiàyǔ (it might rain tomorrow); 要 yào refers to something definite, e.g. 我明天要上班 wǒ míngtiān yào shàngbān (I am going to work tomorrow). 会 huì, 能 néng, and 可以 kěyǐ can all be used to express ability and are sometimes used interchangeably. Strictly, 会 huì should express a learned ability, e.g. 我会说法语 wǒ huì shuō Fǎyǔ (I can speak French), while 能 néng should be used to express physical ability, e.g. 我能跑得很快 wǒ néng pǎo de hěn kuài (I can run very fast).

会话 [huìhuà] VB converse

会见 [huìjiàn] VB meet

会谈 [huìtán] VB hold talks

会议 [huìyì] N **1** (集会) meeting **2** (机构) council

会员 [huìyuán] N member

贿 [huì] N bribe ▶ 贿赂 [huìlù] bribe

昏 [hūn] **I** N dusk **II** ADJ **1** (黑暗) dark ▶ 昏暗 [hūn'àn] dim **2** (迷糊) muddled **III** VB faint

昏迷 [hūnmí] VB be unconscious

荤 [hūn] N meat

婚 [hūn] **I** N marriage **II** VB marry

婚礼 [hūnlǐ] N wedding ceremony

婚姻 [hūnyīn] N marriage

浑 [hún] ADJ **1** (浑浊) muddy **2** (糊涂) muddled

浑蛋 [húndàn] N (讳) bastard

浑身 [húnshēn] ADV from head to toe

浑浊 [húnzhuó] ADJ murky

馄 [hún] *see below*/见下文

馄饨 [húntún] N wonton

馄饨 [húntún]

In Chinese cooking, 馄饨 húntún is a kind of dumpling filled with spiced ground meat and other ingredients such as chopped mushrooms, shrimps, etc. It is usually served in the soup in which it is cooked. The English name for 馄饨 comes from the Cantonese pronunciation, wantan.

魂 [hún] N (灵魂) soul

混 [hùn] **I** VB **1** (搀杂) mix **2** (蒙混) pass off ... as **3** (苟且生活) drift ▷ 混日子 [hùn rìzi] drift through the days **II** ADV aimlessly

混合 [hùnhé] VB mix

混乱 [hùnluàn] ADJ **1** (无秩序) chaotic **2** (无条理) disordered

混淆 [hùnxiáo] VB confuse

活 [huó] **I** VB **1** (生存) live **2** (使生存) keep ... alive **II** ADJ **1** (有生命) alive **2** (不固定) flexible **3** (不死板) lively **4** (逼真) lifelike **III** ADV completely **IV** N **1** (工作) work **2** (产品) product

活动 [huódòng] **I** VB **1** (运动) take exercise **2** (行动) operate **3** (动用关系) use connections **II** N activity **III** ADJ movable

活该 [huógāi] VB (口) serve ... right

活力 [huólì] N vitality

活泼 [huópō] ADJ lively

活期 [huóqī] ADJ current ▷ 活期账号 [huóqī zhànghào] checking account

活跃 [huóyuè] VB **1** (使有生气) invigorate **2** (积极从事) be active

火 [huǒ] **I** N **1** (火焰) fire **2** (枪支弹药) ammunition **3** (医) (指内火) internal heat **4** (喻) (愤怒) rage **II** VB be in a rage **III** ADJ **1** (红色) flaming red ▶ 火红 [huǒhóng] flaming red **2** (兴旺) prosperous

火柴 [huǒchái] N match

火车 [huǒchē] N train

火鸡 [huǒjī] N turkey

火警 [huǒjǐng] N fire alarm

火山 [huǒshān] N volcano

火腿 [huǒtuǐ] N ham

火焰 [huǒyàn] N flame

火药 [huǒyào] N gunpowder

伙 [huǒ] **I** N **1** (同伴) companion **2** (指集体) partnership **3** (伙食) meals (PL) **II** MEAS group

伙伴 [huǒbàn] N companion

伙食 [huǒshi] N meals (PL)

或 [huò] CONJ or

或许 [huòxǔ] ADV perhaps

或者 [huòzhě] **I** ADV maybe **II** CONJ or

货 [huò] N **1** (货币) currency **2** (货物) goods (PL) **3** (人) person ▶ 蠢货 [chǔnhuò] idiot

货币 [huòbì] N currency ▶ 加密货币 [jiāmì huòbì] cryptocurrency

货物 [huòwù] N goods (PL)

获 [huò] VB **1** (捉住) capture **2** (得到) obtain **3** (收割) reap ▶ 收获 [shōuhuò] harvest

获得 [huòdé] VB gain

祸 [huò] N **I** N misfortune **II** VB harm

J

几 [jī] N small table ▸ 茶几 [chájī] tea table
→ *see also*/另见 jǐ
几乎 [jīhū] ADV almost

讥 [jī] VB mock
讥笑 [jīxiào] VB jeer

饥 [jī] I ADJ hungry II N famine
饥饿 [jī'è] ADJ starving

机 [jī] I N 1 (机器) machine ▸ 发动机 [fādòngjī] engine 2 (飞机) airplane ▸ 客机 [kèjī] airliner 3 (枢纽) pivot ▸ 转机 [zhuǎnjī] turning point 4 (机会) opportunity 5 (机能) ▸ 有机体 [yǒujītǐ] organism II ADJ quick-witted ▸ 机智 [jīzhì] ingenious
机场 [jīchǎng] N airport
机关 [jīguān] N 1 (部门) department 2 (机械) mechanism
机会 [jīhuì] N opportunity
机灵 [jīling] ADJ clever
机器 [jīqì] N machine
机械 [jīxiè] I N machinery II ADJ rigid
机遇 [jīyù] N opportunity

肌 [jī] N muscle
肌肉 [jīròu] N muscle

鸡 [jī] N chicken ▸ 公鸡 [gōngjī] cock ▸ 母鸡 [mǔjī] hen
鸡蛋 [jīdàn] N egg

积 [jī] I VB accumulate II ADJ long-standing III N (数) product
积极 [jījí] ADJ 1 (肯定的) positive 2 (热心的) active
积极性 [jījíxìng] N positive attitude
积累 [jīlěi] VB accumulate
积蓄 [jīxù] I VB save II N savings (PL)

基 [jī] I N base II ADJ primary ▸ 基层 [jīcéng] grass roots
基本 [jīběn] I ADJ 1 (根本) basic 2 (主要) essential 3 (基础) elementary II ADV basically
基础 [jīchǔ] I N foundation II ADJ basic
基督教 [Jīdūjiào] N Christianity
基金 [jījīn] N fund

激 [jī] I VB 1 (涌起) surge 2 (刺激) catch a chill 3 (唤起) excite 4 (冰) chill II ADJ violent
激动 [jīdòng] VB excite ▸ 激动的孩子 [jīdòng de háizi] excited child ▸ 令人激动的电影 [lìng rén jīdòng de diànyǐng] exciting film
激光 [jīguāng] N laser
激烈 [jīliè] ADJ intense

及 [jí] I VB 1 (到达) reach 2 (比得上) be as good as 3 (赶上) be in time for II CONJ and
及格 [jígé] VB pass
及时 [jíshí] I ADJ timely II ADV without delay

级 [jí] I N 1 (等级) level 2 (年级) grade 3 (台阶) step II MEAS step ▹ 100多级台阶 [yībǎi duō jí táijiē] a staircase of more than 100 steps

极 [jí] I N 1 (顶点) extreme 2 (指地球或磁体) pole ▸ 南极 [nánjí] the South Pole II VB go to an extreme III ADJ extreme ▸ 极限 [jíxiàn] limit IV ADV very
极其 [jíqí] ADV extremely

即 [jí] I VB 1 (书) (就是) mean 2 (靠近) approach 3 (到) ▸ 即位 [jíwèi] ascend the throne 4 (就着) ▹ 即兴演唱 [jíxìng yǎnchàng] ad-lib II ADJ present ▸ 即日 [jírì] this very day III ADV immediately
即将 [jíjiāng] ADV soon
即使 [jíshǐ] CONJ even if

急 [jí] I ADJ 1 (着急) anxious 2 (急躁) impatient 3 (猛烈) ▹ 水流很急。 [shuǐliú hěn jí] There's a strong current. 4 (紧急) urgent II N priority III VB worry

急救 [jíjiù] VB give first-aid

急忙 [jímáng] ADV hurriedly

急诊 [jízhěn] N emergency treatment

集 [jí] I VB gather II N 1 (集市) market ▸ 赶集 [gǎnjí] go to market 2 (集子) anthology ▸ 诗集 [shījí] an anthology of poems 3 (册) part

集合 [jíhé] VB assemble

集体 [jítǐ] N collective

集团 [jítuán] N group

集中 [jízhōng] VB concentrate

几 [jǐ] NUM 1 (用于疑问句) ▷ 昨天来了几位客人？ [Zuótiān lái le jǐ wèi kèren?] How many customers came yesterday? 2 (用于陈述句) ▷ 几本书 [jǐ běn shū] several books ▷ 十几本书 [shíjǐ běn shū] more than ten books ▷ 几十本书 [jǐshí běn shū] several tens of books
→ *see also*/另见 jī

己 [jǐ] N self ▸ 自己 [zìjǐ] oneself

挤 [jǐ] VB 1 (拥挤) crowd 2 (事情，会议，约会) be close 3 (推人) elbow one's way 4 (贬) (指社交) push one's way 5 (牙膏，颜料) squeeze ... out ▸ 挤奶 [jǐnǎi] milk 6 (时间) make 7 (排斥) rob ... of

计 [jì] I VB 1 (核算) calculate ▸ 共计 [gòngjì] total 2 (打算) plan 3 (考虑) bother II N 1 (计谋) strategy 2 (测量仪器) gauge ▸ 温度计 [wēndùjì] thermometer

计划 [jìhuà] I N plan II VB plan

计算 [jìsuàn] VB 1 (数) calculate 2 (筹划) plan 3 (暗算) scheme

计算机 [jìsuànjī] N computer

计算器 [jìsuànqì] N calculator

记 [jì] I VB 1 (指往事) remember 2 (写) record II N 1 (指书或文章) record ▸ 游记 [yóujì] travel journal ▸ 日记 [rìjì] diary 2 (标志) mark 3 (指皮肤) birthmark

记得 [jìde] VB remember

记号 [jìho] N mark

记录 [jìlù] I VB (写下) write ... down II N 1 (材料) record 2 (指人) secretary 3 (成绩) record

记忆 [jìyì] I VB remember II N memory

记者 [jìzhě] N journalist

纪 [jì] I N 1 age ▸ 中世纪 [zhōngshìjì] the Middle Ages (PL) 2 (指地质) period ▸ 侏罗纪 [zhūluójì] the Jurassic period 3 (纪律) discipline II VB record

纪律 [jìlù] N discipline

纪念 [jìniàn] I VB commemorate II N memento

技 [jì] N 1 (技艺) skill ▸ 技能 [jìnéng] skill ▸ 技巧 [jìqiǎo] technique 2 (本领) ability ▸ 绝技 [juéjì] unique ability

技巧 [jìqiǎo] N technique

技术 [jìshù] N technology

技术员 [jìshùyuán] N technician

季 [jì] N season ▸ 春季 [chūnjì] spring ▸ 旺季 [wàngjì] busy season

季节 [jìjié] N season

既 [jì] I ADV already ▸ 既定 [jìdìng] fixed II CONJ 1 (表示兼而有之) ▷ 他既高又壮。 [Tā jì gāo yòu zhuàng.] He's tall and strong. 2 (既然) since

既然 [jìrán] CONJ since

继 [jì] I ADV 1 (接续) continuously ▸ 继任 [jìrèn] succeed to a post 2 (接连) successively ▸ 相继 [xiāngjì] one after another II VB continue

继承 [jìchéng] VB 1 (遗产，文化等) inherit 2 (遗志，未成事业) take ... on

继续 [jìxù] I VB continue II N continuation

寄 [jì] VB 1 (邮递) mail 2 (付托) place 3 (依附) depend on

加 [jiā] VB 1 (相加) ▷ 2加2等于4。 [Èr

jiā èr děngyú sì.] Two plus two is four. **2** (增加) increase **3** (添加) add

加工 [jiāgōng] VB **1** (制作) process **2** (完善) polish

加拿大 [Jiānádà] N Canada

加强 [jiāqiáng] VB strengthen

加油 [jiāyóu] VB **1** (加燃料) refuel **2** (加劲儿) make more effort ▷ 快，加油！ [Kuài, jiāyóu!] Come on, come on!

夹 [jiā] **I** VB **1** (钳) get hold of **2** (携带) carry ... under one's arm **3** (限制) ▷ 两边高楼夹着一条狭窄的街道。[Liǎngbiān gāolóu jiāzhe yī tiáo xiázhǎi de jiēdào.] A narrow street hemmed in by tall buildings on either side. **4** (带) mix ... with **II** N folder

---

家 [jiā] **I** N **1** (家庭) family **2** (住所) home **3** (学派) school of thought **4** (指人) ▶ 船家 [chuánjiā] boatman ▶ 农家 [nóngjiā] peasant ▶ 专家 [zhuānjiā] expert **II** ADJ **1** (饲养的) domestic ▶ 家畜 [jiāchù] domestic animal **2** (嫡亲的) ▶ 家兄 [jiāxiōng] elder brother **III** MEAS ▷ 一家公司 [yī jiā gōngsī] a company ▷ 两家人 [liǎng jiā rén] two families

measure word, used for families, companies, banks, factories, restaurants, hotels, etc.

家伙 [jiāhuo] N **1** (工具) tool **2** (武器) weapon **3** (人) guy

家具 [jiājù] N furniture

家庭 [jiātíng] N family

家务 [jiāwù] N housework

家乡 [jiāxiāng] N hometown

家长 [jiāzhǎng] N **1** (一家之长) head of the family **2** (父母) parent

---

假 [jiǎ] **I** ADJ **1** (虚伪) false **2** (不真) artificial ▶ 假发 [jiǎfà] wig ▶ 假话 [jiǎhuà] lie **II** CONJ if ▶ 假如 [jiǎrú] if

→ *see also*/另见 jià

假如 [jiǎrú] CONJ if

假设 [jiǎshè] **I** VB suppose **II** N hypothesis

假装 [jiǎzhuāng] VB pretend

价 [jià] N **1** (价格) price ▶ 物价 [wùjià] price **2** (价值) value

价格 [jiàgé] N price

价钱 [jiàqin] N price

价值 [jiàzhí] N value

驾 [jià] **I** VB **1** (驾驭) harness **2** (驾驶) drive **II** PRON (敬) ▶ 劳驾 [láojià] excuse me

驾驶 [jiàshǐ] VB steer

驾照 [jiàzhào] N driver's license

架 [jià] **I** N **1** (架子) frame ▶ 书架 [shūjià] bookshelf ▶ 脚手架 [jiǎoshǒujià] scaffolding **2** (指行为) ▶ 吵架 [chǎojià] quarrel ▶ 打架 [dǎjià] fight **II** VB **1** (撑起) support **2** (招架) ward ... off **3** (绑架) kidnap **4** (搀扶) support ... under the arm **III** MEAS ▷ 5架飞机 [wǔ jià fēijī] five planes ▷ 一架钢琴 [yī jià gāngqín] a piano

measure word, used for pianos, aircraft, machines, etc.

假 [jià] N vacation ▶ 暑假 [shǔjià] summer vacation ▶ 病假 [bìngjià] sick leave

→ *see also*/另见 jiǎ

假条 [jiàtiáo] N note

尖 [jiān] **I** ADJ **1** (锐利) pointed **2** (指声音) shrill **3** (敏锐) sensitive **4** (吝啬) stingy **5** (尖刻) biting **II** N **1** (尖端) tip ▶ 笔尖 [bǐjiān] pen tip **2** (精华) the best

尖锐 [jiānruì] ADJ **1** (锋利) sharp **2** (敏锐) penetrating **3** (刺耳) shrill

---

坚 [jiān] **I** ADJ hard **II** N stronghold **III** ADV firmly ▶ 坚信 [jiānxìn] firmly believe

坚持 [jiānchí] VB go on

坚定 [jiāndìng] ADJ steadfast

坚决 [jiānjué] ADV resolutely
坚强 [jiānqiáng] ADJ strong
坚硬 [jiānyìng] ADJ hard

间 [jiān] **I** PREP between ▶ 课间 [kèjiān] between lessons **II** N **1** (范围) ▶ 晚间 [wǎnjiān] in the evening ▶ 田间 [tiánjiān] field **2** (屋子) room ▶ 房间 [fángjiān] room ▶ 洗手间 [xǐshǒujiān] toilet **III** MEAS ▷ 两间客厅 [liǎng jiān kètīng] two living rooms ▷ 一间病房 [yī jiān bìngfáng] one ward

measure word, used for rooms, lounges, hospital wards, etc.

肩 [jiān] *see below*/见下文
肩膀 [jiānbǎng] N shoulder

艰 [jiān] ADJ difficult ▶ 艰辛 [jiānxīn] hardship
艰巨 [jiānjù] ADJ formidable
艰苦 [jiānkǔ] ADJ harsh
艰难 [jiānnán] ADJ hard

监 [jiān] **I** VB supervise ▶ 监视 [jiānshì] keep watch **II** N **1** (监狱) prison ▶ 探监 [tànjiān] visit a prison **2** (负责人) inspector ▶ 总监 [zǒngjiān] chief inspector
监督 [jiāndū] VB supervise
监狱 [jiānyù] N prison

拣 [jiǎn] VB choose

俭 [jiǎn] ADJ frugal
俭朴 [jiǎnpǔ] ADJ economical

捡 [jiǎn] VB pick ... up

检 [jiǎn] VB **1** (检查) examine ▶ 体检 [tǐjiǎn] medical examination **2** (检点) show restraint
检查 [jiǎnchá] **I** VB examine **II** N self-criticism

减 [jiǎn] VB **1** (减去) subtract **2** (减少) reduce **3** (降低) decrease ▶ 减退 [jiǎntuì] fail
减肥 [jiǎnféi] VB slim
减轻 [jiǎnqīng] VB reduce
减少 [jiǎnshǎo] VB reduce

剪 [jiǎn] **I** N scissors (PL) **II** VB **1** (铰) cut **2** (除去) eliminate
剪刀 [jiǎndāo] N scissors (PL)

简 [jiǎn] **I** ADJ simple **II** VB simplify ▶ 简化 [jiǎnhuà] simplify
简单 [jiǎndān] ADJ **1** (不复杂) simple **2** (草率) casual **3** (平凡) ▷ 这孩子能说两门外语，真不简单。 [Zhè háizi néng shuō liǎng mén wàiyǔ, zhēn bù jiǎndān.] It is quite extraordinary that this child can speak two foreign languages.
简体字 [jiǎntǐzì] N simplified characters (PL)

简体字 [jiǎntǐzì]

简体字 jiǎntǐzì (simplified characters) are the type of Chinese characters used today throughout Mainland China, and mostly derive from the PRC government's efforts during the 1950s and 60s to make the script more accessible and improve literacy. The alternative and older form of the script, known as complex or traditional characters, 繁体字 fántǐzì, is used predominantly in Taiwan, Hong Kong and many overseas Chinese communities. The two systems are closely related, and if you have learnt one, then with a little effort, the other form can be learned without much difficulty.

见 [jiàn] **I** VB **1** (看到) see ▶ 罕见 [hǎnjiàn] rare **2** (接触) come into contact with ▷ 汽油见火就着。 [Qìyóu jiàn huǒ jiù zháo.] Petrol ignites on contact with a flame. **3** (看得出) be visible ▶ 见效 [jiànxiào] take effect **4** (参照) see ▷ 见上图 [jiàn shàngtú] see the above diagram **5** (会见) meet ▶ 接见 [jiējiàn] receive **II** N opinion ▶ 偏见 [piānjiàn] prejudice **III** AUX VB (书) ▷ 请见谅。 [Qǐng jiànliàng.] Please excuse me.

见面 [jiànmiàn] VB meet

件 [jiàn] I MEAS item ▷ 一件衣服 [yī jiàn yīfu] an item of clothing ▷ 两件事 [liǎng jiàn shì] two things II N correspondence ▷ 急件 [jíjiàn] urgent letter

建 [jiàn] VB 1 (建造) build 2 (建立) found 3 (提出) propose ▶ 建议 [jiànyì] propose

建立 [jiànlì] VB establish

建设 [jiànshè] VB build

建议 [jiànyì] VB propose

建筑 [jiànzhù] I VB build II N building

建筑师 [jiànzhùshī] N architect

健 [jiàn] I ADJ ▶ 强健 [qiángjiàn] strong and healthy ▶ 健全 [jiànquán] sound II VB 1 (使强健) strengthen ▶ 健身 [jiànshēn] keep fit 2 (善于) be good at ▶ 健谈 [jiàntán] be good at small talk

健康 [jiànkāng] ADJ healthy

健忘 [jiànwàng] ADJ forgetful

渐 [jiàn] ADV gradually

渐渐 [jiànjiàn] ADV gradually

键 [jiàn] N key

键盘 [jiànpán] N keyboard

箭 [jiàn] N arrow

江 [jiāng] N 1 (大河) river 2 (长江) Yangtze

将 [jiāng] I ADV ▷ 他将成为一名医生。 [Tā jiāng chéngwéi yī míng yīshēng.] He is going to become a doctor. II VB 1 (下棋用语) check 2 (激) egg ... on III PREP with ▷ 请将车停在路边。 [Qǐng jiāng chē tíng zài lùbiān.] Please stop the car by the side of the road.

将军 [jiāngjūn] N general

将来 [jiānglái] N future

将要 [jiāngyào] ADV ▷ 她将要做妈妈了。 [Tā jiāngyào zuò māma le.] She is going to be a mother.

姜 [jiāng] N ginger

讲 [jiǎng] VB 1 (说) speak 2 (解释) explain 3 (谈) discuss 4 (讲求) emphasize ▷ 讲卫生 [jiǎng wèishēng] pay attention to hygiene

讲话 [jiǎnghuà] VB 1 (说话) speak 2 (发言) address

讲台 [jiǎngtái] N dais

讲座 [jiǎngzuò] N course of lectures

奖 [jiǎng] I VB encourage ▶ 夸奖 [kuājiǎng] praise II N award

奖金 [jiǎngjīn] N bonus

奖励 [jiǎnglì] VB encourage and reward

奖品 [jiǎngpǐn] N trophy

奖学金 [jiǎngxuéjīn] N scholarship

降 [jiàng] VB 1 (落下) drop 2 (降低) reduce ▶ 降价 [jiàngjià] reduce prices

降低 [jiàngdī] VB reduce

降落 [jiàngluò] VB land

酱 [jiàng] I N 1 (调味品) soybean paste 2 (糊状食品) paste ▶ 果酱 [guǒjiàng] jam II ADJ ▶ 酱肘子 [jiàngzhǒuzi] knuckle of pork in soy sauce

酱油 [jiàngyóu] N soy sauce

交 [jiāo] I VB 1 (交出) hand ... in 2 (付给) pay 3 (托付) entrust 4 (结交) associate with ▶ 交友 [jiāoyǒu] make friends II N (交情) friendship ▶ 深交 [shēnjiāo] deep friendship

交叉 [jiāochā] I VB 1 (相交) intersect 2 (穿插) alternate II ADJ overlapping

交换 [jiāohuàn] VB exchange

交际 [jiāojì] VB socialize

交警 [jiāojǐng] N traffic police

交流 [jiāoliú] VB exchange

交谈 [jiāotán] VB talk

交通 [jiāotōng] N traffic

交往 [jiāowǎng] VB have contact

交易 [jiāoyì] I VB trade II N

transaction

郊 [jiāo] N suburbs (PL) ▶ 郊外 [jiāowài] outskirts (PL)

郊区 [jiāoqū] N suburbs (PL)

骄 [jiāo] ADJ 1 (骄傲) arrogant ▶ 骄气 [jiāoqì] arrogance 2 (书) (猛烈) fierce

骄傲 [jiāo'ào] I ADJ 1 (傲慢) arrogant 2 (自豪) proud II N pride

胶 [jiāo] I N 1 (黏性物质) glue ▶ 万能胶 [wànnéngjiāo] all-purpose glue 2 (橡胶) rubber ▶ 胶鞋 [jiāoxié] rubber boots (PL) II VB glue

胶卷 [jiāojuǎn] N film

胶囊 [jiāonáng] N capsule

教 [jiāo] VB teach
→ *see also*/另见 jiào

焦 [jiāo] ADJ 1 (成黄黑色) burnt 2 (着急) agitated ▶ 心焦 [xīnjiāo] feel agitated

焦急 [jiāojí] ADJ anxious

角 [jiǎo] N 1 (指动物) horn 2 (军号) bugle 3 (数) angle ▶ 直角 [zhíjiǎo] right angle 4 (角落) corner ▶ 墙角 [qiángjiǎo] corner of a wall

角度 [jiǎodù] N 1 (数) angle 2 (视角) point of view

角落 [jiǎoluò] N corner

饺 [jiǎo] N Chinese dumpling ▶ 水饺 [shuǐjiǎo] Chinese dumpling

饺子 [jiǎozi] N dumpling

饺子 [jiǎozi]

Chinese dumplings, wrapped with a thin doughy skin, are usually filled with ground meat and mixed vegetables. They are normally steamed or boiled, and served with vinegar, soy sauce and other spices.

脚 [jiǎo] N 1 (指人, 动物) foot ▶ 脚印 [jiǎoyìn] footprint 2 (指物体) base ▶ 山脚 [shānjiǎo] foot of a mountain

搅 [jiǎo] VB 1 (搅拌) stir 2 (混杂) mix 3 (搅扰) disturb

搅拌 [jiǎobàn] VB stir

叫 [jiào] VB 1 (喊叫) shout 2 (招呼) call 3 (菜, 车) order 4 (称为) be called 5 (吩咐) order

叫喊 [jiàohǎn] VB yell

叫做 [jiàozuò] VB be called

较 [jiào] VB 1 (比较) compare ▶ 较量 [jiàoliàng] test one's strength 2 (书) (计较) dispute

教 [jiào] I VB teach ▶ 教导 [jiàodǎo] instruct II N religion
→ *see also*/另见 jiāo

教材 [jiàocái] N teaching materials (PL)

教科书 [jiàokēshū] N textbook

教练 [jiàoliàn] N coach

教师 [jiàoshī] N teacher

教室 [jiàoshì] N classroom

教授 [jiàoshòu] I N professor II VB lecture in

教学 [jiàoxué] N 1 (知识传授) teaching 2 (教与学) teaching and study

教训 [jiàoxun] I N lesson II VB teach ... a lesson

教育 [jiàoyù] I N education II VB educate

教员 [jiàoyuán] N teacher

阶 [jiē] N 1 (台阶) step 2 (官阶) rank

阶段 [jiēduàn] N stage

阶级 [jiējí] N class

结 [jiē] VB bear ▶ 结果 [jiéguǒ] bear fruit
→ *see also*/另见 jié

结实 [jiēshi] ADJ 1 (坚固耐用) sturdy 2 (健壮) strong

接 [jiē] VB 1 (靠近) draw near 2 (连接) connect 3 (托住) catch 4 (接收) receive ▷ 接电话 [jiē diànhuà] answer the phone 5 (迎接) meet 6 (接替) take over

接触 [jiēchù] VB (交往) come into contact with

接待 [jiēdài] VB receive

接到 [jiēdào] VB receive

接见 [jiējiàn] VB have an interview with

接近 [jiējìn] I VB approach II ADJ approachable

接受 [jiēshòu] VB accept

接着 [jiēzhe] VB 1 (用手接) catch 2 (紧跟着) follow

街 [jiē] N 1 (街道) street 2 (方) (集市) market

街道 [jiēdào] N 1 (马路) street 2 (社区) neighborhood

节 [jié] I N 1 (连接处) joint 2 (段落) paragraph 3 (节日) festival ▶ 圣诞节 [Shèngdàn Jié] Christmas 4 (事项) item ▶ 细节 [xìjié] details (PL) 5 (节操) moral fiber ▶ 气节 [qìjié] integrity II VB 1 (节约) save 2 (删节) abridge III MEAS 1 (指部分) section ▷ 一节管子 [yī jié guǎnzi] a length of pipe 2 ▷ 三节课 [sān jié kè] three classes ▷ 四节车厢 [sì jié chēxiāng] four carriages ▷ 两节电池 [liǎng jié diànchí] two batteries

measure word, used for school classes, carriages, batteries, etc.

节目 [jiémù] N program

节拍 [jiépāi] N beat

节日 [jiérì] N festival

节省 [jiéshěng] VB conserve

节约 [jiéyuē] VB save

结 [jié] I VB 1 (编织) tie ▶ 结网 [jiéwǎng] weave a net 2 (结合) unite 3 (凝聚) freeze ▶ 结冰 [jiébīng] ice up 4 (了结) settle up ▶ 结账 [jiézhàng] settle up II N 1 (绳扣) knot ▶ 活结 [huójié] slipknot 2 (字据) written undertaking 3 (生理) node

→ *see also*/另见 jiē

结构 [jiégòu] N composition

结果 [jiéguǒ] I N result II ADV in the end

结合 [jiéhé] VB 1 (联系) combine 2 (结为夫妇) become husband and wife

结婚 [jiéhūn] VB get married

结论 [jiélùn] N conclusion

结束 [jiéshù] VB end

捷 [jié] I ADJ quick ▶ 敏捷 [mǐnjié] nimble II N victory

捷径 [jiéjìng] N short cut

姐 [jiě] N elder sister

姐姐 [jiějie] N elder sister

姐妹 [jiěmèi] N sisters (PL)

解 [jiě] VB 1 (分开) divide ▶ 解剖 [jiěpōu] dissect 2 (解开) untie 3 (解除) relieve 4 (解答) answer ▶ 解题 [jiětí] solve a problem 5 (理解) understand

解答 [jiědá] VB answer

解放 [jiěfàng] VB liberate

解雇 [jiěgù] VB fire

解决 [jiějué] VB 1 (处理) resolve 2 (消灭) annihilate

解释 [jiěshì] VB explain

介 [jiè] VB be situated between

介绍 [jièshào] VB 1 (使相识) introduce 2 (推荐) sponsor 3 (使了解) give an introduction to

---

届 [jiè] I VB fall due ▶ 届期 [jièqī] at the appointed time II MEAS 1 (指开始上学的学年) year ▷ 82届毕业生 [bā èr jiè bìyèshēng] the class of '82 2 (指大会, 首脑) ▷ 第10届奥运会 [dì shí jiè Àoyùnhuì] the tenth Olympic Games ▷ 第26届总统 [dì èrshíliù jiè zǒngtǒng] the twenty-sixth president

measure word, used for conferences, sports events, trade fairs, terms of office, etc.

界 [jiè] N 1 (界限) boundary (PL) 2 (阶层) circles (PL) 3 (范围) range 4 (类别) category

借 [jiè] VB **1** (借入) borrow **2** (借出) lend **3** (假托) use ... as a means of **4** (凭借) make use of

借口 [jièkǒu] **I** VB use ... as an excuse **II** N excuse

借助 [jièzhù] VB enlist the help of

斤 [jīn] MEAS *unit of weight, equal to 500 grams*

今 [jīn] **I** ADJ **1** (现在的) present **2** (当前的) current **II** N today

今后 [jīnhòu] ADV from now on

今年 [jīnnián] N this year

今天 [jīntiān] N today

金 [jīn] **I** N **1** (化) gold **2** (金属) metal ▶ 五金 [wǔjīn] hardware **3** (钱) money **II** ADJ golden ▶ 金发 [jīnfà] blonde hair

金融 [jīnróng] N finance

金属 [jīnshǔ] N metal

金子 [jīnzi] N gold

仅 [jǐn] ADV only

仅仅 [jǐnjǐn] ADV just

尽 [jǐn] **I** ADV **1** (尽量) as far as possible ▶ 尽快 [jǐnkuài] as early as possible **2** (最) most **3** (表示继续) constantly **II** VB **1** (不超过) take no more than **2** (考虑在先) give priority to

→ *see also*/另见 jìn

尽管 [jǐnguǎn] **I** ADV without reserve ▷ 有话尽管说。 [Yǒu huà jǐnguǎn shuō.] If there's something you'd like to say please don't hold back. **II** CONJ even though

尽量 [jǐnliàng] ADV to the best of one's ability

尽早 [jǐnzǎo] ADV as soon as possible

紧 [jǐn] **I** ADJ **1** (不松) tight **2** (牢固) secure **3** (接近) close **4** (急迫) pressing **5** (严格) strict **6** (拮据) short of money **II** VB tighten

紧急 [jǐnjí] ADJ urgent

紧张 [jǐnzhāng] ADJ **1** (激烈) intense **2** (不安) nervous **3** (不足) in short supply

尽 [jìn] **I** VB **1** (完) exhaust **2** (达到极限) go to extremes **3** (充分发挥) use ... to the full **4** (努力完成) strive to accomplish **II** ADJ complete

→ *see also*/另见 jǐn

尽力 [jìnlì] VB try one's hardest

尽量 [jìnliàng] VB do all one can

进 [jìn] VB **1** (前进) advance **2** (进入) enter **3** (接纳) bring ... in ▶ 进货 [jìnhuò] stock up **4** (吃食) eat **5** (呈上) submit **6** (攻进) enter ▶ 进球 [jìnqiú] score a goal

进步 [jìnbù] **I** VB improve **II** ADJ advanced

进攻 [jìngōng] VB attack

进化 [jìnhuà] VB evolve

进口 [jìnkǒu] VB import

近来 [jìnlái] VB come in

进去 [jìnqù] VB enter

进入 [jìnrù] VB **1** (走进) enter **2** (到了) reach **3** (到位) get inside

进行 [jìnxíng] VB carry ... out

进修 [jìnxiū] VB take a refresher course

近 [jìn] ADJ **1** (不远) near ▶ 近日 [jìnrì] recently **2** (接近) close **3** (亲近) close to

近来 [jìnlái] ADV recently

近视 [jìnshì] ADJ nearsighted

劲 [jìn] N **1** (力气) strength **2** (情绪) spirit **3** (态度) manner **4** (趣味) fun

禁 [jìn] **I** VB **1** (禁止) forbid **2** (监禁) imprison ▶ 禁闭 [jìnbì] lock ... up **II** N taboo

→ *see also*/另见 jīn

禁止 [jìnzhǐ] VB forbid

京 [jīng] N **1** (首都) capital **2** (北京) Beijing

京剧 [jīngjù] N Beijing opera

京剧 [jīngjù]

京剧 jīngjù is a form of Chinese traditional opera which enjoys a history of over two hundred years, and is regarded as one of the most important Chinese cultural heritages. The performances combine singing, acting, music, dialogue, dancing and acrobatics. Different roles follow different patterns of acting, which are all rather symbolic, suggestive and exaggerated.

经 [jīng] **I** N **1** (经线) warp **2** (指中医) channels (PL) **3** (经度) longitude **4** (经典) scripture ▸ 佛经 [fójīng] Buddhist sutra **II** VB **1** (经营) run ▸ 经商 [jīngshāng] be in business **2** (经受) endure **3** (经过) ▹ 途经西安 [tújīng Xī'ān] go via Xi'an **III** ADJ regular

经常 [jīngcháng] **I** ADJ day-to-day **II** ADV often

经过 [jīngguò] **I** VB **1** (通过) pass **2** (延续) ▹ 经过3年的恋爱, 他们终于结婚了。 [Jīngguò sān nián de liàn'ài, tāmen zhōngyú jiéhūn le.] Having been together for three years, they finally got married. **3** (经历) ▹ 企业经过裁员缩减了经费开支。 [Qǐyè jīngguò cáiyuán suōjiǎn le jīngfèi kāizhī.] Business expenditure was reduced through staff cutbacks. **II** N course

经济 [jīngjì] **I** N **1** (社会生产关系) economy **2** (个人财政状况) financial situation **II** ADJ **1** (有关国民经济) economic **2** (实惠) economical ▹ 经济舱 [jīngjìcāng] economy-class cabin

经理 [jīnglǐ] N manager

经历 [jīnglì] VB experience

经验 [jīngyàn] N experience

惊 [jīng] VB **1** (紧张) start **2** (惊动) startle

惊奇 [jīngqí] ADJ surprised

惊人 [jīngrén] ADJ amazing

惊喜 [jīngxǐ] VB be pleasantly surprised

惊讶 [jīngyà] ADJ astonished

精 [jīng] **I** ADJ **1** (经挑选的) refined ▸ 精兵 [jīngbīng] crack troops **2** (完美) excellent **3** (细密) precise **4** (心细) sharp ▸ 精明 [jīngmíng] shrewd **5** (精通) skilled **II** N **1** (精华) essence ▸ 酒精 [jiǔjīng] alcohol **2** (精力) energy **III** ADV (方) extremely

精彩 [jīngcǎi] ADJ wonderful

精力 [jīnglì] N energy

精确 [jīngquè] ADJ precise

精神 [jīngshén] N **1** (主观世界) mind **2** (宗旨) gist

精神 [jīngshen] **I** N energy **II** ADJ energetic

精通 [jīngtōng] VB be proficient in

井 [jǐng] **I** N **1** (用于取水) well **2** (井状物) ▸ 天井 [tiānjǐng] skylight ▸ 矿井 [kuàngjǐng] mine shaft **II** ADJ neat

景 [jǐng] **I** N **1** (风景) scenery **2** (情形) situation ▸ 背景 [bèijǐng] background **3** (布景) scene ▸ 外景 [wàijǐng] outdoor scene **II** VB admire

景点 [jǐngdiǎn] N scenic spot

景色 [jǐngsè] N scenery

警 [jǐng] **I** ADJ alert ▸ 警惕 [jǐngtì] on the alert **II** VB **1** (使警觉) warn **2** (戒备) be on the alert **III** N **1** (危急) alarm ▸ 报警 [bàojǐng] raise the alarm **2** (警察) police ▸ 巡警 [xúnjǐng] an officer on the beat

警报 [jǐngbào] N alarm

警察 [jǐngchá] N police

警告 [jǐnggào] VB warn

竞 [jìng] VB compete

竞赛 [jìngsài] N competition

竞争 [jìngzhēng] VB compete

敬 [jìng] **I** VB **1** (尊重) respect **2** (恭敬地给) offer **II** ADJ respectful

敬爱 [jìng'ài] VB revere

敬礼 [jìnglǐ] VB salute

静 [jìng] ADJ **1** (不动) still **2** (无声) quiet

镜 [jìng] N **1** (镜子) mirror **2** (指光学器具) lens ▶ 眼镜 [yǎnjìng] glasses

镜子 [jìngzi] N mirror

纠 [jiū] VB **1** (缠绕) entangle **2** (集合) assemble **3** (督察) supervise **4** (改正) correct

纠正 [jiūzhèng] VB correct

究 [jiū] **I** VB investigate **II** ADV actually

究竟 [jiūjìng] **I** N outcome **II** ADV actually

九 [jiǔ] NUM nine

九月 [jiǔyuè] N September

久 [jiǔ] ADJ **1** (时间长) long **2** (时间长短) long

玖 [jiǔ] NUM nine

This is the complex character for "nine", which is mainly used in banks, on receipts, etc. to prevent mistakes and forgery.

酒 [jiǔ] N alcohol ▶ 葡萄酒 [pútaojiǔ] wine ▶ 敬酒 [jìngjiǔ] propose a toast

旧 [jiù] **I** ADJ **1** (过时) old **2** (陈旧) used **II** N old friend

救 [jiù] VB save

救护车 [jiùhùchē] N ambulance

救命 [jiùmìng] VB save a life ▷ 救命啊！ [Jiùmìng a!] Help!

就 [jiù] **I** VB **1** (靠近) move close to **2** (开始) take ... up **3** (完成) accomplish **4** (趁) take the opportunity **5** (搭配着吃) eat ... with **II** ADV **1** (强调时间短) shortly **2** (早已) already **3** (表示紧接着) as soon as **4** (表示条件关系) then **5** (强调数量多) as much as **6** (仅仅) only **7** (原本) already **8** (表示坚决) simply **9** (强调事实) exactly **10** (表示容忍) even though **III** CONJ even if **IV** PREP on

就是 [jiùshì] **I** ADV **1** (表示赞同) exactly **2** (表示坚决) still **3** (表示强调) really **4** (确定范围) only **II** AUX WORD ▷ 你干就是了，没人说你。 [Nǐ gàn jiùshì le, méi rén shuō nǐ.] Just go ahead and do it, no one will blame you! **III** CONJ even if

就算 [jiùsuàn] CONJ even if

舅 [jiù] N **1** (舅父) uncle **2** (妻子的弟兄) brother-in-law

舅舅 [jiùjiu] N uncle

居 [jū] **I** VB **1** (住) live **2** (在) be **II** N house

居住 [jūzhù] VB live

局 [jú] **I** N **1** (棋盘) chessboard **2** (次) game ▶ 平局 [píngjú] a draw **3** (形势) situation ▶ 时局 [shíjú] current political situation **4** (聚会) gathering ▶ 饭局 [fànjú] dinner party **5** (圈套) ruse ▶ 骗局 [piànjú] fraud **6** (部分) part **7** (机关部门) department **8** (业务机构) office **II** MEAS set ▷ 我赢了这局棋。 [Wǒ yíng le zhè jú qí.] I won the chess game.

局长 [júzhǎng] N director

橘 [jú] N tangerine

橘子 [júzi] N orange ▷ 橘子汁 [júzi zhī] orange juice

举 [jǔ] **I** VB **1** (往上托) raise ▶ 举重 [jǔzhòng] weightlifting **2** (兴起) mobilize ▶ 举兵 [jǔbīng] dispatch troops **3** (选举) elect **4** (提出) cite ▶ 举例 [jǔlì] cite an example **II** N act **III** ADJ (书) whole

举办 [jǔbàn] VB hold

举行 [jǔxíng] VB hold

巨 [jù] ADJ huge

巨大 [jùdà] ADJ huge

巨人 [jùrén] N giant

句 [jù] **I** N sentence **II** MEAS ▷ 说几句话 [shuō jǐ jù huà] say a few words ▷ 写两句诗 [xiě liǎng jù shī] write two lines of verse

measure word, used for sentences, and lines in a speech, song, or poem

句子 [jùzi] N sentence

拒 [jù] VB 1 (抵抗) resist 2 (拒绝) refuse

拒绝 [jùjué] VB refuse

具 [jù] I VB have II N utensil ▶ 玩具 [wánjù] toy

具备 [jùbèi] VB have

具体 [jùtǐ] ADJ 1 (明确) detailed 2 (特定) particular

具有 [jùyǒu] VB have

俱 [jù] ADV ▶ 面面俱到 [miàn miàn jù dào] attend to each and every aspect

俱乐部 [jùlèbù] N club

剧 [jù] I N drama ▶ 喜剧 [xǐjù] comedy II ADJ severe ▶ 剧变 [jùbiàn] dramatic change

剧场 [jùchǎng] N theater

剧烈 [jùliè] ADJ severe

剧院 [jùyuàn] N 1 (剧场) theater 2 (剧团) company

据 [jù] I VB 1 (占据) occupy ▶ 盘据 [pánjù] forcibly occupy 2 (凭借) rely on ▶ 据点 [jùdiǎn] stronghold II PREP according to III N evidence ▶ 收据 [shōujù] receipt

据说 [jùshuō] VB be said

距 [jù] N distance

距离 [jùlí] VB be at a distance from

锯 [jù] I N saw II VB saw

卷 [juǎn] I VB 1 (裹成筒形) roll … up 2 (撮起) sweep … up 3 (喻) (牵涉) be swept up in II N roll III MEAS roll ▷ 一卷卫生纸 [yī juǎn wèishēngzhǐ] a roll of toilet paper

决 [jué] I VB 1 (决定) decide 2 (执行死刑) execute 3 (决口) burst 4 (定胜负) decide on a result ▶ 决战 [juézhàn] decisive battle II ADV under any circumstances III ADJ decisive ▶ 果决 [guǒjué] resolute

决定 [juédìng] VB 1 (打定主意) decide 2 (表示条件关系) determine

决心 [juéxīn] N determination

觉 [jué] I VB 1 (感觉) feel 2 (觉悟) become aware of II N sense ▶ 知觉 [zhījué] consciousness

觉得 [juéde] VB 1 (感到) feel 2 (认为) think

觉悟 [juéwù] N awareness

绝 [jué] I VB 1 (断绝) cut … off ▶ 隔绝 [géjué] isolate 2 (穷尽) exhaust 3 (无后代) have no descendants 4 (死) die II ADJ 1 (不通) hopeless ▶ 绝路 [juélù] blind alley 2 (高超) superb III ADV 1 (最) extremely ▶ 绝密 [juémì] top secret 2 (绝对) absolutely

绝对 [juéduì] I ADJ absolute II ADV absolutely

绝望 [juéwàng] VB feel desperate

军 [jūn] I N 1 (军队) army ▶ 参军 [cānjūn] enlist 2 (指军队编制单位) regiment 3 (指集体) forces (PL) II ADJ military ▶ 军费 [jūnfèi] military expenditure

军队 [jūnduì] N troops (PL)

军官 [jūnguān] N officer

军人 [jūnrén] N soldier

军事 [jūnshì] N military affairs (PL)

K

咖 [kā] *see below*/见下文
→ *see also*/另见 gā

咖啡 [kāfēi] N coffee ▷ 速溶咖啡 [sùróng kāfēi] instant coffee

卡 [kǎ] I MEAS (卡路里) calorie II N (卡片) card

卡车 [kǎchē] N truck

卡拉OK [kǎlā'ōukèi] N karaoke

卡通 [kǎtōng] N cartoon

开 [kāi] VB 1 (打开) open ▶ 开门 [kāimén] open the door 2 (银行, 商店) be open 3 (绽放) bloom 4 (松开) come undone 5 (驾驶) drive ▷ 开汽车 [kāi qìchē] drive a car 6 (办) open ... up ▷ 开公司 [kāi gōngsī] start up a business 7 (开始) start ▶ 开课 [kāikè] give a course ▶ 开学 [kāixué] start school ▶ 开演 [kāiyǎn] start the show 8 (举行) hold ▶ 开会 [kāihuì] have a meeting 9 (写出) write ... out 10 (灯, 电器, 煤气) turn on ▷ 开灯 [kāi dēng] turn on the light 11 (沸腾) boil ▷ 水刚开。 [Shuǐ gāng kāi.] The water was just boiled. 12 (饭) serve ▷ 开饭了。 [Kāi fàn le.] Dinner is ready.

开刀 [kāidāo] VB operate on

开放 [kāifàng] VB 1 (解禁) open ▷ 对外开放政策 [duìwài kāifàng zhèngcè] the opening-up policy 2 (开朗) be open-minded

开关 [kāiguān] N switch

开户 [kāihù] VB open an account

开会 [kāihuì] VB have a meeting

开课 [kāikè] VB 1 (开学) start 2 (授课) teach a course

开朗 [kāilǎng] ADJ (指性格) cheerful

开明 [kāimíng] ADJ enlightened

开幕 [kāimù] VB 1 (指演出) start 2 (指会) open

开辟 [kāipì] VB 1 (开通) open ... up 2 (开发) develop

开始 [kāishǐ] I VB start, begin II N beginning

开水 [kāishuǐ] N boiling water

开头 [kāitóu] I VB begin II N beginning

开玩笑 [kāi wánxiào] VB joke ▷ 别拿我开玩笑。 [Bié ná wǒ kāi wánxiào.] Don't make fun of me.

开心 [kāixīn] ADJ happy

开展 [kāizhǎn] VB launch

开支 [kāizhī] VB spend

刊 [kān] I VB (出版) publish II N periodical ▶ 报刊 [bàokān] the press

刊登 [kāndēng] VB publish

刊物 [kānwù] N periodical

看 [kān] VB 1 (照料) look after ▶ 看家 [kānjiā] look after the house 2 (看管) watch over
→ *see also*/另见 kàn

砍 [kǎn] VB 1 (劈) chop 2 (减) cut

看 [kàn] VB 1 (观看) look at ▶ 看到 [kàndào] see ▷ 看电视 [kàn diànshì] watch TV 2 (阅读) read 3 (认为) think ▶ 看成 [kànchéng] consider 4 (拜访) visit ▶ 看望 [kànwàng] visit 5 (照料) look after 6 (对待) treat 7 (诊治) treat ▶ 看病 [kànbìng] see a doctor 8 (取决于) depend on
→ *see also*/另见 kān

看不起 [kàn bu qǐ] VB look down on

看待 [kàndài] VB regard ▷ 当朋友看待 [dāng péngyou kàndài] regard as a friend

看法 [kànfǎ] N opinion

看好 [kànhǎo] VB look good

看见 [kànjiàn] VB see

看来 [kànlái] VB seem

康 [kāng] ADJ (健康) healthy ▶ 康复 [kāngfù] recover

慷 [kāng] *see below*/见下文

慷慨 [kāngkǎi] ADJ (大方) generous

扛 [káng] VB shoulder

抗 [kàng] VB **1** (抵抗) resist **2** (抗拒) refuse

抗议 [kàngyì] VB protest

考 [kǎo] VB **1** (测试) have an exam ▶ 考上 [kǎoshang] pass the entrance exam **2** (检查) check ▶ 考察 [kǎochá] investigate

考虑 [kǎolǜ] VB consider

考试 [kǎoshì] VB sit an exam

考验 [kǎoyàn] VB test

拷 [kǎo] VB (拷贝) copy

烤 [kǎo] VB **1** (指东西) roast ▶ 烤鸭 [kǎoyā] **2** (指人体) warm oneself ▶ 烤火 [kǎohuǒ] warm oneself by a fire

靠 [kào] VB **1** (倚) lean **2** (近) keep to **3** (依赖) rely on **4** (信赖) trust

科 [kē] N **1** (指学术) discipline ▶ 文科 [wénkē] humanities (PL) **2** (指部门) department

科技 [kējì] N science and technology

科目 [kēmù] N subject

科学 [kēxué] **I** N science **II** ADJ scientific

科学家 [kēxuéjiā] N scientist

科研 [kēyán] N scientific research

棵 [kē] MEAS ▷ 一棵水仙 [yī kē shuǐxiān] a narcissus ▷ 三百棵树 [sānbǎi kē shù] three hundred trees

measure word, used for plants, trees, and vegetables

颗 [kē] MEAS ▷ 一颗种子 [yī kē zhǒngzi] a seed ▷ 一颗汗珠 [yī kē hànzhū] a bead of sweat

measure word, used for small, round objects

磕 [kē] VB bump

壳 [ké] N shell

咳 [ké] VB cough

咳嗽 [késou] VB cough

可 [kě] **I** VB (同意) approve **II** AUX VB **1** (可以) can **2** (值得) **III** CONJ but

可爱 [kě'ài] ADJ adorable

可悲 [kěbēi] ADJ lamentable

可靠 [kěkào] ADJ reliable

可乐 [kělè] N Coke

可怜 [kělián] **I** ADJ pitiful **II** VB pity

可能 [kěnéng] **I** ADJ possible **II** ADV maybe **III** N possibility ▶ 可能性 [kěnéngxìng] possibility

可怕 [kěpà] ADJ frightening

可是 [kěshì] CONJ but ▷ 这个小镇不大，可是很热闹。[Zhè gè xiǎozhèn bù dà, kěshì hěn rènào.] This is a small town, but it's very lively.

可惜 [kěxī] **I** ADJ regrettable **II** ADV regrettably

可笑 [kěxiào] ADJ **1** (令人耻笑) ridiculous **2** (引人发笑) funny

可以 [kěyǐ] **I** AUX VB **1** (能够) can **2** (有权) may **II** ADJ (不坏) not bad

可以 kěyǐ, 能 néng, and 会 huì can all be used to express ability and are sometimes used interchangeably. Both 可以 kěyǐ and 能 néng can express being able to do something because you have been granted permission, e.g. 你可以/能借我的照相机 nǐ kěyǐ/néng jiè wǒ de zhàoxiàngjī (you may/can borrow my camera). Strictly, 能 néng should be used to express physical ability, e.g. 我能跑得很快 wǒ néng pǎo de hěn kuài (I can run very fast), while 会 huì should express a learned ability, e.g. 我会说法语 wǒ huì shuō Fǎyǔ (I can speak French).

渴 [kě] **I** ADJ thirsty ▶ 渴望 [kěwàng] long for **II** ADV eagerly

克 [kè] **I** VB **1** (克制) restrain **2** (战胜) overcome **II** MEAS gram

克服 [kèfú] VB (战胜) overcome

克隆 [kèlóng] VB clone

刻 [kè] **I** VB engrave **II** N **1** (雕刻物品) engraving **2** (指十五分钟) quarter

刻苦 [kèkǔ] ADJ hardworking

客 [kè] N **1** (客人) visitor ▶ 客厅 [kètīng] living room **2** (旅客) traveler ▶ 客车 [kèchē] passenger train **3** (顾客) customer ▶ 客户 [kèhù] customer

客观 [kèguān] ADJ objective

客气 [kèqi] **I** ADJ polite **II** VB be polite

客人 [kèrén] N guest

课 [kè] N **1** (学科) subject **2** (学时) class **3** (单元) lesson

课本 [kèběn] N textbook

课程 [kèchéng] N course ▶ 课程表 [kèchéngbiǎo] school timetable

课堂 [kètáng] N classroom

课题 [kètí] N (论题) topic

课文 [kèwén] N text

肯 [kěn] AUX VB be willing

肯定 [kěndìng] **I** VB confirm **II** ADJ **1** (确定的) affirmative **2** (明确的) clear **III** ADV certainly

空 [kōng] **I** ADJ empty ▶ 空虚 [kōngxū] empty **II** N sky ▶ 空中小姐 [kōngzhōng xiǎojiě] stewardess
→ *see also*/另见 kòng

空间 [kōngjiān] N space

空军 [kōngjūn] N air force

空调 [kōngtiáo] N air conditioner

空气 [kōngqì] N (大气) air

空前 [kōngqián] ADJ unprecedented

孔 [kǒng] N hole

孔子 [Kǒngzǐ] N Confucius

孔子 [Kǒngzǐ]

孔子 Kǒngzǐ, Confucius (trad. 551-479 BC), was a hugely influential thinker. A posthumous compilation of his sayings, 《论语》 Lúnyǔ, The Analects, is China's most important philosophical work, and was the key text on which much of the traditional Chinese education system was based.

恐 [kǒng] fear

恐怖 [kǒngbù] **I** ADJ terrifying **II** N terror ▶ 恐怖主义 [kǒngbù zhǔyì] terrorism

恐龙 [kǒnglóng] N dinosaur

恐怕 [kǒngpà] ADV **1** (担心) fearfully **2** (大概) probably

空 [kòng] **I** VB leave ... empty **II** ADJ vacant ▶ 空白 [kòngbái] blank ▶ 空缺 [kòngquē] vacancy **III** N **1** (空间) space **2** (时间) free time ▶ 空儿 [kòngr] spare time ▶ 有空 [yǒu kòng] have free time
→ *see also*/另见 kōng

控 [kòng] VB **1** (控制) control **2** (控告) charge

控制 [kòngzhì] VB control

口 [kǒu] **I** N **1** (嘴) mouth ▶ 口才 [kǒucái] eloquence ▶ 口吃 [kǒuchī] stammering ▶ 口红 [kǒuhóng] lipstick **2** (丁) ▶ 家口 [jiākǒu] family member ▶ 口味 [kǒuwèi] taste **3** (指容器) rim ▶ 瓶口 [píngkǒu] the mouth of a bottle **4** (指端口) ▶ 出口 [chūkǒu] exit ▶ 入口 [rùkǒu] entrance ▶ 窗口 [chuāngkǒu] window **5** (缝) split **II** MEAS ▷ 我家有五口人。 [Wǒ jiā yǒu wǔ kǒu rén.] There are five people in my family.

measure word, used for the number of people in a family

口袋 [kǒudài] N bag

口号 [kǒuhào] N slogan

口气 [kǒuqì] N (语气) tone

口头 [kǒutóu] N **1** (嘴) word **2** (口语) ▷ 口头作文 [kǒutóu zuòwén] oral composition

口信 [kǒuxìn] N message

口音 [kǒuyīn] N (方音) accent

口语 [kǒuyǔ] N spoken language

口罩 [kǒuzhào] N face mask

扣 [kòu] **I** VB **1** (拉紧) fasten **2** (朝下)

put ... upside down 3 (抓) arrest ▶ 扣留 [kòuliú] arrest 4 (减) deduct ▶ 扣除 [kòuchú] **II** N button ▶ 扣子 [kòuzi] button

哭 [kū] VB cry

苦 [kǔ] **I** ADJ **1** (苦涩) bitter **2** (艰苦) hard **II** VB (苦害) be hard on **III** ADV painstakingly ▶ 苦练 [kǔ liàn] train hard **IV** N suffering ▶ 吃苦 [chīkǔ] bear hardships

苦难 [kǔnàn] **I** N hardship **II** ADJ hard

苦恼 [kǔnǎo] ADJ distressed

库存 [kùcún] N stock

裤 [kù] N pants (PL) ▶ 裤子 [kùzi] pants (PL)

夸 [kuā] VB **1** (夸大) exaggerate **2** (夸奖) praise

夸奖 [kuājiǎng] VB praise

夸张 [kuāzhāng] **I** ADJ exaggerated **II** N hyperbole

垮 [kuǎ] VB **1** (坍塌) collapse ▶ 垮台 [kuǎtái] collapse **2** (伤身) wear down

胯 [kuà] N hip

跨 [kuà] VB **1** (迈步) step **2** (骑) mount **3** (超越) surpass ▶ 跨国 [kuàguó] transnational

会 [kuài] N accounting ▶ 财会 [cáikuài] finance and accounting → *see also*/另见 huì

会计 [kuàijì] N **1** (指工作) accounting **2** (指人员) accountant

块 [kuài] **I** N lump **II** MEAS piece ▷ 一块蛋糕 [yī kuài dàngāo] a piece of cake ▷ 一块方糖 [yī kuài fāngtáng] a lump of sugar

快 [kuài] **I** ADJ **1** (快速) fast **2** (赶快) ▷ 快点儿，要不我们就迟到了。Hurry up, or we'll be late. **3** (灵敏) quick ▷ 他脑子快。[Tā nǎozi kuài.] He's quick-witted. **4** (锋利) sharp **5** (直爽) straightforward ▶ 爽快 [shuǎngkuài] frank **II** ADV soon ▶ 快要 [kuàiyào] soon

快餐 [kuàicān] N fast food

快活 [kuàihuo] ADJ delighted

快乐 [kuàilè] ADJ happy

筷 [kuài] N chopsticks (PL) ▶ 筷子 [kuàizi] chopsticks (PL)

宽 [kuān] **I** ADJ **1** (距离大) wide **2** (范围广) broad ▶ 宽敞 [kuānchang] spacious **3** (宽大) lenient ▶ 宽容 [kuānróng] tolerant **II** N width

宽带 [kuāndài] N broadband

款 [kuǎn] N **1** (项目) section **2** (钱) sum of money ▶ 现款 [xiànkuǎn] cash **3** (样式) style ▶ 款式 [kuǎnshì] style

狂 [kuáng] **I** ADJ **1** (疯狂) crazy ▶ 发狂 [fākuáng] go crazy **2** (猛烈) violent ▶ 狂风 [kuángfēng] gale **3** (狂妄) arrogant **4** (狂热) wild **II** ADV wildly

旷 [kuàng] **I** ADJ (空阔) spacious ▶ 旷野 [kuàngyě] wilderness **II** VB neglect ▶ 旷课 [kuàngkè] play truant

况 [kuàng] N situation ▶ 状况 [zhuàngkuàng] condition

况且 [kuàngqiě] CONJ besides

矿 [kuàng] N **1** (矿场) mine **2** (矿石) ore

框 [kuàng] **I** N **1** (框架) frame **2** (方框) box **II** VB **1** (画圈) box **2** (口) (限制) limit

框架 [kuàngjià] N **1** (指建筑) frame **2** (指文书) framework

眶 [kuàng] N socket ▶ 眼眶 [yǎnkuàng] eye socket

亏 [kuī] **I** VB **1** (亏损) lose **2** (欠缺) lack **3** (亏负) allow ... to suffer losses **II** ADV luckily ▷ 亏你把我叫醒，要不我就迟到了。[Kuī nǐ bǎ wǒ jiào xǐng, yào bù wǒ jiù chídào le.] It's lucky you woke me up or I would have been late.

盔 [kuī] N helmet

葵 [kuí] *see below*/见下文

葵花 [kuíhuā] N sunflower

魁 [kuí] **I** N head ▶ 夺魁 [duókuí] win first place **II** ADJ well-built ▶ 魁梧 [kuíwú] tall and sturdy

昆 [kūn] *see below*/见下文

昆虫 [kūnchóng] N insect

捆 [kǔn] **I** VB tie ... up **II** MEAS bundle ▷ 一捆书 [yī kǔn shū] a bundle of books

困 [kùn] **I** VB **1** (困扰) be stricken **2** (限制) trap **II** ADJ **1** (瞌睡) sleepy **2** (困难) difficult

困难 [kùnnan] ADJ **1** (指事情) difficult ▶ 克服困难 [kèfú kùnnan] overcome difficulties **2** (指经济) poor

扩 [kuò] VB expand

扩大 [kuòdà] VB expand

括 [kuò] VB **1** (包括) include **2** (加括号) bracket

括弧 [kuòhú] N bracket

阔 [kuò] ADJ **1** (宽广) wide **2** (阔气) wealthy

L

垃 [lā] *see below*/见下文

垃圾 [lājī] N garbage ▷ 垃圾食品 [lājī shípǐn] junk food

拉 [lā] VB **1** (用力移动) pull **2** (载运) transport ▷ 出租车司机拉我到了机场。 [Chūzūchē sījī lā wǒ dào le jīchǎng.] The taxi driver took me to the airport. **3** (演奏) play ▷ 拉小提琴 [lā xiǎotíqín] play the violin

喇 [lǎ] *see below*/见下文

喇叭 [lǎba] N **1** (管乐器) trumpet **2** (扩音器) loudspeaker

落 [là] VB **1** (遗漏) be missing **2** (忘记) leave
→ *see also*/另见 luò

辣 [là] ADJ (指味道) hot ▶ 辣酱 [làjiàng] chilli sauce ▶ 辣椒 [làjiāo] chillies

蜡 [là] N candle ▶ 蜡烛 [làzhú] candle

啦 [la] AUX WORD ▷ 你回来啦! [Nǐ huílai la!] Hey, you're back!

来 [lái] **I** VB **1** (来到) come ▷ 家里来了几个客人。 [Jiā lǐ lái le jǐ gè kèrén.] Some guests came to the house. **2** (发生) happen ▷ 刚到家，麻烦来了。 [Gāng dào jiā, máfan lái le.] As soon as I got home, the trouble started. **3** (泛指做事) ▷ 请来碗面条。 [Qǐng lái wǎn miàntiáo.] A bowl of noodles, please. ▷ 你累了，让我来。 [Nǐ lèi le, ràng wǒ lái.] You're tired, let me do it. **4** (表示要做) ▷ 请你来帮个忙。 [Qǐng nǐ lái bāng gè máng.] Can you help me with this? **5** (表示目的) ▷ 我要想个法子来对付他。 [Wǒ yào xiǎng gè fǎzi lái duìfu ta.] I must think of a way to deal with him. **6** (表示朝向) ▷ 服务员很快就把饭菜端了上来。 [Fúwùyuán hěnkuài jiù bǎ fàncài duān le shànglai.] Soon the waiter had brought the food to the table. **II** ADJ coming ▶ 来年 [láinián] the coming year **III** AUX WORD **1** (表示持续) ▶ 近来 [jìnlái] lately ▷ 几年来 [jǐ nián lái] in the last few years **2** (表示概数) about ▷ 10来公斤重 [shí lái gōngjīn zhòng] about 10 kilos

来不及 [láibùjí] VB lack sufficient time for

来得及 [láidejí] VB have enough time for

来回 [láihuí] **I** VB **1** (去了再来) make a round trip ▷ 从住宅小区到市中心来回有多远? [Cóng zhùzhái xiǎoqū dào shìzhōngxīn láihuí yǒu duō yuǎn?] How far is it from the residential area to town and back? **2** (来来去去) move back and forth **II** N round trip ▷ 我从学校到家一天跑两个来回。 [Wǒ cóng xuéxiào dào jiā yī tiān pǎo liǎng gè láihuí.] I make the round trip from school to home twice a day.

来往 [láiwǎng] VB have dealings with

来自 [láizì] VB come from

拦 [lán] VB stop

栏 [lán] N **1** (栏杆) fence ▶ 栏杆 [lángān] railing **2** (部分版面) column ▶ 栏目 [lánmù] column

蓝 [lán] ADJ blue ▶ 蓝色 [lánsè] blue ▶ 蓝天 [lántiān] sky

篮 [lán] N (篮子) basket ▶ 篮子 [lánzi] basket

篮球 [lánqiú] N basketball

缆 [lǎn] N (似缆之物) cable

缆车 [lǎnchē] N cable car

懒 [lǎn] ADJ **1** (懒惰) lazy **2** (疲倦) lethargic

懒得 [lǎnde] VB not feel like ▷ 天太热，我懒得出门。 [Tiān tài rè, wǒ lǎn de chūmén.] I don't feel like going out, it's too hot.

懒惰 [lǎnduò] ADJ lazy

烂 [làn] **I** ADJ **1** (破烂) worn-out **2** (头绪乱) messy ▶ 烂摊子 [làn tānzi] a shambles **II** VB be rotten ▷ 西瓜烂了。[Xīguā làn le.] The watermelon has gone off.

狼 [láng] N wolf

廊 [láng] N corridor ▶ 走廊 [zǒuláng] corridor

朗 [lǎng] ADJ **1** (明亮) bright **2** (响亮) clear

朗读 [lǎngdú] VB read ... aloud

朗诵 [lǎngsòng] VB recite

浪 [làng] **I** N wave ▶ 浪潮 [làngcháo] tide **II** ADJ wasteful ▶ 浪费 [làngfèi] squander

浪费 [làngfèi] VB waste

浪漫 [làngmàn] ADJ romantic

捞 [lāo] VB (取) take ▶ 捕捞 [bǔlāo] fish for

劳 [láo] VB **1** (劳动) work **2** (烦劳) trouble ▷ 劳您帮我看下行李。[Láo nín bāng wǒ kān xià xíngli.] Would you mind keeping an eye on my luggage?

劳动 [láodòng] N labor ▷ 脑力劳动 [nǎolì láodòng] brain work

劳动力 [láodònglì] N **1** (劳动能力) labor **2** (人力) workforce

劳驾 [láojià] VB (客套) excuse me

老 [lǎo] **I** ADJ **1** (年岁大的) old **2** (有经验的) experienced ▶ 老手 [lǎoshǒu] veteran **3** (旧的) old ▷ 老同学 [lǎo tóngxué] old school friend **4** (火候大的) over-done **II** N (老人) old people **III** ADV **1** (经常) always **2** (长久) for a long time **3** (非常) very ▶ 老远 [lǎoyuǎn] very far

老百姓 [lǎobǎixìng] N ordinary people

老板 [lǎobǎn] N boss

老虎 [lǎohǔ] N tiger

老家 [lǎojiā] N home ▷ 我老家在上海。[Wǒ lǎojiā zài Shànghǎi.] Shanghai is my hometown.

老练 [lǎoliàn] ADJ experienced

老年 [lǎonián] N old age

老婆 [lǎopo] N (妻子) wife

老师 [lǎoshī] N teacher

老实 [lǎoshi] ADJ **1** (诚实规矩) honest **2** (不聪明) naive

老鼠 [lǎoshǔ] N mouse

老外 [lǎowài] N foreigner

姥 [lǎo] *see below*/见下文

姥姥 [lǎolao] N (口) (母方的) granny

姥爷 [lǎoye] N (口) (母方的) grandpa

乐 [lè] **I** ADJ happy **II** VB **1** (乐于) take pleasure in **2** (笑) laugh
→ *see also*/另见 yuè

乐观 [lèguān] ADJ optimistic

乐趣 [lèqù] N delight

乐意 [lèyì] VB be willing to ▷ 他不乐意帮我们。[Tā bù lèyì bāng wǒmen.] He's unwilling to help us.

了 [le] AUX WORD **1** (表示动作或变化已完成) ▷ 他买了这本书。[Tā mǎi le zhè běn shū.] He's bought this book. **2** (表示对未来的假设已完成) ▷ 下个月我考完了试回家。[Xià gè yuè wǒ kǎo wán le shì huíjiā.] I'll go home next month once my exams are over. **3** (在句尾，表示出现变化) ▷ 下雨了。[Xiàyǔ le.] It's raining. **4** (在句尾，表示提醒, 劝告或催促) ▷ 该回家了。[Gāi huíjiā le.] It's time to go home. ▷ 别喊了！[Bié hǎn le!] Stop shouting!
→ *see also*/另见 liǎo

The usage of 了 le is one of the most complex parts of Chinese grammar, partly because it has two completely different functions. It can indicate completion of an action, e.g. 他喝了三杯啤酒 tā hē le sān bēi píjiǔ (he drank three glasses of beer). Sometimes, when placed at the end of a clause or a sentence, it indicates a change of some kind, e.g. 天黑了 tiān hēi le (it's gone dark).

雷 [léi] N (雷电) thunder ▶ 雷电 [léidiàn] thunder and lightning

累 [lěi] VB (积累) accumulate ▶ 累积 [lěijī] accumulate

累计 [lěijì] VB add up

肋 [lèi] N rib ▶ 肋骨 [lèigǔ] rib

泪 [lèi] N tear ▶ 眼泪 [yǎnlèi] tears (PL) ▶ 流泪 [liúlèi] shed tears

类 [lèi] I N kind ▶ 分类 [fēilèi] classify ▶ 类型 [lèixíng] type II VB be similar to ▶ 类似 [lèisì] similar to

类别 [lèibié] N category

类似 [lèisì] ADJ similar

累 [lèi] I ADJ tired II VB (使劳累) tire ▷ 别累着自己。 [Bié lèizhe zìjǐ.] Don't tire yourself out.
→ *see also*/另见 lěi

冷 [lěng] ADJ 1 (温度低) cold 2 (不热情) frosty ▶ 冷淡 [lěngdàn] give the cold shoulder to

冷藏 [lěngcáng] VB refrigerate

冷冻 [lěngdòng] VB freeze ▶ 冷冻食品 [lěngdòng shípǐn] frozen food

冷静 [lěngjìng] ADJ (沉着) cool-headed

冷饮 [lěngyǐn] N cold drink

厘 [lí] *see below*/见下文

厘米 [límǐ] MEAS centimeter

离 [lí] VB 1 (分离) leave 2 (距离) be far away from ▷ 我家离办公室不太远。 [Wǒ jiā lí bàngōngshì bù tài yuǎn.] My home is quite near to the office.

离 lí is used to express separation of two things, or distance of one thing from another: to say that X is far away from Y, say "X 离Y远", e.g. 我家离火车站不远 wǒ jiā lí huǒchēzhàn bù yuǎn (my home is not far from the train station).

离婚 [líhūn] VB divorce

离开 [líkāi] VB depart

梨 [lí] N pear

礼 [lǐ] N 1 (仪式) ceremony 2 (表示尊敬) courtesy 3 (礼物) present

礼拜 [lǐbài] N (星期) week

礼貌 [lǐmào] N manners (PL)

礼堂 [lǐtáng] N hall

礼物 [lǐwù] N present

里 [lǐ] I N 1 (反面) inside 2 (里边) inner ▶ 里屋 [lǐwū] inner room II PREP in ▷ 屋子里 [wūzi lǐ] in the room III ADV ▶ 这里 [zhèlǐ] here ▶ 那里 [nàlǐ] there IV MEAS lǐ, *a Chinese unit of length, equal to 1/3 of a mile* ▶ 英里 [yīnglǐ] mile

理 [lǐ] I N 1 (道理) reason ▶ 合理 [hélǐ] reasonable 2 (自然科学) natural science ▶ 理科 [lǐkē] science II VB 1 (管理) manage ▶ 理财 [lǐcái] manage the finances 2 (整理) tidy ▶ 理发 [lǐfà] get a haircut 3 (表示态度) acknowledge ▶ 理睬 [lǐcǎi] pay attention

理解 [lǐjiě] VB understand

理论 [lǐlùn] N theory

理想 [lǐxiǎng] I N ideal II ADJ ideal

理由 [lǐyóu] N reason

力 [lì] N 1 (物) force 2 (功能) strength 3 (体力) physical strength

力量 [lìliang] N 1 (力气) strength ▷ 这一拳力量很大。 [Zhè yī quán lìliang hěndà.] That was a very powerful punch. 2 (能力) power 3 (作用) strength ▷ 这种药的力量大。 [Zhèzhǒng yào de lìliang dà.] This medicine is very strong.

力气 [lìqi] N strength

历 [lì] N (经历) experience

历史 [lìshǐ] N history

厉 [lì] ADJ 1 (严格) strict 2 (严肃) stern

厉害 [lìhai] ADJ terrible ▷ 他口渴得厉害。 [Tā kǒukě de lìhai.] He was terribly thirsty.

立 [lì] I VB 1 (站) stand 2 (竖立) stand ... up 3 (建立) ▶ 立功 [lìgōng] make contributions 4 (制定) set ... up ▶ 立法 [lìfǎ] legislate II ADJ upright ▶ 立柜 [lìguì] wardrobe

立方 [lìfāng] I N cube II MEAS cubic ▶ 立方米 [lìfāngmǐ] cubic meter

立即 [lìjí] ADV immediately

立刻 [lìkè] ADV immediately

利 [lì] I ADJ (锋利) sharp II N 1 (利益) interest ▶ 利弊 [lìbì] pros and cons (PL) 2 (利润) profit and interest ▶ 暴利 [bàolì] staggering profits (PL) III VB benefit

利害 [lìhai] ADJ terrible ▷ 天冷得利害。 [Tiān lěng de lìhai.] It's terribly cold today.

利率 [lìlǜ] N interest rate

利润 [lìrùn] N profit

利息 [lìxī] N interest

利益 [lìyì] N benefit

利用 [lìyòng] VB 1 (物) use 2 (人) exploit

例 [lì] N (例子) example ▶ 举例 [jǔlì] give an example

例如 [lìrú] VB give an example ▷ 大商场货物齐全，例如服装，家电，食品等。 [Dà shāngchǎng huòwù qíquán, lìrú fúzhuāng, jiādiàn, shípǐn děng.] The big shopping center sells all kinds of goods, for example, clothes, household appliances, and food.

例外 [lìwài] VB be an exception

例子 [lìzi] N example

荔 [lì] *see below*/见下文

荔枝 [lìzhī] N lychee

栗 [lì] N chestnut ▶ 栗子 [lìzi] chestnut

粒 [lì] MEAS ▷ 一粒珍珠 [yīlì zhēnzhū] a pearl ▷ 三粒种子 [sānlì zhǒngzi] three seeds

measure word, used for small round objects, such as sand, grains, pills, etc.

俩 [liǎ] NUM (口) (两个) two ▷ 我俩 [wǒ liǎ] the two of us

连 [lián] I VB connect ▶ 连接 [liánjiē] link II ADV in succession ▷ 连看了几眼 [lián kàn le jǐ yǎn] glance at several times III PREP 1 (包括) including ▷ 连他4人 [lián tā sì rén] four people, including him 2 (甚至) even

连接 [liánjiē] VB connect

连忙 [liánmáng] ADV at once

连续 [liánxù] VB go on without stopping ▷ 他连续干了3天，觉都没睡。 [Tā liánxù gàn le sān tiān, jiào dōu méi shuì.] He worked for three days in a row without sleeping.

帘 [lián] N drape ▶ 窗帘 [chuānglián] drape

莲 [lián] N lotus ▶ 莲花 [liánhuā] lotus flower

联 [lián] VB unite ▶ 联赛 [liánsài] league match

联合 [liánhé] I VB (人) unite II ADJ joint

联合国 [Liánhéguó] N United Nations, UN

联络 [liánluò] VB contact ▷ 联络方式 [liánluò fāngshì] ways to maintain contact

联系 [liánxì] VB connect ▷ 理论联系实际 [lǐlùn liánxì shíjì] apply theory to practice ▶ 促进经济贸易联系 [cùjìn jīngjì màoyì liánxì] encourage economic and trade relations

脸 [liǎn] N 1 (面部) face 2 (前部) front ▶ 门脸 [ménliǎn] storefront 3 (情面) face ▶ 脸面 [liǎnmiàn] face

脸色 [liǎnsè] N (气色) complexion

练 [liàn] I VB practice ▶ 练武 [liànwǔ] practice martial arts II ADJ experienced ▶ 熟练 [shúliàn] skillful

练习 [liànxí] I VB practice II N exercise

恋 [liàn] VB 1 (恋爱) love ▶ 相恋 [xiāngliàn] fall in love with each other 2 (想念) miss ▶ 恋家 [liànjiā] be homesick

恋爱 [liàn'ài] VB love ▶ 谈恋爱 [tán liàn'ài] be in love

恋人 [liànrén] N lover

良 [liáng] ADJ good

良好 [liánghǎo] ADJ good

良心 [liángxīn] N conscience

凉 [liáng] ADJ (冷) cool
→ *see also*/另见 liàng

凉快 [liángkuai] ADJ cool

量 [liáng] VB (衡量) measure
→ *see also*/另见 liàng

粮 [liáng] N grain

粮食 [liángshi] N food

两 [liǎng] I NUM 1 (表示具体数目) two ▷ 两个小时 [liǎng gè xiǎoshí] two hours 2 (表示不定数目) a few ▷ 说两句 [shuō liǎng jù] say a few words II MEAS liang, *a Chinese unit of weight, equal to 50 grams*

When citing numbers, including cardinal numbers, ordinal numbers, telephone numbers, serial numbers, etc., 二 èr is used for the number two. However, when you want to talk about two things, you must use 两 liǎng and a measure word, e.g. 两个人 liǎng gè rén (2 people), 两杯茶 liǎng bēi chá (2 cups of tea) etc.

亮 [liàng] I ADJ (光线) bright II VB (发光) shine ▷ 灯还亮着。 [Dēng hái liàng zhe.] The lights are still lit.

凉 [liàng] VB let ... cool
→ *see also*/另见 liáng

辆 [liàng] MEAS ▷ 一辆汽车 [yī liàng qìchē] a car ▷ 两辆自行车 [liǎngliàng zìxíngchē] two bicycles

measure word, used for vehicles and bicycles

量 [liàng] N 1 (限度) capacity 2 (数量) quantity
→ *see also*/另见 liáng

晾 [liàng] VB 1 (弄干) dry 2 (晒干) air

聊 [liáo] VB (口) chat ▶ 聊天室 [liáotiānshì] chat room

聊天儿 [liáotiānr] VB (口) chat

了 [liǎo] VB 1 (完毕) finish 2 (放在动词之后表示可能) ▷ 办不了 [bàn bù liǎo] not be able to handle ▷ 受得了 [shòu de liǎo] be able to bear
→ *see also*/另见 le

了不起 [liǎobuqǐ] ADJ amazing

了解 [liǎojiě] VB 1 (知道) understand 2 (打听) find ... out

料 [liào] N (材料) material ▶ 木料 [mùliào] timber

列 [liè] I VB 1 (排列) set ... out 2 (安排) list ▶ 列举 [lièjǔ] list II N 1 (行列) rank 2 (类别) category

列车 [lièchē] N train

劣 [liè] ADJ bad ▶ 恶劣 [èliè] bad

劣质 [lièzhì] ADJ poor-quality

烈 [liè] ADJ (强烈) strong ▶ 激烈 [jīliè] fierce ▶ 烈性酒 [lièxìngjiǔ] strong liquor

猎 [liè] VB hunt ▶ 打猎 [dǎliè] go hunting

裂 [liè] VB split ▶ 分裂 [fēnliè] split ▶ 破裂 [pòliè] break

裂口 [lièkǒu] N split

拎 [līn] VB carry

邻 [lín] N neighbor ▶ 邻居 [línjū] neighbor

邻近 [línjìn] VB be close to

邻居 [línjū] N neighbor

林 [lín] N 1 (树林) wood 2 (林业) forestry ▶ 林业 [línyè] forestry

临 [lín] VB 1 (靠近) face ▶ 临危 [línwēi] face danger 2 (到达) reach ▶ 光临 [guānglín] presence 3 (将要) be about to ▶ 临产 [línchǎn] be in labor

临近 [línjìn] VB be close to ▷ 考试临近了。[Kǎoshì línjìn le.] The exams are approaching.

临时 [línshí] ADV temporarily

淋 [lín] VB drench

淋浴 [línyù] VB take a shower

鳞 [lín] N scale

吝 [lìn] ADJ stingy ▶ 吝啬 [lìnsè] stingy

灵 [líng] I ADJ 1 (灵活) nimble ▶ 灵敏 [língmǐn] agile 2 (灵验) effective II N 1 (灵魂) soul 2 (神灵) deity ▶ 精灵 [jīnglíng] spirit

灵活 [línghuó] ADJ 1 (敏捷的) agile 2 (机动的) flexible

铃 [líng] N 1 (响器) bell ▶ 铃铛 [língdang] small bell 2 (铃状物) ▶ 哑铃 [yǎlíng] dumbbell

零 [líng] I N 1 (零数) zero 2 (零头) odd ▷ 她年纪七十有零。[Tā niánjì qīshí yǒu líng.] She's seventy-odd years old. II ADJ 1 (零碎的) odd ▶ 零活 [línghuó] odd jobs (PL) ▶ 零钱 [língqián] small change 2 (部分的) spare ▶ 零件 [língjiàn] spare parts (PL) III VB CONJ ▷ 两年零三个月 [liǎng nián líng sān gè yuè] two years and three months ▷ 五元零二分 [wǔ yuán líng èr fēn] five yuan two fen

零钱 [língqián] N small change

零食 [língshí] N snack

零售 [língshòu] VB retail

零用钱 [língyòngqián] N allowance

领 [lǐng] I N 1 (衣领) collar 2 (脖颈) neck II VB 1 (带领) lead 2 (占有) possess ▶ 占领 [zhànlǐng] occupy

领带 [lǐngdài] N tie

领导 [lǐngdǎo] I VB lead ▷ 他领导有方。[Tā lǐngdǎo yǒufāng.] He's an effective leader. II N leader

领土 [lǐngtǔ] N territory

领先 [lǐngxiān] VB lead ▷ 他在比赛中遥遥领先。[Tā zài bǐsài zhōng yáoyáo lǐngxiān.] He took a runaway lead in the competition.

领袖 [lǐngxiù] N leader

领养 [lǐngyǎng] VB adopt

另 [lìng] I PRON another II ADV separately

另外 [lìngwài] I PRON other ▷ 我不喜欢这些衣服, 我喜欢另外那些。[Wǒ bù xǐhuan zhèxiē yīfu, wǒ xǐhuan lìngwài nàxiē.] I don't like these clothes, I like the others. II ADV in addition

令 [lìng] I N (命令) order II VB 1 (令) order 2 (使) make

溜 [liū] VB (走开) sneak off

溜达 [liūda] VB go for a stroll

留 [liú] VB 1 (不走) stay 2 (使留) keep ... back ▶ 挽留 [wǎnliú] persuade ... to stay 3 (留意) be careful ▶ 留神 [liúshén] be careful 4 (保留) keep 5 (积蓄) grow ▷ 留胡子 [liú húzi] grow a beard 6 (接受) accept 7 (遗留) leave ... behind 8 (留学) study abroad ▷ 留英 [liú Yīng] study in Britain

留步 [liúbù] VB stop here

留念 [liúniàn] VB keep as a souvenir

留神 [liúshén] VB be on the alert

留心 [liúxīn] VB take note

留学 [liúxué] VB study abroad

留言 [liúyán] VB leave a message

留意 [liúyì] VB look ... out

流 [liú] I VB (流动) flow ▶ 漂流 [piāoliú] drift II N 1 (水流) current ▶ 洪流 [hóngliú] torrent 2 (等级) grade ▶ 一流 [yīliú] first-class

流传 [liúchuán] VB spread

流动 [liúdòng] VB (移动) flow

流感 [liúgǎn] N the flu

流利 [liúlì] ADJ fluent

流氓 [liúmáng] N 1 (下流) perversion 2 (歹徒) hooligan

流水 [liúshuǐ] N (流动水) running water

流行 [liúxíng] VB be fashionable

瘤 [liú] N tumor ▶ 瘤子 [liúzi] tumor

柳 [liǔ] N willow ▶ 柳树 [liǔshù] willow

六 [liù] NUM six

六月 [liùyuè] N June

陆 [liù] NUM six

→ *see also*/另见 lù

This is the complex character for "six", which is mainly used in banks, on receipts, etc. to prevent mistakes and forgery.

遛 [liù] VB 1 (指人) take a stroll 2 (指动物) walk ▶ 遛狗 [liùgǒu] walk the dog

---

龙 [lóng] N dragon

龙卷风 [lóngjuǎnfēng] N tornado

龙头 [lóngtóu] N faucet

聋 [lóng] ADJ deaf

聋子 [lóngzi] N ▷ 他是个聋子。 [Tā shì gè lóngzi.] He's deaf.

笼 [lóng] N (笼子) cage ▶ 笼子 [lóngzi] cage

楼 [lóu] N 1 (楼房) tall building ▷ 教学楼 [jiàoxué lóu] teaching block 2 (楼层) floor

楼房 [lóufáng] N multistory building

楼梯 [lóutī] N stairs (PL)

搂 [lǒu] VB embrace

漏 [lòu] VB 1 (雨, 水) leak 2 (消息, 风声) divulge 3 (词, 句) leave ... out

漏斗 [lòudǒu] N funnel

露 [lòu] VB reveal

→ *see also*/另见 lù

露马脚 [lòumǎjiǎo] VB give oneself away

炉 [lú] N stove

炉灶 [lúzào] N kitchen range

卤 [lǔ] I N 1 (盐卤) bittern 2 (卤汁) thick gravy II VB stew ... in soy sauce

---

陆 [lù] N land

→ *see also*/另见 liù

陆地 [lùdì] N land

录 [lù] I N record II VB 1 (记载) record ▶ 记录 [jìlù] take notes 2 (录音) tape-record

录取 [lùqǔ] VB admit ▷ 她被剑桥大学录取了。 [Tā bèi Jiànqiáo Dàxué lùqǔ le.] She was given a place at the University of Cambridge.

录像 [lùxiàng] VB videotape

录音 [lùyīn] VB record

鹿 [lù] N deer

路 [lù] N 1 (道路) road ▶ 路标 [lùbiāo] signpost 2 (路程) journey ▷ 一路平安 [yī lù píng'ān] have a safe journey 3 (门路) means ▶ 财路 [cáilù] a means of getting rich 4 (条理) sequence ▶ 思路 [sīlù] train of thought 5 (路线) route ▶ 8路车 [bālù chē] No. 8 bus

路程 [lùchéng] N journey

路过 [lùguò] VB pass through

路口 [lùkǒu] N intersection

路线 [lùxiàn] N 1 (指交通) route 2 (指思想) line

露 [lù] I N (水珠) dew II VB reveal ▶ 暴露 [bàolù] expose

→ *see also*/另见 lòu

露天 [lùtiān] N the open air ▷ 露天剧场 [lùtiān jùchǎng] open-air theater

露营 [lùyíng] VB camp out

驴 [lǘ] N donkey

旅 [lǚ] VB travel ▶ 差旅费 [chāilǚfèi]

travel expenses (PL)
旅馆 [lǚguǎn] N hotel
旅客 [lǚkè] N passenger
旅途 [lǚtú] N journey
旅行 [lǚxíng] VB travel
旅游 [lǚyóu] N tour ▷ 旅游业 [lǚyóu yè] tourism ▷ 去国外旅游 [qù guówài lǚyóu] travel abroad

铝 [lǚ] N aluminum

律 [lǜ] N law ▶ 纪律 [jìlǜ] discipline
律师 [lǜshī] N lawyer

绿 [lǜ] ADJ green ▶ 绿灯 [lǜdēng] green light
绿化 [lǜhuà] VB make ... green ▷ 绿化荒山 [lǜhuà huāngshān] plant trees on the mountains
绿卡 [lǜkǎ] N green card
绿洲 [lǜzhōu] N oasis

乱 [luàn] I ADJ 1 (没有秩序的) disorderly ▶ 杂乱 [záluàn] messy 2 (心绪不宁的) disturbed II N (指冲突) chaos ▶ 战乱 [zhuànluàn] war chaos
乱哄哄 [luànhōnghōng] ADJ chaotic
乱七八糟 [luànqībāzāo] in a mess

略 [lè] I N 1 (简述) summary 2 (计谋) plan ▶ 策略 [cèlüè] tactic II VB 1 (夺取) capture ▶ 侵略 [qīnlüè] invade 2 (简化) simplify ▶ 省略 [shěnglüè] omit

伦 [lún] N (人伦) human relationships (PL)
伦敦 [Lúndūn] N London
伦理 [lúnlǐ] N ethics (SG)

轮 [lún] N 1 (轮子) wheel 2 (轮船) steamship
轮船 [lúnchuán] N steamship
轮换 [lúnhuàn] VB take turns
轮廓 [lúnkuò] N outline
轮流 [lúnliú] ADV in turns
轮椅 [lúnyǐ] N wheelchair

论 [lùn] I N 1 (文章) essay 2 (学说) theory ▷ 相对论 [xiāngduì lùn] theory of relativity II VB (分析) discuss ▶ 评论 [pínglùn] comment on
论文 [lùnwén] N dissertation

萝 [luó] N trailing plant
萝卜 [luóbo] N turnip ▶ 胡萝卜 [húluóbo] carrot

逻 [luó] VB patrol
逻辑 [luóji] N logic

螺 [luó] N (指动物) snail
螺钉 [luódīng] N screw

裸 [luǒ] VB expose
裸体 [luǒtǐ] ADJ naked

骆 [luò] *see below*/见下文
骆驼 [luòtuo] N camel

落 [luò] VB 1 (掉下) fall 2 (下降) go down ▶ 降落 [jiàngluò] descend 3 (降下) lower 4 (衰败) decline ▶ 衰落 [shuāiluò] wane 5 (落后) fall behind 6 (归属) fall to
→ *see also*/另见 là
落后 [luòhòu] I VB fall behind II ADJ backward

M

妈 [mā] N (口) (母亲) mom
妈妈 [māma] N (口) mom

抹 [mā] VB (擦) wipe
→ *see also*/另见 mǒ
抹布 [mābù] N cloth

麻 [má] **I** N (指植物) hemp **II** ADJ (麻木) numb
麻烦 [máfan] **I** ADJ problematic **II** N trouble **III** VB trouble ▷ 不好意思，麻烦您了。 [Bùhǎo yìsi, máfan nín le.] Sorry to trouble you.
麻将 [májiàng] N mahjong

麻将 [májiàng]
The game of mahjong is usually played by four people. 144 tiles appearing like dominoes and bearing various designs are drawn and discarded until one player has an entire hand of winning combinations. The game requires strategy as well as luck. In China, mahjong is also a popular gambling game.

麻醉 [mázuì] VB (医) anesthetize

马 [mǎ] N horse
马达 [mǎdá] N motor
马虎 [mǎhu] ADJ careless
马拉松 [mǎlāsōng] N marathon
马路 [mǎlù] N road
马上 [mǎshàng] ADV right away ▷ 他马上就到。 [Tā mǎshàng jiù dào.] He'll be here right away.
马戏 [mǎxì] N circus

码 [mǎ] N numeral ▶ 页码 [yèmǎ] page number
码头 [mǎtou] N pier

蚂 [mǎ] *see below*/见下文
蚂蚁 [mǎyǐ] N ant

骂 [mà] VB **1** (侮辱) insult **2** (斥责) tell ... off

吗 [ma] AUX WORD (表示疑问) ▷ 你去银行吗？ [Nǐ qù yínháng ma?] Are you going to the bank?
吗 ma is added to the end of any statement to turn it into a simple yes/no question, e.g. 你忙吗？ Nǐ máng ma? (Are you busy?), whereas 呢 ne is added to the end of a statement to form a tentative question, or to indicate that a response is expected, e.g. 你好吗？我很好，你呢？Nǐ hǎo ma? Wǒ hěn hǎo, nǐ ne? (How are you? Fine, and you?).

嘛 [ma] AUX WORD **1** (表示显而易见) ▷ 事实就是这样嘛！ [Shìshí jiùshì zhèyàng ma!] That's just the way things are! **2** (表示期望) ▷ 别不高兴嘛！ [Bié bù gāoxìng ma!] Please don't be unhappy.

埋 [mái] VB **1** (盖住) bury **2** (隐藏) hide
→ *see also*/另见 mán
埋葬 [máizàng] VB bury

买 [mǎi] VB **1** (购买) buy ▷ 不是每个人都买得起房。 [Bùshì měigè rén dōu mǎideqǐ fáng.] Not everyone can afford to buy a flat. ▷ 我去市场买东西。 [Wǒ qù shìchǎng mǎi dōngxi.] I'm going shopping in the market. **2** (换取) win ... over ▶ 买通 [mǎitōng] buy ... off
买单 [mǎidān] VB (方) pay a bill ▷ 买单！ [Mǎidān!] The bill, please!
买卖 [mǎimai] N **1** (生意) business **2** (商店) store

迈 [mài] VB step ▶ 迈步 [màibù] stride

麦 [mài] N (麦类粮食) wheat ▶ 燕麦 [yànmài] oats (PL)
麦克风 [màikèfēng] N microphone, mike (口)

卖 [mài] VB (出售) sell ▷ 书都卖完了。 [Shū dōu mài wán le.] The books are all sold out.

卖弄 [màinong] VB show off

脉 [mài] N (脉搏) pulse ▶ 号脉 [hàomài] feel a pulse

脉搏 [màibó] N pulse

埋 [mán] *see below*/见下文
→ *see also*/另见 mái

埋怨 [mányuàn] VB **1** (指责) blame **2** (抱怨) complain

馒 [mán] *see below*/见下文

馒头 [mántou] N steamed bun

瞒 [mán] VB hide the truth from ▷ 别瞒着我们！ [Bié mán zhe wǒmen!] Don't keep us in the dark!

满 [mǎn] **I** ADJ **1** (充实) full **2** (全) complete **II** VB **1** (使充满) fill **2** (到) reach ▷ 孩子刚满六岁。 [Háizi gāng mǎn liùsuì.] The child has just turned six years old. **III** ADV fully

满意 [mǎnyì] VB be satisfied

满足 [mǎnzú] VB **1** (感到满意) be satisfied **2** (使满足) satisfy

漫 [màn] VB overflow

漫长 [màncháng] ADJ endless

漫画 [mànhuà] N comic strip

漫延 [mànyán] VB spread

慢 [màn] **I** ADJ (缓慢) slow **II** VB slow ▷ 慢点儿！ [Màn diǎnr!] Slow down! ▷ 钟慢了十分钟。 [Zhōng màn le shí fēnzhōng.] The clock is ten minutes slow.

忙 [máng] **I** ADJ busy **II** VB be busy with ▷ 你这一段忙什么呢？ [Nǐ zhè yīduàn máng shénme ne?] What's been keeping you busy recently?

盲 [máng] ADJ blind ▶ 文盲 [wénmáng] illiterate

盲目 [mángmù] ADJ blind

盲文 [mángwén] N braille

蟒 [mǎng] N (动物) python

猫 [māo] N cat

猫儿眼 [māoryǎn] N spyhole

毛 [máo] **I** N **1** (毛发) hair ▶ 羽毛 [yǔmáo] feather **2** (指食物上) mold ▶ 面包上长毛了。 [Miànbāo shàng zhǎng máo le.] The bread is moldy. **3** (指动物) fur ▶ 毛皮 [máopí] fur **4** (羊毛) wool ▶ 毛衣 [máoyī] sweater **5** (中国货币单位) mao, *unit of Chinese currency, 1/10 yuan* **II** ADJ (不纯) gross ▶ 毛重 [máozhòng] gross weight

毛笔 [máobǐ] N brush pen

毛病 [máobìng] N **1** (故障) problem **2** (缺点) shortcoming **3** (疾病) illness

毛巾 [máojīn] N towel

毛孔 [máokǒng] N pore

矛 [máo] N spear

矛盾 [máodùn] **I** N **1** (相抵之处) conflict **2** (哲) contradiction **II** ADJ uncertain

锚 [máo] N anchor

茂 [mào] ADJ **1** (茂盛) luxuriant **2** (丰富) abundant

茂盛 [màoshèng] ADJ flourishing

冒 [mào] VB **1** (往外) give ... off ▷ 锅冒烟了。 [Guō mào yān le.] The wok is giving off smoke. **2** (不顾) risk ▷ 冒着生命危险 [màozhe shēngmìng wēixiǎn] putting one's life at risk **3** (假充) pretend to be ▶ 冒牌 [màopái] bogus

冒充 [màochōng] VB pass ... off as

冒牌 [màopái] VB pirate ▷ 冒牌商品 [màopái shāngpǐn] pirated goods

冒险 [màoxiǎn] VB take a risk

贸 [mào] VB trade ▶ 外贸 [wàimào] foreign trade

贸易 [màoyì] N trade

帽 [mào] N (帽子) hat

帽子 [màozi] N (字) hat

貌 [mào] N (相貌, 外表) appearance

没 [méi] **I** VB not have ▶ 没关系 [méiguānxi] it doesn't matter ▷ 屋子里没人。[Wūzi lǐ méi rén.] There's no one in the room. **II** ADV not ▷ 他没看过大海。 [Tā méi kànguò dàhǎi.] He's never seen the sea before.

→ *see also*/另见 mò

Constructing negating sentences in Chinese is very straightforward: just use 不 bù before the verb, e.g. 我不喝酒。Wǒ bù hējiǔ. (I don't drink alcohol). The only exception is the verb 有 yǒu, to have, for which you must use 没 méi, e.g. 我没有钱。 Wǒ méiyǒu qián. (I don't have any money).

没错儿 [méicuòr] VB that's right

没劲 [méijìn] **I** VB have no energy **II** ADJ uninteresting

没门儿 [méiménr] VB (不可能) be impossible

没事 [méishì] VB **1** (有空) be free ▷ 我今晚没事。 [Wǒ jīnwǎn méishì.] I'm free tonight. **2** (不要紧) ▷ 没事。 [Méishì.] It doesn't matter.

没有 [méiyǒu] **I** VB **1** (不具有) not have **2** (不存在) there is not **3** (全都不) ▷ 没有一个答案是正确的。[Méiyǒu yīgè dá'àn shì zhèngquè de.] None of the answers is correct. **4** (不如) be not as ... as ... ▷ 他没有你努力。 [Tā méiyǒu nǐ nǔlì.] He's not as hard-working as you. **5** (不到) be less than ▷ 他们干了没有两个小时就休息了。 [Tāmen gàn le méiyǒu liǎnggè xiǎoshí jiù xiūxi le.] They had been working for less than two hours when they took a rest. **II** ADV **1** (尚未) not yet ▷ 她还没有到。 [Tā hái méiyǒu dào.] She hasn't arrived yet. **2** (未曾) never before ▷ 我没有吃过西餐。 [Wǒ méiyǒu chīguò xīcān.] I have never eaten Western food before.

没辙 [méizhé] VB (方) not be able to do anything about

玫 [méi] *see below*/见下文

玫瑰 [méigui] N rose

眉 [méi] N (眉毛) eyebrow ▶ 眉毛 [méimao] eyebrow

媒 [méi] N **1** (媒人) matchmaker ▶ 做媒 [zuòméi] be a matchmaker **2** (媒介) intermediary

媒体 [méitǐ] N media

煤 [méi] N coal

煤气 [méiqì] N **1** (指燃料) gas **2** (指有毒气体) carbon monoxide ▷ 煤气中毒 [méiqì zhòngdú] carbon monoxide poisoning

霉 [méi] VB **1** (指食物) mold **2** (指衣物) mildew

每 [měi] **I** ADJ every, each ▶ 每次 [měicì] every time ▷ 每个晚上 [měi gè wǎnshang] every evening **II** ADV every time ▷ 每走一步，他的脚都很疼。 [Měi zǒu yī bù, tāde jiǎo dōu hěn téng.] His feet ache with every step he takes.

美 [měi] **I** ADJ **1** (美丽) beautiful **2** (好) good ▷ 我们的明天会更美。[Wǒmen de míngtiān huì gèng měi.] Our future will be even better. **II** N **1** (美丽) beauty **2** (美洲) North and South America ▶ 南美 [Nánměi] South America ▶ 北美 [Běiměi] North America **3** (美国) the USA

美国 [Měiguó] N the US, the USA ▶ 美国人 [Měiguórén] American

美好 [měihǎo] ADJ wonderful

美丽 [měilì] ADJ beautiful

美满 [měimǎn] ADJ perfectly satisfactory

美容 [měiróng] VB make oneself more beautiful ▷ 美容店 [měiróng diàn] beauty salon ▷ 美容手术 [měiróng shǒushù] cosmetic surgery

美食 [měishí] N delicacy

美术 [měishù] N 1 (造型艺术) fine arts (PL) 2 (绘画) painting

美元 [měiyuán] N US dollar

妹 [mèi] N 1 (指同胞) younger sister 2 (指亲戚) ▶ 表妹 [biǎomèi] cousin

妹妹 [mèimei] (指同胞) younger sister

魅 [mèi] N demon

魅力 [mèilì] N charm

闷 [mēn] I ADJ stuffy II VB 1 (盖) cover ... tightly 2 (不出声) keep silent 3 (呆) shut oneself in
→ *see also*/另见 mèn

闷热 [mēnrè] ADJ muggy

门 [mén] I N 1 (指出入口) door ▶ 门口 [ménkǒu] entrance 2 (指开关装置) switch ▶ 电门 [diànmén] switch II MEAS ▷ 5门课 [wǔ mén kè] five courses ▷ 一门新技术 [yī mén xīn jìshù] a new technology

measure word, used for academic subjects, courses, and technology

门类 [ménlèi] N category

门卫 [ménwèi] N guard

门诊 [ménzhěn] N outpatient department

闷 [mèn] ADJ 1 (烦) low 2 (无聊) bored
→ *see also*/另见 mēn

们 [men] SUFFIX ▶ 我们 [wǒmen] we, us ▶ 你们 [nǐmen] you ▶ 他们 [tāmen] they, them

蒙 [mēng] VB 1 (欺骗) deceive 2 (乱猜) make a wild guess
→ *see also*/另见 méng, Měng

蒙骗 [mēngpiàn] VB deceive

蒙 [méng] I VB 1 (遮盖) cover 2 (受到) receive II ADJ ignorant ▶ 启蒙 [qǐméng] enlighten
→ *see also*/另见 mēng, Měng

蒙混 [ménghùn] VB deceive ▷ 蒙混过关 [ménghùn guòguān] muddle through

猛 [měng] I ADJ (凶猛) fierce II ADV 1 (猛烈) fiercely 2 (忽然) suddenly

猛烈 [měngliè] ADJ fierce

蒙 [Měng] N Mongolia ▶ 蒙古 [Měnggǔ] Mongolia ▶ 蒙古人 [Měnggǔrén] Mongolian ▶ 内蒙古 [Nèiměnggǔ] Inner Mongolia
→ *see also*/另见 mēng, méng

梦 [mèng] I N 1 (睡梦) dream ▶ 白日梦 [báirìmèng] daydream ▶ 做梦 [zuòmèng] have a dream 2 (幻想) illusion II VB dream

梦话 [mènghuà] N 1 (字) ▷ 说梦话 [shuō mènghuà] talk in one's sleep 2 (喻) nonsense

梦想 [mèngxiǎng] VB dream

弥 [mí] VB fill

弥补 [míbǔ] VB make ... up

迷 [mí] I VB 1 (迷失) be lost ▶ 迷路 [mílù] lose one's way 2 (迷恋) become obsessed with 3 (迷惑) be deluded II N fan ▶ 球迷 [qiúmí] sports fan ▷ 足球迷 [zúqiú mí] soccer fan

迷你 [mínǐ] ADJ mini ▷ 迷你裙 [mínǐ qún] mini-skirt

迷信 [míxìn] VB 1 (鬼神) be superstitious about 2 (人或事) have blind faith in

猕 [mí] *see below*/见下文

猕猴桃 [míhóutáo] N kiwi fruit

谜 [mí] N 1 (谜语) riddle 2 (神秘) mystery

谜语 [míyǔ] N riddle

米 [mǐ] I N (稻米) rice ▶ 米饭 [mǐfàn] cooked rice II MEAS meter

秘 [mì] I ADJ secret II VB keep ... secret III N secretary

秘密 [mìmì] N secret ▷ 一定要保守秘密！ [Yīdìng yào bǎoshǒu mìmì!] You must keep this a secret!

秘书 [mìshū] N secretary

密 [mì] ADJ 1 (空隙小) dense 2 (关系

近) close ▶ 亲密 [qīnmì] intimate 3 (精致) meticulous ▶ 精密 [jīngmì] precise 4 (秘密) secret ▶ 保密 [bǎomì] keep sth a secret

密度 [mìdù] N density

密封 [mìfēng] VB seal ... tightly

密码 [mìmǎ] N 1 (口令) password 2 (符号系统) code

密切 [mìqiè] ADJ close

幂 [mì] N (数) power

蜜 [mì] I N honey II ADJ sweet

蜜蜂 [mìfēng] N bee

蜜月 [mìyuè] N honeymoon

眠 [mián] VB 1 (睡) sleep ▶ 失眠 [shīmián] suffer from insomnia 2 (冬眠) hibernate

棉 [mián] N cotton

棉花 [miánhua] N (指植物) cotton

棉衣 [miányī] N cotton-padded clothing

免 [miǎn] VB 1 (除去) exempt ▶ 免试 [miǎnshì] be exempt from an exam 2 (避免) avoid ▶ 免不了 [miǎnbùliǎo] be unavoidable 3 (不要) not be allowed ▷ 闲人免进 [xiánrén miǎnjìn] staff only

免费 [miǎnfèi] VB be free of charge ▷ 注册一个免费电子邮箱 [zhùcè yīgè miǎnfèi diànzǐ yǒuxiāng] register for free email

免疫 [miǎnyì] N immunity

勉 [miǎn] VB 1 (努力) strive 2 (勉励) encourage 3 (勉强) force ... to carry on

勉强 [miǎnqiǎng] I VB 1 (尽力) push oneself hard ▷ 做事不要太勉强。 [Zuòshì bùyào tài miǎnqiǎng.] Don't push yourself too hard. 2 (强迫) force ▷ 不要勉强孩子学钢琴。 [Bùyào miǎnqiǎng háizi xué gāngqín.] Don't force the child to study the piano. II ADJ 1 (不情愿) reluctant ▷ 我让他帮忙，他勉强答应了。 [Wǒ ràng tā bāngmáng, tā miǎnqiǎng dāyìng le.] I asked him to help, and he reluctantly agreed. 2 (凑合) barely enough ▷ 他挣的钱勉强够自己花。 [Tā zhèng de qián miǎnqiǎng gòu zìjǐ huā.] The money he earned was barely enough to support himself. 3 (牵强) far-fetched ▷ 这个理论有点勉强。 [Zhègè lǐlùn yǒudiǎn miǎnqiǎng.] This theory is a bit far-fetched.

冕 [miǎn] N 1 (皇冠) crown ▶ 加冕 [jiāmiǎn] be crowned 2 (冠军头衔) title ▶ 卫冕 [wèimiǎn] defend one's title

缅 [miǎn] ADJ (书) remote

缅甸 [Miǎndiàn] N Myanmar

面 [miàn] I N 1 (脸) face 2 (表面) surface 3 (方位) aspect ▶ 前面 [qiánmiàn] front 4 (情面) self-respect 5 (粉末) powder ▶ 辣椒面 [làjiāomiàn] chilli powder 6 (磨成粉的粮食) flour ▶ 面粉 [miànfěn] flour 7 (面条) noodles (PL) II VB (朝) face III MEAS 1 (用于扁平物) ▷ 一面墙 [yī miàn qiáng] a wall ▷ 两面镜子 [liǎng miàn jìngzi] two mirrors

> measure word, used for objects with a flat surface, such as walls, mirrors, drums, etc.

2 (指见面的次数) ▷ 我只见过她一面。 [Wǒ zhǐ jiànguò tā yī miàn.] I've only met her once before. ▷ 我们见过几面。 [Wǒmen jiànguò jǐ miàn.] We've met a few times.

> measure word, used for encounters between two people

面包 [miànbāo] N bread ▶ 面包房 [miànbāofáng] bakery

面对 [miànduì] VB face

面积 [miànjī] N area

面临 [miànlín] VB face

面貌 [miànmào] N 1 (面容) features (PL) 2 (喻) appearance

面前 [miànqián] N ▷ 在困难面前 [zài kùnnan miànqián] in the face of difficulties

面试 [miànshì] VB have an interview

面条 [miàntiáo] N noodles (PL) ▷ 意大利面条 [Yìdàlì miàntiáo] spaghetti

面子 [miànzi] N 1 (体面) face ▷ 丢面子 [diū miànzi] lose face 2 (情面) feelings (PL) ▷ 给我点面子, 你就答应吧！ [Gěi wǒ diǎn miànzi, nǐ jiù dāying ba!] Show some respect for my feelings and say yes!

苗 [miáo] N (指植物) seedling ▶ 树苗 [shùmiáo] sapling

苗条 [miáotiao] ADJ slim

描 [miáo] VB 1 (画) trace 2 (涂抹) touch ... up

描述 [miáoshù] VB describe

描写 [miáoxiě] VB describe

瞄 [miáo] VB fix one's eyes on

瞄准 [miáozhǔn] VB (对准) take aim

秒 [miǎo] MEAS (指时间) second ▷ 5秒 [wǔ miǎo] five seconds

妙 [miào] ADJ 1 (好) wonderful 2 (巧妙) ingenious

庙 [miào] N temple

灭 [miè] VB 1 (熄灭) go out 2 (使熄灭) extinguish ▶ 灭火器 [mièhuǒqì] fire extinguisher 3 (淹没) submerge 4 (消亡) perish 5 (消灭) kill

灭绝 [mièjué] VB (消亡) become extinct

民 [mín] N 1 (人民) the people (PL) 2 (人) person ▶ 网民 [wǎngmín] internet user 3 (民间) folk 4 (非军方) civilian

民歌 [míngē] N folk song

民间 [mínjiān] N 1 (百姓中间) folk ▷ 民间传说 [mínjiān zǔzhī] folklore 2 (非官方) ▷ 民间组织 [mínjiān zǔzhi] non-governmental organization

民警 [mínjǐng] N civil police

民主 [mínzhǔ] I N democracy II ADJ democratic

民族 [mínzú] N nationality ▷ 少数民族 [shǎoshù mínzú] ethnic minority

---

敏 [mǐn] ADJ 1 (快) quick ▶ 敏感 [mǐngǎn] sensitive 2 (聪明) clever ▶ 机敏 [jīmǐn] quick-witted

敏捷 [mǐnjié] ADJ quick

名 [míng] I N 1 (名字) name ▷ 书名 [shū míng] book title 2 (名声) reputation II ADJ famous ▶ 名著 [míngzhù] classics (PL) III MEAS 1 (指人) ▷ 5名工人 [wǔ míng gōngrén] five workers ▷ 10名教师 [shí míng jiàoshī] ten teachers

> measure word, used for people of any profession

2 (指名次) ▷ 期末考试她得了第一名。 [Qīmò kǎoshì tā dé le dìyī míng.] She came first in the end-of-term exams.

> measure word, used for rankings in competitions and exams

名称 [míngchēng] N name

名次 [míngcì] N ranking

名单 [míngdān] N list of names

名额 [míng'é] N quota

名牌 [míngpái] N famous name ▷ 名牌服装 [míngpái fúzhuāng] designer clothing

名片 [míngpiàn] N business card

名气 [míngqi] N fame

名人 [míngrén] N famous person

名声 [míngshēng] N reputation

名胜 [míngshèng] N tourist site

名字 [míngzi] N name ▷ 你叫什么名字？ [Nǐ jiào shénme míngzi?] What's your name?

明 [míng] I ADJ 1 (亮) bright 2 (清楚) clear 3 (公开) open II N 1 (视力) sight ▶ 失明 [shīmíng] lose one's eyesight 2 (光明) light III VB 1 (懂)

understand ▶ 明理 [mínglǐ] be understanding 2 (显示) show ▶ 表明 [biǎomíng] indicate

明白 [míngbai] **I** ADJ **1** (清楚) clear **2** (聪明) sensible **3** (公开) explicit **II** VB understand

明亮 [míngliàng] ADJ **1** (亮堂) bright **2** (发亮) shining **3** (明白) clear

明确 [míngquè] **I** ADJ clear-cut **II** VB clarify

明显 [míngxiǎn] ADJ obvious

明星 [míngxīng] N star

明智 [míngzhì] ADJ sensible

命 [mìng] N **1** (性命) life **2** (命运) fate **3** (寿命) lifespan **4** (命令) order

命令 [mìnglìng] VB order

命名 [mìngmíng] VB name

命运 [mìngyùn] N fate

摸 [mō] VB **1** (触摸) stroke **2** (摸黑行动) feel one's way ▶ 摸索 [mōsuǒ] grope

模 [mó] **I** N model ▶ 模型 [móxíng] model **II** VB imitate
→ *see also*/另见 mú

模范 [mófàn] ADJ model

模仿 [mófǎng] VB imitate

模糊 [móhu] ADJ blurred

模拟 [mónǐ] VB imitate ▶ 模拟考试 [mónǐ kǎoshì] mock exam

模式 [móshì] N pattern

模特儿 [mótèr] N model

模型 [móxíng] N **1** (样品) model **2** (模具) mold

膜 [mó] N (膜状物) film ▶ 保鲜膜 [bǎoxiānmó] Saran wrap®

摩 [mó] VB (摩擦) rub … together

摩擦 [mócā] **I** VB rub **II** N **1** (阻力) friction **2** (冲突) conflict

摩托车 [mótuōchē] N motorbike

磨 [mó] VB **1** (摩擦) rub **2** (指用磨料) grind ▶ 磨刀 [módāo] sharpen a knife **3** (折磨) wear … down **4** (纠缠) pester **5** (拖延) dawdle
→ *see also*/另见 mò

磨擦 [mócā] N rub

磨蹭 [móceng] ADJ sluggish

磨合 [móhé] VB (适应) adapt to each other

磨炼 [móliàn] VB steel

磨损 [mósǔn] VB wear … out

蘑 [mó] N mushroom

蘑菇 [mógu] N mushroom

魔 [mó] **I** N **1** (魔鬼) demon **2** (魔法) magic **II** ADJ magic

魔法 [mófǎ] N magic

魔鬼 [móguǐ] N devil

魔术 [móshù] N magic

魔术师 [móshùshī] N magician

抹 [mǒ] VB **1** (涂抹) apply **2** (擦) wipe **3** (去除) erase
→ *see also*/另见 mā

末 [mò] N (尾) end ▷ 世纪末 [shìjì mò] the end of the century

末尾 [mòwěi] N end

没 [mò] VB **1** (沉没) sink **2** (漫过) overflow **3** (隐没) disappear ▶ 出没 [chūmò] appear and disappear
→ *see also*/另见 méi

没收 [mòshōu] VB confiscate

沫 [mò] N foam ▶ 泡沫 [pàomò] bubble

茉 [mò] *see below*/见下文

茉莉 [mòlì] N jasmine

陌 [mò] N (书) footpath

陌生 [mòshēng] ADJ unfamiliar

陌生人 [mòshēngrén] N stranger

墨 [mò] **I** N (墨汁) ink ▶ 墨汁 [mòzhī] ink **II** ADJ dark ▶ 墨镜 [mòjìng] sunglasses

默 [mò] VB **1** (不出声) do … silently ▶ 默哀 [mò'āi] pay … silent tribute **2** (默写) write … from memory

磨 [mò] **I** N mill ▶ 磨坊 [mòfáng] mill **II** VB grind
→ *see also*/另见 mó

谋 [móu] N plan ▶ 阴谋 [yīnmóu] plot
谋杀 [móushā] VB murder
谋生 [móushēng] VB make a living

某 [mǒu] PRON (指不确定的人或事) ▶ 某人 [mǒurén] somebody

模 [mú] N mold
→ *see also*/另见 mó
模样 [múyàng] N (相貌) looks (PL)

母 [mǔ] I N 1 (母亲) mother 2 (指长辈女子) ▶ 祖母 [zǔmǔ] grandmother 3 (喻) (基础) origin II ADJ (雌性) female ▶ 母牛 [mǔniú] cow
母亲 [mǔqīn] N mother

拇 [mǔ] N *see below*/见下文
拇指 [mǔzhǐ] N 1 (指手) thumb 2 (指脚) big toe

木 [mù] I N 1 (树) tree 2 (木材) wood II ADJ (僵) numb
木材 [mùcái] N timber
木匠 [mùjiang] N carpenter
木偶 [mù'ǒu] N puppet
木头 [mùtou] N wood

目 [mù] N 1 (眼睛) eye 2 (条目) item
目标 [mùbiāo] N 1 (对象) target 2 (目的) goal
目的 [mùdì] N 1 (指地点) destination 2 (结果) aim 3 (企图) intention
目光 [mùguāng] N 1 (视线) gaze 2 (眼神) look
目录 [mùlù] N 1 (指事物) catalog 2 (指书刊中) table of contents
目前 [mùqián] N present ▷ 到目前为止 [dào mùqián wéizhǐ] to date ▷ 我们目前的任务 [wǒmen mùqián de rènwù] our current tasks

牧 [mù] VB herd
牧民 [mùmín] N herdsman
牧师 [mùshī] N priest
牧业 [mùyè] N animal husbandry

募 [mù] VB (钱款) raise
募捐 [mùjuān] VB collect donations

墓 [mù] N grave
墓碑 [mùbēi] N gravestone
墓地 [mùdì] N graveyard

幕 [mù] N (帷幔) curtain ▶ 银幕 [yínmù] the silver screen

睦 [mù] VB get on ▶ 和睦 [hémù] harmonious

穆 [mù] ADJ solemn
穆斯林 [mùsīlín] N Muslim

N

拿 [ná] VB **1** (握) hold **2** (得) get

哪 [nǎ] PRON **1** (什么) which ▷ 你喜欢哪种音乐？ [nǐ xǐhuan nǎ zhǒng yīnyuè?] What kind of music do you like? ▷ 哪个人是李先生？ [nǎ gè rén shì Lǐ Xiānsheng?] Which one is Mr. Li? **2** (任何一个) any ▷ 你哪天来都行。 [nǐ nǎ tiān lái dōu xíng.] You can come any day.

哪个 [nǎge] PRON which

哪里 [nǎli] PRON **1** (用于问处所) ▷ 你住在哪里？ [nǐ zhù zài nǎli?] Where do you live? **2** (指某一地方) ▷ 我们应该在哪里见过。 [wǒmen yīnggāi zài nǎli jiànguo.] I'm sure we've met somewhere before. **3** (谦) ▷ 哪里, 哪里, 你过奖了。 [nǎli, nǎli, nǐ guòjiǎng le.] No, no, it was nothing.

哪些 [nǎxiē] PRON which

那 [nà] **I** PRON that ▷ 那些人 [nàxiē rén] those people **II** CONJ then ▷ 你想买, 那就买吧。 [nǐ xiǎng mǎi, nà jiù mǎi ba.] If you want to buy it, then buy it.

那边 [nàbiān] N that side

那个 [nàge] PRON (指代人, 事或物) that

那里 [nàli] PRON ▷ 我去过那里。 [wǒ qùguo nàli.] I've been there. ▷ 我也要去那里吗? [wǒ yě yào qù nàli ma?] Shall I go over there as well?

那么 [nàme] PRON **1** (表示程度) ▷ 你不该那么相信他。 [nǐ bù gāi nàme xiāngxìn tā.] You shouldn't trust him so much. **2** (表示方式) ▷ 你别那么想。 [nǐ bié nàme xiǎng.] Don't think in that way.

那些 [nàxiē] PRON those

那样 [nàyàng] ADV ▷ 我没有说过那样的话。 [wǒ méiyǒu shuōguo nàyàng de huà.] I never said anything like that.

奶 [nǎi] N milk ▶ 酸奶 [suānnǎi] yoghurt

奶酪 [nǎilào] N cheese

奶奶 [nǎinai] N (父方的) granny

耐 [nài] VB **1** (指人) endure ▶ 耐性 [nàixìng] patience **2** (指材料) be resistant ▶ 耐用 [nàiyòng] enduring

耐力 [nàilì] N stamina

耐心 [nàixīn] ADJ patient

男 [nán] N (男性) male

男孩子 [nánháizi] N boy

男朋友 [nánpéngyou] N boyfriend

男人 [nánrén] N man

南 [nán] N south ▶ 东南 [dōngnán] south-east ▶ 西南 [xīnán] south-west

南边 [nánbiān] N the south

南部 [nánbù] N southern part

南方 [nánfāng] N the South

南极 [nánjí] N South Pole

难 [nán] ADJ **1** (困难) hard **2** (不好) bad, baffle

难道 [nándào] ADV ▷ 你难道还不明白吗？ [nǐ nándào hái bù míngbai ma?] How can you not understand? ▷ 难道你就不累？ [nándào nǐ jiù bù lèi?] Aren't you tired?

难过 [nánguò] **I** VB have a hard time **II** ADJ upset

难看 [nánkàn] ADJ **1** (丑) ugly **2** (不体面) ashamed

难免 [nánmiǎn] VB be unavoidable

难受 [nánshòu] VB **1** (指身体) not feel well **2** (指心情) feel down

脑 [nǎo] N **1** (生理) brain **2** (脑筋) brain **3** (头部) head **4** (头领) leader ▶ 首脑 [shǒunǎo] head

脑袋 [nǎodi] N head

脑子 [nǎozi] N brain

闹 [nào] **I** ADJ noisy **II** VB **1** (吵闹) have a row ▷ 闹别扭 [nào bièniu] fall out **2** (病, 灾难) suffer from ▷ 闹

肚子 [nào dùzi] have diarrhea
闹钟 [nàozhōng] N alarm clock

呢 [ne] AUX WORD 1 (表示疑问) ▷ 你们都走，我呢？ [nǐmen dōu zǒu, wǒ ne?] If you all go, what about me? ▷ 我到底错在哪儿呢？ [wǒ dàodǐ cuò zài nǎr ne?] What did I actually do wrong? 2 (表示陈述) ▷ 离北京还远着呢。 [lí Běijīng hái yuǎnzhe ne.] Beijing is still quite far. 3 (表示持续) ▷ 老师还在办公室呢。 [lǎoshī hái zài bàngōngshì ne.] The teacher is still in the office.
→ *see also*/另见 ní

呢 ne is added to the end of a statement to form a tentative question, or to indicate that a response is expected, e.g. 你好吗？我很好，你呢？ Nǐ hǎo ma? Wǒ hěn hǎo, nǐ ne? (How are you? Fine, and you?). It may also be used to stress continuity, e.g. 我还在吃饭呢 Wǒ hái zài chīfàn ne (I am still eating dinner), whereas 吗 ma is added to the end of any statement to turn it into a simple yes/no question, e.g. 你忙吗？ Nǐ máng ma? (Are you busy?)

内 [nèi] N (里头) inside ▸ 室内 [shìnèi] indoor ▸ 内地 [nèidì] inland ▸ 他在一个月内完成了任务。 [tā zài yī gè yuè nèi wánchéngle rènwu.] He finished the task within a month.
内部 [nèibù] ADJ internal
内服 [nèifú] VB take orally
内行 [neìháng] N expert
内科 [nèikē] N internal medicine
内容 [nèiróng] N content
内向 [nèixiàng] ADJ introverted

能 [néng] I N 1 (能力) ability 2 (物)(能量) energy ▸ 能量 [néngliàng] energy II ADJ capable III AUX VB can

能 néng, 会 huì, and 可以 kěyǐ can all be used to express ability and are sometimes used interchangeably. Strictly, 能 néng should be used to express physical ability, e.g. 我能跑得很快 wǒ néng pǎo de hěn kuài (I can run very fast), while 会 huì should express a learned ability, e.g. 我会说法语 wǒ huì shuō Fǎyǔ (I can speak French). Both 能 néng and 可以 kěyǐ can express being able to do something because you have been granted permission, e.g. 你能/可以借我的照相机 nǐ néng/kěyǐ jiè wǒ de zhàoxiàngjī (you can/may borrow my camera).

能干 [nénggàn] ADJ capable
能够 [nénggòu] VB be able to
能力 [nénglì] N ability
能源 [néngyuán] N energy

呢 [ní] N woolen cloth
→ *see also*/另见 ne
呢子 [nízi] N woolen cloth

泥 [ní] N (指土) mud

你 [nǐ] PRON 1 (称对方) you 2 (你的) your ▸ 你家有几口人？ [nǐ jiā yǒu jǐ kǒu rén?] How many people are there in your family?
你们 [nǐmen] PRON you (PL)

腻 [nì] ADJ (太油) oily

蔫 [niān] ADJ (枯萎) withered

年 [nián] I N 1 (时间单位) year 2 (元旦或春节) New Year 3 (岁数) age II ADJ annual
年代 [niándài] N (时代) period
年级 [niánjí] N grade
年纪 [niánjì] N age
年龄 [niánlíng] N age
年轻 [niánqīng] ADJ young

黏 [nián] ADJ sticky

念 [niàn] VB 1 (读) read 2 (上学)

study

念叨 [niàndao] VB (唠叨) nag

念书 [niànshū] VB study

念头 [niàntou] N idea

鸟 [niǎo] N bird

尿 [niào] I N urine ▶ 撒尿 [sāniào] urinate II VB urinate

镊 [niè] N tweezers (PL) ▶ 镊子 [nièzi] tweezers (PL)

您 [nín] PRON you ▷ 您慢走！ [nín màn zǒu!] Mind how you go!

宁 [níng] ADJ peaceful
→ *see also*/另见 nìng

拧 [níng] VB 1 (毛巾, 衣服) wring 2 (皮肤) pinch

柠 [níng] *see below*/见下文

柠檬 [níngméng] N lemon

宁 [nìng] ADV ▶ 宁愿 [nìngyuàn] would rather
→ *see also*/另见 níng

牛 [niú] N 1 (指动物) cow ▶ 公牛 [gōngniú] bull 2 (指肉) beef ▶ 牛肉 [niúròu] beef

牛奶 [niúnǎi] N milk

牛仔裤 [niúzǎikù] N jeans (PL)

扭 [niǔ] VB 1 (掉转) turn around 2 (拧) twist 3 (崴) sprain

纽 [niǔ] N (扣子) button ▶ 纽扣 [niǔkòu] button

纽约 [Niǔyuē] N New York

农 [nóng] N 1 (农业) agriculture 2 (农民) farmer

农场 [nóngchǎng] N farm

农村 [nóngcūn] N the countryside

农历 [nónglì] N lunar calendar

农民 [nóngmín] N farmer

农业 [nóngyè] N agriculture

浓 [nóng] ADJ 1 (指气味, 味道) strong 2 (指烟雾) thick 3 (指兴趣) great ▷ 他对语言有很浓的兴趣。 [tā duì yǔyán yǒu hěn nóng de xìngqù.] He has a great interest in languages.

浓缩 [nóngsuō] I VB condense II ADJ condensed

弄 [nòng] VB 1 (搞) make 2 (设法取得) get

努 [nǔ] VB (劲儿) make an effort ▷ 我们再努把力。 [wǒmen zài nǔ bǎ lì.] Let's make one last effort.

努力 [nǔlì] VB try hard ▷ 我会尽最大努力。 [wǒ huì jìn zuìdà nǔlì.] I'll try my very best.

怒 [nù] I ADJ (生气) angry ▶ 恼怒 [nǎonù] furious II N anger ▶ 发怒 [fānù] lose one's temper

女 [nǚ] N 1 (女子) woman ▷ 女演员 [nǚyǎnyuán] actress 2 (女儿) daughter ▶ 子女 [zǐnǚ] children (PL)

女儿 [nǚ'ér] N daughter

女孩子 [nǚháizi] N girl

女朋友 [nǚpéngyou] N girlfriend

女人 [nǚrén] N woman

女士 [nǚshì] N 1 (指称呼) Ms. 2 (对妇女的尊称) lady

女婿 [nǚxu] N son-in-law

暖 [nuǎn] I ADJ warm II VB warm

暖和 [nuǎnhuo] I ADJ warm II VB warm up

暖气 [nuǎnqì] N heating

暖水瓶 [nuǎnshuǐpíng] N thermos flask

挪 [nuó] VB move ▶ 挪动 [nuódong] move

O

哦 [ó] INT oh ▷ 哦，他也来了。 [Ó, tā yě láile.] Oh, he's come too.
→ *see also*/另见 ò

哦 [ò] INT oh ▷ 哦，我明白了。 [Ò, wǒ míngbai le.] Oh, now I understand.
→ *see also*/另见 ó

欧 [ōu] N (欧洲) Europe ▶ 欧洲 [Ōuzhōu] Europe
欧元 [ōuyuán] N euro

呕 [ǒu] VB vomit
呕吐 [ǒutù] VB vomit

偶 [ǒu] N **1** (人像) image ▶ 木偶 [mù'ǒu] puppet **2** (双数) even number ▶ 偶数 [ǒushù] even number
偶尔 [ǒu'ěr] ADV occasionally
偶然 [ǒurán] ADJ chance

藕 [ǒu] N lotus root

P

爬 [pá] VB **1** (前移) crawl **2** (上移) climb ▶ 爬山 [páshān] climb a mountain **3** (起床) get up **4** (升迁) be promoted

怕 [pà] VB **1** (惧怕) fear **2** (担心) be afraid **3** (估计) may be

拍 [pāi] **I** VB **1** (击打) beat **2** (拍摄) shoot **3** (发) send **4** (拍马屁) flatter **II** N **1** (用具) paddle **2** (节奏) beat

拍照 [pāizhào] VB take a photograph

拍子 [pāizi] N **1** (用具) paddle ▷ 网球拍子 [wǎngqiú pāizi] tennis racket **2** (节奏) beat

排 [pái] **I** VB **1** (摆放) put ... in order **2** (排演) rehearse **3** (除去) drain **II** N **1** (行列) row **2** (指军队) platoon **3** (指水运) raft **III** MEAS row

排队 [páiduì] VB stand in line

排球 [páiqiú] N volleyball

牌 [pái] N **1** (标志板) board ▶ 门牌 [ménpái] house number ▶ 招牌 [zhāopái] store sign **2** (商标) brand

派 [pài] **I** N **1** (帮派) group ▶ 学派 [xuépài] school of thought **2** (风度) manner **II** VB **1** (分配) set **2** (委派) send **3** (安排) assign

派对 [pàiduì] N party

攀 [pān] VB **1** (向上爬) climb **2** (指关系) seek friends in high places ▶ 高攀 [gāopān] be a social climber **3** (拉扯) chat

攀登 [pāndēng] VB scale

盘 [pán] **I** N **1** (盘子) tray **2** (盘状物) ▶ 棋盘 [qípán] chessboard **3** (行情) quotation **II** VB **1** (绕) wind ▶ 盘旋 [pánxuán] wind **2** (核查) examine ▶ 盘问 [pánwèn] interrogate **3** (清点) make an inventory ▶ 盘货 [pánhuò] stocktake **4** (转让) transfer **III** MEAS **1** (指物量) ▷ 三盘录像带 [sān pán lùxiàngdài] three videotapes **2** (指动量) game measure word, used for videotapes, cassettes, and board games

盘子 [pánzi] N plate

判 [pàn] **I** VB **1** (分辨) distinguish ▶ 判明 [pànmíng] ascertain **2** (评定) judge **3** (裁决) sentence ▶ 审判 [shěnpàn] try **II** ADV clearly

判断 [pànduàn] VB judge

盼 [pàn] VB **1** (盼望) long **2** (看) look ▶ 左顾右盼 [zuǒgù-yòupàn] look around

盼望 [pànwàng] VB long

旁 [páng] **I** N side **II** ADJ (口) other

旁边 [pángbiān] **I** N side **II** ADV beside

胖 [pàng] ADJ fat

抛 [pāo] VB **1** (投掷) throw **2** (丢下) leave ... behind **3** (暴露) bare ▶ 抛头露面 [pāotóu-lùmiàn] appear in public **4** (脱手) dispose of

抛弃 [pāoqì] VB desert

跑 [pǎo] VB **1** (奔) run **2** (逃) escape **3** (奔波) run around **4** (漏) leak

跑步 [pǎobù] VB run

泡 [pào] **I** N **1** (指气体) bubble **2** (泡状物) ▶ 灯泡 [dēngpào] light bulb **II** VB **1** (浸) soak **2** (消磨) dawdle **3** (沏) infuse ▷ 泡茶 [pào chá] make tea

泡沫 [pàomò] N foam

炮 [pào] N **1** (武器) cannon **2** (爆竹) firecracker

陪 [péi] VB **1** (相伴) go with ▷ 我要陪母亲去医院。 [wǒ yào péi mǔqīn qù yīyuàn] I have to go to the hospital with my mother. **2** (协助) assist

陪同 [péitóng] **I** VB accompany **II** N guide

培 [péi] VB foster

培训 [péixùn] VB train
培养 [péiyǎng] VB cultivate
培育 [péiyù] VB 1 (培植养育) cultivate 2 (培养教育) nurture

赔 [péi] VB 1 (赔偿) make good 2 (亏本) make a loss
赔偿 [péicháng] VB compensate

佩 [pèi] VB 1 (佩带) wear 2 (佩服) admire ▶ 钦佩 [qīnpèi] esteem
佩服 [pèifu] VB admire

配 [pèi] I VB 1 (指两性) marry 2 (指动物) mate 3 (调和) mix ▶ 配药 [pèiyào] make up a prescription 4 (分派) allocate ▶ 配售 [pèishòu] ration 5 (衬托) match 6 (符合) fit II N spouse
配合 [pèihé] I VB cooperate II ADJ complementary

喷 [pēn] VB gush
喷泉 [pēnquán] N fountain
喷嚏 [pēntì] N sneeze

盆 [pén] N 1 (盛具) basin ▶ 脸盆 [liǎnpén] washbasin 2 (盆状物) ▶ 骨盆 [gǔpén] pelvis

朋 [péng] N friend
朋友 [péngyou] N 1 (指友谊) friend 2 (女友) girlfriend 3 (男友) boyfriend

捧 [pěng] I VB 1 (托) hold ... in both hands 2 (奉承) flatter II MEAS handful

碰 [pèng] VB 1 (撞击) hit 2 (遇见) bump into 3 (试探) take a chance
碰见 [pèngjiàn] VB encounter
碰巧 [pèngqiǎo] ADV by chance

批 [pī] I VB 1 (批示) comment ▶ 批示 [pīshì] comment 2 (批评) criticize II N wholesale III MEAS 1 (指人) group 2 (指物) batch
批判 [pīpàn] VB 1 (驳斥) repudiate 2 (批评) criticize
批评 [pīpíng] VB criticize
批准 [pīzhǔn] VB approve

披 [pī] VB 1 (搭) drape ... over one's shoulders 2 (开裂) split

皮 [pí] I N 1 (表皮) skin 2 (皮革) leather ▶ 漆皮 [qīpí] patent leather 3 (外皮) covering 4 (表面) surface 5 (薄片) sheet ▶ 奶皮 [nǎipí] skin on the milk 6 (指橡胶) rubber II ADJ 1 (韧) thick-skinned 2 (变韧的) rubbery 3 (顽皮) naughty
皮包 [píbāo] N leather purse
皮肤 [pífū] N skin

疲 [pí] ADJ 1 (疲劳) tired 2 (厌倦) tired of
疲倦 [píjuàn] ADJ tired
疲劳 [píláo] ADJ 1 (劳累) weary 2 (衰退) weakened

啤 [pí] *see below*/见下文
啤酒 [píjiǔ] N beer

脾 [pí] N spleen
脾气 [píqi] N 1 (怒气) temper 2 (性情) temperament

匹 [pǐ] I VB match II MEAS 1 (指动物) ▷ 三匹马 [sān pǐ mǎ] three horses 2 (指布料) bolt

measure word, used for horses, mules, donkeys, and bolts of silk

屁 [pì] I N wind II ADJ meaningless
屁股 [pìgu] N 1 (指人) bottom 2 (指后部) rear

譬 [pì] N analogy ▶ 譬如 [pìrú] for example ▶ 譬喻 [pìyù] metaphor
譬如 [pìrú] VB take ... for example

偏 [piān] ADJ 1 (倾斜的) slanting 2 (不公的) biased
偏见 [piānjiàn] N prejudice
偏偏 [piānpiān] ADV 1 (表示主观) persistently 2 (表示客观) contrary to expectation 3 (表示范围) only

篇 [piān] I N 1 (文章) writing ▶ 篇章 [piānzhāng] sections (PL) 2 (单张纸) sheet ▶ 歌篇儿 [gēpiānr] song sheet II MEAS ▷ 三篇文章 [sān piān wénzhāng] three articles

measure word, used for articles, essays, etc.

便 [pián] *see below*/见下文
→ *see also*/另见 biàn

便便 [piánpián] ADJ fat

便宜 [piányi] I ADJ cheap II N small gains (PL) III VB let … off lightly

片 [piàn] I N 1 (指薄度) piece ▶ 纸片 [zhǐpiàn] scraps of paper 2 (指地区) area II VB slice III ADJ 1 (不全) incomplete ▶ 片面 [piànmiàn] one-sided 2 (简短) brief IV MEAS 1 (指片状物) ▷ 两片药 [liǎng piàn yào] two tablets ▷ 几片树叶 [jǐ piàn shùyè] some leaves ▷ 一片面包 [yī piàn miànbāo] a slice of bread 2 (指水陆) stretch

measure word, used for thin flat objects

片面 [piànmiàn] I N one side II ADJ one-sided

骗 [piàn] VB 1 (欺骗) deceive 2 (骗得) swindle ▶ 骗钱 [piànqián] swindle

骗子 [piànzi] N swindler

漂 [piāo] VB 1 (浮) float 2 (流动) drift
→ *see also*/另见 piào

飘 [piāo] VB 1 (飞扬) flutter 2 (指腿, 脚) wobble

飘扬 [piāoyáng] VB flutter

票 [piào] N 1 (作凭证) ticket 2 (指钞票) bill 3 (指戏曲) amateur performance

漂 [piào] *see below*/见下文
→ *see also*/另见 piāo

漂亮 [piàoliang] ADJ 1 (好看) good-looking 2 (精彩) wonderful

拼 [pīn] VB 1 (合) join together 2 (竭尽全力) go all out ▶ 拼命 [pīnmìng] with all one's might 3 (字, 词) spell ▷ 你能拼一下这个词吗? [nǐ néng pīn yīxià zhègè cí ma?] Can you spell this word?

拼命 [pīnmìng] VB 1 (不要命) risk one's life 2 (努力) go all out

拼音 [pīnyīn] N Pinyin

贫 [pín] I ADJ 1 (穷) poor ▶ 贫民 [pínmín] the poor 2 (少) deficient ▶ 贫血 [pínxuè] anemia II VB (方) be a chatterbox

贫苦 [pínkǔ] ADJ poverty-stricken

贫穷 [pínqióng] ADJ poor

频 [pín] ADV frequently

频繁 [pínfán] ADJ frequent

频率 [pínlǜ] N 1 (物) frequency 2 (指心脏) rate

品 [pǐn] I N 1 (物品) article ▶ 商品 [shāngpǐn] merchandise 2 (等级) grade ▶ 精品 [jīngpǐn] special product 3 (种类) type ▶ 品种 [pǐnzhǒng] variety 4 (品质) character ▶ 品德 [pǐndé] moral character II VB taste

品尝 [pǐncháng] VB savor

品德 [pǐndé] N moral character

品格 [pǐngé] N character

品质 [pǐnzhì] N 1 (品德) character 2 (质量) quality

品种 [pǐnzhǒng] N 1 (动) breed 2 (植) species 3 (指产品) kind

乒 [pīng] I ONO bang II N (*also*: 乒乓球) table tennis

乒乓球 [pīngpāngqiú] N table tennis

平 [píng] I ADJ 1 (平坦) flat ▶ 平原 [píngyuán] plain 2 (安定) calm 3 (普通) ordinary 4 (平均) even ▶ 平分 [píngfēn] fifty-fifty 5 (指比分) ▶ 平局 [píngjú] a draw II VB 1 (夷平) level 2 (指成绩) equal 3 (镇压) suppress

平安 [píng'ān] ADJ safe and sound

平常 [píngcháng] I ADJ common II ADV usually

平等 [píngděng] ADJ equal

平凡 [píngfán] ADJ uneventful

平方 [píngfāng] N 1 (数) square 2 (平

方米) square meter

平衡 [pínghéng] N balance ▶ 平衡收支 [pínghéng shōuzhī] balance revenue and expenditure

平静 [píngjìng] ADJ calm

平均 [píngjūn] ADJ average

平时 [píngshí] ADV usually

平原 [píngyuán] N plain

评 [píng] VB 1 (评论) criticize ▶ 批评 [pīpíng] criticize ▶ 书评 [shūpíng] book review 2 (评判) judge ▶ 评分 [píngfēn] mark 3 (选) select

评价 [píngjià] VB evaluate

评论 [pínglùn] VB review

苹 [píng] *see below*/见下文

苹果 [píngguǒ] N apple

凭 [píng] I VB rely on II N evidence ▶ 凭据 [píngjù] credentials (PL) III CONJ no matter

瓶 [píng] N bottle

瓶子 [píngzi] N bottle

坡 [pō] N slope ▶ 山坡 [shānpō] slope

迫 [pò] I VB 1 (逼迫) force 2 (接近) approach II ADJ urgent

迫切 [pòqiè] ADJ pressing

破 [pò] I ADJ 1 (受损) broken 2 (烂) lousy II VB 1 (受损) cut 2 (破除) break ▶ 破例 [pòlì] make an exception 3 (钱, 工夫) spend 4 (揭穿) expose ▶ 破案 [pò'àn] solve a case 5 (打败) defeat

破坏 [pòhuài] VB 1 (建筑, 环境, 文物, 公物) destroy 2 (团结, 社会秩序) undermine 3 (协定, 法规, 规章) violate 4 (计划) bring ... down 5 (名誉) damage

破裂 [pòliè] VB 1 (谈判) break down 2 (感情) break up 3 (外交关系) break off

扑 [pū] VB 1 (冲向) rush at 2 (专注于) devote 3 (扑打) swat 4 (翅膀) beat

扑克 [pūkè] N poker

铺 [pū] VB 1 (摊开) spread 2 (铺设) lay
→ *see also*/另见 pù

葡 [pú] *see below*/见下文

葡萄 [pútao] N grape

朴 [pǔ] *see below*/见下文

朴实 [pǔshí] ADJ 1 (简朴) simple 2 (诚实) honest

朴素 [pǔsù] ADJ 1 (衣着) plain 2 (生活) simple 3 (语言) plain

普 [pǔ] ADJ general

普遍 [pǔbiàn] I ADJ common II ADV commonly

普通 [pǔtōng] ADJ common

普通话 [pǔtōnghuà] N Mandarin

铺 [pù] N 1 (商店) store ▶ 杂货铺 general store 2 (床) plank bed ▶ 卧铺 berth
→ *see also*/另见 pū

Q

七 [qī] NUM seven

七月 [qīyuè] N July

妻 [qī] N wife ▶ 未婚妻 [wèihūnqī] fiancée

妻子 [qīzǐ] N wife

柒 [qī] NUM seven

This is the complex character for "seven", which is mainly used in banks, on receipts, etc. to prevent mistakes and forgery.

期 [qī] I N 1 (预定时间) time limit ▶ 到期 [dàoqī] expire 2 (一段时间) period of time ▶ 假期 [jiàqī] vacation II MEAS 1 (指训练班) class 2 (指杂志, 报纸) edition III VB expect

期待 [qīdài] VB await

期间 [qījiān] N period of time

期望 [qīwàng] I N expectations (PL) II VB expect

欺 [qī] VB 1 (欺骗) deceive 2 (欺负) bully

欺负 [qīfu] VB bully

欺骗 [qīpiàn] VB deceive

齐 [qí] I ADJ 1 (整齐) neat 2 (一致) joint 3 (完备) ready II VB 1 (达到) reach 2 (取齐) level III ADV at the same time

其 [qí] PRON (书) 1 (他的) his 2 (她的) her 3 (它的) its 4 (他们的, 她们的, 它们的) their 5 (他) him 6 (她) her 7 (它) it 8 (他们, 她们, 它们) them 9 (那个) that

其次 [qícì] PRON 1 (下一个) next ▷ 其次要做的事是什么？ [Qícì yào zuò de shì shì shénme?] What are we going to do next? 2 (次要的) the second

其实 [qíshí] ADV actually

其他 [qítā] PRON other ▷ 我不知道，你问其他人吧。 [Wǒ bù zhīdào, nǐ wèn qítā rén ba.] I don't know, ask someone else. ▷ 还有其他事情没有？ [Háiyǒu qítā shìqing méiyǒu?] Is there anything else?

其余 [qíyú] PRON the rest

其中 [qízhōng] N among which ▷ 他有六套西服，其中两套是黑色的。 [Tā yǒu liù tào xīfú, qízhōng liǎng tào shì hēisè de.] He has six suits, of which two are black.

奇 [qí] I ADJ 1 (非常少见的) strange ▶ 奇闻 [qíwén] fantastic story ▶ 奇事 [qíshì] miracle 2 (出人意料的) unexpected ▶ 奇袭 [qíxí] surprise attack ▶ 奇遇 [qíyù] lucky encounter II VB surprise ▶ 惊奇 [jīngqí] surprise III ADV unusually

奇怪 [qíguài] ADJ strange

奇迹 [qíjì] N miracle

骑 [qí] I VB ride II N cavalry

棋 [qí] N chess ▶ 围棋 [wéiqí] go (*board game*)

旗 [qí] N flag ▶ 锦旗 [jǐnqí] silk banner

旗袍 [qípáo] N cheongsam

旗子 [qízi] N flag

乞 [qǐ] VB beg ▶ 行乞 [xíngqǐ] go begging

乞丐 [qǐgài] N beggar

乞求 [qǐqiú] VB beg

企 [qǐ] VB look forward to

企图 [qǐtú] I VB plan II N (贬) plan

企业 [qǐyè] N enterprise

启 [qǐ] VB 1 (打开) open ▶ 开启 [kāiqǐ] open 2 (开导) enlighten 3 (开始) start

启发 [qǐfā] I VB inspire II N inspiration

起 [qǐ] I VB 1 (起来) rise ▶ 起立 [qǐlì] stand up 2 (取出) remove 3 (长出) form ▷ 脚上起泡 [jiǎoshang qǐ pào]

form a blister on one's foot **4** (产生) become **5** (拟订) sketch out ▶ 起草 [qǐcǎo] draft **6** (建立) establish **II** MEAS ▷ 一起交通事故 [yī qǐ jiāotōng shìgù] a traffic accident ▷ 一起火灾 [yī qǐ huǒzāi] a fire

measure word, used for accidents

起床 [qǐchuáng] VB get up

起点 [qǐdiǎn] N starting point

起飞 [qǐfēi] VB take off ▷ 飞机准时起飞。[Fēijī zhǔnshí qǐfēi.] The plane took off on time.

起来 [qǐlái] VB **1** (站起或坐起) get up **2** (起床) get up

气 [qì] **I** N **1** (气体) gas ▶ 毒气 [dúqì] poison gas **2** (空气) air ▷ 这球没气了。[Zhè qiú méi qì le.] This ball is deflated. **3** (气息) breath **4** (精神) mood **5** (气味) smell ▶ 臭气 [chòuqì] stink **6** (习气) manner ▶ 孩子气 [háiziqì] childishness **7** (怒气) anger **8** (医) qi **II** VB **1** (生气) be angry **2** (使生气) provoke

气氛 [qìfēn] N atmosphere

气功 [qìgōng] N qigong

气候 [qìhòu] N climate ▶ 气候紧急情况 [qìhòu jǐnjí qíngkuàng] climate emergency

气温 [qìwēn] N temperature

气象 [qìxiàng] N **1** (大气现象) weather **2** (气象学) meteorology **3** (情景) atmosphere

汽 [qì] N **1** (气体) vapor **2** (蒸气) steam

汽车 [qìchē] N car ▶ 公共汽车 [gōnggòng qìchē] bus

汽水 [qìshuǐ] N fizzy drink

汽油 [qìyóu] N gasoline

器 [qì] N **1** (器具) utensil ▶ 乐器 [yuèqì] musical instrument ▶ 瓷器 [cíqì] china **2** (器官) organ

器官 [qìguān] N organ

恰 [qià] ADV **1** (适当) appropriately **2** (刚好) exactly

恰当 [qiàdàng] ADJ appropriate

恰好 [qiàhǎo] ADV luckily

千 [qiān] **I** NUM thousand **II** ADJ many

千万 [qiānwàn] **I** NUM ten million **II** ADV ▷ 你千万别做傻事。[Nǐ qiānwàn bié zuò shǎshì.] You absolutely mustn't do anything stupid.

牵 [qiān] VB **1** (拉住) pull **2** (牵涉) involve

铅 [qiān] N (化) lead

铅笔 [qiānbǐ] N pencil

谦 [qiān] ADJ modest

谦虚 [qiānxū] **I** ADJ modest **II** VB speak modestly

签 [qiān] **I** VB **1** (名字) sign **2** (意见) endorse **II** N **1** (指占卜, 赌博, 比赛) lot **2** (标志) label ▶ 书签 [shūqiān] bookmark **3** (细棍子) stick ▶ 牙签 [yáqiān] toothpick

签名 [qiānmíng] VB sign

签证 [qiānzhèng] N visa

签字 [qiānzì] VB sign one's name

前 [qián] **I** ADJ **1** (正面的) front **2** (指次序) first **3** (从前的) former ▶ 前夫 [qiánfū] ex-husband **4** (未来的) future **II** VB advance

前进 [qiánjìn] VB **1** (向前走) advance **2** (发展) make progress

前面 [qiánmian] ADV in front

前年 [qiánnián] N the year before last

前天 [qiántiān] N the day before yesterday

前途 [qiántú] N future

前夕 [qiánxī] N eve

钱 [qián] N money

钱包 [qiánbāo] N **1** (女用) wallet **2** (男用) billfold

浅 [qiǎn] ADJ **1** (指深度) shallow **2** (指难度) easy **3** (指学识) lacking **4** (指颜色) light ▷ 浅蓝色 [qiǎnlánsè] light blue ▷ 浅绿色 [qiǎnlǜsè] pale green 5 (指时间) short

欠 [qiàn] VB 1 (钱, 情) owe 2 (缺乏) lack 3 (移动) raise ... slightly

枪 [qiāng] N 1 (旧兵器) spear 2 (兵器) gun ▸ 手枪 [shǒuqiāng] pistol

强 [qiáng] I ADJ 1 (力量大) strong 2 (程度高) able 3 (好) better 4 (略多于) extra ▹ 三分之一强 [sān fēn zhī yī qiáng] a third extra II VB force → *see also*/另见 qiǎng

强大 [qiángdà] ADJ powerful

强盗 [qiángdào] N robber

强调 [qiángdiào] VB stress

强度 [qiángdù] N intensity

强奸 [qiángjiān] VB rape

强烈 [qiángliè] ADJ intense

墙 [qiáng] N wall

抢 [qiǎng] VB 1 (抢劫) rob 2 (抢夺) grab 3 (抢先) forestall 4 (赶紧) rush

抢劫 [qiǎngjié] VB rob

强 [qiǎng] VB 1 (勉强) make an effort 2 (迫使) force → *see also*/另见 qiáng

强迫 [qiǎngpò] VB force

悄 [qiāo] *see below*/见下文

悄悄 [qiāoqiāo] ADV 1 (悄然无声) quietly 2 (不让知道) stealthily

敲 [qiāo] VB 1 (击) knock 2 (敲诈) blackmail

敲诈 [qiāozhà] VB extort

桥 [qiáo] N bridge

桥梁 [qiáoliáng] N bridge

瞧 [qiáo] VB look

巧 [qiǎo] ADJ 1 (手, 口) nimble 2 (有技能的) skillful 3 (恰好) coincidental 4 (虚浮的) false

巧克力 [qiǎokèlì] N chocolate

巧妙 [qiǎomiào] ADJ clever

切 [qiē] VB cut

茄 [qié] N eggplant

茄子 [qiézi] N eggplant

窃 [qiè] I VB steal II ADV surreptitiously

窃听 [qiètīng] VB eavesdrop

窃贼 [qièzéi] N thief

侵 [qīn] VB invade

侵略 [qīnlüè] VB invade

亲 [qīn] I N 1 (父母) parent 2 (亲戚) relative 3 (婚姻) marriage ▸ 定亲 [dìngqīn] engagement 4 (新娘) bride II ADJ 1 (指血缘近) blood 2 (指感情好) intimate III ADV personally IV VB 1 (亲吻) kiss 2 (亲近) be close to

亲爱 [qīn'ài] ADJ dear

亲近 [qīnjìn] ADJ close

亲密 [qīnmì] ADJ close ▹ 亲密朋友 [qīnmì péngyǒu] close friend ▸ 亲密无间 [qīnmì wújiàn] be as thick as thieves

亲戚 [qīnqi] N relative

亲切 [qīnqiè] ADJ warm

亲热 [qīnrè] ADJ affectionate

亲自 [qīnzì] ADV personally

琴 [qín] N ▸ 钢琴 [gāngqín] piano ▸ 小提琴 [xiǎotíqín] violin

勤 [qín] I ADJ hard-working II ADV regularly III N 1 (勤务) duty ▸ 值勤 [zhíqín] be on duty 2 (到场) attendance ▸ 考勤 [kǎoqín] check attendance

勤奋 [qínfèn] ADJ diligent

勤劳 [qínláo] ADJ hard-working

青 [qīng] I ADJ 1 (指绿色) green 2 (指黑色) black 3 (指年纪) young ▸ 青年 [qīngnián] youth II N 1 (指青草) grass 2 (指庄稼) unripe crops (PL)

青年 [qīngnián] N youth

青少年 [qīngshàonián] N teenager

轻 [qīng] I ADJ 1 (指重量) light 2 (指数量或程度) ▹ 他们年纪很轻。[Tāmen niánjì hěnqīng.] They are quite young. 3 (指无足轻重) not important 4 (指轻松愉快) relaxed ▸ 轻音乐 [qīngyīnyuè] light music

II ADV **1** (指少用力) gently **2** (轻率) rashly **III** VB disparage

轻松 [qīngsōng] ADJ relaxing

轻易 [qīngyì] ADV **1** (容易) easily **2** (随便) rashly

倾 [qīng] **I** VB **1** (斜) lean **2** (塌) collapse **3** (倒出) empty out **4** (用尽) exhaust **II** N tendency

倾向 [qīngxiàng] **I** VB incline to **II** N tendency

清 [qīng] **I** ADJ **1** (纯净) clear **2** (寂静) quiet **3** (清楚) distinct ▶ 分清 [fēnqīng] distinguish **4** (完全) settled **5** (纯洁) pure **II** VB **1** (清除) get rid of **2** (结清) settle **3** (清点) check **4** (清理) put in order

清楚 [qīngchu] **I** ADJ clear **II** VB understand

清洁 [qīngjié] ADJ clean

清静 [qīngjìng] ADJ quiet

清明节 [Qīngmíng Jié] N Tomb Sweeping Festival

清明节 [Qīngmíng Jié]

清明节 Qīngmíng Jié, **Tomb Sweeping Festival**, sometimes translated literally as **Clear and Bright Festival**, is celebrated on April 4th, 5th, or 6th. It is traditionally the time when Chinese families visit graves to honor their dead ancestors.

情 [qíng] N **1** (感情) feeling ▶ 热情 [rèqíng] warmth **2** (情面) kindness **3** (爱情) love **4** (情况) condition ▶ 实情 [shíqíng] true state of affairs

情节 [qíngjié] N **1** (内容) plot **2** (事实) circumstances (PL)

情景 [qíngjǐng] N sight

情况 [qíngkuàng] N **1** (状况) situation **2** (变化) military development

情侣 [qínglǚ] N lovers (PL)

情人节 [Qíngrén Jié] N Valentine's Day

情形 [qíngxíng] N situation

情绪 [qíngxù] N **1** (心理状态) mood **2** (不很开心) moodiness

晴 [qíng] ADJ fine

晴朗 [qínglǎng] ADJ sunny

请 [qǐng] VB **1** (请求) ask ▷ 请他进来。 [Qǐng tā jìnlai.] Ask him to come in. **2** (邀请) invite **3** (敬) ▷ 请这边走。 [Qǐng zhèbiān zǒu.] This way, please. ▷ 请大家安静一下。 [Qǐng dàjiā ānjìng yīxià.] Everyone quiet, please.

请假 [qǐngjià] VB ask for leave

请教 [qǐngjiào] VB consult

请客 [qǐngkè] VB treat

请求 [qǐngqiú] VB ask

请问 [qǐngwèn] VB ▷ 请问怎么出去？ [Qǐngwèn zěnme chūqù?] Could you show me the way out, please?

请勿 [qǐngwù] VB ▷ 请勿吸烟。 [Qǐngwù xīyān.] No smoking.

庆 [qìng] **I** VB celebrate **II** N festival ▶ 国庆 [guóqìng] National Day

庆贺 [qìnghè] VB celebrate

庆祝 [qìngzhù] VB celebrate

穷 [qióng] **I** ADJ poor **II** N limit **III** ADV **1** (彻底) thoroughly **2** (极端) extremely

秋 [qiū] N **1** (指季节) fall **2** (指庄稼) harvest time **3** (指一年) year **4** (指厄运期) period

秋天 [qiūtiān] N fall

求 [qiú] **I** VB **1** (请求) request **2** (追求) strive **II** N demand

球 [qiú] N **1** (数) (球体) sphere **2** (指球状) ball ▶ 雪球 [xuěqiú] snowball **3** (指体育) ball ▶ 篮球 [lánqiú] basketball ▶ 足球 [zúqiú] soccer **4** (指比赛) ball game **5** (地球) the Earth ▶ 全球 [quánqiú] the whole world

球场 [qiúchǎng] N court

球迷 [qiúmí] N fan

区 [qū] **I** VB distinguish **II** N **1** (地区)

area 2 (指行政单位) region ▶ 自治区 [zìzhìqū] autonomous region
区别 [qūbié] VB distinguish
区分 [qūfēn] VB differentiate
区域 [qūyù] N area

趋 [qū] VB 1 (走) hasten 2 (趋向) tend to become
趋势 [qūshì] N trend
趋向 [qūxiàng] I VB tend to II N trend

渠 [qú] N ditch
渠道 [qúdào] N 1 (水道) irrigation ditch 2 (途径) channel

曲 [qǔ] N 1 (指歌曲) song 2 (指乐曲) music
曲子 [qǔzi] N tune

取 [qǔ] 1 (拿到) take 2 (得到) obtain 3 (采取) adopt 4 (选取) choose
取得 [qǔdé] VB get
取消 [qǔxiāo] VB cancel

娶 [qǔ] VB marry

去 [qù] I VB 1 (到) go 2 (除) get rid of 3 (距) be apart 4 (发) send II ADJ past
去年 [qùnián] N last year
去世 [qùshì] VB pass away

趣 [qù] I N interest ▶ 志趣 [zhìqù] interest II ADJ interesting
趣味 [qùwèi] N taste

圈 [quān] I N 1 (环形物) circle ▶ 北极圈 [Běijíquān] Arctic Circle 2 (界) group II VB circle
圈套 [quāntào] N trap

权 [quán] I N 1 (权力) power ▶ 当权 [dāngquán] be in power 2 (权利) right 3 (形势) ▷ 主动权 [zhǔdòngquán] initiative ▷ 控制权 [kòngzhìquán] control 4 (权宜) expediency II ADV for the time being
权力 [quánlì] N power

全 [quán] I ADJ 1 (齐全) complete 2 (整个) whole II ADV entirely III VB keep ... intact
全部 [quánbù] ADJ whole
全面 [quánmiàn] ADJ comprehensive
全体 [quántǐ] N everyone

泉 [quán] N spring ▶ 温泉 [wēnquán] hot spring

拳 [quán] N fist
拳头 [quántou] N fist
拳击 [quánjī] N boxing

鬈 [quán] ADJ curly

劝 [quàn] VB 1 (说服) advise 2 (勉励) encourage
劝告 [quàngào] VB advise

缺 [quē] I VB 1 (缺乏) lack 2 (残破) be incomplete 3 (缺席) be absent II N vacancy ▶ 补缺 [bǔquē] fill a vacancy
缺点 [quēdiǎn] N shortcoming
缺乏 [quēfá] VB lack
缺口 [quēkǒu] N 1 (口子) gap 2 (缺额) shortfall
缺少 [quēshǎo] VB lack
缺席 [quēxí] VB be absent
缺陷 [quēxiàn] N defect

瘸 [qué] VB be lame

却 [què] I VB 1 (后退) step back 2 (使退却) drive ... back 3 (拒绝) decline ▶ 推却 [tuīquè] decline 4 (表示完成) ▶ 冷却 [lěngquè] cool off ▶ 忘却 [wàngquè] forget II ADV however

确 [què] ADV 1 (确实地) really 2 (坚定地) firmly ▶ 确信 [quèxìn] firmly believe
确定 [quèdìng] I VB determine II ADJ definite
确实 [quèshí] I ADJ true II ADV really

裙 [qún] N skirt
裙子 [qúnzi] N skirt

群 [qún] I N crowd II MEAS 1 (指动物) herd, flock ▷ 一群绵羊 [yī qún miányáng] a flock of sheep ▷ 一群

蜜蜂 [yī qún mìfēng] a swarm of bees ▷ 一群奶牛 [yī qún nǎiniú] a herd of cows **2** (指人) group ▷ 一群学生 [yī qún xuésheng] a group of students

群众 [qúnzhòng] N the masses (PL)

R

然 [rán] PRON so
然而 [rán'ér] CONJ however
然后 [ránhòu] CONJ afterwards

燃 [rán] VB 1 (燃烧) burn 2 (点燃) light
燃料 [ránliào] N fuel
燃烧 [ránshāo] VB burn

染 [rǎn] VB 1 (着色) dye 2 (感染) contract 3 (沾染) catch

嚷 [rǎng] VB 1 (喊叫) howl 2 (吵闹) make a racket

让 [ràng] I VB 1 (退让) make allowances 2 (允许) let 3 (转让) transfer II PREP by

扰 [rǎo] VB (搅扰) disturb ▶ 打扰 [dǎrǎo] disturb

绕 [rào] VB 1 (缠绕) wind 2 (围绕) go round 3 (迂回) make a detour

惹 [rě] VB 1 (引起) stir up 2 (触动) provoke 3 (招) make

热 [rè] I N 1 (物) heat 2 (高烧) fever ▶ 发热 [fārè] have a fever II ADJ 1 (温度高) hot 2 (走俏) popular III VB heat
热爱 [rè'ài] VB love
热狗 [règǒu] N hot dog
热烈 [rèliè] ADJ heated
热闹 [rènao] ADJ lively
热情 [rèqíng] I N passion II ADJ enthusiastic
热线 [rèxiàn] N 1 (指电话或电报) hotline 2 (指交通) busy route
热心 [rèxīn] ADJ warm-hearted

人 [rén] N 1 (人类) human being ▶ 人权 [rénquán] human rights (PL) 2 (指某种人) person ▶ 军人 [jūnrén] soldier ▶ 中国人 [Zhōngguórén] a Chinese person/Chinese people 3 (人手) manpower
人才 [réncái] N (指能人) talent
人工 [réngōng] ADJ man-made ▶ 人工智能 [réngōng zhìnéng] artificial intelligence
人口 [rénkǒu] N 1 (地区人数) population 2 (家庭人数) people
人类 [rénlèi] N mankind, humankind
人们 [rénmen] N people
人民 [rénmín] N the people
人民币 [rénmínbì] N Renminbi, RMB
人生 [rénshēng] N life
人体 [réntǐ] N the human body
人物 [rénwù] N 1 (能人) figure 2 (艺术形象) character

忍 [rěn] VB (忍受) endure
忍耐 [rěnnài] VB show restraint
忍受 [rěnshòu] VB bear

认 [rèn] VB 1 (识) know 2 (承认) admit
认得 [rènde] VB be acquainted with
认识 [rènshi] I VB know II N understanding
认为 [rènwéi] VB think
认真 [rènzhēn] I ADJ serious II VB take … seriously

任 [rèn] I VB 1 (聘) appoint ▶ 委任 [wěirèn] appoint 2 (听凭) let II N (职责) responsibility
任何 [rènhé] ADJ any ▷ 任何人都不能迟到。 [Rènhé rén dōu bù néng chídào.] No one can be late.
任务 [rènwu] N task

扔 [rēng] VB 1 (掷) throw 2 (丢) throw … away

仍 [réng] ADV still
仍然 [réngrán] ADV (表示继续) still

日 [rì] N 1 (太阳) sun ▶ 日出 [rìchū] sunrise ▶ 日落 [rìluò] sunset 2 (白天) daytime 3 (天) day ▶ 明日 [míngrì] tomorrow 4 (每天) every day ▷ 城市面貌日见改善。 [Chéngshì miànmào rìjiàn gǎishàn.] The city looks better and better every day.

5 (指某一天) day ▶ 生日 [shēngrì] birthday 6 (*also*: 日本) Japan

日报 [rìbào] N daily paper

日本 [Rìběn] N Japan

日常 [rìcháng] ADJ everyday

日记 [rìjì] N diary

日历 [rìlì] N calendar

日期 [rìqī] N date

日用品 [rìyòngpǐn] N daily necessities

日语 [Rìyǔ] N Japanese

日元 [Rìyuán] N Japanese yen

日子 [rìzi] N **1** (日期) date **2** (时间) day **3** (生活) life

荣 [róng] ADJ (光荣) glorious

荣幸 [róngxìng] ADJ honored ▷ 认识您, 我感到非常荣幸。 [Rèngshi nín wǒ gǎndào fēicháng róngxìng.] I feel honored to know you.

荣誉 [róngyù] N (指名声) honor

容 [róng] **I** VB **1** (容纳) fit ▶ 容纳 [róngnà] hold ▶ 容量 [róngliàng] capacity ▶ 容器 [róngqì] container **2** (容忍) tolerate ▶ 容忍 [róngrěn] tolerate **3** (允许) allow **II** N (相貌) appearance ▶ 容貌 [róngmào] features (PL)

容易 [róngyì] ADJ **1** (简便) easy **2** (较可能) likely

柔 [róu] ADJ **1** (软) soft **2** (柔和) gentle

柔软 [róuruǎn] ADJ soft

揉 [róu] VB (搓) rub

肉 [ròu] N **1** (指人) flesh **2** (指动物) meat ▷ 猪肉 [zhūròu] pork **3** (指瓜果) flesh

如 [rú] VB **1** (好似) be like **2** (比得上) be as good as ▶ 不如 [bùrú] not as good as **3** (例如) ▷ 北京有很多名胜, 如故宫, 天坛等。 Beijing has many tourist attractions, such as the Forbidden City, the Temple of Heaven and so on.

如此 [rúcǐ] PRON so ▷ 他的态度竟如此恶劣。 [Tā de tàidù jìng rúcǐ èliè.] His attitude was so unpleasant.

如果 [rúguǒ] CONJ if

如何 [rúhé] PRON ▷ 此事如何解决? [Cǐ shì rúhé jiějué?] How are we going to sort this out? ▷ 你今后如何打算? [Nǐ jīnhòu rúhé dǎsuàn?] What are your plans for the future?

儒 [rú] N (儒家) Confucianism ▶ 儒家 [Rújiā] Confucianism

入 [rù] VB **1** (进入) enter ▶ 入场 [rùchǎng] enter **2** (参加) join ▶ 入学 [rùxué] enroll

入境 [rùjìng] VB enter a country

入口 [rùkǒu] N (门) entrance

软 [ruǎn] ADJ **1** (柔) soft ▶ 软和 [ruǎnhuo] soft **2** (温和) gentle **3** (柔弱) weak ▶ 软弱 [ruǎnruò] weak

软件 [ruǎnjiàn] N (计算机) software

软卧 [ruǎnwò] N light sleeper

软饮料 [ruǎnyǐnliào] N soft drink

弱 [ruò] ADJ **1** (弱小) weak **2** (年幼) young **3** (软弱) weak

弱点 [ruòdiǎn] N weakness

S

仨 [sā] NUM (口) three ▶ 哥仨 [gēsā] three brothers

撒 [sā] VB **1** (手, 网) let … go **2** (贬) (疯, 野) lose control of oneself ▶ 撒野 [sāyě] have a tantrum
→ *see also*/另见 sǎ

撒谎 [sāhuǎng] VB (口) lie

撒娇 [sājiāo] VB behave like a spoiled child

撒气 [sāqì] VB **1** (球, 车胎) get a puncture **2** (发泄怒气) take one's anger out on ▷ 别拿我撒气! [Bié ná wǒ sāqì!] Don't take your anger out on me!

撒手 [sāshǒu] VB (松手) let go

洒 [sǎ] VB **1** (泼) sprinkle **2** (指不小心) spill

洒脱 [sǎtuo] ADJ carefree

撒 [sǎ] VB **1** (散布) scatter **2** (散落) spill
→ *see also*/另见 sā

腮 [sāi] N cheek

腮帮子 [sāibāngzi] N (口) cheek

塞 [sāi] **I** VB stuff … into **II** N cork

塞子 [sāizi] N cork

赛 [sài] **I** N match ▷ 演讲比赛 [yǎnjiǎng bǐsài] debating contest **II** VB compete

赛车 [sàichē] **I** VB race **II** N (指汽车) race car

赛季 [sàijì] N season

赛跑 [sàipǎo] VB race

三 [sān] NUM **1** (指数目) three ▶ 三月 [sānyuè] March **2** (表示序数) third **3** (表示多数) several ▶ 三思 [sānsī] think twice

三角 [sānjiǎo] N triangle ▷ 三角恋爱 [sānjiǎo liàn'ài] love triangle

三明治 [sānmíngzhì] N sandwich

三围 [sānwéi] N vital statistics (PL)

三心二意 [sān xīn èr yì] half-hearted ▷ 他工作三心二意的。[Tā gōngzuò sān xīn èr yì de.] He's half-hearted about his work.

叁 [sān] NUM three

This is the complex character for "three", which is mainly used in banks, on receipts, etc. to prevent mistakes and forgery.

伞 [sǎn] N umbrella

散 [sǎn] **I** VB loosen **II** ADJ loose
→ *see also*/另见 sàn

散漫 [sǎnmàn] ADJ slack

散文 [sǎnwén] N prose

散 [sàn] VB **1** (分离) break up ▷ 乌云散了。[Wūyún sàn le.] The dark clouds scattered. **2** (散布) give … out **3** (排除) dispel
→ *see also*/另见 sǎn

散布 [sànbù] VB **1** (传单) distribute **2** (谣言) spread

散步 [sànbù] VB go for a stroll

丧 [sāng] N funeral
→ *see also*/另见 sàng

丧事 [sāngshì] N funeral arrangements (PL)

桑 [sāng] N mulberry

桑那浴 [sāngnàyù] N sauna

嗓 [sǎng] N **1** (嗓子) throat **2** (嗓音) voice

嗓门 [sǎngmén] N voice

嗓子 [sǎngzi] N **1** (喉咙) throat **2** (嗓音) voice

丧 [sàng] VB lose
→ *see also*/另见 sāng

丧气 [sàngqì] VB lose heart

丧失 [sàngshī] VB lose

骚 [sāo] VB disturb

骚扰 [sāorǎo] VB harass ▶ 性骚扰 [xìng sāorǎo] sexual harassment

扫 [sǎo] VB **1** (打扫) sweep **2** (除去) clear ... away ▶ 扫黄 [sǎohuáng] anti-pornography campaign
→ *see also*/另见 sào

扫除 [sǎochú] VB **1** (打扫) sweep ... up **2** (除掉) eliminate

扫盲 [sǎománg] VB eliminate illiteracy

扫描 [sǎomiáo] VB scan

扫描仪 [sǎomiáoyí] N scanner

扫兴 [sǎoxìng] ADJ disappointed

嫂 [sǎo] N (哥哥之妻) sister-in-law

嫂子 [sǎozi] N (口) sister-in-law

扫 [sào] *see below*/见下文
→ *see also*/另见 sǎo

扫帚 [sàozhou] N broom

色 [sè] N (颜色) color
→ *see also*/另见 shǎi

色彩 [sècǎi] N **1** (颜色) color **2** (指情调) tone

色盲 [sèmáng] N color blindness

色情 [sèqíng] ADJ pornographic

涩 [sè] ADJ (味道) astringent

森 [sēn] ADJ (形容树多) wooded

森林 [sēnlín] N forest

僧 [sēng] N Buddhist monk ▶ 僧人 [sēngrén] Buddhist monk

杀 [shā] VB **1** (杀死) kill **2** (战斗) fight **3** (削弱) reduce

杀毒 [shādú] VB get rid of a virus ▷ 杀毒软件 [shādú ruǎnjiàn] anti-virus software

杀害 [shāhài] VB murder

杀价 [shājià] VB bargain ▷ 我很会杀价。 [Wǒ hěn huì shājià.] I'm a very good bargainer.

杀手 [shāshǒu] N killer

沙 [shā] N (石粒) sand

沙尘 [shāchén] N dust

沙尘暴 [shāchénbào] N sandstorm

沙发 [shāfā] N sofa

沙锅 [shāguō] N casserole

沙皇 [shāhuáng] N tsar

沙漠 [shāmò] N desert

沙滩 [shātān] N beach

沙哑 [shāyǎ] ADJ hoarse

沙眼 [shāyǎn] N trachoma

沙子 [shāzi] N sand

纱 [shā] N (指织品) gauze

纱布 [shābù] N gauze

刹 [shā] VB brake

刹车 [shāchē] **I** VB **1** (停止机器) brake **2** (喻) (制止) put a stop to **II** N brake

鲨 [shā] N shark ▶ 鲨鱼 [shāyú] shark

傻 [shǎ] ADJ **1** (蠢) stupid **2** (死心眼) inflexible

傻瓜 [shǎguā] N fool

傻子 [shǎzi] N fool

厦 [shà] N tall building ▷ 摩天大厦 [mótiān dàshà] skyscraper

色 [shǎi] N color
→ *see also*/另见 sè

色子 [shǎizi] N dice

晒 [shài] VB **1** (阳光照射) shine upon ▷ 他被晒黑了。 [Tā bèi shài hēi le.] He's tanned. **2** (吸收光热) lie in the sun ▷ 她在沙滩上晒太阳。 [Tā zài shātān shàng shài tàiyang.] She was sunbathing on the beach.

山 [shān] N (地质) mountain ▶ 小山 [xiǎoshān] hill

山村 [shāncūn] N mountain village

山洞 [shāndòng] N cave

山峰 [shānfēng] N peak

山谷 [shāngǔ] N valley

山脚 [shānjiǎo] N foothills (PL)

山林 [shānlín] N wooded hill

山脉 [shānmài] N mountain range

山坡 [shānpō] N mountainside

山区 [shānqū] N mountainous area

山水 [shānshuǐ] N **1** (风景) scenery **2** (画) landscape painting

山珍海味 [shān zhēn hǎi wèi] N exotic delicacies (PL)

删 [shān] VB delete
删除 [shānchú] VB delete

珊 [shān] *see below*/见下文
珊瑚 [shānhú] N coral

扇 [shān] VB 1 (扇子) fan 2 (耳光) slap
→ *see also*/另见 shàn

闪 [shǎn] I VB 1 (闪避) dodge 2 (受伤) sprain 3 (突然出现) flash 4 (闪耀) shine II N lightning ▷ 打闪了。[Dǎshǎn le.] Lightning flashed.
闪电 [shǎndiàn] N lightning
闪动 [shǎndòng] VB flash
闪烁 [shǎnshuò] VB (忽明忽暗) twinkle

扇 [shàn] I N (扇子) fan II MEAS ▷ 一扇窗 [yī shàn chuāng] a window ▷ 两扇门 [liǎng shàn mén] two doors
measure word, used for doors, windows, screens, etc.
→ *see also*/另见 shān

善 [shàn] I ADJ 1 (善良) kind 2 (良好) good ▶ 善事 [shànshì] good deeds 3 (友好) friendly II VB 1 (擅长) be an expert at 2 (容易) be prone to ▶ 善忘 [shànwàng] forgetful
善良 [shànliáng] ADJ kind-hearted
善于 [shànyú] VB be good at

擅 [shàn] VB be expert at
擅长 [shàncháng] VB be skilled in

鳝 [shàn] N eel ▶ 鳝鱼 [shànyú] eel

伤 [shāng] I VB 1 (身体部位) injure ▶ 扭伤 [niǔshāng] sprain 2 (感情) hurt II N injury
伤残 [shāngcán] N the disabled (PL)
伤风 [shāngfēng] VB catch a cold
伤害 [shānghài] VB 1 (感情) hurt 2 (身体) damage
伤痕 [shānghén] N scar
伤口 [shāngkǒu] N wound
伤心 [shāngxīn] ADJ sad

商 [shāng] I VB discuss ▶ 协商 [xiéshāng] negotiate II N 1 (商业) commerce ▶ 经商 [jīngshāng] trade 2 (商人) businessman, businesswoman 3 (数) quotient
商标 [shāngbiāo] N trademark
商场 [shāngchǎng] N shopping center, mall
商店 [shāngdiàn] N store
商量 [shāngliáng] VB discuss
商品 [shāngpǐn] N commodity
商人 [shāngrén] N businessman, businesswoman
商谈 [shāngtán] VB negotiate
商务 [shāngwù] N business ▷ 电子商务 [diànzǐ shāngwù] e-commerce
商业 [shāngyè] N commerce

赏 [shǎng] I VB 1 (赏赐) award 2 (欣赏) admire 3 (赏识) appreciate II N reward
赏识 [shǎngshí] VB think highly of

上 [shàng] I N 1 (指方位) upper part 2 (指等级, 质量) ▶ 上级 [shàngjí] higher authorities (PL) 3 (指时间, 次序) ▷ 上星期 [shàng xīngqī] last week ▷ 上半年 [shàng bànnián] the first half of the year II VB 1 (向上) go up ▷ 上楼 [shànglóu] go upstairs 2 (按点前往) go ▶ 上学 [shàngxué] go to school ▶ 上班 [shàngbān] go to work 3 (去) go to ▷ 他上天津开会去了。 [Tā shàng Tiānjīn kāihuì qù le.] He went to Tianjin to attend a meeting. 4 (出场) make an entrance 5 (添补) fill ▶ 上货 [shànghuò] stock up 6 (饭, 菜) serve ▷ 上菜 [shàng cài] serve food 7 (安装) fix ▷ 上螺丝 [shàng luósī] fix a screw 8 (涂) apply ▷ 上涂料 [shàng túliào] apply paint 9 (登载) appear ▷ 上杂志 [shàng zázhì] appear in a magazine 10 (拧紧) tighten ▷ 我的表已上弦了。 [Wǒde biǎo yǐ shàngxián le.] I've wound up my watch. 11 (车, 船, 飞机) board

12 (表示达到目的) ▷ 当上老师 [dāngshàng lǎoshī] become a teacher **III** PREP **1** (在物体表面) on ▷ 椅子上 [yǐzi shàng] on the chair **2** (表示范围) in ▷ 报纸上 [bàozhǐ shàng] in the newspaper

上当 [shàngdàng] VB be taken in

上等 [shàngděng] ADJ first-class

上帝 [Shàngdì] N God

上吊 [shàngdiào] VB hang oneself

上级 [shàngjí] N higher authorities (PL)

上来 [shànglái] VB **1** (指动作趋向) ▷ 饭菜端上来了。 [Fàncài duān shànglái le.] The meal was brought to the table. **2** (表示成功) ▷ 这个问题我答不上来。 [Zhègè wèntí wǒ dá bù shànglái.] I can't answer this question.

上面 [shàngmian] N **1** (指位置高) ▷ 他住在我上面。 [Tā zhùzài wǒ shàngmian.] He lives above me. **2** (物体表面) ▷ 墙上面挂着相片。 [Qiáng shàngmian guà zhe zhàopiàn.] Photographs were hanging on the walls. **3** (以上的部分) ▷ 上面我们分析了各种可能性。 [Shàngmian wǒmen fénxi le gèzhǒng kěnéngxìng.] As can be seen above, we have made an analysis of all possibilities.

上年纪 [shàng niánji] VB get old

上去 [shàngqù] VB **1** (指由低到高) go up **2** (提高) improve

上身 [shàngshēn] N upper body

上升 [shàngshēng] VB **1** (往高处移) ascend **2** (增加) increase

上市 [shàngshì] VB appear on the market

上司 [shàngsi] N superior

上诉 [shàngsù] VB appeal

上网 [shàngwǎng] VB go online

上午 [shàngwǔ] N morning

上衣 [shàngyī] N top

上瘾 [shàngyǐn] VB be addicted to

上涨 [shàngzhǎng] VB rise

烧 [shāo] VB **1** (着火) burn **2** (加热) heat ▷ 烧水 [shāo shuǐ] boil water **3** (烹) braise **4** (烤) roast ▶ 烧鸡 [shāojī] roast chicken **5** (发烧) have a temperature

烧烤 [shāokǎo] VB barbecue

稍 [shāo] ADV slightly
→ *see also*/另见 shào

稍微 [shāowēi] ADV a little

勺 [sháo] N ladle

少 [shǎo] **I** ADJ few ▷ 屋里家具太少。 [Wū lǐ jiājù tài shǎo.] There is very little furniture in the room. **II** VB **1** (缺) lack ▷ 汤里少了葱。 [Tāng lǐ shǎo le cōng.] There is no onion in the soup. **2** (丢) be missing ▷ 她发现钱包里的钱少了一百块。 [Tā fāxiàn qiánbāo lǐ de qián shǎo le yībǎi kuài.] She discovered that one hundred kuai were missing from her purse.
→ *see also*/另见 shào

少量 [shǎoliàng] N a little

少数 [shǎoshù] N minority

少数民族 [shǎoshù mínzú] N ethnic minorities (PL)

少数民族 [shǎoshù mínzú]

少数民族 shǎoshù mínzú refers to China's ethnic minorities. There are 56 distinct ethnic groups in China, of which the Han is by far the largest, accounting for over 90% of the population. The other 55 minorities are mainly located in the southwestern and north-western provinces. Five regions have been set up as ethnic minorities autonomous regions.

少 [shào] ADJ young ▶ 少女 [shàonǚ] young girl
→ *see also*/另见 shǎo

少年 [shàonián] N youth

哨 [shào] N (哨子) whistle

哨子 [shàozi] N whistle

稍 [shào] *see below*/见下文
→ *see also*/另见 shāo

稍息 [shàoxī] VB stand at ease

奢 [shē] ADJ extravagant

奢侈 [shēchǐ] ADJ luxurious

舌 [shé] N tongue

舌头 [shétou] N tongue

折 [shé] VB (折断) snap ▷ 他的腿折了。[Tāde tuǐ shé le.] He broke his leg.
→ *see also*/另见 zhé

蛇 [shé] N snake

设 [shè] VB **1** (摆) set ... up **2** (想) plan **3** (假定) suppose ▶ 设想 [shèxiǎng] envisage

设备 [shèbèi] N equipment

设计 [shèjì] VB design ▶ 服装设计 [fúzhuāng shèjì] fashion design

设施 [shèshī] N facilities (PL)

社 [shè] N organization ▶ 旅行社 [lǚxíngshè] travel agent

社会 [shèhuì] N society ▷ 社会福利 [shèhuì fúlì] social welfare

社交 [shèjiāo] N social contact ▶ 社交媒体 [shèjiāo méitǐ] social media

社区 [shèqū] N community

舍 [shè] N house ▶ 宿舍 [sùshè] dormitory

射 [shè] VB **1** (发) shoot **2** (喷) spout **3** (放出) emit ▶ 照射 [zhàoshè] shine

射击 [shèjī] **I** VB fire **II** N shooting

射门 [shèmén] VB shoot

射线 [shèxiàn] N (电磁波) ray

涉 [shè] VB (牵涉) involve ▶ 涉嫌 [shèxián] be a suspect

涉及 [shèjí] VB involve

摄 [shè] VB **1** (吸取) absorb **2** (摄影) take a photo

摄像 [shèxiàng] VB make a video

摄影 [shèyǐng] VB **1** (照相) take a photo **2** (拍电影) shoot a movie

谁 [shéi] PRON **1** (表示问人) who ▷ 谁在门外? [Shéi zài mén wài?] Who's at the door? **2** (指任何一个人) whoever ▷ 谁先到谁买票。[Shéi xiān dào shéi mǎipiào.] Whoever arrives first buys the tickets.

申 [shēn] VB express

申请 [shēnqǐng] VB apply ▷ 申请工作 [shēnqǐng gōngzuò] apply for a job

伸 [shēn] VB stretch

伸手 [shēnshǒu] VB (伸出手) hold out one's hand

身 [shēn] N **1** (身体) body **2** (生命) life **3** (自己) oneself

身材 [shēncái] N figure

身份 [shēnfen] N (地位) position

身份证 [shēnfènzhèng] N identity card

身体 [shēntǐ] N body

参 [shēn] N ginseng ▶ 人参 [rénshēn] ginseng
→ *see also*/另见 cān

绅 [shēn] N gentry

绅士 [shēnshì] N gentleman

深 [shēn] **I** ADJ **1** (指深度) deep **2** (指距离) remote **3** (深奥) difficult **4** (深刻) deep ▷ 印象深 [yìnxiàng shēn] a deep impression **5** (密切) close **6** (浓重) dark ▷ 深蓝 [shēnlán] dark blue **7** (指时间久) late ▶ 深夜 [shēnyè] late at night **II** N depth **III** ADV very ▶ 深信 [shēnxìn] firmly believe

深奥 [shēn'ào] ADJ profound

深度 [shēndù] **I** N depth **II** ADJ extreme

深化 [shēnhuà] VB deepen

深刻 [shēnkè] ADJ deep

深入 [shēnrù] **I** VB penetrate **II** ADJ thorough

深远 [shēnyuǎn] ADJ far-reaching

深造 [shēnzào] VB pursue advanced studies

什 [shén] *see below*/见下文

什么 [shénme] PRON 1 (表示疑问) what ▷ 你要什么? [Nǐ yào shénme?] What do you want? 2 (表示虚指) something ▷ 他们在商量着什么。 [Tāmen zài shāngliàng zhe shénme.] They are discussing something. 3 (表示任指) anything ▷ 我什么都不怕。 [Wǒ shénme dōu bùpà.] I'm not afraid of anything. 4 (表示惊讶, 不满) what ▷ 什么! 他拒绝出席会议! [Shénme! Tā jùjué chūxí huìyì!] What! He refused to attend the meeting! 5 (表示责难) ▷ 你在胡说什么! [Nǐ zài húshuō shénme!] What's that rubbish?

什么的 [shénmede] PRON and so on ▷ 餐桌上摆满了香蕉, 李子, 苹果什么的。 [Cānzhuō shàng bǎimǎn le xiāngjiāo, lǐzi, píngguǒ shénme de.] The dining table was loaded with bananas, plums, apples, and so on.

神 [shén] I N 1 (宗) god 2 (精神) spirit ▶ 走神 [zǒushén] be absent-minded II ADJ (高超) amazing ▶ 神奇 [shénqí] magical

神话 [shénhuà] N myth

神经 [shénjīng] N nerve ▶ 神经多样性 [shénjīng duōyàngxìng] neurodiversity

神秘 [shénmì] ADJ mysterious

神气 [shénqì] I N manner II ADJ 1 (精神) impressive 2 (得意) cocky

神圣 [shénshèng] ADJ sacred

神态 [shéntài] N look

神仙 [shénxiān] N immortal

神学 [shénxué] N theology

审 [shěn] VB 1 (审查) go over 2 (审讯) try ▷ 审案子 [shěn ànzi] try a case

审查 [shěnchá] VB examine

审判 [shěnpàn] VB try

审问 [shěnwèn] VB interrogate

婶 [shěn] N aunt

肾 [shèn] N kidney

甚 [shèn] I ADJ extreme II ADV very

甚至 [shènzhì] ADV even

渗 [shèn] VB seep

慎 [shèn] ADJ careful

慎重 [shènzhòng] ADJ cautious

升 [shēng] I VB 1 (由低往高) rise 2 (提升) promote ▶ 升职 [shēngzhí] be promoted II MEAS liter

升级 [shēngjí] VB 1 (升高年级) go up 2 (规模扩大) escalate 3 (指电脑) upgrade

升值 [shēngzhí] VB appreciate

生 [shēng] I VB 1 (生育) give birth to ▷ 生孩子 [shēng háizi] have a baby 2 (长) grow 3 (活) live ▶ 生死 [shēngsǐ] life and death 4 (患) get ▶ 生病 [shēngbìng] get ill 5 (点) light ▶ 生火 [shēnghuǒ] light a fire II N 1 (生命) life 2 (生平) life ▶ 今生 [jīnshēng] this life 3 (学生) student ▶ 新生 [xīnshēng] new student III ADJ 1 (活的) living ▶ 生物 2 (未熟的) unripe 3 (未煮的) raw 4 (生疏) unfamiliar

生产 [shēngchǎn] VB 1 (制造) produce 2 (生孩子) give birth to

生存 [shēngcún] VB survive

生动 [shēngdòng] ADJ lively

生活 [shēnghuó] I N life II VB 1 (居住) live 2 (生存) survive

生计 [shēngjì] N livelihood

生理 [shēnglǐ] N physiology

生命 [shēngmìng] N life

生命力 [shēngmìnglì] N vitality

生气 [shēngqì] VB get angry

生人 [shēngrén] N stranger

生日 [shēngrì] N birthday

生态 [shēngtài] N ecology

生物 [shēngwù] N living things (PL)

生物学 [shēngwùxué] N biology

生肖 [shēngxiào] N animal of the Chinese zodiac

生效 [shēngxiào] VB come into effect

生意 [shēngyi] N business
生育 [shēngyù] VB give birth to
生长 [shēngzhǎng] VB 1 (植物) grow 2 (生物) grow up

声 [shēng] N 1 (声音) sound 2 (名声) reputation ▶ 声誉 [shēngyù] fame 3 (声调) tone (*of Chinese phonetics*)
声波 [shēngbō] N sound wave
声调 [shēngdiào] N tone
声明 [shēngmíng] VB state
声望 [shēngwàng] N prestige
声音 [shēngyīn] N 1 (指人) voice 2 (指物) sound

牲 [shēng] N (家畜) domestic animal
牲畜 [shēngchù] N livestock

甥 [shēng] N nephew ▶ 外甥 [wàishēng] nephew ▶ 外甥女 [wàishēngnǚ] niece

绳 [shéng] N rope
绳子 [shéngzi] N rope

省 [shěng] I VB 1 (节约) save ▷ 省钱 [shěng qián] save money 2 (免掉) leave ... out II N province
省会 [shěnghuì] N provincial capital
省略 [shěnglüè] VB leave ... out
省事 [shěngshì] VB save trouble
省心 [shěngxīn] VB save worry

圣 [shèng] I ADJ holy ▶ 圣诞节 [Shèngdàn Jié] Christmas II N (圣人) sage
圣诞 [Shèngdàn] N Christmas
圣经 [Shèngjīng] N the Bible

胜 [shèng] VB 1 (赢) win 2 (打败) defeat 3 (好于) be better than
胜利 [shènglì] VB 1 (打败对方) be victorious 2 (获得成功) be successful

盛 [shèng] ADJ 1 (兴盛) flourishing 2 (强烈) intense 3 (盛大) grand ▶ 盛宴 [shèngyàn] sumptuous dinner 4 (深厚) abundant ▶ 盛情 [shèngqíng] great kindness 5 (盛行) popular ▶ 盛行 [shèngxíng] be in fashion
→ *see also*/另见 chéng
盛大 [shèngdà] ADJ magnificent

剩 [shèng] VB be left ▶ 剩下 [shèngxià] remain

尸 [shī] N corpse
尸体 [shītǐ] N corpse

失 [shī] I VB 1 (丢失) lose 2 (未得到) fail 3 (背弃) break II N mistake ▶ 过失 [guòshī] error
失败 [shībài] VB fail
失眠 [shīmián] VB be unable to sleep
失眠症 [shīmiánzhèng] N insomnia
失明 [shīmíng] VB go blind
失望 [shīwàng] I ADJ disappointed II VB lose hope
失误 [shīwù] VB slip up
失效 [shīxiào] VB 1 (不起作用) stop working 2 (没有法力) be no longer valid
失信 [shīxìn] VB go back on one's word
失业 [shīyè] VB be unemployed, be out of work
失踪 [shīzōng] VB be missing

师 [shī] N (老师) teacher
师傅 [shīfu] N (口) master

诗 [shī] N poetry
诗歌 [shīgē] N poetry
诗人 [shīrén] N poet

虱 [shī] N louse

狮 [shī] *see below*/见下文
狮子 [shīzi] N lion

施 [shī] VB 1 (实行) carry ... out ▶ 施工 [shīgōng] construct 2 (给予) exert ▶ 施压 [shīyā] exert pressure 3 (肥料) apply ▶ 施肥 [shīféi] spread fertilizer
施行 [shīxíng] VB (执行) implement

湿 [shī] ADJ wet
湿润 [shīrùn] ADJ moist

十 [shí] N ten ▶ 十月 [shíyuè] October ▶ 十一月 [shíyīyuè] November ▶ 十二月 [shí'èryuè] December

十分 [shífēn] ADV extremely

十字路口 [shízì lùkǒu] N crossroads (PL)

石 [shí] N stone

石油 [shíyóu] N oil

时 [shí] N 1 (指时间单位) hour 2 (指规定时间) time ▶ 准时 [zhǔnshí] on time 3 (时常) ▶ 时不时 [shíbùshí] from time to time 4 (时尚) fashion ▶ 入时 [rùshí] fashionable ▶ 过时 [guòshí] out-of-date 5 (时候) time ▶ 当时 [dāngshí] at that time 6 (机会) opportunity 7 (语法) tense ▷ 过去时 [guòqùshí] past tense

时差 [shíchā] N time difference

时常 [shícháng] ADV often

时代 [shídài] N 1 (指时期) age 2 (指人生) period

时候 [shíhou] N time ▷ 你什么时候上班? [Nǐ shénme shíhou shàngbān?] What time do you go to work?

时机 [shíjī] N opportunity

时间 [shíjiān] N time ▷ 时间到了。 [Shíjiān dào le.] Time's up! ▷ 办公时间 [bàngōng shíjiān] working hours

时刻 [shíkè] I N moment II ADV constantly

时刻表 [shíkèbiǎo] N schedule

时髦 [shímáo] ADJ fashionable

时期 [shíqī] N period

时区 [shíqū] N time zone

时事 [shíshì] N current affairs (PL)

时装 [shízhuāng] N fashion

实 [shí] ADJ 1 (实心) solid 2 (真实) true ▶ 实话 [shíhuà] truth

实际 [shíjì] I N reality II ADJ 1 (实有的) real 2 (合乎事实的) practical

实践 [shíjiàn] I VB practice II N practice

实力 [shílì] N strength

实情 [shíqíng] N actual state of affairs

实施 [shíshī] VB implement

实习 [shíxí] VB practice

实习生 [shíxíshēng] N trainee

实现 [shíxiàn] VB realize

实行 [shíxíng] VB put ... into practice

实验 [shíyàn] I VB test II N experiment

实验室 [shíyànshì] N laboratory

实用 [shíyòng] ADJ practical

实在 [shízài] I ADJ honest II ADV really

拾 [shí] I VB pick ... up II NUM ten

> This is the complex character for "ten", which is mainly used in banks, on receipts, etc. to prevent mistakes and forgery.

食 [shí] I VB eat II N 1 (食物) food ▶ 主食 [zhǔshí] staple ▶ 狗食 [gǒushí] dog food 2 (指天体) eclipse ▶ 日食 [rìshí] solar eclipse

食品 [shípǐn] N food

食谱 [shípǔ] N recipe

食堂 [shítáng] N canteen

食物 [shíwù] N food

食欲 [shíyù] N appetite

史 [shǐ] N history

史诗 [shǐshī] N epic

史实 [shǐshí] N historical fact

使 [shǐ] I VB 1 (使用) use 2 (让) make II N envoy ▶ 大使 [dàshǐ] ambassador

使馆 [shǐguǎn] N embassy

使用 [shǐyòng] VB use ▶ 使用说明 [shǐyòng shuōmíng] operating instructions (PL)

始 [shǐ] VB start

始终 [shǐzhōng] ADV all along

屎 [shǐ] N 1 (粪便) excrement 2 (眼, 耳) wax ▶ 耳屎 [ěrshǐ] ear wax

示 [shì] VB show
示范 [shìfàn] VB demonstrate
示威 [shìwēi] VB demonstrate

世 [shì] N 1 (生) life ▶ 来世 [láishì] afterlife 2 (代) generation ▶ 世仇 [shìchóu] family feud 3 (时期) age 4 (世界) world ▶ 世上 [shìshàng] in this world
世纪 [shìjì] N century
世界 [shìjiè] N world

市 [shì] N 1 (城市) city 2 (市场) market
市场 [shìchǎng] N market
市民 [shìmín] N city residents (PL)

式 [shì] N 1 (样式) style 2 (典礼) ceremony 3 (式子) formula ▶ 公式 [gōngshì] formula
式样 [shìyàng] N style

事 [shì] N 1 (事情) thing ▶ 私事 [sīshì] private matter 2 (事故) accident ▶ 出事 [chūshì] have an accident 3 (事端) trouble ▶ 闹事 [nàoshì] make trouble 4 (责任) responsibility 5 (工作) job 6 (用于问答) problem ▷ 有事吗？—没事。 [Yǒu shì ma? —Méishì.] Are you OK? — I'm fine.
事故 [shìgù] N accident
事件 [shìjiàn] N event
事情 [shìqing] N matter
事实 [shìshí] N fact ▷ 事实上 [shìshí shàng] in fact
事务 [shìwù] N work
事物 [shìwù] N thing
事业 [shìyè] N 1 (用于个人) undertaking 2 (用于社会) activity

势 [shì] N 1 (势力) force 2 (姿态) gesture 3 (趋势) tendency
势力 [shìli] N power
势利 [shìli] ADJ snobbish
势利眼 [shìliyǎn] N snob
势头 [shìtóu] N momentum

饰 [shì] I VB 1 (装饰) decorate 2 (扮演) play II N ornament ▶ 首饰 [shǒushì] jewelry
饰物 [shìwù] N ornaments (PL)
饰演 [shìyǎn] VB play

试 [shì] I VB try ▷ 我可以试一下这双鞋吗？ [Wǒ kěyǐ shì yīxià zhè shuāng xié ma?] Can I try on this pair of shoes? II N examination
试卷 [shìjuàn] N exam paper
试题 [shìtí] N exam question
试验 [shìyàn] VB test
试用 [shìyòng] VB try ... out
试用期 [shìyòngqī] N probation

视 [shì] VB 1 (看到) look at 2 (看待) look on
视觉 [shìjué] N vision
视力 [shìlì] N sight

柿 [shì] *see below*/见下文
柿子 [shìzi] N persimmon, sharon fruit

是 [shì] I VB be ▷ 我是学生。 [Wǒ shì xuésheng.] I am a student. II N right ▶ 是非 [shìfēi] right and wrong III ADV yes

> 是 shì is the verb "to be". It is omitted when used with adjectives, e.g. 我很忙 wǒ hěn máng (I am very busy).

适 [shì] ADJ 1 (适合) suitable 2 (恰好) right 3 (舒服) well
适当 [shìdàng] ADJ appropriate
适合 [shìhé] ADJ suitable
适应 [shìyìng] VB adapt

室 [shì] N room ▶ 办公室 [bàngōngshì] office
室外 [shìwài] ADJ outdoor

逝 [shì] VB (人) die
逝世 [shìshì] VB (书) pass away

释 [shì] VB (解释) explain
释放 [shìfàng] VB release

嗜 [shì] VB be addicted to
嗜好 [shìhào] N hobby

誓 [shì] I VB swear ▶ 发誓 [fāshì] vow II N vow

誓言 [shìyán] N oath

收 [shōu] VB 1 (归拢) put … away 2 (取回) take … back 3 (接纳) accept 4 (结束) stop ▸ 收工 [shōugōng] stop work 5 (获得) gain ▸ 收入 [shōurù] income

收获 [shōuhuò] VB 1 (指庄稼) harvest 2 (指成果) gain

收集 [shōují] VB collect

收据 [shōujù] N receipt

收拾 [shōushi] VB 1 (整顿) tidy 2 (修理) repair 3 (口) (惩罚) punish

收缩 [shōusuō] VB 1 (指物理现象) contract 2 (紧缩) cut back

收听 [shōutīng] VB listen to

收音机 [shōuyīnjī] N radio

手 [shǒu] N 1 (指人体) hand 2 (指人) expert ▸ 选手 [xuǎnshǒu] player

手表 [shǒubiǎo] N watch

手电筒 [shǒudiàntǒng] N flashlight

手段 [shǒuduàn] N 1 (方法) method 2 (贬) (花招) trick

手风琴 [shǒufēngqín] N accordion

手工 [shǒugōng] I N craft II VB make … by hand

手机 [shǒujī] N cellphone ▸ 智能手机 [zhìnéng shǒujī] smartphone

手绢 [shǒujuàn] N handkerchief

手铐 [shǒukào] N handcuffs (PL)

手枪 [shǒuqiāng] N pistol

手势 [shǒushì] N sign

手术 [shǒushù] I N operation II VB operate

手套 [shǒutào] N glove ▷ 一副手套 [yī fù shǒutào] a pair of gloves

手腕 [shǒuwàn] N (指人体) wrist

手续 [shǒuxù] N procedure

手语 [shǒuyǔ] N sign language

手掌 [shǒuzhǎng] N palm

手纸 [shǒuzhǐ] N toilet paper

手指 [shǒuzhǐ] N finger

手镯 [shǒuzhuó] N bracelet

守 [shǒu] VB 1 (防卫) guard 2 (遵循) observe ▸ 守法 [shǒufǎ] observe the law

守则 [shǒuzé] N regulation

首 [shǒu] I N 1 (脑袋) head 2 (头领) leader II ADJ 1 (第一) first ▸ 首富 [shǒufù] the richest person 2 (最早) first III MEAS ▷ 一首诗 [yī shǒu shī] one poem ▷ 两首歌 [liǎng shǒu gē] two songs

measure word, used for music, songs, and poems

首都 [shǒudū] N capital

首领 [shǒulǐng] N chief

首脑 [shǒunǎo] N head of state

首饰 [shǒushi] N jewelry

首席 [shǒuxí] ADJ chief

首先 [shǒuxiān] ADV 1 (最早) first 2 (第一) first

首相 [shǒuxiàng] N prime minister

首要 [shǒuyào] ADJ primary

寿 [shòu] N (寿命) lifespan

寿命 [shòumìng] N life

受 [shòu] VB 1 (接受) receive 2 (遭受) suffer 3 (忍受) bear

受罪 [shòuzuì] VB 1 (指苦难) suffer 2 (指不愉快的事) have a hard time

兽 [shòu] N beast

兽医 [shòuyī] N vet

售 [shòu] VB sell

售货员 [shòuhuòyuán] N sales clerk

瘦 [shòu] ADJ 1 (指人) thin 2 (指食用肉) lean 3 (指衣服, 鞋袜) tight

书 [shū] I VB write ▸ 书写 [shūxiě] write II N 1 (册子) book ▸ 书包 [shūbāo] school bag ▸ 书架 [shūjià] bookcase ▸ 书桌 [shūzhuō] desk ▸ 精装书 [jīngzhuāngshū] hardback 2 (书) (信) letter ▸ 情书 [qíngshū] love letter 3 (文件) document ▸ 申请书 [shēnqǐngshū] application documents (PL)

书店 [shūdiàn] N bookstore

书法 [shūfǎ] N calligraphy

书籍 [shūjí] N books (PL)

书记 [shūjì] N secretary
书面语 [shūmiànyǔ] N written language
书信 [shūxìn] N letter
书展 [shūzhǎn] N book fair

叔 [shū] N (指父亲的弟弟) uncle
叔叔 [shūshu] N (口) 1 (指亲戚) uncle 2 (指父辈男性) uncle

梳 [shū] I N comb ▶ 梳子 [shūzi] comb, brush II VB comb

舒 [shū] VB 1 (指身体) stretch out 2 (指心情) relax
舒服 [shūfu] ADJ comfortable
舒适 [shūshì] ADJ cozy

输 [shū] VB 1 (运送) transport 2 (失败) lose
输出 [shūchū] VB (指从内到外) emit
输入 [shūrù] VB (指从外到内) enter
输送 [shūsòng] VB 1 (物品) convey 2 (人员) transfer

蔬 [shū] N vegetable
蔬菜 [shūcài] N vegetable

熟 [shú] ADJ 1 (指果实) ripe 2 (指食物) cooked 3 (熟悉) familiar ▷ 他对北京很熟。 [Tā duì Běijīng hěn shú.] He knows Beijing well. 4 (熟练) skilled
熟练 [shúliàn] ADJ skilled
熟人 [shúrén] N old acquaintance
熟食 [shúshí] N cooked food
熟悉 [shúxī] I VB know well II ADJ familiar

属 [shǔ] I N 1 (生物) genus 2 (家属) family member II VB 1 (隶属) be under 2 (指属相) be ▷ 你属什么? [Nǐ shǔ shénme?] What sign of the Chinese zodiac are you?
属相 [shǔxiang] N (口) sign of the Chinese zodiac
属于 [shǔyú] VB belong to

暑 [shǔ] N 1 (热) heat 2 (盛夏) midsummer
暑假 [shǔjià] N vacation

鼠 [shǔ] N 1 (指家鼠) mouse ▶ 老鼠 [lǎoshǔ] mouse 2 (比家鼠大，尾巴长) rat
鼠标 [shǔbiāo] N mouse

数 [shǔ] VB 1 (数目) count 2 (指名次) rank 3 (列举) list
→ *see also*/另见 shù

薯 [shǔ] N potato ▶ 红薯 [hóngshǔ] sweet potato

术 [shù] N 1 (技艺) skill 2 (策略) tactic
术语 [shùyǔ] N terminology

束 [shù] I VB 1 (捆) tie 2 (约束) restrain II MEAS 1 (指花) bunch ▷ 一束鲜花 [yī shù xiānhuā] a bunch of flowers 2 (指光) ray ▷ 一束阳光 a ray of sunlight
束缚 [shùfù] VB 1 (书) (捆绑) tie 2 (局限) restrain

述 [shù] VB state
述说 [shùshuō] VB give an account

树 [shù] I N tree II VB (建立) establish
树立 [shùlì] VB establish
树林 [shùlín] N wood
树木 [shùmù] N trees (PL)
树阴 [shùyīn] N shade

竖 [shù] I ADJ vertical II VB erect III N vertical stroke

数 [shù] N 1 (数目) number 2 (语法) ▶ 单数 [dānshù] singular ▶ 复数 [fùshù] plural
→ *see also*/另见 shǔ
数据 [shùjù] N data (PL)
数据库 [shùjùkù] N database
数量 [shùliàng] N quantity
数码 [shùmǎ] I N numeral II ADJ digital
数码相机 [shùmǎ xiàngjī] N digital camera
数目 [shùmù] N amount

数学 [shùxué] N mathematics (SG)
数字 [shùzì] N 1 (指系统) numeral 2 (数据) figure

漱 [shù] VB gargle
漱口 [shùkǒu] VB rinse one's mouth out

刷 [shuā] I N brush ▶ 牙刷 [yáshuā] toothbrush II VB (清除) scrub
刷卡 [shuākǎ] VB swipe a card
刷牙 [shuāyá] VB brush one's teeth
刷子 [shuāzi] N brush

耍 [shuǎ] VB 1 (方) (玩) play 2 (戏弄) mess ... around 3 (贬) (施展) play ▷ 别再耍小聪明了。 [Bié zài shuǎ xiǎocōngming le.] Don't play those petty tricks again.
耍花招 [shuǎ huāzhāo] VB play tricks

衰 [shuāi] I ADJ declining II VB decline
衰老 [shuāilǎo] ADJ ageing
衰弱 [shuāiruò] ADJ weak

摔 [shuāi] VB 1 (跌倒) fall 2 (下落) fall out ▷ 他从床上摔了下来。 [Tā cóng chuáng shàng shuāi le xiàlái.] He fell out of bed. 3 (跌坏) break
摔跤 [shuāijiāo] I VB (摔倒) fall over II N wrestling

甩 [shuǎi] VB 1 (抡) swing 2 (扔) fling 3 (抛开) throw ... off
甩卖 [shuǎimài] VB sell at a reduced price

帅 [shuài] I N commander-in-chief II ADJ handsome

率 [shuài] VB command
率领 [shuàilǐng] VB lead

双 [shuāng] I ADJ 1 (两个) two 2 (偶数) even ▶ 双数 [shuāngshù] even number 3 (加倍) double II MEAS pair ▷ 一双鞋 [yī shuāng xié] a pair of shoes ▷ 一双袜子 [yī shuāng wàzi] a pair of socks
双胞胎 [shuāngbāotāi] N twins (PL)
双方 [shuāngfāng] N both sides (PL)
双休日 [shuāngxiūrì] N the weekend

霜 [shuāng] N frost

谁 [shuí] PRON
→ *see also*/另见 shéi

水 [shuǐ] N 1 (物质) water 2 (指江河湖海) waters (PL) 3 (汁) liquid ▶ 消毒水 [xiāodúshuǐ] disinfectant ▶ 墨水 [mòshuǐ] ink
水彩 [shuǐcǎi] N 1 (指颜料) watercolor 2 (指画) watercolor
水果 [shuǐguǒ] N fruit
水晶 [shuǐjīng] N crystal
水库 [shuǐkù] N reservoir
水泥 [shuǐní] N cement
水平 [shuǐpíng] I N standard II ADJ horizontal
水手 [shuǐshǒu] N sailor
水银 [shuǐyín] N mercury
水灾 [shuǐzāi] N flood

税 [shuì] N tax
税收 [shuìshōu] N tax revenue
税务局 [shuìwùjú] N tax office

睡 [shuì] VB sleep
睡觉 [shuìjiào] VB sleep
睡眠 [shuìmián] N sleep

顺 [shùn] I PREP 1 (指方向) with ▶ 顺时针 [shùnshízhēn] clockwise 2 (沿) along 3 (趁便) ▶ 顺便 [shùnbiàn] on the way II VB 1 (朝同一方向) follow 2 (使有条理) put ... in order 3 (顺从) obey 4 (合意) be to one's liking ▶ 顺心 [shùnxīn] as one would wish III ADJ successful ▷ 他找工作很顺。 [Tā zhǎo gōngzuò hěn shùn.] His job hunt has been very successful.
顺便 [shùnbiàn] ADV 1 (指乘方便) on the way 2 (说, 问) by the way ▷ 顺便问一下, 他给你回电话了吗? [Shùnbiàn wèn yīxià, tā gěi nǐ huí diànhuà le ma?] By the way, did he call you back?
顺风 [shùnfēng] VB (指祝福) ▶ 一路

顺风！[Yīlù shùnfēng!] Bon voyage!
顺利 [shùnlì] ADV smoothly
顺序 [shùnxù] N order

说 [shuō] VB 1 (用语言表达意思) say 2 (解释) explain 3 (责备) tell … off
说服 [shuōfú] VB persuade
说话 [shuōhuà] I VB 1 (用语言表达意思) talk 2 (闲谈) chat II ADV (马上) any minute
说明 [shuōmíng] I VB 1 (解释明白) explain 2 (证明) prove II N explanation ▷ 产品使用说明 [chǎnpǐn shǐyòng shuōmíng] instruction manual

硕 [shuò] ADJ large
硕士 [shuòshì] N master's degree

司 [sī] VB take charge of
司机 [sījī] N driver

丝 [sī] N 1 (指蚕) silk 2 (指像丝) thread ▶ 铁丝 [tiěsī] wire
丝绸 [sīchóu] N silk

私 [sī] ADJ 1 (个人的) private ▶ 私事 [sīshì] private affairs 2 (自私的) selfish ▶ 无私 [wúsī] unselfish 3 (暗地里的) secret 4 (非法的) illegal
私人 [sīrén] ADJ 1 (属于个人的) private 2 (人与人之间的) personal
私生活 [sīshēnghuó] N private life
私下 [sīxià] ADV privately
私营 [sīyíng] VB run privately
私有 [sīyǒu] ADJ private ▶ 私有化 [sīyǒuhuà] privatization
私自 [sīzì] ADV without permission

思 [sī] N thought ▶ 思路 [sīlù] train of thought
思考 [sīkǎo] VB think
思念 [sīniàn] I VB miss II N longing
思维 [sīwéi] N thinking
思想 [sīxiǎng] N 1 (指有体系) thought 2 (念头) idea

撕 [sī] VB tear

死 [sǐ] I VB die II ADJ 1 (死亡的) dead 2 (不可调和的) implacable ▶ 死敌 [sǐdí] sworn enemy 3 (不能通过的) impassable ▶ 死胡同 [sǐhutòng] dead end 4 (确切的) fixed 5 (脑筋) slow-witted 6 (规定) rigid 7 (水) still III ADV 1 (拼死) to the death ▶ 死战 [sǐzhàn] fight to the death 2 (表示固执或坚决) stubbornly ▷ 死等 [sǐ děng] wait indefinitely 3 (表示到达极点) extremely ▷ 累死我了。 [Lèi sǐ wǒ le.] I'm completely exhausted.
死机 [sǐjī] VB crash
死尸 [sǐshī] N corpse
死亡 [sǐwáng] VB die
死刑 [sǐxíng] N death penalty
死者 [sǐzhě] N the deceased

四 [sì] NUM four
四季 [sìjì] N the four seasons (PL)
四声 [sìshēng] N *the four tones of Standard Chinese pronunciation*
四月 [sìyuè] N April
四肢 [sìzhī] N limbs (PL)
四周 [sìzhōu] N all sides

寺 [sì] N 1 (指佛教) temple, Tibetan Buddhist temple 2 (指伍斯兰教) mosque ▶ 清真寺 [qīngzhēnsì] mosque

似 [sì] I VB (像) be like ▷ 他的脸似纸一样白。 [Tā de liǎn sì zhǐ yīyàng bái.] His face was as white as a sheet of paper. II ADV apparently
似乎 [sìhū] ADV apparently

饲 [sì] VB raise ▶ 饲养 [sìyǎng] raise
饲料 [sìliào] N fodder

肆 [sì] N four

This is the complex character for "four", which is mainly used in banks, on receipts, etc. to prevent mistakes and forgery.

松 [sōng] I N (树) pine tree II VB 1 (放开) relax 2 (鞋带, 腰带) loosen III ADJ loose

松懈 [sōngxiè] ADJ **1** (放松) relaxed **2** (松散) lax

送 [sòng] VB **1** (信, 邮包, 外卖) deliver **2** (礼物) give ▷ 你准备送他什么结婚礼物? [Nǐ zhǔnbèi sòng tā shénme jiéhūn lǐwù?] What are you going to give him as a wedding present? **3** (送行) see … off ▷ 他把女朋友送到家。 [Tā bǎ nǚpéngyou sòng dào jiā.] He saw his girlfriend home.

送行 [sòngxíng] VB see … off

搜 [sōu] VB search

搜查 [sōuchá] VB search

搜集 [sōují] VB gather

搜索 [sōusuǒ] VB search for

搜索引擎 [sōusuǒ yǐnqíng] N search engine

苏 [sū] VB revive

苏打 [sūdá] N soda

苏格兰 [Sūgélán] N Scotland ▷ 苏格兰短裙 [Sūgélán duǎnqún] kilt

俗 [sú] **I** N (风俗) custom ▶ 民俗 [mínsú] folk custom ▶ 入乡随俗 [rùxiāng suísú] when in Rome, do as the Romans do **II** ADJ **1** (大众的) popular **2** (庸俗) vulgar

俗气 [súqi] ADJ vulgar

俗语 [súyǔ] N common saying

诉 [sù] VB **1** (说给人) tell ▶ 诉说 [sùshuō] tell **2** (倾吐) pour … out ▶ 诉苦 [sùkǔ] complain **3** (控告) accuse ▶ 上诉 [shàngsù] appeal to a higher court

素 [sù] **I** ADJ plain **II** N **1** (蔬菜, 瓜果等食物) vegetable **2** (有根本性质的) element ▶ 维生素 [wéishēngsù] vitamin

素描 [sùmiáo] N sketch

素食 [sùshí] N vegetarian food

素食者 [sùshízhě] N vegetarian

素质 [sùzhì] N character

速 [sù] **I** N speed **II** ADJ quick ▶ 速算 [sùsuàn] quick calculation

速成 [sùchéng] VB take a crash course

速递 [sùdì] VB send by express delivery

速度 [sùdù] N speed

速溶 [sùróng] VB dissolve quickly ▷ 速溶咖啡 [sùróng kāfēi] instant coffee

宿 [sù] VB stay

宿舍 [sùshè] N dormitory

塑 [sù] **I** VB model **II** N mold

塑料 [sùliào] N plastic

塑像 [sùxiàng] N statue

酸 [suān] **I** ADJ **1** (指味道) sour **2** (伤心) sad **3** (迂腐) pedantic **4** (疼) sore **II** N acid

酸奶 [suānnǎi] N yoghurt

蒜 [suàn] N garlic

算 [suàn] VB **1** (计算) calculate **2** (计算进去) count **3** (谋划) plan ▶ 暗算 [ànsuàn] plot against **4** (当作) be considered as **5** (由某人负责) blame **6** (算数) count **7** (作罢) ▷ 算了吧! [Suàn le ba!] Forget it! **8** (推测) suppose

算命 [suànmìng] VB tell sb's fortune ▷ 算命先生 [suànmìng xiānsheng] fortune teller

算盘 [suànpán] N (计算用具) abacus

算术 [suànshù] N math

算账 [suànzhàng] VB **1** (计算账目) work out accounts **2** (把事情扯平) get even with

虽 [suī] CONJ although ▷ 他个子虽小，力气却很大。 [Tā gèzi suī xiǎo, lìqi què hěn dà.] Although he isn't big, he's very strong.

虽然 [suīrán] CONJ although ▷ 虽然她很年轻，可是却很成熟。 [Suīrán tā hěn niánqīng, kěshì què hěn chéngshú.] Although she is very young, she is quite mature.

随 [suí] VB **1** (跟随) follow **2** (顺从) go along with **3** (任凭) let … do as they like ▷ 孩子大了，随他去吧。 [Háizi dà le, suí tā qù ba.] The child's grown up, let him do as he wishes.

随便 [suíbiàn] **I** VB do as one wishes **II** ADJ **1** (随意) casual **2** (欠考虑的) thoughtless **III** ADV ▷ 大家随便坐。 [Dàjiā suíbiàn zuò.] Everyone can sit where they like.

随和 [suíhe] ADJ easygoing

随身 [suíshēn] ADV ▶ 随身行李 [suíshēn xíngli] hand luggage

随时 [suíshí] ADV at any time

随手 [suíshǒu] ADV on one's way ▷ 请随手关门。 [Qǐng suíshǒu guānmén.] Please close the door on your way.

随着 [suízhe] VB follow

岁 [suì] N year ▷ 他20岁了。 [Tā èrshí suì le.] He's 20 years old.

岁数 [suìshu] N age

碎 [suì] **I** VB **1** (破碎) break **2** (使粉碎) smash ▶ 碎纸机 [suìzhǐjī] shredder **II** ADJ (不完整) broken

---

隧 [suì] N tunnel

隧道 [suìdào] N tunnel

孙 [sūn] N grandchild

孙女 [sūnnǚ] N granddaughter

孙子 [sūnzi] N grandson

损 [sǔn] VB **1** (减少) decrease **2** (损害) harm **3** (损坏) damage

损害 [sǔnhài] VB **1** (健康) damage **2** (利益) harm **3** (名誉) ruin **4** (关系) damage

损坏 [sǔnhuài] VB damage

损失 [sǔnshī] **I** VB lose **II** N loss

笋 [sǔn] N bamboo shoot

缩 [suō] VB **1** (收缩) contract **2** (收回去) withdraw

缩减 [suōjiǎn] VB **1** (经费) cut **2** (人员) reduce

缩水 [suōshuǐ] VB shrink

缩写 [suōxiě] **I** N abbreviation **II** VB abridge

所 [suǒ] **I** N **1** (处所) place **2** (用于机构名称) office ▶ 派出所 [pàichūsuǒ] local police station ▶ 诊所 [zěnsuǒ] clinic **II** MEAS ▷ 三所医院 [sān suǒ yīyuàn] three hospitals ▷ 一所大学 [yī suǒ dàxué] a university

> measure word, used for buildings, houses, hospitals, schools, universities, etc.

III AUX WORD **1** (表示被动) ▷ 他被金钱所迷惑。 [Tā bèi jīnqián suǒ míhuò.] He's obsessed with money. **2** (表示强调) ▷ 这正是大家所不理解的。 [Zhè zhèng shì dàjiā suǒ bù lǐjiě de.] This is the bit that no one understands.

所谓 [suǒwèi] ADJ what is known as **1** (通常说的) ▷ 中医所谓 "上火" 不止是指嗓子疼一种症状。 [Zhōngyī suǒwèi"shànghuǒ" bùzhǐ shì zhǐ sǎngzi téng yīzhǒng zhèngzhuàng.] What is known in Chinese medicine as "excess internal heat" covers a lot more than sore throats and the like. **2** (形容不认可) so-called

所以 [suǒyǐ] CONJ (表示结果) so ▷ 路上堵车，所以我迟到了。 [Lù shàng dǔchē, suǒyǐ wǒ chídào le.] There was a lot of traffic, so I am late.

所有 [suǒyǒu] **I** VB own **II** N possession **III** ADJ all

索 [suǒ] **I** N **1** (绳子) rope **2** (链子) chain **II** VB **1** (找) search ▶ 探索 [tànsuǒ] explore **2** (要) request

索赔 [suǒpéi] VB claim damages

索引 [suǒyǐn] N index

锁 [suǒ] **I** N lock **II** VB (用锁锁住) lock

锁链 [suǒliàn] N chain

T

他 [tā] PRON (另一人) he ▷ 他的包 [tā de bāo] his bag ▷ 我还记得他。 [Wǒ hái jìde tā.] I still remember him.

他们 [tāmen] PRON they ▷ 他们的老师 [tāmen de lǎoshī] their teacher ▷ 我给他们写信。 [Wǒ gěi tāmen xiěxìn.] I wrote to them.

他人 [tārén] N others (PL)

它 [tā] PRON it

它们 [tāmen] PRON they

她 [tā] PRON she ▷ 她的帽子 [tā de màozi] her hat ▷ 我给她发了个短信。 [Wǒ gěi tā fā le gè duǎnxìn.] I sent her a text message.

塌 [tā] VB (倒塌) collapse

塌实 [tāshi] ADJ **1** (不浮躁) steady **2** (放心) at peace

塔 [tǎ] N **1** (指佛教建筑物) pagoda **2** (指塔形物) tower

塔楼 [tǎlóu] N high-rise

獭 [tǎ] N otter ▶ 水獭 [shuǐtǎ] otter

踏 [tà] VB (踩) step onto

胎 [tāi] N **1** (母体内的幼体) fetus ▶ 怀胎 [huáitāi] be pregnant **2** (轮胎) tire

胎儿 [tāi'ér] N fetus

台 [tái] **I** N **1** (指建筑) tower ▶ 观测台 [guāncètái] observation tower **2** (指讲话, 表演) stage ▶ 舞台 [wǔtái] stage **3** (指作座子用) stand ▶ 蜡台 [làtái] candlestick **4** (台形物) ▶ 窗台 [chuāngtái] window sill ▶ 站台 [zhàntái] platform **5** (桌子或类似物) table ▶ 梳妆台 [shūzhuāngtái] dressing table ▶ 写字台 [xiězìtái] desk **6** (指电话服务) telephone service ▷ 查号台 [cháhào tái] directory inquiries (PL) **7** (指广播电视) station ▶ 电视台 [diànshìtái] television station **8** (*also*: 台湾) Taiwan **II** MEAS **1** (指机器) ▷ 一台电脑 [yī tái diànnǎo] a computer ▷ 一百台电视 [yībǎi tái diànshì] one hundred TVs **2** (指戏剧, 戏曲) ▷ 两台京剧 [liǎng tái Jīngjù] two Beijing Opera performances ▷ 一台舞剧 [yī tái wǔjù] a ballet

measure word, used for machines, equipment, stage performances, etc.

台风 [táifēng] N typhoon

台阶 [táijiē] N (指建筑) step

台历 [táilì] N desk calendar

台球 [táiqiú] N **1** (指美式) pool **2** (指英式) billiards (SG)

抬 [tái] VB **1** (举) raise **2** (搬) carry

抬头 [táitóu] VB (昂头) raise one's head

太 [tài] **I** ADJ **1** (高或大) highest **2** (指辈分高) senior ▶ 太爷爷 [tài yéye] great-grandfather **II** ADV **1** (指程度过分) too ▷ 这部电影太长。 [Zhè bù diànyǐng tài cháng.] This film is too long. **2** (指程度极高) so ▷ 我太高兴了。 [Wǒ tài gāoxìng le.] I am so happy.

太极拳 [tàijíquán] N Tai-chi

太空 [tàikōng] N space

太平洋 [Tàipíngyáng] N the Pacific Ocean

太太 [tàitai] N **1** (妻子) wife **2** (指对老年妇女) lady **3** (对已婚妇女) Mrs.

太阳 [tàiyáng] N sun

态 [tài] N **1** (状态) state ▶ 常态 [chángtài] normality ▶ 体态 [tǐtài] posture **2** (语言) voice

态度 [tàidu] N **1** (举止神情) manner **2** (看法) attitude

贪 [tān] **I** VB **1** (贪污) be corrupt **2** (不满足) crave **3** (好处, 便宜) covet **II** ADJ greedy

贪吃 [tānchī] be greedy

贪婪 [tānlán] ADJ greedy

贪玩 [tānwán] be too fond of a good time

贪污 [tānwū] VB embezzle

贪心 [tānxīn] I ADJ greedy II N greed

摊 [tān] I VB 1 (摆开) spread ... out ▷ 摊开地图 [tānkāi dìtú] spread out a map 2 (指烹调) fry ▷ 他摊了个鸡蛋。 [Tā tān le gè jīdàn.] He fried an egg. 3 (分担) share II N stall

摊贩 [tānfàn] N street trader

瘫 [tān] I N paralysis II ADJ paralyzed

瘫痪 [tānhuàn] I N paralysis II VB be paralyzed

坛 [tán] N 1 (土台) raised plot ▶ 花坛 [huātán] raised flower bed 2 (台子) platform ▶ 论坛 [lùntán] forum

谈 [tán] I VB talk ▷ 谈生意 [tán shēngyi] discuss business II N talk

谈话 [tánhuà] VB chat

谈论 [tánlùn] VB discuss

谈判 [tánpàn] VB negotiate

谈心 [tánxīn] VB have a heart-to-heart talk

弹 [tán] VB 1 (指弹性) spring ▷ 球弹不起来了。 [Qiú tán bù qǐlái le.] The ball doesn't bounce. 2 (棉花, 羊毛) fluff ... up 3 (土, 灰, 球) flick 4 (乐器) play ▷ 弹钢琴 [tán gāngqín] play the piano

→ *see also*/另见 dàn

弹簧 [tánhuáng] N spring

弹力 [tánlì] N elasticity

弹性 [tánxìng] N 1 (弹力) elasticity 2 (喻) flexibility ▶ 弹性工作制 [tánxìng gōngzuò zhì] flexible working system

痰 [tán] N phlegm

坦 [tǎn] ADJ 1 (平整) flat ▶ 平坦 [píngtǎn] flat 2 (直率) candid 3 (心里安定) calm ▶ 坦然 [tǎnrán] composed

坦白 [tǎnbái] I ADJ candid II VB confess

坦率 [tǎnshuài] ADJ frank

毯 [tǎn] N 1 (指地上) carpet ▶ 地毯 [dìtǎn] carpet 2 (指床上) blanket ▶ 毛毯 [máotǎn] wool blanket 3 (指墙上) tapestry ▶ 壁毯 [bìtǎn] tapestry

叹 [tàn] VB (叹气) sigh

叹气 [tànqì] VB sigh

炭 [tàn] N charcoal

探 [tàn] I VB 1 (试图发现) explore ▶ 探险 [tànxiǎn] explore 2 (看望) visit ▶ 探亲 [tànqīn] visit one's relatives 3 (伸出去) stick ... out 4 (过问) inquire ▶ 打探 [dǎtàn] scout II N scout ▶ 侦探 [zhēntàn] detective

探测 [tàncè] VB survey

探索 [tànsuǒ] VB probe

探讨 [tàntǎo] VB investigate

探望 [tànwàng] VB (看望) visit

碳 [tàn] N carbon

碳中和 [tàn zhōnghé] ADJ carbon-neutral

汤 [tāng] N (指食物) soup

汤药 [tāngyào] N herbal medicine

堂 [táng] I N 1 (房屋) hall ▶ 礼堂 [lǐtáng] auditorium ▶ 课堂 [kètáng] classroom ▶ 教堂 [jiàotáng] church 2 (厅) hall II MEAS ▷ 两堂课 [liǎng táng kè] two lessons

measure word, used for school lessons

糖 [táng] N 1 (指做饭) sugar 2 (糖果) sweet

躺 [tǎng] VB lie

烫 [tàng] I ADJ very hot ▷ 这汤真烫。 [Zhè tāng zhēn tàng.] This soup is boiling hot. II VB 1 (人) scald 2 (加热) heat ... up 3 (熨) iron 4 (头发) perm

烫手 [tàngshǒu] ADJ scalding

趟 [tàng] MEAS 1 (指旅程) ▷ 我已经去了好几趟。 [Wǒ yǐjīng qù le hǎo jǐ tàng.] I've made several trips. 2 (指公车, 地铁等) ▷ 他错过了一趟车。

[Tā cuòguò le yī tàng chē.] He missed the bus.

measure word, used for journeys, visits, scheduled public transport, etc.

掏 [tāo] VB **1** (拿出) take ... out **2** (挖) dig **3** (偷) steal

逃 [táo] VB **1** (逃跑) run away **2** (逃避) flee

逃避 [táobì] VB escape ▷ 逃避责任 [táobì zérèn] shirk responsibility ▷ 逃避关税 [táobì guānshuì] evade customs duties

逃跑 [táopǎo] VB escape

桃 [táo] N peach ▶ 桃子 [táozi] peach

陶 [táo] N pottery

陶瓷 [táocí] N ceramics (PL)

陶器 [táoqì] N pottery

陶醉 [táozuì] VB be intoxicated

淘 [táo] **I** VB **1** (米) wash **2** (金子) pan for ▶ 淘金 [táojīn] pan for gold **II** ADJ naughty

淘气 [táoqì] ADJ naughty

淘汰 [táotài] VB eliminate

讨 [tǎo] VB **1** (债) demand **2** (饭, 钱) beg **3** (讨论) discuss

讨论 [tǎolùn] VB discuss

讨厌 [tǎoyàn] **I** ADJ **1** (可恶) disgusting **2** (指难办) nasty **II** VB dislike

套 [tào] **I** N (套子) cover ▶ 手套 [shǒutào] glove ▶ 避孕套 [bìyùntào] condom **II** VB (罩在外面) slip ... on **III** MEAS set ▷ 一套西装 [yī tào xīzhuāng] a suit ▷ 两套邮票 [liǎng tào yóupiào] two sets of stamps

measure word, used for suits, collections of books, tools, etc.

套餐 [tàocān] N set meal

特 [tè] **I** ADJ special **II** ADV **1** (特地) especially **2** (非常) extremely

特别 [tèbié] **I** ADJ peculiar **II** ADV **1** (格外) exceptionally **2** (特地) specially

特此 [tècǐ] ADV hereby

特地 [tèdì] ADV especially

特点 [tèdiǎn] N characteristic

特价 [tèjià] N bargain price ▷ 特价商品 [tèjià shāngpǐn] bargain

特例 [tèlì] N special case

特区 [tèqū] N special zone

特权 [tèquán] N privilege

特色 [tèsè] N characteristic

特殊 [tèshū] ADJ special

特务 [tèwu] N special agent

特征 [tèzhēng] N characteristic

疼 [téng] **I** ADJ sore ▷ 我牙疼。 [Wǒ yá téng.] I have toothache. **II** VB love

藤 [téng] N vine ▶ 藤椅 [téngyǐ] cane chair

剔 [tī] VB (牙, 指甲) pick

梯 [tī] N ladder ▶ 电梯 [diàntī] elevator ▶ 楼梯 [lóutī] stairs (PL)

踢 [tī] VB kick ▷ 踢足球 [tī zúqiú] play soccer

提 [tí] VB **1** (拿) carry **2** (升) raise ▶ 提拔 [tíbá] promote **3** (提前) bring forward **4** (提出) put ... forward ▷ 他提了个建议。 [Tā tí le gè jiànyì.] He put forward a proposal. **5** (提取) collect **6** (谈起) mention ▷ 别再提那件事了。 [Bié zài tí nà jiàn shì le.] Don't mention that subject again.

提倡 [tíchàng] VB promote

提出 [tíchū] VB put ... forward

提纲 [tígāng] N synopsis

提高 [tígāo] VB raise ▷ 提高效率 [tígāo xiàolǜ] increase efficiency

提供 [tígōng] VB provide

提前 [tíqián] **I** VB bring ... forward **II** ADV early

提问 [tíwèn] VB ask a question

提醒 [tíxǐng] VB remind

提议 [tíyì] **I** VB propose **II** N proposal

题 [tí] **I** N subject ▶ 标题 [biāotí] title **II** VB inscribe

题材 [tícái] N theme

题目 [tímù] N **1** (标题) title **2** (考题) question

蹄 [tí] N hoof

体 [tǐ] N **1** (身体) body ▶ 人体 [réntǐ] human body **2** (物体) substance ▶ 液体 [yètǐ] liquid

体操 [tǐcāo] N gymnastics (SG)

体会 [tǐhuì] **I** VB come to understand **II** N understanding

体积 [tǐjī] N volume

体检 [tǐjiǎn] N physical examination

体力 [tǐlì] N physical strength

体贴 [tǐtiē] VB show consideration for

体温 [tǐwēn] N temperature

体系 [tǐxì] N system

体现 [tǐxiàn] VB embody

体型 [tǐxíng] N physique

体验 [tǐyàn] VB learn from experience

体育 [tǐyù] N **1** (课程) P.E. **2** (运动) sport ▷ 体育比赛 [tǐyù bǐsài] sports event

体育场 [tǐyùchǎng] N stadium

体育馆 [tǐyùguǎn] N gym

体重 [tǐzhòng] N weight

剃 [tì] VB shave

替 [tì] **I** VB (代) replace **II** PREP for ▷ 别替他操心了。 [Bié tì tā cāoxīn le.] Don't worry about him.

替代 [tìdài] VB replace

天 [tiān] **I** N **1** (天空) sky **2** (一昼夜) day ▶ 昨天 [zuótiān] yesterday **3** (一段时间) ▷ 天还早呢。 [Tiān hái zǎo ne.] It's still so early. **4** (季节) season ▶ 秋天 [qiūtiān] fall **5** (天气) weather ▶ 阴天 [yīntiān] overcast weather ▷ 天很热。 [Tiān hěn rè.] It's a very hot day. **6** (自然) nature **7** (造物主) God ▷ 天知道！ [Tiān zhīdao!] God knows! **8** (神的住所) Heaven **II** ADJ (指位于顶部的) overhead ▶ 天桥 [tiānqiáo] overhead walkway

天才 [tiāncái] N **1** (才能) talent **2** (人) genius

天鹅 [tiān'é] N swan

天空 [tiānkōng] N sky

天气 [tiānqì] N weather ▷ 天气预报 [tiānqì yùbào] weather forecast

天然 [tiānrán] ADJ natural

天生 [tiānshēng] ADJ inherent ▷ 这孩子天生聋哑。 [Zhè háizi tiānshēng lóngyǎ.] This child was born deaf and mute.

天使 [tiānshǐ] N angel

天堂 [tiāntáng] N Heaven

天下 [tiānxià] N the world

天线 [tiānxiàn] N aerial

天性 [tiānxìng] N nature

天真 [tiānzhēn] ADJ innocent

添 [tiān] VB (增加) add

田 [tián] N **1** (耕地) field **2** (开采地) field ▶ 油田 [yóutián] oilfield

田径 [tiánjìng] N track and field sports (PL)

田野 [tiányě] N open country

甜 [tián] ADJ **1** (指味道) sweet **2** (指睡觉) sound

甜点 [tiándiǎn] N dessert

甜食 [tiánshí] N sweet

填 [tián] VB **1** (塞满) fill **2** (填写) complete ▷ 填表格 [tián biǎogé] fill in a form

填充 [tiánchōng] VB **1** (填上) stuff **2** (补足) fill ... in

填空 [tiánkòng] VB (指考试) fill in the blanks

填写 [tiánxiě] VB fill ... in

舔 [tiǎn] VB lick

挑 [tiāo] VB **1** (肩扛) carry ... on a carrying pole **2** (挑选) choose **3** (挑剔) nitpick

→ *see also*/另见 tiǎo

挑食 [tiāoshí] VB be a fussy eater
挑剔 [tiāotì] VB nitpick
挑选 [tiāoxuǎn] VB select

条 [tiáo] I N 1 (细树枝) twig 2 (长条) strip 3 (层次) order 4 (分项) item 5 (律令) article 6 (短书信) note II MEAS 1 (用于细长东西) ▷ 两条腿 [liǎng tiáo tuǐ] two legs ▷ 一条烟 [yī tiáo yān] a multipack of cigarettes 2 (指分事项的) ▷ 一条新闻 [yī tiáo xīnwén] an item of news 3 (指与人有关) ▷ 一条人命 [yī tiáo rénmìng] a life

measure word, used for long thin things, news, human lives, etc.

条件 [tiáojiàn] N 1 (客观因素) condition 2 (要求) requirement 3 (状况) circumstances (PL)
条理 [tiáolǐ] N order
条约 [tiáoyuē] N treaty

调 [tiáo] VB 1 (使和谐) harmonize ▶ 失调 [shītiáo] imbalance 2 (使均匀) blend ▷ 给钢琴调音 [gěi gāngqín tiáo yīn] tune a piano 3 (调解) mediate
→ *see also*/另见 diào
调节 [tiáojié] VB adjust
调料 [tiáoliào] N seasoning
调皮 [tiáopí] ADJ (顽皮) naughty
调整 [tiáozhěng] VB adjust

挑 [tiǎo] VB 1 (扯起一头) raise 2 (向上拨) prick
→ *see also*/另见 tiāo
挑战 [tiǎozhàn] VB challenge ▶ 面临新挑战 [miànlín xīn tiǎozhàn] face a new challenge

跳 [tiào] VB 1 (跃) jump ▶ 跳高 [tiàogāo] high jump ▶ 跳水 [tiàoshuǐ] diving ▶ 跳远 [tiàoyuǎn] long jump 2 (弹起) bounce 3 (起伏地动) beat ▶ 心跳 [xīntiào] heartbeat 4 (越过) jump over ▷ 跳过几页 [tiàoguò jǐ yè] skip a few pages
跳槽 [tiàocáo] VB change jobs
跳舞 [tiàowǔ] VB dance
跳跃 [tiàoyuè] VB jump

贴 [tiē] I VB 1 (粘) stick 2 (紧挨) be close to 3 (贴补) subsidize II N allowance

帖 [tiě] N 1 (请帖) invitation ▶ 请帖 [qǐngtiě] invitation 2 (小卡片) card

铁 [tiě] N (金属) iron
铁道 [tiědào] N railroad
铁路 [tiělù] N railroad

厅 [tīng] N 1 (大堂) hall ▶ 客厅 [kètīng] sitting room ▶ 餐厅 [cāntīng] canteen 2 (机关) office

听 [tīng] I VB 1 (收听) listen to 2 (听从) obey ▷ 听老师的话 [tīng lǎoshī de huà] do as the teacher says II N tin III MEAS can ▷ 一听啤酒 [yī tīng píjiǔ] a can of beer
听话 [tīnghuà] I VB obey II ADJ obedient
听见 [tīngjiàn] VB hear
听讲 [tīngjiǎng] VB attend a lecture
听说 [tīngshuō] VB hear
听众 [tīngzhòng] N audience

亭 [tíng] N I (亭子) pavilion II (小房子) kiosk ▶ 电话亭 [diànhuàtíng] phone booth

庭 [tíng] N 1 (书) (厅堂) hall 2 (院子) courtyard
庭院 [tíngyuàn] N courtyard

停 [tíng] VB 1 (止) stop 2 (停留) stop off 3 (停放) park
停车场 [tíngchēchǎng] N car lot
停顿 [tíngdùn] I VB 1 (中止) halt 2 (指说话) pause II N pause
停止 [tíngzhǐ] VB stop ▷ 停止营业 [tíngzhǐ yíngyè] cease trading

挺 [tǐng] ADV very

艇 [tǐng] N boat ▶ 游艇 [yóutǐng] yacht ▶ 救生艇 [jiùshēngtǐng] lifeboat

通 [tōng] **I** VB **1** (连接) connect with ▶ 通商 [tōngshāng] have trade relations with ▶ 通风 [tōngfēng] ventilate **2** (使不堵) clear ... out ▷ 通下水道 [tōng xiàshuǐdào] clear out a drain **3** (传达) inform ▶ 通信 [tōngxìn] correspond by letter ▷ 通电话 [tōng diànhuà] communicate by telephone **4** (通晓) understand ▶ 精通 [jīngtōng] be expert in **II** N expert ▷ 外语通 [wàiyǔ tōng] an expert in foreign languages **III** ADJ **1** (没有障碍) open ▷ 电话打通了。[Diànhuà dǎ tōng le.] The call has been put through. **2** (顺畅) workable **3** (通顺) coherent **4** (普通) common **5** (整个) overall **IV** ADV **1** (全部) completely **2** (一般) normally

通常 [tōngcháng] **I** ADJ normal **II** N normal circumstances (PL) ▷ 我通常7点起床。[Wǒ tōngcháng qīdiǎn qǐchuáng.] Under normal circumstances, I get up at seven o'clock.

通道 [tōngdào] N (指出入) passageway ▷ 地下通道 [dìxià tōngdào] tunnel

通过 [tōngguò] **I** VB **1** (经过) pass ▷ 通过边境线 [tōngguò biānjìngxiàn] cross the border **2** (同意) pass **II** PREP by means of

通俗 [tōngsú] ADJ popular

通宵 [tōngxiāo] N all night

通信 [tōngxìn] VB correspond

通讯 [tōngxùn] **I** N dispatch **II** VB communicate

通用 [tōngyòng] VB be in common use

同 [tóng] **I** VB **1** (一样) be the same ▶ 不同 [bùtóng] be different **2** (共同) do ... together ▶ 同居 [tóngjū] cohabit **II** PREP **1** (跟) with **2** (指比较) as

同伴 [tóngbàn] N companion

同等 [tóngděng] ADJ of the same level

同类 [tónglèi] **I** ADJ of the same kind **II** N the same kind

同盟 [tóngméng] N alliance

同情 [tóngqíng] VB sympathize ▷ 表示同情 [biǎoshì tóngqíng] express sympathy

同时 [tóngshí] **I** N at the same time ▷ 同时发生 [tóngshí fāshēng] occur simultaneously **II** CONJ besides

同事 [tóngshì] N colleague

同性恋 [tóngxìngliàn] N homosexuality

同学 [tóngxué] N **1** (指同校) fellow student **2** (指同班) classmate

同样 [tóngyàng] ADJ **1** (一样) same **2** (情况类似) similar

同意 [tóngyì] VB agree

同志 [tóngzhì] N comrade

铜 [tóng] N copper

铜牌 [tóngpái] N bronze medal

童 [tóng] N (小孩) child ▶ 神童 [shéntóng] child prodigy

童话 [tónghuà] N fairy tale

童年 [tóngnián] N childhood

统 [tǒng] **I** N ▶ 系统 [xìtǒng] system ▶ 血统 [xuètǒng] bloodline **II** VB command **III** ADV all

统计 [tǒngjì] **I** N statistics (PL) ▷ 人口统计 [rénkǒu tǒngjì] census **II** VB count

统统 [tǒngtǒng] ADV entirely

统一 [tǒngyī] **I** VB **1** (使成一体) unite **2** (使一致) unify ▷ 统一思想 [tǒngyī sīxiǎng] reach a common under-standing **II** ADJ unified

统治 [tǒngzhì] VB rule

桶 [tǒng] **I** N bucket ▷ 汽油桶 [qìyóu tǒng] gasoline drum ▷ 啤酒桶 [píjiǔ tǒng] beer barrel **II** MEAS barrel ▷ 一桶柴油 [yī tǒng cháiyóu] a barrel of diesel oil ▷ 两桶牛奶 [liǎng tǒng niúnǎi] two churns of milk

筒 [tǒng] N **1** (竹管) bamboo tube

2 (粗管状物) ▶ 笔筒 [bǐtǒng] pen holder ▶ 邮筒 [yóutǒng] mailbox 3 (指衣服) ▶ 长筒袜 [chángtǒngwà] stockings (PL)

痛 [tòng] I VB 1 (疼) ache ▶ 头痛 [tóutòng] have a headache ▶ 胃痛 [wèitòng] have a stomach ache 2 (悲伤) grieve ▶ 哀痛 [āitòng] sorrow II ADV deeply ▶ 痛打 [tòngdǎ] give a sound beating to

痛苦 [tòngkǔ] ADJ painful

痛快 [tòngkuài] ADJ 1 (高兴) joyful 2 (尽兴) to one's heart's content ▷ 玩个痛快 [wán gè tòngkuài] play to one's heart's content 3 (爽快) straightforward

偷 [tōu] I VB (窃) steal II ADV stealthily

偷空 [tōukòng] VB take time off

偷懒 [tōulǎn] VB be lazy

偷窃 [tōuqiè] VB steal

偷偷 [tōutōu] ADV secretly

头 [tóu] I N 1 (脑袋) head ▶ 点头 [diǎntóu] nod one's head 2 (头发) hair ▶ 分头 [fēntóu] parted hair ▶ 平头 [píngtóu] crew cut ▶ 梳头 [shūtóu] comb one's hair 3 (顶端) tip 4 (开始) beginning 5 (头目) head ▷ 谁是你们的头儿？ [Shéi shì nǐmen de tóur?] Who's your boss? II ADJ 1 (第一) first ▶ 头奖 [tóujiǎng] first prize ▶ 头等 [tóuděng] first class 2 (领头) leading 3 (时间在前) first ▷ 头几年 [tóu jǐ nián] first few years III MEAS 1 (指动物) ▷ 3头母牛 [sān tóu mǔniú] three cows 2 (指蒜) bulb ▷ 一头蒜 [yī tóu suàn] a bulb of garlic

measure word, used for cows, bulls, and vegetable bulbs

头发 [tóufa] N hair

头领 [tóulǐng] N leader

头脑 [tóunǎo] N brains (PL)

头衔 [tóuxián] N title

投 [tóu] VB 1 (扔) throw 2 (放进去) put ... in 3 (跳下去) throw oneself 4 (投射) cast 5 (寄) post

投入 [tóurù] I ADJ 1 (指专注) engrossed 2 (指逼真) realistic II VB 1 (放入) put ... in 2 (参加) throw oneself into

投诉 [tóusù] I VB lodge a complaint II N appeal

投降 [tóuxiáng] VB surrender

投资 [tóuzī] I VB invest II N investment

透 [tòu] I VB 1 (渗透) penetrate 2 (泄露) leak out 3 (显露) appear II ADJ 1 (透彻) thorough 2 (程度深) complete ▷ 我浑身都湿透了。 [Wǒ húnshēn dōu shī tòu le.] I'm soaked to the skin.

透彻 [tòuchè] ADJ incisive

透露 [tòulù] VB disclose

透明 [tòumíng] ADJ transparent

秃 [tū] ADJ 1 (指毛发) bald 2 (指山) barren 3 (指树) bare

秃顶 [tūdǐng] VB be bald

秃子 [tūzi] N (口) baldy

突 [tū] ADV suddenly

突出 [tūchū] I VB give prominence to ▷ 他从不突出自己。 [Tā cóng bù tūchū zìjǐ.] He never pushes himself forward. II ADJ (明显) noticeable ▷ 突出的特点 [tūchū de tèdiǎn] prominent feature

突击 [tūjī] I VB 1 (突然袭击) assault 2 (加快完成) do a rush job II ADV from nowhere

突破 [tūpò] VB 1 (防线, 界线) break through 2 (僵局, 难关) make a breakthrough 3 (限额) surpass 4 (记录) break

突然 [tūrán] I ADJ sudden II ADV suddenly

图 [tú] I N 1 (图画) picture 2 (地图) map 3 (计划) plan II VB 1 (贪图) seek ▷ 图一时痛快 [tú yīshí tòngkuai] seek momentary gratification 2 (谋划) scheme

图案 [tú'àn] N design
图画 [túhuà] N picture
图书 [túshū] N books (PL)
图书馆 [túshūguǎn] N library
图像 [túxiàng] N image
图章 [túzhāng] N seal

徒 [tú] N (徒弟) apprentice ▶ 徒弟 [túdì] apprentice

途 [tú] N way ▶ 旅途 [lǚtú] journey ▶ 前途 [qiántú] prospect
途径 [tújìng] N channel

涂 [tú] VB 1 (抹) spread ... on ▷ 涂油漆 [tú yóuqī] apply paint 2 (乱写乱画) scribble 3 (改动) cross ... out
涂改 [túgǎi] VB alter
涂料 [túliào] N paint

屠 [tú] I VB 1 (动物) slaughter 2 (人) massacre II N butcher
屠夫 [túfū] N (字) butcher
屠杀 [túshā] VB massacre

土 [tǔ] I N 1 (泥) soil 2 (土地) land ▶ 领土 [lǐngtǔ] territory II ADJ 1 (地方) local 2 (民间) folk 3 (不时髦) unfashionable
土地 [tǔdì] N 1 (田地) land 2 (疆域) territory
土豆 [tǔdòu] N potato
土话 [tǔhuà] N local dialect
土壤 [tǔrǎng] N soil
土著 [tǔzhù] N indigenous peoples (PL)

吐 [tǔ] VB (排出口外) spit
→ *see also*/另见 tù

吐 [tù] VB vomit
→ *see also*/另见 tǔ
吐沫 [tùmo] N saliva

兔 [tù] N 1 (野兔) hare 2 (家兔) rabbit

团 [tuán] I N 1 (球形物) ball 2 (组织) group ▶ 剧团 [jùtuán] drama company 3 (军) regiment II VB 1 (聚合) unite ▶ 团聚 [tuánjù] reunite 2 (揉成球状) roll into a ball III ADJ round IV MEAS ▷ 一团面 [yī tuán miàn] a lump of dough ▷ 一团毛线 [yī tuán máoxiàn] a ball of wool

measure word, used for rolled up round things

团伙 [tuánhuǒ] N gang
团结 [tuánjié] VB unite
团体 [tuántǐ] N organization
团圆 [tuányuán] VB reunite

推 [tuī] VB 1 (门, 窗, 车) push 2 (指用工具) scrape ▷ 他推了个光头。 [Tā tuī le gè guāngtóu.] He's shaved his head. 3 (开展) push forward 4 (推断) deduce 5 (辞让) decline 6 (推诿) shift 7 (推迟) postpone 8 (举荐) elect
推测 [tuīcè] VB infer
推辞 [tuīcí] VB decline
推迟 [tuīchí] VB put ... off
推出 [tuīchū] VB bring ... out
推动 [tuīdòng] VB promote
推广 [tuīguǎng] VB popularize
推荐 [tuījiàn] VB recommend
推销 [tuīxiāo] VB promote

腿 [tuǐ] N 1 (下肢) leg ▶ 大腿 [dàtuǐ] thigh ▶ 小腿 [xiǎotuǐ] calf 2 (支撑物) leg

退 [tuì] VB 1 (后移) retreat 2 (使后移) cause ... to withdraw 3 (退出) quit 4 (减退) recede 5 (减弱) fade 6 (退还) return 7 (撤销) cancel
退步 [tuìbù] I VB 1 (落后) lag behind 2 (让步) give way II N leeway
退让 [tuìràng] VB make a concession
退缩 [tuìsuō] VB hold back
退休 [tuìxiū] VB retire

褪 [tuì] VB 1 (衣服) take ... off 2 (毛) shed 3 (颜色) fade

吞 [tūn] VB 1 (整个咽下) swallow 2 (吞并) take over
吞并 [tūnbìng] VB annex
吞没 [tūnmò] VB 1 (据为己有)

misappropriate **2** (淹没) engulf

臀 [tún] N buttock

托 [tuō] **I** VB **1** (撑) support **2** (委托) entrust **3** (依赖) rely on **II** N tray

托儿所 [tuō'érsuǒ] N nursery

托福 [tuōfú] N TOEFL, Test of English as a Foreign Language

托付 [tuōfù] VB entrust

托运 [tuōyùn] VB ship

拖 [tuō] VB **1** (拉) pull **2** (地板) mop **3** (下垂) trail **4** (拖延) delay

拖延 [tuōyán] VB delay

脱 [tuō] VB **1** (皮肤, 毛发) shed **2** (衣服, 鞋帽) take ... off **3** (摆脱) escape **4** (颜色) fade **5** (油脂) skim

脱臼 [tuōjiù] VB dislocate

脱离 [tuōlí] VB **1** (关系) break off **2** (危险) get away from

脱落 [tuōluò] VB **1** (毛发, 牙齿) lose **2** (油漆, 墙皮) come off

脱水 [tuōshuǐ] VB dehydrate

驮 [tuó] VB carry on one's back

驼 [tuó] **I** N camel ▶ 骆驼 [luòtuo] camel **II** ADJ hunchbacked ▶ 驼背 [tuóbèi] be hunchbacked

鸵 [tuó] *see below*/见下文

鸵鸟 [tuóniǎo] N ostrich

妥 [tuǒ] ADJ **1** (适当) appropriate **2** (停当) ready

妥当 [tuǒdang] ADJ appropriate

妥善 [tuǒshàn] ADJ appropriate

妥协 [tuǒxié] VB compromise

椭 [tuǒ] *see below*/见下文

椭圆 [tuǒyuán] N oval

拓 [tuò] VB open ... up

拓展 [tuòzhǎn] VB expand

唾 [tuò] **I** N saliva **II** VB spit

唾沫 [tuòmo] N (口) saliva

W

挖 [wā] VB **1** (掘) dig ▶ 挖掘 [wājué] excavate **2** (耳朵, 鼻子) pick

蛙 [wā] N frog

蛙泳 [wāyǒng] N breaststroke

娃 [wá] N (方) baby

娃娃 [wáwa] N **1** (小孩) baby **2** (玩具) doll

瓦 [wǎ] N tile

瓦斯 [wǎsī] N gas

袜 [wà] N sock ▶ 长筒袜 [chángtǒngwà] stocking

袜子 [wàzi] N sock

歪 [wāi] ADJ (倾斜) slanting

歪斜 [wāixié] ADJ crooked

外 [wài] **I** N **1** (范围以外) outside ▶ 外边 [wàibian] outside **2** (外国) foreign country **II** ADJ **1** (外国的) foreign **2** (其他的) other ▶ 外人 [wàirén] outsider **III** ADV besides

外表 [wàibiǎo] N exterior

外地 [wàidì] N other parts of the country ▶ 外地人 [wàidìrén] person from another part of the country

外公 [wàigōng] N maternal grandfather

外国 [wàiguó] N foreign country

外国人 [wàiguórén] N foreign person

外号 [wàihào] N nickname

外汇 [wàihuì] N (外币) foreign currency

外交 [wàijiāo] N foreign affairs ▶ 外交部 [wàijiāobù] Ministry of Foreign Affairs

外交官 [wàijiāoguān] N diplomat

外科 [wàikē] N surgery ▶ 外科医生 [wàikē yīshēng] surgeon

外卖 [wàimài] N takeout

外贸 [wàimào] N foreign trade

外婆 [wàipó] N maternal grandmother

外企 [wàiqǐ] N foreign enterprise

外伤 [wàishāng] N injury

外商 [wàishāng] N foreign businessman

外甥 [wàisheng] N nephew

外孙 [wàisūn] N grandson

外套 [wàitào] N overcoat

外文 [wàiwén] N foreign language

外向 [wàixiàng] ADJ (指性格) extrovert

外语 [wàiyǔ] N foreign language

弯 [wān] **I** ADJ curved **II** VB bend **III** N bend

湾 [wān] N bay

豌 [wān] *see below*/见下文

豌豆 [wāndòu] N pea

丸 [wán] **I** N (指药) pill ▶ 丸药 [wányào] pill **II** MEAS pill ▷ 他服了一丸药。 [Tā fú le yī wán yào.] He took a pill.

完 [wán] **I** ADJ whole **II** VB **1** (完成) complete **2** (耗尽) run out **3** (了结) finish

完成 [wánchéng] VB complete

完美 [wánměi] ADJ perfect

完全 [wánquán] **I** ADJ complete **II** ADV completely

完整 [wánzhěng] ADJ complete

玩 [wán] VB **1** (玩耍) play **2** (游玩) have a good time ▷ 我去泰国玩了一个星期。 [Wǒ qù Tàiguó wán le yī gè xīngqī.] I went to Thailand on vacation for a week. **3** (做客) visit **4** (表示祝愿) enjoy ▷ 玩得好！ [Wán de hǎo!] Enjoy yourself!

玩具 [wánjù] N toy

玩笑 [wánxiào] N joke ▷ 他喜欢跟人开玩笑。 [Tā xǐhuan gēn rén kāi wánxiào.] He likes to play jokes on people.

玩意儿 [wányìr] N (口) **1** (东西) thing

2 (玩具) toy 3 (器械) gadget

顽 [wán] ADJ 1 (难以摆脱的) stubborn ▶ 顽固 [wángù] stubborn 2 (淘气) naughty ▶ 顽皮 [wánpí] mischievous

挽 [wǎn] VB 1 (拉) hold 2 (卷起) roll ... up

晚 [wǎn] I ADJ late ▶ 晚秋 [wǎnqiū] late autumn ▷ 我起晚了。 [Wǒ qǐ wǎn le.] I got up late. II N evening

晚安 [wǎn'ān] ADJ good night

晚饭 [wǎnfàn] N dinner

晚会 [wǎnhuì] N party

晚年 [wǎnnián] N old age

晚上 [wǎnshang] N evening

碗 [wǎn] N bowl

万 [wàn] NUM ten thousand

万岁 [wànsuì] INT long live

万一 [wànyī] CONJ if by any chance

腕 [wàn] N 1 (指手) wrist 2 (指脚) ankle

腕子 [wànzi] N 1 (指手) wrist 2 (指脚) ankle

亡 [wáng] VB die ▶ 死亡 [sǐwáng] die

王 [wáng] N king

王国 [wángguó] N kingdom

王子 [wángzǐ] N prince

网 [wǎng] N 1 (工具) net 2 (网状物) web 3 (系统) network ▶ 互联网 [Hùliánwǎng] the internet

网吧 [wǎngbā] N internet café

网络 [wǎngluò] N network

网民 [wǎngmín] N internet user

网球 [wǎngqiú] N tennis ▶ 网球场 [wǎngqiúchǎng] tennis court

网页 [wǎngyè] N web page

网站 [wǎngzhàn] N website

网址 [wǎngzhǐ] N web address

往 [wǎng] I PREP to II ADJ past ▶ 往事 [wǎngshì] past events (PL)

往往 [wǎngwǎng] ADV often

忘 [wàng] VB forget

忘记 [wàngjì] VB forget

旺 [wàng] ADJ 1 (火) roaring 2 (人, 生意) flourishing 3 (花) blooming

旺季 [wàngjì] N 1 (指生意) peak season 2 (指水果, 蔬菜) season

旺盛 [wàngshèng] ADJ 1 (精力, 生命力) full of energy 2 (植物) thriving

望 [wàng] VB 1 (向远处看) look into the distance 2 (察看) watch 3 (希望) hope

危 [wēi] I ADJ dangerous II VB endanger

危害 [wēihài] VB harm

危机 [wēijī] N crisis

危险 [wēixiǎn] I ADJ dangerous II N danger

威 [wēi] N power

威力 [wēilì] N power

威士忌 [wēishìjì] N whiskey

威胁 [wēixié] VB threaten

威信 [wēixìn] N prestige

威严 [wēiyán] I ADJ dignified II N dignity

微 [wēi] I ADJ tiny ▶ 微米 [wēimǐ] micron ▶ 微秒 [wēimiǎo] microsecond II ADV slightly

微波炉 [wēibōlú] N microwave oven

微风 [wēifēng] N gentle breeze

微量元素 [wēiliàng yuánsù] N trace element

微妙 [wēimiào] ADJ delicate

微弱 [wēiruò] ADJ faint

微生物 [wēishēngwù] N microorganism

微小 [wēixiǎo] ADJ tiny

微笑 [wēixiào] VB smile

微型 [wēixíng] ADJ mini

为 [wéi] I VB 1 (是) be 2 (充当) act as II PREP by
→ *see also*/另见 wèi

为难 [wéinán] I ADJ embarrassed

II VB make things difficult for
为期 [wéiqī] VB be scheduled for
为生 [wéishēng] VB make a living
为止 [wéizhǐ] VB ▷ 到上周末为止 [dào shàngzhōu mò wéizhǐ] by the end of last week

违 [wéi] VB break ▶ 违章 [wéizhāng] break regulations
违背 [wéibèi] VB go against
违法 [wéifǎ] I VB break the law II ADJ illegal
违反 [wéifǎn] VB go against
违犯 [wéifàn] VB violate

围 [wéi] I VB surround II N 1 (四周) all sides 2 (周长) measurement ▶ 三围 [sānwéi] vital statistics ▶ 胸围 [xiōngwéi] chest measurement
围棋 [wéiqí] N go® (*board game*)

围棋 [wéiqí]

围棋 wéiqí is a popular strategic board game in China, Japan and other East-Asian countries. It originated in ancient China. It is known as go in Japan. It is played by two players alternately placing black and white round stone pieces on the intersections of a square grid on a square game board. To win, the player must control a larger area on the game board than his/her opponent.

围绕 [wéirào] VB 1 (物体) revolve around 2 (话题) center on

惟 [wéi] ADV 1 (单单) only 2 (书) (只是) but only
惟一 [wéiyī] ADJ only

维 [wéi] I VB 1 (连接) hold ... together 2 (保持) maintain II N dimension
维持 [wéichí] VB 1 (保持) maintain 2 (资助) support
维护 [wéihù] VB safeguard
维生素 [wéishēngsù] N vitamin
维修 [wéixiū] VB maintain

伟 [wěi] ADJ great
伟大 [wěidà] ADJ great
伟哥 [wěigē] N (医) Viagra
伟人 [wěirén] N great man

伪 [wěi] ADJ false
伪钞 [wěichāo] N counterfeit bill
伪君子 [wěijūnzǐ] N hypocrite
伪造 [wěizào] VB forge
伪装 [wěizhuāng] I VB disguise II N disguise

尾 [wěi] N 1 (尾巴) tail ▶ 尾巴 [wěiba] tail 2 (末端) end 3 (残余) remainder ▶ 扫尾 [sǎowěi] finish off
尾气 [wěiqì] N tailpipe

纬 [wěi] N (地理) latitude ▶ 纬线 [wěixiàn] latitude
纬度 [wěidù] N latitude

委 [wěi] I VB entrust II N 1 (委员) committee member ▶ 委员 [wěiyuán] committee member 2 (委员会) committee ▶ 委员会 [wěiyuán huì] committee
委屈 [wěiqu] N unjust treatment
委托 [wěituō] VB entrust
委婉 [wěiwǎn] ADJ (指言词) tactful

卫 [wèi] VB protect
卫生 [wèishēng] I N 1 (干净) hygiene 2 (扫除) clean-up II ADJ hygienic
卫生间 [wèishēngjiān] N rest room
卫生纸 [wèishēngzhǐ] N toilet tissue
卫星 [wèixīng] N satellite

为 [wèi] PREP for ▷ 我真为你高兴! [Wǒ zhēn wèi nǐ gāoxìng!] I am really happy for you!
→ *see also*/另见 wéi
为了 [wèile] PREP in order to
为什么 [wèishénme] ADV why

未 [wèi] ADV not
未必 [wèibì] ADV not necessarily
未成年人 [wèichéngniánrén] N minor
未婚夫 [wèihūnfū] N fiancé
未婚妻 [wèihūnqī] N fiancée

未来 [wèilái] N future

位 [wèi] I N 1 (位置) location 2 (地位) position 3 (数学) digit ▷ 两位数 [liǎng wèi shù] two-digit number II MEAS ▷ 两位教授 [liǎng wèi jiàoshòu] two professors ▷ 一位父亲 [yī wèi fùqin] a father

measure word, used for people

位于 [wèiyú] VB be located

位置 [wèizhi] N 1 (地点) location 2 (地位) place 3 (职位) position

位子 [wèizi] N 1 (座位) seat 2 (职位) position

味 [wèi] N 1 (滋味) taste 2 (气味) smell

味道 [wèidao] N (滋味) taste

味精 [wèijīng] N monosodium glutamate

胃 [wèi] N stomach

胃口 [wèikǒu] N 1 (食欲) appetite 2 (喜好) liking

喂 [wèi] I VB feed ▶ 喂养 [wèiyǎng] raise II INT 1 (指打电话) hello 2 (指招呼) hey

温 [wēn] I ADJ 1 (不冷不热) warm 2 (平和) mild II VB (加热) warm ... up III N temperature

温度 [wēndù] N temperature

温和 [wēnhé] ADJ 1 (指性情, 态度) mild 2 (指气候) temperate

温暖 [wēnnuǎn] ADJ warm

温泉 [wēnquán] N hot spring

温柔 [wēnróu] ADJ gentle

温室 [wēnshì] N greenhouse ▷ 温室效应 [wēnshì xiàoyìng] the greenhouse effect

文 [wén] N 1 (字) writing 2 (书面语) written language ▶ 中文 [Zhōngwén] the Chinese language 3 (文章) essay 4 (指社会产物) culture 5 (文科) humanities (PL)

文化 [wénhuà] N 1 (精神财富) culture 2 (知识) education

文件 [wénjiàn] N 1 (公文) document 2 (计算机) file

文具 [wénjù] N stationery

文科 [wénkē] N humanities (PL)

文盲 [wénmáng] ADJ illiterate

文明 [wénmíng] I N civilization II ADJ civilized

文凭 [wénpíng] N diploma

文物 [wénwù] N cultural relic

文学 [wénxué] N literature

文艺 [wényì] N 1 (文学艺术) art and literature 2 (文学) literature 3 (演艺) performing arts (PL)

文章 [wénzhāng] N (著作) essay

文字 [wénzì] N 1 (指符号) script 2 (指文章) writing

闻 [wén] I VB (嗅) smell II N (消息) news (SG) ▶ 新闻 [xīnwén] news

蚊 [wén] N mosquito ▶ 蚊子 [wénzi] mosquito

吻 [wěn] I N kiss II VB kiss

稳 [wěn] I ADJ 1 (平稳) steady 2 (坚定) firm 3 (稳重) composed 4 (可靠) reliable 5 (肯定) sure II VB keep calm

稳定 [wěndìng] I ADJ steady II VB settle

问 [wèn] I VB 1 (提问) ask 2 (问候) send regards to 3 (干预) ask about II N question ▶ 疑问 [yíwèn] doubt

问候 [wènhòu] VB send regards to

问题 [wèntí] N 1 (疑问) question 2 (困难) problem 3 (故障) fault 4 (分项) issue

窝 [wō] N (栖息地) nest

蜗 [wō] *see below/见下文*

蜗牛 [wōniú] N snail

我 [wǒ] PRON 1 (自己, 作主语) I 2 (自己, 作宾语) me

我们 [wǒmen] PRON 1 (作主语) we 2 (作宾语) us

卧 [wò] I VB 1 (躺) lie 2 (趴伏) sit II N berth

卧铺 [wòpù] N berth
卧室 [wòshì] N bedroom

握 [wò] VB 1 (抓) grasp 2 (掌握) master
握手 [wòshǒu] VB shake hands

乌 [wū] I N crow ▶ 乌鸦 [wūyā] crow II ADJ black ▶ 乌云 [wūyún] black cloud
乌龟 [wūguī] N tortoise
乌黑 [wūhēi] ADJ jet-black

污 [wū] ADJ 1 (肮脏) dirty 2 (腐败) corrupt ▶ 贪污 [tānwū] be corrupt
污染 [wūrǎn] VB pollute
污辱 [wūrǔ] VB (侮辱) insult

屋 [wū] N 1 (房子) house 2 (房间) room
屋顶 [wūdǐng] N roof
屋子 [wūzi] N room

无 [wú] I VB (没有) not have ▶ 无效 [wúxiào] invalid ▶ 无形 [wúxíng] invisible II ADV not ▶ 无论如何 [wúlùn rúhé] in any case
无耻 [wúchǐ] ADJ shameless
无辜 [wúgū] I VB be innocent II N the innocent
无关 [wúguān] VB have nothing to do with
无赖 [wúlài] N rascal
无论 [wúlùn] CONJ no matter what
无情 [wúqíng] ADJ 1 (指感情) heartless 2 (不留情) ruthless
无数 [wúshù] I ADJ countless II VB be uncertain
无所谓 [wúsuǒwèi] VB 1 (谈不上) never mind 2 (不在乎) be indifferent
无限 [wúxiàn] ADJ boundless
无线电 [wúxiàndiàn] N radio
无须 [wúxū] ADV needlessly
无知 [wúzhī] ADJ ignorant

五 [wǔ] N five ▶ 五月 [wǔyuè] May ▷ 五分之一 [wǔ fēn zhī yī] one fifth
五官 [wǔguān] N the five sense organs

午 [wǔ] N noon
午饭 [wǔfàn] N lunch
午夜 [wǔyè] N midnight

伍 [wǔ] N (五) five

This is the complex character for "five", which is mainly used in banks, on receipts, etc. to prevent mistakes and forgery.

武 [wǔ] ADJ 1 (军事的) military 2 (勇猛) valiant ▶ 威武 [wēiwǔ] powerful
武力 [wǔlì] N 1 (军事力量) military strength 2 (暴力) force
武器 [wǔqì] N weapon
武士 [wǔshì] N warrior
武术 [wǔshù] N martial arts circles (PL)

侮 [wǔ] VB (侮辱) insult ▶ 侮辱 [wǔrǔ] insult

舞 [wǔ] I N dance II VB (跳舞) dance
舞蹈 [wǔdǎo] N dance
舞台 [wǔtái] N stage

勿 [wù] ADV not ▷ 请勿吸烟 [qǐng wù xīyān] no smoking

务 [wù] I N business ▶ 任务 [rènwù] task II ADV without fail
务必 [wùbì] ADV without fail

物 [wù] N 1 (东西) thing ▶ 物体 [wùtǐ] body 2 (物产) produce ▶ 物产 [wùchǎn] produce 3 (动物) creature 4 (指哲学) matter
物价 [wùjià] N price
物理 [wùlǐ] N (指学科) physics (SG)
物业 [wùyè] N property
物质 [wùzhì] N 1 (哲) matter 2 (非精神) material things (PL)
物种 [wùzhǒng] N species (SG)

误 [wù] I N mistake II ADJ 1 (不正确) erroneous ▶ 误会 [wùhuì] misunderstand 2 (非故意) accidental ▶ 误伤 [wùshāng] accidentally injure **III** VB (耽误) miss ▷ 快点儿，别误了火车！ [Kuàidiǎnr, bié wù le huǒchē!] Hurry up, we don't want to miss the train!

雾 [wù] N fog

X

夕 [xī] N **1** (傍晚) sunset ▶ 夕阳 [xīyáng] setting sun **2** (晚上) evening ▶ 除夕 [chúxī] New Year's Eve

西 [xī] N **1** (方向) west ▶ 西北 [xīběi] northwest ▶ 西南 [xīnán] southwest **2** (疆域) the West ▶ 西藏 [Xīzàng] Tibet

西班牙 [Xībānyá] N Spain ▷ 西班牙人 [Xībānyárén] Spaniard ▷ 西班牙语 [Xībānyáyǔ] the Spanish language

西餐 [xīcān] N Western food

西方 [xīfāng] N the West

西服 [xīfú] N Western clothes

西瓜 [xīguā] N watermelon

西红柿 [xīhóngshì] N tomato

西药 [xīyào] N Western medicine

西医 [xīyī] N (药品) Western medicine

吸 [xī] VB **1** (气, 水等) draw … in ▶ 吸烟 [xīyān] smoke cigarettes **2** (吸收) absorb **3** (吸引) attract

吸尘器 [xīchénqì] N vacuum cleaner

吸收 [xīshōu] VB **1** (摄取) absorb **2** (接纳) recruit

吸引 [xīyǐn] VB attract

希 [xī] VB hope

希望 [xīwàng] **I** VB hope **II** N hope

牺 [xī] *see below*/见下文

牺牲 [xīshēng] VB **1** (献身) sacrifice oneself **2** (放弃) sacrifice

稀 [xī] ADJ **1** (稀有) rare **2** (稀疏) sparse **3** (水多的) watery ▶ 稀饭 [xīfàn] rice porridge

稀少 [xīshǎo] ADJ sparse

稀有 [xīyǒu] ADJ rare

犀 [xī] N rhinoceros ▶ 犀牛 [xīniú] rhinoceros

溪 [xī] N brook

熄 [xī] VB put … out ▶ 熄灯 [xīdēng] put out the light

熄灭 [xīmiè] VB put … out

膝 [xī] N knee ▶ 膝盖 [xīgài] knee

习 [xí] **I** VB **1** (学习) practice ▶ 习武 [xíwǔ] study martial arts **2** (熟悉) be used to ▶ 习以为常 [xí yǐ wéi cháng] become used to **II** N custom ▶ 习俗 [xísú] custom ▶ 习气 [xíqì] bad habit

习惯 [xíguàn] **I** VB be used to **II** N habit

习性 [xíxìng] N habits (PL)

席 [xí] N **1** (编织物) mat ▶ 竹席 [zhúxí] bamboo mat **2** (座位) seat ▶ 席位 [xíwèi] seat ▶ 出席 [chūxí] be present **3** (宴席) feast ▶ 酒席 [jiǔxí] banquet

袭 [xí] VB **1** (攻击) make a surprise attack ▶ 空袭 [kōngxí] air raid **2** (仿做) follow the pattern of ▶ 抄袭 [chāoxí] plagiarize

袭击 [xíjī] VB attack

媳 [xí] N daughter-in-law

媳妇 [xífù] N **1** (儿子的妻子) daughter-in-law **2** (晚辈的妻子) wife

洗 [xǐ] VB **1** (衣, 碗等) wash ▶ 洗衣店 [xǐyīdiàn] Laundromat® **2** (胶卷) develop **3** (录音, 录像) wipe **4** (麻将, 扑克) shuffle

洗衣机 [xǐyījī] N washing machine

洗澡 [xǐzǎo] VB have a bath

喜 [xǐ] **I** ADJ **1** (高兴) happy **2** (可贺的) celebratory **II** VB **1** (爱好) like ▶ 喜好 [xǐhào] like **2** (适宜) suit

喜爱 [xǐ'ài] VB like

喜欢 [xǐhuan] VB like

喜剧 [xǐjù] N comedy

戏 [xì] **I** VB (嘲弄) joke ▶ 戏弄 [xìnòng] tease **II** N show ▶ 京戏 [jīngxì] Beijing Opera ▶ 马戏 [mǎxì] circus

戏法 [xìfǎ] N magic
戏剧 [xìjù] N theater
戏曲 [xìqǔ] N Chinese opera
戏院 [xìyuàn] N theater

系 [xì] **I** N **1** (系统) system **2** (部门) department **II** VB (拴) tie
→ *see also*/另见 jì
系列 [xìliè] N series (SG)
系统 [xìtǒng] N system

细 [xì] **I** ADJ **1** (绳, 线等) thin **2** (沙, 粮等) fine **3** (声, 语等) gentle **4** (节, 则等) detailed ▶ 细节 [xìjié] details (PL) **II** ADV minutely ▶ 细想 [xìxiǎng] consider carefully
细胞 [xìbāo] N cell
细菌 [xìjūn] N germ
细心 [xìxīn] ADJ careful
细致 [xìzhì] ADV meticulously

虾 [xiā] N shrimp ▶ 龙虾 [lóngxiā] lobster ▶ 对虾 [duìxiā] shrimp

瞎 [xiā] ADJ (失明) blind
瞎话 [xiāhuà] N lie

峡 [xiá] N gorge ▶ 海峡 [hǎixiá] strait
峡谷 [xiágǔ] N canyon

狭 [xiá] ADJ narrow ▶ 狭窄 [xiázhǎi] narrow

下 [xià] **I** VB **1** (走下) go down ▷ 下山 [xià shān] go down the mountain ▷ 下楼 [xià lóu] go downstairs ▷ 下船 [xià chuán] disembark from a boat ▷ 下床 [xià chuáng] get out of bed **2** (落下) fall ▶ 下雨 [xiàyǔ] rain ▶ 下雪 [xiàxuě] snow **3** (传发) issue **4** (下锅煮) put ... in **5** (给出) give **6** (开始) begin ▶ 下笔 [xiàbǐ] start to write **7** (结束) finish ▶ 下班 [xiàbān] finish work ▶ 下课 [xiàkè] finish class **8** (生下) ▷ 下蛋 [xià dàn] lay an egg **9** (用于动词后, 表示脱离物体) ▷ 拧下灯泡 [nǐng xià dēngpào] unscrew a light bulb **10** (用于动词后, 表示动作完成) ▷ 记录下会议内容 [jìlù xià huìyì nèiróng] take the minutes at a meeting **II** N **1** (低) ▶ 下层 [xiàcéng] lower level **2** (另) ▶ 下次 [xiàcì] next time ▷ 下个星期 [xià gè xīngqī] next week **3** (指方位或时间) ▶ 楼下 [lóuxià] downstairs ▷ 树下 [shù xià] under the tree **4** (指范围, 情况, 条件) ▷ 在朋友的帮助下 [zài péngyou de bāngzhù xià] with help from friends ▷ 在压力下 [zài yālì xià] under pressure **III** MEAS time ▷ 拍了几下 [pāi le jǐ xià] tapped a few times ▷ 拧了两下 [nǐng le liǎng xià] turned a couple of times

下岗 [xiàgǎng] VB **1** (完工) leave one's post **2** (失业) be laid off

下海 [xiàhǎi] VB (指经商) go into business

下级 [xiàjí] N subordinate

下来 [xiàlai] VB **1** (指由高到低) come down ▷ 我不上去了, 你下来吧。 [Wǒ bù shàngqu le, nǐ xiàlai ba.] I won't come up, you come down. **2** (指作物成熟) be harvested **3** (用于动词后, 指脱离物体) ▷ 他把眼镜摘了下来。 [Tā bǎ yǎnjìng zhāi le xiàlai.] He took off his glasses. **4** (用于动词后, 表示动作完成) ▷ 暴乱平息下来了。 [Bàoluàn píngxī xiàlai le.] The riot has calmed down. **5** (表示出现某种状态) ▷ 灯光暗了下来。 [Dēngguāng àn le xiàlai.] The light started to fade.

下流 [xiàliú] ADJ dirty

下面 [xiàmian] **I** ADV **1** (指位置) underneath **2** (指次序) next **II** N lower levels (PL)

下去 [xiàqu] VB **1** (指由高到低) go down **2** (指时间的延续) continue **3** (用于动词后, 指空间上) ▷ 从楼上跳下去 [cóng lóu shàng tiào xiàqu] jump from a building **4** (时间上的持续) ▷ 唱下去 [chàng xiàqu] keep singing **5** (指数量下降) ▷ 高烧已经退下去了。 [Gāoshāo yǐjīng tuì xiàqu le.] His temperature has already gone down. **6** (指程度深化) ▷ 天气有可能热下去。 [Tiānqì yǒu kěnéng rè xiàqu.] The weather will probably go on getting hotter.

下网 [xiàwǎng] (计算机) go offline

下午 [xiàwǔ] N afternoon

下载 [xiàzǎi] VB download

吓 [xià] VB frighten ▶ 吓人 [xiàrén] scary

吓唬 [xiàhu] VB frighten

夏 [xià] N summer

夏令营 [xiàlìngyíng] N summer camp

夏天 [xiàtiān] N summer

仙 [xiān] N immortal ▶ 仙人 [xiānrén] immortal

先 [xiān] ADJ (指时间) earlier ▶ 事先 [shìxiān] beforehand

先后 [xiānhòu] ADV successively

先进 [xiānjìn] ADJ advanced

先生 [xiānsheng] N 1 (指男士) Mr. 2 (老师) teacher 3 (丈夫) husband

纤 [xiān] ADJ fine

纤维 [xiānwéi] N fiber

掀 [xiān] VB lift

掀起 [xiānqǐ] VB 1 (揭起) lift 2 (涌起) surge

鲜 [xiān] I ADJ 1 (新鲜) fresh 2 (鲜美) delicious II N delicacy ▶ 海鲜 [hǎixiān] seafood

鲜艳 [xiānyàn] ADJ brightly-colored

闲 [xián] I ADJ 1 (不忙) idle 2 (安静) quiet 3 (闲置) unused ▶ 闲房 [xiánfáng] empty house II N leisure

闲话 [xiánhuà] N 1 (流言) gossip 2 (废话) digression

闲事 [xiánshì] N other people's business

弦 [xián] N 1 (指乐器) string 2 (指钟表) spring

咸 [xián] ADJ salted ▶ 咸菜 [xiáncài] pickled vegetables (PL)

嫌 [xián] VB dislike ▷ 他嫌这儿吵，搬走了。 [Tā xián zhèr chǎo, bānzǒu le.] He found it too noisy here and moved away.

嫌弃 [xiánqì] VB cold-shoulder

嫌疑 [xiányí] N suspicion

显 [xiǎn] VB 1 (表现) display 2 (呈现) be apparent

显然 [xiǎnrán] ADV obviously

显示 [xiǎnshì] VB demonstrate

显眼 [xiǎnyǎn] ADJ conspicuous

显著 [xiǎnzhù] ADJ striking

险 [xiǎn] ADJ 1 (险要) strategic 2 (危险) dangerous

县 [xiàn] N county

现 [xiàn] ADJ 1 (现在) present ▶ 现状 [xiànzhuàng] present situation 2 (现有) ready ▶ 现金 [xiànjīn] cash

现场 [xiànchǎng] N scene ▶ 现场报道 [xiànchǎng bàodào] live report

现成 [xiànchéng] ADJ ready-made

现代 [xiàndài] N modern times (PL)

现代化 [xiàndàihuà] N modernization

现实 [xiànshí] N reality

现象 [xiànxiàng] N phenomenon

现在 [xiànzài] N now

现状 [xiànzhuàng] N the current situation

限 [xiàn] I VB limit II N limit

限期 [xiànqī] I VB set a deadline II N deadline

限制 [xiànzhì] VB restrict

线 [xiàn] N 1 (指细长物品) thread ▶ 电线 [diànxiàn] electric wire 2 (交通干线) line

线索 [xiànsuǒ] N clue

宪 [xiàn] N constitution

宪法 [xiànfǎ] N constitution

陷 [xiàn] I N 1 (书) (陷阱) trap 2 (过失) fault ▶ 缺陷 [quēxiàn] defect II VB 1 (沉入) get bogged down 2 (凹进) sink 3 (卷入) get involved

陷害 [xiànhài] VB frame

陷阱 [xiànjǐng] N trap

馅 [xiàn] N stuffing ▷ 饺子馅 [jiǎozi xiàn] *jiaozi* filling

羡 [xiàn] VB admire

羡慕 [xiànmù] VB envy

献 [xiàn] VB 1 (给) give ▶ 献血 [xiànxiě] donate blood 2 (表演) show

腺 [xiàn] N gland

乡 [xiāng] N 1 (乡村) countryside 2 (家乡) home town

乡村 [xiāngcūn] N village

乡下 [xiāngxia] N countryside

相 [xiāng] ADV (互相) mutually ▶ 相差 [xiāngchà] differ → *see also*/另见 xiàng

相处 [xiāngchǔ] VB get along

相当 [xiāngdāng] I VB match II ADJ appropriate III ADV quite

相对 [xiāngduì] I VB be opposite II ADJ 1 (非绝对的) relative 2 (比较的) comparative

相反 [xiāngfǎn] I ADJ opposite II CONJ on the contrary

相关 [xiāngguān] VB be related

相互 [xiānghù] I ADJ mutual II ADV ▷ 相互理解 [xiānghù lǐjiě] understand each other

相识 [xiāngshí] VB be acquainted

相似 [xiāngsì] ADJ similar

相同 [xiāngtóng] ADJ identical

相像 [xiāngxiàng] VB be alike

相信 [xiāngxìn] VB believe

香 [xiāng] I ADJ 1 (芬芳) fragrant 2 (美味) delicious 3 (睡得熟的) sound II N 1 (香料) spice 2 (烧的香) incense

香波 [xiāngbō] N shampoo

香肠 [xiāngcháng] N sausage

香港 [Xiānggǎng] N Hong Kong

香蕉 [xiāngjiāo] N banana

香料 [xiāngliào] N spice

香水 [xiāngshuǐ] N perfume

香烟 [xiāngyān] N (卷烟) cigarette

香皂 [xiāngzào] N soap

箱 [xiāng] N 1 (箱子) box 2 (箱状物) ▶ 信箱 [xìnxiāng] mailbox

箱子 [xiāngzi] N box

详 [xiáng] ADJ detailed

详情 [xiángqíng] N details (PL)

详细 [xiángxì] ADJ detailed

享 [xiǎng] VB enjoy

享受 [xiǎngshòu] VB enjoy

响 [xiǎng] I N 1 (回声) echo 2 (声音) sound II VB sound ▷ 手机响了。[Shǒujī xiǎng le.] The cellphone was ringing. III ADJ loud

响亮 [xiǎngliàng] ADJ loud and clear

响应 [xiǎngyìng] VB respond

想 [xiǎng] VB 1 (思考) think ▷ 想办法 [xiǎng bànfǎ] think of a way 2 (推测) reckon 3 (打算) want to 4 (想念) miss

> In a positive sentence, both 想 xiǎng and 要 yào can be used to express "want to". To express "I don't want to", it is more common to use 不想 bù xiǎng, as the expression 不要 bù yào is stronger and indicates a definite decision, meaning "I shall not (under any circumstances)".

想法 [xiǎngfǎ] N opinion

想念 [xiǎngniàn] VB miss

想像 [xiǎngxiàng] I VB imagine II N imagination

向 [xiàng] I N direction II VB 1 (对着) face 2 (偏袒) side with III PREP to ▷ 我向他表示了感谢。[Wǒ xiàng tā biǎoshì le gǎnxiè.] I expressed my thanks to him.

向导 [xiàngdǎo] N guide

向来 [xiànglái] ADV always

项 [xiàng] I N (项目) item ▶ 事项

[shìxiàng] item **II** MEAS item ▷ 3项要求 [sān xiàng yāoqiú] three requirements ▷ 2项任务 [liǎng xiàng rènwu] two tasks

项链 [xiàngliàn] N necklace

项目 [xiàngmù] N **1** (事项) item **2** (指工程计划) project

巷 [xiàng] N lane

相 [xiàng] N **1** (相貌) appearance **2** (姿势) posture **3** (官位) minister ▶ 外相 [wàixiàng] foreign minister **4** (相片) photograph ▶ 照相 [zhàoxiàng] take a photograph → *see also*/另见 xiāng

相貌 [xiàngmào] N appearance

相片 [xiàngpiàn] N photograph

象 [xiàng] N **1** (大象) elephant **2** (样子) appearance

象棋 [xiàngqí] N Chinese chess

象棋 [xiàngqí]

象棋 xiàngqí is a very popular board game in China. It is a game of skill, played by two players on a board which imitates a battlefield with a river between the two opposing sides. There are some similarities between Chinese chess and international chess.

象牙 [xiàngyá] N ivory

象征 [xiàngzhēng] VB symbolize

像 [xiàng] **I** N portrait ▶ 画像 [huàxiàng] paint portraits ▶ 雕像 [diāoxiàng] statue **II** VB **1** (相似) look like **2** (比如) ▷ 像他这样的好孩子，谁不喜欢呢！ [Xiàng tā zhèyàng de hǎo háizi, shéi bù xǐhuan ne!] Who doesn't like good children like this one! **III** ADV as if ▷ 像要下雪了。 [Xiàng yào xiàxuě le.] It looks as if it might snow.

橡 [xiàng] N **1** (橡树) oak **2** (橡胶树) rubber tree

橡胶 [xiàngjiāo] N rubber

橡皮 [xiàngpí] N eraser

削 [xiāo] VB peel

消 [xiāo] VB **1** (消失) disappear **2** (使消失) remove

消除 [xiāochú] VB eliminate

消防 [xiāofáng] N fire fighting

消费 [xiāofèi] VB consume

消耗 [xiāohào] VB consume

消化 [xiāohuà] VB digest

消极 [xiāojí] ADJ **1** (反面) negative **2** (消沉) demoralized

消灭 [xiāomiè] VB **1** (消失) die out **2** (除掉) eradicate

消失 [xiāoshī] VB vanish

消息 [xiāoxi] N news (SG)

宵 [xiāo] N night ▶ 通宵 [tōngxiāo] all night

销 [xiāo] VB **1** (熔化) melt **2** (除去) cancel **3** (销售) market **4** (消费) spend

销路 [xiāolù] N market

销售 [xiāoshòu] VB sell

小 [xiǎo] ADJ (不大) small ▷ 年龄小 [niánlíng xiǎo] young

小便 [xiǎobiàn] **I** VB urinate **II** N urine

小吃 [xiǎochī] N **1** (非正餐) snack **2** (冷盘) cold dish

小丑 [xiǎochǒu] N (滑稽演员) clown

小儿科 [xiǎo'érkē] N (医) pediatrics department

小费 [xiǎofèi] N tip

小伙子 [xiǎohuǒzi] N lad

小姐 [xiǎojie] N **1** (称呼) Miss **2** (女子) young lady

小看 [xiǎokàn] VB underestimate

小麦 [xiǎomài] N wheat

小名 [xiǎomíng] N pet name

小气 [xiǎoqi] ADJ **1** (气量小) petty **2** (吝啬) stingy

小时 [xiǎoshí] N hour

小说 [xiǎoshuō] N novel

小提琴 [xiǎotíqín] N violin
小偷 [xiǎotōu] N thief
小心 [xiǎoxīn] I VB be careful II ADJ careful
小学 [xiǎoxué] N elementary school
小学生 [xiǎoxuéshēng] N elementary school student
小组 [xiǎozǔ] N group

晓 [xiǎo] I N dawn II VB 1 (知道) know 2 (使人知道) tell
晓得 [xiǎode] VB know

孝 [xiào] I VB be dutiful ▶ 孝子 [xiàozǐ] a filial son II N filial piety
孝顺 [xiàoshùn] I VB show filial obedience II ADJ filial

校 [xiào] N (学校) school
校长 [xiàozhǎng] N principal

哮 [xiào] I N wheezing II VB wheeze
哮喘 [xiàochuǎn] N asthma

笑 [xiào] VB 1 (欢笑) laugh 2 (嘲笑) laugh at
笑话 [xiàohua] I N joke II VB laugh at

效 [xiào] I N effect II VB 1 (仿效) imitate 2 (献出) devote ... to
效果 [xiàoguǒ] N 1 (结果) effect 2 (戏剧) effects (PL)
效率 [xiàolǜ] N efficiency
效益 [xiàoyì] N returns (PL)

些 [xiē] MEAS 1 (不定量) some 2 (略微) a little

歇 [xiē] VB (休息) rest
歇息 [xiēxi] VB 1 (休息) have a rest 2 (睡觉) go to sleep

蝎 [xiē] N scorpion ▶ 蝎子 [xiēzi] scorpion

协 [xié] I VB assist II ADV jointly ▶ 协议 [xiéyì] agree on
协会 [xiéhuì] N association
协调 [xiétiáo] I VB coordinate II ADJ coordinated
协议 [xiéyì] N agreement
协助 [xiézhù] VB help
协作 [xiézuò] VB collaborate

邪 [xié] ADJ (不正当) evil
邪恶 [xié'è] ADJ evil

斜 [xié] I ADJ slanting II VB slant
斜坡 [xiépō] N slope

携 [xié] VB 1 (携带) carry 2 (拉着) hold
携带 [xiédài] VB carry

鞋 [xié] N shoe
鞋匠 [xiéjiàng] N cobbler

写 [xiě] VB 1 (书写) write 2 (写作) write 3 (描写) describe 4 (绘画) draw
写作 [xiězuò] VB write

血 [xiě] N (口) blood
→ *see also*/另见 xuè

泄 [xiè] VB (泄露) let ... out
泄露 [xièlòu] VB let ... out

卸 [xiè] VB 1 (搬下) unload ▶ 卸车 [xièchē] unload a vehicle 2 (除去) remove ▶ 卸妆 [xièzhuāng] remove one's makeup 3 (拆卸) strip 4 (解除) be relieved of ▶ 卸任 [xièrèn] step down

谢 [xiè] VB 1 (感谢) thank ▷ 多谢! [Duōxiè!] Thanks a lot! 2 (认错) apologize 3 (拒绝) decline ▶ 谢绝 [xièjué] decline 4 (脱落) wither
谢谢 [xièxie] VB thank you, thanks (口)

蟹 [xiè] N crab ▶ 螃蟹 [pángxiè] crab

心 [xīn] N 1 (心脏) heart 2 (思想) mind ▶ 用心 [yòngxīn] attentively ▶ 谈心 [tánxīn] heart-to-heart talk 3 (中心) center
心得 [xīndé] N what one has learned
心理 [xīnlǐ] N psychology
心灵 [xīnlíng] N mind
心情 [xīnqíng] N frame of mind
心愿 [xīnyuàn] N one's heart's

desire
心脏 [xīnzàng] N heart
心脏病 [xīnzàngbìng] N heart disease

辛 [xīn] ADJ **1** (辣) hot **2** (辛苦) laborious **3** (痛苦) bitter
辛苦 [xīnkǔ] **I** ADJ laborious **II** VB trouble ▷ 辛苦你了！ [Xīnkǔ nǐ le!] Thanks for taking the trouble!
辛勤 [xīnqín] ADJ hardworking

欣 [xīn] ADJ glad
欣赏 [xīnshǎng] VB **1** (赏识) admire **2** (享受) enjoy

新 [xīn] **I** ADJ (跟旧相对) new **II** ADV newly
新潮 [xīncháo] **I** ADJ fashionable **II** N new trend
新陈代谢 [xīn chén dàixiè] N metabolism
新冠肺炎 [xīnguān fèiyán] N Covid
新郎 [xīnláng] N bridegroom
新年 [xīnnián] N **1** (指一段时间) New Year **2** (指元旦当天) New Year's Day
新娘 [xīnniáng] N bride
新闻 [xīnwén] N news (SG)
新鲜 [xīnxiān] ADJ **1** (指食物) fresh **2** (指植物) tender **3** (清新) fresh **4** (新奇) novel
新颖 [xīnyǐng] ADJ original

薪 [xīn] N (薪水) salary
薪水 [xīnshui] N salary

信 [xìn] **I** VB **1** (相信) believe ▶ 轻信 [qīngxìn] readily believe **2** (信奉) believe in ▶ 信教 [xìnjiào] be religious **II** N **1** (书信) letter ▶ 信箱 [xìnxiāng] mailbox **2** (信息) information ▶ 口信 [kǒuxìn] verbal message **3** (信用) trust ▶ 失信 [shīxìn] lose trust
信贷 [xìndài] N credit
信封 [xìnfēng] N envelope
信号 [xìnhào] N signal
信件 [xìnjiàn] N letter
信赖 [xìnlài] VB trust
信任 [xìnrèn] VB trust
信息 [xìnxī] N information
信心 [xìnxīn] N faith
信仰 [xìnyǎng] VB believe in ▶ 他没有宗教信仰。 [Tā méiyou zōngjiào xìnyǎng.] He has no religious faith.
信用 [xìnyòng] N **1** (指信任) word **2** (指借贷) credit
信用卡 [xìnyòngkǎ] N credit card
信誉 [xìnyù] N reputation

兴 [xīng] VB **1** (旺盛) prosper **2** (流行) be popular **3** (使盛行) promote
→ *see also*/另见 xìng
兴奋 [xīngfèn] VB be excited
兴盛 [xīngshèng] ADJ prosperous
兴旺 [xīngwàng] ADJ prosperous

星 [xīng] N **1** (指天体) star ▶ 星星 [xīngxīng] star **2** (指名人) star ▶ 球星 [qiúxīng] soccer star
星期 [xīngqī] N **1** (周) week **2** (指某天) ▶ 星期天 [xīngqītiān] Sunday ▶ 星期三 [xīngqīsān] Wednesday ▷ 明天星期几？ [Míngtiān xīngqī jǐ?] What day is it tomorrow?

猩 [xīng] N orang-utan ▶ 黑猩猩 [hēixīngxing] chimpanzee

腥 [xīng] ADJ fishy

刑 [xíng] N (刑罚) punishment ▶ 死刑 [sǐxíng] the death penalty

行 [xíng] **I** VB **1** (走) walk ▶ 步行 [bùxíng] go on foot **2** (流通) be current ▶ 发行 [fāxíng] issue **3** (做) do ▶ 行医 [xíngyī] practice medicine **II** ADJ **1** (可以) OK **2** (能干) capable **III** N **1** (旅行) travel **2** (行为) conduct ▶ 暴行 [bàoxíng] act of cruelty
→ *see also*/另见 háng
行动 [xíngdòng] VB (活动) take action
行李 [xíngli] N luggage
行人 [xíngrén] N pedestrian
行驶 [xíngshǐ] VB travel

行为 [xíngwéi] N behavior
行走 [xíngzǒu] VB walk

形 [xíng] N 1 (形状) shape 2 (形体) body
形成 [xíngchéng] VB form
形容 [xíngróng] VB describe
形式 [xíngshì] N form
形象 [xíngxiàng] N image
形状 [xíngzhuàng] N shape

型 [xíng] N type ▶ 体型 [tǐxíng] build ▶ 血型 [xuèxíng] blood group
型号 [xínghào] N model

醒 [xǐng] VB 1 (神志恢复) come to 2 (睡醒) wake up 3 (醒悟) become aware ▶ 提醒 [tíxǐng] remind

兴 [xìng] N excitement
→ *see also*/另见 xīng
兴趣 [xìngqù] N interest ▷ 他对集邮有浓厚的兴趣。 [Tā duì jíyóu yǒu nónghòu de xìngqù.] He has a deep interest in stamp-collecting.

杏 [xìng] N apricot

幸 [xìng] I ADJ lucky II ADV fortunately
幸福 [xìngfú] I N happiness II ADJ happy
幸亏 [xìngkuī] ADV fortunately
幸运 [xìngyùn] I N good luck II ADJ lucky

性 [xìng] N 1 (性格) character ▶ 任性 [rènxìng] stubborn 2 (性能) function ▶ 酸性 [suānxìng] acidity 3 (性别) gender ▶ 男性 [nánxìng] male 4 (情欲) sex 5 (性质) ▶ 可靠性 [kěkàoxìng] reliability ▶ 实用性 [shíyòngxìng] utility 6 (语法) gender ▶ 阳性 [yángxìng] masculine
性别 [xìngbié] N sex
性感 [xìnggǎn] ADJ sexy
性格 [xìnggé] N personality
性质 [xìngzhì] N character

姓 [xìng] I VB ▷ 我姓李。 [Wǒ xìng Lǐ.] My surname is Li. II N surname
姓名 [xìngmíng] N full name

凶 [xiōng] ADJ 1 (不幸的) unlucky 2 (凶恶) ferocious ▶ 凶相 [xiōngxiàng] fierce look 3 (厉害) terrible
凶狠 [xiōnghěn] ADJ vicious
凶手 [xiōngshǒu] N murderer

兄 [xiōng] N brother
兄弟 [xiōngdì] N brother

胸 [xiōng] N 1 (胸部) chest 2 (心胸) heart
胸脯 [xiōngpú] N chest

雄 [xióng] ADJ 1 (公的) male ▶ 雄性 [xióngxìng] male 2 (有气魄的) imposing 3 (强有力的) strong

熊 [xióng] N bear
熊猫 [xióngmāo] N panda

休 [xiū] VB 1 (停止) stop 2 (休息) rest
休息 [xiūxi] VB rest
休闲 [xiūxián] VB (悠闲) be at leisure ▶ 休闲服装 [xiūxián fúzhuāng] casual clothes

修 [xiū] VB 1 (修理) mend 2 (兴建) build 3 (剪) trim
修改 [xiūgǎi] VB alter
修建 [xiūjiàn] VB build
修理 [xiūlǐ] VB repair
修饰 [xiūshì] VB 1 (修整装饰) decorate 2 (修改润饰) polish
修养 [xiūyǎng] N 1 (水平) accomplishments (PL) 2 (指态度) gentility

羞 [xiū] ADJ shy ▶ 害羞 [hàixiū] be shy

秀 [xiù] I ADJ 1 (清秀) elegant 2 (优异) outstanding II N talent ▶ 新秀 [xīnxiù] new talent
秀气 [xiùqi] ADJ 1 (清秀) delicate 2 (文雅) refined

袖 [xiù] N sleeve ▶ 袖子 [xiùzi] sleeve
袖珍 [xiùzhēn] ADJ pocket-sized ▷ 袖珍收音机 [xiùzhēn shōuyīnjī]

pocket radio

绣 [xiù] **I** VB embroider **II** N embroidery

锈 [xiù] N rust ▶ 生锈 [shēngxiù] go rusty

须 [xū] **I** ADV ▶ 必须 [bìxū] must **II** N beard

须要 [xūyào] VB need

须知 [xūzhī] N essentials (PL)

虚 [xū] ADJ **1** (空着) empty **2** (胆怯) timid **3** (虚假) false **4** (虚心) modest **5** (弱) weak

虚构 [xūgòu] VB fabricate

虚假 [xūjiǎ] ADJ false

虚荣 [xūróng] N vanity

虚弱 [xūruò] ADJ frail

虚伪 [xūwěi] ADJ hypocritical

虚心 [xūxīn] ADJ open-minded

需 [xū] **I** VB need **II** N needs (PL) ▶ 军需 [jūnxū] military requirements (PL)

需求 [xūqiú] N demand

需要 [xūyào] **I** VB need **II** N needs (PL) ▷ 日常生活需要 [rìcháng shēnghuó xūyào] necessities of life

许 [xǔ] VB **1** (称赞) praise **2** (答应) promise **3** (允许) allow

许多 [xǔduō] ADJ many ▷ 他养了许多金鱼。 [Tā yǎng le xǔduō jīnyú.] He keeps a lot of goldfish.

叙 [xù] VB **1** (谈) chat **2** (记述) recount

叙事 [xùshì] VB narrate

叙述 [xùshù] VB recount

畜 [xù] VB raise

→ *see also*/另见 chù

畜牧 [xùmù] VB rear ▶ 畜牧业 [xùmùyè] animal husbandry

酗 [xù] *see below*/见下文

酗酒 [xùjiǔ] VB get drunk

婿 [xù] N (女婿) son-in-law ▶ 女婿 [nǚxù] son-in-law

宣 [xuān] VB **1** (宣布) announce **2** (疏导) lead ... off ▶ 宣泄 [xuānxiè] get ... off one's chest

宣布 [xuānbù] VB announce

宣称 [xuānchēng] VB announce

宣传 [xuānchuán] VB disseminate ▶ 宣传工具 [xuānchuán gōngjù] means of dissemination

宣告 [xuāngào] VB proclaim

宣誓 [xuānshì] VB take an oath

宣言 [xuānyán] N declaration

宣扬 [xuānyáng] VB advocate

宣战 [xuānzhàn] VB declare war

喧 [xuān] VB make a noise

喧哗 [xuānhuá] **I** ADJ riotous **II** VB create a disturbance

喧闹 [xuānnào] ADJ rowdy

悬 [xuán] VB **1** (挂) hang **2** (设想) imagine **3** (挂念) be concerned about **4** (未定) be unresolved

悬挂 [xuánguà] VB hang

悬念 [xuánniàn] N suspense

悬崖 [xuányá] N precipice

旋 [xuán] **I** VB **1** (旋转) revolve **2** (返回) return **II** N spiral

→ *see also*/另见 xuàn

旋律 [xuánlǜ] N melody

旋钮 [xuánniǔ] N knob

旋涡 [xuánwō] N whirlpool

旋转 [xuánzhuǎn] VB revolve

选 [xuǎn] **I** VB **1** (挑选) choose **2** (选举) vote **II** N **1** (指人) selection ▶ 人选 [rénxuǎn] selection of people **2** (作品集) collection ▶ 文选 [wénxuǎn] collected works (PL)

选拔 [xuǎnbá] VB select

选举 [xuǎnjǔ] VB elect

选民 [xuǎnmín] N electorate

选手 [xuǎnshǒu] N contestant

选修 [xuǎnxiū] VB choose to study ▶ 选修课程 [xuǎnxiū kèchéng] optional course

选择 [xuǎnzé] VB choose ▶ 别无选择 [biéwú xuǎnzé] have no choice

旋 [xuàn] VB spin
→ *see also*/另见 xuán
旋风 [xuànfēng] N whirlwind

靴 [xuē] N boot
靴子 [xuēzi] N boot

穴 [xué] N **1** (洞) den **2** (穴位) acupuncture point
穴位 [xuéwèi] N acupuncture point

学 [xué] **I** VB **1** (学习) study ▷ 学英语 [xué Yīngyǔ] learn English **2** (模仿) imitate **II** N **1** (学问) learning ▶ 博学 [bóxué] erudition **2** (学科) science ▶ 生物学 [shēngwùxué] biology ▶ 化学 [huàxué] chemistry **3** (学校) school ▶ 大学 [dàxué] university ▶ 中学 [zhōngxué] high school ▶ 小学 [xiǎoxué] elementary school
学费 [xuéfèi] N tuition fee
学科 [xuékē] N subject
学历 [xuélì] N educational background
学生 [xuésheng] N student
学士 [xuéshì] N (指学位) bachelor's degree
学术 [xuéshù] N learning
学说 [xuéshuō] N theory
学位 [xuéwèi] N degree
学问 [xuéwen] N learning
学习 [xuéxí] VB study
学校 [xuéxiào] N school
学业 [xuéyè] N studies (PL)
学者 [xuézhě] N scholar

雪 [xuě] N snow ▶ 下雪 [xiàxuě] to snow
雪花 [xuěhuā] N snowflake

血 [xuè] N (血液) blood
→ *see also*/另见 xiě
血统 [xuètǒng] N blood relation
血型 [xuèxíng] N blood type
血压 [xuèyā] N blood pressure
血液 [xuèyè] N **1** (血) blood **2** (主要力量) lifeblood
血缘 [xuèyuán] N blood relation

熏 [xūn] VB **1** (烟气接触物体) blacken **2** (熏制) smoke ▶ 熏肉 [xūnròu] smoked meat

寻 [xún] VB search
寻常 [xúncháng] ADJ usual
寻求 [xúnqiú] VB seek
寻找 [xúnzhǎo] VB look for

巡 [xún] VB patrol
巡逻 [xúnluó] VB patrol

询 [xún] VB inquire
询问 [xúnwèn] VB ask

循 [xún] VB abide by
循环 [xúnhuán] VB circulate

训 [xùn] **I** VB **1** (教导) teach **2** (训练) train **II** N rule
训练 [xùnliàn] VB train

迅 [xùn] ADJ swift
迅速 [xùnsù] ADJ swift

驯 [xùn] **I** ADJ tame **II** VB tame
驯服 [xùnfú] **I** ADJ tame **II** VB tame

Y

压 [yā] **I** VB **1** (施力) press **2** (超越) outdo **3** (使稳定) control **4** (压制) suppress **5** (积压) put ... off **II** N pressure

压力 [yālì] N **1** (物) pressure **2** (指对人) pressure **3** (负担) burden

压迫 [yāpò] VB **1** (压制) oppress **2** (挤压) put pressure on

压岁钱 [yāsuìqián] N *traditional gifts of money given to children during the Spring Festival*

压抑 [yāyì] VB suppress

呀 [yā] INT (表示惊异) oh ▷ 呀！已经12点了！ [Yā! Yǐjīng shí'èr diǎn le!] Oh! It's 12 o'clock already!

押 [yā] VB (抵押) leave ... as a security

押金 [yājīn] N deposit

鸦 [yā] N crow

鸦片 [yāpiàn] N opium

鸭 [yā] N duck

牙 [yá] N (牙齿) tooth

牙齿 [yáchǐ] N tooth

牙床 [yáchuáng] N gum

牙膏 [yágāo] N toothpaste

牙签 [yáqiān] N toothpick

牙刷 [yáshuā] N toothbrush

牙痛 [yátòng] N toothache

牙医 [yáyī] N dentist

芽 [yá] N (指植物) sprout

崖 [yá] N cliff

哑 [yǎ] ADJ **1** (不能说话) mute **2** (不说话) speechless **3** (嘶哑) hoarse

哑巴 [yǎba] N mute

哑铃 [yǎlíng] N dumbbell

哑语 [yǎyǔ] N sign language

轧 [yà] VB (碾) roll

亚 [yà] **I** ADJ inferior ▶ 亚军 [yàjūn] runner-up **II** N Asia

亚洲 [Yàzhōu] N Asia ▶ 她是亚洲人。[Tā shì Yàzhōurén.] She's Asian.

咽 [yān] N pharynx
→ *see also*/另见 yàn

咽喉 [yānhóu] N (字) throat

烟 [yān] N **1** (指气体) smoke **2** (烟草) tobacco ▶ 香烟 [xiāngyān] cigarette

烟草 [yāncǎo] N **1** (指植物) tobacco plant **2** (烟草制品) tobacco

烟花 [yānhuā] N firework

烟灰缸 [yānhuīgāng] N ashtray

烟民 [yānmín] N smokers (PL)

淹 [yān] VB (淹没) flood

淹没 [yānmò] VB **1** (漫过) submerge **2** (喻) drown ... out

延 [yán] VB **1** (延长) extend **2** (推迟) delay

延长 [yáncháng] VB extend

延迟 [yánchí] VB delay

严 [yán] ADJ **1** (严密) tight **2** (严格) strict

严格 [yángé] ADJ strict

严谨 [yánjǐn] ADJ (严密谨慎) meticulous

严厉 [yánlì] ADJ severe

严肃 [yánsù] ADJ **1** (庄重) solemn **2** (严格认真) severe

严重 [yánzhòng] ADJ serious

言 [yán] **I** VB speak **II** N **1** (话) speech **2** (字) words (PL)

言论 [yánlùn] N speech ▷ 言论自由 [yánlùn zìyóu] freedom of speech

言情片 [yánqíngpiān] N romantic movie

言语 [yányǔ] N language

岩 [yán] N rock

炎 [yán] **I** ADJ scorching **II** N (炎症) inflammation

炎黄子孙 [Yán-Huáng zǐsūn] N Chinese people

炎热 [yánrè] ADJ scorching hot
炎症 [yánzhèng] N inflammation

沿 [yán] I PREP along II VB (依照) follow III N edge
沿岸 [yán'àn] N bank
沿海 [yánhǎi] N coast

研 [yán] VB (研究) research ▶ 研究院 [yánjiūyuàn] research institute ▶ 研究生 [yánjiūshēng] graduate student
研究 [yánjiū] VB 1 (探求) research 2 (商讨) discuss

盐 [yán] N salt

颜 [yán] N 1 (字) face 2 (颜色) color
颜料 [yánliào] N coloring
颜色 [yánsè] N (色彩) color

眼 [yǎn] N 1 (眼睛) eye 2 (小洞) small hole
眼光 [yǎnguāng] N 1 (视线) gaze 2 (观察能力) vision 3 (观点) perspective
眼红 [yǎnhóng] VB be jealous
眼界 [yǎnjiè] N horizons (PL)
眼睛 [yǎnjing] N eye
眼镜 [yǎnjìng] N glasses (PL)
眼泪 [yǎnlèi] N tear
眼力 [yǎnlì] N 1 (视力) eyesight 2 (鉴别能力) judgement
眼神 [yǎnshén] N 1 (指神态) expression 2 (方) (视力) eyesight

演 [yǎn] VB (表演) perform
演出 [yǎnchū] VB perform
演讲 [yǎnjiǎng] VB make a speech
演示 [yǎnshì] VB demonstrate
演说 [yǎnshuō] VB make a speech
演员 [yǎnyuán] N performer
演奏 [yǎnzòu] VB perform

厌 [yàn] VB (厌恶) detest
厌烦 [yànfán] VB be sick of
厌恶 [yànwù] VB loathe

砚 [yàn] N ink stone ▶ 砚台 [yàntai] ink stone

咽 [yàn] VB swallow
→ *see also*/另见 yān

宴 [yàn] VB host a dinner ▶ 宴请 [yànqǐng] invite ... to dinner
宴会 [yànhuì] N banquet

验 [yàn] VB (检查) test
验光 [yànguāng] VB have an eye test
验血 [yànxiě] VB have a blood test

谚 [yàn] N saying ▶ 谚语 [yànyǔ] proverb

雁 [yàn] N wild goose

焰 [yàn] N flame

燕 [yàn] N swallow
燕麦 [yànmài] N oats (PL)
燕尾服 [yànwěifú] N tailcoat

羊 [yáng] N sheep ▶ 山羊 [shānyáng] goat
羊毛 [yángmáo] N wool
羊绒衫 [yángróngshān] N cashmere

阳 [yáng] N 1 (阴的对立面) Yang (*from Yin and Yang*) 2 (太阳) sun ▶ 阳光 [yángguāng] sunlight
阳台 [yángtái] N balcony
阳性 [yángxìng] N 1 (医) positive 2 (语言) masculine

洋 [yáng] I N (海洋) ocean II ADJ (外国的) foreign
洋白菜 [yángbáicài] N cabbage
洋葱 [yángcōng] N onion

仰 [yǎng] VB (脸向上) look up
仰望 [yǎngwàng] VB look up

养 [yǎng] I VB 1 (供给) provide for 2 (饲养) keep ▷ 我爱养花。 [Wǒ ài yǎng huā.] I like growing flowers. 3 (生育) give birth to 4 (培养) form ▷ 养成习惯 [yǎng chéng xíguàn] form a habit II ADJ foster ▶ 养母 [yǎngmǔ] foster mother ▶ 养子 [yǎngzǐ] adopted son
养活 [yǎnghuo] VB (口) 1 (提供生活费用) support 2 (饲养) raise 3 (生

育抚养) give birth to
养料 [yǎngliào] N nourishment
养育 [yǎngyù] VB bring up
养殖 [yǎngzhí] VB breed

氧 [yǎng] N oxygen ▶ 氧气 [yǎngqì] oxygen

痒 [yǎng] VB itch

样 [yàng] **I** N **1** (模样) style **2** (标准物) sample **II** MEAS type ▷ 3样水果 [sān yàng shuǐguǒ] three types of fruit
样品 [yàngpǐn] N sample
样式 [yàngshì] N style
样子 [yàngzi] N **1** (模样) appearance **2** (神情) expression

妖 [yāo] N evil spirit
妖精 [yāojing] N (妖怪) demon

要 [yāo] VB **1** (求) ask **2** (邀请) invite → *see also*/另见 yào

Both 要 yào and 会 huì can be used to express the future tense. 要 yào refers to something definite, e.g. 我明天要上班 wǒ míngtiān yào shàngbān (I am going to work tomorrow); 会 huì is usually used to express a possible, or probable outcome, e.g. 明天会下雨 míngtiān huì xiàyǔ (It might rain tomorrow).

要求 [yāoqiú] **I** VB demand **II** N request

腰 [yāo] N **1** (身体中部) waist **2** (裤腰) waist
腰包 [yāobāo] N billfold
腰带 [yāodài] N belt
腰果 [yāoguǒ] N cashew nut
腰围 [yāowéi] N waistline
腰子 [yāozi] N kidney

邀 [yāo] VB (邀请) invite
邀请 [yāoqǐng] VB invite

谣 [yáo] N **1** (歌谣) folk song ▶ 歌谣 [gēyáo] folk song **2** (谣言) rumor ▶ 谣言 [yáoyán] hearsay
谣传 [yáochuán] **I** VB be rumored **II** N rumor

摇 [yáo] VB shake
摇动 [yáodòng] VB **1** (摇东西) wave **2** (晃) shake
摇滚乐 [yáogǔnyuè] N rock and roll
摇晃 [yáohuàng] VB shake
摇篮 [yáolán] N cradle

遥 [yáo] ADJ distant ▶ 遥控器 [yáokòngqì] remote control
遥控 [yáokòng] VB operate by remote control
遥远 [yáoyuǎn] ADJ **1** (指距离) distant **2** (指时间) far-off

咬 [yǎo] VB **1** (指用嘴) bite **2** (夹住) grip

舀 [yǎo] VB ladle

药 [yào] N **1** (指治病) medicine **2** (指化学物品) chemical
药材 [yàocái] N herbal medicine
药方 [yàofāng] N prescription
药物 [yàowù] N medicine

要 [yào] **I** ADJ important **II** VB **1** (想得到) want ▷ 我女儿要一个新书包。[Wǒ nǚ'ér yào yī gè xīn shūbāo.] My daughter wants a new schoolbag. **2** (要求) ask ▷ 老师要我们安静。[Lǎoshī yào wǒmen ānjìng.] The teacher asked us to be quiet. **III** AUX VB **1** (应该) should ▷ 饭前要洗手。[Fàn qián yào xǐshǒu.] You should wash your hands before you eat. **2** (需要) need ▷ 我要上厕所。[Wǒ yào shàng cèsuǒ.] I need to go to the bathroom. **3** (表示意志) want ▷ 我要学开车。[Wǒ yào xué kāichē.] I want to learn to drive. **4** (将要) be about to ▷ 我们要放暑假了。[Wǒmen yào fàng shǔjià le.] We're about to break for summer vacation. **IV** CONJ (如果) if ▷ 你要碰见他，替我问声好。[Nǐ yào pèngjiàn tā, tì wǒ wèn shēng hǎo.] If you meet him, say hello from me.

→ *see also*/另见 yāo

In a positive sentence, both 要 yào and 想 xiǎng can be used to express "want to". To express "I don't want to", it is more common to use 不想 bù xiǎng, as the expression 不要 bù yào is stronger and indicates a definite decision, meaning "I shall not (under any circumstances)".

要不 [yàobù] CONJ **1** (否则) otherwise ▷ 快点走，要不你要迟到了。[Kuàidiǎn zǒu, yào bù nǐ yào chídào le.] Go quickly, otherwise you'll be late. **2** (表示选择) either ... or ▷ 我们要不去看电影，要不去咖啡厅，你说呢？ [Wǒmen yàobù qù kàn diànyǐng, yàobù qù kāfēitīng, nǐ shuō ne?] We can either go to see a film or go to a coffee shop, which would you prefer?

要紧 [yàojǐn] ADJ **1** (重要) important **2** (严重) serious

要领 [yàolǐng] N **1** (要点) gist **2** (基本要求) main points (PL)

要么 [yàome] CONJ either ... or ▷ 你要么学文，要么学理。[Nǐ yàome xué wén, yàome xué lǐ.] You either study arts or science.

要是 [yàoshi] CONJ if ▷ 要是你不满意，可以随时退货。[Yàoshi nǐ bù mǎnyì, kěyǐ suíshí tuìhuò.] If you're not satisfied, you can return the goods at any time.

钥 [yào] *see below*/见下文

钥匙 [yàoshi] N key

耀 [yào] VB (照射) shine

耶 [yē] *see below*/见下文

耶稣 [Yēsū] N Jesus

椰 [yē] N coconut

椰子 [yēzi] N **1** (树) coconut tree **2** (果实) coconut

噎 [yē] VB (堵塞) choke

爷 [yé] N (祖父) (paternal) grandfather

爷爷 [yéye] N (口) (祖父) (paternal) granddad

也 [yě] ADV **1** (同样) also ▷ 他也去过中国。[Tā yě qùguò Zhōngguó.] He's been to China too. **2** (表示转折) still ▷ 即使他来了，也帮不上忙。[Jíshǐ tā lái le, yě bāng bù shàng máng.] Even if he comes, it still won't be of any use.

也许 [yěxǔ] ADV perhaps

野 [yě] **I** N (野外) open country ▶ 野餐 [yěcān] picnic **II** ADJ **1** (野生) wild ▶ 野菜 [yěcài] wild herbs (PL) **2** (蛮横) rude ▶ 粗野 [cūyě] rough **3** (无约束) unruly

野餐 [yěcān] VB have a picnic

野蛮 [yěmán] ADJ **1** (蒙昧) uncivilized **2** (残暴) brutal

野生 [yěshēng] ADJ wild

野兽 [yěshòu] N wild animal

野外 [yěwài] N open country

野心 [yěxīn] N ambition

野营 [yěyíng] N camp

业 [yè] N **1** (行业) industry ▷ 饮食业 [yǐnshí yè] the food and drink industry **2** (职业) job ▶ 就业 [jiùyè] obtain employment ▶ 失业 [shīyè] be unemployed **3** (学业) studies (PL) ▶ 毕业 [bìyè] graduate **4** (产业) property ▶ 家业 [jiāyè] family property

业务 [yèwù] N profession

业余 [yèyú] **I** N spare time **II** ADJ amateurish

业主 [yèzhǔ] N owner

叶 [yè] N (叶子) leaf

页 [yè] **I** N page **II** MEAS page

页码 [yèmǎ] N page number

夜 [yè] N night

夜班 [yèbān] N night shift

夜猫子 [yèmāozi] N (方) **1** (猫头鹰) owl **2** (喻) (晚睡者) night owl

夜生活 [yèshēnghuó] N nightlife
夜市 [yèshì] N night market
夜宵 [yèxiāo] N late-night snack
夜总会 [yèzǒnghuì] N nightclub

液 [yè] N liquid
液体 [yètǐ] N liquid

腋 [yè] N (夹肢窝) armpit ▶ 腋毛 [yèmáo] underarm hair

一 [yī] NUM 1 (指数目) one ▶ 一辈子 [yībèizi] a lifetime 2 (相同) ▷ 一类人 [yī lèi rén] the same sort of people 3 (全) ▷ 一屋子烟 [yī wūzi yān] full of smoke

一 yī is pronounced as 1st tone when it is used by itself to mean the number one, for example in telephone numbers etc. When it is followed by another syllable it changes its tone depending on the tone of the subsequent syllable. If the subsequent syllable is 1st, 2nd, or 3rd tone then it is pronounced as 4th tone yì. If the subsequent syllable is a 4th tone, then it is pronounced as a 2nd tone yí. For consistency, changes of tone in pinyin are not shown in this book.

一般 [yībān] ADJ 1 (一样) same ▷ 他们俩一般大。 [Tāmen liǎ yībān dà.] The two of them are the same age. 2 (普通) ordinary

一半 [yībàn] N half

一边 [yībiān] I N (一面) side II ADV at the same time

一道 [yīdào] ADV together

一点儿 [yīdiǎnr] MEAS 1 (一些) some ▷ 你行李太多，我帮你提一点儿吧。 [Nǐ xíngli tàiduō, wǒ bāng nǐ tí yīdiǎnr ba.] You've got so much luggage, let me help you with some of it. 2 (很少) a little ▷ 这件事我一点儿都不知道。 [Zhè jiàn shì wǒ yīdiǎnr dōu bù zhīdào.] I know nothing about this.

一定 [yīdìng] I ADJ 1 (规定的) definite 2 (固定的) fixed 3 (相当) certain 4 (特定) given II ADV definitely ▷ 放心，我一定去机场接你。 [Fàngxīn, wǒ yīdìng qù jīchǎng jiē nǐ.] Don't worry, I'll definitely pick you up at the airport.

一共 [yīgòng] ADV altogether ▷ 这套书一共多少本？ [Zhè tào shū yīgòng duōshao běn?] How many books are there in this set?

一…就… [yī…jiù…] ADV as soon as ▷ 我一到家就给你打电话。 [Wǒ yī dào jiā jiù gěi nǐ dǎ diànhuà.] I'll call you as soon as I get home.

一连 [yīlián] ADV on end ▷ 一连下了几个月的雨。 [Yīlián xià le jǐ gè yuè de yǔ.] It's been raining for months on end.

一路 [yīlù] N 1 (行程) journey ▷ 一路顺利吗？ [Yīlù shùnlì ma?] Did you have a good journey? 2 (一起) the same way ▷ 咱俩是一路。 [Zán liǎ shì yīlù.] We're going the same way.

一面 [yīmiàn] I N aspect ▷ 积极的一面 [jījí de yīmiàn] a positive aspect II ADV at the same time ▷ 她一面听音乐，一面看小说。 [Tā yīmiàn tīng yīnyuè, yīmiàn kàn xiǎoshuō.] She was listening to music and reading a novel at the same time.

一齐 [yīqí] ADV simultaneously

一起 [yīqǐ] I N the same place II ADV together

一切 [yīqiè] PRON 1 (全部) all 2 (全部事物) everything

一时 [yīshí] I N 1 (一个时期) time 2 (短暂时间) moment II ADV 1 (临时) for the moment 2 (时而) sometimes

一同 [yītóng] ADV together

一下 [yīxià] I MEAS ▷ 我去问一下。 [Wǒ qù wèn yīxià.] I'll just go and ask.

measure word, used after verbs to indicate one's attempts to do something

II ADV at once ▷ 天一下就冷了。[Tiān yīxià jiù lěng le.] All at once the weather turned cold.

一向 [yīxiàng] ADV always

一些 [yīxiē] MEAS **1** (部分) some **2** (几个) a few **3** (略微) a little ▷ 她感觉好一些了。[Tā gǎnjué hǎo yīxiē le.] She feels a little better.

一样 [yīyàng] ADJ same ▷ 他俩爱好一样。[Tā liǎ àihào yīyàng.] They have the same hobbies.

一再 [yīzài] ADV repeatedly

一直 [yīzhí] ADV **1** (不变向) straight **2** (不间断) always ▷ 大风一直刮了两天两夜。[Dàfēng yīzhí guā le liǎng tiān liǎng yè.] The gale blew for two days and two nights. **3** (指一定范围) all the way ▷ 从南一直到北 [cóng nán yīzhí dào běi] from the north all way to the south

一致 [yīzhì] **I** ADJ unanimous **II** ADV unanimously

衣 [yī] N (衣服) clothing ▶ 衣裳 [yīshang] clothes (PL)

衣服 [yīfu] N clothes (PL)

医 [yī] **I** N **1** (医生) doctor **2** (医) medicine ▶ 中医 [zhōngyī] Chinese traditional medicine **II** VB treat

医疗 [yīliáo] VB treat ▶ 免费医疗制度 [miǎnfèi yīliáo zhìdù] system of free medical care

医生 [yīshēng] N doctor

医术 [yīshù] N medical skill

医务室 [yīwùshì] N clinic

医学 [yīxué] N medicine

医药 [yīyào] N medicine

医院 [yīyuàn] N hospital

医治 [yīzhì] VB cure

依 [yī] VB **1** (依靠) depend on **2** (依从) comply with

依旧 [yījiù] ADV still

依据 [yījù] **I** VB go by **II** N basis

依靠 [yīkào] **I** VB rely on **II** N support

依赖 [yīlài] VB depend on

依然 [yīrán] ADV still

依照 [yīzhào] PREP according to

壹 [yī] NUM one

This is the complex character for "one", which is mainly used in banks, on receipts, etc. to prevent mistakes and forgery.

仪 [yí] N **1** (外表) appearance **2** (礼节) ceremony **3** (仪器) meter

仪器 [yíqì] N meter

仪式 [yíshì] N ceremony

姨 [yí] N **1** (母亲的姐妹) aunt **2** (妻子的姐妹) sister-in-law

移 [yí] VB **1** (移动) move **2** (改变) change

移动 [yídòng] VB move

移民 [yímín] **I** VB emigrate **II** N immigrant

遗 [yí] VB **1** (遗失) lose **2** (留下) leave ... behind

遗产 [yíchǎn] N legacy

遗传 [yíchuán] VB inherit

遗憾 [yíhàn] **I** N regret **II** VB be a pity

遗弃 [yíqì] VB **1** (车, 船等) abandon **2** (妻, 子等) desert

遗书 [yíshū] N (书面遗言) last letter *(of dying man)*

遗体 [yítǐ] N remains (PL)

遗忘 [yíwàng] VB forget

遗址 [yízhǐ] N ruins (PL)

遗嘱 [yízhǔ] N will

疑 [yí] VB doubt

疑难 [yínán] ADJ knotty

疑问 [yíwèn] N question

疑心 [yíxīn] **I** N suspicion **II** VB suspect

已 [yǐ] ADV already

已经 [yǐjīng] ADV already

以 [yǐ] (书) I VB use ▶ 以强凌弱 [yǐ qiáng líng ruò] use one's strength to humiliate the weak II PREP 1 (依照) by 2 (因为) for 3 (表示界限) ▶ 以内 [yǐnèi] within ▷ 以南 [yǐnán] to the south III CONJ ▷ 我们要改进技术，以提高生产效率。 [Wǒmen yào gǎijìn jìshù, yǐ tígāo shēngchǎn xiàolǜ.] We should improve the technology so as to increase production.

以便 [yǐbiàn] CONJ in order that

以后 [yǐhòu] N ▷ 两年以后 [liǎng nián yǐhòu] two years later ▷ 以后我们去看电影。 [Yǐhòu wǒmen qù kàn diànyǐng.] Afterwards we're going to see a film.

以及 [yǐjí] CONJ as well as

以来 [yǐlái] N ▷ 入冬以来 [rù dōng yǐlái] since the beginning of the winter

以免 [yǐmiǎn] CONJ in case

以前 [yǐqián] N ▷ 10年以前 [shí nián yǐqián] ten years ago ▷ 她以前是老师。 [Tā yǐqián shì lǎoshī.] She was a teacher before.

以为 [yǐwéi] VB think

以下 [yǐxià] N (低于某点) ▷ 30岁以下 [sānshí suì yǐxià] under thirty

以致 [yǐzhì] CONJ so that

蚁 [yǐ] N ant ▶ 蚂蚁 [mǎyǐ] ant

椅 [yǐ] N chair

椅子 [yǐzi] N chair

亿 [yì] NUM hundred million

义 [yì] I N 1 (正义) righteousness 2 (情谊) human relationship (PL) 3 (意义) meaning II ADJ 1 (正义的) just 2 (拜认的) adopted ▶ 义父 [yìfù] adoptive father

义卖 [yìmài] VB sell ... for charity

义气 [yìqi] I N loyalty II ADJ loyal

义务 [yìwù] I N duty II ADJ compulsory

艺 [yì] N 1 (技能) skill ▶ 手艺 [shǒuyì] craftsmanship 2 (艺术) art

艺人 [yìrén] N (演员) performer

艺术 [yìshù] I N 1 (文艺) art 2 (方法) skill ▷ 管理艺术 [guǎnlǐ yìshù] management skills II ADJ artistic

艺术家 [yìshùjiā] N artist

忆 [yì] VB remember ▶ 记忆 [jìyì] memory

议 [yì] I N opinion ▶ 建议 [jiànyì] propose II VB discuss ▶ 商议 [shāngyì] discuss

议程 [yìchéng] N agenda

议会 [yìhuì] N parliament

议论 [yìlùn] I VB discuss II N talk

议题 [yìtí] N topic

议员 [yìyuán] N congressman, congresswoman

异 [yì] I ADJ 1 (不同) different ▶ 差异 [chāyì] difference 2 (奇异) strange 3 (另外) other ▶ 异国 [yìguó] foreign country II VB separate ▶ 离异 [líyì] separate

异常 [yìcháng] ADJ unusual

异性 [yìxìng] N (指性别) the opposite sex

译 [yì] VB translate

译文 [yìwén] N translation

译者 [yìzhě] N translator

译制 [yìzhì] VB dub

抑 [yì] VB repress

抑郁 [yìyù] ADJ depressed

抑制 [yìzhì] VB 1 (生理) inhibit 2 (控制) control

易 [yì] ADJ (容易) easy ▷ 易传染 [yì chuánrǎn] easily transmissible

易拉罐 [yìlāguàn] N can

疫 [yì] N epidemic

疫苗 [yìmiáo] N inoculation

益 [yì] I N benefit II ADJ beneficial III VB increase IV ADV increasingly

益处 [yìchù] N benefit

谊 [yì] N friendship ▶ 友谊 [yǒuyì] friendship

意 [yì] N **1** (意思) meaning **2** (心愿) wish ▶ 好意 [hǎoyì] good intention

意见 [yìjiàn] N **1** (看法) opinion **2** (不满) objection

意识 [yìshi] **I** N consciousness **II** VB realize

意思 [yìsi] N **1** (意义) meaning **2** (意见) idea **3** (愿望) wish **4** (趣味) interest ▶ 有意思 [yǒu yìsi] interesting ▶ 没意思 [méi yìsi] boring **5** (心意) token

意图 [yìtú] N intention

意外 [yìwài] **I** N accident **II** ADJ unexpected

意义 [yìyì] N **1** (含义) meaning **2** (作用) significance

毅 [yì] ADJ resolute

毅力 [yìlì] N perseverance

因 [yīn] **I** CONJ because **II** PREP because of ▷ 昨天他因病缺课。[Zuótiān tā yīn bìng quēkè.] He missed a class yesterday because of illness. **III** N cause ▶ 病因 [bìngyīn] cause of the illness

因此 [yīncǐ] CONJ so

因而 [yīn'ér] CONJ therefore

因素 [yīnsù] N **1** (成分) element **2** (原因) factor

因特网 [Yīntèwǎng] N the internet

因为 [yīnwei] CONJ because

阴 [yīn] **I** ADJ **1** (指天气) overcast **2** (阴险的) insidious ▶ 阴谋 [yīnmóu] plot **3** (物) negative ▶ 阴性 [yīnxìng] negative **II** N **1** (阳的对立面) Yin (*from Yin and Yang*) **2** (指月亮) the moon ▶ 阴历 [yīnlì] lunar calendar **3** (阴凉处) shade ▶ 树阴 [shùyīn] the shade

阴暗 [yīn'àn] ADJ gloomy

阴部 [yīnbù] N private parts (PL)

阴凉 [yīnliáng] ADJ shady and cool

音 [yīn] N **1** (声音) sound **2** (消息) news (SG)

音量 [yīnliàng] N volume

音响 [yīnxiǎng] N (指设备) acoustics (PL)

音像 [yīnxiàng] N audio and video

音乐 [yīnyuè] N music

音乐会 [yīnyuèhuì] N concert

银 [yín] **I** N **1** (指) (金属) silver **2** (指) (货币) money ▶ 收银台 [shōuyíntái] cashier's desk **II** ADJ silver

银行 [yínháng] N bank

银河 [yínhé] N the Milky Way

银幕 [yínmù] N screen

银牌 [yínpái] N silver medal

龈 [yín] N gum ▶ 牙龈 [yáyín] gum

引 [yǐn] VB **1** (牵引) draw **2** (引导) lead ▶ 引路 [yǐnlù] lead the way **3** (引起) cause **4** (引用) cite

引导 [yǐndǎo] VB **1** (带领) lead **2** (启发诱导) guide

引进 [yǐnjìn] VB **1** (人) recommend **2** (物) import

引力 [yǐnlì] N gravitation

引起 [yǐnqǐ] VB cause

引擎 [yǐnqíng] N engine

引用 [yǐnyòng] VB (引述) quote

引诱 [yǐnyòu] VB **1** (诱导) induce **2** (诱惑) tempt

饮 [yǐn] **I** VB drink **II** N drink

饮料 [yǐnliào] N drink

饮食 [yǐnshí] N food and drink

饮用水 [yǐnyòngshuǐ] N drinking water

隐 [yǐn] VB conceal

隐藏 [yǐncáng] VB conceal

隐瞒 [yǐnmán] VB cover ... up

隐私 [yǐnsī] N private matters (PL)

瘾 [yǐn] N (嗜好) addiction ▶ 上瘾 [shàngyǐn] be addicted to

印 [yìn] **I** N **1** (图章) stamp **2** (痕迹) print **II** VB (留下痕迹) print

印刷 [yìnshuā] VB print

印象 [yìnxiàng] N impression
印章 [yìnzhāng] N seal

荫 [yìn] ADJ shady
荫凉 [yìnliáng] ADJ shady and cool

应 [yīng] I VB 1 (答应) answer 2 (应允) agree II AUX VB should
→ *see also*/另见 yìng
应当 [yīngdāng] AUX VB should
应该 [yīnggāi] AUX VB should
应允 [yīngyǔn] VB consent

英 [yīng] N 1 (才能出众者) hero ▶ 精英 [jīngyīng] elite 2 (英国) Britain
英镑 [yīngbàng] N pound sterling
英国 [Yīngguó] N Great Britain ▷ 英国的 [Yīngguó de] British
英国人 [Yīngguórén] N the British
英俊 [yīngjùn] ADJ (漂亮的) handsome
英雄 [yīngxióng] I N hero II ADJ heroic
英勇 [yīngyǒng] ADJ brave
英语 [yīngyǔ] N English

婴 [yīng] N baby
婴儿 [yīng'ér] N baby

樱 [yīng] N 1 (樱桃) cherry ▶ 樱桃 [yīngtáo] cherry 2 (樱花) cherry blossom ▶ 樱花 [yīnghuā] cherry blossom

鹦 [yīng] *see below*/见下文
鹦鹉 [yīngwǔ] N parrot

鹰 [yīng] N eagle

迎 [yíng] VB 1 (迎接) welcome 2 (对着) meet
迎合 [yínghé] VB cater to
迎接 [yíngjiē] VB welcome

萤 [yíng] N firefly ▶ 萤火虫 [yínghuǒchóng] firefly

营 [yíng] I VB (经营) operate II N 1 (军队驻地) barracks (PL) 2 (军队编制) battalion 3 (营地) camp ▶ 营地 [yíngdì] camp
营救 [yíngjiù] VB rescue
营销 [yíngxiāo] VB sell
营养 [yíngyǎng] N nourishment
营业 [yíngyè] VB do business

蝇 [yíng] N fly ▶ 苍蝇 [cāngying] fly

赢 [yíng] VB 1 (胜) win 2 (获利) gain
赢利 [yínglì] N gain

影 [yǐng] N 1 (影子) shadow 2 (照片) photograph 3 (电影) movie
影片 [yǐngpiàn] N 1 (胶片) film 2 (电影) movie
影响 [yǐngxiǎng] I VB affect II N influence
影印 [yǐngyìn] VB photocopy

应 [yìng] VB 1 (回答) answer ▶ 回应 [huíyìng] answer 2 (满足) respond to 3 (顺应) comply with 4 (应付) handle ▶ 应急 [yìngjí] handle an emergency
→ *see also*/另见 yīng
应酬 [yìngchou] I VB socialize with II N social engagement
应付 [yìngfu] VB 1 (采取办法) handle 2 (敷衍) do half-heartedly 3 (将就) make do with
应聘 [yìngpìn] VB accept an offer
应用 [yìngyòng] I VB apply II ADJ applied ▶ 应用程序 [yìngyòng chéngxù] app

硬 [yìng] I ADJ 1 (坚固) hard 2 (刚强) firm 3 (能干的) strong II ADV obstinately
硬币 [yìngbì] N coin
硬件 [yìngjiàn] N 1 (计算机) hardware 2 (设备) equipment
硬盘 [yìngpán] N hard disk

哟 [yō] INT (表示轻微的惊异或赞叹) oh

佣 [yōng] I VB hire II N servant ▶ 佣人 [yòngrén] servant
→ *see also*/另见 yòng

拥 [yōng] VB 1 (抱) embrace 2 (围着) gather round 3 (拥挤) swarm 4 (拥护) support
拥抱 [yōngbào] VB embrace

拥护 [yōnghù] VB support
拥挤 [yōngjǐ] I ADJ crowded II VB crowd
拥有 [yōngyǒu] VB have

庸 [yōng] ADJ (不高明) mediocre
庸俗 [yōngsú] ADJ vulgar

永 [yǒng] I ADJ (书) everlasting II ADV forever
永恒 [yǒnghéng] ADJ everlasting
永久 [yǒngjiǔ] ADJ eternal
永远 [yǒngyuǎn] ADV eternally

泳 [yǒng] N swim ▶ 蛙泳 [wāyǒng] breaststroke
泳道 [yǒngdào] N lane

勇 [yǒng] ADJ brave
勇敢 [yǒnggǎn] ADJ brave
勇气 [yǒngqì] N courage

用 [yòng] I VB 1 (使用) use 2 (需要) need 3 (消费) consume ▶ 用餐 [yòngcān] have a meal II N 1 (费用) expense ▶ 家用 [jiāyòng] household expenses (PL) 2 (用处) use ▶ 没用 [méiyòng] useless
用处 [yòngchu] N use
用功 [yònggōng] I ADJ hardworking II VB work hard
用户 [yònghù] N user ▷ 网络用户 [wǎngluò yònghù] internet user
用具 [yòngjù] N tool
用力 [yònglì] VB exert oneself
用品 [yòngpǐn] N goods (PL)
用途 [yòngtú] N use

佣 [yòng] *see below*/见下文
→ *see also*/另见 yōng
佣金 [yòngjīn] N commission

优 [yōu] ADJ (优良) excellent
优点 [yōudiǎn] N strong point
优良 [yōuliáng] ADJ fine
优美 [yōuměi] ADJ elegant
优势 [yōushì] N advantage
优先 [yōuxiān] VB have priority
优秀 [yōuxiù] ADJ outstanding
优越 [yōuyuè] ADJ superior

忧 [yōu] I ADJ anxious II VB worry III N anxiety
忧伤 [yōushāng] ADJ sad
忧郁 [yōuyù] ADJ depressed

幽 [yōu] ADJ (暗) dim ▶ 幽暗 [yōu'àn] gloomy
幽默 [yōumò] ADJ humorous

悠 [yōu] ADJ 1 (久远) remote 2 (闲适) leisurely
悠久 [yōujiǔ] ADJ long-standing
悠闲 [yōuxián] ADJ leisurely

尤 [yóu] ADV especially
尤其 [yóuqí] ADV especially

由 [yóu] I VB 1 (听凭) give in to 2 (经过) go through II PREP 1 (归) by 2 (根据) ▷ 由此可见… [yóu cǐ kě jiàn...] from this we can see... 3 (从) from 4 (由于) due to III N cause ▶ 理由 [lǐyóu] reason
由于 [yóuyú] PREP as a result of

邮 [yóu] I VB mail II N 1 (邮务) mail 2 (邮票) stamp
邮递 [yóudì] VB send ... by mail
邮电 [yóudiàn] N post and telecommunications
邮寄 [yóujì] VB mail
邮件 [yóujiàn] N mail
邮局 [yóujú] N post office
邮票 [yóupiào] N stamp
邮政 [yóuzhèng] N mail service
邮资 [yóuzī] N postage

犹 [yóu] ADV still
犹豫 [yóuyù] ADJ hesitant

油 [yóu] I N oil II ADJ oily
油滑 [yóuhuá] ADJ slippery
油腻 [yóunì] I ADJ greasy II N greasy food
油漆 [yóuqī] I N varnish II VB varnish

鱿 [yóu] N squid
鱿鱼 [yóuyú] N squid

游 [yóu] VB 1 (游泳) swim 2 (游览) tour
游客 [yóukè] N tourist
游览 [yóulǎn] VB tour
游牧 [yóumù] VB live a nomadic life
游说 [yóushuì] VB lobby
游戏 [yóuxì] I N game II VB play
游行 [yóuxíng] VB march
游泳 [yóuyǒng] I VB swim II N swimming
游泳池 [yóuyǒngchí] N swimming pool

友 [yǒu] I N friend ▶ 男友 [nányǒu] boyfriend II ADJ friendly ▶ 友好 [yǒuhǎo] friendly
友爱 [yǒu'ài] ADJ affectionate
友情 [yǒuqíng] N friendship
友人 [yǒurén] N friend
友谊 [yǒuyì] N friendship

有 [yǒu] VB 1 (具有) have 2 (存在) ▷ 院子里有一棵大树。[Yuànzi li yǒu yī kē dàshù.] There's a big tree in the courtyard. 3 (发生) occur ▷ 我的生活有了一些变化。[Wǒ de shēnghuó yǒu le yīxiē biànhuà.] A few changes have occurred in my life. (表示程度) have ▷ 他特别有学问。[Tā tèbié yǒu xuéwèn.] He's extremely knowledgeable. 4 (某) ▶ 有时候 [yǒushíhou] sometimes ▷ 有一次，他得了冠军。[Yǒu yī cì, tā dé le guànjūn.] He won a prize once.
有的 [yǒude] N some ▷ 展出的作品，有的来自本土，有的来自海外。[Zhǎnchū de zuòpǐn, yǒude láizì běntǔ, yǒude láizì hǎiwài.] Of the articles on display, some are local, others are from overseas.
有关 [yǒuguān] VB 1 (有关系) be relevant 2 (涉及到) be about
有利 [yǒulì] ADJ favorable
有趣 [yǒuqù] ADJ interesting
有限 [yǒuxiàn] ADJ limited
有限公司 [yǒuxiàn gōngsī] N limited company
有线电视 [yǒuxiàn diànshì] N cable TV
有幸 [yǒuxìng] ADJ fortunate
有意思 [yǒuyìsi] I ADJ 1 (有意义) significant 2 (有趣味) interesting II VB be interested in

又 [yòu] ADV 1 (重复) again 2 (同时) ▷ 她是一个好教师，又是一个好妈妈。[Tā shì yī gè hǎo jiàoshī, yòu shì yī gè hǎo māma.] She's both a good teacher and a great mother. 3 (也) too 4 (另外) another 5 (再加上) and ▷ 一又三分之二 [yī yòu sān fēn zhī èr] one and two thirds 6 (可是) but

右 [yòu] N 1 (右边) right ▶ 右边 [yòubian] right side ▷ 请向右转。[Qǐng xiàng yòu zhuǎn.] Please turn right. 2 (右翼) the Right

幼 [yòu] I ADJ young II N child ▶ 幼儿园 [yòu'éryuán] kindergarten
幼儿 [yòu'ér] N small child
幼年 [yòunián] N infancy
幼小 [yòuxiǎo] ADJ young
幼稚 [yòuzhì] ADJ 1 (书) (年龄很小) young 2 (头脑简单) naive

诱 [yòu] VB 1 (诱导) guide 2 (引诱) entice
诱饵 [yòu'ěr] N bait
诱惑 [yòuhuò] VB 1 (引诱) entice 2 (吸引) attract

于 [yú] PREP 1 (在) in 2 (向) from 3 (对) to 4 (从) from 5 (比) than ▶ 大于 [dàyú] bigger than
于是 [yúshì] CONJ so

余 [yú] N 1 (零头) ▷ 500余人 [wǔbǎi yú rén] more than five hundred people 2 (指时间) ▶ 课余 [kèyú] extra-curricular
余地 [yúdì] N room

盂 [yú] N jar ▶ 痰盂 [tányú] cuspidor

鱼 [yú] N fish ▶ 鱼肉 [yúròu] fish

娱 [yú] I VB amuse II N amusement

娱乐 [yúlè] I VB have fun II N entertainment

渔 [yú] VB (捕鱼) fish ▶ 渔业 [yúyè] fisheries

愉 [yú] ADJ happy
愉快 [yúkuài] ADJ happy ▷ 祝你旅行愉快！ [Zhù nǐ lǚxíng yúkuài!] Have a pleasant journey!

愚 [yú] I ADJ foolish ▶ 愚蠢 [yúchǔn] foolish II VB fool
愚昧 [yúmèi] ADJ ignorant

舆 [yú] ADJ popular
舆论 [yúlùn] N public opinion

与 [yǔ] I PREP with II CONJ and

宇 [yǔ] N 1 (房屋) house 2 (四方) the universe
宇航 [yǔháng] I VB travel through space II N space travel
宇航员 [yǔhángyuán] N astronaut
宇宙 [yǔzhòu] N universe

羽 [yǔ] N 1 (羽毛) feather 2 (翅膀) wing
羽毛 [yǔmáo] N feather
羽毛球 [yǔmáoqiú] N 1 (指运动) badminton 2 (指球体) shuttlecock

雨 [yǔ] N rain ▶ 下雨 [xiàyǔ] to rain
雨具 [yǔjù] N waterproofs (PL)
雨水 [yǔshuǐ] N (降水) rain

语 [yǔ] I N (语言) language ▶ 手语 [shǒuyǔ] sign language II VB talk
语调 [yǔdiào] N tone
语法 [yǔfǎ] N grammar
语句 [yǔjù] N sentence
语气 [yǔqì] N 1 (口气) tone of voice 2 (语法) mood
语文 [yǔwén] N 1 (语言文字) language 2 (中文) Chinese 3 (语言与文学) language and literature
语言 [yǔyán] N language
语音 [yǔyīn] N pronunciation
语音信箱 [yǔyīn xìnxiāng] N voice mail
语种 [yǔzhǒng] N language

玉 [yù] N (玉石) jade
玉米 [yùmǐ] N (指植物) corn

郁 [yù] ADJ (烦闷) gloomy
郁闷 [yùmèn] ADJ melancholy

育 [yù] I VB 1 (生育) give birth to 2 (养活) raise ▶ 养育 [yǎngyù] bring up II N education ▶ 教育 [jiàoyù] education

狱 [yù] N (监狱) prison ▶ 监狱 [jiānyù] prison

浴 [yù] VB wash
浴盆 [yùpén] N bath
浴室 [yùshì] N bathroom

预 [yù] ADV in advance
预报 [yùbào] VB predict ▶ 天气预报 [tiānqì yùbào] weather forecast
预备 [yùbèi] VB prepare
预测 [yùcè] VB predict
预防 [yùfáng] VB prevent
预感 [yùgǎn] VB have a premonition
预计 [yùjì] VB estimate
预见 [yùjiàn] VB foresee
预科 [yùkē] N foundation course
预料 [yùliào] VB predict
预算 [yùsuàn] N budget
预习 [yùxí] VB prepare for lessons
预言 [yùyán] VB predict

域 [yù] N region ▶ 领域 [lǐngyù] realm

欲 [yù] N desire
欲望 [yùwàng] N desire

遇 [yù] I VB meet ▶ 遇到 [yùdào] meet II N 1 (待遇) treatment 2 (机会) opportunity

寓 [yù] I VB 1 (居住) live 2 (寄托) imply II N residence ▶ 公寓 [gōngyù] apartment
寓言 [yùyán] N fable

鸳 [yuān] N mandarin duck
鸳鸯 [yuānyang] N (指鸟) mandarin duck

冤 [yuān] N 1 (冤枉) injustice ▶ 冤枉 [yuānwang] treat unfairly 2 (冤仇) enmity

元 [yuán] I N 1 (始) first 2 (首) chief ▶ 元首 [yuánshǒu] head of state 3 (主) fundamental ▶ 元素 [yuánsù] element 4 (整体) component ▶ 单元 [dānyuán] unit 5 (圆形货币) coin ▶ 金元 [jīnyuán] gold coin II MEAS yuan ▷ 5元钱 [wǔ yuán qián] five yuan

元旦 [Yuándàn] N New Year's Day

元件 [yuánjiàn] N part

元帅 [yuánshuài] N commander-in-chief

元宵 [yuánxiāo] N *sweet round dumplings made of glutinous rice, usually eaten with the broth in which they are cooked*

元宵节 [Yuánxiāo Jié] N the Lantern Festival

元宵节 [Yuánxiāo Jié]

The Lantern Festival is celebrated on the 15th day of the Lunar Chinese New Year. The traditional food which is eaten at this festival is called 元宵 yuánxiāo or 汤圆 tāngyuán, a traditional sweet dumpling made of glutinous rice, with various sweet fillings.

园 [yuán] N 1 (指菜地或果林) garden 2 (指游乐场所) park

园丁 [yuándīng] N (园艺工人) gardener

园林 [yuánlín] N garden

园艺 [yuányì] N gardening

员 [yuán] N 1 (指工作或学习的人) ▶ 理发员 [lǐfàyuán] hairdresser 2 (成员) member

员工 [yuángōng] N staff (PL)

原 [yuán] ADJ 1 (本来的) original 2 (未加工的) raw ▶ 原油 [yuányóu] crude oil

原来 [yuánlái] I ADJ original II ADV 1 (起初) originally 2 (其实) all along

原理 [yuánlǐ] N principle

原谅 [yuánliàng] VB forgive

原料 [yuánliào] N (指烹饪) ingredient

原始 [yuánshǐ] ADJ 1 (古老) primitive 2 (最初) original

原先 [yuánxiān] I ADJ original II ADV originally

原因 [yuányīn] N reason

原则 [yuánzé] N principle

原著 [yuánzhù] N the original

原子 [yuánzǐ] N atom

圆 [yuán] I ADJ 1 (圆形的) round ▶ 圆圈 [yuánquān] circle 2 (球形的) spherical 3 (圆满的) satisfactory II N (数) (圆周) circle

圆规 [yuánguī] N compasses (PL)

圆满 [yuánmǎn] ADJ satisfactory

圆舞曲 [yuánwǔqǔ] N waltz

援 [yuán] VB (援助) help ▶ 支援 [zhīyuán] support

援救 [yuánjiù] VB rescue

援助 [yuánzhù] VB help

缘 [yuán] N 1 (缘故) cause 2 (缘分) fate 3 (边缘) edge

缘分 [yuánfen] N fate

缘故 [yuángù] N cause

猿 [yuán] N ape

猿猴 [yuánhóu] N apes and monkeys (PL)

猿人 [yuánrén] N ape-man

源 [yuán] N source ▶ 水源 [shuǐyuán] source

远 [yuǎn] ADJ 1 (指距离) far ▶ 远程 [yuǎnchéng] long-distance 2 (指血统) distant 3 (指程度) far

远大 [yuǎndà] ADJ far-reaching

远方 [yuǎnfāng] N afar

远见 [yuǎnjiàn] N foresight

远亲 [yuǎnqīn] N distant relative

远视 [yuǎnshì] N (医) long sightedness

远足 [yuǎnzú] VB hike

院 [yuàn] N 1 (院落) courtyard ▶ 院子 [yuànzi] yard 2 (指机关和处所) ▶ 电影院 [diànyǐngyuàn] movie theater 3 (学院) college 4 (医院) hospital

愿 [yuàn] I N (愿望) wish II AUX VB ▷ 我不愿说。 [Wǒ bù yuàn shuō.] I don't want to say anything.

愿望 [yuànwàng] N wish

愿意 [yuànyì] VB 1 (同意) be willing to 2 (希望) wish

约 [yuē] I VB 1 (束缚) restrict 2 (商定) arrange 3 (邀请) invite II ADJ brief ▶ 简约 [jiǎnyuē] brief III ADV about

约会 [yuēhuì] N 1 (指工作) appointment 2 (指恋人) date

约束 [yuēshù] VB bind

月 [yuè] N 1 (月球) the moon ▶ 满月 [mǎnyuè] full moon 2 (月份) month ▶ 3月 [sānyuè] March 3 (每月) monthly ▶ 月薪 [yuèxīn] monthly salary

月饼 [yuèbing] N mooncake

月饼 [yuèbing]

Mooncakes, the traditional festival food for 中秋节 Zhōngqiū Jié (the Mid-Autumn Festival), are round cakes made of a variety of sweet fillings including beanpaste, egg and peanut.

月份 [yuèfèn] N month

月光 [yuèguāng] N moonlight

月经 [yuèjīng] N (例假) period

月亮 [yuèliang] N the moon

月票 [yuèpiào] N monthly ticket

乐 [yuè] N music ▶ 器乐 [qìyuè] instrumental music ▶ 民乐 [mínyuè] folk music
→ *see also*/另见 lè

乐队 [yuèduì] N band

乐器 [yuèqì] N musical instrument

乐曲 [yuèqǔ] N music

乐团 [yuètuán] N philharmonic orchestra

岳 [yuè] N 1 (高山) mountain 2 (妻子的父母) parents-in-law (PL)

岳父 [yuèfù] N father-in-law

岳母 [yuèmǔ] N mother-in-law

阅 [yuè] VB 1 (看) read 2 (检阅) inspect 3 (经历) experience

阅读 [yuèdú] VB read

阅览 [yuèlǎn] VB read

阅历 [yuèlì] VB experience

跃 [yuè] VB leap ▶ 跳跃 [tiàoyuè] jump

越 [yuè] I VB 1 (跨过) jump over 2 (超过) exceed II ADV ▶ 越发 [yuèfā] increasingly

越来越 [yuèláiyuè] ADV more and more ▷ 天气越来越暖和了。 [Tiānqì yuèláiyuè nuǎnhuo le.] The weather is getting warmer and warmer.

越野 [yuèyě] VB go cross-country

越...越... [yuè...yuè...] ADV the more ... the more ... ▷ 越早越好 [yuè zǎo yuè hǎo] the earlier the better

晕 [yūn] VB 1 (晕眩) feel dizzy 2 (昏迷) faint ▷ 她晕过去了。 [Tā yūn guòqu le.] She passed out.
→ *see also*/另见 yùn

云 [yún] N cloud

云彩 [yúncai] N cloud

匀 [yún] I ADJ even II VB 1 (使均匀) even ... out 2 (分) apportion

匀称 [yúnchèn] ADJ well-proportioned

允 [yǔn] VB allow

允许 [yǔnxǔ] VB allow

孕 [yùn] I VB be pregnant ▶ 怀孕 [huáiyùn] be pregnant II N pregnancy

运 [yùn] I VB 1 (运动) move 2 (搬运) transport 3 (运用) use II N luck ▶ 好运 [hǎoyùn] good luck

运动 [yùndòng] I VB (物) move II N

1 (体育活动) sport 2 (大规模) movement
运动鞋 [yùndòngxié] N trainer
运动员 [yùndòngyuán] N athlete
运河 [yùnhé] N canal
运气 [yùnqi] N luck
运输 [yùnshū] VB transport
运算 [yùnsuàn] VB calculate
运行 [yùnxíng] VB move
运用 [yùnyòng] VB make use of
运转 [yùnzhuǎn] VB (指机器) run
运作 [yùnzuò] VB operate

晕 [yùn] VB feel giddy ▶ 晕机 [yùnjī] be airsick ▶ 晕车 [yùnchē] be carsick ▶ 晕船 [yùnchuán] be seasick → *see also*/另见 yūn

---

熨 [yùn] VB iron
熨斗 [yùndǒu] N iron

Z

杂 [zá] **I** ADJ miscellaneous ▶ 复杂 [fùzá] complicated **II** VB mix

杂货 [záhuò] N groceries (PL)

杂技 [zájì] N acrobatics (PL)

杂志 [zázhì] N magazine

砸 [zá] VB **1** (撞击) pound **2** (打破) break ▷ 杯子砸坏了。[Bēizi záhuài le.] The cup was broken.

灾 [zāi] N **1** (灾害) disaster ▶ 水灾 [shuǐzāi] flood **2** (不幸) misfortune

灾害 [zāihài] N disaster

灾难 [zāinàn] N disaster

栽 [zāi] VB **1** (种) plant ▷ 栽花 [zāi huā] grow flowers **2** (摔倒) tumble

再 [zài] ADV **1** (又) again ▷ 你再说一遍。[Nǐ zài shuō yī biàn.] Say that again. **2** (更) more ▷ 请把音量放得再大些。[Qǐng bǎ yīnliàng fàngde zài dàxiē.] Please turn the volume up a bit. **3** (继续) ▷ 我不能再等了。[Wǒ bùnéng zài děng le.] I can't wait any longer. **4** (接着) then ▷ 你做完功课再看小说。[Nǐ zuòwán gōngkè zài kàn xiǎoshuō.] You can read your book when you've finished your homework. **5** (另外) ▶ 再说 [zàishuō] besides

再见 [zàijiàn] VB say goodbye ▷ 再见! [Zàijiàn!] Goodbye!

再三 [zàisān] ADV again and again

在 [zài] **I** VB **1** (存在) live **2** (处于) be ▷ 你的书在桌子上。[Nǐ de shū zài zhuōzi shang.] Your book is on the table. ▷ 我父母在纽约。[Wǒ fùmǔ zài Niǔyuē.] My parents are in New York. **3** (在于) rest with **II** ADV ▷ 情况在改变。[Qíngkuàng zài gǎibiàn.] Things are changing. ▷ 他们在看电视。[Tāmen zài kàn diànshì.] They're watching TV. **III** PREP at ▷ 在机场等候 [zài jīchǎng děnghòu] wait at the airport ▷ 在历史上 [zài lìshǐ shang] in history

在乎 [zàihu] VB care

在于 [zàiyú] VB (取决于) depend on

咱 [zán] PRON **1** (咱们) we **2** (方) (我) I

咱们 [zánmen] PRON **1** (我们) we **2** (方) (我) I

攒 [zǎn] VB save

暂 [zàn] **I** ADJ brief **II** ADV temporarily

暂时 [zànshí] N ▷ 暂时的需要 [zànshí de xūyào] temporary need

赞 [zàn] VB **1** (帮助) assist ▶ 赞助 [zànzhù] assistance **2** (称颂) commend ▶ 赞赏 [zànshǎng] admire

赞成 [zànchéng] VB approve

赞美 [zànměi] VB praise

赞同 [zàntóng] VB approve of

赞扬 [zànyáng] VB pay tribute to

脏 [zāng] ADJ dirty ▶ 脏话 [zānghuà] dirty word

遭 [zāo] VB meet with ▶ 遭殃 [zāoyāng] suffer

遭到 [zāodào] VB encounter

遭受 [zāoshòu] VB suffer

糟 [zāo] **I** N dregs (PL) **II** VB **1** (浪费) waste ▶ 糟蹋 [zāota] spoil **2** (腌制) flavor with alcohol **III** ADJ **1** (腐烂) rotten **2** (弄坏) messy

糟糕 [zāogāo] ADJ terrible ▷ 真糟糕, 我的钥匙丢了。[Zhēn zāogāo, wǒ de yàoshi diū le.] Oh no, I've lost my key!

早 [zǎo] **I** N morning **II** ADV a long time ago **III** ADJ early

早安 [zǎo'ān] N ▷ 早安! [Zǎo'ān!] Good morning!

早餐 [zǎocān] N breakfast

早晨 [zǎochen] N morning

早饭 [zǎofàn] N breakfast

早晚 [zǎowǎn] I N morning and evening II ADV 1 (迟早) sooner or later 2 (方) (将来) some day
早上 [zǎoshang] N morning

造 [zào] VB 1 (制作) make 2 (瞎编) concoct ▶ 造谣 [zàoyáo] start a rumor
造成 [zàochéng] VB cause
造反 [zàofǎn] VB rebel
造型 [zàoxíng] N model

噪 [zào] VB (嚷) clamor ▶ 噪音 [zàoyīn] noise

责 [zé] I N responsibility ▶ 负责 [fùzé] be responsible for II VB (责备) blame ▶ 指责 [zhǐzé] censure
责备 [zébèi] VB blame
责任 [zérèn] N responsibility

怎 [zěn] PRON (方) ▷ 你怎能相信他的话? [Nǐ zěn néng xiāngxìn tā de huà?] How can you believe him?
怎么 [zěnme] I PRON ▷ 你看这事我该怎么办? [Nǐ kàn zhè shì wǒ gāi zěnme bàn?] What do you think I should do about this? ▷ 你昨天怎么没来上课? [Nǐ zuótiān zěnme méi lái shàngkè?] Why weren't you in class yesterday? II ADV (泛指方式) ▷ 我是怎么想就怎么说。 [Wǒ shì zěnme xiǎng jiù zěnme shuō.] I say whatever I think. ▷ 他最近怎么样? [Tā zuìjìn zénme yàng?] How has he been doing?
怎样 [zěnyàng] ADV how

增 [zēng] VB increase
增加 [zēngjiā] VB increase
增长 [zēngzhǎng] VB increase

赠 [zèng] VB present ▶ 捐赠 [juānzèng] donate
赠品 [zèngpǐn] N gift

扎 [zhā] VB 1 (刺) prick 2 (住下) set up camp 3 (钻进) plunge into
扎实 [zhāshi] ADJ 1 (结实) sturdy 2 (实在) solid

炸 [zhá] VB fry
→ *see also*/另见 zhà

炸 [zhà] VB 1 (爆破) blow ... up 2 (破裂) explode 3 (逃离) run scared
→ *see also*/另见 zhá
炸弹 [zhàdàn] N bomb
炸药 [zhàyào] N explosive

摘 [zhāi] VB 1 (取) pick 2 (选) select 3 (借) borrow

窄 [zhǎi] ADJ 1 (不宽敞) narrow 2 (气量小) narrow-minded 3 (不宽裕) hard up

粘 [zhān] VB stick

盏 [zhǎn] I N small cup II MEAS ▷ 一盏灯 [yī zhǎn dēng] a lamp
measure word, used for lamps and lights

展 [zhǎn] I VB 1 (进行) develop 2 (施展) give free rein to 3 (暂缓) postpone II N exhibition
展出 [zhǎnchū] VB exhibit
展开 [zhǎnkāi] VB 1 (张开) spread 2 (进行) develop
展览 [zhǎnlǎn] N exhibition
展品 [zhǎnpǐn] N exhibit

崭 [zhǎn] *see below*/见下文
崭新 [zhǎnxīn] ADJ brand-new

占 [zhàn] VB (占用) occupy

战 [zhàn] I N war II VB 1 (战斗) fight 2 (发抖) shiver
战斗 [zhàndòu] VB fight
战胜 [zhànshèng] VB overcome
战士 [zhànshì] N soldier
战争 [zhànzhēng] N war

站 [zhàn] I VB 1 (站立) stand 2 (停下) stop II N 1 (停车地点) stop ▷ 公共汽车站 [gōnggòng qìchēzhàn] bus stop 2 (服务机构) center

张 [zhāng] I VB 1 (打开) open 2 (展开) extend ▶ 扩张 [kuòzhāng] stretch 3 (夸大) exaggerate ▶ 夸张 [kuāzhāng] exaggerate 4 (看) look

5 (开业) open for business 6 (陈设) lay ... on **II** MEAS **1** (指平的物体) ▷ 一张海报 [yī zhāng hǎibào] a poster ▷ 一张书桌 [yī zhāng shūzhuō] a desk **2** (指嘴或脸) ▷ 一张大嘴 [yī zhāng dà zuǐ] a big mouth ▷ 一张脸 [yī zhāng liǎn] a face

measure word, used for flat objects such as newspapers, maps, paintings, cards, tickets, pancakes; furniture such as beds, desks, sofas; mouths and faces

章 [zhāng] N **1** (作品) article ▶ 文章 [wénzhāng] article **2** (章节) chapter **3** (条理) order **4** (章程) regulation ▶ 宪章 [xiànzhāng] charter **5** (图章) seal **6** (标志) button

长 [zhǎng] **I** ADJ **1** (大) older ▷ 他年长我3岁。 [Tā niánzhǎng wǒ sān suì.] He's three years older than me. **2** (排行第一) oldest ▶ 长兄 [zhǎngxiōng] oldest brother **II** N **1** (年长者) ▶ 兄长 [xiōngzhǎng] elder brother **2** (头领) head ▶ 校长 [xiàozhǎng] head teacher **III** VB **1** (生) form **2** (发育) grow **3** (增加) acquire

→ *see also*/另见 cháng

涨 [zhǎng] VB increase

掌 [zhǎng] **I** N **1** (手掌) palm **2** (人的脚掌) sole **3** (动物的脚掌) foot **4** (掌形物) ▶ 仙人掌 [xiānrénzhǎng] cactus **5** (U型铁) horseshoe **6** (鞋掌) sole **II** VB **1** (打) slap **2** (钉) sole **3** (主持) be in charge of

掌握 [zhǎngwò] VB control

丈 [zhàng] N (长度单位) *Chinese unit of length, equal to 3.3 meters*

丈夫 [zhàngfu] N husband

帐 [zhàng] N curtain ▶ 蚊帐 [wénzhàng] mosquito net

帐篷 [zhàngpeng] N tent

账 [zhàng] N **1** (账目) accounts (PL) **2** (账簿) ledger **3** (债务) credit ▶ 赊账 [shēzhàng] buy on credit

账单 [zhàngdān] N bill

账号 [zhànghào] N account number

障 [zhàng] **I** N barrier **II** VB hinder

障碍 [zhàng'ài] **I** VB hinder **II** N obstacle

招 [zhāo] **I** VB **1** (挥动) beckon **2** (招收) recruit **3** (引来) attract **4** (惹怒) provoke **5** (坦白) confess **II** N **1** (计谋) trick **2** (指下棋) move

招待 [zhāodài] VB entertain ▶ 招待会 [zhāodàihuì] reception

招呼 [zhāohu] VB **1** (呼唤) call **2** (问候) greet **3** (吩咐) tell

着 [zháo] VB **1** (挨) touch **2** (受到) be affected by **3** (燃烧) be lit **4** (入睡) fall asleep

着急 [zháojí] ADJ worried

找 [zhǎo] VB **1** (寻找) look for **2** (退余额) give change ▶ 找钱 [zhǎoqián] give change **3** (求见) call on

召 [zhào] VB summon

召开 [zhàokāi] VB hold

照 [zhào] **I** VB **1** (照射) light up **2** (映现) reflect **3** (拍摄) take a photograph **4** (照料) look after **5** (对照) contrast **6** (遵照) refer to ▶ 参照 [cānzhào] consult **7** (明白) understand **II** N **1** (照片) photograph **2** (执照) license **III** PREP **1** (按照) according to **2** (向着) in the direction of

照常 [zhàocháng] ADV as usual

照顾 [zhàogu] VB **1** (照料) look after **2** (考虑) consider

照看 [zhàokàn] VB look after

照料 [zhàoliào] VB take care of

照片 [zhàopiàn] N photograph

照相 [zhàoxiàng] VB take a picture

照相机 [zhàoxiàngjī] N camera

折 [zhé] **I** VB **1** (折断) break **2** (损失) lose **3** (弯曲) wind **4** (回转) turn back **5** (使信服) convince **6** (折合) convert ... into **7** (折叠) fold **II** N

1 (折子) notebook ▶ 存折 [cúnzhé] bank book **2** (折扣) discount
→ *see also*/另见 shé

折叠 [zhédié] VB fold

折扣 [zhékòu] N discount

折磨 [zhémó] VB torment

哲 [zhé] **I** ADJ wise **II** N sage

哲学 [zhéxué] N philosophy

这 [zhè] PRON (指人或事物) this

这边 [zhèbian] ADV here

这个 [zhège] PRON this ▷ 这个可比那个好多了。[Zhège kě bǐ nàgè hǎo duō le.] This one is much better than that one.

这么 [zhème] PRON **1** (指程度) so ▷ 今天这么热。[Jīntiān zhème rè.] It's so hot today. **2** (指方式) such ▷ 我看就应该这么做。[Wǒ kàn jiù yīnggāi zhème zuò.] I think it should be done this way.

这儿 [zhèr] ADV here

这些 [zhèxiē] PRON these (PL)

这样 [zhèyàng] PRON **1** (指程度) so ▷ 乡村的风景这样美。[Xiāngcūn de fēngjǐng zhèyàng měi.] The scenery in the countryside is so beautiful. **2** (指状态) such ▷ 再这样下去可不行。[Zài zhèyàng xiàqù kě bùxíng.] It really won't do to carry on like this.

针 [zhēn] N **1** (工具) needle **2** (针状物) ▶ 表针 [biǎozhēn] hand (*on watch*) ▶ 别针 [biézhēn] safety pin **3** (针剂) injection **4** (缝合) stitch

针对 [zhēnduì] VB **1** (对准) be aimed at **2** (按照) have ... in mind

真 [zhēn] **I** ADJ true ▶ 真话 [zhēnhuà] truth ▶ 真品 [zhēnpǐn] genuine product **II** ADV really ▷ 他真勇敢。[Tā zhēn yǒnggǎn.] He is really brave.

真理 [zhēnlǐ] N truth

真实 [zhēnshí] ADJ true

真正 [zhēnzhèng] ADJ true

枕 [zhěn] **I** N pillow **II** VB rest one's head on

枕头 [zhěntou] N pillow

阵 [zhèn] N **1** (军) (阵形) battle formation **2** (军) (阵地) position **3** (时间) a while

振 [zhèn] VB **1** (振动) vibrate **2** (振作) boost

振动 [zhèndòng] VB vibrate

镇 [zhèn] **I** N **1** (城镇) town **2** (重地) garrison **II** VB **1** (抑制) suppress **2** (守卫) guard **3** (安定) calm **4** (冷却) cool **III** ADJ calm ▶ 镇静 [zhènjìng] calm

镇定 [zhèndìng] ADJ calm

正 [zhēng] *see below*/见下文
→ *see also*/另见 zhèng

正月 [zhēngyuè] N *first month of the lunar year*

争 [zhēng] VB **1** (争夺) contend **2** (争论) argue

争论 [zhēnglùn] VB argue

争取 [zhēngqǔ] VB strive for

征 [zhēng] **I** VB **1** (征讨) mount a military expedition **2** (召集) draft ▶ 征兵 [zhēngbīng] conscript **3** (征收) levy ▶ 征税 [zhēngshuì] levy taxes **4** (征求) solicit ▶ 征订 [zhēngdìng] solicit subscriptions **II** N **1** (征程) journey ▶ 长征 [chángzhēng] the Long March **2** (迹象) sign ▶ 特征 [tèzhēng] feature

征服 [zhēngfú] VB conquer

征求 [zhēngqiú] VB solicit

征兆 [zhēngzhào] N sign

睁 [zhēng] VB open

蒸 [zhēng] VB **1** (指烹饪方法) steam **2** (蒸发) evaporate

蒸气 [zhēngqì] N vapor

蒸汽 [zhēngqì] N steam

整 [zhěng] **I** ADJ **1** (完整) whole **2** (规整) tidy **II** VB **1** (整理) sort ... out **2** (修理) repair **3** (刁难) punish

整个 [zhěnggè] ADJ whole

整理 [zhěnglǐ] VB sort ... out

整齐 [zhěngqí] ADJ **1** (有序的) orderly **2** (均匀的) even

正 [zhèng] **I** ADJ **1** (不偏不斜) straight ▷ 正前方 [zhèng qiánfāng] directly ahead ▷ 这照片挂得不正。 [Zhè zhàopiàn guà de bù zhèng.] This photograph is not hung straight. **2** (居中的) main **3** (正面) right **4** (正直) upright ▶ 公正 [gōngzhèng] just **5** (正当) right ▶ 正轨 [zhèngguǐ] the right track **6** (纯正) pure ▷ 这道菜的味儿不正。 [Zhè dào cài de wèir bù zhèng.] This dish does not taste authentic. **7** (规范的) regular **8** (主要的) principal ▶ 正餐 [zhèngcān] main meal **9** (指图形) regular **10** (物) positive **11** (数) (大于零的) positive ▶ 正数 [zhèngshù] positive number **II** VB **1** (使不歪) straighten **2** (改正) put ... right **III** ADV **1** (恰好) just **2** (正在) right now ▷ 天正刮着风。 [Tiān zhèng guā zhe fēng.] It's windy right now.

→ *see also*/另见 zhēng

正常 [zhèngcháng] ADJ normal

正当 [zhèngdāng] ADJ legitimate

正确 [zhèngquè] ADJ correct

正式 [zhèngshì] ADJ official

正在 [zhèngzài] ADV right now

证 [zhèng] **I** VB prove **II** N **1** (证据) evidence ▶ 物证 [wùzhèng] material evidence **2** (证件) ▶ 身份证 [shēnfènzhèng] identity card

证明 [zhèngmíng] **I** VB prove **II** N certificate

政 [zhèng] N **1** (政治) politics (SG) **2** (事务) affairs (PL)

政策 [zhèngcè] N policy

政党 [zhèngdǎng] N political party

政府 [zhèngfǔ] N government

政权 [zhèngquán] N political power

政治 [zhèngzhì] N politics (SG)

挣 [zhèng] VB **1** (赚得) earn ▶ 挣钱 [zhèngqián] earn money **2** (摆脱) break free

---

之 [zhī] AUX WORD (的) ▷ 父母之爱 [fùmǔ zhī ài] parental love

之后 [zhīhòu] PREP after

之间 [zhījiān] PREP **1** (指两者) between **2** (指三者或三者以上) among

之前 [zhīqián] PREP before

之上 [zhīshàng] PREP above

之下 [zhīxià] PREP below

之一 [zhīyī] PRON one of

之中 [zhīzhōng] PREP amid

支 [zhī] **I** VB **1** (支撑) prop ... up **2** (伸出) raise **3** (支持) bear **4** (调度) send **5** (付出) pay ... out **6** (领取) get **II** MEAS **1** (指乐曲) ▷ 一支钢琴曲 [yī zhī gāngqín qǔ] a piano tune **2** (指细长物) ▷ 一支钢笔 [yī zhī gāngbǐ] a pen **3** (指队伍) ▷ 一支部队 [yī zhī bùduì] an army unit

> measure word, used for songs, tunes, troops, and stick-like objects

支持 [zhīchí] VB **1** (鼓励) support **2** (支撑) hold out

支出 [zhīchū] **I** VB spend **II** N expenditure

支付 [zhīfù] VB pay

支票 [zhīpiào] N check ▷ 把支票兑付成现金 [bǎ zhīpiào duìhuàn chéng xiànjīn] cash a check

支援 [zhīyuán] VB help

只 [zhī] MEAS ▷ 一只拖鞋 [yī zhī tuōxié] a slipper ▷ 两只小船 [liǎng zhī xiǎochuán] two boats ▷ 只小鸟 [sān zhī xiǎo niǎo] three birds

→ *see also*/另见 zhǐ

> measure word, used for one of a pair such as gloves, eyes, feet; also used for animals, insects, birds, and boats

---

芝 [zhī] *see below*/见下文

芝麻 [zhīma] N sesame

枝 [zhī] N branch

知 [zhī] **I** VB **1** (知道) know **2** (使知道) inform **II** N knowledge

知道 [zhīdao] VB know ▷ 这事我可不知道。 [Zhè shì wǒ kě bù zhīdao.] I really know nothing about this.

知识 [zhīshi] N knowledge

织 [zhī] VB knit

蜘 [zhī] *see below*/见下文

蜘蛛 [zhīzhū] N spider

执 [zhí] **I** VB **1** (拿着) hold **2** (执掌) take charge of **3** (坚持) stick to **4** (执行) carry out **II** N written acknowledgment ▶ 回执 [huízhí] receipt

执行 [zhíxíng] VB carry out

执照 [zhízhào] N license

直 [zhí] **I** ADJ **1** (不弯曲) straight **2** (竖的) vertical **3** (公正) upstanding **4** (直爽) candid **II** VB straighten **III** ADV **1** (直接) straight **2** (不断地) continuously **3** (简直) simply

直到 [zhídào] PREP until

直接 [zhíjiē] ADJ direct

直升机 [zhíshēngjī] N helicopter

侄 [zhí] N nephew

侄女 [zhínǚ] N niece

侄子 [zhízi] N nephew

值 [zhí] **I** N **1** (价值) value **2** (数) value **II** VB **1** (值得) be worth **2** (碰上) just happen to be **3** (轮到) be on duty

值班 [zhíbān] VB be on duty

值得 [zhíde] VB be worth ▷ 这书值得买。 [Zhè shū zhíde mǎi.] This book is worth buying.

职 [zhí] N **1** (职位) post **2** (职责) duty

职工 [zhígōng] N **1** (员工) staff **2** (工人) blue-collar worker

职业 [zhíyè] N occupation

职员 [zhíyuán] N member of staff

植 [zhí] VB **1** (栽种) plant **2** (树立) establish

植物 [zhíwù] N plant ▷ 草本植物 [cǎoběn zhíwù] herbs

止 [zhǐ] **I** VB **1** (停止) stop **2** (截止) end **II** ADV only

只 [zhǐ] ADV only ▷ 我只在周末有时间。 [Wǒ zhǐ zài zhōumò yǒu shíjiān.] I only have time on the weekend.
→ *see also*/另见 zhī

只好 [zhǐhǎo] ADV have to

只是 [zhǐshì] **I** ADV merely **II** CONJ but

只要 [zhǐyào] CONJ so long as

只有 [zhǐyǒu] ADV only

纸 [zhǐ] N paper

纸币 [zhǐbì] N bill

指 [zhǐ] **I** N finger ▶ 中指 [zhōngzhǐ] middle finger ▶ 无名指 [wúmíngzhǐ] ring finger **II** VB **1** (对着) point to **2** (点明) point ... out **3** (针对) refer to **4** (依靠) rely on

指出 [zhǐchū] VB point ... out

指导 [zhǐdǎo] VB instruct

指挥 [zhǐhuī] **I** VB command **II** N **1** (指挥官) commander **2** (乐队指挥) conductor

指南针 [zhǐnánzhēn] N compass

指示 [zhǐshì] VB instruct

指责 [zhǐzé] VB criticize

至 [zhì] **I** VB arrive **II** PREP to ▷ 从东至西 [cóng dōng zhì xī] from east to west **III** ADV **1** (至于) ▶ 至于 [zhìyú] as to **2** (最) extremely ▶ 至少 [zhìshǎo] at least

至今 [zhìjīn] ADV so far

至少 [zhìshǎo] ADV at least

至于 [zhìyú] PREP as to

制 [zhì] **I** VB **1** (制造) make **2** (拟订) work ... out **3** (约束) restrict **II** N system

制订 [zhìdìng] VB work ... out

制定 [zhìdìng] VB draw ... up

制度 [zhìdù] N system

制造 [zhìzào] VB **1** (物品) manufacture **2** (气氛, 局势) create

制作 [zhìzuò] VB make ▷ 制作网页 [zhìzuò wǎngyè] create a web page ▶ 制作商 [zhìzuòshāng] manufacturer

---

质 [zhì] **I** N **1** (性质) nature ▶ 本质 [běnzhì] nature **2** (质量) quality **3** (物质) matter **4** (抵押品) pledge ▶ 人质 [rénzhì] hostage **II** ADJ simple **III** VB question ▶ 质疑 [zhìyí] cast doubt on

质量 [zhìliàng] N **1** (物) mass **2** (优劣) quality

治 [zhì] VB **1** (治理) control **2** (医治) cure **3** (消灭) exterminate **4** (惩办) punish **5** (研究) research

治安 [zhì'ān] N security ▶ 社会治安 [shèhuì zhì'ān] public order

治疗 [zhìliáo] VB cure

秩 [zhì] N order

秩序 [zhìxù] N sequence

智 [zhì] **I** ADJ wise **II** N wisdom

智慧 [zhìhuì] N intelligence

智力 [zhìlì] N intelligence

智商 [zhìshāng] N IQ

中 [zhōng] **I** N **1** (中心) center ▶ 中央 [zhōngyāng] central **2** (中国) China ▶ 中餐 [zhōngcān] Chinese food **3** **4** (两端之间的) the middle ▶ 中层 [zhōngcéng] mid-level **5** (不偏不倚) impartial ▶ 适中 [shìzhōng] moderate **6** (在过程里的) course **II** VB be suitable for

中国 [Zhōngguó] N China

中国人 [Zhōngguórén] N Chinese person

中华人民共和国 [Zhōnghuá Rénmín Gònghéguó] N People's Republic of China

---

中华人民共和国 [Zhōnghuá Rénmín Gònghéguó]

The People's Republic of China was declared in Tiananmen Square on October 1st 1949 by Chairman Mao Zedong.

中华 [Zhōnghuá] N China

中间 [zhōngjiān] N **1** (中心) middle **2** (之间) ▷ 我站在他俩中间。 [Wǒ zhàn zài tā liǎ zhōngjiān.] I was standing between the two of them.

中介 [zhōngjiè] N agency ▷ 房产中介 [fángchǎn zhōngjiè] estate agent

中年 [zhōngnián] N middle age

中秋节 [Zhōngqiū Jié] N Mid-Autumn Festival

中秋节 [Zhōngqiū Jié]

The Mid-Autumn Festival is celebrated on the 15th day of the 8th month of the Chinese lunar calendar. Traditionally families gather to observe the moon and eat 月饼 yuèbǐng, mooncakes. The roundness of both the full moon and the cakes symbolizes the unity of the family.

中文 [Zhōngwén] N Chinese

中午 [zhōngwǔ] N noon

中心 [zhōngxīn] N center

中学 [zhōngxué] N senior school

中旬 [zhōngxún] N *the middle ten days of a month*

中央 [zhōngyāng] N **1** (中心地) center **2** (最高机构) central government

中药 [zhōngyào] N Chinese medicine

中医 [zhōngyī] N **1** (医学) traditional Chinese medicine **2** (医生) doctor of traditional Chinese medicine

---

终 [zhōng] **I** VB die **II** ADV in the end **III** ADJ all ▶ 终身 [zhōngshēn] all one's life

终点 [zhōngdiǎn] N **1** (尽头) terminus **2** (体育) finish

终于 [zhōngyú] ADV finally

终止 [zhōngzhǐ] VB stop

钟 [zhōng] N **1** (响器) bell **2** (记时器) clock **3** (指时间) ▷ 5点钟 [wǔ diǎnzhōng] five o'clock

钟表 [zhōngbiǎo] N clocks and watches

钟头 [zhōngtóu] N hour

肿 [zhǒng] VB swell

种 [zhǒng] **I** N **1** (物种) species (SG) **2** (人种) race **3** (种子) seed **4** (胆量) courage **II** MEAS kind, type ▷ 各种商品 [gè zhǒng shāngpǐn] all kinds of commodities ▷ 3种选择 [sān zhǒng xuǎnzé] three choices

→ *see also*/另见 zhòng

种子 [zhǒngzi] N seed

种族 [zhǒngzú] N race

种 [zhòng] VB sow ▶ 种田 [zhòngtián] farm ▶ 种痘 [zhòngdòu] vaccinate

→ *see also*/另见 zhǒng

重 [zhòng] **I** N weight **II** ADJ **1** (重量大) heavy **2** (程度深) strong **3** (重要) important ▶ 重任 [zhòngrèn] important task **4** (不轻率) serious ▶ 稳重 [wěnzhòng] staid **III** VB stress ▶ 注重 [zhùzhòng] pay attention to

→ *see also*/另见 chóng

重大 [zhòngdà] ADJ major

重点 [zhòngdiǎn] N key point

重量 [zhòngliàng] N weight

重视 [zhòngshì] VB attach importance to

重要 [zhòngyào] ADJ important

周 [zhōu] **I** N **1** (圈子) circle **2** (星期) week **II** VB **1** (环绕) circle **2** (接济) give ... financial help **III** ADJ **1** (普遍) widespread **2** (完备) thorough

周到 [zhōudào] ADJ thorough

周末 [zhōumò] N weekend

周围 [zhōuwéi] N the vicinity

猪 [zhū] N pig

猪肉 [zhūròu] N pork

竹 [zhú] N bamboo

竹子 [zhúzi] N bamboo

逐 [zhú] **I** VB **1** (追赶) chase **2** (驱逐) drive ... away **II** ADV one after another

逐步 [zhúbù] ADV step by step

逐渐 [zhújiàn] ADV gradually

主 [zhǔ] **I** N **1** (接待者) host ▶ 东道主 [dōngdàozhǔ] host **2** (所有者) owner ▶ 房主 [fángzhǔ] home-owner **3** (当事人) person concerned **4** (主见) idea **5** (上帝) God **II** ADJ main **III** VB **1** (主持) take charge ▶ 主办 [zhǔbàn] take charge of **2** (主张) be in favor of **3** (从自身出发) look at ... subjectively ▶ 主观 [zhǔguān] subjective

主动 [zhǔdòng] ADJ voluntary

主观 [zhǔguān] ADJ subjective

主人 [zhǔren] N **1** (接待者) host **2** (雇佣者) master ▶ 女主人 [nǚzhǔrén] mistress **3** (所有者) owner

主任 [zhǔrèn] N director

主席 [zhǔxí] N chairman, chairwoman

主要 [zhǔyào] ADJ major

主义 [zhǔyì] N doctrine ▶ 社会主义 [shèhuì zhǔyì] socialism ▶ 浪漫主义 [làngmàn zhǔyì] romanticism

主意 [zhǔyi] N **1** (办法) idea **2** (主见) opinion

主张 [zhǔzhāng] **I** VB advocate **II** N standpoint

煮 [zhǔ] VB boil

助 [zhù] VB help

助手 [zhùshǒu] N assistant

住 [zhù] VB **1** (居住) live **2** (停住) stop **3** (用作动词补语)

住宿 [zhùsù] VB stay

住院 [zhùyuàn] VB be hospitalized

住宅 [zhùzhái] N house

住址 [zhùzhǐ] N address

注 [zhù] **I** VB **1** (灌入) pour ▶ 注射 [zhùshè] inject **2** (集中) concentrate **3** (解释) explain **II** N **1** (记载) record

▶ 注册 [zhùcè] enroll **2** (赌注) bet

注意 [zhùyì] VB be careful

祝 [zhù] VB wish

祝贺 [zhùhè] VB congratulate

著 [zhù] **I** ADJ marked **II** VB **1** (显出) show **2** (写作) write **III** N work

著名 [zhùmíng] ADJ famous

著作 [zhùzuò] N writings (PL)

抓 [zhuā] VB **1** (拿住) grab **2** (划过) scratch **3** (捉拿) catch **4** (着重) take control of **5** (吸引) attract **6** (把握住) seize

抓紧 [zhuājǐn] VB make the most of

专 [zhuān] VB **1** (集中) concentrate **2** (独占) dominate ▶ 专卖 [zhuānmài] monopoly

专家 [zhuānjiā] N expert

专门 [zhuānmén] **I** ADJ specialized **II** ADV especially

专心 [zhuānxīn] ADJ single-minded

专业 [zhuānyè] N special field of study

砖 [zhuān] N brick

转 [zhuǎn] VB **1** (改换) turn ▶ 转弯 [zhuǎnwān] turn a corner ▶ 转学 [zhuǎnxué] change schools **2** (传送) pass ... on ▶ 转送 [zhuǎnsòng] deliver
→ *see also*/另见 zhuàn

转变 [zhuǎnbiàn] VB transform

转告 [zhuǎngào] VB pass on

转 [zhuàn] VB turn
→ *see also*/另见 zhuǎn

赚 [zhuàn] VB **1** (获得利润) make a profit **2** (挣钱) earn

庄 [zhuāng] N **1** (指村庄) village **2** (指土地) manor ▶ 庄园 [zhuāngyuán] manor **3** (指商店) ▶ 茶庄 [cházhuāng] teahouse ▶ 饭庄 [fànzhuāng] restaurant

庄稼 [zhuāngjia] N crops (PL)

庄严 [zhuāngyán] ADJ solemn

装 [zhuāng] **I** VB **1** (修饰) dress up ▶ 装饰 [zhuāngshì] decorate **2** (假装) pretend **3** (装载) load **4** (装配) install **II** N (服装) clothing ▶ 套装 [tàozhuāng] matching outfit

状 [zhuàng] N **1** (形状) shape **2** (情况) state ▶ 症状 [zhèngzhuàng] symptom **3** (诉状) complaint ▶ 告状 [gàozhuàng] bring a case **4** (证书) certificate ▶ 奖状 [jiǎngzhuàng] certificate

状况 [zhuàngkuàng] N condition

状态 [zhuàngtài] N condition

撞 [zhuàng] VB **1** (碰撞) collide **2** (碰见) bump into **3** (试探) try **4** (闯) dash

撞车 [zhuàngchē] VB **1** (车辆相撞) collide **2** (发生分歧) clash

追 [zhuī] VB **1** (追赶) chase **2** (追究) investigate **3** (追求) seek **4** (回溯) reminisce

追捕 [zhuībǔ] VB pursue and capture

追求 [zhuīqiú] VB **1** (争取) seek **2** (求爱) chase after

准 [zhǔn] **I** VB **1** (准许) allow ▶ 批准 [pīzhǔn] ratify **2** (依据) be in accord with **II** N standard **III** ADJ **1** (准确) accurate ▶ 准时 [zhǔnshí] punctual **2** (类似) quasi

准备 [zhǔnbèi] VB **1** (筹划) prepare **2** (打算) plan

准确 [zhǔnquè] ADJ accurate

准时 [zhǔnshí] ADJ punctual

捉 [zhuō] VB **1** (握住) clutch **2** (捕捉) catch

桌 [zhuō] **I** N table ▶ 书桌 [shūzhuō] desk **II** MEAS table ▷ 一桌菜 [yī zhuō cài] a table covered with dishes

桌子 [zhuōzi] N table

咨 [zī] VB consult

咨询 [zīxún] VB seek advice from

姿 [zī] N **1** (容貌) looks (PL) **2** (姿势) posture

姿势 [zīshì] N posture

资 [zī] I N 1 (钱财) money ▶ 外资 [wàizī] foreign capital ▶ 邮资 [yóuzī] postage 2 (资质) ability ▶ 天资 [tiānzī] natural ability 3 (资格) qualifications (PL) ▶ 资历 [zīlì] record of service II VB 1 (资助) aid … financially 2 (提供) provide

资本 [zīběn] N (优势)

资格 [zīgé] N 1 (条件) qualifications (PL) 2 (身份) seniority

资金 [zījīn] N funds (PL)

资料 [zīliào] N 1 (必需品) means (PL) 2 (材料) material

资源 [zīyuán] N resources (PL)

子 [zǐ] I N 1 (儿子) son ▶ 母子 [mǔzǐ] mother and son 2 (人) person ▶ 男子 [nánzǐ] man 3 (种子) seed ▶ 瓜子 [guāzǐ] melon seed 4 (卵) egg ▶ 鱼子 [yúzǐ] fish roe 5 (粒状物) ▶ 棋子 [qízǐ] chess piece 6 (铜子) coin II ADJ 1 (幼小) young 2 (附属) affiliated

子女 [zǐnǚ] N children

仔 [zǐ] ADJ young

仔细 [zǐxì] ADJ 1 (细心) thorough 2 (小心) careful

紫 [zǐ] ADJ purple

自 [zì] I PRON oneself II ADV certainly III PREP from

自闭症 [zìbìzhèng] N autism

自从 [zìcóng] PREP since

自动 [zìdòng] ADJ 1 (主动的) voluntary 2 (机械的) automatic

自动取款机 [zìdòng qǔkuǎnjī] N ATM

自费 [zìfèi] ADJ self-funded

自己 [zìjǐ] I PRON oneself II ADJ our

自觉 [zìjué] I VB be aware of II ADJ conscientious

自来水 [zìláishuǐ] N tap water

自然 [zìrán] I N nature II ADJ natural III ADV naturally

自杀 [zìshā] VB commit suicide

自私 [zìsī] ADJ selfish

自我 [zìwǒ] PRON self

自信 [zìxìn] ADJ self-confident

自行车 [zìxíngchē] N bicycle

自学 [zìxué] VB teach oneself

自由 [zìyóu] I N freedom II ADJ free

自愿 [zìyuàn] VB volunteer

自助餐 [zìzhùcān] N self-service buffet

字 [zì] N 1 (文字) character 2 (字音) pronunciation 3 (书法作品) calligraphy ▶ 字画 [zìhuà] painting and calligraphy 4 (字体) script 5 (字据) written pledge

字典 [zìdiǎn] N dictionary

字母 [zìmǔ] N letter

宗 [zōng] N 1 (祖宗) ancestor 2 (家族) clan 3 (宗派) school ▶ 正宗 [zhèngzōng] orthodox school 4 (宗旨) purpose

宗教 [zōngjiào] N religion

综 [zōng] VB summarize ▶ 综述 [zōngshù] sum … up

综合 [zōnghé] I VB synthesize II ADJ comprehensive

总 [zǒng] I VB gather ▶ 总括 [zǒngkuò] sum … up II ADJ 1 (全部的) total 2 (为首的) chief ▶ 总部 [zǒngbù] headquarters (PL) III ADV 1 (一直) always 2 (毕竟) after all

总理 [zǒnglǐ] N premier

总是 [zǒngshì] ADV always

总算 [zǒngsuàn] ADV 1 (最终) finally 2 (大体上) all things considered

总统 [zǒngtǒng] N president

粽 [zòng] N *see below*/见下文

粽子 [zòngzi] N *glutinous rice dumplings*

粽子 [zòngzi]

The traditional festival food for the Dragon Boat Festival is large pyramid-shaped glutinous rice dumplings wrapped in reed or bamboo leaves, often with sweet or meat fillings.

走 [zǒu] VB **1** (行走) walk ▶ 走路 [zǒulù] walk ▷ 出去走走 [chūqu zǒuzǒu] go out for a walk **2** (跑动) run **3** (运行) move **4** (离开) leave ▷ 我先走。 [Wǒ xiān zǒu.] I'll be off. **5** (来往) visit **6** (通过) go through **7** (漏出) leak **8** (改变) depart from **9** (去世) die

走道 [zǒudào] N path

走动 [zǒudòng] VB **1** (行走) walk about **2** (来往) visit each other

走后门 [zǒu hòumén] use one's connections

走廊 [zǒuláng] N corridor

租 [zū] **I** VB **1** (租用) (房屋) rent **2** (租用) (汽车, 自行车, 录像带) hire **3** (出租) rent out **II** N rent ▶ 房租 [fángzū] rent

足 [zú] **I** N foot ▶ 足迹 [zújì] footprint **II** ADJ ample ▶ 充足 [chōngzú] adequate **III** ADV **1** (达到某种程度) as much as **2** (足以) enough

足够 [zúgòu] VB be enough

足球 [zúqiú] N soccer

阻 [zǔ] VB block

阻止 [zǔzhǐ] VB stop

组 [zǔ] **I** VB form **II** N group

组成 [zǔchéng] VB form

组织 [zǔzhī] **I** VB organize **II** N **1** (集体) organization **2** (指器官) tissue **3** (指纱线) weave

祖 [zǔ] N **1** (祖辈) grandparent **2** (祖宗) ancestor **3** (首创者) founder

祖父 [zǔfù] N grandfather

祖国 [zǔguó] N motherland

祖母 [zǔmǔ] N grandmother

祖先 [zǔxiān] N ancestors (PL)

钻 [zuān] VB **1** (打洞) drill **2** (穿过) go through **3** (钻研) bury one's head in

→ *see also*/另见 zuàn

钻研 [zuānyán] VB study ... intensively

钻 [zuàn] N **1** (工具) drill **2** (钻石) diamond

→ *see also*/另见 zuān

钻石 [zuànshí] N **1** (金刚石) diamond **2** (宝石) jewel

嘴 [zuǐ] N **1** (口) mouth **2** (嘴状物) ▷ 茶壶嘴 [cháhú zuǐ] spout of a teapot **3** (话) words (PL) ▶ 插嘴 [chāzuǐ] interrupt

最 [zuì] ADV most ▷ 最难忘的海外之旅 [zuì nánwàng de hǎiwài zhī lǚ] the most unforgettable trip abroad ▷ 这家饭店服务最好。 [Zhè jiā fàndiàn fúwù zuì hǎo.] The service at this restaurant is the best.

最初 [zuìchū] **I** ADJ initial **II** ADV at first

最好 [zuìhǎo] **I** ADJ best **II** ADV had better

最后 [zuìhòu] **I** ADJ final **II** ADV at last

最近 [zuìjìn] ADJ recent

罪 [zuì] **I** N **1** (恶行) crime ▶ 犯罪 [fànzuì] commit a crime **2** (过失) blame **3** (苦难) hardship **4** (刑罚) punishment ▶ 死罪 [sǐzuì] death sentence **II** VB blame

罪犯 [zuìfàn] N criminal

醉 [zuì] **I** ADJ **1** (饮酒过量的) drunk ▶ 醉鬼 [zuìguǐ] drunk **2** (用酒泡制的) steeped in wine **II** VB drink too much

尊 [zūn] **I** ADJ senior **II** VB respect

尊敬 [zūnjìng] VB respect

尊重 [zūnzhòng] **I** VB respect **II** ADJ serious ▷ 放尊重些! [Fàng zūnzhòng xiē!] Behave yourself!

遵 [zūn] VB follow

遵守 [zūnshǒu] VB observe

昨 [zuó] N **1** (昨天) yesterday ▶ 昨日 [zuórì] yesterday **2** (过去) the past

昨天 [zuótiān] N yesterday

左 [zuǒ] **I** N left ▶ 左边 [zuǒbian] the left **II** ADJ **1** (相反的) conflicting

2 (进步的) leftist ▶ 左派 [zuǒpài] left-wing

左边 [zuǒbian] N the left side

左右 [zuǒyòu] I N 1 (左和右) left and right 2 (跟随者) attendants (PL) 3 (上下) ▷ 他身高1点75米左右。[Tā shēngāo yī diǎn qī wǔ mǐ zuǒyòu.] He is about 1.75 meters tall. II VB control

作 [zuò] I VB 1 (起) rise 2 (写) write ▶ 作家 [zuòjiā] writer ▶ 作曲 [zuòqǔ] compose music 3 (装) pretend 4 (犯) do 5 (当) take ... as ▶ 作废 [zuòfèi] become invalid 6 (发作) feel II N work ▶ 杰作 [jiézuò] masterpiece

作罢 [zuòbà] VB drop

作家 [zuòjiā] N writer

作品 [zuòpǐn] N work

作为 [zuòwéi] I N 1 (行为) action 2 (成绩) accomplishment 3 (干头儿) scope II VB (当作) regard ... as

作文 [zuòwén] VB write an essay

作业 [zuòyè] I N work II VB do work

作用 [zuòyòng] I VB affect II N 1 (影响) effect 2 (活动) action

作者 [zuòzhě] N author

坐 [zuò] VB 1 (坐下) sit ▷ 坐在窗口 [zuò zài chuāngkǒu] sit by the window 2 (乘坐) travel by ▷ 坐飞机 [zuò fēijī] travel by plane

座 [zuò] I N 1 (坐位) seat ▶ 座号 [zuòhào] seat number 2 (垫子) stand 3 (星座) constellation ▷ 双子座 [Shuāngzǐ Zuò] Gemini II MEAS ▷ 一座山 [yī zuò shān] a mountain ▷ 三座桥 [sān zuò qiáo] three bridges ▷ 五座办公楼 [wǔ zuò bàngōnglóu] five office buildings

measure word, used for mountains, buildings, bridges, etc.

座谈 [zuòtán] VB discuss

座位 [zuòwèi] N seat

做 [zuò] VB 1 (制造) make 2 (写作) write 3 (从事) do ▷ 做生意 [zuò shēngyi] do business 4 (举行) hold ▷ 做寿 [zuòshòu] hold a birthday party 5 (充当) be ▷ 做大会主席 [zuò dàhuì zhǔxí] chair a meeting 6 (用作) be used as 7 (结成) become ▷ 做朋友 [zuò péngyou] be friends

做法 [zuòfǎ] N method

做客 [zuòkè] VB be a guest

做梦 [zuòmèng] VB dream

English–Chinese Dictionary

A

KEYWORD

a [ə, STRONG eɪ] (*before vowel or silent h:* **an**) INDEF ART **1** (*article*) 一个 yīgè ▶ **a man** 一个男人 yīgè nánrén ▶ **a girl** 一个女孩 yīgè nǚhái ▶ **an elephant** 一只大象 yīzhī dàxiàng ▶ **she's a doctor** 她是一名医生 tā shì yīmíng yīshēng ▶ **they haven't got a television** 他们没有电视 tāmen méiyǒu diànshì
2 (*one*) 一 yī ▶ **a year ago** 一年前 yīnián qián
3 (*expressing ratios, prices etc*) ▶ **five hours a day/week** 一天/一周5个小时 yītiān/yīzhōu wǔgè xiǎoshí ▶ **100 km an hour** 每小时100公里 měi xiǎoshí yībǎi gōnglǐ

abbey [æbi] N [C] 大修道院 dà xiūdàoyuàn [座 zuò]
abbreviation [əbriviейʃən] N [C] 缩写 suōxiě [个 gè]
ability [əbɪlɪti] N [S] ▶ **ability (to do sth)** (做某事的)能力 (zuò mǒushì de) nénglì
able [eɪbəl] ADJ ▶ **to be able to do sth** (*have skill, ability*) 能够做某事 nénggòu zuò mǒushì; (*have opportunity*) 可以做某事 kěyǐ zuò mǒushì
abolish [əbɒlɪʃ] VT (+ *system, practice*) 废止 fèizhǐ
abortion [əbɔrʃən] (*Med*) N [C/U] 流产 liúchǎn [次 cì] ▶ **to have an abortion** 流产 liúchǎn

KEYWORD

about [əbaʊt] **I** PREP (*relating to*) 关于 guānyú ▶ **a book about London** 关于伦敦的一本书 guānyú Lúndūn de yīběn shū ▶ **what's it about?** 这是关于什么的？ zhèshì guānyú shénme de? ▶ **we talked about it** 我们谈到了这事 wǒmen tándào le zhèshì ▶ **to be sorry/pleased/angry about sth** 对某事感到抱歉/开心/生气 duì mǒushì gǎndào bàoqiàn/kāixīn/shēngqì ▶ **what** *or* **how about eating out?** 出去吃怎么样？ chūqù chī zěnmeyàng?
II ADV **1** (*approximately*) 大约 dàyuē ▶ **about a hundred/thousand people** 大约100/1000人 dàyuē yībǎi/yīqiān rén
2 (*place*) 在 zài ▶ **to leave things lying about** 把东西到处乱放 bǎ dōngxi dàochù luànfàng ▶ **to be about to do sth** 正要做某事 zhèng yào zuò mǒushì

above [əbʌv] **I** PREP (*higher than*) 在…上面 zài...shàngmian **II** ADV (*in position*) 在上面 zài shàngmian **III** ADJ ▶ **the above address** 上述地址 shàngshù dìzhǐ ▶ **above all** 首先 shǒuxiān
abroad [əbrɔd] ADV **1** (*be*) 在国外 zài guówài **2** (*go*) 到国外 dào guówài
absence [æbsəns] N **1** [C/U] (*of person*) 缺席 quēxí [次 cì] **2** [S] (*of thing*) 缺乏 quēfá
absent [æbsənt] ADJ 缺席的 quēxí de ▶ **to be absent** 不在 bùzài
absolutely [æbsəlutli] ADV (*utterly*) 绝对地 juéduì de
absorbent cotton [əbzɔrbənt kɒtən] N [U] 脱脂棉 tuōzhīmián
abuse [*n* əbyus, *vb* əbyuz] **I** N **1** [U] (*insults*) 辱骂 rǔmà **2** [U] (*ill-treatment: physical*) 虐待 nüèdài; (*sexual*) 猥亵 wěixiè **3** [C/U] (*misuse: of power, alcohol, drug*) 滥用 lànyòng [种 zhǒng] **II** VT **1** (*ill-treat: physically*) 虐待 nüèdài **2** (*sexually*) (+ *child*) 摧残 cuīcán
academic [ækədɛmɪk] **I** ADJ 学术的 xuéshù de **II** N 大学教师 dàxué jiàoshī
academy [əkædəmi] N [C] **1** 学会

xuéhuì [个 gè] 2 (*school, college*) 学院 xuéyuàn [个 gè]
accelerate [æksɛləreɪt] VI (*Aut*) 加速 jiāsù
accelerator [æksɛləreɪtər] (*Aut*) N [C] 加速器 jiāsùqì [个 gè]
accent [æksɛnt] N [C] 口音 kǒuyīn [种 zhǒng] ▶ **to speak with an (Irish/French) accent** 讲话带(爱尔兰/法国)口音 jiǎnghuà dài (Ài'ěrlán/Fǎguó) kǒuyīn
accept [æksɛpt] VT 接受 jiēshòu
access [æksɛs] I N [U] ▶ **access (to sth)** (*to building, room*) 进入(某物) jìnrù (mǒuwù); (*to information, papers*) (某物的)使用权 (mǒuwù de) shǐyòngquán II VT (*Comput*) 存取 cúnqǔ
accident [æksɪdənt] N [C] 1 (*involving vehicle*) 事故 shìgù [个 gè] 2 (*mishap*) 意外 yìwài [个 gè] ▶ **to have an accident** 出事故 chū shìgù ▶ **by accident** (*unintentionally*) 无意中 wúyì zhōng; (*by chance*) 偶然 ǒurán
accidental [æksɪdɛntᵊl] ADJ 意外的 yìwài de
accommodations [əkɒmədeɪʃᵊnz] N PL 住处 zhùchù
accompany [əkʌmpəni] VT 1 (*frm: escort*) 陪伴 péibàn 2 (*Mus*) 为…伴奏 wèi…bànzòu
according [əkɔrdɪŋ] ▶ **according to** PREP (+ *person*) 据…所说 jù…suǒshuō; (+ *account, information*) 根据 gēnjù
account [əkaʊnt] N [C] 1 (*with bank, at store*) 账户 zhànghù [个 gè] 2 (*report*) 描述 miáoshù [番 fān] ▶ **to take sth into account, take account of sth** 考虑到某事 kǎolǜ dào mǒushì
accountant [əkaʊntənt] N [C] 会计师 kuàijìshī [位 wèi]
accuracy [ækyərəsi] N [U] 1 (*of information, measurements*) 准确 zhǔnquè 2 (*of person, device*) 精确 jīngquè
accurate [ækyərɪt] ADJ (+ *information, measurement, instrument*) 精确的 jīngquè de; (+ *description, account, person, aim*) 准确的 zhǔnquè de
accuse [əkyuz] VT 1 ▶ **to accuse sb of (doing) sth** 指责某人(做)某事 zhǐzé mǒurén (zuò) mǒushì 2 ▶ **to be accused of sth** (*of crime*) 被指控某事 bèi zhǐkòng mǒushì
ache [eɪk] I VI 痛 tòng II N [C] 疼痛 téngtòng [种 zhǒng] ▶ **I have (a) stomach ache/toothache** 我胃/牙痛 wǒ wèi/yá tòng
achieve [ətʃiv] VT (+ *victory, success, result*) 取得 qǔdé
achievement [ətʃivmənt] N [C] 成就 chéngjiù [个 gè]
acid [æsɪd] N [C/U] (*Chem*) 酸 suān [种 zhǒng]
across [əkrɔs] I PREP 1 (*moving from one side to the other of*) 穿过 chuānguò 2 (*situated on the other side of*) 在…对面 zài…duìmiàn 3 (*extending from one side to the other of*) 跨越 kuàyuè II ADV 1 (*from one side to the other*) 从一边到另一边 cóng yībiān dào lìngyībiān 2 ▶ **across from** (*opposite*) 在…对面 zài…duìmiàn 3 ▶ **across at/to** (*towards*) 朝向 cháoxiàng 4 (*in width*) 宽 kuān
act [ækt] I VI 1 (*take action*) 行动 xíngdòng 2 (*behave*) 举止 jǔzhǐ ▶ **They were acting suspiciously.** 他们举止可疑。 tāmen jǔzhǐ kěyí. 3 (*in play, film*) 演戏 yǎnxì II N [C] ▶ **acts of sabotage** 破坏行动 pòhuài xíngdòng
action [ækʃᵊn] N 1 [U] (*steps, measures*) 行动 xíngdòng 2 [C] (*deed*) 行为 xíngwéi [种 zhǒng] ▶ **to take action** 采取行动 cǎiqǔ xíngdòng
active [æktɪv] ADJ 1 活跃的 huóyuè de 2 (+ *volcano*) 活的 huó de
activity [æktɪvɪti] I N [C] 活动 huódòng [项 xiàng] II **activities** N PL 活动 huódòng
actor [æktər] N [C] 演员 yǎnyuán [个 gè]
actress [æktrɪs] N [C] 女演员 nǚ

yǎnyuán [个 gè]
actual [æktʃuəl] ADJ 真实的 zhēnshí de
actually [æktʃuəli] ADV **1** 实际地 shíjì de **2** (*in fact*) 事实上 shìshíshang ▶ **actually, we have the same opinion** 实际上我们有同样的观点 shíjì shàng wǒmen yǒu tóngyàng de guāndiǎn
AD [eɪ di] ADV ABBR (= **Anno Domini**) 公元 gōngyuán
ad [æd] (*inf*) N (*advertisement*) 广告 guǎnggào
adapt [ədæpt] **I** VT 使适合 shǐ shìhé **II** VI ▶ **to adapt (to)** 适应 shìyìng
adaptor [ədæptər] (*Elec*) N [C] 转接器 zhuǎnjiēqì [个 gè]
add [æd] VT **1** (*put in, put on*) 加入 jiārù **2** ▶ **to add (together)** (*calculate total of*) 加(起来) jiā (qǐlái)
addict [ædɪkt] N [C] ▶ **drug/heroin addict** 吸毒/海洛因成瘾的人 xīdú/hǎiluòyīn chéngyǐn de rén [个 gè]
addicted [ədɪktɪd] ADJ ▶ **to be addicted to sth** 对某事上瘾 duì mǒushì shàngyǐn
addition [ədɪʃᵊn] N [U] (*Math*) 加法 jiāfǎ ▶ **in addition to** 除…之外 chú...zhīwài
address [ædrɛs] N [C] 地址 dìzhǐ [个 gè]
adjective [ædʒɪktɪv] N [C] 形容词 xíngróngcí [个 gè]
adjust [ədʒʌst] VT (+ *device, position, setting*) 校准 jiàozhǔn
adjustable [ədʒʌstəbᵊl] ADJ 可调节的 kě tiáojié de
admire [ədmaɪər] VT 钦佩 qīnpèi
admit [ædmɪt] VT **1** (*confess*) 承认 chéngrèn **2** (*accept*) (+ *defeat, responsibility*) 接受 jiēshòu ▶ **he admits that...** 他承认… tā chéngrèn... ▶ **to be admitted to the hospital** 住进医院 zhùjìn yīyuàn
adolescent [ædᵊlɛsᵊnt] N [C] 青少年 qīngshàonián [个 gè]
adopt [ədɒpt] VT **1** (+ *plan, approach, attitude*) 采用 cǎiyòng **2** (+ *child*) 收养 shōuyǎng
adopted [ədɒptɪd] ADJ 被收养的 bèi shōuyǎng de
adoption [ədɒpʃᵊn] N [C/U] (*of child*) 收养 shōuyǎng
adult [ədʌlt] **I** N [C] 成年人 chéngniánrén [个 gè] **II** ADJ (*grown-up*) 成年的 chéngnián de
advance [ædvæns] ADJ (+ *notice, warning*) 预先的 yùxiān de ▶ **in advance** (*book, prepare, plan*) 提前 tíqián
advanced [ædvænst] ADJ **1** (*highly developed*) 先进的 xiānjìn de **2** (*Scol*) (+ *student, pupil*) 高年级的 gāoniánjí de; (+ *course, work*) 高等的 gāoděng de
advantage [ædvɑntɪdʒ, -væn-] N [C] **1** (*benefit*) 好处 hǎochù [种 zhǒng] **2** (*favorable factor*) 有利因素 yǒulì yīnsù [个 gè] ▶ **to take advantage of** (+ *person*) 利用 lìyòng; (+ *opportunity*) 利用 lìyòng
adventure [ædvɛntʃər] N [C] 冒险活动 màoxiǎn huódòng [次 cì]
adverb [ædvɜrb] N [C] 副词 fùcí [个 gè]
advertise [ædvərtaɪz] **I** VI 做广告 zuò guǎnggào **II** VT **1** (+ *product, event*) 为…做广告 wèi...zuò guǎnggào **2** (+ *job*) 刊登 kāndēng
advertisement [ædvərtaɪzmənt] (*Comm*) N [C] 广告 guǎnggào [则 zé]
advice [ædvaɪs] N [U] 忠告 zhōnggào ▶ **a piece of advice** 一条建议 yītiáo jiànyì
advise [ædvaɪz] VT ▶ **to advise sb to do sth** 劝某人做某事 quàn mǒurén zuò mǒushì
aerobics [ɛəroʊbɪks] N [U] 有氧健身操 yǒuyǎng jiànshēncāo
affair [əfɛər] **I** N **1** [S] (*matter, business*) 事情 shìqing **2** [C] (*romance*) 风流韵事 fēngliú yùnshì [桩 zhuāng] **II affairs** N PL **1** (*matters*) 事务 shìwù **2** (*personal concerns*) 私事 sīshì ▶ **to have an affair (with sb)**

(和某人)发生暧昧关系 (hé mǒurén) fāshēng àimèi guānxi

affect [əfɛkt] VT 影响 yǐngxiǎng

afford [əfɔrd] VT ▶ **to be able to afford (to buy/pay) sth** 买/支付得起某物 mǎi/zhīfùdeqǐ mǒuwù

afraid [əfreɪd] ADJ (*frightened*) 害怕的 hàipà de ▶ **to be afraid of sb/sth** 害怕某人/某物 hàipà mǒurén/mǒuwù ▶ **to be afraid to do sth/of doing sth** 怕做某事 pà zuò mǒushì ▶ **to be afraid that...** (*worry, fear*) 担心··· dānxīn...; (*expressing apology, disagreement*) 恐怕··· kǒngpà... ▶ **I'm afraid so/not** 恐怕是/不是的 kǒngpà shì/bùshì de

Africa [æfrɪkə] N 非洲 Fēizhōu

African [æfrɪkən] **I** ADJ 非洲的 Fēizhōu de **II** N [c] (*person*) 非洲人 Fēizhōurén [个 gè]

after [æftər] **I** PREP **1** (*in time*) 在···以后 zài...yǐhòu **2** (*in place, order*) 在···后面 zài...hòumiàn **II** ADV (*afterwards*) 以后 yǐhòu **III** CONJ (*once*) 在···以后 zài...yǐhòu ▶ **the day after tomorrow** 后天 hòutiān ▶ **it's ten after eight** 现在是8点过10分 xiànzài shì bādiǎn guò shífēn ▶ **after all** 毕竟 bìjìng ▶ **after doing sth** 做完某事后 zuòwán mǒushì hòu

> **after, afterwards** 和 **later** 用于表示某事发生在说话的时间，或者某个特定事情之后。**after** 可以和 **not long, shortly** 等连用。*After dinner she spoke to him...Shortly after, she called me.* 在无须指明某个特定时间或事件时，可以用 **afterwards**。*Afterwards we went to a night club... You'd better come and see me later.* **afterwards** 可以和 **soon, shortly** 等连用。*Soon afterwards, he came to the clinic.* **later** 表示某事发生在说话之后，可以和 **a little, much** 或 **not much** 等连用。*A little later, the lights went out... I learned all this much later.* 可以用 **after, afterwards** 和 **later** 后跟表示时间段的词语，表示某事发生的时间。 *... five years after his death...She wrote about it six years later/afterwards.*

afternoon [æftərnuːn] N [c/u] 下午 xiàwǔ [个 gè] ▶ **this afternoon** 今天下午 jīntiān xiàwǔ ▶ **tomorrow/yesterday afternoon** 明天/昨天下午 míngtiān/zuótiān xiàwǔ ▶ **(good) afternoon!** (*hello*) 下午好！ xiàwǔ hǎo!

aftershave (lotion) [æftərʃeɪv (loʊʃᵊn)] N [U] 须后(润肤)水 xūhòu (rùnfū) shuǐ

afterward [æftərwərd] ADV 以后 yǐhòu

again [əgɛn, əgeɪn] ADV 又一次地 yòu yīcì de ▶ **again and again, time and again** 一再 yīzài

against [əgɛnst, əgeɪnst] PREP **1** (*leaning on, touching*) 紧靠在 jǐnkào zài **2** (*opposed to*) 反对 fǎnduì **3** (*in game or competition*) 同···对抗 tóng...duìkàng **4** ▶ **to protect against sth** 保护免受某种伤害 bǎohù miǎnshòu mǒuzhǒng shānghài ▶ **they'll be playing against Australia** 他们将在比赛中同澳大利亚队对抗 tāmen jiāng zài bǐsài zhōng tóng Àodàlìyà duì duìkàng ▶ **against the law/rules** 违反法律/规则 wéifǎn fǎlǜ/guīzé ▶ **against one's will** 违背自己的意愿 wéibèi zìjǐ de yìyuàn

age [eɪdʒ] N **1** [c/u] 年龄 niánlíng **2** [c] (*period in history*) 时代 shídài [个 gè] ▶ **what age is he?** 他多大了？ tā duōdà le? ▶ **at the age of 20** 20岁时 èrshí suì shí ▶ **an age, ages** (*inf*) 很长时间 hěncháng shíjiān ▶ **the Stone/Bronze/Iron Age** 石器/铜器/铁器时代 shíqì/tóngqì/tiěqì shídài

aged[1] [eɪdʒd] ADJ ▶ **aged 10** 10岁 shí suì

aged[2] [eɪdʒɪd] N PL ▶ **the aged** 老人

lǎorén

agent [eɪdʒənt] N [c] 代理人 dàilǐrén [个 gè]

aggressive [əgrɛsɪv] ADJ 好斗的 hàodòu de

ago [əgoʊ] ADV ▶ **2 days ago** 两天前 liǎngtiān qián ▶ **long ago, a long time ago** 很久以前 hěnjiǔ yǐqián ▶ **how long ago?** 多久以前？ duōjiǔ yǐqián?

agony [ægəni] N [c/u] 痛苦 tòngkǔ [种 zhǒng]

agree [əgri] VI **1** (*have same opinion*) 同意 tóngyì **2** ▶ **to agree to sth/to do sth** 同意某事/做某事 tóngyì mǒushì/zuò mǒushì ▶ **to agree with sb about sth** 关于某事赞成某人的看法 guānyú mǒushì zànchéng mǒurén de kànfǎ ▶ **to agree on sth** (+ *price, arrangement*) 商定某事 shāngdìng mǒushì

agreement [əgrimənt] N **1** [c] ▶ **an agreement (on sth)** (*decision, arrangement*) (关于某事的)协议 (guānyú mǒushì de) xiéyì [个 gè] **2** [u] (*consent*) 同意 tóngyì

agricultural [ægrɪkʌltʃərəl] ADJ 农业的 nóngyè de

agriculture [ægrɪkʌltʃər] N [u] 农业 nóngyè

ahead [əhɛd] ADV **1** (*in front*) 在前地 zàiqián de **2** (*in work, achievements*) 提前地 tíqián de **3** (*in competition*) 领先地 lǐngxiān de **4** (*in the future*) 在未来 zài wèilái ▶ **the days/months ahead** 今后几天/几个月 jīnhòu jǐtiān/jǐgè yuè ▶ **ahead of time/schedule** 提前 tíqián ▶ **right** *or* **straight ahead** 笔直向前 bǐzhí xiàngqián ▶ **go ahead!** (*giving permission*) 干吧！ gànba!

AI [eɪ aɪ] N ABBR (= **artificial intelligence**) 人工智能 réngōng zhìnéng

aid [eɪd] N [u] 援助 yuánzhù

AIDS [eɪdz] N ABBR (= **acquired immune deficiency syndrome**) 艾滋病 àizībìng

aim [eɪm] **I** VT ▶ **to aim sth (at sb/sth)** (+ *gun, camera*) 将某物瞄准(某人/某物) jiāng mǒuwù miáozhǔn (mǒurén/mǒuwù) **II** VI (*with weapon*) 瞄准 miáozhǔn **III** N [c] (*objective*) 目标 mùbiāo [个 gè] ▶ **to aim at sth** (*with weapon*) 瞄准某物 miáozhǔn mǒuwù ▶ **to aim to do sth** 打算做某事 dǎsuàn zuò mǒushì

air [ɛər] **I** N [u] 空气 kōngqì **II** CPD (+ *travel*) 乘飞机 chéng fēijī; (+ *fare*) 飞机 fēijī ▶ **in/into/through the air** 在/进入/穿过天空 zài/jìnrù/chuānguò tiānkōng ▶ **by air** (*flying*) 乘飞机 chéng fēijī

air-conditioned [ɛərkəndɪʃənd] ADJ 装有空调的 zhuāngyǒu kōngtiáo de

air conditioning N [u] 空气调节 kōngqì tiáojié

air force N [c] 空军 kōngjūn [支 zhī]

airline [ɛərlaɪn] N [c] 航空公司 hángkōng gōngsī [家 jiā]

airmail [ɛərmeɪl] N [u] ▶ **by airmail** 航空邮寄 hángkōng yóujì

airplane [ɛərpleɪn] N [c] 飞机 fēijī [架 jià]

airport [ɛərpɔrt] N [c] 飞机场 fēijīchǎng [个 gè]

aisle [aɪl] N [c] 过道 guòdào [条 tiáo] ▶ **aisle seat** (*on plane*) 靠过道的座位 kào guòdào de zuòwèi

alarm [əlɑrm] N **1** [c] (*warning device*) 警报 jǐngbào [个 gè] **2** [c] (*on clock*) 闹钟 nàozhōng [个 gè]

alarm clock N [c] 闹钟 nàozhōng [个 gè]

Albania [ælbeɪniə] N 阿尔巴尼亚 Ā'ěrbāníyà

album [ælbəm] N [c] **1** 册子 cèzi [本 běn] **2** (*LP*) 唱片 chàngpiàn [张 zhāng]

alcohol [ælkəhɔl] N [u] 酒 jiǔ

alcoholic [ælkəhɔlɪk] **I** N [c] 酒鬼 jiǔguǐ [个 gè] **II** ADJ (+ *drink*) 含酒精的 hán jiǔjīng de

alert [əlɜrt] N [c] (*situation*) ▶ **a security alert** 安全警戒 ānquán jǐngjiè [个 gè]

Algeria [ældʒɪəriə] N 阿尔及利亚 Ā'ěrjílìyà

alike [əlaɪk] ADJ ▶ **to be/look alike** 是/看起来相似的 shì/kànqǐlái xiāngsì de

alive [əlaɪv] ADJ (*living*) ▸ **to be alive** 活着的 huózhe de ▸ **alive and well** 安然无恙的 ānrán wúyàng de

KEYWORD

all [ɔl] **I** ADJ 所有的 suǒyǒu de ▸ **all day/night** 整日/夜 zhěngrì/yè ▸ **all big cities** 所有的大城市 suǒyǒu de dàchéngshì

II PRON **1** 全部 quánbù ▸ **all I could do was apologize** 我所能做的全部就是道歉 wǒ suǒ néng zuò de quánbù jiùshì dàoqiàn ▸ **I ate it all, I ate all of it** 我把它全都吃了 wǒ bǎ tā quán dōu chīle ▸ **all of us** 我们中的所有人 wǒmen zhōng de suǒyǒu rén ▸ **we all sat down** 我们都坐下了 wǒmen dōu zuòxià le ▸ **is that all?** 那就是全部吗？ nà jiùshì quánbù ma?

2 (*in expressions*) ▸ **after all** (*considering*) 毕竟 bìjìng ▸ **in all** 总共 zǒnggòng ▸ **best of all** 最好不过的是 zuìhǎo bùguò de shì

III ADV **1** (*emphatic*) 完全 wánquán ▸ **he did it all by himself** 他完全是自己做的 tā wánquán shì zìjǐ zuò de ▸ **all alone** 孤零零的 gūlínglíng de

2 (*in scores*) ▸ **the score is 2 all** 比分2比2平 bǐfēn èr bǐ èr píng

allergic [əlɜrdʒɪk] ADJ (+ *reaction, response*) 过敏的 guòmǐn de ▸ **to be allergic to sth** 对某物过敏 duì mǒuwù guòmǐn

allergy [ælərdʒi] (*Med*) N [c/u] 过敏症 guòmǐnzhèng [种 zhǒng] ▸ **to have an allergy to sth** 对某物有过敏症 duì mǒuwù yǒu guòmǐnzhèng

allow [əlaʊ] VT **1** (*permit*) 允许 yǔnxǔ **2** (+ *sum, time, amount*) 留出 liúchū ▸ **to allow sb to do sth** 允许某人做某事 yǔnxǔ mǒurén zuò mǒushì

all right **I** ADJ ▸ **to be all right** (*satisfactory*) 还不错的 hái bùcuò de; (*well, safe*) 安然无恙的 ānrán wúyàng de **II** ADV **1** (*go, work out*) 顺利地 shùnlì de **2** (*see, hear, work*) 没问题地 méi wèntí de **3** (*as answer*) 可以 kěyǐ

almond [ɑmənd, æm-, ælm-] N [c/u] (*nut*) 杏仁 xìngrén [颗 kē]

almost [ɔlmoʊst] ADV 差不多 chàbùduō

alone [əloʊn] **I** ADJ 独自的 dúzì de **II** ADV (*unaided*) 独自地 dúzì de ▸ **to leave sb/sth alone** (*undisturbed*) 不要打扰某人/某物 bùyào dǎrǎo mǒurén/mǒuwù

along [əlɔŋ] **I** PREP **1** 沿着 yánzhe **2** (+ *road, corridor, river*) 沿着 yánzhe **II** ADV 沿着 yánzhe ▸ **along with** (*together with*) 与…一起 yǔ…yīqǐ

alphabet [ælfəbɛt, -bɪt] N ▸ **the alphabet** 字母表 zìmǔbiǎo

already [ɔlrɛdi] ADV 已经 yǐjīng ▸ **I have already started making dinner** 我已经开始做晚餐了 wǒ yǐjīng kāishǐ zuò wǎncān le ▸ **is it five o'clock already?** (*expressing surprise*) 已经到5点了吗？ yǐjīng dào wǔdiǎn le ma?

also [ɔlsoʊ] ADV **1** (*too*) 也 yě **2** (*moreover*) 同样 tóngyàng

alternate [ɔltɜrnɪt] ADJ **1** 交替的 jiāotì de **2** (*alternative*) 供替换的 gōng tìhuàn de

alternative [ɔltɜrnətɪv] **I** ADJ (*nonconventional*) 非常规的 fēi chángguī de **II** N [c] ▸ **(an) alternative (to)** …的替代 ...de tìdài [个 gè] ▸ **to have no alternative (but to)** (除…外)别无选择 (chú...wài) biéwú xuǎnzé

alternatively [ɔltɜrnətɪvli] ADV 或者 huòzhě

although [ɔlðoʊ] CONJ **1** 尽管 jǐnguǎn **2** (*but*) 但是 dànshì

altogether [ɔltəgɛðər] ADV **1** (*completely*) 完全 wánquán **2** (*in total*) 总共 zǒnggòng ▸ **how much is that altogether?** 总共多少钱？ zǒnggòng duōshǎo qián?

aluminum [əlumɪnəm] N [U] 铝 lǚ

always [ɔlweɪz] ADV 总是 zǒngshì ▸ **He's always late** 他总是迟到 tā

zǒngshì chídào
am [əm, STRONG æm] VB *see* **be**
a.m. [eɪ ɛm] ADV ABBR (= **ante meridiem**) 上午 shàngwǔ
amateur [æmətʃɜr, -tʃʊər] N [C] 业余爱好者 yèyú àihàozhě [个 gè]
amaze [əmeɪz] VT 使惊讶 shǐ jīngyà ▸ **to be amazed (at** *or* **by/that...)** (对/被···)惊讶 (duì/bèi...) jīngyà
amazing [əmeɪzɪŋ] ADJ 令人惊讶的 lìng rén jīngyà de
ambassador [æmbæsədər] N [C] 大使 dàshǐ [位 wèi]
ambition [æmbɪʃən] N [C] ▸ **an ambition (to do sth)** (做某事的)志向 (zuò mǒushì de) zhìxiàng [个 gè] ▸ **to achieve one's ambition** 实现自己的抱负 shíxiàn zìjǐ de bàofu
ambitious [æmbɪʃəs] ADJ 雄心勃勃的 xióngxīn bóbó de
ambulance [æmbyələns] N [C] 救护车 jiùhùchē [辆 liàng]
America [əmɛrɪkə] N 美洲 Měizhōu
American [əmɛrɪkən] **I** ADJ 美国的 Měiguó de **II** N [C] (*person*) 美国人 Měiguórén [个 gè]
among(st) [əmʌŋ(st)] PREP 在···当中 zài...dāngzhōng

如果指两个以上的人或物，用 **among** 或 **amongst**。如果只指两个人或物，用 **between**。*...an area between Mars and Jupiter...an opportunity to discuss these issues amongst themselves.* **amongst** 是有些过时的表达方式。注意，如果你 **between** 某些东西或某些人，他们在你的两侧。如果你 **among** 或 **amongst** 某些东西或某些人，他们在你的周围。 *...the bag standing on the floor between us...the sound of a pigeon among the trees...*

amount [əmaʊnt] N [C/U] (*quantity*) 数量 shùliàng; (*of money*) 数额 shù'é [个 gè]; (*of work*) 总量 zǒngliàng [个 gè]
amp [æmp] N [C] 安培 ānpéi
amplifier [æmplɪfaɪər] N [C] 扬声器 yángshēngqì [个 gè]
amuse [əmyuz] VT (*distract, entertain*) 给···消遣 gěi...xiāoqiǎn ▸ **to be amused at** *or* **by sth** 被某事逗乐 bèi mǒushì dòulè
an [ən, STRONG æn] DEF ART *see* **a**
analysis [ənælɪsɪs] (*pl* **analyses**) N [C/U] 分析 fēnxī [种 zhǒng]
analyze [ænəlaɪz] VT 分析 fēnxī
ancestor [ænsɛstər] N [C] 祖先 zǔxiān [位 wèi]
ancient [eɪnʃənt] ADJ **1** (+ *Greece, Rome, monument*) 古代的 gǔdài de **2** (*very old*) 古老的 gǔlǎo de
and [ənd, STRONG ænd] CONJ 和 hé ▸ **men and women** 男人和女人 nánrén hé nǚrén ▸ **better and better** 越来越好 yuè lái yuè hǎo ▸ **to try and do sth** 试着做某事 shìzhe zuò mǒushì
anesthetic [ænɪsθɛtɪk] N [C/U] 麻醉剂 mázuìjì [种 zhǒng] ▸ **local anesthetic** 局部麻醉 júbù mázuì ▸ **general anesthetic** 全身麻醉 quánshēn mázuì
anger [æŋgər] N [U] 生气 shēngqì
angry [æŋgri] ADJ 生气的 shēngqì de ▸ **to be angry with sb/about sth** 对某人/某事生气 duì mǒurén/mǒushì shēngqì ▸ **to make sb angry** 使某人生气 shǐ mǒurén shēngqì
animal [ænɪməl] N [C] 动物 dòngwù [只 zhī]
ankle [æŋkəl] (*Anat*) N [C] 踝 huái [个 gè]
anniversary [ænɪvɜrsəri] N [C] **1** ▸ **anniversary (of sth)** (某事的)周年纪念 (mǒushì de) zhōunián jìniàn [个 gè] **2** (*also*: **wedding anniversary**) 结婚周年纪念 jiéhūn zhōunián jìniàn [个 gè]
announce [ənaʊns] VT 宣布 xuānbù ▸ **the government has announced that...** 政府宣称··· zhèngfǔ xuānchēng...
announcement [ənaʊnsmənt] N

[c] **1** 宣布 xuānbù **2** (*at airport or station*) 通告 tōnggào [个 gè] ▸ **to make an announcement** 发表声明 fābiǎo shēngmíng

annoy [ənɔɪ] VT 使烦恼 shǐ fánnǎo

annoyed [ənɔɪd] ADJ 厌烦的 yànfán de ▸ **to be annoyed at sth/with sb** 对某事/某人感到厌烦 duì mǒushì/mǒurén gǎndào yànfán

annoying [ənɔɪɪŋ] ADJ (+ *noise, habit, person*) 讨厌的 tǎoyàn de

annual [ænyuəl] ADJ **1** (+ *meeting, report*) 每年的 měinián de **2** (+ *sales, income, rate*) 年度的 niándù de

anorak [ænəræk] N [c] 连帽防风夹克 liánmào fángfēng jiákè [件 jiàn]

another [ənʌðər] **I** ADJ **1** ▸ **another book** (*one more*) 另一本书 lìng yī běn shū **2** (*a different one*) 另外的 lìngwài de **3** ▸ **another 5 years/miles/pounds** 再有5年/英里/磅 zài yǒu wǔ nián/yīnglǐ/bàng **II** PRON **1** (*one more*) 再一个 zài yī gè **2** (*a different one*) 不同的一个 bùtóng de yīgè ▸ **one another** 相互 xiānghù

answer [ænsər] **I** N [c] **1** (*reply*) 回答 huídá [个 gè]; (*to letter*) 回信 huíxìn [封 fēng] **2** (*solution*) 答案 dá'àn [个 gè] **II** VI (*reply*) 回答 huídá; (*to telephone ringing, knock at door*) 应答 yìngdá **III** VT (+ *person*) 答复 dáfù; (+ *question*) 回答 huídá; (+ *letter*) 回复 huífù ▸ **to answer the phone** 接听电话 jiētīng diànhuà

answering machine [ænsərɪŋ məʃin] N [c] 电话答录机 diànhuà dálùjī [台 tái]

Antarctic [æntɑrktɪk] N ▸ **the Antarctic** 南极 Nánjí

antenna [æntɛnə] N [c] 天线 tiānxiàn [根 gēn]

anthem [ænθəm] N [c] 赞美诗 zànměishī 国歌 guógē [首 shǒu]

antibiotic [æntibaɪɒtɪk, -taɪ-] N [c] 抗生素 kàngshēngsù [种 zhǒng]

antique [æntik] N [c] 古董 gǔdǒng [件 jiàn]

antiseptic [æntəsɛptɪk] N [c/u] 杀菌剂 shājūnjì [种 zhǒng]

anxious [æŋkʃəs] ADJ 忧虑的 yōulǜ de

KEYWORD

any [ɛni] **I** ADJ **1** (*in negatives, in questions*) 一些的 yīxiē de ▸ **I don't have any chocolate/candy** 我没有巧克力/糖了 wǒ méiyǒu qiǎokèlì/táng le ▸ **there was hardly any food** 几乎没有食物了 jīhū méiyǒu shíwù le ▸ **do you have any chocolate/sweets?** 你有巧克力/糖吗？ nǐ yǒu qiǎokèlì/táng ma?

2 (*in "if" clauses*) 任何的 rènhé de ▸ **if there are any tickets left** 如果有票剩下的话 rúguǒ yǒu piào shèngxia de huà

3 (*no matter which*) 任意的 rènyì de ▸ **take any card you like** 拿你喜欢的任意一张卡 ná nǐ xǐhuan de rènyì yī zhāng kǎ

4 (*in expressions*) ▸ **any day now** 从现在起的任何一天 cóng xiànzài qǐ de rènhé yītiān ▸ **(at) any moment** (在)任何时候 (zài) rèhé shíhou ▸ **any time** (*whenever*) 不论何时 bùlùn héshí; (*also*: **at any time**) 在任何时候 zài rènhé shíhou

II PRON **1** (*in negatives*) 一些 yīxiē ▸ **I didn't eat any (of it)** 我(这)一点也没吃 wǒ (zhè) yīdiǎn yě méi chī ▸ **I don't have any (of them)** 我一个也没有 wǒ yīgè yě méiyǒu

2 (*in questions*) 一些 yīxiē ▸ **have you got any?** 你有吗？ nǐ yǒu ma?

3 (*in "if" clauses*) 任何 rènhé ▸ **if any of you would like to take part, ...** 如果你们中任何人想参加的话，… rúguǒ nǐmen zhōng rènhé rén xiǎng cānjiā de huà, ...

4 (*no matter which ones*) 无论哪一个 wúlùn nǎ yīgè ▸ **help yourself to any of the books** 无论哪本书你随便拿 wúlùn nǎběn shū nǐ suíbiàn ná

III ADV **1** (*with negative*) 丝毫 sīháo ▸ **I don't play tennis any more** 我

不再打网球了 wǒ bùzài dǎ wǎngqiú le ▶ **don't wait any longer** 不再等了 bùzài děng le
2 (*in questions*) …一点 …yīdiǎn ▶ **do you want any more soup/sandwiches?** 你还想再要点汤/三明治吗？ nǐ hái xiǎng zài yào diǎn tāng/sānmíngzhì ma?

anybody [ɛnibɒdi, -bʌdi] PRON = **anyone**
anyhow [ɛnihaʊ] ADV = **anyway**
anyone [ɛniwʌn] PRON **1** (*in negatives, "if" clauses*) 任何人 rènhé rén **2** (*in questions*) 任何一个人 rènhé yīgè rén ▶ **I can't see anyone** 我见不到任何人 wǒ jiànbùdào rènhé rén ▶ **did anyone see you?** 有人看到你吗？ yǒurén kàndào nǐ ma? ▶ **anyone could do it** 任何人都能做到 rènhé rén dōunéng zuòdào
anything [ɛnɪθɪŋ] PRON (*in negatives, questions, "if" clauses*) 任何事 rènhé shì ▶ **I can't see anything** 我什么也看不见 wǒ shénme yě kànbùjiàn ▶ **hardly anything** 几乎没有任何东西 jīhū méiyǒu rènhé dōngxi ▶ **did you find anything?** 你找到些什么吗？ nǐ zhǎodào xiē shénme ma? ▶ **if anything happens to me...** 如果任何事情发生在我身上… rúguǒ rènhé shìqing fāshēng zài wǒ shēnshàng... ▶ **you can say anything you like** 你可以畅所欲言 nǐ kěyǐ chàng suǒ yù yán
anyway [ɛniweɪ] ADV **1** (*besides*) 无论如何 wúlùn rúhé **2** (*all the same*) 还是 háishì **3** (*in short*) 总之 zǒngzhī ▶ **I will go anyway** 不论如何我要走了 bùlùn rúhé wǒ yào zǒu le
anywhere [ɛniwɛər] ADV (*in negatives, questions, "if" clauses*) 任何地方 rènhé dìfāng ▶ **I can't see him anywhere** 我哪里都见不到他 wǒ nǎlǐ dōu jiànbùdào tā
apart [əpɑrt] ADV (*couple, family*) 分开 fēnkāi ▶ **to take sth apart** 拆卸某物 chāixiè mǒuwù ▶ **apart from** (*excepting*) 除去 chúqù
apartment [əpɑrtmənt] N [c] 公寓 gōngyù [处 chù]
apologize [əpɒlədʒaɪz] VI 道歉 dàoqiàn ▶ **to apologize to sb (for sth)** 向某人(为某事)道歉 xiàng mǒurén (wèi mǒushì) dàoqiàn
apology [əpɒlədʒi] N [c/u] 道歉 dàoqiàn [个 gè]
apostrophe [əpɒstrəfi] N [c] 撇号 piěhào [个 gè]
app [æp] N [c] (*Comput: = application*) 应用程序 yìngyòng chéngxù [个 gè]
apparently [əpærəntli] ADV 表面看来 biǎomiàn kànlái
appear [əpɪər] VI **1** (*seem*) 看起来 kànqǐlái **2** (*come into view, begin to develop*) 出现 chūxiàn ▶ **to appear to be/have** 看起来是/有 kànqǐlái shì/yǒu
appendicitis [əpɛndɪsaɪtɪs] N [u] 阑尾炎 lánwěiyán
appetite [æpɪtaɪt] N [c/u] 食欲 shíyù
appetizer [æpɪtaɪzər] N [c] 开胃菜 kāiwèi cài [道 dào]
applause [əplɔz] N [u] 掌声 zhǎngshēng
apple [æpᵊl] N [c] 苹果 píngguǒ [个 gè]
appliance [əplaɪəns] (*frm*) N [c] 器具 qìjù [件 jiàn]
applicant [æplɪkənt] N [c] 申请人 shēnqǐngrén [个 gè]
application [æplɪkeɪʃᵊn] N **1** [c] 申请 shēnqǐng [份 fèn] **2** [c] (*Comput: program*) 应用程序 yìngyòng chéngxù [个 gè]
application form N [c] 申请表格 shēnqǐng biǎogé [份 fèn]
apply [əplaɪ] VI (*make application*) 提出申请 tíchū shēnqǐng ▶ **to apply for sth** (*+ job, grant, membership*) 申请某事 shēnqǐng mǒushì
appointment [əpɔɪntmənt] N [c] (*arranged meeting*) 约会 yuēhuì [个 gè]; (*with hairdresser, dentist, doctor*) 预约 yùyuē [个 gè] ▶ **to make an appointment (with sb)** (*to see hairdresser, dentist, doctor*) (和某人)预约 (hé mǒurén) yùyuē

appreciate [əpriʃieɪt] VT (*be grateful for*) 感谢 gǎnxiè ▸ **I (really) appreciate your help** 我(十分)感谢你的帮助 wǒ (shífēn) gǎnxiè nǐde bāngzhù
approach [əpr<u>oʊ</u>tʃ] **I** VI (*person, car*) 走近 zǒu jìn; (*event, time*) 临近 línjìn **II** VT **1** (*draw near to*) 向…靠近 xiàng...kàojìn **2** (+ *situation, problem*) 处理 chǔlǐ **III** N [c] (*to a problem, situation*) 方式 fāngshì [种 zhǒng]
approval [əpr<u>u</u>vᵊl] N [U] 批准 pīzhǔn
approve [əpr<u>u</u>v] VI 赞成 zànchéng
approximate [əpr<u>ɒ</u>ksɪmət] ADJ 近似的 jìnsì de
apricot [<u>eɪ</u>prɪkɒt] N [C/U] 杏子 xìngzi [个 gè]
April [<u>eɪ</u>prɪl] N [C/U] 四月 sìyuè; *see also* **July**
apron [<u>eɪ</u>prən] N [C] 围裙 wéiqún [条 tiáo]
Aquarius [əkw<u>ɛə</u>riəs] N [U] (*sign*) 宝瓶座 Bǎopíng Zuò
Arab [<u>æ</u>rəb] **I** ADJ 阿拉伯的 Ālābó de **II** N [C] 阿拉伯人 Ālābórén [个 gè]
Arabic [<u>æ</u>rəbɪk] N [U] (*language*) 阿拉伯语 Ālābóyǔ
arch [<u>ɑ</u>rtʃ] N [C] 拱 gǒng [个 gè]
archaeology [<u>ɑ</u>rki<u>ɒ</u>lədʒi] N [U] 考古学 kǎogǔxué
architect [<u>ɑ</u>rkɪtɛkt] N [C] 建筑师 jiànzhùshī [位 wèi]
architecture [<u>ɑ</u>rkɪtɛktʃər] N [U] 建筑学 jiànzhùxué
Arctic [<u>ɑ</u>rktɪk] N ▸ **the Arctic** 北极 Běijí
are [ər, STRONG ɑr] VB *see* **be**
area [<u>ɛə</u>riə] N **1** [C] (*region, zone*) 地区 dìqū [个 gè] **2** [C] (*of room, building etc*) 区 qū [个 gè] **3** [C/U] (*Math, Geom*) 面积 miànjī [个 gè] **4** [C] (*part*) 部分 bùfen [个 gè] ▸ **in the London area** 在伦敦周边地区 zài Lúndūn zhōubiān dìqū
area code N [C] 区号 qūhào [个 gè]
Argentina [ɑrdʒəntinə] N 阿根廷 Āgēntíng
argue [<u>ɑ</u>rgyu] VI (*quarrel*) ▸ **to argue (with sb) (about sth)** (为某事)(和某人)争吵 (wèi mǒushì) (hé mǒurén) zhēngchǎo
argument [<u>ɑ</u>rgyəmənt] N [C/U] (*quarrel*) 争吵 zhēngchǎo [阵 zhèn] ▸ **an argument for/against sth** 赞成/反对某事的论据 zànchéng/fǎnduì mǒushì de lùnjù
Aries [<u>ɛə</u>riz] N [U] (*sign*) 白羊座 Báiyáng Zuò
arithmetic [ər<u>ɪ</u>θmɪtɪk] N [U] (*Math*) 算术 suànshù
arm [<u>ɑ</u>rm] **I** N [C] **1** 胳膊 gēbo [条 tiáo] **2** (*of jacket, shirt etc*) 袖子 xiùzi [只 zhī] **II arms** N PL (*weapons*) 武器 wǔqì
armchair [<u>ɑ</u>rmtʃɛər] N [C] 扶手椅 fúshǒuyǐ [把 bá]
armed [<u>ɑ</u>rmd] ADJ 武装的 wǔzhuāng de
army [<u>ɑ</u>rmi] N ▸ **the army** 军队 jūnduì
around [ər<u>aʊ</u>nd] **I** ADV (*about*) 到处 dàochù **II** PREP **1** (*encircling*) 围绕 wéirào **2** (*near*) 在附近 zài fùjìn **3** (*with numbers, weights, times, dates*) 大约 dàyuē ▸ **to move around the room/sail around the world** 绕房间一周/环球航行 rào fángjiān yī zhōu/huánqiú hángxíng ▸ **all around** 在…周围 zài...zhōuwéi ▸ **to go around (sth)** 绕过(某物) ràoguò (mǒuwù) ▸ **to go around to sb's (house)** 造访某人(的家) zàofáng mǒurén (de jiā) ▸ **I'll be around at 6 o'clock** 我会在6点钟到你家 wǒ huì zài liùdiǎnzhōng dào nǐjiā ▸ **around about** (*approximately*) 大约 dàyuē ▸ **around the clock** 连续24小时 liánxù èrshísì xiáoshí
arrange [ər<u>eɪ</u>ndʒ] **I** VT **1** (*organize*) 安排 ānpái **2** (*put in order*) 整理 zhěnglǐ **II** VI ▸ **to arrange to do sth** 安排做某事 ānpái zuò mǒushì
arrangement [ər<u>eɪ</u>ndʒmənt] **I** N [C] **1** (*agreement*) 约定 yuēdìng [个 gè]

2 (*grouping, layout*) 布置 bùzhì [种 zhǒng] **II arrangements** N PL (*plans, preparations*) 安排 ānpái

arrest [ərɛst] **I** VT 逮捕 dàibǔ **II** N [U] ▶ **to be under arrest** 被逮捕 bèi dàibǔ

arrival [əraɪvᵊl] N [C/U] 到达 dàodá

arrive [əraɪv] VI **1** 到 dào **2** (*letter, meal*) 来 lái

arrow [ærou] N [C] **1** (*weapon*) 箭 jiàn [支 zhī] **2** (*sign*) 箭头标志 jiàntóu biāozhì [个 gè]

art [ɑrt] **I** N **1** [U] 艺术 yìshù **2** [U] (*activity of drawing, painting etc*) 美术 měishù **3** [C] (*skill*) 技艺 jìyì [项 xiàng] **II arts** N PL ▶ **the arts** 艺术活动 yìshù huódòng **III** CPD ▶ **arts** (+ *graduate, student, course*) 文科 wénkē ▶ **work of art** 艺术品 yìshùpǐn

art gallery N [C] 美术馆 měishùguǎn [个 gè]

article [ɑrtɪkᵊl] N [C] **1** (*object, item*) 物品 wùpǐn [件 jiàn] **2** (*in newspaper*) 文章 wénzhāng [篇 piān] **3** (*Ling*) 冠词 guàncí [个 gè]

artificial [ɑrtɪfɪʃᵊl] ADJ 人造的 rénzào de

artist [ɑrtɪst] N [C] 画家 huàjiā [位 wèi]

KEYWORD

as [əz, STRONG æz] **I** CONJ **1** (*referring to time*) 当…时 dāng...shí ▶ **he came in as I was leaving** 我离开时他进来了 wǒ líkāi shí tā jìnlai le

2 (*since, because*) 因为 yīnwèi ▶ **as you can't come, I'll go on my own** 既然你不能来，我就自己去 jìrán nǐ bùnéng lái, wǒ jiù zìjǐ qù

3 (*referring to manner, way*) 像…一样 xiàng...yīyàng ▶ **as you can see** 如你所见到的 rú nǐ suǒ jiàndào de ▶ **it's on the left as you go in** 在你进入时的左侧 zài nǐ jìnrù shí de zuǒcè

II PREP **1** (*in the capacity of*) 作为 zuòwéi ▶ **he works as a salesman** 他做推销员的工作 tā zuò tuīxiāoyuán de gōngzuò

2 (*when*) 在…时 zài...shí ▶ **he was very energetic as a child** 他小时候精力很旺盛 tā xiǎoshíhou jīnglì hěn wàngshèng

III ADV **1** (*in comparisons*) ▶ **as big/good/easy** *etc* **as...** 像…一样大/好/容易{等} xiàng...yīyàng dà/hǎo/róngyì {děng} ▶ **you're as tall as he is** *or* **as him** 你和他一样高 nǐ hé tā yīyàng gāo ▶ **as soon as** 一…就… yī...jiù...

2 (*in expressions*) ▶ **as if** *or* **though** 好像 hǎoxiàng

ash [æʃ] N [U] 灰末 huīmò

ashamed [əʃeɪmd] ADJ ▶ **to be/feel ashamed** 感到羞愧 gǎndào xiūkuì ▶ **to be ashamed of sb/sth** 对某人/某事感到羞愧 duì mǒurén/mǒushì gǎndào xiūkuì

ashtray [æʃtreɪ] N [C] 烟灰缸 yānhuīgāng [个 gè]

Asia [eɪʒə] N 亚洲 Yàzhōu

Asian [eɪʒᵊn] **I** ADJ 亚洲的 Yàzhōu de **II** N [C] (*person*) 亚洲人 Yàzhōurén [个 gè]

ask [ɑsk, æsk] **I** VT **1** ▶ **to ask (sb) a question** 问(某人)一个问题 wèn (mǒurén) yīgè wèntí **2** (*invite*) 邀请 yāoqǐng **II** VI 问 wèn ▶ **to ask (sb) whether/why...** 问(某人)是否/为什么… wèn (mǒurén) shìfǒu/wèishénme... ▶ **to ask sb to do sth** 请求某人做某事 qǐngqiú mǒurén zuò mǒushì ▶ **to ask to do sth** 要求做某事 yāoqiú zuò mǒushì ▶ **to ask sb the time** 向某人询问时间 xiàng mǒurén xúnwèn shíjiān ▶ **to ask sb about sth** 向某人打听某事 xiàng mǒurén dǎtīng mǒushì ▶ **I asked him his name** 我问他叫什么 wǒ wèn tā jiào shénme; **ask for** VT FUS **1** (+ *thing*) 要 yào **2** (+ *person*) 找 zhǎo

asleep [əslip] ADJ 睡着的 shuìzháo de ▶ **to be asleep** 睡着了 shuìzháo le ▶ **to fall asleep** 入睡 rùshuì

aspirin [æspərɪn, -prɪn] N [C] (*tablet*) 阿司匹林药片 āsīpīlín yàopiàn [片 piàn]

assemble [əsɛmbᵊl] **I** VT (+ *machinery, object*) 装配 zhuāngpèi **II** VI (*gather*) 聚集 jùjí

assembly [əsɛmbli] N **1** [C] (*meeting*) 集会 jíhuì [个 gè] **2** [U] (*of vehicles*) 装配 zhuāngpèi

assignment [əsaɪnmənt] N [C] 任务 rènwù [项 xiàng]; (*for student*) 作业 zuòyè [个 gè]

assistance [əsɪstəns] N [U] 帮助 bāngzhù

assistant [əsɪstənt] N [C] (*helper*) 助手 zhùshǒu [个 gè]

assortment [əsɔrtmənt] N [C] ▶ **an assortment of sth** 各种各样的某物 gèzhǒng gèyàng de mǒuwù [件 jiàn]

assume [əsum] VT 假设 jiǎshè

assure [əʃʊər] VT 使确信 shǐ quèxìn

asterisk [æstərɪsk] N [C] 星号 xīnghào [个 gè]

asthma [æzmə] N [U] 哮喘 xiàochuǎn

astonishing [əstɒnɪʃɪŋ] ADJ 惊人的 jīngrén de

astronaut [æstrənɔt] N [C] 宇航员 yǔhángyuán [位 wèi]

astronomy [əstrɒnəmi] N [U] 天文学 tiānwénxué

KEYWORD

at [ət, STRONG æt] PREP **1** (*position, time, age*) 在 zài ▶ **we had dinner at a restaurant** 我们在一家饭店吃了饭 wǒmen zài yījiā fàndiàn chī le fàn ▶ **at home** 在家 zàijiā ▶ **at work** 在工作 zài gōngzuò ▶ **to be sitting at a table/desk** 坐在桌边/书桌边 zuòzài zhuōbiān/shūzhuōbiān ▶ **there's someone at the door** 门口有人 ménkǒu yǒurén

2 (*towards*) ▶ **to throw sth at sb** 向某人扔某物 xiàng mǒurén rēng mǒuwù ▶ **at four o'clock** 在4点钟 zài sìdiǎn zhōng ▶ **at Christmas** 在圣诞节 zài Shèngdànjié

3 (*referring to price, speed*) 以 yǐ ▶ **apples at $2 a pound** 苹果每磅两美元 píngguǒ měi bàng liǎng měiyuán ▶ **at 50 mph** 以每小时50英里的速度 yǐ měi xiǎoshí wǔshí yīnglǐ de sùdù

4 (*in expressions*) ▶ **not at all** (*in answer to question*) 一点也不 yīdiǎn yě bù; (*in answer to thanks*) 别客气 bié kèqi

ate [eɪt] PT *of* **eat**

athlete [æθlit] N [C] 运动员 yùndòngyuán [名 míng]

Atlantic [ətlæntɪk] **I** ADJ 大西洋的 Dàxīyáng de **II** N ▶ **the Atlantic (Ocean)** 大西洋 Dàxīyáng

atlas [ætləs] N [C] 地图册 dìtúcè [本 běn]

atmosphere [ætməsfɪər] N **1** [C] (*of planet*) 大气层 dàqìcéng [个 gè] **2** [S] (*of place*) 气氛 qìfēn

attach [ətætʃ] VT 附上 fùshàng

attachment [ətætʃmənt] N [C] (*of tool, computer file*) 附件 fùjiàn [个 gè]

attack [ətæk] **I** VT **1** (+ *person*) 袭击 xíjī **2** (+ *place, troops*) 攻击 gōngjī **3** (*criticize*) 抨击 pēngjī **II** VI (*Mil, Sport*) 进攻 jìngōng **III** N **1** [C/U] (*on person*) 袭击 xíjī [次 cì] **2** [C/U] (*military assault*) 攻击 gōngjī [次 cì] **3** [C/U] (*of illness*) 发作 fāzuò [阵 zhèn] ▶ **an attack on sb** (*assault*) 袭击某人 xíjī mǒurén; (*criticism*) 抨击某人 pēngjī mǒurén

attempt [ətɛmpt] **I** N [C] (*try*) 尝试 chángshì [个 gè] **II** VI ▶ **to attempt to do sth** 试图做某事 shìtú zuò mǒushì ▶ **an attempt to do sth** 做某事的企图 zuò mǒushì de qǐtú

attend [ətɛnd] VT **1** (+ *school, church, course*) 上 shàng **2** (+ *lecture, conference*) 参加 cānjiā

attention [ətɛnʃᵊn] N [U] **1** (*concentration*) 注意 zhùyì **2** (*care*) 照料 zhàoliào ▶ **to pay attention (to**

sth/sb) 关注(某事/某人) guānzhù (mǒushì/mǒurén)
attitude [ætɪtud] N [c/u] 看法 kànfǎ 态度 tàidù [个 gè]
attorney [ətɜrni] N [c] (*lawyer*) 律师 lǜshī [位 wèi]
attract [ətrækt] VT 吸引 xīyǐn
attraction [ətrækʃ^ən] I N [u] (*charm, appeal*) 吸引力 xīyǐnlì II **attractions** N PL (*also*: **tourist attractions**) (*amusements*) 游览胜地 yóulǎn shèngdì
attractive [ətræktɪv] ADJ (+ *man, woman*) 有魅力的 yǒu mèilì de; (+ *thing, place*) 吸引人的 xīyǐn rén de ▸ **he was very attractive to women** 他对女人很有吸引力 tā duì nǚrén hěnyǒu xīyǐnlì
auburn [ɔbərn] ADJ 赤褐色的 chìhèsè de
auction [ɔkʃ^ən] I N [c] 拍卖 pāimài [次 cì] II VT 拍卖 pāimài
audience [ɔdiəns] N [c] 1 (*in theater*) 观众 guānzhòng [位 wèi] 2 (*Rad, TV*) 听众 tīngzhòng [位 wèi]
August [ɔgəst] N [c/u] 八月 bāyuè; *see also* **July**
aunt [ænt, ɑnt] N [c] (*father's sister*) 姑母 gūmǔ [位 wèi]; (*father's older brother's wife*) 伯母 bómǔ [位 wèi]; (*father's younger brother's wife*) 婶母 shěnmǔ [位 wèi]; (*mother's sister*) 姨母 yímǔ [位 wèi]; (*mother's brother's wife*) 舅母 jiùmǔ [位 wèi]
auntie, aunty [ænti, ɑnti] (*inf*) N = **aunt**
au pair [oʊ pɛər] N [c] 为学习语言而住在当地人家里并提供家政服务的外国年轻人
Australia [ɒstreɪlyə] N 澳大利亚 Àodàlìyà
Australian [ɒstreɪlyən] I ADJ 澳大利亚的 Àodàlìyà de II N [c] (*person*) 澳大利亚人 Àodàlìyàrén [个 gè]
Austria [ɒstriə] N 奥地利 Àodìlì
author [ɔθər] N [c] (*writer: of novel*) 作家 zuòjiā [位 wèi]; (*of text*) 作者 zuòzhě [个 gè]
autism [ɔtɪzəm] N [u] 自闭症 zìbìzhèng
autistic [ɔtɪstɪk] ADJ 患自闭症的 huàn zìbìzhèng de
autobiography [ɔtəbaɪɒgrəfi] N [c] 自传 zìzhuàn [部 bù]
automatic [ɔtəmætɪk] I ADJ 自动的 zìdòng de II N [c] (*car*) 自动挡 zìdòngdǎng [个 gè]
automatically [ɔtəmætɪkli] ADV 1 (*by itself*) 自动地 zìdòng de 2 (*without thinking*) 无意识地 wú yìshi de 3 (*as a matter of course*) 自然而然地 zìrán'érrán de
automobile [ɔtəməbil] N [c] 汽车 qìchē [辆 liàng]
autumn [ɔtəm] N [c/u] 秋季 qiūjì [个 gè] ▸ **in (the) autumn** 在秋季 zài qiūjì
available [əveɪləb^əl] ADJ 1 可用的 kě yòng de 2 (+ *person*) 有空的 yǒukòng de
avalanche [ævəlæntʃ] N [c] 雪崩 xuěbēng [次 cì]
average [ævərɪdʒ, ævrɪdʒ] I N [c] 1 (*Math: mean*) 平均数 píngjūnshù [个 gè] 2 ▸ **the average (for sth/sb)** (某物/某人的)平均水平 (mǒuwù/mǒurén de) píngjūn shuǐpíng [个 gè] II ADJ (*ordinary*) 普通的 pǔtōng de ▸ **on average** 平均 píngjūn ▸ **above/below (the) average** 高于/低于平均水平 gāoyú/dīyú píngjūn shuǐpíng
avoid [əvɔɪd] VT 1 (+ *person, obstacle*) 避免 bìmiǎn 2 (+ *trouble, danger*) 防止 fángzhǐ ▸ **to avoid doing sth** 避免做某事 bìmiǎn zuò mǒushì
awake [əweɪk] ADJ ▸ **to be awake** 醒着的 xǐngzhe de
award [əwɔrd] I N [c] (*prize*) 奖 jiǎng [个 gè] II VT (+ *prize*) 授予 shòuyǔ
aware [əwɛər] ADJ ▸ **to be aware of sth** (*know about*) 意识到某事 yìshi dào mǒushì; (*be conscious of*) 觉察到某事 chájué dào mǒushì ▸ **to be aware that...** 知道… zhīdào...
away [əweɪ] I ADV 1 (*move, walk*) …开 ...kāi 2 (*not present*) 不在 bùzài II ADJ (+ *match, game*) 客场的 kèchǎng de ▸ **a week/month away**

还有一个星期/月 háiyǒu yīgè xīngqī/yuè ▸ **two kilometers away** 离这里两公里远 lí zhèlǐ liǎng gōnglǐ yuǎn

awful [ɔ̲fəl] I ADJ 1 糟糕的 zāogāo de 2 (+ *shock, crime*) 可怕的 kěpà de 3 ▸ **to look/feel awful** (*ill*) 看起来/感觉很糟糕的 kàn qǐlái/gǎnjué hěn zāogāo de II ADV (*inf: very*) 十分地 shífēn de ▸ **an awful lot (of)** (*amount*) 大量的 dàliàng de; (*number*) 非常多的 fēicháng duō de

awkward [ɔ̲kwərd] ADJ 1 (+ *movement*) 笨拙的 bènzhuó de 2 (+ *time, question*) 令人尴尬的 lìng rén gāngà de

ax [æ̲ks] N [C] 斧 fǔ [把 bǎ]

B

baby [beɪbi] N [C] 婴儿 yīng'ér [个 gè] ▶ **to have a baby** 生孩子 shēng háizi
baby carriage [beɪbi kærɪdʒ] N [C] 婴儿车 yīng'ér chē [辆 liàng]
babysit [beɪbisɪt] (*pt, pp* **babysat**) VI 代人照看孩子 dài rén zhàokàn háizi
babysitter [beɪbisɪtər] N [C] 代人照看孩子的人 dài rén zhàokàn háizi de rén [个 gè]
bachelor [bætʃələr] N [C] **1** (*unmarried man*) 单身汉 dānshēnhàn [个 gè] **2** ▶ **Bachelor of Arts/Science** 文/理科学士学位 wén/lǐkē xuéshì xuéwèi [个 gè]
back [bæk] **I** N [C] **1** 背部 bèibù [个 gè] **2** (*of hand, neck, legs*) 背面 bèimiàn [个 gè]; (*of house, door, book*) 后面 hòumiàn [个 gè]; (*of car*) 后部 hòubù [个 gè] **II** VT **1** (*support*) 支持 zhīchí; (*financially*) 资助 zīzhù **2** (*reverse*) 倒 dào **III** ADJ (+ *door, room, wheels*) 后面的 hòumiàn de **IV** ADV **1** (*not forward*) 向后 xiàng hòu **2** (*returned*) 回 huí ▶ **to be back** 回来 huílai ▶ **can I have it back?** 我能要回它吗? wǒ néng yàohuí tā ma?; **back down** VI 做出让步 zuòchū ràngbù; **back out** VI (*withdraw*) 退出 tuìchū; **back up I** VT **1** (+ *statement, theory*) 证实 zhèngshí **2** (*Comput*) (+ *disk*) 备份 bèifèn
backache [bækeɪk] N [C/U] 背痛 bèitòng [阵 zhèn]
background [bækgraʊnd] N **1** [C] (*of picture, scene, events*) 背景 bèijǐng [个 gè] **2** [C/U] (*of person: origins*) 出身 chūshēn [种 zhǒng]; (*experience*) 经验 jīngyàn [种 zhǒng] ▶ **in the background** 在背后 zài bèihòu
backing [bækɪŋ] N [U] (*support*) 支持 zhīchí; (*financial*) 资助 zīzhù
backpack [bækpæk] N [C] 双肩背包 shuāngjiān bēibāo [个 gè]
backpacker [bækpækər] N [C] 背包旅行者 bēibāo lǚxíngzhě [名 míng]

BACKPACKER

backpacker 一词指预算紧张的青年旅行者。他们把全部的随身物品放在一个背包里，尽可能地节俭开支，为的是能延长旅行时间多了解一个地区，多看一些地方。

backstroke [bækstroʊk] N [U] (*also:* **the backstroke**) 仰泳 yǎngyǒng
backup [bækʌp] **I** ADJ (*Comput*) (+ *copy, file, disk*) 备份的 bèifèn de **II** N [U] (*support*) 支持 zhīchí
backward [bækwərd], **backwards** [bækwərdz] ADV 向后地 xiàng hòu de
backyard [bækyɑrd] N [C] 后院 hòuyuàn [个 gè]
bacon [beɪkən] N [U] 腌猪肉 yān zhūròu
bad [bæd] ADJ **1** (+ *weather, health, conditions, temper*) 坏的 huài de; (+ *actor, driver*) 不胜任的 bù shèngrèn de; (+ *behavior, habit*) 不良的 bùliáng de **2** (*wicked*) 恶的 è de **3** (*naughty*) 不听话的 bù tīnghuà de **4** (+ *mistake, accident, headache*) 严重的 yánzhòng de **5** (+ *back, arm*) 有病的 yǒubìng de **6** (*rotten*) 腐烂的 fǔlàn de ▶ **to be bad for sth/sb** 对某事/某物有害 duì mǒushì/mǒuwù yǒuhài ▶ **not bad** 不错 bùcuò
badly [bædli] ADV **1** (*poorly*) 不令人满意地 bù lìng rén mǎnyì de **2** (*damaged, injured*) 严重地 yánzhòng de
badminton [bædmɪntən] N [U] 羽毛球 yǔmáoqiú
bad-tempered [bædtɛmpərd] ADJ 脾气坏的 píqi huài de
bag [bæg] N [C] **1** 袋 dài [个 gè] **2** (*suitcase*) 行李箱 xínglixiāng [个 gè] **3** (*handbag*) 手袋 shǒudài [个

gè] ▶ **to pack one's bags** 准备离开 zhǔnbèi líkāi

baggage [bægɪdʒ] N [U] 行李 xíngli

baggage claim [-kleɪm] N [U] 行李领取 xíngli lǐngqǔ

bake [beɪk] VT 烤 kǎo

baker [beɪkər] N [C] (*also*: **baker's**) 面包店 miànbāodiàn [家 jiā]

bakery [beɪkəri, beɪkri] N [C] 面包房 miànbāofáng [个 gè]

balance [bæləns] N **1** [U] (*of person, object*) 平衡 pínghéng **2** [C] (*in bank account*) 余额 yú'é [笔 bǐ] **3** [S] (*remainder to be paid*) 余欠之数 yúqiàn zhī shù ▶ **to keep/lose one's balance** 保持/失去平衡 bǎochí/shīqù pínghéng

balcony [bælkəni] N [C] (*open*) 露台 lùtái [个 gè]; (*covered*) 阳台 yángtái [个 gè]

bald [bɔld] ADJ 秃的 tū de ▶ **to go bald** 变秃 biàntū

ball [bɔl] N [C] 球 qiú [个 gè]

ballet [bæleɪ] N [U] 芭蕾舞 bāléiwǔ

ballet dancer N [C] 芭蕾舞演员 bāléiwǔ yǎnyuán [位 wèi]

balloon [bəlun] N [C] 气球 qìqiú [只 zhī]

ballpoint (pen) [bɔlpɔɪnt (pɛn)] N [C] 圆珠笔 yuánzhūbǐ [支 zhī]

ban [bæn] **I** N [C] 禁止 jìnzhǐ [种 zhǒng] **II** VT 禁止 jìnzhǐ

banana [bənænə] N [C] 香蕉 xiāngjiāo [只 zhī]

band [bænd] N [C] **1** (*group*) 群 qún **2** (*Mus*) 乐队 yuèduì [个 gè]

bandage [bændɪdʒ] N [C] 绷带 bēngdài [条 tiáo]

Band-Aid® N [C] 邦迪创可贴 Bāngdí chuàngkětiē [贴 tiē]

bang [bæŋ] **I** N [C] **1** (*noise*) 砰的一声 pēng de yīshēng; (*of gun, exhaust*) 爆炸声 bàozhà shēng [阵 zhèn] **2** (*blow*) 撞击 zhuàngjī [下 xià] **II** VT (+ *one's head, elbow*) 撞 zhuàng **III bangs** N PL (*fringe*) 刘海 liúhǎi ▶ **to bang into sth/sb** 猛撞某物/某人 měngzhuàng mǒuwù/mǒurén

Bangladesh [bɑŋglədɛʃ] N 孟加拉国 Mèngjiālāguó

bank [bæŋk] N [C] **1** (*Fin*) 银行 yínháng [家 jiā] **2** (*of river, lake*) 岸 àn [个 gè]

bank account N [C] 银行账户 yínháng zhànghù [个 gè]

bank card N [C] (*credit card*) 银行信用卡 yínháng xìnyòngkǎ [张 zhāng]

banknote [bæŋknoʊt] N [C] 纸币 zhǐbì [张 zhāng]

bar [bɑr] N [C] **1** 酒吧 jiǔbā [个 gè] **2** (*counter*) 吧台 bātái [个 gè] **3** (*of metal*) 条 tiáo **4** (*of soap, chocolate*) 块 kuài

barbecue [bɑrbɪkyu] N [C] 烧烤聚会 shāokǎo jùhuì [次 cì]

barefoot(ed) [bɛərfʊt(ɪd)] ADV 赤脚地 chìjiǎo de

barely [bɛərli] ADV 几乎不 jīhū bù

bargain [bɑrgɪn] N [C] **1** (*good buy*) 廉价品 liánjiàpǐn [件 jiàn] **2** (*deal, agreement*) 协议 xiéyì [个 gè]

barge [bɑrdʒ] N [C] 驳船 bóchuán [艘 sōu]

bark [bɑrk] VI (*dog*) 叫 jiào

barrel [bærəl] N [C] 桶 tǒng [个 gè]

barrier [bæriər] N [C] 关口 guānkǒu [个 gè]

bartender [bɑrtɛndər] N [C] 酒吧侍者 jiǔbā shìzhě [个 gè]

base [beɪs] **I** N [C] **1** (*bottom*) 底部 dǐbù [个 gè] **2** (*basis*) 根基 gēnjī [个 gè] **3** (*military*) 基地 jīdì [个 gè]; (*for individual, organization*) 总部 zǒngbù [个 gè] **II** VT ▶ **to be based on sth** 以某物为根据 yǐ mǒuwù wéi gēnjù ▶ **I'm based in New York** 我长驻纽约 wǒ chángzhù Niǔyuē

baseball [beɪsbɔl] N [U] 棒球 bàngqiú

basement [beɪsmənt] N [C] 地下室 dìxiàshì [间 jiān]

basic [beɪsɪk] ADJ 基本的 jīběn de; *see also* **basics**

basically [beɪsɪkli] ADV **1** (*fundamentally*) 基本上 jīběnshang **2** (*in fact, put simply*) 简而言之 jiǎn ér yán zhī

basics [beɪsɪks] N PL ▸ **the basics** 基本点 jīběndiǎn

basin [beɪsᵊn] N [C] **1** (*bowl*) 盆 pén [个 gè] **2** (*also*: **wash basin**) 洗脸盆 xǐliǎnpén [个 gè] **3** (*of river, lake*) 流域 liúyù [个 gè]

basket [bɑskɪt, bæs-] N [C] 筐 kuāng [个 gè]

basketball [bɑskɪtbɔl, bæs-] N [U] 篮球 lánqiú

bat [bæt] N [C] **1** (*animal*) 蝙蝠 biānfú [只 zhī] **2** (*for baseball*) 球板/棒 qiúbǎn/bàng [只 zhī]

bath [bæθ] N [C] (*act of bathing*) 洗澡 xǐzǎo [次 cì] ▸ **to have** *or* **take a bath** 洗澡 xǐzǎo

bathe [beɪð] VI (*have a bath*) 洗澡 xǐzǎo

bathroom [bæθrum] N [C] **1** 卫生间 wèishēngjiān [个 gè] **2** (*toilet*) 厕所 cèsuǒ [处 chù] ▸ **to go to the bathroom** 去卫生间 qù wèishēngjiān

bathtub [bæθtʌb] N [C] 浴缸 yùgāng [个 gè]

battery [bætəri] N [C] **1** 电池 diànchí [块 kuài] **2** (*in car*) 电瓶 diànpíng [个 gè]

battle [bætᵊl] N [C] **1** (*Mil*) 战役 zhànyì [场 chǎng] **2** (*fig*: *struggle*) 斗争 dòuzhēng [场 chǎng]

bay [beɪ] N [C] 湾 wān [个 gè]

BC [bi si] ADV ABBR (= **before Christ**) 公元前 gōngyuán qián

KEYWORD

be [bi, STRONG bi] (*pt* **was, were**, *pp* **been**) **I** VI **1** (*with complement*) 是 shì ▸ **I'm American/Chinese** 我是美国人/中国人 wǒ shì Měiguórén/Zhōngguórén ▸ **she's tall/pretty** 她长得高/漂亮 tā zhǎngde gāo/piàoliàng ▸ **this is my mother** 这是我妈妈 zhèshì wǒ māma ▸ **who is it?** 是谁啊？ shì shuí a? ▸ **be careful/quiet!** 当心/安静！ dāngxīn/ānjìng!

2 (*referring to time, date*) 是 shì ▸ **it's 5 o'clock** 现在是5点钟 xiànzài shì wǔdiǎnzhōng

3 (*describing weather*) ▸ **it's hot/cold** 天热/冷 tiān rè/lěng

4 (*talking about health*) ▸ **how are you?** 你身体怎么样？ nǐ shēntǐ zěnmeyàng?

5 (*talking about age*) 有 yǒu ▸ **how old are you?** 你多大了？ nǐ duōdà le?

6 (*talking about place*) 在 zài ▸ **Madrid is in Spain** 马德里在西班牙 Mǎdélǐ zài Xībānyá ▸ **the supermarket isn't far from here** 超市离这儿不远 chāoshì lí zhè'er bùyuǎn ▸ **I won't be here tomorrow** 我明天不在这儿 wǒ míngtiān bùzài zhè'er ▸ **have you been to Beijing?** 你去过北京吗？ nǐ qùguò Běijīng ma? ▸ **we've been here for ages** 我们已经在这里好久了 wǒmen yǐjīng zài zhèlǐ hǎojiǔ le ▸ **the meeting will be in the canteen** 会议将在食堂举行 huìyì jiāng zài shítáng jǔxíng

7 (*referring to distance*) 有 yǒu ▸ **it's 10 km to the village** 这儿离村庄有10公里 zhè'er lí cūnzhuāng yǒu shí gōnglǐ

8 (*cost*) 花 huā ▸ **how much was the meal?** 这顿饭花了多少钱？ zhèdùn fàn huāle duōshǎo qián? ▸ **that'll be $5 please** 请付5美元 qǐngfù wǔ měiyuán

9 (*linking clauses*) 是 shì ▸ **the problem is that ...** 问题是… wèntí shì...

II AUX VB **1** (*forming continuous tenses*) ▸ **what are you doing?** 你在干什么？ nǐ zài gàn shénme? ▸ **they're coming tomorrow** 他们明天来 tāmen míngtiān lái

2 (*forming passives*) ▸ **to be murdered** 被谋杀 bèi móushā ▸ **he was killed in a car crash** 他在一场车祸中丧生 tā zài yīchǎng chēhuò zhōng sàngshēng

3 (*in tag questions*) ▸ **it was fun,**

wasn't it? 有意思，是不是？ yǒu yìsi, shì bù shì? ▸ **he's good-looking, isn't he?** 他长得不错，是不是？ tā zhǎngde bùcuò, shìbùshì?

beach [bitʃ] N [C] 海滩 hǎitān [片 piàn]
beads [bidz] N PL (*necklace*) 项链 xiàngliàn
beam [bim] N [C] (*of wood, metal*) 梁 liáng [根 gēn]
bean [bin] N [C] 豆 dòu [粒 lì] ▸ **coffee/cocoa beans** 咖啡/可可豆 kāfēi/kěkě dòu
bear [bɛər] (*pt* **bore**, *pp* **borne**) **I** N [C] 熊 xióng [头 tóu] **II** VT **1** (*tolerate*) 容忍 róngrěn **2** (*endure*) 忍受 rěnshòu
beard [bɪərd] N [C] 胡须 húxū [根 gēn]
beat [bit] (*pt* **beat**, *pp* **beaten**) VT (+ *opponent, record*) 击败 jībài
beaten [bitᵊn] PP *of* **beat**
beautiful [byutɪfəl] ADJ **1** 美丽的 měilì de **2** (+ *shot, performance*) 精彩的 jīngcǎi de
beautifully [byutɪfli] ADV 极好地 jíhǎo de
beauty [byuti] N [U] 美 měi
became [bɪkeɪm] PT *of* **become**
because [bɪkɔz, bɪkɒz] CONJ 因为 yīnwéi ▸ **because of** 因为 yīnwéi

> 我们在解释一件事发生的原因时，可以使用 **because**, **as** 或 **since**。**because** 最为常用，并且是唯一可以回答以 **why** 提出的问题。*"Why can't you come?" – "Because I'm too busy."* 在引出含有原因的从句时，尤其是在书面语中，我们可以用 **as** 或 **since** 代替 **because**。*I was rather nervous, as I hadn't seen her for a long time...Since the juice is quite strong, you should always dilute it.*

become [bɪkʌm] (*pt* **became**, *pp* **become**) VI **1** (+ *noun*) 成为 chéngwéi **2** (+ *adj*) 变 biàn
bed [bɛd] N [C] 床 chuáng [张 zhāng] ▸ **to go to bed** 去睡觉 qù shuìjiào
bed and breakfast N [U] 住宿加早餐 zhùsù jiā zǎocān
bedding [bɛdɪŋ] N [U] 床上用品 chuángshang yòngpǐn
bedroom [bɛdrum] N [C] 卧室 wòshì [间 jiān]
bee [bi] N [C] 蜜蜂 mìfēng [只 zhī]
beef [bif] N [U] 牛肉 niúròu ▸ **roast beef** 烤牛肉 kǎo niúròu
been [bɪn] PP *of* **be**
beer [bɪər] N [U] 啤酒 píjiǔ ▸ **would you like a beer?** 你想喝一瓶啤酒吗? nǐ xiǎng hē yīpíng píjiǔ ma?
beet [bit] N [C] (*red vegetable*) 甜菜根 tiáncàigēn [根 gēn]
beetle [bitᵊl] N [C] 甲虫 jiǎchóng [只 zhī]
before [bɪfɔr] **I** PREP 之前 zhīqián **II** CONJ 在…之前 zài...zhīqián **III** ADV 以前 yǐqián ▸ **before doing sth** 在做某事之前 zài zuò mǒushì zhīqián ▸ **I've never seen it before** 我以前从没见过 wǒ yǐqián cóngméi jiànguò
beg [bɛg] VI (*beggar*) 乞讨 qǐtǎo ▸ **I beg your pardon** (*apologizing*) 对不起 duìbùqǐ; (*not hearing*) 请再说一遍 qǐng zàishuō yībiàn
began [bɪgæn] PT *of* **begin**
beggar [bɛgər] N [C] 乞丐 qǐgài [个 gè]
begin [bɪgɪn] (*pt* **began**, *pp* **begun**) **I** VT 开始 kāishǐ **II** VI 开始 kāishǐ ▸ **to begin doing** *or* **to do sth** 开始做某事 kāishǐ zuò mǒushì
beginner [bɪgɪnər] N [C] 初学者 chūxuézhě [位 wèi]
beginning [bɪgɪnɪŋ] N [C] 开始 kāishǐ [个 gè] ▸ **at the beginning** 开始时 kāishǐ shí
begun [bɪgʌn] PP *of* **begin**
behave [bɪheɪv] VI 表现 biǎoxiàn
behavior [bɪheɪvyər] N [U] 举止 jǔzhǐ
behind [bɪhaɪnd] **I** PREP 在…后面 zài...hòumian **II** ADV (*at/towards the back*) 在/向后面 zài/xiàng hòumian

▶ **to be behind (schedule)** 落后于（计划）luòhòu yú (jìhuà) ▶ **to leave sth behind** (*forget*) 落下 luòxià

beige [beɪʒ] ADJ 灰棕色的 huīzōngsè de

Beijing [beɪʒɪŋ] N 北京 Běijīng

Belgian [bɛldʒᵊn] **I** ADJ 比利时的 Bǐlìshí de **II** N [c] (*person*) 比利时人 Bǐlìshírén [个 gè]

Belgium [bɛldʒᵊm] N 比利时 Bǐlìshí

believe [bɪliv] VT 相信 xiāngxìn ▶ **to believe that ...** 认为… rènwéi…

bell [bɛl] N [c] (*on door*) 门铃 ménlíng [个 gè]

belong [bɪlɔŋ] VI ▶ **to belong to** (+ *person*) 属于 shǔyú; (+ *club, society*) 是…的成员 shì…de chéngyuán

belongings [bɪlɔŋɪŋz] N PL 所有物 suǒyǒuwù

below [bɪloʊ] **I** PREP **1** (*beneath*) 在…之下 zài…zhīxià **2** (*less than*) 低于 dīyú **II** ADV **1** (*beneath*) 下面 xiàmian **2** (*less*) 以下 yǐxià ▶ **below zero** 零度以下 língdù yǐxià ▶ **temperatures below normal** *or* **average** 低于正常{或}平均温度 dīyú zhèngcháng (huò) píngjūn wēndù

belt [bɛlt] N [c] 腰带 yāodài [条 tiáo]

bench [bɛntʃ] N [c] 长椅 chángyǐ [条 tiáo]

bend [bɛnd] (*pt, pp* **bent**) **I** VT 使弯曲 shǐ wānqū **II** VI **1** 屈身 qūshēn **2** (*road, river*) 转弯 zhuǎnwān **III** N [c] (*in road, river*) 弯 wān [个 gè]; **bend down** VI 弯腰 wānyāo

beneath [bɪniθ] **I** PREP 在…之下 zài…zhīxià **II** ADV 在下面 zài xiàmian

benefit [bɛnɪfɪt] **I** N [C/U] 好处 hǎochù [个 gè] **II** VI ▶ **to benefit from sth** 从某事中获益 cóng mǒushì zhōng huòyì

bent [bɛnt] **I** PT, PP *of* **bend II** ADJ 弯曲的 wānqū de

berth [bɜrθ] N [c] (*on boat, train*) 卧铺 wòpù [张 zhāng]

beside [bɪsaɪd] PREP 在…旁边 zài…pángbiān; *see also* **besides**

besides [bɪsaɪdz] **I** ADV (*also*: **beside**) (*in addition*) 另外 lìngwài **II** PREP (*also*: **beside**) (*in addition to, as well as*) 除…之外 chú…zhīwài

> **besides** 引出的事物包括在我们所谈及的事情之内。*She is very intelligent besides being very beautiful.* 不过，当我们说 **the only person besides** 另外某人时，或 **the only thing besides** 另外某物时，我们指在某一特定场合或上下文中的惟一其他人或物。*There was only one person besides me who knew where the money was hidden.* 介词 **except** 后面通常跟我们的陈述中惟独不包括的那些物, 人, 事的名词或代词形式。*She spoke to everyone except me.* **except** 也可作连词，引导从句或副词短语。*There was nothing more to do now except wait.* **except** 还可以引出由连词 **that, when** 或 **if** 引导的从句。*The house stayed empty, except when we came for the holidays.* **except for** 是用在名词前的介词短语，用来引出某人或某物，说明要不是有某人或某物，所陈述的便为全部事实。*Everyone was late except for Richard.*

best [bɛst] **I** ADJ 最好的 zuìhǎo de **II** ADV 最 zuì **III** N ▶ **the best** 最好的事物 zuìhǎo de shìwù ▶ **the best thing to do is ...** 最好是… zuìhǎo shì… ▶ **to do** *or* **try one's best** 尽某人最大的努力 jìn mǒurén zuìdà de nǔlì

bet [bɛt] (*pt, pp* **bet** *or* **betted**) **I** N [c] 赌注 dǔzhù [个 gè] **II** VT **1** ▶ **to bet sb 100 dollars that...** 就…和某人赌100美元 jiù…hé mǒurén dǔ yībǎi měiyuán **2** (*expect, guess*) ▶ **to bet (that)** 断定 duàndìng **III** VI ▶ **to bet on** (+ *horse, result*) 下赌注于 xià

dǔzhù yú
better [bɛtər] **I** ADJ **1** (*comparative of "good"*) 更好的 gènghǎo de **2** (*after an illness or injury*) 好转的 hǎozhuǎn de **II** ADV (*comparative of "well"*) 更好地 gènghǎo de ▸ **to get better** (*improve*) 变得更好 biànde gènghǎo; (*sick person*) 渐愈 jiànyù ▸ **to feel better** 感觉好一些 gǎnjué hǎo yīxiē ▸ **I'd** *or* **I had better go** 我得走了 wǒ děi zǒule
between [bɪtwin] **I** PREP **1** (*in space*) 在…中间 zài...zhōngjiān **2** (*in time*) 介于…之间 jièyú...zhījiān **3** (*in amount, age*) 介于…之间 jièyú...zhījiān **II** ADV ▸ **in between** (*in space*) 在…中间 zài...zhōngjiān; (*in time*) 期间 qījiān ▸ **to choose between** 从中选一个 cóngzhōng xuǎn yīgè ▸ **to be shared/divided between people** 由大家一起分享/分用 yóu dàjiā yīqǐ fēnxiǎng/fēnyòng
beyond [bɪyɒnd] **I** PREP **1** 在…的另一边 zài...de lìng yībiān **2** (+ *time, date, age*) 迟于 chíyú **II** ADV **1** (*in space*) 在另一边 zài lìng yībiān **2** (*in time*) 在…之后 zài...zhīhòu
Bible [baɪbᵊl] (*Rel*) N [C] ▸ **the Bible** 圣经 Shèngjīng [部 bù]
bicycle [baɪsɪkᵊl] N [C] 自行车 zìxíngchē [辆 liàng] ▸ **to ride a bicycle** 骑自行车 qí zìxíngchē
big [bɪg] ADJ **1** 大的 dà de **2** (+ *change, increase, problem*) 大的 dà de
bike [baɪk] N [C] **1** (*bicycle*) 自行车 zìxíngchē [辆 liàng] **2** (*motorcycle*) 摩托车 mótuōchē [部 bù]
bikini [bɪkini] N [C] 比基尼 bǐjīní [套 tào]
bill [bɪl] N [C] **1** (*requesting payment*) 账单 zhàngdān [个 gè] **2** (*banknote*) 钞票 chāopiào [张 zhāng]
billfold [bɪlfoʊld] N [C] 钱夹 qiánjiā [个 gè]
binoculars [bɪnɒkyələrz] N PL 双筒望远镜 shuāngtǒng wàngyuǎnjìng
biochemistry [baɪoʊkɛmɪstri] N [U] 生物化学 shēngwù huàxué
biography [baɪɒgrəfi] N [C] 传记 zhuànjì [部 bù]
biology [baɪɒlədʒi] N [U] 生物学 shēngwùxué
bird [bɜrd] N [C] 鸟 niǎo [只 zhī]
birth [bɜrθ] N [C/U] 出生 chūshēng
birth certificate N [C] 出生证明 chūshēng zhèngmíng [个 gè]
birth control N [U] 节育 jiéyù
birthday [bɜrθdeɪ, -di] **I** N [C] 生日 shēngrì [个 gè] **II** CPD (+ *cake, card, present*) 生日 shēngrì
biscuit [bɪskɪt] N [C] 小圆饼 xiǎoyuánbǐng [块 kuài]
bishop [bɪʃəp] N [C] 主教 zhǔjiào [位 wèi]
bit [bɪt] **I** PT *of* **bite II** N [C] **1** (*piece*) 少许 shǎoxǔ **2** (*part*) 部分 bùfen [个 gè] **3** (*Comput*) 比特 bǐtè [个 gè] ▸ **a bit mad/dangerous** 有点疯狂/危险 yǒudiǎn fēngkuáng/wēixiǎn ▸ **for a bit** (*inf*) 一会儿 yīhuǐ'r ▸ **quite a bit** 不少 bùshǎo
bite [baɪt] (*pt* **bit**, *pp* **bitten**) **I** VT 咬 yǎo **II** N [C] **1** (*mouthful*) 口 kǒu **2** (*from dog*) 咬伤 yǎoshāng [处 chù] **3** (*from snake, mosquito*) 咬痕 yǎohén [个 gè] ▸ **to bite one's nails** 咬指甲 yǎo zhǐjia
bitter [bɪtər] ADJ (+ *taste*) 苦的 kǔ de
black [blæk] **I** ADJ **1** 黑色的 hēisè de **2**; (*person*): **Black** 黑人的 hēirén de **3** (+ *tea, coffee*) 不加牛奶的 bù jiā niúnǎi de **II** N [U] 黑色 hēisè; **black out** VI (*faint*) 暂时失去知觉 zànshí shīqù zhījué
blackboard [blækbɔrd] N [C] 黑板 hēibǎn [个 gè]
blackmail [blækmeɪl] **I** N [U] 敲诈 qiāozhà **II** VT 敲诈 qiāozhà
blade [bleɪd] N [C] 刃 rèn
blame [bleɪm] **I** N [U] (*for mistake, crime*) 责备 zébèi **II** VT ▸ **to blame sb for sth** 为某事责备某人 wèi mǒushì zébèi mǒurén ▸ **to be to blame (for sth)** 该(为某事)负责任 gāi (wèi mǒushì) fù zérèn ▸ **to blame sth on sb** 把某事归咎于某人 bǎ mǒushì

guījiù yú mǒurén
blank [blæŋk] ADJ 空白的 kòngbái de
blanket [blæŋkɪt] N [C] 毛毯 máotǎn [床 chuáng]
blast [blæst] N [C] (*explosion*) 爆炸 bàozhà [次 cì]
blaze [bleɪz] **I** N [C] 大火 dàhuǒ [场 chǎng] **II** VI (*fire*) 熊熊燃烧 xióngxióng ránshāo
blazer [bleɪzər] N [C] 上装 shàngzhuāng [件 jiàn]
bled [blɛd] PT, PP *of* **bleed**
bleed [blid] (*pt, pp* **bled**) VI 流血 liúxuè ▸ **my nose is bleeding** 我流鼻血了 wǒ liú bíxuè le
blender [blɛndər] N [C] 搅拌器 jiǎobànqì [个 gè]
bless [blɛs] VT (*Rel*) 赐福 cìfú ▸ **bless you!** (*after sneeze*) 上帝保佑！shàngdì bǎoyòu!
blew [blu] PT *of* **blow**
blind [blaɪnd] **I** ADJ 失明的 shīmíng de **II** N (*for window*) 向上卷的帘子 xiàng shàng juǎn de liánzi **III the blind** N PL (*blind people*) 盲人 mángrén ▸ **to go blind** 失明 shīmíng
blink [blɪŋk] VI 眨眼睛 zhǎ yǎnjīng
blister [blɪstər] N [C] 水泡 shuǐpào [个 gè]
blizzard [blɪzərd] N [C] 暴风雪 bàofēngxuě [场 chǎng]
block [blɒk] **I** N [C] **1** 街区 jiēqū [个 gè] **2** (*of stone, wood, ice*) 块 kuài **II** VT (+ *entrance, road*) 堵塞 dǔsè ▸ **3 blocks from here** 离这里有3个街区那么远 lí zhèlǐ yǒu sāngè jiēqū nàme yuǎn
blond(e) [blɒnd] ADJ **1** (+ *hair*) 金色的 jīnsè de **2** (+ *person*) 金发的人 jīnfà de rén
blood [blʌd] N [U] 血液 xuèyè
blood pressure N [U] 血压 xuèyā ▸ **to have high/low blood pressure** 有高/低血压 yǒu gāo/dī xuèyā ▸ **to take sb's blood pressure** 量某人的血压 liáng mǒurén de xuèyā
blood test N [C] 验血 yànxuè [次 cì] ▸ **to have a blood test** 验血 yànxuè
blouse [blaʊs] N [C] 女士衬衫 nǚshì chènshān [件 jiàn]
blow [bloʊ] (*pt* **blew**, *pp* **blown**) **I** N [C] **1** (*punch*) 拳打 quándǎ [顿 dùn] **2** (*setback*) 打击 dǎjī [个 gè] **II** VI **1** (*wind, sand, dust etc*) 吹 chuī **2** (*person*) 吹气 chuīqì **III** VT (*wind*) 吹 chuī ▸ **to blow one's nose** 擤鼻子 xǐng bízi; **blow away I** VT 吹走 chuīzǒu **II** VI 刮跑 guāpǎo; **blow down** VT (+ *tree, house*) 刮倒 guādǎo; **blow out** VT (+ *flame, candle*) 吹灭 chuīmiè; **blow up I** VI (*explode*) 爆炸 bàozhà **II** VT **1** (*destroy*) 使爆炸 shǐ bàozhà **2** (*inflate*) 冲气 chōngqì
blow-dry N [C] 吹风定型 chuīfēng dìngxíng
blown [bloʊn] PP *of* **blow**
blue [blu] **I** ADJ 蓝色的 lánsè de **II** N [U] 蓝色 lánsè **III blues** N PL (*Mus*) ▸ **the blues** 蓝调 lándiào
blunt [blʌnt] ADJ **1** (*not sharp*) 钝的 dùn de **2** (+ *person, remark*) 直率的 zhíshuài de
blush [blʌʃ] VI 脸红 liǎnhóng
board [bɔrd] **I** N **1** [C] (*piece of wood*) 木板 mùbǎn [块 kuài] **2** [C] (*also*: **blackboard**) 黑板 hēibǎn [个 gè] **3** [C] (*for chess*) 盘 pán **4** [U] (*at hotel*) 膳食 shànshí **II** VT (+ *ship, train, plane*) 上 shàng **III** VI (*frm: on ship, train, plane*) 登上 dēngshang ▸ **on board** 在船/车/飞机上 zài chuán/chē/fēijī shàng
boarding pass [bɔrdɪŋ pæs] N [C] 登机卡 dēngjīkǎ [张 zhāng]
boarding school [bɔrdɪŋ skul] N [C/U] 寄宿学校 jìsù xuéxiào [个 gè]
boast [boʊst] **I** VI ▸ **to boast (about *or* of)** 说(关于某事的)大话 shuō (guānyú mǒushì de) dàhuà **II** N [C] 自夸 zìkuā [种 zhǒng]
boat [boʊt] N [C] **1** (*small vessel*) 船 chuán [艘 sōu] **2** (*ship*) 轮船 lúnchuán [艘 sōu] ▸ **to go by boat** 乘船去 chéngchuán qù

body [bɒdi] N **1** [c] 身体 shēntǐ [个 gè] **2** [c] (*corpse*) 尸体 shītǐ [具 jù]
bodybuilding [bɒdibɪldɪŋ] N [U] 健身 jiànshēn
bodyguard [bɒdigard] N [c] 保镖 bǎobiāo [个 gè]
boil [bɔɪl] **I** VT **1** (+ *water*) 烧开 shāokāi **2** (+ *eggs, potatoes*) 煮 zhǔ **II** VI (*liquid*) 沸腾 fèiténg **III** N (*Med*) 疖子 jiēzi
boiler [bɔɪlər] N [c] (*device*) 锅炉 guōlú [个 gè]
boiling (hot) [bɔɪlɪŋ hɒt] (*inf*) ADJ ▸ **I'm boiling (hot)** 我太热了 wǒ tài rè le
bolt [boʊlt] N [c] **1** (*to lock door*) 插销 chāxiāo [个 gè] **2** (*used with nut*) 螺钉 luódīng [颗 kē]
bomb [bɒm] **I** N [c] 炸弹 zhàdàn [颗 kē] **II** VT 轰炸 hōngzhà
bomber [bɒmər] N [c] **1** (*Aviat*) 轰炸机 hōngzhàjī [架 jià] **2** (*terrorist*) 投放炸弹的人 tóufàng zhàdàn de rén [个 gè]
bombing [bɒmɪŋ] N [c/U] 轰炸 hōngzhà [阵 zhèn]
bone [boʊn] N **1** [c/U] 骨头 gǔtou [根 gēn] **2** [c] (*in fish*) 刺 cì [根 gēn]
bonfire [bɒnfaɪər] N [c] **1** (*as part of a celebration*) 篝火 gōuhuǒ [堆 duī] **2** (*to burn trash*) 火堆 huǒduī [个 gè]
bonus [boʊnəs] N [c] **1** (*extra payment*) 红利 hónglì [份 fèn] **2** (*additional benefit*) 额外收获 éwài shōuhuò [份 fèn]
book [bʊk] **I** N [c] **1** (*novel etc*) 书 shū [本 běn] **2** (*of stamps, tickets*) 册 cè **II** VT (+ *ticket, table, seat, room*) 预订 yùdìng ▸ **fully booked** 预订一空 yùdìng yīkōng
bookcase [bʊkkeɪs] N [c] 书橱 shūchú [个 gè]
booklet [bʊklɪt] N [c] 小册子 xiǎocèzi [本 běn]
bookshelf [bʊkʃɛlf] N [c] 书架 shūjià [个 gè]
bookstore [bʊkstɔr] N [c] 书店 shūdiàn [家 jiā]
boot [but] **I** N [c] (*for winter*) 靴子 xuēzi [双 shuāng]; (*for football, walking*) 鞋 xié [双 shuāng]; **boot up** (*Comput*) **I** VT 使运行 shǐ yùnxíng **II** VI 开始运行 kāishǐ yùnxíng
border [bɔrdər] N [c] 边界 biānjiè [条 tiáo]
bore [bɔr] **I** PT *of* **bear II** VT **1** (+ *hole*) 钻 zuàn **2** (+ *oil well, tunnel*) 开凿 kāizáo **3** (+ *person*) 使厌烦 shǐ yànfán ▸ **to be bored (with sth)** (对某事)不感兴趣 (duì mǒushì) bùgǎn xìngqù
boring [bɔrɪŋ] ADJ 乏味的 fáwèi de
born [bɔrn] ADJ ▸ **to be born** (*baby*) 出生 chūshēng
borrow [bɒroʊ] VT 借 jiè
boss [bɔs] N [c] **1** (*employer*) 老板 lǎobǎn [个 gè] **2** (*inf: leader*) 领导 lǐngdǎo [位 wèi]
both [boʊθ] **I** ADJ 两者都 liǎngzhě dōu **II** PRON **1** (*things*) 两者 liǎngzhě **2** (*people*) 两个 liǎnggè **III** CONJ ▸ **both A and B** A和B两者都 A hé B liǎngzhě dōu ▸ **both of us went, we both went** 我们两个都去了 wǒmen liǎnggè dōuqù le
bother [bɒðər] **I** VT **1** (*worry*) 烦扰 fánrǎo **2** (*disturb*) 打扰 dǎrǎo **II** VI 在乎 zàihu **III** N [U] (*trouble*) 麻烦 máfan ▸ **don't bother** 不用了 bùyòng le
bottle [bɒtᵊl] N **1** [c] 瓶子 píngzi [个 gè] **2** [c] (*amount contained*) 瓶 píng **3** [c] (*baby's*) 奶瓶 nǎipíng [个 gè] ▸ **a bottle of wine/milk** 一瓶葡萄酒/牛奶 yīpíng pútáojiǔ/niúnǎi
bottle opener [bɒtᵊl oʊpənər] N [c] 开瓶器 kāipíngqì [个 gè]
bottom [bɒtəm] **I** N **1** [c] (*of container, sea*) 底部 dǐbù [个 gè] **2** [c] (*of page, list*) 下端 xiàduān [个 gè] **3** [U/S] (*of class, league*) 最后一名 zuìhòu yīmíng **4** [c] (*of hill, tree, stairs*) 最底部 zuìdǐbù [个 gè] **5** [c] (*buttocks*) 臀部 túnbù [个 gè] **II** ADJ (*lowest*) 最下面的 zuì xiàmian de ▸ **at the bottom**

of 在…的底部 zài...de dǐbù
bought [bɔːt] PT, PP *of* **buy**
bound [baʊnd] ADJ ▶ **to be bound to do sth** (*certain*) 一定做某事 yīdìng zuò mǒushì
boundary [baʊndəri] N [c] 边界 biānjiè [个 gè]
bow¹ [bəʊ] N [c] **1** (*knot*) 蝴蝶结 húdiéjié [个 gè] **2** (*weapon*) 弓 gōng [把 bǎ]
bow² [baʊ] **I** VI (*with head, body*) 鞠躬 jūgōng **II** VT (+ *head*) 低头 dītóu
bowl [boʊl] N [c] **1** 碗 wǎn [个 gè] **2** (*contents*) 一碗的量 yī wǎn de liàng **3** (*for washing clothes/dishes*) 盆 pén [个 gè]
bowling [boʊlɪŋ] N [U] 保龄球 bǎolíngqiú ▶ **to go bowling** 打保龄球 dǎ bǎolíngqiú
bow tie [boʊ taɪ] N [c] 蝶形领结 diéxíng lǐngjié [个 gè]
box [bɒks] **I** N [c] **1** (*container*) 盒子 hézi [个 gè] **2** (*contents*) 盒 hé **3** (*also*: **cardboard box**) 纸箱 zhǐxiāng [个 gè] **4** (*crate*) 箱 xiāng **II** VI (*Sport*) 拳击 quánjī
boxer [bɒksər] N [c] 拳击运动员 quánjī yùndòngyuán [位 wèi]
boxer shorts, boxers N PL 平角裤 píngjiǎokù
boxing [bɒksɪŋ] (*Sport*) N [U] 拳击 quánjī
boy [bɔɪ] N [c] **1** (*male child*) 男孩 nánhái [个 gè] **2** (*young man*) 男青年 nán qīngnián [个 gè]
boyfriend [bɔɪfrɛnd] N [c] 男朋友 nánpéngyou [个 gè]
bra [brɑ] N [c] 胸罩 xiōngzhào [件 jiàn]
bracelet [breɪslɪt] N [c] 手镯 shǒuzhuó [只 zhī]
braid [breɪd] N [c] (*plait*) 辫子 biànzi [条 tiáo]
brain [breɪn] N [c] 脑 nǎo [个 gè]
brainy [breɪni] ADJ (*inf*) 聪明的 cōngming de
brake [breɪk] **I** N [c] (*Aut*) 刹车 shāchē [个 gè] **II** VI (*driver, vehicle*) 刹车 shāchē
branch [bræntʃ] N [c] **1** (*of tree*) 树枝 shùzhī [条 tiáo] **2** (*of store*) 分店 fēndiàn [家 jiā]; (*of bank, company*) 分支机构 fēnzhī jīgòu [个 gè]
brand [brænd] N [c] 牌子 páizi [块 kuài]
brand-new ADJ 全新的 quánxīn de
brandy [brændi] N [c/U] 白兰地酒 báilándìjiǔ [瓶 píng]
brass [bræs] N [U] 铜 tóng
brave [breɪv] ADJ **1** 勇敢的 yǒnggǎn de **2** (+ *attempt, smile, action*) 英勇的 yīngyǒng de
Brazil [brəzɪl] N 巴西 Bāxī
bread [brɛd] N [U] 面包 miànbāo
break [breɪk] (*pt* **broke**, *pp* **broken**) **I** VT **1** 打碎 dǎsuì **2** (+ *leg, arm*) 弄断 nòngduàn **3** (+ *promise, contract*) 违背 wéibèi **4** (+ *law, rule*) 违反 wéifǎn **5** (+ *record*) 打破 dǎpò **II** VI 破碎 pòsuì **III** N **1** [c] (*rest*) 休息 xiūxi [次 cì] **2** [c] (*pause, interval*) 间歇 jiànxiē [个 gè] **3** [c] (*fracture*) 骨折 gǔzhé [次 cì] **4** [c] (*holiday*) 休假 xiūjià [次 cì] ▶ **to break the news to sb** 委婉地向某人透露消息 wěiwǎn de xiàng mǒurén tòulù xiāoxi ▶ **to take a break** (*for a few minutes*) 休息一下 xiūxi yīxià ▶ **without a break** 连续不断 liánxù bùduàn; **break down** VI 坏掉 huàidiào; **break in** VI (*burglar*) 破门而入 pòmén ér rù; **break into** VT FUS (+ *house*) 强行进入 qiángxíng jìnrù; **break off** VT **1** (+ *branch, piece of chocolate*) 折断 zhéduàn **2** (+ *engagement, relationship*) 断绝 duànjué; **break out** VI **1** (*begin*) 爆发 bàofā **2** (*escape*) 逃脱 táotuō; **break up** **I** VI **1** (*couple, marriage*) 破裂 pòliè **2** (*meeting, party*) 纷纷离去 fēnfēn líqù **II** VT **1** (+ *fight*) 调停 tiáotíng **2** (+ *meeting, demonstration*) 驱散 qūsàn ▶ **to break up with sb** 同某人分手 tóng mǒurén fēnshǒu
breakdown [breɪkdaʊn] N [c] **1** (*Aut*) 故障 gùzhàng [个 gè] **2** (*of system, talks*) 中断 zhōngduàn [次

cì] 3 (*of marriage*) 破裂 pòliè [个 gè] 4 (*Med*) (*also*: **nervous breakdown**) 精神崩溃 jīngshén bēngkuì [阵 zhèn] ▶ **to have a breakdown** 精神崩溃 jīngshén bēngkuì

breakfast [brɛkfəst] N [c/U] 早餐 zǎocān [顿 dùn]

break-in N [c] 闯入 chuǎngrù

breast [brɛst] N 1 [c] (*of woman*) 乳房 rǔfáng [个 gè] 2 [c/U] (*of chicken, lamb*) 胸脯肉 xiōngpúròu [块 kuài]

breath [brɛθ] N 1 [c/U] (*intake of air*) 呼吸 hūxī [下 xià] 2 [U] (*air from mouth*) 口气 kǒuqì ▶ **out of breath** 上气不接下气 shàngqì bùjiē xiàqì ▶ **bad breath** 口臭 kǒuchòu ▶ **to hold one's breath** 屏住呼吸 bǐngzhù hūxī

breathe [brið] I VT (+ *air*) 呼吸 hūxī II VI 呼吸 hūxī; **breathe in** VI 吸入 xīrù; **breathe out** VI 呼出 hūchū

breed [brid] (*pt, pp* **bred**) I VT (+ *animals*) 繁殖 fánzhí II N [c] 品种 pǐnzhǒng [个 gè]

breeze [briz] N [c] 微风 wēifēng [阵 zhèn]

brewery [bruəri] N [c] 啤酒厂 píjiǔchǎng [家 jiā]

bribe [braɪb] I N [c] 贿赂 huìlù [种 zhǒng] II VT 行贿 xínghuì ▶ **to bribe sb to do sth** 贿赂某人去做某事 huìlù mǒurén qù zuò mǒushì

brick [brɪk] N [c/U] 砖 zhuān [块 kuài]

bride [braɪd] N [c] 新娘 xīnniáng [个 gè]

bridegroom [braɪdgrum] N [c] 新郎 xīnláng [个 gè]

bridesmaid [braɪdzmeɪd] N [c] 伴娘 bànniáng [个 gè]

bridge [brɪdʒ] N 1 [c] 桥 qiáo [座 zuò] 2 [U] (*Cards*) 桥牌 qiáopái

brief [brif] I ADJ 1 短暂的 duǎnzàn de 2 (+ *description, speech*) 简短的 jiǎnduǎn de II **briefs** N PL 1 (*for men*) 男式三角内裤 nánshì sānjiǎo nèikù 2 (*for women*) 女式三角内裤 nǚshì sānjiǎo nèikù

briefcase [brifkeɪs] N [c] 公事包 gōngshìbāo [个 gè]

briefly [brifli] ADV 简短地 jiǎnduǎn de

bright [braɪt] ADJ 1 (+ *light*) 亮的 liàng de 2 (+ *person*) 聪明的 cōngming de; (+ *idea*) 巧妙的 qiǎomiào de 3 (+ *color*) 鲜亮的 xiānliàng de

brilliant [brɪliənt] ADJ 1 (+ *person, mind*) 才华横溢的 cáihuá héngyì de 2 (+ *idea, performance*) 出色的 chūsè de

bring [brɪŋ] (*pt, pp* **brought**) VT (*with you*) 带来 dàilái; (*to sb*) 拿来 nálái; **bring along** VT 随身携带 suíshēn xiédài; **bring back** VT (*return*) 带回来 dài huílái; **bring forward** VT (+ *meeting*) 提前 tíqián; **bring up** VT 1 (+ *child*) 抚养 fǔyǎng 2 (+ *question, subject*) 提出 tíchū

Britain [brɪtᵊn] N (*also*: **Great Britain**) 英国 Yīngguó ▶ **in Britain** 在英国 zài Yīngguó

BRITAIN

Britain 或 **Great Britain** 由英格兰，威尔士，苏格兰和北爱尔兰组成。如指整个不列颠，应慎用 **England** 和 **English**，以免引起苏格兰和北爱尔兰人的不满。**United Kingdom** 作为王国的官方称谓，常简略为 **the UK**，覆盖大不列颠及北爱尔兰。**British Isles** 包括大不列颠，北爱尔兰，爱尔兰共和国（不隶属 **the UK**）和四周岛屿。

British [brɪtɪʃ] I ADJ 英国的 Yīngguó de II N PL ▶ **the British** 英国人 Yīngguórén

broad [brɔd] ADJ 宽的 kuān de ▶ **in broad daylight** 光天化日之下 guāng tiān huà rì zhīxià

broadband [brɔdbænd] N (*Comput*) 宽带 kuāndài

broadcast [brɔdkæst] (*pt, pp* **broadcast**) I N [c] 广播 guǎngbō [段

duàn] **II** VT 播送 bōsòng
broccoli [brɒkəli] N [U] 花椰菜 huāyēcài
brochure [broʊʃʊr] N [C] 小册子 xiǎocèzi [本 běn]
broil [brɔɪl] VT 烤 kǎo
broke [broʊk] **I** PT *of* **break** **II** ADJ (*inf: penniless*) 身无分文的 shēn wú fēnwén de
broken [broʊkən] **I** PP *of* **break** **II** ADJ **1** 破碎的 pòsuì de **2** (+ *machine*) 坏损的 huàisǔn de ▸ **a broken leg** 折断的腿 zhéduàn de tuǐ
bronchitis [brɒŋkaɪtɪs] N [U] 支气管炎 zhīqìguǎnyán
bronze [brɒnz] N **1** [U] (*metal*) 青铜 qīngtóng **2** [C] (*Sport*) (*also*: **bronze medal**) 铜牌 tóngpái [块 kuài]
brooch [broʊtʃ] N [C] 胸针 xiōngzhēn [枚 méi]
brother [brʌðər] N [C] 兄弟 xiōngdì [个 gè]; (*elder*) 哥哥 gēge [个 gè]; (*younger*) 弟弟 dìdi [个 gè]
brother-in-law [brʌðərɪnlɔ] N [C] (*older sister's husband*) 姐夫 jiěfu [个 gè]; (*younger sister's husband*) 妹夫 mèifu [个 gè]; (*husband's older brother*) 大伯子 dàbǎizi [个 gè]; (*husband's younger brother*) 小叔子 xiǎoshūzi [个 gè]; (*wife's older brother*) 内兄 nèixiōng [个 gè]; (*wife's younger brother*) 内弟 nèidì [个 gè]
brought [brɔt] PT, PP *of* **bring**
brown [braʊn] **I** ADJ **1** 褐色的 hèsè de; (+ *hair, eyes*) 棕色的 zōngsè de **2** (*tanned*) 晒黑的 shàihēi de **II** N [U] (*color*) 褐色 hèsè
browse [braʊz] VI (*on the internet*) 浏览 liúlǎn
bruise [bruz] N [C] 青瘀 qīngyū [块 kuài]
brush [brʌʃ] **I** N [C] (*for cleaning, for decorating*) 刷子 shuāzi [把 bǎ]; (*for hair*) 发刷 fàshuā [把 bǎ]; (*artist's*) 画笔 huàbǐ [支 zhī] **II** VT **1** (+ *carpet etc*) 刷 shuā **2** (+ *hair*) 梳 shū ▸ **to brush one's teeth** 刷牙 shuāyá
Brussels sprout [brʌsəlz spraʊt] N [C] 芽甘蓝 yágānlán [个 gè]
bubble [bʌbəl] N [C] 泡 pào [个 gè]
bubble gum N [U] 泡泡糖 pàopàotáng
bucket [bʌkɪt] N [C] **1** (*pail*) 桶 tǒng [个 gè] **2** (*contents*) 一桶 yītǒng
buckle [bʌkəl] **I** N [C] (*on shoe, belt*) 扣环 kòuhuán [个 gè] **II** VT (+ *shoe, belt*) 扣住 kòuzhù
Buddhism [budɪzəm, bud-] N [U] 佛教 Fójiào
Buddhist [budɪst, bud-] **I** ADJ 佛教的 Fójiào de **II** N [C] 佛教徒 Fójiàotú [个 gè]
buffet [bʌfɪt] [bʊfeɪ] N [C] **1** (*in station*) 餐厅 cāntīng [个 gè] **2** (*food*) 自助餐 zìzhùcān [顿 dùn]
bug [bʌg] N [C] **1** (*insect*) 虫子 chóngzi [只 zhī] **2** (*Comput: in program*) 病毒 bìngdú [种 zhǒng] **3** (*inf: virus*) 病菌 bìngjūn [种 zhǒng]
build [bɪld] (*pt, pp* **built**) **I** N [C/U] (*of person*) 体格 tǐgé [种 zhǒng] **II** VT (+ *house, machine*) 建造 jiànzào; **build up** VI (*accumulate*) 积聚 jījù
builder [bɪldər] N [C] (*worker*) 建筑工人 jiànzhù gōngrén [位 wèi]
building [bɪldɪŋ] N [C] 建筑物 jiànzhùwù [座 zuò]
built [bɪlt] **I** PT, PP *of* **build** **II** ADJ ▸ **well-/heavily-built** (+ *person*) 体态优美/粗笨的 tǐtài yōuměi/cūbèn de
bulb [bʌlb] N [C] **1** (*Elec*) 电灯泡 diàndēngpào [个 gè] **2** (*Bot*) 球茎 qiújīng [个 gè]
Bulgaria [bʌlgɛəriə] N 保加利亚 Bǎojiālìyà
bull [bul] N [C] 公牛 gōngniú [头 tóu]
bullet [bulɪt] N [C] 子弹 zǐdàn [发 fā]
bulletin [bulɪtɪn] N [C] (*news update*) 公告 gōnggào [个 gè]
bulletin board N [C] **1** (*Comput*) 公共留言板 gōnggòng liúyánbǎn **2** (*noticeboard*) 布告栏 bùgàolán
bully [buli] **I** N [C] 恃强凌弱者 shìqiáng língruò zhě [个 gè] **II** VT 欺

侮 qīwǔ

bum [bʌm] (*inf*) N [C] (*tramp*) 流浪汉 liúlànghàn [个 gè]

bump [bʌmp] I N [C] 1 (*on head*) 肿包 zhǒngbāo [个 gè] 2 (*on road*) 隆起物 lóngqǐwù [个 gè] II VT (*strike*) 碰 pèng; **bump into** VT FUS 1 (+ *obstacle, person*) 撞到 zhuàngdào 2 (*inf: meet*) 碰见 pèngjiàn

bumpy [bʌmpi] ADJ 崎岖不平的 qíqū bùpíng de

bunch [bʌntʃ] N [C] 1 (*of flowers*) 束 shù 2 (*of keys, bananas, grapes*) 串 chuàn

bungalow [bʌŋgəloʊ] N [C] 平房 píngfáng [间 jiān]

bunk [bʌŋk] N [C] 铺位 pùwèi [个 gè]

burger [bɜrgər] N [C] 汉堡包 hànbǎobāo [个 gè]

burglar [bɜrglər] N [C] 窃贼 qièzéi [个 gè]

burglary [bɜrgləri] N 1 [C] (*act*) 盗窃 dàoqiè [次 cì] 2 [U] (*crime*) 盗窃罪 dàoqièzuì

burn [bɜrn] (*pt, pp* **burned**) I VT 1 焚烧 fénshāo 2 (+ *fuel*) 燃烧 ránshāo II VI 1 (*fire, flame*) 燃烧 ránshāo 2 (*house, car*) 烧着 shāozháo III N [C] 烧伤 shāoshāng [次 cì] ▶ **I've burnt myself!** 我把自己烫伤了！wǒ bǎ zìjǐ tàngshāng le!; **burn down** VI (*house*) 烧毁 shāohuǐ

burnt [bɜrnt] PT, PP *of* **burn**

burst [bɜrst] (*pt, pp* **burst**) VI (*pipe, tyre*) 爆裂 bàoliè ▶ **to burst into flames** 突然着火 tūrán zháohuǒ ▶ **to burst into tears** 突然大哭起来 tūrán dàkū qǐlái ▶ **to burst out laughing** 突然大笑起来 tūrán dàxiào qǐlái

bury [bɛri] VT 1 掩埋 yǎnmái 2 (+ *dead person*) 埋葬 máizàng

bus [bʌs] N [C] 公共汽车 gōnggòng qìchē [辆 liàng]

bus driver N [C] 公共汽车司机 gōnggòng qìchē sījī [位 wèi]

bush [bʊʃ] N [C] 灌木 guànmù [棵 kē]

business [bɪznɪs] N 1 [C] (*firm*) 公司 gōngsī [家 jiā] 2 [U] (*occupation*) 商业 shāngyè 3 [U] (*trade*) 生意 shēngyì ▶ **to be away on business** 出差 chūchāi ▶ **to do business with sb** 和某人做生意 hé mǒurén zuò shēngyì

businessman [bɪznɪsmæn] (*pl* **businessmen**) N [C] 商人 shāngrén [个 gè]

businesswoman [bɪznɪswʊmən] (*pl* **businesswomen**) N [C] 女商人 nǚ shāngrén [个 gè]

bus station N [C] 公共汽车车站 gōnggòng qìchē chēzhàn [个 gè]

bus stop N [C] 公共汽车站 gōnggòng qìchē zhàn [个 gè]

bust [bʌst] N [C] 胸部 xiōngbù

busy [bɪzi] ADJ 1 忙的 máng de 2 (+ *store, street*) 繁忙的 fánmáng de 3 (+ *schedule, time, day*) 忙碌的 mánglù de 4 (*Tel*) 占线的 zhànxiàn de ▶ **I'm busy** 我正忙着呢 wǒ zhèng mángzhe ne

KEYWORD

but [bət, STRONG bʌt] CONJ (*yet, however*) 但是 dànshì ▶ **I'd love to come, but I'm busy** 我想来，但是有事 wǒ xiǎnglái, dànshì yǒushì ▶ **not only ... but also** 不但…而且 bùdàn...érqiě

butcher [bʊtʃər] N [C] 1 肉商 ròushāng [个 gè] 2 (*store*) (*also*: **butcher's**) 肉铺 ròupù [个 gè]

butter [bʌtər] N [U] 黄油 huángyóu

butterfly [bʌtərflaɪ] N [C] 蝴蝶 húdié [只 zhī]

button [bʌtᵊn] N [C] 1 (*on clothes*) 钮扣 niǔkòu [颗 kē] 2 (*on machine*) 按钮 ànniǔ [个 gè] 3 (*badge*) 徽章 huīzhāng [个 gè]

buy [baɪ] (*pt, pp* **bought**) I VT 买 mǎi II N [C] (*purchase*) 所买之物 suǒ mǎi zhī wù [件 jiàn] ▶ **to buy sb sth** 给某人买某物 gěi mǒurén mǎi mǒuwù

▸ **to buy sth off** *or* **from sb** 从某人处购买某物 cóng mǒurén chù gòumǎi mǒuwù

buzz [bʌz] VI (*insect, machine*) 发出嗡嗡声 fāchū wēngwēngshēng

KEYWORD

by [baɪ] I PREP **1** (*referring to cause, agent*) 被 bèi ▸ **a painting by Picasso** 毕加索的画 Bìjiāsuǒ de huà ▸ **surrounded by a fence** 由篱笆围着 yóu líba wéizhe

2 (*referring to method, manner, means*) ▸ **by bus/car/train** 乘公共汽车/汽车/火车 chéng gōnggòng qìchē/qìchē/huǒchē ▸ **to pay by check** 以支票支付 yǐ zhīpiào zhīfù ▸ **by moonlight/candlelight** 借助月光/烛光 jièzhù yuèguāng/zhúguāng

3 (*via, through*) 经由 jīngyóu ▸ **he came in by the back door** 他从后门进来 tā cóng hòumén jìnlai

4 (*close to, beside*) 靠近 kào jìn ▸ **he was standing by the door** 他正站在门边 tā zhèng zhànzài ménbiān ▸ **the house by the river** 河边的房子 hébiān de fángzi

5 (*with times, dates, years*) 以前 yǐqián ▸ **by 4 o'clock** 4点以前 sìdiǎn yǐqián ▸ **by April 7** 4月7号以前 sì yuè qī hào yǐqián ▸ **by now/then** 到如今/那时 dào rújīn/nàshí

6 (*during*) ▸ **by day/night** 在白天/晚上 zài báitiān/wǎnshang

7 (*specifying degree of change*) 相差 xiāngchā ▸ **crime has increased by 10 percent** 犯罪率上升了10% fànzuìlǜ shàngshēng le bǎi fēn zhī shí

8 (*in measurements*) ▸ **a room 3 meters by 4** 一间长3米宽4米的房间 yī jiān cháng sān mǐ kuān sì mǐ de fángjiān

9 (*Math*) ▸ **to divide/multiply by 3** 被3除/乘 bèi sān chú/chéng

10 ▸ **by myself/himself** *etc* (*unaided*) 我/他{等}自己 wǒ/tā {děng} zìjǐ; (*alone*) 我/他{等}单独 wǒ/tā {děng} dāndú

II ADV *see* **go by, pass by** *etc*

如果你说 *I'll be home by ten o'clock*，你的意思是你要在10点或10点以前到家，但绝不会晚于10点。如果你说 *I'll be home before ten o'clock*，你的意思是10点是你到家的最晚时间，你可能9点以前就到家了。如果你说 *I'll be at home until ten o'clock*，你的意思是10点以前你会在家里，但10点以后就不在了。当我们谈论某人写了一本书或剧本，导演了一部电影，作了一部乐曲或画了一幅画时，我们说一部作品是 **by** 那个人或是 **written by** 那个人。*a collection of piano pieces by Mozart* 当我们谈到某人给你写信或留言时，我们说信或留言是 **from** 那个人。*He received a letter from his brother.*

bye(-bye) [baɪ(baɪ)] (*inf*) INT 再见 zàijiàn

C

cab [kæb] N [c] 出租车 chūzūchē [辆 liàng]
cabbage [kæbɪdʒ] N [c/u] 卷心菜 juǎnxīncài [头 tóu]
cabin [kæbɪn] N [c] **1** (*on ship*) 船舱 chuáncāng [个 gè] **2** (*on plane*) 机舱 jīcāng [个 gè]
cable [keɪbᵊl] N **1** [c/u] (*rope*) 缆绳 lǎnshéng [根 gēn] **2** [c/u] (*Elec*) 电缆 diànlǎn [根 gēn]
cable television N [u] 有线电视 yǒuxiàn diànshì
cactus [kæktəs] (*pl* **cactuses** *or* **cacti**) N [c] 仙人掌 xiānrénzhǎng [棵 kē]
cafeteria [kæfɪtɪəriə] N [c] 自助餐厅 zìzhù cāntīng [个 gè]
cage [keɪdʒ] N [c] 笼子 lóngzi [个 gè]
cake [keɪk] N [c/u] (*large*) 蛋糕 dàngāo [块 kuài]; (*small*) 糕点 gāodiǎn [块 kuài]
calculate [kælkyəleɪt] VT 计算 jìsuàn
calculation [kælkyəleɪʃᵊn] N [c/u] (*Math*) 计算 jìsuàn
calculator [kælkyəleɪtər] N [c] 计算器 jìsuànqì [个 gè]
calendar [kælɪndər] N [c] 日历 rìlì [本 běn]
calf [kæf] (*pl* **calves**) N [c] **1** 小牛 xiǎoniú [头 tóu] **2** (*Anat*) 腿肚 tuǐdù [个 gè]
call [kɔl] **I** VT **1** (*name*) 为…取名 wèi...qǔmíng **2** (*address as*) 称呼 chēnghū **3** (*describe as*) 说成是 shuōchéng shì **4** (*shout*) 喊 hǎn **5** (*Tel*) 打电话 dǎ diànhuà **6** (*summon*) 召唤 zhāohuàn **II** VI (*telephone*) 打电话 dǎ diànhuà **III** N **1** [c] (*shout*) 大喊 dà hǎn **2** [c] (*Tel*) 电话 diànhuà [次 cì] **3** [c] (*visit*) 探访 tànfǎng [次 cì] ▸ **to be called sth** (*person*) 被叫某名 bèijiào mǒumíng; (*object*) 被称为某物 bèi chēngwéi mǒuwù ▸ **who's calling?** (*Tel*) 请问是谁? qǐngwèn shìshuí? ▸ **to make a phone call** 打电话 dǎ diànhuà ▸ **to give sb a call** 打电话给某人 dǎ diànhuà gěi mǒurén; **call back I** VI (*Tel*) 再打电话 zài dǎ diànhuà **II** VT (*Tel*) 给…回电话 gěi...huí diànhuà; **call off** VT 取消 qǔxiāo
call center N [c] (*Tel*) 电话中心 diànhuà zhōngxīn [个 gè]
calm [kɑm] ADJ **1** 冷静的 lěngjìng de **2** (+ *sea*) 平静的 píngjìng de; **calm down I** VT (+ *person, animal*) 使平静 shǐ píngjìng **II** VI (*person*) 平静下来 píngjìng xiàlái
calorie [kæləri] N [c] 卡路里 kǎlùlǐ
calves [kævz] N PL *of* **calf**
Cambodia [kæmboʊdiə] N 柬埔寨 Jiǎnpǔzhài
camcorder [kæmkɔrdər] N [c] 摄像放像机 shèxiàng fàngxiàng jī [部 bù]
came [keɪm] PT *of* **come**
camel [kæmᵊl] N [c] 骆驼 luòtuo [头 tóu]
camera [kæmrə] N [c] **1** (*Phot*) 照相机 zhàoxiàngjī [架 jià] **2** (*Cine, TV*) 摄影机 shèyǐngjī [部 bù]
cameraman [kæmrəmæn] (*pl* **cameramen**) N [c] 摄影师 shèyǐngshī [位 wèi]
camp [kæmp] **I** N [c] (*for refugees, prisoners, soldiers*) 营 yíng **II** VI 扎营 zhāyíng ▸ **to go camping** 外出露营 wàichū lùyíng
campaign [kæmpeɪn] N [c] 运动 yùndòng [场 chǎng]
camper [kæmpər] N [c] **1** (*person*) 野营者 yěyíngzhě [个 gè] **2** (*also*: **camper van**) 野营车 yěyíngchē [辆 liàng]
camping [kæmpɪŋ] N [u] 野营 yěyíng
campsite [kæmpsaɪt] N [c] 营地 yíngdì [个 gè]
campus [kæmpəs] N [c] 校园

xiàoyuán [个 gè]

can[1] [kæn] N [C] 1 (*for food, drinks*) 罐头 guàntou [个 gè]; (*for gasoline, oil*) 罐 guàn [个 gè] 2 (*contents*) 一听所装的量 yītīng suǒ zhuāng de liàng [听 tīng] 3 (*contents and container*) 一罐 yīguàn

KEYWORD

can[2] [kən, STRONG kæn] (*negative* **cannot, can't,** *conditional, pt* **could**) AUX VB 1 (*be able to*) 能 néng ▶ **can I help you?** (*in store*) 您要买点儿什么？ nín yào mǎidiǎn'r shénme?; (*in general*) 我能帮你吗？ wǒ néng bāngnǐ ma? ▶ **you can do it if you try** 如果试试的话你是能做的 rúguǒ shìshì de huà nǐ shì néng zuò de ▶ **I can't hear/see anything** 我什么也听/看不见 wǒ shénme yě tīng/kàn bùjiàn

2 (*know how to*) 会 huì ▶ **I can swim/drive** 我会游泳/开车 wǒ huì yóuyǒng/kāichē

3 (*permission, requests*) 可以 kěyǐ ▶ **can I use your phone?** 我可以用你的电话吗？ wǒ kěyǐ yòng nǐde diànhuà ma? ▶ **can you help me?** 你可以帮我一下吗？ nǐ kěyǐ bāng wǒ yīxià ma?

4 (*possibility*) 可能 kěnéng ▶ **he can be very unpleasant** 他有时会非常不高兴 tā yǒushí huì fēicháng bù gāoxìng

can, could 和 **be able to** 都是用来表示某人有能力做某事，后接原形动词。**can** 或 **be able to** 的现在式都可以指现在，但 **can** 更为常用。*They can all read and write...The snake is able to catch small mammals.* **could** 或 **be able to** 的过去式可用来指过去。**will** 或 **shall** 加 **be able to** 则用于表示将来。指在某一特定时间能够做某事，用 **be able to**。*After treatment he was able to return to work.* **can** 和 **could** 用于表示可能性。**could** 指的是某个特定情况下的可能性，而 **can** 则表示一般情况下的可能性。*Many jobs could be lost...Too much salt can be harmful.* 在谈论过去的时候，使用 **could have** 加过去分词形式。*It could have been much worse.* 在谈论规则或表示许可的时候，用 **can** 表示现在，用 **could** 表示过去。*They can leave at any time.* 注意，当表示请求时，**can** 和 **could** 两者都可。*Can I have a drink?... Could we put the fire on?* 但表示建议时只能使用 **could**。*You could phone her and ask.*

Canada [kænədə] N 加拿大 Jiānádà

Canadian [kəneɪdiən] I ADJ 加拿大的 Jiānádà de II N [C] (*person*) 加拿大人 Jiānádàrén [个 gè]

canal [kənæl] N [C] 运河 yùnhé [条 tiáo]

cancel [kænsᵊl] VT 取消 qǔxiāo

cancer [kænsər] N 1 [C/U] (*Med*) 癌症 áizhèng [种 zhǒng] 2 (*Astrol*) ▶ **Cancer** [U] (*sign*) 巨蟹座 Jùxiè Zuò

candidate [kændɪdeɪt] N [C] 1 (*for job*) 候选人 hòuxuǎnrén [位 wèi] 2 (*in exam*) 报考者 bàokǎozhě [个 gè]

candle [kændᵊl] N [C] 蜡烛 làzhú [根 gēn]

candy [kændi] N [C/U] 糖果 tángguǒ [块 kuài]

canned [kænd] ADJ 罐装的 guànzhuāng de

cannot [kænɒt, kənɒt] = **can not**

canoe [kənu] N [C] 独木船 dúmùchuán [艘 sōu]

canoeing [kənuɪŋ] N [U] 划独木船 huá dúmùchuán

can opener [kæn oʊpᵊnᵊr] N [C] 开罐器 kāi guàn qì [个 gè]

can't [kænt] = **can not**
canvas [kænvəs] N [U] 帆布 fānbù
cap [kæp] N [C] 帽 mào [顶 dǐng]
capable [keɪpəbᵊl] ADJ 有能力的 yǒu nénglì de ▶ **to be capable of doing sth** 有做某事的能力 yǒu zuò mǒushì de nénglì
capacity [kəpæsɪti] N [S] (*of container, ship*) 容量 róngliàng; (*of stadium, theater*) 可容纳人数 kě róngnà rénshù
capital [kæpɪtᵊl] N **1** [C] (*city*) 首都 shǒudū [个 gè] **2** [U] (*money*) 资本 zīběn **3** [C] (*also*: **capital letter**) 大写字母 dàxiě zìmù [个 gè] ▶ **capital R/L** *etc* 大写字母R/L(等) dàxiě zìmǔ R/L (děng)
capitalism [kæpɪtᵊlɪzəm] N [U] 资本主义 zīběn zhǔyì
Capricorn [kæprɪkɔrn] N [U] (*sign*) 摩羯座 Mójié Zuò
captain [kæptɪn] N [C] **1** (*of ship*) 船长 chuánzhǎng [位 wèi] **2** (*of plane*) 机长 jīzhǎng [位 wèi] **3** (*of team*) 队长 duìzhǎng [个 gè]
capture [kæptʃər] VT (+ *animal*) 捕获 bǔhuò; (+ *person*) 俘虏 fúlǔ
car [kɑr] N [C] **1** (*Aut*) 汽车 qìchē [辆 liàng] **2** (*Rail*) 车厢 chēxiāng [节 jié] ▶ **by car** 乘汽车 chéng qìchē
carbon [kɑrbən] N [U] 碳 tàn
carbon-neutral [kɑrbənnutrəl] ADJ 碳中和的 tàn zhōnghé de
card [kɑrd] N **1** [C] 卡片 kǎpiàn [张 zhāng] **2** [C] (*also*: **playing card**) 扑克牌 pūkèpái [张 zhāng] **3** [C] (*greetings card*) 贺卡 hèkǎ [张 zhāng] **4** [C] (*also*: **business card**) 名片 míngpiàn [张 zhāng] **5** [C] (*bank card, credit card*) 信用卡 xìnyòngkǎ [张 zhāng] ▶ **to play cards** 打牌 dǎpái
cardigan [kɑrdɪgən] N [C] 开襟毛衣 kāijīn máoyī [件 jiàn]
care [kɛər] **I** N [U] 照顾 zhàogù **II** VI 关心 guānxīn ▶ **with care** 小心 xiǎoxīn ▶ **take care!** (*saying goodbye*) 慢走! mànzǒu! ▶ **to take care of sb** 照顾某人 zhàogù mǒurén ▶ **to take care of sth** (+ *possession, clothes*) 保管某物 bǎoguǎn mǒuwù; (+ *problem, situation*) 处理某物 chǔlǐ mǒuwù ▶ **I don't care** 我不在乎 wǒ bù zàihu; **care about** VT FUS (+ *person, thing, idea*) 关心 guānxīn; **care for** VT FUS 照顾 zhàogù
career [kərɪər] N [C] **1** (*job, profession*) 事业 shìyè [项 xiàng] **2** (*working life*) 生涯 shēngyá [个 gè]
careful [kɛərfəl] ADJ **1** 小心的 xiǎoxīn de **2** (+ *work, thought, analysis*) 仔细的 zǐxì de ▶ **(be) careful!** 小心! xiǎoxīn! ▶ **to be careful with sth** (+ *money*) 谨慎地使用某物 jǐnshèn de shǐyòng mǒuwù; (+ *fragile object*) 小心对待某物 xiǎoxīn duìdài mǒuwù
carefully [kɛərfəli] ADV **1** (*cautiously*) 小心地 xiǎoxīn de **2** (*methodically*) 用心地 yòngxīn de
careless [kɛərlɪs] ADJ (+ *person, worker*) 粗心的 cūxīn de; (+ *driving*) 疏忽的 shūhu de; (+ *mistake*) 疏忽造成的 shūhu zàochéng de ▶ **it was careless of him to let the dog out** 他真不当心，把狗放了出去 tā zhēn bù dāngxīn, bǎ gǒu fàng le chūqù
car ferry N [C] 汽车渡轮 qìchē dùlún [艘 sōu]
cargo [kɑrgoʊ] (*pl* **cargoes**) N [C/U] 货物 huòwù [批 pī]
Caribbean [kærəbiən, kərɪbiən] N ▶ **the Caribbean (Sea)** 加勒比海 Jiālèbǐhǎi
carnival [kɑrnɪvᵊl] N **1** [C/U] (*festival*) 狂欢节 kuánghuānjié [个 gè] **2** [C] (*traveling show*) 游艺团 yóuyìtuán [个 gè]
carpenter [kɑrpɪntər] N [C] 木匠 mùjiàng [个 gè]
carpet [kɑrpɪt] N [C] (*fitted*) 地毯 dìtǎn [条 tiáo]; (*rug*) 小地毯 xiǎo dìtǎn [块 kuài]
car rental [-rɛntᵊl] N [U] 汽车出租 qìchē chūzū
carrot [kærət] N [C/U] 胡萝卜 húluóbo [根 gēn]
carry [kæri] **I** VT **1** (+ *person*) 抱 bào; (*by hand with the arm down*) 提 tí; (*on one's back*) 背 bēi; (*by hand*) 拿 ná **2** (*transport*) (*ship, plane*) 运载

yùnzài; **carry on I** VI 继续 jìxù **II** VT (*continue*) (+ *work, tradition*) ▸ **to carry on with sth** 继续做某事 jìxù zuò mǒushì ▸ **to carry on doing sth** 继续做某事 jìxù zuò mǒushì; **carry out** VT (+ *order, instruction*) 执行 zhíxíng

cart [kɑrt] N [c] **1** 大车 dàchē [辆 liàng] **2** (*also*: **shopping cart**) 手推车 shǒutuīchē [辆 liàng]

carton [kɑrtᵊn] N [c] **1** (*cardboard box*) 纸箱 zhǐxiāng [个 gè] **2** (*of milk, juice, yoghurt*) 容器 róngqì [个 gè]

cartoon [kartun] N [c] **1** (*drawing*) 漫画 mànhuà [幅 fú] **2** (*animated*) 卡通片 kǎtōngpiàn [部 bù]

cartridge [kɑrtrɪdʒ] N [c] **1** (*for gun*) 弹壳 dànké [个 gè] **2** (*for printer*) 墨盒 mòhé [个 gè]

case [keɪs] N **1** [c] (*instance*) 情况 qíngkuàng [种 zhǒng] **2** [c] (*container*) 盒子 hézi [个 gè] ▸ **lower/upper case** 小/大写 xiǎo/dàxiě ▸ **in case he comes** 以防万一他会来 yǐfáng wànyī tā huì lái ▸ **in any case** 无论如何 wúlùn rúhé ▸ **just in case** 以防万一 yǐfáng wànyī ▸ **in that case** 既然是那样 jìrán shì nàyàng

cash [kæʃ] **I** N [U] **1** (*notes and coins*) 现金 xiànjīn **2** (*money*) 现款 xiànkuǎn **II** VT 兑现 duìxiàn ▸ **to pay (in) cash** 付现金 fù xiànjīn

cashew [kæʃu, kæʃu] N [c] (*also*: **cashew nut**) 腰果 yāoguǒ [颗 kē]

cashier [kæʃɪər] N [c] 出纳员 chūnàyuán [个 gè]

cash register N [c] 收银台 shōuyíntái [个 gè]

casino [kəsinoʊ] N [c] 赌场 dǔchǎng [个 gè]

cassette [kəsɛt] N [c] 磁带 cídài [盘 pán]

cast [kæst] N [c] (*Theat*) 演员表 yǎnyuánbiǎo [份 fèn]

castle [kæsᵊl] N [c] 城堡 chéngbǎo [座 zuò]

casual [kæʒuəl] ADJ **1** (*chance*) 漫不经心的 màn bù jīngxīn de **2** (*unconcerned*) 随便的 suíbiàn de **3** (*informal*) 非正式的 fēizhèngshì de

casualty [kæʒuəlti] N [c] (*of war, accident: injured*) 伤病员 shāngbìngyuán [个 gè]; (*dead*) 伤亡人员 shāngwáng rényuán [批 pī]

cat [kæt] N [c] 猫 māo [只 zhī]

catalog [kætᵊlɒg] N [c] **1** (*for mail order*) 目录 mùlù [个 gè] **2** (*of exhibition*) 目录 mùlù [个 gè] **3** (*of library*) 书目 shūmù [个 gè]

catastrophe [kətæstrəfi] N [c] 大灾难 dàzāinàn [场 chǎng]

catch [kætʃ] (*pt, pp* **caught**) VT **1** (+ *animal, fish*) 捕获 bǔhuò; (+ *thief, criminal*) 抓获 zhuāhuò **2** (+ *ball*) 接 jiē **3** (+ *bus, train, plane*) 赶上 gǎnshang **4** (*discover*) (+ *person*) 发现 fāxiàn **5** (+ *flu, illness*) 染上 rǎnshang ▸ **to catch sb doing sth** 撞见某人做某事 zhuàngjiàn mǒurén zuò mǒushì; **catch up** VI **1** 追上 zhuīshang

category [kætɪgɔri] N [c] 种类 zhǒnglèi [个 gè]

catering [keɪtərɪŋ] N [U] 饮食业 yǐnshíyè

cathedral [kəθidrəl] N [c] 大教堂 dàjiàotáng [个 gè]

Catholic [kæθlɪk] **I** ADJ 天主教的 Tiānzhǔjiào de **II** N [c] 天主教徒 Tiānzhǔjiào tú [个 gè]

cattle [kætᵊl] N PL 牛 niú

caught [kɔt] PT, PP *of* **catch**

cauliflower [kɔliflaʊər] N [c/U] 菜花 càihuā [头 tóu]

cause [kɔz] **I** N [c] 起因 qǐyīn [个 gè] **II** VT 导致 dǎozhì ▸ **to cause sb to do sth** 促使某人做某事 cùshǐ mǒurén zuò mǒushì ▸ **to cause sth to happen** 导致某事发生 dǎozhì mǒushì fāshēng

cautious [kɔʃəs] ADJ 谨慎的 jǐnshèn de

cave [keɪv] N [c] 山洞 shāndòng [个 gè]

CD [si di] N ABBR (= **compact disc**) 激

光唱片 jīguāng chàngpiàn
CD player N [C] 激光唱机 jīguāng chàngjī [部 bù]
CD-ROM [si di rɒm] N ABBR (= **compact disc read-only memory**) 光盘只读存储器 guāngpán zhǐdú cúnchǔ qì ▸ **on CD-ROM** 光盘版 guāngpán bǎn
ceiling [siːlɪŋ] N [C] 天花板 tiānhuābǎn [块 kuài]
celebrate [sɛlɪbreɪt] VT 庆祝 qìngzhù
celebrity [sɪlɛbrɪti] N [C] 名人 míngrén [位 wèi]
cell [sɛl] N [C] **1** (*Bio*) 细胞 xìbāo [个 gè] **2** (*in prison*) 牢房 láofáng [间 jiān]
cellar [sɛlər] N [C] 地下室 dìxiàshì [间 jiān]; (*for wine*) 酒窖 jiǔjiào [个 gè]
cello [tʃɛloʊ] N [C] 大提琴 dàtíqín [把 bá]
cellphone [sɛlfoʊn] N [C] 手机 shǒujī [部 bù]
cement [sɪmɛnt] N [U] (*concrete*) 水泥 shuǐní
cemetery [sɛmətɛri] N [C] 墓地 mùdì [处 chù]
cent [sɛnt] N [C] 分 fēn
center [sɛntər] N **1** [C] 中心 zhōngxīn [个 gè] **2** [C] (*building*) 中心can zhōngxīn [个 gè] ▸ **to be at the center of sth** 是某事的关键 shì mǒushì de guānjiàn ▸ **to center** *or* **be centered on** (*focus on*) 集中于 jízhōng yú
centigrade [sɛntɪgreɪd] ADJ 摄氏的 Shèshì de
centimeter [sɛntɪmitər] N [C] 厘米 límǐ
central [sɛntrəl] ADJ 中心的 zhōngxīn de
central heating N [U] 中央供暖系统 zhōngyāng gōngnuǎn xìtǒng
century [sɛntʃəri] N [C] 世纪 shìjì [个 gè] ▸ **the 21st century** 21世纪 èrshíyī shìjì ▸ **in the twenty-first century** 在21世纪 zài èrshíyī shìjì
cereal [sɪəriəl] N **1** [C] (*plant, crop*) 谷类植物 gǔlèi zhíwù [种 zhǒng] **2** [C/U] (*also*: **breakfast cereal**) 谷类食品 gǔlèi shípǐn [种 zhǒng]
ceremony [sɛrɪmoʊni] N [C] 典礼 diǎnlǐ [个 gè]
certain [sɜrtᵊn] ADJ **1** (*sure*) 肯定的 kěndìng de **2** (*some*) 某些 mǒuxiē ▸ **to be certain that...** 肯定… kěndìng... ▸ **to make certain that...** 证实… zhèngshí... ▸ **to be certain of** 肯定 kěndìng ▸ **a certain amount of sth** 一定量的某物 yīdìngliàng de mǒuwù ▸ **to know sth for certain** 确定某事 quèdìng mǒushì
certainly [sɜrtᵊnli] ADV **1** (*undoubtedly*) 无疑地 wúyí de **2** (*of course*) 当然 dāngrán ▸ **certainly not** 绝对不行 juéduì bùxíng
certificate [sərtɪfɪkɪt] N [C] **1** (*of birth, marriage*) 证 zhèng [张 zhāng] **2** (*diploma*) 结业证书 jiéyè zhèngshū [个 gè]
chain [tʃeɪn] N **1** [C/U] 链条 liàntiáo [根 gēn] **2** [C] (*jewellery*) 链子 liànzi [条 tiáo]
chair [tʃɛər] N [C] 椅子 yǐzi [把 bá]; (*armchair*) 扶手椅 fúshǒuyǐ [把 bá]
chairman [tʃɛərmən] (*pl* **chairmen**) N [C] 主席 zhǔxí [位 wèi]
chairwoman [tʃɛərwʊmən] (*pl* **chairwomen**) N [C] 女主席 nǚ zhǔxí [位 wèi]
chalk [tʃɔk] N [C/U] (*for writing*) 粉笔 fěnbǐ [支 zhī]
challenge [tʃælɪndʒ] **I** N [C/U] **1** (*hard task*) 挑战 tiǎozhàn [个 gè] **2** (*to rival, competitor*) 挑战 tiǎozhàn [个 gè] **II** VT (+ *rival, competitor*) 向…挑战 xiàng...tiǎozhàn ▸ **to challenge sb to a fight/game** 挑战某人打架/比赛 tiǎozhàn mǒurén dǎjià/bǐsài
champagne [ʃæmpeɪn] N [C/U] 香槟酒 xiāngbīn jiǔ [瓶 píng]
champion [tʃæmpiən] N [C] 冠军 guànjūn [位 wèi]
championship [tʃæmpiənʃɪp] N [C] 锦标赛 jǐnbiāo sài [届 jiè]
chance [tʃæns] **I** N **1** [C/U] (*likelihood, possibility*) 可能性 kěnéngxìng [种 zhǒng] **2** [S] (*opportunity*) 机会 jīhuì **3** [U] (*luck*) 运气 yùnqi **II** ADJ

(+ *meeting, discovery*) 偶然的 ǒurán de ▸ **he hasn't much chance of winning** 他赢的机会不大 tā yíng de jīhuì bùdà ▸ **the chance to do sth** 做某事的机会 zuò mǒushì de jīhuì ▸ **by chance** 偶然 ǒurán

change [tʃeɪndʒ] **I** VT **1** 改变 gǎibiàn **2** (+ *wheel, battery*) 换 huàn **3** (+ *trains, buses*) 换 huàn **4** (+ *clothes*) 换 huàn **5** (+ *job, address*) 更改 gēnggǎi **6** (+ *diaper*) 换 huàn **7** (+ *money*) 兑换 duìhuàn **II** VI **1** 变化 biànhuà **2** (*change clothes*) 换衣 huànyī **3** (*on bus, train*) 换车 huànchē **III** N **1** [C/U] (*alteration*) 转变 zhuǎnbiàn [种 zhǒng] **2** [S] (*novelty*) 变化 biànhuà **3** [U] (*coins*) 零钱 língqián; (*money returned*) 找头 zhǎotou ▸ **to change one's mind** 改变主意 gǎibiàn zhǔyì ▸ **for a change** 为了改变一下 wèile gǎibiàn yīxià ▸ **a change of clothes/underwear** 一套换洗的衣服/内衣 yītào huànxǐ de yīfu/nèiyī ▸ **small change** 零钱 língqián ▸ **to give sb change for** *or* **of 10 dollars** 给某人10美元的零钱 gěi mǒurén shí měiyuán de língqián ▸ **keep the change!** 不用找了！ bùyòng zhǎole!

channel [tʃænəl] N [C] **1** (*TV*) 频道 píndào [个 gè] **2** (*for water*) 沟渠 gōuqú [条 tiáo] ▸ **the English Channel** 英吉利海峡 Yīngjílì hǎixiá

chaos [keɪɒs] N [U] 混乱 hùnluàn

chapel [tʃæpəl] N [C] (*in hospital, prison, school*) 附属教堂 fùshǔ jiàotáng [个 gè]

chapter [tʃæptər] N [C] 章 zhāng

character [kærɪktər] N **1** [C] 特性 tèxìng [种 zhǒng] **2** [C] (*in novel, film*) 角色 juésè [个 gè] **3** [C] (*letter, symbol*) 字母 zìmǔ [个 gè]

characteristic [kærɪktərɪstɪk] **I** N [C] 特征 tèzhēng [个 gè] **II** ADJ ▸ **to be characteristic of sb/sth** 反映某人/某物的特性 fǎnyìng mǒurén/mǒuwù de tèxìng

charge [tʃɑrdʒ] **I** N [C] 费用 fèiyòng [笔 bǐ] **II** VT **1** (+ *sum of money*) 要价 yàojià; (+ *customer, client*) 收费 shōufèi **2** (*also*: **charge up**) (+ *battery*) 使充电 shǐ chōngdiàn **III charges** N PL 费 fèi ▸ **free of charge** 免费 miǎnfèi ▸ **to be in charge (of sth/sb)** (*of person, machine*) 主管(某事/某人) zhǔguǎn (mǒushì/mǒurén) ▸ **how much do you charge?** 你收费多少？ nǐ shōufèi duōshǎo? ▸ **to charge sb $20 for sth** 因某物收某人20美元 yīn mǒuwù shōu mǒurén èrshí měiyuán

charity [tʃærɪti] N [C] (*organization*) 慈善机构 císhàn jīgòu [个 gè] ▸ **to give money to charity** 把钱捐给慈善团体 bǎ qián juāngěi císhàn tuántǐ

charm [tʃɑrm] N [C/U] (*of place, thing*) 魅力 mèilì [种 zhǒng]; (*of person*) 迷人的特性 mírén de tèxìng [个 gè]

charming [tʃɑrmɪŋ] ADJ (+ *person*) 迷人的 mírén de; (+ *place, custom*) 吸引人的 xīyǐn rén de

chart [tʃɑrt] N [C] 图表 túbiǎo [个 gè]

chase [tʃeɪs] VT 追赶 zhuīgǎn

chat [tʃæt] **I** VI (*also*: **have a chat**) 聊天 liáotiān **II** N [C] (*conversation*) 聊天 liáotiān [次 cì]

chat room (*Comput*) N [C] 聊天室 liáotiānshì [个 gè]

chauvinist [ʃoʊvɪnɪst] N [C] (*also*: **male chauvinist**) 大男子主义者 dànánzǐzhǔyìzhě [个 gè]

cheap [tʃip] ADJ **1** 便宜的 piányi de **2** (+ *ticket*) 降价的 jiàngjià de; (+ *fare, rate*) 廉价的 liánjià de

cheat [tʃit] **I** VI 作弊 zuòbì **II** VT 欺骗 qīpiàn **III** N [C] (*in games, exams*) 作弊者 zuòbìzhě [个 gè]; **cheat on** (*inf*) VT FUS 不忠实于 bù zhōngshí yú

check [tʃɛk] **I** VT **1** 核对 héduì; (+ *passport, ticket*) 检查 jiǎnchá **2** (*also*: **check in**) (+ *luggage*) 托运 tuōyùn **II** VI (*investigate*) 检查 jiǎnchá **III** N [C] **1** (*inspection*) 检查 jiǎnchá [次 cì] **2** (*in restaurant*) 账单 zhàngdān [张 zhāng] **3** (*Fin*) 支

票 zhīpiào [张 zhāng] 4 (*pattern*: *gen pl*) 方格图案 fānggé tú'àn [个 gè] 5 (*mark*) 勾号 gōuhào [个 gè] **IV** ADJ (*also*: **checked**) (+ *pattern, cloth*) 方格图案的 fānggé tú'àn de ▶ **to check sth against sth** 将某物与某物相比较 jiāng mǒuwù yǔ mǒuwù xiāng bǐjiào ▶ **to check with sb** 向某人证实 xiàng mǒurén zhèngshí ▶ **to keep a check on sb/sth** (*watch*) 监视某人/某物 jiānshì mǒurén/mǒuwù ▶ **to pay by check** 用支票付款 yòng zhīpiào fùkuǎn; **check in** VI (*at hotel, clinic*) 登记 dēngjì; (*at airport*) 办理登机手续 bànlǐ dēngjì shǒuxù; **check into** VT 登记入住 dēngjì rùzhù; **check out** VI (*of hotel*) 结账离开 jiézhàng líkāi

checkbook [tʃɛkbʊk] N [c] 支票簿 zhīpiào bù [本 běn]

checked [tʃɛkt] ADJ *see* **check**

checkers [tʃɛkərz] N PL 西洋跳棋 xīyáng tiàoqí

check-in [tʃɛkɪn] (*also*: **check-in desk**) N [c] 旅客验票台 lǚkè yànpiào tái [个 gè]

checkout [tʃɛkaʊt] N [c] 付款台 fùkuǎntái [个 gè]

check-up N [c] (*by doctor*) 体检 tǐjiǎn [次 cì]; (*by dentist*) 牙科检查 yákē jiǎnchá [次 cì]

cheek [tʃik] N 1 [c] 面颊 miànjiá [个 gè] 2 [U] (*impudence*) 厚颜无耻 hòuyánwúchǐ ▶ **to have the cheek to do sth** 居然有脸做某事 jūrán yǒuliǎn zuò mǒushì

cheeky [tʃiki] ADJ 恬不知耻的 tián bù zhī chǐ de

cheer [tʃɪər] **I** VI 欢呼 huānhū **II** N [c] 喝彩 hècǎi [阵 zhèn] ▶ **cheers!** (*toast*) 干杯! gānbēi!; **cheer up** VI 振作起来 zhènzuò qǐlái

cheerful [tʃɪərfəl] ADJ 兴高采烈的 xìnggāocǎiliè de

cheese [tʃiz] N [c/U] 干酪 gānlào [块 kuài]

chef [ʃɛf] N [c] 厨师 chúshī [位 wèi]

chemical [kɛmɪkᵊl] N [c] 化学剂 huàxué jì [种 zhǒng]

chemist [kɛmɪst] N [c] (*scientist*) 化学家 huàxuéjiā [位 wèi]

chemistry [kɛmɪstri] N [U] 化学 huàxué

cherry [tʃɛri] N [c] 1 (*fruit*) 樱桃 yīngtáo [颗 kē] 2 (*also*: **cherry tree**) 樱桃树 yīngtáo shù [棵 kē]

chess [tʃɛs] N [U] 象棋 xiàngqí

chest [tʃɛst] N [c] 1 胸部 xiōngbù 2 (*box*) 箱子 xiāngzi [个 gè]

chestnut [tʃɛsnʌt, -nət] N [c] 栗子 lìzi [颗 kē]

chew [tʃu] VT 嚼 jiáo

chewing gum [tʃuɪŋ gʌm] N [U] 口香糖 kǒuxiāngtáng

chick [tʃɪk] N [c] 小鸟 xiǎoniǎo [只 zhī]

chicken [tʃɪkɪn] N 1 [c] 鸡 jī [只 zhī] 2 [c/U] (*meat*) 鸡肉 jīròu [块 kuài]

chickenpox [tʃɪkɪnpɒks] N [U] 水痘 shuǐdòu

chief [tʃif] **I** N [c] 首领 shǒulǐng [个 gè] **II** ADJ 首要的 shǒuyào de

child [tʃaɪld] (*pl* **children**) N [c] 1 儿童 értóng [个 gè] 2 (*son, daughter*) 孩子 háizi [个 gè] ▶ **she's just had her second child** 她刚生了第二个孩子 tā gāng shēng le dì'èr gè háizi

children [tʃɪldrən] N PL *of* **child**

Chile [tʃɪli] N 智利 Zhìlì

chili [tʃɪli] N [c/U] 辣椒 làjiāo [个 gè]

chill [tʃɪl] VT (+ *food, drinks*) 使冷冻 shǐ lěngdòng ▶ **to catch a chill** 着凉 zháoliáng

chilly [tʃɪli] ADJ 相当冷的 xiāngdāng lěng de

chimney [tʃɪmni] N [c] 烟囱 yāncōng [节 jié]

chin [tʃɪn] N [c] 下巴 xiàba [个 gè]

China [tʃaɪnə] N 中国 Zhōngguó

china [tʃaɪnə] N [U] (*crockery*) 瓷器 cíqì

Chinese [tʃaɪniz] (*pl* **Chinese**) **I** ADJ 中国的 Zhōngguó de **II** N 1 [c] (*person*) 中国人 Zhōngguórén [个 gè] 2 [U] (*language*) 汉语 Hànyǔ

chip [tʃɪp] N [c] 1 (*snack*) 薯片 shǔpiàn [片 piàn] 2 (*Comput*) (*also*:

microchip) 集成电路片 jíchéng diànlù piàn [块 kuài]

chocolate [tʃɔkəlɪt, tʃɔklɪt] I N 1 [U] 巧克力 qiǎokèlì 2 [C/U] (*drinking chocolate*) 巧克力饮料 qiǎokèlì yǐnliào [瓶 píng] 3 [C] (*piece of confectionery*) 巧克力糖 qiǎokèlì táng [块 kuài] II CPD (+ *cake, pudding, mousse*) 巧克力 qiǎokèlì ▶ **bar of chocolate** 巧克力条 qiǎokèlì tiáo ▶ **piece of chocolate** 一块巧克力 yīkuài qiǎokèlì

choice [tʃɔɪs] N 1 [C/U] (*between items*) 选择 xuǎnzé [个 gè] 2 [C] (*option*) 选择 xuǎnzé [个 gè] ▶ **a wide choice** 多种多样 duōzhǒng duōyàng ▶ **to have no/little choice** 没有/没有太多选择 méiyǒu/méiyǒu tàiduō xuǎnzé

choir [kwaɪər] N [C] 合唱团 héchàngtuán [个 gè]

choke [tʃoʊk] VI (*on food, drink*) 噎住 yēzhù; (*with smoke, dust*) 呛 qiàng ▶ **to choke on sth** 被某物噎了 bèi mǒuwù yēle

choose [tʃuz] (*pt* **chose**, *pp* **chosen**) I VT 挑选 tiāoxuǎn II VI ▶ **to choose between** 在…之间作出选择 zài...zhījiān zuòchū xuǎnzé ▶ **to choose to do sth** 选择做某事 xuǎnzé zuò mǒushì

chop [tʃɒp] I VT (+ *vegetables, fruit, meat*) 切 qiē II N [C] (*Culin*) 排骨 páigǔ [根 gēn]; **chop down** VT (+ *tree*) 砍倒 kǎndǎo; **chop up** VT 切 qiē

chopsticks [tʃɒpstɪks] N PL 筷子 kuàizi

chose [tʃoʊz] PT *of* **choose**

chosen [tʃoʊzᵊn] PP *of* **choose**

Christ [kraɪst] N 耶稣 Yēsū

christening [krɪsᵊnɪŋ] N [C] 洗礼 xǐlǐ [次 cì]

Christian [krɪstʃən] I ADJ 基督教的 Jīdūjiào de II N [C] 基督徒 Jīdūtú [个 gè]

Christian name N [C] 教名 jiàomíng [个 gè]

Christmas [krɪsməs] N [C/U] 1 圣诞节 Shèngdàn Jié [个 gè] 2 (*period*) 圣诞节期间 Shèngdàn Jié qījiān ▶ **Merry Christmas!** 圣诞快乐！ Shèngdàn Kuàilè! ▶ **at Christmas** 在圣诞节 zài Shèngdànjié ▶ **for Christmas** 为了圣诞节 wèile Shèngdànjié

Christmas Eve [krɪsməs iv] N [C/U] 圣诞夜 Shèngdàn Yè [个 gè]

Christmas tree N [C] 圣诞树 Shèngdàn shù [棵 kē]

church [tʃɜrtʃ] N [C/U] 教堂 jiàotáng [座 zuò]

cider [saɪdər] N [C/U] (*non-alcoholic*) 苹果汁 píngguǒ zhī [瓶 píng]

cigar [sɪgɑr] N [C] 雪茄烟 xuějiā yān [支 zhī]

cigarette [sɪgərɛt] N [C] 香烟 xiāngyān [支 zhī]

cinema [sɪnɪmə] N [C] 电影院 diànyǐng yuàn [个 gè]

circle [sɜrkᵊl] N [C] 圆圈 yuánquān [个 gè]

circular [sɜrkyələr] N [C] (*letter*) 供传阅的函件 gōng chuányuè de hánjiàn [封 fēng]

circumstances [sɜrkəmstænsiz] N PL 情况 qíngkuàng ▶ **in** *or* **under the circumstances** 在这种情况下 zài zhèzhǒng qíngkuàng xià

circus [sɜrkəs] N [C] 马戏团 mǎxì tuán [个 gè]

citizen [sɪtɪzᵊn] N [C] 公民 gōngmín [个 gè]

citizenship [sɪtɪzᵊnʃɪp] N [U] 公民身份 gōngmín shēnfèn

city [sɪti] N [C] 城市 chéngshì [座 zuò]

civilization [sɪvɪlɪzeɪʃᵊn] N [C/U] 文明 wénmíng [种 zhǒng]

civilized [sɪvɪlaɪzd] ADJ (+ *society, people*) 文明的 wénmíng de

civil war [sɪvɪl-] N [C/U] 内战 nèizhàn [场 chǎng]

claim [kleɪm] I VT 1 (+ *expenses, rights, inheritance*) 要求 yāoqiú 2 (+ *compensation, damages, benefit*) 索取 suǒqǔ II VI (*for insurance*) 提出索赔 tíchū suǒpéi III N [C] 索赔 suǒpéi [项 xiàng] ▶ **to claim** *or* **make**

a claim on one's insurance 提出保险索赔的要求 tíchū bǎoxiǎn suǒpéi de yāoqiú ▸ **insurance claim** 保险索赔要求 bǎoxiǎn suǒpéi yāoqiú

clap [klæp] VI 鼓掌 gǔzhǎng

clarinet [klærɪnɛt] (*Mus*) N [c] 单簧管 dānhuángguǎn [根 gēn]

class [klæs] **I** N **1** [c] (*Scol: group of pupils*) 班级 bānjí [个 gè]; (*lesson*) 课 kè [堂 táng] **2** [c/U] (*social*) 阶级 jiējí [个 gè] **II** VT (*categorize*) ▸ **to class sb/sth as** 将某人/某物分类为 jiāng mǒurén/mǒuwù fēnlèi wéi

classic [klæsɪk] N [c] 经典 jīngdiǎn [种 zhǒng]

classical [klæsɪkᵊl] ADJ **1** (*traditional*) 传统的 chuántǒng de **2** (*Mus*) 古典的 gǔdiǎn de

classmate [klæsmeɪt] N [c] 同学 tóngxué [位 wèi]

classroom [klæsrum] N [c] 教室 jiàoshì [间 jiān]

claw [klɔ] N [c] 爪子 zhuǎzi [只 zhī]

clay [kleɪ] N [U] 黏土 niántǔ

clean [klin] **I** ADJ 干净的 gānjìng de; (+ *water*) 清洁的 qīngjié de **II** VT (+ *car, cooker*) 弄干净 nòng gānjìng; (+ *room*) 打扫 dǎsǎo ▸ **a clean driving record** 未有违章记录的驾照 wèiyǒu wéizhāng jìlù de jiàzhào; **clean up** VT (+ *room, place*) 打扫干净 dǎsǎo gānjìng; (+ *mess*) 整理 zhěnglǐ

cleaner [klinər] N [c] (*person*) 清洁工 qīngjié gōng [位 wèi]

clear [klɪər] **I** ADJ **1** (+ *explanation, account*) 明确的 míngquè de **2** (*visible*) 清晰的 qīngxī de **3** (*audible*) 清晰的 qīngxī de **4** (*obvious*) 无疑的 wúyí de **5** (*transparent*) 透明的 tòumíng de **6** (*unobstructed*) 畅通的 chàngtōng de **II** VT (+ *place, room*) 清空 qīngkōng **III** VI (*weather, sky*) 变晴 biànqíng; (*fog, smoke*) 消散 xiāosàn ▸ **to be clear about sth** 很明确某事 hěn míngquè mǒushì ▸ **to make o.s. clear** 表达清楚 biǎodá qīngchǔ ▸ **to clear the table** 收拾饭桌 shōushi fànzhuō; **clear away** VT 清除 qīngchú; **clear off** (*inf*) VI (*leave*) 走开 zǒukāi; **clear up I** VT **1** (+ *room, mess*) 清理 qīnglǐ **2** (+ *mystery, problem*) 澄清 chéngqīng **II** VI (*tidy up*) 清理 qīnglǐ

clearly [klɪərli] ADV **1** (*explain*) 明确地 míngquè de; (*think*) 清醒地 qīngxǐng de; (*see*) 清楚地 qīngchu de; (*speak, hear*) 清晰地 qīngxī de **2** (*visible, audible*) 清楚地 qīngchu de **3** (*obviously*) 显然 xiǎnrán

clever [klɛvər] ADJ **1** 聪明的 cōngmíng de **2** (*sly, crafty*) 耍小聪明的 shuǎ xiǎocōngmíng de **3** (+ *device, arrangement*) 巧妙的 qiǎomiào de

click [klɪk] **I** N [c] (*Comput*) ▸ **with a click of one's mouse** 按一下鼠标 àn yīxià shǔbiāo [下 xià] **II** VT ▸ **to click on sth** (*Comput*) 点击某处 diǎnjī mǒuchù

client [klaɪənt] N [c] (*of lawyer*) 委托人 wěituōrén [个 gè]; (*of company, restaurant, shop*) 顾客 gùkè [位 wèi]

cliff [klɪf] N [c] 悬崖 xuányá [个 gè]

climate [klaɪmɪt] N [c/U] 气候 qìhòu [种 zhǒng]

climate emergency N [c] 气候紧急情况 qìhòu jǐnjí qíngkuàng

climb [klaɪm] **I** VT (*also*: **climb up**) (+ *tree*) 爬 pá; (+ *mountain, hill*) 攀登 pāndēng; (+ *ladder*) 登 dēng; (+ *stairs, steps*) 上 shàng **II** VI (*person*) 攀爬 pānpá **III** N [c] 攀登 pāndēng [次 cì] ▸ **to go climbing** 去爬山 qù páshān

climber [klaɪmər] N [c] 登山者 dēngshānzhě [个 gè]

climbing [klaɪmɪŋ] N [U] 攀登 pāndēng

clinic [klɪnɪk] (*Med*) N [c] 诊所 zhěnsuǒ [家 jiā]

cloakroom [kloʊkrum] N [c] (*for coats*) 衣帽间 yīmàojiān [个 gè]

clock [klɒk] N [c] 钟 zhōng [个 gè] ▸ **around the clock** (*work, guard*) 日夜不停 rìyè bùtíng; **clock in** VI (*for work*) 打卡上班 dǎkǎ shàngbān; **clock off** VI (*from work*) 打卡下班 dǎkǎ xiàbān; **clock on** VI = **clock in**;

clock out VI = **clock off**
close[1] [kloʊs] **I** ADJ **1** 近的 jìn de **2** (+ *relative*) 直系的 zhíxì de **3** (+ *contest*) 势均力敌的 shìjūnlìdí de **II** ADV (*near*) 紧紧地 jǐnjǐn de ▶ **close to** (*near*) 近 jìn ▶ **a close friend** 一位密友 yīwèi mìyǒu ▶ **close by, close at hand** 在近旁 zài jìnpáng
close[2] [kloʊz] **I** VT **1** 关 guān **2** (+ *store, factory*) 关闭 guānbì **II** VI **1** 关 guān **2** (*store, library*) 关门 guānmén; **close down** VI (*factory, business*) 关闭 guānbì
closed [kloʊzd] ADJ (+ *door, window*) 关着的 guānzhe de; (+ *store, library*) 关着门的 guānzhe mén de; (+ *road*) 封锁着的 fēngsuǒzhe de
closely [kloʊsli] ADV **1** (*examine, watch*) 仔细地 zǐxì de **2** (*connected*) 密切地 mìqiè de
closet [klɒzɪt] N [c] 壁橱 bìchú [个 gè]
cloth [klɔθ] N **1** [c/U] (*fabric*) 布料 bùliào [块 kuài] **2** [c] (*for cleaning, dusting*) 布 bù [块 kuài] **3** [c] (*tablecloth*) 桌布 zhuōbù [块 kuài]
clothes [kloʊz, kloʊðz] N PL 衣服 yīfu ▶ **to take one's clothes off** 脱衣服 tuō yīfu
cloud [klaʊd] N **1** [c/U] 云 yún [片 piàn] **2** [c] (*of smoke, dust*) 雾 wù [团 tuán]; **cloud over** VI 阴云密布 yīnyún mìbù
cloudy [klaʊdi] ADJ 多云的 duōyún de ▶ **it's cloudy** 天阴 tiānyīn
clown [klaʊn] N [c] 小丑 xiǎochǒu [个 gè]
club [klʌb] N [c] **1** 俱乐部 jùlèbù [个 gè] **2** (*Sport*) 俱乐部 jùlèbù [个 gè] **3** (*nightclub*) 夜总会 yèzǒnghuì [家 jiā]
clue [klu] N [c] **1** (*in investigation*) 线索 xiànsuǒ [条 tiáo] **2** (*in crossword, game*) 提示 tíshì [个 gè] ▶ **I haven't a clue** (*inf*) 我一无所知 wǒ yī wú suǒ zhī
clumsy [klʌmzi] ADJ 笨手笨脚的 bènshǒubènjiǎo de
clutch [klʌtʃ] N [c] (*Aut*) 离合器 líhéqì [个 gè]
coach [koʊtʃ] **I** N [c] (*Sport*) 教练 jiàoliàn [位 wèi] **II** VT (*Sport*) 训练 xùnliàn
coal [koʊl] N [U] 煤 méi
coast [koʊst] N [c] 海岸 hǎi'àn [个 gè]
coat [koʊt] N [c] **1** (*overcoat*) 外套 wàitào [件 jiàn] **2** (*of animal*) 皮毛 pímáo [层 céng]
coat hanger N [c] 衣架 yījià [个 gè]
cocaine [koʊkeɪn] N [U] 可卡因 kěkǎyīn
cocoa [koʊkoʊ] N [U] 可可 kěkě
coconut [koʊkənʌt] N [c] (*nut*) 椰子 yēzi [个 gè]
cod [kɒd] (*pl* **cod** *or* **cods**) N [c] (*fish*) 鳕鱼 xuěyú [条 tiáo]
code [koʊd] N **1** [c] (*cipher*) 密码 mìmǎ [个 gè] **2** [c] (*Tel*) 区号 qūhào [个 gè] **3** [c/U] (*Comput, Sci*) 编码 biānmǎ [个 gè]
coffee [kɔfi] N **1** [U] 咖啡 kāfēi **2** [c] (*cup of coffee*) 一杯咖啡 yībēi kāfēi [杯 bēi] ▶ **black coffee** 黑咖啡 hēi kāfēi ▶ **coffee with milk/cream** 牛奶咖啡 niúnǎi kāfēi
coffin [kɔfɪn] N [c] 棺材 guāncai [口 kǒu]
coin [kɔɪn] N [c] 硬币 yìngbì [枚 méi]
coincidence [koʊɪnsɪdəns] N [c/U] 巧合 qiǎohé [种 zhǒng]
Coke® [koʊk] N [U] (*drink*) 可口可乐 Kěkǒu Kělè
cold [koʊld] **I** ADJ (+ *water, object*) 凉的 liáng de; (+ *weather, room, meat*) 冷的 lěng de **II** N **1** [U] (*weather*) ▶ **the cold** 寒冷天气 hánlěng tiānqì **2** [c] (*illness*) 感冒 gǎnmào [次 cì] ▶ **it's cold** 天气寒冷 tiānqì hánlěng ▶ **to be** *or* **feel cold** (*person*) 感到冷 gǎndào lěng ▶ **to catch (a) cold** 患感冒 huàn gǎnmào
collapse [kəlæps] VI 倒坍 dǎotān; (*person*) 倒下 dǎoxià
collar [kɒlər] N [c] 领子 lǐngzi [个 gè]

collarbone [kɒlərboʊn] N [c] 锁骨 suǒgǔ [根 gēn]
colleague [kɒlig] N [c] 同事 tóngshì [个 gè]
collect [kəlɛkt] VT **1** 采集 cǎijí **2** (*as hobby*) 收集 shōují **3** (+ *money, donations*) 募捐 mùjuān ▸ **to call collect, make a collect call** (*Tel*) 打对方付款的电话 dǎ duìfāng fùkuǎn de diànhuà
collection [kəlɛkʃᵊn] N **1** [c] (*of art, stamps*) 收藏品 shōucáng pǐn [件 jiàn] **2** [c] (*for charity, gift*) 募捐 mùjuān [次 cì]
collector [kəlɛktər] N [c] 收藏家 shōucáng jiā [位 wèi]
college [kɒlɪdʒ] N **1** [c/U] (*for further education*) 学院 xuéyuàn [个 gè] **2** [c] (*of university*) 学院 xuéyuàn [个 gè] ▸ **to go to college** 上大学 shàng dàxué
collide [kəlaɪd] VI 碰撞 pèngzhuàng ▸ **to collide with sth/sb** 与某物/某人碰撞 yǔ mǒuwù/mǒurén pèngzhuàng
collision [kəlɪʒᵊn] N [c/U] (*of vehicles*) 碰撞 pèngzhuàng [下 xià]
colonel [kɜrnᵊl] N [c] 上校 shàngxiào [位 wèi]
color [kʌlər] **I** N **1** [c] 颜色 yánsè [种 zhǒng] **2** [c] (*skin color*) 肤色 fūsè [种 zhǒng] **II** VT 给…着色 gěi...zhuósè **III** CPD (+ *film, photograph, television*) 彩色 cǎisè ▸ **in color** (+ *film, illustrations*) 彩色 cǎisè
colorful [kʌlərfəl] ADJ 色泽鲜艳的 sèzé xiānyàn de
column [kɒləm] N [c] (*Archit*) 支柱 zhīzhù [个 gè]
comb [koʊm] **I** N [c] 梳子 shūzi [把 bǎ] **II** VT 梳理 shūlǐ
combination [kɒmbɪneɪʃᵊn] N [c] 混合 hùnhé [种 zhǒng]
combine [kəmbaɪn] **I** VT ▸ **to combine sth with sth** 将某物与某物结合起来 jiāng mǒuwù yǔ mǒuwù jiéhé qǐlái **II** VI (*qualities, situations*) 结合 jiéhé; (*people, groups*) 组合 zǔhé ▸ **a combined effort** 协力 xiélì

KEYWORD

come [kʌm] (*pt* **came**, *pp* **come**) VI
1 来 lái ▸ **come here!** 到这儿来! dào zhè'r lái! ▸ **can I come too?** 我也能来吗? wǒ yěnéng láima? ▸ **come with me** 跟我来 gēn wǒ lái ▸ **a girl came into the room** 一个女孩进了房间 yīgè nǚhái jìnle fángjiān ▸ **why don't you come to lunch on Saturday?** 何不星期六过来吃午饭呢? hébù xīngqīliù guòlái chī wǔfàn ne? ▸ **he's come here to work** 他已经到了这儿工作 tā yǐjīng dàole zhè'r gōngzuò
2 ▸ **to come to** (*reach*) 到达 dàodá; (*amount to*) 达到 dádào ▸ **to come to a decision** 做出决定 zuòchū juédìng ▸ **the bill came to $40** 账单共计40美元 zhàngdān gòngjì sìshí měiyuán
3 (*be, become*) ▸ **to come first/second/last** *etc* (*in series*) 排在第一/第二/最后{等} páizài dìyī/dì'èr/zuìhòu{děng}; (*in competition, race*) 位居第一/第二/最后{等} wèijū dìyī/dì'èr/zuìhòu{děng}
▸ **come across** VT FUS 偶然发现 ǒurán fāxiàn
▸ **come apart** VI 裂成碎片 lièchéng suìpiàn
▸ **come back** VI (*return*) 回来 huílái
▸ **come down** VI **1** (*price*) 降低 jiàngdī
2 (*plane*) 坠落 zhuìluò
3 (*descend*) 降下 jiàngxià
▸ **come forward** VI (*volunteer*) 自告奋勇 zìgàofènyǒng
▸ **come from** VT FUS 来自 láizì ▸ **I come from New York** 我来自纽约 wǒ láizì Niǔyuē ▸ **where do you come from?** 你是哪里人? nǐ shì nǎlǐ rén?
▸ **come in** VI 进入 jìnrù ▸ **come in!** 进来! jìnlai!
▸ **come off** VI (*button, handle*) 脱落 tuōluò

▶ **come on** VI (*progress*) 进展 jìnzhǎn
▶ **come on!** (*giving encouragement*) 来！ lái!; (*hurry up*) 快一点！ kuàiyīdiǎn!
▶ **come out** VI **1** (*person*) 出去 chūqù
2 (*sun*) 出现 chūxiàn
3 (*book*) 出版 chūbǎn; (*film*) 上映 shàngyìng
▶ **come through** VT FUS (*survive*) 经历…而幸存 jīnglì...ér xìngcún
▶ **come to** VI (*regain consciousness*) 苏醒 sūxǐng
▶ **come up** VI **1** (*approach*) 走近 zǒujìn
2 (*problem, opportunity*) 突然出现 tūrán chūxiàn
▶ **come up to** VT FUS **1** (*approach*) 走近 zǒujìn
2 (*meet*) ▶ **the film didn't come up to our expectations** 电影没有我们预期的那么好 diànyǐng méiyǒu wǒmen yùqī de nàme hǎo

comedian [kəmiːdiən] (*Theat, TV*) N [C] 喜剧演员 xǐjù yǎnyuán [个 gè]
comedy [kɒmədi] N **1** [U] (*humour*) 幽默 yōumò **2** [C] (*play, film*) 喜剧 xǐjù [部 bù]
comfortable [kʌmftəbᵊl, -fərtəbᵊl] ADJ **1** (*person*) ▶ **to be comfortable** 舒服的 shūfu de **2** (+ *furniture, room, clothes*) 使人舒服的 shǐ rén shūfu de ▶ **to make o.s. comfortable** 自在点 zìzài diǎn
comforter [kʌmfərtər] N [C] (*quilt*) 羽绒被 yǔróngbèi [床 chuáng]
comic strip N [C] 系列幽默画 xìliè yōumò huà [套 tào]
comma [kɒmə] N [C] 逗号 dòuhào [个 gè]
command [kəmænd] N **1** [C] (*order*) 命令 mìnglìng [项 xiàng] **2** [C] (*Comput*) 指令 zhǐlìng [个 gè]
comment [kɒmɛnt] **I** N [C/U] 评论 pínglùn [种 zhǒng] **II** VI ▶ **to comment (on sth)** (对某事)发表意见 (duì mǒushì) fābiǎo yìjiàn ▶ **"no comment"** "无可奉告" "wú kě fèng gào"
commentary [kɒmənteri] N [C/U] 实况报道 shíkuàng bàodào [段 duàn]
commentator [kɒmənteɪtər] N [C] 解说员 jiěshuōyuán [位 wèi]
commercial [kəmɜrʃᵊl] **I** ADJ (+ *success, failure*) 从盈利角度出发 cóng yínglì jiǎodù chūfā; (+ *television, radio*) 商业性的 shāngyè xìng de **II** N [C] (*advertisement*) 广告 guǎnggào [则 zé]
commit [kəmɪt] VT 犯 fàn ▶ **to commit suicide** 自杀 zìshā
committee [kəmɪti] N [C] 委员会 wěiyuánhuì [个 gè]
common [kɒmən] ADJ 常见的 chángjiàn de ▶ **to have sth in common** (+ *people*) 有某些共同点 yǒu mǒuxiē gòngtóngdiǎn; (*things*) 有共同的某特征 yǒu gòngtóng de mǒutèzhēng ▶ **to have sth in common with sb/sth** 与某人/某物有某共同点 yǔ mǒurén/mǒuwù yǒu mǒu gòngtóngdiǎn
common sense N [U] 常识 chángshí
communicate [kəmyuːnɪkeɪt] VI 联络 liánluò
communication [kəmyuːnɪkeɪʃᵊn] **I** N [U] 交流 jiāoliú **II communications** N PL 通讯 tōngxùn
communism [kɒmyənɪzəm] N [U] 共产主义 gòngchǎnzhǔyì
community [kəmyuːnɪti] N [C] 社区 shèqū [个 gè]
commute [kəmyuːt] VI 乘车上下班 chéngchē shàngxiàbān ▶ **to commute to/from Manhattan/Baltimore** 去/从曼哈顿/巴尔的摩乘车上下班 qù/cóng Mànhādùn/Bā'ěrdìmó chéngchē shàngxià bān
compact disc N [C] 激光唱片 jīguāng chàngpiàn [张 zhāng]
company [kʌmpəni] N **1** [C] (*firm*) 公司 gōngsī [个 gè] **2** [U] (*companionship*) 交往 jiāowǎng ▶ **to keep sb company** 陪伴某人 péibàn mǒurén

comparatively [kəmpærətɪvli] ADV (+ *easy, safe, peaceful*) 相对地 xiāngduì de

compare [kəmpɛər] I VT 比较 bǐjiào II VI ▸ **to compare favorably/unfavorably (with sth/sb)** 比得上/比不上(某物/某人) bǐdeshang/bǐbùshang (mǒuwù/mǒurén) ▸ **to compare sb/sth to** 把某人/某物比作 bǎ mǒurén/mǒuwù bǐzuò ▸ **compared with** *or* **to** 与…相比 yǔ...xiāngbǐ ▸ **how does he compare with his predecessor?** 和他前任比起来他怎么样？ hé tā qiánrèn bǐ qǐlái tā zěnmeyàng?

comparison [kəmpærɪsən] N [C/U] 比较 bǐjiào [种 zhǒng] ▸ **in** *or* **by comparison (with)** (与…)比较起来 (yǔ...) bǐjiào qǐlái

compartment [kəmpɑrtmənt] N [C] (*Rail*) 隔间 géjiàn [个 gè]

compass [kʌmpəs] N [C] 指南针 zhǐnánzhēn [个 gè]

compatible [kəmpætɪbᵊl] ADJ (+ *people*) 意气相投的 yìqì xiāngtóu de; (*Comput*) 兼容的 jiānróng de ▸ **to be compatible with sth** (*Comput*) 与某物兼容 yǔ mǒuwù jiānróng

compensation [kɒmpənseɪʃᵊn] N [U] 赔偿金 péicháng jīn ▸ **compensation for sth** 因某事而获得的赔偿金 yīn mǒushì ér huòdé de péichángjīn

compete [kəmpit] VI (*companies, rivals*) 竞争 jìngzhēng; (*in contest, game*) 比赛 bǐsài ▸ **to compete for sth** (*companies, rivals*) 争夺某物 zhēngduó mǒuwù; (*in contest, game*) 争夺某物 zhēngduó móuwù ▸ **to compete with sb/sth (for sth)** (*companies, rivals*) 与某人/某物竞争(以得到某物) yǔ mǒurén/mǒuwù jìngzhēng (yǐ dédào mǒuwù); (*in contest, game*) 与某人/某物竞争(以获得某奖项) yǔ mǒurén/mǒuwù jìngzhēng (yǐ huòdé mǒu jiǎngxiàng)

competent [kɒmpɪtənt] ADJ 称职的 chènzhí de; (+ *piece of work*) 合格的 hégé de

competition [kɒmpɪtɪʃᵊn] N 1 [U] (*rivalry*) 竞争 jìngzhēng 2 [C] (*contest*) 竞赛 jìngsài [项 xiàng] ▸ **in competition with** 与…竞争 yǔ...jìngzhēng

competitive [kəmpɛtɪtɪv] ADJ 1 (+ *industry, society*) 竞争性的 jìngzhēngxìng de 2 (+ *person*) 求胜心切的 qiúshèngxīnqìe de

competitor [kəmpɛtɪtər] N [C] 1 (*in business*) 竞争对手 jìngzhēng duìshǒu [个 gè] 2 (*participant*) 参赛者 cānsàizhě [个 gè]

complain [kəmpleɪn] VI ▸ **to complain (about sth)** (就某事)投诉 (jiù mǒushì) tóusù; (*grumble*) (就某事)诉苦 (jiù mǒushì) sùkǔ ▸ **to complain to sb (about sth)** (就某事)向某人投诉 (jiù mǒushì) xiàng mǒurén tóusù

complaint [kəmpleɪnt] N [C] 抱怨 bàoyuàn [个 gè] ▸ **to make a complaint (to sb)** (向某人)投诉 (xiàng mǒurén) tóusù

complete [kəmplit] I ADJ 1 完全的 wánquán de 2 (*whole*) 完整的 wánzhěng de 3 (*finished*) 完成的 wánchéng de II VT 1 完成 wánchéng 2 (+ *form, coupon*) 填写 tiánxiě ▸ **complete with** 附带 fùdài

completely [kəmplitli] ADV (*different, satisfied, untrue*) 完全 wánquán; (*forget, destroy*) 彻底 chèdǐ

complexion [kəmplɛkʃᵊn] N [C] 面色 miànsè [种 zhǒng]

complicated [kɒmplɪkeɪtɪd] ADJ 复杂的 fùzá de

compliment [*n* kɒmplɪmənt, *vb* kɒmplɪmɛnt] I N [C] 赞美 zànměi [种 zhǒng] II VT 赞美 zànměi ▸ **to pay sb a compliment** 赞美某人 zànměi mǒurén ▸ **to compliment sb on sth** 为某事赞美某人 wèi mǒushì zànměi mǒurén

composer [kəmpoʊzər] N [C] 作曲家 zuòqǔjiā [位 wèi]

comprehension [kɒmprɪhɛnʃᵊn]

N 1 [U] (*understanding*) 理解 lǐjiě 2 [C/U] (*Scol*) 理解力练习 lǐjiělì liànxí [项 xiàng]

comprehensive [kɒmprɪhɛnsɪv] ADJ 1 (+ *review, list*) 全面的 quánmiàn de 2 (+ *insurance*) 综合的 zōnghé de

compulsory [kəmpʌlsəri] ADJ 必须的 bìxū de; (+ *course*) 必修的 bìxiū de

computer [kəmpyuːtər] I N [C] 计算机 jìsuànjī [台 tái] II CPD (+ *language, program, system, technology etc*) 电脑 diànnǎo

computer game N [C] 电脑游戏 diànnǎo yóuxì [局 jú]

computer programmer N [C] 电脑编程员 diànnǎo biānchéngyuán [位 wèi]

computer science N [U] 计算机科学 jìsuànjī kēxué

computing [kəmpyuːtɪŋ] I N [U] 计算机运用 jìsuànjī yùnyòng; (*also*: **computing studies**) 计算机学 jìsuànjīxué II CPD (+ *course, skills*) 电脑 diànnǎo

concentrate [kɒnsəntreɪt] VI 集中精力 jízhōng jīnglì ▸ **to concentrate on sth** (*keep attention on*) 全神贯注于某事 quán shén guàn zhù yú mǒushì; (*focus on*) 集中注意力于某事 jízhōng zhùyìlì yú mǒushì

concentration [kɒnsəntreɪʃən] N [U] 专心 zhuānxīn

concern [kənsɜrn] I N [U] (*anxiety*) 担忧 dānyōu II VT (*worry*) 使担忧 shǐ dānyōu ▸ **concern for sb** 为某人担心 wèi mǒurén dānxīn ▸ **as far as I'm concerned** 据我看来 jù wǒ kànlái ▸ **the people concerned** (*in question*) 有关人士 yǒuguān rénshì

concerned [kənsɜrnd] ADJ (*worried*) 担心的 dānxīn de ▸ **to be concerned about sb/sth** 担心某人/某事 dānxīn mǒurén/mǒushì

concerning [kənsɜrnɪŋ] PREP 关于 guānyú

concert [kɒnsərt] N [C] 音乐会 yīnyuèhuì [个 gè]

concert hall N [C] 音乐厅 yīnyuètīng [个 gè]

conclusion [kənkluːʒən] N 1 [S] (*end*) 结尾 jiéwěi 2 [C] (*deduction*) 结论 jiélùn [个 gè] ▸ **to come to the conclusion that...** 得出的结论是… déchū de jiélùn shì...

concrete [kɒŋkrit] I N [U] 混凝土 hùnníngtǔ II ADJ 1 (+ *block, floor*) 混凝土的 hùnníngtǔ de 2 (+ *proposal, evidence*) 确实的 quèshí de

condemn [kəndɛm] VT (*denounce*) 谴责 qiǎnzé

condition [kəndɪʃən] I N 1 [S] (*state*) 状态 zhuàngtài 2 [C] (*stipulation*) 条件 tiáojiàn [个 gè] II **conditions** N PL 环境 huánjìng ▸ **in good/poor condition** 状况良好/不好 zhuàngkuàng liánghǎo/bùhǎo ▸ **weather conditions** 天气形势 tiānqì xíngshì ▸ **on condition that...** 在…条件下 zài...tiáojiàn xià

conditional [kəndɪʃənəl] I ADJ 有条件的 yǒu tiáojiàn de II N (*Ling*) ▸ **the conditional** 条件从句 tiáojiàn cóngjù

conditioner [kəndɪʃənər] N [C/U] 护发素 hùfàsù [种 zhǒng]

condom [kɒndəm] N [C] 安全套 ānquán tào [只 zhī]

conduct [kəndʌkt] VT (+ *orchestra, choir*) 指挥 zhǐhuī

conductor [kəndʌktər] N [C] 1 (*of orchestra*) 指挥家 zhǐhuījiā [位 wèi] 2 (*on train*) 列车员 lièchēyuán [位 wèi]

cone [koʊn] N [C] 1 (*shape*) 圆锥体 yuánzhuītǐ [个 gè] 2 (*also*: **ice cream cone**) 锥形蛋卷冰淇淋 zhuīxíng dànjuǎn bīngqílín [个 gè]

conference [kɒnfərəns, -frəns] N [C] 会议 huìyì [次 cì]

confess [kənfɛs] VI 坦白 tǎnbái ▸ **to confess to sth/to doing sth** 承认某事/做了某事 chéngrèn mǒushì/zuòle mǒushì

confession [kənfɛʃən] N [C/U] (*admission*) 坦白 tǎnbái [种 zhǒng]

▶ **to make a confession** 坦白 tǎnbái
confidence [kɒnfɪdəns] N **1** [U] (*faith*) 信赖 xìnlài **2** [U] (*self-assurance*) 自信 zìxìn ▶ **in confidence** 秘密地 mìmì de
confident [kɒnfɪdənt] ADJ (*self-assured*) 自信的 zìxìn de ▶ **to be confident that...** 有信心… yǒu xìnxīn...
confidential [kɒnfɪdɛnʃᵊl] ADJ 机密的 jīmì de
confirm [kənfɜrm] VT 肯定 kěndìng; (+ *appointment, date*) 确认 quèrèn
confiscate [kɒnfɪskeɪt] VT 没收 mòshōu ▶ **to confiscate sth from sb** 没收某人的某物 mòshōu mǒurén de mǒuwù
confuse [kənfyuz] VT **1** (*perplex*) 把…弄糊涂 bǎ...nòng hútu **2** (*mix up*) 混淆 hùnxiáo
confused [kənfyuzd] ADJ 困惑的 kùnhuò de
confusing [kənfyuzɪŋ] ADJ 含混不清的 hánhùn bùqīng de
confusion [kənfyuʒᵊn] N **1** [C/U] (*uncertainty*) 惶惑 huánghuò [种 zhǒng] **2** [U] (*mix-up*) 混淆 hùnxiáo
congratulate [kəngrætʃəleɪt] VT 祝贺 zhùhè ▶ **to congratulate sb on sth/on doing sth** 祝贺某人某事/做某事 zhùhè mǒurén mǒushì/zuò mǒushì
congratulations [kəngrætʃəleɪʃᵊnz] N PL 祝贺 zhùhè ▶ **congratulations on your engagement!** 祝贺你订婚了! zhùhè nǐ dìnghūn le!
Congress [kɒŋgres] N 国会 guóhuì

Congress

国会是美国的立法机构，由参议院和众议院组成。各州在参议院中均有两名议员作为其代表；而众议院的435个席位则按各州人口比例分配。国会议案需在参、众两院讨论通过，出现的分歧由一个两院联席协调委员会做出调解。参、众两院均可以三分之二多数票推翻总统否决。

congressman [kɒŋgrɪsmən] (*pl* **congressmen**) N [C] 国会议员 guóhuì yìyuán [位 wèi]
congresswoman [kɒŋgrɪswʊmən] (*pl* **congresswomen**) N [C] 女国会议员 nǚ guóhuì yìyuán [位 wèi]
connection [kənɛkʃᵊn] N **1** [C/U] (*link*) 联系 liánxì [种 zhǒng] **2** [C] (*Elec*) 接头 jiētóu [个 gè] **3** [C] (*train, plane*) 联运 liányùn [种 zhǒng] ▶ **what is the connection between them?** 他们之间有什么关系? tāmen zhījiān yǒu shénme guānxi?
conscience [kɒnʃᵊns] N [C] 是非感 shìfēi gǎn [种 zhǒng] ▶ **to have a guilty/clear conscience** 感到内疚/问心无愧 gǎndào nèijiù/wèn xīn wú kuì
conscientious [kɒnʃiɛnʃəs] ADJ 认真的 rènzhēn de
conscious [kɒnʃəs] ADJ **1** (*awake*) 清醒的 qīngxǐng de **2** (+ *decision, effort*) 蓄意的 xùyì de ▶ **to be conscious of sth** 意识到某事 yìshi dào mǒushì
consciousness [kɒnʃəsnɪs] N [U] (*Med*) 知觉 zhījué ▶ **to lose consciousness** 失去知觉 shīqù zhījué
consequence [kɒnsɪkwɛns, -kwəns] N [C] 后果 hòuguǒ [种 zhǒng]
consequently [kɒnsɪkwɛntli, -kwəntli] ADV 所以 suǒyǐ
conservation [kɒnsərveɪʃᵊn] N [U] (*of environment*) 环保 huánbǎo; (*of energy*) 节约 jiéyuē
conservative [kənsɜrvətɪv] ADJ (*traditional*) 保守的 bǎoshǒu de
conservatory [kənsɜrvətɔri] N [C] 暖房 nuǎnfáng [间 jiān]
consider [kənsɪdər] VT **1** (*think about*) 考虑 kǎolǜ **2** (*take into account*) 考虑到 kǎolǜ dào
considerate [kənsɪdərɪt] ADJ 体贴的 tǐtiē de
considering [kənsɪdərɪŋ] **I** PREP 考

虑到 kǎolǜ dào **II** CONJ ▶ **considering (that)...** 考虑到… kǎolǜ dào...
consist [kənsɪst] VI ▶ **to consist of** 由…组成 yóu...zǔchéng
consonant [kɒnsənənt] N [C] 辅音 fǔyīn [个 gè]
constant [kɒnstənt] ADJ **1** (+ *threat, pressure, pain, reminder*) 不断的 bùduàn de **2** (+ *interruptions, demands*) 重复的 chóngfù de **3** (+ *temperature, speed*) 恒定的 héngdìng de
constantly [kɒnstəntli] ADV **1** (*repeatedly*) 不断地 bùduàn de **2** (*uninterruptedly*) 持续地 chíxù de
constipated [kɒnstɪpeɪtɪd] ADJ 便秘的 biànmì de
construct [kənstrʌkt] VT 建造 jiànzào
construction [kənstrʌkʃ°n] N **1** [U] (*of building, road, machine*) 建造 jiànzào **2** [C] (*structure*) 建筑 jiànzhù [座 zuò]
consult [kənsʌlt] VT (+ *doctor, lawyer, friend*) 咨询 zīxún; (+ *book, map*) 查阅 cháyuè
consumer [kənsumər] N [C] (*of goods, services*) 消费者 xiāofèizhě [个 gè]; (*of resources*) 使用者 shǐyòngzhě [个 gè]
contact [kɒntækt] **I** N **1** [C/U] (*communication*) 联络 liánluò [种 zhǒng] **2** [C] (*person*) 熟人 shúrén [个 gè] **II** VT 联系 liánxì ▶ **to be in contact with sb** 与某人有联络 yǔ mǒurén yǒu liánluò
contact lenses N PL 隐形眼镜 yǐnxíng yǎnjìng
contactless [kɒntæktlɪs] ADJ (*payment, technology*) 非接触式的 fēi jiēchù shì de
contain [kənteɪn] VT (+ *objects*) 装有 zhuāngyǒu; (+ *component, ingredient*) 含有 hányǒu
container [kənteɪnər] N [C] **1** (*box, jar etc*) 容器 róngqì [个 gè] **2** (*for transport*) 集装箱 jízhuāngxiāng [个 gè]
content[1] [kɒntɛnt] **I** N [U] 内容 nèiróng **II contents** N PL (*of bottle, packet*) 所含之物 suǒhán zhī wù
content[2] [kəntɛnt] ADJ 满足的 mǎnzú de
contest [kɒntɛst] N [C] 比赛 bǐsài [项 xiàng]
contestant [kəntɛstənt] N [C] 参赛者 cānsàizhě [位 wèi]
context [kɒntɛkst] N [C/U] (*of word, phrase*) 上下文 shàngxiàwén [个 gè]
continent [kɒntɪnənt] N [C] 大陆 dàlù [个 gè]
continental breakfast [kɒntɪnɛnt°l-] N [C] 欧洲大陆式早餐 Ōuzhōu dàlù shì zǎocān [顿 dùn]
continue [kəntɪnyu] VI **1** 继续 jìxù **2** (*speaker*) 继续说 jìxù shuō ▶ **to continue to do sth** *or* **doing sth** 持续做某事 chíxù zuò mǒushì ▶ **to continue with sth** 继续某事 jìxù mǒushì
continuing education [kəntɪnyuɪŋ ɛdʒʊkeɪʃ°n] N [U] 继续教育 jìxù jiàoyù
continuous [kəntɪnyuəs] ADJ 连续不停的 liánxù bù tíng de
contraception [kɒntrəsɛpʃ°n] N [U] 避孕 bìyùn
contraceptive [kɒntrəsɛptɪv] N [C] (*drug*) 避孕药 bìyùn yào [片 piàn]; (*device*) 避孕工具 bìyùn gōngjù [种 zhǒng]
contract [kɒntrækt] N [C] 合同 hétong [份 fèn]
contradict [kɒntrədɪkt] VT 驳斥 bóchì
contradiction [kɒntrədɪkʃ°n] N [C/U] 矛盾 máodùn [种 zhǒng]
contrary [kɒntrɛri] N [C/U] ▶ **the contrary** 相反 xiāngfǎn ▶ **on the contrary** 正相反 zhèng xiāngfǎn
contrast [*n* kɒntræst, *vb* kəntræst] **I** N [C/U] **1** 明显的差异 míngxiǎn de chāyì [种 zhǒng] **2** ▶ **to be a contrast to sth** 与某物截然不同 yǔ mǒuwù jiérán bùtóng [个 gè] **II** VI ▶ **to contrast with sth** 与某事形成对照 yǔ mǒushì xíngchéng duìzhào ▶ **to contrast sth with sth** 将某物与某物进行对比 jiāng mǒuwù yǔ mǒuwù

jìnxíng duìbǐ

contribute [kəntrɪbyut] **I** VI ▶ **to contribute (to sth)** (*with money*) (给某事)捐助 (gěi mǒushì) juānzhù **II** VT ▶ **to contribute 10 dollars (to sth)** (给某事)捐献10美元 (gěi mǒushì) juānxiàn shí měiyuán

contribution [kɒntrɪbyuʃᵊn] N [C] 捐献 juānxiàn [次 cì]

control [kəntroʊl] **I** VT (+ *country, organization*) 统治 tǒngzhì; (+ *person, emotion, disease, fire*) 控制 kòngzhì **II** N [U] (*of country, organization*) 控制权 kòngzhì quán **III controls** N PL (*of vehicle, machine, TV*) 操纵装置 cāozòng zhuāngzhì ▶ **to control o.s.** 克制自己 kèzhì zìjǐ ▶ **to be in control (of sth)** (*of situation, car*) 控制着(某事) kòngzhì zhe (mǒushì) ▶ **to be under control** (*fire, situation*) 处于控制之下 chǔyú kòngzhì zhīxià ▶ **circumstances beyond our control** 不在我们控制之中的情况 bùzài wǒmen kòngzhì zhīzhōng de qíngkuàng

controversial [kɒntrəvɜrʃᵊl] ADJ 有争议的 yǒu zhēngyì de; (+ *book, film*) 引起争论的 yǐnqǐ zhēnglùn de

convenient [kənvinyənt] ADJ (+ *method, system, time*) 方便的 fāngbiàn de; (+ *place*) 近便的 jìnbiàn de

conventional [kənvɛnʃənᵊl] ADJ 符合习俗的 fúhé xísú de; (+ *method, product*) 传统的 chuántǒng de

conversation [kɒnvərseɪʃᵊn] N [C/U] 交谈 jiāotán [次 cì] ▶ **to have a conversation (about sth/with sb)** (和某人)谈(某事) (hé mǒurén) tán (mǒushì)

convert [kənvɜrt] VT (*transform*) (+ *substance*) 使转化 shǐ zhuǎnhuà; (+ *building*) 改建 gǎijiàn ▶ **to convert sth into sth** (+ *substance*) 将某物转化成某物 jiāng mǒuwù zhuǎnhuà chéng mǒuwù; (+ *building*) 将某建筑改建成某建筑 jiāng mǒujiànzhù gǎijiàn chéng mǒujiànzhù

convince [kənvɪns] VT **1** (*cause to believe*) 使信服 shǐ xìnfú **2** (*persuade*) 说服 shuōfú ▶ **to convince sb to do sth** 说服某人去做某事 shuōfú mǒurén qù zuò mǒushì

cook [kʊk] **I** VT (+ *food, meat, vegetables*) 烹调 pēngtiáo; (+ *meal*) 做 zuò **II** VI **1** (*person*) 做饭 zuòfàn **2** (*food*) 烧 shāo **III** N [C] 厨师 chúshī [位 wèi] ▶ **a good cook** 会做饭的人 huì zuòfàn de rén

cookie [kʊki] N [C] **1** (*for eating*) 小甜饼 xiǎotiánbǐng [块 kuài] **2** (*Comput*) 记忆块 jìyì kuài [个 gè]

cooking [kʊkɪŋ] N [U] 烹调 pēngtiáo

cool [kul] **I** ADJ **1** 凉的 liáng de **2** (*calm, unemotional*) 冷静的 lěngjìng de **3** (*inf*: *good*) 顶呱呱的 dǐngguāguā de; (*fashionable*) 酷的 kù de **II** VT 使变凉 shǐ biànliáng **III** VI 冷下来 lěngxiàlái **IV** N ▶ **to keep/lose one's cool** (*inf*) 保持冷静/失去自制而激动起来 bǎochí lěngjìng/shīqù zìzhì ér jīdòng qǐlái ▶ **to keep sth cool** 保持某物的凉度 bǎochí mǒuwù de liángdù; **cool down** VI 变凉 biànliáng

cooperate [koʊɒpəreɪt] VI **1** (*collaborate*) 合作 hézuò **2** (*be helpful*) 配合 pèihé

cope [koʊp] VI 对付 duìfù

copper [kɒpər] N [U] 铜 tóng

copy [kɒpi] **I** N **1** [C] 复制品 fùzhìpǐn [件 jiàn] **2** [C] (*of book, record, newspaper*) 本/张/份 běn/zhāng/fèn **II** VT 模仿 mófǎng ▶ **to make a copy of sth** 复印某物 fùyìn mǒuwù

cork [kɔrk] N [C] 瓶塞 píngsāi [个 gè]

corkscrew [kɔrkskru] N [C] 瓶塞钻 píngsāizuàn [个 gè]

corn [kɔrn] N [U] 玉米 yùmǐ ▶ **corn on the cob** 玉米(棒子) yùmǐ (bàngzi)

corner [kɔrnər] N [C] **1** 角落 jiǎoluò [个 gè] **2** (*of road*) 街角 jiējiǎo [个 gè]

corpse [kɔrps] N [C] 死尸 sǐshī [具 jù]

correct [kərɛkt] **I** ADJ 正确的 zhèngquè de; (+ *decision, means, procedure*) 适当的 shìdàng de **II** VT (+ *mistake, fault, person*) 纠正 jiūzhèng

correction [kərɛkʃᵊn] N [C] 修改 xiūgǎi [次 cì]

corridor [kɒrɪdər, -dɔr] N [C] (*in house, building*) 走廊 zǒuláng [条 tiáo]; (*on train*) 车厢过道 chēxiāng guòdào [个 gè]

corruption [kərʌpʃᵊn] N [U] 贪赃舞弊 tānzāng wǔbì

cosmetics N PL (*beauty products*) 化妆品 huàzhuāng pǐn

cost [kɔst] (*pt, pp* **cost**) **I** N [C] 价格 jiàgé [种 zhǒng] **II** VT 价格为 jiàgé wéi ▸ **how much does it cost?** 这多少钱？ zhè duōshǎo qián? ▸ **it costs 5 dollars/too much** 价格为5美元/太高 jiàgé wéi wǔ meǐyuán/tàigāo ▸ **the cost of living** 生活费用 shēnghuó fèiyòng

costume [kɒstum] N [C/U] 戏装 xìzhuāng [套 tào]

costume party N [C] 化装舞会 huàzhuāng wǔhuì [个 gè]

cot [kɒt] N [C] (*bed*) 帆布床 fānbù chuáng [张 zhāng]

cottage [kɒtɪdʒ] N [C] 村舍 cūnshè [个 gè]

cotton [kɒtᵊn] **I** N [U] **1** (*fabric*) 棉布 miánbù **2** (*thread*) 棉线 miánxiàn **II** CPD (+ *dress, sheets*) 棉布 miánbù

couch [kaʊtʃ] N [C] 长沙发 cháng shāfā [个 gè]

cough [kɔf] **I** VI 咳嗽 késou **II** N [C] 咳嗽 késou [阵 zhèn] ▸ **to have a cough** 咳嗽 késou

KEYWORD

could [kəd, STRONG kʊd] AUX VB

1 (*referring to past*) ▸ **we couldn't go to the party** 我们没能去参加聚会 wǒmen méi néng qù cānjiā jùhuì ▸ **he couldn't read or write** 他不会读也不会写 tā bùhuì dú yě bùhuì xiě

2 (*possibility*) ▸ **he could be in the library** 他可能在图书馆 tā kěnéng zài túshūguǎn ▸ **you could have been killed!** 可能你连命都没了！ kěnéng nǐ lián mìng dōu méile!

3 (*in conditionals with "if"*) ▸ **if we had more time, I could finish this** 如果有更多时间，我能够完成的 rúguǒ yǒu gèngduō shíjiān, wǒ nénggòu wánchéng de ▸ **we'd take a vacation, if we could afford it** 如果能支付得起的话，我们就去度假了 rúguǒ néng zhīfù de qǐ de huà, wǒmen jiù qù dùjià le

4 (*in offers, suggestions, requests*) 可以 kěyǐ ▸ **I could call a doctor** 我可以叫个医生 wǒ kěyǐ jiào gè yīshēng ▸ **could I borrow the car?** 我可以借一下车吗？ wǒ kěyǐ jiè yīxià chē ma? ▸ **he asked if he could make a phone call** 他问是否可以打个电话 tā wèn shìfǒu kěyǐ dǎgè diànhuà

council [kaʊnsᵊl] N [C] 议会 yìhuì [个 gè]

count [kaʊnt] **I** VT **1** (*also*: **count up**) 数 shǔ **2** (*include*) 把…计算在内 bǎ...jìsuàn zàinèi **II** VI **1** 数 shǔ **2** (*matter*) 有价值 yǒu jiàzhí ▸ **to count (up) to 10** 数到10 shǔdào shí;

count on VT FUS (+ *support, help*) 指望 zhǐwàng; (+ *person*) 依靠 yīkào

counter [kaʊntər] N [C] 柜台 guìtái [个 gè]

country [kʌntri] N **1** [C] (*nation*) 国家 guójiā [个 gè] **2** (*countryside*) ▸ **the country** 乡下 xiāngxià [个 gè] **3** [C] (*native land*) 家乡 jiāxiāng [个 gè]

countryside [kʌntrisaɪd] N [U] 农村 nóngcūn

couple [kʌpᵊl] N [C] **1** (*married*) 夫妻 fūqī [对 duì]; (*living together*) 情侣 qínglǚ [对 duì] **2** ▸ **a couple of** (*two*) 两个 liǎnggè

courage [kɜrɪdʒ] N [U] 勇气 yǒngqì

courier [kʊəriər, kɜr-] N [C] **1** (*messenger*) 信使 xìnshǐ [个 gè]

2 (*rep*) 旅游团的服务员 lǚyóutuán de fúwùyuán [个 gè]

course [kɔrs] N 1 [C] 课程 kèchéng [个 gè] 2 (*of meal*) ▶ **first/next/last course** 第一/下一/最后一道菜 dìyī/xiàyī/zuìhòu yīdào cài [道 dào] 3 [C] (*for golf, horseracing*) 场 chǎng ▶ **of course** (*naturally*) 自然 zìrán; (*certainly*) 当然 dāngrán ▶ **of course!** 没问题！ méi wèntí! ▶ **of course not!** 当然不行！ dāngrán bùxíng!

court [kɔrt] N [C] 1 (*Law*) 法庭 fǎtíng [个 gè] 2 (*for tennis, badminton*) 球场 qiúchǎng [个 gè]

courthouse [kɔrthaʊs] N [C] 法院 fǎyuàn [个 gè]

courtyard [kɔrtyard] N [C] 庭院 tíngyuàn [个 gè]

cousin [kʌzᵊn] N [C] (*older male on father's side*) 堂兄 tángxiōng [个 gè]; (*younger male on father's side*) 堂弟 tángdì [个 gè]; (*older female on father's side*) 堂姐 tángjiě [个 gè]; (*younger female on father's side*) 堂妹 tángmèi [个 gè]; (*older male on mother's side*) 表兄 biǎoxiōng [个 gè]; (*younger male on mother's side*) 表弟 biǎodì [个 gè]; (*older female on mother's side*) 表姐 biǎojiě [个 gè]; (*younger female on mother's side*) 表妹 biǎomèi [个 gè]

cover [kʌvər] I VT 1 ▶ **to cover sth (with sth)** (用某物) 盖着某物 (yòng mǒuwù) gàizhe mǒuwù 2 (*in insurance*) ▶ **to cover sb (against sth)** 给某人保(某事的)险 gěi mǒurén bǎo (mǒushì de) xiǎn II N 1 [C] 套子 tàozi [个 gè] 2 [C] (*of book, magazine*) 封面 fēngmiàn [个 gè] 3 [U] (*insurance*) 保险 bǎoxiǎn III **covers** N PL (*on bed*) 铺盖 pūgai ▶ **to be covered in** *or* **with sth** 被某物覆盖 bèi mǒuwù fùgài; **cover up** I VT (+ *facts, feelings, mistakes*) (用某事) 掩饰某事 (yòng mǒushì) yǎnshì mǒushì

Covid [koʊvɪd] N ABBR (= **coronavirus disease 2019**) 新冠肺炎 xīn guān fèiyán

cow [kaʊ] N [C] 奶牛 nǎiniú [头 tóu]

coward [kaʊərd] N [C] 胆小鬼 dǎnxiǎoguǐ [个 gè]

cowboy [kaʊbɔɪ] N [C] 牛仔 niúzǎi [个 gè]

crab [kræb] N 1 [C] (*creature*) 螃蟹 pángxiè [只 zhī] 2 [U] (*meat*) 蟹肉 xièròu

crack [kræk] N [C] 裂缝 lièfèng [条 tiáo]; **crack down on** VT FUS 对…严惩不贷 duì…yánchéng bùdài

cracked [krækt] ADJ 破裂的 pòliè de

cracker [krækər] N [C] 薄脆饼干 báocuì bǐnggān [块 kuài]

cradle [kreɪdᵊl] N [C] 摇篮 yáolán [个 gè]

craft [kræft] N [C] (*weaving, pottery etc*) 工艺 gōngyì [道 dào]

cramp [kræmp] N [C/U] 抽筋 chōujīn [阵 zhèn]

crane [kreɪn] N [C] 起重机 qǐzhòngjī [部 bù]

crash [kræʃ] I N [C] 1 (*of car*) 撞击 zhuàngjī [下 xià]; (*of plane*) 坠机 zhuìjī [次 cì] 2 (*noise*) 哗啦声 huālā shēng [声 shēng] II VT (+ *car, plane*) 使撞毁 shǐ zhuànghuǐ III VI 1 (*car, driver*) 撞击 zhuàngjī; (*plane*) 坠毁 zhuìhuǐ 2 (*Comput*) 死机 sǐjī ▶ **a car/plane crash** 撞车/飞机失事 zhuàngchē/fēijī shīshì ▶ **to crash into sth** 猛地撞上某物 měngde zhuàngshàng mǒuwù

crawl [krɔl] VI 爬 pá

crazy [kreɪzi] (*inf*) ADJ 发疯的 fāfēng de ▶ **to go crazy** 发疯 fāfēng

cream [krim] I N 1 [U] (*dairy cream*) 奶油 nǎiyóu 2 [C/U] (*for skin*) 乳霜 rǔshuāng [瓶 píng] II ADJ (*in color*) 乳白色的 rǔbáisè de

crease [kris] N [C] (*in cloth, paper: fold*) 折痕 zhéhén [道 dào]; (*wrinkle*) 皱纹 zhòuwén [条 tiáo]

create [krieɪt] VT 创造 chuàngzào

creative [krieɪtɪv] ADJ 有创造力的 yǒu chuàngzàolì de

creature [kritʃər] N [C] 动物 dòngwù [种 zhǒng]

credit [krɛdɪt] N 1 [U] (*financial*) 贷

款 dàikuǎn **2** [U] (*recognition*) 赞扬 zànyáng **3** [C] (*Scol, Univ*) 学分 xuéfēn [个 gè] ▶ **on credit** 赊账 shēzhàng
credit card N [C] 信用卡 xìnyòng kǎ [张 zhāng]
crew [kru] N **1** [C] 全体工作人员 quántǐ gōngzuò rényuán **2** [C] (*TV*) 组 zǔ [个 gè]
crib [krɪb] N [C] 有围栏的童床 yǒu wéilán de tóngchuáng [张 zhāng]
cricket [krɪkɪt] N [U] (*sport*) 板球 bǎnqiú; (*insect*) 蟋蟀 xīshuài
crime [kraɪm] N **1** [C] (*illegal act*) 罪行 zuìxíng [种 zhǒng] **2** [U] (*illegal activities*) 犯罪活动 fànzuì huódòng
criminal [krɪmɪnᵊl] N [C] 罪犯 zuìfàn [个 gè]
crisis [kraɪsɪs] (*pl* **crises**) N [C/U] 危机 wēijī [种 zhǒng]
critical [krɪtɪkᵊl] ADJ **1** (*crucial*) 关键的 guānjiàn de **2** (*serious*) 危急的 wēijí de
criticism [krɪtɪsɪzəm] N **1** [U] (*censure*) 批评 pīpíng **2** [C] (*complaint*) 指责 zhǐzé [种 zhǒng]
criticize [krɪtɪsaɪz] VT 批评 pīpíng
Croatia [kroʊeɪʃə] N 克罗地亚 Kèluódìyà
crocodile [krɒkədaɪl] N [C] 鳄鱼 èyú [只 zhī]
crooked [krʊkɪd] ADJ (*off-center*) 歪的 wāi de
crop [krɒp] N **1** [C] (*plants*) 庄稼 zhuāngjia [种 zhǒng] **2** [C] (*amount produced*) 收成 shōuchéng [个 gè]
cross [krɔs] **I** N [C] **1** (*x shape*) 交叉符号 jiāochā fúhào [个 gè]; (*showing disagreement*) 叉号 chāhào [个 gè] **2** (*crucifix shape*) 十字 shízì [个 gè] **3** (*Rel*) 十字架 shízìjià [个 gè] **II** VT (+ *street, room*) 横穿 héngchuān **III** VI (*roads, lines*) 相交 xiāngjiāo **IV** ADJ (*angry*) 生气的 shēngqì de; **cross out** VT (*delete*) 取消 qǔxiāo; **cross over** VI (*cross the street*) 过马路 guò mǎlù
crossing [krɔsɪŋ] N [C] (*voyage*) 横渡 héngdù [次 cì]
crossroads [krɔsroʊdz] (*pl* **crossroads**) N [C] 十字路口 shízì lùkǒu [个 gè]
crosswalk [krɔswɔk] N [C] 人行横道 rénxíng héngdào [个 gè]
crossword [krɔswɜrd] N [C] (*also*: **crossword puzzle**) 填字游戏 tiánzì yóuxì [个 gè]
crowd [kraʊd] N [C] 人群 rénqún [个 gè] ▶ **crowds of people** 大批人群 dàpī rénqún
crowded [kraʊdɪd] ADJ 拥挤的 yōngjǐ de
crown [kraʊn] N [C] 皇冠 huángguān [个 gè]
cruel [kruəl] ADJ 残忍的 cánrěn de; (+ *treatment, behavior*) 恶毒的 èdú de ▶ **to be cruel to sb** 残酷地对待某人 cánkù de duìdài mǒurén
cruelty [kruəlti] N [U] 残忍 cánrěn
cruise [kruz] N [C] 游船 yóuchuán [艘 sōu] ▶ **to be/go on a cruise** 乘游船旅行 chéng yóuchuán lǚxíng
crush [krʌʃ] VT **1** (+ *garlic*) 压碎 yāsuì **2** (+ *person*) 使挤在一起 shǐ jǐzài yīqǐ
cry [kraɪ] VI (*weep*) 哭 kū ▶ **what are you crying about?** 你哭什么？ nǐ kū shénme?
cryptocurrency [krɪptoʊkɛrənsi] N [C/U] 加密货币 jiāmì huòbì
cub [kʌb] N [C] **1** 幼兽 yòushòu [只 zhī] **2** (*also*: **Cub Scout**) 幼童军 yòutóngjūn [名 míng]
cube [kyub] N [C] 立方体 lìfāngtǐ [个 gè]
cucumber [kyukʌmbər] N [C/U] 黄瓜 huángguā [根 gēn]
cuddle [kʌdᵊl] **I** VT, VI 搂抱 lǒubào **II** N [C] 拥抱 yōngbào [个 gè]
cultural [kʌltʃərəl] ADJ 文化的 wénhuà de
culture [kʌltʃər] N [C/U] 文化 wénhuà [种 zhǒng]
cunning [kʌnɪŋ] ADJ 狡猾的 jiǎohuá de
cup [kʌp] N [C] **1** (*for drinking*) 杯子 bēizi [个 gè] **2** (*trophy*) 奖杯 jiǎngbēi [个 gè] ▶ **a cup of tea** 一杯茶 yībēi chá

cupboard [kʌbərd] N [C] 柜子 guìzi [个 gè]
curb [kɜrb] N [C] 路缘 lùyuán [个 gè]
cure [kyʊər] **I** VT (*Med*) 治好 zhìhǎo; (+ *patient*) 治愈 zhìyù **II** N [C] (*Med*) 疗法 liáofǎ [种 zhǒng]
curious [kyʊəriəs] ADJ 好奇的 hàoqí de ▶ **to be curious about sb/sth** 对某人/某物感到好奇 duì mǒurén/mǒuwù gǎndào hàoqí
curl [kɜrl] N [C] 卷发 juǎnfà [头 tóu]
curly [kɜrli] ADJ 卷曲的 juǎnqū de
currant [kɜrənt] N [C] 无子葡萄干 wúzǐ pútao gān [粒 lì]
currency [kɜrənsi] N [C/U] 货币 huòbì [种 zhǒng]
current [kɜrənt] **I** N [C] **1** (*of air, water*) 流 liú [股 gǔ] **2** (*Elec*) 电流 diànliú [股 gǔ] **II** ADJ (+ *situation, tendency, policy*) 目前的 mùqián de
current affairs N PL 时事 shíshì ▶ **a current affairs program** 时事讨论节目 shíshì tǎolùn jiémù
curriculum [kərɪkyələm] (*pl* **curriculums** *or* **curricula**) N [C] **1** 全部课程 quánbù kèchéng **2** (*for particular subject*) 课程 kèchéng [门 mén]
curriculum vitae [kərɪkyələm vaɪti] N [C] 简历 jiǎnlì [份 fèn]
curry [kɜri] N [C/U] (*dish*) 咖哩 gālí [种 zhǒng]
cursor [kɜrsər] (*Comput*) N [C] 光标 guāngbiāo [个 gè]
curtain [kɜrtᵊn] N [C] 窗帘 chuānglián [幅 fú] ▶ **to draw the curtains** (*together*) 拉上窗帘 lāshàng chuānglián; (*apart*) 拉开窗帘 lākāi chuānglián
cushion [kʊʃᵊn] N [C] 靠垫 kàodiàn [个 gè]
custom [kʌstəm] **I** N **1** [C/U] (*tradition*) 传统 chuántǒng [个 gè] **2** [C/U] (*convention*) 惯例 guànlì [个 gè] **II customs** N PL 海关 hǎiguān ▶ **to go through customs** 过海关 guò hǎiguān
customer [kʌstəmər] N [C] 顾客 gùkè [位 wèi]
customs officer N [C] 海关官员 hǎiguān guānyuán [位 wèi]
cut [kʌt] (*pt, pp* **cut**) **I** VT **1** 切 qiē **2** (*injure*) ▶ **to cut one's hand/knee** 割破手/膝盖 gēpò shǒu/xīgài **3** (+ *grass, hair, nails*) 修剪 xiūjiǎn **4** (+ *scene, episode, paragraph*) 删剪 shānjiǎn **5** (+ *prices, spending*) 削减 xiāojiǎn **II** N **1** [C] (*injury*) 伤口 shāngkǒu [个 gè] **2** [C] (*reduction*) 削减 xuējiǎn [次 cì] ▶ **to cut sth in half** 将某物切成两半 jiāng mǒuwù qiēchéng liǎngbàn ▶ **to cut o.s.** 割破自己 gēpò zìjǐ ▶ **to get** *or* **have one's hair cut** 剪发 jiǎnfà ▶ **a cut and blow-dry** 剪发吹干 jiǎnfà chuīgān; **cut down** VT **1** (+ *tree*) 砍倒 kǎndǎo **2** (*reduce*) 减少 jiǎnshǎo; **cut down on** VT FUS (+ *alcohol, coffee, cigarettes*) 减少 jiǎnshǎo; **cut off** VT **1** (+ *part of sth*) 切掉 qiēdiào **2** (+ *supply*) 停止供应 tíngzhǐ gōngyìng; **cut up** VT 切碎 qiēsuì
cute [kyut] (*inf*) ADJ **1** (+ *child, dog, house*) 可爱的 kě'ài de **2** (*attractive*) 迷人的 mírén de
cybercafé [saɪbərkæfeɪ] N [C] 网吧 wǎngbā [家 jiā]
cycle [saɪkᵊl] **I** N [C] 自行车 zìxíngchē [辆 liàng] **II** VI 骑自行车 qí zìxíngchē **III** CPD (+ *shop, helmet, ride*) 自行车 zìxíngchē ▶ **to go cycling** 骑自行车 qí zìxíngchē
cycling [saɪklɪŋ] N [U] 骑自行车 qí zìxíngchē
cyclist [saɪklɪst] N [C] 骑自行车的人 qí zìxíngchē de rén [个 gè]
cylinder [sɪlɪndər] N [C] (*of gas*) 罐 guàn [个 gè]
cynical [sɪnɪkᵊl] ADJ 愤世嫉俗的 fènshìjísú de
Cyprus [saɪprəs] N 塞浦路斯 Sàipǔlùsī
Czech Republic [tʃɛk-] N ▶ **the Czech Republic** 捷克共和国 Jiékègònghéguó

D

dad [dæd] (*inf*) N [C] 爸爸 bàba [个 gè]
daffodil [dæfədɪl] N [C] 黄水仙 huángshuǐxiān [支 zhī]
daily [deɪli] I ADJ 每日的 měirì de II ADV 每日 měirì
daisy [deɪzi] N [C] 雏菊 chújú [朵 duǒ]
dam [dæm] N [C] 水坝 shuǐbà [个 gè]
damage [dæmɪdʒ] I N [U] 1 损坏 sǔnhuài 2 (*dents, scratches*) 损伤 sǔnshāng II VT 毁坏 huǐhuài
damp [dæmp] ADJ 潮湿的 cháoshī de
dance [dæns] I N 1 [C] (*waltz, tango*) 舞蹈 wǔdǎo [曲 qǔ] 2 [C] (*social event*) 舞会 wǔhuì [个 gè] II VI 跳舞 tiàowǔ
dancer [dænsər] N [C] 舞蹈演员 wǔdǎo yǎnyuán [位 wèi]
dancing [dænsɪŋ] N [U] 跳舞 tiàowǔ
dandruff [dændrəf] N [U] 头皮屑 tóupíxiè
danger [deɪndʒər] N 1 [U] (*unsafe situation*) 危险 wēixiǎn 2 [C] (*hazard, risk*) 威胁 wēixié [个 gè] ▸ **there is a danger of/that...** 有…的危险 yǒu...de wēixiǎn ▸ **to be in danger of doing sth** 有…的危险 yǒu...de wēixiǎn
dangerous [deɪndʒərəs, deɪndʒrəs] ADJ 危险的 wēixiǎn de ▸ **it's dangerous to...** …是危险的 ...shì wēixiǎn de
Danish [deɪnɪʃ] I ADJ 丹麦的 Dānmài de II N [U] (*language*) 丹麦语 Dānmàiyǔ
dare [dɛər] I VT ▸ **to dare sb to do sth** 激某人做某事 jī mǒurén zuò mǒushì II VI ▸ **to dare (to) do sth** 敢做某事 gǎn zuò mǒushì ▸ **I dare say** (*I suppose*) 我相信 wǒ xiāngxìn ▸ **how dare you!** 你怎敢！ nǐ zěngǎn!
daring [dɛərɪŋ] ADJ 勇敢的 yǒnggǎn de
dark [dɑrk] I ADJ 1 (+ *room, night*) 黑暗的 hēi'àn de 2 (+ *eyes, hair, skin*) 黑色的 hēisè de; (+ *person*) 头发和皮肤深色的 tóufa hé pífū shēnsè de 3 (+ *suit, fabric*) 深色的 shēnsè de II N ▸ **the dark** 黑暗 hēi'àn ▸ **dark blue/green** 深蓝色/绿色 shēnlán sè/lǜsè ▸ **it is getting dark** 天黑了 tiān hēile
darling [dɑrlɪŋ] N 亲爱的 qīn'àide
darts [dɑrts] N PL 投镖游戏 tóubiāo yóuxì
data [deɪtə, dætə] N PL 数据 shùjù
database [deɪtəbeɪs, dætə-] N [C] 数据库 shùjùkù [个 gè]
date [deɪt] I N [C] 1 日期 rìqī [个 gè] 2 (*meeting with friend*) 约会 yuēhuì [个 gè] 3 (*fruit*) 红枣 hóngzǎo [颗 kē] II VT (+ *letter, check*) 给…注明日期 gěi...zhùmíng rìqī ▸ **what's the date today?, what's today's date?** 今天几号？ jīntiān jǐhào? ▸ **date of birth** 出生日期 chūshēng rìqī ▸ **to be out of date** (*old-fashioned*) 落伍 luòwǔ; (*expired*) 过期 guòqī ▸ **to be up to date** (*modern*) 时新 shíxīn
daughter [dɔtər] N [C] 女儿 nǚ'ér [个 gè]
daughter-in-law [dɔtərɪnlɔ] (*pl* **daughters-in-law**) N [C] 媳妇 xífu [个 gè]
dawn [dɔn] N [C/U] 黎明 límíng [个 gè]
day [deɪ] N 1 [C] 天 tiān 2 [C/U] (*daylight hours*) 白天 báitiān [个 gè] ▸ **during the day** 在白天 zài báitiān ▸ **the day before/after** 前/后一天 qián/hòu yītiān ▸ **the day after tomorrow** 后天 hòutiān ▸ **these days** (*nowadays*) 现在 xiànzài ▸ **the following day** 第二天 dì'èrtiān ▸ **one day/some day/one of these days** 有一天 yǒu yītiān ▸ **by day** 在白天 zài

báitiān ▸ **all day (long)** 一天到晚 yītiān dàowǎn ▸ **to work an 8 hour day** 每天工作8小时 měitiān gōngzuò bā xiǎoshí

day care center N [C] 托儿所 tuō'érsuǒ [个 gè]

daylight [deɪlaɪt] N [U] 白昼 báizhòu

dead [dɛd] ADJ **1** 死的 sǐ de **2** (+ *battery*) 不能再用的 bùnéng zài yòng de ▸ **over my dead body!** (*inf*) 绝对不行！ juéduì bùxíng!

deadline [dɛdlaɪn] N [C] 截止日期 jiézhǐ rìqī [个 gè] ▸ **to meet a deadline** 如期 rúqī

deaf [dɛf] ADJ 聋的 lóng de; (*partially*) 耳背的 ěrbèi de

deafening [dɛfənɪŋ] ADJ (+ *noise*) 震耳欲聋的 zhèn ěr yù lóng de

deal [dil] (*pt, pp* **dealt**) N [C] 协议 xiéyì [个 gè] ▸ **to do** *or* **make** *or* **strike a deal with sb** 和某人做买卖 hé mǒurén zuò mǎimài ▸ **it's a deal!** (*inf*) 成交！ chéngjiāo! ▸ **a good** *or* **great deal (of)** 大量(的…) dàliàng(de...); **deal with** VT FUS (+ *problem*) 处理 chǔlǐ

dealer [dilər] N [C] **1** 商人 shāngrén [个 gè] **2** (*in drugs*) 毒品贩子 dúpǐn fànzi [个 gè]

dealt [dɛlt] PT, PP *of* **deal**

dear [dɪər] **I** ADJ **1** 亲爱的 qīn'ài de **2** (*expensive*) 昂贵的 ángguì de **II** N ▸ **(my) dear** 亲爱的 qīn'ài de **III** INT ▸ **oh dear/dear dear/dear me!** 呵/哎呀！ hè/āiyā! ▸ **Dear Sir/Madam** (*in letter*) 亲爱的先生/女士 qīn'ài de xiānshēng/nǚshì ▸ **Dear Peter/Jane** 亲爱的彼得/简 qīn'ài de Bǐdé/Jiǎn

death [dɛθ] N [C/U] 死亡 sǐwáng [个 gè] ▸ **(a matter of) life and death** 生死攸关(的事情) shēngsǐ yōuguān (de shìqing) ▸ **to scare/bore sb to death** 吓死某人/使某人感到无聊之极 xiàsǐ mǒurén/shǐ mǒurén gǎndào wúliáo zhī jí

death penalty N ▸ **the death penalty** 死刑 sǐxíng

debate [dɪbeɪt] N [C/U] 讨论 tǎolùn [次 cì]

debt [dɛt] N **1** [C] (*sum of money owed*) 债务 zhàiwù [笔 bǐ] **2** [U] (*state of owing money*) 欠债 qiànzhài ▸ **to be in/get into debt** 负债 fùzhài

decade [dɛkeɪd] N [C] 十年 shínián [个 gè]

decaffeinated [dikæfɪneɪtɪd, -kæfiə-] ADJ 不含咖啡因的 bù hán kāfēiyīn de

deceive [dɪsiv] VT 欺骗 qīpiàn

December [dɪsɛmbər] N [C/U] 十二月 shí'èryuè; *see also* **July**

decent [disᵊnt] ADJ (+ *person*) 受尊重的 shòu zūnzhòng de

decide [dɪsaɪd] **I** VT (+ *question, argument*) 解决 jiějué **II** VI 决定 juédìng ▸ **to decide to do sth** 决定做某事 juédìng zuò mǒushì ▸ **I can't decide whether...** 我无法决定是否… wǒ wúfǎ juédìng shìfǒu...

decimal [dɛsɪmᵊl] **I** ADJ (+ *system, currency*) 十进位的 shíjìnwèi de **II** N [C] 小数 xiǎoshù [个 gè]

decision [dɪsɪʒᵊn] N [C] 决定 juédìng [个 gè] ▸ **to make a decision** 作出决定 zuòchū juédìng

deck [dɛk] N [C] 甲板 jiǎbǎn [个 gè]

deck chair N [C] 折叠式躺椅 zhédiéshì tǎngyǐ [把 bǎ]

declare [dɪklɛər] VT **1** (+ *intention, attitude*) 宣布 xuānbù; (+ *support*) 表明 biǎomíng **2** (*at customs*) 报关 bàoguān ▸ **to declare war (on sb)** (向某人)宣战 (xiàng mǒurén) xuānzhàn

decorate [dɛkəreɪt] VT **1** ▸ **to decorate (with)** (用…)装饰 (yòng...) zhuāngshì **2** (*paint etc*) 装潢 zhuānghuáng

decoration [dɛkəreɪʃᵊn] N [C/U] 装饰 zhuāngshì [种 zhǒng]

decrease [*vb* dɪkris, *n* dɪkris] **I** N [C] ▸ **decrease (in sth)** (某物的)减少 (mǒuwù de) jiǎnshǎo **II** VT, VI 减少 jiǎnshǎo

deduct [dɪdʌkt] VT ▸ **to deduct sth (from sth)** (从某物中)减去某物

(cóng mǒuwùzhōng) jiǎnqù mǒuwù

deep [dip] I ADJ 1 深的 shēn de 2 (+ *voice, sound*) 低沉的 dīchén de 3 (+ *sleep*) 酣睡的 hānshuì de II ADV 深 shēn ▶ **it is 1 m deep** 它有1米深 tā yǒu yīmǐ shēn ▶ **to take a deep breath** 深呼吸 shēn hūxī

deeply [dipli] ADV 1 (*breathe, sigh*) 深深地 shēnshēn de 2 (*sleep*) 沉沉地 chénchén de

deer [dɪər] (*pl* **deer**) N [C] 鹿 lù [头 tóu]

defeat [dɪfit] I N [C/U] 1 (*of army*) 战败 zhànbài [次 cì] 2 (*of team*) 击败 jībài [次 cì] II VT 1 (+ *enemy, opposition*) 战胜 zhànshèng 2 (+ *team*) 击败 jībài

defect [difɛkt] N [C] 缺点 quēdiǎn [个 gè]

defend [dɪfɛnd] VT 防御 fángyù ▶ **to defend o.s.** 自卫 zìwèi

defender [dɪfɛndər] N [C] (*in team*) 防守队员 fángshǒu duìyuán [个 gè]

defense [difɛns] N 1 [U] (*protection*) 防御 fángyù 2 [U] (*Mil*) 国防措施 guófáng cuòshī ▶ **the Department of Defense** 国防部 Guófángbù

definite [dɛfɪnɪt] ADJ 1 (+ *plan, answer, views*) 明确的 míngquè de 2 (+ *improvement, possibility, advantage*) 肯定的 kěndìng de ▶ **is that definite?** 肯定吗？ kěndìng ma?

definitely [dɛfɪnɪtli] ADV 确定地 quèdìng de

defy [dɪfaɪ] VT (+ *law, ban*) 蔑视 mièshì

degree [dɪgri] N [C] 1 ▶ **degree (of sth)** (*level*) (某事的)程度 (mǒushì de) chéngdù [种 zhǒng] 2 (*measure of temperature, angle, latitude*) 度 dù 3 (*at university*) 学位 xuéwèi [个 gè] ▶ **to some degree/a certain degree** 从某种/一定程度上来说 cóng mǒuzhǒng/yīdìng chéngdù shàng lái shuō ▶ **10 degrees below (zero)** 零下10度 língxià shídù ▶ **a degree in math** 数学学位 shùxué xuéwèi

delay [dɪleɪ] I VT 1 (+ *decision, ceremony*) 推迟 tuīchí 2 (+ *person*) 耽搁 dānge; (+ *plane, train*) 延误 yánwù II VI 耽搁 dānge III N [C/U] 延误 yánwù [个 gè] ▶ **to be delayed** (*person, flight, departure*) 被耽搁了 bèi dānge le ▶ **without delay** 立即 lìjì

delete [dɪlit] VT 删除 shānchú

deliberate [dɪlɪbərɪt] ADJ 故意的 gùyì de ▶ **it wasn't deliberate** 那不是故意的 nà bùshì gùyì de

deliberately [dɪlɪbərɪtli] ADV 故意地 gùyì de

delicate [dɛlɪkɪt] ADJ 1 (*fragile*) 易碎的 yìsuì de 2 (+ *problem, situation, issue*) 微妙的 wēimiào de 3 (+ *color, flavor, smell*) 清淡可口的 qīngdàn kěkǒu de

delicious [dɪlɪʃəs] ADJ 美味的 měiwèi de

delight [dɪlaɪt] N [U] 快乐 kuàilè

delighted [dɪlaɪtɪd] ADJ ▶ **delighted (at** *or* **with sth)** (对某事)感到高兴 (duì mǒushì) gǎndào gāoxìng ▶ **to be delighted to do sth** 乐意做某事 lèyì zuò mǒushì

deliver [dɪlɪvər] VT 1 (+ *letter, parcel*) 传送 chuánsòng 2 (+ *baby*) 接生 jiēshēng

delivery [dɪlɪvəri] N 1 [U] 传送 chuánsòng 2 [C] (*consignment*) 递送的货物 dìsòng de huòwù [件 jiàn]

demand [dɪmænd] I VT (+ *apology, explanation, pay rise*) 要求 yāoqiú II N 1 [C] (*request*) 要求 yāoqiú [个 gè] 2 [U] (*for product*) 需求量 xūqiúliàng ▶ **to make demands on sb/sth** 对某人/某事提出要求 duì mǒurén/mǒushì tíchū yāoqiú ▶ **to be in demand** 受欢迎 shòu huānyíng

democracy [dɪmɒkrəsi] N 1 [U] (*system*) 民主 mínzhǔ 2 [C] (*country*) 民主国 mínzhǔ guó [个 gè]

democratic [dɛməkrætɪk] ADJ 民主的 mínzhǔ de

demolish [dɪmɒlɪʃ] VT 拆毁 chāihuǐ

demonstrate [dɛmənstreɪt] I VT

(+ *skill, appliance*) 演示 yǎnshì **II** VI ▶ **to demonstrate (for/against sth)** 示威(支持/反对某事) shìwēi (zhīchí/fǎnduì mǒushì) ▶ **to demonstrate how to do sth** 演示如何做某事 yǎnshì rúhé zuò mǒushì

demonstration [dɛmənstreɪʃᵊn] N [C] **1** 示威 shìwēi [次 cì] **2** (*of appliance, cooking*) 演示 yǎnshì [个 gè]

demonstrator [dɛmənstreɪtər] N [C] 示威者 shìwēizhě [个 gè]

denim [dɛnɪm] N [U] 斜纹粗棉布 xiéwén cū miánbù

Denmark [dɛnmark] N 丹麦 Dānmài

dent [dɛnt] N [C] 凹部 āobù [个 gè]

dental [dɛntᵊl] ADJ 牙齿的 yáchǐ de

dentist [dɛntɪst] N [C] **1** (*person*) 牙医 yáyī [位 wèi] **2** ▶ **the dentist('s)** 牙医诊所 yáyī zhěnsuǒ [家 jiā]

deny [dɪnaɪ] VT 否定 fǒudìng

deodorant [dioʊdərənt] N [C/U] 除臭剂 chúchòujì [种 zhǒng]

depart [dɪpɑrt] VI ▶ **to depart (from/for somewhere)** (从某地)出发/出发(赶往某地) (cóng mǒudì) chūfā/chūfā (gǎnwǎng mǒudì)

department [dɪpɑrtmənt] N [C] **1** (*in store*) 部 bù [个 gè] **2** (*in school or college*) 系 xì [个 gè]

department store N [C] 百货商店 bǎihuò shāngdiàn [家 jiā]

departure [dɪpɑrtʃər] N [C/U] 出发 chūfā

departure lounge N [C] 候机厅 hòujītīng [个 gè]

depend [dɪpɛnd] VI **1** ▶ **to depend on sth** 依某物而定 yī mǒuwù ér dìng **2** ▶ **you can depend on me/him** (*rely on, trust*) 你可以信赖我/他 nǐ kěyǐ xìnlài wǒ/tā **3** ▶ **to depend on sb/sth** (*for survival*) 依靠某人/某物为生 yīkào mǒurén/mǒuwù wéishēng ▶ **it (all) depends** 要看情况而定 yào kàn qíngkuàng érdìng

deposit [dɪpɒzɪt] N [C] (*in account*) 储蓄 chǔxù [笔 bǐ]; (*on house, bottle, when hiring*) 押金 yājīn [份 fèn] ▶ **to put down a deposit of 50 dollars** 支付50美元的保证金 zhīfù wǔshí měiyuán de bǎozhèngjīn

depressed [dɪprɛst] ADJ 沮丧的 jǔsàng de

depressing [dɪprɛsɪŋ] ADJ 令人沮丧的 lìng rén jǔsàng de

deprive [dɪpraɪv] VT ▶ **to deprive sb of sth** 剥夺某人某物 bōduó mǒurén mǒuwù

depth [dɛpθ] N [C/U] 深 shēn ▶ **at/to/from a depth of 3 meters** 在/到/从3米深处 zài/dào/cóng sānmǐ shēnchù ▶ **to study/analyze sth in depth** 深入研究/分析某事 shēnrù yánjiū/fēnxī mǒushì

descend [dɪsɛnd] VI (*frm*) 下来 xiàlai ▶ **to be descended from** 是…的后裔 shì…de hòuyì

describe [dɪskraɪb] VT 描述 miáoshù

description [dɪskrɪpʃᵊn] N [C/U] 描述 miáoshù [种 zhǒng]

desert [*n* dɛzᵊrt, *vb* dɪzɜrt] N **1** [C/U] (*Geo*) 沙漠 shāmò [片 piàn] **2** [C] (*fig: wasteland*) 荒地 huāngdì [片 piàn]

deserve [dɪzɜrv] VT 应受 yīng shòu ▶ **to deserve to do sth** 应该获得某事 yīnggāi huòdé mǒuwù

design [dɪzaɪn] **I** N **1** [U] (*art, process, layout, shape*) 设计 shèjì **2** [C] (*pattern*) 图案 tú'àn [种 zhǒng] **II** VT 设计 shèjì ▶ **to be designed for sb/to do sth** 专门为某人/做某事设计 zhuānmén wèi mǒurén/zuò mǒushì shèjì

designer [dɪzaɪnər] **I** N [C] 设计者 shèjìzhě [位 wèi] **II** CPD (+ *clothes, label, jeans*) 名师设计的 míngshī shèjì de

desk [dɛsk] N [C] **1** (*in office*) 办公桌 bàngōngzhuō [张 zhāng] **2** (*for pupil*) 书桌 shūzhuō [张 zhāng] **3** (*in hotel, at airport, hospital*) 服务台 fúwùtái [个 gè]

desk clerk N [C] 接待员 jiēdàiyuán [位 wèi]

despair [dɪspɛər] N [U] 绝望 juéwàng ▸ **in despair** 绝望地 juéwàng de
desperate [dɛspərɪt] ADJ **1** (+ *person*) 绝望的 juéwàng de **2** (+ *attempt, effort*) 铤而走险的 tǐng ér zǒu xiǎn de **3** (+ *situation*) 危急的 wēijí de
desperately [dɛspərɪtli] ADV (*struggle, shout*) 拼命地 pīnmìng de
despise [dɪspaɪz] VT 鄙视 bǐshì
despite [dɪspaɪt] PREP 尽管 jǐnguǎn
dessert [dɪzɜrt] N [C/U] 饭后甜点 fànhòu tiándiǎn [份 fèn]
destination [dɛstɪneɪʃən] N [C] 目的地 mùdìdì [个 gè]
destroy [dɪstrɔɪ] VT 破坏 pòhuài
destruction [dɪstrʌkʃən] N [U] 破坏 pòhuài
detail [diteɪl] **I** N [C] 细节 xìjié [个 gè] **II details** N PL 详情 xiángqíng ▸ **in detail** 详细地 xiángxì de
detailed [dɪteɪld] ADJ 详细的 xiángxì de
detective [dɪtɛktɪv] N [C] 侦探 zhēntàn [个 gè]
detective story, detective novel N [C] 侦探小说 zhēntàn xiǎoshuō [部 bù]
detergent [dɪtɜrdʒənt] N [C/U] 清洁剂 qīngjiéjì [种 zhǒng]
determined [dɪtɜrmɪnd] ADJ 坚定的 jiāndìng de ▸ **to be determined to do sth** 决心做某事 juéxīn zuò mǒushì
detour [ditʊər] N [C] **1** ▸ **to make a detour** 绕道 ràodào [次 cì] **2** (*on road*) 绕行道路 ràoxíng dàolù [条 tiáo]
develop [dɪvɛləp] **I** VT **1** (+ *business, idea, relationship*) 发展 fāzhǎn; (+ *land, resource*) 开发 kāifā **2** (+ *product, weapon*) 开发 kāifā **3** (*Phot*) 冲洗 chōngxǐ **II** VI (*person*) 成长 chéngzhǎng; (*country, situation, friendship, skill*) 发展 fāzhǎn
development [dɪvɛləpmənt] N **1** [U] (*growth*) 成长 chéngzhǎng; (*political, economic*) 发展 fāzhǎn **2** [C] (*event*) 新形势 xīn xíngshì [种 zhǒng]
devil [dɛvəl] N 魔鬼 móguǐ ▸ **the Devil** 撒旦 Sādàn [个 gè]
devoted [dɪvoʊtɪd] ADJ **1** (+ *husband, daughter*) 忠诚的 zhōngchéng de **2** ▸ **devoted to sth** (*specializing in*) 致力于某事的 zhìlì yú mǒushì de
diabetes [daɪəbitɪs, -tiz] N [U] 糖尿病 tángniàobìng
diabetic [daɪəbɛtɪk] N [C] 糖尿病患者 tángniàobìng huànzhě [个 gè]
diagonal [daɪægənəl, -ægnəl] ADJ 斜的 xié de
diagram [daɪəgræm] N [C] 图解 tújiě [个 gè]
dial [daɪəl] **I** N [C] (*on clock or meter*) 标度盘 biāodùpán [个 gè] **II** VT (+ *number*) 拨 bō **III** VI 拨号 bōhào
dialog [daɪəlɔːg] N [C/U] (*conversation*) 对话 duìhuà [次 cì]
diamond [daɪmənd, daɪə-] N [C] 钻石 zuànshí [颗 kē]
diaper [daɪpər, daɪə-] N [C] 尿布 niàobù [块 kuài]
diarrhea [daɪəriə] N [U] 腹泻 fùxiè ▸ **to have diarrhea** 腹泻 fùxiè
diary [daɪəri] N [C] **1** 日记簿 rìjìbù [个 gè] **2** (*daily account*) 日记 rìjì [篇 piān]
dice [daɪs] (*pl* **dice**) N [C] 骰子 tóuzi [个 gè]
dictionary [dɪkʃənɛri] N [C] 词典 cídiǎn [本 běn]
did [dɪd] PT *of* **do**
die [daɪ] VI **1** 死 sǐ ▸ **to die of** *or* **from sth** 死于某事 sǐyú mǒushì ▸ **to be dying** 奄奄一息 yǎn yǎn yī xī ▸ **to be dying for sth/to do sth** 渴望某事/做某事 kěwàng mǒushì/zuò mǒushì;
die out VI **1** (*custom, way of life*) 灭亡 mièwáng **2** (*species*) 灭绝 mièjué
diesel [dizəl] N **1** [U] (*also*: **diesel oil**) 柴油 cháiyóu **2** [C] (*vehicle*) 柴油机驱动的车辆 cháiyóujī qūdòng de chēliàng [辆 liàng]
diet [daɪɪt] **I** N **1** [C/U] 饮食 yǐnshí [种 zhǒng] **2** [C] (*slimming*) 减肥饮食 jiǎnféi yǐnshí [份 fèn] **II** VI 节食 jiéshí ▸ **to be on a diet** 实行减肥节食 shíxíng jiǎnféi jiéshí

difference [dɪfərəns, dɪfrəns] N [C] 差异 chāyì [种 zhǒng] ▶ **the difference in size/color** 尺寸/颜色上的差异 chǐcùn/yánsè shàng de chāyì ▶ **to make a/no difference (to sb/sth)** (对某人/某事)有/无影响 (duì mǒurén/mǒushì) yǒu/wú yǐngxiǎng

different [dɪfərənt, dɪfrənt] ADJ 不同的 bùtóng de

difficult [dɪfɪkʌlt, -kəlt] ADJ **1** 困难的 kùnnan de **2** (+ *person, child*) 执拗的 zhíniù de ▶ **it is difficult for us to understand her** 我们很难理解她 wǒmen hěnnán lǐjiě tā

difficulty [dɪfɪkʌlti, -kəlti] N [C] 困难 kùnnan [个 gè] ▶ **to have difficulty/difficulties** 有困难 yǒu kùnnan

dig [dɪg] (*pt, pp* **dug**) **I** VT **1** (+ *hole*) 挖 wā **2** (+ *garden*) 掘土 juétǔ **II** VI (*with spade*) 挖掘 wājué; **dig up** VT (+ *plant, body*) 挖出 wāchū

digital [dɪdʒɪtᵊl] ADJ **1** (+ *clock, watch*) 数字的 shùzì de **2** (+ *recording, technology*) 数码的 shùmǎ de

digital camera N [C] 数码相机 shùmǎ xiàngjī [台 tái]

digital television N [U] 数字电视 shùzì diànshì

dim [dɪm] ADJ **1** 暗淡的 àndàn de **2** (*inf: stupid*) 迟钝的 chídùn de

dime [daɪm] N [C] 一角银币 yījiǎo yínbì [枚 méi]

dimension [dɪmɛnʃᵊn, daɪ-] **I** N [C] (*aspect*) 方面 fāngmiàn [个 gè] **II dimensions** N PL (*measurements*) 面积 miànjī

diner [daɪnər] N [C] (*restaurant*) 廉价餐馆 liánjià cānguǎn [家 jiā]

dinghy [dɪŋgi] N [C] (*also*: **rubber dinghy**) 橡皮筏 xiàngpífá [个 gè]

dining room [daɪnɪŋ rum] N [C] **1** (*in house*) 饭厅 fàntīng [个 gè] **2** (*in hotel*) 餐厅 cāntīng [个 gè]

dinner [dɪnər] N **1** [C/U] 晚餐 wǎncān [顿 dùn] **2** [C] (*formal meal*) 正餐 zhèngcān [顿 dùn]

dinner party N [C] 宴会 yànhuì [个 gè]

dinnertime N [C/U] 晚饭时间 wǎnfàn shíjiān [段 duàn]

dinosaur [daɪnəsɔr] N [C] 恐龙 kǒnglóng [只 zhī]

dip [dɪp] VT 蘸 zhàn

diploma [dɪploʊmə] N [C] 毕业文凭 bìyè wénpíng [张 zhāng]

direct [dɪrɛkt, daɪ-] **I** ADJ 直达的 zhídá de **II** VT **1** (*show*) 给…指路 gěi...zhǐlù **2** (*manage*) 管理 guǎnlǐ **3** (+ *play, film, program*) 导演 dǎoyǎn **III** ADV (*go, write, fly*) 直接地 zhíjiē de

direction [dɪrɛkʃᵊn, daɪ-] **I** N [C] 方向 fāngxiàng [个 gè] **II directions** N PL **1** (*to get somewhere*) 指路说明 zhǐlù shuōmíng **2** (*for doing something*) 用法说明 yòngfǎ shuōmíng ▶ **in the direction of** 朝 cháo

director [dɪrɛktər, daɪ-] N [C] **1** (*of company*) 经理 jīnglǐ [位 wèi] **2** (*of organization, public authority*) 主任 zhǔrèn [位 wèi] **3** (*of play, film*) 导演 dǎoyǎn [位 wèi]

directory [dɪrɛktəri, daɪ-] N [C] **1** 电话号码簿 diànhuà hàomǎbù [个 gè] **2** (*on computer*) 文件名录 wénjiàn mínglù [个 gè]

dirt [dɜrt] N [U] 污物 wūwù

dirty [dɜrti] ADJ 脏的 zāng de

disabled [dɪseɪbᵊld] ADJ **1** 伤残的 shāngcán de **2** (*with learning difficulties*) 有缺陷的 yǒu quēxiàn de

disadvantage [dɪsədvæntɪdʒ] N [C/U] (*drawback*) 不利 bùlì [种 zhǒng]

disagree [dɪsəgri] VI ▶ **to disagree (with sb)** 不同意(某人的观点) bù tóngyì (mǒurén de guāndiǎn) ▶ **to disagree (with sth)** (对某事表示)不同意 (duì mǒushì biǎoshì) bù tóngyì

disagreement [dɪsəgrimənt] N [C] (*argument*) 争执 zhēngzhí [个 gè]

disappear [dɪsəpɪər] VI **1** (*from view*) 消失 xiāoshī **2** (*go missing*) 失踪 shīzōng **3** (*cease to exist*) 消失 xiāoshī

disappearance [dɪsəpɪərəns] N [C/U] (*of person*) 失踪 shīzōng [次 cì]

disappoint [dɪsəpɔɪnt] VT (+ *person*) 使失望 shǐ shīwàng
disappointed [dɪsəpɔɪntɪd] ADJ 失望的 shīwàng de
disappointment [dɪsəpɔɪntmənt] N 1 [U] (*emotion*) 失望 shīwàng 2 [C] (*cause*) 令人失望的人/事 lìng rén shīwàng de rén/shì [个/件 gè/jiàn]
disapprove [dɪsəpruv] VI ▶ **to disapprove (of sb/sth)** 不同意(某人/某事) bù tóngyì (mǒurén/mǒushì)
disaster [dɪzæstər] N [C/U] 1 (*earthquake, flood*) 灾难 zāinàn [次 cì] 2 (*accident, crash etc*) 灾祸 zāihuò [场 cháng] 3 (*fiasco*) 惨败 cǎnbài [次 cì] 4 (*serious situation*) 灾难 zāinàn [个 gè]
disastrous [dɪzæstrəs] ADJ 1 (*catastrophic*) 灾难性的 zāinànxìng de 2 (*unsuccessful*) 惨败的 cǎnbài de
discipline [dɪsɪplɪn] N [U] 纪律 jìlǜ
disc jockey N [C] 简称为DJ，意为广播电台或迪斯科舞厅流行音乐唱片播放及介绍人
disco [dɪskoʊ] N (*event*) 迪斯科 dísīkē
disconnect [dɪskənɛkt] VT 1 (+ *pipe, tap, hose*) 拆开 chāikāi 2 (+ *computer, cooker, TV*) 断开 duànkāi
discount [dɪskaʊnt] N [C/U] 折扣 zhékòu [个 gè]
discourage [dɪskɜrɪdʒ] VT 使泄气 shǐ xièqì
discover [dɪskʌvər] VT 发现 fāxiàn
discovery [dɪskʌvəri] N 1 [C/U] (*of treasure, cure*) 发现 2 [C] (*thing found*) 被发现的事物 bèi fāxiàn de shìwù [个 gè]
discrimination [dɪskrɪmɪneɪʃᵊn] N [U] 歧视 qíshì ▶ **racial/sexual discrimination** 种族/性别歧视 zhǒngzú/xìngbié qíshì
discuss [dɪskʌs] VT 讨论 tǎolùn
discussion [dɪskʌʃᵊn] N [C/U] 讨论 tǎolùn [次 cì]
disease [dɪziz] N [C/U] (*illness*) 病 bìng [场 chǎng]
disgraceful [dɪsgreɪsfəl] ADJ 可耻的 kěchǐ de
disguise [dɪsgaɪz] I N [C] 伪装品 wěizhuāngpǐn [件 jiàn] II VT ▶ **(to be) disguised (as sth/sb)** (+ *person*) 假扮成(某物/某人) jiǎbànchéng (mǒuwù/mǒurén) ▶ **in disguise** 乔装着 qiáozhuāng zhe
disgusted [dɪsgʌstɪd] ADJ 感到厌恶的 gǎndào yànwù de
disgusting [dɪsgʌstɪŋ] ADJ 1 (+ *food, habit*) 令人作呕的 lìng rén zuò'ǒu de 2 (+ *behavior, situation*) 讨厌的 tǎoyàn de
dish [dɪʃ] I N [C] 1 (*for serving*) 盘 pán [个 gè]; (*for eating*) 碟 dié [个 gè] 2 (*recipe, food*) 一道菜 yī dào cài [道 dào] 3 (*also*: **satellite dish**) 盘形物 pánxíngwù [个 gè] II **dishes** N PL 碗碟 wǎndié ▶ **to do** *or* **wash the dishes** 刷洗碗碟 shuāxǐ wǎndié
dishonest [dɪsɒnɪst] ADJ 1 不诚实的 bù chéngshí de 2 (+ *behavior*) 不正直的 bù zhèngzhí de
dishtowel [dɪʃtaʊəl] N [C] 擦拭布 cāshìbù [块 kuài]
dishwasher [dɪʃwɒʃər] N [C] 洗碗机 xǐwǎnjī [台 tái]
dishwashing liquid [dɪʃwɒʃɪŋ lɪkwɪd] N [U] 洗洁剂 xǐjiéjì
disinfectant [dɪsɪnfɛktənt] N [C/U] 消毒剂 xiāodújì [种 zhǒng]
disk [dɪsk] N [C] 1 圆盘 yuánpán [个 gè] 2 (*Comput: hard*) 硬盘 yìngpán [个 gè]; (*floppy*) 软盘 ruǎnpán [张 zhāng]
dislike [dɪslaɪk] I VT 不喜欢 bù xǐhuān II N [C] ▶ **one's likes and dislikes** 某人的爱好和厌恶 mǒurén de àihào hé yànwù
dismiss [dɪsmɪs] VT 解雇 jiěgù
disobedient [dɪsəbidiənt] ADJ 不服从的 bù fúcóng de
disobey [dɪsəbeɪ] VT 1 不顺从 bù shùncóng 2 (+ *order*) 不服从 bù fúcóng
display [dɪspleɪ] I N 1 [C] (*in store, at exhibition*) 陈列 chénliè [种 zhǒng]

2 [c] (*information on screen*) 显示 xiǎnshì [个 gè] 3 [c] (*screen*) 显示屏 xiǎnshìpíng [个 gè] II VT 1 (+ *exhibits*) 陈列 chénliè 2 (+ *results, information*) 显示 xiǎnshì

disposable [dɪspoʊzəbᵊl] ADJ 一次性的 yīcìxìng de

dispute [dɪspyut] N (*industrial*) 争执 zhēngzhí

disqualify [dɪskwɒlɪfaɪ] VT 取消资格 qǔxiāo zīgé

disrupt [dɪsrʌpt] VT 1 (+ *conversation, meeting*) 扰乱 rǎoluàn 2 (+ *plan, process*) 妨碍 fáng'ài

dissolve [dɪzɒlv] VI (*in liquid*) 溶解 róngjiě

distance [dɪstəns] N [c/u] 距离 jùlí [个 gè] ▶ **within walking distance** 步行可到 bùxíng kě dào

distinct [dɪstɪŋkt] ADJ (+ *advantage, change*) 明确的 míngquè de

distinguish [dɪstɪŋgwɪʃ] VT ▶ **to distinguish one thing from another** 将一事物与另一事物区别开来 jiāng yīshìwù yǔ lìngyī shìwù qūbié kāilái

distract [dɪstrækt] VT (+ *person*) 使分心 shǐ fēnxīn ▶ **to distract sb's attention** 分散某人的注意力 fēnsàn mǒurén de zhùyìlì

distribute [dɪstrɪbyut] VT 1 (*hand out*) 分发 fēnfā 2 (*share out*) 分配 fēnpèi

district [dɪstrɪkt] N [c] 地区 dìqū [个 gè]

disturb [dɪstɜrb] VT (*interrupt*) 打扰 dǎrǎo

disturbing [dɪstɜrbɪŋ] ADJ 令人不安的 lìng rén bù'ān de

ditch [dɪtʃ] N [c] 沟 gōu [条 tiáo]

dive [daɪv] VI (*into water*) 跳水 tiàoshuǐ; (*under water*) 潜水 qiánshuǐ

diver [daɪvər] N [c] 潜水员 qiánshuǐyuán [位 wèi]

divide [dɪvaɪd] I VT 1 ▶ **to divide (up)** (*into groups, areas*) 划分 huàfēn 2 (*in math*) 除 chú 3 ▶ **to divide sth between/among sb/sth** (*share*) 在两个/3个以上的人/物之间分配某物 zài liǎnggè/sāngè yǐshàng de rén/wù zhījiān fēnpèi mǒuwù II VI (*into groups*) 分开 fēnkāi ▶ **to divide sth in half** 将某物一分为二 jiāng mǒuwù yī fēn wéi èr ▶ **40 divided by 5** 40除以5 sìshí chúyǐ wǔ

diving [daɪvɪŋ] N [U] 1 (*underwater*) 潜水 qiánshuǐ 2 (*from board*) 跳水 tiàoshuǐ

division [dɪvɪʒᵊn] N 1 [U] (*Math*) 除法 chúfǎ 2 [U] (*sharing out: of labor, resources*) 分配 fēnpèi

divorce [dɪvɔrs] I N [c/U] 离婚 líhūn [次 cì] II VT (+ *spouse*) 与…离婚 yǔ...líhūn III VI 离婚 líhūn

divorced [dɪvɔrst] ADJ 离异的 líyì de ▶ **to get divorced** 离婚 líhūn

dizzy [dɪzi] ADJ ▶ **to feel dizzy** 感到头晕 gǎndào tóuyūn

DJ [di dʒeɪ] N ABBR (= **disc jockey**) 简称为DJ，意为广播电台或迪斯科舞厅流行音乐唱片播放及介绍人

KEYWORD

do [də, STRONG du] (*pt* **did**, *pp* **done**)
I VT 1 做 zuò ▶ **what are you doing?** 你在做什么呢？ nǐ zài zuò shénme ne? ▶ **are you doing anything tomorrow evening?** 你明晚有什么打算？ nǐ míngwǎn yǒu shénme dǎsuàn? ▶ **what did you do with the money?** (*how did you spend it*) 你怎么用这笔钱的？ nǐ zěnme yòng zhèbǐ qián de? ▶ **what are you going to do about this?** 你打算对此怎么办？ nǐ dǎsuàn duìcǐ zěnmebàn?

2 (*for a living*) ▶ **what do you do?** 你做什么工作？ nǐ zuò shénme gōngzuò?

3 (*with noun*) ▶ **to do the cooking** 做饭 zuòfàn

4 (*referring to speed, distance*) ▶ **the car was doing 100** 汽车以100英里的时速行进 qìchē yǐ yībǎi yīnglǐ de shísù xíngjìn ▶ **we've done 200 km already** 我们的时速已达到了200公

里 wǒmen de shísù yǐjīng dádào le èrbǎi gōnglǐ
5 (*cause*) ▶ **the explosion did a lot of damage** 爆炸造成了很大损失 bàozhà zàochéng le hěndà sǔnshī ▶ **a vacation will do you good** 休次假会对你有好处 xiū cì jià huì duì nǐ yǒu hǎochù
II VI **1** (*act, behave*) 做 zuò ▶ **do as I tell you** 按我告诉你的做 àn wǒ gàosù nǐ de zuò
2 (*get on*) 进展 jìnzhǎn ▶ **he's doing well/badly at school** 他的学习成绩很好/很差 tāde xuéxí chéngjī hěnhǎo/hěnchà ▶ **"how do you do?" – "how do you do?"** "你好" "你好" "nǐhǎo""nǐhǎo"
3 (*suit*) 行 xíng ▶ **will it do?** 行吗? xíngma?
4 (*be sufficient*) 足够 zúgòu ▶ **will $15 do?** 15美元够吗? shíwǔ měiyuán gòuma?
III AUX VB **1** (*in negative constructions*) ▶ **I don't understand** 我不懂 wǒ bùdǒng ▶ **she doesn't want it** 她不想要这个 tā bùxiǎng yào zhège ▶ **don't be silly!** 别傻了! bié shǎ le!
2 (*to form questions*) ▶ **do you like jazz?** 你喜欢爵士乐吗? nǐ xǐhuān juéshìyuè ma? ▶ **what do you think?** 你怎么想? nǐ zěnme xiǎng? ▶ **why didn't you come?** 你为什么没来? nǐ wèishénme méilái?
3 (*for emphasis, in polite expressions*) ▶ **do sit down/help yourself** 赶快坐啊/千万别客气 gǎnkuài zuò a/qiānwàn bié kèqi
4 (*used to avoid repeating vb*) 用于避免动词的重复 ▶ **they say they don't care, but they do** 他们说不在乎，但实际是在乎的 tāmen shuō bù zàihu, dàn shíjì shì zàihu de ▶ **(and) so do I** 我也是 wǒ yěshì ▶ **and neither did we** 我们也不 wǒmen yěbù ▶ **"who made this mess?" – "I did"** "是谁弄得乱七八糟的?" "是我" "shì shuí nòngde luàn qī bā zāo de""shì wǒ"
5 (*in question tags*) ▶ **I don't know him, do I?** 我不认识他，是吗? wǒ bù rènshi tā, shìma? ▶ **she lives in Washington, doesn't she?** 她住在华盛顿，不是吗? tā zhùzài Huáshèngdùn, bùshì ma?
▶ **do up** VT FUS (+ *laces*) 系紧 jìjǐn; (+ *dress, coat, buttons*) 扣上 kòu shàng
▶ **do with** VT FUS **1** (*need*) ▶ **I could do with a drink/some help** 我想喝一杯/需要帮助 wǒ xiǎng hē yībēi/xūyào bāngzhù
2 (*be connected*) ▶ **to have to do with** 与…有关 yǔ…yǒuguān ▶ **what has it got to do with you?** 这跟你有什么关系? zhè gēn nǐ yǒu shénme guānxi?
▶ **do without** VT FUS 没有…也行 méiyǒu…yě xíng

dock [dɒk] N [C] (*Naut*) 船坞 chuánwù [个 gè]
doctor [dɒktər] N [C] **1** 医生 yīshēng [位 wèi] **2** ▶ **the doctor's** 诊所 zhěnsuǒ [家 jiā]
document [dɒkyəmənt] N [C] **1** 文件 wénjiàn [份 fèn] **2** (*Comput*) 文档 wéndàng [个 gè]
documentary [dɒkyəmɛntəri, -tri] N [C] 纪录片 jìlùpiàn [部 bù]
does [dəz, STRONG dʌz] VB *see* **do**
doesn't [dʌzᵊnt] = **does not**
dog [dɔg] N [C] **1** 狗 gǒu [只 zhī] **2** (*male*) 雄兽 xióngshòu [头 tóu]
do-it-yourself [duːɪtyɔrsɛlf] **I** N [U] 自己动手的活计 zìjǐ dòngshǒu de huójì
II ADJ (+ *store*) 出售供购买者自行装配物品的 chūshòu gòng gòumǎizhě zìxíng zhuāngpèi wùpǐn de
doll [dɒl] N [C] 娃娃 wáwa [个 gè]
dollar [dɒlər] N [C] 元 yuán
dolphin [dɒlfɪn] N [C] 海豚 hǎitún [只 zhī]
dominoes [dɑmənoʊz] N [U] 多米诺骨牌游戏 duōmǐnuò gǔpái yóuxì
donate [doʊneɪt] VT **1** ▶ **to donate (to sb)** (+ *money, clothes*) 捐赠(给某人) juānzèng (gěi mǒurén) **2** (+ *blood, organs*) 捐献 juānxiàn

done [dʌn] PP *of* **do**
donkey [dɒŋki] N [c] 驴 lǘ [头 tóu]
don't [doʊnt] = **do not**
donut [doʊnʌt, -nət] N [c] 炸面饼圈 zhá miànbǐngquān [个 gè]
door [dɔr] N [c] 门 mén [扇 shàn] ▸ **to answer the door** 应门 yìngmén
doorbell [dɔrbɛl] N [c] 门铃 ménlíng [个 gè]
dormitory [dɔrmɪtɔri] N [c] **1** (*room*) 宿舍 sùshè [间 jiān] **2** (*building*) 宿舍楼 sùshèlóu [座 zuò]
dose [doʊs] N [c] 一剂 yījì
dot [dɒt] N [c] 圆点 yuándiǎn [个 gè] ▸ **on the dot** (*punctually*) 准时地 zhǔnshí de
dot-com N [c] 网络公司 wǎngluò gōngsī [家 jiā]
double [dʌbᵊl] **I** ADJ 双份的 shuāngfèn de **II** VI (*population, size*) 变成两倍 biànchéng liǎngbèi ▸ **it's spelled with a double "M"** 它的拼写中有两个 "M" tāde pīnxiě zhōng yǒu liǎnggè"M" ▸ **double the size/number (of sth)** (是某物)大小/数量的两倍 (shì mǒuwù) dàxiǎo/shùliàng de liǎngbèi
double bass [dʌbᵊl beɪs] N [c/U] 低音提琴 dīyīn tíqín [把 bǎ]
double-click VI 双击 shuāngjī
double room N [c] 双人房 shuāngrénfáng
doubt [daʊt] **I** N [c/U] (*uncertainty*) 怀疑 huáiyí [种 zhǒng] **II** VT (+ *person's word*) 不信 bùxìn ▸ **to doubt if** *or* **whether...** 拿不准是否… nábùzhǔn shìfǒu... ▸ **I doubt it (very much)** 我(很)怀疑 wǒ (hěn) huáiyí
doubtful [daʊtfəl] ADJ **1** (*questionable*) ▸ **it is doubtful that/whether...** 不能确定…/是否… bùnéng quèdìng.../shìfǒu... **2** (*unconvinced*) ▸ **to be doubtful that/whether...** 怀疑…/是否… huáiyí.../shìfǒu... ▸ **to be doubtful about sth** 对某事有怀疑 duì mǒushì yǒu huáiyí
down [daʊn] **I** ADV **1** (*downwards*) 向下 xiàngxià **2** (*in a lower place*) 在下面 zài xiàmian **II** PREP **1** (*towards lower level*) 沿着…往下 yánzhe...wǎng xià **2** (*at lower part of*) 在下面 zài xiàmian **3** (*along*) 沿着 yánzhe ▸ **she looked down** 她向下看 tā xiàngxià kàn ▸ **he walked down the road** 他沿街走去 tā yánjiē zǒuqù ▸ **down there** 在那儿 zài nàr ▸ **the team was two goals down** (*behind*) 该队落后两分 gāi duì luòhòu liǎng fēn
download [daʊnloʊd] VT 下载 xiàzái
downstairs [daʊnstɛərz] ADV **1** (*on or to floor below*) 楼下 lóuxià **2** (*on or to ground level*) 在一层 zài yī céng
downtown [daʊntaʊn] **I** ADV **1** (*be, work*) 在市中心 zài shì zhōngxīn **2** (*go*) 去市中心 qù shì zhōngxīn **II** ADJ ▸ **downtown Chicago** 芝加哥的市中心 Zhījiāgē de shì zhōngxīn
dozen [dʌzᵊn] N [c] 一打 yīdá ▸ **two dozen eggs** 两打鸡蛋 liǎngdá jīdàn ▸ **dozens of** 许多 xǔduō
draft [dræft] N **1** [c] (*first version*) 草稿 cǎogǎo **2** [c] (*bank draft*) 汇票 huìpiào [张 zhāng] **3** [c] (*of air*) 气流 qìliú [股 gǔ]
drag [dræg] VT (*pull*) (+ *large object, body*) 拖 tuō
dragon [drægən] N [c] 龙 lóng [条 tiáo]
drain [dreɪn] **I** N [c] (*in street*) 排水沟 páishuǐgōu [条 tiáo] **II** VT (+ *vegetables*) 使…流干 shǐ...liúgān **III** VI (*liquid*) 流入 liúrù
drama [drɑmə, dræmə] N **1** [U] (*theater*) 戏剧 xìjù **2** [c] (*play*) 一出戏剧 yīchū xìjù [幕 mù] **3** [c/U] (*excitement*) 戏剧性 xìjùxìng [种 zhǒng]
dramatic [drəmætɪk] ADJ **1** (*marked, sudden*) 戏剧性的 xìjùxìng de **2** (*exciting, impressive*) 激动人心的 jīdòng rénxīn de **3** (*theatrical*) 戏剧的 xìjù de
drank [dræŋk] PT *of* **drink**

drapes [dreɪps] N PL 窗帘 chuānglián
draw [drɔ] (*pt* **drew**, *pp* **drawn**) I VT 1 画 huà 2 (+ *curtains, blinds*) (*close*) 拉上 lāshang; (*open*) 拉开 lākāi II VI 1 (*with pen, pencil etc*) 画画 huàhuà 2 ▶ **to draw (with/against sb)** (*Sport*) (与某人)打成平局 (yǔ mǒurén) dǎ chéng píngjú III N [c] 1 (*Sport*) 平局 píngjú [个 gè] 2 (*lottery*) 抽奖 chōujiǎng [次 cì]; **draw up** VT (+ *document, plan*) 草拟 cǎonǐ
drawback [drɔbæk] N [c] 欠缺 qiànquē [个 gè]
drawer [drɔr] N [c] 抽屉 chōuti [个 gè]
drawing [drɔɪŋ] N 1 [c] (*picture*) 素描 sùmiáo [幅 fú] 2 [U] (*skill, discipline*) 绘画 huìhuà
drawn [drɔn] PP *of* **draw**
dread [drɛd] VT (*fear*) 惧怕 jùpà
dreadful [drɛdfəl] ADJ 糟透的 zāotòu de
dream [drim] (*pt, pp* **dreamed** *or* **dreamt**) I N [c] 1 梦 mèng [场 chǎng] 2 (*ambition*) 梦想 mèngxiǎng [个 gè] II VI ▶ **to dream about** (*when asleep*) 梦到 mèngdào
dreamt [drɛmt] PT, PP *of* **dream**
drench [drɛntʃ] VT (*soak*) 使湿透 shǐ shītòu
dress [drɛs] I N [c] 连衣裙 liányīqún [条 tiáo] II VT 1 (+ *child*) 给…穿衣 gěi...chuān yī 2 (+ *salad*) 拌 bàn III VI 穿衣 chuān yī ▶ **to dress o.s., get dressed** 穿好衣服 chuānhǎo yīfu; **dress up** VI 1 (*wear best clothes*) 穿上盛装 chuānshang shèngzhuāng 2 ▶ **to dress up as** 化装成 huàzhuāng chéng
dresser [drɛsər] N [c] (*chest of drawers*) 梳妆台 shūzhuāngtái [个 gè]
dressing gown N [c] 晨衣 chényī [套 tào]
dressing table N [c] 梳妆台 shūzhuāngtái [个 gè]
drew [dru] PT *of* **draw**
dried [draɪd] ADJ (+ *fruit, herbs*) 干的 gān de; (+ *eggs, milk*) 粉状的 fěnzhuàng de
drier [draɪər] N = **dryer**
drill [drɪl] I N [c] (*for DIY etc*) 钻 zuàn [个 gè]; (*of dentist*) 钻头 zuàntóu [个 gè] II VT 在…上钻孔 zài...shang zuānkǒng
drink [drɪŋk] (*pt* **drank**, *pp* **drunk**) I N 1 [c] (*tea, water etc*) 饮料 yǐnliào [种 zhǒng] 2 [c] (*alcoholic*) 酒 jiǔ [瓶 píng] II VT 喝 hē III VI (*drink alcohol*) 喝酒 hējiǔ ▶ **to have a drink** 喝一杯 hē yībēi; (*alcoholic*) 喝酒 hējiǔ
drive [draɪv] (*pt* **drove**, *pp* **driven**) I N 1 [c] (*journey*) 车程 chēchéng [段 duàn] 2 [c] (*also*: **driveway**) 私家车道 sījiā chēdào [条 tiáo] 3 [c] (*also*: **CD ROM/disk drive**) 驱动器 qūdòngqì [个 gè] II VT 1 (+ *vehicle*) 驾驶 jiàshǐ 2 ▶ **to drive sb to the station/airport** 驱车送某人去车站/飞机场 qūchē sòng mǒurén qù chēzhàn/fēijīchǎng III VI 开车 kāichē ▶ **to go for a drive** 开车兜风 kāichē dōufēng ▶ **it's a 3-hour drive from Chicago** 到芝加哥要3个小时的车程 dào Zhījiāgē yào sāngè xiǎoshí de chēchéng ▶ **to drive sb mad/to desperation** 逼得某人发疯/绝望 bīde mǒurén fāfēng/juéwàng ▶ **to drive at 50 km an hour** 以每小时50公里的速度驾车 yǐ měi xiǎoshí wǔshí gōnglǐ de sùdù jiàchē
driver [draɪvər] N [c] 1 (*of own car*) 驾驶员 jiàshǐyuán [位 wèi] 2 (*of taxi, bus, lorry, train*) 司机 sījī [位 wèi]
driver's license N [c] 驾驶执照 jiàshǐ zhízhào [本 běn]
driveway [draɪvweɪ] N [c] 车道 chēdào [条 tiáo]
driving instructor N [c] 驾驶教练 jiàshǐ jiàoliàn [位 wèi]
driving test N [c] 驾驶执照考试 jiàshǐ zhízhào kǎoshì [次 cì]
drizzle [drɪzᵊl] VI ▶ **it is drizzling** 下着毛毛雨 xiàzhe máomáoyǔ
drop [drɒp] I N 1 [c] (*of liquid*) 滴 dī 2 (*reduction*) ▶ **a drop in sth** 某物的

下降 mǒuwù de xiàjiàng **II** VT **1** 失手落下 shīshǒu luòxià; (*deliberately*) 放 fàng **2** (*set down from car*) 将…送到 jiāng...sòng dào **III** VI (*amount, level*) 下降 xiàjiàng; (*object*) 落下 luòxià; **drop in** (*inf*) VI ▸ **to drop in (on sb)** 顺便拜访(某人) shùnbiàn bàifǎng (mǒurén); **drop off I** VI (*fall asleep*) 睡着 shuìzháo **II** VT (+ *passenger*) 将…送到 jiāng...sòng dào; **drop out** VI (*of college, university*) 辍学 chuòxué

drought [draʊt] N [C/U] 旱灾 hànzāi [场 chǎng]

drove [droʊv] PT *of* **drive**

drown [draʊn] **I** VT ▸ **to be drowned** 被淹死 bèi yānsǐ **II** VI (*person, animal*) 溺死 nìsǐ

drug [drʌg] N [C] **1** (*prescribed*) 药 yào [片 piàn] **2** (*recreational*) 毒品 dúpǐn [种 zhǒng] ▸ **to take drugs** 吸毒 xīdú ▸ **hard/soft drugs** 硬/软毒品 yìng/ruǎn dúpǐn

drug addict N [C] 吸毒成瘾者 xīdú chéngyǐnzhě [个 gè]

drug dealer N [C] 毒品贩子 dúpǐn fànzi

druggist [drʌgɪst] N [C] **1** (*person*) 药剂师 yàojìshī [位 wèi] **2** ▸ **druggist('s)** (*store*) 药店 yàodiàn [家 jiā]

drugstore [drʌgstɔr] N [C] 杂货店 záhuòdiàn [家 jiā]

drum [drʌm] **I** N [C] 鼓 gǔ [面 miàn] **II drums** N PL (*kit*) 鼓 gǔ

drummer [drʌmər] N [C] 鼓手 gǔshǒu [位 wèi]

drunk [drʌŋk] **I** PP *of* **drink II** ADJ 醉的 zuì de ▸ **to get drunk** 喝醉了 hēzuì le

dry [draɪ] **I** ADJ **1** 干的 gān de **2** (+ *climate, weather, day*) 干燥的 gānzào de **II** VT 把…弄干 bǎ...nòng gān **III** VI (*paint, washing*) 变干 biàn gān ▸ **to dry one's hands/hair** 擦干手/头发 cāgān shǒu/tóufa

dry cleaner N [C] 干洗店 gānxǐdiàn [家 jiā]

dryer [draɪər] N [C] **1** (*tumble dryer, spin-dryer*) 干衣机 gānyījī [台 tái] **2** (*hair dryer*) 吹风机 chuīfēngjī [个 gè]

duck [dʌk] N **1** [C] (*bird*) 鸭 yā [只 zhī] **2** [U] (*as food*) 鸭肉 yāròu

due [du] **I** ADJ ▸ **to be due** (*person, train, bus*) 应到 yīng dào; (*baby*) 预期 yùqī; (*rent, payment*) 应支付 yīng zhīfù **II** ADV ▸ **due north/south** 正北方/南方 zhèng běifāng/nánfāng ▸ **due to...** (*because of*) 由于… yóuyú...

dug [dʌg] PT, PP *of* **dig**

dull [dʌl] ADJ **1** (+ *weather, day*) 阴沉的 yīnchén de **2** (*boring*) 单调乏味的 dāndiào fáwèi de

dumb [dʌm] ADJ (*pej: stupid, foolish*) 愚蠢的 yúchǔn de

dump [dʌmp] **I** N [C] (*for rubbish*) 垃圾场 lājīchǎng [个 gè] **II** VT **1** (*get rid of*) 倾倒 qīngdào **2** (+ *computer data*) 转储 zhuǎn chǔ

Dumpster® [dʌmpstər] N [C] (用以装运工地废料的无盖)废料筒 (yòngyǐ zhuāngyùn gōngdì fèiliào de wú gài) fèiliàotǒng [个 gè]

during [dʊərɪŋ] PREP **1** 在…期间 zài...qījiān **2** (*at some point in*) 在…时候 zài...shíhou

dusk [dʌsk] N [U] 黄昏 huánghūn ▸ **at dusk** 黄昏时刻 huánghūn shíkè

dust [dʌst] N [U] (*dirt: outdoors*) 尘土 chéntǔ; (*indoors*) 灰尘 huīchén

dusty [dʌsti] ADJ 满是尘土的 mǎn shì chéntǔ de

Dutch [dʌtʃ] **I** ADJ 荷兰的 Hélán de **II** N [U] (*language*) 荷兰语 Hélányǔ **III the Dutch** N PL (*people*) 荷兰人 Hélánrén

duty [duti] **I** N [C/U] **1** (*responsibility*) 责任 zérèn [个 gè] **2** (*tax*) 税 shuì [种 zhǒng] **II duties** N PL (*tasks*) 任务 rènwù

duty-free ADJ (+ *drink, cigarettes*) 免税的 miǎnshuì de ▸ **duty-free shop** 免税商店 miǎnshuì shāngdiàn

DVD player N [C] DVD播放器 DVD bōfàngqì [台 tái]

dye [daɪ] **I** N [C/U] 染料 rǎnliào [种 zhǒng] **II** VT 染色 rǎnsè

dynamic [daɪnæmɪk] ADJ 生气勃勃的 shēngqì bóbó de

dyslexia [dɪslɛksiə] N [U] 诵读困难 sòngdú kùnnan

dyslexic [dɪslɛksɪk] ADJ 诵读有困难的 sòngdú yǒu kùnnan de

E

each [it∫] I ADJ 每 měi II PRON (*each one*) 每个 měigè ▸ **each one of them** 他们中的每一个 tāmen zhōngde měiyīgè ▸ **each other** 互相 hùxiāng ▸ **they have 2 books each** 他们每人有两本书 tāmen měirén yǒu liǎngběnshū ▸ **they cost 5 dollars each** 每个售价5美元 měigè shòujià wǔ měiyuán

> **each** 表示一个群体中的每一个人或物，强调的是每一个个体。**every** 指由两个以上的个体组成的群体中的所有的人或物，强调的是整体。*He listened to every news bulletin...an equal chance for every child...* 注意 **each** 指两个当中的任何一个。*Each apartment has two bedrooms...We each carried a suitcase.* **each** 和 **every** 后面都只能跟名词单数形式。

ear [ɪər] N [c] 耳朵 ěrduo [只 zhī]

earache [ɪəreɪk] N [c/u] 耳朵痛 ěrduo tòng

earlier [ɜrliər] I ADJ (+ *date, time*) 较早的 jiàozǎo de II ADV (*leave, go*) 提早 tízǎo ▸ **earlier this year** 本年初 běnnián chū

early [ɜrli] I ADV 1 (*in day, month*) 在初期 zài chūqī 2 (*before usual time: get up, go to bed, arrive, leave*) 早 zǎo II ADJ (+ *stage, career*) 早期的 zǎoqī de ▸ **I usually get up early** 我通常早起床。 wǒ tōngcháng zǎo qǐchuáng ▸ **early this morning** 今天一大早 jīntiān yīdàzǎo ▸ **early in the morning** 清早 qīngzǎo ▸ **you're early!** 你怎么这么早！ nǐ zěnme zhème zǎo!

earn [ɜrn] VT 挣得 zhèngdé ▸ **to earn one's** *or* **a living** 谋生 móushēng

earnings [ɜrnɪŋz] N PL 收入 shōurù

earphones [ɪərfoʊnz] N PL 耳机 ěrjī

earring [ɪərɪŋ] N [c] 耳环 ěrhuán [只 zhī]

earth [ɜrθ] N 1 [u/s] (*also*: **the Earth**) 地球 dìqiú 2 [u] (*land surface*) 陆地 lùdì 3 [u] (*soil*) 泥土 nítǔ

earthquake [ɜrθkweɪk] N [c] 地震 dìzhèn [次 cì]

easily [izɪli] ADV 不费力地 bù fèilì de

east [ist] I N 1 [s/u] 东方 dōngfāng 2 ▸ **the East** (*the Orient*) 东方国家 dōngfāng guójiā II ADJ 东部的 dōngbù de III ADV 向东方 xiàng dōngfāng ▸ **the east of Spain** 西班牙东部 Xībānyá dōngbù ▸ **to the east** 以东 yǐdōng ▸ **east of ...** …以东 ...yǐdōng

Easter [istər] N [u] 复活节 Fùhuó Jié ▸ **the Easter vacation** 复活节假期 Fùhuó Jié jiàqī

eastern [istərn] ADJ 1 (*Geo*) 东部的 dōngbù de 2 ▸ **Eastern** (*oriental*) 东方的 Dōngfāng de

easy [izi] ADJ 1 容易的 róngyì de 2 (+ *life, time*) 安逸的 ānyì de ▸ **dogs are easy to train** 狗很容易训练 gǒu hěn róngyì xùnliàn ▸ **it's easy to train dogs** 训狗是容易的 xùngǒu shì róngyì de

eat [it] (*pt* **ate**, *pp* **eaten**) I VT 吃 chī II VI 1 吃 chī 2 (*have a meal*) 吃饭 chīfàn

eaten [itᵊn] PP *of* **eat**

echo [ɛkoʊ] (*pl* **echoes**) N [c] 回音 huíyīn [个 gè]

ecology [ɪkɒlədʒi] N [u] 1 (*environment*) 生态 shēngtài 2 (*subject*) 生态学 shēngtàixué

economic [ɛkənɒmɪk, ik-] ADJ 1 经济的 jīngjì de 2 (*profitable*) 有利可图的 yǒulì kětú de

economical [ɛkənɒmɪkᵊl, ik-] ADJ 节约的 jiéyuē de

economics [ɛkənɒmɪks, ik-] N [u] 经济学 jīngjìxué

economy [ɪkɒnəmi] N 1 [c] 经济

jīngjì [种 zhǒng] **2** [U] (*thrift*) 节约 jiéyuē

eczema [ɛksəmə, ɛgzə-, ɪgzi-] N [U] 湿疹 shīzhěn

edge [ɛdʒ] N [C] **1** (*of road, town*) 边缘 biānyuán [个 gè] **2** (*of table, chair*) 棱 léng

editor [ɛdɪtər] N [C] 编辑 biānjí [个 gè]

educate [ɛdʒʊkeɪt] VT 教育 jiàoyù

education [ɛdʒʊkeɪʃᵊn] N [U/S] 教育 jiàoyù

effect [ɪfɛkt] **I** N [C/U] 影响 yǐngxiǎng [个 gè] **II effects** N PL (*Cine*) 特别效果 tèbié xiàoguǒ ▸ **to take effect** (*drug*) 见效 jiànxiào ▸ **to have an effect on sb/sth** 对某人/某事产生影响 duì mǒurén/mǒushì chǎnshēng yǐngxiǎng

effective [ɪfɛktɪv] ADJ 有效的 yǒuxiào de

efficiency [ɪfɪʃᵊnsi] N [U] 效率 xiàolǜ

efficient [ɪfɪʃᵊnt] ADJ 效率高的 xiàolǜ gāo de

effort [ɛfərt] N **1** [U] 努力 nǔlì **2** [C] (*attempt*) 尝试 chángshì [个 gè] **3** [U/S] ▸ **to make an effort to do sth** 努力做某事 nǔlì zuò mǒushì

e.g. [i dʒi] ADV ABBR (= **exempli gratia**) (*for example*) 举例来说 jǔlì lái shuō

egg [ɛg] N [C] 蛋 dàn [个 gè]

eggplant [ɛgplænt] N [C/U] 茄子 qiézi [个 gè]

Egypt [idʒɪpt] N 埃及 Āijí

eight [eɪt] NUM 八 bā; *see also* **five**

eighteen [eɪtin] NUM 十八 shíbā; *see also* **fifteen**

eighteenth [eɪtinθ] NUM 第十八 dì shíbā; *see also* **fifth**

eighth [eɪtθ] NUM **1** 第八 dì bā **2** (*fraction*) 八分之一 bā fēn zhī yī; *see also* **fifth**

eighty [eɪti] NUM 八十 bāshí; *see also* **fifty**

Eire [ɛrə] N 爱尔兰共和国 Ài'ěrlán Gònghéguó

KEYWORD

either [iðər, aɪðər] **I** ADJ **1** (*one or other*) 两者任一的 liǎngzhě rènyī de **2** (*both, each*) 两者中每一方的 liǎngzhě zhōng měiyīfāng de ▸ **on either side** 在两边 zài liǎngbiān

II PRON **1** (*after negative*) 两者之中任何一个 liǎngzhě zhī zhōng rènhé yīgè ▸ **I don't like either of them** 两个我都不喜欢 liǎnggè wǒ dōu bù xǐhuān **2** (*after interrogative*) 两者之中任何一个 liǎngzhě zhī zhōng rènhé yīgè

III ADV (*in negative statements*) 也 yě

IV CONJ ▸ **either... or...** 要么…要么… yàome...yàome... ▸ **no, I don't either** 不，我也不 bù, wǒ yě bù

elastic [ɪlæstɪk] N [U] 橡皮 xiàngpí

elbow [ɛlboʊ] N [C] (*Anat*) 肘 zhǒu [个 gè]

elder [ɛldər] ADJ (+ *brother, sister*) 年龄较大的 niánlíng jiào dà de

elderly [ɛldərli] **I** ADJ 年长的 niánzhǎng de **II** N PL ▸ **the elderly** 老人家 lǎorenjia

eldest [ɛldɪst] **I** ADJ 年龄最大的 niánlíng zuìdà de **II** N [S/PL] 年龄最大的孩子 niánlíng zuìdà de háizi

elect [ɪlɛkt] VT 选举 xuǎnjǔ

election [ɪlɛkʃᵊn] N [C] 选举 xuǎnjǔ [次 cì] ▸ **to hold an election** 举行选举 jǔxíng xuǎnjǔ

electric [ɪlɛktrɪk] ADJ **1** 电动的 diàndòng de **2** (+ *current, charge, socket*) 电的 diàn de

electrical [ɪlɛktrɪkᵊl] ADJ 电动的 diàndòng de

electric guitar N [C/U] 电吉他 diànjítā [把 bǎ]

electrician [ɪlɛktrɪʃᵊn, ilɛk-] N [C] 电工 diàngōng [个 gè]

electricity [ɪlɛktrɪsɪti, ilɛk-] N [U] **1** (*energy*) 电 diàn **2** (*supply*) 供电 gòngdiàn

electric shock N [C] 触电 chùdiàn [次 cì]

electronic [ɪlɛktrɒnɪk, i-] ADJ 电子的 diànzǐ de
electronics [ɪlɛktrɒnɪks, i-] N [U] 电子学 diànzǐxué
elegant [ɛlɪgənt] ADJ 优雅的 yōuyǎ de
elementary school [ɛlɪmɛntəri skul] N [C/U] 小学 xiǎoxué
elephant [ɛlɪfənt] N [C] 大象 dàxiàng [头 tóu]
elevator [ɛlɪveɪtər] N [C] 电梯 diàntī [部 bù]
eleven [ɪlɛvᵊn] NUM 十一 shíyī; *see also* **five**
eleventh [ɪlɛvᵊnθ] NUM 第十一 dì shíyī; *see also* **fifth**
eliminate [ɪlɪmɪneɪt] VT **1** (+ *poverty*) 消除 xiāochú **2** (+ *team, contestant, candidate*) 淘汰 táotài
else [ɛls] ADV ▶ **or else** (*otherwise*) 否则 fǒuzé; (*threatening*) 要不然 yàobùrán ▶ **Don't talk to me like that again, or else!** 别这么跟我说话，要不够你受的！ bié zhème gēn wǒ shuōhuà, yàobù gòu nǐ shòu de! ▶ **something else** 其他东西 qítā dōngxi ▶ **anything else** 任何其他东西 rènhé qítā dōngxi ▶ **what else?** 其他什么？ qítā shénme ▶ **everywhere else** 其他任何地方 qítā rènhé dìngfāng ▶ **everyone else** 其他人 qítā rén ▶ **nobody else** 没有其他人 méiyǒu qítā rén
elsewhere [ɛlswɛər] ADV **1** (*be*) 在别处 zài biéchù **2** (*go*) 到别处 dào biéchù
email [imeɪl] **I** N [C/U] 电子邮件 diànzǐ yóujiàn [封 fēng] **II** VT **1** (+ *person*) 给…发电子邮件 gěi...fā diànzǐ yóujiàn **2** (+ *file, document*) 用电子邮件寄 yòng diànzǐ yóujiàn jì
email account N [C] 电子邮件账号 diànzǐ yóujiàn zhànghào [个 gè]
email address N [C] 电子邮件地址 diànzǐ yóujiàn dìzhǐ [个 gè]
embarrassed [ɪmbærəst] ADJ ▶ **to be embarrassed** 不好意思的 bùhǎo yìsi de
embarrassing [ɪmbærəsɪŋ] ADJ 令人尴尬的 lìng rén gāngà de
embassy [ɛmbəsi] N [C] 大使馆 dàshǐguǎn [个 gè]
emergency [ɪmɜrdʒᵊnsi] N [C] (*crisis*) 紧急情况 jǐnjí qíngkuàng [个 gè] ▶ **in an emergency** 在紧急情况下 zài jǐnjí qíngkuàng xià
emergency room N [C] 急诊室 jízhěnshì [个 gè]
emigrate [ɛmɪgreɪt] VI 移居外国 yíjū wàiguó
emotion [ɪmoʊʃᵊn] N [C/U] 感情 gǎnqíng [种 zhǒng]
emotional [ɪmoʊʃənᵊl] ADJ 易动感情的 yì dòng gǎnqíng de
emperor [ɛmpərər] N [C] 皇帝 huángdì [个 gè]
emphasize [ɛmfəsaɪz] VT 强调 qiángdiào
empire [ɛmpaɪər] N [C] 帝国 dìguó [个 gè]
employ [ɪmplɔɪ] VT 雇用 gùyòng ▶ **he was employed as a technician** 他受雇做技师 tā shòugù zuò jìshī
employee [ɪmplɔɪi] N [C] 雇员 gùyuán [个 gè]
employer [ɪmplɔɪər] N [C] 雇主 gùzhǔ [个 gè]
employment [ɪmplɔɪmənt] N [U] 工作 gōngzuò
empty [ɛmpti] **I** ADJ 空的 kōng de **II** VT 倒空 dào kōng
encourage [ɪnkɜrɪdʒ] VT **1** (+ *person*) 鼓励 gǔlì **2** (+ *activity, attitude*) 支持 zhīchí **3** (+ *growth, industry*) 助长 zhùzhǎng ▶ **to encourage sb to do sth** 鼓励某人去做某事 gǔlì mǒurén qùzuò mǒushì
encouragement [ɪnkɜrɪdʒmənt] N [U] 鼓励 gǔlì
encyclopedia [ɪnsaɪkləpidiə] N [C] 百科全书 bǎikē quánshū
end [ɛnd] **I** N **1** [S] (*of period, event*) 末期 mòqī **2** [S] (*of film, book*) 末尾 mòwěi **3** [C] (*of street, line, rope, table*) 尽头 jìntóu [个 gè] **4** [C] (*of town*) 端 duān **II** VT (*finish, stop*)

终止 zhōngzhǐ **III** VI (*meeting, film, book*) 结束 jiéshù ▸ **at the end of August** 在8月末 zài bāyuè mò ▸ **to come to an end** 完结 wánjié ▸ **in the end** 最终 zuìzhōng; **end up** VI ▸ **to end up in/at** (+ *place*) 最终到了 zuìzhōng dào le

ending [ɛndɪŋ] N [C] 结局 jiéjú [个 gè] ▸ **a happy ending** 美满结局 měimǎn jiéjú

enemy [ɛnəmi] N [C] 敌人 dírén [个 gè]

energetic [ɛnərdʒɛtɪk] ADJ **1** 精力充沛的 jīnglì chōngpèi de **2** (+ *activity*) 生机勃勃的 shēngjī bóbó de

energy [ɛnərdʒi] N [U] 能源 néngyuán

engaged [ɪngeɪdʒd] ADJ (*to be married*) 已订婚的 yǐ dìnghūn de ▸ **to get engaged (to)** (与…)订婚 (yǔ...) dìnghūn

engagement [ɪngeɪdʒmənt] N [C] (*to marry*) 婚约 hūnyuē [个 gè]

engagement ring N [C] 订婚戒指 dìnghūn jièzhǐ [枚 méi]

engine [ɛndʒɪn] N [C] **1** (*Aut*) 发动机 fādòngjī [台 tái] **2** (*Rail*) 机车 jīchē [部 bù]

engineer [ɛndʒɪnɪər] N [C] **1** (*who designs machines, bridges*) 工程师 gōngchéngshī [位 wèi] **2** (*who repairs machines, phones etc*) 机械师 jīxièshī [位 wèi]

engineering [ɛndʒɪnɪərɪŋ] N [U] **1** (*of roads, bridges, machinery*) 工程 gōngchéng **2** (*science*) 工程学 gōngchéngxué

England [ɪŋglənd] N 英格兰 Yīnggélán

English [ɪŋglɪʃ] **I** ADJ 英国的 Yīngguó de **II** N (*language*) 英语 Yīngyǔ **III the English** N PL (*people*) 英国人 Yīngguórén ▸ **an English speaker** 一个讲英语的人 yīgè jiǎng yīngyǔ de rén

Englishman [ɪŋglɪʃmən] (*pl* **Englishmen**) N [C] 英格兰男人 Yīnggélán nánrén [个 gè]

Englishwoman [ɪŋglɪʃwʊmən] (*pl* **Englishwomen**) N [C] 英格兰女人 Yīnggélán nǚrén [个 gè]

enjoy [ɪndʒɔɪ] VT (*take pleasure in*) 享受…的乐趣 xiǎngshòu...de lèqù ▸ **to enjoy doing sth** 喜欢做某事 xǐhuān zuò mǒushì ▸ **to enjoy o.s.** 过得快活 guòde kuàihuó ▸ **enjoy your meal!** 吃好！ chīhǎo!

enjoyable [ɪndʒɔɪəbᵊl] ADJ 有乐趣的 yǒu lèqù de

enormous [ɪnɔrməs] ADJ **1** 庞大的 pángdà de **2** (+ *pleasure, success, disappointment*) 巨大的 jùdà de

enough [ɪnʌf] **I** ADJ (+ *time, books, people*) 足够的 zúgòu de **II** PRON (*sufficient, more than desired*) 足够的东西 zúgòu de dōngxi **III** ADV ▸ **big/old/tall enough** 足够大/到年龄了/足够高 zúgòu dà/ dào niánlíng le/ zúgòu gāo ▸ **enough time/money to do sth** 有足够的时间/金钱去做某事 yǒu zúgòu de shíjiān/jīnqián qùzuò mǒushì ▸ **have you got enough?** 你够吗？ nǐ gòuma ▸ **enough to eat** 够吃 gòuchī ▸ **will 5 be enough?** 5个够吗？ wǔgè gòuma ▸ **I've had enough!** 我受够了！ wǒ shòugòu le! ▸ **that's enough, thanks** 足已，谢谢 zúyǐ, xièxiè

enquiry [ɪnkwaɪəri] N = **inquiry**

enroll [ɪnroʊl] **I** VT **1** 招…入学 zhāo...rùxué **2** (*in course, in club*) 注册 zhùcè **II** VI (*at school, university, in course, in club*) 注册 zhùcè

ensure [ɪnʃʊər] (*frm*) VT 保证 bǎozhèng

enter [ɛntər] **I** VT **1** (+ *room, building*) 进入 jìnrù **2** (+ *race, competition*) 参加 cānjiā **3** (*Comput*) (+ *data*) 输入 shūrù **II** VI (*come or go in*) 进来 jìnlái

entertain [ɛntərteɪn] VT **1** (*amuse*) 给…娱乐 gěi...yúlè **2** (*invite*) (+ *guest*) 招待 zhāodài

entertainment [ɛntərteɪnmənt] N [U] 娱乐活动 yúlè huódòng

enthusiasm [ɪnθuziæzəm] N [U] 热

情 rèqíng ▶ **enthusiasm for sth** 对某事的热情 duì mǒushì de rèqíng
enthusiastic [ɪnθuziæstɪk] ADJ 极感兴趣的 jí gǎn xìngqù de; (+ *response, reception*) 热情的 rèqíng de ▶ **to be enthusiastic about sth** 对某事满怀热情 duì mǒushì mǎnhuái rèqíng
entire [ɪntaɪər] ADJ 整个的 zhěnggè de
entirely [ɪntaɪərli] ADV 完全地 wánquán de
entrance [ɛntrəns] N [c] 入口 rùkǒu [个 gè] ▶ **the entrance to sth** 某处的入口 mǒuchù de rùkǒu
entry [ɛntri] N **1** [c] (*way in*) 入口 rùkǒu [个 gè] **2** [c] (*in competition*) 登记 dēngjì [个 gè] **3** [c] (*item: in diary*) 项目 xiàngmù [个 gè]; (*Comput*) 输入 shūrù [项 xiàng] ▶ **"no entry"** (*to land, room*) "禁止入内" jìnzhǐ rùnèi; (*Aut*) "禁止通行" jìnzhǐ tōngxíng
envelope [ɛnvəloʊp, ɒn-] N [c] 信封 xìnfēng [个 gè]
environment [ɪnvaɪrənmənt, -vaɪərn-] N [c/U] 环境 huánjìng [个 gè] ▶ **the environment** (*natural world*) 自然环境 zìrán huánjìng
environmental [ɪnvaɪrənmɛntᵊl, -vaɪərn-] ADJ 环境保护的 huánjìng bǎohù de
environmentally friendly [ɪnvaɪrənmɛntᵊli frɛndli] ADJ 不污染环境的 bù wūrǎn huánjìng de
envy [ɛnvi] **I** N [U] 羡慕 xiànmù **II** VT (*be jealous of*) 羡慕 xiànmù ▶ **to envy sb sth** 羡慕某人的某物 xiànmù mǒurénde mǒuwù
epilepsy [ɛpɪlɛpsi] N [U] 癫痫 diānxián
episode [ɛpɪsoʊd] N [c] (*TV*) 集 jí
equal [ikwəl] **I** ADJ **1** 相等的 xiāngděng de **2** (+ *intensity, importance*) 同样的 tóngyàng de **II** VT **1** (+ *number, amount*) 等于 děngyú **2** (*match, rival*) 比得上 bǐdéshàng ▶ **they are roughly equal in size** 它们大小差不多 tāmen dàxiǎo chàbùduō ▶ **to be equal to** (*the same as*) 与…相同 yǔ...xiāngtóng ▶ **79 minus 14 equals 65** 79减14等于65 qīshíjiǔ jiǎn shísì děngyú liùshíwǔ
equality [ɪkwɒlɪti] N [U] 平等 píngděng
equally [ikwəli] ADV **1** (*share, divide*) 平等地 píngděng de **2** (*good, important*) 同样地 tóngyàng de
equator [ɪkweɪtər] N ▶ **the equator** 赤道 chìdào
equipment [ɪkwɪpmənt] N [U] 设备 shèbèi
equivalent [ɪkwɪvələnt] **I** ADJ 相同的 xiāngtóng de **II** N [c] 相当的人/物 xiāngdāng de rén/wù [个 gè]
ER [i ɑr] N ABBR (*Med*) (= **emergency room**) 急诊室 jízhěnshì [个 gè]
eraser [ɪreɪsər] N [c] 橡皮 xiàngpí [块 kuài]
error [ɛrər] N [c/U] 差错 chācuò [个 gè] ▶ **to make an error** 犯错误 fàn cuòwù
escalator [ɛskəleɪtər] N [c] 自动扶梯 zìdòng fútī [部 bù]
escape [ɪskeɪp] **I** VI **1** (*get away*) 逃走 táozǒu **2** (*from jail*) 逃跑 táopǎo **3** (*from accident*) ▶ **to escape unhurt** 安然逃脱 ānrán táotuō **II** VT (+ *injury*) 避免 bìmiǎn ▶ **to escape from** (+ *place*) 从…逃跑 cóng... táopǎo; (+ *person*) 避开 bìkāi
especially [ɪspɛʃᵊli] ADV 尤其 yóuqí
essay [ɛseɪ] N [c] (*Scol*) 论文 lùnwén
essential [ɪsɛnʃᵊl] **I** ADJ **1** (*necessary, vital*) 必要的 bìyào de **2** (*basic*) 基本的 jīběn de **II essentials** N PL (*necessities*) 必需品 bìxūpǐn ▶ **it is essential to...** 必须… bìxū...
estate [ɪsteɪt] N [c] (*land*) 庄园 zhuāngyuán [个 gè]
estimate [*n* ɛstɪmɪt, *vb* ɛstɪmeɪt] **I** N [c] 估计 gūjì [种 zhǒng] **II** VT (*reckon, calculate*) 估计 gūjì ▶ **the damage was estimated at 300 million dollars** 估计损失为3亿美元 gūjì sǔnshī wéi sānyì měiyuán
etc. [ɛt sɛtərə, -sɛtrə] ABBR (= **et**

cetera) 等等 děngděng

Ethiopia [iθioupiə] N 埃塞俄比亚 Āisài'ébǐyà

ethnic [ɛθnɪk] ADJ 种族的 zhǒngzú de

EU [i yu] N ABBR (= **European Union**) ▸ **the EU** 欧洲联盟 Ōuzhōu Liánméng

euro [yʊəroʊ] (*pl* **euros**) N [c] 欧元 Ōuyuán [个 gè]

Europe [yʊərəp] N 欧洲 Ōuzhōu

European [yʊərəpiən] **I** ADJ 欧洲的 Ōuzhōu de **II** N [c] (*person*) 欧洲人 Ōuzhōurén [个 gè]

European Union N ▸ **the European Union** 欧洲联盟 Ōuzhōu Liánméng

evacuate [ɪvækyueɪt] VT **1** (+ *people*) 疏散 shūsàn **2** (+ *place*) 撤离 chèlí

evaluate [ɪvælyueɪt] VT 评估 pínggū

even [ivᵊn] **I** ADV 甚至 shènzhì **II** ADJ **1** (*flat*) 平坦的 píngtǎn de **2** (+ *number*) 偶数的 ǒushù de ▸ **he didn't even hear what I said** 他甚至根本没听见我的话 tā shènzhì gēnběn méi tīngjiàn wǒ de huà ▸ **even more** 甚至更多 shènzhì gèngduō ▸ **even if** 即使 jíshǐ ▸ **even though** 尽管 jǐnguǎn ▸ **not even** 连…也不 lián... yěbù ▸ **even on Sundays** 甚至星期天 shènzhì xīngqītiān

evening [ivnɪŋ] N [c/u] **1** (*early*) 傍晚 bàngwǎn [个 gè] **2** (*late*) 晚上 wǎnshang [个 gè] **3** (*whole period, event*) 晚上 wǎnshang [个 gè] ▸ **in the evening** 在晚上 zài wǎnshang ▸ **this evening** 今晚 jīnwǎn ▸ **tomorrow/yesterday evening** 明/昨晚 míng/zuówǎn

evening class N [c] 夜校 yèxiào [个 gè]

event [ɪvɛnt] N [c] 事件 shìjiàn [个 gè]

eventually [ɪvɛntʃuəli] ADV **1** (*finally*) 终于 zhōngyú **2** (*ultimately*) 最终 zuìzhōng

> 请勿将 **eventually** 和 **finally** 混淆。如果某事拖延了很久 ，或者经历了相当复杂的过程后终于发生了，可以说它 **eventually** 发生了，*Eventually, they got to the hospital... I found Victoria Avenue eventually.* **eventually** 还可以表示发生的一系列事情中的最后一件事 ，通常这最后的一件事是前面一系列事情的结果。，*Eventually, they were forced to return to England.* 在经历了长期等待或期盼后，某事终于发生了，可以说它 **finally** 发生了。 *Finally, I went to bed... The heat of the sun finally became too much for me.* **finally** 还可以表示发生的一系列事情当中最后的一件事。 *The sky turned red, then purple, and finally black.*

ever [ɛvər] ADV 从来 cónglái ▸ **have you ever seen it/been there** *etc*? 你曾经见过它/去过那儿 {等} 吗? nǐ céngjīng jiànguò tā/qùguò nàr (děng) ma? ▸ **ever since** (*adv*) 从…以来 cóng...yǐlái; (*conj*) 自从 zìcóng ▸ **we have been friends ever since** 我们从那时以来一直是朋友 wǒmen cóng nàshí yǐlái yīzhí shì péngyǒu ▸ **Jack has loved trains ever since he was a boy** 杰克自小就喜爱火车 Jiékè zìxiǎo jiù xǐ'ài huǒchē ▸ **the best ever** 迄今最佳 qìjīn zuìjiā ▸ **hardly ever** 几乎从不 jīhū cóngbù

KEYWORD

every [ɛvri] ADJ **1** (*each*) 每个 měigè ▸ **every village should have a post office** 每个村庄都应该有一个邮局 měigè cūnzhuāng dōu yīnggāi yǒu yīgè yóujú
2 (*all possible*) 一切可能的 yīqiè kěnéng de ▸ **recipes for every occasion** 各个场合均适用的菜谱 gègè chǎnghé jūn shìyòng de càipǔ
3 (*with time words*) 每 měi ▸ **every day/week** 每天/周 měitiān/zhōu

▸ **every Sunday** 每个星期天 měigè xīngqītiān ▸ **every now and then** *or* **again** 不时地 bùshí de

everybody [ɛvribɒdi, -bʌdi] PRON 每人 měirén ▸ **everybody knows about it** 谁都知道 shuí dōu zhīdào ▸ **everybody else** 其他所有人 qítā suǒyǒurén

everyone [ɛvriwʌn] PRON = **everybody**

请勿将 **everyone** 和 **every one** 混淆。**everyone** 总是指人 ,并且用作单数名词。*Everyone likes him... On behalf of everyone in the school, I'd like to thank you.* 在短语 **every one** 中，**one** 是代词 ，在不同的上下文当中，它能够指代任何人或事物。其后经常紧随单词 **of**，*We've saved seeds from every one of our plants...Every one of them phoned me.* 在这些例子当中，**every one** 是表达 **all** 的含义，而且语气更强烈。

everything [ɛvriθɪŋ] PRON 所有事物 suǒyǒu shìwù ▸ **is everything OK?** 都还好吧？ dōu hái hǎo ba ▸ **everything is ready** 所有都准备就绪 suǒyǒu dōu zhǔnbèi jiùxù ▸ **he did everything possible** 他尽了最大努力 tā jìnle zuìdà nǔlì

everywhere [ɛvriwɛər] **I** ADV 各处 gèchù **II** PRON 所有地方 suǒyǒu dìfang ▸ **there's trash everywhere** 到处都是垃圾 dàochù dōushì lājī ▸ **everywhere you go** 无论你去哪里 wúlùn nǐ qù nǎlǐ

evidence [ɛvɪdəns] N [U] **1** (*proof*) 根据 gēnjù **2** (*signs, indications*) 迹象 jìxiàng

evil [iv^əl] ADJ 邪恶的 xié'è de

ex- [ɛks-] PREFIX (+ *husband, president etc*) 前 qián ▸ **my ex-wife** 我的前妻 wǒde qiánqī

exact [ɪgzækt] ADJ 确切的 quèqiè de

exactly [ɪgzæktli] ADV **1** (*precisely*) 确切地 quèqiè de **2** (*indicating agreement*) 一点不错 yīdiǎn bùcuò ▸ **at 5 o'clock exactly** 在5点整时 zài wǔdiǎnzhěng shí ▸ **not exactly** 不完全是 bù wánquán shì

exaggerate [ɪgzædʒəreɪt] **I** VI 夸张 kuāzhāng **II** VT (*overemphasize*) 夸大 kuādà

exam [ɪgzæm] N 测验 cèyàn

pass an exam 表示考试通过，若没通过，则说 **fail an exam**。参加考试，用动词 **take**，在英式英语中则用 **sit an exam**。

examination [ɪgzæmɪneɪʃ^ən] N **1** [C] (*frm*) (*Scol, Univ*) 考试 kǎoshì [次 cì] **2** [C/U] (*Med*) 体检 tǐjiǎn [次 cì]

examine [ɪgzæmɪn] VT **1** (*inspect*) 检查 jiǎnchá **2** (*Scol, Univ*) 对…进行测验 duì...jìnxíng cèyàn **3** (*Med*) 检查 jiǎnchá

example [ɪgzæmp^əl] N [C] 例子 lìzi [个 gè] ▸ **for example** 例如 lìrú ▸ **an example of sth** 某物的例子 mǒuwù de lìzi

excellence [ɛksələns] N [U] 卓越 zhuóyuè

excellent [ɛksələnt] **I** ADJ 极好的 jíhǎo de **II** INT ▸ **excellent!** 太好了！ tài hǎo le!

except [ɪksɛpt] PREP 除了 chúle ▸ **except for** 除了…外 chúle...wài ▸ **except if/when** …时例外 ...shí lìwài

exception [ɪksɛpʃ^ən] N [C] 例外 lìwài [个 gè]

exchange [ɪkstʃeɪndʒ] **I** VT **1** (+ *gifts, addresses*) 交换 jiāohuàn **2** ▸ **to exchange sth (for sth)** (+ *goods*) 用某物交换（某物） yòng mǒuwù jiāohuàn (mǒuwù) **II** N [C/U] (*of students, sportspeople*) 交流 jiāoliú [次 cì] ▸ **in exchange (for)** 作为(对…的)交换 zuòwéi (duì...de) jiāohuàn

exchange rate N [C] 汇率 huìlǜ [个 gè]

excited [ɪksaɪtɪd] ADJ 兴奋的 xīngfèn

de ▶ **to be excited about sth/about doing sth** 对某事/做某事感到激动 duì mǒushì/zuò mǒushì gǎndào jīdòng ▶ **to get excited** 激动兴奋 jīdòng xīngfèn
excitement [ɪksaɪtmənt] N [U] 兴奋 xīngfèn
exciting [ɪksaɪtɪŋ] ADJ 令人兴奋的 lìng rén xīngfèn de
exclamation point [ɛkskləmeɪʃən pɔɪnt] N [C] 感叹号 gǎntànhào [个 gè]
excluding [ɪkskludɪŋ] PREP 不包括 bù bāokuò
excuse [*n* ɪkskyus, *vb* ɪkskyuz] I N [C/U] 借口 jièkǒu [个 gè] II VT 1 (*justify*) 是…的正当理由 shì... de zhèngdàng lǐyóu 2 (*forgive*) 原谅 yuánliàng ▶ **to make an excuse** 找借口 zhǎo jièkǒu ▶ **excuse me!** (*attracting attention*) 劳驾！ láojià; (*as apology*) 对不起！ duìbùqǐ ▶ **excuse me, please** 请原谅 qǐng yuánliàng ▶ **excuse me?** 对不起，你说什么？ duìbùqǐ, nǐ shuō shénme?
exercise [ɛksərsaɪz] I N 1 [U] (*physical exertion*) 运动 yùndòng 2 [C] (*series of movements*) 练习 liànxí [个 gè] 3 [C] (*Scol, Mus*) 练习 liànxí [个 gè] II VT (+ *muscles*) 锻炼 duànliàn; (+ *mind*) 运用 yùnyòng III VI (*person*) 锻炼 duànliàn ▶ **to take** *or* **get exercise** 做健身活动 zuò jiànshēn huódòng ▶ **to do exercises** (*Sport*) 锻炼身体 duànliàn shēntǐ
exhaust [ɪgzɔst] N 1 [C] (*also*: **exhaust pipe**) 排气管 páiqìguǎn [根 gēn] 2 [U] (*fumes*) 废气 fèiqì
exhausted [ɪgzɔstɪd] ADJ 精疲力竭的 jīng pí lì jié de
exhibition [ɛksɪbɪʃən] N [C] 展览会 zhǎnlǎnhuì [个 gè]
exist [ɪgzɪst] VI 1 (*be present*) 存在 cúnzài 2 (*live, subsist*) 生存 shēngcún
exit [ɛgzɪt, ɛksɪt] I N [C] 出口 chūkǒu [个 gè] II VT (*Comput*) 退出 tuìchū III VI ▶ **to exit from sth** (+ *room, motorway*) 离开某处 líkāi mǒuchù
expect [ɪkspɛkt] I VT 1 (*anticipate*) 预料 yùliào 2 (*await*) 期待 qīdài 3 (+ *baby*) 怀有 huáiyǒu 4 (*suppose*) 料想 liàoxiǎng II VI ▶ **to be expecting** (*be pregnant*) 怀孕 huáiyùn ▶ **to expect sth to happen** 预期某事将发生 yùqī mǒushì jiāng fāshēng ▶ **I expect so** 我想会的 wǒ xiǎng huìde
expense [ɪkspɛns] I N [C/U] 费用 fèiyòng [笔 bǐ] II **expenses** N PL 经费 jīngfèi
expensive [ɪkspɛnsɪv] ADJ 1 昂贵的 ángguì de 2 (+ *mistake*) 代价高的 dàijià gāo de
experience [ɪkspɪəriəns] I N 1 [U] (*in job*) 经验 jīngyàn 2 [U] (*of life*) 阅历 yuèlì 3 [C] (*individual event*) 经历 jīnglì [个 gè] II VT (+ *feeling, problem*) 体验 tǐyàn
experienced [ɪkspɪəriənst] ADJ 有经验的 yǒu jīngyàn de
experiment [*n* ɪkspɛrɪmənt, *vb* ɪkspɛrɪmɛnt] I N [C] 1 (*Sci*) 实验 shíyàn [个 gè] 2 (*trial*) 试用 shìyòng [次 cì] II VI 试验 shìyàn ▶ **to perform** *or* **conduct** *or* **carry out an experiment** 做实验 zuò shíyàn
expert [ɛkspɜrt] I N [C] 专家 zhuānjiā [位 wèi] II ADJ (+ *opinion, help, advice*) 专家的 zhuānjiā de ▶ **an expert on sth** 某事的专家 mǒushì de zhuānjiā
expertise [ɛkspɜrtiz] N [U] 专门知识 zhuānmén zhīshi
expire [ɪkspaɪər] VI (*passport, license*) 过期 guòqī
explain [ɪkspleɪn] VT 1 (+ *situation, contract*) 解释 jiěshì 2 (+ *decision, actions*) 阐明 chǎnmíng ▶ **to explain why/how** *etc* 解释为什么/如何{等} jiěshì wèishénme/rúhé(děng) ▶ **to explain sth to sb** 向某人解释某事 xiàng mǒurén jiěshì mǒushì
explanation [ɛkspləneɪʃən] N 1 [C/U] (*reason*) ▶ **explanation (for)** (对…的)解释 (duì...de) jiěshì [个 gè]

2 [c] (*description*) ▸ **explanation (of)** (…的) 说明 (...de) shuōmíng [个 gè]

explode [ɪksplo͟ʊd] **I** VI 爆炸 bàozhà **II** VT (+ *bomb, tank*) 使爆炸 shǐ bàozhà

exploit [ɪksplo͟ɪt] VT (+ *resources*) 开发 kāifā; (+ *person, idea*) 剥削 bōxuē

explore [ɪksplo͟r] **I** VT 探索 tànsuǒ **II** VI 探险 tànxiǎn

explosion [ɪksplo͟ʊʒᵊn] N [c] **1** 爆炸 bàozhà [个 gè] **2** (*of population*) 激增 jīzēng [个 gè]

export [*vb* ɪkspo͟rt, *n* e͟kspɔrt] **I** VT 输出 shūchū **II** N **1** [U] (*process*) 出口 chūkǒu **2** [c] (*product*) 出口物 chūkǒuwù [宗 zōng]

express [ɪksprɛ͟s] VT 表达 biǎodá; (+ *service, mail*) 特快的 tèkuài de ▸ **to express o.s.** 表达自己的意思 biǎodá zìjǐ de yìsi

expression [ɪksprɛ͟ʃᵊn] N **1** [c] (*word, phrase*) 言辞 yáncí [种 zhǒng] **2** [c/U] (*on face*) 表情 biǎoqíng [种 zhǒng]

extension [ɪkstɛ͟nʃᵊn] N [c] **1** (*of building*) 扩建部分 kuòjiàn bùfen [个 gè] **2** (*of contract, visa*) 延期 yánqī [次 cì] **3** (*Tel*) 分机 fēnjī [部 bù] ▸ **extension 3718** (*Tel*) 3718分机 sān qī yī bā fēnjī

extent [ɪkstɛ͟nt] N [U/S] (*of problem, damage*) 程度 chéngdù ▸ **to a certain extent** 在一定程度上 zài yīdìng chéngdù shàng

extinct [ɪkstɪ͟ŋkt] ADJ (+ *animal, plant*) 灭绝的 mièjué de

extra [ɛ͟kstrə] **I** ADJ 额外的 éwài de **II** ADV (*in addition*) 额外地 éwài de **III** N [c] **1** (*luxury*) 额外的事物 éwài de shìwù [件 jiàn] **2** (*surcharge*) 另外的收费 lìngwài de shōufèi [项 xiàng] ▸ **wine will cost extra** 酒另外收钱 jiǔ lìngwài shōuqián

extraordinary [ɪkstro͟rdᵊnɛri] ADJ 非凡的 fēifán de

extreme [ɪkstri͟m] ADJ **1** 极度的 jídù de **2** (+ *opinions, methods*) 极端的 jíduān de

extremely [ɪkstri͟mli] ADV 非常 fēicháng

extremist [ɪkstri͟mɪst] N [c] 过激分子 guòjī fènzǐ [个 gè]

eye [a͟ɪ] N [c] (*Anat*) 眼睛 yǎnjing [只 zhī] ▸ **to keep an eye on sb/sth** 密切注意某人/某事 mìqiè zhùyì mǒurén/mǒushì

eyebrow [a͟ɪbraʊ] N [c] 眉毛 méimao [个 gè]

eyelash [a͟ɪlæʃ] N [c] 眼睫毛 yǎnjiémáo [根 gēn]

eyelid [a͟ɪlɪd] N [c] 眼皮 yǎnpí [个 gè]

eyeliner [a͟ɪlaɪnər] N [c/U] 眼线笔 yǎnxiànbǐ

eyeshadow [a͟ɪʃædoʊ] N [c/U] 眼影 yǎnyǐng

eyesight [a͟ɪsaɪt] N [U] 视力 shìlì

F

fabric [fæbrɪk] N [C/U] 织物 zhīwù [件 jiàn]
fabulous [fæbyələs] ADJ (*inf*) 极好的 jíhǎo de
face [feɪs] I N 1 [C] (*Anat*) 脸 liǎn [张 zhāng] 2 [C] (*expression*) 表情 biǎoqíng [个 gè] II VT 1 (+ *direction*) 面向 miànxiàng 2 (+ *unpleasant situation*) 面对 miànduì ▸ **I can't** *or* **couldn't face it** 我应付不了 wǒ yìngfù bùliǎo ▸ **to come face to face with** (+ *person*) 与…面对面 yǔ...miàn duì miàn; **face up to** VT FUS 1 (+ *truth, facts*) 接受 jiēshòu 2 (+ *responsibilities, duties*) 承担 chéngdān
face mask N [C] (*also Med*) 口罩 kǒuzhào [个 gè]
facility [fəsɪlɪti] N [C] (*service*) 设施 shèshī [种 zhǒng]
fact [fækt] N [C] 真相 zhēnxiàng [个 gè] ▸ **in (actual) fact, as a matter of fact** (*for emphasis*) 实际上 shíjì shàng ▸ **facts and figures** 精确的资料 jīngquè de zīliào
factory [fæktəri, -tri] N [C] 工厂 gōngchǎng [家 jiā]
fail [feɪl] I VT (+ *exam, test*) 没有通过 méiyǒu tōngguò II VI 1 (*candidate*) 没通过 méi tōngguò 2 (*attempt, plan, remedy*) 失败 shībài ▸ **to fail to do sth** 未能做某事 wèinéng zuò mǒushì
failure [feɪlyər] N 1 [C/U] (*lack of success*) 失败 shībài [次 cì] 2 [C] ▸ **failure to do sth** 没有做某事 méiyǒu zuò mǒushì
faint [feɪnt] I ADJ 1 (+ *sound, light, smell, hope*) 微弱的 wēiruò de 2 (+ *mark, trace*) 隐约的 yǐnyuē de II VI 晕倒 yūndǎo ▸ **to feel faint** 感到眩晕 gǎndào xuànyūn
fair [fɛər] I ADJ 1 (*just, right*) 公平的 gōngpíng de 2 (*quite large*) 相当的 xiāngdāng de 3 (*quite good*) 大体的 dàtǐ de 4 (+ *skin, complexion*) 白皙的 báixī de; (+ *hair*) 金色的 jīnsè de II N [C] (*trade fair*) 交易会 jiāoyìhuì [届 jiè] ▸ **it's not fair!** 太不公平了! tài bù gōngpíng le!
fairground [fɛərgraʊnd] N [C] 游乐场 yóulèchǎng [座 zuò]
fairly [fɛərli] ADV 1 (*justly*) 公平地 gōngpíng de 2 (*quite*) 相当 xiāngdāng
faith [feɪθ] N 1 [U] (*trust*) 信任 xìnrèn 2 [U] (*religious belief*) 信仰 xìnyǎng ▸ **to have faith in sb/sth** 相信某人/某事 xiāngxìn mǒurén/mǒushì
faithful [feɪθfəl] ADJ 忠实的 zhōngshí de
fake [feɪk] I N [C] 赝品 yànpǐn [件 jiàn] II ADJ 假的 jiǎ de
fall [fɔl] (*pt* **fell**, *pp* **fallen**) VI 掉 diào 2 (*snow, rain*) 下 xià 3 (*price, temperature, currency*) 下降 xiàjiàng II N 1 [C] (*of person*) 摔倒 shuāidǎo [次 cì] 2 [C] (*in price, temperature*) 下降 xiàjiàng [次 cì] 3 [C/U] (*season*) 秋天 qiūtiān [个 gè] ▸ **to fall in love (with sb/sth)** 爱上(某人/某事) àishàng (mǒurén/mǒushì); **fall down** VI 1 (*person*) 摔倒 shuāidǎo 2 (*building*) 倒塌 dǎotā; **fall off** VI (*person, object*) 掉下 diàoxià; **fall over** VI (*person, object*) 跌倒 diēdǎo; **fall through** VI (*plan*) 落空 luòkōng
fallen [fɔlən] PP *of* **fall**
false [fɔls] ADJ 假的 jiǎ de
fame [feɪm] N [U] 声誉 shēngyù
familiar [fəmɪlyər] ADJ 熟悉的 shúxī de ▸ **to be familiar with** 对…熟悉 duì...shúxī
family [fæmɪli, fæmli] N [C] 1 (*relations*) 家庭 jiātíng [个 gè] 2 (*children*) 孩子 háizi [个 gè]
famine [fæmɪn] N [C/U] 饥荒 jīhuāng [阵 zhèn]
famous [feɪməs] ADJ 著名的 zhùmíng de
fan [fæn] N [C] 1 (*of pop star*) 迷

mí [个 gè]; (*Sport*) 球迷 qiúmí [个 gè] 2 (*Elec*) 风扇 fēngshàn [台 tái] 3 (*handheld*) 扇子 shànzi [把 bǎ]

fanatic [fənætɪk] N [C] 狂热者 kuángrè zhě [名 míng]

fantastic [fæntæstɪk] ADJ 1 极好的 jíhǎo de 2 (+ *sum, amount, profit*) 巨大的 jùdà de

FAQ [fæk] N ABBR (= **frequently asked question**) 常见问题 chángjiàn wèntí

far [fɑr] I ADJ 1 远的 yuǎn de 2 ▶ **the far end/side** 尽头的 jìntóu de II ADV 1 (*in space*) 远 yuǎn; (*in time*) 久远地 jiǔyuǎn de 2 (*much, greatly*) …得多 …de duō ▶ **as far as I know** 据我所知 jùwǒ suǒzhī ▶ **by far** …得多 …de duō ▶ **so far** 迄今为止 qìjīn wéizhǐ ▶ **it's not far from here** 离这里不远 lí zhèlǐ bùyuǎn ▶ **how far?** 多远? duōyuǎn? ▶ **far away** 遥远 yáoyuǎn ▶ **far better** 好得多 hǎodeduō

fare [fɛər] N [C] 票价 piàojià [种 zhǒng]; (*in taxi*) 乘客 chéngkè [位 wèi] ▶ **half/full fare** 半/全价 bàn/quánjià

Far East N ▶ **the Far East** 远东 Yuǎndōng

farm [fɑrm] N [C] 农场 nóngchǎng [个 gè]

farmer [fɑrmər] N [C] 农民 nóngmín [个 gè]

farming [fɑrmɪŋ] N [U] 农业 nóngyè

fascinating [fæsɪneɪtɪŋ] ADJ 迷人的 mírén de

fashion [fæʃᵊn] N [U/S] 流行的式样 liúxíng de shìyàng ▶ **in fashion** 流行 liúxíng

fashionable [fæʃənəbᵊl] ADJ 流行的 liúxíng de

fast [fæst] I ADJ 快的 kuài de II ADV 快 kuài ▶ **my watch is 5 minutes fast** 我的表快5分钟。 wǒde biǎo kuài wǔfēnzhōng ▶ **fast asleep** 酣睡 hānshuì

fasten [fæsᵊn] VT (+ *coat, jacket, belt*) 系 jì

fast food N [U] 快餐 kuàicān

fat [fæt] I ADJ 肥胖的 féipàng de; (+ *animal*) 肥的 féi de II N 1 [U] (*on person, animal, meat*) 脂肪 zhīfáng 2 [C/U] (*for cooking*) 食用油 shíyòng yóu [桶 tǒng]

> 用 **fat** 形容某人胖，显得过于直接，甚至有些粗鲁。比较礼貌而又含蓄的说法是 **plump** 或 **chubby**，后者更为正式。**overweight** 和 **obese** 暗示某人因为肥胖而有健康问题。**obese** 是医学术语，表示某人极度肥胖或超重。一般而言，应尽量避免当面使用任何表示肥胖的词语。

fatal [feɪtᵊl] ADJ 1 致命的 zhìmìng de 2 (+ *mistake*) 严重的 yánzhòng de

father [fɑðər] N [C] 父亲 fùqin [位 wèi]

father-in-law [fɑðərɪnlɔ] (*pl* **fathers-in-law**) N [C] (*of woman*) 公公 gōnggong [位 wèi]; (*of man*) 岳父 yuèfù [位 wèi]

faucet [fɔsɪt] N [C] 水龙头 shuǐlóngtou [个 gè]

fault [fɔlt] N 1 [S] 错误 cuòwù 2 [C] (*defect: in person*) 缺点 quēdiǎn [个 gè]; (*in machine*) 故障 gùzhàng [个 gè] ▶ **it's my fault** 是我的错 shì wǒde cuò

fava bean [fɑvə bin] N [C] 蚕豆 cándòu [颗 kē]

favor [feɪvər] N [C] 恩惠 ēnhuì [种 zhǒng] ▶ **to do sb a favor** 帮某人的忙 bāng mǒurén de máng ▶ **to be in favor of sth/doing sth** 赞成某事/做某事 zànchéng mǒushì/zuò mǒushì

favorite [feɪvərɪt, feɪvrɪt] I ADJ 最喜欢的 zuì xǐhuan de II N [C] 偏爱 piān'ài [种 zhǒng]

fax [fæks] I N [C] 1 传真 chuánzhēn [份 fèn] 2 (*also*: **fax machine**) 传真机 chuánzhēnjī [台 tái] II VT (+ *document*) 用传真发送 yòng chuánzhēn fāsòng

fear [fɪər] N 1 [C/U] (*terror*) 害怕 hàipà [种 zhǒng] 2 [C/U] (*anxiety*) 焦虑 jiāolǜ [种 zhǒng]

feather [fɛðər] N [c] 羽毛 yǔmáo [根 gēn]
feature [fitʃər] N [c] 特点 tèdiǎn [个 gè]
February [fɛbyuɛri, fɛbru-] N [c/u] 二月 èryuè; *see also* **July**
fed [fɛd] PT, PP *of* **feed**
fed up (*inf*) ADJ ▶ **to be fed up** 厌倦 yànjuàn
fee [fi] N [c] 费 fèi [种 zhǒng]; (+ *of doctor, lawyer*) 费用 fèiyòng [项 xiàng]
feeble [fibᵊl] ADJ **1** 虚弱的 xūruò de **2** (+ *attempt, excuse, argument*) 无力的 wúlì de
feed [fid] (*pt, pp* **fed**) VT 喂 wèi
feel [fil] (*pt, pp* **felt**) VT **1** (*touch*) (+ *object, face*) 摸 mō **2** (+ *pain*) 感到 gǎndào **3** (*think, believe*) 认为 rènwéi ▶ **to feel that...** 感到… gǎndào... ▶ **to feel hungry** 觉得饿 juéde è ▶ **to feel cold** 觉得冷 juéde lěng ▶ **to feel lonely/better** 感到孤独/感觉好多了 gǎndào gūdú/gǎnjué hǎo duō le ▶ **I don't feel well** 我觉得身体不适 wǒ juéde shēntǐ bùshì ▶ **to feel sorry for sb** 同情某人 tóngqíng mǒurén ▶ **to feel like** (*want*) 想要 xiǎng yào
feeling [filɪŋ] **I** N **1** [c] (*emotion*) 感受 gǎnshòu [种 zhǒng] **2** [c] (*physical sensation*) 感觉 gǎnjué [种 zhǒng] **3** [s] (*impression*) 感觉 gǎnjué **II feelings** N PL **1** (*attitude*) 看法 kànfǎ **2** (*emotions*) 情感 qínggǎn ▶ **I have a feeling that...** 我有种感觉… wǒ yǒuzhǒng gǎnjué... ▶ **to hurt sb's feelings** 伤害某人的感情 shānghài mǒurén de gǎnqíng
feet [fit] N PL *of* **foot**
fell [fɛl] PT *of* **fall**
felt [fɛlt] PT, PP *of* **feel**
felt-tip pen, felt-tip N [c] 毡头墨水笔 zhāntóu mòshuǐbǐ [支 zhī]
female [fimeɪl] **I** N [c] **1** (*Zool*) 雌兽 císhòu [头 tóu] **2** (*woman*) 女性 nǚxìng [位 wèi] **II** ADJ **1** (*Zool*) 雌性的 cíxìng de **2** (*relating to women*) 妇女的 fùnǚ de ▶ **male and female students** 男女学生 nánnǚ xuéshēng
feminine [fɛmɪnɪn] ADJ **1** 女性的 nǚxìng de **2** (*Ling*) 阴性的 yīnxìng de
feminist [fɛmɪnɪst] N [c] 女权主义者 nǚquán zhǔyìzhě [位 wèi]
fence [fɛns] N [c] 篱笆 líba [道 dào]
fencing [fɛnsɪŋ] N [u] (*Sport*) 击剑 jījiàn
ferry [fɛri] N [c] (*small*) 摆渡 bǎidù [个 gè]; (*large*) (*also*: **ferryboat**) 渡船 dùchuán [艘 sōu]
festival [fɛstɪvᵊl] N [c] **1** (*Rel*) 节日 jiérì [个 gè] **2** (*Theat, Mus*) 艺术节 yìshù jié [届 jiè]
fetch [fɛtʃ] VT 去拿来 qù nálái ▶ **to fetch sth for sb, fetch sb sth** 去给某人拿来某物 qù gěi mǒurén nálái mǒuwù
fever [fivər] N [c/u] (*Med*) 发烧 fāshāo [次 cì]
few [fyu] **I** ADJ **1** (*not many*) 少数的 shǎoshù de **2** ▶ **a few** (*some*) 几个 jǐge **II** PRON **1** ▶ **a few** (*some*) 几个 jǐge **2** ▶ **in the next few days** 在接下来的几天里 zài jiēxiàlái de jǐtiān lǐ ▶ **in the past few days** 在过去的几天里 zài guòqù de jǐtiān lǐ ▶ **a few of us/them** 我们/他们中的几个 wǒmen/tāmen zhōng de jǐgè ▶ **a few more** 再多几个 zài duō jǐgè ▶ **very few survive** 极少幸存 jíshǎo xìngcún
fewer [fyuər] ADJ 较少的 jiàoshǎo de ▶ **no fewer than** 不少于 bù shǎoyú
fiancé [fiɑnseɪ, fiɑnseɪ] N [c] 未婚夫 wèihūnfū [个 gè]
fiancée [fiɑnseɪ, fiɑnseɪ] N [c] 未婚妻 wèihūnqī [个 gè]
fiction [fɪkʃᵊn] N [u] 小说 xiǎoshuō
field [fild] N [c] **1** (*grassland*) 草地 cǎodì [块 kuài] **2** (*cultivated*) 田地 tiándì [片 piàn] **3** (*Sport*) 场地 chǎngdì [个 gè] **4** (*subject, area of interest*) 领域 lǐngyù [个 gè]
fierce [fɪərs] ADJ **1** 凶猛的 xiōngměng de **2** (+ *loyalty, resistance, competition*) 强烈的 qiángliè de

fifteen [fɪfti̲n] NUM 十五 shíwǔ ▶ **she's fifteen (years old)** 她15岁了 tā shíwǔ suì le

fifteenth [fɪfti̲nθ] NUM 第十五 dì shíwǔ; *see also* **fifth**

fifth [fɪ̲fθ] NUM **1** (*in series*) 第五 dìwǔ **2** (*fraction*) 五分之一 wǔfēnzhīyī ▶ **on July fifth** 在7月5日 zài qīyuè wǔrì

fifty [fɪ̲fti] NUM 五十 wǔshí ▶ **he's in his fifties** 他50多岁 tā wǔshí duō suì

fight [fa̲ɪt] (*pt, pp* **fought**) **I** N [c] **1** 斗殴 dòu'ōu [场 chǎng] **2** (*against disease, alcoholism, prejudice*) 斗争 dòuzhēng [场 chǎng] **II** VT 与…对打 yǔ...duìdǎ **III** VI **1** 战斗 zhàndòu **2** (*struggle*) 奋斗 fèndòu ▶ **to fight for/against sth** 为支持/反对某事而斗争 wèi zhīchí/fǎnduì mǒushì ér dòuzhēng

figure [fɪ̲gyər] **I** N [c] **1** (*number, statistic*) 统计数字 tǒngjì shùzì [个 gè] **2** (*digit*) 数字 shùzì [个 gè] **3** (*body, shape*) 身材 shēncái [种 zhǒng] **II** VT (*inf: reckon*) 估计 gūjì ▶ **that figures** (*inf*) 那不足为怪 nà bùzú wéiguài

file [fa̲ɪl] **I** N [c] **1** (*dossier*) 档案 dàng'àn [份 fèn] **2** (*folder*) 文件夹 wénjiànjiā [个 gè] **3** (*Comput*) 文件 wénjiàn [份 fèn] **II** VT **1** (*also*: **file away**) (+ *papers, document*) 把…归档 bǎ...guīdàng **2** (+ *wood, metal, fingernails*) 把…锉平 bǎ...cuòpíng

fill [fɪ̲l] VT **1** (+ *container*) 装满 zhuāngmǎn **2** (+ *space, area*) 占满 zhànmǎn **3** (+ *tooth*) 补 bǔ ▶ **to fill sth with sth** 用某物填满某物 yòng mǒuwù tiánmǎn mǒuwù; **fill out** VT (+ *form*) 填写 tiánxiě

filling [fɪ̲lɪŋ] N [c] (*in tooth*) 填补物 tiánbǔ wù [种 zhǒng]

film [fɪ̲lm] **I** N **1** [c] (*movie*) 影片 yǐngpiàn [部 bù] **2** [c/U] (*Phot*) 胶卷 jiāojuǎn [卷 juǎn] **II** VT 把…拍成影片 bǎ...pāichéng yǐngpiàn

filthy [fɪ̲lθi] ADJ 污秽的 wūhuì de

final [fa̲ɪnᵊl] **I** ADJ **1** 最后的 zuìhòu de **2** (+ *decision, offer*) 不可变更的 bùkě biàngēng de **II** N [c] (*Sport*) 决赛 juésài [场 chǎng]

finally [fa̲ɪnᵊli] ADV **1** (*eventually*) 终于 zhōngyú **2** (*lastly*) 最后 zuìhòu **3** (*in conclusion*) 总之 zǒngzhī

find [fa̲ɪnd] (*pt, pp* **found**) **I** VT **1** (+ *person, object, exit*) 找到 zhǎodào; (+ *lost object*) 找回 zhǎohuì **2** (*discover*) (+ *answer, solution*) 找出 zhǎochū; (+ *object, person*) 发现 fāxiàn **3** (+ *work, job*) 得到 dédào; (+ *time*) 有 yǒu ▶ **to find sb guilty/not guilty** 判决某人有罪/无罪 pànjué mǒurén yǒuzuì/wúzuì ▶ **to find one's way** 认得路 rènde lù; **find out I** VT (+ *fact, truth*) 查明 chámíng **II** VI ▶ **to find out about sth** (*deliberately*) 获知某事 huòzhī mǒushì; (*by chance*) 偶然发现某物 ǒurán fāxiàn mǒuwù

fine [fa̲ɪn] **I** ADJ **1** (*satisfactory*) 还不错的 hái bùcuò de **2** (*excellent*) 好的 hǎo de **3** (*in texture*) 细的 xì de **4** (+ *weather, day*) 晴朗的 qínglǎng de **II** ADV (*well*) 不错地 bùcuò de **III** N [c] (*Law*) 罚款 fákuǎn [笔 bǐ] **IV** VT (*Law*) 处…以罚金 chǔ...yǐ fájīn ▶ **(I'm) fine** (我)很好 (wǒ) hěnhǎo ▶ **(that's) fine** (那)好吧 (nà) hǎoba ▶ **you're doing fine** 你做得很好 nǐ zuòde hěnhǎo

finger [fɪ̲ŋgər] N [c] 手指 shǒuzhǐ [根 gēn]

finish [fɪ̲nɪʃ] **I** N **1** [s] (*end*) 结束 jiéshù **2** [c] (*Sport*) 终点 zhōngdiǎn [个 gè] **II** VT (+ *work*) 结束 jiéshù; (+ *task, report, book*) 完成 wánchéng **III** VI **1** (*course, event*) 结束 jiéshù **2** (*person*) 说完 shuōwán ▶ **to finish doing sth** 做完某事 zuòwán mǒushì

Finland [fɪ̲nlənd] N 芬兰 Fēnlán

fir [f3̲r] N [c] (*also*: **fir tree**) 冷杉 lěngshān [棵 kē]

fire [fa̲ɪər] **I** N **1** [U] (*flames*) 火 huǒ **2** [c] (*in fireplace, hearth*) 炉火 lúhuǒ [团 tuán] **3** [c/U] (*accidental*) 火灾 huǒzāi [场 cháng] **II** VT **1** (*shoot*) 射出 shèchū **2** (*inf: dismiss*) 解雇 jiěgù

III VI (*shoot*) 开火 kāihuǒ ▶ **on fire** 起火 qǐhuǒ ▶ **to catch fire** 着火 zháohuǒ

fire alarm N [C] 火警警报 huǒjǐng jǐngbào [个 gè]

fire department N [C] 消防队 xiāofáng duì [支 zhī]

firefighter [faɪərfaɪtər] N [C] 消防队员 xiāofáng duìyuán [位 wèi]

fireman [faɪərmən] (*pl* **firemen**) N [C] 消防队员 xiāofáng duìyuán [位 wèi]

fire station N [C] 消防站 xiāofángzhàn [个 gè]

fire truck N [C] 救火车 jiùhuǒchē [辆 liàng]

firework [faɪərwɜrk] **I** N [C] 烟火 yānhuǒ [团 tuán] **II fireworks** N PL (*display*) 烟火表演 yānhuǒ biǎoyǎn

firm [fɜrm] **I** ADJ **1** (+ *mattress, ground*) 硬实的 yìngshi de **2** (+ *person*) 坚定的 jiāndìng de **II** N [C] 公司 gōngsī [家 jiā]

first [fɜrst] **I** ADJ **1** (*in series*) 第一的 dìyī de **2** (+ *reaction, impression*) 最初的 zuìchū de **3** (+ *prize, division*) 头等的 tóuděng de **II** ADV **1** (*before anyone else*) 首先 shǒuxiān **2** (*before other things*) 首先 shǒuxiān **3** (*when listing reasons*) 第一 dìyī **4** (*for the first time*) 第一次 dìyīcì **5** (*in race, competition*: *come, finish*) 第一名 dìyīmíng ▶ **at first** 起先 qǐxiān ▶ **January first** 1月1号 yīyuè yīhào

first aid N [U] 急救 jíjiù

first-class I ADJ **1** (*excellent*) 第一流的 dìyīliú de **2** (+ *seat, ticket, stamp*) 一类的 yīlèi de **II** ADV (*travel, send*) 作为一类 zuòwéi yīlèi

firstly [fɜrstli] ADV 首先 shǒuxiān

first name N [C] 名 míng [个 gè]

fish [fɪʃ] **I** N **1** [C] 鱼 yú [条 tiáo] **2** [U] (*food*) 鱼肉 yúròu **II** VI (*commercially*) 捕鱼 bǔyú; (*as sport, hobby*) 钓鱼 diàoyú ▶ **to go fishing** 去钓鱼 qù diàoyú

fisherman [fɪʃərmən] (*pl* **fishermen**) N [C] 渔民 yúmín [位 wèi]

fishing [fɪʃɪŋ] N [U] 钓鱼 diàoyú

fishing boat N [C] 渔船 yúchuán [条 tiáo]

fist [fɪst] N [C] 拳 quán [个 gè]

fit [fɪt] **I** ADJ (*healthy*) 健康的 jiànkāng de **II** VI **1** (*clothes, shoes*) 合身 héshēn **2** (*in space, gap*) 适合 shìhé ▶ **to keep fit** 保持健康 bǎochí jiànkāng ▶ **to have a fit** (*Med*) 癫痫病发作 diānxiánbìng fāzuò ▶ **to be a good fit** 很合身 hěn héshēn;

fit in I VI (*lit*) 容纳 róngnà **II** VT (+ *appointment, visitor*) 定时间于 dìng shíjiān yú

fitness [fɪtnɪs] N [U] 健康 jiànkāng

five [faɪv] NUM 五 wǔ ▶ **that will be five dollars, please** 请付5美元 qǐng fù wǔ měiyuán ▶ **she's five (years old)** 她5岁了 tā wǔsuì le ▶ **it's five o'clock** 5点了 wǔdiǎn le

fix [fɪks] VT **1** (+ *date, price, meeting*) 确定 quèdìng **2** (*mend*) 修理 xiūlǐ **3** (+ *problem*) 解决 jiějué

flag [flæg] N [C] 旗 qí [面 miàn]

flame [fleɪm] N [C/U] 火焰 huǒyàn [团 tuán] ▶ **in flames** 燃烧着 ránshāo zhe

flash [flæʃ] **I** VI 闪光 shǎnguāng **II** N [C] **1** 闪光 shǎnguāng [阵 zhèn] **2** (*Phot*) 闪光灯 shǎnguāngdēng [个 gè] ▶ **to flash one's headlights** 亮起车头灯 liàngqǐ chētóudēng

flashlight [flæʃlaɪt] N [C] 手电筒 shǒudiàn tǒng [个 gè]

flask [flæsk] N [C] 保温瓶 bǎowēnpíng [个 gè]

flat [flæt] ADJ **1** 平的 píng de **2** (+ *tyre, ball*) 气不足的 qì bùzú de

flatter [flætər] VT 奉承 fèngchéng

flavor [fleɪvər] **I** N [C/U] 味 wèi [种 zhǒng] **II** VT 给…调味 gěi...tiáowèi

flea [fli] N [C] 跳蚤 tiàozao [只 zhī]

flew [flu] PT *of* **fly**

flexible [flɛksɪbᵊl] ADJ **1** 柔韧的 róurèn de **2** (+ *person, schedule*) 机动的 jīdòng de

flight [flaɪt] N **1** [C] (*journey*) 航班 hángbān [个 gè] **2** [C] (*also*: **flight**

of stairs, flight of steps) 一段楼梯 yīduàn lóutī [段 duàn]
flight attendant [flaɪt ətɛndənt] N [c] (*male*) 男空服人员 nán kōngfú rényuán [位 wèi]; (*female*) 空姐 kōngjiě [位 wèi]
float [floʊt] VI **1** 漂浮 piāofú **2** (*stay afloat*) 浮着 fúzhe
flock [flɒk] N [c] 群 qún
flood [flʌd] **I** N [c/U] 洪水 hóngshuǐ [次 cì] **II** VT 淹没 yānmò
floor [flɔr] N **1** [c] 地板 dìbǎn [块 kuài] **2** [c] (*story*) 楼层 lóucéng [个 gè] ▸ **on the floor** 在地板上 zài dìbǎn shàng ▸ **first floor** 一楼 yī lóu
floppy [flɒpi] N [c] (*also*: **floppy disk**) 软盘 ruǎnpán [张 zhāng]
florist [flɔrɪst] N [c] **1** 花商 huāshāng [个 gè] **2** (*also*: **florist's**) 花店 huādiàn [家 jiā]
flour [flaʊər] N [U] 面粉 miànfěn
flow [floʊ] **I** VI 流动 liúdòng **II** N [c/U] **1** 流动 liúdòng **2** (*of traffic*) 川流不息 chuānliú bùxī
flower [flaʊər] **I** N [c] 花 huā [朵 duō] **II** VI 开花 kāihuā ▸ **in flower** 正开着花 zhèng kāizhe huā
flown [floʊn] PP *of* **fly**
flu [flu] N [U] 流感 liúgǎn
fluent [fluənt] ADJ (+ *speech, reading, writing*) 流畅的 liúchàng de ▸ **to speak fluent French, be fluent in French** 讲流利的法语 jiǎng liúlì de Fǎyǔ
flush [flʌʃ] VT ▸ **to flush the toilet** 冲厕所 chōng cèsuǒ
flute [flut] N [c] 长笛 chángdí [支 zhī]
fly [flaɪ] (*pt* **flew**, *pp* **flown**) **I** VT (+ *plane*) 驾驶 jiàshǐ **II** VI **1** (*bird, insect, plane*) 飞 fēi **2** (*passengers*) 乘飞机 chéng fēijī **III** N [c] (*insect*) 苍蝇 cāngying [只 zhī]; **fly away** VI 飞走 fēizǒu
focus [foʊkəs] (*pl* **focuses**) **I** N **1** [U] (*Phot*) 聚焦 jùjiāo **2** [c] (*subject*) 重点 zhòngdiǎn [个 gè] **II** VI ▸ **to focus (on)** (*with camera*) 聚焦（于） jùjiāo (yú); (*concentrate on*) 集中（于） jízhōng (yú) ▸ **in focus/out of focus** 焦点对准/没对准 jiāodiǎn duìzhǔn/méi duìzhǔn ▸ **to be the focus of attention** 为关注的焦点 wéi guānzhù de jiāodiǎn
fog [fɒg] N [c/U] 雾 wù [场 chǎng]
foggy [fɒgi] ADJ (+ *day, climate*) 有雾的 yǒuwù de ▸ **it's foggy** 今天有雾 jīntiān yǒu wù
fold [foʊld] VT (*also*: **fold up**) 折叠 zhédié
folder [foʊldər] N [c] 文件夹 wénjiàn jiā [个 gè]
follow [fɒloʊ] VT **1** 跟随 gēnsuí **2** (+ *example, advice, instructions*) 遵循 zūnxún **3** (+ *route, path*) 沿着…行进 yánzhe...xíngjìn ▸ **I don't quite follow you** 我不太理解你的意思 wǒ bùtài lǐjiě nǐde yìsi ▸ **as follows** (*when listing*) 如下 rúxià; (*in this way*) 按如下方式 àn rúxià fāngshì ▸ **followed by** 接着是 jiēzhe shì
following [fɒloʊɪŋ] **I** PREP (*after*) 在…之后 zài...zhīhòu **II** ADJ **1** (+ *day, week*) 接着的 jiēzhe de **2** (*next-mentioned*) 下述的 xiàshù de
fond [fɒnd] ADJ ▸ **to be fond of** (+ *person*) 喜爱 xǐ'ài; (+ *food, walking*) 喜欢 xǐhuan
food [fud] N [c/U] 食物 shíwù [种 zhǒng]
fool [ful] **I** N [c] 白痴 báichī [个 gè] **II** VT (*deceive*) 欺骗 qīpiàn
foot [fʊt] (*pl* **feet**) N **1** [c] (*measure*) 英尺 yīngchǐ **2** [c] (*of person*) 脚 jiǎo [只 zhī] ▸ **on foot** 步行 bùxíng
football [fʊtbɔl] N **1** [c] (*ball*) 足球 zúqiú [只 zhī] **2** [U] (*sport*) 美式足球 měishì zúqiú
footpath [fʊtpæθ] N [c] 人行小径 rénxíng xiǎojìng [条 tiáo]
footprint [fʊtprɪnt] N [c] 足迹 zújì [个 gè]

KEYWORD

for [fər, STRONG fɔr] PREP **1** 为 wèi

▶ **is this for me?** 这是为我准备的吗？ zhèshì wèi wǒ zhǔnbèi de ma? ▶ **a table for two** 供两人用的桌子 gòng liǎngrén yòng de zhuōzi
2 (*purpose*) 为了 wèile ▶ **what's it for?** 它有什么用途？ tā yǒu shénme yòngtú ▶ **it's time for lunch** 该吃午饭了 gāi chī wǔfàn le ▶ **what for?** 为什么呢？ wèi shénme ne? ▶ **a knife for chopping vegetables** 用于切菜的刀 yòngyú qiēcài de dāo
3 (*time*) ▶ **he was away for two years** 他离开两年了 tā líkāi liǎngnián le ▶ **it hasn't rained for three weeks** 已经有3周没下雨了 yǐjīng yǒu sānzhōu méi xiàyǔ le ▶ **the trip is scheduled for June 5** 旅行安排在6月5日 lǚxíng ānpái zài liùyuè wǔrì
4 (*in exchange for*) ▶ **I sold it for $50** 我以五十美元卖掉了它 wǒ yǐ wǔshí měiyuán màidiào le tā ▶ **to pay 50 cents for a ticket** 花50美分买张票 huā wǔshí měifēn mǎi zhāng piào
5 (*reason*) 因为 yīnwèi
6 (*on behalf of, representing*) 为 wèi ▶ **he works for a local firm** 他为一家当地公司工作 tā wèi yījiā dāngdì gōngsī gōngzuò ▶ **G for George** George中的G George zhōng de G
7 (*destination*) 前往 qiánwǎng ▶ **he left for Rome** 他前往罗马 tā qiánwǎng Luómǎ
8 (*with infinitive clause*) ▶ **it is not for me to decide** 这不是由我来决定的 zhè bùshì yóu wǒ lái juédìng de ▶ **there is still time for you to do it** 你还有时间去做 nǐ hái yǒu shíjiān qù zuò
9 (*in favor of*) 赞成 zànchéng
10 (*referring to distance*) 达 dá ▶ **there is road construction for 50 mi** 长跑练习长达50公里 chángpǎo liànxí chángdá wǔshí gōnglǐ

> **for** 和 **to** 都可用于表示某人的目的，但后接不同的语言结构。**for** 用于表示目的时，后面必须跟名词。*Occasionally I go to the bar for a drink.* **for** 通常不用在动词前面。不能说 *I go to the bar for to have a drink*。**for** 用在 **-ing** 形式前表示某物的用途。 *...a small machine for weighing the letters...* 与动词连用时，不定式前不加 **for**。*She went off to fetch help.*

forbade [fərbæd, fɔr-] PT *of* **forbid**
forbid [fərbɪd, fɔr-] (*pt* **forbade**, *pp* **forbidden**) VT 禁止 jìnzhǐ ▶ **to forbid sb to do sth** 禁止某人做某事 jìnzhǐ mǒurén zuò mǒushì
forbidden [fərbɪdᵊn, fɔr-] PP *of* **forbid**
force [fɔrs] **I** N **1** [U] (*violence*) 武力 wǔlì **2** [U] (*strength*) 力量 lìliàng **II** VT 强迫 qiǎngpò **III forces** N PL (*Mil*) 部队 bùduì ▶ **to force sb to do sth** 强迫某人做某事 qiǎngpò mǒurén zuò mǒushì
forecast [fɔrkæst] (*pt, pp* **forecast** *or* **forecasted**) **I** N [C] 预报 yùbào [个 gè] **II** VT (*predict*) 预测 yùcè
forehead [fɔrhɛd, fɔrɪd] N [C] 额 é [个 gè]
foreign [fɔrɪn] ADJ 外国的 wàiguó de
foreigner [fɔrɪnər] N [C] 外国人 wàiguórén [个 gè]
forest [fɔrɪst] N [C/U] 森林 sēnlín [片 piàn]
forever [fɔrɛvər, fər-] ADV 永远 yǒngyuǎn
forgave [fərgeɪv] PT *of* **forgive**
forge [fɔrdʒ] VT (+ *signature, banknote*) 伪造 wěizào
forget [fərgɛt] (*pt* **forgot**, *pp* **forgotten**) **I** VT **1** 忘记 wàngjì **2** (*leave behind*) (+ *object*) 忘带 wàng dài **II** VI (*fail to remember*) 忘记 wàngjì ▶ **to forget to do sth** 忘记做某事 wàngjì zuò mǒushì ▶ **to forget that...** 忘记⋯ wàngjì...
forgive [fərgɪv] (*pt* **forgave**, *pp* **forgiven**) VT 原谅 yuánliàng ▶ **to forgive sb for sth** 原谅某人某事

yuánliàng mǒurén mǒushì
forgot [fərgɒt] PT *of* **forget**
forgotten [fərgɒtᵊn] PP *of* **forget**
fork [fɔrk] N [C] **1** 餐叉 cānchā [把 bǎ] **2** (*in road, river, railway*) 岔路 chàlù [条 tiáo]
form [fɔrm] **I** N **1** [C] (*type*) 类型 lèixíng [种 zhǒng] **2** [C] (*document*) 表格 biǎogé [张 zhāng] **II** VT **1** (*make*) 组成 zǔchéng **2** (*create*) (+ *group, organization, company*) 成立 chénglì ▸ **in the form of** 通过…方式 tōngguò...fāngshì
formal [fɔrmᵊl] ADJ 正式的 zhèngshì de
former [fɔrmər] ADJ 前任的 qiánrèn de ▸ **in former times/years** 以前 yǐqián
fortunate [fɔrtʃənɪt] ADJ 幸运的 xìngyùn de
fortunately [fɔrtʃənɪtli] ADV 幸运的是 xìngyùn de shì
fortune [fɔrtʃən] N [C] 大笔钱 dàbǐqián ▸ **to make a fortune** 发大财 fā dàcái
forty [fɔrti] NUM 四十 sìshí
forward [fɔrwərd], **forwards** [fɔrwərdz] ADV 向前 xiàngqián
fought [fɔt] PT, PP *of* **fight**
found [faʊnd] **I** PT, PP *of* **find II** VT (+ *organization, company*) 创办 chuàngbàn
fountain [faʊntɪn] N [C] 喷泉 pēnquán [个 gè]
four [fɔr] NUM 四 sì; *see also* **five**
fourteen [fɔrtin] NUM 十四 shísì; *see also* **fifteen**
fourteenth [fɔrtinθ] NUM 第十四 dì shísì; *see also* **fifth**
fourth [fɔrθ] NUM **1** 第四 dìsì **2** (*quarter*) 四分之一 sìfēnzhīyī; *see also* **fifth**
fox [fɒks] N [C] 狐狸 húli [只 zhī]
fragile [frædʒᵊl] ADJ 易损的 yìsǔn de
frame [freɪm] N [C] **1** 框 kuàng [个 gè] **2** (*also*: **frames**) (*of spectacles*) 眼镜架 yǎnjìngjià [副 fù]
France [fræns] N 法国 Fǎguó
fraud [frɔd] N [C/U] 诈骗 zhàpiàn [种 zhǒng]
freckle [frɛkᵊl] N [C] 雀斑 quèbān [个 gè]
free [fri] ADJ **1** (*costing nothing*) 免费的 miǎnfèi de **2** (+ *person*) 自由的 zìyóu de **3** (+ *time*) 空闲的 kòngxián de **4** (+ *seat, table*) 空余的 kòngyú de ▸ **free (of charge), for free** 免费 miǎnfèi ▸ **to be free of** *or* **from sth** 没有某物 méiyǒu mǒuwù ▸ **to be free to do sth** 随意做某事 suíyì zuò mǒushì
freedom [fridəm] N [U] 自由 zìyóu
freeway [friweɪ] N [C] 高速公路 gāosù gōnglù [条 tiáo]
freeze [friz] (*pt* **froze**, *pp* **frozen**) **I** VI **1** (*liquid, weather*) 结冰 jiébīng **2** (*pipe*) 冻住 dòngzhù **II** VT (+ *food*) 冷冻 lěngdòng
freezer [frizər] N [C] 冰柜 bīngguì [个 gè]
freezing [frizɪŋ] ADJ (*also*: **freezing cold**) (+ *day, weather*) 极冷的 jílěng de; (+ *person, hands*) 冰凉的 bīngliáng de ▸ **I'm freezing** 冻死我了 dòngsǐ wǒ le
French [frɛntʃ] **I** ADJ 法国的 Fǎguó de **II** N [U] (*language*) 法语 Fǎyǔ **III the French** N PL (*people*) 法国人 Fǎguórén
french fries N PL 炸薯条 zhá shǔtiáo
Frenchman [frɛntʃmən] (*pl* **Frenchmen**) N [C] 法国男人 Fǎguó nánrén [个 gè]
Frenchwoman [frɛntʃwʊmən] (*pl* **Frenchwomen**) N [C] 法国女人 Fǎguó nǚrén [个 gè]
frequent [frikwənt] ADJ 频繁的 pínfán de
fresh [frɛʃ] ADJ **1** 新鲜的 xīnxiān de **2** (+ *approach, way*) 新颖的 xīnyǐng de ▸ **fresh air** 新鲜空气 xīnxiān kōngqì
Friday [fraɪdeɪ, -di] N [C/U] 星期五 xīngqīwǔ [个 gè]; *see also* **Tuesday**
fried [fraɪd] **I** PT, PP *of* **fry II** ADJ (+ *food*) 炒的 chǎo de

friend [frɛnd] N [C] 朋友 péngyou [个 gè] ▸ **to make friends with sb** 与某人交朋友 yǔ mǒurén jiāo péngyou
friendly [frɛndli] ADJ 友善的 yǒushàn de ▸ **to be friendly with** 跟…友好 gēn...yǒuhǎo
friendship [frɛndʃɪp] N [C] 友情 yǒuqíng [种 zhǒng]
fright [fraɪt] N [C] 惊吓 jīngxià [个 gè] ▸ **to give sb a fright** 吓唬某人一下 xiàhu mǒurén yīxià
frighten [fraɪtᵊn] VT 使惊恐 shǐ jīngkǒng
frightened [fraɪtᵊnd] ADJ ▸ **to be frightened** 被吓倒 bèi xiàdǎo ▸ **to be frightened of sth/of doing sth** *or* **to do sth** 害怕某事/做某事 hàipà mǒushì/zuò mǒushì
frightening [fraɪtᵊnɪŋ] ADJ 令人恐惧的 lìngrén kǒngjù de
frog [frɔg] (*Zool*) N [C] 青蛙 qīngwā [只 zhī]

KEYWORD

from [frəm, STRONG frʌm] PREP
1 (*indicating starting place*) 来自 láizì ▸ **where are you from?** 你来自哪里？ nǐ láizì nǎlǐ? ▸ **from San Francisco to Los Angeles** 从旧金山到洛杉矶 cóng Jiùjīnshān dào Luòshānjī
2 (*indicating origin*) 来自 láizì ▸ **a present/telephone call/letter from sb** 来自某人的礼物/电话/信 láizì mǒurén de lǐwù/diànhuà/xìn
3 (*with time, distance, price, numbers*) 从 cóng ▸ **from one o'clock to** *or* **until two** 从1点直到2点 cóng yīdiǎn zhídào liǎngdiǎn ▸ **it's 1 km from the beach** 从海滩到这儿有1公里 cóng hǎitān dào zhèr yǒu yī gōnglǐ

front [frʌnt] **I** N [C] (*of house, dress*) 前面 qiánmiàn; (*of coach, train, car*) 前部 qiánbù [个 gè] **II** ADJ 前面的 qiánmiàn de ▸ **in front** 在前面 zài qiánmiàn ▸ **in front of** (*facing*) 在…前面 zài...qiánmiàn; (*in the presence of*) 在…面前 zài...miànqián
front door N [C] 前门 qiánmén [个 gè]
frontier [frʌntɪər, frɒn-] N [C] 国界 guójiè [个 gè]
front page N [C] (*Publishing*) 头版 tóubǎn [个 gè]
frost [frɔst] N [C] 霜 shuāng [次 cì]
frosty [frɔsti] ADJ 有霜冻的 yǒu shuāngdòng de
froze [froʊz] PT *of* **freeze**
frozen [froʊzᵊn] **I** PP *of* **freeze II** ADJ **1** (+ *food*) 冷冻的 lěngdòng de; (+ *ground, lake*) 结冰的 jiébīng de **2** (+ *person, fingers*) 冰冷的 bīnglěng de
fruit [frut] (*pl* **fruit** *or* **fruits**) N [C/U] 水果 shuǐguǒ [种 zhǒng]
frustrated [frʌstreɪtɪd] ADJ 泄气的 xièqì de
fry [fraɪ] (*pt, pp* **fried**) **I** VT 油煎 yóujiān **II fries** N PL (*Culin*) = **french fries**
frying pan [fraɪɪŋ pæn] N [C] 平底煎锅 píngdǐ jiānguō [个 gè]
fuel [fyuəl] N [C/U] 燃料 ránliào [种 zhǒng]
full [fʊl] ADJ **1** (+ *place, container*) 满的 mǎn de **2** (+ *details*) 全部的 quánbù de; (+ *information, name*) 完全的 wánquán de ▸ **I'm full (up)** 我吃饱了 wǒ chībǎo le ▸ **full of** 充满 chōngmǎn
full-time I ADJ (+ *work, study*) 全职的 quánzhí de; (+ *student, staff*) 全日制的 quánrìzhì de **II** ADV (*work, study*) 全日地 quánrì de
fully [fʊli] ADV 完全地 wánquán de
fumes [fyumz] N PL 浓烈的烟气 nóngliè de yānqì
fun [fʌn] N [U] 乐趣 lèqù ▸ **to have fun** 玩得开心 wánde kāixīn ▸ **to do sth for fun** 为找乐而做某事 wèi zhǎolè ér zuò mǒushì ▸ **to make fun of sb/sth** 取笑某人/某事 qǔxiào mǒurén/mǒushì
fund [fʌnd] **I** N [C] 基金 jījīn [项

xiàng] **II funds** N PL (*money*) 资金 zījīn

funeral [fyunərəl] N [C] 葬礼 zànglǐ [个 gè]

funny [fʌni] ADJ **1** (*amusing*) 可笑的 kěxiào de **2** (*strange*) 奇怪的 qíguài de

fur [fɜr] N [C/U] 毛 máo [根 gēn]

furious [fyʊəriəs] ADJ 大发雷霆的 dà fā léitíng de

furniture [fɜrnɪtʃər] N [U] 家具 jiājù ▶ **a piece of furniture** 一件家具 yījiàn jiājù

further [fɜrðər] ADV (*in distance, time*) 更远地 gèngyuǎn de ▶ **how much further is it?** 还有多远？háiyǒu duōyuǎn?

fuss [fʌs] N [S/U] 大惊小怪 dàjīng xiǎoguài ▶ **to make** *or* **kick up a fuss (about sth)** （对某事）小题大做 (duì mǒushì) xiǎo tí dà zuò

future [fyutʃər] **I** ADJ 将来的 jiānglái de **II** N **1** ▶ **the future** 未来 wèilái **2** (*Ling*) (*also*: **future tense**) ▶ **the future** 将来时 jiāngláishí ▶ **in (the) future** (*from now on*) 从今以后 cóngjīn yǐhòu ▶ **in the near/foreseeable future** 在不久/可预见的未来 zài bùjiǔ/kě yùjiàn de wèilái

fuze [fyuz] N [C] 保险丝 bǎoxiǎnsī [根 gēn] ▶ **a fuze has blown** 保险丝烧断了 bǎoxiǎnsī shāoduàn le

G

gallery [gæləri] N [c] (*also*: **art gallery**) 美术馆 měishùguǎn [个 gè]
gamble [gæmbᵊl] **I** VI **1** (*bet*) 赌博 dǔbó **2** (*take a risk*) 投机 tóujī **II** N [c] (*risk*) 冒险 màoxiǎn [次 cì] ▶ **to gamble on sth** 对某事打赌 duì mǒushì dǎdǔ; (+ *success, outcome*) 对某事冒险 duì mǒushì màoxiǎn
gambling [gæmblɪŋ] N [U] 赌博 dǔbó
game [geɪm] N **1** [c] (*sport*) 运动 yùndòng [项 xiàng] **2** [c] (*activity*: *children's*) 游戏 yóuxì [个 gè] **3** [c] (*also*: **board game**) 棋盘游戏 qípán yóuxì [项 xiàng]; (*also*: **computer game**) 电脑游戏 diànnǎo yóuxì [项 xiàng] **4** [c] (*match*) 比赛 bǐsài [场 chǎng] ▶ **a game of soccer/tennis** 一场足球/网球赛 yīchǎng zúqiú/wǎngqiú sài
gang [gæŋ] N [c] 一帮 yī bāng
gangster [gæŋstər] N [c] 歹徒 dǎitú [个 gè]
gap [gæp] N [c] 缝隙 fèngxì [个 gè]
garage [gərɑʒ] N [c] **1** (*of private house*) 车库 chēkù [个 gè] **2** (*for car repairs*) 汽车修理厂 qìchē xiūlǐchǎng [个 gè]
garbage [gɑrbɪdʒ] N [U] **1** (*rubbish*) 垃圾 lājī **2** (*nonsense*) 废话 fèihuà
garbage can N [c] 垃圾箱 lājīxiāng [个 gè]
garbage man (*pl* **garbage men**) N [c] 清洁工 qīngjiégōng [位 wèi]
garden [gɑrdᵊn] N [c] 花园 huāyuán [个 gè]
gardener [gɑrdənər] N [c] (*professional*) 园丁 yuándīng [位 wèi]; (*amateur*) 园艺爱好者 yuányì àihàozhě [个 gè]
gardening [gɑrdənɪŋ] N [U] 园艺 yuányì
garlic [gɑrlɪk] N [U] 大蒜 dàsuàn
gas [gæs] N **1** [U] (*for cooking, heating*) 煤气 méiqì **2** [U] (*also*: **gasoline**) 汽油 qìyóu
gasoline [gæsəlin] N [U] 汽油 qìyóu
gas station N [c] 加油站 jiāyóuzhàn [个 gè]
gate [geɪt] N [c] **1** 门 mén [个 gè]; (*of building*) 大门 dàmén [个 gè] **2** (*at airport*) 登机口 dēngjīkǒu [个 gè]
gather [gæðər] **I** VT (*understand*) ▶ **to gather (that)...** 获悉… huòxī... **II** VI 聚集 jùjí
gave [geɪv] PT *of* **give**
gay [geɪ] ADJ 同性恋的 tóngxìngliàn de
gear [gɪər] N **1** [c] (*of car, bicycle*) 排挡 páidǎng [个 gè] **2** [U] (*equipment*) 装备 zhuāngbèi **3** [U] (*clothing*) 服装 fúzhuāng ▶ **to shift gear** 换挡 huàndǎng
gender [dʒɛndər] N [c/U] (*person, language*) 性 xìng
geese [gis] N PL *of* **goose**
gel [dʒɛl] N [c/U] 啫喱 zhělí [瓶 píng] ▶ **bath/shower gel** 浴液 yùyè
Gemini [dʒɛmɪni] N [U] (*sign*) 双子座 Shuāngzǐ Zuò
general [dʒɛnrəl] ADJ **1** (*overall*) (+ *situation*) 总的 zǒng de; (+ *decline, standard*) 一般的 yībān de **2** (+ *terms, outline, idea*) 笼统的 lǒngtǒng de
general election N [c] 大选 dàxuǎn [届 jiè]
generally [dʒɛnrəli] ADV **1** (*on the whole*) 大体上 dàtǐshang **2** (*usually*) 通常 tōngcháng
generation [dʒɛnəreɪʃᵊn] N [c] 一代人 yīdàirén [代 dài]
generous [dʒɛnərəs] ADJ 大方的 dàfāng de
genius [dʒinyəs] N [c] 天才 tiāncái [位 wèi]
gentle [dʒɛntᵊl] ADJ 温和的 wēnhé de
gentleman [dʒɛntᵊlmən] (*pl* **gentlemen**) N [c] 先生 xiānsheng [位 wèi]
genuine [dʒɛnyuɪn] ADJ (*real*) 真正

的 zhēnzhèng de; (+ *emotion, interest*) 实实在在的 shíshí zàizài de

geography [dʒiɒgrəfi] N [U] **1** 地理 dìlǐ **2** (*school/university subject*) 地理学 dìlǐxué

germ [dʒɜrm] (*Bio*) N [C] 细菌 xìjūn [种 zhǒng]

German [dʒɜrmən] **I** ADJ 德国的 Déguó de **II** N **1** [C] (*person*) 德国人 Déguórén [个 gè] **2** [U] (*language*) 德语 Déyǔ

Germany [dʒɜrməni] N 德国 Déguó

KEYWORD

get [gɛt] (*pt* **got**, *pp* **got, gotten**) **I** VT

1 ▸ **to have got** *see* **have, got**

2 (+ *money, permission, results, information*) 获得 huòdé; (+ *job, flat, room*) 得到 dédào ▸ **he got a job in Boston** 他在波士顿得到一份工作 tā zài Bōshìdùn dédào yīfèn gōngzuò

3 (*fetch*) 去拿 qùná ▸ **to get sth for sb** 为某人去拿某物 wèi mǒurén qù ná mǒuwù ▸ **can I get you some coffee?** 要我给你拿杯咖啡吗？ yào wǒ gěi nǐ ná bēi kāfēi ma? ▸ **I'll come and get you** 我会来接你的 wǒ huì lái jiē nǐ de

4 (+ *present, letter, prize, TV channel*) 收到 shōudào ▸ **what did you get for your birthday?** 你生日时得到了什么礼物？ nǐ shēngrìshí dédào le shénme lǐwù?

5 (+ *plane, bus*) 乘坐 chéngzuò ▸ **I'll get the bus** 我会乘坐公共汽车 wǒ huì chéngzuò gōnggòng qìchē

6 (*cause to be/become*) ▸ **to get sth/sb ready** 使某事/某人准备就绪 shǐ mǒurén/mǒushì zhǔnbèi jiùxù

7 (*take, move*) 把…送到 bǎ...sòngdào ▸ **we must get him to the hospital** 我们必须把他送到医院 wǒmen bìxū bǎ tā sòngdào yīyuàn

8 (*buy*) 买 mǎi; (*regularly*) 买到 mǎidào ▸ **I'll get some milk from the supermarket** 我要去超市买牛奶 wǒ yào qù chāoshì mǎi niúnǎi

9 (*be infected by*) (+ *cold, measles*) 染上 rǎnshang ▸ **you'll get a cold** 你会得感冒的 nǐ huì dé gǎnmào de

10 (+ *time, opportunity*) 有 yǒu

11 ▸ **to get sth done** (*do oneself*) 做某事 zuò mǒushì; (*have done*) 完成某事 wánchéng mǒushì ▸ **to get one's hair cut** 理发 lǐfà ▸ **to get sb to do sth** 让某人做某事 ràng mǒurén zuò mǒushì

II VI **1** (*become, be: adj*) 变得 biàn de ▸ **to get old/tired/cold/dirty** 变老/变得疲倦/变冷/变脏 biànlǎo/biànde píjuàn/biànlěng/biànzāng ▸ **to get drunk** 喝醉了 hēzuì le

2 (*go*) ▸ **to get to work/the airport/Beijing** *etc* 到办公室/到达机场/到达北京{等} dào bàngōngshì/dàodá jīchǎng/dàodá Běijīng {děng} ▸ **how did you get here?** 你是怎么到这儿的？ nǐ shì zěnme dào zhèr de? ▸ **he didn't get home till 10pm** 他直到晚上10点才到家 tā zhídào wǎnshàng shídiǎn cái dàojiā ▸ **how long does it take to get from New York to Paris?** 从纽约到巴黎需要多久？ cóng Niǔyuē dào Bālí xūyào duōjiǔ?

3 (*begin*) ▸ **to get to know sb** 开始了解某人 kāishǐ liǎojiě mǒurén ▸ **let's get going** *or* **started!** 开始吧！ kāishǐ ba!

III AUX VB **1** ▸ **to have got to** *see* **have, got**

2 (*passive use*) 作为构成被动语态的助动词 ▸ **to get killed** 被杀 bèishā

▸ **get away** VI 逃跑 táopǎo

▸ **get back I** VI (*return*) 回来 huílái **II** VT (*reclaim*) 重新得到 chóngxīn dédào

▸ **get back to** VT FUS (*return to*) (+ *activity, work*) 回到 huídào; (+ *subject*) 重新回到 chóngxīn huídào ▸ **to get back to sleep** 重又睡着 chóng yòu shuìzháo

▸ **get in** VI (*train, bus, plane*) 抵达 dǐdá

2 (*arrive home*) 到家 dàojiā

▸ **get into** VT FUS (+ *vehicle*) 乘坐

chéngzuò
▶ **get off I** VI (*from train, bus*) 下车 xiàchē
II VT (*as holiday*) 放假 fàngjià ▶ **we get three days off at Christmas** 圣诞节时我们放了3天假 Shèngdànjié shí wǒmen fàngle sāntiānjià
III VT FUS (+ *train, bus*) 从…下来 cóng...xiàlái
▶ **get on I** VI **1** (*be friends*) 和睦相处 hémù xiāngchǔ ▶ **to get on well with sb** 与某人相处融洽 yǔ mǒurén xiāngchǔ róngqià
2 (*progress*) 进展 jìnzhǎn ▶ **how are you getting along?** 你过得怎么样？nǐ guòde zěnmeyàng?
II VT FUS (+ *bus, train*) 上 shàng
▶ **get out I** VI (*of vehicle*) 下车 xiàchē
II VT (*take out*) 拿出 náchū
▶ **get out of** VT FUS (+ *vehicle*) 从…下来 cóng...xiàlái
▶ **get over** VT FUS (+ *illness, shock*) 从…中恢复过来 cóng...zhōng huīfù guòlái
▶ **get through I** VI (*Tel*) 接通 jiētōng
II VT FUS (+ *work, book*) 完成 wánchéng
▶ **get together** VI (*people*) 聚在一起 jùzài yīqǐ
▶ **get up** VI (*from chair, sofa*) 站起来 zhànqǐlái; (*out of bed*) 起床 qǐchuáng

ghost [goʊst] N [C] 鬼神 guǐshén [种 zhǒng]
giant [dʒaɪənt] **I** N [C] 巨人 jùrén [个 gè] **II** ADJ (*huge*) 巨大的 jùdà de
gift [gɪft] N [C] **1** 礼物 lǐwù [件 jiàn] **2** (*talent*) 天赋 tiānfù [种 zhǒng]
gin [dʒɪn] N [U] 杜松子酒 dùsōngzǐjiǔ
ginger [dʒɪndʒər] **I** N [U] (*spice*) 姜 jiāng **II** ADJ (*color*) 姜色的 jiāngsè de
girl [gɜrl] N [C] **1** (*child*) 女孩 nǚhái [个 gè]; (*young woman, woman*) 姑娘 gūniang [个 gè] **2** (*daughter*) 女儿 nǚ'ér [个 gè]
girlfriend [gɜrlfrɛnd] N **1** [C] (*of girl*) 女性朋友 nǚxìng péngyǒu [个 gè] **2** (*of boy*) 女朋友 nǚ péngyǒu [个 gè]

KEYWORD

give [gɪv] (*pt* **gave**, *pp* **given**) **I** VT **1** ▶ **to give sb sth, give sth to sb** 给某人某物 gěi mǒurén mǒuwù; (*as gift*) 送给某人某物 sònggěi mǒurén mǒuwù ▶ **I gave David the book, I gave the book to David** 我把这本书送给了戴维 wǒ bǎ zhèběn shū sònggěi le Dàiwéi ▶ **give it to him** 把它送给他 bǎ tā sònggěi tā
2 (+ *advice, details*) 提供 tígōng ▶ **to give sb sth** (+ *opportunity, surprise, shock, job*) 给某人某物 gěi mǒurén mǒuwù
3 (*deliver*) ▶ **to give a speech/a lecture** 做演讲/讲座 zuò yǎnjiǎng/jiǎngzuò
4 (*organize*) ▶ **to give a party/dinner party** *etc* 做东办一个聚会/宴会 {等} zuòdōng bàn yī gè jùhuì/yànhuì {děng}
▶ **give back** VT 交还 jiāohuán ▶ **to give sth back to sb** 把某物交还给某人 bǎ mǒuwù jiāohuán gěi mǒurén
▶ **give in** VI (*yield*) 屈服 qūfú
▶ **give up I** VI 放弃 fàngqì
II VT (+ *job*) 辞掉 cídiào ▶ **to give up smoking** 戒烟 jièyān

glad [glæd] ADJ 高兴的 gāoxìng de ▶ **I'd be glad to help you** 我很愿意帮助你 wǒ hěn yuànyì bāngzhù nǐ
glamorous [glæmərəs] ADJ 富有魅力的 fùyǒu mèilì de
glass [glɑs, glæs] **I** N **1** [U] (*substance*) 玻璃 bōli **2** [C] (*container*) 玻璃杯 bōlibēi [个 gè] **3** [C] (*glassful*) 一杯 yī bēi **II glasses** N PL (*spectacles*) 眼镜 yǎnjìng ▶ **a pair of glasses** 一副眼镜 yīfù yǎnjìng
global [gloʊbᵊl] ADJ 全球的 quánqiú

de

global warming [gloʊbᵊl wɔrmɪŋ] N [U] 全球变暖 quánqiú biànnuǎn

glove [glʌv] N [C] 手套 shǒutào [副 fù] ▶ **a pair of gloves** 一副手套 yīfù shǒutào

glue [glu] N [C/U] 胶 jiāo [种 zhǒng]

KEYWORD

go [goʊ] (*pt* **went**, *pp* **gone**, *pl* **goes**)

I VI **1** 去 qù ▶ **he's going to New York** 他要去纽约 tā yào qù Niǔyuē ▶ **where's he gone?** 他去哪儿了？ tā qù nǎr le? ▶ **shall we go by car or train?** 我们开车去还是坐火车去？ wǒmen kāichē qù háishì zuò huǒchē qù?

2 (*depart*) 离开 líkāi ▶ **let's go** 我们走吧 wǒmen zǒuba ▶ **I must be going** 我必须得走了 wǒ bìxū děi zǒu le ▶ **our plane goes at 11pm** 我们的飞机晚上11点起飞 wǒmen de fēijī wǎnshàng shíyīdiǎn qǐfēi

3 (*disappear*) 消失 xiāoshī ▶ **all her jewelry had gone** 她所有的珠宝首饰都不见了 tā suǒyǒu de zhūbǎo shǒushì dōu bùjiàn le

4 (*attend*) ▶ **to go to school/college** 上学/上大学 shàngxué/shàng dàxué

5 (*with activity*) ▶ **to go for a walk** 去散步 qù sànbù ▶ **to go on a trip** 去旅行 qù lǚxíng

6 (*work*) 运转 yùnzhuǎn

7 (*become*) ▶ **to go pale/moldy/bald** 变得苍白/发霉/秃顶 biàn de cāngbái/fāméi/tūdǐng

8 (*be about to, intend to*) ▶ **are you going to come?** 你要来吗？ nǐ yào lái ma? ▶ **I think it's going to rain** 我想天要下雨了 wǒxiǎng tiān yào xiàyǔ le

9 (*progress*) 进行 jìnxíng ▶ **how did it go?** 这事进展如何？ zhèshì jìnzhǎn rúhé?

10 (*lead*) (*road, path*) 通向 tōngxiàng

11 (*in other expressions*) ▶ **there's still a week to go before the exams** 考试前还有一个星期的时间 kǎoshì qián háiyǒu yī gè xīngqī de shíjiān ▶ **to keep going** 继续下去 jìxù xiàqù

II N **1** [C] (*try*) 尝试 chángshì [次 cì] ▶ **to have a go (at sth/at doing sth)** 试一下（某事/做某事） shì yīxià (mǒushì/zuò mǒushì)

2 [C] (*turn*) 轮流 lúnliú [次 cì] ▶ **whose go is it?** 轮到谁了？ lúndào shuí le?

▶ **go ahead** VI **1** (*event*) 发生 fāshēng

2 (*press on*) ▶ **to go ahead with sth** 着手做某事 zhuóshǒu zuò mǒushì ▶ **go ahead!** (*encouraging*) 干吧！ gànba!

▶ **go around** VI **1** (*news, rumor*) 传播 chuánbō

2 (*revolve*) 转动 zhuàndòng

▶ **go away** VI **1** (*leave*) 离开 líkāi

2 (*on holiday*) 外出 wàichū

▶ **go back** VI 返回 fǎnhuí

▶ **go back to** VT FUS (+ *activity, work, school*) 回到 huídào

▶ **go down** VI **1** (*price, level, amount*) 下降 xiàjiàng

2 (*sun*) 落下 luòxià

3 (*computer*) 死机 sǐjī

II VT FUS (+ *stairs, ladder*) 从…下来 cóng...xiàlái

▶ **go for** VT FUS (*fetch*) 去取 qùqǔ

▶ **go in** VI 进去 jìnqù

▶ **go in for** VT FUS (+ *competition*) 参加 cānjiā

▶ **go into** VT FUS (*enter*) 进入 jìnrù

▶ **go off** VI **1** (*leave*) 离去 líqù ▶ **he's gone off to work** 他已经去上班了 tā yǐjīng qù shàngbān le

2 (*explode*) 爆炸 bàozhà

3 (*alarm*) 响起 xiǎngqǐ

4 (*lights*) 熄灭 xīmiè

▶ **go on** VI (*continue*) 继续 jìxù ▶ **to go on with one's work** 继续自己的工作 jìxù zìjǐ de gōngzuò ▶ **to go on doing sth** 继续做某事 jìxù zuò mǒushì

2 (*happen*) 发生 fāshēng ▶ **what's**

going on here? 这里发生什么事了？ zhèlǐ fāshēng shénme shì le?
▶ **go out** VI 1 (*person*) 离开 líkāi; (*to party, club*) 出去消遣 chūqù xiāoqiǎn ▶ **are you going out tonight?** 你今晚出去吗？ nǐ jīnwǎn chūqù ma?
2 (*couple*) 和…交往 hé...jiāowǎng ▶ **to go out with sb** 和某人交往 hé mǒurén jiāowǎng
3 (*light, fire*) 熄灭 xīmiè
▶ **go over** VI 过去 guòqù
▶ **go round** VI = **go around**
▶ **go through** VT FUS (+ *place, town*) 路过 lùguò
▶ **go up** VI 1 (*price, level, value*) 上涨 shàngzhǎng
2 (*go upstairs*) 上楼 shànglóu
▶ **go up to** VT FUS 向…走过去 xiàng...zǒuguòqù
▶ **go with** VT FUS (*accompany*) 与…相伴共存 yǔ...xiāngbàn gòngcún
▶ **go without** VT FUS (+ *food, treats*) 没有 méiyǒu...

goal [goʊl] N [C] 1 (*Sport*) 进球得分 jìnqiú défēn [次 cì] 2 (*aim*) 目标 mùbiāo [个 gè] ▶ **to score a goal** 进一球 jìn yīqiú

goalkeeper [goʊlkipər] N [C] 守门员 shǒuményuán [个 gè]

goat [goʊt] N [C] 山羊 shānyáng [只 zhī]

God [gɒd] N 上帝 Shàngdì

goggles [gɒgᵋlz] N PL 护目镜 hùmùjìng

gold [goʊld] I N [U] (*metal*) 黄金 huángjīn II ADJ (+ *ring, watch, tooth*) 金的 jīn de

golf [gɒlf] N [U] 高尔夫球 gāo'ěrfūqiú ▶ **to play golf** 打高尔夫球 dǎ gāo'ěrfūqiú

golf course N [C] 高尔夫球场 gāo'ěrfūqiúchǎng [个 gè]

gone [gɔn] I PP *of* **go** II ADJ 离去的 líqù de ▶ **the food's all gone** 食物都没了 shíwù dōu méi le

good [gʊd] I ADJ 1 (*pleasant*) 令人愉快的 lìng rén yúkuài de 2 (+ *food, school, job*) 好的 hǎo de 3 (*well-behaved*) 乖的 guāi de 4 (+ *idea, reason, advice*) 好的 hǎode 5 (*skillful*) 好的 hǎode 6 (+ *news, luck, example*) 好的 hǎo de 7 (*morally correct*) 公正的 gōngzhèng de II N [U] (*right*) 善 shàn ▶ **good!** 好！ hǎo! ▶ **to be good at (doing) sth** 精于（做）某事 jīngyú (zuò) mǒushì ▶ **to be no good at (doing) sth** 不擅长（做）某事 bù shàncháng (zuò) mǒushì ▶ **it's no good doing...** 做…没有用 zuò...méiyǒu yòng ▶ **it's good for you** 对你有益 duì nǐ yǒuyì ▶ **it's good to see you** 很高兴见到你 hěn gāoxìng jiàndào nǐ ▶ **good morning/afternoon!** 早上/下午好！ zǎoshàng/xiàwǔ hǎo! ▶ **good night!** (*before going home*) 再见！ zàijiàn!; (*before going to bed*) 晚安！ wǎn'ān! ▶ **for good** (*forever*) 永久地 yǒngjiǔ de; *see also* **goods**

goodbye [gʊdbaɪ] INT 再见 zàijiàn ▶ **to say goodbye** 告别 gàobié

good-looking [gʊdlʊkɪŋ] ADJ 好看的 hǎokàn de

goods [gʊdz] N PL 商品 shāngpǐn

goose [gus] (*pl* **geese**) N [C] 鹅 é [只 zhī]

gorgeous [gɔrdʒəs] ADJ (+ *weather, day*) 宜人的 yírén de

gossip [gɒsɪp] I N [U] (*rumors*) 流言蜚语 liúyán fēiyǔ II VI (*chat*) 闲谈 xiántán

got [gɒt] PT, PP *of* **get** ▶ **have you got your umbrella?** 你有伞吗？ nǐ yǒu sǎn ma? ▶ **he has got to accept the situation** 他只得接受现状 tā zhǐdé jiēshòu xiànzhuàng

gotten [gɒtᵊn] PP *of* **get**

government [gʌvərnmənt] N [C] (*institution*) 政府 zhèngfǔ [届 jiè]

GP [dʒi pi] N ABBR [C] (= **general practitioner**) 家庭医生 jiātíng yīshēng [位 wèi]

graceful [greɪsfəl] ADJ 优美的 yōuměi de

grade [greɪd] N [C] 1 (*school mark*)

分数 fēnshù [个 gè] **2** (*school class*) 年级 niánjí [个 gè]
grade crossing N [C] 铁路线与公路交叉处
grade school N [C/U] 小学 xiǎoxué [座 zuò]
gradual [grædʒuəl] ADJ 逐渐的 zhújiàn de
gradually [grædʒuəli] ADV 逐渐地 zhújiàn de
gram [græm] N [C] 克 kè
grammar [græmər] N [U] 语法 yǔfǎ
grand [grænd] ADJ 壮丽的 zhuànglì de
grandchild [græntʃaɪld] (*pl* **grandchildren**) N [C] (*male on father's side*) 孙子 sūnzi [个 gè]; (*female on father's side*) 孙女 sūnnǚ [个 gè]; (*male on mother's side*) 外孙 wàisūn [个 gè]; (*female on mother's side*) 外孙女 wàisūnnǚ [个 gè]
granddaughter ['gr[ʷae]nd˘:t↓] N [C] (*on father's side*) 孙女 sūnnǚ; (*on mother's side*) 外孙女 wàisūnnǚ
grandfather [grænfaðər] N [C] (*on mother's side*) 外公 wàigōng [位 wèi]; (*on father's side*) 爷爷 yéye [位 wèi]
grandmother [grænmʌðər] N [C] (*on father's side*) 外婆 wàipó [位 wèi]; (*on father's side*) 奶奶 nǎinai [位 wèi]
grandson [grænsʌn] N [C] (*on father's side*) 孙子 sūnzi [个 gè]; (*on mother's side*) 外孙 wàisūn [个 gè]
grape [greɪp] N [C] 葡萄 pútáo [串 chuàn] ▸ **a bunch of grapes** 一串葡萄 yīchuàn pútáo
grapefruit [greɪpfrut] (*pl* **grapefruit** *or* **grapefruits**) N [C/U] 柚子 yòuzi [个 gè]
graph [græf] N [C] 图表 túbiǎo [幅 fú]
graphics I N [U] (*design*) 制图学 zhìtúxué II N PL (*images*) 图形 túxíng
grass [græs] N [C/U] (*Bot*) 草 cǎo [株 zhū] ▸ **the grass** (*the lawn*) 草坪 cǎopíng
grate [greɪt] VT (+ *food*) 磨碎 mósuì
grateful [greɪtfəl] ADJ 感激的 gǎnjī de ▸ **to be grateful to sb for sth** 为某事感激某人 wèi mǒushì gǎnjī mǒurén
grave [greɪv] N [C] 坟墓 fénmù [座 zuò]
graveyard [greɪvyard] N [C] 墓地 mùdì [块 kuài]
gray [greɪ] I ADJ **1** 灰色的 huīsè de; (+ *hair*) 灰白的 huībái de **2** (+ *weather, day*) 阴沉的 yīnchén de II N [C/U] 灰色 huīsè [种 zhǒng]
gray-haired [greɪ(hɛərd)] ADJ 灰白头发的 huībái tóufa de
greasy [grisi, -zi] ADJ **1** (+ *food*) 油腻的 yóunì de **2** (+ *skin, hair*) 多油脂的 duō yóuzhīde
great [greɪt] I ADJ **1** (*large*) 巨大的 jùdà de **2** (+ *success, achievement*) 重大的 zhòngdà de; (+ *pleasure, difficulty, value*) 极大的 jídà de; (+ *risk*) 超乎寻常的 chāohū xúncháng de **3** (+ *city, person, work of art*) 伟大的 wěidà de **4** (*terrific*) (+ *person, place*) 好极了的 hǎojíle de; (+ *idea*) 棒极了的 bàngjíle de II INT ▸ **great!** 太好了！ tàihǎole! ▸ **we had a great time** 我们玩得很快活 wǒmen wánde hěn kuàihuo
Great Britain [greɪt brɪtᵊn] N 大不列颠 Dàbùlièdiān
Greece [gris] N 希腊 Xīlà
greedy [gridi] ADJ 贪心的 tānxīn de
Greek [grik] I ADJ 希腊的 Xīlà de II N **1** [C] (*person*) 希腊人 Xīlàrén [个 gè] **2** [U] (*modern language*) 希腊语 Xīlàyǔ
green [grin] I ADJ **1** 绿色的 lǜsè de **2** (*environmental*) 环保的 huánbǎo de II N [C/U] 绿色 lǜsè [抹 mǒ]
greenhouse [grinhaʊs] I N [C] 暖房 nuǎnfáng [间 jiān] II CPD (+ *gas, emissions*) 温室 wēnshì
grew [gru] PT *of* **grow**
grief [grif] N [U] 悲痛 bēitòng
grit [grɪt] N [U] 沙粒 shālì

groan [groʊn] VI 呻吟 shēnyín
grocer [groʊsər] N [c] **1** (*person*) 食品杂货商 shípǐn záhuòshāng [个 gè] **2** (*store*) (*also*: **grocer's**) 食品杂货店 shípǐn záhuòdiàn [家 jiā]
grocery [groʊsəri, groʊsri] **I** N [c] (*also*: **grocery store**) 食品杂货店 shípǐn záhuòdiàn [家 jiā] **II groceries** N PL (*provisions*) 食品杂货 shípǐn záhuò
groom [grum] N [c] (*also*: **bridegroom**) 新郎 xīnláng [位 wèi]
ground [graʊnd] **I** PT, PP *of* **grind II** N **1** (*floor*) ▶ **the ground** 地面 dìmiàn **2** (*earth, soil, land*) ▶ **the ground** 土地 tǔdì **3** [c] (*Sport*) 场 chǎng ▶ **on the ground** 在地面上 zài dìmiàn shàng
group [grup] N [c] **1** 组 zǔ [个 gè] **2** (*also*: **pop group, rock group**) 组合 zǔhé [个 gè] ▶ **in groups** 成组地 chéngzǔ de
grow [groʊ] (*pt* **grew**, *pp* **grown**) **I** VI **1** (*plant, tree*) 生长 shēngzhǎng; (*person, animal*) 长大 zhǎngdà **2** (*amount, feeling, problem*) 扩大 kuòdà **II** VT (+ *flowers, vegetables*) 栽种 zāizhòng ▶ **to grow by 10%** 增长10% zēngzhǎng bǎi fēn zhī shí; **grow up** VI (*be brought up*) 长大 zhǎngdà; (*be mature*) 成熟 chéngshú
grown [groʊn] PP *of* **grow**
grown-up N [c] 成年人 chéngniánrén [个 gè]
growth [groʊθ] N **1** [U/S] (*of economy, industry*) 发展 fāzhǎn **2** [U] (*of child, animal, plant*) 生长 shēngzhǎng ▶ **a growth in sth** 某方面的发展 mǒu fāngmiàn de fāzhǎn
grumble [grʌmbᵊl] VI (*complain*) 抱怨 bàoyuàn
guarantee [gærənti] N [c] (*Comm: warranty*) 质保承诺 zhìbǎo chéngnuò [个 gè]
guard [gɑrd] **I** N [c] (*sentry*) 警卫 jǐngwèi [个 gè] **II** VT (+ *building, entrance, door*) 守卫 shǒuwèi; (+ *person*) 保护 bǎohù ▶ **to be on one's guard (against)** 提防 dīfáng
guess [gɛs] **I** VT, VI (*conjecture*) 猜测 cāicè **II** N [c] 猜测 cāicè [种 zhǒng] ▶ **I guess so** 我想是吧 wǒxiǎng shìba?
guest [gɛst] N [c] (*at home*) 客人 kèrén [位 wèi]; (*at special event*) 宾客 bīnkè [位 wèi]; (*in hotel*) 房客 fángkè [位 wèi]
guide [gaɪd] **I** N [c] **1** (*tour guide*) 导游 dǎoyóu [位 wèi] **2** (*local guide*) 向导 xiàngdǎo [位 wèi] **3** (*also*: **guide book**) 指南 zhǐnán [本 běn] **II** VT **1** (*round city, museum*) 给…导游 gěi...dǎoyóu **2** (*lead*) 给…领路 gěi...lǐnglù
guidebook [gaɪdbʊk] N [c] 旅游指南 lǚyóu zhǐnán [本 běn]
guided tour [gaɪdɪd tʊər] N [c] 有导游的游览 yǒu dǎoyóu de yóulǎn [次 cì]
guilty [gɪlti] ADJ **1** (+ *person, feelings*) 内疚的 nèijiù de **2** (+ *secret, conscience*) 自知有过错的 zìzhī yǒu guòcuò de **3** (*responsible*) 有过失的 yǒu guòshī de **4** (*Law*) 有罪的 yǒuzuì de ▶ **guilty of murder/manslaughter** 谋杀/误杀罪 móushā/wùshā zuì
guitar [gɪtɑr] N [c] 吉他 jítā [把 bǎ]
gum [gʌm] N **1** [c] (*Anat*) 牙床 yáchuáng [个 gè] **2** [U] (*also*: **chewing gum/bubblegum**) 口香糖 kǒuxiāngtáng
gun [gʌn] N [c] (*small, medium-sized*) 枪 qiāng [支 zhī]; (*large*) 炮 pào [架 jià]
guy [gaɪ] N [c] (*man*) 家伙 jiāhuo [个 gè] ▶ **(you) guys** 伙计们 huǒjìmen
gym [dʒɪm] N **1** [c] (*also*: **gymnasium**) 健身房 jiànshēnfáng [个 gè] **2** [U] (*also*: **gymnastics**) 体操 tǐcāo
gymnast [dʒɪmnæst] N [c] 体操运动员 tǐcāo yùndòngyuán [位 wèi]
gymnastics [dʒɪmnæstɪks] N [U] 体操 tǐcāo
Gypsy [dʒɪpsi] N [c] (*inf!*) 吉卜赛人 Jípǔsàirén [个 gè]

H

habit [hæbɪt] N [C/U] 习惯 xíguàn [个 gè] ▸ **to be in the habit of doing sth** 有做某事的习惯 yǒu zuò mǒushì de xíguàn ▸ **a bad habit** 坏习惯 huài xíguàn

hacker [hækər] (*Comput*) N [C] 黑客 hēikè

had [həd, STRONG hæd] PT, PP *of* **have**

hadn't [hædᵊnt] = **had not**

hail [heɪl] **I** N [U] 冰雹 bīngbáo **II** VI 下雹 xiàbáo

hair [hɛər] N **1** [U] 头发 tóufa **2** [C] (*single strand*) 毛发 máofà [根 gēn] ▸ **to do one's hair** 梳头 shūtóu ▸ **to have** *or* **get one's hair cut** 剪头发 jiǎn tóufa

hairbrush [hɛərbrʌʃ] N [C] 发刷 fàshuā [把 bǎ]

haircut [hɛərkʌt] N [C] **1** 理发 lǐfà [次 cì] **2** (*hairstyle*) 发型 fàxíng [种 zhǒng] ▸ **to have** *or* **get a haircut** 剪头发 jiǎn tóufa

hairdresser [hɛərdrɛsər] N [C] **1** 美发师 měifàshī [位 wèi] **2** (*also:* **hairdresser's**) 发廊 fàláng [个 gè]

hairdryer [hɛərdraɪər] N [C] 吹风机 chuīfēngjī [个 gè]

hair gel N [U] 发胶 fàjiāo

hairspray [hɛərspreɪ] N [U] 喷发定型剂 pēnfà dìngxíngjì

hairstyle [hɛərstaɪl] N [C] 发型 fàxíng [种 zhǒng]

half [hæf] (*pl* **halves**) **I** N, PRON [C] 一半 yībàn **II** ADJ (+ *bottle*) 一半的 yībàn de **III** ADV (*empty, closed, open, asleep*) 半 bàn ▸ **to cut sth in half** 把某物切成两半 bǎ mǒuwù qiēchéng liǎngbàn ▸ **two/three** *etc* **and a half** 二/三{等}点五 èr/sān (děng) diǎn wǔ ▸ **half a pound/kilo/mile** 半磅/公斤/英里 bànbàng/gōngjīn/yīnglǐ ▸ **a day/week/pound** *etc* **and a half** 一天/星期/磅{等}半 yītiān/xīngqī/bàng (děng) bàn ▸ **half an hour** 半小时 bàn xiǎoshí ▸ **half past three/four** *etc* 三/四{等}点半 sān/sì (děng) diǎn bàn

half hour N [C] 半小时 bàn xiǎoshí [个 gè]

half price **I** ADJ 半价的 bànjià de **II** ADV 半价地 bànjià de

half time (*Sport*) N [U] 半场 bànchǎng ▸ **at halftime** 半场时 bànchǎng shí

halfway [hæfweɪ] ADV (*between two points*) 到一半 dào yībàn ▸ **halfway through sth** 在某事过了一半时 zài mǒushì guòle yībàn shí

hall [hɔl] N **1** [C] (*entrance*) 门厅 méntīng [个 gè] **2** [C] (*room*) 礼堂 lǐtáng [个 gè]

ham [hæm] **I** N 火腿 huǒtuǐ **II** CPD (+ *sandwich, roll, salad*) 火腿 huǒtuǐ

hamburger [hæmbɜrgər] N [C] 汉堡包 hànbǎobāo [个 gè]

hammer [hæmər] N [C] 锤子 chuízi [把 bǎ]

hand [hænd] **I** N **1** [C] 手 shǒu [双 shuāng] **2** [C] (*of clock*) 指针 zhǐzhēn [个 gè] **II** VT 递 dì ▸ **to do sth by hand** 手工制作 shǒugōng zhìzuò ▸ **to give** *or* **lend sb a hand (with sth)** 帮某人(做某事) bāng mǒurén (zuò mǒushì) ▸ **on the one hand..., on the other hand...** 一方面…，另一方面… yī fāngmiàn..., lìngyī fāngmiàn...; **hand in** VT 上交 shàngjiāo; **hand out** VT 分配 fēnpèi; **hand over** VT 交给 jiāogěi

handcuffs [hændkʌfs] N PL 手铐 shǒukào ▸ **in handcuffs** 带手铐 dài shǒukào

handkerchief [hæŋkərtʃɪf] N [C] 手帕 shǒupà [条 tiáo]

handle [hændᵊl] **I** N [C] (*of bag*) 把手 bǎshǒu [个 gè]; (*of cup, knife, paintbrush, broom, spade*) 柄 bǐng [个 gè]; (*of door, window*) 拉手 lāshǒu [个 gè] **II** VT (+ *problem, job, responsibility*) 处理 chǔlǐ

handlebars [hændᵊlbarz] N PL 把手

bǎshǒu

handmade [hændmeɪd] ADJ 手工制作的 shǒugōng zhìzuò de

handsome [hænsəm] ADJ 英俊的 yīngjùn de

handwriting [hændraɪtɪŋ] N [U] 笔迹 bǐjì

handy [hændi] ADJ **1** (*useful*) 方便的 fāngbiàn de **2** (*close at hand*) 手边的 shǒubiān de

hang [hæŋ] (*pt, pp* **hung**) **I** VT 挂 guà **II** VI (*be suspended*) 悬挂 xuánguà; **hang around** (*inf*) VI 闲荡 xiándàng; **hang on** VI (*wait*) 稍等 shāoděng; **hang up I** VI (*Tel*) 挂断电话 guàduàn diànhuà **II** VT (+ *coat, hat, clothes*) 挂起 guàqǐ

hanger [hæŋər] N [C] (*also*: **coat hanger**) 衣架 yījià [个 gè]

hangover [hæŋoʊvər] N [C] 宿醉 sùzuì [次 cì]

happen [hæpən] VI 发生 fāshēng ▸ **what will happen if...?** 如果…会怎么样？ rúguǒ...huì zěnmeyàng? ▸ **tell me what happened** 告诉我发生了什么事 gàosù wǒ fāshēng le shénme shì

happiness [hæpinɪs] N [U] 幸福 xìngfú

happy [hæpi] ADJ **1** 高兴的 gāoxìng de **2** (+ *life, childhood, marriage, place*) 美满的 měimǎn de ▸ **to be happy with sth** (*satisfied*) 对某事满意 duì mǒushì mǎnyì ▸ **to be happy to do sth** (*willing*) 乐意做某事 lèyì zuò mǒushì ▸ **happy birthday!** 生日快乐！ shēngrì kuàilè!

harassment [həræsmənt, hærəs-] N [U] 骚扰 sāorǎo

harbor [hɑrbər] N [C] 港口 gǎngkǒu [个 gè]

hard [hɑrd] **I** ADJ **1** (+ *surface, object*) 硬的 yìng de **2** (+ *question, problem*) 困难的 kùnnan de; (+ *work*) 费力的 fèilì de **3** (+ *push, punch, kick*) 用力的 yònglì de **II** ADV **1** (*work, try, think*) 努力地 nǔlì de **2** (*hit, punch, kick*) 用力地 yònglì de ▸ **it's hard to tell/say/know** 很难讲/说/知道 hěnnán jiǎng/shuō/zhīdào ▸ **such events are hard to understand** 这种事很难理解 zhèzhǒng shì hěnnán lǐjiě ▸ **it's hard work being a waitress** 女服务员的工作不好做 nǚ fúwùyuán de gōngzuò bù hǎo zuò

hard disk N [C] (*Comput*) 硬盘 yìngpán [个 gè]

hardly [hɑrdli] ADV **1** (*scarcely*) 几乎不 jīhū bù **2** (*no sooner*) ▸ **he had hardly sat down when the door burst open** 他一坐下门就被猛地打开了 tā yī zuòxià mén jiù bèi měng de dǎkāi le ▸ **hardly ever/any/anyone** 几乎从不/没有/没有任何人 jīhū cóngbù/méiyǒu/méiyǒu rènhé rén ▸ **I can hardly believe it** 我简直不能相信 wǒ jiǎnzhí bùnéng xiāngxìn

hardware [hɑrdwɛr] N [U] (*Comput*) 硬件 yìngjiàn

hardworking [hɑrdwɜrkɪŋ] ADJ 勤奋的 qínfèn de

harm [hɑrm] VT **1** (*damage*) 损坏 sǔnhuài **2** (*injure*) 伤害 shānghài

harmful [hɑrmfəl] ADJ 有害的 yǒuhài de

harp [hɑrp] N [C] (*Mus*) 竖琴 shùqín [架 jià]

harvest [hɑrvɪst] N **1** [C/U] (*harvest time*) 收获 shōuhuò [种 zhǒng] **2** [C] (*crop*) 收成 shōucheng [个 gè]

has [həz, STRONG hæz] VB *see* **have**

hasn't [hæzᵊnt] = **has not**

hat [hæt] N [C] 帽子 màozi [顶 dǐng]

hate [heɪt] VT (+ *person*) 恨 hèn; (+ *food, activity, sensation*) 讨厌 tǎoyàn ▸ **to hate doing** *or* **to do sth** 不喜欢做某事 bù xǐhuān zuò mǒushì

hatred [heɪtrɪd] N [U] 仇恨 chóuhèn

KEYWORD

have [həv, STRONG hæv] (*pt, pp* **had**) **I** VT **1** 有 yǒu ▸ **he has** *or* **he has got blue eyes/dark hair** 他长着蓝眼睛/黑头发 tā zhǎngzhe lán yǎnjīng/hēi tóufa ▸ **do you have** *or* **have you**

got a car/phone? 你有车/电话吗? nǐ yǒu chē/diànhuà ma? ▸ **to have** *or* **have got sth to do** 有必须得做的事 yǒu bìxū děi zuò de shì ▸ **she had her eyes closed** 她闭上了眼睛 tā bìshàng le yǎnjīng
2 ▸ **to have breakfast** 吃早饭 chī zǎofàn ▸ **to have a drink/a cigarette** 喝一杯/抽支烟 hē yībēi/chōu zhī yān
3 ▸ **to have a swim/bath** 游泳/洗澡 yóuyǒng/xǐzǎo ▸ **to have a meeting/party** 开会/开派对 kāihuì/kāi pàiduì
4 (*receive, obtain*) 得到 dédào ▸ **can I have your address?** 能告诉我你的地址吗? néng gàosù wǒ nǐde dìzhǐ ma? ▸ **you can have it for $5** 你可以$5买走 nǐ kěyǐ wǔ měiyuán mǎi zǒu
5 ▸ **to have a baby** 生孩子 shēng háizi
6 ▸ **to have sth done** 指使/安排做某事 zhǐshǐ/ānpái zuò mǒushì ▸ **to have one's hair cut** 理发 lǐfà
7 ▸ **to have a headache** 头痛 tóutòng ▸ **to have an operation** 动手术 dòng shǒushù
II AUX VB **1** ▸ **to have arrived/gone** 已到了/走了 yǐ dàole/zǒule ▸ **has he told you?** 他已经告诉你了吗? tā yǐjīng gàosù nǐ le ma? ▸ **when she had dressed, she went downstairs** 穿好衣服后，她下了楼 chuānhǎo yīfu hòu, tā xiàle lóu ▸ **I haven't seen him for ages/since July** 我已经很久/自7月以来就没见过他了 wǒ yǐjīng hěnjiǔ/zì qīyuè yǐlái jiù méi jiànguò tā le
2 (*in tag questions*) ▸ **you've done it, haven't you?** 你已经做了，是不是? nǐ yǐjīng zuò le, shì bùshì?
3 (*in short answers and questions*) ▸ **yes, I have** 是的，我有/已做了 shìde, wǒ yǒu/yǐzuò le ▸ **no I haven't!** 不，我还没有/没做呢! bù, wǒ hái méiyǒu/méizuò ne! ▸ **so have I!** 我也一样! wǒ yě yīyàng! ▸ **neither have I** 我也没有过 wǒ yě méiyǒu guò ▸ **I've finished, have you?** 我已经完成了，你呢? wǒ yǐjīng wánchéng le, nǐne?
4 (*be obliged*) ▸ **to have (got) to do sth** 不得不做某事 bùdébù zuò mǒushì ▸ **she has (got) to do it** 她必须得这么做 tā bìxū děi zhème zuò
▸ **have on** VT (+ *clothes*) 穿着 chuānzhe ▸ **he didn't have anything on** 他什么都没穿 tā shénme dōu méi chuān

haven't [hævᵊnt] = **have not**
hay fever N [U] 花粉病 huāfěnbìng
hazel [heɪzᵊl] ADJ (+ *eyes*) 淡褐色的 dàn hèsè de
he [hi, STRONG hi] PRON 他 tā
head [hɛd] **I** N [C] **1** 头 tóu [个 gè] **2** (*of company, organization, department*) 领导 lǐngdǎo [个 gè]
II VT **1** (+ *list, group*) 以…打头 yǐ…dǎtóu **2** (*Soccer*) (+ *ball*) 用头顶 yòng tóu dǐng ▸ **10 dollars a** *or* **per head** 每人10美元 měirén shí měiyuán ▸ **from head to foot** *or* **toe** 从头到脚 cóng tóu dào jiǎo ▸ **heads or tails?** 正面还是反面? zhèngmiàn háishì fǎnmiàn?; **head for** VT FUS 前往 qiánwǎng ▸ **to be heading** *or* **headed for Glasgow** 正前往格拉斯哥 zhèng qiánwǎng Gélāsīgē
headache [hɛdeɪk] N [C] 头痛 tóutòng [阵 zhèn] ▸ **to have a headache** 头痛 tóutòng
headlight [hɛdlaɪt] N [C] 前灯 qiándēng [个 gè]
headline [hɛdlaɪn] N [C] 标题 biāotí [个 gè] ▸ **the headlines** (*Publishing*) 头条新闻 tóutiáo xīnwén; (*TV, Rad*) 内容提要 nèiróng tíyào
head office N [C/U] (*of company*) 总部 zǒngbù
headphones [hɛdfoʊnz] N PL 耳机 ěrjī
headquarters [hɛdkwɔrtərz] N PL 总部 zǒngbù
heal [hil] VI 痊愈 quányù
health [hɛlθ] N [U] 健康 jiànkāng ▸ **to be good/bad for one's health** 对某人的健康有益/不利 duì mǒurén

de jiànkāng yǒuyì/bùlì ▶ **to drink (to) sb's health** 举杯祝某人健康 jǔbēi zhù mǒurén jiànkāng

healthy [hɛlθi] ADJ **1** 健康的 jiànkāng de **2** (+ *diet, lifestyle*) 对健康有益的 duì jiànkāng yǒuyì de

heap [hip] N [C] 堆 duī [个 gè]

hear [hɪər] (*pt, pp* **heard**) VT **1** 听见 tīngjiàn **2** (+ *news, lecture, concert*) 听 tīng ▶ **to hear sb doing sth** 听见某人做某事 tīngjiàn mǒurén zuò mǒushì ▶ **to hear that...** 听说… tīngshuō... ▶ **to hear about sth/sb** 听说某事/某人 tīngshuō mǒushì/mǒurén ▶ **to hear from sb** 得到某人的消息 dédào mǒurén de xiāoxi ▶ **I've never heard of him** 我从来没听说过他 wǒ cónglái méi tīngshuō guò tā

heart [hɑrt] N **1** [C] 心脏 xīnzàng [颗 kē] **2** [C] (*emotions*) 感情 gǎnqíng [种 zhǒng] **3** [C] (*shape*) 心形物 xīnxíng wù [个 gè] ▶ **to learn/know sth (off) by heart** 背诵某事 bèisòng mǒushì ▶ **to break sb's heart** 使某人伤心 shǐ mǒurén shāngxīn

heart attack N [C] 心脏病发作 xīnzàngbìng fāzuò [阵 zhèn] ▶ **to have a heart attack** 心脏病发作 xīnzàngbìng fāzuò

heat [hit] I N **1** [U] 热 rè **2** [U] (*temperature*) 热度 rèdù **3** [C] (*Sport*) (*also*: **qualifying heat**) 预赛 yùsài [场 chǎng] **II** VT (+ *water, food*) 加热 jiārè; (+ *room, house*) 取暖 qǔnuǎn ▶ **I find the heat unbearable** 热得我实在受不了 rède wǒ shízài shòubùliǎo; **heat up** VT (+ *food*) 加热 jiārè

heater [hitər] N [C] (*electric heater, gas heater*) 供暖装置 gōngnuǎn zhuāngzhì [个 gè]; (*in car*) 暖气设备 nuǎnqì shèbèi [套 tào]

heating [hitɪŋ] N [U] (*system*) 暖气 nuǎnqì

heat wave [hitweɪv] N [C] 酷暑时期 kùshǔ shíqī [段 duàn]

heaven [hɛvən] N [U] 天堂 tiāntáng

heavy [hɛvi] ADJ **1** 重的 zhòng de **2** (+ *traffic*) 拥挤的 yōngjǐ de; (+ *fine, penalty, sentence*) 重的 zhòng de; (+ *drinking, smoking, gambling*) 过度的 guòdù de; (+ *rain, snow*) 大的 dà de ▶ **how heavy are you/is it?** 你/它有多重? nǐ/tā yǒu duōzhòng?

he'd [hid, STRONG hid] = **he would, he had**

hedge [hɛdʒ] N [C] 树篱 shùlí [道 dào]

heel [hil] N [C] **1** (*of foot*) 脚后跟 jiǎohòugēn [个 gè] **2** (*of shoe*) 鞋跟 xiégēn [个 gè]

height [haɪt] N **1** [C/U] 高度 gāodù [个 gè] **2** [C] (*altitude*) 高处 gāochù ▶ **of average/medium height** 平均/中等高度 píngjūn/zhōngděng gāodù

held [hɛld] PT, PP *of* **hold**

helicopter [hɛlikɒptər] N [C] 直升飞机 zhíshēng fēijī [架 jià]

hell [hɛl] I N [U] 地狱 dìyù **II** INT (*inf!*) 天啊 tiān a ▶ **it was hell** (*inf*) 糟糕极了 zāogāo jíle

he'll [hɪl, hil] = **he will, he shall**

hello [hɛloʊ] INT (*as greeting*) 你好 nǐhǎo; (*Tel*) 喂 wèi; (*to attract attention*) 劳驾 láojià

helmet [hɛlmɪt] N [C] 头盔 tóukuī [个 gè]; (*of soldier, police officer, firefighter*) 钢盔 gāngkuī [个 gè]

help [hɛlp] I N [U] 帮助 bāngzhù **II** VT (+ *person*) 帮助 bāngzhù **III** VI **1** (*assist*) 帮忙 bāngmáng **2** (*be useful*) 有用 yǒuyòng ▶ **thanks, you've been a great help** 谢谢，你帮了很大忙 xièxiè, nǐ bāngle hěndà máng ▶ **I helped him (to) fix his car** 我帮助他修了他的车 wǒ bāngzhù tā xiūle tāde chē ▶ **help!** 救命！ jiùmìng! ▶ **can I help you?** (*in shop*) 我能为您效劳吗? wǒ néng wèi nín xiàoláo ma? ▶ **I can't help feeling sorry for him** 我情不自禁地同情他 wǒ qíng bù zì jīn de tóngqíng tā ▶ **it can't be helped** 没办法 méi bànfǎ

helpful [hɛlpfʊl] ADJ 有用的 yǒuyòng de; (+ *advice, suggestion*) 有建设性的 yǒu jiànshèxìng de

helping [hɛlpɪŋ] N [C] (*of food*) 一

份 yīfèn

helpless [hɛlplɪs] ADJ 无依无靠的 wúyīwúkào de

hen [hɛn] N [C] 母鸡 mǔjī [只 zhī]

her [hər, STRONG hɜr] **I** PRON 她 tā **II** ADJ 她的 tā de ▸ **I haven't seen her** 我还没见到她。 wǒ hái méi jiàndào tā ▸ **they gave her the job** 他们给了她那份工作 tāmen gěile tā nàfèn gōngzuò ▸ **her face was very red** 她的脸很红 tāde liǎn hěnhóng

herb [ɜrb] N [C] 草本植物 cǎoběn zhíwù [株 zhū]

herd [hɜrd] N [C] 牧群 mùqún [群 qún]

here [hɪər] ADV **1** (*in/to this place*) 在这里 zài zhèlǐ **2** (*near me*) 到这里 dào zhèlǐ ▸ **here's my phone number** 这是我的电话号码 zhèshì wǒde diànhuà hàomǎ ▸ **here he is** 他到了 tā dào le ▸ **here you are** (*take this*) 给你 gěi nǐ ▸ **here and there** 各处 gèchù

hero [hɪəroʊ] (*pl* **heroes**) N [C] **1** 男主人公 nán zhǔréngōng [个 gè] **2** (*of battle, struggle*) 英雄 yīngxióng [位 wèi]

heroin [hɛroʊɪn] N [U] 海洛因 hǎiluòyīn

heroine [hɛroʊɪn] N [C] **1** 女主人公 nǚ zhǔréngōng [个 gè] **2** (*of battle, struggle*) 女英雄 nǚ yīngxióng [位 wèi]

hers [hɜrz] PRON 她的 tā de ▸ **this is hers** 这是她的 zhèshì tāde ▸ **a friend of hers** 她的一个朋友 tāde yīgè péngyou

herself [hərsɛlf] PRON **1** 她自己 tā zìjǐ **2** (*emphatic*) 她本人 tā běnrén ▸ **she hurt herself** 她伤了自己 tā shāngle zìjǐ ▸ **she made the dress herself** 她自己做的这件连衣裙 tā zìjǐ zuòde zhèjiàn liányīqún ▸ **she lives by herself** 她独自一人住 tā dúzì yīrén zhù

he's [hiz, STRONG hɪz] = **he is, he has**

hesitate [hɛzɪteɪt] VI 犹豫 yóuyù ▸ **he did not hesitate to take action** 他毫不迟疑地采取了行动 tā háobù chíyí de cáiqǔ le xíngdòng ▸ **don't hesitate to contact me** 请务必和我联系 qǐng wùbì héwǒ liánxì

heterosexual [hɛtəroʊsɛkʃuəl] **I** ADJ (+ *person, relationship*) 异性的 yìxìng de **II** N [C] 异性恋者 yìxìngliànzhě [个 gè]

hi [haɪ] INT (*as greeting*) 嘿 hēi; (*in email*) 你好 nǐhǎo

hiccup [hɪkʌp] **hiccups** N PL ▸ **to have/get (the) hiccups** 打嗝 dǎgé

hid [hɪd] PT *of* **hide**

hidden [hɪdᵊn] PP *of* **hide**

hide [haɪd] (*pt* **hid**, *pp* **hidden**) **I** VT 隐藏 yǐncáng; (+ *feeling, information*) 隐瞒 yǐnmán **II** VI 藏起来 cáng qǐlái ▸ **to hide from sb** 躲着某人 duǒzhe mǒurén

hi-fi [haɪfaɪ] N [C] 高保真音响设备 gāobǎozhēn yīnxiǎng shèbèi [套 tào]

high [haɪ] **I** ADJ 高的 gāo de **II** ADV (*reach, throw*) 高高地 gāogāo de; (*fly, climb*) 高 gāo ▸ **it is 20 m high** 有20米高 yǒu èrshímǐ gāo ▸ **foods that are high in fat** 脂肪含量高的食品 zhǐfáng hánliàng gāo de shípǐn ▸ **safety has always been our highest priority** 安全一直是我们最重视的问题 ānquán yīzhí shì wǒmen zuì zhòngshì de wèntí ▸ **high up** 离地面高的 lí dìmiàn gāo de

> **high** 不能用于描写人,动物和植物，而应用 **tall**。*She was rather tall for a woman.* **tall** 还可以用来描写建筑物，如摩天大楼等，以及其他高度大于宽度的东西。*...tall pine trees...a tall glass vase...*

higher education [haɪər ɛdʒʊkeɪʃᵊn] N [U] 高等教育 gāoděng jiàoyù

high-rise **I** ADJ 高层的 gāocéng de **II** N [C] 高楼大厦 gāolóu dàshà [座 zuò]

high school N [C/U] 中学 zhōngxué [所 suǒ]

hijack [haɪdʒæk] VT 劫持 jiéchí

hijacker [haɪdʒækər] N [c] 劫持者 jiéchízhě [个 gè]
hike [haɪk] **I** VI 步行 bùxíng **II** N [c] (*walk*) 徒步旅行 túbù lǚxíng [次 cì] ▸ **to go hiking** 做徒步旅行 zuò túbù lǚxíng
hiking [haɪkɪŋ] N [U] 步行 bùxíng
hill [hɪl] N [c] 小山 xiǎoshān [座 zuò]; (*slope*) 坡 pō [个 gè]
him [hɪm] PRON 他 tā ▸ **I haven't seen him** 我还没看见他 wǒ hái méi kànjiàn tā ▸ **they gave him the job** 他们给了他那份工作 tāmen gěile tā nàfèn gōngzuò
himself [hɪmsɛlf] PRON **1** 他自己 tā zìjǐ **2** (*emphatic*) 他本人 tā běnrén ▸ **he hurt himself** 他伤了自己 tā shāngle zìjǐ ▸ **he prepared the supper himself** 他自己准备了晚餐 tā zìjǐ zhǔnbèi le wǎncān ▸ **he lives by himself** 他独自一人住。 tā dúzì yīrén zhù
Hindu [hɪndu] **I** N [c] 印度教信徒 Yìndùjiào xìntú [位 wèi] **II** ADJ 与印度教有关的 yǔ Yìndùjiào yǒuguān de
hip [hɪp] N [c] 髋部 kuānbù [个 gè]
hippie [hɪpi] N [c] 嬉皮士 xīpíshì [个 gè]
hire [haɪər] VT 租用 zūyòng; (+ *worker*) 雇用 gùyòng
his [*det* hɪz, *pron* hɪz] **I** ADJ 他的 tā de **II** PRON 他的 tā de ▸ **his face was very red** 他的脸很红 tāde liǎn hěnhóng ▸ **these are his** 这些是他的 zhèxiē shì tāde ▸ **a friend of his** 他的一个朋友 tāde yīgè péngyǒu
history [hɪstəri, -tri] N [U] 历史 lìshǐ
hit [hɪt] (*pt, pp* **hit**) **I** VT **1** (*strike*) 打 dǎ **2** (*collide with*) 碰撞 pèngzhuàng **3** (+ *target*) 击中 jīzhòng **II** N [c] **1** (*on website*) 点击 diǎnjī [次 cì] **2** (*hit song*) 成功而风行一时的事物 chénggōng ér fēngxíng yīshí de shìwù [个 gè]
hitchhike [hɪtʃhaɪk] VI 搭便车旅行 dā biànchē lǚxíng
hitchhiker [hɪtʃhaɪkər] N [c] 搭便车旅行者 dā biànchē lǚxíngzhě [个 gè]
HIV [eɪtʃ aɪ vi] N ABBR (= **human immunodeficiency virus**) 艾滋病病毒 àizībìng bìngdú
hoarse [hɔrs] ADJ 嘶哑的 sīyǎ de
hobby [hɒbi] N [c] 爱好 àihào [种 zhǒng]
hockey [hɒki] N [U] (*on ice*) 冰球 bīngqiú
hold [hoʊld] (*pt, pp* **held**) **I** VT **1** 拿 ná **2** (*contain*) 容纳 róngnà **II** VI (*Tel*) 等着 děngzhe **III** N [c] (*of ship, plane*) 货舱 huòcāng [个 gè] ▸ **hold the line!** (*Tel*) 别挂线！ bié guàxiàn! ▸ **to hold sb prisoner/hostage** 扣留某人作为囚犯/人质 kòuliú mǒurén zuòwéi qiúfàn/rénzhì ▸ **to get/grab/take hold of sb/sth** 紧紧拿着/抓着/握着某人/某物 jǐnjǐn názhe/zhuāzhe/wòzhe mǒurén/mǒuwù ▸ **I need to get hold of Bob** 我需要找到鲍勃 wǒ xūyào zhǎodào Bàobó; **hold on** VI **1** (*keep hold*) 抓牢 zhuāláo **2** (*wait*) 等一会儿 děng yīhuìr; **hold up** VT **1** (*lift up*) 举起 jǔqǐ **2** (*delay*) 阻碍 zǔ'ài
hold-up N [c] **1** (*robbery*) 持械抢劫 chíxiè qiǎngjié [次 cì] **2** (*delay*) 延搁 yángē [次 cì]; (*in traffic*) 交通阻塞 jiāotōng zǔsè [阵 zhèn]
hole [hoʊl] N [c] **1** (*space, gap*) 洞 dòng [个 gè] **2** (*tear*) 破洞 pòdòng [个 gè]
holiday [hɒlɪdei] N [c/U] 假期 jiàqī [个 gè]
Holland [hɒlənd] N 荷兰 Hélán
hollow [hɒloʊ] ADJ (*not solid*) 空的 kōng de
holy [hoʊli] ADJ 神圣的 shénshèng de
home [hoʊm] **I** N **1** [c/U] (*house*) 家 jiā [个 gè] **2** [c/U] (*country, area*) 家乡 jiāxiāng [个 gè] **3** [c] (*institution*) 收容院 shōuróngyuàn [个 gè] **II** ADV (*be, go, get etc*) 在家 zàijiā ▸ **at home** (*in house*) 在家 zàijiā
homeless [hoʊmlɪs] **I** ADJ 无家可归的 wújiā kěguī de **II** N PL ▸ **the homeless** 无家可归的人 wújiā kěguī

de rén

homepage [hoʊmpeɪdʒ] N [c] 主页 zhǔyè [个 gè]

homesick [hoʊmsɪk] ADJ 想家的 xiǎngjiā de

homework [hoʊmwɜrk] N [u] 家庭作业 jiātíng zuòyè

homosexual [hoʊmoʊsɛkʃuəl] **I** ADJ 同性恋的 tóngxìngliàn de **II** N [c] 同性恋者 tóngxìngliànzhě [个 gè]

honest [ɒnɪst] ADJ 诚实的 chéngshí de ▸ **to be honest,...** 说实话，··· shuō shíhuà, ...

honesty [ɒnɪsti] N [u] 诚实 chéngshí

honey [hʌni] N [u] 蜂蜜 fēngmì

honeymoon [hʌnimun] N [c] 蜜月 mìyuè [个 gè]

Hong Kong [hɒŋ kɒŋ] N 香港 Xiānggǎng

hood [hʊd] N [c] **1** 兜帽 dōumào [个 gè] **2** (*Aut*) 发动机罩 fādòngjī zhào [个 gè]

hoof [hʊf, huf] (*pl* **hooves**) N 蹄 tí

hook [hʊk] N [c] 钩 gōu [个 gè] ▸ **to take the phone off the hook** 不把电话听筒挂上 bùbǎ diànhuà tīngtǒng guàshàng

hooray [hʊreɪ] INT 好哇 hǎo wa

hooves [huvz] N PL *of* **hoof**

hop [hɒp] VI 单脚跳 dānjiǎo tiào

hope [hoʊp] **I** VT 希望 xīwàng **II** VI 盼望 pànwàng **III** N [u] 希望 xīwàng ▸ **I hope so/not** 希望是这样/希望不会 xīwàng shì zhèyàng/xīwàng bùhuì ▸ **to hope that...** 希望··· xīwàng... ▸ **to hope to do sth** 希望能做某事 xīwàng néng zuò mǒushì

hopefully [hoʊpfəli] ADV ▸ **hopefully,...** 如果运气好··· rúguǒ yùnqì hǎo...

hopeless [hoʊplɪs] ADJ **1** (+ *situation, position*) 糟糕的 zāogāo de **2** (*inf: useless*) 无能的 wúnéng de

horizon [həraɪzᵊn] N ▸ **the horizon** 地平线 dìpíngxiàn

horizontal [hɔrɪzɒntᵊl] ADJ 水平的 shuǐpíng de

horn [hɔrn] N **1** [c] (*of animal*) 角 jiǎo [个 gè] **2** [c] (*Aut*) 喇叭 lǎba [个 gè]

horoscope [hɔrəskoʊp] N [c] 占星术 zhānxīngshù [种 zhǒng]

horrible [hɔrɪbᵊl, hɒr-] ADJ (+ *color, food, mess*) 糟透的 zāotòu de; (+ *accident, crime*) 可怕的 kěpà de; (+ *experience, moment, situation, dream*) 令人恐惧的 lìng rén kǒngjù de

horror movie [hɔrər-] N [c] 恐怖片 kǒngbù piān [部 bù]

horse [hɔrs] N [c] 马 mǎ [匹 pǐ]

horseracing N [u] 赛马 sàimǎ

hose [hoʊz] N [c] (*also*: **hosepipe**) 输水软管 shūshuǐ ruǎnguǎn [根 gēn]

hospital [hɒspɪtᵊl] N [c/u] 医院 yīyuàn [家 jiā] ▸ **to be in the hospital** 住院 zhùyuàn

hospitality [hɒspɪtælɪti] N [u] 好客 hàokè

host [hoʊst] N [c] 主人 zhǔrén [位 wèi]

hostage [hɒstɪdʒ] N [c] 人质 rénzhì [个 gè] ▸ **to be taken/held hostage** 被绑架/扣押做人质 bèi bǎngjià/kòuyā zuò rénzhì

hostel [hɒstᵊl] N [c] 招待所 zhāodàisuǒ [个 gè]

hostess [hoʊstɪs] N [c] 女主人 nǚ zhǔrén [位 wèi]

hot [hɒt] ADJ **1** (+ *object*) 烫的 tàng de; (+ *weather, person*) 热的 rè de **2** (*spicy*) 辣的 là de

hotel [hoʊtɛl] N [c] 旅馆 lǚguǎn [个 gè] ▸ **to stay at a hotel** 住旅馆 zhù lǚguǎn

hour [aʊər] **I** N [c] 小时 xiǎoshí [个 gè] **II hours** N PL (*ages*) 很长时间 hěncháng shíjiān ▸ **the buses leave on the hour** 每小时正点有一班公共汽车 měi xiǎoshí zhèngdiǎn yǒu yībān gōnggòng qìchē ▸ **for three/four hours** 三/四个小时 sān/sìgè xiǎoshí ▸ **(at) 60 kilometers/miles an** *or* **per hour** 每小时60公里/英里 měi xiǎoshí liùshí gōnglǐ/

yīnglǐ ▸ **to pay sb by the hour** 按小时付费给某人 àn xiǎoshí fùfèi gěi mǒurén ▸ **lunch hour** 午餐时间 wǔcān shíjiān

house [haʊs] N [c] 家 jiā [个 gè] ▸ **at/to my house** 在/到我家 zài/dào wǒjiā

housewife [haʊswaɪf] (*pl* **housewives**) N [c] 家庭主妇 jiātíng zhǔfù [个 gè]

housework [haʊswɜrk] N [U] 家务劳动 jiāwù láodòng

hovercraft [hʌvərkræft] (*pl* **hovercraft**) N [c] 气垫船 qìdiàn chuán [艘 sōu]

KEYWORD

how [haʊ] I ADV 1 (*in questions*) 怎样 zěnyàng ▸ **how did you do it?** 你是怎么做的？ nǐ shì zěnme zuòde? ▸ **how are you?** 你好吗？ nǐ hǎo ma? ▸ **how long have you lived here?** 你在这儿住了多久了？ nǐ zài zhèr zhùle duōjiǔ le? ▸ **how much milk/many people?** 有多少奶/人？ yǒu duōshǎo nǎi/rén? ▸ **how old are you?** 你多大了？ nǐ duōdà le? ▸ **how tall is he?** 他有多高？ tā yǒu duō gāo?
2 (*in suggestions*) ▸ **how about a cup of coffee/a walk etc?** 来杯咖啡/去走走怎么样？ lái bēi kāfēi/qù zǒuzou zěnmeyàng?
II CONJ 怎么 zěnme ▸ **I know how you did it** 我知道你怎么做的 wǒ zhīdào nǐ zěnme zuòde ▸ **to know how to do sth** 知道如何做某事 zhīdào rúhé zuò mǒushì

however [haʊɛvər] ADV 1 (*but*) 但是 dànshì 2 (*with adj, adv*) 不管怎样 bùguǎn zěnyàng 3 (*in questions*) 究竟怎样 jiūjìng zěnyàng

hug [hʌg] I VT (+ *person*) 拥抱 yōngbào II N [c] 拥抱 yōngbào [个 gè] ▸ **to give sb a hug** 拥抱某人 yōngbào mǒurén

huge [hyudʒ] ADJ 巨大的 jùdà de; (+ *amount, profit, debt*) 巨额的 jù'é de; (+ *task*) 庞大的 pángdà de

human [hyumən] I ADJ 人的 rén de II N [c] (*also*: **human being**) 人 rén [个 gè] ▸ **the human race** 人类 rénlèi ▸ **human nature** 人性 rénxìng

humor [hyumər] N [U] 幽默 yōumò ▸ **sense of humor** 幽默感 yōumògǎn

hundred [hʌndrɪd] I NUM 百 bǎi II **hundreds** N PL 几百 jǐbǎi ▸ **a** *or* **one hundred books/people/dollars** 一百本书/个人/美元 yībǎiběn shū/gè rén/měiyuán

hung [hʌŋ] PT, PP *of* **hang**

Hungary [hʌŋgᵊri] N 匈牙利 Xiōngyálì

hungry [hʌŋgri] ADJ 饥饿的 jī'è de ▸ **to be hungry** 饿了 èle

hunt [hʌnt] I VT (*for food, sport*) 打猎 dǎliè II VI (*for food, sport*) 打猎 dǎliè III N [c] 1 (*for food, sport*) 狩猎 shòuliè [次 cì] 2 (*for missing person*) 搜寻 sōuxún [次 cì] 3 (*for criminal*) 追捕 zhuībǔ [次 cì]

hunting [hʌntɪŋ] N [U] (*for food, sport*) 打猎 dǎliè ▸ **job/house/bargain hunting** 到处找工作/住房/便宜货 dàochù zhǎo gōngzuò/zhùfáng/piányi huò

hurricane [hɜrɪkeɪn, hʌr-] N [c] 飓风 jùfēng [场 chǎng] ▸ **hurricane Charley/Tessa** 查理/特萨号台风 Chálǐ/Tèsàhào táifēng

hurry [hɜri, hʌr-] I VI 赶紧 gǎnjǐn II N ▸ **to be in a hurry (to do sth)** 急于（做某事） jí yú (zuò mǒushì) ▸ **to do sth in a hurry** 匆忙地做某事 cōngmángde zuò mǒushì; **hurry up** VI 赶快 gǎnkuài

hurt [hɜrt] (*pt, pp* **hurt**) I VT 1 (*cause pain to*) 弄痛 nòngtòng 2 (*injure*) 使受伤 shǐ shòushāng 3 (*emotionally*) 使伤心 shǐ shāngxīn II VI (*be painful*) 痛 tòng III ADJ 1 (*injured*) 受伤的 shòushāng de 2 (*emotionally*) 受委屈的 shòu wěiqū de ▸ **to hurt o.s.** 伤了自己 shāngle zìjǐ ▸ **I didn't want to**

hurt your feelings 我并不想伤害你的感情 wǒ bìng bùxiǎng shānghài nǐ de gǎnqíng ▸ **where does it hurt?** 哪儿疼？ nǎr téng?

husband [hʌzbənd] N [c] 丈夫 zhàngfu [个 gè]

hut [hʌt] N [c] (*shed*) 木棚 mùpéng [个 gè]

hyphen [haɪfᵊn] N [c] 连字符 liánzìfú [个 gè]

I

I [aɪ] PRON 我 wǒ

ice [aɪs] N [U] 冰 bīng; (*for drink*) 冰块 bīngkuài

iceberg [aɪsbɜrg] N [C] 冰山 bīngshān [座 zuò] ▶ **the tip of the iceberg** (*fig*) 冰山一角 bīngshān yījiǎo

ice cream N [C/U] 冰淇淋 bīngqílín [个 gè]

ice cube N [C] 冰块 bīngkuài [块 kuài]

Iceland [aɪslənd] N 冰岛 Bīngdǎo

ice rink N [C] 溜冰场 liūbīngchǎng [个 gè]

ice-skating N [U] 溜冰 liūbīng

icing [aɪsɪŋ] (*Culin*) N [U] 糖霜 tángshuāng

icon [aɪkɒn] N [C] (*Comput*) 图符 túfú [个 gè]

I'd [aɪd] = **I would, I had**

ID [aɪ di] N ABBR (= **identification**) 身份证明 shēnfèn zhèngmíng ▶ **do you have any ID?** 你有证件吗？ nǐ yǒu zhèngjiàn ma?

ID card N [C] 身份证 shēnfènzhèng [个 gè]

idea [aɪdiə] N **1** [C] (*scheme*) 主意 zhǔyì [个 gè] **2** [C] (*opinion, theory*) 看法 kànfǎ [种 zhǒng] **3** [C/U] (*notion*) 概念 gàiniàn [个 gè] ▶ **(what a) good idea!** （真是个）好主意！ (zhēnshì gè)hǎo zhǔyì! ▶ **I haven't the slightest** *or* **faintest idea** 我根本就不知道 wǒ gēnběn jiù bù zhīdào

ideal [aɪdiəl] ADJ 理想的 lǐxiǎng de

identical [aɪdɛntɪkᵊl] ADJ 完全相同的 wánquán xiāngtóng de ▶ **identical to** 和…完全相同 hé…wánquán xiāngtóng

identification [aɪdɛntɪfɪkeɪʃᵊn] N [U] (*proof of identity*) 身份证明 shēnfèn zhèngmíng

identify [aɪdɛntɪfaɪ] VT (*recognize*) 识别 shíbié

idiot [ɪdiət] N [C] 傻子 shǎzi [个 gè]

i.e. [aɪ i] ABBR (= **id est**) 也就是 yě jiùshì

KEYWORD

if [ɪf] CONJ **1** (*conditional use*) 如果 rúguǒ ▶ **I'll go if you come with me** 如果你和我一起的话我就去 rúguǒ nǐ hé wǒ yīqǐde huà wǒ jiù qù ▶ **if I were you** 如果我是你的话 rúguǒ wǒ shì nǐ de huà ▶ **if necessary** 如有必要 rúyǒu bìyào ▶ **if so** 如果是这样的话 rúguǒ shì zhèyàng de huà ▶ **if not** 如果不行的话 rúguǒ bùxíng de huà

2 (*whenever*) 无论何时 wúlùn héshí ▶ **if we are in Hong Kong, we always go to see her** 我们无论何时去香港，都会去看她 wǒmen wúlùn héshí qù xiānggǎng, dōuhuì qù kàntā

3 (*whether*) 是否 shìfǒu ▶ **ask him if he can come** 问他是否能来 wèn tā shìfǒu nénglái

4 (*in expressions*) ▶ **if only we had more time!** 要是我们再多点时间就好了！ yàoshì wǒmen zài duōdiǎn shíjiān jiù hǎo le!

ignore [ɪgnɔr] VT (+ *person*) 不理 bù lǐ; (+ *advice, event*) 不顾 bù gù

I'll [aɪl] = **I will, I shall**

ill [ɪl] **I** ADJ 有病的 yǒubìng de **II the ill** N PL ▶ **the mentally/terminally ill** 精神/晚期病人 jīngshén/wǎnqī bìngrén ▶ **to fall** *or* **be taken ill** 生病 shēngbìng

单词 **ill** 和 **sick** 在语意上很相近，但使用方法略有不同。**ill** 通常不用在名词前，但可用在动词词组中，比如 **fall ill** 和 **be taken ill**。*He fell ill shortly before Christmas...One of the jury members was taken ill.* **sick** 经常用在名词前。*...sick children...* 在英式英语中，**ill** 比 **sick** 更为文雅和委婉。**sick**

常常指实际的身体病痛，例如晕船或呕吐。*I spent the next 24 hours in bed, groaning and being sick.* 美式英语中，**sick** 经常用在英国人说 **ill** 的地方。*Some people get hurt in accidents or get sick.*

illegal [ɪliːɡəl] ADJ 非法的 fēifǎde

illness [ɪlnɪs] N [c/u] 病 bìng [场 chǎng]

illusion [ɪluːʒən] N [c] 幻想 huànxiǎng [个 gè]

illustration [ɪləstreɪʃən] N [c] 插图 chātú [幅 fú]

imagination [ɪmædʒɪneɪʃən] N **1** [c/u] 想象力 xiǎngxiànglì [种 zhǒng] **2** [c] (*mind's eye*) 想象 xiǎngxiàng [个 gè]

imagine [ɪmædʒɪn] VT **1** (*envisage*) 想象 xiǎngxiàng **2** (*suppose*) 设想 shèxiǎng

imitate [ɪmɪteɪt] VT **1** (*copy*) 效仿 xiàofǎng **2** (+ *person, sound, gesture*) 模仿 mófǎng

imitation [ɪmɪteɪʃən] **I** N [c] 仿制品 fǎngzhìpǐn [件 jiàn] **II** ADJ 仿制的 fǎngzhì de

immediate [ɪmiːdiɪt] ADJ 立即的 lìjí de

immediately [ɪmiːdiɪtli] **I** ADV (*at once*) 立即地 lìjí de **II**

immigrant [ɪmɪɡrənt] N [c] 移民 yímín [个 gè]

immigration [ɪmɪɡreɪʃən] **I** N [u] **1** (*process*) 移民 yímín **2** (*also*: **immigration control**) 移民局检查 yímínjú jiǎnchá **II** CPD (+ *authorities, policy, controls, officer*) 移民 yímín

impatient [ɪmpeɪʃənt] ADJ 急躁的 jízào de ▸ **to get impatient (at** *or* **with sth)** （对某事）不耐烦 (duì mǒushì) bù nàifán

import [ɪmpɔrt] VT 进口 jìnkǒu

importance [ɪmpɔrtəns] N [u] **1** (*significance*) 重要性 zhòngyàoxìng **2** (*influence*) 影响 yǐngxiǎng

important [ɪmpɔrtənt] ADJ **1** 重要的 zhòngyào de **2** (*influential*) 有影响的 yǒu yǐngxiǎng de ▸ **it is important to eat sensibly** 合理进食是很重要的 hélǐ jìnshí shì hěn zhòngyào de ▸ **it's not important** 不重要的 bù zhòngyào de

impossible [ɪmpɒsɪbəl] ADJ 不可能的 bù kěnéng de ▸ **it is impossible to understand what's going on** 不可能了解事情的进展情况 bù kěnéng liǎojiě shìqíng de jìnzhǎn qíngkuàng

impress [ɪmprɛs] VT (+ *person*) 给…极深的印象 gěi...jíshēn de yìnxiàng ▸ **to be impressed by** *or* **with sb/sth** 对某人/某物印象深刻 duì mǒurén/mǒuwù yìnxiàng shēnkè

impression [ɪmprɛʃən] N [c] 印象 yìnxiàng [个 gè] ▸ **to make** *or* **create a good/bad impression** 留下好/不良印象 liúxià hǎo/bùliáng yìnxiàng

impressive [ɪmprɛsɪv] ADJ 给人深刻印象的 gěi rén shēnkè yìnxiàng de

improve [ɪmpruːv] **I** VT 改进 gǎijìn **II** VI (*weather, situation*) 改善 gǎishàn; (*pupil, performance*) 进步 jìnbù

improvement [ɪmpruːvmənt] N [c/u] 改进 gǎijìn [个 gè] ▸ **improvement in** (+ *person, thing*) 进步 jìnbù

KEYWORD

in [*prep* ɪn, *adv* ɪn] **I** PREP **1** 在…里 zài...lǐ ▸ **it's in the house/garden/box** 它在房子/花园/盒子里 tā zài fángzi/huāyuán/hézi lǐ ▸ **put it in the house/garden/box** 把它放在房子/花园/盒子里 bǎ tā fàngzài fángzi/huāyuán/hézi lǐ ▸ **in here/there** 在这儿/那儿 zài zhè'r/nà'r

2 (*with place names*) 在 zài ▸ **in Boston/America** 在波士顿/美国 zài Bōshìdùn/měiguó

3 (*time*: *during*) 在 zài; (*within*: *referring to future*) 在…之后 zài...zhīhòu; (*referring to past*) 在…之内 zài...zhīnèi ▸ **in 1988/May** 在1988年/5月 zài yī jiǔ bā bā nián/wǔyuè ▸ **in the morning/afternoon**

在上午/下午 zài shàngwǔ/xiàwǔ ▶ **I'll see you in two weeks** 我两周后见你 wǒ liǎngzhōu hòu jiàn nǐ ▶ **I did it in 3 hours/days** 我花了3小时/天完成 wǒ huāle sān xiǎoshí/tiān wánchéng
4 (*indicating manner, style etc*) 以 yǐ ▶ **in pencil/ink** 用铅笔/墨水笔 yòng qiānbǐ/mòshuǐbǐ ▶ **the boy in the blue shirt** 穿蓝衬衫的男孩儿 chuān lán chènshān de nánhái'r ▶ **in the sun/rain** 在阳光下/雨中 zài yángguāng xià/yǔzhōng
5 (*with languages*) 用 yòng ▶ **in English/French** 用英语/法语 yòng yīngyǔ/fǎyǔ
6 (*with ratios, numbers*) 每 měi ▶ **one in ten people** 十分之一的人 shí fēn zhī yī de rén
7 (*amongst*) (+ *group, collection*) 在…中 zài...zhōng ▶ **the best athlete in the team** 该队中最好的运动员 gāiduì zhōng zuìhǎo de yùndòngyuán
II ADV ▶ **to be in** (*at home, work*) 在 zài ▶ **to ask sb in** 把某人请到家中 bǎ mǒurén qǐngdào jiāzhōng

inch [ɪntʃ] N [c] 英寸 yīngcùn
include [ɪnklud] VT 包括 bāokuò
including [ɪnkludɪŋ] PREP 包括 bāokuò ▶ **nine people were injured, including two Americans** 九人受伤，其中有两名美国人 jiǔ rén shòushāng, qízhōng yǒu liǎng míng Měiguórén
income [ɪnkʌm] N [c/u] 收入 shōurù [笔 bǐ]
income tax N [u] 所得税 suǒdéshuì
inconvenient [ɪnkənvinyənt] ADJ (+ *time, moment*) 不合时宜的 bùhé shíyí de
incorrect [ɪnkərɛkt] ADJ 错误的 cuòwù de
increase [*n* ɪnkris, *vb* ɪnkris] **I** N [c] 增长 zēngzhǎng [成 chéng] **II** VI 增长 zēngzhǎng **III** VT (+ *price, number, level*) 提高 tígāo ▶ **a 5% increase, an increase of 5%** 百分之五的增长 bǎi fēn zhī wǔ de zēngzhǎng
incredible [ɪnkrɛdɪbᵊl] ADJ (*amazing, wonderful*) 不可思议的 bùkě sīyì de
indeed [ɪndid] ADV (*as a reply*) 是的 shì de ▶ **yes indeed!** 的确如此！díquè rúcǐ!
independence [ɪndɪpɛndəns] N [u] 独立 dúlì
independent [ɪndɪpɛndənt] ADJ 独立的 dúlì de
index [ɪndɛks] (*pl* **indexes**) N [c] 索引 suǒyǐn [条 tiáo]
India [ɪndiə] N 印度 Yìndù
Indian [ɪndiən] **I** ADJ 印度的 Yìndù de **II** N [c] (*person from India*) 印度人 Yìndùrén [个 gè]
indicate [ɪndɪkeɪt] VT **1** 表明 biǎomíng **2** (*point to*) 指向 zhǐxiàng
indifferent [ɪndɪfərənt] ADJ **1** 没兴趣的 méi xìngqù de **2** (*mediocre*) 平庸的 píngyōng de
indigestion [ɪndɪdʒɛstʃᵊn, -daɪ-] N [u] 消化不良 xiāohuà bù liáng
individual [ɪndɪvɪdʒuᵊl] **I** N 个人 gèrén **II** ADJ (*personal*) 个人的 gèrén de
indoor [ɪndɔr] ADJ 室内的 shìnèi de
indoors [ɪndɔrz] ADV 在室内 zài shì nèi
industrial [ɪndʌstriəl] ADJ 工业的 gōngyè de; (+ *accident*) 因工的 yīngōng de
industrial park N [c] 工业区 gōngyè qū [个 gè]
industry [ɪndəstri] N **1** [u] (*manufacturing*) 工业 gōngyè **2** [c] (*business*) 行业 hángyè [种 zhǒng]
inevitable [ɪnɛvɪtəbᵊl] ADJ 不可避免的 bùkě bìmiǎn de
infection [ɪnfɛkʃᵊn] N [c] 感染 gǎnrǎn [处 chù] ▶ **to have an ear/a throat infection** 耳朵/咽喉感染 ěrduo/yānhóu gǎnrǎn
infectious [ɪnfɛkʃəs] ADJ 传染的 chuánrǎn de
inflation [ɪnfleɪʃᵊn] N [u] 通货膨胀 tōnghuò péngzhàng
influence [ɪnfluəns] **I** N **1** [c/u]

(*power*) 权势 quánshì [种 zhǒng] **2** [c] (*effect*) 影响 yǐngxiǎng [个 gè] **II** VT 影响 yǐngxiǎng

inform [ɪnfɔ̲rm] VT 告诉 gàosù ▶ **to inform sb that...** 告诉某人… gàosù mǒurén...

informal [ɪnfɔ̲rmᵊl] ADJ **1** (*relaxed*) 不拘礼节的 bùjū lǐjié de **2** (+ *clothes, party*) 日常的 rìcháng de **3** (+ *meeting, discussions, agreement*) 非正式的 fēizhèngshì de

information [ɪ̲nfərme̲ɪʃᵊn] N [U] 信息 xìnxī ▶ **a piece of information** 一条信息 yītiáo xìnxī

information technology N [U] 信息技术 xìnxī jìshù

ingredient [ɪngri̲diənt] N [C] 配料 pèiliào [种 zhǒng]

inhabitant [ɪnhæ̲bɪtənt] N [C] 居民 jūmín [个 gè]

inherit [ɪnhɛ̲rɪt] VT 继承 jìchéng

initial [ɪnɪ̲ʃᵊl] **I** N [C] (*letter*) 首字母 shǒuzìmǔ [个 gè] **II initials** N PL (*of name*) 首字母 shǒuzìmǔ

injection [ɪndʒɛ̲kʃᵊn] N [C] 注射 zhùshè ▶ **to give sb an injection** 给某人注射 gěi mǒurén zhùshè

injure [ɪ̲ndʒər] VT (+ *person*) 伤害 shānghài ▶ **he was badly injured in the attack** 他在进攻中受了重伤 tā zài jìngōng zhōng shòule zhòngshāng

injury [ɪ̲ndʒəri] N [C/U] (*wound*) 伤害 shānghài [个 gè] ▶ **to escape without injury** 安然脱险 ānrán tuōxiǎn

ink [ɪ̲ŋk] N [C/U] 墨水 mòshuǐ [瓶 píng]

in-laws [ɪ̲nlɔz] N PL 姻亲 yīnqīn

innocent [ɪ̲nəsənt] ADJ 清白的 qīngbái de

inquiry [ɪn'kwaɪrɪ] N **1** [C] (*question*) 询问 xúnwèn; (*about advertisement*) 咨询 zīxún **2** [C] (*investigation*) 调查 diàochá

insect [ɪ̲nsɛkt] N [C] 昆虫 kūnchóng [只 zhī]

insect repellent [-rɪpɛ̲lᵊnt] N [C/U] 杀虫剂 shāchóngjì [瓶 píng]

inside [ɪnsa̲ɪd] **I** N 内部 nèibù **II** ADJ (+ *wall, surface*) 内部的 nèibù de **III** ADV **1** (*go*) 里面 lǐmiàn; (*be*) 在里面 zài lǐmiàn **2** (*indoors*) 在屋内 zài wū nèi **IV** PREP (+ *place, container*) 在…的里面 zài...de lǐmiàn

insist [ɪnsɪ̲st] VI, VT 坚持 jiānchí ▶ **to insist on sth/doing sth** 坚持要求某事/做某事 jiānchí yāoqiú mǒushì/zuò mǒushì

inspector [ɪnspɛ̲ktər] N [C] (*official*) 检查员 jiǎncháyuán [位 wèi]

install, instal [ɪnstɔ̲l] VT 安装 ānzhuāng

installment [ɪnstɔ̲lmənt] N [C] 分期付款 fēnqī fùkuǎn [期 qī]

instance [ɪ̲nstəns] N [C] (*example*) 例子 lìzi [个 gè] ▶ **for instance** 例如 lìrú

instant [ɪ̲nstənt] **I** N [C] (*moment*) 瞬息 shùnxī [个 gè] **II** ADJ **1** (+ *reaction, success*) 立即的 lìjí de **2** (+ *coffee, soup, noodles*) 速食的 sùshí de ▶ **for an instant** 一瞬间 yī shùnjiān

instantly [ɪ̲nstᵊntli] ADV 立即 lìjí

instead [ɪnstɛ̲d] ADV 代替 dàitì ▶ **instead of** 而不是 ér bùshì

instinct [ɪ̲nstɪŋkt] N [C/U] 本能 běnnéng [种 zhǒng]

instruct [ɪnstrʌ̲kt] VT ▶ **to instruct sb to do sth** 命令某人做某事 mìnglìng mǒurén zuò mǒushì

instruction [ɪnstrʌ̲kʃᵊn] **I** CPD (+ *manual, leaflet*) 说明 shuōmíng **II instructions** N PL **1** (*on label, in manual*) 说明 shuōmíng **2** (*teaching*) 教学 jiàoxué **3** (*fees*) 学费 xuéfèi

instructor [ɪnstrʌ̲ktər] N [C] 教员 jiàoyuán [位 wèi]

instrument [ɪ̲nstrəmənt] N [C] **1** 器械 qìxiè [件 jiàn] **2** (*Mus*) 乐器 yuèqì [件 jiàn]

insulin [ɪ̲nsəlɪn] N [U] 胰岛素 yídǎosù

insult [*n* ɪ̲nsʌlt, *vb* ɪnsʌ̲lt] **I** N [C] 侮辱 wǔrǔ [个 gè] **II** VT 侮辱 wǔrǔ

insurance [ɪnʃʊ̲ərəns] N [U] 保险 bǎoxiǎn ▶ **fire/life/health insurance** 火/人寿/健康险 huǒ/rénshòu/

jiànkāng xiǎn
insure [ɪnʃʊər] VT (+ *house, car*) 给…保险 gěi...bǎoxiǎn
intelligent [ɪntɛlɪdʒᵊnt] ADJ 聪明的 cōngmíng de
intend [ɪntɛnd] VT ▸ **to intend to do sth** 打算做某事 dǎsuàn zuò mǒushì
intense [ɪntɛns] ADJ (+ *heat, pain*) 剧烈的 jùliè de; (+ *competition*) 激烈的 jīliè de
intensive care [ɪntɛnsɪv kɛər] N ▸ **to be in intensive care** 接受重病特别护理 jiēshòu zhòngbìng tèbié hùlǐ
intention [ɪntɛnʃᵊn] N [C/U] 打算 dǎsuàn [个 gè]
interest [ɪntrɪst, -tərɪst] N **1** [U/S] (*in subject, idea, person*) 兴趣 xìngqù **2** [C] (*pastime, hobby*) 爱好 àihào [个 gè] **3** [U] (*on loan, savings*) 利息 lìxī ▸ **to take an interest in sth/sb** 对某事/某人感兴趣 duì mǒushì/mǒurén gǎn xìngqù
interested [ɪntərɛstɪd, -trɪstɪd] ADJ ▸ **to be interested (in sth/doing sth)** 对（某事/做某事）有兴趣 duì (mǒushì/zuò mǒushì) yǒu xìngqù

> 请勿将 **interested** 和 **interesting** 混淆。如果你 **interested in** 某事，说明你对它很感兴趣，很想了解或知道更多关于它的事情，或者想花更多的时间来做这件事。*Not all of the children were interested in animals... She asked him how he became interested in politics.* 如果你发现某事**interesting**，表示它令人感兴趣，引人注意，使你乐于更多地了解这件事或者去做这件事。*It must be an awfully interesting job...The interesting thing is that this is exactly the answer we got before.*

interesting [ɪntərɛstɪŋ, -trɪstɪŋ] ADJ 有趣的 yǒuqù de
interfere [ɪntərfɪər] VI (*meddle*) 干涉 gānshè ▸ **to interfere with sth** (+ *plans, career, duty*) 妨碍某事 fángài mǒushì
interior [ɪntɪəriər] N [C] 内部 nèibù
intermission [ɪntərmɪʃᵊn] N [C] **1** (*break, pause*) 间隔 jiàngé [个 gè] **2** (*Cine*) 休息时间 xiūxi shíjiān [段 duàn]
international [ɪntərnæʃənᵊl] ADJ 国际的 guójì de
internet [ɪntərnɛt] N ▸ **the internet** 因特网 yīntèwǎng
internet café N [C] 网吧 wǎngbā [个 gè]
interpret [ɪntɜrprɪt] VI 口译 kǒuyì
interpreter [ɪntɜrprɪtər] N [C] 口译者 kǒuyìzhě [位 wèi]
interrupt [ɪntərʌpt] **I** VT **1** 打断 dǎduàn **2** (+ *activity*) 中断 zhōngduàn **II** VI (*in conversation*) 打岔 dǎchà
interruption [ɪntərʌpʃᵊn] N [C/U] 打扰 dǎrǎo [种 zhǒng]
intersection [ɪntərsɛkʃᵊn] N [C] 交叉点 jiāochādiǎn [个 gè]
interview [ɪntərvyu] **I** N [C/U] **1** (*for job*) 面试 miànshì [次 cì] **2** (*Publishing, Rad, TV*) 采访 cǎifǎng [次 cì] **II** VT **1** (*for job*) 面试 miànshì **2** (*Publishing, Rad, TV*) 采访 cǎifǎng ▸ **to go for/have an interview** 参加面试 cānjiā miànshì
interviewer [ɪntərvyuər] N [C] 采访者 cǎifǎngzhě [位 wèi]
intimidate [ɪntɪmɪdeɪt] VT 恐吓 kǒnghè
into [ɪntu] PREP 到…里面 dào...lǐmiàn ▸ **come into the house/garden** 走进房子/花园里 zǒujìn fángzi/huāyuán lǐ ▸ **get into the car** 进入车子 jìnrù chēzi ▸ **let's go into town** 我们进城吧 wǒmen jìnchéng ba ▸ **to translate Chinese into French** 把汉语翻译成法语 bǎ Hànyǔ fānyì chéng Fǎyǔ ▸ **research into cancer** 对癌症的深入研究 duì áizhèng de shēnrù yánjiū ▸ **I'd like to change some dollars into euros** 我想把一些美元换成欧元 wǒ xiǎng bǎ yīxiē měiyuán

huànchéng ōuyuán
introduce [ɪntrədus] VT **1** (+ *new idea, measure, technology*) 引进 yǐnjìn **2** ▸ **to introduce sb (to sb)** 给某人介绍（某人） gěi mǒurén jièshào (mǒurén) ▸ **may I introduce you (to...)?** 让我介绍你（认识…）好吗？ ràng wǒ jièshào nǐ (rènshi...) hǎo ma?
introduction [ɪntrədʌkʃᵊn] N **1** [U] (*of new idea, measure, technology*) 引进 yǐnjìn **2** [C] (*of person*) 介绍 jièshào [个 gè] **3** [C] (*of book, talk*) 引言 yǐnyán [个 gè]
invade [ɪnveɪd] VT 侵略 qīnlüè
invalid [ɪnvəlɪd] N [C] 病弱者 bìngruòzhě [个 gè]
invent [ɪnvɛnt] VT 发明 fāmíng
invention [ɪnvɛnʃᵊn] N [C] 发明 fāmíng [项 xiàng]
investigate [ɪnvɛstɪgeɪt] VT 调查 diàochá
investigation [ɪnvɛstɪgeɪʃᵊn] N [C/U] 调查 diàochá [项 xiàng]
invisible [ɪnvɪzɪbᵊl] ADJ 看不见的 kànbùjiàn de
invitation [ɪnvɪteɪʃᵊn] N **1** [C] 邀请 yāoqǐng [个 gè] **2** [C] (*card*) 请柬 qǐngjiǎn [封 fēng]
invite [ɪnvaɪt] VT 邀请 yāoqǐng ▸ **to invite sb to do sth** 邀请某人做某事 yāoqǐng mǒurén zuò mǒushì ▸ **to invite sb to dinner** 请某人赴宴 qǐng mǒurén fùyàn
involve [ɪnvɒlv] VT **1** (*entail*) 包含 bāohán **2** (*concern, affect*) 使卷入 shǐ juǎnrù ▸ **to involve sb (in sth)** 使某人参与（某事） shǐ mǒurén cānyù (mǒushì)
iPad® [aɪpæd] 苹果随身播放器 Píngguǒ suíshēn bōfàng qì [个 gè]
Iran [ɪræn, ɪrɑn] N 伊朗 Yīlǎng
Iraq [ɪræk, ɪrɑk] N 伊拉克 Yīlākè
Iraqi [ɪræki, ɪrɑki] **I** ADJ 伊拉克的 Yīlākè de **II** N [C] (*person*) 伊拉克人 Yīlākèrén [名 míng]
Ireland [aɪərlənd] N 爱尔兰 Ài'ěrlán ▸ **the Republic of Ireland** 爱尔兰共和国 Ài'ěrlán Gònghéguó
Irish [aɪrɪʃ] **I** ADJ 爱尔兰的 Ài'ěrlán de **II** N [U] (*language*) 爱尔兰语 Ài'ěrlányǔ **III the Irish** N PL 爱尔兰人 Ài'ěrlánrén
Irishman [aɪrɪʃmən] (*pl* **Irishmen**) N [C] 爱尔兰男人 Ài'ěrlán nánrén [个 gè]
Irishwoman [aɪrɪʃwʊmən] (*pl* **Irishwomen**) N [C] 爱尔兰女人 Ài'ěrlán nǚrén [个 gè]
iron [aɪərn] **I** N **1** [U] (*metal*) 铁 tiě **2** [C] (*for clothes*) 熨斗 yùndǒu [个 gè] **II** ADJ (+ *bar, railings*) 铁的 tiě de **III** VT (+ *clothes*) 熨 yùn
irresponsible [ɪrɪspɒnsɪbᵊl] ADJ (+ *person, driver*) 无责任感的 wú zérèngǎn de; (+ *attitude, behavior*) 不负责任的 bù fù zérèn de
irritating [ɪrɪteɪtɪŋ] ADJ 烦人的 fánrén de
is [ɪz] VB *of* **be**
Islam [ɪslɑm] N [U] 伊斯兰教 Yīsīlánjiào
Islamic [ɪslæmɪk, -lɑ-] ADJ (+ *law, faith*) 伊斯兰教的 Yīsīlánjiào de; (+ *country*) 伊斯兰的 Yīsīlán de
island [aɪlənd] N [C] 岛 dǎo [个 gè]
isolated [aɪsəleɪtɪd] ADJ **1** (+ *place*) 孤零零的 gūlínglíng de **2** (+ *person*) 孤立的 gūlì de **3** (+ *incident, case, example*) 个别的 gèbié de
Israel [ɪzriəl] N 以色列 Yǐsèliè
Israeli [ɪzreɪli] **I** ADJ 以色列的 Yǐsèliè de **II** N [C] (*person*) 以色列人 Yǐsèlièrén [名 míng]
issue [ɪʃu] N [C] (*problem, subject*) 问题 wèntí [个 gè]
IT [aɪ ti] N ABBR (= **Information Technology**) 信息技术 xìnxī jìshù
it [ɪt] PRON **1** (*object or animal*) 它 tā; (*referring to baby*) 他/她 tā/tā **2** (*weather, date, time*) ▸ **it's raining** 正在下雨 zhèngzài xiàyǔ **3** (*impersonal*) ▸ **it doesn't matter** 没关系 méiguānxi ▸ **I can't find it** 我找不到 wǒ zhǎo bù dào ▸ **what is it?** (*thing*) 是什么东西？ shì shénme

dōngxi?; (*what's the matter?*) 怎么了？ zěnme le? ▸ **"who is it?" – "it's me"** "是谁？" "是我" "shì shuí?""shìwǒ"

Italian [ɪtælian] I ADJ 意大利的 Yìdàlì de II N 1 [c] (*person*) 意大利人 Yìdàlìrén [名 míng] 2 [U] (*language*) 意大利语 Yìdàlìyǔ

Italy [ɪtəli] N 意大利 Yìdàlì

itch [ɪtʃ] VI 发痒 fāyǎng

itchy [ɪtʃi] ADJ 发痒的 fāyǎng de

it'd [ɪtəd] = **it would, it had**

item [aɪtəm] N [C] 项目 xiàngmù [个 gè]; (*on bill*) 项 xiàng ▸ **items of clothing** 几件衣服 jǐjiàn yīfu

it'll [ɪtᵊl] = **it will**

its [ɪts] ADJ 1 (*of animal*) 它的 tā de 2 (*of baby*) 他/她的 tā/tā de

it's [ɪts] = **it is, it has**

itself [ɪtsɛlf] PRON 1 (*reflexive*) 它自己 tāzìjǐ 2 (*emphatic*) 本身 běnshēn ▸ **it switches itself on automatically** 它自动接通 tā zìdòng jiētōng ▸ **I think life itself is a learning process** 我认为生活本身是个学习的过程 wǒ rènwéi shēnghuó běnshēn shì gè xuéxí de guòchéng ▸ **by itself** (*alone*) 单独地 dāndú de

I've [aɪv] = **I have**

J

jack [dʒæk] N [C] (*Aut*) 千斤顶 qiānjīndǐng [个 gè]
jacket [dʒækɪt] N [C] 夹克 jiākè [件 jiàn]
jail [dʒeɪl] **I** N [C/U] 监狱 jiānyù [个 gè] **II** VT 监禁 jiānjìn
janitor [dʒænɪtər] N [C] 看门人 kānménrén [个 gè]
January [dʒænyuɛri] N [C/U] 一月 yīyuè; *see also* **July**
Japan [dʒəpæn] N 日本 Rìběn
Japanese [dʒæpəniz] (*pl* **Japanese**) **I** ADJ 日本的 Rìběn de **II** N **1** [C] (*person*) 日本人 Rìběnrén [个 gè] **2** [U] (*language*) 日语 Rìyǔ
jar [dʒɑr] N [C] 广口瓶 guǎngkǒupíng [个 gè]
jaw [dʒɔ] (*Anat*) **I** N [C] 颌 hé [个 gè] **II jaws** N PL 嘴巴 zuǐba
jazz [dʒæz] N [U] (*Mus*) 爵士乐 juéshìyuè
jealous [dʒɛləs] ADJ **1** (+ *husband, wife*) 爱妒忌的 ài dùjì de **2** (*envious*) 妒忌的 dùjì de
jeans [dʒinz] N PL 牛仔裤 niúzǎikù ▸ **a pair of jeans** 一条牛仔裤 yītiáo niúzǎikù
jelly [dʒɛli] N [C/U] 果酱 guǒjiàng [瓶 píng]
jersey [dʒɜrzi] N [C] (*pullover*) 针织毛衫 zhēnzhī máoshān [件 jiàn]
Jesus [dʒizəs] N (*Rel*) 耶稣 Yēsū ▸ **Jesus Christ** 耶稣基督 Yēsū Jīdū
jet [dʒɛt] N [C] (*airplane*) 喷气式飞机 pēnqìshì fēijī [架 jià]
jet lag N [U] 时差反应 shíchā fǎnyìng
Jew [dʒu] N [C] 犹太人 Yóutàirén [个 gè]
jewel [dʒuəl] N [C] 宝石 bǎoshí [块 kuài]
jewelry [dʒuəlri] N [U] 首饰 shǒushì
Jewish [dʒuɪʃ] ADJ 犹太的 Yóutài de
jigsaw [dʒɪgsɔ] N [C] (*also*: **jigsaw puzzle**) 拼图玩具 pīntú wánjù [套 tào]
job [dʒɒb] N [C] **1** (*position*) 工作 gōngzuò [份 fèn] **2** (*task*) 任务 rènwù [项 xiàng] ▸ **Gladys got a job as a secretary** 格拉迪斯找到了一份秘书工作 Gélādísí zhǎodào le yīfèn mìshū gōngzuò ▸ **a part-time/full-time job** 半职/全职工作 bànzhí/quánzhí gōngzuò
jockey [dʒɒki] N [C] (*Sport*) 赛马骑师 sàimǎ qíshī [位 wèi]
jog [dʒɒg] VI 慢跑 mànpǎo
jogging [dʒɒgɪŋ] N [U] 慢跑 mànpǎo
join [dʒɔɪn] **I** VT **1** (+ *club, party, army, navy, line*) 加入 jiārù **2** (+ *person*) 会面 huìmiàn ▸ **will you join us for dinner?** 你想不想和我们一起吃晚饭？ nǐ xiǎngbùxiǎng hé wǒmen yīqǐ chīwǎnfàn?; **join in** VI 参与 cānyù
joint [dʒɔɪnt] N [C] 关节 guānjié [个 gè]
joke [dʒoʊk] **I** N [C] 笑话 xiàohua [个 gè] **II** VI 开玩笑 kāi wánxiào ▸ **you're joking** *or* **you must be joking!** (*inf*) 你在开玩笑{或}你一定在开玩笑吧！ nǐ zài kāi wánxiào {huò} nǐ yīdìng zài kāi wánxiào ba!
Jordan [dʒɔrdᵊn] N 约旦 Yuēdàn
journalist [dʒɜrnəlɪst] N [C] 新闻工作者 xīnwén gōngzuòzhě [位 wèi]
journey [dʒɜrni] N [C] 旅程 lǚchéng [段 duàn] ▸ **a 5-hour journey** 5个小时的路程 wǔgè xiǎoshí de lùchéng ▸ **to go on a journey** 去旅行 qù lǚxíng

> 请勿将 **journey, voyage** 和 **trip** 混淆。**journey** 是指从一地搭乘车船或飞机到另一地的过程。*...a journey of over 2000 miles...* 如果你 **journey to** 某地，你就是去那里。这是书面的用法。*The nights became colder as they journeyed north.* **voyage** 是指从一地到另一地的长途行程，通常指乘船旅行或者太空旅行。*...the*

voyage to the moon in 1972... **trip** 是指从一地到另一地的旅行过程，在目的地做短暂的停留后返回。*...a business trip to Milan...*

joy [dʒɔɪ] N [U] 快乐 kuàilè

judge [dʒʌdʒ] **I** N [C] **1** (*Law*) 法官 fǎguān [位 wèi] **2** (*in competition*) 裁判 cáipàn [个 gè] **II** VT (+ *exhibits, competition*) 评定 píngdìng

judo [dʒudoʊ] N [U] 柔道 róudào

jug [dʒʌg] N [C] 壶 hú [把 bǎ]

juice [dʒus] N [C/U] 汁 zhī [杯 bēi]

July [dʒʊlaɪ] N [C/U] 七月 qīyuè ▸ **July first** 七月一日 qīyuè yīrì ▸ **at the beginning/end of July** 在七月初/末 zài qīyuè chū/mò ▸ **each** *or* **every July** 每年七月 měinián qīyuè

jump [dʒʌmp] **I** VI 跳 tiào **II** N [C] 跳 tiào ▸ **to jump over sth** 跳过某物 tiào guò mǒuwù ▸ **to jump out of a window** 从窗户跳下 cóng chuānghu tiàoxià ▸ **to jump on/off sth** 跳上/下某物 tiàoshàng/xià mǒuwù

June [dʒun] N [C/U] 六月 liùyuè; *see also* **July**

jungle [dʒʌŋgᵊl] N [C/U] 丛林 cónglín [片 piàn]

junior [dʒuniər] ADJ 级别低的 jíbié dī de ▸ **Martin Luther King Jr.** 小马丁・路德・金 xiǎo Mádīng lùdé jīn

junior high (school) N [C/U] 初中 chūzhōng [所 suǒ]

junk [dʒʌŋk] N [U] (*inf*) 废旧杂物 fèijiù záwù

jury [dʒʊəri] N [C] **1** (*Law*) 陪审团 péishěntuán [个 gè] **2** (*in competition*) 评审团 píngshěn tuán [个 gè]

just [dʒʌst] **I** ADJ (*frm*) (+ *decision, punishment, reward*) 公平的 gōngpíng de; (+ *society, cause*) 公正的 gōngzhèng de **II** ADV **1** (*exactly*) 正好 zhènghǎo **2** (*merely*) 仅仅 jǐnjǐn **3** (*for emphasis*) 简直 jiǎnzhí **4** (*in instructions, requests*) 只是 zhǐshì ▸ **it's just right** 正合适 zhèng héshì ▸ **I'm just finishing this** 我马上就做完了 wǒ mǎshàng jiù zuòwán le ▸ **we were just going** 我们正要走 wǒmen zhèngyào zǒu ▸ **to have just done sth** 刚刚做完某事 gānggāng zuòwán mǒushì ▸ **just now** (*a moment ago*) 刚才 gāngcái; (*at the present time*) 现在 xiànzài ▸ **just about everything/everyone** 差不多所有东西/所有人 chàbùduō suǒyǒu dōngxi/suǒyǒu rén ▸ **just before/after...** 就在…以前/以后 jiùzài...yǐqián/yǐhòu ▸ **just enough time/money** 时间/钱正好够 shíjiān/qián zhènghǎo gòu ▸ **just a minute, just one moment** (*asking someone to wait*) 等一下 děng yīxià; (*interrupting*) 慢着 mànzhe

justice [dʒʌstɪs] N **1** [U] (*Law: system*) 司法 sīfǎ **2** [U] (*fairness*) 正义 zhèngyì

K

K [keɪ] ABBR **1** (*inf*) (= **thousands**) 千 qiān **2** (*Comput*) (= **kilobytes**) 千字节 qiānzìjié
kangaroo [kæŋgəru] N [C] 袋鼠 dàishǔ [只 zhī]
karaoke [kærioʊki] N [U] 卡拉OK kǎlā ōukèi
karate [kərɑti] N [U] 空手道 kōngshǒudào
keen [kin] ADJ 热衷的 rèzhōng de ▸ **to be keen to do sth** 渴望做某事 kěwàng zuò mǒushì ▸ **to be keen on sth** 热衷于某事 rèzhōng yú mǒushì
keep [kip] (*pt, pp* **kept**) **I** VT **1** (+ *receipt, money, job*) 保留 bǎoliú **2** (*store*) 保存 bǎocún **3** (*detain*) 留 liú ▸ **to keep doing sth** (*repeatedly*) 总是做某事 zǒngshì zuò mǒushì; (*continuously*) 不停做某事 bùtíng zuò mǒushì ▸ **to keep sb waiting** 让某人等着 ràng mǒurén děngzhe ▸ **to keep the room tidy** 保持房间整洁 bǎochí fángjiān zhěngjié ▸ **to keep a promise** 履行诺言 lǚxíng nuòyán ▸ **can you keep a secret?** 你能保守秘密吗？ nǐ néng bǎoshǒu mìmì ma? ▸ **to keep a record (of sth)** 记录(某事) jìlù (mǒushì) ▸ **how are you keeping?** (*inf*) 你还好吗？ nǐ hái hǎo ma?; **keep away** VI ▸ **to keep away (from sth)** 不接近(某处) bù jiējìn (mǒuchù); **keep off** VT FUS ▸ **keep off the grass!** 请勿进入草坪！ qǐng wù jìnrù cǎopíng!; **keep on** VI ▸ **to keep on doing sth** 继续做某事 jìxù zuò mǒushì; **keep up** VI 跟上 gēnshang ▸ **to keep up with sb** (*walking, moving*) 跟上某人 gēnshàng mǒurén; (*in work*) 跟上某人 gēnshàng mǒurén
kept [kɛpt] PT, PP *of* **keep**
ketchup [kɛtʃəp, kætʃ-] N [U] 番茄酱 fānqiéjiàng
key [ki] N [C] **1** (*for lock, mechanism*) 钥匙 yàoshi [把 bǎ] **2** (*of computer, typewriter, piano*) 键 jiàn [个 gè]
keyboard [kibɔrd] N [C] 键盘 jiànpán [个 gè]
keyhole [kihoʊl] N [C] 钥匙孔 yàoshikǒng [个 gè]
kick [kɪk] **I** VT (+ *person, ball*) 踢 tī **II** N [C] 踢 tī [顿 dùn]; **kick off** VI 开赛 kāisài
kickoff [kɪkɔf] N [S] 开场时间 kāichǎng shíjiān
kid [kɪd] N [C] (*inf: child*) 小孩 xiǎohái [个 gè]; (*teenager*) 年轻人 niánqīngrén [个 gè] **II** VI ▸ **you're kidding!** 你一定是在开玩笑吧！ nǐ yīdìng shì zài kāi wánxiào ba!
kidnap [kɪdnæp] VT 绑架 bǎngjià
kidney [kɪdni] N **1** [C] (*Anat*) 肾脏 shènzàng [个 gè] **2** [C/U] (*Culin*) 腰子 yāozi [个 gè]
kill [kɪl] VT **1** (+ *person, animal, plant*) 致死 zhìsǐ **2** (*murder*) 谋杀 móushā ▸ **my back's killing me** (*inf*) 我的背疼死了 wǒde bèi téngsǐ le
killer [kɪlər] N [C] 凶手 xiōngshǒu [个 gè]
kilo [kiloʊ] N [C] 公斤 gōngjīn
kilometer [kɪləmitər, kɪlɒmɪtər] N [C] 公里 gōnglǐ
kind [kaɪnd] **I** ADJ 友好的 yǒuhǎo de **II** N [C] (*type, sort*) 种类 zhǒnglèi [个 gè] ▸ **an opportunity to meet all kinds of people** 与各种各样的人见面的机会 yǔ gèzhǒng gèyàng de rén jiànmiàn de jīhuì ▸ **it was kind of them to help** 他们来帮忙真是太好了 tāmen lái bāngmáng zhēnshì tàihǎo le
kindness [kaɪndnɪs] N [U] 仁慈 réncí
king [kɪŋ] N [C] 国王 guówáng [位 wèi]
kingdom [kɪŋdəm] N [C] 王国 wángguó [个 gè]
kiss [kɪs] **I** N [C] 吻 wěn [个 gè] **II** VT 吻 wěn ▸ **to give sb a kiss** 吻某人

一下 wěn mǒurén yīxià ▶ **to kiss sb goodbye/goodnight** 与某人吻别/吻某人一下，道晚安 yǔ mǒurén wěnbié/wěn mǒurén yīxià, dào wǎn'ān

kitchen [kɪtʃᵊn] N [C] 厨房 chúfáng [个 gè]

kite [kaɪt] N [C] 风筝 fēngzhēng [个 gè]

kitten [kɪtᵊn] N [C] 小猫 xiǎomāo [只 zhī]

knee [ni] N [C] 膝盖 xīgài [个 gè]

kneel [nil] (*pt, pp* **knelt**) VI (*also:* **kneel down**) 跪下 guìxià

knelt [nɛlt] PT, PP *of* **kneel**

knew [nu] PT *of* **know**

knife [naɪf] (*pl* **knives**) N [C] 刀 dāo [把 bǎ] ▶ **knife and fork** 刀叉 dāochā

knit [nɪt] VI 织 zhī

knives [naɪvz] N PL *of* **knife**

knob [nɒb] N [C] 球形把手 qiúxíng bǎshǒu [个 gè]

knock [nɒk] **I** VT (*strike*) 碰撞 pèngzhuàng **II** VI (*on door, window*) 敲 qiāo **III** N [C] **1** (*blow, bump*) 碰撞 pèngzhuàng [下 xià] **2** (*on door*) 敲门声 qiāoménshēng [声 shēng] ▶ **to knock sb unconscious** (*blow, blast*) 把某人打昏 bǎ mǒurén dǎhūn; **knock down** VT **1** (*run over*) 撞倒 zhuàngdǎo **2** (*demolish*) 拆除 chāichú; **knock out** VT **1** (*make unconscious*) 打昏 dǎhūn **2** (*Boxing*) 击昏 jīhūn **3** (*eliminate: in game, competition*) 淘汰 táotài; **knock over** VT 撞倒 zhuàngdǎo

knot [nɒt] N [C] 结 jié [个 gè] ▶ **to tie a knot** 打个结 dǎ gè jié

know [noʊ] (*pt* **knew**, *pp* **known**) VT **1** (+ *facts, dates*) 知道 zhīdào **2** (+ *language*) 懂 dǒng **3** (+ *person, place, subject*) 认识 rènshi ▶ **to know that...** 知道… zhīdào... ▶ **to know where/when** 知道何处/何时… zhīdào héchù/héshí... ▶ **to get to know sb** 逐渐开始了解某人 zhújiàn kāishǐ liǎojiě mǒurén ▶ **to know about sth** 听说过某事 tīngshuō guò mǒushì ▶ **yes, I know** 对，的确如此 duì, díquè rúcǐ ▶ **you never know** 很难讲 hěn nánjiǎng ▶ **you know** (*used for emphasis*) 你得知道 nǐ děi zhīdào

knowledge [nɒlɪdʒ] N [U] 知识 zhīshi ▶ **to (the best of) my knowledge** 据我所知 jù wǒ suǒzhī

known [noʊn] PP *of* **know**

Koran [kɔran] N ▶ **the Koran** 《古兰经》 Gǔlánjīng

Korea [kɔriə] N *see* **North Korea, South Korea**

Korean [kɔriən] **I** ADJ 韩国的 Hánguó de **II** N **1** (*person*) 韩国人 Hánguórén **2** (*language*) 韩语 Hányǔ

L

label [leɪbᵊl] **I** N [c] 标签 biāoqiān [个 gè] **II** VT 用标签标明 yòng biāoqiān biāomíng
labor [leɪbər] N [U] (*manpower*) 劳动力 láodònglì ▸ **to be in labor** (*Med*) 处于阵痛期 chǔyú zhèntòng qī
laboratory [læbrətɔri] N [c] 研究室 yánjiūshì [个 gè]
labor union N [c] 工会 gōnghuì [个 gè]
lace [leɪs] N **1** [U] (*fabric*) 花边 huābiān **2** [c] (*of shoe*) 系带 jìdài [根 gēn]
lack [læk] **I** N [S/U] 缺乏 quēfá **II** VT (+ *means, skills, experience, confidence*) 缺乏 quēfá
ladder [lædər] N [c] 梯子 tīzi [个 gè]
lady [leɪdi] N [c] 女士 nǚshì [位 wèi] ▸ **ladies and gentlemen...** 女士们，先生们… nǚshìmen, xiānshēngmen... ▸ **the ladies' room** 女厕所 nǚ cèsuǒ
laid [leɪd] PT, PP *of* **lay**
lain [leɪn] PP *of* **lie**
lake [leɪk] N [c] 湖 hú [个 gè]
lamb [læm] N **1** [c] (*animal*) 羔羊 gāoyáng [只 zhī] **2** [U] (*meat*) 羔羊肉 gāoyángròu
lamp [læmp] N [c] 灯 dēng [盏 zhǎn]
lampshade [læmpʃeɪd] N [c] 灯罩 dēngzhào [个 gè]
land [lænd] **I** N **1** [U] (*area of open ground*) 土地 tǔdì **2** [U] (*not sea*) 陆地 lùdì **II** VI **1** (*Aviat, Space*) 降落 jiàngluò **2** (*from ship*) 登陆 dēnglù
landing [lændɪŋ] N [c/U] (*Aviat*) 降落 jiàngluò [次 cì]
landlady [lændleɪdi] N [c] 女房东 nǚfángdōng [位 wèi]
landlord [lændlɔrd] N [c] 男房东 nánfángdōng [位 wèi]
landscape [lændskeɪp] N [c/U] 风景 fēngjǐng [道 dào]
lane [leɪn] N [c] **1** (*in country*) 小路 xiǎolù [条 tiáo] **2** (*Aut: of road*) 车道 chēdào [条 tiáo]
language [læŋgwɪdʒ] N **1** [c] (*English, Russian etc*) 语言 yǔyán [种 zhǒng] **2** [U] (*speech*) 语言表达能力 yǔyán biǎodá nénglì
language laboratory N [c] 语言实验室 yǔyán shíyànshì [个 gè]
lap [læp] N [c] **1** (*of person*) 大腿的上方 dàtuǐ de shàngfāng **2** (*in race*) 圈 quān
laptop [læptɒp] N [c] (*also*: **laptop computer**) 笔记本电脑 bǐjìběn diànnǎo [个 gè]
large [lɑrdʒ] ADJ (+ *house, person*) 大的 dà de; (+ *number, amount*) 大量的 dàliàng de
laser [leɪzər] N **1** [c/U] (*beam*) 激光 jīguāng [束 shù] **2** [c] (*machine*) 激光器 jīguāngqì [台 tái]
last [læst] **I** ADJ **1** (*most recent*) 最近的 zuìjìn de; (+ *Monday, July, weekend etc*) 上 shàng **2** (*final*) 最后的 zuìhòu de; (*of series, row*) 最后的 zuìhòu de **II** PRON (*final one*) 最后一个 zuìhòu yī gè **III** ADV **1** (*most recently*) 最近 zuìjìn **2** (*at the end*) 最后 zuìhòu **3** (*in final position*) 最后 zuìhòu **IV** VI (*continue*) 持续 chíxù ▸ **last week** 上个星期 shàng gè xīngqī ▸ **last night** (*yesterday evening*) 昨晚 zuówǎn; (*during the night*) 昨天夜里 zuótiān yèli ▸ **the last time** (*the previous time*) 上一次 shàng yīcì ▸ **at (long) last** (*finally*) 终于 zhōngyú ▸ **our house is the second to last one** 我们的房子是倒数第二个 wǒmen de fángzi shì dàoshǔ dì'èrgè ▸ **it lasts (for) 2 hours** 持续了两个小时 chíxù le liǎnggè xiǎoshí
lastly [læstli] ADV 最后 zuìhòu
late [leɪt] **I** ADJ **1** (*not on time*) 迟的 chí de **2** (*after the usual time*) 稍晚的 shāowǎn de **II** ADV **1** (*not on time*) 迟 chí **2** (*after the usual time*) 晚 wǎn ▸ **we're late** 我们迟到了 wǒmen

chídào le ▶ **sorry I'm late** 对不起，我迟到了 duìbuqǐ, wǒ chídào le ▶ **to be 10 minutes late** 迟到10分钟 chídào shí fēnzhōng ▶ **in late May** 5月下旬 wǔyuè xiàxún

lately [leɪtli] ADV 最近 zuìjìn

later [leɪtər] ADV 以后 yǐhòu ▶ **some time/weeks/years later** 一些时候/几个星期/几年以后 yīxiē shíhou/jǐgè xīngqī/jǐnián yǐhòu ▶ **later on** 以后 yǐhòu

latest [leɪtɪst] ADJ **1** (+ *book, film, news*) 最新的 zuìxīn de **2** (*most up-to-date*) 最新式的 zuì xīnshì de ▶ **at the latest** 最迟 zuìchí

Latin [lætɪn, -tᵊn] N [U] 拉丁语 Lādīngyǔ

Latin America [lætɪn əmɛrɪkə] N 拉丁美洲 Lādīngměizhōu

Latin American [lætɪn əmɛrɪkən] **I** ADJ 拉丁美洲的 Lādīngměizhōu de **II** N [C] (*person*) 拉丁美洲人 Lādīngměizhōurén [个 gè]

latter [lætər] N ▶ **the latter** 后者 hòuzhě

laugh [læf] **I** N [C] 笑 xiào [阵 zhèn] **II** VI 笑 xiào; **laugh at** VT FUS 对…发笑 duì...fāxiào

launch [lɔntʃ] VT **1** (+ *rocket, missile, satellite*) 发射 fāshè **2** (+ *product, publication*) 推出 tuīchū

laundry [lɔndri] N [U] (*dirty washing*) 待洗的衣物 dàixǐ de yīwù; (*clean washing*) 洗好的衣物 xǐhǎo de yīwù

laundry detergent [lɔndri dɪtɜrdʒᵊnt] N [U/C] 洗衣粉 xǐyīfěn

law [lɔ] N **1** [S/U] (*legal system*) 法律 fǎlǜ **2** [C] (*regulation*) 法规 fǎguī [条 tiáo] ▶ **against the law** 违法 wéifǎ ▶ **to break the law** 违法 wéifǎ ▶ **by law** 依照法律 yīzhào fǎlǜ ▶ **to study law** 学习法律 xuéxí fǎlǜ

lawn [lɔn] N [C] 草坪 cǎopíng [片 piàn]

lawn mower [lɔnmoʊər] N [C] 割草机 gēcǎojī [部 bù]

lawyer [lɔɪər, lɔyər] N [C] 律师 lǜshī [位 wèi]

lay [leɪ] (*pt, pp* **laid**) **I** PT *of* **lie II** VT **1** (*put*) 放 fàng; **lay down** VT (*put down*) 放下 fàngxià; **lay off** VT 解雇 jiěgù

layer [leɪər] N [C] 层 céng

layout [leɪaʊt] N [C] 布局 bùjú [个 gè]

lazy [leɪzi] ADJ 懒惰的 lǎnduò de

lead¹ [lid] (*pt, pp* **led**) **I** N **1** [C] (*for dog*) 皮带 pídài [条 tiáo] **2** [C] (*Elec*) 导线 dǎoxiàn [根 gēn] **II** VT **1** (*guide*) 带领 dàilǐng **2** (+ *group, party, organization*) 领导 lǐngdǎo; (+ *march, demonstration, parade*) 带领 dàilǐng **III** VI (*in race, competition*) 领先 lǐngxiān ▶ **to be in the lead** 领先 lǐngxiān ▶ **to lead the way** (*lit*) 引路 yǐnlù; (*fig*) 率先 shuàixiān; **lead away** VT (+ *prisoner*) 带走 dàizǒu; **lead to** VT FUS (*result in*) 导致 dǎozhì

lead² [lɛd] N [U] 铅 qiān

leader [lidər] N [C] 领导人 lǐngdǎorén [位 wèi]

leaf [lif] (*pl* **leaves**) N [C] 叶 yè [片 piàn]

leaflet [liflɪt] N [C] (*booklet*) 小册子 xiǎocèzi [本 běn]; (*single sheet*) 传单 chuándān [份 fèn]

league [lig] N [C] (*Sport*) 联赛 liánsài [季 jì]

leak [lik] **I** N [C] (*of liquid, gas*) 裂隙 lièxì [条 tiáo] **II** VI (*shoes, pipe, liquid, gas*) 漏 lòu

lean [lin] (*pt, pp* **leaned**) **I** VT ▶ **to lean sth on** *or* **against sth** 把某物靠在某物上 bǎ mǒuwù kàozài mǒuwù shang **II** ADJ (+ *meat*) 瘦的 shòu de ▶ **to lean against sth** (*person*) 靠在某物上 kàozài mǒuwù shàng ▶ **to lean forward/back** 向前/后倾 xiàngqián/hòu qīng; **lean on** VT FUS 倚 yǐ

leap year N [C] 闰年 rùnnián [个 gè]

learn [lɜrn] **I** VT (*study*) (+ *skill*) 学学 xué; (+ *poem, song*) 背 bèi **II** VI 学 xué ▶ **to learn about sth** (*study*) 学到某物 xuédào mǒuwù ▶ **to learn to do sth/how to do sth** 学做某事/怎样做某事 xuézuò mǒushì/zěnyàng zuò mǒushì

least [li̲st] **I** ADJ (+ *noun*) 最少的 zuìshǎo de **II** ADV **1** (+ *adjective*) ▸ **the least expensive/attractive/interesting** 最便宜/没有魅力/没趣的 zuì piányi/méiyǒu mèilì/méi qù de **2** (+ *verb*) 最不 zuìbù **III** PRON ▸ **the least** 最少 zuìshǎo ▸ **at least** (*in expressions of quantity, comparisons*) 至少 zhìshǎo

leather [lɛ̲ðər] **I** N [U] 皮革 pígé **II** CPD (+ *jacket, shoes, chair*) 皮 pí

leave [li̲v] (*pt, pp* **left**) **I** VT **1** (+ *place*) 离开 líkāi **2** (+ *school, job, group*) 放弃 fàngqì **3** (*leave behind*: *deliberately*) 留下 liúxià; (*accidentally*) 落 luò **4** (+ *message*) 留 liú **II** VI **1** (*depart*) (*person*) 离开 líkāi; (*bus, train*) 出发 chūfā **2** (*give up school*) 辍学 chuòxué; (*give up job*) 辞职 cízhí **III** N [U] 休假 xiūjià; (*Mil*) 假期 jiàqī ▸ **to leave sth to sb** 把某物留给某人 bǎ mǒuwù liúgěi mǒurén ▸ **to leave sb/sth alone** 不理会某人/某物 bù lǐhuì mǒurén/mǒuwù ▸ **to leave for** (+ *destination*) 前往 qiánwǎng; **leave behind** VT (*forget*) 忘带 wàngdài; **leave on** VT (+ *light, heating*) 开着 kāizhe; **leave out** VT 删掉 shāndiào

leaves [li̲vz] N PL *of* **leaf**

Lebanon [lɛ̲bənɒn] N 黎巴嫩 Líbānèn

lecture [lɛ̲ktʃər] N [C] (*talk*) 讲座 jiǎngzuò [个 gè] ▸ **to give a lecture (on sth)** 作(某方面的)讲座 zuò (mǒu fāngmiàn de) jiǎngzuò

lecturer [lɛ̲ktʃərər] N [C] 讲师 jiǎngshī [位 wèi]

led [lɛ̲d] PT, PP *of* **lead**[1]

left[1] [lɛ̲ft] **I** ADJ (*not right*) 左的 zuǒ de **II** N ▸ **the left** 左侧 zuǒcè **III** ADV (*turn, go, look*) 向左 xiàngzuǒ ▸ **on the left** 在左边 zài zuǒbiān ▸ **to the left** 靠左边 kào zuǒbiān

left[2] [lɛ̲ft] **I** PT, PP *of* **leave II** ADJ ▸ **to be left over** 剩下 shèngxià

left-hand [lɛ̲fthæ̲nd] ADJ (+ *side, corner*) 左侧的 zuǒcè de

left-handed [lɛ̲fthæ̲ndɪd] ADJ 左撇子的 zuǒpiězi de

leg [lɛ̲g] N **1** [C] 腿 tuǐ [条 tiáo] **2** [C/U] (*of lamb, chicken*) 腿 tuǐ [根 gēn]

legal [li̲gᵊl] ADJ **1** (+ *system, requirement*) 法律的 fǎlǜ de **2** (+ *action, situation*) 合法的 héfǎ de

legal holiday N [C] 法定假期 fǎdìng jiàqī [个 gè]

leisure [li̲ʒər, lɛ̲ʒ-] N [U] 闲暇 xiánxiá

lemon [lɛ̲mən] N [C] 柠檬 níngméng [个 gè]

lemonade [lɛ̲məne̲ɪd] N [U] 柠檬汽水 níngméng qìshuǐ

lend [lɛ̲nd] (*pt, pp* **lent**) VT **1** ▸ **to lend sth to sb** 把某物借给某人 bǎ mǒuwù jiègěi mǒurén **2** (*bank*) 贷 dài

length [lɛ̲ŋθ] N **1** [C/U] (*of object, animal*) 长度 chángdù [个 gè]; (*of sentence, article*) 篇幅 piānfu [个 gè] **2** [C/U] (*duration*) 期间 qījiān [个 gè]

lens [lɛ̲nz] N [C] (*of spectacles*) 镜片 jìngpiàn [片 piàn]; (*of telescope, camera*) 镜头 jìngtóu [个 gè]

Lent [lɛ̲nt] N [U] 大斋节 Dàzhāijié

lent [lɛ̲nt] PT, PP *of* **lend**

lentil [lɛ̲ntɪl, -tᵊl] N [C] 小扁豆 xiǎobiǎndòu [颗 kē]

Leo [li̲oʊ] N [U] (*sign*) 狮子座 Shīzi Zuò

leopard [lɛ̲pərd] N [C] 豹 bào [只 zhī]

lesbian [lɛ̲zbiən] **I** ADJ 女同性恋的 nǚ tóngxìngliàn de **II** N [C] 女同性恋者 nǚ tóngxìngliànzhě [个 gè]

less [lɛ̲s] **I** ADJ (+ *noun*) 更少的 gèng shǎo de **II** ADV **1** (+ *adjective/adverb*) 较少地 jiàoshǎo de **2** (+ *verb*) 较少 jiàoshǎo **III** PRON 较少的东西 jiàoshǎo de dōngxi **IV** PREP ▸ **less tax/10% discount** 去掉税/10%的折扣 qùdiào shuì/bǎifēnzhīshí de zhékòu ▸ **less than half** 不到一半 bùdào yībàn

lesson [lɛ̲sᵊn] N [C] 课 kè [堂 táng]

let [lɛt] (*pt, pp* **let**) VT **1** ▶ **to let sb do sth** (*give permission*) 允许某人做某事 yǔnxǔ mǒurén zuò mǒushì **2** ▶ **to let sth happen** 让某事发生 ràng mǒushì fāshēng ▶ **to let sb know that...** 告诉某人… gàosù mǒurén... **3** ▶ **to let sb in/out** 让某人进去/出去 ràng mǒurén jìnqù/chūqù ▶ **let's go/eat** 我们走/吃吧 wǒmen zǒu/chībā ▶ **"to let"** "现房待租" "xiànfáng dàizū" ▶ **to let go** (*release one's grip*) 松开 sōngkāi ▶ **to let sb/sth go** (*release*) 放走某人/某物 fàngzǒu mǒurén/mǒuwù; **let down** VT (+ *person*) 令…失望 lìng...shīwàng; **let in** VT **1** (+ *water, air*) 允许进来 yǔnxǔ jìnlái **2** (+ *person*) 给…开门 gěi...kāimén

letter [lɛtər] N [c] **1** (*note*) 信 xìn [封 fēng] **2** (*of alphabet*) 字母 zìmǔ [个 gè]

lettuce [lɛtɪs] N [c/u] 生菜 shēngcài [棵 kē]

level [lɛvᵊl] **I** ADJ 平的 píng de **II** N [c] **1** (*standard*) 水平 shuǐpíng [种 zhǒng] **2** (*height*) 水位 shuǐwèi [个 gè]

lever [livər, lɛv-] N [c] 杆 gǎn [根 gēn]

liar [laɪər] N [c] 说谎者 shuōhuǎngzhě [个 gè]

liberal [lɪbərəl, lɪbrəl] **I** ADJ (+ *person, attitude*) 开明的 kāimíng de **II** N [c] (*Pol*) ▶ **Liberal** 自由党党员 Zìyóudǎng dǎngyuán [名 míng]

Libra [librə] N [u] (*sign*) 天秤座 Tiānchèng Zuò

librarian [laɪbrɛəriən] N [c] 图书管理员 túshū guǎnlǐyuán [位 wèi]

library [laɪbrɛri] N [c] 图书馆 túshūguǎn [个 gè]

license [laɪsᵊns] N **1** [c] (*permit*) 许可证 xǔkězhèng [张 zhāng] **2** [c] (*also*: **driver's license**) 驾驶执照 jiàshǐ zhízhào [本 běn]

license plate N [c] 车牌照 chēpáizhào [个 gè]

lick [lɪk] VT 舔 tiǎn

lid [lɪd] N [c] **1** (*of box, case, pan*) 盖 gài [个 gè] **2** (*eyelid*) 眼睑 yǎnjiǎn [个 gè]

lie[1] [laɪ] (*pt* **lay**, *pp* **lain**) VI **1** (*person*) 躺 tǎng; **lie around** VI **1** 乱放 luànfàng; **lie down** VI (*person*) 躺下 tǎngxià

lie[2] [laɪ] **I** 说谎 shuōhuǎng **II** N [c] 谎言 huǎngyán [个 gè] ▶ **to tell lies** 说谎 shuōhuǎng

life [laɪf] (*pl* **lives**) N **1** [c/u] (*living, existence*) 生命 shēngmìng [个 gè] **2** [c] (*lifespan*) 一生 yīshēng [个 gè] ▶ **his personal/working life** 他的个人/工作生活 tāde gèrén/gōngzuò shēnghuó

lifeboat [laɪfboʊt] N [c] 救生船 jiùshēngchuán [艘 sōu]

life preserver [-prɪzɜrvər] N [c] (*lifebelt*) 救生用具 jiùshēng yòngjù [件 jiàn]; (*life jacket*) 救生衣 jiùshēngyī [件 jiàn]

lifestyle [laɪfstaɪl] N [c/u] 生活方式 shēnghuó fāngshì [种 zhǒng]

lift [lɪft] VT 举起 jǔqǐ; **lift up** VT (+ *person, thing*) 举起 jǔqǐ

light [laɪt] (*pt, pp* **lit**) **I** N **1** [u] (*from sun, moon, lamp, fire*) 光 guāng **2** [c] (*Elec, Aut*) 灯 dēng [盏 zhǎn] **3** [s] (*for cigarette*) 打火机 dǎhuǒjī **II** VT (+ *candle, fire, cigarette*) 点燃 diǎnrán **III** ADJ **1** (+ *color*) 淡的 dàn de **2** (*not heavy*) 轻的 qīng de **IV lights** N PL (*also*: **traffic lights**) 交通指示灯 jiāotōng zhǐshìdēng ▶ **to turn** *or* **switch the light on/off** 开/关灯 kāi/guān dēng

light bulb N [c] 灯泡 dēngpào [个 gè]

lighter [laɪtər] N [c] (*also*: **cigarette lighter**) 打火机 dǎhuǒjī [个 gè]

lighthouse [laɪthaʊs] N [c] 灯塔 dēngtǎ [座 zuò]

lightning [laɪtnɪŋ] N [u] 闪电 shǎndiàn

like[1] [laɪk, laɪk] PREP **1** (*similar to*) 像 xiàng **2** (*in similes*) 像…一样 xiàng...yīyàng **3** (*such as*) 如 rú ▶ **a house like ours** 像我们这样的房

子 xiàng wǒmen zhèyàng de fángzi ▶ **to be like sth/sb** 像某物/某人 xiàng mǒuwù/mǒurén ▶ **what's he/the weather like?** 他/天气怎么样? tā/tiānqì zěnmeyàng? ▶ **to look like** (+ *person*) 长得像 zhǎngde xiàng; (+ *thing*) 类似 lèisì ▶ **what does it look/sound/taste like?** 看/听/尝起来怎么样? kàn/tīng/chángqǐlái zěnmeyàng? ▶ **like this** 像这样 xiàng zhèyàng

like[2] [laɪk] **I** VT (+ *person, thing*) 喜欢 xǐhuan **II** N ▶ **his likes and dislikes** 他的好恶 tā de hàowù ▶ **to like doing sth** 喜欢做某事 xǐhuān zuò mǒushì ▶ **I would** *or* **I'd like an ice-cream/to go for a walk** 我想吃个冰激凌/去散步 wǒxiǎng chīgè bīngjilíng/qù sànbù ▶ **would you like some coffee?** 你想不想来杯咖啡? nǐ xiǎngbùxiǎng láibēi kāfēi? ▶ **if you like** (*in offers, suggestions*) 如果你愿意的话 rúguǒ nǐ yuànyì de huà

likely [laɪkli] ADJ 很可能的 hěn kěnéng de ▶ **it is likely that...** 有可能… yǒu kěnéng... ▶ **to be likely to do sth** 很有可能做某事 hěnyǒu kěnéng zuò mǒushì

lime [laɪm] N [C] (*fruit*) 酸橙 suānchéng [个 gè]

limit [lɪmɪt] N [C] **1** (*maximum point*) 限度 xiàndù [个 gè] **2** (*on time, money*) 限定 xiàndìng [种 zhǒng]

limp [lɪmp] VI 跛行 bǒxíng

line [laɪn] N [C] **1** (*long thin mark*) 线 xiàn [条 tiáo] **2** (*of people, things*) 排 pái **3** (+ *of words*) 行 háng **4** (*Tel*) 线路 xiànlù [条 tiáo] **5** (*railway*) 铁路线路 tiělù xiànlù [条 tiáo] ▶ **hold the line please!** (*Tel*) 请稍等! qǐng shāoděng! ▶ **to stand** *or* **wait in line** 排队等候 páiduì děnghòu ▶ **on the right lines** 大体正确 dàtǐ zhèngquè

linen [lɪnɪn] **I** N [U] **1** (*cloth*) 亚麻布 yàmábù **2** (*tablecloths, sheets*) 亚麻制品 yàmá zhìpǐn **II** CPD (+ *jacket, sheets*) 亚麻料 yàmáliào

lining [laɪnɪŋ] N [C/U] 衬里 chènlǐ [个 gè]

link [lɪŋk] **I** N [C] **1** (*between people, organizations*) 联系 liánxì [种 zhǒng] **2** (*Comput*) (*also*: **hyperlink**) 超链接 chāoliànjiē [个 gè] **II** VT **1** (+ *places, objects*) 连接 liánjiē **2** (+ *people, situations*) 联系 liánxì

lion [laɪən] N [C] 狮子 shīzi [头 tóu]

lip [lɪp] N [C] 唇 chún [个 gè]

lip-read [lɪprid] VI 唇读 chúndú

lipstick [lɪpstɪk] N [C/U] 口红 kǒuhóng [支 zhī]

liquid [lɪkwɪd] N [C/U] 液体 yètǐ [种 zhǒng]

liquor [lɪkər] N [U] 酒 jiǔ

list [lɪst] **I** N [C] 单子 dānzi [个 gè] **II** VT **1** (*record*) (*person*) 列出 lièchū **2** (*Comput*) 列出 lièchū

listen [lɪsən] VI **1** (*to sound, music*) 听 tīng; (*to speaker*) 听…说 tīng...shuō **2** (*follow advice*) 听从 tīngcóng ▶ **to listen to sb** (*pay attention to*) 留神听某人说话 liúshén tīng mǒurén shuōhuà; (*follow advice of*) 听从某人 tīngcóng mǒurén ▶ **to listen to sth** 听某事 tīng mǒushì

lit [lɪt] PT, PP *of* **light**

liter [lɪtər] N [C] 升 shēng

literature [lɪtərətʃər, -tʃʊr] N [U] 文学 wénxué

litter [lɪtər] N [U] 垃圾 lājī

little [lɪtəl] **I** ADJ **1** (*small*) 小的 xiǎo de **2** (*young*) (+ *child*) 小的 xiǎo de **3** (*younger*) ▶ **little brother/sister** 弟弟/妹妹 dìdi/mèimei **4** (*quantifier*) ▶ **to have little time/money** 没有多少时间/金钱 méiyǒu duōshao shíjiān/jīnqián **II** ADV 少 shǎo ▶ **a little** (*small amount*) 一点 yīdiǎn; (+ *noun*) 一点 yīdiǎn; (*sleep, eat*) 一点 yīdiǎn ▶ **a little boy of 8** 一个8岁的小男孩 yīgè bāsuì de xiǎo nánhái ▶ **a little bit** (*adj*) 有点 yǒudiǎn ▶ **little by little** 逐渐地 zhújiàn de

live[1] [lɪv] **I** VI **1** (*reside*) 住 zhù **2** (*lead one's life*) 生活 shēnghuó **II** VT (+ *life*) 过 guò; **live on** VT FUS (+ *money*) 靠…维持生活 kào...wéichí shēnghuó; **live**

together VI 同居 tóngjū; **live with** VT FUS (+ *partner*) 与…同居 yǔ...tóngjū
live² [laɪv] **I** ADJ (+ *animal, plant*) 活的 huó de **II** ADV (*broadcast*) 实况地 shíkuàng de
lively [laɪvli] ADJ (+ *person*) 活泼的 huópo de; (+ *place, event, discussion*) 活跃的 huóyuè de
liver [lɪvər] N **1** [C] 肝脏 gānzàng [个 gè] **2** [C/U] (*Culin*) 肝 gān [个 gè]
lives [laɪvz] N PL *of* **life**
living [lɪvɪŋ] N [U] (*life*) 生活 shēnghuó ▶ **for a living** 作为谋生之道 zuòwéi móushēng zhīdào ▶ **to earn** *or* **make a/one's living** 谋生 móushēng
living room N [C] 起居室 qǐjūshì [间 jiān]
load [loʊd] **I** N [C] (*thing carried*: *of vehicle*) 装载量 zhuāngzàiliàng [车 chē] **II** VT **1** (*also*: **load up**) (+ *vehicle, ship*) 装 zhuāng **2** (+ *program, data*) 下载 xiàzài ▶ **loads of** *or* **a load of money/people** (*inf*) 很多钱/人 hěnduō qián/rén
loaf [loʊf] (*pl* **loaves**) N [C] ▶ **a loaf (of bread)** 一条(面包) yītiáo (miànbāo)
loan [loʊn] **I** N [C] 贷款 dàikuǎn [笔 bǐ] **II** VT ▶ **to loan sth (out) to sb** (+ *money, thing*) 把某物借给某人 bǎ mǒuwù jiègěi mǒurén
loaves [loʊvz] N PL *of* **loaf**
local [loʊkᵊl] ADJ (+ *council, newspaper, library*) 当地的 dāngdì de; (+ *residents*) 本地的 běndì de
lock [lɒk] **I** N [C] 锁 suǒ [把 bǎ] **II** VT **1** 锁 suǒ **2** (+ *screen*) 锁 suǒ; **lock out** VT **1** (+ *person*) (*deliberately*) 把…锁在外面 bǎ...suǒ zài wàimian ▶ **to lock o.s. out** 把自己锁在外面 bǎ zìjǐ suǒ zài wàimian; **lock up** VT 锁好 suǒhǎo
locker [lɒkər] N [C] 小柜 xiǎoguì [个 gè]
lodger [lɒdʒər] N [C] 房客 fángkè [个 gè]
loft [lɔft] N [C] (*attic*) 阁楼 gélóu [座 zuò]
log [lɔg] N [C] (*for fuel*) 木柴 mùchái [根 gēn]; **log in, log on** (*Comput*) VI 登录 dēnglù; **log into** (*Comput*) VT FUS 登入 dēngrù; **log out, log off** (*Comput*) VI 退出系统 tuìchū xìtǒng
logical [lɒdʒɪkᵊl] ADJ (+ *argument, analysis*) 逻辑的 luójí de; (+ *conclusion, result*) 合逻辑的 hé luójí de; (+ *course of action*) 合乎情理的 héhū qínglǐ de
London [lʌndᵊn] N 伦敦 Lúndūn
lonely [loʊnli] ADJ **1** (+ *person*) 孤独的 gūdú de **2** (+ *place*) 人迹罕至的 rénjì hǎn zhì de
long [lɔŋ] **I** ADJ **1** (+ *rope, hair, table, tunnel*) 长的 cháng de **2** (+ *meeting, discussion, film, time*) 长的 cháng de **3** (+ *book, poem*) 长的 cháng de **II** ADV (*time*) 长久 chángjiǔ ▶ **how long is the lesson?** 这节课多长时间? zhèjiékè duōcháng shíjiān? ▶ **6 meters long** 6米长 liùmǐ cháng ▶ **so** *or* **as long as** (*provided*) 只要 zhǐyào ▶ **long ago** 很久以前 hěnjiǔ yǐqián ▶ **it won't take long** 这不需花很多时间 zhè bù xūyào huā hěnduō shíjiān ▶ **a long way** 很远 hěnyuǎn
look [lʊk] **I** VI **1** (*glance, gaze*) 看 kàn **2** (*search*) 找 zhǎo **3** (*seem, appear*) 看起来 kànqǐlái **II** N (*expression*) 表情 biǎoqíng [副 fù] ▶ **to look out of the window** 望向窗外 wàngxiàng chuāngwài ▶ **look out!** 当心! dāngxīn! ▶ **to look like sb** 长得像某人 zhǎngde xiàng mǒurén ▶ **to look like sth** 看起来像某物 kànqǐlái xiàng mǒuwù ▶ **it looks as if...** 看来… kànlái... ▶ **to have** *or* **take a look at** 看一看 kànyīkàn; **look after** VT FUS 照顾 zhàogù; **look around, look round I** VI **1** (*turn head*) 环顾 huángù **2** (*in building*) 看看 kànkan **II** VT FUS (+ *place, building*) 游览 yóulán; **look at** VT FUS 看一看 kàn yī kàn; **look for** VT FUS (+ *person, thing*) 寻找 xúnzhǎo; **look forward to** VT FUS 盼望 pànwàng ▶ **to look forward to doing sth** 盼望做某事 pànwàng

zuò mǒushì ▸ **we look forward to hearing from you** 我们盼望收到你的回音 wǒmen pànwàng shōudào nǐde huíyīn; **look into** VT FUS (*investigate*) 调查 diàochá; **look through** VT FUS (+ *book, magazine, papers*) 翻阅 fānyuè; **look up** VT (+ *information, meaning*) 查 chá

loose [lu̲s] ADJ **1** (+ *screw, connection, tooth*) 松动的 sōngdòng de **2** (+ *hair*) 散开的 sǎnkāi de **3** (+ *clothes, trousers*) 宽松的 kuānsōng de

lose [lu̲z] (*pt, pp* **lost**) **I** VT **1** (*mislay*) 丢失 diūshī **2** (*not win*) (+ *contest, fight, argument*) 输 shū **3** (*through death*) (+ *relative, wife etc*) 失去 shīqù **II** VI 输 shū ▸ **to lose weight** 减重 jiǎnzhòng

loss [lɔ̲s] N [C/U] 丧失 sàngshī [种 zhǒng]

lost [lɔ̲st] **I** PT, PP *of* **lose II** ADJ (+ *object*) 丢失的 diūshī de; (+ *person, animal*) 走失的 zǒushī de ▸ **to get lost** 迷路 mílù

lost and found N [U] **1** (*things*) 招领的失物 zhāolǐng de shīwù **2** (*office*) 失物招领处 shīwù zhāolǐngchù

lot [lɒ̲t] N [C] ▸ **a lot** (*many*) 许多 xǔduō; (*much*) 很多 hěnduō ▸ **a lot of** 许多 xǔduō ▸ **lots of** 许多 xǔduō ▸ **he reads/smokes a lot** 他书读得/烟抽得很多 tā shū dúde/yān chōude hěnduō

lottery [lɒ̲təri] N [C] 彩票 cǎipiào [张 zhāng]

loud [la̲ʊd] **I** ADJ 响亮的 xiǎngliàng de **II** ADV (*speak*) 大声地 dàshēng de

loudly [la̲ʊdli] ADV 大声地 dàshēng de

loudspeaker [la̲ʊdspi̲kər] N [C] 扬声器 yángshēngqì [个 gè]

lounge [la̲ʊndʒ] N [C] **1** (*in hotel*) 休息室 xiūxishì [间 jiān] **2** (*at airport, station*) 等候室 děnghòushì [间 jiān]

love [lʌ̲v] **I** N [U] (*for partner, sweetheart*) 爱情 àiqíng; (*for child, pet*) 爱 ài **II** VT (+ *partner, child, pet*) 爱 ài; (+ *thing, food, activity*) 热爱 rè'ài ▸ **to be in love (with sb)** (与某人)恋爱 (yǔ mǒurén) liàn'ài ▸ **to fall in love (with sb)** 爱上(某人) àishàng (mǒurén) ▸ **to make love** 做爱 zuò'ài ▸ **love (from) Anne** (*on letter*) 爱你的，安妮 àinǐde, Ānní ▸ **to love doing/to do sth** 喜爱做某事 xǐ'ài zuò mǒushì ▸ **I'd love to come** 我非常想来 wǒ fēicháng xiǎng lái

lovely [lʌ̲vli] ADJ **1** (+ *place, person, music*) 漂亮的 piàoliang de **2** (+ *vacation, meal, present*) 令人愉快的 lìng rén yúkuài de; (+ *person*) 可爱的 kě'ài de

lover [lʌ̲vər] N [C] 情人 qíngrén [个 gè] ▸ **a lover of art** *or* **an art lover** 钟爱艺术的人 zhōng'ài yìshù de rén

low [lo̲ʊ] ADJ **1** (+ *wall, hill, heel*) 矮的 ǎi de **2** (+ *temperature, price, level, speed*) 低的 dī de **3** (+ *standard, quality*) 低劣的 dīliè de ▸ **low in calories/salt/fat** 低卡路里/盐/脂肪 dī kǎlùlǐ/yán/zhīfáng

lower [lo̲ʊər] VT (*reduce*) 降低 jiàngdī

loyal [lɔ̲ɪəl] ADJ 忠实的 zhōngshí de

loyalty [lɔ̲ɪəlti] N [U] 忠诚 zhōngchéng

luck [lʌ̲k] N [U] **1** (*chance*) 运气 yùnqì **2** (*good fortune*) 幸运 xìngyùn ▸ **good luck** 好运 hǎoyùn ▸ **good luck!** *or* **best of luck!** 祝你好运！zhùnǐ hǎoyùn! ▸ **bad luck** 不走运 bù zǒuyùn

luckily [lʌ̲kɪli] ADV 幸运的是 xìngyùn de shì

lucky [lʌ̲ki] ADJ (+ *person*) 幸运的 xìngyùn de ▸ **to be lucky** 走运 zǒuyùn ▸ **it is lucky that...** 侥幸的是… jiǎoxìng de shì... ▸ **to have a lucky escape** 侥幸逃脱 jiǎoxìng táotuō

luggage [lʌ̲gɪdʒ] N [U] 行李 xíngli ▸ **piece of luggage** 一件行李 yījiàn xíngli

lunch [lʌ̲ntʃ] N **1** [C/U] (*meal*) 午餐

wǔcān [顿 dùn] **2** [U] (*lunchtime*) 午餐时间 wǔcān shíjiān ▸ **to have lunch (with sb)** (与某人)共进午餐 (yǔ mǒurén) gòngjìn wǔcān
lung [lʌŋ] N [C] 肺 fèi [片 piàn]
Luxembourg [lʌksᵊmbɜrg] N 卢森堡 Lúsēnbǎo
luxurious [lʌgʒʊəriəs] ADJ 豪华的 háohuá de
luxury [lʌkʃəri, lʌgʒə-] **I** N [U] (*comfort*) 奢华 shēhuá **II** CPD (+ *hotel, car, goods*) 豪华 háohuá
lying [laɪɪŋ] VB *see* **lie**[1], **lie**[2]
lyrics [lɪrɪks] N PL 词句 cíjù

M

machine [məʃiːn] N [C] 机器 jīqì [台 tái]
machine gun N [C] 机关枪 jīguānqiāng [架 jià]
machinery [məʃiːnəri] N [U] 机器 jīqì
mad [mæd] ADJ **1** (*insane*) 精神失常的 jīngshén shīcháng de **2** (*inf: angry*) 恼怒的 nǎonù de ▸ **to go mad** (*go insane*) 发疯 fāfēng; (*get angry*) 发火 fāhuǒ ▸ **to be mad about** *or* **on sth** (*inf*) 狂热地爱好某物 kuángrè de àihào mǒuwù
madam [mædəm] N 女士 nǚshì ▸ **Dear Madam** 尊敬的女士 zūnjìng de nǚshì
made [meɪd] PT, PP *of* **make**
madness [mædnɪs] N [U] **1** (*insanity*) 疯狂 fēngkuáng **2** (*foolishness*) 愚蠢 yúchǔn
magazine [mægəziːn, -ziːn] N [C] 杂志 zázhì [份 fèn]
magic [mædʒɪk] **I** N [U] 魔法 mófǎ **II** ADJ **1** (+ *formula, solution, cure*) 神奇的 shénqí de **2** (*supernatural*) 魔法的 mófǎ de
magnet [mægnɪt] N [C] 磁铁 cítiě [块 kuài]
maid [meɪd] N [C] (*servant*) 女仆 nǚpú [个 gè]
maiden name [meɪdᵊn-] N [C] 娘家姓 niángjiā xìng [个 gè]
mail [meɪl] **I** N [U] **1** ▸ **the mail** 邮政 yóuzhèng **2** (*letters*) 邮件 yóujiàn **3** (*email*) 电子邮件 diànzǐ yóujiàn **II** VT **1** (*post*) 寄出 jìchū **2** (*email*) 发电邮给 fā diànyóu gěi ▸ **by mail** 以邮寄方式 yǐ yóujì fāngshì
mailbox [meɪlbɒks] N [C] **1** (*for letters*) 信箱 xìnxiāng [个 gè] **2** (*in street*) 邮筒 yóutǒng [个 gè] **3** (*Comput*) 电子信箱 diànzǐ xìnxiāng [个 gè]
mail carrier N [C] 邮递员 yóudìyuán [位 wèi]
mailman [meɪlmæn] (*pl* **mailmen**) N [C] 邮差 yóuchāi [个 gè]
main [meɪn] ADJ 主要的 zhǔyào de
main course N [C] 主菜 zhǔcài [道 dào]
mainly [meɪnli] ADV 主要地 zhǔyào de
main road N [C] 主干道 zhǔ gàndào [条 tiáo]
majesty [mædʒɪsti] N (*title*) ▸ **Your/His/Her Majesty** 陛下 bìxià
major [meɪdʒər] **I** ADJ 重要的 zhòngyào de **II** N [C] **1** (*Mil*) 少校 shàoxiào [位 wèi] **2** (*main subject*) 专业 zhuānyè [个 gè]
majority [mədʒɔrɪti] N [S + PL VB] 大多数 dàduōshù
make [meɪk] (*pt, pp* **made**) **I** VT **1** (+ *object, clothes, cake*) 做 zuò; (+ *noise*) 制造 zhìzào; (+ *mistake*) 犯 fàn **2** (*manufacture*) 生产 shēngchǎn **3** (*cause to be*) ▸ **to make sb sad** 使某人难过 shǐ mǒurén nánguò **4** (*force*) ▸ **to make sb do sth** 促使某人做某事 cùshǐ mǒurén zuò mǒushì **5** (+ *money*) 挣 zhèng **6** (*equal*) ▸ **2 and 2 make 4** 2加2等于4 èrjiā'èr děngyú sì **II** N [C] (*brand*) 牌子 páizi [个 gè] ▸ **to make a profit/loss** 赢利/赔钱 yínglì/péiqián ▸ **what time do you make it?** 你表几点了？ nǐ biǎo jǐdiǎn le ▸ **it's made (out) of glass** 是玻璃做的 shì bōli zuò de; **make out** VT (+ *cheque*) 开出 kāichū; **make up** VT **1** (+ *story, excuse*) 捏造 niēzào **2** (*with cosmetics*) 化妆 huàzhuāng ▸ **to make up one's mind** 下定决心 xià dìng juéxīn ▸ **to make o.s. up** 化妆 huàzhuāng
makeup N [U] (*cosmetics*) 化妆品 huàzhuāngpǐn
Malaysia [məleɪʒə] N 马来西亚 Mǎláixīyà
male [meɪl] ADJ (+ *employee, child, model, friend, population*) 男的 nán

de; (+ *animal, insect, plant, tree*) 雄性的 xióngxìng de

mall [mɔl] N [C] (*also*: **shopping mall**) 大型购物中心 dàxíng gòuwù zhōngxīn [个 gè]

Malta [mɔltə] N 马耳他 Mǎ'ěrtā

mammal [mæməl] N [C] 哺乳动物 bǔrǔ dòngwù [个 gè]

man [mæn] (*pl* **men**) N **1** [C] (*person*) 男人 nánrén [个 gè] **2** [U] (*mankind*) 人类 rénlèi

manage [mænɪdʒ] **I** VT (+ *business, shop, time, money*) 管理 guǎnlǐ **II** VI (*cope*) 应付 yìngfù ▶ **to manage to do sth** 设法做到某事 shèfǎ zuòdào mǒushì

management [mænɪdʒmənt] N **1** [U] (*managing*) 管理 guǎnlǐ **2** [U/S] (*managers*) 管理人员 guǎnlǐ rényuán

manager [mænɪdʒər] N [C] **1** 经理 jīnglǐ [位 wèi] **2** (*Sport*) 球队经理 qiúduì jīnglǐ [位 wèi]

mandarin [mændərɪn] N **1** [U] ▶ **Mandarin (Chinese)** 普通话 Pǔtōnghuà **2** [C] (*also*: **mandarin orange**) 柑橘 gānjú [个 gè]

maniac [meɪniæk] N [C] (*lunatic*) 疯子 fēngzi [个 gè]

manner [mænər] **I** N [S] (*way*) 方式 fāngshì **II manners** N PL 礼貌 lǐmào ▶ **it's good/bad manners to arrive on time** 准时是有礼貌/无礼的表现 zhǔnshí shì yǒu lǐmào/wúlǐ de biǎoxiàn

manual [mænyuəl] N [C] (*handbook*) 手册 shǒucè [本 běn]

manufacture [mænyəfæktʃər] VT 生产 shēngchǎn

manufacturer [mænyəfæktʃərər] N [C] 制造商 zhìzàoshāng [个 gè]

many [mɛni] **I** ADJ (*a lot of*) 许多的 xǔduō de **II** PRON 许多的 xǔduō de ▶ **how many** (*direct question*) 多少 duōshǎo ▶ **twice as many (as)** (是…的)两倍 (shì...de) liǎngbèi

map [mæp] N [C] 地图 dìtú [张 zhāng]

marathon [mærəθɒn] N [C] (*race*) 马拉松长跑 mǎlāsōng chángpǎo [次 cì]

marble [mɑrbəl] **I** N [U] 大理石 dàlǐshí **II marbles** N PL (*game*) 弹子游戏 dànzǐ yóuxì

March [mɑrtʃ] N [C/U] 三月 sānyuè; *see also* **July**

march [mɑrtʃ] VI 行军 xíngjūn

margarine [mɑrdʒərɪn] N [U] 人造黄油 rénzào huángyóu

marijuana [mærɪwɑnə] N [U] 大麻 dàmá

mark [mɑrk] **I** N **1** [C] (*cross, tick*) 记号 jìhao [个 gè] **2** [C] (*stain*) 污点 wūdiǎn [个 gè] **II** VT (*indicate*) (+ *place*) 标示 biāoshì

market [mɑrkɪt] N [C] 集市 jíshì [个 gè]

marketing [mɑrkɪtɪŋ] N [U] 市场营销 shìchǎng yíngxiāo

marriage [mærɪdʒ] N **1** [C/U] (*relationship, institution*) 婚姻 hūnyīn [个 gè] **2** [C] (*wedding*) 婚礼 hūnlǐ [场 chǎng]

married [mærid] ADJ 已婚的 yǐhūn de ▶ **to be married to sb** 和某人结婚 hé mǒurén jiéhūn ▶ **to get married** 结婚 jiéhūn

marry [mæri] VT 和…结婚 hé...jiéhūn

marvelous [mɑrvələs] ADJ 极好的 jíhǎo de

masculine [mæskyəlɪn] ADJ **1** (+ *characteristic, value*) 男性的 nánxìng de **2** (*Ling*) (+ *pronoun*) 阳性的 yángxìng de

mashed potato [mæʃt-] N [C/U] 土豆泥 tǔdòuní [份 fèn]

mask [mæsk] N [C] **1** (*disguise*) 面罩 miànzhào [个 gè] **2** (*protection*) 口罩 kǒuzhào [个 gè]

mass [mæs] N [C] (*large amount, number*) 大量 dàliàng ▶ **masses of** (*inf*) 大量 dàliàng

massage [məsɑʒ] N [C/U] 按摩 ànmó [次 cì]

massive [mæsɪv] ADJ (+ *amount,*

increase) 巨大的 jùdà de; (+ *explosion*) 大规模的 dà guīmó de
master [mæstər] VT (*learn*) (+ *skill, language*) 掌握 zhǎngwò
masterpiece [mæstərpis] N [C] 杰作 jiézuò [部 bù]
mat [mæt] N [C] 席 xí [张 zhāng]
match [mætʃ] **I** N **1** [C] (*game*) 比赛 bǐsài [场 chǎng] **2** [C] (*for lighting fire*) 火柴 huǒchái [根 gēn] **II** VI (*go together*) (*colors, materials*) 相配 xiāngpèi
mate [meɪt] N [C] (*animal*) 配偶 pèi'ǒu [个 gè]
material [mətɪəriəl] **I** N **1** [C/U] (*cloth*) 衣料 yīliào [块 kuài] **2** [U] (*information, data*) 资料 zīliào **II materials** N PL (*equipment*) 用具 yòngjù
math [mæθ] N [U] 数学 shùxué
mathematics [mæθəmætɪks] (*frm*) N [U] 数学 shùxué
matter [mætər] **I** N [C] 事件 shìjiàn [个 gè] **II** VI (*be important*) 要紧 yàojǐn ▸ **what's the matter (with...)?** (…)怎么了？ (...)zěnme le? ▸ **it doesn't matter** 没关系 méi guānxi
mattress [mætrɪs] N [C] 床垫 chuángdiàn [个 gè]
maximum [mæksɪməm] **I** ADJ (+ *speed, height*) 最高的 zuìgāo de; (+ *weight*) 最重的 zuìzhòng de **II** N [C] 最大量 zuìdàliàng
May [meɪ] N [C/U] 五月 wǔyuè; *see also* **July**

KEYWORD

may [meɪ] AUX VB **1** (*possibility*) ▸ **it may rain later** 等会儿可能要下雨 děnghuì'r kěnéng yào xiàyǔ ▸ **we may not be able to come** 我们可能来不了 wǒmen kěnéng lái bùliǎo ▸ **he may have hurt himself** 他可能伤了自己 tā kěnéng shāngle zìjǐ **2** (*permission*) ▸ **may I come in?** 我可以进来吗？ wǒ kěyǐ jìnlái ma?

maybe [meɪbi] ADV **1** 可能 kěnéng **2** (*making suggestions*) 也许 yěxǔ **3** (*estimating*) 大概 dàgài ▸ **maybe so/not** 也许如此/不是 yěxǔ rúcǐ/bùshì
mayor [meɪər, mɛər] N [C] 市长 shìzhǎng [位 wèi]
me [mi, STRONG mi] PRON 我 wǒ ▸ **it's me** 是我 shì wǒ
meal [mil] N **1** [C] (*occasion*) 一餐 yīcān [顿 dùn] **2** [C] (*food*) 膳食 shànshí [顿 dùn] ▸ **to go out for a meal** 出去吃饭 chūqù chīfàn
mean [min] (*pt, pp* **meant**) **I** VT **1** (*signify*) 表示…意思 biǎoshì...yìsī **2** (*refer to*) 意指 yìzhǐ **3** (*intend*) ▸ **to mean to do sth** 意欲做某事 yìyù zuò mǒushì **II** ADJ **1** (*not generous*) 吝啬的 lìnsè de **2** (*unkind*) 刻薄的 kèbó de ▸ **what does "imperialism" mean?** "imperialism" 是什么意思？ "imperialism" shì shénme yìsi? ▸ **what do you mean?** 你什么意思？ nǐ shénme yìsi?; *see also* **means**
meaning [minɪŋ] N [C/U] (*of word, expression*) 意思 yìsi [层 céng]; (*of symbol, dream, gesture*) 含义 hányì [个 gè]
means [minz] (*pl* **means**) N [C] (*method*) 方法 fāngfǎ [个 gè]
meant [mɛnt] PT, PP *of* **mean**
meanwhile [minwaɪl] ADV 同时 tóngshí
measles [mizᵊlz] N [U] 麻疹 mázhěn
measure [mɛʒər] VT 测量 cèliáng
measurement [mɛʒərmənt] **I** N [C] (*length, width etc*) 尺寸 chǐcùn **II measurements** N PL (*of person*) 三围 sānwéi
meat [mit] N [U] 肉 ròu
Mecca [mɛkə] N 麦加 Màijiā
mechanic [mɪkænɪk] N [C] 机械工 jīxiègōng [位 wèi]
medal [mɛdᵊl] N [C] 奖章 jiǎngzhāng [枚 méi]
media [midiə] N PL ▸ **the media** 媒体 méitǐ
medical [mɛdɪkᵊl] **I** ADJ 医疗的

yīliáo de **II** N [c] (*examination*) 体格检查 tǐgé jiǎnchá [次 cì]

medicine [mɛdɪsɪn] N **1** [U] (*science*) 医学 yīxué **2** [c/U] (*medication*) 药 yào [种 zhǒng]

Mediterranean [mɛdɪtəreɪniən] N ▶ **the Mediterranean** (*sea*) 地中海 Dìzhōnghǎi; (*region*) 地中海沿岸地区 Dìzhōnghǎi yán'àn dìqū

medium [midiəm] ADJ **1** (*average*) 中等的 zhōngděng de **2** (*clothing size*) 中码的 zhōngmǎ de

medium-sized [midiəmsaɪzd] ADJ 中等大小的 zhōngděng dàxiǎo de

meet [mit] (*pt, pp* **met**) **I** VT **1** (*accidentally*) 遇见 yùjiàn; (*by arrangement*) 和…见面 hé...jiànmiàn **2** (*for the first time*) 结识 jiéshí; (*be introduced to*) 认识 rènshi **3** (*at station, airport*) 接 jiē **II** VI **1** (*accidentally*) 相遇 xiāngyù; (*by arrangement*) 见面 jiànmiàn **2** (*for the first time*) 认识 rènshi ▶ **pleased to meet you** 见到你很高兴 jiàndào nǐ hěn gāoxìng; **meet up** VI 会面 huìmiàn

meeting [mitɪŋ] N **1** [c] (*of club, committee*) 会议 huìyì [次 cì] **2** [c] (*encounter*) 会面 huìmiàn [次 cì]

megabyte [mɛgəbaɪt] N [c] 兆字节 zhàozìjié [个 gè]

melon [mɛlən] N [c/U] 瓜 guā [个 gè]

melt [mɛlt] **I** VI 融化 rónghuà **II** VT (+ *metal, ice, snow, butter, chocolate*) 使融化 shǐ rónghuà

member [mɛmbər] N [c] **1** (*of family, staff, public*) 一员 yīyuán **2** (*of club, party*) 成员 chéngyuán [个 gè]

memorial [mɪmɔriəl] N [c] 纪念碑 jìniànbēi [座 zuò]

memorize [mɛməraɪz] VT 记住 jìzhù

memory [mɛməri] N **1** [c/U] (*ability to remember*) 记忆力 jìyìlì [种 zhǒng] **2** [c] (*thing remembered*) 记忆 jìyì [个 gè] **3** [c/U] (*Comput*) 存储器 cúnchǔqì [个 gè] ▶ **to have a good/bad memory (for sth)** (对某事)记忆力好/差 (duì mǒushì)jìyìlì hǎo/chà

men [mɛn] N PL *of* **man**

mend [mɛnd] VT 修理 xiūlǐ

mental [mɛntᵊl] ADJ (+ *illness, health*) 精神的 jīngshén de

mental hospital N [c] (*o.f. inf!*) 精神病院 jīngshénbìngyuàn [个 gè]

mention [mɛnʃᵊn] VT 提到 tídào ▶ **don't mention it!** 不客气! bù kèqi!

menu [mɛnyu] N [c] **1** 菜单 càidān [个 gè] **2** (*Comput*) 选择菜单 xuǎnzé càidān [个 gè]

merry [mɛri] ADJ ▶ **Merry Christmas!** 圣诞快乐! Shèngdàn Kuàilè!

mess [mɛs] N **1** [s/U] (*untidiness*) 凌乱 língluàn **2** [s/U] (*chaotic situation*) 混乱的局面 hùnluàn de júmiàn; **mess around** (*inf*) VI 混日子 hùn rìzi

message [mɛsɪdʒ] N [c] 消息 xiāoxi [条 tiáo] ▶ **to leave (sb) a message** (给某人)留个信 (gěi mǒurén) liú gè xìn

met [mɛt] PT, PP *of* **meet**

metal [mɛtᵊl] N [c/U] 金属 jīnshǔ [种 zhǒng]

meter [mitər] N [c] **1** (*for gas, water, electricity*) 仪表 yíbiǎo [个 gè]; (*also*: **parking meter**) 停车计时器 tíngchē jìshíqì [个 gè] **2** (*unit*) 米 mǐ

method [mɛθəd] N [c/U] 方法 fāngfǎ [种 zhǒng]

metric [mɛtrɪk] ADJ 公制的 gōngzhì de

Mexico [mɛksɪkoʊ] N 墨西哥 Mòxīgē

mice [maɪs] N PL *of* **mouse**

microchip [maɪkroʊtʃɪp] N [c] 集成电路块 jíchéng diànlù kuài [个 gè]

microphone [maɪkrəfoʊn] N [c] 话筒 huàtǒng [个 gè]

microscope [maɪkrəskoʊp] N [c] 显微镜 xiǎnwēijìng [个 gè]

microwave [maɪkroʊweɪv] N [c] (*also*: **microwave oven**) 微波炉 wēibōlú [个 gè]

midday [mɪddeɪ] N [U] 正午 zhèngwǔ

▸ **at midday** 在正午 zài zhèngwǔ
middle [mɪdᵊl] **I** N **1** [c] (*center*) 中央 zhōngyāng [个 gè] **2** [s] (*of month, event*) 中 zhōng **II** ADJ (+ *position, event, period*) 中间的 zhōngjiān de ▸ **in the middle of the night** 在半夜 zài bànyè
middle-aged [mɪdᵊleɪdʒd] ADJ 中年的 zhōngnián de
middle class ADJ (*also*: **middle-class**) 中层社会的 zhōngcéng shèhuì de
Middle East N ▸ **the Middle East** 中东 Zhōngdōng
middle name N [c] 中间名字 zhōngjiān míngzi [个 gè]

MIDDLE NAME

first name 是由父母取的名字。**last name** 或 **surname** 是家族的姓氏。在说英语的国家中，名在姓之前。在 **first name** 和 **last name** 之间，还可能有 **middle name**（中名），这是你父母给你取的第二个"名"。**middle name** 通常只用于正式场合，例如，选课或签署文件时。

midnight [mɪdnaɪt] N [U] 半夜 bànyè ▸ **at midnight** 在午夜 zài wǔyè
midwife [mɪdwaɪf] (*pl* **midwives**) N [c] 助产士 zhùchǎnshì [位 wèi]
might [maɪt] AUX VB (*possibility*) ▸ **I might get home late** 我可能会晚回家 wǒ kěnéng huì wǎn huíjiā ▸ **it might have been an accident** 可能是个事故 kěnéng shì gè shìgù
migraine [maɪgreɪn] N [c/U] 偏头痛 piāntóutòng [阵 zhèn]
mild [maɪld] ADJ **1** (+ *infection, illness*) 轻微的 qīngwēi de **2** (+ *climate, weather*) 温暖的 wēnnuǎn de
mile [maɪl] **I** N [c] 英里 yīnglǐ **II miles** N PL (*inf: a long way*) 很远的距离 hěnyuǎn de jùlí ▸ **70 miles per** *or* **an hour** 每小时70英里 měi xiǎoshí qīshí yīnglǐ
military [mɪlɪtɛri] ADJ 军事的 jūnshì de
milk [mɪlk] N [U] 奶 nǎi
milkshake [mɪlkʃeɪk] N [c/U] 奶昔 nǎixī [份 fèn]
millimeter [mɪlɪmitər] N [c] 毫米 háomǐ
million [mɪlyən] **I** NUM 百万 bǎiwàn **II millions** N PL (*lit*) 数百万 shùbǎiwàn; (*inf: fig*) 无数 wúshù ▸ **a** *or* **one million books/people/dollars** 100万本书/个人/元 yībǎiwàn běn shū/gè rén/yuán
millionaire [mɪlyənɛər] N [c] 百万富翁 bǎiwàn fùwēng [个 gè]
mind [maɪnd] **I** N [c] 智力 zhìlì [种 zhǒng] **II** VT **1** (*be careful of*) 当心 dāngxīn **2** (*object to*) 介意 jièyì **3** (*have a preference*) ▸ **I don't mind (what/who...)** 我不在乎(什么/谁…) wǒ bù zàihu (shénme/shéi...) **4** ▸ **do/would you mind (if...)?** (如果…)你介意吗？ (rúguǒ...) nǐ jièyì ma? ▸ **to make up one's mind** *or* **make one's mind up** 下定决心 xiàdìng juéxīn ▸ **to change one's/sb's mind** 改变主意 gǎibiàn zhǔyì ▸ **I wouldn't mind a coffee** 我挺想喝杯咖啡 wǒ tǐngxiǎng hē bēi kāfēi ▸ **mind the step** 小心脚下 xiǎoxīn jiǎoxià

KEYWORD

mine¹ [maɪn] PRON 我的 wǒ de ▸ **this is mine** 这是我的 zhèshì wǒde ▸ **these are mine** 这些是我的 zhèxiē shì wǒde

mine² [maɪn] N [c] 矿 kuàng [座 zuò]
mineral water [mɪnərəl wɔtər] N [U/c] 矿泉水 kuàngquánshuǐ
miniature [mɪniətʃər, -tʃʊər] ADJ 微型的 wēixíng de
minibus [mɪnibʌs] N [c] 小公共汽车 xiǎo gōnggòng qìchē [辆 liàng]
minimum [mɪnɪməm] **I** ADJ 最低的 zuìdī de **II** N [c] 最少量 zuìshǎoliàng

miniskirt [mɪnɪskɜrt] N [C] 超短裙 chāoduǎnqún [条 tiáo]
minister [mɪnɪstər] N [C] (*Rel*) 牧师 mùshī [位 wèi]
minor [maɪnər] ADJ (+ *repairs, changes*) 不重要的 bù zhòngyào de; (+ *injuries*) 不严重的 bù yánzhòng de
minority [mɪnɔrɪti, maɪ-] N 1 [S + PL VB] (*of group, society*) 少数 shǎoshù 2 [C] (*ethnic, cultural, religious*) 少数民族 shǎoshù mínzú [个 gè]
mint [mɪnt] N 1 [U] (*plant*) 薄荷 bòhe 2 [U] (*sweet*) 薄荷糖 bòhe táng
minus [maɪnəs] PREP (*inf: without*) 没有 méiyǒu ▶ **12 minus 3 (is** *or* **equals 9)** 12减3(等于9) shí'èr jiǎn sān (děngyú jiǔ) ▶ **minus 24 (degrees C/F)** (*temperature*) 零下24(摄氏/华氏度) língxià èrshísì (shèshì/huáshì dù) ▶ **B minus** (*Scol*) B减 bì jiǎn
minute [mɪnɪt] N [C] 1 (*unit*) 分钟 fēnzhōng 2 (*short time*) 一会儿 yīhuìr ▶ **wait** *or* **just a minute!** 等一会儿！ děng yīhuì'r!
miracle [mɪrəkᵊl] N [C] 1 (*Rel*) 圣迹 shèngjì [处 chù] 2 (*marvel*) 奇迹 qíjì [个 gè]
mirror [mɪrər] N [C] 镜子 jìngzi [面 miàn]; (*in car*) 后视镜 hòushìjìng [个 gè]
misbehave [mɪsbɪheɪv] VI 行为无礼 xíngwéi wúlǐ
miscellaneous [mɪsəleɪniəs] ADJ 形形色色的 xíngxíng sèsè de
miserable [mɪzərəbᵊl] ADJ 1 (+ *person*) 痛苦的 tòngkǔ de 2 (+ *weather, day*) 恶劣的 èliè de
Miss [mɪs] N 1 小姐 xiǎojiě 2 (*as form of address*) 小姐 xiǎojiě ▶ **Dear Miss Smith** 亲爱的史密斯小姐 qīn'ài de Shǐmìsī Xiǎojiě

MISS, MRS., MS.

在说英语的国家中，**Mrs.** (夫人)用于已婚女士的姓名前。**Miss** (小姐)用于未婚女士的姓名前。有些女士认为，让人们知道她是否结婚并不重要，所以往往用 **Ms.** (女士)称呼自己。与 **Mr.** (先生)类似，**Ms.** 不表明任何婚姻状况。

miss [mɪs] VT 1 (*fail to hit*) 未击中 wèi jīzhòng 2 (+ *train, bus, plane*) 错过 cuòguò 3 (+ *chance, opportunity*) 错过 cuòguò ▶ **you can't miss it** 你不会找不到 nǐ bùhuì zhǎo bùdào
missing [mɪsɪŋ] ADJ (+ *person*) 失踪的 shīzōng de; (+ *object*) 丢失的 diūshī de
mist [mɪst] N [C/U] 薄雾 bówù [场 cháng]
mistake [mɪsteɪk] N [C] 1 (*error*) 错误 cuòwù [个 gè] 2 (*blunder*) 过失 guòshī [个 gè] ▶ **to make a mistake** 犯错 fàncuò ▶ **to do sth by mistake** 误做某事 wùzuò mǒushì
mistaken [mɪsteɪkən] I PP *of* **mistake** II ADJ ▶ **to be mistaken (about sth)** (*person*) (把某事)搞错 (bǎ mǒushì)gǎocuò
mistook [mɪstʊk] PT *of* **mistake**
misty [mɪsti] ADJ 有雾的 yǒuwù de
misunderstand [mɪsʌndərstænd] (*pt, pp* **misunderstood**) VT, VI 误解 wùjiě
misunderstanding [mɪsʌndərstændɪŋ] N [C/U] 误会 wùhuì [个 gè]
misunderstood [mɪsʌndərstʊd] PT, PP *of* **misunderstand**
mix [mɪks] I VT 混合 hùnhé II VI (*socially*) ▶ **to mix (with sb)** (和某人)相处 (hé mǒurén) xiāngchǔ III N [C] 混合 hùnhé [种 zhǒng] ▶ **to mix sth with sth** (+ *activities*) 将某物同某物混淆 jiāng mǒuwù tóng mǒuwù hùnxiáo;
mix up VT (+ *people*) 分辨不出 fēnbiàn bùchū; (+ *things*) 混淆 hùnxiáo
mixed [mɪkst] ADJ 1 (+ *salad, herbs*) 什锦的 shíjǐn de 2 (+ *group, community*) 形形色色的 xíngxíng sèsè de 3 (+ *school, education*) 男女混合的 nánnǚ hùnhé de

mixture [mɪkstʃər] N [c/U] 混合物 hùnhéwù [种 zhǒng]
mix-up (*inf*) N [c] 混乱 hùnluàn [种 zhǒng]
model [mɒdᵊl] **I** N [c] **1** (*of boat, building*) 模型 móxíng [个 gè] **2** (*fashion model*) 时装模特 shízhuāng mótè [位 wèi] **II** ADJ (*miniature*) ▸ **model aircraft/train** 模型飞机/火车 móxíng fēijī/huǒchē **III** VT (+ *clothes*) 展示 zhǎnshì
modem [moʊdəm, -dɛm] N [c] 调制解调器 tiáozhì jiětiáo qì [个 gè]
moderate [mɒdərɪt] ADJ 中庸的 zhōngyōng de
modern [mɒdərn] ADJ **1** (+ *world, times, society*) 现代的 xiàndài de **2** (+ *technology, design*) 新式的 xīnshì de
modernize [mɒdərnaɪz] VT 使现代化 shǐ xiàndàihuà
modern languages N PL 现代语言 xiàndài yǔyán
modest [mɒdɪst] ADJ 谦虚的 qiānxū de
moisturizer [mɔɪstʃəraɪzər] N [c/U] 保湿霜 bǎoshīshuāng [瓶 píng]
mom [mɒm] N (*inf*) 妈妈 māma
moment [moʊmənt] N **1** [c] (*period of time*) 片刻 piànkè **2** [c] (*point in time*) 瞬间 shùnjiān ▸ **at the/this (present) moment** 此刻/当前 cǐkè/dāngqián ▸ **at the last moment** 在最后一刻 zài zuìhòu yīkè
mommy [mɒmi] N [c] (*inf*) 妈妈 māma [位 wèi]
Monday [mʌndeɪ, -di] N [c/U] 星期一 xīngqīyī [个 gè]; *see also* **Tuesday**
money [mʌni] N [U] **1** (*cash*) 钱 qián **2** (*in the bank*) 存款 cúnkuǎn **3** (*currency*) 货币 huòbì ▸ **to make money** (*person, business*) 赚钱 zhuànqián
monitor [mɒnɪtər] N [c] 显示屏 xiǎnshìpíng [个 gè]
monkey [mʌŋki] N [c] (*Zool*) 猴 hóu [只 zhī]
monotonous [mənɒtᵊnəs] ADJ (+ *life, job etc, voice, tune*) 单调的 dāndiào de
month [mʌnθ] N [c] 月 yuè [个 gè] ▸ **every month** 每个月 měigè yuè
monthly [mʌnθli] **I** ADJ 每月的 měiyuè de **II** ADV (*every month*) 按月 ànyuè
monument [mɒnyəmənt] N [c] 纪念碑 jìniànbēi [座 zuò]
mood [mud] N [c] 心情 xīnqíng [种 zhǒng] ▸ **to be in a good/bad/awkward mood** 心情好/坏/不痛快 xīnqíng hǎo/huài/bù tòngkuài
moon [mun] N ▸ **the moon** 月球 yuèqiú
moonlight [munlaɪt] N [U] 月光 yuèguāng
moped [moʊpɛd] N [c] 机动自行车 jīdòng zìxíngchē [辆 liàng]
moral [mɔrᵊl] ADJ (+ *issues, values*) 道德的 dàodé de; (+ *behavior, person*) 品行端正的 pǐnxíng duānzhèng de

KEYWORD

more [mɔr] **I** ADJ **1** 更多的 gèngduō de ▸ **I get more money/vacation days than you do** 我比你有更多的钱/假期 wǒ bǐ nǐ yǒu gèngduōde qián/jiàqī
2 (*additional*) 再一些的 zài yīxiē de ▸ **would you like some more tea/peanuts?** 你要再来点茶/花生吗？ nǐ yào zài lái diǎn chá/huāshēng ma ▸ **is there any more wine?** 还有酒吗？ háiyǒu jiǔ ma? ▸ **a few more weeks** 再几个星期 zài jǐgè xīngqī
II PRON **1** (*in comparisons*) 更多的量 gèngduō de liàng ▸ **there's/there are more than I thought** 比我想得更多 bǐ wǒ xiǎngde gèngduō ▸ **more than 20** 大于20 dàyú èrshí ▸ **she's got more than I** 她比我得到的多 tā bǐ wǒ dédào de duō
2 (*further, additional*) 额外的量 éwài de liàng ▸ **is there/are there any more?** 还有多的吗？ háiyǒu duōde ma? ▸ **have you got any more**

of it/them? 你还有吗？ nǐ háiyǒu ma? ▸ **much/many more** 多得多 duōdeduō

III ADV **1** (*to form comparative*) 更 gèng ▸ **more dangerous/difficult (than)** (比…)更危险/难 (bǐ...)gèng wēixiǎn/nán

2 (*in expressions*) ▸ **more and more** 越来越 yuèláiyuè ▸ **more or less** (*adj, adv*) 差不多 chàbùduō ▸ **more than ever** 空前的多 kōngqián de duō ▸ **once more** 再一次 zài yīcì

morning [mɔ̲rnɪŋ] N [c/ʊ] (*early in the morning*) 早晨 zǎochén [个 gè]; (*later in the morning*) 上午 shàngwǔ [个 gè] ▸ **good morning!** 早上好！ zǎoshàng hǎo! ▸ **at 3 o'clock/7 o'clock in the morning** 凌晨3点/早上7点 língchén sāndiǎn/zǎoshàng qīdiǎn ▸ **this morning** 今天上午 jīntiān shàngwǔ ▸ **on Monday morning** 星期一上午 Xīngqīyī shàngwǔ

Morocco [mərɒ̲koʊ] N 摩洛哥 Móluògē

mortgage [mɔ̲rgɪdʒ] N [c] 抵押贷款 dǐyā dàikuǎn [笔 bǐ]

Moslem [mɒ̲zləm, mʊ̲zlɪm] ADJ, N = **Muslim**

mosque [mɒ̲sk] N [c] 清真寺 qīngzhēnsì [座 zuò]

mosquito [məski̲toʊ] (*pl* **mosquitoes**) N [c] 蚊 wén [只 zhī]

KEYWORD

most [moʊ̲st] **I** ADJ **1** (*almost all*) 大部分的 dàbùfen de ▸ **most people** 大多数人 dàduōshù rén

2 (*in comparisons*) ▸ **(the) most** 最 zuì ▸ **who won the most money/prizes?** 谁赢了最多的钱/奖品？ shuí yíngle zuìduō de qián/jiǎngpǐn?

II PRON 大部分 dàbùfen; (*plural*) 大多数 dàduōshù ▸ **most of it/them** 它/他们的大部分 tā/tāmen de dà bùfen ▸ **I paid the most** 我付了大部分 wǒ fùle dà bùfen ▸ **to make the most of sth** 充分利用某物 chōngfèn lìyòng mǒuwù ▸ **at the (very) most** 顶多 dǐngduō

III ADV (*superlative*) **1** (*with verb*) ▸ **(the) most** 最 zuì ▸ **what I miss (the) most is...** 我最想念的是… wǒ zuì xiǎngniàn de shì...

2 (*with adj*) ▸ **the most comfortable/expensive sofa in the shop** 店里最舒服/贵的沙发 diǎnlǐ zùi shūfu/guì de shāfā

3 (*with adv*) ▸ **most efficiently/effectively** 最有效率/有效地 zuì yǒuxiàolǜ/yǒuxiào de ▸ **most of all** 最起码的 zuì qǐmǎ de

mother [mʌ̲ðər] N [c] 母亲 mǔqīn [位 wèi]

mother-in-law [mʌ̲ðərɪnlɔ] (*pl* **mothers-in-law**) N [c] (*of woman*) 婆婆 pópo [位 wèi]; (*of man*) 岳母 yuèmǔ [位 wèi]

Mother's Day N [c/ʊ] 母亲节 Mǔqīn Jié [个 gè]

motivated ADJ 士气高涨的 shìqì gāozhǎng de

motor [moʊ̲tər] N [c] 发动机 fādòngjī [个 gè]

motorbike [moʊ̲tərbaɪk] N [c] 摩托车 mótuōchē [辆 liàng]

motorboat [moʊ̲tərboʊt] N [c] 摩托艇 mótuōtǐng [艘 sōu]

motorcycle [moʊ̲tərsaɪkᵊl] (*frm*) N [c] 摩托车 mótuōchē [辆 liàng]

motorcyclist [moʊ̲tərsaɪklɪst] N [c] 摩托车手 mótuōchēshǒu [位 wèi]

motorist [moʊ̲tərɪst] N [c] 开汽车的人 kāi qìchē de rén [个 gè]

mountain [maʊ̲ntᵊn] N [c] 山 shān [座 zuò]

mountain bike N [c] 山地自行车 shāndì zìxíngchē [辆 liàng]

mountainous [maʊ̲ntᵊnəs] ADJ 多山的 duōshān de

mouse [maʊ̲s] (*pl* **mice**) N [c] **1** 鼠 shǔ [只 zhī] **2** (*Comput*) 鼠标 shǔbiāo [个 gè]

mouse pad N [C] 鼠标垫 shǔbiāo diàn [个 gè]
mouth [maʊθ] N [C] **1** 嘴 zuǐ [张 zhāng] **2** (*of river*) 河口 hékǒu [个 gè]
mouthful [maʊθfʊl] N [C] 一口 yīkǒu
move [muv] **I** VI **1** (*vehicle*) 行进 xíngjìn; (*person, object*) 动 dòng **2** (*relocate*) 搬家 bānjiā; (*from activity*) 改换 gǎihuàn **II** VT **1** (+ *furniture, car*) 挪动 nuódòng **2** (*affect emotionally*) 感动 gǎndòng **III** N [C] **1** (*relocation*) 搬家 bānjiā [次 cì] **2** (*in game*) 一步 yībù ▶ **to get a move on** (*inf*) 快点 kuàidiǎn; **move away** VI (*from town, area*) 离开 líkāi; (*from window, door*) 走开 zǒukāi; **move back** VI **1** (*return*) 回来 huílái **2** (*backwards*) 后退 hòutuì; **move forward** VI (*person, troops, vehicle*) 向前移动 xiàngqián yídòng; **move in** VI (*into house*) 搬入 bānrù; **move into** VT FUS (*house, area*) 搬进 bānjìn; **move out** VI (*of house*) 搬出去 bān chūqù; **move over** VI (*to make room*) 让开些 ràngkāixiē
movement [muvmənt] N **1** [C] (*group of people*) 团体 tuántǐ [个 gè] **2** [C] (*gesture*) 动作 dòngzuò [个 gè]
movie [muvi] N [C] 电影 diànyǐng [部 bù] ▶ **the movies** 电影 diànyǐng
movie star N [C] 影星 yǐngxīng [位 wèi]
movie theater N [C] 电影院 diànyǐngyuàn [个 gè]
moving [muvɪŋ] ADJ **1** (*emotionally*) 动人的 dòngrén de **2** (*not static*) 活动的 huódòng de
MP3 [ɛm pi θri] N **1** (*format*) 一种音频压缩格式 **2** (*file*) 以这种音频压缩格式储存的声音文件
mph ABBR (= **miles per hour**) 每小时…英里 měi xiǎoshí...yīnglǐ
Mr. [mɪstər] N ▶ **Mr. Smith** 史密斯先生 Shǐmìsī xiānsheng
Mrs. [mɪsɪz] N ▶ **Mrs. Smith** 史密斯太太 Shǐmìsī tàitai
Ms. [mɪz] N (*Miss or Mrs*) ▶ **Ms. Smith** 史密斯女士 Shǐmìsī nǚshì

KEYWORD

much [mʌtʃ] **I** ADJ 大量的 dàliàng de ▶ **we haven't got much time/money** 我们没有多少时间/钱 wǒmen méiyǒu duōshǎo shíjiān/qián
II PRON 大量 dàliàng ▶ **there isn't much left** 剩下的不多了 shèngxià de bùduō le ▶ **he doesn't do much on the weekend** 他周末不干什么 tā zhōumò bù gàn shénme
III ADV **1** (*a great deal*) 许多 xǔduō ▶ **he hasn't changed much** 他没变很多 tā méi biàn hěnduō ▶ **"did you like her?" – "not much"** "你喜欢她吗?" "不太喜欢" "nǐ xǐhuan tā ma?" "bùtài xǐhuan"
2 (*far*) …得多 ...deduō ▶ **I'm much better now** 我感觉好多了 wǒ gǎnjué hǎoduō le
3 (*often*) 经常 jīngcháng ▶ **do you go out much?** 你经常出去吗? nǐ jīngcháng chūqù ma?

mud [mʌd] N [U] 泥 ní
muddle [mʌdᵊl] N [C/U] **1** (*of papers, figures, things*) 混乱状态 hùnluàn zhuàngtài [个 gè] **2** (*situation*) 糟糕局面 zāogāo júmiàn [个 gè] ▶ **to be in a muddle** 一片混乱 yīpiàn hùnluàn
muddy [mʌdi] ADJ 沾满烂泥的 zhānmǎn lànní de
muesli [myuzli] N [U] 穆兹利，和干水果混在一起的燕麦早餐
mug [mʌg] **I** N [C] 大杯子 dà bēizi [个 gè] **II** VT (*rob*) 行凶抢劫 xíngxiōng qiǎngjié
mugging [mʌgɪŋ] N [C/U] 行凶抢劫 xíngxiōng qiǎngjié [次 cì]
multiply [mʌltɪplaɪ] **I** VT (*Math*) ▶ **to multiply sth (by sth)** (某数)乘以某数 (mǒushù) chéngyǐ mǒushù **II** VI (*increase*) 增加 zēngjiā
murder [mɜrdər] **I** N [C/U] 谋杀

móushā [个 gè] **II** VT 谋杀 móushā

murderer [mɜrdərər] N [C] 凶手 xiōngshǒu [个 gè]

muscle [mʌsᵊl] N [C/U] 肌肉 jīròu [块 kuài]

museum [myuziəm] N [C] 博物馆 bówùguǎn [个 gè]

mushroom [mʌʃrum] N [C] 蘑菇 mógu [个 gè]

music [myuzɪk] N [U] **1** 音乐 yīnyuè **2** (*Scol, Univ*) 音乐课 yīnyuè kè

musical [myuzɪkᵊl] ADJ **1** (*related to music*) 音乐的 yīnyuè de **2** (*musically gifted*) 有音乐天赋的 yǒu yīnyuè tiānfù de

musical instrument N [C] 乐器 yuèqì [件 jiàn]

musician [myuzɪʃᵊn] N [C] 音乐家 yīnyuèjiā [位 wèi]

Muslim [mʌzlɪm, mʊs-], **Moslem** **I** N [C] 穆斯林 Mùsīlín [个 gè] **II** ADJ 穆斯林的 Mùsīlín de

must [məst, STRONG mʌst] AUX VB **1** (*expressing importance or necessity*) 必须 bìxū **2** (*expressing intention*) 得 děi **3** (*expressing presumption*) 一定 yīdìng **4** ▶ **you must be joking** 你准是在开玩笑 nǐ zhǔn shì zài kāi wánxiào ▶ **the doctor must allow the patient to decide** 医生必须让病人来决定。 yīshēng bìxū ràng bìngrén lái juédìng. ▶ **I really must be getting back** 我真得回去了。 wǒ zhēnděi huíqù le

mustache [mʌstæʃ] N [C] 髭 zī [根 gēn]

mustard [mʌstərd] N [U] 芥末 jièmo

mustn't [mʌsᵊnt] = **must not**

my [maɪ] ADJ 我的 wǒ de

myself [maɪsɛlf] PRON **1** 我自己 wǒ zìjǐ **2** (*me*) 我 wǒ ▶ **I hurt myself** 我伤了自己。 wǒ shāngle zìjǐ ▶ **by myself** (*unaided*) 我独力地 wǒ dúlì de; (*alone*) 我独自 wǒ dúzì

mysterious [mɪstɪəriəs] ADJ 神秘的 shénmì de

mystery [mɪstəri, mɪstri] N **1** [C] (*puzzle*) 谜 mí [个 gè] **2** [C] (*story*) 推理作品 tuīlǐ zuòpǐn [部 bù]

myth [mɪθ] N [C] **1** (*legend, story*) 神话 shénhuà [个 gè] **2** (*fallacy*) 谬论 miùlùn [个 gè]

N

nail [neɪl] N [C] **1** (*of finger, toe*) 指甲 zhǐjia [个 gè] **2** (*for hammering*) 钉子 dīngzi [个 gè]

nail file N [C] 指甲锉 zhǐjia cuò [个 gè]

nail polish N [U] 指甲油 zhǐjia yóu

naked [neɪkɪd] ADJ 裸体的 luǒtǐ de

name [neɪm] N [C] 名字 míngzi [个 gè] ▸ **what's your name?** 你叫什么名字? nǐ jiào shénme míngzi? ▸ **my name is Peter** 我叫彼得 wǒ jiào bǐdé ▸ **to give one's name and address** 留下姓名和地址 liúxià xìngmíng hé dìzhǐ

nanny [næni] N [C] 保姆 bǎomǔ [个 gè]

napkin [næpkɪn] N [C] 餐巾 cānjīn [张 zhāng]

narrow [næroʊ] ADJ 窄的 zhǎi de

nasty [næsti] ADJ **1** (+ *taste, smell*) 恶心的 ěxīn de **2** (+ *injury, accident, disease*) 严重的 yánzhòng de

nation [neɪʃᵊn] N [C] 国家 guójiā [个 gè]

national [næʃənᵊl] **I** ADJ 国家的 guójiā de **II** N [C] 公民 gōngmín [个 gè]

national anthem N [C] 国歌 guógē [首 shǒu]

national holiday N [C] 法定假期 fǎdìng jiàqī [个 gè]

nationality [næʃənælɪti] N [C/U] 国籍 guójí [个 gè]

national park N [C] 国家公园 guójiā gōngyuán [个 gè]

native [neɪtɪv] ADJ (+ *country*) 本国的 běnguó de; (+ *language, tongue*) 母语的 mǔyǔ de

natural [nætʃərəl, nætʃrəl] ADJ **1** (*normal*) 正常的 zhèngcháng de **2** (+ *material, product, food*) 天然的 tiānrán de

naturally [nætʃərəli, nætʃrəli] ADV **1** (*unsurprisingly*) 自然地 zìrán de **2** (*occur, happen*) 自然而然地 zìrán ér rán de

nature [neɪtʃər] N [U] (*also*: **Nature**) 自然界 zìránjiè

naught [nɔt] NUM 零 líng

naughty [nɔti] ADJ 淘气的 táoqì de

navy [neɪvi] **I** N **1** ▸ **the navy** (*service*) 海军 hǎijūn **2** [U] (*also*: **navy-blue**) 藏青色 zàngqīngsè **II** ADJ (*also*: **navy-blue**) 藏青色的 zàngqīngsè de

near [nɪər] **I** ADJ 近的 jìn de **II** ADV (*close*) 近 jìn **III** PREP (*also*: **near to**) **1** (*physically*) 近 jìn **2** (*just before/after*) 临近 línjìn ▸ **the nearest shops are 5 km away** 最近的商店离这里有5公里远。 zuìjìn de shāngdiàn lí zhèlǐ yǒu wǔ gōnglǐ yuǎn ▸ **in the near future** 在不远的将来 zài bùyuǎn de jiānglái

nearby [nɪərbaɪ] **I** ADJ 附近的 fùjìn de **II** ADV 在附近 zài fùjìn

nearly [nɪərli] ADV 差不多 chà bù duō ▸ **you're nearly as tall as I am** 你跟我差不多高了 nǐ gēn wǒ chàbùduō gāole ▸ **nearly always** 几乎总是 jīhū zǒngshì

nearsighted [nɪərsaɪtɪd] ADJ 近视的 jìnshì de

neat [nit] ADJ **1** 整洁的 zhěngjié de; (+ *handwriting*) 工整的 gōngzhěng de **2** (*inf*: *great*) 绝妙的 juémiào de

neatly [nitli] ADV 整齐地 zhěngqí de

necessarily [nɛsɪsɛərɪli] ADV 必然 bìrán

necessary [nɛsɪsɛri] ADJ 必要的 bìyào de ▸ **if/when/where necessary** 如有必要/必要时/在必要处 rú yǒu bìyào/bìyào shí/zài bìyào chù

neck [nɛk] N [C] **1** (*Anat*) 颈 jǐng **2** (*of shirt, dress, sweater*) 领子 lǐngzi [个 gè]

necklace [nɛklɪs] N [C] 项链 xiàngliàn [条 tiáo]

necktie [nɛktaɪ] N [C] 领带 lǐngdài [条 tiáo]

need [nid] VT **1** (*require*) 需要 xūyào

2 (*want*) (+ *drink, vacation, cigarette*) 想要 xiǎngyào 3 (+ *a haircut, a bath, a wash*) 得 děi ▶ **to need to do sth** 必须做某事 bìxū zuò mǒushì ▶ **the car needs servicing** 这辆车需要维修了 zhèliàng chē xūyào wéixiū le

needle [nidᵊl] N [C] 1 (*for sewing*) 针 zhēn [根 gēn] 2 (*for injections*) 注射针 zhùshèzhēn [只 zhī]

negative [nɛgətɪv] I ADJ 1 (+ *test, result*) 阴性的 yīnxìng de 2 (+ *person, attitude, view*) 消极的 xiāojí de 3 (+ *answer, response*) 否定的 fǒudìng de II N [C] (*Ling*) 否定词 fǒudìngcí [个 gè]

negotiate [nɪgoʊʃieɪt] VI 商讨 shāngtǎo

neighbor [neɪbər] N [C] 邻居 línjū [个 gè]

neighborhood [neɪbərhʊd] N [C] 地区 dìqū [个 gè]

neither [niðər, naɪ-] I PRON (*person*) 两人都不 liǎngrén dōu bù; (*thing*) 两者都不 liǎngzhě dōu bù II CONJ ▶ **I didn't move and neither did John** 我和约翰都没动 wǒ hé Yuēhàn dōu méi dòng ▶ **neither do/have I** 我也不/没 wǒ yě bù/méi ▶ **neither... nor...** 既不…也不… jìbù...yěbù...

> **neither** 和 **none** 作代词的时候用法不同。用 **neither** 指两个人或事物，表示否定含义。*Neither had close friends at college.* **neither of** 的用法与之相同，后接代词或名词词组。*Neither of them spoke... Neither of these options is desirable.* 注意，也可以把 **neither** 用在单数可数名词之前。*Neither side can win.* **none** 可以指代三个或者三个以上的人或事物，表示否定含义。*None could afford the food.* **none of** 的用法与之相同，后接代词或名词词组。*None of them had learned anything.*

nephew [nɛfyu] N [C] (*brother's son*) 侄子 zhízi [个 gè]; (*sister's son*) 外甥 wàisheng [个 gè]

nerve [nɜrv] N 1 [C] (*Anat*) 神经 shénjīng [根 gēn] 2 [U] (*courage*) 勇气 yǒngqì ▶ **to get on sb's nerves** 使某人心烦 shǐ mǒurén xīnfán

nervous [nɜrvəs] ADJ 紧张的 jǐnzhāng de ▶ **to be nervous about sth/about doing sth** 对某事/做某事感到紧张不安 duì mǒushì/zuò mǒushì gǎndào jǐnzhāng bù'ān

nest [nɛst] N [C] 巢 cháo [个 gè]

net [nɛt] N 1 [C] 网 wǎng [张 zhāng] 2 (*Comput*) ▶ **the Net** 网络 wǎngluò [个 gè]

Netherlands [nɛðərləndz] N PL ▶ **the Netherlands** 荷兰 Hélán

network [nɛtwɜrk] N [C] 1 网状系统 wǎngzhuàng xìtǒng [个 gè] 2 (*system*) 网络 wǎngluò [个 gè]

neurodiverse [nuroʊdaɪvəs] ADJ (*person, condition*) 神经多样性的 shénjīng duōyàngxìng de

never [nɛvər] ADV 从未 cóngwèi ▶ **we never saw him again** 我们再没有见过他 wǒmen zài méiyǒu jiànguò tā

new [nu] ADJ 1 崭新的 zhǎnxīn de 2 (+ *product, system, method*) 新式的 xīnshì de 3 (+ *job, address, boss, president*) 新的 xīn de ▶ **this concept is new to me** 我对这个概念不熟悉 wǒ duì zhègè gàiniàn bù shúxi

news [nuz] N [U] 消息 xiāoxi ▶ **a piece of news** 一条消息 yītiáo xiāoxi ▶ **good/bad news** 好/坏消息 hǎo/huài xiāoxi ▶ **the news** (*TV, Rad*) 新闻 xīnwén

newspaper [nuzpeɪpər, nus-] N [C] 报纸 bàozhǐ [份 fèn]

New Year N [U] ▶ **(the) New Year** 新年 Xīnnián ▶ **in the New Year** 在新的一年中 zài xīnde yīnián zhōng ▶ **Happy New Year!** 新年快乐！ Xīnnián Kuàilè!

New Year's N [U] (*also*: **New Year's Day**) 元旦 Yuándàn; (*also*: **New Year's Eve**) 元旦前夜 Yuándàn qiányè

New Zealand [-zilənd] I N 新西兰 Xīnxīlán II ADJ 新西兰的 Xīnxīlán de

next [nɛkst] I ADJ 1 下一个的 xiàyīgè de 2 (+ *house, street, room*) 旁边的 pángbiān de II ADV 接下来地 jiēxiàlái de ▶ **the next day/morning** 第二天/天早晨 dì'èrtiān/tiān zǎochén ▶ **the next five years/weeks will be very important** 接下来的5年/周将是至关重要的 jiēxiàlái de wǔnián/zhōu jiāngshì zhì guān zhòng yào de ▶ **the next flight/prime minister** 下一次航班/下一任首相 xià yīcì hángbān/xià yīrèn shǒuxiàng ▶ **next time, be a bit more careful** 下一次，要更谨慎些 xià yīcì, yào gèng jǐnshèn xiē ▶ **who's next?** 下一位是谁? xià yīwèi shì shuí? ▶ **the week after next** 下下个星期 xiàxiàgè xīngqī ▶ **next to** (*beside*) 旁边 pángbiān

next door ADV 隔壁 gébì

nice [naɪs] ADJ 1 好的 hǎo de 2 (+ *person*) (*likeable*) 和蔼的 hé'ǎi de; (*friendly*) 友好的 yǒuhǎo de ▶ **to look nice** 看上去不错 kànshàngqù bùcuò ▶ **it's nice to see you** 很高兴见到你 hěn gāoxìng jiàndào nǐ

nickname [nɪkneɪm] N [C] 绰号 chuòhào [个 gè]

niece [nis] N [C] (*brother's daughter*) 侄女 zhínǚ [个 gè]; (*sister's daughter*) 甥女 shēngnǚ [个 gè]

Nigeria [naɪdʒɪəriə] N 尼日利亚 Nírìlìyà

night [naɪt] N 1 [C/U] 黑夜 hēiyè [个 gè] 2 [C] (*evening*) 晚上 wǎnshang [个 gè] ▶ **at night** 夜间 yèjiān ▶ **in/during the night** 夜里 yèlǐ

nightclub [naɪtklʌb] N [C] 夜总会 yèzǒnghuì [个 gè]

nightie [naɪti] N [C] 睡衣 shuìyī [件 jiàn]

nightmare [naɪtmɛər] N [C] 恶梦 èmèng [场 chǎng]

nil [nɪl] N ▶ **their chances of survival are nil** 他们没有幸存的可能 tāmen méiyǒu xìngcún de kěnéng

nine [naɪn] NUM 九 jiǔ; *see also* **five**

nineteen [naɪntin] NUM 十九 shíjiǔ; *see also* **fifteen**

ninety [naɪnti] NUM 九十 jiǔshí; *see also* **fifty**

KEYWORD

no [noʊ] (*pl* **noes**) I ADV (*opposite of "yes"*) 不 bù ▶ **"did you see it?" – "no (I didn't)"** "你看见了吗?" "不(我没见到)" "nǐ kànjiàn le má?" bù (wǒ méi jiàndào)" ▶ **no thank you, no thanks** 不用，谢谢你 bùyòng, xièxie nǐ

II ADJ (*not any*) 没有 méiyǒu ▶ **I have no milk/books** 我没有牛奶/书 wǒ méiyǒu niúnǎi/shū ▶ **"no smoking"** "严禁吸烟" "yánjìn xīyān" ▶ **no way!** 没门儿! méiménr!

nobody [noʊbɒdi, -bʌdi] PRON 没有人 méiyǒu rén

noise [nɔɪz] N 1 [C] (*sound*) 响声 xiǎngshēng [阵 zhèn] 2 [U] (*din*) 噪音 zàoyīn

noisy [nɔɪzi] ADJ 嘈杂的 cáozá de; (+ *place*) 喧闹的 xuānnào de

none [nʌn] PRON 1 (*not one*) 没有一个 méiyǒu yī gè 2 (*not any*) 没有一点儿 méiyǒu yīdiǎnr ▶ **none of us/them** 我们/他们谁也没 wǒmen/tāmen shuí yě méi ▶ **I've/there's none left** 我一点也没有了/一点也没剩 wǒ yīdiǎn yě méiyǒu le/yīdiǎn yě méi shèng

nonsense [nɒnsɛns, -səns] N [U] 胡说八道 húshuō bādào

nonsmoking [nɒnsmoʊkɪŋ] ADJ 禁烟的 jìn yān de

nonstop ADV 1 (*ceaselessly*) 不断地 bùduàn de 2 (*fly, drive*) 不停地 bù tíng de

noodles [nudᵊlz] N PL 面条 miàntiáo

noon [nun] N [U] 中午 zhōngwǔ ▶ **at noon** 中午 zhōngwǔ

no one PRON = **nobody**

nor [nɔr] CONJ 也不 yěbù; *see also* **neither**

normal [nɔrmᵊl] ADJ 正常的 zhèngcháng de ▶ **more/higher/worse than normal** 比正常的多/高/糟糕 bǐ

zhèngchángde duō/gāo/zāogāo
normally [nɔrməli] ADV (*usually*) 通常地 tōngcháng de
north [nɔrθ] **I** N [U/S] 北方 běifāng **II** ADJ 北部的 běibù de **III** ADV 向北方 xiàng běifāng ▶ **to the north** 以北 yǐběi ▶ **north of** …以北 ...yǐběi
North America N 北美 Běiměi
northeast I N 东北 dōngběi **II** ADJ 东北的 dōngběi de **III** ADV 向东北 xiàng dōngběi
northern [nɔrðərn] ADJ 北方的 běifāng de ▶ **the northern hemisphere** 北半球 běibànqiú
Northern Ireland N 北爱尔兰 Běi'ài'ěrlán
North Korea N 朝鲜 Cháoxiǎn
North Pole N ▶ **the North Pole** 北极 Běijí
northwest I N 西北 xīběi **II** ADJ 西北的 xīběi de **III** ADV 向西北 xiàng xīběi
Norway [nɔrweɪ] N 挪威 Nuówēi
nose [noʊz] N [C] 鼻子 bízi [个 gè]
not [nɒt] ADV 不 bù ▶ **he is not** *or* **isn't here** 他不在这儿 tā bùzài zhèr ▶ **it's too late, isn't it?** 现在太晚了，不是吗？ xiànzài tàiwǎn le, bùshì ma? ▶ **he asked me not to do it** 他叫我不要这么做 tā jiào wǒ bùyào zhème zuò ▶ **are you coming or not?** 你来不来？ nǐ láibùlái? ▶ **not at all** (*in answer to thanks*) 不客气 bù kèqi ▶ **not yet/now** 还没/现在不 háiméi/xiànzài bù ▶ **not really** 并不是的 bìng bùshì de
note [noʊt] **I** N [C] (*message*) 便条 biàntiáo [张 zhāng] **II** VT (*observe*) 留意 liúyì **III notes** N PL (*from or for lecture*) 笔记 bǐjì ▶ **to make a note of sth** 记下某事 jìxià mǒushì ▶ **to take notes** 记笔记 jì bǐjì
notebook [noʊtbʊk] N [C] 笔记本 bǐjìběn [个 gè]
notepad [noʊtpæd] N [C] **1** (*pad of paper*) 记事本 jìshìběn [个 gè] **2** (*Comput*) 记事簿 jìshìbù [个 gè]
nothing [nʌθɪŋ] PRON 什么也没有 shénme yě méiyǒu ▶ **nothing new/serious/to worry about** 没有什么新的/要紧的/值得担忧的 méiyǒu shénme xīnde/yàojǐn de/zhídé dānyōu de ▶ **nothing else** 没有别的 méiyǒu biéde ▶ **for nothing** 免费 miǎnfèi ▶ **nothing at all** 什么也没有 shénme yě méiyǒu
notice [noʊtɪs] **I** VT 注意到 zhùyì dào **II** N [C] 公告 gōnggào [个 gè] ▶ **to notice that...** 注意到… zhùyì dào... ▶ **to take no notice of sb/sth** 不理某人/某事 bùlǐ mǒurén/mǒushì ▶ **without notice** 不事先通知 bù shìxiān tōngzhī
noun [naʊn] N [C] 名词 míngcí [个 gè]
novel [nɒvᵊl] N [C] 小说 xiǎoshuō [部 bù]
novelist [nɒvəlɪst] N [C] 小说家 xiǎoshuōjiā [位 wèi]
November [noʊvɛmbər] N [C/U] 十一月 shíyīyuè [个 gè]; *see also* **July**
now [naʊ] **I** ADV **1** 现在 xiànzài **2** (*these days*) 如今 rújīn **II** CONJ ▶ **now (that)** 既然 jìrán ▶ **right now** 这时 zhèshí ▶ **by now** 到现在 dào xiànzài ▶ **just now** 眼下 yǎnxià ▶ **from now on** 从现在起 cóng xiànzài qǐ ▶ **that's all for now** 就到这里 jiùdào zhèli
nowhere [noʊwɛər] ADV 无处 wúchù ▶ **nowhere else** 没有其他地方 méiyǒu qítā dìfang
nuclear [nukliər] ADJ 核能的 hénéng de
nuisance [nusᵊns] N ▶ **to be a nuisance** (*thing*) 讨厌的东西 tǎoyàn de dōngxi
numb [nʌm] ADJ 麻木的 mámù de
number [nʌmbər] **I** N **1** [C] (*Math*) 数 shù [个 gè] **2** [C] (*telephone number*) 电话号码 diànhuà hàomǎ [个 gè] **3** [C] (*of house, bank account, bus*) 号 hào [个 gè] **4** [C/U] (*quantity*) 数量 shùliàng **II** VT (+ *pages*) 给…标号码 gěi...biāo hàomǎ ▶ **a number of** (*several*) 几个 jǐgè ▶ **a large/small number of** 大量/少数 dàliàng/shǎoshù

nun [nʌn] N [c] 修女 xiūnǚ [名 míng]
nurse [nɜrs] N [c] 护士 hùshi [位 wèi]
nursery [nɜrsəri] N [c] 幼儿园 yòu'éryuán [个 gè]
nursery school N [c/u] 幼儿园 yòu'éryuán [个 gè]
nut [nʌt] N [c] **1** (*Bot, Culin*) 坚果 jiānguǒ [枚 méi] **2** (*Tech*) 螺母 luómǔ [个 gè]
nylon [naɪlɒn] N [u] 尼龙 nílóng

O

oak [oʊk] N **1** [C] (*also*: **oak tree**) 橡树 xiàngshù [棵 kē] **2** [U] (*wood*) 橡木 xiàngmù
oar [ɔr] N [C] 桨 jiǎng [只 zhī]
oats [oʊts] N PL 燕麦 yànmài
obedient [oʊbidiənt] ADJ 顺从的 shùncóng de
obey [oʊbeɪ] **I** VT (+ *person, orders*) 听从 tīngcóng; (+ *law, regulations*) 服从 fúcóng **II** VI 服从 fúcóng
object [*n* ɒbdʒɪkt, *vb* əbdʒɛkt] **I** N [C] **1** (*thing*) 物体 wùtǐ [个 gè] **2** (*Ling*) 宾语 bīnyǔ [个 gè] **II** VI 反对 fǎnduì
objection [əbdʒɛkʃᵊn] N [C] 异议 yìyì [个 gè]
obsess [əbsɛs] VT 使着迷 shǐ zháomí
obsession [əbsɛʃᵊn] N [C] 着迷 zháomí [种 zhǒng]
obtain [əbteɪn] VT 获得 huòdé
obvious [ɒbviəs] ADJ 明显的 míngxiǎn de
obviously [ɒbviəsli] ADV (*of course*) 显然地 xiǎnrán de
occasion [əkeɪʒᵊn] N [C] **1** (*moment*) 时刻 shíkè [个 gè] **2** (*event, celebration*) 场合 chǎnghé [种 zhǒng]
occasionally [əkeɪʒənᵊli] ADV 偶尔地 ǒu'ěr de
occupation [ɒkyəpeɪʃᵊn] N [C] 职业 zhíyè [种 zhǒng]
occupy [ɒkyəpaɪ] VT **1** (*inhabit*) (+ *house, office*) 占用 zhànyòng **2** ▶ **to be occupied** (*seat, place etc*) 被占用 bèi zhànyòng **3** (*fill*) (+ *time*) 占用 zhànyòng
occur [əkɜr] VI 发生 fāshēng ▶ **to occur to sb** 某人想到 mǒurén xiǎngdào
ocean [oʊʃᵊn] N [C] 海洋 hǎiyáng [片 piàn]
o'clock [əklɒk] ADV ▶ **six o'clock** 6点钟 liùdiǎnzhōng
October [ɒktoʊbər] N [C/U] 十月 shíyuè; *see also* **July**
octopus [ɒktəpəs] N [C] 章鱼 zhāngyú [只 zhī]
odd [ɒd] ADJ **1** (*strange*) 奇怪的 qíguài de **2** (+ *number*) 奇数的 jīshù de
odor [oʊdər] N [C/U] 气味 qìwèi [种 zhǒng]

KEYWORD

of [əv, STRONG ʌv] PREP **1** (*gen*) 的 de ▶ **the history of China** 中国历史 Zhōngguó lìshǐ ▶ **at the end of the street** 在街的尽头 zài jiēde jìntóu ▶ **the city of New York** 纽约城 Niǔyuēchéng
2 (*expressing quantity, amount*) ▶ **a pound of flour** 一磅面粉 yī bàng miànfěn ▶ **a cup of tea/vase of flowers** 一杯茶/一瓶花 yībēi chá/yīpíng huā ▶ **there were three of them** 他们有3个 tāmen yǒu sāngè ▶ **an annual income of $30,000** 每年3万美元的收入 měinián sānwàn měiyuán de shōurù
3 (*in dates*) ▶ **the 5th of July** 7月5日 qīyuè wǔrì
4 (*in times*) ▶ **at five minutes to three** 3点差5分 sāndiǎn chà wǔfēn

KEYWORD

off [*prep* ɔf, *adv* ɔf] **I** ADJ **1** (*not turned on*) 关着的 guānzhe de
2 (*canceled*) 取消的 qǔxiāo de
II ADV **1** (*away*) ▶ **I must be off** 我必须得走了 wǒ bìxū děi zǒu le ▶ **where are you off to?** 你上哪儿去？ nǐ shàng nǎ'r qù?
2 (*not at work*) ▶ **to have a day off** (*as holiday*) 休假一天 xiūjià yītiān; (*because ill*) 休病假一天 xiūbìngjià yītiān
3 (*Comm*) ▶ **10% off** 10%的折扣

bǎifēn zhī shí de zhékòu
III PREP (*indicating motion, removal etc*) ▸ **to take a picture off the wall** 把画像从墙上取下来 bǎ huàxiàng cóng qiáng shang qǔ xiàlái

offend [əfɛnd] VT (*upset*) 得罪 dézuì
offense [əfɛns] N [C] (*crime*) 罪行 zuìxíng [种 zhǒng]
offer [ɔfər] **I** VT **1** 给 gěi **2** (*bid*) 出价 chūjià **II** N [C] **1** 提议 tíyì [项 xiàng] **2** (*special deal*) 特价 tèjià [个 gè]
office [ɔfɪs] N **1** [C] (*room*) 办公室 bàngōngshì [间 jiān] **2** [C] (*department*) 部门 bùmén [个 gè] **3** [C] (*of doctor, dentist*) 诊所 zhěnsuǒ [家 jiā]
office building N [C] 办公大楼 bàngōng dàlóu [座 zuò]
officer [ɔfɪsər] N [C] **1** (*Mil*) 军官 jūnguān [位 wèi] **2** (*also*: **police officer**) 警官 jǐngguān [位 wèi]
office worker N [C] 职员 zhíyuán [个 gè]
official [əfɪʃᵊl] ADJ 官方的 guānfāng de
often [ɔfᵊn] ADV (*frequently*) 经常 jīngcháng ▸ **how often do you wash the car?** 你多久洗一次车? nǐ duōjiǔ xǐ yīcì chē?
oil [ɔɪl] **I** N [C/U] 油 yóu [桶 tǒng] **II** VT (+ *engine, machine*) 给…加油 gěi...jiāyóu
oil rig [-rɪg] N [C] (*on land*) 石油钻塔 shíyóu zuàntǎ [个 gè]; (*at sea*) 钻井平台 zuànjǐng píngtái [个 gè]
okay [oʊkeɪ] **I** ADJ **1** (*acceptable*) 可以的 kěyǐ de **2** (*safe and well*) 好的 hǎo de **II** ADV (*acceptably*) 不错 bùcuò **III** INT **1** (*expressing agreement*) 行 xíng **2** (*in questions*) 好吗 hǎo ma ▸ **are you okay?** 你还好吗? nǐ hái hǎoma? ▸ **it's okay with** *or* **by me** 这对我没问题 zhè duìwǒ méi wèntí
old [oʊld] ADJ **1** (+ *person*) 年老的 niánlǎo de **2** (*not new, not recent*) 古老的 gǔlǎo de **3** (*worn out*) 破旧的 pòjiù de **4** (*former*) 以前的 yǐqián de **5** (+ *friend, enemy, rival*) 老的 lǎo de ▸ **how old are you?** 你多大了? nǐ duōdà le? ▸ **he's 10 years old** 他10岁了 tā shísuì le ▸ **older brother/sister** 哥哥/姐姐 gēge/jiějie
old-fashioned [oʊldfæʃᵊn] ADJ (+ *object, custom, idea*) 老式的 lǎoshì de; (+ *person*) 守旧的 shǒujiù de
olive [ɒlɪv] N [C] 橄榄 gǎnlǎn [棵 kē]
olive oil N [U] 橄榄油 gǎnlǎnyóu
Olympic [əlɪmpɪk] **I** ADJ 奥林匹克的 Àolínpǐkè de **II the Olympics** N PL 奥林匹克运动会 Àolínpǐkè Yùndònghuì
omelet [ɒmlɪt, ɒməlɪt] N [C] 煎蛋饼 jiāndànbǐng [个 gè]

KEYWORD

on [ɒn] **I** PREP **1** (*indicating position*) 在…上 zài...shang ▸ **it's on the table/wall** 它在桌上/墙上 tā zài zhuōshàng/qiángshàng ▸ **the house is on the main road** 房子在主路旁 fángzi zài zhǔlù páng ▸ **on the left/right** 在左边/右边 zài zuǒbiān/yòubiān ▸ **on the top floor** 在顶楼 zài dǐnglóu
2 (*indicating means, method, condition etc*) ▸ **on foot** 步行 bùxíng ▸ **on the train/bus** (*be, sit*) 在火车/公共汽车上 zài huǒchē/gōnggòng qìchē shàng; (*travel, go*) 乘坐 chéngzuò ▸ **on the television/radio** 在电视上/广播中 zài diànshì shàng/guāngbō zhōng ▸ **on the internet** 在因特网上 zài Yīntèwǎng shàng ▸ **to be on antibiotics** 定期服用抗生素 dìngqī fúyòng kàngshēngsù
3 (*referring to time*) 在 zài ▸ **on Friday** 在星期五 zài xīngqīwǔ ▸ **on Friday, June 20th** 在6月20日，星期五 zài liùyuè èrshí rì, xīngqīwǔ
II ADV **1** (*clothes*) ▸ **to have one's coat on** 穿着外套 chuānzhe wàitào ▸ **what's she got on?** 她穿着什么? tā chuānzhe shénme?
2 (*covering, lid etc*) ▸ **screw the lid on tightly** 把盖子旋紧 bǎ gàizi xuánjǐn

III ADJ **1** (*turned on*) 打开的 dǎkāi de **2** (*happening*) ▸ **is the meeting still on?** 会议还在进行吗？ huìyì háizài jìnxíng ma? ▸ **there's a good movie on at the movie theater** 电影院正在上映一部好电影 diànyǐngyuàn zhèngzài shàngyìng yībù hǎo diànyǐng

once [wʌns] **I** ADV **1** (*one time only*) 一次 yīcì **2** (*at one time*) 曾经 céngjīng **3** (*on one occasion*) 有一次 yǒu yīcì **II** CONJ (*as soon as*) 一旦 yīdàn ▸ **at once** (*immediately*) 立刻 lìkè ▸ **once a** *or* **every month** 每月一次 měiyuè yīcì ▸ **once upon a time** (*in stories*) 很久以前 hěnjiǔ yǐqián ▸ **once in a while** 偶尔 ǒu'ěr ▸ **once or twice** (*a few times*) 一两次 yīliǎng cì

KEYWORD

one [wʌn] **I** ADJ **1** (*number*) 一 yī ▸ **it's one o'clock** 现在1点 xiànzài yīdiǎn ▸ **one hundred/thousand children** 100/1000个孩子 yībǎi/yīqiān gè háizi
2 (*same*) 同一的 tóngyī de ▸ **shall I put it all on the one plate?** 要我把它都放在同一个盘子里吗？ yào wǒ bǎ tā dōu fàngzài tóngyīgè pánzi lǐ ma?
II PRON **1** (*number*) 一 yī ▸ **I've already got one** 我已经有一个了 wǒ yǐjīng yǒu yīgè le ▸ **one of them/of the boys** 他们中的一个/男孩中的一个 tāmen zhōng de yīgè/nánhái zhōng de yīgè ▸ **one by one** 一个一个地 yīgè yīgè de
2 (*with adj*) 一个 yīgè ▸ **I've already got a red one** 我已经有一个红的了 wǒ yǐjīng yǒu yīgè hóngde le
3 (*in generalizations*) 人人 rénrén ▸ **what can one do?** 一个人能做什么呢？ yīgèrén néng zuò shénme ne? ▸ **this one** 这个 zhègè ▸ **that one** 那个 nàgè
III N (*numeral*) 一 yī

KEYWORD

oneself [wʌnsɛlf] PRON 自己 zìjǐ ▸ **to hurt oneself** 伤了自己 shāngle zìjǐ ▸ **by oneself** (*unaided*) 独力地 dúlì de; (*alone*) 独自 dúzì

one-way ADJ **1** (+ *street, traffic*) 单行的 dānxíng de **2** (+ *ticket, trip*) 单程的 dānchéng de

onion [ʌnyən] N [C] 洋葱 yángcōng [个 gè]

online [ɒnlaɪn] (*Comput*) ADV (*on the internet*) 网上 wǎngshang

only [oʊnli] **I** ADV **1** 仅仅 jǐnjǐn **2** (*emphasizing insignificance*) 只 zhǐ **II** ADJ (*sole*) 唯一的 wéiyī de **III** CONJ (*but*) 可是 kěshì ▸ **I was only joking** 我只是在开玩笑 wǒ zhǐshì zài kāi wánxiào ▸ **not only... but (also)...** 不但…而且… bùdàn...érqiě... ▸ **an only child** 独生子女 dúshēng zǐnǚ

onto, on to [ɒntu] PREP 到…上 dào...shàng

open [oʊpən] **I** ADJ **1** (+ *door, window*) 开着的 kāizhe de; (+ *mouth, eyes*) 张着的 zhāngzhe de **2** (+ *store*) 营业的 yíngyè de **II** VT (+ *container*) 打开 dǎkāi; (+ *door, lid*) 开 kāi; (+ *letter*) 拆开 chāikāi; (+ *book, hand, mouth, eyes*) 开 kāi **III** VI **1** (*door, lid*) 开 kāi **2** (*public building*) 开门 kāimén ▸ **in the open (air)** 在户外 zài hùwài

open-minded [oʊpənmaɪndɪd] ADJ 开明的 kāimíng de

opera [ɒpərə, ɒprə] N [C] 歌剧 gējù [部 bù]

operate [ɒpəreɪt] **I** VT (+ *machine, vehicle, system*) 操作 cāozuò **II** VI **1** (*machine, vehicle, system*) 工作 gōngzuò; (*company, organization*) 运作 yùnzuò **2** (*Med*) 动手术 dòngshǒushù ▸ **to operate on sb** (*Med*) 给某人动手术 gěi mǒurén dòng shǒushù

operation [ɒpəreɪʃᵊn] N **1** [C] (*procedure*) 实施步骤 shíshī bùzhòu [个 gè] **2** [C] (*Med*) 手术 shǒushù [次

cì] ▸ **to have an operation** (*Med*) 接受手术 jiēshòu shǒushù

operator [ɒpəreɪtər] N [c] (*Tel*) 接线员 jiēxiànyuán [位 wèi]

opinion [əpɪnyən] N [c] (*individual view*) 观点 guāndiǎn [个 gè] ▸ **in my/her opinion** 按我的/她的意见 àn wǒde/tāde yìjiàn

opinion poll [əpɪnyən poʊl] N [c] 民意测验 mínyì cèyàn [次 cì]

opponent [əpoʊnənt] N [c] 对手 duìshǒu [个 gè]

opportunity [ɒpərtunɪti] N [c/U] 机会 jīhuì [个 gè] ▸ **to take the opportunity of doing sth** *or* **to do sth** 趁机会做某事 chèn jīhuì zuò mǒushì

oppose [əpoʊz] VT (+ *person, idea*) 反对 fǎnduì ▸ **to be opposed to sth** 反对某事 fǎnduì mǒushì

opposite [ɒpəzɪt] I ADJ 1 (+ *side, house*) 对面的 duìmiàn de 2 (+ *end, corner*) 最远的 zuìyuǎn de 3 (+ *meaning, direction*) 相反的 xiāngfǎn de II ADV (*live, work, sit*) 在对面 zài duìmiàn III PREP 在…的对面 zài...de duìmiàn IV N ▸ **the opposite** 对立面 duìlìmiàn ▸ **the opposite sex** 异性 yìxìng

opposition [ɒpəzɪʃən] N [U] 反对 fǎnduì

optimistic [ɒptɪmɪstɪk] ADJ 乐观的 lèguān de

option [ɒpʃən] N [c] (*choice*) 选择 xuǎnzé [种 zhǒng]

optometrist [ɒptɒmətrɪst] N [c] 1 眼镜商 yǎnjìngshāng [个 gè] 2 (*also*: **optometrist's**) 眼镜店 yǎnjìngdiàn [家 jiā]

or [ər, STRONG ɔr] CONJ 1 还是 háishì 2 (*also*: **or else**) 否则 fǒuzé

oral [ɔrəl] I ADJ (+ *test, report*) 口头的 kǒutóu de II N [c] 口试 kǒushì [次 cì]

orange [ɔrɪndʒ] I N [c] (*fruit*) 柑橘 gānjú [只 zhī] II ADJ (*in color*) 橙色的 chéngsè de

orange juice N [U] 橘子汁 júzizhī

orchard [ɔrtʃərd] N [c] 果园 guǒyuán [个 gè]

orchestra [ɔrkɪstrə] N [c] 管弦乐队 guǎnxián yuèduì [支 zhī]

order [ɔrdər] I N 1 [c] (*command*) 命令 mìnglìng [个 gè] 2 [c] (*Comm: in restaurant*) 点菜 diǎncài [份 fèn] 3 [U] (*sequence*) 次序 cìxù II VT 1 (*command*) 命令 mìnglìng 2 (*Comm: from store, company*) 定购 dìnggòu; (*in restaurant*) 点菜 diǎncài III VI (*in restaurant*) 点菜 diǎncài ▸ **in alphabetical/numerical order** 按字母/数字顺序 àn zìmǔ/shùzì shùnxù ▸ **out of order** (*not working*) 已坏停用 yǐhuài tíngyòng ▸ **in order to do sth** 为了做某事 wèile zuò mǒushì ▸ **to order sb to do sth** 命令某人做某事 mìnglìng mǒurén zuò mǒushì

ordinary [ɔrdənɛri] ADJ 普通的 pǔtōng de

organ [ɔrgən] N [c] 1 (*Anat*) 器官 qìguān [个 gè] 2 (*Mus*) 管风琴 guǎnfēngqín [架 jià]

organic [ɔrgænɪk] ADJ 1 (+ *food, farming*) 有机的 yǒujī de 2 (+ *substance*) 有机物的 yǒujīwù de

organization [ɔrgənɪzeɪʃən] N [c] 组织 zǔzhī [个 gè]

organize [ɔrgənaɪz] VT 组织 zǔzhī

original [ərɪdʒɪnəl] ADJ 1 (*first, earliest*) 最初的 zuìchū de 2 (*imaginative*) 独创的 dúchuàng de

originally [ərɪdʒɪnəli] ADV 起初 qǐchū

ornament [ɔrnəmənt] N [c] 装饰物 zhuāngshìwù [件 jiàn]

orphan [ɔrfən] N [c] 孤儿 gū'ér [个 gè]

other [ʌðər] I ADJ 1 (*additional*) 另外的 lìngwài de 2 (*not this one*) 其他的 qítā de 3 ▸ **the other...** (*of two things or people*) 另一… lìngyī... 4 (*apart from oneself*) 其他的 qítā de II PRON 1 (*additional one, different one*) 其他 qítā 2 (*of two things or people*) ▸ **the other** 另一个 lìng yīgè ▸ **the other**

day/week (*inf*: *recently*) 几天/星期前 jǐtiān/xīngqī qián

otherwise [ʌðərwaɪz] ADV **1** (*if not*) 否则 fǒuzé **2** (*apart from that*) 除此以外 chúcǐ yǐwài

ought [ɔt] (*pt* **ought**) AUX VB **1** (*indicating advisability*) ▸ **you ought to see a doctor** 你应该去看医生 nǐ yīnggāi qù kàn yīshēng **2** (*indicating likelihood*) ▸ **he ought to be there now** 他现在应该到那儿了 tā xiànzài yīnggāi dào nàr le

our [aʊər] ADJ 我们的 wǒmen de

ours [aʊərz] PRON 我们的 wǒmen de

ourselves [aʊərsɛlvz] PRON PL 我们自己 wǒmen zìjǐ ▸ **we didn't hurt ourselves** 我们没伤到自己 wǒmen méi shāngdào zìjǐ ▸ **by ourselves** (*unaided*) 我们独力地 wǒmen dúlì de; (*alone*) 我们单独地 wǒmen dāndú de

KEYWORD

out [aʊt] **I** ADV **1** (*outside*) 在外面 zài wàimiàn ▸ **out here/there** 这儿/那儿 zhè'r/nà'r
2 (*absent, not in*) 不在 bù zài ▸ **Mr Green is out at the moment** 格林先生这会儿不在 Gélín xiānshēng zhèhuìr bùzài ▸ **to have a day/night out** 外出玩一天/一晚 wàichū wán yītiān/yīwǎn
3 (*Sport*) ▸ **the ball was out** 球出界了 qiú chūjiè le
II ADJ ▸ **to be out** (*out of game*) 出局的 chūjú de; (*extinguished*) (*fire, light, gas*) 熄灭的 xīmiè de
III ▸ **out of** PREP **1** (*outside*: *with movement*) 出 chū; (*beyond*) 朝…外 cháo...wài ▸ **to go/come out of the house** 从房子里走出去/来 cóng fángzi lǐ zǒu chūqù/lái
2 (*from among*) …中的 ...zhōng de ▸ **one out of every three smokers** 每3个烟民中的1个 měi sāngè yānmín zhōng de yīgè
3 (*without*) ▸ **to be out of milk/gas** 牛奶喝完了/汽油用完了 niúnǎi hē wán le/qìyóu yòng wán le

outdoor [aʊtdɔr] ADJ **1** (+ *activity*) 户外的 hùwài de **2** (+ *swimming pool, toilet*) 露天的 lùtiān de

outdoors [aʊtdɔrz] ADV 在户外 zài hùwài

outing [aʊtɪŋ] N [c] 出游 chūyóu [次 cì]

outlet [aʊtlɛt, -lɪt] N [c] **1** (*hole, pipe*) 排放口 páifàngkǒu [个 gè] **2** (*Elec*) 电源插座 diànyuán chāzuò [个 gè]

outline [aʊtlaɪn] N [c] **1** (*shape*) 轮廓 lúnkuò [个 gè] **2** (*brief explanation*) 概要 gàiyào [篇 piān]

outside [aʊtsaɪd] **I** N [c] (*of container*) 外面 wàimiàn [个 gè]; (*of building*) 外表 wàibiǎo [个 gè] **II** ADJ (*exterior*) 外部的 wàibù de **III** ADV **1** (*be, wait*) 在外面 zài wàimiàn **2** (*go*) 向外面 xiàng wàimiàn **IV** PREP **1** (+ *place*) 在…外 zài...wài; (+ *organization*) 在…以外 zài...yǐwài **2** (+ *larger place*) 在…附近 zài...fùjìn

outskirts [aʊtskɜrts] N PL ▸ **the outskirts** 郊区 jiāoqū ▸ **on the outskirts of...** 在…的郊区 zài...de jiāoqū

outstanding [aʊtstændɪŋ] ADJ 杰出的 jiéchū de

oval [oʊvəl] ADJ 椭圆形的 tuǒyuánxíng de

oven [ʌvən] N [c] 烤箱 kǎoxiāng [个 gè]

KEYWORD

over [oʊvər] **I** ADJ (*finished*) 结束的 jiéshù de
II PREP **1** (*more than*) 超过 chāoguò ▸ **over 200 people came** 超过二百人来了 chāoguò èrbǎirén láile
2 (*above, on top of*) 在…上 zài...shang; (*spanning*) 横跨 héngkuà; (*across*) 穿过 chuānguò; (*on the other side of*) 在…对面 zài...duìmiàn ▸ **a bridge**

over the river 横跨河流的一座桥 héngkuà héliú de yīzuò qiáo
3 (*during*) 在…期间 zài...qījiān ▶ **we talked about it over dinner** 我们边吃晚饭边讨论 wǒmen biān chī wǎnfàn biān tǎolùn
4 (+ *illness, shock, trauma*) 康复 kāngfù
5 ▶ **all over the town/house/floor** 全镇/满屋子/满地 quánzhèn/mǎn wūzi/mǎndì
III ADV **1** (*walk, jump, fly etc*) 过 guò ▶ **over here/there** 在这里/那里 zài zhèlǐ/nàlǐ
2 (*more, above*) 超过 chāoguò ▶ **people aged 65 and over** 65岁及以上年龄的人 liùshíwǔ suì jí yǐshàng niánlíng de rén
3 (*again*) 再 zài
4 ▶ **all over** (*everywhere*) 到处 dàochù

overcast [oʊvərkæst] ADJ 多云的 duōyún de
overdose [oʊvərdoʊs] N [C] 过量用药 guòliàng yòngyào [剂 jì]
overseas [oʊvərsiz] ADV 向海外 xiàng hǎiwài
overtake [oʊvərteɪk] (*pt* **overtook**, *pp* **overtaken**) **I** VT (*Aut*) 超过 chāoguò **II** VI (*Aut*) 超车 chāochē
overtaken [oʊvərteɪkᵊn] PP *of* **overtake**
overtime [oʊvərtaɪm] N [U] 加班时间 jiābān shíjiān
overtook [oʊvərtʊk] PT *of* **overtake**
overweight [oʊvərweɪt] ADJ 超重的 chāozhòng de
owe [oʊ] VT (+ *money*) 欠 qiàn ▶ **to owe sb sth** 欠某人某物 qiàn mǒurén mǒuwù
owl [aʊl] N [C] 猫头鹰 māotóuyīng [只 zhī]
own [oʊn] **I** ADJ 自己的 zìjǐ de **II** VT (+ *house, land, car etc*) 拥有 yōngyǒu ▶ **a room of my own** 我自己的房间 wǒ zìjǐ de fángjiān ▶ **on one's own** (*alone*) 独自地 dúzì de; (*without help*) 独立地 dúlì de; **own up** VI (*confess*) 坦白 tǎnbái
owner [oʊnər] N [C] 物主 wùzhǔ [位 wèi]
oxygen [ɒksɪdʒən] N [U] 氧气 yǎngqì
oyster [ɔɪstər] N [C] 蚝 háo 牡蛎 mǔlì [个 gè]
ozone layer [oʊzoʊn-] N [C] 臭氧层 chòuyǎngcéng [层 céng]

P

Pacific [pəsɪfɪk] N ▶ **the Pacific (Ocean)** 太平洋 Tàipíngyáng
pack [pæk] **I** VT **1** (+ *clothes*) 把…打包 bǎ...dǎbāo **2** (+ *suitcase, bag*) 把…装箱 bǎ...zhuāngxiāng **II** VI 打点行装 dǎdiǎn xíngzhuāng **III** N (*of cards*) 副 fù
package [pækɪdʒ] N [C] **1** 包裹 bāoguǒ [个 gè] **2** (*Comput*) 程序包 chéngxùbāo [个 gè]
packed [pækt] ADJ 拥挤的 yōngjǐ de
pad [pæd] N [C] 便笺簿 biànjiānbù [个 gè]
paddle [pædᵊl] N [C] **1** (*for canoe*) 短桨 duǎnjiǎng [个 gè] **2** (*for table tennis*) 球拍 qiúpāi [只 zhī]
padlock [pædlɒk] N [C] 挂锁 guàsuǒ [个 gè]
page [peɪdʒ] N [C] 页 yè
pain [peɪn] N [C/U] 疼痛 téngtòng [阵 zhèn] ▶ **to have a pain in one's chest/arm** 胸痛/胳膊疼 xiōngtòng/gēbo téng ▶ **to be in pain** 在苦恼中 zài kǔnǎo zhōng
painful [peɪnfəl] ADJ (+ *back, joint, swelling*) 疼痛的 téngtòng de
painkiller [peɪnkɪlər] N [C] 止痛药 zhǐtòngyào [片 piàn]
paint [peɪnt] **I** N [C/U] **1** (*decorator's*) 油漆 yóuqī [桶 tǒng] **2** (*artist's*) 颜料 yánliào [罐 guàn] **II** VT **1** (+ *wall, door, house*) 油漆 yóuqī **2** (+ *person, object*) 描绘 miáohuì **3** (+ *picture, portrait*) 用颜料画 yòng yánliào huà **III** VI (*creatively*) 绘画 huìhuà ▶ **a can of paint** 一罐颜料 yīguàn yánliào ▶ **to paint sth blue/white** *etc* 把某物涂成蓝色/白色{等} bǎ mǒuwù túchéng lánsè/báisè {děng}
paintbrush [peɪntbrʌʃ] N [C] **1** (*decorator's*) 漆刷 qīshuā [个 gè] **2** (*artist's*) 画笔 huàbǐ [支 zhī]
painter [peɪntər] N [C] **1** (*artist*) 画家 huàjiā [位 wèi] **2** (*decorator*) 油漆工 yóuqīgōng [个 gè]
painting [peɪntɪŋ] N **1** [U] (*artistic*) 绘画 huìhuà; (*decorating walls, doors etc*) 上油漆 shàng yóuqī **2** [C] (*picture*) 画 huà [幅 fú]
pair [pɛər] N [C] **1** (*of shoes, gloves, socks*) 双 shuāng **2** (*two people*) 对 duì ▶ **a pair of scissors** 一把剪刀 yībǎ jiǎndāo ▶ **a pair of pants** 一条裤子 yītiáo kùzi
pajamas [pədʒɑməz] N PL 睡衣裤 shuìyīkù ▶ **a pair of pajamas** 一套睡衣裤 yītào shuìyīkù
Pakistan [pækɪstæn] N 巴基斯坦 Bājīsītǎn
Pakistani [pækɪstæni, pɑkɪstɑni] **I** ADJ 巴基斯坦的 Bājīsītǎn de **II** N [C] 巴基斯坦人 Bājīsītǎn rén [个 gè]
palace [pælɪs] N [C] 宫殿 gōngdiàn [座 zuò]
pale [peɪl] ADJ **1** (+ *color*) 淡的 dàn de **2** (+ *skin, complexion*) 白皙的 báixī de **3** (*from sickness, fear*) 苍白的 cāngbái de ▶ **pale blue/pink/green** 淡蓝色/粉红色/绿色 dàn lánsè/fěnhóngsè/lǜsè
Palestine [pælɪstaɪn] N 巴勒斯坦 Bālèsītǎn
Palestinian [pælɪstɪniən] **I** ADJ 巴勒斯坦的 Bālèsītǎn de **II** N [C] 巴勒斯坦人 Bālèsītǎn rén [个 gè]
pan [pæn] N [C] (*also*: **saucepan**) 炖锅 dùnguō [口 kǒu]
pancake [pænkeɪk] N [C] 薄煎饼 báo jiānbing [张 zhāng]
panda [pændə] N [C] 熊猫 xióngmāo [只 zhī]
panic [pænɪk] **I** N [U] 惊恐 jīngkǒng **II** VI 惊慌 jīnghuāng
panties [pæntiz] N PL (*underwear*) 内裤 nèikù
pants [pænts] N PL 裤子 kùzi
pantyhose [pæntihoʊz] N PL 连裤袜 liánkùwà ▶ **a pair of pantyhose** 一条连裤袜 yītiáo liánkùwà
paper [peɪpər] N **1** [U] 纸 zhǐ **2** [C]

(*also*: **newspaper**) 报纸 bàozhǐ [份 fèn] ▸ **a piece of paper** (*odd bit, sheet*) 一张纸 yīzhāng zhǐ
paperback [peɪpərbæk] N [C] 平装书 píngzhuāng shū [本 běn]
paper clip N [C] 回形针 huíxíngzhēn [枚 méi]
parachute [pærəʃut] N [C] 降落伞 jiàngluòsǎn [个 gè]
parade [pəreɪd] N [C] 游行 yóuxíng [次 cì]
paradise [pærədaɪs] N **1** [U] (*Rel*) 天堂 tiāntáng **2** [C/U] (*fig*) 乐园 lèyuán [个 gè]
paragraph [pærəgræf] N [C] 段落 duànluò [个 gè]
parallel [pærəlɛl] ADJ **1** 平行的 píngxíng de **2** (*Comput*) 并行的 bìngxíng de
paramedic [pærəmɛdɪk] N [C] 护理人员 hùlǐ rényuán [位 wèi]
parcel [parsᵊl] N [C] 包裹 bāoguǒ [个 gè]
pardon [pardᵊn] N [C] ▸ **pardon me?** 请问您刚才说什么？ qǐngwèn nín gāngcái shuō shénme?
parent [pɛərənt, pær-] **I** N [C] **1** (*father*) 父亲 fùqīn [位 wèi] **2** (*mother*) 母亲 mǔqīn [位 wèi] **II parents** N PL 父母 fùmǔ
park [park] **I** N [C] 公园 gōngyuán [个 gè] **II** VT 停放 tíngfàng **III** VI 停车 tíngchē
parking [parkɪŋ] N [U] 停车 tíngchē ▸ **"no parking"** "严禁停车" "yánjìn tíngchē"
parking lot N [C] 停车场 tíngchēchǎng [个 gè]
parking meter N [C] 停车计时器 tíngchē jìshíqì [个 gè]
parking ticket N [C] 违章停车罚款单 wéizhāng tíngchē fákuǎndān [张 zhāng]
parrot [pærət] N [C] 鹦鹉 yīngwǔ [只 zhī]
part [part] N **1** [C/U] (*section, division*) 部分 bùfen [个 gè] **2** [C] (*of machine, vehicle*) 部件 bùjiàn [个 gè] ▸ **to take part in** (*participate in*) 参加 cānjiā;
part with VT FUS (+ *possessions*) 放弃 fàngqì; (+ *money, cash*) 花 huā
participate [partɪsɪpeɪt] VI 参与 cānyù ▸ **to participate in sth** (+ *activity, discussion*) 参加某事 cānjiā mǒushì
particular [pərtɪkyələr] ADJ 特定的 tèdìng de
partly [partli] ADV 部分地 bùfen de
partner [partnər] N [C] **1** (*wife, husband, girlfriend, boyfriend*) 伴侣 bànlǚ [个 gè] **2** (*in firm*) 合伙人 héhuǒrén [个 gè] **3** (*Sport*) 搭档 dādàng [个 gè] **4** (*for cards, games*) 对家 duìjiā [个 gè] **5** (*at dance*) 舞伴 wǔbàn [个 gè]
part-time **I** ADJ 兼职的 jiānzhí de **II** ADV (*work, study*) 部分时间地 bùfen shíjiān de
party [parti] N [C] **1** (*Pol*) 党 dǎng [个 gè] **2** (*social event*) 聚会 jùhuì [次 cì] ▸ **birthday party** 生日聚会 shēngrì jùhuì
pass [pæs] **I** VT **1** (*hand*) ▸ **to pass sb sth** (+ *salt, glass, newspaper, tool*) 把某物递给某人 bǎ mǒuwù dìgěi mǒurén **2** (*go past*) 经过 jīngguò **3** (+ *exam, test*) 通过 tōngguò **II** VI **1** (*go past*) 经过 jīngguò **2** (*in exam*) 及格 jígé ▸ **to get a pass (in sth)** (*Scol, Univ*) (某考试)达到及格标准 (mǒu kǎoshì) dádào jígé biāozhǔn;
pass away VI (*die*) 去世 qùshì
passage [pæsɪdʒ] N [C] 走廊 zǒuláng [条 tiáo]
passenger [pæsɪndʒər] N [C] 乘客 chéngkè [位 wèi]
passive [pæsɪv] N [U] ▸ **the passive** (*Ling*) 被动语态 bèidòng yǔtài
passport [pæspɔrt] N [C] 护照 hùzhào [本 běn]
password [pæswɜrd] N [C] 密码 mìmǎ [个 gè]
past [pæst] **I** PREP (*in front of, beyond, later than*) 过 guò **II** ADV (*by*) ▸ **to go/walk/drive past** 经/走/开过 jīng/zǒu/kāiguò **III** ADJ (+ *week,*

month, year) 刚过去的 gāng guòqù de **IV** N [c] ▶ **the past** 过去 guòqù [个 gè]; (*tense*) 过去时 guòqùshí ▶ **it's past midnight** 过了午夜 guòle wǔyè ▶ **ten/(a) quarter past eight** 8点10/15分 bādiǎn shí/shíwǔ fēn ▶ **for the past few/3 days** 过去几/3天以来 guòqù jǐ/sāntiān yǐlái ▶ **the past tense** 过去时 guòqù shí ▶ **in the past** (*before now*) 在过去 zài guòqù

pasta [pɑstə] N [U] 意大利面食 Yìdàlì miànshí

pastry [peɪstri] N **1** [U] (*dough*) 油酥面团 yóusū miàntuán **2** [c] (*cake*) 酥皮糕点 sūpí gāodiǎn [块 kuài]

patch [pætʃ] N [c] **1** (*piece of material*) 补丁 bǔding [个 gè] **2** (*area*) 斑片 bānpiàn [块 kuài]

path [pæθ] N [c] (*track*) 小路 xiǎolù [条 tiáo]; (*in garden*) 小径 xiǎojìng [条 tiáo]

pathetic [pəθɛtɪk] ADJ (+ *excuse, effort, attempt*) 不足道的 bùzúdào de

patience [peɪʃᵊns] N [U] 耐心 nàixīn

patient [peɪʃᵊnt] **I** N [c] (*Med*) 病人 bìngrén [个 gè] **II** ADJ (+ *person*) 耐心的 nàixīn de

patrol [pətroʊl] VT 在…巡逻 zài...xúnluó ▶ **to be on patrol** 在巡逻中 zài xúnluó zhōng

pattern [pætərn] N [c] **1** (*on material, carpet*) 花样 huāyàng [种 zhǒng] **2** (*for sewing, knitting*) 样式 yàngshì [个 gè]

pause [pɔz] VI (*when speaking*) 停顿 tíngdùn; (*when doing sth*) 暂停 zàntíng

pay [peɪ] (*pt, pp* **paid**) **I** N [U] 工资 gōngzī **II** VT **1** (+ *debt, bill, tax*) 付 fù **2** (+ *person*) ▶ **to get paid** 发工资 fā gōngzī **3** ▶ **to pay sb sth** (*as wage, salary, for goods, services*) 付给某人某物 fùgěi mǒurén mǒuwù ▶ **how much did you pay for it?** 你买那个花了多少钱? nǐ mǎi nàgè huāle duōshǎo qián?; **pay back** VT **1** (+ *money, loan*) 偿还 chánghuán **2** (+ *person*) (*with money*) 还给 huángěi; **pay for** VT FUS 买 mǎi

payment [peɪmənt] N [c] 付款额 fùkuǎn é [笔 bǐ]

pay phone [peɪfoʊn] N [c] 公用电话 gōngyòng diànhuà [部 bù]

PC [pi si] N ABBR (= **personal computer**) 个人电脑 gèrén diànnǎo

PDA [pi di eɪ] N ABBR (= **personal digital assistant**) 掌上电脑 zhǎngshàng diànnǎo

PE [pi i] (*Scol*) N ABBR (= **physical education**) 体育 tǐyù

pea [pi] N [c] 豌豆 wāndòu [粒 lì]

peace [pis] N [U] **1** (*not war*) 和平 hépíng **2** (*of place, surroundings*) 宁静 níngjìng

peaceful [pisfəl] ADJ 安静的 ānjìng de

peach [pitʃ] N [c] 桃 táo [个 gè]

peak [pik] **I** N [c] 山顶 shāndǐng [个 gè] **II** ADJ (+ *level, times*) 高峰的 gāofēng de

peanut [pinʌt, -nət] N [c] 花生 huāshēng [粒 lì]

pear [pɛər] N [c] 梨 lí [个 gè]

pearl [pɜrl] N [c] 珍珠 zhēnzhū [颗 kē]

pebble [pɛbᵊl] N [c] 卵石 luǎnshí [块 kuài]

peculiar [pɪkyulyər] ADJ 奇怪的 qíguài de

pedal [pɛdᵊl] N [c] **1** (*on bicycle*) 脚蹬子 jiǎodēngzi [个 gè] **2** (*in car, on piano*) 踏板 tàbǎn [个 gè]

pedestrian [pɪdɛstriən] N [c] 行人 xíngrén [个 gè]

pedophile [pidəfaɪl] N [c] 恋童癖者 liàntóngpǐzhě [个 gè]

pee [pi] (*inf*) VI 撒尿 sāniào

peel [pil] **I** N [U] 皮 pí **II** VT (+ *vegetables, fruit*) 削 xiāo

peg [pɛg] N [c] (*for coat, hat, bag*) 挂钉 guàdīng [枚 méi]

pen [pɛn] N [c] 笔 bǐ [支 zhī]; (*also*: **fountain pen**) 自来水笔 zìláishuǐbǐ [支 zhī]; (*also*: **ballpoint pen**) 圆珠笔 yuánzhūbǐ [支 zhī]

penalty [pɛn°lti] N [C] **1** 处罚 chǔfá [次 cì] **2** (*Soccer*) 罚球 fáqiú [个 gè]

pencil [pɛns°l] N [C] 铅笔 qiānbǐ [支 zhī]

pencil sharpener [-ʃɑrpnər] N [C] 铅笔刀 qiānbǐdāo [把 bǎ]

penguin [pɛŋgwɪn] N [C] 企鹅 qǐ'é: [只 zhī]

penicillin [pɛnɪsɪlɪn] N [U] 青霉素 qīngméisù

penknife [pɛnnaɪf] (*pl* **penknives**) N [C] 小刀 xiǎodāo [把 bǎ]

penny [pɛni] (*pl* **pennies**) N [C] 便士 biànshì [枚 méi]

pension [pɛnʃ°n] N [C] (*from state*) 养老金 yǎnglǎojīn [份 fèn]; (*from employer*) 退休金 tuìxiūjīn [份 fèn]

people [pipəl] N PL **1** 人 rén **2** (*generalizing*) 人们 rénmen ▶ **old people** 老人 lǎorén ▶ **many people** 许多人 xǔduō rén ▶ **people say that...** 有人说… yǒurén shuō...

pepper [pɛpər] N **1** [U] (*spice*) 胡椒粉 hújiāofěn **2** [C] (*vegetable*) 胡椒 hújiāo [个 gè]

peppermint [pɛpərmɪnt] N [C] 薄荷糖 bòhe táng [块 kuài]

per [pər, STRONG pɜr] PREP 每 měi ▶ **per day** 每天 měitiān ▶ **per person** 每人 měirén ▶ **per annum** 每年 měinián

percent [pərsɛnt] (*pl* **percent**) N [C] 百分之… bǎifēnzhī... ▶ **by 15 percent** 以百分之15 yǐ bǎifēnzhī shíwǔ

perfect [*adj* pɜrfɪkt, *vb* pərfɛkt] **I** ADJ **1** (+ *weather, behavior*) 完美的 wánměi de; (+ *sauce, skin, teeth*) 无瑕的 wúxiá de **2** (+ *crime, solution, example*) 理想的 lǐxiǎng de **II** N ▶ **the perfect (tense)** 完成(时) wánchéng(shí)

perfectly [pɜrfɪktli] ADV **1** 非常好地 fēicháng hǎo de **2** (*honest, reasonable, clear*) 绝对地 juéduì de

perform [pərfɔrm] **I** VT 表演 biǎoyǎn **II** VI (*function*) (*actor, musician, singer, dancer*) 演出 yǎnchū

performance [pərfɔrməns] N **1** [C] (*Theat*: *by actor, musician, singer, dancer*) 表演 biǎoyǎn [次 cì]; (*of play, show*) 演出 yǎnchū [场 chǎng] **2** [U] (*of employee, surgeon, athlete, team*) 表现 biǎoxiàn

perfume [pɜrfyum, pərfyum] N **1** [C/U] 香水 xiāngshuǐ [瓶 píng] **2** [C] (*smell*) 芳香 fāngxiāng [种 zhǒng]

perhaps [pərhæps, præps] ADV 可能 kěnéng ▶ **perhaps not** 未必 wèibì

period [pɪəriəd] N [C] **1** (*interval, stretch*) 周期 zhōuqī [个 gè] **2** (*time*) 时期 shíqī [段 duàn] **3** (*era*) 时代 shídài [个 gè] **4** (*punctuation mark*) 句号 jùhào [个 gè] **5** (*also*: **menstrual period**) 月经期 yuèjīngqī [个 gè] ▶ **to have one's period** 来例假 lái lìjià

permanent [pɜrmənənt] ADJ 持久的 chíjiǔ de; (+ *damage*) 永久的 yǒngjiǔ de; (+ *state, job, position*) 长期的 chángqī de

permission [pərmɪʃ°n] N [U] **1** (*consent*) 准许 zhǔnxǔ **2** (*official authorization*) 批准 pīzhǔn

permit [pɜrmɪt] N [C] (*authorization*) 许可证 xǔkězhèng [个 gè]

persecute [pɜrsɪkyut] VT 迫害 pòhài

person [pɜrs°n] (*pl gen* **people**) N [C] 人 rén [个 gè] ▶ **in person** 亲自 qīnzì ▶ **first/second/third person** 第一/二/三人称 dìyī/èr/sān rénchēng

personal [pɜrsən°l] ADJ **1** (+ *telephone number, bodyguard*) 私人的 sīrén de; (+ *opinion, habits*) 个人的 gèrén de; (+ *care, contact, appearance, appeal*) 亲自的 qīnzì de **2** (+ *life, matter, relationship*) 私人的 sīrén de

personality [pɜrsənælɪti] N [C/U] 个性 gèxìng [种 zhǒng]

personally [pɜrsənəli] ADV 就我个人来说 jiù wǒ gèrén láishuō

perspiration [pɜrspɪreɪʃ°n] N [U] 汗 hàn

persuade [pərsweɪd] VT ▶ **to persuade sb to do sth** 劝说某人做某事 quànshuō mǒurén zuò mǒushì

pessimistic [pɛsɪmɪstɪk] ADJ 悲观的

bēiguān de

pest [pɛst] N [c] (*insect*) 害虫 hàichóng [只 zhī]

pester [pɛstər] VT 烦扰 fánrǎo

pet [pɛt] N [c] 宠物 chǒngwù [只 zhī]

pharmacy [fɑrməsi] N **1** [c] (*shop*) 药店 yàodiàn [家 jiā] **2** [U] (*science*) 药学 yàoxué

philosophy [fɪlɒsəfi] N [U] (*subject*) 哲学 zhéxué

phone [foʊn] **I** N [c] 电话 diànhuà [部 bù] **II** VT 打电话给 dǎ diànhuà gěi **III** VI 打电话 dǎ diànhuà ▸ **to be on the phone** (*be calling*) 在通话 zài tōnghuà ▸ **by phone** 通过电话 tōngguò diànhuà

phone bill N [c] 话费单 huàfèi dān [张 zhāng]

phone book N [c] 电话簿 diànhuà bù [本 běn]

phone call N [c] 电话 diànhuà [部 bù] ▸ **to make a phone call** 打电话 dǎ diànhuà

phone card [foʊnkard] N [c] (*o.f.*) 电话卡 diànhuà kǎ [张 zhāng]

phone number N [c] 电话号码 diànhuà hàomǎ [个 gè]

photo [foʊtoʊ] N [c] 照片 zhàopiàn [张 zhāng] ▸ **to take a photo (of sb/sth)** 给(某人/某物)拍照片 gěi (mǒurén/mǒuwù) pāi zhàopiàn

photocopier [foʊtəkɒpiər] N [c] 影印机 yǐngyìnjī [台 tái]

photocopy [foʊtəkɒpi] **I** N [c] 影印本 yǐngyìnběn [个 gè] **II** VT (+ *document, picture*) 影印 yǐngyìn

photograph [foʊtəgræf] N [c] 照片 zhàopiàn [张 zhāng]

photographer [fətɒgrəfər] N [c] 摄影师 shèyǐngshī [位 wèi]

photography [fətɒgrəfi] N [U] 摄影 shèyǐng

phrase [freɪz] N [c] **1** (*expression*) 习语 xíyǔ [个 gè] **2** (*in phrase book, dictionary*) 短语 duǎnyǔ [个 gè]

phrase book N [c] 常用词手册 chángyòngcí shǒucè [本 běn]

physical [fɪzɪkᵊl] ADJ 生理的 shēnglǐ de

physical therapist [-θɛrəpɪst] N [c] 理疗师 lǐliáoshī [位 wèi]

physical therapy [-θɛrəpi] N [U] 物理疗法 wùlǐ liáofǎ

physician [fɪzɪʃᵊn] N [c] 医生 yīshēng [位 wèi]

physicist [fɪzɪsɪst] N [c] 物理学家 wùlǐxué jiā [位 wèi]

physics [fɪzɪks] N [U] 物理学 wùlǐxué

pianist [piænɪst, piənɪst] N [c] (*professional*) 钢琴家 gāngqínjiā [位 wèi]; (*amateur*) 钢琴演奏者 gāngqín yǎnzòuzhě [位 wèi]

piano [piænoʊ, pyænoʊ] N [c] 钢琴 gāngqín [架 jià]

pick [pɪk] **I** VT **1** (*choose*) 选择 xuǎnzé **2** (+ *fruit, flowers*) 采摘 cǎizhāi **II** N ▸ **take your pick** 随意挑选 suíyì tiāoxuǎn; **pick out** VT (*select*) (+ *person, thing*) 挑中 tiāozhòng; **pick up** VT **1** (+ *object*) (*take hold of*) 拿起 náqǐ; (*from floor, ground*) 捡起 jiǎnqǐ **2** (*collect*) (+ *person, parcel*) 接 jiē

pickpocket [pɪkpɒkɪt] N [c] 扒手 páshǒu [个 gè]

picnic [pɪknɪk] N [c] (*meal*) 野餐 yěcān [顿 dùn]

picture [pɪktʃər] N [c] **1** (*painting, drawing, print*) 画 huà [幅 fú] **2** (*photograph*) 照片 zhàopiàn [张 zhāng] **3** (*film, movie*) 电影 diànyǐng [部 bù]

picture messaging [pɪktʃər mɛsɪdʒɪŋ] N [U] 彩信 cǎixìn

piece [pis] N [c] **1** (*fragment*) 块 kuài **2** (*of string, ribbon, sticky tape*) 段 duàn **3** (*of cake, bread, chocolate*) 块 kuài ▸ **a piece of paper** 一张纸 yīzhāng zhǐ

pierced [pɪərst] ADJ (+ *ears, nose, lip*) 穿孔的 chuānkǒng de

piercing [pɪərsɪŋ] N [c] 人体穿孔 réntǐ chuānkǒng [个 gè]

pig [pɪg] N [C] 猪 zhū [头 tóu]
pigeon [pɪdʒɪn] N [C] 鸽子 gēzi [只 zhī]
pile [paɪl] **I** N [C] 堆 duī [个 gè] **II** VT 堆起 duīqǐ ▸ **piles of** *or* **a pile of sth** (*inf*) 一大堆某物 yīdàduī mǒuwù
pill [pɪl] N [C] 药丸 yàowán [粒 lì] ▸ **the pill** (*contraceptive pill*) 避孕药 bìyùnyào ▸ **to be on the pill** 服避孕药 fú bìyùnyào
pillow [pɪloʊ] N [C] 枕头 zhěntou [个 gè]
pilot [paɪlət] N [C] 飞行员 fēixíngyuán [个 gè]
PIN [pɪn] N ABBR (= **personal identification number**) 密码 mìmǎ
pin [pɪn] **I** N [C] **1** (*used in sewing*) 大头针 dàtóuzhēn [枚 méi] **2** (*badge*) 饰针 shìzhēn [枚 méi] **II** VT (*on wall, door, board*) 钉住 dìngzhù ▸ **pins and needles** 发麻 fāmá
pinch [pɪntʃ] VT (+ *person*) 捏 niē
pine [paɪn] N **1** [C] (*also*: **pine tree**) 松树 sōngshù [棵 kē] **2** [U] (*wood*) 松木 sōngmù
pineapple [paɪnæpᵊl] N [C] 凤梨 fènglí 菠萝 bōluó [个 gè]
pink [pɪŋk] **I** ADJ 粉红色的 fěnhóngsè de **II** N [C/U] 粉红色 fěnhóngsè [种 zhǒng]
pint [paɪnt] N [C] (*measure*: *473 cc*) 品脱 pǐntuō
pipe [paɪp] N [C] **1** (*for water, gas*) 管子 guǎnzi [根 gēn] **2** (*for smoking*) 烟斗 yāndǒu [个 gè]
pirate [paɪrɪt] N [C] 海盗 hǎidào [个 gè]
pirated (*Comm*) ADJ 盗版的 dàobǎn de
Pisces [paɪsiz] N [U] (*sign*) 双鱼座 Shuāngyú Zuò
pity [pɪti] **I** N **1** [U] (*compassion*) 同情 tóngqíng **2** (*misfortune*) ▸ **it is a pity that...** 真遗憾··· zhēn yíhàn... **II** VT (+ *person*) 同情 tóngqíng ▸ **what a pity!** 真可惜！zhēn kěxī!
pizza [pitsə] N [C] 比萨饼 bǐsàbǐng [个 gè]
place [pleɪs] **I** N **1** [C] (*location*) 地方 dìfang [个 gè] **2** [C] (*space*) 空位 kòngwèi [个 gè]; (*seat*) 座位 zuòwèi [个 gè]; (*at college, on course, on committee, in team*) 名额 míng'é [个 gè] **3** [C] (*in competition*) 名次 míngcì [个 gè] **4** (*inf*) ▸ **some/every/no/any place** 某些/每个/没有/任何地方 mǒuxiē/měigè/méiyǒu/rènhé dìfang **II** VT (*put*) 放 fàng; (*classify*) ▸ **in places** 有几处 yǒu jǐchù ▸ **at sb's place** (*home*) 在某人的家里 zài mǒurén de jiālǐ ▸ **to take sb's/sth's place** 代替某人/某物 dàitì mǒurén/mǒuwù ▸ **to take place** (*happen*) 发生 fāshēng
plain [pleɪn] **I** ADJ (*not patterned*) 无图案花纹的 wú tú'àn huāwén de **II** N [C] (*area of land*) 平原 píngyuán [个 gè]
plan [plæn] **I** N [C] **1** (*scheme, project*) 计划 jìhuà [个 gè] **2** (*drawing*) 详图 xiángtú [张 zhāng] **II** VT 计划 jìhuà **III** VI (*think ahead*) 打算 dǎsuàn **IV plans** N PL (*intentions*) 计划 jìhuà ▸ **to plan to do sth** 计划做某事 jìhuà zuò mǒushì
plane [pleɪn] N [C] 飞机 fēijī [架 jià]
planet [plænɪt] N [C] 行星 xíngxīng [个 gè]
plant [plænt] **I** N **1** [C] 植物 zhíwù [株 zhū] **2** [C] (*factory, power station*) 工厂 gōngchǎng [个 gè] **II** VT 栽种 zāizhòng
plaster [plæstər] N [U] 灰泥 huīní
plastic [plæstɪk] **I** N [C/U] 塑料 sùliào [种 zhǒng] **II** ADJ (+ *bucket, chair, cup*) 塑料的 sùliào de
plastic wrap N [U] 保鲜膜 bǎoxiān mó
plate [pleɪt] N [C] 碟 dié [个 gè]
platform [plætfɔrm] N [C] **1** (*stage*) 平台 píngtái [个 gè] **2** (*Rail*) 站台 zhàntái [个 gè] ▸ **the train leaves from platform 7** 火车从7号站台出发 huǒchē cóng qīhào zhàntái chūfā
play [pleɪ] **I** N [C] 戏剧 xìjù [出 chū]

II VT **1** (+ *game, chess*) 玩 wán; (+ *football*) 踢 tī; (+ *baseball, tennis*) 打 dǎ **2** (+ *team, opponent*) 同…比赛 tóng...bǐsài **3** (+ *part, role, character*) 扮演 bànyǎn **4** (+ *instrument, piece of music*) 演奏 yǎnzòu **5** (+ *CD, record, tape*) 播放 bōfàng **III** VI **1** (*children*) 玩耍 wánshuǎ **2** (*orchestra, band*) 演奏 yǎnzòu ▶ **to play cards** 玩纸牌 wán zhǐpái; **play back** VT 回放 huífàng

player [pleɪər] N [C] **1** (*Sport*) 选手 xuǎnshǒu [名 míng] **2** (*Mus*) ▶ **a trumpet/flute/piano player** 小号/长笛/钢琴演奏者 xiǎohào/chángdí/gāngqín yǎnzòuzhě [位 wèi]

playground [pleɪgraʊnd] N [C] (*at school*) 运动场 yùndòng chǎng [个 gè]; (*in park*) 游戏场 yóuxì chǎng [个 gè]

playing card [pleɪɪŋ kard] N [C] 纸牌 zhǐpái [张 zhāng]

pleasant [plɛzᵊnt] ADJ **1** (*agreeable*) 令人愉快的 lìngrén yúkuài de **2** (*friendly*) 友善的 yǒushàn de

please [pliz] **I** INT 请 qǐng **II** VT (*satisfy*) 使高兴 shǐ gāoxìng ▶ **yes, please** 好的 hǎode

pleased [plizd] ADJ 开心的 kāixīn de ▶ **pleased to meet you** 见到你很高兴 jiàndào nǐ hěn gāoxìng ▶ **pleased with sth** 对某事满意 duì mǒushì mǎnyì

pleasure [plɛʒər] N **1** [U] (*happiness, satisfaction*) 高兴 gāoxìng **2** [U] (*fun*) 享乐 xiǎnglè ▶ **"it's a pleasure", "my pleasure"** "乐意效劳" "lèyì xiàoláo"

plenty [plɛnti] PRON **1** (*lots*) 大量 dàliàng **2** (*sufficient*) 充足 chōngzú ▶ **plenty of** (+ *food, money, time*) 很多 hěnduō; (+ *jobs, people, houses*) 许多 xǔduō

plot [plɒt] **I** N **1** [C] (*secret plan*) ▶ **a plot (to do sth)** (做某事的)阴谋 (zuò mǒushì de) yīnmóu [个 gè] **2** [C/U] (*of story, play, film*) 情节 qíngjié [个 gè] **II** VI (*conspire*) 密谋 mìmóu ▶ **to plot to do sth** 密谋做某事 mìmóu zuò mǒushì

plug [plʌg] N [C] **1** (*Elec: on appliance*) 插头 chātóu [个 gè]; (*socket*) 插座 chāzuò [个 gè] **2** (*in sink, bath*) 塞子 sāizi [个 gè]; **plug in** (*Elec*) VT 插上…的插头 chāshang...de chātóu

plum [plʌm] N [C] (*fruit*) 梅子 méizi [颗 kē]

plumber [plʌmər] N [C] 管子工 guǎnzi gōng [位 wèi]

plural [plʊərəl] **I** ADJ 复数的 fùshù de **II** N [C] 复数 fùshù [个 gè]

plus [plʌs] **I** CONJ **1** (*added to*) 加 jiā **2** (*as well as*) 和 hé **II** ADV (*additionally*) 此外 cǐwài **III** N [C] (*inf*) ▶ **it's a plus** 这是个附加的好处 zhè shì gè fùjiā de hǎochù [个 gè] ▶ **B plus** (*Scol*) B加 bìjiā

p.m. [pi ɛm] ADV ABBR (= **post meridiem**) 下午 xiàwǔ

pneumonia [nʊmoʊnyə, -moʊniə] N [U] 肺炎 fèiyán

pocket [pɒkɪt] N [C] 口袋 kǒudài [个 gè]

pocketbook [pɒkitbʊk] N [C] (*purse*) 手提包 shǒutíbāo [个 gè]

poet [poʊɪt] N [C] 诗人 shīrén [位 wèi]

poetry [poʊɪtri] N [U] **1** (*poems*) 诗 shī **2** (*form of literature*) 诗歌 shīgē

point [pɔɪnt] **I** N **1** [C] (*in report, lecture, interview*) 论点 lùndiǎn [个 gè] **2** [S] (*significant part: of argument, discussion*) 要害 yàohài **3** [S] (*purpose: of action*) 目的 mùdì **4** [C] (*place*) 位置 wèizhi [个 gè] **5** [S] (*moment*) 时刻 shíkè **6** [C] (*sharp end*) 尖端 jiānduān [个 gè] **7** [C] (*in score, competition, game, sport*) 分 fēn **8** [C] (*also*: **decimal point**) 小数点 xiǎoshùdiǎn [个 gè] **II** VI (*with finger, stick*) 指出 zhǐchū **III** VT ▶ **to point sth at sb** 把某物瞄准某人 bǎ mǒuwù miáozhǔn mǒurén ▶ **there's no point (in doing that)** (那样做)毫无意义 (nàyàng zuò) háowú yìyì ▶ **two point five** (*2.5*) 二点五 èrdiǎnwǔ ▶ **to point at sth/sb** (*with finger, stick*) 指着某物/某人 zhǐzhe mǒuwù/mǒurén; **point out** VT 指出 zhǐchū ▶ **to point out that...** 指出… zhǐchū...

pointless [pɔɪntlɪs] ADJ 无意义的 wú yìyì de

poison [pɔɪzᵊn] I N [C/U] 毒药 dúyào [种 zhǒng] II VT 下毒 xiàdú

poisonous [pɔɪzᵊnəs] ADJ (*lit*) (+ *animal, plant, fumes, chemicals*) 有毒的 yǒudú de

poker [poʊkər] N [U] 扑克牌 pūkèpái

Poland [poʊlənd] N 波兰 Bōlán

polar bear [poʊlər-] N [C] 北极熊 běijíxióng [头 tóu]

Pole [poʊl] N [C] 波兰人 Bōlánrén [个 gè]

pole [poʊl] N [C] 1 (*stick*) 杆 gān [根 gēn] 2 (*Geo*) 地极 dìjí [个 gè]

police [pəlis] N PL 1 (*organization*) 警方 jǐngfāng 2 (*members*) 警察 jǐngchá

policeman [pəlismən] (*pl* **policemen**) N [C] 男警察 nán jǐngchá [个 gè]

police officer N [C] 警察 jǐng chá [名 míng]

police station N [C] 警察局 jǐngchá jú [个 gè]

policewoman [pəliswʊmən] (*pl* **policewomen**) N [C] 女警察 nǚ jǐngchá [个 gè]

Polish [poʊlɪʃ] I ADJ 波兰的 Bōlán de II N [U] (*language*) 波兰语 Bōlányǔ

polish [pɒlɪʃ] I N [C/U] 上光剂 shàngguāng jì [盒 hé] II VT (+ *shoes*) 擦亮 cāliàng; (+ *furniture, floor*) 上光 shàngguāng

polite [pəlaɪt] ADJ 有礼貌的 yǒu lǐmào de

political [pəlɪtɪkᵊl] ADJ 政治的 zhèngzhì de

politician [pɒlɪtɪʃᵊn] N [C] 政治家 zhèngzhì jiā [位 wèi]

politics [pɒlɪtɪks] N [U] 1 (*activity*) 政治 zhèngzhì 2 (*subject*) 政治学 zhèngzhì xué

pollute [pəlut] VT 污染 wūrǎn

polluted [pəlutɪd] ADJ 被污染的 bèi wūrǎn de

pollution [pəluʃᵊn] N [U] 1 (*process*) 污染 wūrǎn 2 (*substances*) 污染物 wūrǎn wù

pond [pɒnd] N [C] 池塘 chítáng [个 gè]

pony [poʊni] N [C] 小马 xiǎomǎ [匹 pǐ]

ponytail [poʊniteɪl] N [C] 马尾辫 mǎwěibiàn [条 tiáo]

pool [pul] N 1 [C] (*pond*) 水塘 shuǐtáng [个 gè] 2 [C] (*also*: **swimming pool**) 游泳池 yóuyǒngchí [个 gè] 3 [U] (*game*) 美式台球 měishì táiqiú

poor [pʊər] I ADJ 1 (+ *person*) 贫穷的 pínqióng de; (+ *country, area*) 贫困的 pínkùn de 2 (*bad*) (+ *quality, performance*) 低水平的 dī shuǐpíng de; (+ *wages, conditions, results, attendance*) 差的 chà de II N PL ▶ **the poor** 穷人 qióngrén ▶ **poor (old) Bill** 可怜的(老)比尔 kělián de (lǎo) Bǐ'ěr

pop [pɒp] N 1 [U] (*Mus*) 流行音乐 liúxíng yīnyuè 2 [C] (*inf*: *father*) 爸爸 bàba [个 gè]

popcorn [pɒpkɔrn] N [U] 爆米花 bàomǐhuā

pope [poʊp] N [C] 教皇 jiàohuáng [位 wèi]

popular [pɒpyələr] ADJ 1 (+ *person, place, thing*) 流行的 liúxíng de 2 (+ *name, activity*) 时髦的 shímáo de

population [pɒpyəleɪʃᵊn] N [C] 人口 rénkǒu [个 gè]

pork [pɔrk] N [U] 猪肉 zhūròu

port [pɔrt] N 1 [C] (*harbor*) 港口 gǎngkǒu [个 gè] 2 [C] (*town*) 港市 gǎngshì [座 zuò]

portable [pɔrtəbᵊl] ADJ 便携式的 biànxiéshì de

porter [pɔrtər] N [C] (*on train*) 列车员 lièchēyuán [位 wèi]

portion [pɔrʃᵊn] N [C] 份 fèn

portrait [pɔrtrɪt, -treɪt] N [C] (*picture*)

画像 huàxiàng [幅 fú]
Portugal [pɔrtʃʊgᵊl] N 葡萄牙 Pútáoyá
Portuguese [pɔrtʃʊgiz] (*pl* **Portuguese**) **I** ADJ 葡萄牙的 Pútáoyá de **II** N **1** [C] (*person*) 葡萄牙人 Pútáoyárén [个 gè] **2** [U] (*language*) 葡萄牙语 Pútáoyáyǔ
posh [pɒʃ] (*inf*) ADJ (+ *hotel, restaurant, car*) 豪华的 háohuá de
position [pəzɪʃᵊn] N [C] **1** (*of house, person, thing*) 位置 wèizhi [个 gè] **2** (*posture: of person's body*) 姿势 zīshì [种 zhǒng]
positive [pɒzɪtɪv] ADJ **1** (*good*) 有益的 yǒuyì de **2** (*affirmative*) (+ *test, result*) 阳性的 yángxìng de **3** (*sure*) ▶ **to be positive (about sth)** 确信(某事) quèxìn (mǒushì)
possession [pəzɛʃᵊn] **I** N [U] 拥有 yōngyǒu **II possessions** N PL 财产 cáichǎn
possibility [pɒsɪbɪlɪti] N [C] **1** (*that sth is true*) 可能性 kěnéngxìng [种 zhǒng]; (*of sth happening*) 可能的事 kěnéng de shì [件 jiàn] **2** (*option*) 可选性 kěxuǎnxìng [种 zhǒng]
possible [pɒsɪbᵊl] ADJ (+ *event, reaction, effect, consequence*) 可能的 kěnéng de; (+ *risk, danger*) 潜在的 qiánzài de; (+ *answer, cause, solution*) 可接受的 kě jiēshòu de ▶ **it's possible (that...)** 可能(…) kěnéng... ▶ **if possible** 如有可能 rúyǒu kěnéng ▶ **as soon as possible** 尽快 jǐnkuài
possibly [pɒsɪbli] ADV (*perhaps*) 大概 dàgài
post [poʊst] N **1** [C] (*pole*) 柱子 zhùzi [根 gēn] **2** [C] (*job*) 职位 zhíwèi [个 gè]
postcard [poʊstkard] N [C] 明信片 míngxìnpiàn [张 zhāng]
poster [poʊstər] N [C] 海报 hǎibào [张 zhāng]
post office N [C] 邮局 yóujú [个 gè]
postpone [poʊstpoʊn, poʊspoʊn] VT 推迟 tuīchí
pot [pɒt] N **1** [C] (*for cooking*) 锅 guō [口 kǒu] **2** [C] (*also*: **teapot**) 茶壶 cháhú [个 gè] **3** [C] (*also*: **coffeepot**) 咖啡壶 kāfēihú [个 gè] **4** [C] (*for paint, jam, marmalade, honey*) 罐 guàn [个 gè] **5** [C] (*also*: **flowerpot**) 花盆 huāpén [个 gè]
potato [pəteɪtoʊ] (*pl* **potatoes**) N [C/U] 马铃薯 mǎlíngshǔ [个 gè] 土豆 tǔdòu [个 gè]
potato chips N PL 薯片 shǔpiàn
pottery [pɒtəri] N **1** [U] (*work, hobby*) 陶艺 táoyì **2** [C] (*factory, workshop*) 制陶厂 zhìtáo chǎng [家 jiā]
pound [paʊnd] N [C] **1** (*unit of weight*) 磅 bàng **2** (*unit of money*) 镑 bàng ▶ **half a pound (of sth)** 半磅(某物) bànbàng (mǒuwù)
pour [pɔr] VT ▶ **to pour sth (into/onto sth)** 灌某物(到某物里/上) guàn mǒuwù (dào mǒuwù lǐ/shang) ▶ **it is pouring (down) rain** 大雨如注 dàyǔ rúzhù
poverty [pɒvərti] N [U] 贫穷 pínqióng
powder [paʊdər] N [C/U] 粉 fěn [袋 dài]
power [paʊər] N [U] **1** (*over people, activities*) 权力 quánlì **2** (*electricity*) 电力 diànlì
powerful [paʊərfəl] ADJ **1** (*influential*) 有影响力的 yǒu yǐngxiǎnglì de **2** (*physically strong*) 强健的 qiángjiàn de **3** (+ *engine, machine*) 大功率的 dà gōnglǜ de
practical [præktɪkᵊl] ADJ **1** (+ *difficulties, experience*) 实践的 shíjiàn de **2** (+ *ideas, methods, advice, suggestions*) 切合实际的 qièhé shíjì de **3** (+ *person, mind*) 有实际经验的 yǒu shíjì jīngyàn de
practically [præktɪkli] ADV 几乎 jīhū
practice [præktɪs] **I** N **1** [U] (*exercise, training*) 练习 liànxí **2** [C] (*training session*) 实习 shíxí [次 cì] **II** VT 练习 liànxí **III** VI 练习 liànxí ▶ **in practice** (*in reality*) 实际上 shíjì shàng ▶ **2**

hours of piano practice 2小时的练琴时间 èr xiǎoshí de liànqín shíjiān

praise [preɪz] VT 称赞 chēngzàn

pray [preɪ] VI 祷告 dǎogào

prayer [prɛər] (*Rel*) N [c] (*words*) 祈祷文 qídǎowén [篇 piān]

precaution [prɪkɔːʃᵊn] N [c] 预防措施 yùfáng cuòshī [项 xiàng]

precious [prɛʃəs] ADJ (+ *time, resource, memories*) 宝贵的 bǎoguì de; (*financially*) 贵重的 guìzhòng de

precise [prɪsaɪs] ADJ **1** (+ *time, nature, position, circumstances*) 精确的 jīngquè de; (+ *figure, definition*) 准确的 zhǔnquè de; (+ *explanation*) 清晰的 qīngxī de **2** (+ *instructions, plans*) 详尽的 xiángjìn de

precisely [prɪsaɪsli] ADV (*exactly*) 确切地 quèqiè de; (*referring to time*) 正好 zhènghǎo

predict [prɪdɪkt] VT 预言 yùyán

prediction [prɪdɪkʃᵊn] N [c] 预言 yùyán [种 zhǒng]

prefer [prɪfɜr] VT 偏爱 piān'ài ▸ **to prefer coffee to tea** 喜欢咖啡胜于茶 xǐhuān kāfēi shèngyú chá ▸ **I'd prefer to go by train** 我宁愿坐火车去 wǒ nìngyuàn zuò huǒchē qù

pregnant [prɛgnənt] ADJ 怀孕的 huáiyùn de ▸ **3 months pregnant** 怀孕3个月 huáiyùn sāngèyuè

prejudice [prɛdʒədɪs] N [c/u] 偏见 piānjiàn [个 gè]

preparation [prɛpəreɪʃᵊn] **I** N [U] 准备 zhǔnbèi **II preparations** N PL (*arrangements*) ▸ **preparations (for sth)** (为某事的)准备工作 (wèi mǒushì de) zhǔnbèi gōngzuò ▸ **in preparation for sth** 为某事而准备的 wèi mǒushì ér zhǔnbèi de

prepare [prɪpɛər] **I** VT 准备 zhǔnbèi; (+ *food, meal*) 预备 yùbèi **II** VI ▸ **to prepare (for sth)** (为某事)做准备 (wèi mǒushì) zuò zhǔnbèi ▸ **to prepare to do sth** (*get ready*) 准备好做某事 zhǔnbèi hǎo zuò mǒushì

prepared [prɪpɛərd] ADJ ▸ **to be prepared to do sth** (*willing*) 有意做某事 yǒuyì zuò mǒushì ▸ **prepared (for sth)** (*ready*) (对某事)有所准备的 (duì mǒushì) yǒu suǒ zhǔnbèi de

prescribe [prɪskraɪb] VT (*Med*) 开 kāi

prescription [prɪskrɪpʃᵊn] N [c] (*Med: slip of paper*) 处方 chǔfāng [个 gè]; (*medicine*) 药方 yàofāng [个 gè]

present [prɛzᵊnt] **I** ADJ **1** (*current*) 现有的 xiànyǒu de **2** (*in attendance*) 在场的 zàichǎng de **II** N **1** (*not past*) ▸ **the present** 目前 mùqián **2** [c] (*gift*) 礼物 lǐwù [件 jiàn] **3** ▸ **the present** (*also*: **the present tense**) 现在时态 xiànzài shítài [个 gè] ▸ **to be present at sth** 出席某事 chūxí mǒushì ▸ **at present** 现在 xiànzài ▸ **to give sb a present** 给某人礼物 gěi mǒurén lǐwù

president [prɛzɪdənt] N [c] (*Pol*) 总统 zǒngtǒng [位 wèi]

press [prɛs] **I** N ▸ **the press** 新闻界 xīnwén jiè **II** VT **1** (+ *button, switch, bell*) 按 àn **2** (*iron*) 熨平 yùnpíng ▸ **to be pressed for time/money** 时间紧迫/手头紧 shíjiān jǐnpò/shǒutóu jǐn

pressure [prɛʃər] N **1** [U] (*physical force*) 压力 yālì **2** [U] (*coercion*) ▸ **pressure (to do sth)** (做某事的)压力 (zuò mǒushì de) yālì **3** [c/u] (*stress*) 压力 yālì [种 zhǒng] ▸ **to put pressure on sb (to do sth)** 对某人施加压力(去做某事) duì mǒurén shījiā yālì (qù zuò mǒushì)

pretend [prɪtɛnd] VT ▸ **to pretend to do sth/pretend that...** 假装做某事/假装⋯ jiǎzhuāng zuò mǒushì/jiǎzhuāng...

pretty [prɪti] **I** ADJ 漂亮的 piàoliang de **II** ADV (*quite*) (*good, happy, soon etc*) 相当 xiāngdāng

prevent [prɪvɛnt] VT (+ *war, disease, situation*) 阻止 zǔzhǐ; (+ *accident, fire*) 防止 fángzhǐ ▸ **to prevent sb (from) doing sth** 阻止某人做某事 zǔzhǐ mǒurén zuò mǒushì ▸ **to**

prevent sth (from) happening 防止某事发生 fángzhǐ mǒushì fāshēng
previous [priviəs] ADJ **1** (+ *marriage, relationship, experience, owner*) 前的 qián de **2** (+ *chapter, week, day*) 以前的 yǐqián de
previously [priviəsli] ADV **1** 以前 yǐqián **2** ▸ **10 days previously** 10天前 shí tiān qián
price [praɪs] N [C/U] 价格 jiàgé [种 zhǒng]
pride [praɪd] N [U] 自豪 zìháo ▸ **to take (a) pride in sb/sth** 因某人/某事而自豪 yīn mǒurén/mǒushì ér zìháo
priest [prist] N [C] 神职人员 shénzhí rényuán [位 wèi]
primarily [praɪmɛrɪli] ADV 主要地 zhǔyào de
Prime Minister [praɪm mɪnɪstər] N [C] 总理 Zǒnglǐ [位 wèi]
prince [prɪns] N [C] 王子 wángzǐ [位 wèi]
princess [prɪnsɪs, -sɛs] N [C] 公主 gōngzhǔ [位 wèi]
principal [prɪnsɪpᵊl] **I** ADJ 主要的 zhǔyào de **II** N [C] (*of school*) 校长 xiàozhǎng [位 wèi]
principle [prɪnsɪpᵊl] N [C/U] 准则 zhǔnzé [个 gè] ▸ **in principle** (*in theory*) 原则上 yuánzé shàng
print [prɪnt] **I** N [C] (*photograph*) 照片 zhàopiàn [张 zhāng] **II** VT **1** (+ *story, article*) 出版 chūbǎn **2** (*stamp*) 印 yìn **3** (*write*) 用印刷体写 yòng yìnshuātǐ xiě **4** (*Comput*) 打印 dǎyìn; **print out** VT 打印出 dǎyìn chū
printer [prɪntər] N [C] 打印机 dǎyìnjī [台 tái]
printout [prɪntaʊt] N [C] 打印输出 dǎyìn shūchū [次 cì]
priority [praɪɔrɪti] **I** N [C] (*concern*) 重点 zhòngdiǎn [个 gè] **II priorities** N PL 优先考虑的事 yōuxiān kǎolǜ de shì ▸ **to give priority to sth/sb** 给某事/某人以优先权 gěi mǒushì/mǒurén yǐ yōuxiān quán
prison [prɪzᵊn] N **1** [C/U] (*institution*) 监狱 jiānyù [个 gè] **2** [U] (*imprisonment*) 坐牢 zuòláo ▸ **in prison** 坐牢 zuòláo
prisoner [prɪzənər] N [C] 囚犯 qiúfàn [个 gè]
private [praɪvɪt] ADJ **1** (+ *property, land, plane*) 私人的 sīrén de **2** (+ *education, housing, health care, industries*) 私有的 sīyǒu de **3** (*confidential*) 秘密的 mìmì de **4** (+ *life, thoughts, plans, affairs, belongings*) 私人的 sīrén de ▸ **in private** 私下 sīxià
prize [praɪz] N [C] 奖 jiǎng [个 gè]
prizewinner [praɪzwɪnər] N [C] 获奖者 huòjiǎngzhě [位 wèi]
pro [proʊ] PREP (*in favor of*) 赞成 zànchéng
probability [prɒbəbɪlɪti] N [C/U] ▸ **probability (of sth/that...)** (某事/…的)可能性 (mǒushì/...de) kěnéngxìng [种 zhǒng]
probable [prɒbəbᵊl] ADJ 可能的 kěnéng de
probably [prɒbəbli] ADV 可能 kěnéng
problem [prɒbləm] N [C] 难题 nántí [个 gè] ▸ **what's the problem?** 有什么问题吗？ yǒu shénme wèntí ma? ▸ **I had no problem finding her** 我要找她不难 wǒ yào zhǎo tā bùnán ▸ **no problem!** (*inf*) 没问题！ méi wèntí!
process [prɒsɛs] **I** N [C] (*procedure*) 过程 guòchéng [个 gè] **II** VT (*Comput*) (+ *data*) 处理 chǔlǐ ▸ **to be in the process of doing sth** 在从事某事的过程中 zài cóngshì mǒushì de guòchéng zhōng
produce [prədus] VT **1** (+ *effect, result*) 促成 cùchéng **2** (+ *goods, commodity*) 生产 shēngchǎn **3** (+ *play, movie, program*) 上演 shàngyǎn
producer [prədusər] N [C] **1** (*of movie, play, program*) 制片人 zhìpiànrén [位 wèi] **2** (*of food, material: country*) 产地 chǎndì [个 gè]; (*company*) 制造商 zhìzào shāng [个 gè]
product [prɒdʌkt] N [C] 产品 chǎnpǐn [个 gè]

production [prədʌkʃᵊn] N **1** [U] (*process*) 生产 shēngchǎn; (*amount produced, amount grown*) 产量 chǎnliàng **2** [C] (*play, show*) 作品 zuòpǐn [部 bù]

profession [prəfɛʃᵊn] N [C] 职业 zhíyè [种 zhǒng]

professional [prəfɛʃənᵊl] ADJ **1** (+ *photographer, musician, football player*) 职业的 zhíyè de; (+ *advice, help*) 专业的 zhuānyè de **2** (*skillful*) 专业水平的 zhuānyè shuǐpíng de

professor [prəfɛsər] N [C] 教员 jiàoyuán [位 wèi]

profit [prɒfɪt] N [C/U] 利润 lìrùn ▸ **to make a profit** 赚钱 zhuànqián

profitable [prɒfɪtəbᵊl] ADJ 有利润的 yǒu lìrùn de

program [proʊgræm, -grəm] **I** N [C] **1** (*Rad, TV*) 节目 jiémù [个 gè] **2** (*also*: **computer program**) 程序 chéngxù [个 gè] **3** (*for theater, concert*) 节目宣传册 jiémù xuānchuáncè [本 běn] **4** (*of talks, events, performances*) 节目单 jiémù dān [个 gè] **II** VT ▸ **to program sth (to do sth)** (*Comput*) 为某物编程(做某事) wèi mǒuwù biānchéng (zuò mǒushì); (+ *machine, system*) 设定某事(做某事) shèdìng mǒushì (zuò mǒushì)

programmer [proʊgræmər] (*Comput*) N [C] 程序员 chéngxùyuán [位 wèi]

progress [prɒgrɛs] N [U] **1** (*headway*) 进展 jìnzhǎn **2** (*advances*) 进步 jìnbù ▸ **to make progress (with sth)** (对某事)取得进步 (duì mǒushì) qǔdé jìnbù

project [prɒdʒɛkt] N [C] 工程 gōngchéng [个 gè]

promise [prɒmɪs] **I** N [C] 许诺 xǔnuò [个 gè] **II** VI 保证 bǎozhèng **III** VT ▸ **to promise sb sth, promise sth to sb** 保证给某人某物 bǎozhèng gěi mǒurén mǒuwù ▸ **to break/keep a promise (to do sth)** 违背/遵守(做某事的)诺言 wéibèi/zūnshǒu (zuò mǒushì de) nuòyán ▸ **to promise to do sth** 保证做某事 bǎozhèng zuò mǒushì

promotion [prəmoʊʃᵊn] N [C/U] 晋级 jìnjí [次 cì]

prompt [prɒmpt] **I** ADJ **1** (*on time*) 干脆的 gāncuì de **2** (*rapid*) (+ *action, response*) 迅速的 xùnsù de **II** N [C] (*Comput*) 提示符 tíshì fú [个 gè] ▸ **at 8 o'clock prompt** 8点整 bādiǎn zhěng

pronoun [proʊnaʊn] N [C] 代词 dàicí [个 gè]

pronounce [prənaʊns] VT 发音 fāyīn

pronunciation [prənʌnsieɪʃᵊn] N [C/U] 发音 fāyīn [个 gè]

proof [pruf] N [U] 证据 zhèngjù

proper [prɒpər] ADJ (+ *procedure, place, word*) 恰当的 qiàdàng de

properly [prɒpərli] ADV **1** (*eat, work, concentrate*) 充分地 chōngfèn de **2** (*behave*) 体面地 tǐmiàn de

property [prɒpərti] N **1** [U] (*possessions*) 财产 cáichǎn **2** [C/U] (*buildings and land*) 地产 dìchǎn [处 chù]

prostitute [prɒstɪtut] N [C] (*female*) 妓女 jìnǚ [个 gè] ▸ **a male prostitute** 男妓 nánjì

protect [prətɛkt] VT 保护 bǎohù ▸ **to protect sb/sth from** *or* **against sth** 保护某人/某物不受某物的伤害 bǎohù mǒurén/mǒuwù bùshòu mǒuwù de shānghài

protection [prətɛkʃᵊn] N [C/U] ▸ **protection (from** *or* **against sth)** (免受某物侵害的)保护 (miǎnshòu mǒuwù qīnhài de) bǎohù [种 zhǒng]

protest [*n* proʊtɛst, *vb* prətɛst] **I** N [C/U] 抗议 kàngyì [个 gè] **II** VT (*voice opposition to*) 示威 shìwēi

Protestant [prɒtɪstənt] **I** N [C] 新教徒 Xīnjiàotú [个 gè] **II** ADJ 新教的 Xīnjiào de

protester [prətɛstər] N [C] 抗议者 kàngyìzhě [名 míng]

proud [praʊd] ADJ **1** (+ *parents, owner*) 自豪的 zìháo de **2** (*arrogant*)

骄傲的 jiāo'ào de ▸ **to be proud of sb/sth** 为某人/某事感到自豪 wèi mǒurén/mǒushì gǎndào zìháo
prove [pruv] **I** VT (+ *idea, theory*) 证明 zhèngmíng **II** VI ▸ **to prove that...** (*person*) 证明… zhèngmíng...; (*situation, experiment, calculations*) 显示… xiǎnshì... ▸ **to prove sb right/wrong** 证明某人是对的/错的 zhèngmíng mǒurén shì duìde/cuòde
provide [prəvaɪd] VT (+ *food, money, shelter*) 供应 gōngyìng; (+ *answer, opportunity, details*) 提供 tígōng ▸ **to provide sb with sth** 提供某人某物 tígōng mǒurén mǒuwù
provided (that) [prəvaɪdɪd (ðæt)] CONJ 假如 jiǎrú
PS [pi ɛs] ABBR (= **postscript**) 附言 fùyán
psychiatrist [sɪkaɪətrɪst] N [C] 精神病医生 jīngshénbìng yīshēng [位 wèi]
psychological [saɪkəlɒdʒɪkəl] ADJ 心理的 xīnlǐ de
psychologist [saɪkɒlələdʒɪst] N [C] 心理学家 xīnlǐxué jiā [位 wèi]
psychology [saɪkɒlədʒi] N [U] 心理学 xīnlǐxué
PTO ABBR (= **please turn over**) 请翻过来 qǐng fān guòlái
public [pʌblɪk] **I** ADJ **1** (+ *support, opinion, interest*) 公众的 gōngzhòng de **2** (+ *building, service, library*) 公共的 gōnggòng de **3** (+ *announcement, meeting*) 公开的 gōngkāi de **II** N [S + PL VB] ▸ **the (general) public** 民众 mínzhòng
public holiday N [C] 法定假期 fǎdìng jiàqī [个 gè]
publicity [pʌblɪsɪti] N [U] **1** (*information, advertising*) 宣传 xuānchuán **2** (*attention*) 关注 guānzhù
public school N [C/U] 公立学校 gōnglì xuéxiào [所 suǒ]
public transportation N [U] 公共交通 gōnggòng jiāotōng
publish [pʌblɪʃ] VT (+ *book, magazine*) 出版 chūbǎn
publisher [pʌblɪʃər] N [C] (*company*) 出版社 chūbǎnshè [家 jiā]
puddle [pʌdəl] N [C] 水坑 shuǐkēng [个 gè]
pull [pʊl] **I** VT **1** (+ *rope, hair*) 拖 tuō; (+ *handle, door, cart, carriage*) 拉 lā **2** (+ *trigger*) 扣 kòu **II** VI 猛拉 měnglā ▸ **to pull a muscle** 扭伤肌肉 niǔshāng jīròu ▸ **to pull sb's leg** (*fig*) 开某人的玩笑 kāi mǒurén de wánxiào; **pull down** VT (+ *building*) 拆毁 chāihuǐ; **pull in** VI (*at curb*) 停了下来 tíngle xiàlái; **pull out** VI **1** (*Aut: from curb*) 开出 kāichū; (*when overtaking*) 超车 chāochē **2** (*from agreement, contest*) 退出 tuìchū; **pull through** VI (*from illness*) 恢复健康 huīfù jiànkāng; (*from difficulties*) 渡过难关 dùguò nánguān; **pull up I** VI (*stop*) 停下 tíngxià **II** VT **1** (*raise*) (+ *socks, trousers*) 拉起 lāqǐ **2** (+ *plant, weed*) 拔除 báchú
pullover [pʊloʊvər] N [C] 套头衫 tàotóushān [件 jiàn]
pulse [pʌls] N [C] (*Anat*) 脉搏 màibó [下 xià] ▸ **to take** *or* **feel sb's pulse** 给某人诊脉 gěi mǒurén zhěnmài
pump [pʌmp] N [C] **1** (*for liquid, gas*) 泵 bèng [个 gè] **2** (*for getting water*) 抽水机 chōushuǐjī [台 tái] **3** (*for inflating sth*) 打气筒 dǎqìtǒng [个 gè] ▸ **water/gas pump** 水/油泵 shuǐ/yóubèng; **pump up** VT 打气 dǎqì
punch [pʌntʃ] **I** N [C] 拳打 quándǎ [顿 dùn] **II** VT **1** (*hit*) 用拳打击 yòng quán dǎjī **2** (+ *button, keyboard*) 敲击 qiāojī **3** (+ *ticket, paper*) 在…上打孔 zài...shang dǎkǒng; **punch in** VT 敲入 qiāorù
punctual [pʌŋktʃuəl] ADJ 准时的 zhǔnshí de
punctuation [pʌŋktʃueɪʃən] N [U] 标点 biāodiǎn
puncture [pʌŋktʃər] **I** N [C] 刺孔 cìkǒng [个 gè] **II** VT (+ *tire, lung*) 戳破 chuōpò ▸ **to have a puncture** 轮胎被扎破了 lúntāi bèi zhāpò le

punish [pʌnɪʃ] VT 惩罚 chéngfá ▸ **to punish sb for sth/for doing sth** 因某事/做某事而惩罚某人 yīn mǒushì/zuò mǒushì ér chéngfá mǒurén

punishment [pʌnɪʃmənt] N **1** [U] 惩罚 chéngfá **2** [C/U] (*penalty*) 处罚 chǔfá [次 cì]

pupil [pyu̲pɪl] N [C] 学生 xuéshēng [名 míng]

puppy [pʌpi] N [C] 小狗 xiǎogǒu [只 zhī]

purchase [pɜrtʃɪs] (*frm*) VT 购买 gòumǎi

pure [pyʊ̲ər] ADJ **1** (+ *silk, gold, wool*) 纯的 chún de **2** (*clean*) 纯净的 chúnjìng de

purple [pɜrpəl] **I** ADJ 紫色的 zǐsè de **II** N [C/U] 紫色 zǐsè [种 zhǒng]

purpose [pɜrpəs] N [C] **1** (*of person*) 目的 mùdì [个 gè] **2** (*of act, meeting, visit*) 意义 yìyì [个 gè] ▸ **on purpose** 故意地 gùyì de

purse [pɜrs] N (*handbag*) 手袋 shǒudài [个 gè]

push [pʊ̲ʃ] **I** N [C] 推 tuī **II** VT **1** (+ *button*) 按 àn **2** (+ *car, door, person*) 推 tuī **III** VI **1** (*press*) 按 àn **2** (*shove*) 推 tuī ▸ **at the push of a button** 只要按一下按钮 zhǐyào àn yīxià ànniǔ ▸ **to push one's way through the crowd** 挤过人群 jǐguò rénqún ▸ **to push sth/sb out of the way** 把某物/某人推开 bǎ mǒuwù/mǒurén tuīkāi ▸ **to push a door open/shut** 把门推开/上 bǎ mén tuīkāi/shàng ▸ **to be pushed for time/money** (*inf*) 赶时间/缺钱 gǎn shíjiān/quēqián ▸ **to push forward/push through the crowd** 挤向/过人群 jǐxiàng/guò rénqún; **push in** VI (*in queue*) 插队 chāduì; **push over** VT (+ *person, wall, furniture*) 推倒 tuīdǎo; **push up** VT (+ *total, prices*) 提高 tígāo

put [pʊ̲t] (*pt, pp* **put**) VT **1** (+ *thing*) 放 fàng; (+ *person*) (*in institution*) 安置 ānzhì **2** (*write, type*) 写 xiě ▸ **to put a lot of time/energy/effort into sth/into doing sth** 投入大量的时间/精力/努力于某事/做某事 tóurù dàliàng de shíjiān/jīnglì/nǔlì yú mǒushì/zuò mǒushì ▸ **how shall I put it?** 我该怎么说呢？ wǒ gāi zěnme shuō ne?; **put across, put over** VT (+ *ideas, argument*) 讲清 jiǎngqīng; **put away** VT 把…收起 bǎ...shōuqǐ; **put back** VT **1** (*replace*) 放回 fànghuí **2** (+ *watch, clock*) 倒拨 dàobō; **put down** VT **1** (*on floor, table*) 放下 fàngxià **2** (*in writing*) 写下 xiěxià; **put forward** VT (+ *ideas, proposal, name*) 提出 tíchū; **put in** VT **1** (+ *request, complaint, application*) 提出 tíchū **2** (*install*) 安装 ānzhuāng; **put off** VT (*delay*) 推迟 tuīchí; (*distract*) 使分心 shǐ fēnxīn; (*discourage*) 使失去兴趣 shǐ shīqù xìngqù ▸ **to put off doing sth** (*postpone*) 推迟做某事 tuīchí zuò mǒushì; **put on** VT **1** (+ *clothes, makeup, glasses*) 穿戴 chuāndài **2** (+ *light, TV, radio, oven*) 开 kāi; (+ *CD*) 放 fàng ▸ **to put on weight/three kilograms** *etc* 增重/增加了3公斤{等} zēngzhòng/zēngjiā le sān gōngjīn {děng}; **put out** VT **1** (+ *candle, cigarette*) 熄灭 xīmiè; (+ *fire, blaze*) 扑灭 pūmiè **2** (*switch off*) 关 guān **3** (*inconvenience*) 麻烦 máfan; **put over** VT = **put across**; **put through** VT (*Tel*) 接通 jiētōng ▸ **put me through to Miss Blair** 请帮我接布莱尔小姐 qǐng bāng wǒ jiē Bùlái'ěr xiǎojiě; **put up** VT **1** (+ *fence, building, tent*) 建造 jiànzào; (+ *poster, sign*) 张贴 zhāngtiē **2** (+ *umbrella, hood*) 撑起 chēngqǐ **3** (+ *price, cost*) 增加 zēngjiā **4** (*accommodate*) 为…提供住宿 wèi...tígōng zhùsù ▸ **to put up one's hand** 举手 jǔshǒu; **put up with** VT FUS 容忍 róngrěn

puzzle [pʌzəl] N **1** [C] (*riddle, conundrum*) 谜 mí [个 gè]; (*toy*) 测智玩具 cèzhì wánjù [套 tào] **2** [S] (*mystery*) 谜团 mítuán

puzzled [pʌzəld] ADJ 茫然的 mángrán de

pylon [paɪlɒn] N [C] 电缆塔 diànlǎn tǎ [个 gè]

pyramid [pɪrəmɪd] N [C] 金字塔 jīnzì tǎ [座 zuò]

Q

qualification [kwɒlɪfɪkeɪʃᵊn] N [c] 资格证明 zīgé zhèngmíng [个 gè]

qualified [kwɒlɪfaɪd] ADJ 合格的 hégé de ▸ **fully qualified** 完全合格的 wánquán hégé de

qualify [kwɒlɪfaɪ] VI **1** (*pass examinations*) 取得资格 qǔdé zīgé **2** (*in competition*) 具备资格 jùbèi zīgé ▸ **to qualify as an engineer/a nurse** *etc* 取得工程师/护士{等}的资格 qǔdé gōngchéngshī/hùshì {děng} de zīgé

quality [kwɒlɪti] N **1** [U] (*standard*) 质量 zhìliàng **2** [c] (*characteristic: of person*) 素质 sùzhì [种 zhǒng] ▸ **quality of life** 生活质量 shēnghuó zhìliàng

quantity [kwɒntɪti] N **1** [c/U] (*amount*) 数量 shùliàng **2** [U] (*volume*) 容量 róngliàng ▸ **in large/small quantities** 大/少量 dà/shǎoliàng

quarantine [kwɔrəntin] N [U] 检疫 jiǎnyì ▸ **in quarantine** 被隔离 bèi gélí

quarrel [kwɔrəl] **I** N [c] 吵架 chǎojià [场 chǎng] **II** VI 争吵 zhēngchǎo

quarry [kwɔri] N [c] 采石场 cǎishí chǎng [座 zuò]

quarter [kwɔrtər] N [c] 四分之一 sìfēnzhīyī ▸ **to cut/divide sth into quarters** 把某物切/分为4份 bǎ mǒuwù qiē/fēnwéi sìfèn ▸ **a quarter of an hour** 一刻钟 yīkèzhōng ▸ **it's a quarter of three** 现在是三点差一刻 xiànzài shì sāndiǎn chà yīkè ▸ **it's a quarter after three** 现在是三点一刻 xiànzài shì sāndiǎn yīkè

quarterfinal N [c] 四分之一决赛 sìfēnzhīyī juésài [场 chǎng]

quay [ki] N [c] 码头 mǎtóu [个 gè]

queen [kwin] N [c] **1** (*monarch*) 女王 nǚwáng [位 wèi] **2** (*king's wife*) 王后 wánghòu [位 wèi]

query [kwɪəri] **I** N [c] 疑问 yíwèn [个 gè] **II** VT (+ *figures, bill, expenses*) 询问 xúnwèn

question [kwɛstʃᵊn] **I** N **1** [c] (*query*) 问题 wèntí [个 gè] **2** [c] (*issue*) 议题 yìtí [项 xiàng] **3** [c] (*in written exam*) 试题 shìtí [道 dào] **II** VT (*interrogate*) 盘问 pánwèn ▸ **to ask sb a question, to put a question to sb** 问某人一个问题，向某人提出问题 wèn mǒurén yīgè wèntí, xiàng mǒurén tíchū wèntí ▸ **to be out of the question** 不可能的 bù kěnéng de

question mark N [c] 问号 wènhào [个 gè]

questionnaire [kwɛstʃənɛər] N [c] 问卷 wènjuàn [份 fèn]

quick [kwɪk] **I** ADJ **1** (*fast*) 快的 kuài de **2** (+ *look*) 快速的 kuàisù de; (+ *visit*) 短时间的 duǎn shíjiān de **3** (+ *reply, response, decision*) 迅速的 xùnsùde **II** ADV (*inf: quickly*) 快地 kuài de ▸ **be quick!** 快点！ kuàidiǎn!

quickly [kwɪkli] ADV **1** (*walk, grow, speak, work*) 快地 kuài de **2** (*realize, change, react, finish*) 迅速地 xùnsù de

quiet [kwaɪɪt] ADJ **1** (+ *voice, music*) 悄声的 qiāoshēng de; (+ *place*) 安静的 ānjìng de **2** (+ *person*) 平静的 píngjìng de **3** (*silent*) ▸ **to be quiet** 沉默的 chénmò de ▸ **be quiet!** 请安静！ qǐng ānjìng!

quietly [kwaɪɪtli] ADV **1** (*speak, play*) 安静地 ānjìng de **2** (*silently*) 默默地 mòmò de

quilt [kwɪlt] N [c] 被子 bèizi [床 chuáng]

quit [kwɪt] (*pt, pp* **quit**) **I** VT **1** (*give up*) (+ *habit, activity*) 摆脱 bǎituō **2** (*inf: leave*) (+ *job*) 辞去 cíqù **II** VI **1** (*give up*) 放弃 fàngqì **2** (*resign*) 辞职 cízhí

quite [kwaɪt] ADV **1** (*rather*) 相当 xiāngdāng **2** (*completely*) 十分

shífēn ▸ **I see them quite a lot** 我常常见到他们 wǒ chángcháng jiàndào tāmen ▸ **quite a lot of money** 很多钱 hěnduō qián ▸ **quite a few** 相当多 xiāngdāng duō ▸ **it's not quite finished** 像是还没结束 xiàng shì hái méi jiéshù ▸ **quite (so)!** 的确(是这样)！ díquè (shì zhèyàng)! ▸ **it was quite a sight** 景色十分了得 jǐngsè shífēn liǎodé

> **quite** 可用在 **a** 或 **an** 之前，后接形容词加名词结构。例如，可以说 *It's quite an old car* 或者 *The car is quite old*，以及 *It was quite a warm day* 或者 *The day was quite warm*。如前例所示，**quite** 应放在不定冠词之前。例如，不能说 *It's a quite old car*。**quite** 可以用来修饰形容词和副词，而且程度比 **fairly** 更强烈，但是比 **very** 弱。**quite** 暗示某事物的某种特性超出预料。*Nobody here's ever heard of it but it is actually quite common.* 注意，不要混淆 **quite** 和 **quiet**。

quiz [kwɪz] N [C] (*game*) 测验 cèyàn [次 cì]

quotation [kwoʊteɪʃᵊn] N [C] **1** 引语 yǐnyǔ [句 jù] **2** (*estimate*) 报价 bàojià [个 gè]

quote [kwoʊt] **I** VT (+ *politician, author*) 引用 yǐnyòng; (+ *line*) 引述 yǐnshù **II** N [C] 引语 yǐnyǔ [句 jù] **III quotes** N PL (*inf*: *quotation marks*) 引号 yǐnhào ▸ **in quotes** 在引号里 zài yǐnhào lǐ

R

rabbi [ræbaɪ] N [C] 拉比(犹太教教师或法学导师)
rabbit [ræbɪt] N [C] 兔子 tùzi [只 zhī]
rabies [reɪbiz] N [U] 狂犬病 kuángquǎnbìng
race [reɪs] I N 1 [C] (*speed contest*) 速度竞赛 sùdù jìngsài [场 chǎng] 2 [C/U] (*ethnic group*) 种族 zhǒngzú [个 gè] II VI 参赛 cānsài III VT 与…进行速度竞赛 yǔ...jìnxíng sùdù jìngsài ▸ **a race against time** 抢时间 qiǎng shíjiān
race car N [C] sàichē
racehorse [reɪshɔrs] N [C] 赛马 sàimǎ [匹 pǐ]
racetrack [reɪstræk] N [C] (*for cars*) 赛道 sàidào [条 tiáo]; (*for horses*) 赛马场 sàimǎchǎng [个 gè]
racial [reɪʃəl] ADJ 种族的 zhǒngzú de
racism [reɪsɪzəm] N [U] 种族歧视 zhǒngzú qíshì
racist [reɪsɪst] I ADJ (+ *policy, attack, behavior, idea*) 种族主义的 zhǒngzú zhǔyì de; (+ *person, organization*) 有种族偏见的 yǒu zhǒngzú piānjiàn de II N [C] 种族主义者 zhǒngzú zhǔyìzhě [个 gè]
rack [ræk] N [C] 1 (*also*: **luggage rack**) 行李架 xínglijià [个 gè] 2 (*for hanging clothes, dishes*) 架 jià [个 gè]
racket [rækɪt] N [C] 球拍 qiúpāi [副 fù]
racquet [rækɪt] N [C] 球拍 qiúpāi [副 fù]
radar [reɪdar] N [C/U] 雷达 léidá [个 gè]
radiation [reɪdieɪʃən] N [U] 辐射 fúshè
radiator [reɪdieɪtər] N [C] 暖气片 nuǎnqìpiàn [个 gè]
radio [reɪdioʊ] N 1 [C] (*receiver*) 收音机 shōuyīnjī [台 tái] 2 [U] (*broadcasting*) 广播 guǎngbō ▸ **on the radio** 广播中 guǎngbō zhōng
radioactive [reɪdioʊæktɪv] ADJ 放射性的 fàngshèxìng de
radio station N [C] 广播电台 guǎngbō diàntái [个 gè]
rag [ræg] N [C/U] 破布 pòbù [块 kuài]
rage [reɪdʒ] N [C/U] 盛怒 shèngnù [阵 zhèn]
raid [reɪd] VT (*soldiers, police*) 突袭 tūxí; (*criminal*) 袭击 xíjī
rail [reɪl] N [C] 1 (*for safety on stairs*) 扶手 fúshǒu [个 gè]; (*on bridge, balcony*) 横栏 hénglán [个 gè] 2 (*for hanging clothes*) 横杆 hénggān [根 gēn] 3 (*for trains*) 铁轨 tiěguǐ [条 tiáo] ▸ **by rail** 乘火车 chéng huǒchē
railroad [reɪlroʊd] N [C] 1 (*system*) 铁路 tiělù 2 (*line*) 铁道 tiědào [条 tiáo]
railroad crossing N [C] 平交道口 píngjiāodàokǒu [个 gè]
rain [reɪn] I N [U] 雨 yǔ II VI 下雨 xiàyǔ ▸ **in the rain** 在雨中 zài yǔzhōng ▸ **it's raining** 正在下雨 zhèngzài xiàyǔ
rainbow [reɪnboʊ] N [C] 彩虹 cǎihóng [条 tiáo]
raincoat [reɪnkoʊt] N [C] 雨衣 yǔyī [件 jiàn]
rain forest N [C/U] 雨林 yǔlín [片 piàn]
rainy [reɪni] ADJ 多雨的 duōyǔ de
raise [reɪz] I VT 1 (*lift*) (+ *hand, glass*) 举起 jǔqǐ 2 (*increase*) (+ *salary, rate, speed limit*) 增加 zēngjiā; (+ *morale, standards*) 提高 tígāo 3 (*rear*) (+ *child, family*) 抚养 fǔyǎng II N [C] (*payrise*) 加薪 jiāxīn [次 cì]
rally [ræli] N [C] 1 (*public meeting*) 集会 jíhuì [次 cì] 2 (*Aut*) 拉力赛 lālìsài [场 chǎng]
ramp [ræmp] N [C] 坡道 pōdào [条 tiáo]
ran [ræn] PT *of* **run**
rang [ræŋ] PT *of* **ring**
range [reɪndʒ] I N [C] 1 [C] (*of ages,*

prices) 范围 fànwéi [个 gè]; (*of subjects, possibilities*) 系列 xìliè [个 gè] **2** (*also*: **mountain range**) 山脉 shānmài [个 gè] **II** VI ▶ **to range from... to...** 在…到…之间 zài...dào...zhījiān

rape [reɪp] **I** N [c/U] 强奸 qiángjiān [次 cì] **II** VT 强奸 qiángjiān

rapids [ræpɪdz] N PL 湍流 tuānliú

rare [rɛər] ADJ **1** 稀有的 xīyǒu de **2** (+ *steak*) 半熟的 bànshóu de

rarely [rɛərli] ADV 很少 hěnshǎo

raspberry [ræzbɛri] N [c] 山莓 shānméi [只 zhī]

rat [ræt] N [c] 田鼠 tiánshǔ [只 zhī]

rather [ræðər] ADV 相当 xiāngdāng ▶ **rather a lot** 相当多 xiāngdāng duō ▶ **I would rather go than stay** 我宁愿走而不愿留下来 wǒ nìngyuàn zǒu ér bùyuàn liúxià lái ▶ **I'd rather not say** 我宁可不说 wǒ nìngkě bùshuō

raw [rɔ] ADJ 生的 shēng de

raw materials N PL 原材料 yuáncáiliào

razor [reɪzər] N [c] **1** (*also*: **safety razor**) 剃须刀 tìxūdāo [个 gè] **2** (*also*: **electric razor**) 电动剃须刀 diàndòng tìxūdāo [个 gè]

razor blade N [c] 剃须刀刀片 tìxūdāo dāopiàn [个 gè]

reach [ritʃ] **I** VT (+ *place, destination*) 到达 dàodá; (+ *conclusion, agreement, decision*) 达成 dáchéng; (+ *stage, level, age*) 达到 dádào **II** N [U] ▶ **within easy reach of...** 离…很近 lí...hěnjìn

react [riækt] VI 反应 fǎnyìng

reaction [riækʃ^ən] N [c/U] 反应 fǎnyìng [种 zhǒng]

reactor [riæktər] N [c] 反应器 fǎnyìngqì [个 gè]

read [rid] (*pt, pp* **read**) [rɛd] **I** VI 阅读 yuèdú **II** VT **1** 读 dú; **read through** VT **1** (*quickly*) 浏览 liúlǎn **2** (*thoroughly*) 仔细阅读 zǐxì yuèdú

reading [ridɪŋ] N [U] 阅读 yuèdú

ready [rɛdi] ADJ 做好准备的 zuòhǎo zhǔnbèi de ▶ **to get ready** 准备好 zhǔnbèi hǎo ▶ **to get sb/sth ready** 使某人/某物准备就绪 shǐ mǒurén/mǒuwù zhǔnbèi jiùxù ▶ **to be ready to do sth** (*prepared*) 准备做某事 zhǔnbèi zuò mǒushì; (*willing*) 愿意做某事 yuànyì zuò mǒushì

real [ril] ADJ **1** (+ *leather, gold*) 真正的 zhēnzhèng de **2** (+ *reason, interest, name*) 真实的 zhēnshí de **3** (+ *life, feeling*) 真实的 zhēnshí de

realistic [riəlɪstɪk] ADJ **1** 现实的 xiànshí de **2** (*convincing*) (+ *book, film, portrayal*) 逼真的 bīzhēn de

reality [riælɪti] N [U] (*real things*) 现实 xiànshí ▶ **in reality** 事实上 shìshí shàng

realize [riəlaɪz] VT 意识到 yìshídào ▶ **to realize that...** 意识到… yìshí dào...

really [riəli] ADV **1** (*very*) ▶ **really good/delighted** 真好/真高兴 zhēnhǎo/zhēn gāoxìng **2** (*genuinely*) 确实 quèshí **3** (*after negative*) 真正地 zhēnzhèng de ▶ **really?** (*indicating surprise, interest*) 真的吗？ zhēnde ma?

Realtor® [riəltər, -tɔr] N [c] 房地产商 fángdìchǎn shāng [个 gè]

rear [rɪər] N [s] (*back*) 后面 hòumian

reason [riz^ən] N [c] 原因 yuányīn [个 gè] ▶ **the reason for sth** 某事的动机 mǒushì de dòngjī ▶ **the reason why** …的原因 ...de yuányīn

reasonable [rizənəb^əl] ADJ **1** (+ *person, decision*) 合情合理的 héqíng hélǐ de; (+ *number, amount*) 相当的 xiāngdāng de; (+ *price*) 合理的 hélǐ de **2** (*not bad*) 凑合的 còuhe de ▶ **be reasonable!** 理智些！ lǐzhì xie!

reasonably [rizənəbli] ADV (*moderately*) 相当地 xiāngdāng de

reassure [riəʃʊər] VT 使安心 shǐ ānxīn

receipt [rɪsit] N [c] 收据 shōujù [张 zhāng]

receive [rɪsiv] VT 收到 shōudào

recent [ris^ənt] ADJ 最近的 zuìjìn de

recently [ri̲sᵊntli] ADV 最近 zuìjìn ▶ **until recently** 直到最近 zhídào zuìjìn
reception [rɪsɛ̲pʃᵊn] N **1** [s] (*in public building*) 接待处 jiēdàichù **2** [c] (*party*) 欢迎会 huānyínghuì [个 gè] **3** [c] (*welcome*) 反响 fǎnxiǎng [种 zhǒng]
recipe [rɛ̲sɪpi] (*Culin*) N [c] 食谱 shípǔ [个 gè]
recognize [rɛ̲kəgnaɪz] VT 认出 rènchū
recommend [rɛ̲kəmɛ̲nd] VT 推荐 tuījiàn
record [*n, adj* rɛ̲kərd, *vb* rɪkɔ̲rd] **I** N [c] **1** (*sound recording*) 唱片 chàngpiàn [张 zhāng] **2** (*unbeaten statistic*) 记录 jìlù [个 gè] **II records** N PL 记录 jìlù **III** VT (*make recording of*) 录制 lùzhì **IV** ADJ (+ *sales, profits, levels*) 创记录的 chuàng jìlù de ▶ **in record time** 破记录地 pò jìlù de ▶ **to keep a record of sth** 记录某事 jìlù mǒushì
recover [rɪkʌ̲vər] VI 恢复 huīfù
recovery [rɪkʌ̲vəri] N [c/u] 康复 kāngfù
recycle [ri̲saɪ̲kᵊl] VT 再生利用 zàishēng lìyòng
recycling [ri̲saɪ̲kᵊlɪŋ] N [u] 循环利用 xúnhuán lìyòng
red [rɛ̲d] **I** ADJ **1** 红色的 hóngsè de **2** (+ *face, person*) 涨红的 zhànghóng de **3** (+ *hair*) 红褐色的 hónghèsè de **4** (+ *wine*) 红的 hóng de **II** N [c/u] 红色 hóngsè [种 zhǒng]
Red Cross N ▶ **the Red Cross** 红十字会 Hóngshízìhuì
red-haired [rɛ̲dhɛ̲ərd] ADJ 红棕色头发的 hóngzōngsè tóufa de
reduce [rɪdu̲s] VT 减少 jiǎnshǎo ▶ **to reduce sth by/to** 将某物减少…/将某物减少到… jiāng mǒuwù jiǎnshǎo…/jiāng mǒuwù jiǎnshǎo dào…
reduction [rɪdʌ̲kʃᵊn] N **1** [c/u] (*decrease*) 减少 jiǎnshǎo **2** [c] (*discount*) 减价 jiǎnjià [次 cì]
refer [rɪfɜ̲r] VT ▶ **to refer sb to** (+ *book*) 叫某人参看 jiào mǒurén cānkàn; **refer to** VT FUS 提到 tídào
referee [rɛ̲fəri̲] N [c] (*Sport*) 裁判员 cáipànyuán [位 wèi]
reference [rɛ̲fərəns, rɛ̲frəns] N [c] **1** (*mention*) 提到 tídào [次 cì] **2** (*for job application: letter*) 证明人 zhèngmíngrén [位 wèi]
refill [ri̲fɪ̲l] VT 再装满 zàizhuāngmǎn
reflect [rɪflɛ̲kt] VT (+ *image*) 映出 yìngchū; (+ *light, heat*) 反射 fǎnshè
reflection [rɪflɛ̲kʃᵊn] N **1** [c] (*image*) 影像 yǐngxiàng [个 gè] **2** [u] (*thought*) 沉思 chénsī
refreshing [rɪfrɛ̲ʃɪŋ] ADJ 提神的 tíshén de
refreshments [rɪfrɛ̲ʃmənts] N PL 饮料及小吃 yǐnliào jí xiǎochī
refrigerator [rɪfrɪ̲dʒəreɪtər] N [c] 冰箱 bīngxiāng [个 gè]
refugee [rɛ̲fyudʒi̲] N [c] 难民 nànmín [批 pī] ▶ **a political refugee** 政治难民 zhèngzhì nànmín
refund [*n* ri̲fʌnd, *vb* rɪfʌ̲nd] **I** N [c] 退款 tuìkuǎn [笔 bǐ] **II** VT 偿还 chánghuán
refuse[1] [rɪfyu̲z] VT, VI 拒绝 jùjué ▶ **to refuse to do sth** 拒绝做某事 jùjué zuò mǒushì ▶ **to refuse sb permission** 不批准某人 bù pīzhǔn mǒurén
refuse[2] [rɛ̲fyus] N [u] 垃圾 lājī
regard [rɪga̲rd] **I** VT (*consider, view*) 认为 rènwéi **II** N ▶ **to give one's regards to** 向…表示问候 xiàng…biǎoshì wènhòu
region [ri̲dʒᵊn] N [c] 区域 qūyù [个 gè]
regional [ri̲dʒənᵊl] ADJ 地区的 dìqū de
register [rɛ̲dʒɪstər] N [c] **1** (*at hotel*) 登记 dēngjì [个 gè] **2** (*in school*) 注册 zhùcè [个 gè]
registered [rɛ̲dʒɪstərd] ADJ (*Mail*) 挂号的 guàhào de
registration [rɛ̲dʒɪstreɪ̲ʃᵊn] N [c/u] (*of birth, death, students*) 登记 dēngjì [个 gè]

regret [rɪgrɛt] I VT 后悔 hòuhuǐ II N [c] ▶ **to have no regrets** 没有遗憾 méiyǒu yíhàn ▶ **to regret that...** 对…感到后悔 duì...gǎndào hòuhuǐ

regular [rɛgyələr] ADJ 1 (+ *breathing, intervals*) 有规律的 yǒu guīlǜ de 2 (+ *event*) 有规律的 yǒu guīlǜ de; (+ *visitor*) 经常的 jīngcháng de 3 (*normal*) 正常的 zhèngcháng de

regularly [rɛgyələrli] ADV 经常 jīngcháng

regulation [rɛgyəleɪʃ^ən] N [c] 规章 guīzhāng [套 tào]

rehearsal [rɪhɜrs^əl] N [c/u] 排练 páiliàn [次 cì]

rehearse [rɪhɜrs] VT, VI 排练 páiliàn

reject [rɪdʒɛkt] VT 1 拒绝接受 jùjué jiēshòu 2 (+ *applicant, admirer*) 拒绝 jùjué

related [rɪleɪtɪd] ADJ (+ *people*) 有亲缘关系的 yǒu qīnyuán guānxì de ▶ **to be related to sb** 和某人有关连 hé mǒurén yǒu guānlián

relation [rɪleɪʃ^ən] N [c] 1 (*relative*) 亲戚 qīnqi [个 gè] 2 (*connection*) 关系 guānxì [种 zhǒng] ▶ **in relation to** 与…相比 yǔ...xiāngbǐ

relationship [rɪleɪʃ^ənʃɪp] N [c] 1 (*connection*) 关系 guānxì [个 gè] 2 (*rapport: between two people, countries*) 关系 guānxì [种 zhǒng] 3 (*affair*) 亲密的关系 qīnmì de guānxì [种 zhǒng] ▶ **to have a good relationship** 关系亲密 guānxi qīnmì

relative [rɛlətɪv] N [c] 亲戚 qīnqi [个 gè]

relatively [rɛlətɪvli] ADV 相对 xiāngduì

relax [rɪlæks] VI 放松 fàngsōng

relaxation [rilækseɪʃ^ən] N [u] 消遣 xiāoqiǎn

relaxed [rɪlækst] ADJ 放松的 fàngsōng de; (+ *discussion, atmosphere*) 轻松的 qīngsōng de

relaxing [rɪlæksɪŋ] ADJ 令人放松的 lìng rén fàngsōng de

release [rɪlis] I N [c] 释放 shìfàng [次 cì] II VT 1 释放 shìfàng 2 (+ *record, film*) 发行 fāxíng

relevant [rɛləv^ənt] ADJ 切题的 qiètí de ▶ **relevant to** 和…有关的 hé...yǒuguān de

reliable [rɪlaɪəb^əl] ADJ 可靠的 kěkào de; (+ *method, machine*) 可信赖的 kěxìnlài de

relief [rɪlif] N [u] 如释重负 rú shì zhòng fù

relieved [rɪlivd] ADJ 宽慰的 kuānwèi de ▶ **to be relieved that...** 对…感到放心 duì...gǎndào fàngxīn

religion [rɪlɪdʒ^ən] N 1 [u] (*belief*) 宗教信仰 zōngjiào xìnyǎng 2 [c] (*set of beliefs*) 宗教 zōngjiào [种 zhǒng]

religious [rɪlɪdʒəs] ADJ 1 (+ *activities, faith*) 宗教的 zōngjiào de 2 (+ *person*) 笃信宗教的 dǔxìn zōngjiào de

reluctant [rɪlʌktənt] ADJ 不情愿的 bùqíngyuàn de ▶ **to be reluctant to do sth** 不愿做某事 bùyuàn zuò mǒushì

reluctantly [rɪlʌktəntli] ADV 不情愿地 bùqíngyuàn de

rely on [rɪlaɪ ɒn] VT FUS 1 (*be dependent on*) 依赖 yīlài 2 (*trust*) 信赖 xìnlài

remain [rɪmeɪn] VI 1 (*continue to be*) 仍然是 réngrán shì 2 (*stay*) 逗留 dòuliú ▶ **to remain silent/in control** 保持沉默/仍然控制局面 bǎochí chénmò/réngrán kòngzhì júmiàn

remaining [rɪmeɪnɪŋ] ADJ 剩下的 shèngxià de

remark [rɪmark] N [c] (*comment*) 评论 pínglùn [个 gè]

remarkable [rɪmarkəb^əl] ADJ 不寻常的 bù xúncháng de

remarkably [rɪmarkəbli] ADV 极其地 jíqí de

remember [rɪmɛmbər] VT 1 (+ *person, name, event*) 记住 jìzhù 2 (*bring back to mind*) 回想起 huíxiǎngqǐ 3 (*bear in mind*) 牢记 láojì ▶ **she remembered to do it** 她记得要做某事 tā jìdé yào zuò mǒushì

remind [rɪmaɪnd] VT 提醒 tíxǐng ▶ **to remind sb to do sth** 提醒某人做

某事 tíxǐng mǒurén zuò mǒushì ▸ **to remind sb of sb/sth** 使某人想起某人/某事 shǐ mǒurén xiǎngqǐ mǒurén/mǒushì
remote [rɪmoʊt] ADJ 遥远的 yáoyuǎn de
remote control N [C] 遥控器 yáokòngqì [个 gè]
remove [rɪmuv] VT **1** (+ *object, organ*) 移走 yízǒu **2** (+ *clothing, bandage*) 脱下 tuōxià **3** (+ *stain*) 清除 qīngchú
renew [rɪnu] VT (+ *loan, contract*) 延长 yáncháng
rent [rɛnt] **I** N [C/U] 租金 zūjīn [笔 bǐ] **II** VT **1** 租用 zūyòng **2** (*also*: **rent out**) (+ *house, room*) 出租 chūzū
reorganize [riɔrgənaɪz] VT 重组 chóngzǔ
rep [rɛp] N (*also*: **sales rep**) 商品经销代理 shāngpǐn jīngxiāo dàilǐ [位 wèi]
repaid [rɪpeɪd] PT, PP *of* **repay**
repair [rɪpɛər] **I** N [C/U] 修理 xiūlǐ [次 cì] **II** VT **1** 修补 xiūbǔ **2** (+ *damage*) 维修 wéixiū
repay [rɪpeɪ] (*pt, pp* **repaid**) VT 偿还 chánghuán
repeat [rɪpit] VT **1** 重复 chóngfù **2** (+ *action, mistake*) 重做 chóngzuò
repeatedly [rɪpitɪdli] ADV 反复地 fǎnfù de
replace [rɪpleɪs] VT **1** (*put back*) 将…放回 jiāng…fànghuí **2** (*take the place of*) 代替 dàitì
replay [*n* ripleɪ, *vb* ripleɪ] **I** N [C] (*of game*) 重新比赛 chóngxīn bǐsài [场 chǎng] **II** VT (+ *track, song, etc*) 重新播放 chóngxīn bōfàng ▸ **to replay a game** 重新比赛 chóngxīn bǐsài
reply [rɪplaɪ] **I** N [C] 回答 huídá [个 gè] **II** VI 答复 dáfù ▸ **there's no reply** (*Tel*) 无人接听 wúrén jiētīng
report [rɪpɔrt] **I** N [C] (*account*) 报告 bàogào [个 gè] **II** VT (+ *theft, accident, death*) 报案 bào'àn; (+ *person*) 告发 gàofā
report card N [C] 学生成绩报告单 xuéshēng chéngjì bàogàodān [份 fèn]
reporter [rɪpɔrtər] N [C] 记者 jìzhě [名 míng]
represent [rɛprɪzɛnt] VT (+ *person, nation*) 代表 dàibiǎo
representative [rɛprɪzɛntətɪv] N [C] 代表 dàibiǎo [个 gè]
republic [rɪpʌblɪk] N [C] 共和国 gònghéguó [个 gè]
reputation [rɛpyəteɪʃᵊn] N [C] 名声 míngshēng [种 zhǒng]
request [rɪkwɛst] **I** N [C] 要求 yāoqiú [个 gè] **II** VT 要求 yāoqiú
require [rɪkwaɪər] VT (*need*) 需要 xūyào ▸ **to be required** (*approval, permission*) 必须有 bìxū yǒu
rescue [rɛskyu] **I** N [C/U] 营救 yíngjiù [次 cì] **II** VT 解救 jiějiù
research [rɪsɜrtʃ, risɜrtʃ] N [U] 研究 yánjiū ▸ **to do research** 从事研究 cóngshì yánjiū
resemblance [rɪzɛmbləns] N [C/U] 相似 xiāngsì [种 zhǒng]
reservation [rɛzərveɪʃᵊn] N [C] 预定 yùdìng [个 gè] ▸ **to make a reservation** (*in hotel, restaurant, on train*) 预定 yùdìng
reservation desk N [C] 预定台 yùdìngtái [个 gè]
reserve [rɪzɜrv] VT 预定 yùdìng
reserved [rɪzɜrvd] ADJ **1** (+ *seat*) 已预定的 yǐ yùdìng de **2** (*restrained*) 矜持的 jīnchí de
resident [rɛzɪdənt] N [C] 居民 jūmín [位 wèi]
resign [rɪzaɪn] VI 辞职 cízhí
resist [rɪzɪst] VT (+ *temptation, urge*) 克制 kèzhì
resolution [rɛzəluʃᵊn] N [C/U] 决心 juéxīn [个 gè] ▸ **New Year's resolution** 新年决心 Xīnnián juéxīn
resort [rɪzɔrt] N [C] (*also*: **holiday resort**) 度假胜地 dùjià shèngdì [个 gè] ▸ **a seaside/winter sports resort** 海边/冬季运动胜地 hǎibiān/dōngjì yùndòng shèngdì ▸ **as a last resort** 作为最后手段 zuòwéi zuìhòu shǒuduàn

resource [risɔrs] **resources** N PL **1** (*coal, iron, oil*) 资源 zīyuán **2** (*money*) 财力 cáilì ▶ **natural resources** 自然资源 zìrán zīyuán
respect [rɪspɛkt] **I** N [U] 尊敬 zūnjìng **II** VT 尊敬 zūnjìng ▶ **to have respect for sb/sth** 对某人/某事怀有敬意 duì mǒurén/mǒushì huáiyǒu jìngyì
respectable [rɪspɛktəbᵊl] ADJ **1** (+ *area, background*) 体面的 tǐmiàn de **2** (+ *person*) 受人尊敬的 shòurén zūnjìng de
responsibility [rɪspɒnsɪbɪlɪti] **I** N **1** [S] (*duty*) 职责 zhízé **2** [U] (*obligation*) 义务 yìwù **II responsibilities** N PL 责任 zérèn
responsible [rɪspɒnsɪbᵊl] ADJ **1** (*at fault*) 负有责任的 fùyǒu zérèn de **2** (*in charge*) 负责的 fùzé de **3** (*sensible, trustworthy*) 可靠的 kěkào de
rest [rɛst] **I** N **1** [U] (*relaxation*) 休息 xiūxi **2** [C] (*break*) 休息 xiūxi [次 cì] **3** [S] (*remainder*) 剩余 shèngyú **II** VI (*relax*) 休息 xiūxi **III** VT (+ *eyes, legs, muscles*) 休息 xiūxi ▶ **to rest sth on/against sth** (*lean*) 把某物靠在某物上 bǎ mǒuwù kàozài mǒuwù shàng ▶ **the rest (of them)** (他们当中)其余的 (tāmen dāngzhōng)qíyú de
rest area N [C] 路边服务站 lùbiān fúwùzhàn [个 gè]
restaurant [rɛstərənt, -tərant, -trant] N [C] 餐馆 cānguǎn [家 jiā]
restless [rɛstlɪs] ADJ (*fidgety*) 坐立不安的 zuòlì bù'ān de
restore [rɪstɔr] VT 修复 xiūfù
restrict [rɪstrɪkt] VT **1** (+ *growth, membership, privilege*) 限制 xiànzhì **2** (+ *activities*) 约束 yuēshù
restroom N [C] 洗手间 xǐshǒujiān [个 gè]
result [rɪzʌlt] **I** N [C] (*of event, action*) 后果 hòuguǒ [种 zhǒng]; (*of match, election, exam, competition*) 结果 jiéguǒ [个 gè]; (*of calculation*) 答案 dá'àn [个 gè] **II** VI 产生 chǎnshēng ▶ **to result in** 导致 dǎozhì ▶ **as a result of** 由于 yóuyú ▶ **to result from** 因…而产生 yīn...ér chǎnshēng
résumé [rɛzʊmeɪ] N [C] (*curriculum vitae*) 简历 jiǎnlì [份 fèn]
retire [rɪtaɪər] VI 退休 tuìxiū
retired [rɪtaɪərd] ADJ 退休的 tuìxiū de
retiree [rɪtaɪəri] N [C] 领养老金的人 lǐng yǎnglǎojīn de rén [位 wèi]
retirement [rɪtaɪərmənt] N [C/U] 退休 tuìxiū
return [rɪtɜrn] **I** VI 返回 fǎnhuí **II** VT 归还 guīhuán **III** N **1** [S] (*of person*) 返回 fǎnhuí **2** [S] (*of something borrowed or stolen*) 归还 guīhuán **3** [U] (*Comput: key*) 回车键 huíchējiàn ▶ **in return (for)** 作为(对…)的回报 zuòwéi(duì...)de huíbào
reunion [riyuniən] N [C] 团聚 tuánjù [次 cì]
reveal [rɪvil] VT (*make known*) 透露 tòulù
revenge [rɪvɛndʒ] N [U] 复仇 fùchóu ▶ **to take (one's) revenge (on sb)** (对某人)进行报复 (duì mǒurén) jìnxíng bàofù
review [rɪvyu] N [C] (*of book, film*) 评论 pínglùn [个 gè]
revise [rɪvaɪz] VT (*study*) 复习 fùxí
revolution [rɛvəluʃᵊn] N **1** [C/U] (*Pol*) 革命 gémìng [场 chǎng] **2** [C] (*in industry, education*) 变革 biàngé [场 chǎng]
reward [rɪwɔrd] **I** N [C] 奖励 jiǎnglì [种 zhǒng] **II** VT 奖赏 jiǎngshǎng
rewarding [rɪwɔrdɪŋ] ADJ 值得做的 zhídé zuò de
rewind [riwaɪnd] (*pt, pp* **rewound**) VT 倒带 dàodài
rewound [riwaʊnd] PT, PP *of* **rewind**
rhythm [rɪðəm] N [C/U] 节奏 jiézòu [个 gè]
rib [rɪb] N [C] 肋骨 lèigǔ [根 gēn]
ribbon [rɪbən] N [C/U] 饰带 shìdài [条 tiáo]
rice [raɪs] N [C/U] **1** (*grain*) 大米 dàmǐ [粒 lì] **2** (*when cooked*) 米饭 mǐfàn [碗 wǎn]

rich [rɪtʃ] ADJ (+ *person, country*) 富有的 fùyǒu de

rid [rɪd] (*pt, pp* **rid**) VT ▶ **to get rid of sth/sb** (+ *smell, dirt, car etc*) 摆脱某物/某人 bǎituō mǒuwù/mǒurén

ride [raɪd] (*pt* **rode**, *pp* **ridden**) **I** N [C] **1** (*in car, on bicycle*) 兜风 dōufēng [次 cì] **2** (*on horse, bus, train*) 出行 chūxíng [次 cì] **II** VI (*on horse*) 骑马 qímǎ; (*on bicycle*) 骑车 qíchē; (*in car*) 乘坐 chéngzuò **III** VT **1** (+ *horse, bicycle, motorcycle*) 骑 qí **2** (+ *distance*) 行进 xíngjìn ▶ **to give sb a ride** 让某人搭车 ràng mǒurén dāchē

ridden [rɪdᵊn] PP *of* **ride**

ridiculous [rɪdɪkyələs] ADJ 荒谬的 huāngmiù de

rifle [raɪfᵊl] N [C] 步枪 bùqiāng [支 zhī]

right [raɪt] **I** ADJ **1** (*not left*) 右边的 yòubiān de **2** (*correct*) 正确的 zhèngquè de; (+ *person, place, clothes*) 合适的 héshì de; (+ *decision, direction, time*) 最适宜的 zuì shìyí de **II** N **1** [S] (*not left*) 右边 yòubiān **2** [C] (*entitlement*) 权利 quánlì [个 gè] **III** ADV **1** (*correctly*) 正确地 zhèngquè de **2** (*properly, fairly*) 恰当 qiàdàng **3** (*not to/on the left*) 右边地 yòubiān de **IV** INT 好 hǎo ▶ **do you have the right time?** 你的表几点了？ nǐde biǎo jǐdiǎn le? ▶ **to be right** (*person*) 正确 zhèngquè; (*answer, fact*) 对 duì; (*clock*) 准确 zhǔnquè ▶ **you did the right thing** 你做得对 nǐ zuòde duì ▶ **to** *or* **on the right** (*position*) 靠{或}在右侧 kào{huò}zài yòucè ▶ **to the right** (*movement*) 向右 xiàngyòu

right-handed [raɪthændɪd] ADJ 惯用右手的 guànyòng yòushǒu de

ring [rɪŋ] (*pt* **rang**, *pp* **rung**) **I** N [C] (*on finger*) 戒指 jièzhi [枚 méi] **II** VI **1** (*bell*) 鸣响 míngxiǎng **2** (*telephone*) 响 xiǎng **III** VT (+ *bell, doorbell*) 使…响 shǐ...xiǎng ▶ **there was a ring at the door, the doorbell rang** 有人按门铃 yǒurén àn ménlíng

rinse [rɪns] VT (+ *dishes, clothes*) 漂洗 piǎoxǐ

riot [raɪət] **I** N [C] (*disturbance*) 暴乱 bàoluàn [次 cì] **II** VI 闹事 nàoshì

ripe [raɪp] ADJ 成熟的 chéngshú de

rise [raɪz] (*pt* **rose**, *pp* **risen**) **I** N [C] (*in prices, temperature, crime rate*) 上升 shàngshēng [次 cì] **II** VI **1** (*move upwards*) 上升 shàngshēng **2** (*prices, numbers*) 上升 shàngshēng **3** (*sun, moon*) 升起 shēngqǐ **4** (*from chair*) 起身 qǐshēn

risen [rɪzᵊn] PP *of* **rise**

risk [rɪsk] **I** N **1** [C/U] (*danger*) 危险 wēixiǎn [个 gè] **2** [C] (*possibility, chance*) 风险 fēngxiǎn [种 zhǒng] **II** VT (*take the chance of*) 冒险做 màoxiǎn zuò ▶ **to take a risk** 担风险 dān fēngxiǎn ▶ **to risk it** (*inf*) 冒险一试 màoxiǎn yīshì

rival [raɪvᵊl] **I** N [C] 竞争对手 jìngzhēng duìshǒu [个 gè] **II** ADJ (+ *teams, groups, supporters*) 对立的 duìlì de

river [rɪvər] N [C] 河 hé [条 tiáo]

river bank N [C] 河岸 hé'àn [个 gè]

road [roʊd] N [C] **1** (*in country*) 公路 gōnglù [条 tiáo] **2** (*in town*) 路 lù [条 tiáo] ▶ **it takes four hours by road** 要花4小时的车程 yào huā sì xiǎoshí de chēchéng

road map N [C] 道路图 dàolùtú [张 zhāng]

road sign N [C] 交通标志 jiāotōng biāozhì [个 gè]

roast [roʊst] VT 烤 kǎo

rob [rɒb] VT 抢劫 qiǎngjié ▶ **to rob sb of sth** 剥夺某人的某物 bōduó mǒurén de mǒuwù

robber [rɒbər] N [C] 强盗 qiángdào [个 gè]

robbery [rɒbəri] N [C/U] 抢劫 qiǎngjié [次 cì]

robot [roʊbət, -bɒt] N [C] 机器人 jīqìrén [个 gè]

rock [rɒk] N **1** [C] (*boulder*) 巨石 jùshí [块 kuài] **2** [C] (*small stone*) 小石子

xiǎoshízǐ [块 kuài] 3 [U] (*Mus*) (*also*: **rock music**) 摇滚乐 yáogǔnyuè
rocket [rɒkɪt] N [C] 1 (*Space*) 火箭 huǒjiàn [支 zhī] 2 (*firework*) 火箭式礼花 huǒjiànshì lǐhuā [个 gè]
rod [rɒd] N [C] 1 (*pole*) 杆 gān [根 gēn] 2 (*also*: **fishing rod**) 钓鱼竿 diàoyúgān [根 gēn]
rode [roʊd] PT *of* **ride**
role [roʊl] N [C] 1 (*function*) 作用 zuòyòng [个 gè] 2 (*Theat*: *part*) 角色 juésè [个 gè]
roll [roʊl] I N [C] 1 一卷 yī juǎn [个 gè] 2 (*also*: **bread roll**) 小圆面包 xiǎoyuánmiànbāo [个 gè] II VT 使滚动 shǐ gǔndòng III VI (*ball, stone*) 滚动 gǔndòng ▸ **cheese/ham roll** 奶酪/火腿面包卷 nǎilào/huǒtuǐ miànbāojuǎn
Rollerblade® [roʊlərbleɪd] N 直排轮溜冰鞋 zhípáilún liūbīngxié
roller coaster [roʊlər koʊstər] N [C] (*at carnival*) 过山车 guòshānchē [辆 liàng]
roller skates N PL 旱冰鞋 hànbīngxié
roller-skating [roʊlərskeɪtɪŋ] N [U] 穿旱冰鞋滑行 chuān hànbīngxié huáxíng
Roman [roʊmən] I ADJ 1 (*of ancient Rome*) 古罗马的 gǔ Luómǎ de 2 (*of modern Rome*) 罗马的 Luómǎ de II N [C] (*in ancient Rome*) 古罗马人 gǔ Luómǎrén [个 gè]
Roman Catholic I ADJ 天主教的 Tiānzhǔjiào de II N [C] 天主教教徒 Tiānzhǔjiào Jiàotú [个 gè]
romance [roʊmæns, roʊmæns] N 1 [C] (*affair*) 恋情 liànqíng [种 zhǒng] 2 [U] (*charm, excitement*) 迷人之处 mírén zhī chù
Romania [roʊmeɪniə] N 罗马尼亚 Luómǎníyà
Romanian [roʊmeɪniən] I ADJ 罗马尼亚的 Luómǎníyà de II N 1 [C] (*person*) 罗马尼亚人 Luómǎníyàrén [个 gè] 2 [U] (*language*) 罗马尼亚语 Luómǎníyàyǔ
romantic [roʊmæntɪk] ADJ 1 (+ *person*) 浪漫的 làngmàn de 2 (*connected with love*) (+ *play, story etc*) 爱情的 àiqíng de 3 (*charming, exciting*) (+ *setting, holiday, dinner etc*) 浪漫的 làngmàn de
roof [ruf] N [C] 1 (*of building*) 屋顶 wūdǐng [个 gè] 2 (*of cave, mine, vehicle*) 顶 dǐng [个 gè]
room [rum] N 1 [C] (*in house*) 室 shì [个 gè] 2 [C] (*also*: **bedroom**) 卧室 wòshì [个 gè] 3 [U] (*space*) 空间 kōngjiān ▸ **single/double room** 单人/双人间 dānrén/shuāngrén jiān ▸ **room and lodging** 食宿 shísù
root [rut] N [C] 根 gēn [个 gè]
rope [roʊp] N [C/U] 绳子 shéngzi [根 gēn]
rose [roʊz] I PT *of* **rise** II N [C] (*flower*) 玫瑰 méigui [朵 duǒ]
rot [rɒt] I VT (*cause to decay*) 使腐坏 shǐ fǔhuài II VI (*decay*) (*teeth, wood, fruit*) 腐烂 fǔlàn
rotten [rɒtᵊn] ADJ 1 (*decayed*) 腐烂的 fǔlàn de 2 (*inf*: *awful*) 糟透的 zāotòu de
rough [rʌf] ADJ 1 (+ *skin, surface, cloth*) 粗糙的 cūcāo de 2 (+ *terrain*) 崎岖的 qíqū de 3 (+ *sea, crossing*) 波涛汹涌的 bōtāo xiōngyǒng de 4 (*violent*) (+ *person*) 粗鲁的 cūlǔ de; (+ *town, area*) 治安混乱的 zhì'ān hùnluàn de 5 (+ *outline, plan, idea*) 粗略的 cūlüè de
roughly [rʌfli] ADV 1 (*violently*) 粗暴地 cūbào de 2 (*approximately*) 大约 dàyuē ▸ **roughly speaking** 粗略地说 cūlüè de shuō
round [raʊnd] I ADJ 1 (*circular*) 圆的 yuán de 2 (*spherical*) 球形的 qiúxíng de 3 (+ *figure, sum*) 不计尾数的 bù jì wěishù de II N [C] 1 (*stage*: *in competition*) 一轮 yī lún 2 (*Golf*) 一场 yī chǎng III PREP 1 (*surrounding*) 围绕 wéirào 2 (*near*) 在…附近 zài...fùjìn 3 (*on or from the other side of*) 绕过 ràoguò ▸ **all (the) year round** 一年到头 yīnián dàotóu ▸ **a round**

of applause 掌声雷动 zhǎngshēng léidòng; **round off** VT **1** (+ *meal, evening*) 圆满结束 yuánmǎn jiéshù; **round up** VT **1** (+ *cattle, sheep*) 驱拢 qūlǒng **2** (+ *people*) 围捕 wéibǔ **3** (+ *price, figure*) 把…调高为整数 bǎ...tiáogāo wéi zhěngshù

round trip I N [C] 往返旅行 wǎngfǎn lǚxíng [次 cì] **II** ADJ 往返的 wǎngfǎn de

route [rut, raʊt] N [C] **1** (*path, journey*) 路 lù [条 tiáo] **2** (*of bus, train*) 路线 lùxiàn [条 tiáo]

routine [rutin] N [C/U] 例行公事 lìxíng gōngshì [次 cì]

row [roʊ] **I** N [C] **1** (*of people, houses*) 一排 yī pái **2** (*of seats in theater, cinema*) 一排 yī pái **II** VI (*in boat*) 划船 huáchuán **III** VT (+ *boat*) 划 huá ▸ **in a row** 连续 liánxù

rowboat [roʊboʊt] N [C] 划艇 huátǐng [艘 sōu]

rowing [roʊɪŋ] (*Sport*) N [U] 赛艇运动 sàitǐng yùndòng

royal [rɔɪəl] ADJ 皇家的 huángjiā de

rub [rʌb] VT (*with hand, fingers*) 揉 róu; (*with cloth, substance*) 擦 cā

rubber [rʌbər] N [U] (*substance*) 橡胶 xiàngjiāo

rubber band N [C] 橡皮筋 xiàngpíjīn [根 gēn]

rubber boot N [C] 橡胶长统靴 xiàngjiāo chángtǒngxuē [双 shuāng]

rude [rud] ADJ **1** 无礼的 wúlǐ de **2** (+ *word, joke, noise*) 粗鄙的 cūbǐ de ▸ **to be rude to sb** 对某人无礼 duì mǒurén wúlǐ

rug [rʌg] N [C] 小地毯 xiǎodìtǎn [块 kuài]

rugby [rʌgbi] N [U] (*also*: **rugby football**) 英式橄榄球 yīngshì gǎnlǎnqiú

ruin [ruɪn] **I** N [U] 毁坏 huǐhuài **II** VT (+ *clothes, carpet*) 毁坏 huǐhuài; (+ *plans, prospects*) 葬送 zàngsòng **III ruins** N PL (*of building, castle*) 废墟 fèixū ▸ **to be in ruins** (*building, town*) 破败不堪 pòbài bùkān

rule [rul] N **1** [C] (*regulation*) 规则 guīzé [条 tiáo] **2** [C] (*of language, science*) 规则 guīzé [条 tiáo] ▸ **it's against the rules** 这是不合规定的 zhèshì bùhé guīdìng de ▸ **as a rule** 通常 tōngcháng

ruler [rulər] N [C] (*for measuring*) 直尺 zhíchǐ [把 bǎ]

rum [rʌm] N [U] 朗姆酒 lǎngmǔjiǔ

rumor [rumər] N [C/U] 谣言 yáoyán [个 gè]

run [rʌn] (*pt* **ran**, *pp* **run**) **I** N [C] **1** (*as exercise, sport*) 跑步 pǎobù [次 cì] **2** (*Baseball*) 跑动得分 pǎodòng défēn [次 cì] **II** VT **1** (+ *race, distance*) 跑 pǎo **2** (*operate*) (+ *business, store, country*) 经营 jīngyíng **3** (+ *water, bath*) 流 liú **4** (+ *program, test*) 进行 jìnxíng **III** VI **1** 跑 pǎo **2** (*flee*) 逃跑 táopǎo **3** (*bus, train*) 行驶 xíngshǐ **4** (*in combination*) 变得 biànde ▸ **to go for a run** (*as exercise*) 跑步锻炼 pǎobù duànliàn ▸ **in the long run** 终究 zhōngjiū ▸ **I'll run you to the station** 我开车送你去车站 wǒ kāichē sòng nǐ qù chēzhàn ▸ **to run on gas/to run off batteries** 以汽油/电池为能源 yǐ qìyóu/diànchí wéi néngyuán; **run after** VT FUS (*chase*) 追赶 zhuīgǎn; **run away** VI (*from home, situation*) 出走 chūzǒu; **run into** VT FUS (*meet*) (+ *person*) 偶然碰见 ǒurán pèngjiàn; (+ *trouble, problems*) 遭遇 zāoyù; **run off** VI 跑掉 pǎodiào; **run out** VI **1** (*time, money, luck*) 用完 yòngwán **2** (*lease, passport*) 到期 dàoqī; **run out of** VT FUS 耗尽 hàojìn; **run over** VT (*Aut*) (+ *person*) 撞倒 zhuàngdǎo

rung [rʌŋ] PP *of* **ring**

runner [rʌnər] N [C] (*in race*) 赛跑者 sàipǎozhě [个 gè]

runner-up N [C] 亚军 yàjūn [个 gè]

running [rʌnɪŋ] **I** N [U] (*sport*) 赛跑 sàipǎo **II** ADJ ▸ **6 days running** 连续6天 liánxù liùtiān

run-up N ▸ **the run-up to...** (+ *election etc*) …的前期 ...de qiánqī

runway [rʌnweɪ] N [C] 跑道 pǎodào [条 tiáo]

rush [rʌʃ] **I** N [S] (*hurry*) 匆忙 cōngmáng **II** VI (*person*) 急速前往 jísù qiánwǎng
rush hour N [C] 高峰时间 gāofēng shíjiān [段 duàn]
Russia [rʌʃᵊ] N 俄罗斯 Éluósī
Russian [rʌʃᵊn] **I** ADJ 俄罗斯的 Éluósī de **II** N **1** [C] (*person*) 俄罗斯人 Éluósīrén [个 gè] **2** [U] (*language*) 俄语 Éyǔ
rust [rʌst] N [U] 铁锈 tiěxiù
rusty [rʌsti] ADJ **1** (+ *surface, object*) 生锈的 shēngxiù de **2** (+ *skill*) 荒疏的 huāngshū de
RV [ɑr vi] N ABBR (= **recreational vehicle**) 娱乐车 yúlèchē
rye [raɪ] N [U] (*cereal*) 黑麦 hēimài

S

sack [sæk] **I** N [c] 麻袋 mádài [个 gè] **II** VT 解雇 jiěgù

sad [sæd] ADJ **1** 伤心的 shāngxīn de **2** (*distressing*) 令人悲伤的 lìngrén bēishāng de

saddle [sædᵊl] N [c] (*for horse*) 马鞍 mǎ'ān [副 fù]; (*on bike, motorbike*) 车座 chēzuò [个 gè]

safe [seɪf] **I** ADJ **1** (*not dangerous*) 安全的 ānquán de **2** (*out of danger*) 脱险的 tuōxiǎn de **3** (+ *place*) 保险的 bǎoxiǎn de **II** N [c] 保险箱 bǎoxiǎnxiāng [个 gè]

safety [seɪfti] N [U] **1** 安全 ānquán **2** (*of person, crew*) 平安 píng'ān

Sagittarius [sædʒɪtɛəriəs] N [U] (*sign*) 人马座 Rénmǎ Zuò

said [sɛd] PT, PP *of* **say**

sail [seɪl] **I** N [c] 帆 fān [张 zhāng] **II** VI (*ship*) 航行 hángxíng; (*passenger*) 乘船航行 chéngchuán hángxíng ▶ **to go sailing** 去航行 qù hángxíng

sailing [seɪlɪŋ] N [U] 帆船运动 fānchuán yùndòng

sailor [seɪlər] N [c] 水手 shuǐshǒu [位 wèi]

saint [seɪnt] N [c] 圣徒 shèngtú [个 gè]

salad [sæləd] N [c/U] 色拉 sèlā [份 fèn]

salary [sæləri] N [c/U] 薪水 xīnshuǐ [份 fèn]

sale [seɪl] **I** N **1** [s] (*selling*) 出售 chūshòu **2** [c] (*with reductions*) 贱卖 jiànmài [次 cì] **II sales** N PL (*quantity sold*) 销售量 xiāoshòuliàng ▶ **to be (up) for sale** 待售 dàishòu ▶ **to be on sale** (*reduced*) 廉价出售 liánjià chūshòu

sales clerk N [c] 店员 diànyuán [位 wèi]

salesman [seɪlzmən] (*pl* **salesmen**) N [c] 推销员 tuīxiāo yuán [位 wèi]

salmon [sæmən] (*pl* **salmon**) N [c/U] 大马哈鱼 dà mǎhā yú [条 tiáo]

salon [səlɑn] N [c] 美发廊 měifà láng [家 jiā]

salt [sɔlt] N [U] 盐 yán

salty [sɔlti] ADJ (+ *food*) 咸的 xián de

same [seɪm] **I** ADJ **1** (+ *size, color, age*) 相同的 xiāngtóng de **2** (+ *place, person, time*) 同一个的 tóngyīgè de **II** PRON ▶ **the same 1** (*similar*) 一样 yīyàng **2** (*also*: **the same thing**) 同样 tóngyàng ▶ **the same as** 与…一样 yǔ…yīyàng ▶ **the same book/place as** 与…一样的书/地方 yǔ…yīyàng de shū/dìfang ▶ **at the same time** 同时 tóngshí

sample [sæmpᵊl] N [c] 样品 yàngpǐn [件 jiàn]; (*of blood, urine*) 采样 cǎiyàng [个 gè]

sand [sænd] N [U] 沙子 shāzi

sandal [sændᵊl] N [c] 凉鞋 liángxié [双 shuāng]

sandwich [sænwɪtʃ, sænd-] N [c] 三明治 sānmíngzhì [份 fèn] ▶ **a cheese/ham/jelly sandwich** 奶酪/火腿/果酱三明治 nǎilào/huǒtuǐ/guǒjiàng sānmíngzhì

sang [sæŋ] PT *of* **sing**

sanitary napkin [sænɪtɛri næpkɪn] N [c] 卫生巾 wèishēng jīn [块 kuài]

sank [sæŋk] PT *of* **sink**

Santa (Claus) [sæntə (klɔz)] N 圣诞老人 Shèngdàn Lǎorén

Saran Wrap® [səræn ræp] N [U] 保鲜纸 bǎoxiān zhǐ

sardine [sardin] N [c] 沙丁鱼 shādīng yú [条 tiáo]

SARS [sarz] N ABBR (= **severe acute respiratory syndrome**) 非典型性肺炎 fēi diǎnxíngxìng fèiyán

SAT [ɛs eɪ ti] N ABBR (= **Scholastic Aptitude Test**) 学业能力倾向测试 Xuéyè Nénglì Qīngxiàng Cèshì

sat [sæt] PT, PP *of* **sit**

satellite [sætᵊlaɪt] N **1** [c] 人造卫星 rénzào wèixīng [颗 kē] **2** [U]

(*also*: **satellite television**) 卫星电视 wèixīng diànshì
satisfactory [sætɪsfæktəri] ADJ 令人满意的 lìngrén mǎnyì de
satisfied [sætɪsfaɪd] ADJ 满足的 mǎnzú de ▶ **to be satisfied with sth** 对某事满意 duì mǒushì mǎnyì
Saturday [sætərdeɪ, -di] N [c/u] 星期六 xīngqīliù [个 gè]; *see also* **Tuesday**
sauce [sɔs] N [c/u] 酱 jiàng [种 zhǒng]
saucepan [sɔspæn] N [c] 深平底锅 shēn píngdǐ guō [个 gè]
saucer [sɔsər] N [c] 茶杯碟 chábēi dié [个 gè]
Saudi Arabia [saʊdi əreɪbiə] N 沙特阿拉伯 Shātè Ālābó
sausage [sɔsɪdʒ] N [c/u] 香肠 xiāngcháng [根 gēn]
save [seɪv] **I** VT **1** (+ *person*) 救 jiù **2** (*also*: **save up**) 积攒 jīzǎn **3** (*economize on*) (+ *money, time*) 节省 jiéshěng **4** (*Comput*) 存储 cúnchǔ **II** VI (*also*: **save up**) 积攒 jīzǎn ▶ **to save sb's life** 挽救某人的生命 wǎnjiù mǒurén de shēngmìng
savings [seɪvɪŋz] N PL (*money*) 存款 cúnkuǎn
savory [seɪvəri] ADJ 咸辣的 xiánlà de
saw [sɔ] (*pt* **sawed**, *pp* **sawed** *or* **sawn**) **I** PT *of* **see II** VT 锯 jù **III** N [c] 锯子 jùzi [把 bǎ]
sawn [sɔn] PP *of* **saw**
saxophone [sæksəfoʊn] N [c] 萨克斯管 sàkèsī guǎn [根 gēn]
say [seɪ] (*pt, pp* **said**) VT **1** 说 shuō **2** (*clock, watch*) 表明 biǎomíng; (*sign*) 写着 xiězhe ▶ **to say sth to sb** 告诉某人某事 gàosù mǒurén mǒushì ▶ **to say yes/no** 同意/不同意 tóngyì/bù tóngyì
scale [skeɪl] **I** N [s] (*size, extent*) 规模 guīmó **II scales** N PL 秤 chèng ▶ **on a large/small scale** 以大/小规模 yǐ dà/xiǎo guīmó
scandal [skændᵊl] N [c] 丑闻 chǒuwén [条 tiáo]
Scandinavia [skændɪneɪviə] N 斯堪的纳维亚 Sīkāndìnàwéiyà
scanner [skænər] N [c] (*Comput*) 扫描仪 sǎomiáo yí [台 tái]
scar [skɑr] N [c] 伤疤 shāngbā [个 gè]
scarce [skɛərs] ADJ 短缺的 duǎnquē de
scarcely [skɛərsli] ADV 几乎不 jīhūbù
scare [skɛər] VT 使害怕 shǐ hàipà
scared [skɛərd] ADJ ▶ **to be scared (of sb/sth)** 害怕（某人/某物） hàipà (mǒurén/mǒuwù)
scarf [skɑrf] (*pl* **scarfs** *or* **scarves**) N [c] (*long*) 围巾 wéijīn [条 tiáo]; (*square*) 头巾 tóujīn [块 kuài]
scarves [skɑrvz] N PL *of* **scarf**
scenery [sinəri] N [U] 风景 fēngjǐng
schedule [skɛdʒul, -uəl] N [c] **1** (*agenda*) 日程安排 rìchéng ānpái [个 gè] **2** (*of trains, buses*) 时间表 shíjiān biǎo [个 gè] ▶ **on schedule** 准时 zhǔnshí ▶ **to be ahead of/behind schedule** 提前/落后于计划 tíqián/luòhòu yú jìhuà
scheme [skim] N [c] (*plan*) 方案 fāng'àn [个 gè]
scholarship [skɒlərʃɪp] N [c] 奖学金 jiǎngxué jīn [项 xiàng]
school [skul] N **1** [c/u] (*place*) 学校 xuéxiào [所 suǒ]; (*pupils and staff*) 全体师生 quántǐ shīshēng **2** [c/u] (*university*) 大学 dàxué [所 suǒ] ▶ **to go to school** (*child*) 上学 shàngxué ▶ **to leave school** (*child*) 结束义务教育 jiéshù yìwù jiàoyù
schoolboy [skulbɔɪ] N [c] 男生 nánshēng [个 gè]
schoolchildren [skultʃɪldrən] N PL 学童 xuétóng
schoolgirl [skulgɜrl] N [c] 女生 nǚshēng [个 gè]
science [saɪəns] N **1** [U] (*scientific study*) 科学 kēxué **2** [c/u] (*branch of science, school subject*) 学科 xuékē [个 gè]
science fiction N [U] 科幻小说

kēhuàn xiǎoshuō
scientific [saɪəntɪfɪk] ADJ 科学的 kēxué de
scientist [saɪəntɪst] N [c] 科学家 kēxué jiā [位 wèi]
scissors [sɪzərz] N PL 剪刀 jiǎndāo ▸ **a pair of scissors** 一把剪刀 yībǎ jiǎndāo
scooter [skutər] N [c] (*also*: **motor scooter**) 小型摩托车 xiǎoxíng mótuō chē [辆 liàng]
score [skɔr] **I** N [c] 比分 bǐfēn [个 gè] **II** VT (+ *goal, point*) 得 dé **III** VI (*in game, sport*) 得分 défēn
Scorpio [skɔrpioʊ] N [U] (*sign*) 天蝎座 Tiānxiē Zuò
Scotch® tape [skɒtʃ-] N [U] 透明胶带 tòumíng jiāodài
Scotland [skɒtlənd] N 苏格兰 Sūgélán
Scottish [skɒtɪʃ] ADJ 苏格兰的 Súgélán de
scrambled egg [skræmbᵊld-] N [c/U] 炒鸡蛋 chǎo jīdàn [盘 pán]
scrap [skræp] VT **1** (+ *car, ship*) 报废 bàofèi **2** (+ *project, idea, system, tax*) 废弃 fèiqì
scratch [skrætʃ] **I** N [c] **1** (*on car, furniture*) 刮痕 guāhén [条 tiáo] **2** (*on body*) 擦伤 cāshāng [处 chù] **II** VT **1** (*damage*) 划破 huápò **2** (*because of itch*) 搔 sāo
scream [skrim] VI 尖声喊叫 jiānshēng hǎnjiào
screen [skrin] N [c] **1** (*at cinema*) 银幕 yínmù [个 gè] **2** (*of television, computer*) 屏幕 píngmù [个 gè]
screw [skru] N [c] 螺丝 luósī [个 gè]
screwdriver [skrudraɪvər] N [c] 螺丝起子 lúosīqǐzi [把 bá]
sculpture [skʌlptʃər] N [U] 雕塑 diāosù
sea [si] N ▸ **the sea** 海洋 hǎiyáng ▸ **by sea** 由海路 yóu hǎilù
seafood [sifud] N [U] 海味 hǎiwèi
seagull [sigʌl] N [c] 海鸥 hǎi'ōu [只 zhī]
seal [sil] N [c] 海豹 hǎibào [只 zhī]
search [sɜrtʃ] **I** N [c] **1** (*for missing person*) 搜寻 sōuxún [次 cì] **2** (*Comput*) 检索 jiǎnsuǒ [次 cì] **II** VT 搜查 sōuchá
seashore [siʃɔr] N [c] 海岸 hǎi'àn [个 gè]
seasick [sisɪk] ADJ 晕船的 yūnchuán de ▸ **to be** *or* **feel seasick** 感到晕船恶心 gǎndào yùnchuán ěxīn
season [sizᵊn] N [c] 季节 jìjié [个 gè]
seat [sit] N [c] **1** (*chair*) 椅子 yǐzi [把 bǎ]; (*in car, theater*) 座 zuò [个 gè] **2** (*place: in theater, bus, train*) 座位 zuòwèi [个 gè] ▸ **to take a/one's seat** 就座 jiùzuò ▸ **to be seated** (*be sitting*) 坐下 zuòxia
seat belt N [c] 安全带 ānquán dài [条 tiáo]
sea turtle [-tɜrtᵊl] N [c] 龟 guī [只 zhī]
second [sɛkənd] **I** ADJ 第二的 dì'èr de **II** ADV (*come, finish*) 第二名地 dì'èrmíng de **III** N [c] (*unit of time*) 秒 miǎo ▸ **second floor** 二层 èrcéng
secondary school N [c/U] 中学 zhōngxué [所 suǒ]
second-hand ADJ 二手的 èrshǒu de
secondly [sɛkəndli] ADV 其次 qícì
secret [sikrɪt] **I** ADJ 秘密的 mìmì de **II** N [c] 秘密 mìmì [个 gè]
secretary [sɛkrɪtɛri] N [c] 秘书 mìshū [位 wèi]
section [sɛkʃᵊn] N [c] 部分 bùfen [个 gè]
security [sɪkyʊərɪti] N [U] 保安措施 bǎo'ān cuòshī
see [si] (*pt* **saw**, *pp* **seen**) VT **1** 看见 kànjiàn **2** (*meet*) 见 jiàn **3** (+ *movie, play*) 看 kàn **4** (*notice*) 意识到 yìshí dào ▸ **to see sb doing** *or* **do sth** 看见某人做某事 kànjiàn mǒurén zuò mǒushì ▸ **to go and see sb** 去见某人 qùjiàn mǒurén ▸ **see you later!** 一会儿见！ yīhuǐr jiàn! ▸ **I see** 我明白 wǒ míngbai
seed [sid] N [c/U] 籽 zǐ [粒 lì]
seem [sim] VI 似乎 sìhū ▸ **it seems**

that... 看来… kànlái...
seen [sin] PP *of* **see**
seldom [sɛldəm] ADV 不常 bùcháng
select [sɪlɛkt] VT 挑选 tiāoxuǎn
selection [sɪlɛkʃᵊn] N [C] (*range*) 供选择的范围 gōng xuǎnzéde fànwéi [个 gè]
self-confidence [sɛlfkɒnfɪdəns] N [U] 自信心 zìxìn xīn
selfish [sɛlfɪʃ] ADJ 自私的 zìsī de
self-service [sɛlfsɜrvɪs] ADJ 自助的 zìzhù de
sell [sɛl] (*pt, pp* **sold**) VT 卖 mài ▶ **to sell sb sth, sell sth to sb** 将某物卖给某人 jiāng mǒuwù màigěi mǒurén
semifinal N [C] 半决赛 bàn juésài [场 chǎng]
send [sɛnd] (*pt, pp* **sent**) VT **1** ▶ **to send sth (to sb)** 将某物发送（给某人） jiāng mǒuwù fāsòng (gěi mǒurén) **2** (+ *person*) 派遣 pàiqiǎn
senior [sinyər] ADJ 高级的 gāojí de
senior citizen N [C] 已届退休年龄的公民 yǐjiè tuìxīu niánlíng de gōngmín [位 wèi]
senior high (school) N [C] 高中 gāozhōng [所 suǒ]
sense [sɛns] N **1** [C] (*of smell, taste*) 感觉官能 gǎnjué guānnéng [种 zhǒng] **2** [U] (*good sense*) 明智 míngzhì **3** [C] (*meaning*) 释义 shìyì [个 gè]
sensible [sɛnsɪbᵊl] ADJ 通情达理的 tōngqíng dálǐ de; (+ *decision, suggestion*) 明智的 míngzhì de
sensitive [sɛnsɪtɪv] ADJ **1** 善解人意的 shànjiě rényì de **2** (+ *skin*) 敏感的 mǐngǎn de
sent [sɛnt] PT, PP *of* **send**
sentence [sɛntəns] N [C] (*Ling*) 句子 jùzi [个 gè]
separate [*adj, n* sɛpərɪt, *vb* sɛpəreɪt] **I** ADJ (+ *section, piece, pile*) 分开的 fēnkāi de; (+ *rooms*) 单独的 dāndú de **II** VT (*split up*) 分开 fēnkāi **III** VI (*parents, couple*) 分居 fēnjū ▶ **to be separated** (*couple*) 分居 fēnjū
September [sɛptɛmbər] N [C/U] 九月 jiǔyuè; *see also* **July**
serial [sɪəriəl] N [C] 连续剧 liánxùjù [部 bù]; (*in magazine*) 连载 liánzǎi [个 gè]
series [sɪəriz] (*pl* **series**) N [C] **1** 一系列 yīxìliè [个 gè] **2** (*on TV, radio*) 系列节目 xìliè jiémù [个 gè]
serious [sɪəriəs] ADJ **1** 严重的 yánzhòng de **2** (*sincere*) 当真的 dàngzhēn de; (*solemn*) 严肃的 yánsù de
serve [sɜrv] VT **1** (*in shop, bar*) 招待 zhāodài **2** (+ *food, drink, meal*) 端上 duānshang
service [sɜrvɪs] N **1** [C] 服务 fúwù [项 xiàng] **2** [C] (*train/bus service*) 火车/公共汽车营运 huǒchē/gōnggòng qìchē yíngyùn [种 zhǒng] **3** [C] (*Rel*) 仪式 yíshì [个 gè] ▶ **service included/not included** 含/不含小费 hán/bùhán xiǎofèi
service charge N [C] 服务费 fúwùfèi [笔 bǐ]
service station N [C] 加油站 jiāyóu zhàn [座 zuò]
set [sɛt] (*pt, pp* **set**) **I** N **1** [C] (*of silverware, saucepans, books, keys*) 套 tào **2** [C] (*TV, Rad*) 电视机 diànshìjī [台 tái] **II** ADJ (+ *routine, time, price*) 规定的 guīdìng de **III** VT **1** (*put*) 放 fàng **2** (+ *table*) 摆放 bǎifàng **3** (+ *time, price, rules*) 确定 quèdìng **4** (+ *alarm*) 设定 shèdìng; (+ *heating, volume*) 调整 tiáozhěng **IV** VI (*sun*) 落山 luòshān ▶ **a chess set** 一副国际象棋 yīfù guójì xiàngqí;
set off I VI ▶ **to set off (for)** 启程（前往） qǐchéng (qiánwǎng) **II** VT (+ *alarm*) 触发 chùfā; **set out** VI 出发 chūfā
settee [sɛti] N [C] 长沙发椅 cháng shāfāyǐ [个 gè]
settle [sɛtᵊl] VT (+ *bill, account, debt*) 支付 zhīfù
seven [sɛvᵊn] NUM 七 qī; *see also* **five**
seventeen [sɛvᵊntin] NUM 十七 shíqī; *see also* **fifteen**
seventh [sɛvᵊnθ] NUM 第七 dìqī; *see also* **fifth**

seventy [sɛvᵊnti] NUM 七十 qīshí; *see also* **fifty**
several [sɛvrəl] ADJ, PRON 几个 jǐgè
severe [sɪvɪər] ADJ **1** (+ *pain, damage, shortage*) 严重的 yánzhòng de **2** (+ *punishment, criticism*) 严厉的 yánlì de
sew [soʊ] (*pt* **sewed**, *pp* **sewn**) VI, VT 缝 féng
sewing [soʊɪŋ] N [U] 缝纫 féngrèn
sewn [soʊn] PP *of* **sew**
sex [sɛks] N **1** [C] (*gender*) 性别 xìngbié [种 zhǒng] **2** [U] (*lovemaking*) 性交 xìngjiāo ▶ **to have sex (with sb)** （和某人）性交 (hé mǒurén) xìngjiāo
sexism [sɛksɪzəm] N [U] 性别歧视 xìngbié qíshì
sexist [sɛksɪst] ADJ 性别歧视的 xìngbié qíshì de
sexual [sɛkʃuəl] ADJ 性的 xìng de
sexy [sɛksi] ADJ 性感的 xìnggǎn de
shade [ʃeɪd] N **1** [U] 阴凉处 yīnliáng chù **2** [C] (*of color*) 色度 sèdù [种 zhǒng] **3** [C] (*blind*) 遮阳窗帘 zhēyáng chuānglián [副 fù]
shadow [ʃædoʊ] N [C] 影子 yǐngzi [个 gè]
shake [ʃeɪk] (*pt* **shook**, *pp* **shaken**) **I** VT (+ *bottle, cocktail, medicine*) 摇晃 yáohuàng; (+ *buildings, ground*) 使震动 shǐ zhèndòng **II** VI (*person, part of the body*) 发抖 fādǒu; (*building, table*) 震动 zhèndòng; (*ground*) 震颤 zhènchàn ▶ **to shake one's head** 摇头拒绝 yáotóu jùjué ▶ **to shake hands (with sb)** （和某人）握手 (hé mǒurén) wòshǒu
shaken [ʃeɪkᵊn] PP *of* **shook**
shall [ʃəl, STRONG ʃæl] AUX VB **1** (*indicating future in 1st person*) ▶ **I shall go** 我要走了 wǒ yào zǒule **2** (*in 1st person questions*) ▶ **shall I/we open the door?** 我/我们把门打开好吗？ wǒ/wǒmen bǎ mén dǎkāi hǎoma?
shallow [ʃæloʊ] ADJ 浅的 qiǎn de
shame [ʃeɪm] N [U] 耻辱 chǐrǔ ▶ **it is a shame that...** …真遗憾 ...zhēn yíhàn ▶ **what a shame!** 太遗憾了！ tài yíhàn le!
shampoo [ʃæmpu] N [C/U] 洗发液 xǐfàyè [瓶 píng]
shape [ʃeɪp] N [C] 形状 xíngzhuàng [种 zhǒng]
share [ʃɛər] **I** N [C] **1** (*part*) 一份 yīfèn **2** (*Comm, Fin*) 股票 gǔpiào [支 zhī] **II** VT **1** (+ *room, bed, taxi*) 合用 héyòng **2** (+ *job, cooking, task*) 分担 fēndān; **share out** VT 平均分配 píngjūn fēnpèi
shark [ʃark] N [C/U] 鲨鱼 shāyú [条 tiáo]
sharp [ʃarp] **I** ADJ **1** (+ *knife, teeth*) 锋利的 fēnglì de; (+ *point, edge*) 尖锐的 jiānruì de **2** (+ *curve, bend*) 急转的 jízhuǎn de **II** ADV (*precisely*) ▶ **at 2 o'clock sharp** 两点整 liǎng diǎn zhěng
shave [ʃeɪv] **I** VT (+ *head, legs*) 剃毛发 tìmáofà **II** VI 刮脸 guāliǎn
shaving cream [ʃeɪvɪŋ-] N [U] 剃须膏 tìxūgāo
she [ʃɪ, STRONG ʃi] PRON 她 tā
she'd [ʃid, ʃɪd] = **she had, she would**
sheep [ʃip] (*pl* **sheep**) N [C] 绵羊 miányáng [只 zhī]
sheet [ʃit] N [C] **1** 床单 chuángdān [床 chuáng] **2** (*of paper*) 一张 yīzhāng
shelf [ʃɛlf] (*pl* **shelves**) N [C] (*bookshelf*) 架子 jiàzi [个 gè]; (*in cabinet*) 搁板 gēbǎn [块 kuài]
shell [ʃɛl] N [C] **1** 贝壳 bèiké [只 zhī] **2** (*of tortoise, snail, crab, egg, nut*) 壳 ké [个 gè]
she'll [ʃil, ʃɪl] = **she will**
shellfish [ʃɛlfɪʃ] (*pl* **shellfish**) **I** N [C/U] 贝类海产 bèilèi hǎichǎn [种 zhǒng] **II** N PL (*as food*) 贝类海鲜 bèilèi hǎixiān
shelter [ʃɛltər] **I** N [C] (*building*) 遮蔽处 zhēbìchù [个 gè] **II** VI 躲避 duǒbì
shelves [ʃɛlvz] N PL *of* **shelf**
she's [ʃiz, ʃɪz] = **she is, she has**
shift [ʃɪft] VT 移动 yídòng

shin [ʃɪn] N [c] 胫部 jìngbù
shine [ʃaɪn] (*pt, pp* **shone**) VI 照耀 zhàoyào
ship [ʃɪp] N [c] 船 chuán [艘 sōu]
shirt [ʃɜrt] N [c] 衬衫 chènshān [件 jiàn]
shiver [ʃɪvər] VI 发抖 fādǒu
shock [ʃɒk] **I** N **1** [c] 震骇 zhènhài [种 zhǒng] **2** [U] (*Med*) 休克 xiūkè **3** [c] (*also*: **electric shock**) 触电 chùdiàn [次 cì] **II** VT 使厌恶 shǐ yànwù
shocked [ʃɒkt] ADJ 感到不快的 gǎndào bùkuài de
shoe [ʃu] N [c] 鞋 xié [双 shuāng] ▸ **a pair of shoes** 一双鞋 yīshuāng xié
shone [ʃoʊn] PT, PP *of* **shine**
shook [ʃʊk] PT *of* **shake**
shoot [ʃut] (*pt, pp* **shot**) **I** VT (*kill*) 向…开枪 xiàng...kāiqiāng **II** VI **1** (*with gun, bow*) ▸ **to shoot (at sb/sth)** （朝某人/某物）射击 (cháo mǒurén/mǒuwù) shèjī **2** (*Soccer etc*) 射门 shèmén
shop [ʃɒp] VI 购物 gòuwù ▸ **to go shopping** 去买东西 qù mǎi dōngxi
shopping [ʃɒpɪŋ] N [U] **1** (*activity*) 购物 gòuwù **2** (*goods*) 所购之物 suǒgòu zhī wù; *see also* **shop**
shopping center N [c] 购物中心 gòuwù zhōngxīn [个 gè]
shore [ʃɔr] N [c] 岸 àn [个 gè]
short [ʃɔrt] **I** ADJ **1** (*in time*) 短暂的 duǎnzàn de **2** (*in length*) 短的 duǎn de **3** (*not tall*) 矮的 ǎi de **II shorts** N PL **1** (*short pants*) 短裤 duǎnkù **2** (*underpants*) 男用短衬裤 nányòng duǎnchènkù ▸ **a pair of shorts** 一条短裤 yītiáo duǎnkù
shortage [ʃɔrtɪdʒ] N [C/U] 短缺 duǎnquē [种 zhǒng]
shortly [ʃɔrtli] ADV 马上 mǎshàng ▸ **shortly after/before sth** 某事后/前不久 mǒushì hòu/qián bùjiǔ
shot [ʃɒt] **I** PT, PP *of* **shoot II** N **1** [c] 射击 shèjī [阵 zhèn] **2** [c] (*Football*) 射门 shèmén [次 cì] **3** [c] (*injection*) 皮下注射 píxià zhùshè [针 zhēn]
should [ʃəd, STRONG ʃʊd] AUX VB **1** (*indicating advisability*) ▸ **I should go now** 我现在应该走了 wǒ xiànzài yīnggāi zǒule **2** (*indicating obligation*) 应当 yīngdāng **3** (*indicating likelihood*) ▸ **he should be there by now/he should get there soon** 他现在该到那儿了/他该很快就到那儿了 tā xiànzài gāi dào nàrle/tā gāi hěnkuài jiù dào nàrle ▸ **you should have been more careful** 你本该更加小心 nǐ běngāi gèngjiā xiǎoxīn ▸ **he should have arrived by now** 他现在应该到了 tā xiànzài yīnggāi dàole
shoulder [ʃoʊldər] N [c] 肩膀 jiānbǎng [个 gè]
shout [ʃaʊt] VI (*also*: **shout out**) 喊叫 hǎnjiào
show [ʃoʊ] (*pt* **showed**, *pp* **shown**) **I** N [c] **1** (*exhibition*) 展览 zhǎnlǎn [个 gè] **2** (*TV, Rad*) 节目 jiémù [个 gè] **II** VT **1** 表明 biǎomíng ▸ **to show sb sth** *or* **to show sth to sb** 给某人看某物{或}把某物给某人看 gěi mǒurén kàn mǒuwù {huò} bǎ mǒuwù gěi mǒurén kàn **2** (*illustrate, depict*) 描述 miáoshù ▸ **on show** 在展览中 zài zhǎnlǎn zhōng ▸ **to show that...** 表明… biǎomíng... ▸ **to show sb how to do sth** 示范某人如何做某事 shìfàn mǒurén rúhé zuò mǒushì; **show around** VT 带…参观 dài...cānguān
shower [ʃaʊər] **I** N [c] **1** 阵雨 zhènyǔ [场 chǎng] **2** (*for washing*) 淋浴器 línyùqì [个 gè] **II** VI 洗淋浴 xǐ línyù ▸ **to have** *or* **take a shower** 洗淋浴 xǐ línyù
shown [ʃoʊn] PP *of* **show**
shrank [ʃræŋk] PT *of* **shrink**
shrimp [ʃrɪmp] N [c] (*small*) 小虾 xiǎoxiā [只 zhī]; (*bigger*) 虾 xiā [只 zhī]
shrink [ʃrɪŋk] (*pt* **shrank**, *pp* **shrunk**) VI 缩水 suōshuǐ
shrunk [ʃrʌŋk] PP *of* **shrink**
shut [ʃʌt] (*pt, pp* **shut**) **I** VT 关上 guānshang; (+ *store*) 关门 guānmén; (+ *mouth, eyes*) 闭上 bìshang **II** VI (*shop*) 打烊 dǎyàng **III** ADJ (+ *door,*

drawer) 关闭的 guānbì de; (+ *shop*) 打烊的 dǎyàng de; (+ *mouth, eyes*) 闭着的 bìzhe de; **shut up** VI (*inf*) 住口 zhùkǒu ▶ **shut up!** (*inf*) 闭嘴! bìzuǐ!

shuttle [ʃʌtᵊl] N [C] (*plane, bus*) 穿梭班机/班车 chuānsuō bānjī/bānchē [架/辆 jià/liàng]

shy [ʃaɪ] ADJ 害羞的 hàixiū de

sick [sɪk] ADJ **1** (*physically*) 患病的 huànbìng de; (*mentally*) 令人讨厌的 lìngrén tǎoyàn de **2** ▶ **to be sick** (*vomit*) 呕吐 ǒutù ▶ **to feel sick** 感觉恶心 gǎnjué ěxīn

sickness [sɪknɪs] N [U] 患病 huànbìng

side [saɪd] **I** N [C] **1** 边 biān [个 gè] **2** (*of building, vehicle*) 侧面 cèmiàn [个 gè]; (*of body*) 体侧 tǐcè [边 biān] **3** (*of paper, face, brain*) 一面 yīmiàn [个 gè]; (*of tape, record*) 面 miàn [个 gè] **4** (*of road, bed*) 边缘 biānyuán [个 gè] **5** (*of hill, valley*) 坡 pō [个 gè] **6** (*in conflict, contest*) 一方 yīfāng **II** ADJ (+ *door, entrance*) 旁边的 pángbiān de ▶ **on the other side of sth** 在某物的另一边 zài mǒuwù de lìngyībiān

side effect N [C] 副作用 fù zuòyòng [个 gè]

sidewalk [saɪdwɔk] N [C] 人行道 rénxíngdào [条 tiáo]

sigh [saɪ] VI 叹气 tànqì

sight [saɪt] **I** N **1** [U] 视力 shìlì **2** [C] (*spectacle*) 景象 jǐngxiàng [种 zhǒng] **II sights** N PL ▶ **the sights** 景点 jǐngdiǎn

sightseeing [saɪtsiɪŋ] N [U] 观光 guānguāng ▶ **to go sightseeing** 观光游览 guānguāng yóulǎn

sign [saɪn] **I** N **1** [C] 指示牌 zhǐshìpái [块 kuài] **2** [C] (*also*: **road sign**) 路标 lùbiāo [个 gè] **3** [C/U] (*indication, evidence*) 迹象 jìxiàng [种 zhǒng] **II** VT 签署 qiānshǔ ▶ **it's a good/bad sign** 这是个好/坏兆头 zhèshì gè hǎo/huài zhàotou

signal [sɪgnəl] **I** N [C] **1** (*to do sth*) 信号 xìnhào [个 gè] **2** (*Rail*) 信号机 xìnhàojī [部 bù] **3** (*Elec*) 信号 xìnhào [个 gè] **II** VI (*with gesture, sound*) ▶ **to signal (to sb)** (向某人)示意 (xiàng mǒurén) shìyì

signature [sɪgnətʃər, -tʃʊər] N [C] 签名 qiānmíng [个 gè]

sign language N [C/U] 手语 shǒuyǔ [种 zhǒng]

signpost [saɪnpoʊst] N [C] 路标 lùbiāo [个 gè]

silence [saɪləns] N [C/U] 寂静 jìjìng [片 piàn] ▶ **in silence** 鸦雀无声 yā què wú shēng

silent [saɪlənt] ADJ (+ *person*) 沉默的 chénmò de

silk [sɪlk] N [C/U] 丝绸 sīchóu [块 kuài]

silly [sɪli] ADJ 愚蠢的 yúchǔn de; (+ *idea, object*) 可笑的 kěxiào de

silver [sɪlvər] **I** N [U] 银 yín **II** ADJ (+ *spoon, necklace*) 银的 yín de

silverware [sɪlvərwɛər] N [U] 餐具 cānjù

SIM card [sɪm kard] N [C] 手机智能卡 shǒujī zhìnéngkǎ [张 zhāng]

similar [sɪmɪlər] ADJ 相似的 xiāngsì de ▶ **to be similar to sth** 和某事物类似 hé mǒu shìwù lèisì

simple [sɪmpᵊl] ADJ **1** (*easy*) 简单的 jiǎndān de **2** (+ *meal, life, cottage*) 简朴的 jiǎnpǔ de

simply [sɪmpli] ADV **1** (*merely*) 仅仅 jǐnjǐn **2** (*absolutely*) 完全 wánquán

since [sɪns] **I** ADV (*from then onwards*) 此后 cǐhòu **II** PREP **1** (*from*) 自…以来 zì...yǐlái **2** (*after*) 从…以后 cóng...yǐhòu **III** CONJ **1** (*from when*) 自从 zìcóng **2** (*after*) 从…以后 cóng...yǐhòu **3** (*as*) 因为 yīnwèi ▶ **since then** *or* **ever since** 从那时起 cóng nàshí qǐ ▶ **I've been here since the end of June** 我自6月底以来一直在这儿。 wǒ zì liùyuè dǐ yǐlái yīzhí zài zhèr ▶ **since it was Saturday, he stayed in bed an extra hour** 因为是星期六，他在床上多呆了一小时。 yīnwéi shì xīngqīliù, tā zài chuángshàng duō dāile yī xiǎoshí

sincere [sɪnsɪər] ADJ 真诚的 zhēnchéng de

sincerely [sɪnsɪərli] ADV 由衷地 yóuzhōng de ▶ **Sincerely yours** 谨上 jǐnshàng

sing [sɪŋ] (*pt* **sang**, *pp* **sung**) **I** VI (*person*) 唱歌 chànggē; (*bird*) 鸣 míng **II** VT (+ *song*) 唱 chàng

Singapore [sɪŋəpɔr] N 新加坡 Xīnjiāpō

singer [sɪŋər] N [C] 歌手 gēshǒu [位 wèi]

singing [sɪŋɪŋ] N [U] 唱歌 chànggē

single [sɪŋgəl] ADJ **1** (*solitary*) 单个的 dāngè de **2** (*unmarried*) 单身的 dānshēn de

singular [sɪŋgyələr] **I** ADJ 单数的 dānshù de **II** N ▶ **the singular** 单数形式 dānshù xíngshì ▶ **in the singular** 用单数

sink [sɪŋk] (*pt* **sank**, *pp* **sunk**) **I** N [C] 洗涤槽 xǐdí cáo [个 gè] **II** VI (*ship*) 沉没 chénmò

sir [sɜr] N 先生 xiānsheng ▶ **Dear Sir** 亲爱的先生 Qīn'ài de Xiānsheng ▶ **Dear Sir or Madam** 亲爱的先生或女士 Qīn'ài de xiānsheng huò nǚshì

siren [saɪrən] N [C] 警报器 jǐngbàoqì [个 gè]

sister [sɪstər] N [C] 姐妹 jiěmèi [对 duì]; (*elder*) 姐姐 jiějie [个 gè]; (*younger*) 妹妹 mèimei [个 gè] ▶ **my brothers and sisters** 我的兄弟姐妹们 wǒde xiōngdì jiěmèi men

sister-in-law [sɪstərɪnlɔ] (*pl* **sisters-in-law**) N [C] (*husband's sister*) 姑子 gūzi [个 gè]; (*wife's sister*) 姨子 yízi [个 gè]; (*older brother's wife*) 嫂子 sǎozi [位 wèi]; (*younger brother's wife*) 弟媳 dìxí [个 gè]

sit [sɪt] (*pt, pp* **sat**) VI **1** (*also*: **sit down**) 坐下 zuòxià **2** (*be sitting*) 坐 zuò; **sit down** VI 坐下 zuòxià ▶ **to be sitting down** 就座 jiùzuò

site [saɪt] N [C] (*also*: **website**) 网址 wǎngzhǐ [个 gè]

situated [sɪtʃueɪtɪd] ADJ ▶ **to be situated in/on/near sth** 位于某物中/上/旁 wèiyú mǒuwù zhōng/shàng/páng

situation [sɪtʃueɪʃən] N [C] 情况 qíngkuàng [种 zhǒng]

six [sɪks] NUM 六 liù; *see also* **five**

sixteen [sɪkstin] NUM 十六 shíliù; *see also* **fifteen**

sixth [sɪksθ] NUM **1** (*in series*) 第六 dìliù **2** (*fraction*) 六分之一 liùfēnzhī yī; *see also* **fifth**

sixty [sɪksti] NUM 六十 liùshí; *see also* **fifty**

size [saɪz] N **1** [C/U] (*of object*) 大小 dàxiǎo [种 zhǒng]; (*of clothing, shoes*) 尺码 chǐmǎ [个 gè] **2** [U] (*of area, building, task, loss*) 大 dà ▶ **what size shoes do you take?** 你穿几号的鞋? nǐ chuān jǐhào de xié?

skate [skeɪt] VI **1** (*ice skate*) 溜冰 liūbīng **2** (*roller skate*) 溜旱冰 liūhànbīng

skateboard [skeɪtbɔrd] N [C] 滑板 huábǎn [个 gè]

skating [skeɪtɪŋ] N [U] (*ice-skating*) 冰上运动 bīngshàng yùndòng; *see also* **skate**

skeleton [skɛlɪtən] N [C] 骨骼 gǔgé [副 fù]

sketch [skɛtʃ] N [C] (*drawing*) 素描 sùmiáo [张 zhāng]

ski [ski] VI 滑雪 huáxuě ▶ **to go skiing** 去滑雪 qù huáxuě

skiing [skiɪŋ] N [U] 滑雪 huáxuě; *see also* **ski**

skill [skɪl] N **1** [U] (*ability*) 技巧 jìqiǎo **2** [C] (*acquired*) 技能 jìnéng [项 xiàng]

skillful [skɪlfəl] ADJ 老练的 lǎoliàn de; (+ *use, choice, management*) 技巧娴熟的 jìqiǎo xiánshú de

skin [skɪn] N [C/U] 皮肤 pífū; (*of animal*) 皮 pí [张 zhāng]; (*complexion*) 肤色 fūsè [种 zhǒng]

skip [skɪp] VT (+ *lunch, lecture*) 故意不做 gùyì bùzuò

skirt [skɜrt] N [C] 裙子 qúnzi [条 tiáo]

skull [skʌl] N [C] 颅骨 lúgǔ [个 gè]
sky [skaɪ] N [C/U] 天空 tiānkōng [片 piàn]
skyscraper [skaɪskreɪpər] N [C] 摩天大厦 mótiān dàshà [座 zuò]
slap [slæp] I N [C] 掌击 zhǎngjī [次 cì] II VT 掴 guó
sled [slɛd] N [C] 雪橇 xuěqiāo [副 fù]
sleep [slip] (*pt, pp* **slept**) I N 1 [U] 睡眠 shuìmián 2 [C] (*nap*) 睡觉 shuìjiào II VI (*be asleep*) 睡 shuì; (*spend the night*) 过夜 guòyè ▶ **to go to sleep** 去睡觉 qù shuìjiào; **sleep with** VT FUS 和…有性关系 hé...yǒu xìngguānxì
sleeping bag [slipɪŋ bæg] N [C] 睡袋 shuìdài [个 gè]
sleeping pill [slipɪŋ pɪl] N [C] 安眠药 ānmiányào [片 piàn]
sleet [slit] N [U] 雨夹雪 yǔjiāxuě
sleeve [sliv] N [C] 袖子 xiùzi [个 gè]
slept [slɛpt] PT, PP *of* **sleep**
slice [slaɪs] N [C] 片 piàn
slide [slaɪd] (*pt, pp* **slid**) I N [C] (*in playground*) 滑梯 huátī [个 gè] II VI ▶ **to slide down/off/into sth** 滑下/离/进某物 huáxià/lí/jìn mǒuwù
slight [slaɪt] ADJ 微小的 wēixiǎo de
slightly [slaɪtli] ADV 略微地 lüèwēi de
slim [slɪm] I ADJ 苗条的 miáotiáo de II VI 节食减肥 jiéshí jiǎnféi
slip [slɪp] I VI (*person*) 滑跤 huájiāo; (*object*) 滑落 huáluò II N [C] (*mistake*) 差错 chācuò [个 gè]
slipper [slɪpər] N [C] 拖鞋 tuōxié [只 zhī]
slippery [slɪpəri] ADJ 滑的 huá de
slot machine [slɒt məʃin] N [C] 投币机 tóubìjī [个 gè]; (*for gambling*) 吃角子老虎机 chījiǎozi lǎohǔjī [部 bù]
slow [sloʊ] I ADJ 慢的 màn de II ADV (*inf*) 缓慢地 huǎnmàn de ▶ **my watch is 20 minutes slow** 我的表慢了20分钟 wǒde biǎo mànle èrshí fēnzhōng; **slow down** I VI 放松 fàngsōng
slowly [sloʊli] ADV 慢慢地 mànmàn de
smack [smæk] VT (*as punishment*) 打 dǎ
small [smɔl] ADJ 1 小的 xiǎo de 2 (*young*) 年幼的 niányòu de 3 (+ *mistake, problem, change*) 微不足道的 wēibùzúdào de
smart [smɑrt] ADJ 1 (*neat, tidy*) 漂亮的 piàoliang de 2 (*fashionable*) 时髦的 shímáo de 3 (*clever*) 聪明的 cōngmíng de
smartphone [smɑrtfoʊn] N [C] 智能手机 zhìnéng shǒujī [部 bù]
smash [smæʃ] VT 打碎 dǎsuì
smell [smɛl] (*pt, pp* **smelled** *or* **smelt**) I N [C] 气味 qìwèi [种 zhǒng] II VT 闻到 wéndào III VI 1 (*have unpleasant odor*) 发臭 fāchòu 2 ▶ **to smell nice/delicious/spicy** *etc* 闻起来香/好吃/辣{等} wén qǐlái xiāng/hǎochī/là {děng} ▶ **to smell of** 有…气味 yǒu...qìwèi
smelt [smɛlt] PT, PP *of* **smell**
smile [smaɪl] I N [C] 微笑 wēixiào [个 gè] II VI ▶ **to smile (at sb)** （对某人）微笑 (duì mǒurén) wēixiào
smoke [smoʊk] I N [U] 烟 yān II VI (*person*) 吸烟 xīyān III VT (+ *cigarette, cigar, pipe*) 抽 chōu
smoker [smoʊkər] N [C] 吸烟者 xīyānzhě [个 gè]
smoking [smoʊkɪŋ] N [U] 吸烟 xīyān ▶ **"no smoking"** "禁止吸烟" "jìnzhǐ xīyān"
smooth [smuð] ADJ (*not rough*) 光滑的 guānghuá de
smother [smʌðər] VT 使窒息 shǐ zhìxī
SMS [ɛs ɛm ɛs] N ABBR (= **short message service**) 短信息服务 duǎn xìnxī fúwù
smuggle [smʌgᵊl] VT 走私 zǒusī ▶ **to smuggle sth in/out** 走私进口/出口某物 zǒusī jìnkǒu/chūkǒu mǒuwù
snack [snæk] N [C] 小吃 xiǎochī [份 fèn]
snail [sneɪl] N [C] 蜗牛 wōniú [只 zhī]
snake [sneɪk] N [C] 蛇 shé [条 tiáo]
snapshot [snæpʃɒt] N [C] 快照 kuàizhào [张 zhāng]

sneakers [sni̱kərz] N PL 胶底运动鞋 jiāodǐ yùndòngxié
sneeze [sni̱z] VI 打喷嚏 dǎ pēntì
snob [snɒ̱b] (*pej*) N [C] 势利小人 shìlì xiǎorén [个 gè]
snooker [snʊ̱kər] N [U] (*Sport*) 英式台球 yīngshì táiqiú
snore [snɔ̱r] VI 打鼾 dǎhān
snow [snoʊ̱] I N [U] 雪 xuě II VI 下雪 xiàxuě ▸ **it's snowing** 下雪了 xiàxuě le
snowball [snoʊ̱bɔl] N [C] 雪球 xuěqiú [个 gè]

KEYWORD

so [soʊ̱] I ADV 1 (*thus, likewise*) 这样 zhèyàng ▸ **they do so because...** 他们这样做是因为… tāmen zhèyàng zuò shì yīnwéi... ▸ **if you don't want to go, say so** 如果你不想去，就说你不想去 rúguǒ nǐ bùxiǎng qù, jiù shuō nǐ bùxiǎng qù ▸ **if so** 如果这样 rúguǒ zhèyàng ▸ **I hope/think so** 我希望/认为如此 wǒ xīwàng/rènwéi rúcǐ ▸ **so far** 迄今为止 qìjīn wéizhǐ ▸ **and so on** 等等 děngděng
2 (*also*) ▸ **so do I/so am I** 我也一样 wǒ yě yīyàng
3 (*to such a degree*) 如此 rúcǐ ▸ **so quickly/big (that)** 如此快/大（以至于） rúcǐ kuài/dà(yǐzhì yú)
4 (*very*) 非常 fēicháng ▸ **so much** 那么多 nàme duō ▸ **so many** 那么多 nàme duō
5 (*linking events*) 于是 yúshì ▸ **so I was right after all** 那终究我是对的 nà zhōngjiū wǒ shì duìde
II CONJ 1 (*expressing purpose*) ▸ **so (that)** 为的是 wèi de shì ▸ **I brought it so (that) you could see it** 我带过来给你看 wǒ dàiguò lái gěi nǐ kàn
2 (*expressing result*) 因此 yīncǐ ▸ **he didn't come so I left** 他没来，因此我走了 tā méilái, yīncǐ wǒ zǒule

soaking [soʊ̱kɪŋ] ADJ (*also*: **soaking wet**) (+ *person*) 湿透的 shītòu de; (+ *clothes*) 湿淋淋的 shīlínlín de
soap [soʊ̱p] N [C/U] 1 肥皂 féizào [块 kuài] 2 = **soap opera**
soap opera N [C] 肥皂剧 féizào jù [部 bù]
sober [soʊ̱bər] ADJ 未醉的 wèizuìde
soccer [sɒ̱kər] N [U] 足球 zúqiú
soccer player [sɒ̱kər pleɪər] N [C] 足球运动员 zúqiú yùndòngyuán [位 wèi]
social [soʊ̱ʃəl] ADJ 1 社会的 shèhuì de 2 (+ *event, function*) 社交的 shèjiāo de
socialism [soʊ̱ʃəlɪzəm] N [U] 社会主义 shèhuì zhǔyì
socialist [soʊ̱ʃəlɪst] I ADJ 社会主义的 shèhuì zhǔyì de II N [C] 社会主义者 shèhuì zhǔyìzhě [位 wèi]
social media N PL 社交媒体 shèjiāo méitǐ
social worker N [C] 社会福利工作者 shèhuì fúlì gōngzuòzhě [位 wèi]
society [səsa̱ɪɪti] N [U] 社会 shèhuì
sock [sɒ̱k] N [C] 袜子 wàzi [双 shuāng]
sofa [soʊ̱fə] N [C] 沙发 shāfā [个 gè]
soft [sɔ̱ft] ADJ 1 (+ *towel*) 松软的 sōngruǎn de; (+ *skin*) 柔软的 róuruǎn de 2 (+ *bed, paste*) 柔软的 róuruǎn de
soft drink N [C] 软性饮料 ruǎnxìng yǐnliào [瓶 píng]
software [sɔ̱ftwɛər] N [U] 软件 ruǎnjiàn
soil [sɔ̱ɪl] N [C/U] 土壤 tǔrǎng [种 zhǒng]
solar power [soʊ̱lər-] N [U] 太阳能 tàiyáng néng
sold [soʊ̱ld] PT, PP *of* **sell**
soldier [soʊ̱ldʒər] N [C] 士兵 shìbīng [位 wèi]
sole [soʊ̱l] N [C] 底 dǐ [个 gè]
solid [sɒ̱lɪd] ADJ 1 (*not soft*) 坚实的 jiānshí de 2 (*not liquid*) 固体的 gùtǐ de 3 (+ *gold, oak*) 纯质的 chúnzhì de
solution [səlu̱ʃən] N [C] 解决方案 jiějué fāng'àn [个 gè]
solve [sɒ̱lv] VT 1 (+ *mystery, case*) 破

解 pòjiě **2** (+ *problem*) 解决 jiějué

KEYWORD

some [səm, STRONG sʌm] **I** ADJ **1** (*a little, a few*) 一些 yīxiē ▶ **some milk/books** 一些牛奶/书 yīxiē niúnǎi/shū **2** (*certain, in contrasts*) 某些 mǒuxiē ▶ **some people say that...** 有些人说… yǒuxiē rén shuō...
II PRON (*a certain amount, certain number*) 一些 yīxiē ▶ **I've got some** 我有一些 wǒ yǒu yīxiē ▶ **there was/were some left** 还剩下一些 hái shèngxià yīxiē ▶ **some of it/them** 它的一部分/他们中的一些 tāde yī bùfen/tāmen zhōng de yīxiē

somebody [sʌmbadi, -bʌdi] PRON = **someone**

somehow [sʌmhaʊ] ADV 不知怎样地 bùzhī zěnyàng de

someone [sʌmwʌn] PRON 某人 mǒurén ▶ **I saw someone in the garden** 我看见花园里有人 wǒ kànjiàn huāyuán lǐ yǒurén ▶ **someone else** 别人 biérén

someplace [sʌmpleɪs] ADV = **somewhere**

something [sʌmθɪŋ] PRON 某事物 mǒushìwù ▶ **something else** 其他事情 qítā shìqing ▶ **would you like a sandwich or something?** 你要来点三明治或其他什么东西吗？ nǐ yào lái diǎn sānmíngzhì huò qítā shénme dōngxi ma?

sometime [sʌmtaɪm] ADV 某个时候 mǒugè shíhòu

> 请勿将 **sometimes** 和 **sometime** 混淆。**sometimes** 表示某事物只发生在某些时候，而不是总是发生。*Do you visit your sister? – Sometimes... Sometimes I wish I still lived in Australia.* **sometimes** 还可以表示某事物发生在特定情况下，而不是在任何情况下都会发生。*Sometimes they stay for a week, sometimes just for the weekend.* **sometime** 表示未来或过去某个不确定或未指明的时间。*Can I come and see you sometime? ...He started his new job sometime last month.*

sometimes [sʌmtaɪmz] ADV 有时 yǒushí

somewhere [sʌmwɛər] ADV 在某处 zài mǒuchù ▶ **I need somewhere to live** 我需要找个地方住 wǒ xūyào zhǎogè dìfang zhù ▶ **I must have lost it somewhere** 我一定把它丢在哪儿了 wǒ yīdìng bǎ bā diūzài nǎr le ▶ **let's go somewhere quiet** 我们去个安静的地方吧 wǒmen qù gè ānjìng de dìfang ba ▶ **somewhere else** 别的地方 biéde dìfang

son [sʌn] N [C] 儿子 érzi [个 gè]

song [sɔŋ] N [C] 歌曲 gēqǔ [首 shǒu]

son-in-law [sʌnɪnlɔ] (*pl* **sons-in-law**) N [C] 女婿 nǚxu [个 gè]

soon [sun] ADV **1** (*in a short time*) 不久 bùjiǔ **2** (*a short time later*) 很快 hěnkuài **3** (*early*) 早 zǎo ▶ **soon afterwards** 不久后 bùjiǔ hòu ▶ **as soon as** 一…就… yī...jiù... ▶ **quite soon** 很快 hěnkuài ▶ **see you soon!** 再见！ zàijiàn!

sooner [sunər] ADV ▶ **sooner or later** 迟早 chízǎo ▶ **the sooner the better** 越快越好 yuè kuài yuè hǎo

sophomore [sɒfəmɔr] N [C] 二年级学生 èr niánjí xuéshēng [个 gè]

sore [sɔr] ADJ 痛的 tòng de

sorry [sɒri] ADJ 懊悔的 àohuǐ de ▶ **(I'm) sorry!** (*apology*) 对不起！ duìbùqǐ! ▶ **sorry?** (*pardon?*) 请再讲一遍 qǐng zài jiǎng yībiàn ▶ **to feel sorry for sb** 对某人表示同情 duì mǒurén biǎoshì tóngqíng ▶ **to be sorry about sth** 对某事表示歉意 duì mǒushì biǎoshì qiànyì ▶ **I'm sorry to hear that...** 听到…我很伤心 tīngdào...wǒ hěn shāngxīn

sort [sɔrt] **I** N **1** [C] ▶ **sort (of)** 种类

zhǒnglèi [个 gè] **2** [c] (*make, brand*) 品牌 pǐnpái [个 gè] **II** VT **1** (+ *papers, mail, belongings*) 把…分类 bǎ...fēnlèi **2** (*Comput*) 整理 zhěnglǐ ▶ **sort of** (*inf*) 有点儿 yǒu diǎnr ▶ **all sorts of** 各种不同的 gèzhǒng bùtóng de; **sort out** VT **1** (+ *problem*) 解决 jiějué

sound [saʊnd] **I** N [c] 声音 shēngyīn [种 zhǒng] **II** VI **1** (*alarm, bell*) 响 xiǎng **2** (*seem*) 听起来 tīng qǐlái ▶ **to make a sound** 出声 chūshēng ▶ **that sounds like an explosion** 听起来像是爆炸声的 tīngqǐlái xiàngshì bàozhàshēng de ▶ **that sounds like a great idea** 这主意听起来妙极了 zhè zhǔyì tīngqǐlái miàojí le ▶ **it sounds as if...** 听起来似乎… tīngqǐlái sìhū...

soup [sup] N [c/u] 汤 tāng [份 fèn]

sour [saʊər] ADJ **1** (*bitter-tasting*) 酸的 suān de **2** (+ *milk*) 酸的 suān de

south [saʊθ] **I** N [s/u] 南方 nánfāng **II** ADJ 南部的 nánbù de **III** ADV 向南方 xiàng nánfāng ▶ **to the south** 以南 yǐnán ▶ **south of...** 在…以南 zài...yǐnán

South Africa N 南非 Nánfēi

South America N 南美洲 Nán měizhōu

southeast I N 东南 dōngnán **II** ADJ 东南的 dōngnán de **III** ADV 向东南 xiàng dōngnán

southern [sʌðərn] ADJ 南方的 nánfāng de ▶ **the southern hemisphere** 南半球 nán bànqiú

South Korea N 韩国 Hánguó

South Pole N ▶ **the South Pole** 南极 Nánjí

southwest I N [s/u] 西南 xīnán **II** ADJ 西南的 xīnán de **III** ADV 向西南 xiàng xīnán

souvenir [suvənɪər] N [c] 纪念品 jìniàn pǐn [件 jiàn]

soy sauce [sɔɪ-] N [u] 酱油 jiàngyóu

space [speɪs] N **1** [c/u] (*gap, place*) 空隙 kòngxì [个 gè] **2** [u] (*beyond Earth*) 太空 tàikōng ▶ **to clear a space for sth** 为某物腾地方 wèi mǒuwù téng dìfang

spade [speɪd] N [c] 锹 qiāo [把 bǎ]

spaghetti [spəgɛti] N [u] 意大利面 yìdàlì miàn

Spain [speɪn] N 西班牙 Xībānyá

spam [spæm] (*Comput*) N [u] 垃圾邮件 lājī yóujiàn

Spanish [spænɪʃ] **I** ADJ 西班牙的 Xībānyá de **II** N [u] (*language*) 西班牙语 Xībānyáyǔ

spare [spɛər] **I** ADJ **1** (*free*) 多余的 duōyú de **2** (*extra*) 备用的 bèiyòng de **II** N [c] = **spare part**

spare part N [c] 备件 bèijiàn [个 gè]

spare time N [u] 业余时间 yèyú shíjiān

spat [spæt] PT, PP *of* **spit**

speak [spik] (*pt* **spoke**, *pp* **spoken**) **I** VT (+ *language*) 讲 jiǎng **II** VI 讲话 jiǎnghuà ▶ **to speak to sb about sth** 和某人谈某事 hé mǒurén tán mǒushì

special [spɛʃᵊl] ADJ **1** (*important*) 特别的 tèbié de **2** (*particular*) 专门的 zhuānmén de ▶ **we only use these plates on special occasions** 我们只在特别场合才用这些碟子 wǒmen zhǐzài tèbié chǎnghé cái yòng zhèxiē diézi ▶ **it's nothing special** 没什么特别的 méi shénme tèbié de

specially [spɛʃəli] ADV 专门地 zhuānmén de

specialty [spɛʃᵊlti] N [c] (*food*) 特制品 tèzhìpǐn [种 zhǒng]; (*product*) 特产 tèchǎn [种 zhǒng]

species [spiʃiz] N [c] 种 zhǒng [个 gè]

specific [spɪsɪfɪk] ADJ **1** (*fixed*) 特定的 tèdìng de **2** (*exact*) 具体的 jùtǐ de

spectacles [spɛktəkᵊlz] N PL 眼镜 yǎnjìng

spectacular [spɛktækyələr] ADJ (+ *view, scenery*) 壮丽的 zhuànglìde; (+ *rise, growth*) 惊人的 jīngrénde; (+ *success, result*) 引人注目的 yǐnrén zhùmù de

spectator [spɛkteɪtər] N [c] 观众 guānzhòng [个 gè]

sped [spɛd] PT, PP *of* **speed**

speech [spiːtʃ] N [C] 演说 yǎnshuō [场 chǎng]

speed [spiːd] (*pt, pp* **sped**) N **1** [C/U] (*rate, promptness*) 速度 sùdù [种 zhǒng] **2** [U] (*fast movement*) 快速 kuàisù **3** [C] (*rapidity*) 迅速 xùnsù ▸ **at a speed of 70mph** 以时速70英里 yǐ shísù qīshí yīnglǐ

speed limit (*Law*) N [C] 速度极限 sùdù jíxiàn [个 gè]

spell [spɛl] (*pt, pp* **spelled** *or* **spelt**) VT 用字母拼 yòng zìmǔ pīn ▸ **he can't spell** 他不会拼写 tā bùhuì pīnxiě

spelling [spɛlɪŋ] N [C] (*of word*) 拼法 pīnfǎ [种 zhǒng] ▸ **spelling mistake** 拼写错误 pīnxiě cuòwù

spelt [spɛlt] PT, PP *of* **spell**

spend [spɛnd] (*pt, pp* **spent**) VT **1** (+ *money*) 花费 huāfèi **2** (+ *time, life*) 度过 dùguò ▸ **to spend time/energy on sth** 在某事上花时间/精力 zài mǒushì shàng huā shíjiān/jīnglì ▸ **to spend time/energy doing sth** 花时间/精力做某事 huā shíjiān/jīnglì zuò mǒushì ▸ **to spend the night in a hotel** 在旅馆度过一晚 zài lǚguǎn dùguò yīwǎn

spent [spɛnt] PT, PP *of* **spend**

spicy [spaɪsi] ADJ 辛辣的 xīnlà de

spider [spaɪdər] N [C] 蜘蛛 zhīzhū [只 zhī] ▸ **spider's web** 蜘蛛网 zhīzhū wǎng

spill [spɪl] (*pt, pp* **spilled** *or* **spilt**) **I** VT 使溢出 shǐ yìchū **II** VI 溢出 yìchū ▸ **to spill sth on/over sth** 将某物洒在某物上 jiāng mǒuwù sǎzài mǒuwù shàng

spilt [spɪlt] PT, PP *of* **spill**

spinach [spɪnɪtʃ] N [U] 菠菜 bōcài

spine [spaɪn] N [C] 脊柱 jǐzhù [根 gēn]

spit [spɪt] (*pt, pp* **spat**) **I** N [U] (*saliva*) 唾液 tuòyè **II** VI 吐唾液 tǔ tuòyè

spite [spaɪt] N [U] 恶意 èyì ▸ **in spite of** 尽管 jǐnguǎn

splendid [splɛndɪd] ADJ (*excellent*) 极好的 jíhǎo de

split [splɪt] (*pt, pp* **split**) **I** VT **1** (*divide*) 把…划分 bǎ...huàfēn **2** (+ *work, profits*) 平分 píngfēn; **split up I** VI 分手 fēnshǒu

spoil [spɔɪl] (*pt, pp* **spoiled** *or* **spoilt**) VT **1** (*damage*) 损害 sǔnhài **2** (+ *child*) 溺爱 nì'ài

spoilt [spɔɪlt] **I** PT, PP *of* **spoil II** ADJ 宠坏的 chǒnghuài de

spoke [spoʊk] PT *of* **speak**

spoken [spoʊkən] PP *of* **speak**

spokesman [spoʊksmən] (*pl* **spokesmen**) N [C] 男发言人 nán fāyánrén [位 wèi]

spokeswoman [spoʊkswʊmən] (*pl* **spokeswomen**) N [C] 女发言人 nǚ fāyánrén [位 wèi]

sponge [spʌndʒ] N [U] 海绵 hǎimián

spoon [spuːn] N [C] 匙 chí [把 bǎ]

sport [spɔrt] N **1** [C] (*particular game*) 运动 yùndòng [项 xiàng] **2** [U] (*generally*) 体育 tǐyù

sportswear [spɔrtswɛər] N [U] 运动服 yùndòngfú

spot [spɒt] N [C] **1** (*mark*) 斑点 bāndiǎn [个 gè] **2** (*dot*) 点 diǎn [个 gè] ▸ **on the spot** (*in that place*) 在现场 zài xiànchǎng; (*immediately*) 当场 dāngchǎng

sprain [spreɪn] VT ▸ **to sprain one's ankle/wrist** 扭伤脚踝/手腕 niǔshāng jiǎohuái/shǒuwàn

spray [spreɪ] VT **1** (+ *liquid*) 喷 pēn **2** (+ *crops*) 向…喷杀虫剂 xiàng...pēn shāchóng jì

spread [sprɛd] (*pt, pp* **spread**) VT **1** ▸ **to spread sth on/over** 把某物摊在…上 bǎ mǒuwù tānzài...shang **2** (+ *disease*) 传播 chuánbō

spreadsheet [sprɛdʃit] N [C] 电子表格 diànzǐ biǎogé [份 fèn]

spring [sprɪŋ] N **1** [C/U] (*season*) 春季 chūnjì [个 gè] **2** [C] (*wire coil*) 弹簧 tánhuáng [个 gè] ▸ **in (the) spring** 在春季 zài chūnjì

spy [spaɪ] N [C] 间谍 jiàndié [个 gè]

spying N [U] 当间谍 dāng jiàndié

square [skwɛər] **I** N [C] **1** 正方形 zhèngfāng xíng [个 gè] **2** (*in town*)

广场 guǎngchǎng [个 gè] 3 (*Math*) 平方 píngfāng [个 gè] II ADJ 正方形的 zhèngfāng xíng de ▶ **2 square meters** 2平方米 èr píngfāngmǐ

squash [skwɒʃ] I N [U] (*Sport*) 壁球 bìqiú II VT 把…压碎 bǎ...yāsuì

squeeze [skwiːz] VT 用力捏 yònglì niē

stab [stæb] VT 刺 cì

stable [steɪbᵊl] I ADJ 稳定的 wěndìng de II N [C] 马厩 mǎjiù [个 gè]

stadium [steɪdiəm] (*pl* **stadia** *or* **stadiums**) N [C] 体育场 tǐyùchǎng [个 gè]

staff [stæf] N [C] 职员 zhíyuán [名 míng]

stage [steɪdʒ] N [C] 1 (*in theater*) 舞台 wǔtái [个 gè] 2 (*platform*) 平台 píngtái [个 gè] ▶ **in the early/final stages** 在早/晚期 zài zǎo/wǎnqī

stain [steɪn] I N [C] 污迹 wūjì [处 chù] II VT 沾污 zhānwū

stainless steel [steɪnlɪs stiːl] N [U] 不锈钢 bùxiù gāng

stair [stɛər] I N [C] (*step*) 梯级 tījí [层 céng] II **stairs** N PL (*flight of steps*) 楼梯 lóutī

stall [stɔːl] N [C] 货摊 huòtān [个 gè]

stamp [stæmp] I N [C] 1 邮票 yóupiào [枚 méi] 2 (*in passport*) 章 zhāng [个 gè] II VT (+ *passport, visa*) 盖章于 gàizhāng yú

stand [stænd] (*pt, pp* **stood**) I VI 1 (*be upright*) 站立 zhànlì 2 (*rise*) 站起来 zhàn qǐlái 3 ▶ **to stand aside/back** 让开/退后 ràngkāi/tuìhòu II VT ▶ **I can't stand him/it** 我无法容忍他/它 wǒ wúfǎ róngrěn tā/tā; **stand for** VT FUS (*abbreviation*) 代表 dàibiǎo; **stand out** VI 醒目 xǐngmù; **stand up** VI (*rise*) 起立 qǐlì

standard [stændərd] I N [C] 1 (*level*) 水平 shuǐpíng [种 zhǒng] 2 (*norm, criterion*) 标准 biāozhǔn [个 gè] II ADJ 1 (+ *size*) 普通的 pǔtōng de 2 (+ *procedure, practice*) 标准的 biāozhǔn de 3 (+ *model, feature*) 规范的 guīfàn de

stank [stæŋk] PT *of* **stink**

star [stɑr] N [C] 1 星 xīng [颗 kē] 2 (*celebrity*) 明星 míngxīng [个 gè] ▶ **a 4-star hotel** 4星级旅馆 sì xīngjí lǚguǎn

stare [stɛər] VI ▶ **to stare (at sb/sth)** 盯着（某人/某物） dīngzhe (mǒurén/mǒuwù)

start [stɑrt] I N [C] 开始 kāishǐ [个 gè] II VT 1 (*begin*) 开始 kāishǐ 2 (+ *business*) 创建 chuàngjiàn 3 (+ *engine, car*) 启动 qǐdòng III VI (*begin*) 开始 kāishǐ ▶ **to start doing** *or* **to do sth** 开始做某事 kāishǐ zuò mǒushì; **start on** VT FUS 开始 kāishǐ; **start over** VI, VT 重新开始 chóngxīn kāishǐ; **start up** VT 创办 chuàngbàn

starve [stɑrv] VI 1 (*be very hungry*) 挨饿 ái'è 2 (*die from hunger*) 饿死 èsǐ ▶ **I'm starving** 我饿极了 wǒ è jí le

state [steɪt] I N 1 [C] (*condition*) 状态 zhuàngtài [种 zhǒng] 2 [C] (*country*) 国家 guójiā [个 gè] 3 [C] (*part of country*) 州 zhōu [个 gè] II **the States** N PL (*inf*) 美国 Měiguó ▶ **state of affairs** 事态 shìtài

statement [steɪtmənt] N [C] 声明 shēngmíng [个 gè]

station [steɪʃᵊn] N [C] 1 (*railway station*) 车站 chēzhàn [个 gè] 2 (*on radio*) 电台 diàntái [个 gè]

statue [stætʃu] N [C] 塑像 sùxiàng [尊 zūn]

stay [steɪ] I N [C] 逗留 dòuliú [次 cì] II VI 1 (*in place, position*) 呆 dāi 2 (*in town, hotel, someone's house*) 逗留 dòuliú 3 (*in state, situation*) 保持 bǎochí III VT ▶ **to stay the night** 过夜 guòyè ▶ **to stay with sb** 在某人家暂住 zài mǒurén jiā zànzhù; **stay in** VI 呆在家里 dāizài jiālǐ; **stay up** VI 不去睡 bùqùshuì

steady [stɛdi] ADJ 1 (+ *progress, increase, fall*) 稳定的 wěndìng de 2 (+ *job, income*) 固定的 gùdìng de

steak [steɪk] N [C/U] 牛排 niúpái [份 fèn]

steal [stil] (*pt* **stole**, *pp* **stolen**) I VT 偷窃 tōuqiè II VI 行窃 xíngqiè ▸ **he stole it from me** 他从我这里把它偷走了 tā cóng wǒ zhèlǐ bǎ tā tōuzǒu le

steam [stim] I N [U] 蒸汽 zhēngqì II VT 蒸 zhēng

steel [stil] I N [U] 钢铁 gāngtiě II CPD 钢制 gāngzhì

steep [stip] ADJ 陡的 dǒu de

steering wheel [stɪərɪŋ-] N [C] 方向盘 fāngxiàng pán [个 gè]

step [stɛp] I N 1 [C] (*stage*) 阶段 jiēduàn [个 gè] 2 [C] (*of stairs*) 梯级 tījí [层 céng] II VI ▸ **to step forward/backward** *etc* 向前/后{等}迈步 xiàngqián/hòu {děng} màibù; **step aside, step down** VI 辞职 cízhí

stepbrother [stɛpbrʌðər] N [C] (*with shared father*) 异母兄弟 yìmǔ xiōngdì [个 gè]; (*with shared mother*) 异父兄弟 yìfù xiōngdì [个 gè]

stepdaughter [stɛpdɔtər] N [C] 继女 jìnǚ [个 gè]

stepfather [stɛpfɑðər] N [C] 继父 jìfù [位 wèi]

stepmother [stɛpmʌðər] N [C] 继母 jìmǔ [位 wèi]

stepsister [stɛpsɪstər] N [C] (*with shared father*) 异母姐妹 yìmǔ jiěmèi [个 gè]; (*with shared mother*) 异父姐妹 yìfù jiěmèi [个 gè]

stepson [stɛpsʌn] N [C] 继子 jìzǐ [个 gè]

stereo [stɛrioʊ, stɪər-] N [C] 立体声装置 lìtǐ shēng zhuāngzhì [套 tào]

sterling [stɜrlɪŋ] N [U] 英国货币 Yīngguó huòbì ▸ **one pound sterling** 一英镑 yī yīngbàng

stew [stu] N [C/U] 炖的食物 dùn de shíwù [种 zhǒng]

stewardess [stuərdɪs] N [C] 女乘务员 nǚ chéngwù yuán [位 wèi]

stick [stɪk] (*pt, pp* **stuck**) I N [C] 1 (*of wood*) 枯枝 kūzhī [根 gēn] 2 (*walking stick*) 拐杖 guǎizhàng [根 gēn] II VT ▸ **to stick sth on** *or* **to sth** (*with glue etc*) 将某物粘贴在某物上 jiāng mǒuwù zhāntiē zài mǒuwù shang; **stick out** VI 伸出 shēnchū

sticker [stɪkər] N [C] 不干胶标签 bù gānjiāo biāoqiān [个 gè]

sticky [stɪki] ADJ 1 (+ *substance*) 黏的 nián de 2 (+ *tape, paper*) 黏性的 niánxìng de

stiff [stɪf] I ADJ 1 (+ *person*) 酸痛的 suāntòng de; (+ *neck, arm etc*) 僵硬的 jiāngyìng de 2 (+ *competition*) 激烈的 jīliè de II ADV ▸ **to be bored/scared stiff** 讨厌/害怕极了 tǎoyàn/hàipà jíle

still [stɪl] I ADJ (+ *person, hands*) 不动的 bùdòng de II ADV 1 (*up to the present*) 仍然 réngrán 2 (*even*) 更 gèng 3 (*yet*) 还 hái 4 (*nonetheless*) 尽管如此 jǐnguǎn rúcǐ ▸ **to stand/keep still** 站着别动/别动 zhànzhe biédòng/biédòng ▸ **he still hasn't arrived** 他还没到 tā hái méi dào

sting [stɪŋ] (*pt, pp* **stung**) I N [C] 刺 cì [根 gēn] II VT 刺 cì

stink [stɪŋk] (*pt* **stank**, *pp* **stunk**) I N [C] 恶臭 èchòu [种 zhǒng] II VI 发臭 fāchòu

stir [stɜr] VT 搅动 jiǎodòng

stitch [stɪtʃ] N [C] (*Med*) 缝针 féngzhēn [枚 méi]

stock [stɒk] N [C] 供应物 gōngyìng wù [种 zhǒng]; **stock up** VI ▸ **to stock up (on** *or* **with sth)** 储备（某物）chǔbèi (mǒuwù)

stock exchange N [C] 股票交易所 gǔpiào jiāoyì suǒ [个 gè]

stocking [stɒkɪŋ] N [C] 长统袜 chángtǒng wà [双 shuāng]

stole [stoʊl] PT *of* **steal**

stolen [stoʊlᵊn] PP *of* **steal**

stomach [stʌmək] N [C] 1 (*organ*) 胃 wèi [个 gè] 2 (*abdomen*) 腹部 fùbù [个 gè]

stomachache [stʌməkeɪk] N [C/U] 胃痛 wèitòng [阵 zhèn]

stone [stoʊn] N 1 [U] 石头 shítou 2 [C] (*pebble*) 石子 shízǐ [块 kuài]

stood [stʊd] PT, PP *of* **stand**

stop [stɒp] I VT 1 停止 tíngzhǐ 2 (*prevent*) 阻止 zǔzhǐ II VI 1 (*person,* *vehicle*) 停下来 tíng xiàlái **2** (*rain, noise, activity*) 停 tíng **III** N [c] (*for bus, train*) 车站 chēzhàn [个 gè] ▸ **to stop doing sth** 停止做某事 tíngzhǐ zuò mǒushì ▸ **to stop sb (from) doing sth** 阻止某人做某事 zǔzhǐ mǒurén zuò mǒushì ▸ **stop it!** 住手！ zhùshǒu!

stoplight [stɒplaɪt] N [c] (*in road*) 交通信号灯 jiāotōng xìnhào dēng [个 gè]

store [stɔr] **I** N [c] (*shop*) 店铺 diànpù [家 jiā] **II** VT **1** (+ *provisions, information*) 存放 cúnfàng **2** (*computer, brain*) (+ *information*) 存储 cúnchǔ

store window N [c] 商店橱窗 shāngdiàn chúchuāng [个 gè]

storm [stɔrm] N [c] 暴风雨 bàofēngyǔ [场 chǎng]

stormy [stɔrmi] ADJ 有暴风雨的 yǒu bàofēngyǔ de

story [stɔri] N [c] **1** (*account*) 描述 miáoshù [种 zhǒng] **2** (*tale*) 故事 gùshì [个 gè] **3** (*in newspaper, on news broadcast*) 报道 bàodào [条 tiáo] **4** (*of building*) 层 céng

stove [stoʊv] N [c] 炉子 lúzi [个 gè]

straight [streɪt] **I** ADJ **1** 笔直的 bǐzhí de **2** (+ *hair*) 直的 zhí de **II** ADV **1** (*walk, stand, look*) 直 zhí **2** (*immediately*) 直接地 zhíjiē de

straightforward [streɪtfɔrwərd] ADJ 简单的 jiǎndān de

strain [streɪn] **I** N **1** [c/u] (*pressure*) 负担 fùdān [个 gè] **2** [c/u] ▸ **back/muscle strain** 背部/肌肉扭伤 bèibù/jīròu niǔshāng [处 chù] **II** VT (+ *back, muscle*) 扭伤 niǔshāng

strange [streɪndʒ] ADJ **1** (*odd*) 奇怪的 qíguài de **2** (*unfamiliar*) (+ *person, place*) 陌生的 mòshēng de

stranger [streɪndʒər] N [c] 陌生人 mòshēng rén [个 gè]

strap [stræp] N [c] (*of watch, bag*) 带 dài [根 gēn]

straw [strɔ] N **1** [u] 稻草 dàocǎo **2** [c] (*drinking straw*) 吸管 xīguǎn [根 gēn]

strawberry [strɔbɛri] N [c] 草莓 cǎoméi [个 gè]

stream [strim] **I** N [c] 溪流 xīliú [条 tiáo] **II** VI (*on internet*) 在线观看或收听 zàixiàn guānkàn huò shōutīng

street [strit] N [c] 街道 jiēdào [条 tiáo]

streetcar [stritkɑr] N [c] 有轨电车 yǒuguǐ diànchē [部 bù]

strength [strɛŋkθ, strɛŋθ] N **1** [u] 力气 lìqi **2** [u] (*of object, material*) 强度 qiángdù

stress [strɛs] **I** N [c/u] 压力 yālì [个 gè] **II** VT (+ *point, importance*) 强调 qiángdiào

stressful [strɛsfəl] ADJ 紧张的 jǐnzhāng de

stretch [strɛtʃ] **I** VI 伸懒腰 shēn lǎnyāo **II** VT (+ *arm, leg*) 伸直 shēnzhí; **stretch out** VT (+ *arm, leg*) 伸出 shēnchū

strict [strɪkt] ADJ **1** (+ *rule, instruction*) 严格的 yángé de **2** (+ *person*) 严厉的 yánlì de

strike [straɪk] (*pt, pp* **struck**) **I** N [c] 罢工 bàgōng [场 chǎng] **II** VI **1** 罢工 bàgōng **2** (*clock*) 报时 bàoshí ▸ **to be on strike** 在罢工 zài bàgōng

striker [straɪkər] N [c] **1** (*person on strike*) 罢工者 bàgōng zhě [名 míng] **2** (*Soccer*) 前锋 qiánfēng [个 gè]

string [strɪŋ] (*pt, pp* **strung**) N **1** [c/u] 细绳 xìshéng [根 gēn] **2** [c] (*on guitar, violin*) 弦 xián [根 gēn]

strip [strɪp] **I** N [c] (*of paper, cloth*) 狭条 xiátiáo [条 tiáo] **II** VI (*undress*) 脱光衣服 tuōguāng yīfu; (*as entertainer*) 表演脱衣舞 biǎoyǎn tuōyī wǔ

stripe [straɪp] N [c] 条纹 tiáowén [个 gè]

striped [straɪpt] ADJ 有条纹的 yǒu tiáowén de

stroke [stroʊk] **I** N [c] (*Med*) 中风 zhòngfēng [次 cì] **II** VT (+ *person, animal*) 抚摸 fǔmō

stroller [stroʊlər] N [c] 婴儿小推车 yīng'ér xiǎo tuīchē [辆 liàng]

strong [strɔŋ] ADJ **1** (+ *person, arms,*

grip) 有力的 yǒulì de **2** (+ *object, material*) 牢固的 láogù de **3** (+ *wind, current*) 强劲的 qiángjìn de
struck [strʌk] PT, PP *of* **strike**
struggle [strʌgᵊl] VI **1** (*try hard*) 尽力 jìnlì **2** (*fight*) 搏斗 bódòu
stubborn [stʌbərn] ADJ 倔强的 juéjiàng de
stuck [stʌk] **I** PT, PP *of* **stick II** ADJ ▸ **to be stuck** (*object*) 卡住 qiǎzhù; (*person*) 陷于 xiànyú
student [studᵊnt] N [C] **1** (*at university*) 大学生 dà xuéshēng [名 míng] **2** (*at school*) 中学生 zhōng xuéshēng [名 míng] ▸ **a law/medical student** 一名法律/医学学生 yīmíng fǎlǜ/yīxué xuéshēng
studio [studioʊ] N [C] **1** (*TV, Rad, Mus*) 摄影室 shèyǐng shì [个 gè] **2** (*of artist*) 画室 huàshì [个 gè]
study [stʌdi] **I** N [C] (*room*) 书房 shūfáng [间 jiān] **II** VT (+ *subject*) 攻读 gōngdú **III** VI 学习 xuéxí
stuff [stʌf] **I** N [U] **1** (*things*) 物品 wùpǐn **2** (*substance*) 东西 dōngxi **II** VT (+ *peppers, mushrooms*) 给…装馅 gěi...zhuāngxiàn; (+ *chicken, turkey*) 把填料塞入 bǎ tiánliào sāirù
stuffy [stʌfi] ADJ 闷热的 mēnrè de
stung [stʌŋ] PT, PP *of* **sting**
stunk [stʌŋk] PP *of* **stink**
stunning [stʌnɪŋ] ADJ **1** (*impressive*) 惊人的 jīngrén de **2** (*beautiful*) 极漂亮的 jí piàoliàng de
stupid [stupɪd] ADJ **1** 笨的 bèn de **2** (+ *question, idea, mistake*) 愚蠢的 yúchǔn de
style [staɪl] N **1** [C] (*type*) 方式 fāngshì [种 zhǒng] **2** [U] (*elegance*) 风度 fēngdù **3** [C/U] (*design*) 样式 yàngshì [种 zhǒng]
subject [sʌbdʒɪkt] N [C] **1** (*matter*) 主题 zhǔtí [个 gè] **2** (*Scol*) 科目 kēmù [个 gè] **3** (*Gram*) 主语 zhǔyǔ [个 gè]
submarine [sʌbmərin] N [C] 潜水艇 qiánshuǐtǐng [艘 sōu]
substance [sʌbstəns] N [C] 物质 wùzhì [种 zhǒng]
substitute [sʌbstɪtut] **I** N [C] **1** (*person*) 代替者 dàitì zhě [位 wèi] **2** (*thing*) 代用品 dàiyòngpǐn [件 jiàn] **II** VT ▸ **to substitute sth (for sth)** 用某物代替（某物） yòng mǒuwù dàitì (mǒuwù)
subtitles [sʌbtaɪtᵊlz] N PL 字幕 zìmù
subtract [səbtrækt] VT ▸ **to subtract sth (from sth)** （从某数中）减去某数 (cóng mǒushù zhōng) jiǎnqù mǒushù
suburb [sʌbɜrb] N [C] 郊区 jiāoqū [个 gè]
subway [sʌbweɪ] N [C] (*underground railway*) 地铁 dìtiě [条 tiáo]
succeed [səksid] VI 成功 chénggōng ▸ **to succeed in doing sth** 成功地做某事 chénggōng de zuò mǒushì
success [səksɛs] N [U/C] 成功 chénggōng ▸ **without success** 一无所成 yī wú suǒ chéng
successful [səksɛsfəl] ADJ 成功的 chénggōng de
successfully [səksɛsfəli] ADV 成功地 chénggōng de
such [sʌtʃ] ADJ **1** (*of this kind*) 此类的 cǐlèi de **2** (*so much*) 这么 zhème ▸ **such a lot of** 那么多 nàme duō ▸ **such as** (*like*) 像 xiàng
suck [sʌk] VT 含在嘴里舔吃 hánzài zuǐlǐ tiǎnchī
sudden [sʌdᵊn] ADJ 意外的 yìwài de
suddenly [sʌdᵊnli] ADV 突然 tūrán
suede [sweɪd] N [U] 仿麂皮 fǎng jǐpí
suffer [sʌfər] VI **1** (*due to pain, illness, poverty*) 受损失 shòu sǔnshī **2** (*be badly affected*) 受苦难 shòu kǔnàn
sugar [ʃʊgər] N [U/C] 糖 táng [勺 sháo]
suggest [səgdʒɛst] VT 建议 jiànyì ▸ **to suggest that...** (*propose*) 建议… jiànyì...
suggestion [səgdʒɛstʃᵊn] N [C] 建议 jiànyì [条 tiáo] ▸ **to make a suggestion** 提建议 tí jiànyì
suicide [suɪsaɪd] N [C/U] 自杀 zìshā ▸ **a suicide bomber** 人肉炸弹 rénròu zhàdàn ▸ **to commit suicide** 自杀

zìshā

suit [sut] I N [C] 西装 xīzhuāng [套 tào] II VT 1 (*be convenient, appropriate*) 对…合适 duì...héshì 2 (*color, clothes*) 适合 shìhé

suitable [sutəbᵊl] ADJ 1 (+ *time, place*) 合适的 héshì de 2 (+ *person, clothes*) 适合的 shìhé de

suitcase [sutkeɪs] N [C] 手提箱 shǒutíxiāng [个 gè]

sum [sʌm] I N [C] 1 (*amount*) 数额 shù'é [笔 bǐ] 2 (*calculation*) 算术题 suànshù tí [道 dào] ▸ **to do a sum** 算算术 suàn suànshù; **sum up** VI 总结 zǒngjié

summarize [sʌməraɪz] VT 概括 gàikuò

summary [sʌməri] N [C] 摘要 zhāiyào [个 gè]

summer [sʌmər] N [C/U] 夏季 xiàjì [个 gè] ▸ **in (the) summer** 在夏季 zài xiàjì

summit [sʌmɪt] N [C] 峰顶 fēngdǐng [个 gè]

sun [sʌn] N 1 [S/C] (*in the sky*) 太阳 tàiyáng [轮 lún] 2 [U] (*heat*) 太阳的光和热 tàiyáng de guāng hé rè; (*light*) 阳光 yángguāng

sunbathe [sʌnbeɪð] VI 晒日光浴 shài rìguāngyù

sunburn [sʌnbɜrn] N [U] 晒斑 shàibān

sunburned [sʌnbɜrnd], **sunburnt** [sʌnbɜrnt] ADJ 晒伤的 shàishāng de

Sunday [sʌndeɪ, -di] N [C/U] 星期天 xīngqītiān [个 gè]; *see also* **Tuesday**

sung [sʌŋ] PP *of* **sing**

sunglasses [sʌnglæsɪz] N PL 墨镜 mòjìng

sunk [sʌŋk] PP *of* **sink**

sunny [sʌni] ADJ 晴朗的 qínglǎng de ▸ **it is sunny** 天气晴朗 tiānqì qínglǎng

sunrise [sʌnraɪz] N [U] 拂晓 fúxiǎo

sunscreen [sʌnskrin] N [C/U] 遮光屏 zhēguāng píng [个 gè]

sunset [sʌnsɛt] N 1 [U] (*time*) 傍晚 bàngwǎn 2 [C] (*sky*) 日落 rìluò [次 cì]

sunshine [sʌnʃaɪn] N [U] 阳光 yángguāng

suntan [sʌntæn] I N [C] 晒黑 shàihēi [处 chù] II CPD (+ *lotion, cream*) 防晒 fángshài

supermarket [supərmarkɪt] N [U] 超级市场 chāojí shìchǎng

supervise [supərvaɪz] VT 监督 jiāndū

supper [sʌpər] N [C/U] 1 (*early evening*) 晚餐 wǎncān [顿 dùn] 2 (*late evening*) 夜宵 yèxiāo [顿 dùn]

supply [səplaɪ] I VT 提供 tígōng II N [C/U] 供应量 gōngyìng liàng ▸ **to supply sb/sth with sth** 为某人/某物提供某物 wèi mǒurén/mǒuwù tígōng mǒuwù

support [səpɔrt] VT 1 (*morally*) 支持 zhīchí 2 (*financially*) 供养 gōngyǎng 3 (+ *football team*) 支持 zhīchí

supporter [səpɔrtər] N [C] 支持者 zhīchí zhě [个 gè]

suppose [səpoʊz] VT 认为 rènwéi ▸ **I suppose** 我想 wǒ xiǎng ▸ **I suppose so/not** 我看是/不是这样 wǒ kàn shì/bùshì zhèyàng ▸ **he's supposed to be an expert** 人们以为他是个专家 rénmen yǐwéi tā shì gè zhuānjiā

supposing [səpoʊzɪŋ] CONJ 假使 jiǎshǐ

sure [ʃʊər] ADJ 1 有把握的 yǒu bǎwò de 2 ▸ **to be sure to do sth** (*certain*) 肯定做某事 kěndìng zuò mǒushì ▸ **to make sure that...** (*take action*) 保证… bǎozhèng...; (*check*) 查明… chámíng... ▸ **sure!** (*inf: of course*) 当然了！ dāngrán le! ▸ **I'm sure of it** 我确信 wǒ quèxìn ▸ **I'm not sure how/why/when** 我不能肯定如何/为什么/什么时候 wǒ bùnéng kěndìng rúhé/wèishénme/shénme shíhou

surf [sɜrf] I N [U] 拍岸的浪花 pāi'àn de lànghuā II VT ▸ **to surf the internet** 网上冲浪 wǎngshang chōnglàng ▸ **to go surfing** 去冲浪 qù chōnglàng

surface [sɜrfɪs] N **1** [c] (*of object*) 表面 biǎomiàn [个 gè] **2** [c] (*top layer*) 表层 biǎocéng [个 gè] ▶ **on the surface** 在表面上 zài biǎomiàn shàng
surfboard [sɜrfbɔrd] N [c] 冲浪板 chōnglàng bǎn [块 kuài]
surgeon [sɜrdʒᵊn] N [c] 外科医师 wàikē yīshī [位 wèi]
surgery [sɜrdʒəri] N [U] (*treatment*) 外科手术 wàikē shǒushù
surname [sɜrneɪm] N [c] 姓 xìng [个 gè]
surprise [sərpraɪz] **I** N **1** [c] (*unexpected event*) 意想不到的事物 yìxiǎng bùdào de shìwù [个 gè] **2** [U] (*astonishment*) 诧异 chàyì **II** VT 使感到意外 shǐ gǎndào yìwài ▶ **to my (great) surprise** 使我（很）惊奇的是 shǐ wǒ (hěn) jīngqí de shì
surprised [sərpraɪzd] ADJ 惊讶的 jīngyà de
surprising [sərpraɪzɪŋ] ADJ 出人意外的 chūrén yìwài de
surrender [sərɛndər] VI 投降 tóuxiáng
surround [səraʊnd] VT 包围 bāowéi
surroundings [səraʊndɪŋz] N PL 环境 huánjìng
survey [sɜrveɪ] N [c] 民意测验 mínyì cèyàn [项 xiàng]
survive [sərvaɪv] VI 幸存 xìngcún
survivor [sərvaɪvər] N [c] 幸存者 xìngcúnzhě [个 gè]
suspect [*n* sʌspɛkt, *vb* səspɛkt] **I** N [c] 嫌疑犯 xiányí fàn [个 gè] **II** VT **1** (+ *person*) 怀疑 huáiyí **2** (+ *sb's motives*) 质疑 zhìyí **3** (*think*) 猜想 cāixiǎng ▶ **to suspect that...** 怀疑… huáiyí...
suspense [səspɛns] N [U] 焦虑 jiāolǜ
suspicious [səspɪʃəs] ADJ (+ *circumstances, death, package*) 可疑的 kěyí de ▶ **to be suspicious of** *or* **about sb/sth** 对某人/某事起疑心 duì mǒurén/mǒushì qǐ yíxīn
swallow [swɒloʊ] VT 吞下 tūnxià
swam [swæm] PT *of* **swim**
swan [swɒn] N [c] 天鹅 tiān'é [只 zhī]
swap [swɒp] VT ▶ **to swap sth (for)** (*exchange for*) （以某物）作交换 (yǐ mǒuwù) zuò jiāohuàn; (*replace with*) 以…替代某物 yǐ...tìdài mǒuwù ▶ **to swap places (with sb)** （与某人）换位子 (yǔ mǒurén) huàn wèizi
swear word [swɛər-] N [c] 骂人的话 màrén de huà [句 jù]
sweat [swɛt] VI 出汗 chūhàn
sweater [swɛtər] N [c] 毛衣 máoyī [件 jiàn]
sweatshirt [swɛtʃɜrt] N [c] 棉毛衫 miánmáoshān [件 jiàn]
Sweden [swidᵊn] N 瑞典 Ruìdiǎn
sweep [swip] (*pt, pp* **swept**) VT 扫 sǎo
sweet [swit] ADJ **1** (*sugary*) 甜的 tián de **2** (*cute*) 可爱的 kě'ài de ▶ **sweet and sour** 糖醋 tángcù
swept [swɛpt] PT, PP *of* **sweep**
swerve [swɜrv] VI 突然转向 tūrán zhuǎnxiàng
swim [swɪm] (*pt* **swam**, *pp* **swum**) **I** VI **1** (*person, animal*) 游水 yóushuǐ **2** (*as sport*) 游泳 yóuyǒng **II** VT (+ *distance*) 游 yóu **III** N [c] ▶ **to go for a swim** 去游泳 qù yóuyǒng [次 cì] ▶ **to go swimming** 去游泳 qù yóuyǒng
swimming [swɪmɪŋ] N [U] 游泳 yóuyǒng
swimming pool N [c] 游泳池 yóuyǒng chí [个 gè]
swimsuit [swɪmsut] N [c] 游泳衣 yóuyǒng yī [套 tào]
swing [swɪŋ] (*pt, pp* **swung**) **I** N [c] 秋千 qiūqiān [副 fù] **II** VT (+ *arms, legs*) 摆动 bǎidòng **III** VI **1** (*pendulum*) 晃动 huàngdòng **2** (*door*) 转动 zhuǎndòng
switch [swɪtʃ] **I** N [c] 开关 kāiguān [个 gè] **II** VT (*change*) 改变 gǎibiàn; **switch off** VT 关掉 guāndiào; **switch on** VT (+ *light, engine, radio*) 开启 kāiqǐ

Switzerland [swɪtsərlənd] N 瑞士 Ruìshì
swollen [swoʊlᵊn] ADJ 肿胀的 zhǒngzhàng de
sword [sɔrd] N [C] 剑 jiàn [把 bǎ]
swum [swʌm] PP *of* **swim**
swung [swʌŋ] PT, PP *of* **swing**
symbol [sɪmbᵊl] N [C] **1** (*sign*) 象征 xiàngzhēng [种 zhǒng] **2** (*Math, Chem*) 符号 fúhào [个 gè]
sympathetic [sɪmpəθɛtɪk] ADJ 有同情心的 yǒu tóngqíngxīn de
sympathy [sɪmpəθi] N [U] 同情心 tóngqíng xīn
syringe [sɪrɪndʒ] N [C] 注射器 zhùshè qì [支 zhī]
system [sɪstəm] N [C] **1** (*organization, set*) 系统 xìtǒng [个 gè] **2** (*method*) 方法 fāngfǎ [种 zhǒng]

T

table [teɪbəl] N [C] 桌子 zhuōzi [张 zhāng] ▸ **to set the table** 摆餐桌 bǎi cānzhuō
tablecloth [teɪbəlklɔθ] N [C] 桌布 zhuōbù [块 kuài]
tablespoon [teɪbəlspun] N [C] 餐匙 cānchí [把 bǎ]
tablet [tæblɪt] N [C] **1** (*Med*) 药片 yàopiàn [片 piàn] **2** (*Comput*) 平板电脑 píngbǎn diànnǎo [个 gè]
table tennis N [U] 乒乓球 pīngpāngqiú
tact [tækt] N [U] 机智 jīzhì
tactful [tæktfəl] ADJ 老练的 lǎoliàn de
tactics [tæktɪks] N PL 策略 cèlüè
tadpole [tædpoʊl] N [C] 蝌蚪 kēdǒu [只 zhī]
taffy [tæfi] N [U] 太妃糖 tàifēitáng
tag [tæg] N [C] **1** (*label*) 标签 biāoqiān [个 gè] **2** (*electronic*) 标签 biāoqiān [个 gè]
tail [teɪl] N [C] 尾巴 wěiba [条 tiáo] ▸ **"heads or tails?" – "tails"** "正面还是背面？" "背面" "zhèngmiàn háishì bèimiàn?" "bèimiàn"
tailor [teɪlər] N [C] 裁缝 cáifeng [个 gè]
take [teɪk] (*pt* **took**, *pp* **taken**) **I** VT **1** (+ *vacation*) 度 dù; (+ *shower, bath*) 洗 xǐ **2** (*take hold of*) 拿 ná **3** (*steal*) 偷走 tōuzǒu **4** (*accompany*) 送 sòng **5** (*carry, bring*) 携带 xiédài **6** (+ *road*) 走 zǒu **7** (+ *bus, train*) 乘坐 chéngzuò **8** (+ *size*) 穿 chuān **9** (+ *time*) 花费 huāfèi **10** (+ *exam, test*) 参加 cānjiā **11** (+ *drug, pill*) 服用 fúyòng ▸ **don't forget to take your umbrella** 别忘了带雨伞。bié wàngle dài yǔsǎn; **take apart** VT (*dismantle*) (+ *bicycle, radio, machine*) 拆开 chāikāi; **take away** VT **1** (*remove*) 拿走 názǒu **2** (*carry off*) 带走 dàizǒu; **take back** VT (+ *goods*) 退回 tuìhuí; **take down** VT **1** (*write down*) 记录 jìlù; **take off I** VI 起飞 qǐfēi **II** VT (+ *clothes, glasses, makeup*) 脱下 tuōxià; **take out** VT (+ *person*) 邀请 yāoqǐng; **take up** VT **1** (+ *hobby, sport*) 开始 kāishǐ **2** (+ *time, space*) 占用 zhànyòng
taken [teɪkən] PP *of* **take**
takeoff [teɪkɔf] N [C] 起飞 qǐfēi [次 cì]
takeout [teɪkoʊt] N [C] **1** (*shop, restaurant*) 外卖店 wàimàidiàn [家 jiā] **2** (*food*) 外卖 wàimài [个 gè]
tale [teɪl] N [C] 故事 gùshi [个 gè]
talent [tælənt] N [C/U] 才能 cáinéng [种 zhǒng]
talented [tæləntɪd] ADJ 有才能的 yǒu cáinéng de
talk [tɔk] **I** N **1** [C] (*prepared speech*) 讲话 jiǎnghuà [次 cì] **2** [U] (*gossip*) 谣言 yáoyán **3** [C] (*discussion*) 交谈 jiāotán [次 cì] **II** VI **1** (*speak*) 说话 shuōhuà **2** (*chat*) 聊 liáo ▸ **to talk to** *or* **with sb** 跟某人谈话 gēn mǒurén tánhuà ▸ **to talk about sth** 谈论某事 tánlùn mǒushì; **talk over, talk through** VT 仔细商讨 zǐxì shāngtǎo
talkative [tɔkətɪv] ADJ 健谈的 jiàntán de
talk show N [C] 脱口秀 tuōkǒuxiù [个 gè]
tall [tɔl] ADJ 高的 gāo de ▸ **he's 6 feet tall** 他6英尺高 tā liù yīngchǐ gāo
tame [teɪm] ADJ 驯服的 xùnfú de
tampon [tæmpɒn] N [C] 月经棉栓 yuèjīng miánshuān [个 gè]
tan [tæn] N [C] 晒黑的肤色 shàihēi de fūsè [种 zhǒng]
tangerine [tændʒərin] N [C] 红橘 hóngjú [个 gè]
tank [tæŋk] N [C] **1** (*Mil*) 坦克 tǎnkè [部 bù] **2** (*for gasoline, water*) 箱 xiāng [个 gè]

tanker [tæŋkər] N [c] **1** (*ship*) 油轮 yóulún [艘 sōu] **2** (*truck*) 油罐车 yóuguànchē [辆 liàng]
tanned [tænd] ADJ 晒黑的 shàihēi de
tap [tæp] N [c] 龙头 lóngtóu [个 gè]
tap-dancing N [U] 踢踏舞 tītàwǔ
tape [teɪp] **I** N **1** [c] (*cassette*) 磁带 cídài [盘 pán] **2** [U] (*adhesive*) 胶带 jiāodài **II** VT **1** (*record*) 录制 lùzhì **2** (*attach*) 贴 tiē
tape measure N [c] 卷尺 juǎnchǐ [把 bǎ]
tar [tɑr] N [U] 沥青 lìqīng
target [tɑrgɪt] N [c] **1** (*of missile*) 目标 mùbiāo [个 gè] **2** (*aim*) 目标 mùbiāo [个 gè]
tart [tɑrt] N [c] 果馅饼 guǒxiànbǐng [个 gè]
tartan [tɑrtᵊn] **I** N [c/U] 苏格兰方格呢 Sūgélán fānggéní [块 kuài] **II** ADJ (+ *rug, scarf etc*) 苏格兰方格的 Sūgélán fānggé de
task [tæsk] N [c] 任务 rènwù [项 xiàng]
taste [teɪst] **I** N **1** [c] (*flavor*) 味道 wèidao [种 zhǒng] **2** [c] (*sample*) 尝试 chángshì [次 cì] **3** [U] (*choice, liking*) 品位 pǐnwèi **II** VI ▸ **to taste of/like sth** 有/像某物的味道 yǒu/xiàng mǒuwù de wèidao
tasty [teɪsti] ADJ 味美的 wèiměi de
tattoo [tætu] N [c] 纹身 wénshēn [个 gè]
taught [tɔt] PT, PP *of* **teach**
Taurus [tɔrəs] N [U] 金牛座 Jīnniú Zuò
tax [tæks] N [c/U] 税 shuì [种 zhǒng]
taxi [tæksi] N [c] 出租车 chūzūchē [辆 liàng]
taxi stand N [c] 出租车候客站 chūzūchē hòukèzhàn [个 gè]
TB [ti bi] N ABBR (= **tuberculosis**) 肺结核 fèijiéhé
tea [ti] N [c/U] **1** (*drink*) 茶 chá [杯 bēi] **2** (*dried leaves*) 茶叶 cháyè [片 piàn]

TEA

英国人和美国人喝的茶大多是红茶。通常茶里要加牛奶，可能还加糖，当然也可以在茶里只放一小片柠檬。花草茶（**herbal tea**），如薄荷或甘菊茶，正风行起来。**tea** 还可以指下午小餐，通常有三明治, 蛋糕，还有茶。在英国的一些地方，**tea** 还可以指晚上的正餐。

teach [titʃ] (*pt, pp* **taught**) **I** VT **1** ▸ **to teach sb sth, teach sth to sb** 教某人某事，将某事教给某人 jiāo mǒurén mǒushì, jiāng mǒushì jiāogěi mǒurén **2** (+ *pupils, subject*) 教 jiāo **II** VI (*be a teacher*) 教书 jiāoshū ▸ **to teach sb to do sth/how to do sth** 教某人做某事/怎样做某事 jiāo mǒurén zuò mǒushì/zěnyàng zuò mǒushì
teacher [titʃər] N [c] 教师 jiàoshī [位 wèi]
teakettle [tikɛtᵊl] N [c] 水壶 shuǐhú [把 bǎ]
team [tim] N [c] **1** (*of people, experts, horses*) 组 zǔ [个 gè] **2** (*Sport*) 队 duì [个 gè]
teapot [tipɒt] N [c] 茶壶 cháhú [个 gè]
tear[1] [tɛər] (*pt* **tore**, *pp* **torn**) **I** N [c] (*rip, hole*) 裂口 lièkǒu [个 gè] **II** VT 撕裂 sīliè; **tear down** VT (+ *building*) 拆毁 chāihuǐ; **tear up** VT 撕毁 sīhuǐ
tear[2] [tɪər] N [c] (*when crying*) 眼泪 yǎnlèi [滴 dī] ▸ **to burst into tears** 哭起来 kū qǐlái
tease [tiz] VT 逗弄 dòunong
teaspoon [tispun] N [c] 茶匙 cháchí [把 bǎ]
technical [tɛknɪkᵊl] ADJ **1** (+ *problems, advances*) 技术的 jìshù de **2** (+ *terms, language*) 专业的 zhuānyè de
technician [tɛknɪʃᵊn] N [c] 技师 jìshī [位 wèi]
technological [tɛknəlɒdʒɪkᵊl] ADJ 工艺的 gōngyì de
technology [tɛknɒlədʒi] N [c/U] 工

艺学 gōngyìxué [门 mén]
teddy (bear) [tɛ̲di-] N [C] 玩具熊 wánjùxióng [只 zhī]
teenage [ti̲neɪdʒ] ADJ 十几岁的 shíjǐsuì de
teenager [ti̲neɪdʒər] N [C] 青少年 qīngshàonián [个 gè]
tee-shirt [ti̲ʃɜrt] N = **T-shirt**
teeth [ti̲θ] N PL *of* **tooth**
telephone [tɛ̲lɪfoʊn] N [C] 电话 diànhuà [部 bù]
telephone book, telephone directory N [C] 电话簿 diànhuàbù [个 gè]
telescope [tɛ̲lɪskoʊp] N [C] 望远镜 wàngyuǎnjìng [架 jià]
television [tɛ̲lɪvɪʒᵊn, -vɪ̲ʒ-] N **1** [C] (*also*: **television set**) 电视机 diànshìjī [台 tái] **2** [U] (*system*) 电视 diànshì
tell [tɛ̲l] (*pt, pp* **told**) VT **1** (*inform*) ▸ **to tell sb sth** 告诉某人某事 gàosù mǒurén mǒushì **2** (+ *story, joke*) 讲 jiǎng ▸ **to tell sb to do sth** 指示某人做某事 zhǐshì mǒurén zuò mǒushì ▸ **to tell sb that...** 告诉某人说… gàosù mǒurén shuō...; **tell off** VT ▸ **to tell sb off** 斥责某人 chìzé mǒurén
teller [tɛ̲lər] N [C] (*in bank*) 出纳员 chūnàyuán [个 gè]
temper [tɛ̲mpər] N [C/U] 脾气 píqì [种 zhǒng] ▸ **to lose one's temper** 发怒 fānù
temperature [tɛ̲mprətʃər, -tʃʊər] N **1** [C/U] (*of place*) 气温 qìwēn **2** [U] (*of person*) 体温 tǐwēn ▸ **to have** *or* **be running a temperature** 发烧 fāshāo
temple [tɛ̲mpᵊl] N [C] 庙宇 miàoyǔ [座 zuò]
temporary [tɛ̲mpərɛri] ADJ 临时的 línshí de
temptation [tɛmpteɪ̲ʃᵊn] N [C/U] 诱惑 yòuhuò [种 zhǒng]
tempting [tɛ̲mptɪŋ] ADJ 诱人的 yòurén de
ten [tɛ̲n] NUM 十 shí
tend [tɛ̲nd] VI ▸ **to tend to do sth** 倾向于做某事 qīngxiàng yú zuò mǒushì
tennis [tɛ̲nɪs] N [U] 网球运动 wǎngqiú yùndòng
tennis court N [C] 网球场 wǎngqiúchǎng [个 gè]
tennis player N [C] 网球手 wǎngqiúshǒu [位 wèi]
tense [tɛ̲ns] **I** ADJ 紧张的 jǐnzhāng de **II** N [C] (*Ling*) 时态 shítài [种 zhǒng]
tension [tɛ̲nʃᵊn] N **1** [C/U] (*of situation*) 紧张的局势 jǐnzhāng de júshì [个 gè] **2** [U] (*of person*) 焦虑 jiāolǜ
tent [tɛ̲nt] N [C] 帐篷 zhàngpeng [顶 dǐng]
tenth [tɛ̲nθ] NUM **1** (*in series*) 第十 dì shí **2** (*fraction*) 十分之一 shífēn zhī yī; *see also* **fifth**
term [tɜ̲rm] N [C] 学期 xuéqī [个 gè] ▸ **in the short/long term** 短/长期 duǎn/chángqī ▸ **to be on good terms with sb** 与某人关系好 yǔ mǒurén guānxi hǎo
terminal [tɜ̲rmɪnᵊl] **I** ADJ 晚期的 wǎnqī de **II** N [C] **1** (*Comput*) 终端 zhōngduān [个 gè] **2** (*at airport*) 终点站 zhōngdiǎnzhàn [个 gè]
terminally [tɜ̲rmɪnᵊli] ADV ▸ **terminally ill** 病入膏肓的 bìng rù gāo huāng de
terrace [tɛ̲rɪs] N [C] (*patio*) 平台 píngtái [个 gè]
terraced [tɛ̲rɪst] ADJ (+ *house*) 成排的 chéngpái de
terrible [tɛ̲rɪbᵊl] ADJ **1** (+ *accident, winter*) 可怕的 kěpà de **2** (*very poor*) 糟糕的 zāogāo de **3** (*awful*) 糟透的 zāotòu de
terribly [tɛ̲rɪbli] ADV **1** (*very*) 非常 fēicháng **2** (*very badly*) 差劲地 chàjìn de
terrific [tərɪ̲fɪk] ADJ **1** (+ *amount, thunderstorm, speed*) 惊人的 jīngrén de **2** (+ *time, party, idea*) 极好的 jíhǎo de
terrified [tɛ̲rɪfaɪd] ADJ 吓坏的 xiàhuài de
terror [tɛ̲rər] N [U] 恐惧 kǒngjù

terrorism [tɛrərɪzəm] N [U] 恐怖主义 kǒngbù zhǔyì

terrorist [tɛrərɪst] I N [C] 恐怖分子 kǒngbù fènzǐ [个 gè] II ADJ 恐怖分子的 kǒngbù fènzǐ de

test [tɛst] I N [C] 1 (*trial, check*) 试验 shìyàn [次 cì] 2 (*Med*) 检验 jiǎnyàn [次 cì] 3 (*Scol*) 测验 cèyàn [个 gè] 4 (*also*: **driving test**) 驾驶考试 jiàshǐ kǎoshì [次 cì] II VT 1 (*try out*) 试验 shìyàn 2 (*Scol*) 测试 cèshì

test tube N [C] 试管 shìguǎn [根 gēn]

text [tɛkst] I N 1 [U] (*written material*) 正文 zhèngwén 2 [C] (*book*) 课本 kèběn [本 běn] 3 [C] (*also*: **text message**) 手机短信 shǒujī duǎnxìn [条 tiáo] II VT (*on mobile phone*) 发短消息 fā duǎnxiāoxi

textbook [tɛkstbʊk] N [C] 课本 kèběn [本 běn]

text message N [C] 短信 duǎnxìn [条 tiáo]

than [ðən, STRONG ðæn] PREP (*in comparisons*) 比 bǐ ▶ **it's smaller than a matchbox** 它比一个火柴盒还小 tā bǐ yīggè huǒcháihé hái xiǎo ▶ **more/less than Paul** 比保罗多/少 bǐ Bǎoluó duō/shǎo ▶ **more than 20** 多于20 duōyú èrshí ▶ **she's older than you think** 她比你想的年纪要大 tā bǐ nǐ xiǎngde niánjì yào dà

thank [θæŋk] VT (+ *person*) 感谢 gǎnxiè ▶ **thank you (very much)** (非常)感谢你 (fēicháng) gǎnxiè nǐ ▶ **no, thank you** 不，谢谢 bù, xièxie ▶ **to thank sb for (doing) sth** 感谢某人(做)某事 gǎnxiè mǒurén (zuò) mǒushì

thanks [θæŋks] I N PL 感谢 gǎnxiè II INT 谢谢 xièxie ▶ **many thanks, thanks a lot** 多谢 duōxiè ▶ **no, thanks** 不了，谢谢 bùle, xièxie ▶ **thanks to sb/sth** 多亏某人/某事 duōkuī mǒurén/mǒushì

Thanksgiving (Day) [θæŋksgɪvɪŋ-] N [C/U] 感恩节 Gǎn'ēnjié [个 gè]

KEYWORD

that [ðæt] (*demonstrative adj, pron: pl* **those**) I ADJ 那 nà ▶ **that man/woman/book** 那个男人/女人/那本书 nàgè nánrén/nǚrén/nàběnshū ▶ **that one** 那一个 nàyīgè

II PRON 1 (*demonstrative*) 那 nà ▶ **who's/what's that?** 那是谁/那是什么？ nàshì shuí/nàshì shénme? ▶ **is that you?** 是你吗？ shì nǐ ma? ▶ **that's my house** 那是我的房子 nàshì wǒde fángzi

2 (*relative*) …的 ...de ▶ **the man that I saw** 我见过的那个男的 wǒ jiànguò de nàgè nánde ▶ **the woman that you spoke to** 和你说过话的那个女的 hé nǐ shuōguò huà de nàgè nǚde

III CONJ 引导宾语从句的关系代词 ▶ **he thought that I was ill** 他以为我病了 tā yǐwéi wǒ bìngle

IV ADV (*so*) 如此 rúcǐ ▶ **that much/bad/high** 如此多/糟糕/高 rúcǐ duō/zāogāo/gāo

KEYWORD

the [ðə, ði] DEF ART 1 定冠词，用于指代已知的人或物 ▶ **the man/girl/house/book** 男人/女孩/房子/书 nánrén/nǚhái/fángzi/shū ▶ **the men/women/houses/books** 男人/女孩/房子/书 nánrén/nǚhái/fángzi/shū ▶ **the best solution** 最好的解决方案 zuìhǎo de jiějué fāng'àn

2 (*in dates, decades*) 表示具体时间 ▶ **the fifth of March** 3月5日 sānyuè wǔrì ▶ **the nineties** 90年代 jiǔshí niándài

3 (*in titles*) 用于称谓中 ▶ **Elizabeth the First** 伊丽莎白一世 Yīlìshābái Yīshì

theater [θi̱ətər] N 1 [C] (*building*) 剧院 jùyuàn [座 zuò] 2 [C] (*Med*) (*also*: **operating theater**) 手术室 shǒushùshì [间 jiān] 3 [C] (*also*: **movie theater**) 电影院 diànyǐngyuàn [家 jiā]

theft [θɛft] N [c/u] 盗窃 dàoqiè [次 cì]

their [ðɛər] ADJ **1** (*of men, boys, mixed group*) 他们的 tāmen de; (*of women, girls*) 她们的 tāmen de; (*of things, animals*) 它们的 tāmen de **2** (*his or her*) 他/她的 tā/tā de

theirs [ðɛərz] PRON (*of men, boys, mixed group*) 他们的 tāmen de; (*of women, girls*) 她们的 tāmen de; (*of animals*) 它们的 tāmen de ▶ **a friend of theirs** 他们/她们的一个朋友 tāmen/tāmen de yīgè péngyou

them [ðəm, STRONG ðɛm] PRON (*plural referring to men, boys, mixed group*) 他们 tāmen; (*referring to women, girls*) 她们 tāmen; (*referring to things and animals*) 它们 tāmen

theme park [θim-] N [c] 主题公园 zhǔtí gōngyuán [座 zuò]

themselves [ðəmsɛlvz] PL PRON **1** (*referring to men, boys, mixed group*) 他们自己 tāmen zìjǐ; (*referring to girls, women*) 她们自己 tāmen zìjǐ; (*referring to animals*) 它们自己 tāmen zìjǐ **2** (*emphatic: referring to men, boys, mixed group*) 他们本人 tāmen běnrén; (*referring to women, girls*) 她们本人 tāmen běnrén ▶ **they all enjoyed themselves** 他们/她们都玩得很开心 tāmen/tāmen dōu wánde hěn kāixīn ▶ **by themselves** (*unaided*) 他/她们独立地 tā/tāmen dúlì de; (*alone*) 他/她们独自地 tā/tāmen dúzì de

then [ðɛn] ADV **1** (*at that time: past*) 当时 dāngshí; (*future*) 那时 nàshí **2** (*after that*) 之后 zhīhòu ▶ **by then** 到那时 dào nàshí ▶ **before then** 在那之前 zài nà zhīqián ▶ **until then** 直到那时 zhídào nàshí ▶ **since then** 自从那时 zìcóng nàshí ▶ **well/OK then** 好吧 hǎoba

there [ðɛər] ADV 那儿 nàr ▶ **they've lived there for 30 years** 他们在那儿住了30年 tāmen zài nàr zhùle sānshí nián ▶ **is Shirley there please?** (*on telephone*) 请问雪莉在吗？ qǐngwèn Xuělì zàima? ▶ **it's over there** 在那边 zài nàbiān ▶ **there he is!** 他在那儿呐！ tā zài nàr ne! ▶ **there you are** (*offering something*) 给你 gěinǐ ▶ **there is/there are** 有 yǒu ▶ **there has been an accident** 发生了一个事故 fāshēng le yīgè shìgù

therefore [ðɛərfɔr] ADV 因此 yīncǐ

there's [ðɛərz] = **there is, there has**

thermometer [θərmɒmɪtər] N [c] 温度计 wēndùjì [个 gè]

these [*det* ðiz, *pron* ðiz] **I** PL ADJ (*demonstrative*) 这些 zhèxiē **II** PL PRON 这些 zhèxiē ▶ **these days** 目前 mùqián

they [ðeɪ] PL PRON **1** (*referring to men, boys, mixed group*) 他们 tāmen; (*referring to women, girls*) 她们 tāmen; (*referring to animals, things*) 它们 tāmen **2** (*in generalizations*) 人们 rénmen

they'd [ðeɪd] = **they had, they would**

they'll [ðeɪl] = **they shall, they will**

they're [ðɛər] = **they are**

they've [ðeɪv] = **they have**

thick [θɪk] ADJ **1** (+ *slice, line, book, clothes*) 厚的 hòu de **2** (+ *sauce, mud, fog*) 浓的 nóng de ▶ **it's 20 cm thick** 有20厘米粗 yǒu èrshí límǐ cū

thief [θif] (*pl* **thieves**) N [c] 贼 zéi [个 gè]

thieves [θivz] PL *of* **thief**

thigh [θaɪ] N [c] 大腿 dàtuǐ [条 tiáo]

thin [θɪn] ADJ **1** (+ *slice, line, book, material*) 薄的 báo de **2** (+ *person, animal*) 瘦的 shòu de

thing [θɪŋ] **I** N [c] **1** 事 shì [件 jiàn] **2** (*physical object*) 物品 wùpǐn [件 jiàn] **II things** N PL **1** (*belongings*) 东西 dōngxi **2** (*in general*) 情形 qíngxíng ▶ **a strange thing happened** 发生了一件很奇怪的事 fāshēng le yījiàn hěn qíguài de shì ▶ **how are things going?** 情形如何？ qíngxíng rúhé?

think [θɪŋk] (*pt, pp* **thought**) **I** VI **1** (*reflect*) 思考 sīkǎo **2** (*reason*) 想 xiǎng **II** VT **1** (*be of the opinion, believe*) 认为 rènwéi **2** (*believe*) 以为

yǐwéi ▸ **what do you think of...?** 你认为…怎么样? nǐ rènwéi...zěnmeyàng? ▸ **to think about sth/sb** 想着某事物/某人 xiǎngzhe mǒu shìwù/mǒurén ▸ **to think of doing sth** 考虑做某事 kǎolǜ zuò mǒushì ▸ **I think so/not** 我想是/不是的 wǒ xiǎng shì/bùshì de; **think over** VT (+ *offer, suggestion*) 仔细考虑 zǐxì kǎolǜ

third [θɜrd] NUM **1** (*in series*) 第三 dì sān **2** (*fraction*) 三份 sānfèn ▸ **a third of** 三分之一 sān fēn zhī yī; *see also* **fifth**

thirdly [θɜrdli] ADV 第三 dì sān

Third World I N ▸ **the Third World** 第三世界 Dì Sān Shìjiè **II** ADJ (+ *country, debt*) 第三世界的 Dì Sān Shìjiè de

thirst [θɜrst] N [C/U] 口渴 kǒukě [阵 zhèn]

thirsty [θɜrsti] ADJ 渴的 kě de

thirteen [θɜrtin] NUM 十三 shísān; *see also* **fifteen**

thirteenth [θɜrtinθ] NUM 第十三 dì shísān; *see also* **fifth**

thirty [θɜrti] NUM 三十 sānshí; *see also* **fifty**

KEYWORD

this [ðɪs] (*pl* **these**) **I** ADJ **1** (*demonstrative*) 这 zhè ▸ **this man** 这个男人 zhègè nánrén ▸ **this house** 这座房子 zhèzuò fángzi ▸ **this one is better than that one** 这个比那个好 zhègè bǐ nàgè hǎo
2 (*with days, months, years*) 这个 zhège ▸ **this Sunday/month/year** 这个星期天/月/今年 zhègè xīngqītiān/yuè/jīnnián
II PRON 这个 zhège ▸ **who's/what's this?** 这是谁/什么? zhèshì shuí/shénme? ▸ **this is Janet** (*in introduction*) 这是珍妮特 zhèshì Zhēnnítè; (*on telephone*) 我是珍妮特 wǒshì Zhēnnítè ▸ **like this** 像这个一样的 xiàng zhègè yīyàng de
III ADV (*demonstrative*) ▸ **this much/high/long** 这么多/高/长 zhème duō/gāo/cháng

thorn [θɔrn] N [C] 刺 cì [根 gēn]

thorough [θɜroʊ] ADJ **1** (+ *search, investigation*) 彻底的 chèdǐ de **2** (*methodical*) (+ *person*) 细致的 xìzhì de

those [*adj* ðoʊz, *pron* ðoʊz] **I** PL ADJ 那些 nàxiē **II** PL PRON 那些 nàxiē ▸ **those people/books** 那些人/书 nàxiē rén/shū ▸ **are those yours?** 那些是你的吗? nàxiē shì nǐde ma?

though [ðoʊ] **I** CONJ (*although*) 虽然 suīrán **II** ADV 但是 dànshì ▸ **even though** 尽管 jǐnguǎn

thought [θɔt] **I** PT, PP *of* **think II** N [C] 想法 xiǎngfǎ [个 gè]

thoughtful [θɔtfəl] ADJ **1** (*deep in thought*) 深思的 shēnsī de **2** (*considerate*) 体贴的 tǐtiē de

thoughtless [θɔtlɪs] ADJ (+ *behavior, words, person*) 不体贴的 bù tǐtiē de

thousand [θaʊzᵊnd] NUM ▸ **a** *or* **one thousand** 一千 yī qiān ▸ **thousands of** 许许多多 xǔ xǔ duō duō

thread [θrɛd] N [C/U] 线 xiàn [根 gēn]

threat [θrɛt] N [C/U] 威胁 wēixié [个 gè]

threaten [θrɛtᵊn] VT **1** (*make a threat against*) (+ *person*) 威胁 wēixié **2** (*endanger*) (+ *life, livelihood*) 使受到威胁 shǐ shòudào wēixié

three [θri] NUM 三 sān; *see also* **five**

three-quarters [θrikwɔrtərz] **I** N PL 四分之三 sìfēn zhī sān **II** ADV ▸ **three-quarters full/empty** 四分之三满/空 sìfēn zhīsān mǎn/kōng **III** PRON 四分之三 sìfēn zhī sān ▸ **three-quarters of an hour** 45分钟 sìshíwǔ fēnzhōng

threw [θru] PT *of* **throw**

thriller [θrɪlər] N [C] 惊险 jīngxiǎn [场 chǎng]

thrilling [θrɪlɪŋ] ADJ 令人兴奋的 lìng rén xīngfèn de

throat [θroʊt] N [C] **1** (*gullet*) 咽喉 yānhóu [个 gè] **2** (*neck*) 脖子 bózi [个 gè] ▸ **to have a sore throat** 嗓子疼 sǎngzi téng

through [θru] **I** PREP **1** (+ *place*) 穿

过 chuānguò 2 (*throughout*) (+ *time*) 整个 zhěnggè 3 (*coming from the other side of*) 穿过 chuānguò **II** ADJ (+ *ticket, train*) 直达的 zhídá de ▶ **(from) Monday through Friday** (从)周一到周五 (cóng) zhōuyī dào zhōuwǔ

throughout [θruaʊt] PREP **1** (+ *place*) 遍及 biànjí **2** (+ *time*) 贯穿 guànchuān

throw [θroʊ] (*pt* **threw**, *pp* **thrown**) VT **1** (*toss*) (+ *stone, ball*) 丢 diū **2** (+ *person*) 抛 pāo; **throw away** VT **1** (+ *trash*) 扔掉 rēngdiào **2** (+ *opportunity*) 错过 cuòguò; **throw out** VT **1** (+ *trash*) 扔掉 rēngdiào **2** (*from team, organization*) 赶走 gǎnzǒu; **throw up** (*inf*) VI (*vomit*) 呕吐 ǒutù

thrown [θroʊn] PP *of* **throw**

thru [θru] = **through**

thumb [θʌm] N [C] 大拇指 dàmǔzhǐ [个 gè]

thumbtack [θʌmtæk] N [C] 图钉 túdīng [颗 kē]

thunder [θʌndər] N [U] 雷 léi

thunderstorm [θʌndərstɔrm] N [C] 雷雨 léiyǔ [阵 zhèn]

Thursday [θɜrzdeɪ, -di] N [C/U] 星期四 xīngqīsì [个 gè]; *see also* **Tuesday**

tick [tɪk] **I** N [C] (*mark*) 勾号 gōuhào [个 gè] **II** VI (*clock, watch*) 嘀嗒作响 dīdā zuòxiǎng **III** VT (+ *item on list*) 打勾 dǎgōu; **tick off** VT (+ *item on list*) 打勾 dǎgōu

ticket [tɪkɪt] N **1** [C] (*for public transport, theater, raffle*) 票 piào [张 zhāng] **2** [C] (*Aut*) (*also*: **parking ticket**) 违章停车罚单 wéizhāng tíngchē fádān [张 zhāng]

ticket inspector N [C] 查票员 chápiàoyuán [位 wèi]

ticket office N [C] 售票处 shòupiàochù [个 gè]

tickle [tɪkᵊl] VT 挠 náo

tide [taɪd] N [C] 潮汐 cháoxī ▶ **high/low tide** 涨/落潮 zhǎng/luò cháo

tidy [taɪdi] **I** ADJ 整洁的 zhěngjié de **II** VT (*also*: **tidy up**) 整理 zhěnglǐ; **tidy up** VT, VI 整理 zhěnglǐ

tie [taɪ] **I** N [C] **1** (*clothing*) 领带 lǐngdài [条 tiáo] **2** (*Sport*) 淘汰赛 táotàisài [局 jú] **3** (*draw: in competition*) 平局 píngjú [个 gè] **II** VT (*also*: **tie up**) 扎 zā; **tie up** VT **1** (+ *parcel*) 捆绑 kǔnbǎng **2** (+ *dog*) 拴 shuān **3** (+ *person*) 捆绑 kǔnbǎng

tiger [taɪgər] N [C] 老虎 lǎohǔ [只 zhī]

tight [taɪt] **I** ADJ **1** (+ *shoes, clothes*) 紧身的 jǐnshēn de **2** (*strict*) (+ *budget, schedule*) 紧张的 jǐnzhāng de; (+ *security, controls*) 严格的 yángé de **II** ADV (*hold, squeeze, shut*) 紧紧地 jǐnjǐn de

tightly [taɪtli] ADV 紧紧地 jǐnjǐn de

tile [taɪl] N [C] **1** (*on roof*) 瓦 wǎ [片 piàn] **2** (*on floor, wall*) 砖 zhuān [块 kuài]

till [tɪl] PREP, CONJ = **until**

time [taɪm] N **1** [U] 时间 shíjiān **2** [U] (*period*) 时候 shíhou **3** [S] (*by clock*) 时间 shíjiān **4** [C] (*occasion*) 次 cì ▶ **to have a good/bad time** 度过一段愉快/不愉快的时光 dùguò yīduàn yúkuài/bù yúkuài de shíguāng ▶ **to spend one's time doing sth** 花时间做某事 huā shíjiān zuò mǒushì ▶ **three times a day** 一日三次 yīrì sāncì ▶ **all the time** 总是 zǒngshì ▶ **at the same time** (*simultaneously*) 同时 tóngshí ▶ **at times** (*sometimes*) 有时 yǒushí ▶ **in time (for)** 正好赶上(…) zhènghǎo gǎnshàng (...) ▶ **in a week's/month's time** 一周/月以后 yīzhōu/yuè yǐhòu ▶ **on time** 准时 zhǔnshí ▶ **5 times 5 is 25** 5乘5等于25 wǔ chéng wǔ děngyú èrshíwǔ ▶ **what time is it?, what's the time?** 几点了？ jǐdiǎn le? ▶ **time off** 休假 xiūjià

timetable [taɪmteɪbᵊl] N [C] (*program of events*) 计划表 jìhuàbiǎo [个 gè]

tin [tɪn] N [U] (*metal*) 锡 xī

tiny [taɪni] ADJ 极小的 jíxiǎo de

tip [tɪp] **I** N [C] **1** (*of branch,*

paintbrush) 顶端 dǐngduān [个 gè]
2 (*to waiter*) 小费 xiǎofèi [笔 bǐ]
3 (*advice*) 提示 tíshì [个 gè] **II** VT
1 (+ *waiter*) 给…小费 gěi...xiǎofèi
2 (*pour*) 倒出 dàochū

tiptoe [tɪptoʊ] VI 踮着脚走 diǎnzhe jiǎo zǒu ▸ **on tiptoe** 踮着脚走 diǎnzhe jiǎo zǒu

tire [taɪər] N [C] 轮胎 lúntāi [个 gè]

tired [taɪərd] ADJ 累的 lèi de ▸ **to be tired of (doing) sth** 厌倦于(做)某事 yànjuàn yú (zuò) mǒushì

tiring [taɪərɪŋ] ADJ 令人疲劳的 lìng rén píláo de

tissue [tɪʃu] N [C] (*paper handkerchief*) 纸巾 zhǐjīn [张 zhāng]

title [taɪtᵊl] N **1** [C] (*of book, play*) 标题 biāotí [个 gè] **2** [C] (*Sport*) 冠军 guànjūn [个 gè]

KEYWORD

to [tə, tu] **I** PREP **1** (*direction*) 到 dào ▸ **to France/Boston/school/the station** 去法国/波士顿/学校/车站 qù Fǎguó/Bōshìdùn/xuéxiào/chēzhàn
2 (*as far as*) ▸ **from here to New York** 从这儿到伦敦 cóng zhèr dào Lúndūn
3 (*position*) 向 xiàng ▸ **to the left/right** 向左/右 xiàng zuǒ/yòu
4 (*in time expressions*) ▸ **it's five/ten/a quarter to five** 差5分/10分/一刻5点 chà wǔfēn/shífēn/yīkè wǔ diǎn
5 (*for, of*) 的 de ▸ **a letter to his wife** 给他妻子的一封信 gěi tā qīzi de yīfēng xìn
6 (*indirect object*) ▸ **to give sth to sb** 给某人某物 gěi mǒurén mǒuwù ▸ **to talk to sb** 对某人说 duì mǒurén shuō ▸ **a danger to sb** 对某人的危险 duì mǒurén de wēixiǎn
7 (*towards*) ▸ **to be friendly/kind/loyal to sb** 对某人友好/仁慈/忠实 duì mǒurén yǒuhǎo/réncí/zhōngshí
8 (*in relation to*) ▸ **30 miles to the gallon** 每加仑可行30英里 měi jiālún kě xíng sānshí yīnglǐ ▸ **three goals to two** 3比2 sān bǐ èr
9 (*purpose, result*) ▸ **to come to sb's aid** 来帮某人的忙 lái bāng mǒurén de máng
10 (*indicating range, extent*) ▸ **from... to...** 从…到… cóng...dào... ▸ **from May to September** 从5月到9月 cóng wǔyuè dào jiǔyuè
II WITH VERB **1** (*simple infinitive*) 与原形动词一起构成动词不定式 ▸ **to go/eat** 走/吃 zǒu/chī
2 (*with vb omitted*) 用来代替动词不定式或不定式短语，避免重复 ▸ **I don't want to** 我不想 wǒ bù xiǎng
3 (*in order to*) 为了 wèile ▸ **I did it to help you** 我这么做是为了帮你 wǒ zhème zuò shì wèile bāngnǐ
4 (*equivalent to relative clause*) 用作定语 ▸ **I have things to do** 我有事要做 wǒ yǒushì yào zuò
5 (*after adjective etc*) 用于某些动词，名词，形容词后构成不定式 ▸ **to be ready to go** 准备走 zhǔnbèi zǒu ▸ **too old/young to do sth** 年纪太大/太小以至于不能做某事 niánjì tàidà/tàixiǎo yǐzhì yú bùnéng zuò mǒushì ▸ **to and fro** 来来回回地 lái lái huí huí de

toast [toʊst] N **1** [U] (*Culin*) 烤面包 kǎomiànbāo **2** [C] (*drink*) 祝酒 zhùjiǔ [次 cì] ▸ **a piece** *or* **slice of toast** 一片烤面包 yīpiàn kǎo miànbāo ▸ **to drink a toast to sb** 为某人干杯 wèi mǒurén gānbēi

toaster [toʊstər] N [C] 烤面包机 kǎo miànbāo jī [台 tái]

tobacco [təbækoʊ] N [U] 烟草 yāncǎo

today [tədeɪ] **I** ADV 今天 jīntiān **II** N [U] 今天 jīntiān ▸ **what day is it today?** 今天星期几？ jīntiān xīngqījǐ? ▸ **today is March 4th** 今天是3月4日 jīntiān shì sānyuè sìrì

toddler [tɒdlər] N [C] 学步的小孩 xuébù de xiǎohái [个 gè]

toe [toʊ] N [C] **1** (*of foot*) 脚趾 jiǎozhǐ [个 gè] **2** (*of shoe, sock*) 脚趾处 jiǎozhǐchù [个 gè] ▸ **big/little toe** 大/

小脚趾 dà/xiǎo jiǎozhǐ

together [təgɛðər] ADV **1** (*with each other*) 一起 yīqǐ **2** (*at the same time*) 同时 tóngshí **3** (*combined*) 加起来 jiā qǐlái ▸ **together with** 连同 liántóng

toilet [tɔɪlɪt] N [c] (*apparatus*) 抽水马桶 chōushuǐ mǎtǒng [个 gè]

toilet paper [tɔɪlɪt peɪpər] N [U] 卫生纸 wèishēngzhǐ

toiletries [tɔɪlətriz] N PL 卫生用品 wèishēng yòngpǐn

told [toʊld] PT, PP *of* **tell**

toll [toʊl] N [c] (*on road, bridge*) 通行费 tōngxíngfèi [笔 bǐ]

tomato [təmeɪtoʊ] (*pl* **tomatoes**) N [c/U] 西红柿 xīhóngshì 番茄 fānqié [个 gè]

tomorrow [təmɔroʊ] **I** ADV 明天 míngtiān **II** N [U] 明天 míngtiān ▸ **the day after tomorrow** 后天 hòutiān ▸ **tomorrow morning** 明天早晨 míngtiān zǎochén

ton [tʌn] N [c] **1** (*also*: **short ton**) 美吨 měidūn **2** (*metric ton*) 公吨 gōngdūn

tongue [tʌŋ] N [c] (*Anat*) 舌头 shétou [个 gè]

tonic [tɒnɪk] N [U] (*also*: **tonic water**) 奎宁水 kuíníngshuǐ

tonight [tənaɪt] ADV, N [U] 今晚 jīnwǎn

tonsil [tɒnsᵊl] N [c] 扁桃体 biǎntáotǐ [个 gè]

tonsillitis [tɒnsɪlaɪtɪs] N [U] 扁桃腺炎 biǎntáoxiànyán

too [tu] ADV **1** (*excessively*) 太 tài **2** (*also*) 也 yě ▸ **you're from Brooklyn? Me too!** 你从布鲁克林来？我也是！ nǐ cóng Bùlǔkèlín lái? Wǒ yěshì!

took [tʊk] PT *of* **take**

tool [tul] N [c] 用具 yòngjù [种 zhǒng]

tooth [tuθ] (*pl* **teeth**) N [c] 牙齿 yáchǐ [颗 kē]

toothache [tuθeɪk] N [c/U] 牙痛 yátòng [阵 zhèn] ▸ **to have toothache** 牙痛 yátòng

toothbrush [tuθbrʌʃ] N [c] 牙刷 yáshuā [把 bǎ]

toothpaste [tuθpeɪst] N [c/U] 牙膏 yágāo [管 guǎn]

top [tɒp] **I** N **1** [c] (*of mountain, building, tree, stairs*) 顶部 dǐngbù [个 gè] **2** [c] (*of page*) 顶端 dǐngduān [个 gè] **3** [c] (*of surface, table*) 表面 biǎomiàn [个 gè] **4** [c] (*lid*: *of box, jar, bottle*) 盖子 gàizi [个 gè] **5** [c] (*blouse*) 上衣 shàngyī [件 jiàn] **II** ADJ **1** (+ *shelf, step, storey, marks*) 最高的 zuìgāo de **2** (+ *executive, golfer*) 顶级的 dǐngjí de ▸ **at the top of the stairs/page** 在楼梯/页面的顶端 zài lóutī/yèmiàn de dǐngduān

topic [tɒpɪk] N [c] 话题 huàtí [个 gè]

tore [tɔr] PT *of* **tear**[1]

torn [tɔrn] PP *of* **tear**[1]

tortoise [tɔrtəs] N [c] 乌龟 wūguī [只 zhī]

torture [tɔrtʃər] **I** N [U] 酷刑 kùxíng **II** VT 对…施以酷刑 duì...shīyǐ kùxíng

total [toʊtᵊl] **I** ADJ 总的 zǒng de **II** N [c] 总数 zǒngshù [个 gè] ▸ **in total** 总共 zǒnggòng

totally [toʊtᵊli] ADV **1** (*agree, destroy*) 完全地 wánquán de **2** (*different, new*) 绝对地 juéduì de

touch [tʌtʃ] **I** N [c] (*contact*) 触摸 chùmō [次 cì] **II** VT **1** (*with hand, foot*) 触摸 chùmō **2** (*move*: *emotionally*) 感动 gǎndòng **III** VI (*be in contact*) 接触 jiēchù ▸ **to get in touch with sb** 与某人联系 yǔ mǒurén liánxì ▸ **to lose touch (with sb)** (与某人)失去联系 (yǔ mǒurén) shīqù liánxì

tough [tʌf] ADJ **1** (*strong, hard-wearing*) (+ *material*) 坚韧的 jiānrèn de **2** (+ *meat*) 老的 lǎo de **3** (*physically*) 强壮的 qiángzhuàng de **4** (*rough*) 无法无天的 wú fǎ wú tiān de

tour [tʊər] **I** N [c] **1** (*journey*) 旅行 lǚxíng [次 cì] **2** (*of town, factory, museum*) 观光 guānguāng [次 cì]

3 (*by pop group, sports team*) 巡回表演 xúnhuí biǎoyǎn [个 gè] **II** VT (+ *country, city*) 观光 guānguāng ▶ **to go on a tour of** (+ *region*) 去…旅行 qù...lǚxíng

tourism [tʊərɪzəm] N [U] 旅游业 lǚyóuyè

tourist [tʊərɪst] **I** N [C] 游客 yóukè [位 wèi] **II** CPD (+ *season, attraction*) 旅游 lǚyóu

tow [toʊ] VT (+ *vehicle, trailer*) 拖 tuō; **tow away** VT (+ *vehicle*) 拖走 tuōzǒu

toward(s) [təwɔrd(z)] PREP **1** (*in direction of*) 朝着 cháozhe **2** (*with regard to*) 对于 duìyú **3** (*near*) 接近 jiējìn

towel [taʊəl] N [C] 毛巾 máojīn [条 tiáo]

tower [taʊər] N [C] 塔 tǎ [座 zuò]

town [taʊn] N [C] 城镇 chéngzhèn [个 gè]

tow truck N [C] 拖车 tuōchē [部 bù]

toy [tɔɪ] **I** N [C] 玩具 wánjù [个 gè] **II** CPD (+ *train, car*) 玩具 wánjù

trace [treɪs] N [C] (*of substance*) 痕迹 hénjì [个 gè]; (*of person*) 踪迹 zōngjì [个 gè]

track [træk] N [C] **1** (*path*) 小径 xiǎojìng [条 tiáo] **2** (*Rail*) 轨道 guǐdào [条 tiáo] **3** (*on record*) 曲目 qǔmù [首 shǒu]

track and field N [U] 田径运动 tiánjìng yùndòng

tractor [træktər] N [C] 拖拉机 tuōlājī [部 bù]

trade [treɪd] **I** N **1** [U] (*buying and selling*) 贸易 màoyì **2** [C] (*skill, job*) 谋生之道 móushēng zhī dào [种 zhǒng] **II** VT (*exchange*) ▶ **to trade sth (for sth)** 用某物交换(某物) yòng mǒuwù jiāohuàn (mǒuwù)

trademark [treɪdmark] N [C] 商标 shāngbiāo [个 gè]

tradition [trədɪʃᵊn] N [C/U] 传统 chuántǒng [个 gè]

traditional [trədɪʃənᵊl] ADJ 传统的 chuántǒng de

traffic [træfɪk] N [U] 交通 jiāotōng

traffic circle N [C] 转盘 zhuànpán [个 gè]

traffic jam N [C] 交通阻塞 jiāotōng zǔsè [阵 zhèn]

traffic lights N PL 红绿灯 hónglǜdēng

tragedy [trædʒɪdi] N [C/U] **1** (*disaster*) 极大的不幸 jídà de bùxìng [个 gè] **2** (*Theat*) 悲剧 bēijù [个 gè]

tragic [trædʒɪk] ADJ 悲惨的 bēicǎn de

trailer [treɪlər] N [C] **1** (*Aut*) 拖车 tuōchē [部 bù] **2** (*mobile home*) 房式拖车 fángshì tuōchē [辆 liàng]

train [treɪn] **I** N [C] (*Rail*) 火车 huǒchē [辆 liàng] **II** VT **1** (*teach skills to*) 培训 péixùn **2** (+ *athlete*) 培养 péiyǎng **III** VI **1** (*learn a skill*) 受训练 shòu xùnliàn **2** (*Sport*) 锻炼 duànliàn

trained [treɪnd] ADJ 经专门训练的 jīng zhuānmén xùnliàn de

trainee [treɪni] N [C] **1** (*apprentice*) 受训者 shòuxùnzhě [位 wèi] **2** (*in office, management job*) 实习生 shíxíshēng [个 gè]

trainer [treɪnər] N [C] (*Sport*) 教练 jiàoliàn

training [treɪnɪŋ] N [U] **1** (*for occupation*) 培训 péixùn **2** (*Sport*) 训练 xùnliàn

training course N [C] 培训班 péixùnbān [个 gè]

tramp [træmp] N [C] 流浪者 liúlàngzhě [个 gè]

trampoline [træmpəlin] N [C] 蹦床 bèngchuáng [个 gè]

transfer [trænsfɜr] N **1** [C/U] (*of money, documents*) 转移 zhuǎnyí [次 cì] **2** [C] (*Sport*) 转会 zhuǎnhuì [次 cì]

transgender [trænzdʒɛndər] ADJ 跨性别的 kuàxìngbié de

transit [trænzɪt] N **1** ▶ **in transit** (*people*) 在途中 zài túzhōng **2** [U] 运输 yùnshū

translate [trænzleɪt] VT 翻译 fānyì

translation [trænzleɪʃᵊn] N **1** [C] (*text*) 译文 yìwén [篇 piān] **2** [U] (*act of translating*) 翻译 fānyì

translator [trænzleɪtər] N [C] 译者 yìzhě [个 gè]
transparent [trænspɛərənt, -pær-] ADJ 透明的 tòumíng de
transplant [*vb* trænsplænt, *n* trænsplænt] **I** VT (*Med*) 移植 yízhí **II** N [C/U] (*Med*: *operation*) 移植 yízhí [次 cì]
transport [*n* trænspɔrt, *vb* trænspɔrt] **I** N [U] 交通工具 jiāotōng gōngjù **II** VT 运送 yùnsòng
transportation [trænspərteɪʃən] N [U] (*transport*) 运输 yùnshū
trap [træp] **I** N [C] 陷阱 xiànjǐng [个 gè] **II** VT **1** (+ *animal*) 诱捕 yòubǔ **2** (*in building*) 困住 kùnzhù
trash [træʃ] N [U] 废物 fèiwù
trash can N [C] 垃圾桶 lājītǒng [个 gè]
travel [trævəl] **I** N [U] (*traveling*) 旅行 lǚxíng **II** VI 前往 qiánwǎng **III** VT (+ *distance*) 走过 zǒuguò
travel agency N [C] 旅行社 lǚxíngshè [个 gè]
travel agent N [C] **1** (*shop, office*) 旅行中介 lǚxíng zhōngjiè [个 gè] **2** (*person*) 旅行代理人 lǚxíng dàilǐrén [个 gè]
traveler [trævələr] N [C] 旅行者 lǚxíngzhě [位 wèi]
traveler's check N [C] 旅行支票 lǚxíng zhīpiào [张 zhāng]
traveling [trævəlɪŋ] N [U] 行程 xíngchéng
travel sickness N [U] 晕车/船/机症 yùnchē/chuán/jī zhèng
tray [treɪ] N [C] 托盘 tuōpán [个 gè]
treasure [trɛʒər] N [U] 宝藏 bǎozàng
treat [trit] VT **1** (*behave towards*) (+ *person, object*) 对待 duìdài **2** (*Med*) (+ *patient, illness*) 医治 yīzhì
treatment [tritmənt] N [C/U] (*Med*) 治疗 zhìliáo [次 cì]
tree [tri] N [C] 树 shù [棵 kē]
tremble [trɛmbəl] VI (*with fear, cold*) 战栗 zhànlì
tremendous [trɪmɛndəs] ADJ **1** (*enormous*) 极大的 jídà de **2** (*excellent*) 极棒的 jíbàng de
trend [trɛnd] N [C] **1** (*tendency*) 趋势 qūshì [种 zhǒng] **2** (*fashion*) 潮流 cháoliú [个 gè]
trendy [trɛndi] (*inf*) ADJ 时髦的 shímáo de
trial [traɪəl] N [C/U] (*Law*) 审理 shěnlǐ [次 cì] ▶ **on trial** (*Law*) 受审 shòushěn; (*on approval*) 试验 shìyàn
triangle [traɪæŋgəl] N [C] (*Math*) 三角 sānjiǎo [个 gè]
tribe [traɪb] N [C] 部落 bùluò [个 gè]
trick [trɪk] **I** N [C] **1** (*by conjuror*) 戏法 xìfǎ [个 gè] **2** (*deception*) 伎俩 jìliǎng [个 gè] **II** VT (*deceive*) 耍花招 shuǎ huāzhāo
tricky [trɪki] ADJ 棘手的 jíshǒu de
tricycle [traɪsɪkəl] N [C] 三轮车 sānlúnchē [辆 liàng]
trillion [trɪlyən] N [C] 十亿 shíyì
trip [trɪp] **I** N [C] **1** (*journey*) 出行 chūxíng [次 cì] **2** (*outing*) 外出 wàichū [次 cì] **II** VI (*also*: **trip up**) 绊倒 bàndǎo ▶ **to go on a trip** 外出旅行 wàichū lǚxíng
triple [trɪpəl] **I** ADJ 三部分的 sān bùfen de **II** VI 三倍于 sānbèi yú
triplets [trɪplɪts] N PL 三胞胎 sānbāotāi
triumph [traɪʌmf] N [C] 巨大的成功 jùdà de chénggōng [个 gè]
trivial [trɪviəl] ADJ 琐碎的 suǒsuì de
trolley [trɒli] N [C] (*vehicle*) 电车 diànchē [辆 liàng]
trombone [trɒmboʊn] N [C] 长号 chánghào [只 zhī]
troop [trup] **I** N [C] (*of people, animals*) 群 qún **II troops** N [C] PL (*Mil*) 部队 bùduì [支 zhī]
trophy [troʊfi] N [C] 奖品 jiǎngpǐn [个 gè]
tropical [trɒpɪkəl] ADJ 热带的 rèdài de
trouble [trʌbəl] N **1** [C/U] (*difficulties, bother, effort*) 麻烦 máfan [个 gè] **2** [S] (*problem*) 问题 wèntí **3** [U] (*unrest*) 骚乱 sāoluàn ▶ **to be in**

trouble (*with police, authorities*) 惹麻烦 rě máfan ▶ **the trouble is...** 问题是… wèntí shì... ▶ **stomach/back trouble** 胃部/背部毛病 wèibù/bèibù máobìng

trout [traʊt] N [C/U] 鳟鱼 zūnyú [条 tiáo]

truck [trʌk] N [C] 卡车 kǎchē [辆 liàng]

truck driver N [C] 卡车司机 kǎchē sījī [位 wèi]

true [truː] ADJ 真实的 zhēnshí de

truly [truːli] ADV (*genuinely*) 确实地 quèshí de ▶ **yours truly** (*in letter*) 您忠诚的 nín zhōngchéng de

trumpet [trʌmpɪt] N [C] 小号 xiǎohào [把 bǎ]

trunk [trʌŋk] N [C] **1** (*of tree*) 树干 shùgàn [个 gè] **2** (*of elephant*) 象鼻 xiàngbí [个 gè] **3** (*of car*) 后备箱 hòubèixiāng [个 gè]

trust [trʌst] VT 信任 xìnrèn

truth [truːθ] N [U] 事实 shìshí

try [traɪ] **I** N [C] 尝试 chángshì [个 gè] **II** VT (*attempt*) 试 shì **III** VI (*make effort*) 努力 nǔlì ▶ **to try to do sth, try doing sth** 尽力做某事 jìnlì zuò mǒushì; **try on** VT 试穿 shìchuān; **try out** VT 试验 shìyàn

T-shirt [tiʃɜrt] N [C] 短袖衫 duǎnxiùshān [件 jiàn]

tub [tʌb] N [C] **1** (*container*) 缸 gāng [个 gè] **2** (*bathtub*) 浴缸 yùgāng [个 gè]

tube [tuːb] N **1** [C] (*pipe*) 管子 guǎnzi [根 gēn] **2** [C] (*container*) 筒 tǒng [个 gè]

tuberculosis [tubɜrkyəloʊsɪs] N [U] 肺结核 fèijiéhé

Tuesday [tuːzdeɪ, -di] N [C/U] 星期二 xīngqī'èr [个 gè] ▶ **it is Tuesday March 23rd** 今天是3月23号，星期二 jīntiān shì sānyuè èrshísān hào, xīngqī'èr ▶ **on Tuesday** 在星期二 zài xīngqī'èr ▶ **on Tuesdays** 每个星期二 měigè xīngqī'èr ▶ **every Tuesday** 每逢星期二 měiféng xīngqī'èr ▶ **last/next Tuesday** 上个/下个星期二 shànggè/xiàgè xīngqī'èr ▶ **Tuesday morning/afternoon/evening** 星期二早晨/下午/晚上 xīngqī'èr zǎochén/xiàwǔ/wǎnshàng

tummy [tʌmi] (*inf*) N [C] 肚子 dùzi [个 gè]

tuna [tuːnə] N [C/U] (*also*: **tuna fish**) 金枪鱼 jīnqiāngyú [条 tiáo]

tune [tuːn] N [C] 曲调 qǔdiào [个 gè]

Tunisia [tuniːʒə] N 突尼斯 Tūnísī

tunnel [tʌnᵊl] N [C] 隧道 suìdào [条 tiáo]

Turk [tɜrk] N [C] 土耳其人 Tǔ'ěrqírén [个 gè]

Turkey [tɜrki] N 土耳其 Tǔ'ěrqí

turkey [tɜrki] N **1** [C] (*bird*) 火鸡 huǒjī [只 zhī] **2** [U] (*meat*) 火鸡肉 huǒjī ròu

Turkish [tɜrkɪʃ] **I** ADJ 土耳其的 Tǔ'ěrqí de **II** N [U] (*language*) 土耳其语 Tǔ'ěrqíyǔ

turn [tɜrn] **I** N [C] (*in game, series*) 机会 jīhuì [个 gè] **II** VT **1** (+ *part of body*) 转动 zhuàndòng **2** (+ *object*) 调转 diàozhuǎn **3** (+ *handle, key*) 转动 zhuǎndòng **4** (+ *page*) 翻 fān **5** (*in road*) 拐弯 guǎiwān [个 gè] **III** VI **1** (*rotate*) (*object, wheel*) 旋转 xuánzhuǎn **2** (*change direction*) (*person*) 转身 zhuǎnshēn **3** (*vehicle*) 转向 zhuǎnxiàng ▶ **it's my turn to...** 轮到我做… lúndào wǒ zuò... ▶ **to take turns** *or* **to take it in turns (to do sth)** 轮流做(某事) lúnliú zuò (mǒushì); **turn around, turn round** VI (*person, vehicle*) 调转 diàozhuǎn; **turn back** VI 往回走 wǎnghuí zǒu; **turn down** VT (+ *heat, sound*) 调低 tiáodī; **turn into** VT FUS 变成 biànchéng; **turn off** VT **1** (+ *light, radio, tap*) 关 guān **2** (+ *engine*) 关掉 guāndiào; **turn on** VT (+ *light, radio, tap*) 打开 dǎkāi; **turn out** VT (+ *light, gas*) 关掉 guāndiào ▶ **to turn out to be** (*prove to be*) 原来是 yuánlái shì; **turn up I** VI **1** (*person*) 露面 lòumiàn **2** (*lost object*) 出现 chūxiàn **II** VT (+ *radio, heater*) 开大 kāidà

turn-out N [C] 路侧停车处 lùcè tíngchēchù [个 gè]
turn signal N [U] 指示器 zhǐshìqì
turquoise [tɜrkwɔɪz] ADJ (+ *color*) 青绿色的 qīnglǜsè de
tutor [tutər] N [C] (*private tutor*) 家庭教师 jiātíng jiàoshī [位 wèi]
tuxedo [tʌksidoʊ] N [C] 男式晚礼服 nánshì wǎnlǐfú [件 jiàn]
TV [ti vi] N ABBR (= **television**) 电视 diànshì [台 tái]
tweezers [twizərz] N PL 镊子 nièzi ▸ **a pair of tweezers** 一把镊子 yībǎ nièzi
twelfth [twɛlfθ] NUM (*in series*) 第十二 dì shí'èr; *see also* **fifth**
twelve [twɛlv] NUM 十二 shí'èr ▸ **at twelve (o'clock)** (*midday*) 中午12点 zhōngwǔ shí'èr diǎn; (*midnight*) 凌晨零点 língchén língdiǎn; *see also* **five**
twentieth [twɛntiəθ] NUM 第二十 dì èrshí
twenty [twɛnti] NUM 二十 èrshí ▸ **twenty-one** 二十一 èrshíyī; *see also* **fifty**
twice [twaɪs] ADV 两次 liǎngcì ▸ **twice as much/long as** 多/长至两倍 duō/chángzhì liǎngbèi
twin [twɪn] **I** ADJ (+ *sister, brother*) 孪生的 luánshēng de **II** N [C] **1** (*person*) 双胞胎 shuāngbāotāi [对 duì] **2** (*also*: **twin room**) 双人房 shuāngrénfáng [间 jiān]
twist [twɪst] VT **1** (*turn*) 扭 niǔ **2** (+ *ankle*) 扭伤 niǔshāng
two [tu] NUM 二 èr; *see also* **five**
two-percent milk [tupərsɛnt mɪlk] N [U] 半脱脂奶 bàn tuōzhīnǎi
type [taɪp] **I** N **1** [C] (*sort, kind*) 类型 lèixíng [种 zhǒng] **2** [U] (*Typ*) 字体 zìtǐ **II** VT, VI 打字 dǎzì; **type into** VT 录入 lùrù
typewriter [taɪpraɪtər] N [C] 打字机 dǎzìjī [台 tái]
typical [tɪpɪkᵊl] ADJ 典型的 diǎnxíng de

U

UFO [yu ɛf oʊ, yufoʊ] N ABBR (= **unidentified flying object**) 不明飞行物 bùmíng fēixíngwù

ugly [ʌgli] ADJ 丑陋的 chǒulòu de

UK [yu keɪ] N ABBR (= **United Kingdom**) ▶ **the UK** 大不列颠及北爱尔兰联合王国 Dàbùlièdiān jí Běi'ài'ěrlán Liánhéwángguó

ulcer [ʌlsər] N [c] 溃疡 kuìyáng [处 chù]

umbrella [ʌmbrɛlə] N [c] 伞 sǎn [把 bǎ]

umpire [ʌmpaɪr] N [c] (*Baseball, Tennis*) 裁判员 cáipànyuán [位 wèi]

UN [yu ɛn] N ABBR (= **United Nations**) ▶ **the UN** 联合国 Liánhéguó

unable [ʌneɪbᵊl] ADJ ▶ **to be unable to do sth** 不能做某事 bùnéng zuò mǒushì

unanimous [yunænɪməs] ADJ 一致同意的 yīzhì tóngyì de

unavoidable [ʌnəvɔɪdəbᵊl] ADJ 不可避免的 bùkě bìmiǎn de

unbearable [ʌnbɛərəbᵊl] ADJ 难以忍受的 nányǐ rěnshòu de

uncertain [ʌnsɜrtᵊn] ADJ 不确定的 bù quèdìng de ▶ **to be uncertain about sth** 对某事心无定数 duì mǒushì xīn wú dìng shù

uncle [ʌŋkᵊl] N [c] (*father's older brother*) 伯父 bófù [位 wèi]; (*father's younger brother*) 叔父 shūfù [位 wèi]; (*father's sister's husband*) 姑父 gūfù [位 wèi]; (*mother's brother*) 舅父 jiùfù [位 wèi]; (*mother's sister's husband*) 姨父 yífù [位 wèi]

uncomfortable [ʌnkʌmftəbᵊl, -kʌmfərtə-] ADJ (+ *person*) 不舒服的 bù shūfu de; (+ *chair, room, journey*) 不舒适的 bù shūshì de

unconscious [ʌnkɒnʃəs] ADJ 失去知觉的 shīqù zhījué de

under [ʌndər] **I** PREP **1** (*beneath*) 在…下面 zài...xiàmian **2** (*less than*) (+ *age, price*) 不到 bùdào **II** ADV **1** (*go, fly*) 从下面 cóng xiàmian **2** (*in age, price etc*) 以下 yǐxià

underground [ʌndərgraʊnd] ADJ 地下的 dìxià de

underneath [ʌndərniθ] **I** ADV 在下面 zài xiàmian **II** PREP **1** 在…下面 zài...xiàmian **2** (*fig*) 在…背后 zài...bèihòu

underpants [ʌndərpænts] N PL 内裤 nèikù

underpass [ʌndərpæs] N [c] 地下通道 dìxià tōngdào [条 tiáo]

undershirt [ʌndərʃɜrt] N [c] 贴身内衣 tiēshēn nèiyī [件 jiàn]

understand [ʌndərstænd] (*pt, pp* **understood**) VT 明白 míngbai; (+ *foreign language*) 懂 dǒng

understanding [ʌndərstændɪŋ] ADJ 通情达理的 tōngqíng dálǐ de

understood [ʌndərstʊd] PT, PP *of* **understand**

underwater [ʌndərwɔtər] ADV 在水下 zài shuǐxià

underwear [ʌndərwɛər] N [U] 内衣 nèiyī

undid [ʌndɪd] PT *of* **undo**

undo [ʌndu] (*pt* **undid**, *pp* **undone**) VT 解开 jiěkāi

undone [ʌndʌn] PP *of* **undo**

undress [ʌndrɛs] VI 脱衣服 tuō yīfu

uneasy [ʌnizi] ADJ 不安的 bù'ān de ▶ **to be uneasy about sth** 为某事忧虑 wèi mǒushì yōulǜ

unemployed [ʌnɪmplɔɪd] **I** ADJ 失业的 shīyè de **II** N PL ▶ **the unemployed** 失业者 shīyèzhě

unemployment [ʌnɪmplɔɪmənt] N [U] 失业 shīyè

unexpected [ʌnɪkspɛktɪd] ADJ 意外的 yìwài de

unexpectedly [ʌnɪkspɛktɪdli] ADV 意外地 yìwài de

unfair [ʌnfɛər] ADJ 不公平的 bù gōngpíng de

unfamiliar [ʌnfəmɪlyər] ADJ 陌生的

mòshēng de
unfashionable [ʌnfæʃənəbᵊl] ADJ 过时的 guòshí de
unfit [ʌnfɪt] ADJ 不太健康的 bù tài jiànkāng de
unfold [ʌnfoʊld] VT 展开 zhǎnkāi
unforgettable [ʌnfərgɛtəbᵊl] ADJ 难忘的 nánwàng de
unfortunately [ʌnfɔrtʃənɪtli] ADV 可惜 kěxī
unfriendly [ʌnfrɛndli] ADJ 不友善的 bù yǒushàn de
unhappy [ʌnhæpi] ADJ 愁苦的 chóukǔ de
unhealthy [ʌnhɛlθi] ADJ **1** (+ *person*) 身体不佳的 shēntǐ bùjiā de **2** (+ *place, diet, lifestyle*) 不利于健康的 bù lìyú jiànkāng de
uniform [yunɪfɔrm] N [C/U] 制服 zhìfú [套 tào]
uninhabited [ʌnɪnhæbɪtɪd] ADJ 无人居住的 wúrén jūzhù de
union [yunyən] N [C] (*also*: **labor union**) 工会 gōnghuì [个 gè]
Union Jack N [C] 英国国旗 Yīngguó guóqí [面 miàn]
unique [yunik] ADJ 罕有的 hǎnyǒu de
unit [yunɪt] N [C] **1** (*single whole*) 单位 dānwèi [个 gè] **2** (*group, center*) 小组 xiǎozǔ [个 gè] **3** (*in course book*) 单元 dānyuán [个 gè]
United Kingdom [yunaɪtɪd kɪŋdəm] N ▸ **the United Kingdom** 大不列颠及北爱尔兰联合王国 Dàbùlièdiān Jí Běi'àiěr'lán Liánhéwángguó
United Nations [yunaɪtɪd neɪʃᵊnz] N ▸ **the United Nations** 联合国 Liánhéguó
United States (of America) [yunaɪtɪd steɪts (əv əmɛrɪkə)] N ▸ **the United States (of America)** 美利坚合众国 Měilìjiān Hézhòngguó
universe [yunɪvɜrs] N [C] 宇宙 yǔzhòu [个 gè]
university [yunɪvɜrsɪti] **I** N [C/U] 大学 dàxué [所 suǒ] **II** CPD (+ *student, professor, education, year*) 大学 dàxué
unkind [ʌnkaɪnd] ADJ 刻薄的 kèbó de
unknown [ʌnnoʊn] ADJ **1** (+ *fact, number*) 未知的 wèizhī de **2** (+ *writer, artist*) 名不见经传的 míng bù jiàn jīngzhuàn de
unleaded [ʌnlɛdɪd] **I** ADJ 无铅的 wúqiān de **II** N [U] 无铅燃料 wúqiān ránliào
unless [ʌnlɛs] CONJ 除非 chúfēi
unlikely [ʌnlaɪkli] ADJ 未必会发生的 wèibì huì fāshēng de ▸ **he is unlikely to win** 他获胜的希望不大 tā huòshèng de xīwàng bùdà
unload [ʌnloʊd] VT **1** (+ *objects*) 卸 xiè **2** (+ *car, truck*) 从…上卸货 cóng...shang xièhuò
unlock [ʌnlɒk] VT 开 kāi
unlucky [ʌnlʌki] ADJ **1** (+ *person*) 不幸的 bùxìng de **2** (+ *object, number*) 不吉利的 bù jílì de
unmarried [ʌnmærid] ADJ 未婚的 wèihūn de
unnatural [ʌnnætʃərᵊl] ADJ 反常的 fǎncháng de
unnecessary [ʌnnɛsəsɛri] ADJ 不必要的 bù bìyào de
unpack [ʌnpæk] **I** VI 开包 kāibāo **II** VT (+ *suitcase, bag*) 打开…取出东西 dǎkāi...qǔchū dōngxi
unpleasant [ʌnplɛzᵊnt] ADJ 使人不愉快的 shǐ rén bù yúkuài de; (+ *person, manner*) 令人讨厌的 lìng rén tǎoyàn de
unplug [ʌnplʌg] VT 拔去…的插头 báqù...de chātóu
unpopular [ʌnpɒpyʊlər] ADJ 不受欢迎的 bù shòu huānyíng de
unrealistic [ʌnriəlɪstɪk] ADJ 不切实际的 bù qiè shíjì de ▸ **it is unrealistic to expect that...** 指望…是不切实际的 zhǐwàng...shì bùqiè shíjì de
unreasonable [ʌnrizənəbᵊl] ADJ 无理的 wúlǐ de
unreliable [ʌnrɪlaɪəbᵊl] ADJ **1** (+ *person, firm*) 不可信赖的 bù kě xìnlài de **2** (+ *machine, method*) 不可

靠的 bù kěkào de

unroll [ʌnroʊl] VT 展开 zhǎnkāi

unscrew [ʌnskru] VT 旋开 xuánkāi

unsuccessful [ʌnsəksɛsfəl] ADJ 1 (+ *attempt, application*) 失败的 shībài de 2 (+ *person, applicant*) 不成功的 bù chénggōng de

unsuitable [ʌnsutəbᵊl] ADJ 1 (+ *place, time, clothes*) 不适宜的 bù shìyí de 2 (+ *candidate, applicant*) 不合适的 bù héshì de ▶ **to be unsuitable for sth/for doing sth** 不适于某事/做某事 bù shìyú mǒushì/zuò mǒushì

untidy [ʌntaɪdi] ADJ 1 (+ *room*) 不整洁的 bù zhěngjié de 2 (+ *person, appearance*) 邋遢的 lātā de

until [ʌntɪl] I PREP 直到…时 zhídào...shí II CONJ 到…为止 dào...wéizhǐ ▶ **until now** 直到现在 zhídào xiànzài ▶ **until then** 届时 jièshí

unusual [ʌnyuʒuəl] ADJ 不寻常的 bù xúncháng de

unwilling [ʌnwɪlɪŋ] ADJ ▶ **to be unwilling to do sth** 不愿做某事 bùyuàn zuò mǒushì

unwrap [ʌnræp] VT 打开…的包装 dǎkāi...de bāozhuāng

KEYWORD

up [*prep* ʌp, *adv* ʌp] I PREP 1 (*to higher point on*) 沿…向上 yán...xiàngshàng ▶ **he went up the stairs/the hill/the ladder** 他上了楼/山/梯子 tā shàngle lóu/shān/tīzi
2 (*along*) 沿着 yánzhe
3 (*at higher point on*) 在…高处 zài...gāochù; (+ *road*) 在…高远处 zài...gāoyuǎnchù ▶ **they live further up the street** 他们住在这条街那边儿 tāmen zhùzài zhètiáo jiē nàbiānr
II ADV 1 (*towards higher point*) 往上 wǎngshàng ▶ **the lift only goes up to the 12th floor** 电梯只到12层楼以上 diàntī zhǐdào shí'èr céng lóu yǐshàng
2 (*at higher point*) 高高地 gāogāo de ▶ **up here/there** 这/那上面 zhè/nà shàngmiàn
3 ▶ **to be up** (*be out of bed*) 起床 qǐchuáng
4 (*to/in the north*) 在/向北方 zài/xiàng běifāng ▶ **he often comes up to Scotland** 他常北上去苏格兰 tā cháng běishàng qù Sūgélán
5 (*approaching*) ▶ **to go/come/run up (to sb)** (朝某人)走去/过来/跑去 (cháo mǒurén) zǒuqù/guòlái/pǎoqù
6 ▶ **up to** (*as far as*) 直到 zhídào; (*in approximations*) 多达 duōdá ▶ **I can spend up to $100** 我可以花到100美元 wǒ kěyǐ huādào yībǎi měiyuán
7 ▶ **up to** *or* **until** 直到 zhídào ▶ **I'll be here up to** *or* **until 5.30 pm** 我会一直呆到下午5点30分 wǒ huì yīzhí dāidào xiàwǔ wǔdiǎn sānshífēn ▶ **up to now** 直到现在 zhídào xiànzài
8 ▶ **it is up to you (to decide)** 随便你(决定) suíbiàn nǐ (juédìng)
9 ▶ **to feel up to sth/to doing sth** 感到能胜任某事/感到有力气做某事 gǎndào néng shèngrèn mǒushì/gǎndào yǒu lìqi zuò mǒushì

update [ʌpdeɪt] I VT 更新 gēngxīn II N [C] 最新信息 zuìxīn xìnxī [条 tiáo]

uphill [ʌphɪl] ADV (*walk, push*) 往坡上 wǎng pōshang

upright [ʌpraɪt] ADV (*sit, stand*) 挺直地 tǐngzhí de

upset [ʌpsɛt] (*pt, pp* **upset**) I VT (+ *person*) 使苦恼 shǐ kǔnǎo II ADJ 1 (*unhappy*) 心烦意乱的 xīnfán yìluàn de 2 (+ *stomach*) 不舒服的 bù shūfu de ▶ **to be upset about sth** 为某事感到烦恼 wèi mǒushì gǎndào fánnǎo

upside down [ʌpsaɪd daʊn] ADV 上下颠倒地 shàngxià diāndǎo de

upstairs [ʌpstɛərz] ADV 1 (*be*) 在楼上 zài lóushang 2 (*go*) 往楼上 wǎng lóushang

up-to-date ADJ 最新的 zuìxīn de

upwards [ʌpwərdz] ADV 向上 xiàngshàng

urgent [ɜrdʒ^ə^nt] ADJ 紧急的 jǐnjí de

US [yu ɛs] N ABBR (= **United States**) ▶ **the US** 美国 Měiguó

us [əs, STRONG ʌs] PRON 我们 wǒmen

USA [yu ɛs eɪ] N ABBR (= **United States of America**) ▶ **the USA** 美国 Měiguó

use [*n* yus, *vb* yuz] **I** N [C/U] (*purpose*) 用途 yòngtú [种 zhǒng] **II** VT **1** (+ *object, tool*) 使用 shǐyòng **2** (+ *word, phrase*) 应用 yìngyòng ▶ **to make use of sth** 利用某物 lìyòng mǒuwù ▶ **it's no use** 没用的 méiyòng de ▶ **it's no use arguing/crying** *etc* 吵/哭{等}是没用的 chǎo/kū {děng} shì méiyòng de ▶ **to be no use (to sb)** (对某人)毫无用处 (duì mǒurén) háowú yòngchù ▶ **she used to do it** 她过去是这么做的 tā guòqù shì zhème zuò de ▶ **I didn't use to** *or* **I used not to worry so much** 我过去不这么焦虑 wǒ guòqù bù zhème jiāolǜ ▶ **to be used to sth/to doing sth** 习惯于某事/做某事 xíguàn yú mǒushì/zuò mǒushì ▶ **to get used to sth/to doing sth** 开始习惯于某事/做某事 kāishǐ xíguàn yú mǒushì/zuò mǒushì; **use up** VT 用完 yòngwán

useful [yusfəl] ADJ 有用的 yǒuyòng de ▶ **to be useful for sth/doing sth** 对某事/做某事有帮助的 duì mǒushì/zuò mǒushì yǒu bāngzhù de

useless [yuslɪs] ADJ (*pointless*) 徒劳的 túláo de

user [yuzər] N [C] 使用者 shǐyòngzhě [位 wèi]

user-friendly ADJ 易于使用的 yìyú shǐyòng de

usual [yuʒuəl] ADJ 惯常的 guàncháng de ▶ **as usual** 像往常一样 xiàng wǎngcháng yīyàng ▶ **warmer/colder than usual** 比平常暖和/冷 bǐ píngcháng nuǎnhe/lěng

usually [yuʒuəli] ADV 通常地 tōngcháng de

V

vacancy [veɪkənsi] N [c] (*job*) 空缺 kòngquē [个 gè]; (*hotel room*) 空房 kòngfáng [间 jiān] ▸ **"no vacancies"** "客满" "kèmǎn"

vacant [veɪkənt] ADJ 空着的 kòngzhe de

vacation [veɪkeɪʃᵊn] N [c] 休假 xiūjià [次 cì] ▸ **to take a vacation** 休假 xiūjià ▸ **to be/go on vacation** 在/去度假 zài/qù dùjià

vaccinate [væksɪneɪt] VT ▸ **to vaccinate sb (against sth)** 给某人接种疫苗(预防某疾病) gěi mǒurén jiēzhòng yìmiáo (yùfáng mǒu jíbìng)

vacuum cleaner [vækyum-] N [c] (*also*: **vacuum**) 真空吸尘器 zhēnkōng xīchénqì [台 tái]

vague [veɪg] ADJ 不清楚的 bù qīngchǔ de

vain [veɪn] ADJ (+ *person*) 自负的 zìfù de ▸ **in vain** 徒然 túrán

Valentine's Day [væləntaɪnz-] N [c/u] 情人节 Qíngrénjié [个 gè]

valid [vælɪd] ADJ 有效的 yǒuxiào de

valley [væli] N [c] 山谷 shāngǔ [个 gè]

valuable [vælyuəbᵊl] ADJ 贵重的 guìzhòng de

value [vælyu] N **1** [c/u] (*financial worth*) 价值 jiàzhí [种 zhǒng] **2** [u] (*worth in relation to price*) 价格 jiàgé

van [væn] N [c] (*Aut*) 厢式运货车 xiāngshì yùnhuòchē [辆 liàng]

vandalism [vændᵊlɪzəm] N [u] 蓄意破坏公物的行为 xùyì pòhuài gōngwù de xíngwéi

vandalize [vændᵊlaɪz] VT 肆意毁坏 sìyì huǐhuài

vanish [vænɪʃ] VI 消失 xiāoshī

variety [vəraɪɪti] N **1** [u] (*diversity*) 多样性 duōyàngxìng **2** [s] (*range: of objects*) 若干 ruògān

various [vɛəriəs] ADJ 不同的 bùtóng de

vary [vɛəri] **I** VT (*make changes to*) 更改 gēnggǎi **II** VI (*be different*) 有差异 yǒu chāyì

vase [veɪs, vaz] N [c] 花瓶 huāpíng [个 gè]

VCR [vi si ar] N ABBR (= **video cassette recorder**) (*o.f.*) 录像机 lùxiàngjī

VDT [vi di ti] N ABBR (= **visual display terminal**) 视频显示装置 shìpín xiǎnshì zhuāngzhì

veal [vil] N [u] 小牛肉 xiǎoniúròu

vegan [vigən] N [c] 纯素食主义者 chún sùshí zhǔyìzhě [个 gè]

vegetable [vɛdʒtəbᵊl, vɛdʒɪ-] N [c] 蔬菜 shūcài [种 zhǒng]

vegetarian [vɛdʒɪtɛəriən] **I** N [c] 素食者 sùshízhě [个 gè] **II** ADJ (+ *diet, restaurant etc*) 素的 sù de

vehicle [viɪkᵊl] N [c] 机动车 jīdòngchē [辆 liàng]

vein [veɪn] N [c] 静脉 jìngmài [条 tiáo]

velvet [vɛlvɪt] N [c/u] 天鹅绒 tiān'éróng [块 kuài]

vending machine [vɛndɪŋ məʃin] N [c] 自动售货机 zìdòng shòuhuòjī [部 bù]

verb [vɜrb] N [c] 动词 dòngcí [个 gè]

versus [vɜrsəs] PREP 对 duì

vertical [vɜrtɪkᵊl] ADJ 垂直的 chuízhí de

very [vɛri] ADV **1** 很 hěn **2** ▸ **the very end/beginning** 最终/一开始 zuìzhōng/yī kāishǐ ▸ **very much so** 确实如此 quèshí rúcǐ ▸ **very little** 极少的 jíshǎo de ▸ **there isn't very much (of...)** (…)不太多了 (...)bùtài duōle

vest [vɛst] N [c] 马甲 mǎjiǎ [件 jiàn]

veterinarian [vɛtərɪnɛəriən] N [c] 兽医 shòuyī [个 gè]

via [vaɪə, viə] PREP 经由 jīngyóu

vicar [vɪkər] N [c] 教区牧师 jiàoqū mùshī [位 wèi]

vicious [vɪʃəs] ADJ **1** (+ *attack, blow*)

剧烈的 jùliè de 2 (+ *person, dog*) 凶残的 xiōngcán de
victim [vɪktəm] N [c] 受害者 shòuhàizhě [个 gè] ▶ **to be the victim of** 成为…的受害者 chéngwéi...de shòuhàizhě
victory [vɪktəri, vɪktri] N [c/U] 胜利 shènglì [次 cì]
video [vɪdioʊ] N (*o.f.*) 1 [c] (*film*) 录像 lùxiàng [段 duàn] 2 [U] (*system*) 录像 lùxiàng 3 [c] (*cassette*) 录像带 lùxiàngdài [盘 pán]
video camera N [c] 摄像机 shèxiàngjī [台 tái]
video game N [c] 电子游戏 diànzǐ yóuxì [种 zhǒng]
video recorder [vɪdioʊ rɪkɔrdər] N [c] (*o.f.*) 录像机 lùxiàngjī [台 tái]
Vietnam [viɛtnɑm] N 越南 Yuènán
Vietnamese [viɛtnəmiz] (*pl* **Vietnamese**) **I** ADJ 越南的 Yuènán de **II** N 1 [c] (*person*) 越南人 Yuènánrén [个 gè] 2 [U] (*language*) 越南语 Yuènányǔ
view [vyu] N [c] 1 景色 jǐngsè [道 dào] 2 (*opinion*) 看法 kànfǎ [种 zhǒng]
village [vɪlɪdʒ] N [c] 村庄 cūnzhuāng [个 gè]
vine [vaɪn] N [c] 葡萄藤 pútáoténg [条 tiáo]
vinegar [vɪnɪgər] N [c/U] 醋 cù [瓶 píng]
vineyard [vɪnyərd] N [c] 葡萄园 pútáoyuán [座 zuò]
violence [vaɪələns] N [U] 暴力 bàolì
violent [vaɪələnt] ADJ 暴力的 bàolì de
violin [vaɪəlɪn] N [c] 小提琴 xiǎotíqín [把 bǎ]
violinist [vaɪəlɪnɪst] N [c] 小提琴手 xiǎotíqínshǒu [个 gè]
virgin [vɜrdʒɪn] N [c] 处女 chǔnǚ [个 gè]
Virgo [vɜrgoʊ] N [U] (*sign*) 处女座 Chǔnǚ Zuò
virus [vaɪrəs] (*Med, Comput*) N [c] 病毒 bìngdú [种 zhǒng]
visa [vizə] N [c] 签证 qiānzhèng [个 gè]
visit [vɪzɪt] **I** N [c] 1 (*to person*) 拜访 bàifǎng [次 cì] 2 (*to place*) 访问 fǎngwèn [次 cì] **II** VT 1 (+ *person*) 拜访 bàifǎng 2 (+ *place*) 游览 yóulǎn;
visit with VT FUS 拜访 bàifǎng
visitor [vɪzɪtər] N [c] 1 (*to city, country*) 游客 yóukè [位 wèi] 2 (*to person, house*) 来客 láikè [位 wèi]
visual [vɪʒuəl] ADJ 视觉的 shìjué de
vital [vaɪtᵊl] ADJ 至关重要的 zhìguān zhòngyào de
vitamin [vaɪtəmɪn] N [c] 维生素 wéishēngsù [种 zhǒng]
vivid [vɪvɪd] ADJ 1 生动的 shēngdòng de 2 (+ *color, light*) 鲜艳的 xiānyàn de
vocabulary [voʊkæbyəlɛri] N 1 [c/U] (*of person*) 词汇量 cíhuìliàng 2 [c] (*of language*) 词汇 cíhuì [个 gè]
vodka [vɒdkə] N [c/U] 伏特加酒 fútèjiā jiǔ [瓶 píng]
voice [vɔɪs] N [c] 嗓音 sǎngyīn [种 zhǒng]
voice mail N [U] 语音留言 yǔyīn liúyán
volcano [vɒlkeɪnoʊ] (*pl* **volcanoes**) N [c] 火山 huǒshān [座 zuò]
volleyball [vɒlibɔl] N [U] 排球 páiqiú
volume [vɒlyum] N [U] (*of TV, radio, stereo*) 音量 yīnliàng ▶ **volume one/two** (*of book*) 第一/二册 dìyī/èrcè
voluntary [vɒlənteri] ADJ 1 (*not compulsory*) 自愿的 zìyuàn de 2 (+ *work, worker*) 志愿的 zhìyuàn de
volunteer [vɒləntɪər] N [c] (*unpaid worker*) 志愿者 zhìyuànzhě [个 gè] ▶ **to volunteer to do sth** 自愿做某事 zìyuàn zuò mǒushì
vomit [vɒmɪt] **I** N [U] 呕吐物 ǒutùwù **II** VT 吐 tù **III** VI 呕吐 ǒutù
vote [voʊt] **I** N [c] 选票 xuǎnpiào [张 zhāng] **II** VI 投票 tóupiào ▶ **to take a vote on sth** 就某事进行表决 jiù mǒushì jìnxíng biǎojué ▶ **to vote**

for sb 投某人票 tóu mǒurén piào ▶ to vote for/against sth 投票支持/反对某事 tóupiào zhīchí/fǎnduì mǒushì

voucher [vaʊtʃər] N [c] 代金券 dàijīnquàn [张 zhāng]

vowel [vaʊəl] N [c] 元音 yuányīn [个 gè]

W

wage [weɪdʒ] N [C] (*also*: **wages**) 工资 gōngzī [份 fèn]

waist [weɪst] N [C] **1** 腰 yāo [个 gè] **2** (*of clothing*) 腰身 yāoshēn [个 gè]

wait [weɪt] **I** VI 等待 děngdài **II** N [C] (*interval*) 等待时间 děngdài shíjiān [段 duàn] ▸ **to wait for sb/sth** 等候某人/某物 děnghòu mǒurén/mǒuwù ▸ **wait a minute!** 等一下！ děngyīxià! ▸ **to keep sb waiting** 让某人等着 ràng mǒurén děngzhe

waiter [weɪtər] N [C] 男服务员 nán fúwùyuán [位 wèi]

waiting list [weɪtɪŋ lɪst] N [C] 等候者名单 děnghòuzhě míngdān [个 gè]

waiting room [weɪtɪŋ rum] N [C] 等候室 děnghòushì [间 jiān]

waitress [weɪtrɪs] N [C] 女服务员 nǚ fúwùyuán [位 wèi]

wake [weɪk] (*pt* **woke** *or* **waked**, *pp* **woken** *or* **waked**) **wake up I** VT 唤醒 huànxǐng **II** VI 醒来 xǐnglái

Wales [weɪlz] N 威尔士 Wēi'ěrshì ▸ **the Prince of Wales** 威尔士王子 Wēi'ěrshì Wángzǐ

walk [wɔk] **I** N [C] 散步 sànbù [次 cì] **II** VI 走 zǒu **III** VT (+ *distance*) 走 zǒu ▸ **it's 10 minutes' walk from here** 从这儿走有10分钟的路程 cóng zhèr zǒu yǒu shífēnzhōng de lùchéng ▸ **to go for a walk** 去散步 qù sànbù

walking [wɔkɪŋ] N [U] 步行 bùxíng

wall [wɔl] N [C] **1** (*of building, room*) 墙 qiáng [堵 dǔ] **2** (*around garden, field*) 围墙 wéiqiáng [圈 quān]

wallet [wɒlɪt] N [C] (*for money*) 钱包 qiánbāo [个 gè]

wallpaper [wɔlpeɪpər] N [C/U] 墙纸 qiángzhǐ [张 zhāng]

walnut [wɔlnʌt, -nət] N [C] (*nut*) 核桃 hétao [个 gè]

wander [wɒndər] VI 漫游 mànyóu

want [wɒnt] VT **1** (*wish for*) 想要 xiǎngyào **2** (*inf*: *need*) 需要 xūyào ▸ **to want to do sth** 想要做某事 xiǎngyào zuò mǒushì ▸ **to want sb to do sth** 希望某人做某事 xīwàng mǒurén zuò mǒushì

war [wɔr] N [C/U] 战争 zhànzhēng [场 chǎng]

wardrobe [wɔrdroʊb] N [C] 衣橱 yīchú [个 gè]

warehouse [wɛərhaʊs] N [C] 仓库 cāngkù [间 jiān]

warm [wɔrm] **I** ADJ **1** (+ *meal, soup, water*) 温热的 wēnrè de; (+ *day, weather*) 暖和的 nuǎnhe de **2** (+ *clothes, blankets*) 保暖的 bǎonuǎn de **3** (+ *applause, welcome*) 热情的 rèqíng de ▸ **it's warm** 天很暖和 tiān hěn nuǎnhe ▸ **are you warm enough?** 你觉得够暖和吗？nǐ juéde gòu nuǎnhe ma?; **warm up I** VI (*athlete, pianist*) 热身 rèshēn **II** VT (+ *food*) 加热 jiārè

warn [wɔrn] VT ▸ **to warn sb that** 警告某人… jǐnggào mǒurén... ▸ **to warn sb not to do sth** 告诫某人不要做某事 gàojiè mǒurén bùyào zuò mǒushì

warning [wɔrnɪŋ] N **1** [C] (*action, words, sign*) 警告 jǐnggào [个 gè] **2** [C/U] (*notice*) 预兆 yùzhào [个 gè]

was [wəz, STRONG wʌz, wɒz] PT *of* **be**

wash [wɒʃ] **I** VT 洗 xǐ **II** VI (*person*) 洗净 xǐjìng ▸ **to wash one's face/hands/hair** 洗脸/手/头发 xǐliǎn/shǒu/tóufa; **wash up** VI (*have a wash*) 洗一洗 xǐyīxǐ

washbasin [wɒʃbeɪsᵊn] N [C] 脸盆 liǎnpén [个 gè]

washcloth [wɒʃklɔθ] N [C] 毛巾 máojīn [条 tiáo]

washing [wɒʃɪŋ] N [U] **1** (*dirty*) 待洗衣物 dàixǐ yīwù **2** (*clean*) 洗好的衣物 xǐhǎo de yīwù ▸ **to do the washing** 洗衣服 xǐ yīfu

washing machine N [C] 洗衣机 xǐyījī [台 tái]

wasn't [wʌzᵊnt, wɒz-] = **was not**

wasp [wɒsp] N [C] 黄蜂 huángfēng [只 zhī]

waste [weɪst] I N 1 [S/U] (*of resources, food, money*) 浪费 làngfèi 2 [U] (*trash*) 废料 fèiliào II VT (+ *money, energy, time*) 浪费 làngfèi; (+ *opportunity*) 失去 shīqù ▸ **it's a waste of time** 这是浪费时间 zhèshì làngfèi shíjiān

watch [wɒtʃ] I N [C] 手表 shǒubiǎo [块 kuài] II VT 1 (*look at*) 注视 zhùshì; (+ *match, program, TV*) 看 kàn 2 (*pay attention to*) 关注 guānzhù III VI 注视 zhùshì ▸ **to watch sb do/doing sth** 看着某人做某事 kànzhe mǒurén zuò mǒushì; **watch out** VI 提防 dīfang ▸ **watch out!** (*inf*) 小心! xiǎoxīn!

water [wɔtər] I N [U] 水 shuǐ II VT (+ *plant*) 给…浇水 gěi...jiāoshuǐ ▸ **a drink of water** 一杯水 yībēishuǐ

waterfall [wɔtərfɔl] N [C] 瀑布 pùbù [条 tiáo]

watermelon [wɔtərmɛlən] N [C] 西瓜 xīguā [个 gè]

waterproof [wɔtərpruf] ADJ 防水的 fángshuǐ de

water-skiing N [U] ▸ **to go water-skiing** 去滑水 qùhuáshuǐ

wave [weɪv] I N [C] 1 (*of hand*) 挥动 huīdòng [下 xià] 2 (*on water*) 波浪 bōlàng [个 gè] II VI 挥手示意 huīshǒu shìyì III VT (+ *hand*) 挥 huī ▸ **to wave goodbye to sb, wave sb goodbye** 向某人挥手告别 xiàng mǒurén huīshǒu gàobié

wax [wæks] N [U] 蜡 là

way [weɪ] I N 1 [C] (*route*) 路 lù [条 tiáo] 2 [S] (*distance*) 距离 jùlí 3 [C] (*direction*) 方向 fāngxiàng [个 gè] 4 [C] (*manner*) 方式 fāngshì [种 zhǒng] 5 [C] (*method*) 方法 fāngfǎ [个 gè] II **ways** N PL (*habits*) 习俗 xísú ▸ **"which way?" – "this way"** "往哪边?" "这边" "wǎng nǎbiān?" "zhèbiān" ▸ **on the way** 在路上 zài lùshàng ▸ **it's a long way away** 离这儿很远 lí zhèr hěnyuǎn ▸ **to lose one's way** 迷路 mílù ▸ **the way back** 回去的路 huíqù de lù ▸ **to give way** (*break, collapse*) 倒塌 dǎotā ▸ **in a way** 在某种程度上 zài mǒuzhǒng chéngdù shàng ▸ **by the way...** 顺便提一下… shùnbiàn tíyīxià... ▸ **way of life** 生活方式 shēnghuó fāngshì ▸ **do it this way** 这么做 zhème zuò

we [wɪ, STRONG wi] PL PRON 我们 wǒmen

weak [wik] ADJ 1 虚弱的 xūruò de 2 (+ *tea, coffee, substance*) 淡的 dàn de

wealthy [wɛlθi] ADJ 富有的 fùyǒu de

weapon [wɛpən] N [C] 武器 wǔqì [种 zhǒng]

wear [wɛər] (*pt* **wore**, *pp* **worn**) I VT 穿着 chuānzhe; (+ *glasses, jewelry*) 戴着 dàizhe ▸ **I can't decide what to wear** 我拿不定主意该穿什么 wǒ nábùdìng zhǔyì gāi chuān shénme; **wear out** VI 耗尽 hàojìn

weather [wɛðər] N [U] 天气 tiānqì ▸ **what's the weather like?** 天气怎么样? tiānqì zěnmeyàng?

weather forecast N [C] 天气预报 tiānqì yùbào [个 gè]

web [wɛb] N [C] ▸ **the Web** 互联网 hùliánwǎng [个 gè] ▸ **on the Web** 在互联网上 zài hùliánwǎng shàng

Web page N [C] 网页 wǎngyè [个 gè]

website [wɛbsaɪt] N [C] 网址 wǎngzhǐ [个 gè]

we'd [wɪd, STRONG wid] = **we had, we would**

wedding [wɛdɪŋ] N [C] 婚礼 hūnlǐ [场 chǎng]

Wednesday [wɛnzdeɪ, -di] N [C/U] 星期三 xīngqīsān [个 gè]; *see also* **Tuesday**

week [wik] N [C] 星期 xīngqī [个 gè] ▸ **this/next/last week** 本/下/上周 běn/xià/shàngzhōu ▸ **once/twice a week** 一周一次/两次 yīzhōu yīcì/liǎngcì

weekday [wikdeɪ] N [C] 工作日 gōngzuòrì [个 gè] ▸ **on weekdays** 在工作日 zài gōngzuòrì

weekend [wiːkɛnd] N [c] 周末 zhōumò [个 gè] ▸ **at the weekend** 在周末 zài zhōumò ▸ **this/next/last weekend** 这个周末/下周末/上周末 zhègè zhōumò/xiàzhōu mò/shàngzhōu mò

weigh [weɪ] I VT 称…的重量 chēng...de zhòngliàng II VI ▸ **she weighs 50kg** 她的体重为50公斤 tāde tǐzhòng wéi wǔshí gōngjīn

weight [weɪt] I N [U] 重量 zhòngliàng II **weights** N PL (*in gym*) 举重器械 jǔzhòng qìxiè ▸ **to lose weight** 体重减轻 tǐzhòng jiǎnqīng

welcome [wɛlkəm] I N [c] 欢迎 huānyíng II VT 欢迎 huānyíng ▸ **welcome to Beijing!** 欢迎到北京来！ huānyíng dào Běijīng lái! ▸ **"thank you" – "you're welcome!"** "谢谢你" "别客气！" "xièxie nǐ" "bié kèqi!" ▸ **to give sb a warm welcome** 热烈欢迎某人 rèliè huānyíng mǒurén

well [wɛl] I N [c] 井 jǐng [口 kǒu] II ADV 1 (*to a high standard*) 好 hǎo 2 (*completely*) 充分地 chōngfèn de III ADJ (*healthy*) 身体好的 shēntǐ hǎo de IV INT 唔 ńg ▸ **to do well** (*person*) 做得好 zuòde hǎo; (*business*) 进展顺利 jìnzhǎn shùnlì ▸ **well done!** 棒极了！ bàngjí le! ▸ **as well** (*in addition*) 也 yě ▸ **I don't feel well** 我觉得不舒服 wǒ juéde bù shūfu ▸ **get well soon!** 早日康复！ zǎorì kāngfù! ▸ **well, as I was saying...** 那么，像我刚才所说的… nàme, xiàng wǒ gāngcái suǒshuō de...

we'll [wɪl, STRONG wiːl] = **we will, we shall**

well-known [wɛlnoʊn] ADJ (+ *person*) 有名的 yǒumíng de; (+ *fact, brand*) 众所周知的 zhòng suǒ zhōu zhī de

well-off [wɛlɔf] ADJ 富裕的 fùyù de

Welsh [wɛlʃ] I ADJ 威尔士的 Wēi'ěrshì de II N [U] (*language*) 威尔士语 Wēi'ěrshìyǔ III N PL ▸ **the Welsh** 威尔士人 Wēi'ěrshìrén

went [wɛnt] PT *of* **go**

were [wər, STRONG wɜr] PT *of* **be**

we're [wɪər] = **we are**

weren't [wɜrnt, wɜrənt] = **were not**

west [wɛst] I N 1 [U/S] (*direction*) 西方 xīfāng 2 ▸ **the West** (*Pol*) 西方国家 xīfāng guójiā II ADJ 西部的 xībù de III ADV 向西 xiàng xī ▸ **west of** …以西 ...yǐxī

western [wɛstərn] I ADJ (*Geo*) 西部的 xībù de II N [c] 西部影片 xībù yǐngpiàn [部 bù]

West Indian I ADJ 西印度群岛的 Xīyìndù Qúndǎo de II N [c] 西印度群岛人 Xīyìndù Qúndǎorén [个 gè]

West Indies [-ɪndiz] N PL ▸ **the West Indies** 西印度群岛 Xīyìndù Qúndǎo

wet [wɛt] ADJ 1 (+ *person, clothes*) 湿的 shī de; (+ *paint, cement, glue*) 未干的 wèigān de 2 (*rainy*) (+ *weather, day*) 多雨的 duōyǔ de ▸ **to get wet** 弄湿 nòngshī

we've [wɪv, STRONG wiv] = **we have**

whale [weɪl] N [c] 鲸 jīng [头 tóu]

KEYWORD

what [wʌt, wɒt] I PRON 1 什么 shénme ▸ **what is happening?** 发生了什么事？ fāshēng le shénme shì? ▸ **what is it?** 那是什么？ nàshì shénme? ▸ **what are you doing?** 你在干什么？ nǐ zài gànshénme? ▸ **what did you say?** 你说什么？ níshuō shénme?

2 (*in indirect questions/speech subject, object*) 什么 shénme ▸ **do you know what's happening?** 你知道发生了什么事吗？ nǐ zhīdào fāshēng le shénme shì ma?

3 (*relative*) 所…的 suǒ...de ▸ **I saw what was on the table** 我看见了桌上的东西 wǒ kànjiàn le zhuōshàng de dōngxi

II ADJ 1 什么 shénme ▸ **what time is it?** 几点了？ jǐdiǎn le? ▸ **what size is this shirt?** 这件衬衫是几码的？ zhèjiàn chènshān shì jǐmǎ de?

2 (*in exclamations*) 多么 duōme

▶ **what a mess!** 真是一团糟！ zhēnshì yītuán zāo! ▶ **what a lovely day!** 多么好的天气啊！ duōme hǎo de tiānqì a!
III INT 什么 shénme ▶ **what, no coffee!** 什么，没咖啡了！ shénme, méi kāfēi le!

whatever [wʌtɛvər, wɒt-] **I** ADV (*whatsoever*) 任何 rènhé **II** PRON ▶ **do whatever is necessary/you want** 做任何必要的/你想做的事情 zuò rènhé bìyào de/nǐ xiǎngzuò de shìqing
wheat [wit] N [U] 小麦 xiǎomài
wheel [wil] N [C] **1** 轮 lún [个 gè] **2** (*also*: **steering wheel**) 方向盘 fāngxiàngpán [个 gè]
wheelchair [wiltʃɛər] N [C] 轮椅 lúnyǐ [部 bù]

KEYWORD

when [wɛn] **I** ADV (*interrogative*) 什么时候 shénme shíhou ▶ **when did it happen?** 什么时候发生的？ shénme shíhou fāshēng de?
II PRON (*relative*) ▶ **the day when** 当…的那一天 dāng…de nà yī tiān
III CONJ (*in time clauses*) 当…时 dāng…shí ▶ **be careful when you cross the road** 过马路时要当心 guò mǎlù shí yào dāngxīn ▶ **she was reading when I came in** 当我进来时她正在阅读 dāng wǒ jìnlái shí tā zhèngzài yuèdú ▶ **I know when it happened** 我知道什么时候发生的 wǒ zhīdào shénme shíhou fāshēng de

where [wɛər] **I** ADV (*in or to what place*) 在哪里 zài nǎli **II** CONJ (*the place in which*) 哪里 nǎli ▶ **where are you from?** 你是哪里人？ nǐ shì nǎlǐ rén?
whether [wɛðər] CONJ 是否 shìfǒu ▶ **I don't know whether to accept or not** 我不知道是接受还是不接受 wǒ bù zhīdào shì jiēshòu háishì bù jiēshòu

KEYWORD

which [wɪtʃ] **I** ADJ **1** (*interrogative singular*) 哪个 nǎge; (*plural*) 哪些 nǎxiē ▶ **which picture do you want?** 你要哪幅画？ nǐ yào nǎfú huà? ▶ **which one/ones?** 哪个/些？ nǎgè/xiē?
2 (*in indirect questions/speech singular*) 哪个 nǎge; (*plural*) 哪些 nǎxiē ▶ **he asked which book I wanted** 他问我要哪本书 tā wènwǒ yào nǎběn shū
II PRON **1** (*interrogative subject, object*) 哪个 nǎge ▶ **which of these is yours?** 这些中的哪个是你的？ zhèxiē zhōng de nǎgè shì nǐde?
2 (*in indirect questions/speech subject, object*) 哪个 nǎge ▶ **ask him which of the models is the best** 问他哪种型号是最好的 wèn tā nǎzhǒng xínghào shì zuìhǎo de
3 (*relative subject, object*) …的那个… …de nàge… ▶ **the shot which you heard/which killed him** 你听到的那一枪/杀死他的那一枪 nǐ tīngdào de nàyīqiāng/shāsǐ tā de nàyīqiāng

while [waɪl] **I** N [S] 一会儿 yīhuìr **II** CONJ **1** (*during the time that*) 在…时 zài…shí **2** (*although*) 虽然 suīrán ▶ **while I'm very fond of him, I don't actually want to marry him** 虽然我很喜欢他，但我真的不想嫁给他 suīrán wǒ hěn xǐhuān tā, dàn wǒ zhēnde bùxiǎng jiàgěi tā ▶ **for a while** 有一会儿 yǒu yīhuǐr
whiskey [wɪski] N [C/U] 威士忌酒 wēishìjì jiǔ [瓶 píng]
whisper [wɪspər] VI 低语 dīyǔ
whistle [wɪsᵊl] **I** VI 吹口哨 chuī kǒushào **II** N [C] **1** (*device*) 哨子 shàozi [个 gè] **2** (*sound*) 口哨声 kǒushàoshēng [声 shēng]
white [waɪt] **I** ADJ **1** 雪白的 xuěbái de; (+ *wine*) 白的 bái de **2** (+ *coffee*) 加奶的 jiā nǎi de **3** (*person*): **White** 白种

人的 báizhǒngrén de **II** N [U] (*color*) 白色 báisè

WHITE HOUSE

白宫是美国总统在华盛顿特区的官邸。自1800年约翰·亚当斯总统以来，那里一直是美国历届在任总统的住所。1814年它曾被英国人焚毁，但随后进行了重建和扩充。1902年罗斯福总统正式将该建筑命名为“白宫”。如今每年都会有约一百五十万人前往那里参观。

KEYWORD

who [hu] PRON **1** 谁 shéi ▸ **who is it?** 是谁？ shì shuí? ▸ **who did you discuss it with?** 你和谁讨论了？ nǐ hé shuí tǎolùn le?
2 (*in indirect questions/speech subject, object, after preposition*) 谁 shéi ▸ **I told her who I was** 我告诉了她我是谁 wǒ gàosù le tā wǒ shì shuí ▸ **I don't know who he gave it to** 我不知道他把它给了谁 wǒ bù zhīdào tā bǎ tā gěile shuí
3 (*relative subject, object*) …的那个… ...de nàge... ▸ **the girl who came in** 进来的那个女孩 jìnlai de nàgè nǚhái ▸ **the man who we met in Sydney** 我们在悉尼遇到的那个男子 wǒmen zài Xīní yùdào de nàgè nánzǐ

whole [houl] **I** ADJ 整个的 zhěnggè de **II** N **1** [U] (*entirety*) 整体 zhěngtǐ [个 gè] **2** ▸ **the whole of sth** 某物的全部 mǒuwù de quánbù [个 gè] ▸ **the whole (of the) time** 所有的时间 suǒyǒu de shíjiān ▸ **on the whole** 大体上 dàtǐ shàng

whom [hum] (*frm*) PRON **1** (*interrogative*) 谁 shéi **2** (*relative*) 所…的那个… suǒ...de nàge... ▸ **the man whom I saw/to whom I spoke** 我见到的/我跟他说过话的那个男的 wǒ jiàndào de/wǒ gēn tā shuō guò huà de nàgè nánde

whose [huz] **I** ADJ **1** (*interrogative*) 谁的 shéi de **2** (*relative*) …的 ...de **II** PRON 谁的 shéi de ▸ **whose is this?** 这是谁的？ zhè shì shéi de? ▸ **whose book is this/coats are these?** 这本书是谁的/这些外套是谁的？ zhèběnshū shì shuíde/zhèxiē wàitào shì shuíde? ▸ **the woman whose car was stolen** 汽车给偷走的那个女的 qìchē gěi tōuzǒu de nàgè nǚde

KEYWORD

why [waɪ] **I** ADV 为什么 wèishénme ▸ **why is he always late?** 为什么他总是迟到？ wèishénme tā zǒngshì chídào? ▸ **why not?** 为什么不呢？ wèishénme bù ne? ▸ **I don't know why** 我不知道为什么 wǒ bù zhīdào wèishénme
II CONJ 为什么 wèishénme ▸ **I wonder why he said that** 我想知道他为什么那么说 wǒxiǎng zhīdào tā wèishénme nàme shuō ▸ **the reason why he did it** 他那么做的原因 tā nàme zuò de yuányīn

wicked [wɪkɪd] ADJ (*evil*) (+ *person*) 邪恶的 xié'è de; (+ *act, crime*) 罪恶的 zuì'è de

wide [waɪd] **I** ADJ **1** 宽的 kuān de **2** (+ *range, variety, publicity, choice*) 广泛的 guǎngfàn de **II** ADV ▸ **to open sth wide** 张大某物 zhāngdà mǒuwù

widow [wɪdoʊ] N [C] 寡妇 guǎfù [个 gè]

widower [wɪdoʊər] N [C] 鳏夫 guānfū [个 gè]

width [wɪdθ, wɪtθ] N [C/U] 宽度 kuāndù [个 gè]

wife [waɪf] (*pl* **wives**) N [C] 妻子 qīzi [个 gè]

wild [waɪld] ADJ **1** 野生的 yěshēng de **2** (+ *person, behavior*) 狂野的 kuángyě de

wildlife [waɪldlaɪf] N [U] 野生动物 yěshēng dòngwù

KEYWORD

will [wɪl] I AUX VB 1 ▸ **I will call you tonight** 我今晚会给你打电话的 wǒ jīnwǎn huì gěi nǐ dǎ diànhuà de ▸ **what will you do next?** 下面你要做什么？ xiàmiàn nǐ yào zuò shénme?
2 (*in conjectures, predictions*) 该是 gāishì ▸ **he'll be there by now** 他现在该到了 tā xiànzài gāidào le
3 (*in commands, requests, offers*) ▸ **will you be quiet!** 你安静点！ nǐ ānjìng diǎn!
II N 1 (*volition*) 意志 yìzhì ▸ **against his will** 违背他的意愿 wéibèi tāde yìyuàn
2 (*testament*) 遗嘱 yízhǔ [个 gè] ▸ **to make a will** 立遗嘱 lì yízhǔ

willing [wɪlɪŋ] ADJ ▸ **to be willing to do sth** 愿意做某事 yuànyì zuò mǒushì
win [wɪn] (*pt, pp* **won**) I N [c] 胜利 shènglì [个 gè] II VT 1 在…中获胜 zài...zhōng huòshèng 2 (+ *prize, medal*) 赢得 yíngdé III VI 获胜 huòshèng
wind [wɪnd] N [c/u] 风 fēng [阵 zhèn]
window [wɪndoʊ] N [c] 1 窗户 chuānghu [扇 shàn]; (*in store*) 橱窗 chúchuāng [个 gè]; (*in car, train*) 窗 chuāng [个 gè] 2 (*Comput*) 视窗 shìchuāng [个 gè]
windshield [wɪndʃild] N [c] 挡风玻璃 dǎngfēng bōlí [块 kuài]
windsurfing [wɪndsɜrfɪŋ] N [u] 帆板运动 fānbǎn yùndòng
windy [wɪndi] ADJ (+ *weather, day*) 有风的 yǒufēng de ▸ **it's windy** 今天风很大 jīntiān fēng hěndà
wine [waɪn] N [c/u] 葡萄酒 pútáojiǔ [瓶 píng]
wing [wɪŋ] N [c] 1 翅膀 chìbǎng [个 gè]; (*of airplane*) 机翼 jīyì [个 gè] 2 (*of building*) 侧楼 cèlóu [座 zuò]
wink [wɪŋk] VI (*person*) 眨眼 zhǎyǎn ▸ **to give sb a wink, wink at sb** 向某人眨了眨眼 xiàng mǒurén zhǎlezhǎ yǎn
winner [wɪnər] N [c] 获胜者 huòshèngzhě [位 wèi]
winter [wɪntər] I N [c/u] 冬季 dōngjì [个 gè] II VI 过冬 guòdōng ▸ **in (the) winter** 在冬季 zài dōngjì
wipe [waɪp] VT (*dry, clean*) 擦 cā ▸ **to wipe one's nose** 擦鼻子 cā bízi; **wipe up** VT 把…擦干净 bǎ...cā gānjìng
wire [waɪər] N [c] (*Elec: uninsulated*) 电线 diànxiàn [根 gēn]; (*insulated*) 电缆 diànlǎn [条 tiáo]
wise [waɪz] ADJ 睿智的 ruìzhì de
wish [wɪʃ] I N [c] 愿望 yuànwàng [个 gè] II VT 但愿 dànyuàn ▸ **best wishes** 良好的祝愿 liánghǎo de zhùyuàn ▸ **with best wishes** 祝好 zhùhǎo ▸ **give her my best wishes** 代我向她致意 dài wǒ xiàng tā zhìyì ▸ **to wish to do sth** 想要做某事 xiǎngyào zuò mǒushì

KEYWORD

with [wɪð, wɪθ] PREP 1 和…在一起 hé...zài yīqǐ ▸ **I was with him** 我和他在一起 wǒ hé tā zài yīqǐ ▸ **I'll be with you in a minute** 请稍等 qǐng shāoděng ▸ **we stayed with friends** 我们和朋友们呆在一起 wǒmen hé péngyǒumen dāizài yīqǐ
2 (*indicating feature, possession*) 有 yǒu ▸ **the man with the gray hat/blue eyes** 戴着灰帽子/有蓝眼睛的男人 dàizhe huī màozi/yǒu lán yǎnjīng de nánrén
3 (*indicating means, substance*) 用 yòng ▸ **to walk with a stick** 拄着拐杖走 zhǔzhe guǎizhàng zǒu ▸ **to fill sth with water** 在某物里装满水 zài mǒuwù lǐ zhuāngmǎn shuǐ
4 (*indicating cause*) ▸ **red with anger** 气得涨红了脸 qìde zhànghóngle liǎn

without [wɪðaʊt, wɪθ-] PREP 没有 méiyǒu ▸ **without a coat** 未穿外套 wèichuān wàitào ▸ **without speaking**

不曾说话 bùcéng shuōhuà

witness [wɪtnɪs] N [c] (*gen, also in court*) 目击者 mùjīzhě [位 wèi]

witty [wɪti] ADJ 诙谐的 huīxié de

wives [waɪvz] N PL *of* **wife**

woke [woʊk] PT *of* **wake**

woken [woʊkən] PP *of* **wake**

wolf [wʊlf] (*pl* **wolves**) N [c] 狼 láng [条 tiáo]

woman [wʊmən] (*pl* **women**) N [c] 妇女 fùnǚ [位 wèi]

won [wʌn] PT, PP *of* **win**

wonder [wʌndər] I VT ▸ **to wonder whether/why** *etc* 想知道是否/为什么{等} xiǎng zhīdào shìfǒu/wèishénme {děng} II VI 感到奇怪 gǎndào qíguài

wonderful [wʌndərfəl] ADJ 绝妙的 juémiào de

won't [woʊnt] = **will not**

wood [wʊd] N 1 [U] 木材 mùcái 2 [c] (*forest*) 树林 shùlín [棵 kē]

wool [wʊl] N [U] 羊毛 yángmáo

word [wɜrd] N 1 [c] 词 cí [个 gè] 2 [s] (*promise*) 诺言 nuòyán ▸ **what's the word for "pen" in French?** "钢笔"这个词在法语里怎么说? "gāngbǐ" zhègè cí zài Fǎyǔ lǐ zěnme shuō? ▸ **in other words** 换句话说 huàn jù huà shuō

word processing [wɜrd prɒsɛsɪŋ] N [U] 文字处理 wénzì chǔlǐ

word processor [wɜrd prɒsɛsər] N [c] (*machine*) 文字处理器 wénzì chǔlǐqì [个 gè]

wore [wɔr] PT *of* **wear**

work [wɜrk] I N 1 [U] (*tasks, duties*) 事情 shìqing 2 [U] (*job*) 工作 gōngzuò II VI 1 (*have job, do tasks*) 工作 gōngzuò 2 (*function*) 运行 yùnxíng 3 (*be successful*) (*idea, method*) 起作用 qǐ zuòyong ▸ **to go to work** 去上班 qù shàngbān ▸ **to be out of work** 失业 shīyè ▸ **to work hard** 努力工作 nǔlì gōngzuò; **work out** I VI (*Sport*) 锻炼 duànliàn II VT (+ *answer, solution*) 努力找出 nǔlì zhǎochū; (+ *plan, details*) 制订出 zhìdìng chū

worker [wɜrkər] N [c] 工人 gōngrén [位 wèi] ▸ **a hard/good worker** 工作努力/良好的人 gōngzuò nǔlì/liánghǎo de rén

work experience N [U] 工作经历 gōngzuò jīnglì

workstation [wɜrksteɪʃᵊn] N [c] 1 (*desk*) 工作台 gōngzuòtái [个 gè] 2 (*computer*) 工作站 gōngzuòzhàn [个 gè]

world [wɜrld] I N ▸ **the world** 世界 shìjiè II CPD (+ *champion, record, power, authority*) 世界 shìjiè; (+ *tour*) 环球 huánqiú ▸ **all over the world** 全世界 quán shìjiè

World Wide Web N ▸ **the World Wide Web** 万维网 Wànwéiwǎng

worn [wɔrn] PP *of* **wear**

worried [wɜrid] ADJ 闷闷不乐的 mènmèn bù lè de ▸ **to be worried about sth/sb** 担心某事/某人 dānxīn mǒushì/mǒurén

worry [wɜri] I N 1 [U] (*feeling of anxiety*) 忧虑 yōulǜ 2 [c] (*cause of anxiety*) 担心 dānxīn [种 zhǒng] II VT 使担心 shǐ dānxīn III VI 担心 dānxīn

worse [wɜrs] I ADJ 更坏的 gènghuài de II ADV (*comparative of badly*) 更糟地 gèngzāo de ▸ **to get worse** 逐渐恶化 zhújiàn èhuà

worst [wɜrst] I ADJ 最坏的 zuì huài de II ADV (*superlative of badly*) 最糟地 zuì zāo de III N [s/U] 最坏的事 zuì huài de shì ▸ **at worst** 在最坏的情况下 zài zuìhuài de qíngkuàng xià

worth [wɜrθ] I N [U] 价值 jiàzhí II ADJ ▸ **to be worth $50** 值50美元 zhí wǔshí měiyuán ▸ **it's worth it** 这是值得的 zhèshì zhídé de ▸ **400 dollars' worth of damage** 价值400美元的损失 jiàzhí sìbǎi měiyuán de sǔnshī ▸ **it would be (well) worth doing...** (很)值得做… (hěn) zhídé zuò...

KEYWORD

would [wəd, STRONG wʊd] AUX VB 1 ▸ **I would love to go to Italy** 我很愿

意去意大利 wǒ hěn yuànyì qù Yìdàlì ▸ **I'm sure he wouldn't do that** 我确定他不会那么做的 wǒ quèdìng tā bùhuì nàme zuòde
2 (*in offers, invitations, requests*) ▸ **would you like a cookie?** 你要来块饼干吗？ nǐ yào lái kuàn bǐnggān ma? ▸ **would you ask him to come in?** 你要叫他进来吗？ nǐ yào jiàotā jìnlai ma?
3 (*be willing to*) ▸ **she wouldn't help me** 她不愿意帮助我 tā bù yuànyì bāngzhù wǒ
4 (*in indirect speech*) ▸ **he said he would be at home later** 他说他晚点儿会在家的 tā shuō tā wǎndiǎnr huì zàijiā de

wouldn't [wʊdᵊnt] = **would not**
wrap [ræp] I VT (*cover*) 包 bāo; **wrap up** VT (*pack*) 包起来 bāo qǐlái
wrapping paper [ræpɪŋ peɪpər] N [U] (*gift wrap*) 包装纸 bāozhuāngzhǐ
wreck [rɛk] I N [C] 1 (*wreckage: of vehicle, ship*) 残骸 cánhái [个 gè] 2 (*accident*) 事故 shìgù [次 cì] II VT (+ *car, building*) 摧毁 cuīhuǐ
wrestling [rɛslɪŋ] N [U] 摔跤 shuāijiāo
wrinkled [rɪŋkᵊld] ADJ 布满皱纹的 bùmǎn zhòuwén de
wrist [rɪst] N [C] 手腕 shǒuwàn [个 gè]
write [raɪt] (*pt* **wrote**, *pp* **written**) I VT 1 (+ *address, number*) 写下 xiěxià 2 (+ *letter, note*) 写 xiě 3 (+ *novel, music*) 创作 chuàngzuò 4 (+ *check, receipt, prescription*) 开 kāi II VI 写字 xiězì ▸ **to write to sb** 写信给某人 xiěxìn gěi mǒurén; **write down** VT 记下 jìxià
writer [raɪtər] N [C] 作家 zuòjiā [位 wèi]
writing [raɪtɪŋ] N [U] 1 (*sth written*) 文字 wénzì 2 (*handwriting*) 笔迹 bǐjì ▸ **in writing** 以书面形式 yǐ shūmiàn xíngshì
written [rɪtᵊn] PP *of* **write**
wrong [rɔŋ] I ADJ 1 (+ *person, equipment, kind, job*) 不合适的 bù héshì de 2 (+ *answer, information, report*) 错误的 cuòwù de 3 (*morally bad*) 不道德的 bù dàodé de II ADV (*incorrectly*) 错误地 cuòwù de ▸ **to be wrong** (*answer*) 是错的 shì cuòde; (*person*) 弄错的 nòng cuò de ▸ **what's wrong?** 出了什么事？ chūle shénme shì? ▸ **what's wrong with you?** 你怎么了？ nǐ zěnme le? ▸ **to go wrong** (*plan*) 失败 shībài; (*machine*) 发生故障 fāshēng gùzhàng
wrote [roʊt] PT *of* **write**
WWW [dʌbᵊlyu dʌbᵊlyu dʌbᵊlyu] (*Comput*) N ABBR (= **World Wide Web**) 万维网 Wànwéiwǎng

Xmas [ɛksməs] N ABBR (= **Christmas**) 圣诞节 Shèngdànjié

X-ray [ɛksreɪ] **I** N [C] (*photo*) X光照片 X guāng zhàopiàn [张 zhāng] **II** VT 用X光检查 yòng X guāng jiǎnchá ▶ **to have an X-ray** 做一次X光检查 zuò yīcì X guāng jiǎnchá

Y

yacht [yɒt] N [c] **1** (*sailing boat*) 帆船 fānchuán [艘 sōu] **2** (*luxury craft*) 游艇 yóutǐng [艘 sōu]

yard [yɑrd] N [c] **1** 庭院 tíngyuàn [座 zuò] **2** (*measure*) 码，长度单位。一码等于3英尺或0.9144米

yawn [yɔn] **I** VI 打呵欠 dǎ hēqiàn **II** N [c] 呵欠 hēqiàn [个 gè]

year [yɪər] N [c] **1** 年 nián **2** (*Scol, Univ*) 学年 xuénián [个 gè] ▸ **every year** 每年 měinián ▸ **this year** 今年 jīnnián ▸ **last year** 去年 qùnián ▸ **a** *or* **per year** 每年 měinián ▸ **we lived there for years** 我们住在那儿有好多年了 wǒmen zhùzài nàr yǒu hǎoduō nián le

yellow [yɛloʊ] **I** ADJ 黄色的 huángsè de **II** N [c/U] 黄色 huángsè [种 zhǒng]

yes [yɛs] **I** ADV 是的 shìde **II** N [c] (*answer*) 是 shì

yesterday [yɛstərdeɪ, -di] **I** ADV 昨天 zuótiān **II** N [U] 昨天 zuótiān ▸ **the day before yesterday** 前天 qiántiān

yet [yɛt] **I** ADV (*up to now: with negative*) 还 hái; (*in questions*) 已经 yǐjīng **II** CONJ 然而 rán'ér ▸ **they haven't finished yet** 他们还没完工 tāmen hái méi wángōng ▸ **yet again** 又一次 yòu yīcì

yogurt [yoʊgərt] N [c/U] 酸奶 suānnǎi [瓶 píng]

you [yu] PRON **1** (*singular*) 你 nǐ; (*plural*) 你们 nǐmen **2** (*one*) 任何人 rènhérén ▸ **you never know** 谁知道 shuí zhīdào

young [yʌŋ] ADJ 幼小的 yòuxiǎo de ▸ **my younger brother/sister** 我的弟弟/妹妹 wǒde dìdi/mèimei

your [yɔr, yʊər] ADJ (*of one person*) 你的 nǐ de; (*of more than one person*) 你们的 nǐmen de

yours [yɔrz, yʊərz] PRON (*of one person*) 你的 nǐ de; (*of more than one person*) 你们的 nǐmen de ▸ **is this yours?** 这是你/你们的吗？ zhèshì nǐ/nǐmen de ma? ▸ **yours sincerely/faithfully** 你真挚的/忠实的 nǐ zhēnzhì de/zhóngshí de

yourself [yɔrsɛlf, yʊər-] PRON **1** 你自己 nǐzìjǐ **2** (*you*) 你 nǐ ▸ **by yourself** (*unaided*) 独立地 dúlì de; (*alone*) 独自地 dúzì de

yourselves [yɔrsɛlvz, yʊər-] PL PRON **1** 你们自己 nǐmen zìjǐ **2** (*you*) 你们 nǐmen ▸ **by yourselves** (*unaided*) 独力地 dúlì de; (*alone*) 独自地 dúzì de

youth club [yuθ klʌb] N [c] 青年俱乐部 qīngnián jùlèbù [个 gè]

youth hostel [yuθ hɒstᵊl] N [c] 青年招待所 qīngnián zhāodàisuǒ [个 gè]

Z

zero [zɪə̲roʊ] (*pl* **zero** *or* **zeroes**) N **1** [U/C] (*number*) 零 líng [个 gè] **2** [U] (*nothing*) 没有 méiyǒu ▸ **5 degrees below zero** 零下5度 língxià wǔdù

zip code [zɪ̲p koʊd] N [C] 邮政编码 yóuzhèng biānmǎ [个 gè]

zipper [zɪ̲pər] N [C] 拉链 lāliàn [条 tiáo]

zone [zo̲ʊ̲n] N [C] (*area*) 地带 dìdài [个 gè]

zoo [zu̲] (*pl* **zoos**) N [C] 动物园 dòngwùyuán [个 gè]

zucchini [zuki̲ni] (*pl* **zucchini** *or* **zucchinis**) N [C/U] 绿皮西葫芦 lùpí xīhúlu [个 gè]